The Ismāʿīlīs constitute the second largest Shīʿī community in the Muslim world. They are scattered over many parts of the world, including India, Pakistan, East Africa, Central Asia, Afghanistan, Iran, Syria, Yaman, Continental Europe, the United Kingdom, and North America. Almost all recognize the Aga Khan as their imām or spiritual leader. This authoritative book, the product of twenty years' research … the history and doctrinal development … its origins to the present day, a perio… rst comprehensive synthesis of the scatte… on the subject and draws on numerou… s, particularly on a number of Ismāʿīlī … ly become available.

All the major phases of Ismāʿīlī history are covered. Beginning at the pre-Fāṭimid period, Dr Daftary conducts a detailed investigation through the Fāṭimid 'golden age' and the troubled Mustaʿlī-Ṭayyibī period up to the spiritual and physical strengths of Nizārī Ismāʿīlism in Iran and Syria before the onslaught of the Mongols. The final part of the book traces the modern developments of the Ismāʿīlī community, explaining the revival of Nizārī Ismāʿīlism, particularly in Iran and on the Indian subcontinent, and the socio-economic progress of the Nizārī communities.

For all students of Islamic and Middle Eastern history, *The Ismāʿīlīs: their history and doctrines* will serve as the most definitive account yet of the history of the Ismāʿīlīs and their movement.

The Ismāʿīlīs : their history and doctrines

The Ismāʿīlīs: their history and doctrines

Farhad Daftary

The right of the University of Cambridge to print and sell all manner of books was granted by Henry VIII in 1534. The University has printed and published continuously since 1584.

CAMBRIDGE UNIVERSITY PRESS

Cambridge
New York Port Chester
Melbourne Sydney

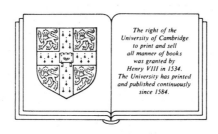

Published by the Press Syndicate of the University of Cambridge
The Pitt Building, Trumpington Street, Cambridge CB2 1RP
40 West 20th Street, New York, NY 10011, USA
10 Stamford Road, Oakleigh, Victoria 3166, Australia

First published 1990
Reprinted 1992
First paperback edition 1992

Printed in Great Britain at
the University Press, Cambridge

British Library cataloguing in publication data

Daftary, Farhad
The Isma'ilis.
1. Ismailis
I. Title
297'.822

Library of Congress cataloging in publication data

Daftary, Farhad.
The Ismāʿīlīs: their history and doctrines / Farhad Daftary.
p. cm.
Bibliography: p.
Includes index.
ISBN 0 521 37019 1
1. Ismailites. I. Title.
BP195.I8D33 1990
297'.822 – dc20 89–7257CIP

ISBN 0 521 37019 1 hardback
ISBN 0 521 42974 9 paperback

To Fereshteh

CONTENTS

ILLUSTRATIONS

Plates

Map

FOREWORD

The study of the history of the Isma'ili religion, which for long had depended largely on the polemical and often distorted accounts of its opponents, has been transformed since the time of the First World War by the discovery of large private collections of authentic Isma'ili works in the Soviet Union and India. Many of the original texts, previously kept secret from outsiders by the Isma'ili communities, have now been published or are accessible in manuscript to scholarly research. Although a relatively small number of scholars in East and West have actively pursued such research, progress in uncovering the story of the Isma'ili movement in its various branches and the development of Isma'ili religious thought has been steady. The major aspects and characteristics of this thought and its transformations in the course of often catastrophic events affecting the scattered Isma'ili communities have become evident. There are, to be sure, still large gaps left in our knowledge of these developments, some of which may prove difficult to fill because of a lack of sources. Moreover, on some fundamental questions, especially concerning the early stages of Isma'ilism, consensus has not yet been reached among scholars. Yet these problems must not obscure the remarkable advances made in the study of Isma'ilism, which provide both a general outline of the history of one of the major branches of Shi'ite Islam and a sound basis for further detailed research.

In the present volume, Dr F. Daftary offers a first comprehensive and detailed synthesis of the complex history of Isma'ilism. His presentation fully reflects the progress of recent research, widely scattered in editions of texts, monographs and articles, and integrates it into an evenly readable account. In some areas, especially on the modern developments, entirely new ground is covered. The book will no doubt be widely appreciated as a general reference work by students and by all readers interested in aspects of Ismaʿili history from a scholarly point of view.

Wilferd Madelung
Laudian Professor of Arabic
The University of Oxford

PREFACE

The Ismāʿīlīs constitute the second largest Shīʿī community after the Twelvers in the Muslim world and are now scattered in more than twenty countries of Asia, Africa, Europe and America. This book traces the history and doctrines of the Ismāʿīlī movement from its origins to the present time, a period of approximately twelve centuries.

The origins of Sunnism and Shīʿism, the two main divisions of Islam, may be traced to the crisis of succession faced by the nascent Muslim community following the death of the Prophet Muḥammad, though the doctrinal bases of these divisions developed gradually in the course of several centuries. In time, Shīʿī Islam, the minoritarian view, became subdivided into different groups, many of which proved short-lived. But Imāmī Shīʿism, providing the common early heritage for several Shīʿī sects, notably the Twelvers and the Ismāʿīlīs, was a major exception.

The Ismāʿīlīs have had a long and eventful history. In mediaeval times, they twice established states of their own and played important parts for relatively long periods on the historical stage of the Muslim world. During the second century of their history, the Ismāʿīlīs founded the first Shīʿī caliphate under the Fāṭimid caliph-imāms. They also made important contributions to Islamic thought and culture during the Fāṭimid period. Later, after a schism that split Ismāʿīlism into its two major Nizārī and Mustaʿlian branches, the Nizārī leaders succeeded in founding a cohesive state, with numerous mountain strongholds and scattered territories stretching from eastern Persia to Syria. The Nizārī state collapsed only under the onslaught of the all-conquering Mongols. Thereafter, the Ismāʿīlīs never regained any political prominence and survived in many lands as a minor Shīʿī Muslim sect. By the second half of the eighteenth century, however, the spiritual leaders or imāms of the Nizārī majority came out of their obscurity and actively participated in certain political events in Persia and, then, in British India; later they acquired international prominence under their hereditary title of Āghā Khān (Aga Khan).

The Ismāʿīlīs have almost continuously faced the hostility of the majority of Muslim dynasties and groups. Indeed, they have been amongst the most severely persecuted communities in the Islamic world. As a result, the Ismāʿīlīs have been obliged for the most part to live clandestinely, also guarding secretly their religious beliefs and literature.

Under such circumstances, the Ismāʿīlīs were until a few decades ago studied and judged mainly on the basis of the hostile accounts produced by their enemies, including the writings of the majority of the mediaeval Muslim historians, theologians, heresiographers and polemists as well as the fanciful stories related by the occidental chroniclers of the Crusaders. Having had confrontations with the Nizārīs of Syria, the Crusaders were also responsible for making these sectarians, followers of the Old Man of the Mountain, known in Europe as the Assassins; an unfortunate misnomer that is still occasionally applied by some writers to the entire Nizārī branch of Ismāʿīlism. The same anti-Ismāʿīlī sources provided the basis for the studies of the nineteenth-century orientalists on different aspects of the Ismāʿīlī movement.

However, Ismāʿīlī studies have been revolutionized in the present century, especially since the 1930s, mainly by the discovery and study of a large number of Ismāʿīlī manuscripts preserved in India, Central Asia and Yaman. Many of these Ismāʿīlī texts, including the classical treatises of the Fāṭimid period, have been gradually edited and published. The new availability of genuine Ismāʿīlī sources has enabled a small group of specialists, initially led by the late Wladimir Ivanow, to produce important studies in the field. As a result of the modern progress in Ismāʿīlī studies, we have now acquired a much better understanding of the true nature of the Ismāʿīlī movement, necessitating a drastic revision of previously held ideas on the subject.

This study aims to present, in a connected manner, the results of modern scholarship on the history and doctrines of the Ismāʿīlīs. Drawing on a large number of Ismāʿīlī texts and other primary sources, as well as the contributions of the modern authorities, it seeks to cover all the major phases and events in the development of Ismāʿīlism.

The genesis of this book dates back to more than two decades ago when I was a graduate student at the University of California, Berkeley, and began to correspond with Wladimir Ivanow, who was the original inspirer of my interest in Ismāʿīlī studies. The bulk of the manuscript was, however, written in Tehran between 1979 and 1987, the turbulent years of the Islamic revolution in Iran. Subsequently, some sections were revised and many additions were made to the notes and references. In conducting my research, I utilized, over the years, the collections of several private and public libraries in Tehran, Paris, London and elsewhere. I am particularly indebted to the Institute of Ismaili Studies, London, for placing at my disposal their Ismāʿīlī manuscripts.

Professor Wilferd Madelung of the University of Oxford read the entire typescript of the book and made many valuable suggestions for its improvement, also saving me from several errors and inaccuracies; I owe him a very special debt of gratitude.

A number of friends accompanied me on field trips to Alamūt, Lamasar, Girdkūh, Anjudān, Dizbād, and other Ismāʿīlī sites in Iran, or in different ways contributed to the completion of this book; I am grateful to all of them. I am particularly indebted to Mithra Razmjoo for her literary judgement and keen editing; to Mohammad R. Moghtader for preparing an earlier draft of the map; to Azizeh Azodi for letting me benefit from her profound knowledge of the German and Russian languages; and to Susan van de Ven for carefully preparing the final typescript for the Press. Iradj Bagherzade, extremely busy with his own publishing schedule in London, always found time to advise me on publishing matters; I should like to express my warm thanks to him. And I am deeply thankful to Farideh Agha Khan, who has been a constant source of inspiration and assistance over the years.

Finally, there is Fereshteh who not only encouraged the writing of this book and then bore with me while I was writing it, but who also photographed many Ismāʿīlī sites for me, at times with great risk to her safety, and typed the various drafts of the book. I can never thank her adequately; this book is dedicated to her as a token of my deep sense of appreciation.

NOTE ON THE TEXT

The system of transliteration used in this book for the Arabic script is essentially that of the new edition of the *Encyclopaedia of Islam*, with two modifications, namely, *j* for *dj*, and *q* for *ḳ*. To maintain consistency, the same system is utilized for transliterating Persian names and terms, except that *č* is replaced by *ch*, and sometimes *v* is used for *w*. Furthermore, an attempt has been made to reproduce the more elaborate vowel system of Turkish and Mongol names, thus Hülegü and not Hūlāgū. Common geographical names and certain Islamic terms which have acquired standard usage in the English language have not been transliterated.

The lunar years of the Islamic calendar are generally followed throughout the text and the endnotes (with the exception of chapter 1) by the corresponding Gregorian solar years (e.g., 6th/12th century). The years of the Islamic era, initiated by the emigration (*hijra*) of the Prophet Muḥammad from Mecca to Medina in July 622, commonly abbreviated in the Latin form A.H. (= *Anno Hegirae*), have been converted to the corresponding dates of the Christian era, abbreviated as A.D. (= *Anno Domini*), on the basis of the conversion tables given in Greville S. P. Freeman-Grenville, *The Muslim and Christian Calendars* (London, 1963). In Iran (Persia), a solar Islamic calendar was officially adopted in the 1920s. The Islamic dates of the sources published in modern Iran are, therefore, solar, coinciding with the corresponding Christian years starting on 21 March.

A few standardized abbreviations have been used in this book, notably, b. for *ibn*, and less frequently for born; ca. for *circa*, indicating an approximate date; d. for died; ed. for editor or edition; fl. for flourished, and tr. or trans. for translator or translation. The list of the abbreviations used for certain frequently cited periodicals and other sources appears at the head of the endnotes to the text of the book.

1

Introduction: Western progress in Ismāʿīlī studies

The Ismāʿīlīs, or al-Ismāʿīliyya, constitute a major sect of Shīʿī Islam. The origins of Islam's two main divisions, namely Sunnism and Shīʿism, date back to the crisis of succession to the Prophet Muḥammad. The varying viewpoints of the then nascent Islamic community on the important question of succession in effect became crystallized into two different interpretations of the same Islamic message. The Muslim majority developed and supported what eventually became characterized as the Sunnī perspective of Islam, while a minority partisan group worked out the Shīʿī interpretation that had its own distinctive doctrinal features. In time the Shīʿīs themselves, upholding particular conceptions of leadership and religious authority in the community, were further subdivided into a number of sects; not only because they disagreed on who was to be their rightful imām or leader from amongst the members of the Prophet's family, but also because divergent trends of thought and policy were involved. The Ismāʿīlīs, or more correctly the proto-Ismāʿīlīs, were one such Shīʿī sect, coming into existence in the middle of the 2nd/8th century. From its earliest beginnings, the Ismāʿīlī movement, which derived its name retrospectively from Ismāʿīl, the son of the Shīʿī Imām Jaʿfar al-Ṣādiq (d. 148/765), represented the most important revolutionary wing of Shīʿism. As such, the Ismāʿīlīs had separated from the moderate Shīʿīs whose central body eventually became known as the Twelvers or the Ithnāʿashariyya.

The first century of Ismāʿīlī history remains rather obscure. But starting in the second half of the 3rd/9th century, following the emergence of Ismāʿīlism as a centrally organized and dynamic movement, the Ismāʿīlīs rapidly acquired a prominence far exceeding that of any other Shīʿī movement of mediaeval times. For several centuries thereafter, the Ismāʿīlīs played an important part in the historical events of the Muslim world, also making noteworthy contributions to Islamic thought and culture.

By the opening decades of the 4th/10th century, the Ismāʿīlī movement had already succeeded in establishing a powerful state, the Fāṭimid Caliphate, which for almost two centuries challenged the position of numerous dynasties in the Islamic world. During this 'golden age' of Ismāʿīlism, when the Ismāʿīlī religious propaganda activity or mission (*daʿwa*) with its secret hierarchical organization was successfully spreading from North Africa to Sind, Ismāʿīlī thought and literature attained their fullest developments. The celebrated Ismāʿīlī authors and missionaries (singular, *dāʿī*) of this period produced numerous theological and theosophical treatises, which also represented important efforts towards synthesizing various Islamic and Hellenistic trends of thought. In particular, the Ismāʿīlī cosmology of the Fāṭimid period came to contain elements adapted from Neoplatonism. Indeed, from the earliest times in their history, the Ismāʿīlīs, with their distinctive esotericism and allegorical exegesis, concentrated on offering a comprehensive view of the universe, as well as a cyclical interpretation of religious history. These endeavours found their full expression during the Fāṭimid period, in an elaborate gnostic system, the so-called *ḥaqāʾiq*, embodying the unchangeable truths of religion. Simultaneously, Cairo, the capital city founded by the Fāṭimids, was developed into a renowned centre of intellectual activity in the Muslim world.

Subsequently, at the end of the 5th/11th century, when the Fāṭimid state had already begun to disintegrate, Ismāʿīlism witnessed its greatest internal conflict, as a result of which the movement was split into its two major branches, the Nizāriyya and the Mustaʿlawiyya. The Mustaʿlians or the Western Ismāʿīlīs continued the traditions of Fāṭimid Ismāʿīlism, never acquiring any particular political prominence. But the Nizārīs or the Eastern Ismāʿīlīs, who were to become known as the Assassins to the mediaeval Europeans, under the capable leadership of Ḥasan-i Ṣabbāḥ (d. 518/1124), founded a vigorous state in Persia. This territorially scattered state, with its seat at the mountainous fortress of Alamūt, posed a serious challenge to the powerful and ardently Sunnī Saljūqid empire. At the same time, an affiliated Nizārī state in Syria confronted the Christian Crusaders. The Nizārī state in Persia, which had played a perceptible role in the cultural life of the time, collapsed in the middle of the 7th/13th century, only under the assault of the all-conquering Mongols; shortly afterwards, the Syrian Nizārīs were finally subdued by the Mamlūk Turks.

Following the collapse of the Fāṭimid and the Nizārī states, Ismāʿīlism never regained its earlier prominence, and the Ismāʿīlīs took refuge in the remotest corners of the Muslim world, especially in Yaman and in the Indian subcontinent. At present, the Ismāʿīlīs, the second largest Shīʿī group after the Twelvers, are to be found mainly in India, Pakistan, and East Africa where Indian Ismāʿīlīs settled in the nineteenth century; smaller numbers of Ismāʿīlīs live in Yaman, Syria, Persia (Iran), Afghanistan, the Soviet Central Asia and the Chinese Pāmīr. Since the 1970s, an increasing number of Ismāʿīlīs have also immigrated to several countries in the West, notably Canada, the United States and the United Kingdom. Today's Nizārī Ismāʿīlīs, including those better known in India as the Khojas, mostly recognize H.H. Karīm Āghā Khān IV as their 49th imām; while the Mustaʿlian Ismāʿīlīs, represented in India by the Bohras, continue to await the reappearance of their hidden imām.

Students of Ismāʿīlism are well acquainted with the numerous dark periods and obscure issues regarding the origin, history and doctrines of the Ismāʿīlī movement. Some of the research problems in this complex field of study stem from the very nature of the Ismāʿīlī movement, while others have been due to the fact that at least until recent times, study of the Ismāʿīlīs was limited mainly to anti-Ismāʿīlī sources. The Ismāʿīlīs have been almost continuously treated as heretics by the Sunnī and most Shīʿī Muslims. As a result, they have been among the most ruthlessly persecuted minorities of the Muslim world, being frequently subjected to massacre. In such hostile surroundings, the Ismāʿīlīs have been obliged from the earliest times in their history, to adhere rather strictly to the Shīʿī principle of *taqiyya*, the precautionary dissimulation of one's true belief in the face of danger. Consequently, the Ismāʿīlī movement, in particular its important religious hierarchy and propaganda organization, evolved under utmost secrecy. The Ismāʿīlīs were, in effect, coerced into what may be termed an underground existence; understandably, they categorically refused to disclose their sectarian beliefs to the uninitiated. It should be noted, then, that the adverse circumstances under which Ismāʿīlism has evolved, together with the esoteric nature of Ismāʿīlī teachings, have not permitted the production of any substantial volume of sectarian literature. The so-called 'classical' Fāṭimid period is the major exception. Nevertheless, as shall be seen, the breakthrough of modern scholarship in Ismāʿīlī studies came to be based on the discovery and study of this meagre literary heritage.

Other distinguishing features of Ismāʿīlism, too, have contributed to research difficulties of this field. The forced underground survival of the Ismāʿīlī movement has been sustained mainly in the form of a fairly large number of local communities dispersed over a wide region. Thus, pronounced socio-economic as well as linguistic and ethnological differences have combined to further separate the Ismāʿīlī communities from one another. There have also been interruptions in the history of many an Ismāʿīlī community, with some communities like that of the Druzes even drifting away from the movement. Moreover, in the course of its long history, stretching over some twelve centuries, Ismāʿīlism has undergone several major and minor schisms, with all that these developments imply in terms of causing still greater differentiations in the Ismāʿīlī tenets. In sum, the Ismāʿīlī communities have not evolved in any uniform manner or with strict historical continuity; and numerous factors have been at work to prevent the consolidation of Ismāʿīlī doctrines into what might readily be regarded as the orthodox or representative form during any extended period of time. Considerations of temporal and locational factors and peculiarities are, indeed, of utmost importance in any specific investigation of Ismāʿīlism.

It was under such circumstances that the Ismāʿīlīs were, until about the 1920s, studied and judged almost entirely in the light of evidence collected, or often fabricated, by their adversaries. It is therefore not surprising that the orientalists of the nineteenth century, in line with the Crusaders and the majority of Muslim theologians, historians, and heresiographers of the mediaeval times, painted such a distorted picture of the Ismāʿīlīs. In particular, the Nizārī Ismāʿīlīs of Persia and Syria had come to be viewed as a scheming secret band of depraved assassins, and numerous hostile and legendary accounts were fabricated in an aura of mystery and misconception to explain the various facets of their existence. This distorted image of the Ismāʿīlīs has, however, now undergone drastic revision, as modern scholarship has shed light on the true nature of their movement.

The investigation of progress made in the study of Ismāʿīlism is an interesting subject in its own right. Here, it will suffice to review the main highlights of Western scholarship in this field, attained prior to the recent breakthroughs. This review is indispensable for any meaningful appreciation of the achievements of modern scholarship in Ismāʿīlī studies. Indeed, it is due to these very achievements that it has at last become possible to convey an overall view of the evolution of Ismāʿīlism.

Westerners first became aware of the existence of the Ismāʿīlīs in the opening decades of the twelfth century, when the Christian Crusaders, setting out to liberate the Holy Land from the domination of the Muslims, or the so-called Saracen infidels, came into contact with the Nizārī branch of the sect. But it was not until the second half of that century that occidental travellers and chroniclers of the Crusades began to collect information and write about these strange sectarians, the followers of a mysterious 'Old Man of the Mountain', or, '*le Vieux de la Montagne*'.[1] These Ismāʿīlīs, first encountered in the Levant, were to become designated in different European languages by the variant forms of the word *Assassin*.

Benjamin of Tudela, the Spanish rabbi and traveller who was in Syria in 1167, is one of the very first Europeans to have written about the Ismāʿīlīs.[2] He noted that in Syria there existed a people strongly devoted to their chief or elder, whom they also regarded as their prophet. These people, whom he called the *Hashishin*, had their principal seat at Kadmus and were dreaded by their neighbours, he added, because they would kill even kings at the expense of their own lives. Benjamin also referred, again for the first time, to the Persian Ismāʿīlīs who, according to him, lived in the mountainous district of *Mulhet*;[3] obviously a corruption of the Arabic *mulḥid* (plural, *malāḥida*), a Muslim term of abuse for a religious deviant or heretic and the most common anti-Ismāʿīlī epithet. It is interesting to note, however, that though recognizing the existence of some connection between the Syrian and Persian branches of the sect, Benjamin failed to realize that the people he was describing were actually Muslims.

Another early description of the sect is contained in a diplomatic report dated 1175, of an envoy sent to Egypt and Syria by the Holy Roman emperor Frederick I Barbarossa.[4] The envoy, a certain Burchard or Gerhard, reports that 'on the confines of Damascus, Antioch and Aleppo there is a certain race of Saracens in the mountains, who in their own vernacular are called *Heyssessini* and in Roman *segnors de montana*. This race of men live without laws... They dwell in the mountains and are quasi impregnable, because of their fortified castles... They have among them, a lord who inspires the greatest fear in the Saracen princes near and far, and also in the neighbouring Christians, because he is accustomed to killing them in a strange manner.' The report then goes on to explain how the chief of the sect trained the many sons of his peasants, raised from childhood in his mountain palaces, in strict obedience to his commands for the exclusive purpose of carrying out these killing missions.

William, archbishop of Tyre, the famous historian who spent the greater part of his life in the Latin East and died in Rome in or about 1186, is the first occidental chronicler of the Crusades to have described the Ismāʿīlīs. He included a general account of the sect in his history of Palestine, which also covers the Crusader events from their very inception in 1095 to 1184. He states that these sectarians, living in the diocese of Tortosa, numbered some 60,000 and possessed ten castles with their surrounding villages. Emphasizing the high degree of obedience of these people towards their non-hereditarily selected chief, William of Tyre further notes that both the Christians and Muslims called these sectarians *Assissini*, the origin of which name admittedly remained unknown to him.[5]

In 1192, Conrad of Montferrat, the titular king of the Latin kingdom of Jerusalem, fell victim in Tyre to the daggers of two Christian monks who were allegedly Nizārī emissaries in disguise, sent by the Old Man. This event, occurring just before the death of Rāshid al-Dīn Sinān himself, the original Old Man of the Mountain who ruled the Syrian Nizārīs for some thirty years, greatly impressed the Frankish circles. It came to be discussed, usually with some explanatory notes on the sect, by most of the occidental historians of the Third Crusade (1189–1192).[6] The narrative of the German chronicler Arnold of Lübeck (d. 1212) is of particular interest because it also seems to be the earliest Western source referring to an intoxicating potion administered by the Old Man to the would-be killers from amongst the Syrian sectarians; Arnold adds that these Saracens are called *Heissessin* in their own language.[7] Soon afterwards in 1194, a meeting reportedly took place between count Henry of Champagne (d. 1197), the effective ruler of the kingdom of Jerusalem after Conrad, and the Old Man who had just succeeded Sinān in the latter's castle at Kahf. The most impressive story, first related by the continuators of William of Tyre and repeated by many later European writers, such as the Venetian historian Marino Sanudo Torsello and the Dominican friar Francesco Pipino of Bologna, of how the Ismāʿīlīs would leap to their deaths from high towers in a show of loyalty to their chief, dates back to this meeting.[8]

Gradually, the Crusaders and their chroniclers acquired more information about the Ismāʿīlīs. Official contacts increased between the Franks and the sectarians, including those arising from the payment of tributes by the Syrian Ismāʿīlīs to the Templars and the Hospitallers. However, Western historians of the first half of the thirteenth century added few new details to the knowledge of the sect then held by the Europeans. James of Vitry (d. 1240), who became bishop of Acre in 1217 and also participated in the Fifth

Crusade (1217–1221), while discussing the Syrian Ismāʿīlīs and putting their number at 40,000, merely noted that the sect had originated in Persia.[9] Thus, in contrast to Benjamin of Tudela, James had now correctly recognized the dependency of the Syrian Ismāʿīlīs on the Persian branch of the sect. But he committed an error of his own by contending that the Ismāʿīlīs descended from the Jews. The same point was repeated by Thietmar, a German traveller who visited the Holy Land in the first quarter of that century.[10] Shortly thereafter, Matthew Paris (d. 1259), the English monk and historian who is noted for his knowledge of European events between 1235 and 1259, made several references to the Ismāʿīlīs. Of particular importance is his account of the arrival in Europe in 1238 of a mission sent by the Old Man of the Mountain to ask assistance of Louis IX and Henry III, the kings of France and England, against the imminent threat of the Tartars, as the Mongols were to be called for a long time to come.[11]

By the middle of the thirteenth century, however, more direct information began to appear about the Ismāʿīlīs of both Syria and Persia, mainly as a result of the activities and the diplomatic designs of Louis IX, better known as Saint Louis (d. 1270). St Louis, the same king who had been approached earlier in Europe by an Ismāʿīlī mission, now led the Seventh Crusade (1249–1250) to the Holy Land. But after his early defeat in Egypt, he went to Acre and remained in Palestine for almost four years (May 1250–April 1254). It was during this period that the French king exchanged embassies with the Old Man of the Mountain and established friendly relations with the Ismāʿīlīs. We have an invaluable account of his dealings with the Syrian Nizārīs from the vivid pen of the French chronicler Jean de Joinville (d. 1317), who accompanied the king on his Crusade and became his intimate companion in the Holy Land.[12]

Joinville, who interestingly enough refers to the Nizārī Ismāʿīlīs as both the *Assacis* and the Bedouins,[13] relates that 'during the king's residence at Acre, there came likewise to him ambassadors from the prince of the Bedouins, called the Old Man of the Mountain', demanding of him gifts, 'in like manner as the emperor of Germany, the king of Hungary, the sultan of Babylon, and many other princes, have yearly done; for they know, that they would not be allowed to exist or reign, but during his good pleasure'. The ambassadors made it known, however, that their chief (*seigneur*) would be equally satisfied if the king were to 'acquit him of the tribute he pays annually to the grand master of the Temple, or the Hospital'. On the intervention of the said grand masters, the Nizārī emissaries failed to win the king's approval for either of their requests, notwithstanding a second meeting which took place a fortnight later. St Louis, in his search for new alliances, encouraged these contacts and reciprocated by sending his own envoys, accompanied by an Arabic-speaking friar, Yves le Breton, to the Nizārī chief. During their meetings, which probably took place in 1250 and at the main Nizārī stronghold of Maṣyāf in central Syria, Yves conversed with the sectarian chief on 'the articles of his faith'. According to Joinville, Yves later reported to the king some details on the religious beliefs of the Nizārīs, as he had understood them. The Old Man, he said, 'did not believe in Mahomet, but followed the religion of Aly'. They also maintained, Yves related, that 'when any one is killed by the command or in the service of his superior, the soul of the person so killed goes into another body of higher rank, and enjoys more comforts than before'. Yves cited this belief in metempsychosis as the main reason why the Nizārīs were eager to be killed in the service of their chief. Joinville himself collected some information about the Ismāʿīlīs, and notes that 'their numbers are not to be counted; for they dwell in the kingdoms of Jerusalem, Egypt, and throughout all the lands of the Saracens and infidels'.[14]

The main diplomatic ambition of king Louis IX of France, however, was to secure an alliance with the Mongols against the Muslims. In pursuit of this objective and encouraged by the news of the Mongols' tendencies towards Nestorian Christianity, the king entrusted William of Rubruck (Rubruquis), a Franciscan friar at his court, with an informal mission to the Great Khan in Mongolia. We have several references to the Persian Ismāʿīlīs in William's account of his journey, which he embarked upon in 1253.[15] He took the northern route to Mongolia, and passed north of the Caspian Sea which, he notes, 'has the Caspian mountains and Persia to the south, the Mulihec mountains, that is the mountains of the Axasins to the east'. The word *Mulihec*, which he also writes as *Mulidet* and which in some versions appears as *Muliech* or *Musihet*, is obviously a corruption for the Arabic *mulḥid* or *malāḥida*. By placing the sectarians to the east of the Caspian, William might actually have been referring to the Nizārīs of Girdkūh, in the district of Qūmis, or some other strongholds in eastern Persia. He also seems to have been amongst the first Europeans to have designated the Persian Ismāʿīlīs by names such as *Axasins* and *Hacsasins*, hitherto used only in connection with the Syrian Ismāʿīlīs. Doubtless, William had heard these terms from the Crusaders and was himself aware of the ties between the Syrian and the Persian Nizārīs.

William of Rubruck passed the first half of 1254 at the court of the Great Khan Möngke (d. 1259), in and near his capital at Karakorum. There, he noticed strict security measures against foreigners, because 'it had been reported to Mangu Chan that forty Hacsasins had entered the city under various guises to kill him'. This, as William learned, might have been in reprisal for the fact that the Great Khan had already sent one of his brothers 'to the country of the Hacsasins, whom they call Mulidet, and he ordered him to put them all to death'. The brother in question, it will be recalled, was Hülegü, who had left Mongolia in 1253 at the head of a major expedition. While Hülegü was proceeding westward at a leisurely pace, William himself had started on his homeward journey in 1254 and on reaching Acre in August 1255 learned that St Louis had returned to France the previous year.

Hülegü finally crossed the Oxus in January 1256, and in the course of that year managed to destroy the Nizārī state in Persia. The efforts of the Mongols to conquer Syria in 1260, however, proved abortive, in spite of initial victories in Aleppo and Damascus. After the collapse of the Nizārī state in Persia, the Syrian Nizārīs at first maintained their independence and joined other Muslims to repel the Mongol invaders from Syria. But the Nizārī fortresses in Syria survived the Mongols only to be taken by the Mamlūks of Egypt. In 1270, Baybars I (1260–1277), the strong Mamlūk sultan who withstood the Mongols and inflicted decisive defeats on the Crusaders, conducted negotiations with the Old Man of the Mountain, forcing him to pay tribute. By 1273, he had seized all the fortresses of the Syrian Nizārīs. Henceforth, the Syrian Nizārīs became the obedient subjects (though as an autonomous community) of the Mamlūks, and later, after 1517, of the Ottoman Turks.

Meanwhile, the most celebrated of all the mediaeval European travellers, the Venetian Marco Polo (1254–1324), had embarked on his famous journey to China. According to his travel accounts, the youthful Marco accompanied his father and uncle in their second journey to the court of Qubilai (1260–1294), Möngke's brother and successor. The Polos started from Acre in 1271, and on their way passed through Persia in 1272, about fifteen years after the collapse of the Nizārī state there. Marco Polo, who committed his itinerary to writing through a scribe in 1298, after having spent some seventeen years in China and finally returning to Venice in 1295, relates what he had heard in Persia from several natives of that country concerning the Old Man of the Mountain and the Persian Ismāʿīlīs,[16] whom he calls the *Mulehet*, *Mulcete*, etc.[17]

The Old Man was called in their language ALOADIN. He had caused a certain valley between two mountains to be enclosed, and had turned it into a garden, the largest and most beautiful that ever was seen, filled with every variety of fruit. In it were erected pavilions and palaces the most elegant that can be imagined, all covered with gilding and exquisite painting. And there were runnels too, flowing freely with wine and milk and honey and water; and numbers of ladies and of the most beautiful damsels in the world, who could play on all manner of instruments, and sung most sweetly, and danced in a manner that it was charming to behold. For the Old Man desired to make his people believe that this was actually Paradise. So he had fashioned it after the description that Mahommet gave of his Paradise, to wit, that it should be a beautiful garden running with conduits of wine and milk and honey and water, and full of lovely women for the delectation of all its inmates. And sure enough the Saracens of those parts believed that it *was* Paradise!

Now no man was allowed to enter the Garden save those whom he intended to be his ASHISHIN. There was a Fortress at the entrance to the Garden, strong enough to resist all the world, and there was no other way to get in. He kept at his Court a number of the youths of the country, from 12 to 20 years of age, such as had a taste for soldiering, and to these he used to tell tales about Paradise, just as Mahommet had been wont to do, and they believed in him just as the Saracens believe in Mahommet. Then he would introduce them into his garden, some four, or six, or ten at a time, having first made them drink a certain potion which cast them into a deep sleep, and then causing them to be lifted and carried in. So when they awoke, they found themselves in the Garden.

It is then related, in respect to the training of these Assassins or *Ashishin*, which is the English rendering of *Asciscin* adopted by Sir Henry Yule (1820–1889),[18] the learned translator and commentator of Marco Polo, that

Now this Prince whom we call the Old One kept his Court in grand and noble style, and made those simple hill-folks about him believe firmly that he was a great Prophet. And when he wanted one of his *Ashishin* to send on any mission, he would cause that potion whereof I spoke to be given to one of the youths in the garden, and then had him carried into his Palace. So when the young man awoke, he found himself in the Castle, and no longer in that Paradise; whereat he was not over well pleased. He was then conducted to the Old Man's presence, and bowed before him with great veneration as believing himself to be in the presence of a true Prophet. The Prince would then ask whence he came, and he would reply that he came from Paradise! and that it was exactly such as Mahommet had described it in the Law. This of course gave the others who stood by, and who had not been admitted, the greatest desire to enter therein.

So when the Old Man would have any Prince slain, he would say to such a youth: 'Go thou and slay So and So; and when thou returnest my Angels shall bear thee into Paradise. And shouldst thou die, natheless even so will I send my Angels to carry thee back into Paradise.' So he caused them to believe; and thus there was no order of his that they would not affront any peril to execute, for the great desire they had to get back into that Paradise of his. And in this manner the Old One got his people to murder any one whom he desired to get rid of. Thus, too, the great dread that he inspired all Princes withal, made them become his tributaries in order that he might abide at peace and amity with them.

At the end of his narrative, Marco Polo states that the Old Man had had his deputies in the territories of Damascus and Curdistan, who copied him exactly in the same manner. And, that the end of the Old Man came when, after being besieged for three years, he and all his men were put to death by the Mongols who also destroyed his castle with its garden of paradise. Several points are noteworthy in connection with Marco Polo's narrative which has been read and often repeated by generations of Westerners during the last 700 years.

Marco Polo's description of the Old Man's castle may appear to refer to one of the Nizārī fortresses in the Alamūt valley.[19] But, as Yule was perhaps the first person to point out, 'there is no reason to suppose that Polo visited Alamūt, which would have been quite out of the road that he is following'.[20] The then eighteen-year-old traveller may actually have heard some details about the locality of Alamūt, as his entire account of the Persian Ismāʿīlīs is admittedly not based on personal observation. It is almost certain, however, that he did visit a ruined Nizārī castle somewhere in Persia,[21] although it has not been possible to identify the site. It is in eastern Persia, around Ṭabas and Tūn in Quhistān, the barren region in the south of Khurāsān, that Marco Polo interrupts his itinerary to discuss the Old Man; a digression probably triggered by seeing a Nizārī fortress.[22] It may, therefore, be inferred that the castle in question was either the mountainous stronghold of Girdkūh near Dāmghān, which had finally surrendered to the Mongols in 1270, about two years before the Polo party crossed Khurāsān into northern Afghanistan; or, more probably, some fortress in eastern Quhistān. It will be recalled that the Nizārī Ismāʿīlīs had previously controlled several main towns in that region where they had also developed an elaborate network of fortresses.

Marco Polo, like William of Rubruck before him, uses various forms of the name *Assassin* in reference to the Persian Ismāʿīlīs.[23] However, he adopts this name only in connection with those sectarians selected for the murderous missions, as distinct from the Ismāʿīlīs in general, whom he designates by the corrupted forms of *mulḥid* and *malāḥida*. In this exclusive sense, the term *Assassin* denotes those sectarians who were called *fidāʾīs*, or *fidāwīs*, by the Nizārī Ismāʿīlīs. Furthermore, Marco Polo is responsible for putting into circulation the most developed version of the tale of the Old Man's garden of paradise in relation to the training of the special Nizārī devotees or *fidāʾī*s who risked their lives to kill the enemies of their sect. Finally, it may be noted that Marco Polo also uses, perhaps in the first instance of its kind, the Syrian title 'Old Man of the Mountain' in reference to the chief of the Persian Ismāʿīlīs whose supremacy over their Syrian co-religionists he had distinctly acknowledged. Needless to add that ʿAlāʾ al-Dīn Muḥammad III (d. 653/1255), Marco Polo's Old Man Aloadin, was only the penultimate ruler of the Nizārī state centred in Persia. The last ruler was his son Rukn al-Dīn who surrendered to the Mongols in 1256 and was killed by them shortly afterwards on Möngke's orders.

As noted, the political prominence of the Nizārīs was finally brought to an end when the last of their strongholds in Syria surrendered to the Mamlūks. The Franks of the Levant met a similar fate at the hands of Baybars I who, by 1277, reduced the dominion of the Crusaders to a small strip of coastland in Syria. Subsequently in 1291, Acre, the last remaining stronghold of Christendom in the Holy Land, was stormed by the Mamlūk troops. These developments also marked the end of relations between the Crusaders and the Syrian Nizārīs. By that time, however, the name *Assassin* in its different forms, and the stories about the sectarians who bore it, had been carried to Europe by the Crusaders and European travellers returning from the Holy Land.[24] Indeed, by the turn of the thirteenth century, Provençal poets already made comparisons between their own romantic devotion and the fanatical loyalty of the Assassins to the Old Man of the Mountain.[25] But it was the murderous method of struggle of the Nizārīs against their enemies, rather than self-sacrificing devotion to their chief, that eventually impressed the Europeans and gave the word *Assassin* a new meaning. By the first half of the fourteenth century, instead of signifying the name of a sect in the Near East, the word had come to mean a professional killer. The earliest European examples of this usage, retained to the present day, apparently occurred in Italy. The great Italian poet Dante (1265–1321), in his *La Divina Commedia*, speaks of the treacherous assassin (*Le perfido assassin*). The Florentine historian Giovanni Villani (d. 1348) relates how the lord of Lucca sent his assassins (*i suoi assassini*) to Pisa to kill an enemy.[26] The occidental observers of the Nizārī Ismāʿīlīs had thus introduced a new common noun to most Western European languages.

When the Crusaders spoke of the Assassins, they originally referred to the Nizārī Ismāʿīlīs of Syria. Later, the term was also commonly applied to the Persian sectarians by European travellers and chroniclers. It should be noted, however, that the Persian Nizārīs had also been called *ḥashīshīs* by some of their contemporary Muslim opponents, notably the Caspian Zaydīs. The title 'Old Man of the Mountain' has a similar history. It was initially used by the Crusaders only in respect to the Syrian leader of the sect. Bernard Lewis, who has investigated these terminological matters more thoroughly than any other modern scholar, has observed that it would not be unnatural for the Ismāʿīlīs to use the common Muslim term of respect *shaykh*, also meaning 'Old Man' or 'Elder', in reference to their leader.[27] However, the Crusaders misunderstood the term *shaykh*, rendering it on the basis of its secondary meaning into Latin as *Vetus*, *Vetulus* or *Senex*, rather than by its more relevant equivalents *Senior* or *Dominus*. In any event, the meaning of this title was also linked with the mountainous fortresses in which the Syrian Nizārī leaders lived. It should be added, however, that the Syrian title 'Old Man of the Mountain' seems to have been used only by the Crusaders and other occidental sources, since thus far it has not come to light in any contemporary Arabic or Persian sources. Consequently, the full Arabic equivalent of this title, *Shaykh al-Jabal*, may represent a later translation from the Latin forms used by the occidental chroniclers of the Crusades;[28] forms such as *Vetus de Montanis*.

Europeans then, continued to maintain an interest in the Ismāʿīlīs. Marco Polo particularly stirred the imagination of his contemporaries, and his garden of paradise story was adopted by several writers in the early fourteenth century. Mention should be made of the romance of Bauduin de Sebourc,[29] and also of friar Pipino, who, having produced a Latin translation of Marco Polo, cannot be excused for thinking that the Mongols destroyed the Syrian Nizārīs as well. There is also Jacopo d'Acqui, a Dominican friar who confusingly mixes Marco Polo's narrative with a number of unrelated events about the Tartars.[30] Of greater fame, however, is the account of the traveller Odoric of Pordenone (d. 1331), the Franciscan missionary from northern Italy who visited China during 1323–1327. On his return, Odoric apparently passed, around 1328, through northern Persia along the coast of the Caspian Sea where he visited a certain country called *Melistorte* or *Millistorte* (probably corruptions of *malāḥida*).[31] In his account,[32] which may refer to the Alamūt valley, Odoric repeats Marco Polo's narrative almost in its entirety.

And in this country there was a certain aged man called Senex de monte, who round about two mountains had built a wall to enclose the said mountains. Within this wall there were the fairest and most crystal fountains in the whole world: and about the said fountains there were most beautiful virgins in great number, and goodly horses also, and in a word, everything that could be devised for bodily solace and delight, and therefore the inhabitants of the country call the same place by the name of Paradise. The said old Senex, when he saw any proper and valiant young man, he would admit him into his paradise. Moreover by certain conduits he makes wine and milk to flow abundantly. This Senex, when he hath a mind to revenge himself or to slay any king or baron... And therefore all the kings of the East stood in awe of the said old man, and gave unto him great tribute.

A few years later in 1332, a treatise was submitted to King Philip VI of France who was then preparing for a new military expedition into the Holy Land. This work, which meant to serve as a guidebook, offered the French king detailed recommendations based on the prolonged stay of its author in Armenia and other parts of the Near East. The author, variously said to have been a certain Brocardus, the French Dominican Raymond Étienne, or perhaps William Adam (Guillelmus Adae), the second archbishop of Sulṭāniyya in northwestern Persia during 1322–1324, includes the Assassins amongst the dangerous peoples of the region. Admittedly, the author had had no direct contacts with these sectarians who would kill the innocent for a price, nor does he place them in any specific locality. After being told of their innumerable crimes, however, the king was cautioned to protect himself against them by requiring ample security clearances from the staff of his royal household.[33] These advices, however, had no chance of implementation since the planned Crusade never took place.

By the sixteenth century, when the centres of the Ismāʿīlī movement had moved farther away to Yaman and India, the greatly reduced number of Nizārīs of the Near East were now either living in secrecy, as in Persia, or had become obedient subjects of the Ottoman empire. As a result, European documentation of the Ismāʿīlīs during the Renaissance, became few and far in between. They were now referred to mainly by an occasional missionary or traveller to the Holy Land. But, Western scholarship continued to be based on the earlier impressions of the Crusaders. For instance, the Dominican friar Felix Fabri, who visited the Holy Land twice between 1480 and 1484, mentions the Assassins amongst the peoples of the region,[34] and fancifully repeats that

their captain causes their young men to be taught diverse languages, and sends them out into other kingdoms to serve the kings thereof; to the end that, when the time requires it, each king's servant may kill him by poison or otherwise. If after slaying a king the servant makes good his escape to his own land, he is rewarded with honors, riches and dignities; if he is taken and put to death, he is worshipped in his own country as a martyr.[35]

Soon, first-hand accounts came to be supplemented by more scholarly investigations. The first Western monograph devoted entirely to the subject of the Ismāʿīlīs seems to be that of Denis Lebey de Batilly, a French official at the court of Henry IV.[36] The author had become deeply concerned about the revival of political murders in Europe, after the 1589 stabbing of Henry III of France at the hands of a Jacobin friar, whom he refers to as '*un religieux assasin-porte-couteau*'. Apprehensive about the existence of would-be assassins in the religious orders of Christendom, he set out in 1595, to compose a short treatise on the true origin of the word *assasin*, which had acquired new currency in France, and the history of the Muslim sect to which it originally belonged, calling these sectarians '*les premiers et anciens assasins d'entre les Sarrasins et Mahometans*'. This work, however, was based almost exclusively on the occidental chronicles, the accounts of which were combined in a confusing manner with Marco Polo's narrative, and it did not add any new detail to what had been known on the subject in Europe some three centuries earlier.

The next important publication appeared in 1659, when Henricus Bengertus produced his edition of the *Chronicle* of Arnold of Lübeck. In his explanatory notes, the learned German editor briefly discusses the sect and enumerates the name of almost every Latin author who, to his knowledge, had mentioned the Assassins.[37] However, Bengertus, too, thought that it was the Mongols who destroyed the power of the Syrian Nizārīs. For some time, this error was repeated by many scholars, including the prodigious Johann Philipp Baratier (1721–1740). But in his French translation of Benjamin of Tudela's itinerary, he rectified that traveller's wrong notion of making the Persian Nizārīs subservient to the chief of the Syrian sectarians.[38] It should be added that, by the seventeenth century, the etymology of the word *Assassin* had long been forgotten in Europe. Consequently, an increasing number of philologists and lexicographers now started to collect the variants of this term used in occidental sources, such as *Accini*, *Arsasini*, *Assassi*, *Assassini*, *Assessini*, *Assissini*, *Hesesin*, *Heyssessini*, etc., as well as the form *Hashishin* mentioned only by Benjamin of Tudela. Many additional etymologies were also proposed. Charles du Fresne du Cange (1610–1668), who discussed *Assassini* in his glossary of mediaeval Latin[39] first published in 1678, is one of the most famous pioneers in this respect; he was joined by several contemporaries, such as Gilles Ménages (1613–1692), and a host of later scholars who included similar entries in their etymological dictionaries.

The first important advance in the study of the Ismāʿīlīs appeared in 1697, with the posthumous publication of the encyclopaedic work of

Barthélemy d'Herbelot (1625–1695).[40] This pioneer work of Western orientalism, which covered all fields of the Muslim East, was to remain the standard reference work in Europe until the early nineteenth century. The noted French orientalist d'Herbelot, who never visited the orient, had read and utilized in his encyclopaedia a variety of Arabic, Persian and Turkish sources. As a result, he now offered details on the history and religion of Islam hitherto unknown to Europeans. He was also able to identify the Ismāʿīlīs more correctly, studying them within the broader context of Islam. In a number of entries, such as 'Bathania', 'Carmath', 'Fathemiah', 'Ismaelioun', 'Molahedoun', and 'Schiah', d'Herbelot showed clearly that the Ismāʿīlīs were in fact one of the main sects of Shīʿī Islam, and that they themselves had been further subdivided into two main groups: the Ismāʿīlīs of Africa and Egypt (Fatémites) and those of Asia (also called Melahedah Kouhestan). The latter group, he noted, had its seat at Alamūt and was founded by Ḥasan-i Ṣabbāḥ who was succeeded by seven more princes.

During the eighteenth century, European scholarship made little further progress in the field beyond what d'Herbelot had presented. Thomas Hyde of Oxford, whilst discussing his own etymology of *Assassini*, assured his readers that the Mount Lebanon used to be inhabited by many sectarians coming from the region of Kurdistān, and that the so-called *Assassins* were in fact of Kurdish origin.[41] Joseph Simonius Assemani (1687–1768), belonging to the famous Syrian Maronite family of orientalists and a custodian of the Vatican Library, made brief references to the Assassins and suggested his own peculiar etymology.[42] There were other incidental references to the sectarians by the European missionaries, travellers and historians of that century.[43] A more detailed account was produced by Pierre Alexandre de la Ravalière (1697–1762), a French bishop who, however, concerned himself exclusively with the murder of Conrad of Montferrat and the two unsuccessful assassination plots alleged to have been planned by the Syrian Nizārīs against kings Philip II Augustus and St Louis of France.[44] The Druzes, an offshoot of the Ismāʿīlīs, were now also investigated for the first time.[45] But the most important contribution of the eighteenth century was contained in two memoirs read in 1743 by a French non-orientalist, Camille Falconet (1671–1762), to the Académie Royale des Inscriptions et Belles Lettres. In these memoirs, published in 1751 in the previously cited article, Falconet, after reviewing the works of his Western predecessors, presented a summary account of the history and religion of the Persian and Syrian Nizārīs with references to the origins of the Ismāʿīlīs and yet another etymology of the name *Assassin*. Knowing no oriental languages, Falconet relied mainly on d'Herbelot and on translations of some Eastern sources.

By the early years of the nineteenth century, the Ismāʿīlīs were still being investigated almost strictly from the limited and biased viewpoint of the Crusaders, mainly because Eastern sources had not yet started to be utilized on any meaningful scale in Europe. Joseph's grandnephew abbot Simone Assemani (1752–1821), who had spent the earlier part of his life in Tripoli where he had heard about the contemporary Syrian Ismāʿīlīs, and who later became a professor of oriental languages at a seminary in Padua, published in 1806 a hostile article on the sect.[46] He also proposed an etymology for *Assissana*, which he believed to be the original name of the Nizārī sectarians. According to him, the word *Assassini*, a corruption of *Assissani*, was connected with the Arabic word *assissath* (*al-ṣīṣa*), meaning rock or fortress; thus, *Assissani* (*al-ṣīṣānī*) referred to someone who dwelt in a rock fortress. Assemani also favoured an earlier etymological explanation which connected the word *Assassini*, a corruption of *Hassassini*, to the name of the sect's founder, Ḥasan. This was followed first by another so-called historical memoir on the Assassins, a confused account which again traced the Nizārīs as descendants of the Kurds,[47] and then by what was to be the last unsuccessful attempt at proposing an explanation for the name *Assassin*.[48]

Meanwhile, scientific orientalism had begun in France with the establishment in 1795 of the École des Langues Orientales Vivantes in Paris. Baron Antoine Isaac Silvestre de Sacy (1758–1838), the most distinguished orientalist of his time, became the first professor of Arabic in the newly founded School of Oriental Languages and was appointed in 1806 to the new chair of Persian at the Collège de France; later, he became the director of both these institutions as well as the president and permanent secretary of the Académie des Inscriptions. With an ever-increasing number of students and a wide circle of correspondents and disciples, de Sacy also acquired the distinction of being the teacher of the most prominent orientalists of the first half of the nineteenth century.[49] At the same time, oriental studies had received an important boost from the Napoleonic expedition of 1798–1799 to Egypt and Syria. In the aftermath of these developments there were significant increases in the number of orientalists, particularly in France and Germany, and oriental chairs in European universities. This enhanced interest in orientalism found expression also in the publication of specialized periodicals, beginning in

1809 with the *Fundgruben des Orients*, and also in the foundation of learned societies. The Société Asiatique was formed in 1822 with de Sacy as its first president, and was followed by other societies which played important roles in facilitating the research activities of the orientalists.

It was Silvestre de Sacy, who maintained a life-long interest in the religion of the Druzes,[50] who finally solved the mystery of the name *Assassin*. Utilizing the collection of Arabic manuscripts at the Bibliothèque Nationale in Paris, de Sacy prepared an important memoir which he read before the Institut de France in May 1809.[51] In this memoir, he examined and rejected previous explanations and showed, once and for all, that the word *Assassin* was connected with the Arabic word *ḥashīsh*; referring to the Indian hemp, a narcotic product of *cannabis sativa*. More specifically, he suggested that the main variant forms (such as *Assissini* and *Assassini*) occurring in base-Latin documents of the Crusaders and in different European languages were derived from two alternative Arabic forms, *ḥashīshī* (plural, *ḥashīshiyya* or *ḥashīshiyyīn*) and *ḥashshāsh* (plural, *ḥashshāshīn*). While de Sacy was able to cite Arabic texts, notably by the Syrian chronicler Abū Shāma (599–665/1203–1267), in which the sectarians are called *ḥashīshī*, he was unable to do the same for the second Arabic form of his suggested etymology. Nor have any texts come to light since then, employing the form *ḥashshāsh*, the common epithet for a *ḥashīsh*-consumer. Therefore, as Lewis has argued, this part of de Sacy's theory, with all that it implies, must be abandoned; and it would seem that all the European variants of the name *Assassin* are corruptions of *ḥashīshī* and its plural forms.[52]

De Sacy also made some conjectures on the reason for the application of the name to the Nizārīs. He had no doubt that *ḥashīsh*, or rather a *ḥashīsh*-containing potion was, in some manner, used by the Nizārīs. But, unlike some other orientalists, he did not subscribe to the opinion that the sectarians were called the Assassins because they were addicts to the euphoria-producing potion. Similarly, he excluded the possibility of any habitual use of this debilitating drug by the Nizārī *fidāʾīs* to whom alone he thought the term originally applied. De Sacy believed that *ḥashīsh* was, at the time, the secret possession of the Nizārī chiefs who used it in a regulated manner on the *fidāʾīs* to inspire them with dreams of paradise and blind obedience. In other words, while not necessarily accepting the reality of a garden of paradise into which the drugged devotees would be led, de Sacy nevertheless linked his own interpretation to the famous tale told by Marco Polo and others about the alleged practices of the Nizārīs.[53]

The tale of how the Nizārī chiefs secretly administered *ḥashīsh* to the *fidāʾīs* in order to control and motivate them has been accepted by many scholars since Arnold of Lübeck. But the fact remains that neither the Ismāʿīlī texts which have come to light in modern times nor any serious contemporary Muslim source in general attest to the actual use of *ḥashīsh*, with or without gardens of paradise, by the Nizārīs. Therefore, as Lewis and Hodgson have summed up the relevant arguments, it would seem that the various versions of this once popular tale should now be dismissed as fictitious.[54]

The use and effects of *ḥashīsh* were known at the time, as best witnessed by the existence of the name *ḥashīshiyya*. Therefore the drug could not have been the secret property of the Nizārī chiefs, as suggested by de Sacy. Furthermore, the name is rarely used by the Muslim authors who, in contrast to the Crusaders and other Europeans, prefer to designate the sectarians by religious names such as Bāṭiniyya and Taʿlīmiyya, or simply as the Ismāʿīliyya and Nizāriyya, if not using terms of abuse like *malāḥida*. However, few contemporary Muslim historians, mainly from the thirteenth century, occasionally use the term *ḥashīshiyya* in reference to the Nizārīs of Syria (al-Shām); while the Nizārīs of Persia are also called *ḥashīshīs* in some Caspian Zaydī texts.[55] Evidently, the term has been used only once in any known Ismāʿīlī source; namely, in the second half of the highly polemical epistle issued in the 1120s, by the Fāṭimid caliph al-Āmir against his Nizārī adversaries who eventually assassinated him in 1130. But in this epistle too, the word *ḥashīshiyya* is used of the Syrian Nizārīs without any derivative explanation.[56]

In all probability, the name *ḥashīshiyya* was applied to the Nizārīs as a term of abuse and reproach. The Nizārīs were already despised by other Muslims and would easily qualify for every sort of contemptuous judgement on their beliefs and behaviour. In other words, it seems that the name *ḥashīshiyya* reflected a criticism of the Nizārīs rather than an accurate description of their secret practices. And it was the name that gave rise to the imaginative tale which supplied some justification of the behaviour that would otherwise seem rather irrational to Westerners. Even abstracting from the ascetic morality of Ḥasan-i Ṣabbāḥ, the obedience and devotion of the Nizārī *fidāʾīs* is not without its equivalents amongst the earlier Shīʿī groups such as the Mughīriyya and the Manṣūriyya, who were similarly imbued with elitism and a strong sense of devotion. In modern times, similar behaviour has been displayed by certain Muslim groups thriving on Shīʿī martyrology, notably the Persian Fidāʾiyyān-i Islām.

Despite its deficiencies, de Sacy's memoir was a landmark in Ismāʿīlī studies in Europe, and it paved the way for more systematic endeavours based on Eastern sources and a number of more strictly historical studies during the next few decades. Étienne Marc Quatremère (1782–1852) published a few short works on the Fāṭimids and the Nizārīs.[57] This great orientalist, it will be recalled, also made available for the first time in printed form a portion of Rashīd al-Dīn's famous history which, together with that of Juwaynī, represents the earliest Persian historical sources on the Nizārīs. Another French orientalist, Jourdain, who in 1813 had edited and translated the section on the Persian Nizārīs contained in another important Persian history by Mīrkhwānd, produced a summary account of the Nizārīs.[58] Meanwhile, de Sacy had continued his broader investigation of the Ismāʿīlīs. In what was to be his final work, and the result of over thirty years' study of the Druze religion, he devoted a long introduction to the origins and the early history of the Ismāʿīlī movement.[59] It was there that de Sacy also discussed at some length Ismāʿīlī doctrine, including a so-called nine-degree initiation process for the adepts, and presented the controversial ʿAbd Allāh b. Maymūn al-Qaddāḥ as the real 'founder' of Ismāʿīlism, basing his case mainly on the lost anti-Ismāʿīlī polemical work of Akhū Muḥsin as preserved in excerpts by al-Nuwayrī. Indeed, de Sacy's treatment of early Ismāʿīlism continued to be maintained by the bulk of the subsequent orientalists until more recent times.[60]

Of all the Western works on the Ismāʿīlīs produced during the first half of the nineteenth century, however, the most widely read came from the pen of the Austrian orientalist diplomat Joseph von Hammer-Purgstall (1774–1856). Like many other orientalists of his time, especially in Germany and Austria under the Habsburg monarchy, von Hammer had started his career in the diplomatic service, as a dragoman in Istanbul and a consul in the Balkans. In 1818, by utilizing the various chronicles of the Crusades as well as the Eastern manuscript sources in the Imperial Library, Vienna, and in his own private collection, he published a book in German devoted entirely to the Nizārīs of the Alamūt period.[61] This book traced for the first time, in a detailed manner, the entire history of the Nizārī state in Persia, with briefer references to the Syrian Nizārīs. Von Hammer's book achieved great success; it was soon translated into French and English[62] and continued to serve, until as recently as the 1930s, as the standard interpretation of the subject.[63]

It should be noted, however, that von Hammer was strongly biased against the Nizārīs, and had accepted Marco Polo's narrative in its entirety, together with all the criminal acts attributed to the Nizārīs.[64] Thus, he treated the Nizārīs as 'that union of imposters and dupes which, under the mask of a more austere creed and severer morals, undermined all religion and morality; that order of murderers, beneath whose daggers the lords of nations fell; all powerful, because, for the space of three centuries, they were universally dreaded, until the den of ruffians fell with the khaliphate, to whom, as the centre of spiritual and temporal power, it had at the outset sworn destruction'.[65] This view, in turn, reflected a tacit purpose. Writing not too long after the French revolution, von Hammer apparently wanted to use the Nizārīs as an example to produce a tract for the times that would warn against 'the pernicious influence of secret societies in weak governments, and of the dreadful prostitution of religion to the horrors of unbridled ambition'.[66] In line with this scheme, he drew close analogies between the 'order of the Assassins' on the one hand, and the European secret orders of his time, which he detested, such as the Templars, the Jesuits, the Illuminati, and the Freemasons, on the other. He emphasized parallels in terms of their 'various grades of initiation; the appellations of master, companions, and novices; the public and the secret doctrine; the oath of unconditional obedience to unknown superiors, to serve the ends of the order.'[67]

With a few exceptions, European scholarship made little further progress in Ismāʿīlī studies during the second half of the nineteenth century. The outstanding exception was provided by the contributions of the French orientalist Charles François Defrémery (1822–1883) who collected a large number of references from various Muslim chronicles on the Nizārīs of Persia and Syria. Having already translated the section on the Persian Nizārī state, contained in the fourteenth-century Persian history of Ḥamd Allāh Mustawfī,[68] Defrémery then published the results of his Nizārī studies in two long articles.[69] A few years later, Reinhart Dozy (1820–1883) investigated the early history of the Ismāʿīlīs,[70] a subject that was more thoroughly pursued, especially with respect to the Carmatians or Qarmaṭīs, by another famous Dutch orientalist, Michael Jan de Goeje (1836–1909).[71] There also appeared for the first time a history of the Fāṭimids, which was, however, a compilation from various Arabic chronicles;[72] several new works on the Druzes also appeared.[73]

De Sacy's treatment of early Ismāʿīlism and von Hammer's interpretation of the Nizārīs continued to set the perspective within which European orientalists collected any reference to the Ismāʿīlīs. As a result, though some progress was slowly being made, the distorted image of Ismāʿīlism, reflecting the earlier impressions, was nevertheless maintained through the opening decades of the twentieth century by anyone interested in the subject, including even the eminent Edward Granville Browne (1862–1926) who summarized the contributions of his predecessors.[74] This should not cause any particular surprise since very few Ismāʿīlī sources had been available to the orientalists of the nineteenth and early twentieth century.

The earliest Ismāʿīlī-related sources known to the West were the Druze manuscripts which found their way in the eighteenth century from the Levant to the Bibliothèque Royale and then to other major European libraries.[75] Similarly, the first Ismāʿīlī manuscripts to become known to orientalists came from Syria, the first area of Western interest in the Ismāʿīlīs. Jean Baptiste L. J. Rousseau (1780–1831), the French consul-general in Aleppo from 1809 to 1816 and a long-time resident of the Near East, who was also interested in oriental studies and maintained a close professional relationship with Silvestre de Sacy, was the first person to draw the attention of European orientalists to the existence of the contemporary Ismāʿīlīs as well as to their local traditions and literature. In 1810, he prepared a memoir on the Syrian Nizārīs of his time, which contained many interesting historical, social and religious details obtainable only through direct contact with the Nizārīs themselves.[76] This memoir, which also underlined the miserable conditions of the Syrian Nizārīs especially after their 1809 massacre at the hands of their neighbours and arch-enemies, the Nuṣayrīs, was published in Paris in 1811. It immediately received much publicity in Europe, mainly because of de Sacy's association with it. Rousseau also supplied information to Europe about the Persian Nizārīs. He had visited Persia in 1807–1808 as a member of an official French mission sent to the court of the second Qājār monarch Fatḥ ʿAlī Shāh (1797–1834), and whilst there he had enquired about the Ismāʿīlīs of that country. Rousseau was surprised to find out that there were many Ismāʿīlīs in Persia and that they still had their imām (thought to be a descendant of Ismāʿīl b. Jaʿfar), whose name was Shāh Khalīl Allāh. This imām, he was further told, resided at Kahak, a small village near Maḥallāt, and was revered almost like a god by his followers, including those Indian Ismāʿīlīs who came regularly from the banks of the Ganges to receive his blessings. Rousseau also mentions that this imām was detested by the Persian clergy, meaning the Ithnāʿasharī clergy, but protected and respected by the Qājār king because of the annual revenues brought to the country by the Ismāʿīlī pilgrims from India.[77] In 1825, Rousseau's account was confirmed, and new details were added to it by James Baillie Fraser (1783–1856), the Scottish traveller who in the course of a journey through Persia had heard, in 1822, about the Ismāʿīlīs.[78] Fraser notes that

> every one is acquainted with the devotion of his followers to Hussun Soubah, and his successors; and even at this day the sheikh or head of the sect is most blindly revered by those who yet remain, though their zeal has lost the deep and terrific character which it once bore. It is but lately that one of these, by name Shah Khuleel Oollah, resided at Yezd... He was a person of high respectability, and great influence, keeping an hundred gholaums of his own in pay; but he was put to death by the inhabitants of Yezd, in a riot... The Bhoras, from India, were particularly devoted to their saint; and many that day sacrificed themselves in his cause.

Shāh Khalīl Allāh, whose Indian followers in this passage are wrongly believed to have been the Bohras instead of the Khojas, was in fact murdered in 1817 in Yazd, where he had transferred his residence about two years earlier from Kahak. Fraser concludes his remarks by relating that these sectarian devotees were 'so eager to pour in presents upon their ghostly chief, that he had accumulated great riches. He was succeeded in his religious capacity by one of his sons, who meets with a similar respect from the sect.' The son and successor in question, it may be noted, was to become known as the Āghā Khān, properly Āqā Khān, the first of the Nizārī Imāms to bear this title and the one who eventually led an unsuccessful revolt in Persia and then left for India in the early 1840s.[79]

Rousseau played another pioneering role in supplying direct evidence of the Ismāʿīlīs to contemporary Europe. This diplomat, who was an avid collector of oriental manuscripts and who, in the 1820s, sold 700 such manuscripts from his private collection to the newly-founded Asiatic Museum in St Petersburg, had obtained an anonymous Ismāʿīlī work from Maṣyāf, one of the main Ismāʿīlī centres in Syria. This Arabic manuscript, containing a number of fragments bearing on the religious doctrines of the Nizārīs, had been actually procured for Rousseau soon after the pillage of the Ismāʿīlī villages in 1809 by the noted Swiss orientalist and explorer John Lewis Burckhardt (1784–1817), who produced some travel notes of his own on the Syrian sectarians.[80] In 1812, as the first instance of its kind, some extracts from this manuscript, as translated by Rousseau and communicated to de Sacy, were published in Paris.[81] Rousseau later sent this Nizārī source to the Société Asiatique and the full text of it was, in due course, printed and translated into French by Stanislas Guyard (1846–1884).[82] A few years later, this young orientalist published, together with a valuable introduction and notes, the text and translation of yet another Nizārī work, which was the first sectarian source containing historical information to find its way to Europe.[83] This Arabic manuscript on the life and the miraculous deeds of Rāshid al-Dīn Sinān, composed around 1324, had been discovered in Syria in 1848 and then donated to the library of the Société Asiatique, where it was re-discovered some thirty years later by Guyard himself.[84] Meanwhile, a few other Ismāʿīlī texts of the Syrian provenance had been sent by a missionary to distant America, where they were translated into English and published in 1851–1852.[85] These early discoveries of Ismāʿīlī sources were, however, few and far between, and it was largely scholars in Paris, the capital of orientalism in the nineteenth century, who had access to them.

Direct information about the Ismāʿīlīs reflecting their viewpoint continued to become available. The travelogue of Nāṣir-i Khusraw was published for the first time, accompanied by a French translation, as were some other Persian works of this famous traveller, poet, theosophist and Ismāʿīlī *dāʿī* of the 5th/11th century.[86] In 1898, Paul Casanova (1861–1926) announced his discovery at the Bibliothèque Nationale of a manuscript containing the last section of the famous encyclopaedic work, *Rasāʾil Ikhwān al-Ṣafāʾ* (*The Epistles of the Brethren of Purity*).[87] This French orientalist, who later made some important studies on the Fāṭimids and had already published some numismatic notes on the Nizārīs,[88] was the first European to recognize the Ismāʿīlī origin of this work. Before this, several copies of the *Epistles* had been known to Europe, and the German orientalist Friedrich Dieterici (1821–1903) had published some portions of the *Rasāʾil*, without realizing their Ismāʿīlī character.[89]

Other types of information about the Ismāʿīlīs now started to appear. Earlier in the nineteenth century, some brief notes had been published on Alamūt by British officers who had visited the ruins of the fortress or its vicinity,[90] but Max van Berchem (1863–1921), while travelling in Syria in 1895, read and studied almost all of the epigraphic evidence of the Syrian Nizārī fortresses.[91] Different types of archaeological evidence from the Fāṭimid period had already been presented by van Berchem himself.[92] Much information on the Khojas and the first Āghā Khān also became available in the course of a peculiar case investigated by the High Court of Bombay, culminating in the famous legal judgement of 1866.[93] All these developments, together with progress in the publication of new Muslim sources and the reinterpretation of the old ones, were paving the way for a revaluation of the Ismāʿīlīs.

In the opening decades of the twentieth century, Ismāʿīlī manuscripts began to be discovered from other regions and, though still on a limited basis, more systematically. In 1903, Giuseppe Caprotti, an Italian merchant who had spent some thirty years in Yaman, brought a collection of sixty Arabic manuscripts from Ṣanʿāʾ to Italy. Between 1906 and 1909, he sold these and more than 1,500 other manuscripts of south Arabian origin to the Ambrosiana Library in Milan. While being catalogued, the Caprotti collection was found by Eugenio Griffini (1878–1925), the famous Milanese Islamist, to contain several works on Ismāʿīlī doctrine.[94] Of greater importance were the efforts of some Russian scholars and officials who, having become aware of the existence of Ismāʿīlī communities within their own domains in Central Asia, now tried to establish direct contacts with the sectarians. The Central Asian Ismāʿīlīs, it may be noted, belong to the Nizārī branch of the sect and are to be found mainly in western Pāmīr, an area lying north and east of the Panj river, a major upper headwater of the Āmū Daryā (Oxus). Since 1895, this area had come under the effective control of Russian military officials, although an Anglo-Russian boundary commission in that year had formally handed the region on the right bank of the Panj to the Khanate of Bukhārā, while designating the left-bank region, or Badakhshān proper, as Afghan territory. Indeed, in the 1860s the Russians had secured a firm footing in Bukhārā and other Central Asian Khanates and this was officially recognized during the reign of ʿAbd al-Aḥad (1885–1910) who, as the *amīr* of Bukhārā, had to submit to Russian imperial power.

It was under these circumstances that Russians travelled freely in the upper Oxus region. Count Alexis A. Bobrinskoy, a Russian scholar who studied the inhabitants of Wakhān and Ishkāshim, and visited these districts of western Pāmīr in 1898, published in 1902 a short account of the Ismāʿīlīs living in the Russian and Bukhārā districts of Central Asia.[95] In the same year, A. Polovtsev, an official in Turkistān who was interested in Ismāʿīlism and later became the Russian consul-general in Bombay, while travelling in the upper Oxus, acquired a copy of the *Umm al-kitāb*, the most secret book of the Central Asian Ismāʿīlīs. A second manuscript copy of this enigmatic work written in Persian was obtained, in 1911, from Wakhān by J. Lutsch, another Russian official in Turkistān. Photostats of both these copies were taken to St Petersburg and deposited in the Asiatic Museum of the Imperial Russian Academy of Sciences, an institution which by that time, despite its name, had become a library. Carl Salemann, the director of the Museum and a renowned specialist in Iranian languages, was preparing an edition of this work when he died in 1916. This task was later accomplished by Wladimir Ivanow,[96] of whom we shall have more to say.

Meanwhile in 1914, Ivan I. Zarubin (1887–1964), the well-known Russian ethnologist and specialist in Tājik dialects (which are spoken in the Pāmīr), acquired a small collection of Ismāʿīlī manuscripts from the western Pāmīr districts of Shughnān and Rushān, which in 1916 he presented to the Asiatic Museum. In 1918, the Museum came into the possession of a second collection of Nizārī Ismāʿīlī texts written in the Persian language. These manuscripts had been procured a few years earlier, again from districts in the upper Oxus region, by the orientalist Aleksandr Aleksandrovich Semenov (1873–1958), the Russian pioneer in Ismāʿīlī studies from Tashkent. He had already investigated certain beliefs of the Shughnānī Ismāʿīlīs whom he had first visited in 1901.[97] It is interesting to note that the Zarubin and Semenov collections of the Asiatic Museum, though altogether comprising less than twenty genuine items, represented the then largest holding of Ismāʿīlī manuscripts in any Western library.[98] The generally meagre number of such sectarian titles known to orientalists by 1922 is well reflected in the first Western bibliography of Ismāʿīlī works, both published and unpublished, which appeared in that year.[99] Little further progress was made in Ismāʿīlī studies during the 1920s, aside from the publication of some of Nāṣir-i Khusraw's works, including his *Wajh-i dīn* from the manuscript in the Zarubin collection, and a few studies by Semenov and Ivanow.[100] Indeed, by 1927, when the article 'Ismāʿīlīya' by Clément Huart (1854–1926) appeared in the second volume of the *Encyclopaedia of Islam*, European orientalism on the subject still displayed the negative biases of the Crusaders. But Ismāʿīlī studies were now about to witness a breakthrough, as the work of discovering the sectarian manuscripts was gaining momentum, and a new generation of scholars led by Ivanow and some Indian Ismāʿīlīs were preparing to make their contributions.

Remarkable modern progress in Ismāʿīlī studies began in the 1930s.[101] This progress has already necessitated a drastic revision of our ideas concerning the history and doctrines of the Ismāʿīlīs, as well as the significance of Ismāʿīlism within the general context of Islamic civilization. This long-awaited breakthrough, arising from the discovery of genuine Ismāʿīlī sources on a scale unknown before, has been made possible through access to the secretly-guarded private collections of manuscripts preserved in Yaman, the greater Badakhshān and above all, India. In 1931, a small number of Ismāʿīlī manuscripts was procured by the School of Oriental Studies in London.[102] Since then, the discovery of Ismāʿīlī manuscripts has proceeded at an astonishing pace. More libraries, including those at the American University of Beirut, the Tübingen University and, most importantly, the Institute of Ismaili Studies, London, have come to hold Ismāʿīlī collections. The largest single success to date in this respect was perhaps attained during the period 1959–1963, when a Soviet expedition discovered some 250 Ismāʿīlī manuscripts in the Gorno-Badakhshān region, which has since 1925 formed part of the Soviet Socialist Republic of Tājikistān. These manuscripts had been preserved by the Nizārīs of Shughnān in western Pāmīr, mainly in the valleys of Ghund, Bartang and Shākh-dara on the right bank of the Panj. The photostats of these Persian manuscripts, thirty of which are evidently unique, are presently kept at the Department of Oriental Studies of the Tājik Academy of Sciences in Dushanbe.[103] The recovery of a substantial portion of the surviving Ismāʿīlī literature, although rather disappointing in terms of historical information, has also dispelled the once popular belief that Ismāʿīlī texts had been totally destroyed upon the collapse of the Fāṭimid Caliphate in Egypt and the Nizārī state in Persia with its celebrated library at Alamūt.

The acquisition of Ismāʿīlī manuscripts by public libraries, as well as the readier access of scholars to private collections where such works are mainly found, are in turn reflections of a drastic change in the mentality of many modern-day Ismāʿīlīs. These liberal sectarians no longer subscribe to the traditional view that the community needs to protect its literature from uninitiated outsiders, not only non-Ismāʿīlīs but also Ismāʿīlīs belonging to different branches and groups. Fortunately for the students of Ismāʿīlism, increasing numbers of Ismāʿīlīs, especially in India, the main literary storehouse of the sect, are becoming agreeable to divulging the contents of their spiritual riches and to entrusting these possessions to the hands of scholars and researchers.[104] The most noteworthy instance of this new outlook was manifested in 1957 in the generous donation of some 200 Ismāʿīlī manuscripts to the library of the Bombay University by Asaf Ali Asghar Fyzee, a Sulaymānī Ismāʿīlī and the foremost modern authority on Ismāʿīlī jurisprudence.[105] Furthermore, some Ismāʿīlīs, notably in India and Syria, have taken the initiative of publishing their sectarian sources and doing research on the subject. This change in attitude of contemporary Ismāʿīlīs is well accounted for in the prefatory acknowledgements appearing in the editions of the many Ismāʿīlī texts published over the last three decades.

It should be noted at this juncture that modern progress in Ismāʿīlī studies, perhaps more so than in any comparable field of Islamic studies, has been due to the efforts of a small group of scholars. The Western pioneers of this group include Rudolph Strothmann (1877–1960), Louis Massignon (1883–1962), Marius Canard (1888–1982), Henry Corbin (1903–1978), Paul Kraus (1904–1944), Bernard Lewis, and more recently Samuel Miklos Stern (1920–1969), Marshall G. S. Hodgson (1922–1968) and Wilferd Madelung. Notable Eastern pioneers have been Zāhid ʿAlī, Ḥusayn ibn Fayḍ Allāh al-Hamdānī (1901–1962), Asaf Ali Asghar Fyzee (1899–1981), Muḥammad Kāmil Ḥusayn (1901–1961), and more recently ʿĀrif Tāmir, Muṣṭafā Ghālib and Abbas Hamdani; all except Ḥusayn being Ismāʿīlīs themselves. Finally, there is Vladimir Alekseevich Ivanov (1886–1970), better known as W. Ivanow, who belongs in a special category by himself; not only because he was the foremost pioneer in Ismāʿīlī studies, but also because he was the only Westerner in the field who spent his entire scholarly life in the East.

Ivanow studied Arabic and Persian at St Petersburg. Later he specialized in modern Persian dialects and Ṣūfism, pursuing his studies under the greatest Russian scholars of the time, Victor Rosen (1849–1908) and Valentin A. Zhukovsky (1858–1918). In 1915, Ivanow became associated with the Asiatic Museum as an assistant keeper of oriental manuscripts. He travelled widely in Central Asia and procured more than a thousand Arabic and Persian manuscripts for the Museum. It was also at the Asiatic Museum that, on examining the Zarubin collection, he had his first major contact with Ismāʿīlī literature. Ivanow left his native Russia, never to return, in 1918. Henceforth, he devoted his life exclusively to Ismāʿīlī studies, mainly in India and Persia.

It was in Bombay, starting in the 1930s, that Ivanow acquired a multitude of Ismāʿīlī friends and found access to their collections of manuscripts. Ivanow's close relations with the sectarians expanded rapidly and reached out to the remotest corners of the Ismāʿīlī world in Badakhshān and in the adjoining Chitral, Gilgit and Hunza districts, where the Nizārī Ismāʿīlīs are known as Mawlāʾīs. It was also in Bombay that, together with some of his Ismāʿīlī friends including Fyzee, Ivanow founded in 1933 the Islamic Research Association, which produced a series of publications devoted mainly to Ismāʿīlī works. Similarly, he played a major part in the creation of the Ismaili Society of Bombay in 1946, under the patronage of the late Āghā Khān III, Sir Sulṭān Muḥammad Shāh (1877–1957), with the aim of promoting independent and critical studies of all matters Ismāʿīlī. The library of the Ismaili Society, mainly through the efforts of Ivanow, came to possess a large number of Ismāʿīlī manuscripts. The Society's series of publications, a landmark in modern Ismāʿīlī studies, were edited by Ivanow and came to be devoted mainly to his own works which included the publication of first editions of numerous Nizārī texts. In the same series also appeared, in 1963, Ivanow's magnum opus, a bio-bibliographical survey of Ismāʿīlī literature[106] which was the amplified edition of a work published thirty years earlier.[107] This survey work remained indispensable through its two editions for more than four decades for students of Ismāʿīlism. Many of the titles described, especially those relating to the Nizārī branch, were actually discovered by Ivanow himself. Ivanow's survey was superseded only in 1977 by the more comprehensive bibliography of Ismāʿīl Qurbān Ḥusayn Poonawala, an Indian Ismāʿīlī scholar who has had direct access to many private collections of manuscripts preserved by the Ismāʿīlīs of India.[108]

Ivanow's work was indeed his life, and, as Fyzee observed, in every branch of Ismāʿīlism his work constitutes the basis for further studies.[109] Nevertheless, it was Nizārī Ismāʿīlism, especially as developed in Persia, that occupied the centre of his research efforts. Ever since his first major publication on the subject in 1922,[110] Ivanow indefatigably recovered, studied, edited and translated into English most of the extant literature of the Persian Nizārīs; a literature written entirely in the Persian language. It is, therefore, to his publications that reference is commonly made by anyone investigating the Nizārīs. In no small measure, it is also due to his contributions that the Nizārīs are no longer groundlessly judged as a detestable order of drugged assassins. As Hodgson, another authority on the Nizārīs, has observed, Ivanow stands unchallenged as the founder of modern Nizārī studies.[111]

The main objective of this survey is to present the results of modern scholarship on the origins, history and doctrines of the Ismāʿīlī movement. As already noted, it is rather difficult to select any specific order of phases in the history of Ismāʿīlism. It is, however, possible on the basis of a mixture of chronological, doctrinal, geographical as well as literary and ethnological considerations, to distinguish five phases, some running parallel to others. These major phases, which will provide the framework for our survey, are as follows:

1 Early Ismāʿīlism; or, the initial phase of the movement, from its earliest proto-Ismāʿīlī origins in the middle of the 2nd/8th century until the foundation of the Fāṭimid Caliphate in North Africa.

2 Fāṭimid Ismāʿīlism; or, the so-called 'classical' Fāṭimid period, from 297/909 until the death of the eighth Fāṭimid caliph-imām al-Mustanṣir in 487/1094, and the ensuing Nizārī-Mustaʿlī schism in the movement. This phase also covers the history of some dissident Ismāʿīlī groups, especially the Qarmaṭīs of southern ʿIrāq and Baḥrayn.

3 Mustaʿlian Ismāʿīlism; or, the phase of development of one of the two major branches of Ismāʿīlism, from the Nizārī-Mustaʿlī schism to the present time. This phase, which is essentially the continuation of the traditions of the Fāṭimid Ismāʿīlīs, can be traced in terms of an initial period and the subsequent histories of the Ḥāfiẓī and Ṭayyibī factions of the Mustaʿliyya. While the Ḥāfiẓiyya disintegrated soon after the fall of the Fāṭimid dynasty in 567/1171, the Ṭayyibiyya survived through their Yamanī and Indian periods and are currently represented by the Dā'ūdīs and the Sulaymānīs, residing chiefly in India where they are commonly known as the Bohorās (Bohras).

4 Nizārī Ismāʿīlism of the Alamūt period; or, the phase of Ismāʿīlism of the Nizārī tradition, from around 483/1090 until the destruction of the Nizārī state in Persia by the Mongols in 654/1256. This phase also covers the history of the Syrian Nizārīs. The Ismāʿīlīs of the Saljūq territories and Syria succeeded, mainly through the initial efforts of Ḥasan-i Ṣabbāḥ, to establish a vigorous state, stretching from Syria to eastern Persia. These Ismāʿīlīs, who came to uphold the rights of Nizār and his descendants to the imāmate, launched an open revolt throughout the Saljūq realm even before the Nizārī-Mustaʿlī schism; a revolt based on the seizure of mountain fortresses and the assassination of prominent political enemies. On al-Mustanṣir's death, the Nizārīs severed their ties with the Fāṭimid headquarters in Cairo. The Nizārīs also introduced or elaborated several important doctrines.

5 The post-Alamūt phase of Nizārī Ismāʿīlism, from the second half of the 7th/13th century to the present time. This phase covers three distinct periods; namely, the obscure early post-Alamūt, the so-called Anjudān, and the modern periods. With the collapse of the Nizārī state, the Nizārīs

soon reorganized themselves and, after experiencing a schism, survived in Persia mainly under the guise of Ṣūfism. Later, the Nizārīs achieved new successes in the Indian subcontinent and Central Asia. Starting in the 9th/15th century, Nizārī Ismāʿīlism experienced a revival, which lasted almost two centuries. This renaissance of Nizārī Ismāʿīlism, led by the imāms of the so-called Qāsim-Shāhī line, has been designated as the Anjudān period by Ivanow.[112] In the second half of the 12th/18th century, while the line of the Muḥammad-Shāhī Imāms was nearing its end, the Qāsim-Shāhī Nizārī Imāms who by then had acquired some ties with certain Ṣūfī orders, emerged from their underground existence in Persia. Subsequently in the nineteenth century, while the seat of the Nizārī Imāmate was transferred from Persia to India, the Nizārī Ismāʿīlīs entered the modern period of their history under the leadership of the Āghā Khāns.

The plan of our study follows the above-mentioned classification scheme. But before taking up the subject of early Ismāʿīlism, it is necessary to review certain developments of early Islam and, more specifically, early Shīʿism. This review of the formative period of Shīʿī Islam is indispensable as the proper perspective, not only because the Ismāʿīlīs adopted much of the heritage of the early Shīʿīs but also because it explains the religio-political milieu within which proto-Ismāʿīlism originated.

2

Origins and early development of Shīʿism

It was not until the latter part of the nineteenth century that Islamic studies was established as a separate field within general orientalism in the West. Since then, much progress and specialization has occurred in the field, and recent works have particularly enhanced our knowledge of the formative period of Islam. This rather gradual progress has resulted from the publication and study of numerous Islamic sources, and from the cumulative contributions of a large number of Islamists, such as Julius Wellhausen (1844–1918), Ignaz Goldziher (1850–1921), Carl H. Becker (1876–1933), and Leone Caetani (1869–1935), to name but a few of the greatest pioneers of the last generation; as well as Sir Hamilton A. R. Gibb (1895–1971), William Montgomery Watt and Laura Veccia Vaglieri, amongst others of the present generation. The study of Shīʿism, however, whether viewed as a major Islamic perspective or as a heterodoxical religious movement, has not received its deserved share of modern scholarship. This shortage becomes more evident when the overall meagre studies devoted to different aspects of Shīʿism are compared with the investigation of studies of Sunnī Islam, which continues to occupy the focus of attention of the majority of Eastern and Western Islamists.

The study of Shīʿism was indeed, until recent times, one of the most neglected branches within Islamic studies. In this century, Israel Friedlaender was perhaps the first person to have noted that 'we have a very imperfect notion of the rise and development of the *religious* tendencies in Shiism and the sources from which they were derived'.[1] Edward G. Browne, too, writing in 1924, once again deplored the lack of knowledge concerning the Shīʿī creed and its evolution, and rightly added that 'we still possess no comprehensive and authoritative statement of the Shīʿa doctrine in any European language'.[2] Still later, in 1934, Rudolph Strothmann, an important European authority on Shīʿī studies, found it necessary to re-state that 'there is no thorough account of the Shīʿa'.[3] Similar statements have continued to be made, especially with respect to early Shīʿism,[4] despite the progress of more recent scholarship in certain aspects of the subject.

However, during the last few decades, an extremely selective group of scholars have sought to devote more serious and specialized efforts towards the study of Shīʿī Islam. Louis Massignon, the multi-dimensional dean of modern French Islamists, should be regarded as the pioneer and guide of this group in the West, while the untiring efforts of Henry Corbin, his student and successor at the École Pratique des Hautes Études, at the Sorbonne in Paris, occupy a unique place in the modern annals of Shīʿī studies. The contributions of Corbin, who devoted a lifetime to the study of Shīʿism, especially to its two major Twelver and Ismāʿīlī branches, are invaluable in understanding Shīʿī thought in general, and its theosophical and metaphysical aspects as developed in Persia in particular. Corbin's works, reflecting the benefit of his close association with several leading Twelver Shīʿī religious scholars, or *ʿulamāʾ*, of Persia, undoubtedly provide the most important single source in any Western language on many intellectual aspects of Shīʿism. The bulk of Corbin's major works, including his editions of numerous texts, appeared in his own well-known Bibliothèque Iranienne series, published by the Département d'Iranologie of the Institut Franco-Iranien, Tehran, where he lectured every fall during the last twenty-five years of his life.[5] Meanwhile in Persia, where Twelver Shīʿism has predominated as the state religion for almost five centuries, a number of contemporary Shīʿī authorities, notably ʿAllāma Ṭabāṭabāʾī (1903–1981), have taken the initiative of elaborating their religious views on a more systematic, though still traditional, basis.[6] These scholars, by holding classes at the religious institutions of the country, especially in the holy cities of Qumm and Mashhad, or at their homes, have trained a number of younger disciples and students, such as Sayyid Jalāl al-Dīn Āshtiyānī, who are making contributions to the study of Shīʿism.

In spite of recent researches, the early history and doctrinal development of Shīʿism, especially during the first century of Islam, continue to be obscure and controversial. This review, then, is based on what should rightly be regarded as the tentative and fragmentary results of modern scholarship concerning the origins and early development of Shīʿism. More specifically, we shall trace the early development of Shīʿism, with special reference to the Shīʿī tendencies and movements that eventually evolved, in the middle of the 2nd/8th century, into what retrospectively came to be designated as the Ismāʿīlī movement. Needless to add that in a similar retrospective sense, the earliest history of Shīʿism, until the death of the Imām Jaʿfar al-Ṣādiq in 148/765, is shared by the Ismāʿīlī Shīʿīs who recognize the same first six imāms as the Twelver Shīʿīs, although with a somewhat different enumeration.

Muḥammad, the Messenger of God (*rasūl Allāh*), between his emigration (*hijra*) from Mecca to Medina in the September of 622 which marks the initiation of the Islamic era (Latin, *Anno Hegirae*) and his death on 13 Rabīʿ I 11/8 June 632, succeeded in founding a state of considerable power and prestige according to Arabian standards of the time. During this short ten-year period, most of the desert-dwelling bedouin tribes of Arabia had pledged their allegiance to the Prophet of Islam, who thus laid the foundation for the subsequent expansion of the new faith (*īmān*) in God beyond the Arabian peninsula. The death of the Prophet after a brief illness, however, confronted the nascent Islamic community (*umma*) with its first major crisis. This crisis of succession marks the beginning of what was eventually to develop into a permanent Sunnī–Shīʿī division in the Islamic community.

As long as the Prophet was alive, Muslims had taken it for granted that he would provide them the best guidance according to the revealed message of Islam. However, aside from delivering and guarding his Prophetic message, Muḥammad had also acted as the head of the Muslim community. His death in Medina left the Muslims in a state of serious confusion, because, at least in view of the majority, the Prophet had left neither formal instruction nor a testament regarding his successor. In the ensuing discussions, there was immediate consensus of opinion on one point only. The successor to the Prophet could not be another prophet or *nabī* (although soon several persons were to appear with such claims), as it had already been made known through divine revelation that Muḥammad was the Seal of the Prophets (*khātim al-anbiyāʾ*). However, it was still essential to choose a successor in order to have effective leadership and ensure the continuation of the Islamic community and state. Consequently, amidst much debate, mainly between the Meccan Emigrants (Muhājirūn) and the Medinese Helpers (Anṣār), Abū Bakr, one of the earliest converts to Islam and a trusted Companion of the Prophet, was elected as the successor. Abū Bakr's election was effectuated on the suggestion of ʿUmar b. al-Khaṭṭāb, himself another of the Muhājirūn, and by the acclamation of other leading Companions of the Prophet, the Ṣaḥāba, who accorded Abū Bakr their oath of allegiance (*bayʿa*).

Abū Bakr, as the new leader of the Islamic community, took the title of *Khalīfat Rasūl Allāh*, Successor of the Messenger of God, a title which was soon simplified to *khalīfa* (whence the word *caliph* in Western languages). Thus, by electing the first successor to the Prophet, the unique Islamic institution of the caliphate was also founded. From its very inception, the caliphate came to embody both the religious and the political leadership of the community.[7] This unique arrangement was to be expected from the very nature of Islam's teachings and the limited experience of the early Islamic community under the leadership of the Prophet. The early Muslims recognized neither distinction between religion and state nor between religious and secular authorities and organizations, distinctions so familiar to modern-day Westerners. Indeed, a strictly theocratic conception of order, in which Islam is not merely a religion but a complete system ordained by God for the socio-political as well as the moral and spiritual governance of mankind, had been an integral part of Muḥammad's message and practice.

Abū Bakr's caliphate lasted just over two years, and before his death in 13/634, he personally selected ʿUmar as his successor. This selection, however, was preceded by an informal consultation with several of the leading Muslims and followed by the acclamation and *bayʿa* of the community. ʿUmar, who was assassinated in 23/644, introduced a new procedure for the election of his successor; he had decided that a council (*shūrā*) of six of the early Companions was to choose the new caliph from amongst themselves. In due time, ʿUthmān b. ʿAffān, a member of the important Meccan clan of the Banū Umayya, was selected, and, upon receiving the customary *bayʿa*, became the third caliph.

In the meantime, immediately upon the death of the Prophet, there had appeared a minority group in Medina who believed that ʿAlī b. Abī Ṭālib, first cousin and son-in-law of the Prophet and bound in matrimony to his daughter Fāṭima, was better qualified than any other candidate, including Abū Bakr, to succeed the Prophet. This minority group, originally comprised of some of ʿAlī's friends and supporters, in time came to be known as the *Shīʿat ʿAlī*, or the party of ʿAlī, and then simply as the Shīʿa. But ʿAlī eventually succeeded as the fourth caliph, instead of fulfilling the aspiration of the Shīʿa in becoming the immediate successor to the Prophet. In any event, the powers of authority exercised by the first four caliphs, known as *al-khulafāʾ al-rāshidūn* or the Rightly-Guided Caliphs, also called the Orthodox Caliphs, essentially seem to have consisted of the implementation of the all-embracing regulations of the message of Islam, as expressed in the revelations contained in the Qur'ān. When necessary, however, the Qur'ān, the standard written text of which came to be issued during ʿUthmān's caliphate, was to be supplemented in the governing affairs of the community by the *sunna*, or practice, established in the nascent Islamic community during the lifetime of the Prophet.

It is not known what role ʿAlī played in the succession claim put forth on his behalf by his partisans. Matters are particularly vague in that after a delay of about six months, ʿAlī finally recognized Abū Bakr's caliphate; a lapse of time also coinciding with Fāṭima's death. It should be added parenthetically that Fāṭima had been involved in a rather complicated inheritance dispute with Abū Bakr over an estate held by the Prophet.[8] Regardless, ʿAlī's candidacy continued to be supported by his partisans in Medina, both among the Muhājirūn and the Anṣār; in due time, the Shīʿa developed a doctrinal view and their cause received wider recognition. According to non-Shīʿī sources, the chief consideration initially underlying the position of the Shīʿa was basically related to the special significance they attached to ʿAlī's being the foremost member of the Ahl al-Bayt or the People of the House, referring to the Prophet's family.

The view on the origins of the caliphate and Shīʿism outlined above is essentially that held by the Sunnī Muslims and accepted by the majority of Western Islamists. But there is also the Shīʿī version which significantly differs from that of the Sunnīs. However, Shīʿism, or the minority position, should not be regarded as a 'heterodoxy', a late revolt against, or a deviation from, an established 'orthodoxy'. In fact, both Sunnism and Shīʿism constitute an integral part of Islam; and they should more correctly be regarded as different interpretations of the same Islamic message.[9] Needless to say that the objective validity of one or the other perspective, as in most religious controversies, is hardly a debatable matter. The differences cannot be resolved on the basis of the various categories of primary sources, notably the theological, historical and the so-called heresiographical works. This is not only because these sources reflect Sunnī or Shīʿī biases, but also because according to the Shīʿa, the possibility of the Shīʿī perspective in Islam existed, as we shall see, from the very beginning.

There are, however, those Western Islamists who are of the opinion that the Shīʿī point of view, in time, led to a re-writing of the early history of Islam. They argue that the Twelvers in particular, from the last quarter of the 3rd/9th century onwards when Twelver Shīʿism started to acquire its now familiar form, attempted to present a version of events relating to the period from the death of the Prophet until 260/874, the date of the occultation of their twelfth imām, which supported their doctrinal position but was not necessarily in accordance with the facts.[10] Our purpose does not hold in delving into polemics or defending either of the two major divisions of Islam; after all, the main points have already been debated throughout the centuries, leading to an abundancy of theological treatises supporting one view or refuting the other. Rather, our purpose here is to present the Shīʿī view on the origins of Shīʿism,[11] irrespective of the possibility that some of the beliefs involved might not have been entertained by the earliest Shīʿīs.

The Shīʿīs, on the basis of specific Qur'ānic verses and certain *ḥadīths*, have maintained that the Prophet did in fact appoint a successor, or an imām as they have preferred to call the spiritual guide and leader of the *umma*. The central Shīʿī evidence of ʿAlī's succession legitimacy is, however, the event of Ghadīr Khumm.[12] On 18 Dhu'l-Ḥijja 10/16 March 632 when returning from his Farewell Pilgrimage, the Prophet stopped at a site by that name between Mecca and Medina to make an announcement to the pilgrims who accompanied him. Taking ʿAlī by the hand, he uttered the famous sentence *man kuntu mawlāhu fa-ʿAlī mawlāhu* (He of whom I am the patron, of him ʿAlī is also the patron), which, according to the Shīʿa, made ʿAlī his successor. Furthermore, it is the Shīʿī belief that the Prophet had received the designation (*naṣṣ*) in question, nominating ʿAlī as the imām of the Muslims after his own death, through divine revelation. This event of the spiritual investiture of ʿAlī b. Abī Ṭālib continues to be celebrated as one of the most important Shīʿī feasts.

As a result, after the Prophet's death, a number of pious Muslims, including especially Salmān al-Fārisī, Abū Dharr al-Ghiffārī, al-Miqdād b. al-Aswad al-Kindī and ʿAmmār b. Yāsir, four of the Ṣaḥāba who came to be known collectively as the four pillars of the early Shīʿa, zealously maintained that the succession to the Prophet was the legitimate right of ʿAlī. This contention was opposed by the Muslim majority who supported the caliphate of Abū Bakr. The latter group, while refusing to concede that the Prophet had specified a successor, considered the decision on the caliphate to be a matter for the *ijmāʿ* or consensus of the community. Consequently, ʿAlī and his partisans became obliged to protest against the act of choosing the Prophet's successor through elective methods. It was this very protest, raised by the pious circle supporting ʿAlī, which separated the Shīʿa from the majority of Muslims.

As the case of the Shīʿa was ignored by the rest of the community, including the majority of the Companions, the Shīʿa persisted that all religious matters should be referred to ʿAlī, who in their opinion was the sole person possessing religious authority. Indeed, the Shīʿa did hold a particular conception of religious authority; a conception that occupies a central position in Shīʿī thought, but which should not be taken to imply any intended separation between the religious and political domains in Shīʿī Islam. Such a distinction, as noted, was meaningless to the early Muslims. According to the Shīʿī view, from the very beginning the partisans of ʿAlī believed that the most important question facing the Muslims after the Prophet was the elucidation of Islamic teachings and religious tenets. This was because they were aware that the teachings of the Qur'ān and the sacred law of Islam (Sharīʿa), having emanated from sources beyond the comprehension of the ordinary man, contained truths and inner purposes that could not be grasped directly through human reason. Therefore, in order to understand the true meaning of the Islamic revelation, the Shīʿa had realized the necessity for a religiously authoritative person, namely the imām. According to this view then, the very possibility of a Shīʿī perspective existed within the message of Islam, and the possibility was only actualized by the genesis of Shīʿism.

It was due to such Shīʿī ideas that there eventually arose in the Muslim community two different conceptions of succession to the Prophet. The majority came to consider the *khalīfa* as being the administrator of the Sharīʿa and leader of the community. The Shīʿa, on the other hand, while also holding that the successor must rule justly over the community, saw in the succession an important spiritual function, a function connected with the interpretation of the Islamic message. As a result, the successor would for them also have to possess legitimate authority for elucidating the teachings of Islam and for providing spiritual guidance for the Muslims. A person with such qualifications, according to the Shīʿa, could come only from amongst the Ahl al-Bayt, as they alone possessed religious authority and provided the sole channel for transmitting the original message of Islam. There were, of course, differences regarding the precise composition of the Ahl al-Bayt, later defined to include only certain members of the Prophet's immediate family, especially ʿAlī and Fāṭima and their progeny. Nevertheless, ʿAlī was from the beginning regarded by his devoted partisans as the most prominent member of the Prophet's family, and as such, was believed to have inherited the Prophet's undivulged teachings and religious knowledge or *ʿilm*. He was, indeed, held to be the Prophet's *waṣī* or legatee. In the eyes of the Shīʿa, ʿAlī's unique qualifications as successor held yet another important dimension in that he was believed to have been nominated by divine command (*amr*) as expressed through the Prophet's testament. This meant that ʿAlī was also divinely inspired and immune from error and sin (*maʿṣūm*), thus making him infallible both in his knowledge and as a teaching authority after the Prophet. As a result of such beliefs, the Shīʿa maintained that the two ends of governing the community and exercising religious authority could be accomplished only by ʿAlī.

The Shīʿī point of view on the origins of Shīʿism contains distinctive doctrinal elements that admittedly cannot be attributed in their entirety to the early Shīʿīs, especially the original partisans of ʿAlī. Needless to say that many Western Islamists are of the opinion that Shīʿism, during its first half-century when it was a purely political movement, did not maintain any religious beliefs different from those held by the non-Shīʿī Muslims. The fact remains that very little is known with historical certainty concerning the earliest Shīʿī ideas and tendencies. But, taking once again the Shīʿī sources and traditions as points of reference, it may be said that perhaps the earliest Shīʿī ideas centred broadly around a particular notion of religious knowledge connected with the Prophet's own *ʿilm*. There were probably also ideas on the possession of this knowledge regarded as a qualification for leading the community. Moreover, it may be added that the partisans of ʿAlī, by contrast to the majority, seem to have been more inclined in their thinking towards the hereditary attributes of individuals. The idea that certain special qualities were hereditary was of course in line with the pre-Islamic Arab notion that outstanding human attributes were transmitted through tribal stock. It was, therefore, rather natural for ʿAlī's religiously learned followers, who also had special respect for the Prophet's family, to believe that some of Muḥammad's special attributes, notably his *ʿilm*, would be inherited by the members of his clan, the Banū Hāshim, and his immediate family. Such beliefs might have been particularly held by those Shīʿīs with south Arabian origins, since they had been accustomed to the Yamanī traditions of divine and semi-divine kingship and its hereditary sanctity.

The earliest Shīʿī currents of thought, whatever their precise nature, developed gradually over time, finding their full expression and consolidation in the doctrine of the imāmate. The stages through which this doctrine passed remain rather obscure. But it is generally known that the basic conception of this distinctive Shīʿī doctrine, which embodies the fundamental beliefs of Shīʿī Islam, came to be postulated in the time of the

Imām Jaʿfar al-Ṣādiq. Later on in this chapter, more will be said on certain aspects of this doctrine; for now we shall commence our discussion of the early development of Shīʿism.

After their initial defeat, the Shīʿa lost much of their enthusiasm. Shīʿism remained in a practically dormant state during the caliphates of both Abū Bakr and ʿUmar, when ʿAlī himself maintained a passive and secluded attitude. During this early period (11–23/632–644), ʿAlī's behaviour is best illustrated by his lack of participation in the affairs of the community and in the ongoing wars of conquest. This was a marked departure from his earlier active role in the community, and his appearance in the forefront of all the battles fought in the Prophet's time, except the battle of Tabūk. He actually retreated, during this period, to his house in Medina. This behaviour should not however be taken as an indication of ʿAlī's reluctance to be involved in public affairs, since the first two caliphs did in fact attempt to exclude him from any position of importance. He was, nevertheless, appointed along with ʿUthmān, Ṭalḥa and al-Zubayr, to the six-member council of the Companions that was to select ʿUmar's successor.[13]

These stagnating conditions changed rather drastically for ʿAlī and his partisans in the caliphate of ʿUthmān (23–35/644–656). During this period of strife and discontent in the community, the turn of events was such as to activate Shīʿī aspirations and tendencies. The mounting grievances against ʿUthmān, which related mainly to economic issues, evolved around the opposition of the provincials and the Medinese Anṣār whose earlier position of influence had now been curtailed.[14] ʿUthmān distributed the governorships of all the major provinces as well as the important garrison towns (singular, *miṣr*) of Kūfa and Baṣra amongst his close relatives. These governors, in turn, adopted policies aimed at enhancing the power and financial interests of the Umayyads and their wealthy Meccan allies. As a result, the tribal leaders whose claims were mainly based on the strengths of their tribes, having been kept in control under ʿUmar's caliphate, were now restored to positions of influence in the provinces. As a corollary to this, many of the early Muslims who lacked tribal stature came to be displaced by the so-called traditional tribal aristocracy or the *ashrāf al-qabāʾil*. This policy created discontent among the Anṣār and the lesser tribal groups of the provinces; groups which had developed claims of their own based on the principle of Islamic *sābiqa* or priority; viz., priority in acceptance of and service to Islam.

The provincial grievances against ʿUthmān's rule had other causes too.

By the time of ʿUthmān, Islam's period of rapid expansion had effectively terminated. But the Arab soldier-tribesmen (*muqātila*) of the garrison towns that had hitherto served as military bases for numerous conquests, were now to remain permanently in their encampments, even though the booty on the battlefield no longer provided any lucrative source of income. These changed realities of the post-conquest period, by themselves created dissatisfaction with the regime. To make matters worse, the central authority of the caliphate in Medina, itself no longer satisfied with the diminishing size of its customary one-fifth of the movable booty (*ghanīma*), became compelled to seek new provincial sources of revenue to compensate for the falling receipts of the Muslim state treasury, the *bayt al-māl*.

Another particular grievance related to the abandoned Sāsānid lands in Mesopotamia. Of the various groups aspiring to the ownership of these agriculturally rich lands in the Sawād district of Kūfa, the so-called *qurrāʾ* posed the strongest claim. The *qurrāʾ* evidently represented those participants in the early wars (*ahl al-ayyām*) against the Sāsānid empire who had occupied the vacated estates of southern ʿIrāq; but some later Muslim historians referred to these groups of villagers as 'reciters of the Qur'ān', which in time became the widely adopted definition of the term *qurrāʾ*. ʿUthmān's policy of gradually allocating the disputed lands to those enjoying his favour, therefore, came to be particularly resented by the *qurrāʾ*, whose leaders had furthermore lost their positions of influence to the strong tribal leaders of Kūfa. The Kūfan *qurrāʾ*, in response to this double assault, generated the first provincial opposition to ʿUthmān's caliphate.

As noted, the provincial opposition was centred in the garrison towns, especially in Kūfa and Baṣra. Kūfa soon came to acquire also a special place in the annals of early Shīʿism. It would, therefore, be in order to say a few words on certain aspects of these garrison towns.[15] The Islamic empire, during its phase of rapid expansion in the caliphate of ʿUmar, came into possession of many ancient cities within the domains of the former Byzantine and Sāsānid empires. Numerous new towns were also founded by the conquering Arabs. These towns were originally conceived as military camps for the invading Arab warriors, who were not allowed to settle in the old cities of the conquered lands and mingle with the non-Arab natives. As the main advances of the Arab armies had been directed towards the Sāsānid territories, the most important garrison towns had now come to be located in the eastern lands of the caliphate, particularly in

ʿIrāq. Kūfa, in the region of Ctesiphon (Madāʾin), the capital of the Sāsānids, and Baṣra, situated strategically between the desert and the Persian Gulf ports, were the two main garrison towns in that region, both having been founded in or about 17/638. It was, therefore, to these two towns that the bulk of Arab migration from all parts of northern and southern Arabia, later supplanted by non-Arabs, had gone to join the victorious armies, especially after 20/641 when the conquest of Mesopotamia had been assured.

The organizations of Kūfa and Baṣra were strongly based on the tribal pattern prevailing in the Arab society. This meant that their inhabitants were divided into a number of tribal groups, each having its own separate military district and tribal leader. In Kūfa, in contrast to Baṣra, the tribal composition of the population was extremely heterogeneous with a predominance of southern Arabs, or Yamanī tribal groups. This was among the chief factors that made Kūfa an important recruiting ground for the Shīʿa, while non-Shīʿī sentiments prevailed in Baṣra. The soldier-tribesmen of the garrison towns, aside from receiving booty of conquest, lived on stipends allotted to them on the basis of an elaborate system of distribution created under ʿUmar. According to this system, itself based on a registry or stipend-roll (*dīwān*), the size of the stipend (*ʿaṭāʾ*) would be determined by the already-noted criterion of *sābiqa*, reflecting ʿUmar's desire to displace traditional Arab claims, based on tribal affiliation and authority, by Islamic ones.

As the opposition to ʿUthmān's policies gained momentum during the latter years of his caliphate, the partisans of ʿAlī found it opportune to revive their subdued aspirations. The Shīʿīs were still led at this time by some of the original partisans of ʿAlī, such as Abū Dharr who died in 31/651–652 in exile under ʿUthmān, as punishment for his protests; and ʿAmmār who would be killed soon afterwards in 37/657 in the battle of Ṣiffīn. But, a number of new partisans were now appearing and the Shīʿa drew general support also from the Banū Hāshim, whose interests had been ignored by the Umayyads. Simultaneous with the emergence of the Shīʿa as a more active party, ʿAlī found himself approached by the various discontented provincials; groups that started becoming more systematically organized around 34/654, and, as such, needed an effective and acceptable spokesman in the capital. The Shīʿa and the discontented provincials, two groups differing in the nature of their opposition to ʿUthmān's rule but with similar objectives, joined forces unintentionally. As a result of this complex alliance, the unpopularity of ʿUthmān grew side by side with the pro-Shīʿī sentiments and the partisanship for ʿAlī, who at the same time mediated with the opposition on behalf of the distressed caliph. The situation deteriorated rapidly, soon exploding into open rebellion, when rebel contingents from Kūfa, Baṣra and Egypt converged on Medina under the overall leadership of the Kūfan *qurrāʾ*. The chaos finally culminated in the murder of ʿUthmān in 35/656, at the hands of a group of mutineers from the Arab army of Egypt.

In the aftermath of this regicide, the Islamic community became badly torn over the question of ʿUthmān's guilt and hence on the justification of the mutineers' action. In an emotionally tense and confused atmosphere, ʿAlī was acclaimed as the new caliph in Medina. This was a notable victory for the Shīʿa whose imām had now succeeded, though with a delay of some twenty-four years, to caliphal authority. ʿAlī drew support from virtually every group opposed to conditions under ʿUthmān. The emergence of the new coalition of groups supporting ʿAlī, together with the austere state of affairs expected under his rule, were naturally alarming to the traditional tribal aristocracy, particularly the Banū Umayya and other influential Meccan clans. Due to such conflicts of interest, ʿAlī was confronted from the start with difficulties which soon erupted into the first civil war in Islam, lasting through his short-lived caliphate. He never succeeded in enforcing his caliphal authority throughout the Islamic empire, especially in the territories of ʿUthmān's relative Muʿāwiya b. Abī Sufyān, who had governed Syria for almost twenty years.

The first challenge to ʿAlī came in the form of a revolt led under the pretext of demanding vengeance for ʿUthmān, by Ṭalḥa and al-Zubayr, two of the most influential of the Companions. They were joined by ʿĀʾisha, Abū Bakr's daughter and the Prophet's widow who nurtured a long-felt hatred for ʿAlī. The three rebel leaders, along with a contingent of the Quraysh, went to Baṣra to organize support for their rebellion. ʿAlī reacted swiftly and left Medina to gather support for his own forces at Kūfa, whose inhabitants had shown their inclinations towards him. The rebels were easily defeated in 36/656, at the so-called battle of the Camel (al-Jamal) near Baṣra, in which Ṭalḥa and al-Zubayr were killed. This rebellion had some significant and enduring consequences, however. Henceforth, the Muslims were to fight amongst themselves and the central authority of the caliphate came to be transferred from Medina to the provinces, ʿIrāq and Syria, where the military effectiveness of the empire was now concentrated. It was in this new setting that the Umayyad challenge to ʿAlī's authority unfolded.

Almost immediately upon ʿAlī's rise to power, Muʿāwiya, at the head of a pro-ʿUthmān party, had launched a campaign against the new caliph to whom he refused to give his allegiance. He, too, particularly as ʿUthmān's kinsman, had found the call for avenging the slain caliph a convenient pretext for covering his real intention of seeing Umayyad rule established throughout the empire. ʿAlī was trapped in an unenviable situation. The actual murderers had fled Medina, while many of the *qurrā*ʾ surrounding him were equally implicated. As ʿAlī was either unable or unwilling to punish those directly responsible, Muʿāwiya rose in rebellion and challenged the very legitimacy of his caliphate.

ʿAlī had, in the meantime, entered Kūfa to mobilize support for the anticipated confrontation with Muʿāwiya. As an important measure towards consolidating his power base there, ʿAlī reorganized the Kūfan tribal groups with a two-fold result. First, by reshuffling tribes and clans from one group to another, he changed the composition of the then existing seven tribal groups in favour of the Yamanīs who, unlike the northern or Nizārī Arabs, were more disposed towards him and the Shīʿī ideal of leadership. Second, and more important, through this very reshuffling he in effect attempted to re-establish the Islamic leadership in Kūfa at the expense of the tribal leadership that had emerged there under ʿUthmān. Accordingly, men like Mālik al-Ashtar, Ḥujr b. ʿAdī al-Kindī and ʿAdī b. Ḥātim, leaders of the early Kūfan *qurrā*ʾ who had been eclipsed by the *ashrāf al-qabāʾil*, were restored to positions of authority. These men, with similarly situated Kūfans, along with their following, provided the backbone of ʿAlī's forces and became the new leaders of the Shīʿa.[16] The Shīʿī leaders urged ʿAlī to attack Muʿāwiya's forces without any delay. On the other hand, the Kūfan *ashrāf* advised against such haste since they were more interested in seeing a stalemate between the contending parties. Doubtless, ʿAlī's victory and egalitarian policies would undermine their privileged positions, while Syrian domination would deprive them of their independent status in ʿIrāq. It was under such circumstances that, after the failure of lengthy negotiations, ʿAlī eventually set out from Kūfa and encountered the Syrian forces at Ṣiffīn on the upper Euphrates, in the spring of 37/657. A long battle ensued, perhaps the most controversial one in the history of early Islam.

The events of the battle of Ṣiffīn, the Syrian arbitration proposal and ʿAlī's acceptance of it, and the resulting arbitration verdict of Adhruḥ issued about a year later, have all been critically examined by a number of modern scholars; as have the intervening circumstances leading to the secession of different groups from ʿAlī's forces, the seceders being subsequently designated as the Khawārij.[17] These events irrevocably undermined ʿAlī's position. His popularity was particularly damaged when he finally decided to check the growing menace of the Khawārij by attacking their camp along the canal of al-Nahrawān in 38/658, inflicting heavy losses on the dissenters. This action, far from destroying the Khawārij, caused large scale defections from ʿAlī's already faltering forces. Failing in his efforts to mobilize a new army, ʿAlī was compelled to retreat to Kūfa and virtually ignore the mounting campaign of Muʿāwiya. During the final two years of the civil war, while many Muslims continued to be hesitant in taking sides, ʿAlī rapidly lost ground to his arch-enemy. Finally, ʿAlī b. Abī Ṭālib, Commander of the Faithful (*Amīr al-Mu'minīn*), fourth caliph and first Shīʿī Imām, was struck with the poisoned sword of a Khārijī in the mosque of Kūfa. He died a few days later, on 21 Ramaḍān 40/25 January 661.

The Islamic community emerged from its first civil war severely tested and split into factions that were to confront one another throughout subsequent centuries. The main factions had already begun to take shape during the final years of ʿUthmān's rule. But they crystallized more explicitly into two opposing parties in the aftermath of the murder of ʿUthmān and the battles of the Jamal and Ṣiffīn. Henceforth, these parties acquired denominations which, in an eclectic sense, revealed their personal loyalties as well as their regional attachments. The supporters of ʿAlī came to be called the *Ahl al-ʿIrāq* (People of ʿIrāq) as well as the *Shīʿat ʿAlī* (Party of ʿAlī), while their adversaries were designated the *Shīʿat ʿUthmān* (Party of ʿUthmān), or more commonly the ʿUthmāniyya. The latter party, after Ṣiffīn, constituted mainly the *Ahl al-Shām* (People of Syria), also referred to as the *Shīʿat Muʿāwiya* (Party of Muʿāwiya). From the time of the first civil war onwards, the partisans of ʿAlī, the Shīʿa *par excellence*, also referred to themselves by terms with more precise religious connotations such as the *Shīʿat Ahl al-Bayt* or its equivalent the *Shīʿat āl Muḥammad* (Party of the Prophet's Household). Starting with the battle of Ṣiffīn, a third faction, the Khawārij, appeared in the community. The Khawārij, seriously opposed to the other two factions, were initially also called the Ḥarūriyya, after the locality Ḥarūrā' to which the first seceders from ʿAlī's forces had retreated, as well as the Shurāt (singular, *shārī*, the vendor), signifying those who sold their soul for the cause of God. As we know, they managed to organize a rapidly spreading movement that many times in the later history of Islam challenged any form of legitimacy and dynastic privilege.[18]

It was during ʿAlī's caliphate that important changes occurred in the composition and influence of the Shīʿa. At the time of ʿAlī's accession to power, the Shīʿa still represented a small personal party comprised chiefly of the original partisans. But during the next few years, the Shīʿa expanded by absorbing some of the most pious Muslims, such as the leaders of the early Kūfan *qurrāʾ* who were to persist in their devotion to ʿAlī. The new partisans were not numerically significant, but they made much difference, as subsequent events showed, to the cause of the Shīʿa, in terms of their unwavering loyalty to ʿAlī and his descendants the ʿAlids. These devout partisans are, indeed, amongst those reported to have sworn to ʿAlī that they would be 'friends of those he befriended, and enemies of those to whom he was hostile';[19] reminiscent of the very words used by the Prophet himself with regard to ʿAlī at Ghadīr Khumm.

As a possible explanation of this deep devotion, W. M. Watt has suggested an interesting hypothesis, arguing that the attachment of the Shīʿa to ʿAlī had acquired a more strictly theological dimension precisely during this same period of his caliphate. The civil war, according to this hypothesis, was a period of crisis and general insecurity in the community, when the nomadic tribesmen of Arabia were experiencing the strains of their new lives in the unstable conditions of Kūfa and other rapidly growing garrison towns. These displaced and insecure Arabs naturally tended to search for salvation which could be attained through different channels. In the case of the Shīʿa, they were already exposed to the idea of the hereditary sanctity of the Prophet's family, while the Yamanī partisans amongst them were particularly familiar with the tradition of divine kingship and the superhuman qualities of kings. It was, therefore, not difficult for them to develop the distinct feeling that their salvation and delivery from distress might best be guaranteed by following a so-called charismatic leader, a person possessing certain superhuman, or divinely ordained, attributes. Thus, the Shīʿa came to find the charismata of inerrancy and infallibility in ʿAlī, and he became a charismatic leader to whom his partisans were deeply attached for their salvation.[20]

The very existence of this zealous party of supporters largely explains how Shīʿism managed to survive ʿAlī's death and numerous subsequent tragic events and defeats. The Shīʿa proper should, however, be distinguished from the other groups in ʿAlī's following. In the confusing milieu of the civil war, several heterogeneous groups, devoid of any particular devotion to ʿAlī, had rallied behind him. They were united in their opposition to ʿUthmān and other mutual adversaries and in the hope of receiving a variety of politico-economic benefits. As a result, the *Shīʿat ʿAlī* came to be loosely and temporarily aligned with all those more appropriately considered the pro-Shīʿī or non-Shīʿī supporters of ʿAlī. It was in this broader sense that Shīʿism was established among the mixed population of southern ʿIrāq, especially in Kūfa. In effect, ʿAlī portrayed the symbol of the ʿIrāqī opposition to Syrian domination, and for a long time the ʿIrāqīs continued to consider his brief rule as a 'golden age', when Kūfa and not Damascus was the capital of the caliphate. But, starting with the events of Ṣiffīn, the situation changed against the hitherto spreading form of broad Shīʿism. Different non-Shīʿī groups in ʿAlī's following, including the Kūfan *ashrāf* who had earlier found it expedient to support him after a dubious fashion, now began to desert him. However, by the time of his murder, the Shīʿa still drew support from certain non-Shīʿī groups. Furthermore, while the ʿIrāqīs in general had remained hesitant in taking sides during the civil war, the Arab settlers of Kūfa, being dominated by the Yamanīs, remained sympathetic towards the Shīʿī ideal of leadership. As we shall see, the Persians too, who soon came to account for an important proportion of Kūfa's non-Arab population, were to express similar pro-Shīʿī inclinations.

It was in these circumstances that al-Ḥasan b. ʿAlī, the elder son of ʿAlī and Fāṭima, was acclaimed as caliph by some forty thousand Kūfans, immediately after his father's death. But the young grandson of the Prophet was no match for the shrewd Muʿāwiya who had endeavoured for many years to win the office for himself. Indeed, Muʿāwiya's power had now become quite unchallengeable, and he easily succeeded in inducing al-Ḥasan to abdicate from the caliphate. The chronology of the events and the circumstances surrounding the brief struggle between al-Ḥasan and Muʿāwiya, as well as the terms under which al-Ḥasan abdicated and retired to Medina, remain rather obscure.[21] The fact remains, however, that after al-Ḥasan's withdrawal, the caliphate easily fell to the Umayyad contender, who was speedily recognized as the new caliph in all provinces and by the majority of the Muslims, except the Shīʿīs and the Khawārij. Having skilfully seized power under the pretext of avenging ʿUthmān, Muʿāwiya also succeeded in founding the Umayyad Caliphate that was destined to rule the Islamic empire on a dynastic basis for nearly a century (41–132/661–750). With these developments, Shīʿism entered into the most difficult period of its early history, being severely persecuted by the Umayyads.

With Muʿāwiya's final victory, the remnants of the non-Shīʿī supporters of ʿAlī and his family either defected to the victorious party, or else scattered. Consequently, eclectic Shīʿism of ʿAlī's time was now reduced to the true Shīʿīs who continued as a small but zealous opposition party in Kūfa. On the other hand, it was the expanding party of Muʿāwiya that eventually came to represent the central body of the community, also called the 'assembly of the believers' (*jamāʿat al-muʾminīn*). By the early ʿAbbāsid times, the majority of the Muslims upholding the caliphates of the Umayyads and the ʿAbbāsids, became known as *Ahl al-Sunna wa'l-Jamāʿa* (people of the *sunna* and of the community), or simply as the Sunnīs. This designation was used not because the majority were more attached than others to the '*sunna* of the Prophet', but because they claimed to be the adherents of correct Prophetic practice and as such, they stood opposed to those who deviated from the common ways and principles of the *Jamāʿa*.[22]

The acquiescent attitude of al-Ḥasan must have been a source of disappointment to many Shīʿīs in whose eyes his abdication from the caliphate did not invalidate his position as their imām. The Shīʿīs continued to regard him as their leader after ʿAlī, while the ʿAlids considered him the head of their family. However, now the spokesman for the Shīʿa was not to be al-Ḥasan, who in accordance with his treaty with Muʿāwiya, abstained from all non-personal activities, but rather Ḥujr b. ʿAdī al-Kindī. This loyal ʿAlid partisan became the moving spirit behind Shīʿī sentiments in Kūfa and never ceased to protest against the official cursing of ʿAlī from the pulpit after the Friday prayers, a policy instituted by Muʿāwiya. On a few occasions, the Shīʿīs from Kūfa visited al-Ḥasan in Medina, the permanent domicile of the ʿAlids, attempting in vain to persuade him to rise against Muʿāwiya. The latter, who was ruling with an iron fist, had meanwhile taken various precautionary measures, including his own reorganization of the Kūfan tribal groups, to prevent any serious Shīʿī insurrection. On the whole, the Shīʿī movement remained subdued during the period between al-Ḥasan's renouncement of caliphal authority and his early death in 49/669.

After al-Ḥasan, the Shīʿīs revived their aspirations for restoring the caliphate to the ʿAlids, now headed by al-Ḥasan's younger and full-brother, al-Ḥusayn b. ʿAlī. They invited their new imām to rise against the Umayyads. However al-Ḥusayn made it known that, in observance of his brother's abdication agreement, he would not respond to such summons so long as Muʿāwiya was still alive. Yet the most zealous Shīʿīs could no longer remain inactive. In 51/671, soon after Muʿāwiya's adopted brother Ziyād b. Abīhi had become the governor of both Kūfa and Baṣra, Ḥujr and a handful of die-hard Shīʿīs attempted to instigate a revolt in Kūfa.[23] The revolt never actually materialized as the Shīʿīs were not yet sufficiently numerous and organized, and as the Kūfan tribal support they had relied on was not forthcoming. Ḥujr and his associates were arrested, and they chose to sacrifice their lives rather than denounce ʿAlī and be pardoned. The tragedy of Ḥujr in effect initiated the Shīʿī martyrology and became the prelude to that of the principal Shīʿī martyr al-Ḥusayn, called *Sayyid al-Shuhadāʾ*, or Lord of the Martyrs.

Muʿāwiya died in 60/680, and according to his unprecedented testament for which he had previously obtained the consent of the notables of the empire, his son Yazīd succeeded to the caliphate. The Shīʿī leaders of Kūfa, such as Sulaymān b. Ṣurad al-Khuzāʿī, Ḥabīb b. Muẓāhir and Muslim b. ʿAwsaja, loyal partisans who had fought on ʿAlī's side at the battles of the Camel and Ṣiffīn, wrote to al-Ḥusayn inviting him to lead his Kūfan followers in wresting the caliphate from Yazīd. Similar invitations were sent out by other Kūfans, especially the Yamanīs, in the hope that al-Ḥusayn would organize a revolt against Umayyad rule and end the Syrian domination of ʿIrāq. Before making a decision, however, al-Ḥusayn, who had already refused to accord the *bayʿa* to Yazīd and had withdrawn to Mecca, thought it prudent to assess the situation through his cousin Muslim b. ʿAqīl. On his arrival in Kūfa, Muslim soon collected thousands of pledges of support, and, assured of the situation, advised al-Ḥusayn to assume the active leadership of the Shīʿīs and their sympathizers in Kūfa. Finally, al-Ḥusayn decided to respond to the pressing summons.

Yazīd, on his part, having become weary of mounting Shīʿī sentiments, reacted swiftly. He appointed his strongman ʿUbayd Allāh b. Ziyād, then governing Baṣra, to also take charge of Kūfa, with strict orders to crush the pro-Ḥusayn disturbances there. Ibn Ziyād's severe retaliatory measures and punishments soon terrified the Kūfans, including the Yamanīs and other Shīʿī sympathizers. This is not surprising, since the Kūfans had time and again shown a characteristic lack of resolve. Thus abandoned by the Kūfans, and failing in his efforts to start an immediate uprising, Muslim was arrested and executed. Kūfa was once again brought under the full control of the Umayyads. But al-Ḥusayn had already embarked on the route to Kūfa.

On his fatal journey, al-Ḥusayn was accompanied by a small group of relatives and companions. Before reaching their destination, they were intercepted in the plain of Karbalāʾ, near Kūfa, by an Umayyad army of 4,000 men. It was there that, refusing one last time to yield to Yazīd, al-Ḥusayn and his company of some 72 men were brutally massacred on 10 Muḥarram 61/10 October 680. Only women and some children were spared. ʿAlī b. al-Ḥusayn, who was to receive the honorific title Zayn al-ʿĀbidīn, being sick and confined to his tent, was one of the survivors. Amongst the 54 non-ʿAlid martyrs of Karbalāʾ, there were only a few of the Kūfan Shīʿīs who had somehow managed to penetrate Ibn Ziyād's tight blockade of Kūfa to be with their imām in his hour of need. The Shīʿīs have particular reverence for these martyrs, notably the aged Muslim b. ʿAwsaja, ʿĀbis b. Abī Ḥabīb, Saʿīd b. ʿAbd Allāh al-Ḥanafī, and Ḥabīb b. Muẓāhir, who commanded the left flank of al-Ḥusayn's company, the right one having been held by Zuhayr b. al-Qayn, a faithful companion. Thus concluded a legend of heroism, the most tragic episode in the early history of Shīʿism, and indeed, of Islam.[24] This event is still commemorated devoutly in the Shīʿī world, by special ceremonies and a type of popular religious play (*taʿziya*).

The heroic martyrdom of the Prophet's grandson infused a new religious fervour in the Shīʿa. This event, solidly establishing the Shīʿī martyrology, was destined to play a significant role in the consolidation of the Shīʿī identity. In the immediate aftermath of Karbalāʾ, the Shīʿīs and many other Kūfans who had so persistently invited al-Ḥusayn into their midst, were deeply moved. A sense of repentance set in, and they felt the urge to avenge the murder of al-Ḥusayn and to expiate their own failure to support him. Hence, these people called themselves the Tawwābūn or the Penitents. Towards the end of 61/680, they formally began to organize a movement, with an original membership of one-hundred die-hard Shīʿīs of Kūfa, none of whom was under sixty years of age. Old and devoted, these partisans were doubtless reacting on the basis of their conscience. The Tawwābūn did not openly proclaim any of the ʿAlids as their imām.[25] Sulaymān b. Ṣurad, then in the forefront of all the Shīʿī activities in Kūfa, was selected as their leader; and for three years, while Yazīd was alive, the movement proceeded with extreme caution and secrecy.

With Yazīd's sudden death in 64/683, the Tawwābūn found it opportune to come into the open and expand their recruiting efforts. This was mainly because the unrest of Yazīd's rule had now erupted into outright civil war, the second one for Islam. Yazīd was succeeded by his sickly son,

Muʿāwiya II, and when the latter died some six months later, the aged Marwān b. al-Ḥakam (d. 65/685), the most prominent member of the ruling family, became the new caliph. This immediately led to a serious conflict between the two major rival tribes of Syria, Kalb and Qays, making it impossible for the Umayyads to maintain their control over ʿIrāq. Meanwhile, in the Ḥijāz, ʿAbd Allāh b. al-Zubayr, who like al-Ḥusayn had refused to pay homage to Yazīd and had revolted, was now successfully claiming the caliphate for himself. In particular, he had gained general recognition by the ʿIrāqīs who were attempting to acquire their independence from Syria. They expelled Ibn Ziyād, the Umayyad governor of both Kūfa and Baṣra, who bore chief responsibility for the massacre at Karbalāʾ. In the prevailing chaos, the Tawwābūn managed to solicit pledges of support from some 16,000 persons, not all of whom were Shīʿīs. Sulaymān b. Ṣurad, contrary to the advice of some of his associates, decided to attack the Umayyad forces of Ibn Ziyād, who was then near the Syrian border in order to reconquer ʿIrāq for Marwān. The Tawwābūn congregated at Nukhayla, near Kūfa, in Rabīʿ II 65/November 684, as planned. But to their disappointment, only 4,000 men showed up. Regardless, they proceeded, and some two months later met Ibn Ziyād's much larger army at ʿAyn al-Warda. By the end of the three-day battle, the majority of the Tawwābūn, including Sulaymān himself, fulfilled their pledge of sacrificing their lives for al-Ḥusayn.

The movement of the Tawwābūn, representing yet another defeat for the Shīʿa, marks the end of what may be regarded as the Arab and the unified phase of Shīʿism. During its first half-century, from 11/632 until around 65/684, Shīʿism maintained an almost exclusively Arab nature, with a limited appeal to non-Arab Muslims. The Tawwābūn who fell in battle were all Arabs, including a significant number of the early Kūfan *qurrāʾ* who provided the leading personalities of the movement. These Arabs belonged mainly to various Yamanī tribes settled in Kūfa, although northern Arabs were also amongst them. In addition, during this initial phase, the Shīʿī movement consisted of a single party, without any internal division. These features were to change drastically with the next event in the history of Shīʿism, the revolt of al-Mukhtār.[26]

Al-Mukhtār b. Abī ʿUbayd al-Thaqafī was an ambitious and controversial man devoted to the cause of the ʿAlids. He had participated in the premature insurrection of Muslim b. ʿAqīl. He had then gone to the Ḥijāz, hoping in vain to collaborate with Ibn al-Zubayr. Subsequently, with the rising Shīʿī sentiments in Kūfa, he again appeared there in 64/684, a few months after Yazīd's death. There, he strove to acquire a leading position among the Shīʿīs, who lacked an active imām. However, he did not have much success while Sulaymān b. Ṣurad was still alive. The latter refused either to join forces with al-Mukhtār or to pay heed to his warnings against the futility of any poorly-organized entanglement with the Umayyads.

With the demise of the Tawwābūn, the long-awaited opportunity finally arose for al-Mukhtār's own plans. He launched a vigorous campaign, again with a general call for avenging al-Ḥusayn's murder, in the name of Muḥammad b. al-Ḥanafiyya, ʿAlī's son by Khawla, a woman from the Banū Ḥanīfa. Al-Mukhtār tactfully claimed to be the trusted agent and representative, *amīn* and *wazīr*, of Ibn al-Ḥanafiyya. It is not clear to what extent such claims had the prior approval of Ibn al-Ḥanafiyya, who resided in Medina and remained a mere figurehead in the unfolding revolt. Of greater consequence was al-Mukhtār's proclamation of Ibn al-Ḥanafiyya as al-Mahdī, 'the divinely guided one', the saviour imām who would establish justice on earth and thus deliver the oppressed from tyranny (*ẓulm*). This title had already been applied in a purely honorific sense to ʿAlī, al-Ḥasan and al-Ḥusayn, but its first use in a messianic sense now derived from al-Mukhtār. The concept of the Imām-Mahdī was a very important doctrinal innovation, and it proved particularly appealing to the non-Arab Muslims, the so-called *mawālī* who constituted the bulk of the oppressed masses of Kūfa.

Al-Mukhtār soon won the support of the Shīʿī majority, including the survivors of the Tawwābūn and the influential Ibrāhīm b. al-Ashtar (d. 72/691), the leader of the hard-core Shīʿīs who, like his father, was a loyal ʿAlid partisan. Having collected a sufficient army, the open revolt took place in Rabīʿ I 66/October 685. Without much bloodshed, al-Mukhtār speedily won control of Kūfa. The *ashrāf* who had not sided with the revolt surrendered and paid homage to al-Mukhtār, as did other Kūfans. Initially, al-Mukhtār adopted a conciliatory policy. He chose his officials primarily from amongst the Arab ruling class, while concern for the weak and the oppressed, which in fact meant the *mawālī*, constituted an important part of his socio-economic programme. For instance, he accorded the *mawālī* rights to booty and also entitled them to army stipends. But the Arab Muslims were reluctant to see their privileged positions curbed for the benefit of the *mawālī* whom they considered to be of an altogether inferior status. Consequently, the Arabs, especially the Kūfan tribal chiefs who were never inclined towards Shīʿism in the first place, soon came to resent al-Mukhtār's policies, and began to desert him.

Subjected to a triple assault by the Kūfan *ashrāf*, the Umayyads, and eventually the Zubayrids, al-Mukhtār's victory was to be short-lived.

The Syrian forces, now in the caliphate of ʿAbd al-Malik b. Marwān (65–86/685–705), the most celebrated member of the Umayyad dynasty, were once again directed against ʿIrāq towards the end of 66/685. But Ibrāhīm b. al-Ashtar, leading al-Mukhtār's army, succeeded in defeating them in a fierce battle in Muḥarram 67/August 686, in which their commander, the famous Ibn Ziyād, was slain. In the meantime, the Kūfan *ashrāf* had risen against al-Mukhtār; they, too, were easily defeated by Ibn al-Ashtar. After this episode, al-Mukhtār gave free rein to the hitherto restrained Shīʿīs to take their revenge on the *ashrāf*. Most of those guilty for the tragedy of al-Ḥusayn, including Shamir b. Dhi'l-Jawshan and ʿUmar b. Saʿd, were routed out and beheaded. Many of the *ashrāf*, however, managed to flee to Baṣra, seeking protection from its governor, Muṣʿab, the younger brother of the Meccan anti-caliph. With these developments, many of the Kūfan Arabs who until then had supported al-Mukhtār, defected to the side of the *ashrāf*. The tribal leaders, on their part, were now openly aligning themselves with Ibn al-Zubayr in order to re-establish their position *vis-à-vis* al-Mukhtār and the Syrians. Henceforth, al-Mukhtār was forced to rely almost completely on the *mawālī*, who called themselves the *Shīʿat al-Mahdī*.

The *ashrāf* finally induced Muṣʿab to fight against the Kūfan Shīʿīs. The Baṣran forces, in the company of the Kūfan tribal leaders, defeated al-Mukhtār's army in two encounters, the second one taking place in Jumādā I 67/December 686 in which many *mawālī* were killed. Al-Mukhtār retreated to the citadel of Kūfa where he and the remnants of his *mawālī* soldiers were besieged by Muṣʿab's troops for about four months. Finally, al-Mukhtār and a group of his most devoted supporters, refusing to surrender unconditionally, were killed whilst attempting a sortie, in Ramaḍān 67/April 687. Kūfa was brought under the control of Ibn al-Zubayr to the satisfaction of the *ashrāf* who took their own revenge on the *mawālī*.

With al-Mukhtār out of the way, the two claimants to the caliphate, ʿAbd al-Malik and Ibn al-Zubayr, found themselves in direct confrontation. ʿAbd al-Malik's most trusted lieutenant, al-Ḥajjāj b. Yūsuf, after defeating Muṣʿab in 72/691, conquered Mecca and killed Ibn al-Zubayr in battle in 73/692. The collapse of the Zubayrid anti-caliphate also ended the second civil war, and unity was again restored to the Islamic state. In 75/694, al-Ḥajjāj became the governor of ʿIrāq and ruled that province and its eastern dependencies with an iron fist for the next twenty years, using Syrian troops when necessary. He built the fortified garrison town of Wāsiṭ, midway between Kūfa and Baṣra, in 83/702, as the new provincial seat of government where he stationed his loyal Syrian militia. Al-Ḥajjāj's efforts brought peace and economic prosperity to ʿIrāq and also resulted in new Islamic conquests in Transoxiana and the Indus valley, during the caliphate of ʿAbd al-Malik's son and successor al-Walīd (86–96/705–715), who gave still greater authority to this most able Umayyad governor. Al-Ḥajjāj died in 95/714, almost a year before al-Walīd's own death. This brief digression explains why there were no Shīʿī revolts in Kūfa during al-Ḥajjāj's long rule. Indeed, with the solid control of the Umayyads re-established in ʿIrāq in 72/691, the Shīʿīs, who now lacked effective leaders, were deprived of any opportunity for open activity for about the next fifty years. Nevertheless, Shīʿī ideas and tendencies continued to take shape, especially amongst the *mawālī*. It is, therefore, useful to take a closer look at the *mawālī* and their grievances, which provided the necessary motivation for their effective participation in the Shīʿī movement.

The *mawālī* (singular, *mawlā*) essentially comprised of the non-Arab Muslims who, in early Islam, represented an important intermediary class between the Arab Muslims and the non-Muslim subjects of the empire.[27] By the third Islamic century, however, with their greater integration within the Islamic society under the ʿAbbāsids, the *mawālī* could no longer be identified as a distinct social class, and consequently the term lost its significance and disappeared.

In the wake of the Islamic conquests, a need had been felt for a term to describe the new converts from amongst the Persian, Aramaean, Berber and other non-Arab natives of the conquered lands. For this purpose, the old term *mawlā*, which was originally used in Arab society in reference to certain types of kinship as well as relationship by covenant particularly between individuals and tribes, was adopted. In its new sense, *mawlā* meant a Muslim of non-Arab origin attached as client to an Arab tribe; because, non-Arabs on embracing Islam were expected to become affiliated as clients to Arab tribes. This requirement was indicative of the fact that the tribal pattern characterizing the pre-Islamic Arab society had continued to shape the social structure of the Islamic state. According to this type of clientage, or *walāʾ*, a special relationship would be established between the protected client, often a liberated prisoner of war or slave, and his protector, normally his former patron or an influential Arab.

The *mawālī* represented different cultures and religious traditions. In ʿIrāq, they were comprised mainly of Aramaeans, though Persians and other non-Arabs representing the older strata of the province's population were also amongst them. Upon the destruction of the Sāsānid empire, Aramaeans and Persians had flocked in large numbers to the ʿIrāqī garrison towns, as these were the most rapidly growing administrative, economic and urban centres of the new Islamic empire. Kūfa in particular, as the foremost of such centres in the east, was the recipient of the bulk of these uprooted emigrants who came from different socio-economic backgrounds and, in due course, formed various *mawlā* categories.[28] First, there were those craftsmen, tradesmen, shopkeepers and other skilled persons, who had swarmed into the prospering new towns to offer their services to the Arab garrisons. These *mawālī*, probably the largest *mawlā* category in Kūfa, were subject to a special type of clientage whereby they were almost independent members of the tribes with which they were associated. Second, there were the freed slaves, the original non-Arab *mawālī*, who had been brought to the garrison towns in successive waves as prisoners of war and as part of the Arabs' spoils. They had acquired their freedom upon conversion to Islam, but as *mawālī* they continued to be affiliated to their former patrons. In Kūfa, these freed slaves constituted the second largest *mawlā* category. In the third largest category were those petty landowners and cultivators who, with the collapse of the Sāsānid feudal system and the destruction of their villages by the invading Arabs, had found the cultivation of their lands no longer economical. The problems of these rural people, including those engaged in the villages and estates around Kūfa, were further aggravated due to the high level of the land tax, or *kharāj*. Consequently, an increasing number of them were continuously obliged to abandon the fields in search of alternative employment in the garrison towns. Finally, there was the numerically insignificant group of Persian *mawālī* who claimed noble extraction and were permitted to share some of the privileges reserved for the Arab ruling class.

In line with the spread of Islamization, the total number of the *mawālī* increased very rapidly. In fact, within a few decades, they came to outnumber the Arab Muslims. As Muslims, the *mawālī* expected the same rights and privileges as their Arab co-religionists. After all, the Prophet himself had declared the equality of all believers before God, despite possible differences stemming from descent, race and tribal affiliation. But the Islamic teaching of equality was not conceded by the Arab rulers under the Umayyads, although in the earliest years of Islam and prior to ʿUmar's caliphate, when the *mawālī* were still a minority group, the precepts of Islam had been observed more closely.

In all its categories, a *mawlā* had come to represent a socially and racially inferior status, a second-class citizen as compared to an Arab Muslim. The *mawālī* were, however, set apart from the non-Muslim subjects of the empire who were accorded an even more inferior status. These so-called people of protection, *ahl al-dhimma* or simply *dhimmīs*, were the followers of certain recognized religions, notably Judaism, Christianity and, later, Zoroastrianism. They received the protection (*dhimma*) of the Muslim state in return for the payment of a distinguishing tribute called *jizya*, which later developed into a precise poll-tax. A *dhimmī*, who was subject to certain social restrictions as well, would acquire *mawlā* status by converting to Islam and becoming duly attached to an Arab tribe. The Arabs discriminated, in various ways, especially economically, against the *mawālī*. The *mawālī* were often deprived of any share of the booty accruing in wars to the tribes with which they were associated; nor were they entitled to the customary army stipends. More significantly, the taxes paid by the new converts were often similar to the *jizya* and *kharāj*, required of the non-Muslim subjects. This provided perhaps the most important single cause of their discontent, since many of them had converted precisely in order to be less heavily taxed.

As a large and underprivileged social class concentrated in the urban milieus, and aspiring for a state and society which would be more sensitive to the teachings of Islam, the *mawālī* provided a valuable recruiting ground for any movement opposed to the exclusively Arab order under the Umayyads. They did, in fact, participate in the Khārijī revolts and some 100,000 of them joined Ibn al-Ashʿath's unsuccessful rebellion against al-Ḥajjāj in 82/701. But above all, they were to be involved in the more important Shīʿī opposition centred in Kūfa, not only because Shīʿism proved to have a greater appeal to the oppressed masses but also because the backgrounds of some *mawālī* made them more inclined towards the Shīʿī ideal of leadership. For instance, the Persian *mawālī* of southern ʿIrāq had had a religio-political tradition of divine kingship and hereditary leadership almost similar to that of the Yamanīs. Consequently, they were readily responsive to the summons of the Shīʿa and to their promise to overthrow the impious Umayyads and install the Ahl al-Bayt to the caliphate, so as to fulfil the egalitarian teachings of Islam.[29]

As noted previously, al-Mukhtār was the first person who identified the growing political importance of the *mawālī* and their potential receptivity to the cause of the Shīʿa. By attempting to remove their grievances, and through the appeal of the idea of the Mahdī, he easily succeeded in mobilizing them in his revolt. But more significantly, al-Mukhtār had now drawn these discontented non-Arabs into the Shīʿī movement, whereby Shīʿism acquired a much broader base of social support. As a result of this development, representing a vital turning point in the history of Shīʿism, the superficially Islamized *mawālī* brought many ideas into Shīʿī Islam from their old Babylonian, Judaeo-Christian, and Irano-Zoroastrian backgrounds, including those derived from the Iranian religious heresies such as Manichaeism and Mazdakism, ideas foreign to early Islam. In terms of their numbers, ideas and revolutionary zeal, the *mawālī* played a major role in the transformation of Shīʿism from an Arab party of limited membership and doctrinal basis into an active sectarian movement.

For the sixty-odd years intervening between the revolt of al-Mukhtār and the ʿAbbāsid revolution, Shīʿism did not represent a unified and coherent movement. During this period, different Shīʿī groups co-existed, each having its own imām, and developing its own doctrines, while individuals moved freely and frequently between them. Furthermore, the Shīʿī Imāms now came not only from amongst the ʿAlids who had become quite numerous by this time,[30] but also from other branches of the Prophet's clan of Hāshim. There were also those Shīʿī leaders who, like al-Mukhtār, claimed to have derived their authority from various imāms. Thus, Shīʿism of this period, by contrast to the previous half a century, did not accord general recognition to any single succession of imāms, from which various dissident groups would diverge in favour of alternative claimants.

An important factor responsible for the internal division of the Shīʿa revolved around differences of opinion on the composition of the Ahl al-Bayt. As noted, the Shīʿa from the beginning believed in the sanctity of the Prophet's family and the special hereditary attributes of its members. These very attributes distinguished the Shīʿī Imām from the Ahl al-Bayt, and qualified him to lead the Muslims under divine guidance along the right path. But in this formative period, though the imāms who succeeded al-Ḥusayn continued to come chiefly from amongst the ʿAlids, the Prophet's family was still defined more broadly in its old tribal sense. It covered the various branches of the Banū Hāshim, the leading Quraysh clan, regardless of direct descent from the Prophet Muḥammad himself.[31]

The Ahl al-Bayt, then, included the progeny of Muḥammad through Fāṭima and ʿAlī as well as those of his two paternal uncles; not only the Ṭālibids, the descendants of Abū Ṭālib (d. ca. 619) through his sons ʿAlī and Jaʿfar (d. 8/629), but even the ʿAbbāsids, the descendants of al-ʿAbbās (d. ca. 32/653) who had embraced Islam only in 8/630. For analogous reasons, ʿAlī's family was the centre of much diversity in allegiance, with Shīʿīs rallying to the side of all its three major branches: the Ḥanafids, the Ḥusaynids, and the Ḥasanids. In other words, the Fāṭimid and non-Fāṭimid ʿAlids as well as many non-ʿAlid Hāshimids, all descendants of the Prophet's paternal grandfather ʿAbd al-Muṭṭalib b. Hāshim, apparently qualified for being members of the Ahl al-Bayt.

It was later, after the accession of the ʿAbbāsids, that the Shīʿīs came to define the Ahl al-Bayt more restrictively to include only the descendants of the Prophet through Fāṭima, known as the Fāṭimids (covering both the Ḥasanids and the Ḥusaynids); while the bulk of the non-Zaydī Shīʿīs had come to acknowledge chiefly the Ḥusaynid Fāṭimids. The latter definition was the one adopted by the Twelver and Ismāʿīlī Shīʿīs. The lack of consensus on the composition of the Prophet's family had not created any disagreements amongst the Shīʿīs until al-Ḥusayn's death, whilst the ʿAlids had readily accepted al-Ḥasan and al-Ḥusayn as the heads of their family after ʿAlī. But now, prevailing circumstances led to diversity.

In this confusing setting, the development of Shīʿism took place in terms of two main branches or trends. First, and until the accession of the ʿAbbāsids the more predominant of the two, there was a radical branch comprised of several inter-related groups which, beginning with al-Mukhtār's movement, recognized the Ḥanafids, and later other Hāshimids (notably the ʿAbbāsids) deriving their claims from Ibn al-Ḥanafiyya's son, as their imāms. This trend, designated by Lewis also as *mawlā* Shīʿism,[32] drew mainly on the support of the *mawālī* in southern ʿIrāq and elsewhere, who upheld extremist doctrines and revolutionary objectives, though many Arabs were also amongst them, often in leading positions. There was, secondly, a moderate branch which remained essentially removed from any anti-regime activity. This branch, later known as the Imāmiyya, followed a Ḥusaynid line of imāms. Eventually, both trends converged, though each one maintained its own identity, in the latter part of the imāmate of the Ḥusaynid Jaʿfar al-Ṣādiq who succeeded in consolidating Shīʿism to a large extent. However, the radical trend was once again retrieved mainly by the proto-Ismāʿīlī Imāmīs, while the moderate trend ultimately crystallized into Twelver Shīʿism, representing the majority body of the Shīʿa. A few words are required now regarding the circumstances under which these two trends originated.

After Karbalāʾ, the young Zayn al-ʿĀbidīn, al-Ḥusayn's only surviving son and the progenitor of all the Ḥusaynids, retired to Medina and adopted a quiescent attitude towards the Umayyads and the Zubayrid anti-caliphate, and later towards al-Mukhtār's movement and the Ḥanafids. He kept aloof from all political activity, a policy which was to be maintained and in fact justified doctrinally by his successors in the moderate branch. The later Shīʿī supporters of the Ḥusaynid line claimed that al-Ḥusayn had personally designated Zayn al-ʿĀbidīn as his successor. But the fact remains that after al-Ḥusayn's death, Zayn al-ʿĀbidīn did not acquire any following. On the other hand, al-Mukhtār's campaign for Ibn al-Ḥanafiyya as the Mahdī, had an unprecedented popular appeal among the Kūfan masses. As a result, the overwhelming majority of the Shīʿīs, both Arabs and *mawālī*, joined his active movement and recognized the imāmate of Ibn al-Ḥanafiyya. It should also be recalled that Ibn al-Ḥanafiyya now enjoyed a particular position of honour and seniority amongst the ʿAlids. Some Islamists have even argued that as ʿAlī's eldest surviving son and the eldest ʿAlid, being some twenty years older than his nephew Zayn al-ʿĀbidīn, Ibn al-Ḥanafiyya was considered as the *shaykh* or head of the ʿAlid family; a position which was never publicly challenged by Zayn al-ʿĀbidīn.[33] With these beginnings, the moderate trend came to be eclipsed for some time by the radical branch of Shīʿism, to which we shall now turn.

The movement started by al-Mukhtār survived the suppression of his rule in Kūfa. It rapidly spread under its own *mawlā* dynamism, as witnessed by a state founded in Niṣībīn by some of al-Mukhtār's adherents shortly after his death, and which collapsed in 71/690 under the attacks of the Umayyad forces. The followers of al-Mukhtār, upholding the imāmate of Ibn al-Ḥanafiyya, were initially called the Mukhtāriyya. But they were soon more commonly referred to as the Kaysāniyya. The origin of this designation, like the names of some other Shīʿī groups, can be traced to the heresiographical works written about the internal divisions and the sects of Islam; notably those by al-Ashʿarī (d. 324/935–936), al-Malaṭī (d. 377/987), al-Baghdādī (d. 429/1037), and Ibn Ḥazm (d. 456/1064), who were devout Sunnīs; al-Shahrastānī (d. 548/1153), and the earliest sources on Shīʿī sub-sects produced by Shīʿī authors al-Nawbakhtī (d. between 300 and 310/912–922) and al-Qummī (d. 301/913–914).[34] At any rate, the name Kaysāniyya seems to have been based either on the *kunya* of al-Mukhtār himself or, more probably, on the highly controversial figure of Abū ʿAmra Kaysān, a prominent *mawlā* and chief of al-Mukhtār's personal guard.[35] The latter etymology emphasizes the role of the *mawālī* in the movement.

The Kaysānīs were left without active leadership and organization after al-Mukhtār, while Ibn al-Ḥanafiyya maintained some contacts with them and, though submitting to the Umayyad caliph ʿAbd al-Malik in 73/692, did not openly dissociate himself from the movement.[36] But when Ibn al-Ḥanafiyya died in 81/700, the Kaysāniyya split into at least three distinct groups, commonly designated as sects (singular, *firqa*) by the heresiographers who use the term indiscriminately for an independent group, a subgroup, a school of thought, or even a minor doctrinal position.[37] One group, refusing to acknowledge Ibn al-Ḥanafiyya's death, believed he was concealed (*ghāʾib*) in the Raḍwā mountains near Medina, whence he would eventually emerge as the Mahdī to fill the earth with justice and equity, as it had formerly been filled with injustice and oppression. These partisans were called the Karibiyya or Kuraybiyya, after their leader Abū Karib (Kurayb) al-Ḍarīr. Initially, the renowned extremist Ḥamza b. ʿUmāra al-Barbarī also belonged to this group, and was a disciple of Abū Karib. Later, while asserting divinity for Ibn al-Ḥanafiyya and prophethood for himself, Ḥamza separated and acquired some supporters in Medina and Kūfa. Among the other original adherents of the Karibiyya, the heresiographers also mention Bayān b. Samʿān al-Tamīmī, the controversial extremist Shīʿī who later headed a group of his own in Kūfa. The views of the Karibiyya have been vividly preserved in the poetry of Kuthayyir (d. 105/723), and al-Sayyid al-Ḥimyarī (d. 173/789) who subsequently turned to the Imām Jaʿfar al-Ṣādiq. A second group, apparently under the leadership of a certain Ḥayyān al-Sarrāj, while affirming Ibn al-Ḥanafiyya's death, maintained that he and his partisans would return to life in time, when he would establish justice on earth.

In these early Kaysānī beliefs, circulated mainly amongst the *mawālī*, we have the first Shīʿī statements of the eschatological doctrines of *ghayba*, the absence or occultation of an imām whose life has been miraculously prolonged and who is due to reappear as the Mahdī; and *rajʿa*, the return of a messianic personality from the dead, or from occultation, sometime before the Day of Resurrection (*qiyāma*). The closely related concept of the Mahdī had now also acquired, for the first time, an eschatological meaning, with the implication that no further imāms would succeed the Mahdī during his period of *ghayba*.[38] It is not clear why the title al-Mahdī, to which the participle 'expected' (*al-muntaẓar*) was sometimes attached, came to be adopted for the messianic deliverer in Islam. As the term does not occur in the Qur'ān, the origin of this eschatological idea has been the subject of varied explanations. Some modern scholars, citing the ultimate Zoroastrian saviour (Saoshyant) who is destined to carry out what in Zoroastrian eschatology is called the final transfiguration or renovation of the world (*frashkart*), ascribe its origins to Iranian sources.[39] Still others have attributed its roots to the Judaeo-Christian messianic teachings.[40] Regardless, henceforth the idea of a future deliverer who would eventually appear before the end of time, became a doctrinal feature common to most Muslim groups. This included the early Ismāʿīlīs and the Ithnāʿasharīs who are still awaiting the parousia of their twelfth imām.

The majority of Ibn al-Ḥanafiyya's followers, however, accepting his death, now recognized the imāmate of his eldest son Abū Hāshim ʿAbd Allāh, whom they believed to have been personally designated by Ibn al-Ḥanafiyya as his successor.[41] This probably marks the first instance of the important Shīʿī principle of *naṣṣ* imāmate, whereby an imām is appointed through the explicit designation (*naṣṣ*) of a preceding imām. Abū Hāshim, who was slightly younger than his cousin Zayn al-ʿĀbidīn, thus became the imām of the Shīʿī majority. He was also regarded as the head of the Ḥanafids, though he did not exert undisputed authority over the entire ʿAlid family who could no longer agree on the selection of a *shaykh*. There exist no details on the nature of the doctrines held by Abū Hāshim and his partisans, known as the Hāshimiyya. All that may be inferred is that there was continuity from al-Mukhtār's movement to the Hāshimiyya. It is also known that from their base in Kūfa, the Hāshimiyya managed to recruit adherents in other provinces, especially among the *mawālī* in Khurāsān.

Abū Hāshim died in 98/716, in the village of Ḥumayma on the border separating Palestine and Arabia, on his return from a visit to the court of al-Walīd's brother and successor Sulaymān (96–99/715–717). On Abū Hāshim's death, his partisans split into four main groups. One group, adhering to the belief that the then-approaching second Islamic century would be a turning point in the realization of the Shīʿī messianic expectations, professed that Abū Hāshim remained alive and concealed, and would soon reappear as the Mahdī. Bayān b. Samʿān now joined this group and acquired a leading position among them. He taught many extremist ideas and also speculated on the nature of God in crudely anthropomorphic terms, maintaining that God is a man of light. His followers, later forming a group known as the Bayāniyya, at first affirmed that Abū Hāshim would emerge as the Mahdī. Subsequently, they asserted that Abū Hāshim had in fact conferred prophethood on Bayān on behalf of God, while some of them regarded him as an imām. Indeed, the Bayāniyya, as a separate group, came to hold a multitude of extremist views, such as ascribing prophethood to the imāms on the basis of an indwelling divine light transmitted through them.[42] A second group maintained that Abū Hāshim, who left no male progeny, had appointed his younger brother ʿAlī as his successor. They recognized this Ḥanafid ʿAlī as their new imām, after whose death they traced the imāmate through his son al-Ḥasan and then the latter's son and grandson, ʿAlī and al-Ḥasan respectively. This group, called the 'pure Kaysāniyya' by al-Nawbakhtī,[43] affirmed that the imāmate belonged exclusively to the descendants of Ibn al-Ḥanafiyya, from amongst whom the Mahdī would eventually arise. When the last-mentioned al-Ḥasan died without leaving any sons some members of this group separated, claiming that Ibn al-Ḥanafiyya himself would return as their awaited Mahdī.

The bulk of the Hāshimiyya, however, recognized Muḥammad b. ʿAlī b. ʿAbd Allāh b. al-ʿAbbās, the great-grandson of the Prophet's uncle, as their imām after Abū Hāshim. They held that Abū Hāshim, shortly before dying in Ḥumayma, then the residence of the ʿAbbāsids, had bequeathed his rights to the imāmate to this ʿAbbāsid. But as he was a minor at the time, the testament had been entrusted to his father ʿAlī b. ʿAbd Allāh (d. 118/736), the head of the ʿAbbāsid family in whose house Abū Hāshim had died, apparently of food poisoning. On the death of Muḥammad b. ʿAlī in 125/743, his partisans accepted the imāmate of his son Ibrāhīm, the brother of the first two ʿAbbāsid caliphs. This party, supported by the majority of the extremist Shīʿīs until the accession of the ʿAbbāsids, continued to be known as the Hāshimiyya and later also as the Rāwandiyya, after an obscure sectarian leader, ʿAbd Allāh al-Rāwandī.[44]

The matter of Abū Hāshim's testament in favour of the ʿAbbāsid Muḥammad b. ʿAlī has been the subject of much controversy throughout the centuries.[45] Some scholars believe that the testament in question was fabricated by the ʿAbbāsids themselves, so as to win the support of the Shīʿīs who normally favoured the ʿAlid candidates; they have also argued that Abū Hāshim may actually have been poisoned by the ʿAbbāsids, rather than on the alleged orders of the Umayyad caliph Sulaymān.[46] On the other hand, certain modern Islamists, notably Cahen and Lewis, have rightly stated that the determination of the authenticity of this testament, even if it were possible, is not a question of vital importance.[47] The undisputed fact remains that the majority of Abū Hāshim's partisans did transfer their allegiance to Muḥammad b. ʿAlī; and more significantly, with this transference the ʿAbbāsids inherited the party and the propaganda organization of the Hāshimiyya. In sum, it was the utilization of the testament rather than its authenticity that is of historical relevance, since it was the party of the Hāshimiyya which became the main instrument of the ʿAbbāsid movement, and eventually of the overthrow of the Umayyads.

Finally, there was another distinct group, the special partisans of ʿAbd Allāh b. Muʿāwiya, the great-grandson of Jaʿfar b. Abī Ṭālib, ʿAlī's brother. Jaʿfar, known as al-Ṭayyār and Dhu'l-Janāḥayn, and his son ʿAbd Allāh and grandson Muʿāwiya were highly respected figures for the Shīʿīs. No special partisans, however, were attached to any of these individuals belonging to the Jaʿfarid branch of the Ṭālibid family. But on the death of Abū Hāshim, a certain faction of the Hāshimiyya maintained that the deceased imām had designated his distant cousin Ibn Muʿāwiya as his successor and, since the latter was a minor, the testament had been consigned to a certain Ṣāliḥ b. Mudrik. This group became known as the Ḥarbiyya or Ḥārithiyya, after a leader whose name is variously mentioned as ʿAbd Allāh (b. ʿAmr) b. al-Ḥarb (or al-Ḥārith) al-Kindī.[48] Ibn Ḥarb, who had previously founded a group of his own and taught antinomianism, had now joined Ibn Muʿāwiya and later expressed many extremist ideas about him. The heresiographers ascribe a prominent role to this somewhat enigmatic personality for introducing some key doctrines, including metempsychosis and a cyclical history of eras (*adwār*) and aeons (*akwār*), into the radical trend of Shīʿism. The Ḥarbiyya and the pro-ʿAbbāsid Hāshimiyya disputed over Abū Hāshim's testament, each party claiming its own candidate to be the true beneficiary of the bequest. The disputing parties finally agreed to submit the matter to the arbitration of one of their trusted leaders, Abū Riyāḥ. The latter decided in favour of the ʿAbbāsids, and thereupon, the bulk of Ibn Muʿāwiya's supporters seceded and joined the ʿAbbāsid party, the seceders becoming known as the Riyāḥiyya. Those who continued to recognize the imāmate of Ibn Muʿāwiya from amongst the former Ḥarbiyya, subsequently became known as the Janāḥiyya.[49]

These, then, were the main groups in the extremist branch of Shīʿism evolving out of al-Mukhtār's movement. By the end of the Umayyad period, some of these groups comprising the majority of the radical Shīʿīs had already fallen captive to the successful ʿAbbāsid movement, while others were rapidly disintegrating as separate bodies. In the aftermath of the ʿAbbāsid revolution in southern ʿIrāq the remnants of the groups that had branched out of the Kaysāniyya came to be absorbed by the various Shīʿī sects formed after the imāmate of Jaʿfar al-Ṣādiq. In Persia and Transoxiana on the other hand, such survivors, especially from amongst the Ḥarbiyya-Janāḥiyya, gradually merged into various syncretic sects, often generically termed the Khurramiyya or Khurramdīniyya.[50] The radical Shīʿīs of the Umayyad period, however, had made a lasting contribution to the development of Shīʿī thought.

It was due to their free religious speculations that many of the early radical Shīʿī leaders and groups, such as the Bayāniyya and the Ḥarbiyya, retrospectively came to be termed as the so-called Ghāliya or Ghulāt (singular, *ghālī*, exaggerator).[51] This was a general term of disapproval, probably coined by some early Shīʿī authors and adopted by the heresiographers, in reference to those Shīʿīs accused of exaggeration (*ghuluww*) in religion and in respect to the imāms and other Shīʿī personalities. The criteria of *ghuluww* were determined by the Shīʿīs themselves, since the Sunnīs remained basically uninterested in the divergencies within Shīʿism. Furthermore, these criteria changed in time. But practically all the early speculative Shīʿīs whose doctrinal innovations (singular, *bidʿa*) came to be rejected by the Twelver or the Imāmī Shīʿīs of the end of the 3rd/9th century and thereafter qualified for the designation; although some of the ideas of these Ghulāt, who were to be found also in the moderate branch of Shīʿism, had by that time become accepted as proper Shīʿī tenets. Accordingly, the earliest Shīʿī heresiographers who also belonged to the Imāmī sect categorized as *ghuluww* much of the strictly religious speculations of the radical Shīʿīs of this formative period. This applied in particular to the first half of the second Islamic century. The Sunnī heresiographers, with their general hostility towards the Shīʿa, used the Shīʿī criteria of *ghuluww* even more harshly, often treating the Ghulāt as unbelievers and excluding them from the Muslim community.

The common feature of the earliest ideas propagated by the Ghulāt was an exaggerated reverence towards the imāms on whom superhuman attributes were conferred. The heresiographers usually trace the origins of the Shīʿī Ghulāt to a certain ʿAbd Allāh b. Sabaʾ whose object of exaltation was ʿAlī.[52] The basic *ghuluww* of this highly controversial figure, and his followers known as the Sabaʾiyya, seems to have consisted of the denial of ʿAlī's death and the belief that he would remain alive until he had driven out his enemies.[53] Ibn Sabaʾ is also alleged to have preached ʿAlī's divinity, which would qualify him more readily as a *ghālī*. Modern scholarship, however, has dismissed this allegation as a later attribution.[54] In any event, Ibn Saba' was banished to Madā'in on ʿAlī's orders, probably for his public condemnation of the first two caliphs. Subsequently, he and some of his followers are said to have been burned to death. The survivors of the Saba'iyya later joined al-Mukhtār's movement in Kūfa, which may explain why in some sources the Mukhtāriyya are sometimes identified with the Saba'iyya.

In the opening decades of the second Islamic century, following Abū Hāshim's death, the Shīʿīs became still further divided in their allegiance, as pretenders to the imāmate had become quite numerous. Under such circumstances, when the identity of the rightful imām was a disputed matter, it became necessary for each of the relatively closed Shīʿī groups to seek additional justification, other than just ʿAlid or even Hāshimid descent, to legitimize their imāms. Some adhered to the principle of *naṣṣ* imāmate which proved ineffective during this period, when several candidates claimed to be the recipients of the *naṣṣ* of the same imām, with similar claims generating in respect to the heritage of other imāms. Consequently, the more radical Shīʿīs, especially the Ghulāt theorists who had already established the tradition of conferring superhuman qualities on their imāms, began to think even more freely about the person and authority of the imām. Simultaneously, they found themselves speculating on wider issues of religious importance, such as the nature of God, the soul and afterlife. The speculations of the Ghulāt soon brought about many more doctrinal innovations. As a result, the earlier eschatological doctrines of *ghayba*, *rajʿa*, and Mahdism, which in any case were to become accepted Shīʿī views, in themselves no longer represented *ghuluww*.[55] Thus the Ghulāt became delineated from other Shīʿīs on the basis of more pronounced divergencies, the accounts of which are related with much variation and confusion by the heresiographers. Here, we can only take note of some of the more important of these ideas attributed to the Ghulāt of the first half of the second Islamic century, which is the period of our concentration.[56]

The Ghulāt speculated on the nature of God, often with strong tendencies towards anthropomorphism (*tashbīh*) inspired by certain Qur'ānic passages. Several of them, notably al-Mughīra b. Saʿīd and Abū Manṣūr al-ʿIjlī, are particularly known for their descriptions of God in terms of human features. More commonly, many of the Ghulāt maintained that Allāh, in His essence (*dhāt*), is the divine spirit or light, which may be manifested in diverse forms and creatures. Consequently, they believed in the infusion or incarnation (*ḥulūl*) of the divine essence in the human body, especially in the body of the imāms. They also allowed for *badāʾ*, or change in God's will; a doctrine first expounded by al-Mukhtār to rationalize the failures of his predictions.

The Ghulāt were equally interested in thinking about divination and the various types of divine inspiration. Accordingly, they revived the notion of prophecy (*nubuwwa*) and conceived of the recurrent possibility that God may continue to speak to man through other intermediaries and messengers after the Prophet Muḥammad. Therefore, they often ascribed a prophetic authority to their imāms, though one secondary to that of Muḥammad's and without expecting a new divine revelation replacing the message of Islam. Indeed, the imām above all others, was the focus of much of these speculations, though he himself did not directly encourage them. According to a multitude of extremist ideas, expressed to legitimize the imām's authority, he was thought to have a special relation to God. While some believed in the *ḥulūl* of the divine spirit in his person, others went so far as to deify him, perhaps as a lesser god on earth. More frequently, the Ghulāt, if not attributing a prophetic authority to the imām, felt that he received at least some form of divine guidance and protection. As a result, the imām was thought to be innately endowed with some divinely bestowed attributes, such as sinlessness and infallibility (*ʿiṣma*).

These notions provided a perspective for the speculations about the soul and its relation to the body, death and afterlife, as well as the status of the true believer and the Day of Judgement. Many of the Ghulāt thought of the soul in terms of the doctrine of metempsychosis or transmigration (*tanāsukh*), namely the passing of the soul (*rūḥ* or *nafs*) from one body to another, presupposing the belief in the independent existence of the soul from the body. Some further maintained that this process of the transmigration of souls would take place in cycles, perhaps indefinitely; each cycle (*dawr*) consisting of a specific number of thousands of years. Due to these new ideas, for many the doctrine of *rajʿa*, the return from the dead in the same body, was now replaced by that of *tanāsukh*, the reincarnation of the soul in a different human body or in a different creature. The Ghulāt also conceived of the spirit of one imām transmigrating into the body of his successor. This belief provided an important justification for legitimizing a candidate's imāmate, while simultaneously making it unnecessary to await the emergence (*ẓuhūr*) of an Imām–Mahdī.

By ascribing an exclusive role to the soul, which was capable of transmigration, some of the Ghulāt advocated the eternity of life, or rather the successive lives of a person. As a corollary, they did not believe in corporeal death, or afterlife, and denied the resurrection of the dead at the end of time. For similar reasons, they refuted the existence of Paradise, Hell, and the Day of Judgement, in their conventional sense. Instead, by emphasizing the idea of an immortal soul, they believed in a purely spiritual resurrection in this world, whereby reward and punishment would fall on the soul. According to one's goodness or evilness, his soul would be reincarnated into the bodies of pious persons, or lower and sub-human creatures (*maskh*). The main criterion by which the piety or sinfulness of a person was judged related essentially to his recognition or ignorance of the rightful imām.

In such a perspective, when the *maʿrifa* or knowledge of the imām was held to be the most essential religious obligation of the true believer, the role of the developing Sharīʿa became less important, especially for the Ghulāt who were excessively concerned with loyalty to the Shīʿī cause. These fervent Shīʿīs seem to have regarded the details and the ritual prescriptions of the sacred law of Islam, such as prayer, fasting and pilgrimage, as not binding on those who knew and were devoted to the true imām. They were equally cited for dispensing with the prohibitions of law and morality. Consequently, the Ghulāt were often accused of advocating *ibāḥa* or antinomianism, and of endorsing libertinism. These and many similar charges, however, may well reflect the inferences and hostilities of the heresiographers, both the Sunnī and the Twelver ones. No doubt such accusations were encouraged by the fact that the early Ghulāt did venerate their imāms as almost superhuman beings who alone were destined by divine ordinance to lead the believers. It was during this period of oppressive Umayyad rule that the radical Shīʿīs, out of their exaltation of the ʿAlids, began to curse not only ʿUthmān and other Umayyads, but also Abū Bakr and ʿUmar, as usurpers of ʿAlī's rights. This public condemnation of the Companions (*sabb al-Ṣaḥāba*), especially of the first two caliphs, which probably originated with Ibn Sabaʾ but in due time was to be adopted by almost all Shīʿī groups, has always remained the chief offence of Shīʿism in the eyes of Sunnī Muslims.

Certain points should be singled out with respect to the early Ghulāt and their heritage. Practically no Shīʿī group of this formative period, especially in the first half of the second Islamic century, remained completely free of some Ghulāt thinkers, although the radical branch attracted the greatest number. Initially, many of the Ghulāt leaders were Arabs and it is possible that some of their ideas had pre-Islamic Arab origins; the expectation that a dead hero might return to life being one probable instance. A few of their notions may even be traced to Islamic teachings and the Qur'ān. However, the Ghulāt soon arose also from amongst the *mawālī*, who then comprised the bulk of the radical Shīʿīs. The non-Arab Ghulāt, along with the *mawālī* in general, brought with them a multitude of ideas from their varied backgrounds. The speculations on the soul and the nature of its reward and punishment probably originated from Manichaeism which, in turn, might have derived them from earlier sources.[57] Another point is that the Ghulāt initially devoted their efforts solely to religious speculations. Subsequently, however, as the Umayyad Caliphate began to show signs of disintegration, some of the leaders of the Ghulāt embarked on political activities against the regime. Finally, the spiritual independence of the early Ghulāt and their daring ideas contributed significantly to giving Shīʿism its distinctive religious basis and identity.

By the middle of the 3rd/9th century, with the gradual formation of the various Shīʿī sects which were acquiring their own sectarian names, the term Ghulāt began to lose its earlier importance. In the ʿAbbāsid period, religious deviations which posed political dangers to the state stemmed from the more widespread and sectarian movements, such as the one organized by the Ismāʿīlīs. At any rate, the heresiographers use the term Ghulāt sparingly in reference to individuals or groups appearing after the imāmate of Jaʿfar al-Ṣādiq, although this usage of the term was maintained by the later Muslim authorities producing bio-bibliographical works. For instance, al-Nawbakhtī mentions as the last of the Ghulāt groups the Khaṭṭābiyya, identified by some authorities as the earliest Ismāʿīlīs. These were the followers of Abu'l-Khaṭṭāb, the leading *ghālī* in Jaʿfar's entourage. The fact, however, remains that much of the heritage of the early radical Shīʿīs, especially the Ghulāt amongst them, was in due time absorbed into the main Shīʿī sects. In particular, their ideas on the imāmate and on eschatology were adopted and elaborated by the Twelvers and the Ismāʿīlīs. On the other hand, those of their teachings which implied any compromise of the unity of God, such as their belief in *ḥulūl* and in the divinity of the imāms, were disciplined, especially in the Imāmī branch of Shīʿism. But such doctrines were maintained by the Nuṣayrīs and some other extremist Shīʿī circles; and in later centuries, these and other notions of the early Ghulāt found new expression in the doctrines of the Druzes and other Muslim groups.

We shall now resume our discussion of the moderate branch of Shīʿism. The Ḥusaynid Zayn al-ʿĀbidīn persisted in his quiescence and did not claim the imāmate for himself. However, after Ibn al-Ḥanafiyya's death, Zayn al-ʿĀbidīn, now as the eldest ʿAlid, began to enjoy a more influential position within the ʿAlid family. In addition, due to his renowned piety, which had won him his honorific title 'the Ornament of the Pious', he had gradually come to be held in great esteem, especially by the pious circles of Medina. But since he refrained from any form of political activity and devoted his time mainly to praying (whence his additional title al-Sajjād), he did not acquire any following. By the closing years of his life, Zayn al-ʿĀbidīn had, however, developed an entourage, consisting of some relatives and a few piety-minded Arabs. In sum, during Zayn al-ʿĀbidīn's lifetime, the moderate Imāmī branch was clearly eclipsed by the radical branch, then represented mainly by the Hāshimiyya. Having survived his father by some thirty-four years, ʿAlī b. al-Ḥusayn Zayn al-ʿĀbidīn died in 95/714, shortly before the death of his cousin and rival, Abū Hāshim.

According to the later Twelver and Ismāʿīlī Shīʿīs, Zayn al-ʿĀbidīn had designated his eldest son Muḥammad, later called al-Bāqir, as his successor. Some modern Islamists, too, have argued that it was evidently in al-Bāqir's time that the idea of *naṣṣ* imāmate became more widespread amongst the Shīʿīs.[58] At any event, al-Bāqir seems to have considered himself the sole legitimate ʿAlid authority, and he acquired followers who regarded him as such.[59] Al-Bāqir continued his father's quiescent attitude towards the Umayyads and contented himself, as a matter of policy, with the religious aspects of his authority. Nevertheless, from the very beginning, his authority was challenged by some of his close Fāṭimid relatives. The new claimants to the imāmate provided yet more diverse outlets for the allegiance of the Shīʿīs, who were already divided into numerous groups. Of particular importance was the movement started by al-Bāqir's half-brother Zayd b. ʿAlī. There also started at this time the movement of ʿAbd Allāh b. al-Ḥasan al-Muthannā b. al-Ḥasan b. ʿAlī, with whom the Ḥasanid branch of the ʿAlid family came into prominence. This Ḥasanid movement, which like that of Zayd acquired its importance after al-Bāqir's imāmate, was in effect launched in the name of ʿAbd Allāh's son Muḥammad, known as al-Nafs al-Zakiyya (the Pure Soul). We shall now turn to the background of Zayd's movement which eventually resulted in the separate Zaydiyya sect of Shīʿism.

Few details are available on the ideas held by Zayd and his original followers. According to some later and unreliable reports, Zayd was an associate of Wāṣil b. ʿAṭāʾ (d. 131/748–749), one of the reputed founders of the theological school of the Muʿtazila, originally a religio-political movement. The Muʿtazilīs, as far as we know, initially aimed at reuniting the Muslim community on a compromise solution of the disputes among the various religio-political parties; however they focused their attention on theological principles with only a secondary interest in the doctrine of the imāmate. Modern scholarship has increasingly shown that the doctrinal positions of the early Shīʿīs and the Muʿtazilīs were rather incompatible with one another during the 2nd/8th century; and it was only in the latter part of the 3rd/9th century that Zaydism, as well as Imāmī Shīʿism, came under the influence of Muʿtazilism.[60] Therefore, it can no longer be maintained that the earliest Zaydīs were influenced by Muʿtazilī ideas.

Zayd appears to have emphasized the need for a just imām and the community's obligation to remove an unjust one. He also paid special attention to the Islamic principle of 'commanding the good and prohibiting the evil' (*al-amr bi'l-maʿrūf wa'l-nahy ʿan al-munkar*). Furthermore, he is reported to have stated that if an imām wanted to be recognized, he had to assert his rights publicly, sword in hand if need be. In other words, Zayd was not prepared to accept the idea of a concealed Mahdī or a quiescent imām; nor did he attach any significance to hereditary succession and to *naṣṣ* imāmate. Accordingly, the Zaydīs originally maintained that the imāmate might legitimately be held by any member of the Ahl al-Bayt, though later restricting it to the Fāṭimids. This was under the condition that the claimant possessed the required religious learning along with certain other pious qualities; he would also have to be able to launch an uprising (*khurūj*), as Zayd was to do, against the illegitimate ruler of the time. The combination of Zayd's activist policy and his otherwise conservative views, appealed to many Shīʿīs, preventing them from joining the Imāmī branch of Shīʿism. At the same time, Zayd had realized that in order to be successful against the Umayyads, he would need the support of the main body of the Muslims. To this end, and reflecting the position of the moderate Shīʿa in Kūfa, he made an important doctrinal compromise. He asserted that, though ʿAlī was the most excellent (*al-afḍal*) to succeed the Prophet, the allegiance given to Abū Bakr and ʿUmar who were less excellent (*al-mafḍūl*) was, nevertheless, valid. This view, it may be noted, was repudiated by the later Zaydīs. Zayd's recognition of the rule of the first two caliphs, or of the *imāmat al-mafḍūl*, which was repellent to the radical Shīʿīs who were then condemning these Companions, won him the general sympathy of all those Muslims upholding the *Jamāʿa* principle of unity.[61]

Meanwhile, al-Bāqir contented himself with teaching and thinking about the rudiments of some of the ideas which were to become the legitimist principles of the Imāmī branch. Above all, he seems to have concerned himself with explaining the functions and the divinely bestowed attributes of the imāms. He is also credited with introducing the principle of *taqiyya*, dissimulation of one's true belief under adverse circumstances; a principle which was quite alien to Zayd's thinking but was later adopted by both the Twelvers and the Ismāʿīlīs. In spite of many difficulties, al-Bāqir did manage in the course of his imāmate of almost twenty years to expand his circle of partisans. He also acquired a number of adherents from amongst the famous traditionists and jurists of Kūfa, notably Zurāra b. Aʿyan who had initially supported Zayd, and Muḥammad b. Muslim al-Ṭā'ifī. The renowned poet al-Kumayt b. Zayd al-Asadī (d. 126/743) was another follower of al-Bāqir. The names of the adherents of al-Bāqir and other imāms of the Ḥusaynid line have been recorded in the earliest biographical compendium of Shīʿī personalities, by the Imāmī traditionist al-Kashshī who flourished in the first half of the 4th/10th century.[62] Later works, belonging to the same category of the *kutub al-rijāl* (bio-bibliographical books), compiled by other prominent Twelver Shīʿī scholars al-Najāshī (d. 450/1058), al-Ṭūsī (d. 460/1067), one of the leading Shīʿī authorities who has preserved an abridged version of al-Kashshī's work, and Ibn Shahrāshūb (d. 588/1192), also contain valuable information on the Imāmī Shīʿīs.[63]

It may be pointed out here that al-Bāqir's imāmate also coincided with the initial stages of the Islamic science of law (*ʿilm al-fiqh*). It was, however, in the final decades of the second Islamic century that the old Arabian concept of *sunna*, the normative custom or the established practice of the community, which had reasserted itself under Islam, came to be explicitly identified by the piety-minded Muslims with the *sunna* of the Prophet. This identification, in turn, necessitated the collection of those *ḥadīth*s or traditions which claimed to be the reports on the sayings and actions of the Prophet, handed down orally through an uninterrupted chain of trustworthy authorities. The activity of collecting and studying *ḥadīth*, which had initially arisen mainly in opposition to the extensive use of human reasoning by the Islamic judges (singular, *qāḍī*), and for citing the authority of the Prophet to determine proper legal practices, soon became a major field of Islamic learning, complementing the science of Islamic jurisprudence.[64] In this formative period of the Islamic religious sciences, al-Bāqir has been mentioned as a reporter of *ḥadīth*, particularly of those supporting the Shīʿī cause and derived from ʿAlī. The Imāms al-Bāqir and al-Ṣādiq, however, interpreted the law mostly on their own authority, without much recourse to *ḥadīth* from earlier authorities. It should be added that in Shīʿism, *ḥadīth* is reported on the authority of the imāms and it includes the sayings of the imāms in addition to the Prophetic traditions. Al-Bāqir was also the first imām of the Ḥusaynid line to attract a few Ghulāt theorists to his side. The most prominent of these Ghulāt who were originally in al-Bāqir's following were al-Mughīra b. Saʿīd, mentioned variously as a *mawlā* or an Arab from the tribe of ʿIjl, and Abū Manṣūr al-ʿIjlī. It is useful to consider the highlights of their ideas, some of which anticipated certain distinguishing aspects of early Ismāʿīlī thought.

The heresiographers provide many details on the ideas propagated by al-Mughīra.[65] According to these sometimes contradictory accounts, he seems to have combined a variety of pre-Islamic beliefs of the Near East into his teaching, reflecting particularly the influences of Mandaean and Manichaean gnostic doctrines.[66] Indeed, al-Mughīra, with his spiritualism and pronounced dualism, has been credited for being the first Shīʿī gnostic.[67] One of the most distinctive features of his teaching was his anthropomorphic description of God. He asserted that God is a man of light with a crown of light on his head, a concept closely resembling the Mandaean doctrine of their deity, referred to as the 'king of light'.[68] He further added that God has limbs which correspond to the letters of the Arabic alphabet, and that these letters (*ḥurūf*) themselves derived from the Greatest Name of God, spoken at the time of creation. These ideas are clearly reminiscent of the teaching of Marcus the Gnostic, one of the leading exponents of Valentinian Gnosticism, for whom the body of the 'supreme truth' (*Aletheia*) was composed of the letters of the Greek alphabet.[69] Al-Mughīra may, in fact, be considered as the first Shīʿī, or the first Muslim for that matter, who thought about the mystical and symbolic nature of the alphabet and thus, anticipated the more elaborate views of the early Ismāʿīlīs. It was probably also due to al-Mughīra's ideas, further developed by others, that the extremist Shīʿīs came to attribute certain occult properties to the twenty-eight letters of the Arabic alphabet.[70] Al-Mughīra is equally noted for his theory of the creation of the world and the first beings. His cosmogony, too, reflects the influence of ancient gnostic systems and, like his anthropomorphism, seems to have been inspired by the allegorical interpretation or *ta'wīl* of certain Qur'ānic passages; a method distinctively associated with the Ismāʿīlīs. The fundamental aspect of this cosmogony is its gnostic dualism, characterized by the eternal conflict between light and darkness which, in close affinity with the basic tenet of Manichaeism, symbolize good and evil.

In time, al-Mughīra acquired followers of his own in Kūfa, from amongst both the Arabs and the *mawālī*. They became known as the Mughīriyya, representing one of the most important of the Ghulāt groups. Al-Mughīra imbued his followers with a sense of exclusiveness and devotion to his leadership, which may explain why they were also referred to as the Wuṣafā', the Servants. The origins of religious elitism among the extremist Shīʿīs may, indeed, be traced to the Mughīriyya.[71] The elitist feelings of the Mughīriyya, which made them hostile towards their enemies, in turn, laid the foundation of religious militancy. The sources do, in fact, attest to the use of terrorist methods by the Mughīriyya; methods of struggle which were more characteristic of Abū Manṣūr's group, and which, some four centuries later, became an established practice with the Nizārī Ismāʿīlīs of Persia and Syria.

Abū Manṣūr, who interestingly enough was illiterate, also preached the imāmate of al-Bāqir and, like al-Mughīra, founded his own group, the Manṣūriyya.[72] He advocated, now as a matter of policy, the use of assassination in dealing with adversaries.[73] After al-Bāqir's death, Abū Manṣūr asserted that the imāmate had been bequeathed to him by al-Bāqir, whose legatee he claimed to be. Still later, he claimed prophethood, maintaining that he had ascended to Heaven where God patted him on his head, addressed him in Syriac, and charged him with delivering a prophetic message. Abū Manṣūr, too, speculated about the creation,[74] and certain aspects of his teaching anticipate, in embryonic form, important Ismāʿīlī parallels. He held the belief in the uninterrupted succession of prophets; adding that, after himself, prophethood would continue in his progeny for six generations, the last of whom (the seventh one counting from Abū Manṣūr) would be the Mahdī. Furthermore, he resorted to the allegorical interpretation of the Qur'ān and maintained that whereas Muḥammad had delivered the message of Islam, it was now his own divinely inspired duty to explain it allegorically. He also denied the resurrection and interpreted Paradise and Hell symbolically in terms of the experiences of this world.

It has been reported that al-Bāqir disavowed both al-Mughīra and Abū Manṣūr, though each one later claimed his heritage. Jaʿfar al-Ṣādiq, too, renounced the most prominent of the Ghulāt in his entourage. But the undisputed fact remains that from the time of al-Bāqir, the Ghulāt were drawn into the following of the Ḥusaynid Imāms. This was a significant event causing a lasting influence on the doctrinal basis of the Imāmī branch of Shīʿism. Having taken important preliminary steps towards establishing the identity of Imāmī Shīʿism, the Imām Abū Jaʿfar Muḥammad b. ʿAlī al-Bāqir died around 114/732–733,[75] one century after the death of the Prophet. In the meantime, after the short reigns of Sulaymān, the pious ʿUmar II (99–101/717–720) who paid greater attention to the precepts of Islam and was more friendly towards the ʿAlids, terminating also the condemnation of ʿAlī from the pulpits, and Yazīd II (101–105/720–724), the caliphate had passed to the capable Hishām b. ʿAbd al-Malik (105–125/724–743). One of Hishām's first acts was to appoint the skilful Khālid b. ʿAbd Allāh al-Qasrī as the governor of ʿIrāq, in which post he remained for almost fifteen years (106–120/724–738), longer than any other Umayyad governor with the exception of al-Ḥajjāj. Khālid maintained a strict surveillance over the Kūfan Shīʿīs who were continuing their clandestine activities. As it soon became apparent, however, Hishām's long caliphate was to mark the final period of stability of Umayyad rule.

On the death of al-Bāqir, his following split into several groups.[76] One group, the Bāqiriyya, awaited his reappearance as the Mahdī, while another group went over to the Ḥasanid al-Nafs al-Zakiyya. There were also those who transferred their allegiance to al-Mughīra and Abū Manṣūr. But a faithful group of al-Bāqir's partisans now recognized his eldest son Abū ʿAbd Allāh Jaʿfar, later called al-Ṣādiq (the Trustworthy), as their new imām designated by *naṣṣ*. This group of Imāmī Shīʿīs continued to support Jaʿfar and in time expanded significantly. Jaʿfar al-Ṣādiq's long imāmate of some thirty odd years, coinciding with the most turbulent epoch of early Islamic history, may best be studied in terms of two periods. During the first period, lasting until shortly after the accession of the ʿAbbāsids, he remained overshadowed by certain other claimants to the imāmate, while the ʿAbbāsid movement was successfully unfolding. It was during the second period, covering roughly the final decade of his imāmate, that Jaʿfar acquired a unique prominence. We shall now turn to the events of the first two decades of Jaʿfar's imāmate; events which also resulted in the elimination of his most active Hāshimid rivals.

By the time of Jaʿfar al-Ṣādiq, the movement of Zayd b. ʿAlī was already well-established. Jaʿfar continued his father's passive policy towards his elder uncle, and even displayed public reverence for him. Soon afterwards, however, some of Zayd's followers abandoned him and joined the Imām Jaʿfar, probably due to the attraction of the latter's *naṣṣ* imāmate. According to one account, Zayd designated these deserters as Rawāfiḍ or Rejectors, because of their refusal to support his revolt,[77] a term subsequently applied abusively to other Shīʿī groups and in particular to the Imāmiyya. The movement of Muḥammad al-Nafs al-Zakiyya also began to gain momentum during the earlier years of Jaʿfar's imāmate. This movement, as noted, had been launched by Muḥammad's father ʿAbd Allāh who, being a Ḥasanid through his father and a Ḥusaynid through his mother Fāṭima bint al-Ḥusayn b. ʿAlī, had earned the by-name of al-Maḥḍ (of Pure Blood). ʿAbd Allāh was the *shaykh* of the Ḥasanids and was also held in high esteem within the entire ʿAlid family.[78] He had ambitious designs for his son, Muḥammad, whom he had designated from the time of his birth, supposedly in 100/718, for the role of the expected Mahdī. This was probably encouraged by a tradition circulated by the Shīʿīs, to the effect that the Mahdī who in time would arise from amongst the Ahl al-Bayt would carry the same name, Muḥammad b. ʿAbd Allāh, as the Prophet himself.

Meanwhile, the Umayyad regime had begun to show signs of collapse during the final years of Hishām's rule. The Shīʿīs, quick in noticing the changed conditions and having refrained from all open activity for almost half a century, staged a number of risings in Kūfa.[79] All these attempts ended in failure since they lacked sufficient organization and support. In 119/737, al-Mughīra and Bayān, who had apparently joined forces after al-Bāqir's death, were arrested together with a handful of their followers and burned in Kūfa on the orders of Khālid b. ʿAbd Allāh. It is not clear whether this action was taken to suppress a premature rising or to bring the suspected rebels into the open. In 124/742, Abū Manṣūr met a similar fate at the hands of Khālid's successor Yūsuf b. ʿUmar al-Thaqafī, who governed ʿIrāq from 120/738 to 126/744. The bulk of the supporters of these three martyred Ghulāt, from amongst the Bayāniyya, the Mughīriyya and the Manṣūriyya, subsequently joined al-Nafs al-Zakiyya.

More significantly, in Ṣafar 122/January 740, Zayd b. ʿAlī staged his open revolt in Kūfa, which was actually the first Shīʿī attempt of its kind since that of al-Mukhtār's and the second one led hitherto by an ʿAlid after Karbalāʾ. The revolt proved abortive, not only because the Kūfans had once again displayed their unreliability and failed to recruit 100,000 armed men for Zayd as promised, but also because Yūsuf b. ʿUmar had discovered the plot in time and took severe measures to repress it. Zayd and the small band of the zealous partisans who fought with him were massacred by the Syrian troops; a tragic end reminiscent of that of Zayd's grandfather al-Ḥusayn.[80] Soon afterwards, the caliph Hishām commanded that all prominent Ṭālibids should publicly condemn Zayd and dissociate themselves from all anti-Umayyad activities. ʿAbd Allāh al-Maḥḍ and Ibn Muʿāwiya, amongst others, complied; the Imām Jaʿfar was apparently spared the ordeal, as his name does not appear in connection with this episode in any known source. This may indicate that by the time of Zayd's revolt, the Imām Jaʿfar had already been explicit about his opposition to any militant Shīʿī activity. Zayd's movement, however, was continued by his son Yaḥyā, whose Ḥanafid mother was one of Abū Hāshim's daughters. Yaḥyā concentrated his activities in Khurāsān, where many Kūfan Shīʿīs had been exiled by the governors of ʿIrāq. But after three years of futile efforts, he was overtaken by the troops of the governor of Khurāsān, Naṣr b. Sayyār. Yaḥyā was killed in battle near Jūzjān in 125/743.[81] The Zaydīs were later led by al-Nafs al-Zakiyya, Yaḥyā's brother ʿĪsā b. Zayd (d. 166/783), and then by Aḥmad b. ʿĪsā (d. 247/861) and others whom they recognized as their imāms.

The disintegration of the Umayyad regime accentuated upon Hishām's death in 125/743. Scarcely a year had passed when the caliphate of Hishām's nephew and successor al-Walīd II was brought to an end in 126/744, by a *coup d'état* engineered by the Syrian army and with the cooperation of the Umayyad family. This event, which amounted to political suicide for the ruling dynasty, marked the imminent end of what Wellhausen has called the 'Arab Kingdom'. The rule of the next caliph, Yazīd III, the choice of the rebellious generals, lasted less than six months, and on his sudden death further dynastic rivalries led to a civil war. Ibrāhīm b. al-Walīd I was acknowledged as the new caliph only in southern Syria, and during his short reign of some three months, general conditions deteriorated into complete chaos. The ambitious Marwān, known as Marwān II al-Ḥimār, from an offshoot of the Umayyad family, was now the only person with sufficient military power to enforce some semblance of order in the empire. Consequently, he marched to Damascus, deposed Ibrāhīm and proclaimed himself the new caliph in 127/744. By that time, however, the task of rescuing Umayyad rule had become all but an impossibility, as revolts were raging in almost every province.

The prevailing chaos encouraged the Shīʿīs of Kūfa and elsewhere to make yet bolder efforts towards wresting the caliphate. At a gathering of the Hāshimids held at al-Abwāʾ near Medina in 126/744, ʿAbd Allāh al-Maḥḍ succeeded in persuading all the participants to accord their oath of allegiance to al-Nafs al-Zakiyya and to recognize him as the most suitable candidate for the caliphate.[82] Amongst those who complied were Ibrāhīm b. Muḥammad, the head of the ʿAbbāsids, and his two brothers Abu'l-ʿAbbās and Abū Jaʿfar, future ʿAbbāsid caliphs, who complied under false pretences. Only the Imām Jaʿfar, the most respected Ḥusaynid after Zayd's martyrdom, is reported to have withheld his approval. While ʿAbd Allāh al-Maḥḍ may have attributed Jaʿfar's opposition to the then existing rivalries between the Ḥasanids and the Ḥusaynids, it should be recalled that Jaʿfar was not prepared to accept the claims of his Ḥasanid cousin or any other ʿAlid since he clearly regarded himself as the rightful imām of the time. After this family reunion, al-Nafs al-Zakiyya and his brother Ibrāhīm embarked on a vigorous campaign, which received the support of many Muʿtazilīs and Zaydīs, as well as several Ghulāt groups.[83] Their movement, however, lacked foresight and organization and was easily overtaken and then crushed by the ʿAbbāsids.

The last unsuccessful revolt of the Umayyad period, which was Shīʿī in the broadest sense, was launched by the Ṭālibid ʿAbd Allāh b. Muʿāwiya who, as noted, had his own extremist Shīʿī partisans, the Janāḥiyya. But now Ibn Muʿāwiya was to lead a movement of much greater social significance, supported by a multitude of Shīʿī and non-Shīʿī groups.[84] In the confusing aftermath of al-Walīd II's murder, the Kūfan Shīʿīs had urged Ibn Muʿāwiya, then sojourning in their city, to rebel against ʿAbd Allāh b. ʿUmar, the son of the pious Umayyad caliph, who governed ʿIrāq under the caliphs Yazīd III and Ibrāhīm. However, Ibn Muʿāwiya's open revolt, which took place in Muḥarram 127/October 744, was easily suppressed by Ibn ʿUmar, as the Kūfans turned out to be as unreliable as ever. Only the Zaydīs in his following fought bravely for a few days, until Ibn Muʿāwiya was given a safe-conduct out of Kūfa. He withdrew to western Persia, where he soon acquired a large number of supporters, especially from amongst the Persian *mawālī*. In 128/745, he established himself at Iṣṭakhr in the Fārs province, from where he ruled for a few years over a vast territory in Persia.

Ibn Muʿāwiya gathered an extremely varied coalition of groups around himself. In fact, the outstanding feature of his rebellious movement was the peculiar diversity of its composition. Aside from the *mawālī*, it included several Shīʿī groups, many Khārijīs, the notable ʿAbbāsids, and even some discontented Umayyads. This reveals how widespread the anti-regime sentiments had now become; it also indicates that Ibn Muʿāwiya's movement did not have any particular ideological basis, Shīʿī or otherwise. Ibn Muʿāwiya himself seems to have been more concerned with political power than with doctrinal issues, as attested by his willingness to receive support from heterogeneous religio-political factions. The lack of ideology proved to be a fundamental shortcoming of this movement. Ibn Muʿāwiya was finally defeated in 130/748, by a large army sent after him by Marwān II who, having established his authority in Syria and ʿIrāq, had now turned his attention to the eastern provinces which were no longer controlled effectively by the Umayyads. ʿAbd Allāh b. Muʿāwiya fled from his enemies and sought asylum in Khurāsān, where he was killed in 131/748–749 by his friends, probably on the orders of Abū Muslim al-Khurāsānī, the chief architect of the ʿAbbāsid victory.

The ʿAbbāsids had, meanwhile, learned important lessons from the many abortive Shīʿī revolts of the Umayyad period. Consequently, while awaiting their own turn to make a bid for power, they paid particular attention to developing the organization of their movement, concentrating their activities in the remote eastern province of Khurāsān.[85] As noted, the ʿAbbāsid Muḥammad b. ʿAlī took over the claims of the Ḥanafid Abū Hāshim and his propaganda organization, and party, the Hāshimiyya. With these valuable assets, the active propaganda or mission, *daʿwa*, of the ʿAbbāsids seems to have begun around the year 100/718, soon after Abū Hāshim's death.[86] From headquarters in Kūfa, numerous emissaries were sent to Khurāsān, where there was widespread support for Shīʿism among both the Arab settlers in the province and the native Persian *mawālī*. Khurāsān, with its capital at Marw, soon became the main recruiting ground for, and the revolutionary base of, the ʿAbbāsid movement. The ʿAbbāsid *daʿwa* was cleverly preached in the name of *al-riḍā min āl Muḥammad*, a phrase which spoke of an unidentified personage belonging to the Prophet's family. Aside from being a precautionary measure, this aimed at drawing maximum support from the Shīʿīs who upheld the leadership of the Ahl al-Bayt.

Initially, the ʿAbbāsid *daʿwa* in Khurāsān was organized mainly in the form of small clandestine groups, but still many of the ʿAbbāsid *dāʿīs* were discovered and killed by the Umayyads. Therefore, it soon became necessary to create a more formal organization. A supreme council of twelve chiefs, the so-called *nuqabāʾ*, was set up at Marw to direct the activities of a large number of newly appointed *dāʿīs*; a method of organization adopted by the Ismāʿīlīs. These changes proved successful, especially when ʿAmmār b. Yazīd, better known as Khidāsh, was sent to Khurāsān to head the new *daʿwa* organization. He was apparently inclined towards the ʿAlids and taught extremist doctrines, which may explain why he was later disavowed by the ʿAbbāsids. Khidāsh, who was arrested and executed in 118/736, was succeeded by Sulaymān b. Kathīr. Contact between the partisans in Khurāsān and the imām, who resided in Ḥumayma but remained nameless, continued to be maintained through the leader of the ʿAbbāsids' Kūfan organization, a post held by Bukayr b. Māhān from 105/723.

Muḥammad b. ʿAlī died in 125/743, and his son Ibrāhīm, known as al-Imām, became the new imām of the Hāshimiyya-ʿAbbāsiyya party and, hence, the leader of the movement. Ibrāhīm intensified the ʿAbbāsid *daʿwa* and initiated its more militant phase. In the prevailing confusion and in the aftermath of the defeats of Zayd and of his son Yaḥyā, the movement began to meet with increasing success. In 128/745–746, Ibrāhīm sent his Persian *mawlā*, Abū Muslim, the celebrated personality with an obscure background who earlier had apparently followed al-Mughīra and had also in vain offered his services to the Imām Jaʿfar, as his personal representative to Khurāsān to organize and lead the final phase of the movement.[87] Meanwhile, Abū Salama al-Khallāl, a prominent Shīʿī leader, had become the new head of the Kūfan organization, following the death of Bukayr in 127/744. Abū Muslim's success was astonishingly rapid, and by 129/747 he had unfurled the black banners that were to become the emblem of the ʿAbbāsids, signifying open revolt. His revolutionary army, the Khurāsāniyya, comprised of both Persian *mawālī* and Arabs, especially Yamanīs, expanded significantly in a short period. It was also in Abū Muslim's army that complete integration of Arab and non-Arab Muslims was attained for the first time.

In 130/748, Abū Muslim entered Marw and then seized all of Khurāsān, driving out the aged Umayyad governor Naṣr b. Sayyār. In the same year, the Khurāsānī army under the command of Qaḥṭaba b. Shabīb, one of the original *nuqabāʾ*, started its swift advance westward, defeating the Umayyad armies along the way.[88] In Muḥarram 132/August 749, the forces of Ibn Hubayra, the last Umayyad governor of ʿIrāq, were defeated in a battle near Kūfa, in which Qaḥṭaba lost his life. A few days later, the victorious Khurāsānīs entered Kūfa. Thereupon, power was handed to Abū Salama who was immediately acknowledged as *wazīr āl Muḥammad*. The idea of *wazīr*, first introduced with a vague connotation to the Arab

Muslims by al-Mukhtār, was now about to develop into an important administrative office under the ʿAbbāsids.

The time had finally come for disclosing the name of *al-riḍā* from the Prophet's family, who would be acceptable to all. Just before the fall of Kūfa, Ibrāhīm al-Imām died in Marwān II's prison in Ḥarrān, where he had been confined for several months upon the Umayyad caliph's discovery of his role in the ʿAbbāsid *daʿwa*. It was now left to Abū Salama to reveal the identity of Ibrāhīm's successor, who was to be installed as the new caliph. Abū Salama personally favoured seeing an ʿAlid succeed to the caliphate.[89] He contacted three of the leading ʿAlids of the time, amongst them the Imām Jaʿfar and ʿAbd Allāh al-Maḥḍ. Abū Salama's offer of caliphal authority was rejected by them, as was his request for the formation of an ʿAlid council to select a suitable candidate. Finally, after two months of waiting watchfully, the Khurāsāniyya took matters into their own hands and decided on Ibrāhīm's half-brother Abu'l-ʿAbbās, as the new caliph. He and other members of the ʿAbbāsid family had shortly before moved from Ḥumayma to Kūfa, where they had remained in hiding on Abū Salama's instructions. The whereabouts of Abu'l-ʿAbbās was, however, discovered by the loyal agents of Abū Muslim, who himself had stayed behind in Khurāsān. On 12 Rabīʿ II 132/28 November 749, Abu'l-ʿAbbās was proclaimed as the first ʿAbbāsid caliph, with the title al-Saffāḥ, in the mosque of Kūfa. Abū Salama was obliged to pay homage and continued as *wazīr*. Soon afterwards, he was executed on the caliph's orders and with Abū Muslim's complicity.

In 132/750, the Khurāsānī troops achieved their final victory, in the battle of the Greater Zāb, against the Umayyad forces. The defeated Marwān II fled towards Egypt, where he was killed in the same year. Thus, after more than thirty years of meticulous planning, the ʿAbbāsids had finally succeeded in sealing the fate of the Umayyads. They installed their own dynasty to the caliphate and ruled over a varying portion of the Islamic world for five centuries, until they were overthrown in 656/1258 by the Mongols. The struggle between ʿIrāq and Syria, an important factor in the anti-Umayyad activities of the Shīʿīs since ʿAlī's time, had now also ended in the defeat of the Syrians. The early ʿAbbāsids, who relied on the Persians and their Sāsānid models of centralized administration in the governing affairs of the state, established the seat of the caliphate in ʿIrāq, at first in the small town of Hāshimiyya and other localities near Kūfa and later, after 145/762, in the new city of Baghdād.

The ʿAbbāsid revolution marked a turning point in the history of early

Islam, representing not only a change of dynasty but other important changes as well. With the fall of the Umayyads, their social order, which assigned a privileged position to the Arabs, also collapsed. The ʿAbbāsids distributed political power more widely and removed the distinction between the Arabs and the *mawālī*, many of whom no longer had any affiliation with an Arab tribe. During the first half-century of ʿAbbāsid rule, the hegemony of the Arab aristocracy rapidly came to an end, and those privileges derived from birth, race or tribal affiliation, ceased to have their earlier significance. Now, a new multi-racial ruling class, with Islam as its unifying feature, emerged to replace the Arab ruling class of the Umayyad period. With the emancipation of the *mawālī* and the new alignment of classes on non-racial grounds, some of the most pressing demands of the opposition movements, notably those of the radical Shīʿīs, were satisfied. As a result, revolutionary Shīʿism henceforth ceased to be identified with the aspirations of the *mawālī*, who had at last acquired their equality and were soon to disappear as a distinct social class. Instead, it came to provide a suitable outlet for a wider spectrum of the oppressed and economically underprivileged masses.

The ʿAbbāsid victory, however, was to be a source of disappointment in other respects, especially for the Shīʿīs, who had remained loyal to the ʿAlid cause. The ʿAbbāsids had conducted their secret propaganda in the name of the Ahl al-Bayt and on a largely Shīʿī basis. Their success, therefore, was expected to bring about the long-awaited Shīʿī triumph. But from the very beginning of ʿAbbāsid rule, the Shīʿīs became greatly disillusioned when the hitherto unnamed *al-riḍā*, now installed to the caliphate, turned out to belong to the ʿAbbāsid branch of the Banū Hāshim instead of being an ʿAlid Hāshimid. The Shīʿī disappointment was further aggravated when the ʿAbbāsids chose to adhere to the *Jamāʿa*, the community as a body, and became staunch supporters of Sunnī Islam. The ʿAbbāsids realized that in order to be accepted as legitimate rulers by the majority of the Muslims, they had to renounce their extremist past. Consequently, almost immediately upon their accession, they began to sever all ties with their more strictly Shīʿī supporters and the revolutionary leaders who had brought them to power. Abū Salama and Sulaymān b. Kathīr were summarily executed; and, in 133/750–751, a Shīʿī revolt led by a certain Sharīk b. Shaykh al-Mahrī, the first of its kind in the ʿAbbāsid times, was ruthlessly suppressed in Bukhārā.[90] Soon afterwards in 137/755, Abū Muslim was lured to ʿIrāq and murdered on the orders of Abū Jaʿfar al-Manṣūr (136–158/754–775), the elder and stronger brother and successor of Abu'l-ʿAbbās who consolidated ʿAbbāsid rule and established the permanent capital of the Islamic empire in the newly founded city of Baghdād, built near the ruins of Ctesiphon, the capital of the Sāsānid empire.

The caliph al-Manṣūr adopted still more repressive measures against the ʿAlids and the Shīʿīs. In 141/758, he massacred a group of the Rāwandiyya who besieged his palace and hailed him as the incarnation of divinity.[91] A few years later, he had many of the ʿAlids, notably from the Ḥasanid branch, imprisoned or killed. The ʿAbbāsids' breach with their Shīʿī origins and their efforts to legitimize their own rights to the caliphate were finally completed by the caliph Muḥammad al-Mahdī (158–169/775–785), who abandoned the ʿAbbāsid claim to Abū Hāshim's inheritance and instead declared that the Prophet had actually appointed al-ʿAbbās as his successor. This, of course, implied the repudiation of the analogous claims of the ʿAlids. With these adverse developments, those of the extremist Shīʿī followers of the ʿAbbāsids who did not scatter became alienated. Some of them in Persia and Central Asia found an outlet in a series of religio-political movements termed the Khurramiyya. Still others in ʿIrāq rallied to the side of the Fāṭimids, who were now the leading ʿAlids, and later many joined the Ismāʿīlī movement, which was to resume the interrupted development of revolutionary Shīʿism.

Under these circumstances, the time had come for the rise to prominence of the imāmate of Jaʿfar, now called al-Ṣādiq, which occurred roughly during the last decade of his life and the first decade of al-Manṣūr's caliphate. There are diverse reasons for this phenomenon. As noted, the extremist *mawlā* Shīʿism of the Umayyad times, upheld by the various Kaysānī groups which supported the Ḥanafid line of imāms or others deriving their claims from these imāms, had finally aborted mainly in the ʿAbbāsid cause; and those who survived were ready to join other ʿAlid claimants. At the same time, with the Ḥanafids out of the way, the ʿAlid family had been reduced to its Ḥusaynid and Ḥasanid branches, of which Jaʿfar al-Ṣādiq and Muḥammad al-Nafs al-Zakiyya were, respectively, the chief figures. In other words, the bulk of the Shīʿīs were now obliged to follow either one of these two Fāṭimid Imāms. It was as of then that increasing stress was laid on direct descent from the Prophet through Fāṭima and ʿAlī, and Fāṭimid ancestry acquired its special significance for the Shīʿīs, being also used as the criterion for determining the composition of the Ahl al-Bayt. No doubt, the messianic claims and militant attitude of al-Nafs al-Zakiyya, who had refused to render homage to al-Manṣūr and had subsequently gone into hiding to prepare for a rebellion, held greater attraction for at least some of the more activist Shīʿīs. But this Ḥasanid movement soon ended in defeat. The open revolt of Muḥammad al-Nafs al-Zakiyya in the Ḥijāz and that of his supporting brother Ibrāhīm in ʿIrāq were subdued and the two brothers were killed in 145/762–763, by the forces of the ʿAbbāsid ʿĪsā b. Mūsā, who governed Kūfa for fifteen years from 132/750 to 147/764. With the removal of al-Nafs al-Zakiyya, Jaʿfar al-Ṣādiq emerged as the main rallying point for the allegiance of the Shīʿīs, especially in southern ʿIrāq; and his imāmate provided the basis for the most important Shīʿī sects, the Twelvers and the Ismāʿīlīs, while the Zaydīs continued to follow their own imāms. By that time, however, the Imām Jaʿfar had already become prominent, which, aside from the aforementioned factors, may be attributed to his own personality and fame for learning, and to the appeal of certain ideas taught by him and his associates.

Jaʿfar al-Ṣādiq, of superior intellectual quality to his ʿAlid relatives and predecessors, had gradually acquired a widespread reputation for religious learning.[92] He was a reporter of *ḥadīth* and is cited respectfully as such in the chains of authorities (*isnāds*) accepted by the Sunnīs. Additionally, he taught *fiqh* and is credited with founding, after the work of his father, what was to become the Shīʿī school of religious law or *madhhab*, which differs somewhat from the four Sunnī schools.[93] Hence, the Twelvers, when referring to their *madhhab*, have called it the Jaʿfarī. It is important to note that Jaʿfar al-Ṣādiq was accepted as a teaching authority not only by his own partisans, but by a much wider circle, including the piety-minded Muslims of Medina and Kūfa. For instance, Abū Ḥanīfa al-Nuʿmān (d. 150/767) and Mālik b. Anas (d. 179/795), the famous jurists and eponyms of the Ḥanafī and Mālikī Sunnī schools of law, reportedly studied or consulted with him. In time, Jaʿfar collected a noteworthy group of thinkers around himself, and became the object of more Ghulāt speculations than any other ʿAlid. He is, indeed, one of the most respected Shīʿī Imāms and religious authorities both among the Twelvers and the Ismāʿīlīs.

Throughout the tumultuous years preceding the ʿAbbāsid revolution, and also following it, when as a result of the great Shīʿī disappointment a fundamental re-orientation in Shīʿism was called for, Jaʿfar al-Ṣādiq was quietly propounding his views regarding the imāmate. Some of these views had already been formulated in rudimentary form by the Imām Muḥammad al-Bāqir, but it remained for Jaʿfar and his associates, notably the eminent Imāmī authority Hishām b. al-Ḥakam (d. 179/795–796), to develop them more precisely and systematically into the basic conception of the doctrine of the imāmate. Here we are concerned only with certain principles embodied in this central Shīʿī doctrine; principles that were emphasized by Jaʿfar in response to the challenging needs of the time and, as such, proved effective in strengthening his imāmate.[94]

The first principle was that of imāmate by *naṣṣ*, defined as a prerogative bestowed by God upon a chosen person from the Ahl al-Bayt, who before his death and with divine guidance, transfers the imāmate to his successor by an explicit designation or *naṣṣ*. As noted, others too had claimed a *naṣṣ* imāmate; but the distinguishing feature of Jaʿfar al-Ṣādiq's teaching was its emphasis to the effect that, on the authority of the *naṣṣ*, the imāmate remained located in a specific individual, whether or not he claimed the caliphate. Thus, Jaʿfar maintained that there was always in existence a true imām designated by *naṣṣ* who possessed all the authority of the sole legitimate imām, whether or not he was at the time ruling over the community. Furthermore, the antecedence of the Imām Jaʿfar's own *naṣṣ* was traced back to ʿAlī, who was believed to have been appointed as the Prophet's *waṣī* and successor. This first *naṣṣ*, initiated by the Prophet under divine command or inspiration, had remained in the Ḥusaynid line of imāms, having been transmitted successively from ʿAlī to al-Ḥasan, and then to al-Ḥusayn, Zayn al-ʿĀbidīn, and al-Bāqir until it had reached Jaʿfar al-Ṣādiq, now the only claimant to a *naṣṣ* imāmate within the ʿAlid family. The principle of the *naṣṣ* had two important results. First, it made it no longer necessary for an imām to rebel against the established regimes in order to become the actual ruler. In other words, the institutions of the imāmate and the caliphate were separated from one another, by allowing for a non-ruling imām who was not required to seize the caliphal authority if circumstances did not permit it. This explains why Jaʿfar al-Ṣādiq himself remained so non-committal in all the ʿAlid risings of his time, while the Ḥusaynids were largely spared the persecutions of al-Manṣūr against the Ḥasanids.[95] Secondly, as noted by Hodgson, *naṣṣ* imāmate provided an important basis for the sectarian continuity of Shīʿism, since 'it made possible a continuing dissident body of people attached to a continuing line of imāms regardless of the fate of particular political movements. It also encouraged a systematic development of special religious ideas which could gain acceptance among such dissident bodies without competing for the attention of all Muslims generally'.[96]

The second fundamental principle embodied in the doctrine of the imāmate, closely related to the *naṣṣ* principle and emphasized by Jaʿfar al-Ṣādiq, was that of an imāmate based on *ʿilm* or special religious knowledge. In the light of this *ʿilm*, which is divinely inspired and transmitted through the *naṣṣ* of the preceding imām, the rightful imām becomes the exclusively authorized source of the knowledge on how to decide points of conscience for the Muslims and lead them along the right path. Consequently, the imām will acquire the all-important functions of providing spiritual guidance for his adherents and explaining the inner meaning and significance of the Qur'ān and the religious injunctions, even when he is not occupied with the temporal function of ruling over the community. As Hodgson has observed, 'this was the time of the rise of *ḥadīth*, and the attempt to construct total systems of the pious life – which eventually issued in the full *sharīʿa* law'.[97] In this context, Jaʿfar al-Ṣādiq, by virtue of his *naṣṣ* imāmate and Fāṭimid descent, had acquired a unique position amongst all the authorities who were then concerned with working out the details of a pious life. His followers, too, attributed to him a uniquely authoritative *ʿilm*, necessary to guide the conscience and the lives of the true believers. As in the case of the *naṣṣ*, the Imām Jaʿfar's *ʿilm* was traced back in the Ḥusaynid line to ʿAlī, who had acquired it from the Prophet.

It may be added that, in line with his passivity and prudence, the Imām al-Ṣādiq refined the closely-related principle of *taqiyya*, or precautionary dissimulation, and made it an absolute article of Shīʿī faith.[98] No doubt, it must have been dangerous for the imāms and their followers to openly propagate their minoritarian beliefs, and to publicly announce that certain individuals, other than the ruling caliphs, were the divinely appointed religious leaders of the Muslims. The practice of *taqiyya* conveniently protected the Shīʿīs, especially the later Ismāʿīlīs, from persecution, and served in the preservation of their sectarian existence under hostile circumstances. In sum, by placing emphasis on an imāmate based on *naṣṣ* and *ʿilm*, and recommending the use of *taqiyya*, Jaʿfar al-Ṣādiq had presented a new interpretation of the imām's attributes and functions. This interpretation, which concerned itself with a non-ruling imām who until such time as God desired it, would solely act as spiritual guide and religious teacher, proved invaluable in preventing the absorption of Shīʿism into the Sunnī synthesis of Islam that was simultaneously being worked out by the representative groups of the *Jamāʿa*. At the same time, by underlining the hereditary and the divinely-bestowed attributes of both *naṣṣ* and *ʿilm*, the Imām Jaʿfar had now restricted the sanctity of the Ahl al-Bayt not only to the ʿAlids and especially the Fāṭimids amongst them, to the exclusion of the ʿAbbāsids and all other non-ʿAlid Hāshimids, but more specifically to his own Ḥusaynid line of imāms. This was because al-Ḥusayn had inherited the imāmate from al-Ḥasan, whose progeny had never claimed a *naṣṣ* imāmate.

The fundamental conception of the Imāmī doctrine of the imāmate is embodied in numerous traditions reported mainly from Jaʿfar al-Ṣādiq, preserved in the earliest corpus of Shīʿī *ḥadīth* by Abū Jaʿfar Muḥammad b. Yaʿqūb al-Kulaynī (d. 329/940–941).[99] This conception, also retained by the Ismāʿīlīs,[100] is founded on the permanent need of mankind for a divinely guided, sinless and infallible (*maʿṣūm*) imām who would act as the authoritative teacher and guide of men in all their religious and spiritual affairs. However, the imām can practise *taqiyya*, and, unlike Muḥammad who was the Seal of the Prophets, he does not receive divine revelation (*waḥy*), nor does he bring a new message and sacred law as did a messenger prophet. Although the imām is entitled to temporal leadership as much as to religious authority, his mandate does not depend on his actual rule or any attempt at gaining it. It is further maintained that the Prophet Muḥammad had designated ʿAlī b. Abī Ṭālib as his *waṣī* and successor, by an explicit designation (*naṣṣ*) under divine command; but the majority of the Companions apostatized by ignoring this testament. After ʿAlī, the imāmate was to be transmitted from father to son by *naṣṣ*, among the descendants of ʿAlī and Fāṭima; and after al-Ḥasan and al-Ḥusayn, in the progeny of the latter until the end of time. This imām, who is also the inheritor of Muḥammad's secret knowledge, is endowed by God with special *ʿilm*, and has perfect understanding of the outward or exoteric (*ẓāhir*) and the inward or esoteric (*bāṭin*) aspects and meanings of the Qur'ān and the sacred law of Islam. Indeed, the world cannot exist for a moment without an imām, the proof (*ḥujja*) of God on earth. Even if only two men were left upon the face of the earth, one of them would be the imām. And there can only be a single imām at one and the same time, though there may be a silent one (*ṣāmit*), his successor, beside him; an idea reflecting the influence of Abu'l-Khaṭṭāb's teaching. In sum, the imām's existence in the terrestrial world is so essential that his recognition and obedience is made the absolute duty of every believer; hence, the famous *ḥadīth* reported from the Imām al-Ṣādiq that 'whoever dies without having acknowledged the true imām of his time dies as an unbeliever (*kāfir*)'.[101]

In Shīʿī thought, the imām's all-important spiritual function of interpreting the inner meaning of the revelations announced by the Prophet is known as *ta'wīl*. The term *walāya* (Persian, *walāyat*), meaning devotion to the imāms, is sometimes also used in this sense. No adequate equivalent exists in any of the Western languages for this sense of the term *walāya*, adopted in modern times especially by Corbin, but it may roughly be translated as 'initiation'.[102] According to the Shīʿīs, the cycle of prophecy (*dāʾirat al-nubuwwa*), representing the deliverance of new sacred laws by different prophets who thus discharged an exoteric prophetic function, came to its end with the Prophet Muḥammad; but then, there arose the permanent need for the initiatic function connected with explaining the secret meaning of the Islamic message. And the person whose duty it is in every age to fulfil the function of *taʾwīl* (or *walāya*), inseparable from imāmate, is the rightful imām. It is through this function that the imāms become the *awliyāʾ Allāh*, or the friends of Allāh.[103] As we shall see, the notion of *taʾwīl* affirms the Shīʿī belief in the existence of the separate exoteric and esoteric dimensions in all religious scriptures and teachings, necessitating the spiritual comprehension of, and initiation into, their hidden and true meaning. Herein lies the essence of the imām's role, and the justification for the importance assigned to esotericism and gnosis (*ʿirfān*) by some Shīʿī groups. Shīʿī esotericism found its fullest development in Ismāʿīlism, by far the most representative of the Shīʿī sects designated with the term Bāṭiniyya; referring to those who give primacy to the inner, esoteric, or *bāṭinī* meaning behind the literal wording of all religious texts and formulations.

Finally, another factor which contributed to the strength of Jaʿfar al-Ṣādiq's imāmate revolved around the activities of the circle of thinkers surrounding him and his own ability to discipline the more extremist trends of thought within his following. Imām Jaʿfar attracted an active group of thinkers who vigorously dealt with the intellectual issues and problems of the time. Most of these individuals lived in Kūfa, like the bulk of Jaʿfar's partisans from amongst both the ordinary Imāmī Shīʿīs upholding the legitimacy of the Ḥusaynid line of imāms, and the more radical ones representing the heritage of the earlier extremist Shīʿīs. At the same time that the Imām Jaʿfar encouraged the speculations of his disciples and associates, he made a point of keeping them within tolerable bounds, by imposing a certain doctrinal discipline. This formal disciplining seems to have been particularly enforced after the accession of al-Manṣūr, in response to the latter's anti-Shīʿī policies. As a result, while the imāmate of Jaʿfar was invigorated by the ideas of the Ghulāt and other types of thinkers in his entourage, such ideas were kept in check, and often reconciled with one another, so as not to permit them to go too far beyond the limits acceptable to the *Jamāʿa* and to Sunnī Islam. This policy ultimately proved invaluable in making the Ḥusaynid line of imāms the most widely recognized by the Shīʿīs.

Besides a number of jurists-traditionists who concentrated mainly on legal problems,[104] Jaʿfar's close circle of associates included some of the most famous speculative theologians (*mutakallimūn*) of the time. These theologians, such as Zurāra b. Aʿyan, Mu'min al-Ṭāq, Hishām b. Sālim al-Jawāliqī, ʿAlī b. Ismāʿīl al-Maythamī, and above all Hishām b. al-Ḥakam, the foremost representative of Imāmī *kalām* or scholastic theology, made significant contributions to the formulation of the Imāmī doctrine of the imāmate.[105] Separate mention may be made of the enigmatic Jābir b. Ḥayyān, the renowned alchemist, who regarded Jaʿfar al-Ṣādiq as his master and who was greatly influenced by the gnosticism of the early Shīʿī Ghulāt. There has been much debate concerning the authorship of the corpus of writings attributed to him; some of these works, in which the occult properties of the letters of the alphabet play an important part, were probably produced by circles close to the Ismāʿīlīs of much later times.[106] There were also several noteworthy Ghulāt contributing to the rich and varied intellectual life of Jaʿfar's coterie; not only individuals such as Jābir al-Juʿfī (d. 128/745–746),[107] whom Jafri has classified among the so-called semi-Ghulāt,[108] but most significantly, Abu'l-Khaṭṭāb Muḥammad b. Abī Zaynab Miqlāṣ al-Ajdaʿ al-Asadī, the most prominent of all the early Ghulāt.

Abu'l-Khaṭṭāb, a Kūfan and a *mawlā* of the tribe of Asad, was the first Shīʿī to have organized a movement of a specifically *bāṭinī* type, namely, esoteric and gnostic.[109] For quite some time, he was an intimate associate of Jaʿfar al-Ṣādiq, who had appointed him as his chief *dāʿī* in Kūfa, the centre of Jaʿfar's partisans whom the imām visited occasionally from Medina. Abu'l-Khaṭṭāb acquired many followers of his own, known as the Khaṭṭābiyya, while he remained a zealous disciple of the Imām Jaʿfar and made exaggerated claims about him, in addition to holding other extremist views. As expected, the situation of this outspoken disciple eventually became intolerably dangerous to his quiescent and dissimulating imām. Consequently, Abu'l-Khaṭṭāb, who had apparently found one of the imām's sons, Ismāʿīl, responsive to his militant views and objectives, was accused of erring and was publicly cursed by Jaʿfar al-Ṣādiq. This repudiation, which probably took place soon after al-Manṣūr's accession in Dhu'l-Ḥijja 136/June 754, caused great consternation among the imām's followers. Shortly afterwards, in 138/755–756, seventy of Abu'l-Khaṭṭāb's enthusiastic supporters, in the company of their denounced leader, assembled in the mosque of Kūfa under obscure circumstances and possibly for rebellious purposes. They were attacked and massacred by the troops of the city's alert governor, ʿĪsā b. Mūsā, who later crushed the revolt of the Ḥasanid brothers. Abu'l-Khaṭṭāb was arrested and then crucified on the governor's orders. On the death of Abu'l-Khaṭṭāb, who had remained loyal to Jaʿfar al-Ṣādiq till the very end, the Khaṭṭābiyya, identified by al-Nawbakhtī and al-Qummī with the nascent Ismāʿīliyya, split into several groups. Some of the Khaṭṭābīs transferred their allegiance to Ismāʿīl b. Jaʿfar, the eponym of the Ismāʿīliyya and a close associate of the radical Shīʿīs in his father's following, and to the latter's son Muḥammad b. Ismāʿīl. Further discussion of these developments belongs in our next chapter. Suffice it to say here that with Abu'l-Khaṭṭāb, the early Khaṭṭābiyya, and Ismāʿīl we are already dealing with the immediate milieu that gave rise to proto-Ismāʿīlism.

Only fragmentary information is available on the doctrines upheld by Abu'l-Khaṭṭāb and the early Khaṭṭābīs. Before being disavowed, Abu'l-Khaṭṭāb claimed to be the deputy and *waṣī* of the Imām Jaʿfar who had allegedly taught him the Greatest Name of God (*ism Allāh al-aʿẓam*), with its miraculous implications. Aside from speculating about broad issues, like other Ghulāt, Abu'l-Khaṭṭāb and his disciples seem to have been particularly concerned with spiritual ranking and spiritual adoption. They ranked persons as angels, prophets, divine messengers, or even gods, though not in real rivalry with the one God, Allāh, but rather as His representatives.[110] Abu'l-Khaṭṭāb is said to have taught that at all times there must be two prophets, one speaking (*nāṭiq*) and the other silent (*ṣāmit*); in Muḥammad's time, he had been the speaking prophet and ʿAlī the silent one, and now Jaʿfar and Abu'l-Khaṭṭāb were, respectively, the speaking and silent prophets. The early Khaṭṭābīs preached the divinity of the imāms, on the basis of the divine light or *nūr* inherited by them. They are also credited with emphasizing the *bāṭinī ta'wīl*, the esoteric or allegorical interpretation of the Qur'ān and the sacred prescriptions; a method adopted and refined to its fullest extent by the Ismāʿīlīs. In cosmogony, they replaced the use of the letters of the alphabet, as introduced by al-Mughīra, by their corresponding numerical values. Some of the ideas or terminologies introduced or utilized by Abu'l-Khaṭṭāb were also adopted by the early Ismāʿīlīs who, like the Khaṭṭābīs, were preoccupied with esotericism, cyclicism, hierarchism, and symbolical exegesis.

Such were the circumstances under which Jaʿfar al-Ṣādiq appealed to the diffuse Shīʿī sentiments, following decades of defeats, tragedies and martyrdom for the loyal partisans of the ʿAlid cause. They served to strengthen his imāmate, while setting Imāmī Shīʿism well on its way towards acquiring its sectarian character. Having consolidated Shīʿism and established a solid foundation for its further doctrinal development, Abū ʿAbd Allāh Jaʿfar b. Muḥammad al-Ṣādiq, the last imām recognized by both the Twelvers and the Ismāʿīlīs, being the sixth one for the former and the fifth for the latter, died (or was poisoned according to some Shīʿīs, on the orders of the caliph al-Manṣūr) in 148/765. He was buried in Medina, in the Baqīʿ cemetery, next to his father, grandfather and al-Ḥasan b. ʿAlī, whose tombs were destroyed by the Wahhābīs in modern times. The dispute over the Imām Jaʿfar al-Ṣādiq's succession, causing historic splits in his following, marks the official beginning of what was to become known as the Ismāʿīlī movement.

3

Early Ismāʿīlism

Early Ismāʿīlism, which in Corbin's words represents the period of fermentation and incubation of the Ismāʿīlī movement,[1] is the most obscure major phase in the entire history of Ismāʿīlism. It extends from the proto-Ismāʿīlī origins of the movement, in the middle of the 2nd/8th century, to the establishment of the Fāṭimid Caliphate in the year 297/909, a period of almost one and a half centuries. Little reliable information is available on the history and doctrines of the early Ismāʿīlīs who contributed so much to the success and intellectual development of their movement. As a result, many aspects of early Ismāʿīlism continue to be shrouded in uncertainty, causing irreconcilable disagreements among scholars regarding some vital issues. The late Asaf Fyzee summed up this situation well in 1969, noting that 'we are faced not so much with fact and history as with legend and myth; conjecture and hypothesis; the passions and prejudices of the historians...'[2] Needless to recall that at least until a few decades ago, research problems were accentuated by the fact that anti-Ismāʿīlī texts constituted the main sources of information on the subject.

The particular difficulties of studying the early Ismāʿīlīs stem partly from the general dearth of accurate information on Shīʿism during the early ʿAbbāsid period, when the major Shīʿī sects of Ithnāʿashariyya and Ismāʿīliyya, then in the process of being formed, were for the most part severely persecuted and as such had to resort to *taqiyya* and underground existence. More significantly, however, the persistence of research difficulties has been due to the fact that few genuine Ismāʿīlī sources have survived from this early period. It is highly probable that the early Ismāʿīlīs, living in an extremely hostile milieu, did not produce any substantial volume of literature, preferring instead to propagate their doctrines mainly by word of mouth. The modern rediscovery of Ismāʿīlī literature has confirmed this suspicion. It seems that the early Ismāʿīlīs produced only a few treatises which circulated mainly among the most trusted members of their community. Even then, however, utmost effort was made to conceal the identity of the authors. Another point to be noted here is that the meagre literary output of the early Ismāʿīlīs soon became obsolete and was subjected to censorship by the Fāṭimids; not only because the earlier works appeared rather crude compared to the elaborate treatises of the Fāṭimid period but, more importantly, because some of the views contained in them were in conflict with the official Fāṭimid doctrines. Nevertheless, a small collection of Ismāʿīlī texts from the pre-Fāṭimid period has survived to the present day. These include some fragments from the *Kitāb al-rushd wa'l-hidāya*,[3] attributed to the celebrated Ismāʿīlī *dāʿī* Ibn Ḥawshab, known as Manṣūr al-Yaman (d. 302/914); and the *Kitāb al-ʿālim wa'l-ghulām* which, if not written by Ibn Ḥawshab or his son Jaʿfar, does apparently belong to the same school that produced the preceding item.[4]

At any rate, the production of Ismāʿīlī literature on a much larger scale occurred only after the accession of the Fāṭimids when the great Ismāʿīlī authors and *dāʿīs* embarked on their activities. A good portion of this literature has now become available to researchers. Unfortunately, it has also become clear that Ismāʿīlī sources, being essentially religious and philosophical in their character, contain little historical information, especially on the initial period of the movement. The earliest historical work in Ismāʿīlī literature is the *Iftitāḥ al-daʿwa* of the famous al-Qāḍī al-Nuʿmān (d. 363/974), who served the first four Fāṭimid caliphs in different capacities.[5] This work, completed in 346/957, covers the immediate background to the establishment of the Fāṭimid Caliphate; it was used as the main source in all the subsequent Ismāʿīlī (and some non-Ismāʿīlī) writings on the subject. Furthermore, only one general history of Ismāʿīlism seems to have been written by an Ismāʿīlī; the *ʿUyūn al-akhbār* of Idrīs ʿImād al-Dīn (d. 872/1468), the 19th Ṭayyibī *dāʿī* in Yaman. This is a seven-volume history from the time of the Prophet until the opening phases of the Ṭayyibī *daʿwa* in Yaman.[6] In all these Ismāʿīlī historical works, the opening stage of the Ismāʿīlī movement is treated with great obscurity. For this earliest phase, the brief accounts of the Imāmī heresiographers al-Nawbakhtī and al-Qummī provide our main sources of information.

The first Western orientalist who collected much valuable information on the early Ismāʿīlīs, particularly on the so-called Qarmaṭīs (al-Qarāmiṭa) of Baḥrayn, was de Goeje. But the meticulous researches of this Dutch scholar, who also edited a number of Muslim historical and geographical works, anteceded the modern access to Ismāʿīlī sources. Consequently, like de Sacy and other leading orientalists of the nineteenth century, he had to rely mainly on anti-Ismāʿīlī writings. With modern progress in Ismāʿīlī studies, we have now acquired a much better understanding of early Ismāʿīlism, thanks especially to the pioneering labours of Massignon, Ivanow and Lewis, and to the more recent contributions of Stern[7] and Madelung.[8] The latter two specialists have also done much to clarify the picture of early Ismāʿīlism produced by the later Ismāʿīlīs, who no longer subscribed to all the aims and doctrines of the earlier revolutionary phase of the movement.

Before commencing our detailed discussion of early Ismāʿīlism, a few words are in order concerning the name al-Ismāʿīliyya, which apparently was never used by the early Ismāʿīlīs themselves. This designation, as we shall see, owes its origins to heresiographical works, notably those of al-Nawbakhtī and al-Qummī. It may be added that the name al-Qarāmiṭa, originally belonging to only one section of the movement, had soon come to be applied in a wider and derogatory sense to the entire Ismāʿīlī movement. The early Ismāʿīlīs, when not referred to abusively as the *malāḥida*, were normally denominated as Qarmaṭīs or Bāṭinīs by their contemporaries. They themselves, however, seem to have designated their movement simply as *al-daʿwa*, 'the mission', or more formally as *al-daʿwa al-hādiya*, 'the rightly-guiding mission'.[9] Such expressions, stressing the attitude of the sectarians towards their movement and their divine duty to appeal for the allegiance of other Muslims, continued to be utilized by the Ismāʿīlīs, in preference to al-Ismāʿīliyya, through the Fāṭimid and later times. For instance, aside from appearing in the works of al-Qāḍī al-Nuʿmān, who used the title *Iftitāḥ al-daʿwa* for his book describing the beginnings of Ismāʿīlī propaganda in Yaman and North Africa, they are mentioned in some letters or epistles of the eighth Fāṭimid caliph al-Mustanṣir, written between 469/1076 and 481/1089 to the pro-Fāṭimid Ṣulayḥid rulers of Yaman;[10] in the already-noted epistle of another Fāṭimid caliph, al-Āmir, addressed around 516/1122 to the Nizārī Ismāʿīlīs,[11] and in numerous earlier and later Ismāʿīlī works.[12]

The history of Ismāʿīlism as an independent movement may be traced to the dispute over the succession to the Imām Jaʿfar al-Ṣādiq, who died in 148/765. According to the majority of the available sources, Jaʿfar al-Ṣādiq had designated his son Ismāʿīl as his successor, by the rule of the *naṣṣ*. There can be no doubt about the authenticity of this designation, which forms the basis of the claims of the Ismāʿīliyya and which should have settled the question of al-Ṣādiq's succession in due course. But, as related in the majority of the sources, Ismāʿīl died before his father, and his death raised some questions in the minds of some of al-Ṣādiq's followers who did not understand how a divinely guided imām could be fallible regarding so crucial a matter as *naṣṣ*. A group of these Imāmī Shīʿīs, having become doubtful about al-Ṣādiq's *ʿilm* and his own claim to the imāmate, had already left him during his lifetime.[13] Anti-Ismāʿīlī sources also add that Ismāʿīl had been deprived of his succession rights due to his indulgence in drink. Such reports about Ismāʿīl's dipsomania and his disavowal by his father, especially as related by the Twelver sources, may represent later fabrications by those who did not accept the Ismāʿīlī line of imāms.[14] As shall be seen, the Imām al-Ṣādiq had been apprehensive of Ismāʿīl for the reason of the latter's association with extremist circles. It is not absolutely certain whether Jaʿfar al-Ṣādiq designated another of his sons after Ismāʿīl's death, although the later Twelver Shīʿīs claimed such a *naṣṣ* for Mūsā b. Jaʿfar, the younger half-brother of Ismāʿīl, producing several *ḥadīth*s to this effect.[15] However, the fact remains that three of al-Ṣādiq's surviving sons simultaneously claimed his succession, while none of them could convincingly prove to have been the beneficiary of a second *naṣṣ*. As a result, the Imām al-Ṣādiq's Shīʿī partisans split into six groups, two of which constituted the nucleus of the nascent Ismāʿīliyya.[16]

A small group refused to believe in al-Ṣādiq's death and awaited his reappearance as the Mahdī; they were called the Nāwūsiyya after their leader, a certain ʿAbd Allāh (or ʿIjlān) b. al-Nāwūs. A few others recognized Muḥammad b. Jaʿfar, known as al-Dībāj, the younger full-brother of Mūsā; they became denominated as the Shumayṭiyya (Sumayṭiyya), after their leader Yaḥyā b. Abi'l-Shumayṭ (al-Sumayṭ). Muḥammad al-Dībāj revolted unsuccessfully in 200/815–816 against the caliph al-Maʾmūn (198–218/813–833), and died soon afterwards in 203/818. But the majority of al-Ṣādiq's partisans now accepted his eldest surviving son ʿAbd Allāh al-Afṭaḥ, the full-brother of Ismāʿīl, as their new imām. ʿAbd Allāh seems to have claimed a second *naṣṣ* from his father; and his adherents, the Afṭaḥiyya, or Faṭḥiyya, cited a *ḥadīth* from the Imām al-Ṣādiq to the effect that the imāmate must be transmitted through the eldest son of the imām. At any rate, when ʿAbd Allāh died, about seventy days after the death of his father, the bulk of his supporters went over to Mūsā b. Jaʿfar, later called al-Kāẓim, who had already been acknowledged as his father's successor by some of the Imāmiyya.

Thus, Mūsā al-Kāẓim soon received the allegiance of the majority of the

Imāmī Shīʿīs, including the most renowned scholars in al-Ṣādiq's entourage, such as Hishām b. al-Ḥakam and Mu'min al-Ṭāq who had supported Mūsā from the start. Mūsā, later counted as the seventh imām of the Twelvers, refrained from all political activity and was more quiescent than his father. He was, in fact, one of the two ʿAlids who reportedly refused to support al-Ḥusayn b. ʿAlī, known as Ṣāḥib Fakhkh. This Ḥasanid, a grandnephew of ʿAbd Allāh al-Maḥḍ, revolted in the Ḥijāz during the short caliphate of al-Hādī (169–170/785–786), and was killed at Fakhkh near Mecca, together with many other ʿAlids, in 169/786.[17] Nevertheless, Mūsā was not spared the Shīʿī persecutions of the ʿAbbāsids. He was arrested several times and finally died (possibly having been poisoned) in 183/799, whilst imprisoned at Baghdād on the caliph Hārūn al-Rashīd's orders. Subsequently, one group of Mūsā's partisans acknowledged the imāmate of his eldest son ʿAlī b. Mūsā al-Riḍā, who later became the heir apparent and son-in-law of the caliph al-Ma'mūn.[18] ʿAlī al-Riḍā died in Ṭūs in 203/818, and most of his followers traced the imāmate through four more imāms, the direct descendants of al-Riḍā, namely, Muḥammad al-Taqī (d. 220/835), ʿAlī al-Naqī (d. 254/868), al-Ḥasan al-ʿAskarī (d. 260/874), and Muḥammad al-Mahdī (b. 255/869). This sub-sect of the Imāmiyya eventually became known as the Ithnāʿashariyya, or the Twelver Shīʿa; referring to those Imāmīs who recognize a line of twelve imāms, starting with ʿAlī b. Abī Ṭālib and ending with Muḥammad b. al-Ḥasan al-Mahdī, Lord of the Time (*Ṣāḥib al-Zamān*) whose emergence or *ẓuhūr* is still being awaited.[19]

Two other groups supporting the claims of Ismāʿīl b. Jaʿfar and constituting the proto-Ismāʿīlīs, issued from amongst the Imāmī Shīʿī following of the Imām al-Ṣādiq. These Kūfan groups had actually come into being earlier, on the death of Ismāʿīl; a date mentioned by Ivanow and Corbin as the official beginning of Ismāʿīlism.[20] However, these pro-Ismāʿīl or proto-Ismāʿīlī groups seceded from the rest of the Imāmiyya only after al-Ṣādiq's death. One group, denying the death of Ismāʿīl during his father's lifetime, maintained that he was the true imām after al-Ṣādiq; they further believed that Ismāʿīl remained alive and would eventually return as the Mahdī. These Shīʿīs defended their claims by noting that al-Ṣādiq, who as an imām could speak only the truth, had done nothing to revoke Ismāʿīl's succession rights to the imāmate; accordingly, they had no reason for renouncing their allegiance to Ismāʿīl. They believed that the Imām al-Ṣādiq had announced Ismāʿīl's death merely as a ruse to protect his son, whom he had hidden because he feared for his safety. Al-Nawbakhtī and al-Qummī call the members of this group, recognizing Ismāʿīl as their Imām-Mahdī, the 'pure Ismāʿīliyya' (*al-Ismāʿīliyya al-khāliṣa*).[21] Some later heresiographers, notably al-Shahrastānī, designate this group as *al-Ismāʿīliyya al-wāqifa*, referring to those who stopped their line of imāms with Ismāʿīl.[22]

There was a second group of pro- Ismāʿīl Shīʿīs who, affirming Ismāʿīl's death during the lifetime of al-Ṣādiq, now recognized Muḥammad b. Ismāʿīl as their imām. They held that he was the rightful successor to Ismāʿīl and that the Imām al-Ṣādiq had personally designated him as such, after Ismāʿīl's death. According to these partisans of Muḥammad, the imāmate could not be transferred from brother to brother after the case of the Imāms al-Ḥasan and al-Ḥusayn. This was why they rejected the claims of Mūsā and other brothers of Ismāʿīl, as they did that of Muḥammad b. al-Ḥanafiyya, who, according to them, had falsely claimed the imāmate in rivalry with ʿAlī b. al-Ḥusayn Zayn al-ʿĀbidīn. The Imāmī heresiographers call this group the Mubārakiyya, named supposedly after their leader al-Mubārak, a *mawlā* of Ismāʿīl.[23] However, Ivanow has shown that in all probability al-Mubārak (meaning 'The Blessed') was the epithet of Ismāʿīl himself, citing some passages from the famous Ismāʿīlī *dāʿī* of the 4th/10th century, al-Sijistānī, in which Ismāʿīl is repeatedly referred to by this name.[24] More instances of the application of the name al-Mubārak to Ismāʿīl have now come to light, lending strong support to Ivanow's hypothesis.[25] It seems likely then that the Mubārakiyya were at first the upholders of Ismāʿīl's imāmate, and it was only after al-Ṣādiq's death that the bulk of Ismāʿīl's supporters rallied to the side of Muḥammad b. Ismāʿīl and recognized him as their new imām. At the same time, Ismāʿīl had to be elevated retrospectively to the imāmate.[26] In other words, it was maintained that while al-Ṣādiq was still alive, the imāmate had passed from him to Ismāʿīl. At any rate, it is certain that al-Mubārakiyya was the original name of the nascent Ismāʿīliyya.

Al-Qummī identifies *al-Ismāʿīliyya al-khāliṣa* with the Khaṭṭābiyya; and al-Nawbakhtī has a similar statement.[27] Furthermore, both authors, intent on showing the influence of the Khaṭṭābīs on the nascent Ismāʿīliyya, report that a group of Abu'l-Khaṭṭāb's followers after his death joined the supporters of Muḥammad b. Ismāʿīl, claiming that the spirit of the Imām al-Ṣādiq had passed into Abu'l-Khaṭṭāb and from him, to Muḥammad b. Ismāʿīl.[28] Many later sources, too, speak of close connections between the early Ismāʿīlīs and the Khaṭṭābīs.[29] The exact nature of the relationships between *al-Ismāʿīliyya al-khāliṣa* and the Mubārakiyya on the one hand, and the Khaṭṭābiyya on the other, remains rather obscure. It is certain, however, that all these groups in the following of the Imām al-Ṣādiq were comprised of radical Shīʿīs who provided the milieus in which proto-Ismāʿīlism originated.

It will be useful at this juncture to know more about the life and activities of Ismāʿīl himself. For the Ismāʿīlīs, he is an imām; the sixth one in the series. As such, he is highly revered by them, but unfortunately, Ismāʿīlī sources such as the *ʿUyūn al-akhbār* contain little historical information of any value concerning him. On the other hand, the Twelver sources, which are better informed than the Sunnī sources regarding the Shīʿī sub-sects, are basically hostile towards Ismāʿīl and the claims raised on his behalf. The Twelvers, who recognize Mūsā al-Kāẓim as their imām after al-Ṣādiq, are interested in upholding Mūsā's rights against Ismāʿīl.[30] It is not surprising, therefore, that they regard Ismāʿīl as a reprobate. We have to keep these reservations in mind in utilizing the Twelver references to Ismāʿīl, about whom our knowledge is extremely limited.

Abū Muḥammad Ismāʿīl b. Jaʿfar (al-Mubārak) and his full-brother ʿAbd Allāh were the eldest sons of the Imām al-Ṣādiq by his first wife Fāṭima, a granddaughter of the Imām al-Ḥasan b. ʿAlī. It is related that al-Ṣādiq did not take a second wife as long as Fāṭima was alive. As a result, there was a significant age difference between ʿAbd Allāh and Ismāʿīl on the one hand, and Mūsā, Isḥāq and Muḥammad, al-Ṣādiq's sons from a slave concubine called Ḥamīda, on the other. Ismāʿīl's birth date is unknown; but apparently he was the second son of al-Ṣādiq, born between 80 and 83/699–702, and was also some twenty-five years older than Mūsā, who was born in 128/745–746. It seems likely then that Ismāʿīl was born sometime during the initial years of the second Islamic century.[31] The exact date and the circumstances of Ismāʿīl's death also remain unknown. According to some Ismāʿīlī authors, Ismāʿīl survived the Imām al-Ṣādiq. However, the majority of sources report that he predeceased his father in Medina, and was buried in the Baqīʿ cemetery. Ḥasan b. Nūḥ al-Bharūchī, an Indian Ismāʿīlī author, relates visiting Ismāʿīl's grave in 904/1498.[32] Many Ismāʿīlī and non-Ismāʿīlī sources repeat the story of how, before and during Ismāʿīl's funeral procession, the Imām al-Ṣādiq made deliberate attempts to show the face of his dead son to witnesses,[33] though some of the same sources also relate reports indicating that Ismāʿīl was seen in Baṣra soon afterwards. There are few other indisputable facts available on Ismāʿīl's biography. Al-Kashshī relates several versions of an event regarding how Ismāʿīl acted on behalf of his father to protest against the killing of al-Muʿallā b. Khunays, one of Jaʿfar al-Ṣādiq's extremist followers.[34] The execution of al-Muʿallā, which greatly angered the imām, had been ordered by the governor of Medina, Dā'ūd b. ʿAlī. As the latter's term of office lasted only a few months during 133/750, it is possible to infer that Ismāʿīl was still alive in that year. One source actually places his death in the year 133 A.H.[35] Other sources, however, mention later years, the latest one being 145/762–763.[36] In addition, in the accounts of Ismāʿīl's death and burial, al-Manṣūr, who succeeded his brother in 136/754, is usually named as the ruling ʿAbbāsid caliph. It is, therefore, safe to conclude that Ismāʿīl's premature death occurred sometime during 136–145/754–763, probably soon after 136 A.H.

Regarding Ismāʿīl's activities, reference has already been made to his contacts with the extremist Shīʿīs in his father's following. These contacts are clearly alluded to in several traditions reported by al-Kashshī,[37] showing Ismāʿīl's popularity amongst the radical Shīʿīs and his close association with them, especially with al-Mufaḍḍal b. ʿUmar al-Juʿfī, a money lender. At the same time, these traditions reveal al-Ṣādiq's dissatisfaction with the radical Shīʿīs who were leading his son astray. Al-Mufaḍḍal, the supposed author of several works,[38] was the transmitter of certain gnostic teachings and the cyclical history associated with the earlier Kaysānīs; he was an extremist disciple of al-Ṣādiq and initially an associate of Abu'l-Khaṭṭāb. He is also mentioned as the leader of one of the sub-groups, the Mufaḍḍaliyya, into which the Khaṭṭābiyya split after Abu'l-Khaṭṭāb's disavowal by the Imām al-Ṣādiq.[39] However, unlike the other four Khaṭṭābī sub-groups, the Mufaḍḍaliyya repudiated Abu'l-Khaṭṭāb. And Jaʿfar al-Ṣādiq, though making some uncomplimentary remarks about him, never openly denounced al-Mufaḍḍal, as he did in the case of other Khaṭṭābī leaders. In fact, there are reports to the effect that Jaʿfar al-Ṣādiq appointed al-Mufaḍḍal to guide his Kūfan followers, or at least those amongst them who had supported Abu'l-Khaṭṭāb, subsequent to the imām's rift with the latter. In any event, al-Mufaḍḍal later became an adherent of Mūsā al-Kāẓim during whose imāmate he died, although he did not lend support to the condemnation of Ismāʿīl by certain Imāmī circles. According to another report, Ismāʿīl was evidently involved in a militant anti-regime plot in collaboration with several others, including Bassām b. ʿAbd Allāh al-Ṣayrafī, another extremist Shīʿī engaged in money lending in Kūfa.[40] The caliph al-Manṣūr summoned Ismāʿīl along with the Imām al-Ṣādiq, as well as Bassām, to his administrative capital at al-Ḥīra near Kūfa. The suspected plotters were taken before the caliph, who had Bassām executed but spared Ismāʿīl. Massignon places the date of this event in the year 138/755, and suggests that Bassām had the responsibility of financing the alleged plot.[41] This is one of the occasions reported by the Imāmī sources, during which al-Ṣādiq expressed his strong disapproval of Ismāʿīl's activities.

All this evidence confirms the existence of close relations between Ismāʿīl and the radical circles in al-Ṣādiq's following; and it definitely places the young Ismāʿīl amongst those Shīʿīs who were not satisfied with their imām's conservatism and passivity. Jaʿfar al-Ṣādiq could not approve of such activities that were at variance with his efforts to consolidate Shīʿism on a quiescent basis. As noted, some Imāmī sources do identify the early Khaṭṭābiyya, one of the most extremist Shīʿī groups, with the nascent Ismāʿīliyya. In modern times, too, this identification has been maintained by certain scholars, notably Massignon and Corbin.[42] Massignon has in fact suggested that Abu'l-Khaṭṭāb was the spiritual or adoptive father of Ismāʿīl, whence his *kunya* of Abū Ismāʿīl.[43] In this connection, he formulated a general hypothesis, contending that since the beginning of the second Islamic century, the expression *anta minnā ahl al-bayt* (you are from the Prophet's family) purportedly used by the Prophet in reference to Salmān al-Fārisī, and as reported in a *ḥadīth*, had acquired a ritual value indicating 'spiritual adoption' amongst the revolutionary Shīʿīs, for whom real family ties were established through spiritual parentage, adoption or initiation. Lewis, too, accepts the idea of 'spiritual adoption' and envisages a close collaboration between Ismāʿīl and Abu'l-Khaṭṭāb who, according to him, worked for the creation of a revolutionary Shīʿī sect comprised of all the minor Shīʿī groups, around the imāmate of Ismāʿīl and his descendants.[44]

However, such inter-connections as may have existed between the proto-Ismāʿīlīs and the early Khaṭṭābīs should not be exaggerated, especially in the doctrinal domain, although certain ideas and terminologies attributed to Abu'l-Khaṭṭāb and his followers were subsequently adopted by the early Ismāʿīlīs.[45] The Khaṭṭābiyya, as noted, believed in the divinity of the imāms and also held that al-Ṣādiq's spirit had passed to Abu'l-Khaṭṭāb, while some of them maintained that after the latter's death this spirit had devolved to Muḥammad b. Ismāʿīl. The Mubārakiyya and their successors, on the other hand, did not entertain such beliefs; they simply upheld the imāmate of Muḥammad b. Ismāʿīl, who later came to be regarded as the awaited Mahdī by the bulk of the early Ismāʿīlīs. Fāṭimid

Ismāʿīlism, in fact, regarded Abu'l-Khaṭṭāb as a heretic and repudiated the Khaṭṭābiyya.[46]

There is, moreover, the enigmatic *Umm al-kitāb*,[47] preserved by the Nizārī Ismāʿīlīs of Central Asia, in which the Khaṭṭābīs are mentioned as the founders of Ismāʿīlism. More specifically, it states that the Ismāʿīlī religion (*madhhab*) is that founded by the children (*farzandān*, referring probably to disciples) of Abu'l-Khaṭṭāb, who gave their lives for love of Ismāʿīl, the son of Jaʿfar al-Ṣādiq, and it will continue through the cycle of cycles (*dawr-i dawāʾir*).[48] This book, extant only in an archaic Persian, contains the discourses of the Imām Muḥammad al-Bāqir in response to questions raised by an anachronistic group of disciples, including Jābir b. ʿAbd Allāh al-Anṣārī, Jaʿfar (Jābir) al-Juʿfī and Muḥammad b. al-Mufaḍḍal. The Imām al-Bāqir appears here in the guise of a five-year-old child, strongly reminiscent of certain apocryphal Gospels relating to Jesus.[49] The *Umm al-kitāb*, containing the doctrines of certain Shīʿī Ghulāt, is a syncretic work reflecting the influences of diverse non-Islamic religious traditions and schools of thought, such as Valentinian Gnosticism and Manichaeism. However, the author (or authors) and the date of the composition of this treatise remain unknown. According to Ivanow, it must have been written before the beginning of the 5th/11th century. Corbin assigns its origins to those Shīʿī milieus in the 2nd/8th century which produced proto-Ismāʿīlism, while Madelung is of the opinion that the final redaction of this book probably dates from the earlier part of the 6th/12th century.[50]

Recent scholarship, by examining the terminology and the cosmogony of the *Umm al-kitāb* which is expressed in the form of a gnostic myth, has revealed that the treatise was in all probability produced by an early Shīʿī group called al-Mukhammisa.[51] This inference is supported by other doctrinal features of the treatise, such as its endorsement of metempsychosis, and by the important role it assigns to Salmān al-Fārisī, whose gnostic name here is al-Salsal. In fact Salmān and Abu'l-Khaṭṭāb are mentioned jointly and repeatedly in a sacred formula throughout the text. The Mukhammisa or the Pentadists were a group of the Shīʿī Ghulāt who originated in Kūfa during the second half of the 2nd/8th century, and subsequently survived for some time, like the Khaṭṭābiyya, on the fringe of the Imāmiyya. Al-Qummī, the only early heresiographer who discusses the Mukhammisa in some detail, identifies them with the Khaṭṭābiyya.[52] According to his account, they preached that the Prophet Muḥammad was God, who had appeared in five different bodies or persons, namely, Muḥammad, ʿAlī, Fāṭima, al-Ḥasan and al-Ḥusayn. In this divine pentad, however, only the person of Muḥammad was real and represented the true meaning (*maʿnā*); for he was the first person created and the first speaker (*nāṭiq*). They also maintained that Muḥammad had been Ādam, Nūḥ, Ibrāhīm, Mūsā and ʿĪsā, appearing continuously among the Arabs and non-Arabs; and Salmān was the *bāb*, or gate, who always appeared with Muḥammad. These and other doctrines of the Mukhammisa are strongly represented in the *Umm al-kitāb*.

Al-Qummī describes a variant of the Mukhammisa, the so-called ʿUlyā'iyya or ʿAlbā'iyya, followers of Bashshār al-Shaʿīrī, a Kūfan *ghālī* who was reportedly repudiated by Jaʿfar al-Ṣādiq.[53] The members of this group upheld the divinity of ʿAlī instead of that of Muḥammad, and this was the main point distinguishing them from the rest of the Mukhammisa. The doctrines of the Mukhammisa, especially those held by the ʿUlyā'iyya, provided the basis of the beliefs of the later Nuṣayriyya, one of the most famous extremist Shīʿī sects.[54] The cosmological and eschatological ideas of the Nuṣayrīs, named after Muḥammad b. Nuṣayr (d. 270/883) who initially followed the tenth imām of the Twelvers but who later made exaggerated claims for himself, are equally present in the *Umm al-kitāb*. The Nuṣayrīs, who are still found in Syria, where for centuries they have maintained rivalries with their Nizārī Ismāʿīlī neighbours, worship ʿAlī as God and maintain that Muḥammad was his prophet. Besides these two, Salmān assumes a special rank for them.[55] If ʿAlī is the original sense or the true meaning (*maʿnā*), and Muḥammad his name (*ism*), then Salmān is the gate (*bāb*) leading to the 'name' and the 'meaning'. In Nuṣayrī thought, this triad is designated symbolically by *ʿayn–mīm–sīn*, standing for the first letters of the names ʿAlī, Muḥammad and Salmān, and corresponding to *maʿnā–ism–bāb*. Such gnostic designations, and the use of the mystical properties of the letters of the alphabet, are also important features of the *Umm al-kitāb*.

The technical terminology of the Mukhammisa-ʿUlyā'iyya tradition is equally incorporated into the already-noted *Kitāb al-haft*, which is essentially a Mufaḍḍalī-Nuṣayrī text. This book, also known amongst the Ṭayyibīs, found its way to the Nizārī Ismāʿīlīs, who seized the Nuṣayrī fortresses and settlements of central Syria, recruiting also new converts from the defeated community, in the first half of the 6th/12th century. The Ismāʿīlīs came to view the book in question as their own, though no Ismāʿīlī ideas are found in it. The *Umm al-kitāb* of the Central Asian Nizārīs may have had a similar fate. It is safe to conclude that the *Umm al-kitāb* originated, probably during the second half of the 2nd/8th century, in the

Shīʿī Ghulāt milieus of southern ʿIrāq which gave rise to the Mukhammisa and later to the Nuṣayriyya traditions. It represents the earliest extant Shīʿī record of the Mukhammisa–ʿUlyā'iyya type, which is quite distinct from the beliefs of the early Ismāʿīlīs, especially regarding creation. Evidently, this text was eventually adopted into Ismāʿīlī literature, and, under obscure circumstances, found its way into the private libraries of the Nizārīs of Shughnān, Wakhān and Chitral in the upper Oxus, where these sectarians have claimed the book as their own. Filippani-Ronconi has postulated a complex hypothesis regarding the origins of this work and how it came to be located in Central Asia.[56]

As in the case of Ismāʿīl, little is known about Muḥammad b. Ismāʿīl, the seventh imām of the Ismāʿīliyya. No specific details are related about him in Muslim historical literature, as he did not participate in any anti-ʿAbbāsid revolt. In Ismāʿīlī literature, he is treated briefly and with numerous anachronisms. The relevant information contained in Ismāʿīlī sources has been collected by Idrīs ʿImād al-Dīn, who provides the most detailed biographical account of him.[57] Muḥammad was the eldest son of Ismāʿīl who had at least one other son named ʿAlī. He was also the eldest grandson of the Imām al-Ṣādiq and, according to Ismāʿīlī tradition, was twenty-six years old at the time of the latter's death.[58] Furthermore, all sources agree that he was older than his uncle Mūsā by about eight years. On the basis of these details, Muḥammad must have been born around 120/738. The *Dastūr al-munajjimīn*, in fact, places his birth in Dhu'l-Ḥijja 121/November 739.[59] He was the imām of the Mubārakiyya and the eldest male member of the Imām al-Ṣādiq's family, after the death of his uncle ʿAbd Allāh al-Afṭaḥ. As such, he enjoyed a certain degree of respect and seniority in this Fāṭimid branch of the ʿAlid family.[60] However, after the recognition of the imāmate of Mūsā al-Kāẓim by the majority of al-Ṣādiq's followers, Muḥammad's position became rather untenable in his native Ḥijāz where his uncle and chief rival Mūsā also lived. It was probably then, not long after al-Ṣādiq's death, that Muḥammad left Medina for the east and went into hiding; henceforth, he acquired the epithet al-Maktūm, the Hidden. As a result, he was saved from persecution by the ʿAbbāsids, while continuing to maintain close contacts with the Mubārakiyya who like most other radical Shīʿī groups of the time were centred in Kūfa. Different sources mention various localities and regions as Muḥammad's final destination; but it is certain that he first went to southern ʿIrāq and then to Persia.[61] According to the later Ismāʿīlīs, this emigration marks the beginning of the period of concealment (*dawr al-satr*) in early Ismāʿīlism, the concealment ending with the establishment of the Fāṭimid Caliphate.

Muḥammad b. Ismāʿīl seems to have spent the latter part of his life in Khūzistān, in southwestern Persia, where he had a certain number of supporters and from where he despatched his own *dāʿīs* to adjoining areas. The exact date of Muḥammad's death remains unknown. But it is almost certain that he died during the caliphate of the celebrated Hārūn al-Rashīd (170–193/786–809), perhaps soon after 179/795–796,[62] the year in which al-Rashīd, continuing the anti-ʿAlid policy of his predecessors, arrested Mūsā al-Kāẓim in Medina and banished him to ʿIrāq as a prisoner. The Twelver sources, which are hostile to Muḥammad b. Ismāʿīl, maintain that it was he who betrayed Mūsā to the ʿAbbāsids, though they also relate the story of a reconciliation between these two Fāṭimids prior to Muḥammad's departure for ʿIrāq.[63] Muḥammad had at least two sons, Ismāʿīl and Jaʿfar, while he lived openly in Medina; after his emigration, he had four more sons, including ʿAbd Allāh, who, according to the later Ismāʿīlīs, was his rightful successor.[64]

Almost nothing is known about the early history of Ismāʿīlism after these proto-Ismāʿīlī beginnings. On the basis of the opening remarks of al-Nawbakhtī and al-Qummī on the Qarāmiṭa, and in view of the later history of the sect, however, it may be assumed that the Mubārakiyya split into two groups on the death of Muḥammad b. Ismāʿīl.[65] One small and obscure group apparently traced the imāmate in the posterity of the deceased imām. However, the separate existence of this group has not been recorded in any contemporary source, until ʿUbayd Allāh – or ʿAbd Allāh according to the Ismāʿīlīs who reject the diminutive form of his name – the future leader of the movement, openly claimed the imāmate of the Ismāʿīlīs for himself and his ancestors. It should be mentioned in passing that in using the name ʿUbayd Allāh instead of ʿAbd Allāh in this book, in accordance with popular usage, we do not intend to be pejorative. There was a second group, still small but comprising the bulk of the Mubārakiyya, who refused to acknowledge the death of Muḥammad b. Ismāʿīl. For these sectarians, identified by the Imāmī heresiographers as the immediate predecessors of the Qarmaṭīs, Muḥammad b. Ismāʿīl was regarded as their seventh and last imām, who was expected to reappear as the Mahdī or Qāʾim, 'riser'. It should be added that the terms al-Mahdī and al-Qāʾim are basically synonymous in their Shīʿī usage, though al-Qāʾim came to be preferred by the Ismāʿīlīs, especially after the accession of ʿUbayd Allāh to the Fāṭimid Caliphate.[66] Such sects of the so-called *Wāqifiyya*, 'those who stand fast' by their last imām, upholding his imminent return as the Mahdī to fill the earth with justice, were quite numerous during the 2nd/8th century. Muḥammad b. Ismāʿīl, who had a considerable following, could easily have qualified for the position of the eschatological Mahdī.

More details of the original beliefs of the Ismāʿīlīs can be derived from what al-Nawbakhtī and al-Qummī relate about the Qarmaṭīs.[67] These writers do not mention any other specific Ismāʿīlī group of their time, and their accounts antedate ʿUbayd Allāh's open claim to the imāmate and the splitting up of the movement in 286/899. According to their accounts, the Qarmaṭīs, who had issued from the Mubārakiyya, limited the number of their imāms to seven, which also explains why the Ismāʿīliyya later acquired the additional denomination of the Sabʿiyya or the Seveners.[68] These imāms were ʿAlī b. Abī Ṭālib, who was both an imām and a messenger-prophet (*rasūl*), al-Ḥasan, al-Ḥusayn, ʿAlī b. al-Ḥusayn, Muḥammad b. ʿAlī, Jaʿfar b. Muḥammad, and finally Muḥammad b. Ismāʿīl b. Jaʿfar, who was the Imām al-Qāʾim al-Mahdī and also a messenger-prophet. It is interesting to note that in order to keep within the limit of seven, and starting with ʿAlī, both authors omit the name of Ismāʿīl b. Jaʿfar from the series of the imāms recognized by the Qarmaṭīs. As a result, Muḥammad b. Ismāʿīl ranks as the seventh imām in the series. At the same time, however, these Imāmī heresiographers contradict themselves by adding that according to the Qarmaṭīs, the imāmate had in effect been transferred during the lifetime of the Imām al-Ṣādiq to his son Ismāʿīl, just as the position of God's emissary and messenger-prophet had passed by divine command at Ghadīr Khumm, from Muḥammad to ʿAlī, while the former was still alive. On the basis of this reckoning, Ismāʿīl would have to be counted as an imām, the seventh one, with the result that his son Muḥammad would now become the eighth imām in the series. The matter is not very clear, however. It seems that some Qarmaṭīs or early Ismāʿīlīs included Ismāʿīl as an imām, while others omitted him. In later Ismāʿīlī literature, ʿAlī acquires a higher rank than that of an ordinary imām, being regarded as the foundation of the imāmate (*asās al-imāma*), and Ismāʿīl is always included in the list of the imāms. According to this enumeration, still maintained by the Mustaʿlians, al-Ḥasan is counted as the first imām, with Ismāʿīl and Muḥammad occupying, respectively, the sixth and seventh positions. The latter system of enumeration was somewhat modified by the Nizārīs who, emphasizing the equality of all imāms, counted ʿAlī as the first and al-Ḥusayn as the second imām. The Nizārīs exclude al-Ḥasan who according to them was a temporary or trustee (*mustawdaʿ*) imām as distinct from the permanent (*mustaqarr*) imāms.

In any event, the Qarmaṭīs and their predecessors maintained that Muḥammad b. Ismāʿīl, who remained alive, was the Qā'im and the last of the great messenger-prophets. On his reappearance, he would bring a new religious law, abrogating the one announced by the Prophet Muḥammad. The Qarmaṭīs recognized a series of seven such law-announcing (*shāriʿ*) prophets, the so-called *ūlu'l-ʿazm* or the prophets 'with resolution', namely, Nūḥ, Ibrāhīm, Mūsā, ʿĪsā, Muḥammad, ʿAlī, and Muḥammad b. Ismāʿīl, the last being the seal of the series. The inclusion of ʿAlī in this sequence cannot easily be understood. As the early Ismāʿīlīs emphasized the distinction between the inward and outward aspects of the religious scriptures and commandments, this inclusion may have been due to the role conceived for ʿAlī as the revealer of the all-important inner (*bāṭin*) meaning of the Sharīʿa delivered by Muḥammad, rather than his having promulgated a religious law of his own, replacing Muḥammad's. The latter role was clearly reserved for the Qā'im Muḥammad b. Ismāʿīl. Indeed, it cannot be doubted that the bulk of the Ismāʿīlīs (Qarmaṭīs) originally preached the Mahdism of Muḥammad b. Ismāʿīl. Aside from the testimony of our Imāmī heresiographers, this is confirmed by the already-mentioned letter of the first Fāṭimid caliph,[69] as well as by the few other extant early Ismāʿīlī sources. The *Kitāb al-rushd*, for instance, centres around the idea of the reappearance of the Mahdī, the seventh *nāṭiq* and the eighth imām whose name is Muḥammad.[70] There is another pre-Fāṭimid Ismāʿīlī text, the *Kitāb al-kashf*, a collection of six short treatises, written separately but attributed to Jaʿfar b. Manṣūr al-Yaman who apparently acted only in the capacity of the compiler and editor of the collection. In this work, too, the expectation of the return of the seventh speaker-prophet (*nāṭiq*) as the Mahdī or Qā'im, often referred to as the *Ṣāḥib al-Zamān*, plays a significant part.[71] In close affinity with the ideas of the early Ismāʿīlīs, the final chapter of the *Umm al-kitāb* also contains brief references to the cycles of the seven prophets, the names here being Ādam, Nūḥ, Ibrāhīm, Mūsā, ʿĪsā, Muḥammad, and the Qā'im who, as the last of the prophets, will on his return initiate the seventh and the final cycle (*dawr*).[72]

After these obscure and underground beginnings, lasting for almost a century, the Ismāʿīlī movement suddenly appeared on the historical stage shortly after the middle of the 3rd/9th century. The movement now emerged as a dynamic, revolutionary organization conducting intensive *daʿwa* activity through a network of *dāʿīs*. Behind this outburst of activity, one can clearly discern the guiding hands of an energetic and secret central leadership. Stern denies the existence of strict historical continuity between this Ismāʿīlī movement and the earlier Ismāʿīlī (or proto-Ismāʿīlī) group or groups of the 2nd/8th century, although he does allow for some such continuity as best manifested in the role assigned to the figure of Muḥammad b. Ismāʿīl in early Ismāʿīlī thought.[73] In any event, the Ismāʿīlīs who were awaiting the reappearance of Muḥammad b. Ismāʿīl as the Qā'im now began to attract the attention of the ʿAbbāsid officials and the public at large, under the name of al-Qarāmiṭa. In fact, al-Nawbakhtī and al-Qummī, who as well-informed contemporary writers, describe the situation of the Ismāʿīlīs prior to the year 286/899, when a schism occurred in the movement, mention no other Ismāʿīlī group besides the Qarmaṭīs. They report that at the time they were writing, there were some 100,000 Qarmaṭīs concentrated chiefly in the Sawād of Kūfa, Yaman and Yamāma;[74] this figure and the designation al-Qarāmiṭa were obviously meant to refer to the whole movement. The Ismāʿīlī *daʿwa* soon met with unprecedented success; it managed, in a few decades, to spread rapidly from southwestern Persia and southern ʿIrāq to several other parts of the Muslim world, including Yaman, Baḥrayn, Syria, the Jibāl, Khurāsān, Transoxiana, Sind, and North Africa, where the Ismāʿīlī Imām was finally installed to a new caliphate.

There are diverse accounts on the beginnings of the Ismāʿīlī *daʿwa* of the 3rd/9th century, and on the exact religious functions and pedigree of the central leaders who were responsible for organizing and directing the movement. There is the brief and vague official version, sponsored by the Fāṭimid caliphs who censured the extremist aspects of the origins of the sect. This version is summed up in the fourth volume of the *ʿUyūn al-akhbār* of the *dāʿī* Idrīs who based himself on the few Ismāʿīlī historical sources produced during the 4th/10th century. There is, on the other hand, the anti-Ismāʿīlī version of the Sunnī pamphleteers and polemists who gave rise to a fanciful 'black legend' regarding early Ismāʿīlism and its alleged founder, a diabolical non-ʿAlid bent on destroying Islam from within. This hostile account can be traced in its main outline to a work written in the refutation of Ismāʿīlism by Abū ʿAbd Allāh Muḥammad b. ʿAlī b. Rizām (or Razzām) al-Ṭā'ī al-Kūfī who flourished in the opening decades of the 4th/10th century.[75] There is, furthermore, al-Ṭabarī's narrative of the opening phase of the Qarmaṭī movement in ʿIrāq.[76] This narrative is based on the report of the interrogation of an Ismāʿīlī captive (a relative of the *dāʿī* Zikrawayh b. Mihrawayh) by an ʿAbbāsid official,

Muḥammad b. Dā'ūd al-Jarrāḥ (d. 296/908); an event which took place around 291/903–904.

According to the official Fāṭimid version, the founder of the Fāṭimid dynasty, ʿUbayd Allāh (ʿAbd Allāh) al-Mahdī, was preceded by a series of 'hidden imāms' (*al-a'imma al-mastūrīn*) who were descendants of Muḥammad b. Ismāʿīl.[77] Al-Nawbakhtī and al-Qummī, it is true, refer to a subgroup of the Mubārakiyya who maintained the imāmate in the progeny of Muḥammad b. Ismāʿīl. However, as the same writers indicate, the majority of the nascent Ismāʿīliyya, known as the Qarāmiṭa by the middle of the 3rd/9th century, did not recognize any imāms after Muḥammad b. Ismāʿīl. As we shall see later on, it seems that the ancestors of the Fāṭimids, the central leaders of the Ismāʿīlī movement, were initially regarded as the lieutenants or representatives of the Qā'im; and it was only due to the reform of ʿUbayd Allāh that the imāmate came to be openly claimed for these past leaders. According to this official version, Muḥammad b. Ismāʿīl appointed as his successor his eldest son ʿAbd Allāh, the first of the second heptad of the Ismāʿīlī Imāms. In order to escape ʿAbbāsid persecution, ʿAbd Allāh, who later received the surname al-Raḍī, sought refuge in different parts of Persia and did not reveal his identity and place of residence except to a few trusted associates. Eventually, he settled in Ahwāz, in the province of Khūzistān, whence he later fled to ʿIrāq and then to Salamiyya in central Syria. In Salamiyya, the residence of the imāms and the headquarters of the Ismāʿīlī *daʿwa* for the next few decades, he posed as an ordinary Hāshimid, of whom there were many in that locality, and as a merchant.[78] Before dying in about 212/827–828,[79] ʿAbd Allāh had designated his son Aḥmad as his successor. Aḥmad, who according to Ismāʿīlī tradition was the author of the famous *Rasā'il Ikhwān al-Ṣafā'*, was, in turn, succeeded by his son al-Ḥusayn, and then by the latter's son ʿAbd Allāh (ʿAlī), also called Saʿīd, who later became known as ʿUbayd Allāh al-Mahdī. ʿUbayd Allāh was born in 259 or 260/873–874, and he was about eight years of age when his father died around 268/881–882.[80] In fact, ʿUbayd Allāh spent many years under the care and tutelage of his paternal uncle and future father-in-law Muḥammad b. Aḥmad, known as Saʿīd al-Khayr and al-Ḥakīm with the additional *kunya* Abu'l-Shalaghlagh (or Shalaʿlaʿ). It is not clear whether or not Muḥammad b. Aḥmad himself had meanwhile succeeded to the leadership of the movement.[81] However, it is reported that before ʿUbayd Allāh took charge of the leadership, his uncle Muḥammad had attempted several times, in vain, to usurp the leadership for his own sons, all of whom died prematurely.[82]

It is necessary to point out at this juncture that the issue of the genealogy of the Fāṭimid caliphs has been the centre of numerous controversies, some of which seem to defy satisfactory solution. The ancestors of the Fāṭimids, according to the later official doctrine, were the Ismāʿīlī Imāms who descended from Muḥammad b. Ismāʿīl. However, the Ismāʿīlī sources are very reluctant to mention the names of these so-called 'hidden imāms', the links between ʿUbayd Allāh (ʿAbd Allāh) and Muḥammad b. Ismāʿīl b. Jaʿfar; individuals who lived under obscure circumstances. Their names are, in fact, not to be found in the earliest Ismāʿīlī sources which have so far come to light. Ivanow has interpreted this silence as reflecting an Ismāʿīlī prejudice against 'uncovering those whom God has veiled'.[83] Consequently, there has developed some disagreement among the Ismāʿīlīs concerning the names, number, sequence and the actual descendance of the 'hidden imāms',[84] notwithstanding the traditional Fāṭimid version, namely, Muḥammad b. Ismāʿīl, ʿAbd Allāh b. Muḥammad, Aḥmad b. ʿAbd Allāh, al-Ḥusayn b. Aḥmad, and ʿUbayd Allāh (ʿAbd Allāh) b. al-Ḥusayn. The difficulties have been accentuated by the fact that the ancestors of the Fāṭimids who led the Ismāʿīlī movement used pseudonyms to protect their identity, while the enemies of the sect produced their own non-ʿAlid pedigrees of the Fāṭimid dynasty.

The Fāṭimid caliphs did not clarify matters by their persistent refusal to publish any official genealogy. ʿUbayd Allāh (ʿAbd Allāh), the only one among them who did make such an attempt, simply added to the confusion. In his letter to the Ismāʿīlī community in Yaman, reproduced from memory at a later date by Jaʿfar b. Manṣūr al-Yaman, ʿUbayd Allāh explains the *nasab* or genealogy of the Fāṭimid caliphs, divulging the names of the 'hidden imāms', in the manner he desired them to be known. He does claim Fāṭimid ancestry by declaring himself to be ʿAlī b. al-Ḥusayn b. Aḥmad b. ʿAbd Allāh b. ʿAbd Allāh b. Jaʿfar al-Ṣādiq. But strangely enough, instead of tracing his descent to Ismāʿīl b. Jaʿfar and his son Muḥammad, he names Jaʿfar's eldest surviving son ʿAbd Allāh as his progenitor, whom he regards as the *Ṣāḥib al-Ḥaqq* or the legitimate successor of the Imām al-Ṣādiq.[85] We shall have more to say on this important letter. Here it suffices to add that, according to ʿUbayd Allāh al-Mahdī, ʿAbd Allāh b. Jaʿfar had called himself Ismāʿīl b. Jaʿfar, for the sake of *taqiyya*; and similarly each of his successors had assumed the name Muḥammad. Be it as it may, ʿUbayd Allāh's explanation of his ancestry, whatever its merits or authenticity, was not eventually accepted as the official genealogy of the Fāṭimid dynasty by ʿUbayd Allāh's successors.

As noted, there is also an anti-Ismāʿīlī version of events and of the Fāṭimid genealogy which can be traced back to Ibn Rizām who, it seems, had access to some early Ismāʿīlī sources. The original polemical treatise of Ibn Rizām has been lost, though excerpts of it have been preserved in some later works. It is quoted directly by Ibn al-Nadīm in his famous catalogue of Arabic books completed in 377/987–988.[86] Above all, it was utilized extensively in another anti-Ismāʿīlī book written in about 370/980 by the Sharīf Abu'l-Ḥusayn Muḥammad b. ʿAlī, known as Akhū Muḥsin, an ʿAlid from Damascus and a descendant of Muḥammad b. Ismāʿīl.[87] Akhū Muḥsin, who died around 375/985–986, was a polemist and one of the early genealogists of the ʿAlid family. His book, which contained historical and doctrinal parts, is also lost. However, substantial portions of it have been preserved by the Egyptian historians al-Nuwayrī (d. 732/1332),[88] Ibn al-Dawādārī, in a chronicle completed in 736/1335,[89] and al-Maqrīzī (d. 845/1442),[90] who was the first authority to have identified Ibn Rizām as the principal source of Akhū Muḥsin while condemning both writers as unreliable. The unreliability of Ibn Rizām had already been pointed out by his contemporary chronicler al-Masʿūdī, who included him in his list of the anti-Qarmaṭī writers.[91] The Ibn Rizām–Akhū Muḥsin account which aimed at discrediting the whole Ismāʿīlī movement, provided the basis for most subsequent Sunnī writings on the subject.[92] It also influenced the famous anti-Fāṭimid manifesto of Baghdād, issued in 402/1011, by a number of ʿAlids and jurists.[93] This declaration, sponsored by the reigning ʿAbbāsid caliph al-Qādir (381–422/991–1031), was a public denunciation of the ʿAlid descent of the Fāṭimid caliphs. In short, this anti-Ismāʿīlī account became the standard treatment of the rise of Ismāʿīlism, and, as such, it came to be adopted also by the majority of the nineteenth-century orientalists; eminent scholars like de Sacy and de Goeje.

The most derogatory and lasting aspect of the Ibn Rizām-Akhū Muḥsin narrative has been the allegation that a certain non-ʿAlid, ʿAbd Allāh b. Maymūn al-Qaddāḥ, was the founder of Ismāʿīlism as well as the progenitor of the Fāṭimid caliphs. According to this allegation, Maymūn al-Qaddāḥ was a follower of Abu'l-Khaṭṭāb and founded a sect called al-Maymūniyya. He was also a Dayṣānī (Bardesanian), an adherent of Ibn Dayṣān (Bar Dīṣān or Bardesanes), the celebrated heresiarch of Edessa and a dualist who founded the Christian Gnostic sect of the Bardesanians or Dayṣāniyya and died at the beginning of the third century A.D.[94] This explains why in some later sources, following Akhū Muḥsin, Maymūn was referred to as the son of Dayṣān, while the Baghdād manifesto names a certain Dayṣān b. Saʿīd as the ancestor of the Fāṭimids. Maymūn's son, ʿAbd Allāh, claimed to be a prophet, and supported his claim by conjuring tricks. He organized a movement and instituted a system of belief, consisting of seven stages that culminated in libertinism and atheism; he pretended to preach on behalf of Muḥammad b. Ismāʿīl as the expected Mahdī. ʿAbd Allāh came originally from the vicinity of Ahwāz, but later moved to ʿAskar Mukram[95] and then to Baṣra, fleeing from the Shīʿīs and the Muʿtazilīs, and accompanied by an associate al-Ḥusayn al-Ahwāzī. In Baṣra, he sought refuge with the family of the Hāshimid ʿAqīl b. Abī Ṭālib. Later, he fled to Salamiyya, where he remained in hiding until his death sometime after 261/874. From Salamiyya, *dāʿīs* were sent to ʿIrāq, one of whom converted a certain Ḥamdān Qarmaṭ. ʿAbd Allāh was succeeded by his son Aḥmad, and then by the latter's descendants who extended the *daʿwa* to many regions, as their *dāʿīs* operated in ʿIrāq, Yaman, Baḥrayn, Rayy, Ṭabaristān, Khurāsān and Fārs. Eventually, one of ʿAbd Allāh's Qaddāḥid successors, Saʿīd b. al-Ḥusayn, went to the Maghrib in North Africa and founded the Fāṭimid dynasty. He claimed to be a descendant of Muḥammad b. Ismāʿīl, and called himself ʿUbayd Allāh al-Mahdī.

This is essentially what Akhū Muḥsin and his source, Ibn Rizām, have to say on Ibn al-Qaddāḥ and the origins of Ismāʿīlism. Akhū Muḥsin also included in his book an outline of the doctrine of the Ismāʿīlīs. He quotes long passages on the procedures observed by the *dāʿīs* for winning new converts and the various degrees of initiation into Ismāʿīlism, from an allegedly Ismāʿīlī book entitled the *Kitāb al-siyāsa*.[96] Ibn al-Nadīm also claims to have seen such works describing the degrees of attainment through which a proselyte was gradually initiated.[97] However, the Ismāʿīlī tradition knows the book in question only through the polemics of the enemies of the sect;[98] and, as quoted by Akhū Muḥsin, it seems to represent a malevolent forgery.[99] Nevertheless, the doctrinal part of Akhū Muḥsin's work still holds some accurate details, though its attribution of libertinism and atheism to the sectarians should be dismissed as totally unfounded. The doctrine of the imāmate which it describes agrees almost completely with that ascribed to the Qarmaṭīs by al-Nawbakhtī and al-Qummī. Akhū Muḥsin lists the same series of seven imāms, starting with ʿAlī b. Abī Ṭālib and ending with Muḥammad b. Ismāʿīl, and states that the seventh imām was the expected Qāʾim. However, by counting ʿAlī as the first imām, he faces the same problem as the Imāmī heresiographers, and like them, mentions that some included while others omitted Ismāʿīl as an imām. Another important piece of information is Akhū Muḥsin's reference to a schism in the movement, resulting from some doctrinal changes. In this connection, he notes, there was a change of opinion about Muḥammad b. Ismāʿīl, for whom they had first demanded recognition as the Imām-Mahdī, but whom they then replaced by a descendant of ʿAbd Allāh b. Maymūn al-Qaddāḥ, whose progeny have ruled in the Maghrib, Egypt and Syria.[100]

The modern progress in Ismāʿīlī studies has, indeed, shown that the Ibn Rizām–Akhū Muḥsin account, despite its hostile intentions and false accusations, sheds valuable light on early Ismāʿīlism. Aside from containing certain valid points of doctrine, it also provides the main source of information on the history of the Ismāʿīlī movement during the second half of the 3rd/9th century. But the section which treats Ibn al-Qaddāḥ as the founder of Ismāʿīlism and the ancestor of ʿUbayd Allāh, the most controversial part of the account, seems to have been motivated by strongly anti-Ismāʿīlī sentiments. Al-Nawbakhtī and al-Qummī, as well as many other important early authorities such as al-Ṭabarī (d. 310/923) and ʿArīb b. Saʿd (d. 370/980), do not mention Ibn al-Qaddāḥ in connection with the Ismāʿīliyya; nor is he named in the anti-Fāṭimid Baghdād manifesto of 402/1011. Massignon, Qazvīnī and Lewis were the first modern scholars to have clarified the biographies of Maymūn al-Qaddāḥ and his son ʿAbd Allāh.[101] It was Ivanow, however, who produced the most detailed study of the true personalities of these individuals, based on a comprehensive survey of various types of Twelver Shīʿī sources.[102] In fact, Ivanow made every effort to refute what he called the myth of Ibn al-Qaddāḥ; a myth which, according to him, was probably invented by Ibn Rizām himself.[103]

Maymūn b. al-Aswad al-Qaddāḥ al-Makkī, a *mawlā* of the Banū Makhzūm and a resident of Mecca, was actually a disciple of the Imām Muḥammad al-Bāqir, from whom he reported a few *ḥadīth*s. Maymūn's son ʿAbd Allāh, who died sometime during the second half of the 2nd/8th century, was a companion of the Imām al-Ṣādiq and a reporter (*rāwī*) of numerous traditions from him. These Qaddāḥids may also have taken care of the properties of the imāms in Mecca. In any event, Maymūn al-Qaddāḥ and ʿAbd Allāh are known in the Twelver literature as respected Shīʿī traditionists from the Ḥijāz,[104] and not as Bardesanians originating in Khūzistān. It is, therefore, important to know why this Ibn al-Qaddāḥ, who lived in the 2nd/8th century, was chosen by Ibn Rizām as the organizer of a movement that occurred in the 3rd/9th century, several decades after his death. Recent access to Ismāʿīlī sources has made it possible to formulate a plausible answer to this question.

As noted, the early leaders of the Ismāʿīlī movement lived under utmost secrecy and kept their identity hidden, in order to escape persecution. In his letter to the Yamanī Ismāʿīlīs, ʿUbayd Allāh (ʿAbd Allāh) explains that the true imāms after Jaʿfar al-Ṣādiq indeed assumed names other than their own; calling themselves Mubārak (the Blessed One), Maymūn (the Fortunate One), and Saʿīd (the Happy One).[105] It has become evident that Mubārak was the epithet of Ismāʿīl b. Jaʿfar; and, according to numerous Ismāʿīlī and non-Ismāʿīlī sources, Saʿīd was ʿUbayd Allāh's pseudonym prior to his advent in North Africa. Now, the myth of ʿAbd Allāh b. Maymūn can be solved if it is shown that Maymūn was the sobriquet of Muḥammad b. Ismāʿīl. This conclusion is strongly implied by ʿUbayd Allāh's letter.[106] It is also suggested by a report,[107] dating back to the 6th/12th century, naming Muḥammad b. Ismāʿīl as the imām of the Maymūniyya, a sect which according to Ibn Rizām was founded by Maymūn al-Qaddāḥ. In all probability, then, the Maymūniyya, like the Mubārakiyya, must have been one of the original designations of the nascent Ismāʿīliyya; in this case named after the epithet of Muḥammad b. Ismāʿīl.

There is, furthermore, the epistle of the fourth Fāṭimid caliph al-Muʿizz, written in 354/965, and sent to the chief *dāʿī* of Sind, Ḥalam (or Jalam) b. Shaybān.[108] This document, which represents perhaps the earliest official refutation of the myth of Ibn al-Qaddāḥ, reasserts the ʿAlid ancestry of the Fāṭimid caliphs. It states that when the *daʿwa* on behalf of Muḥammad b. Ismāʿīl spread, the ʿAbbāsids sought the person who was acknowledged as its leader. Therefore, the imāms went into hiding and the *dāʿīs*, to protect the imāms, called them by pseudonyms (or esoteric names); referring, for instance, to ʿAbd Allāh, the son and successor of Muḥammad b. Ismāʿīl, as the son of Maymūn al-Qaddāḥ. This was true, the epistle affirms, since ʿAbd Allāh was the son of *maymūn al-naqība* (the one with the happy disposition) and *al-qādiḥ zand al-hidāya* (striking the spark of right guidance). Similar names were applied to the imāms succeeding ʿAbd Allāh, according to the instructions of the imāms to their *dāʿīs*. But then, such code-names reached those who did not understand their real meaning, and so they erred and misled others. The substance of this epistle is confirmed by an earlier document, preserved in one of al-Qāḍī al-Nuʿmān's books, reporting a conversation between al-Muʿizz and some envoys sent by a *dāʿī* from a distant land.[109] In this audience, which took place about the year 348/959–960, the Fāṭimid caliph again explains that Maymūn and Qādiḥ had been the pseudonyms of the true imāms from the family of the Prophet. In short, al-Muʿizz emphasizes that in reality ʿAbd Allāh b. Maymūn al-Qaddāḥ had been a code-name for ʿAbd Allāh, the son of Muḥammad b. Ismāʿīl, the 'hidden imām' whom the Fāṭimids regarded as their ancestor. It is, therefore, not surprising that the name of this Fāṭimid ʿAbd Allāh b. Muḥammad, esoterically called ʿAbd Allāh b. Maymūn, should have been confused, deliberately or accidentally, with the Shīʿī traditionist of the earlier times, ʿAbd Allāh b. Maymūn al-Qaddāḥ.

Finally, it is interesting to review the manner in which Ibn al-Qaddāḥ has been treated in Ismāʿīlī tradition.[110] The earliest Ismāʿīlī sources do not mention Maymūn al-Qaddāḥ and his son ʿAbd Allāh. Later, after Ibn Rizām had already produced his account, the official Fāṭimid doctrine consistently denied any connection between these persons and the Ismāʿīlī movement. Nevertheless, in the time of al-Muʿizz, certain Ismāʿīlī circles from amongst his adherents deviated from the official position and held that the leadership of the movement had passed, after Muḥammad b. Ismāʿīl, to ʿAbd Allāh b. Maymūn al-Qaddāḥ and his Qaddāḥid descendants; but that it had later reverted to the progeny of Muḥammad b. Ismāʿīl, who ruled as the Fāṭimid caliphs.[111] As noted, al-Muʿizz had found it necessary to refute the views of these dissident eastern Ismāʿīlīs. The sectarians in question seem to have been influenced by some Qarmaṭī groups who had persisted in not recognizing any imāms after Muḥammad b. Ismāʿīl. Still later, around the beginning of the 5th/11th century, Ḥamīd al-Dīn al-Kirmānī, one of the most learned Ismāʿīlī *dāʿīs*, produced his own refutation of the Qaddāḥid ancestry of the Fāṭimids. He wrote a short treatise rejecting the views of a certain Zaydī Imām, al-Mu'ayyad bi'llāh Aḥmad b. al-Ḥusayn b. Hārūn al-Buṭḥānī al-Hārūnī (333–411/944–1020), who had attacked the claims of the Fāṭimid caliph al-Ḥākim to the imāmate while accepting Ibn al-Qaddāḥ as the progenitor of the Fāṭimids.[112] At about the same time, highly complex and often contradictory ideas concerning Ibn al-Qaddāḥ began to appear in the sacred literature of the Druzes, who split off from the Ismāʿīlīs. According to these ideas,[113] there had been seven 'hidden imāms', not all genuine ʿAlids. ʿAbd Allāh b. Maymūn al-Qaddāḥ, possibly an ʿAlid, was an associate and the *asās* of Muḥammad b. Ismāʿīl, the seventh *nāṭiq*; he was also the progenitor of some of the latter's successors, including ʿUbayd Allāh. But the second Fāṭimid caliph was a genuine descendant of Muḥammad b.

Ismāʿīl. Ibn Rizām had already stated that the second Fāṭimid caliph was not the son of ʿUbayd Allāh.[114] He had, thus, implied that only the 'hidden imāms' and ʿUbayd Allāh were descended from Maymūn al-Qaddāḥ, without clarifying the ancestry of the second Fāṭimid caliph al-Qā'im.

The idea that al-Qā'im was not the son of ʿUbayd Allāh (ʿAbd Allāh) al-Mahdī reappears in the post-Fāṭimid Ismāʿīlī works of some Yamanī *dāʿīs* who assigned a compromise role to al-Qaddāḥ and his son. Al-Khaṭṭāb b. al-Ḥasan al-Hamdānī (d. 533/1138), in his esoteric work the *Ghāyat al-mawālīd*, sought to establish historical precedents supporting his ideas on the need for a substitute or guardian when the rightful imām was under age; the particular minor in point being al-Ṭayyib, the son of the Mustaʿlian Imām al-Āmir. He says that Ismāʿīl b. Jaʿfar entrusted his infant son and heir Muḥammad to the care of Maymūn al-Qaddāḥ, who was his *ḥujja*.[115] Upon attaining maturity, Muḥammad took up his responsibilities and the imāmate continued in his lineage from father to son, until it reached ʿAlī b. al-Ḥusayn b. Aḥmad b. ʿAbd Allāh b. Muḥammad b. Ismāʿīl. It should be noted that al-Khaṭṭāb here introduces ʿAlī b. al-Ḥusayn as the fourth hidden imām after the usual sequence of three, and adds that this imām, before dying on the way to the Maghrib, handed over the charge of the *daʿwa*, as a trust or *wadīʿa*, to his *ḥujja* al-Saʿīd, known as al-Mahdī. Later, al-Mahdī, whose own descent is not specified, returned the trust to its legitimate *mustaqarr* holder, Muḥammad b. ʿAlī al-Qā'im, and the imāmate continued in his progeny. It is not possible to evaluate the historical truth of these important statements which appear for the first time in the literature of the Mustaʿlian Ismāʿīlīs. Suffice it to note that in his obvious zeal to prove that ʿUbayd Allāh (ʿAbd Allāh) was the temporary substitute for, rather than the true imām and the father of, the second Fāṭimid caliph whom he reports to have been the son of ʿAlī b. al-Ḥusayn, al-Khaṭṭāb overlooked the fact that ʿAlī had been one of the names, besides Saʿīd and ʿAbd Allāh, used by ʿUbayd Allāh himself. Al-Khaṭṭāb presents the cases of al-Qaddāḥ and ʿUbayd Allāh as sufficient proof that the *ḥujja* of an under-age imām can take temporary charge of the imāmate. Similarly, al-Khaṭṭāb's younger contemporary and the second Yamanī *dāʿī* Ibrāhīm b. al-Ḥusayn al-Ḥāmidī (d. 557/1162) briefly refers to ʿAbd Allāh b. Maymūn as the tutor of the Imām Muḥammad b. Ismāʿīl, adding that the latter was succeeded by his son ʿAbd Allāh b. Muḥammad.[116] But he regards ʿUbayd Allāh as the father of the second Fāṭimid caliph, whom he names as Muḥammad b. ʿAbd Allāh al-Mahdī. The divergencies between al-Khaṭṭāb's account and the official Fāṭimid version of the sequence of the 'hidden imāms' proved to be particularly confusing some three centuries later, for the learned *dāʿī* Idrīs, who mentions Maymūn al-Qaddāḥ and his son as the guardians and the *ḥujja*s of the successive Imāms Ismāʿīl b. Jaʿfar, Muḥammad, ʿAbd Allāh and Aḥmad.[117] In his exoteric historical work *ʿUyūn al-akhbār*, he adopts the official version, according to which the Imāms al-Ḥusayn b. Aḥmad, ʿUbayd Allāh al-Mahdī and al-Qā'im are of the same lineage. But in his esoteric work *Zahr al-maʿānī*, he attempts to reconcile this version with al-Khaṭṭāb's ideas, which he follows closely; the results are very ambiguous indeed.[118]

The available evidence, both Ismāʿīlī and non-Ismāʿīlī, does not prove that ʿUbayd Allāh (ʿAbd Allāh) al-Mahdī was not the father of al-Qā'im, nor does it lend support to the alleged Qaddāḥid origin of the Fāṭimid dynasty. Amongst the modern authorities, Ivanow laboured indefatigably to show the absence of any connection between the Shīʿī traditionists Maymūn al-Qaddāḥ and his son and the Ismāʿīlī movement. On the other hand, following the earlier suggestion of Qazvīnī, Stern believes that the basis for the story about Maymūn and ʿAbd Allāh is to be sought in the role that some of their descendants played in the Ismāʿīlī movement of the 3rd/9th century.[119] There is also the interpretation of B. Lewis who accepts the historicity of the roles of the non-ʿAlid Maymūn and his son in early Ismāʿīlism.[120] By relying mainly on the allusions of the Druze scriptures and the *Ghāyat al-mawālīd* and by emphasizing the significance of spiritual parentage and the distinction between *mustaqarr* and *mustawdaʿ* imāms in Ismāʿīlism, Lewis is of the opinion that there existed actually two lines of imāms during the period of concealment. According to this interpretation, Maymūn al-Qaddāḥ was the chief *dāʿī* and guardian of Muḥammad b. Ismāʿīl; and ʿAbd Allāh b. Maymūn, who succeeded his father in the role of chief *dāʿī*, received the imāmate in trust and bequeathed it to his own descendants down to ʿUbayd Allāh al-Mahdī. These were the *mustawdaʿ* or trustee imāms who were of Qaddāḥid origin but were spiritually associated to the ʿAlids. There was, however, a second line of 'hidden imāms', the genuine ʿAlid and *mustaqarr* imāms, starting with Muḥammad b. Ismāʿīl and ending with the second Fāṭimid caliph al-Qā'im, with whom the imāmate returned to the Fāṭimids. In other words, while attributing a Qaddāḥid ancestry to ʿUbayd Allāh, al-Qā'im and his successors are thought to have been genuine Fāṭimids. This interesting theory has been adopted, with slight variations, by some other modern authorities,[121] although it, too, presents its own shortcomings.[122] Finally, we should recall again at this juncture the already-mentioned hypothesis of Hamdani and de Blois who argue that the official version of the genealogy of the 'hidden imāms' and the Fāṭimid caliphs was, in fact, constructed by combining two parallel lines of descendants of Jaʿfar al-Ṣādiq, viz., the descendants of ʿAbd Allāh and Ismāʿīl b. Jaʿfar; thus this official genealogy reflected a rearrangement of the genealogy claimed by ʿUbayd Allāh al-Mahdī, who was a descendant of ʿAbd Allāh b. Jaʿfar.

Resuming our discussion of the history of Ismāʿīlism during the second half of the 3rd/9th century, it should be recalled that the main sources of information are still the Ibn Rizām-Akhū Muḥsin account, along with al-Ṭabarī's statements on the Qarmaṭī movement in ʿIrāq. It is certain that after Muḥammad b. Ismāʿīl, ʿAbd Allāh and his descendants organized and led the Ismāʿīlī *daʿwa*, first from Khūzistān and eventually from Salamiyya. Shortly after the middle of the 3rd/9th century, the Ismāʿīlī leadership intensified its activities by sending numerous *dāʿīs* to various regions, especially to southern ʿIrāq and the adjoining areas where earlier forms of revolutionary Shīʿism had been successful. Ibn al-Nadīm quotes Ibn Rizām as saying that the *daʿwa* in ʿIrāq was organized in 261 A.H., soon after the death of the Twelvers' eleventh imām and the occultation of their twelfth imām. It was in that year, or in 264/877–878 according to Akhū Muḥsin,[123] that Ḥamdān Qarmaṭ, the son of al-Ashʿath, was converted to Ismāʿīlism by al-Ḥusayn al-Ahwāzī. This prominent *dāʿī* had been sent to southern ʿIrāq to propagate the doctrines of the sect; he met and converted Ḥamdān, a carrier, in the latter's native locality, the Sawād of Kūfa.[124] Ḥamdān's surname Qarmaṭ (or Qarmaṭūya), which is probably of Aramaic origin, is variously explained as meaning short-legged or red-eyed, amongst other descriptions and etymologies.

Ḥamdān organized the *daʿwa* in the villages around Kūfa and in other parts of southern ʿIrāq, appointing *dāʿīs* for the major districts. Soon, he succeeded in winning many converts who were named Qarmaṭī (plural, Qarāmiṭa) after their first local leader. This term came to be applied also to the sections of the Ismāʿīlī movement not organized by Ḥamdān. At the time, there was one unified *daʿwa* centrally directed from Syria; and Ḥamdān, having his own headquarters at Kalwādhā near Baghdād, accepted the authority of the central leaders with whom he corresponded but whose identity continued to remain a well-kept secret. A major factor contributing to the rapid success of Ḥamdān was the revolt of the Zanj, the rebellious black slaves who for fifteen years (255–270/869–883), terrorized southern ʿIrāq and distracted the attention of the ʿAbbāsid officials at Baghdād. The Qarmaṭīs of ʿIrāq had become quite numerous by 267/880, when Ḥamdān found it opportune to make an offer of alliance to the leader of the Zanj, ʿAlī b. Muḥammad al-Zanjī; the latter, however, being at the height of his own power, declined the offer.[125] The rapid success of the *daʿwa* in ʿIrāq is attested by the fact that references to the Qarmaṭīs began to appear soon after 261/874–875. However, Ḥamdān's activities may have started earlier than that year, which is the earliest date mentioned in our sources, though probably still during the caliphate of al-Muʿtamid (256–279/870–892). This is because al-Faḍl b. Shādhān, the great Imāmī scholar of Nīshāpūr who died in 260/873–874, had already written a refutation of the Qarāmiṭa.[126] The revolutionary, messianic movement of the Ismāʿīlīs (Qarmaṭīs) achieved particular success amongst those Imāmīs who had become increasingly dissatisfied with the quietism and political powerlessness of Imāmī Shīʿism. Furthermore, with the death of their eleventh imām in 260 A.H., who had left no apparent successor, the Imāmīs had been left in disarray. Under such circumstances, the Ismāʿīlī *daʿwa*, then promising the imminent advent of Muḥammad b. Ismāʿīl as the Mahdī and the restorer of religion and justice, had obvious appeals for them. As a result, many dissatisfied Imāmīs in southern ʿIrāq and elsewhere converted to Ismāʿīlism, contributing significantly to the success of the Ismāʿīlī movement during the second half of the 3rd/9th century.

Ḥamdān's chief assistant and one of the most celebrated early Ismāʿīlī *dāʿīs* was his brother-in-law ʿAbdān.[127] ʿAbdān, who enjoyed a high degree of independence, appointed many of the *dāʿīs* in ʿIrāq and probably also in southern Persia and Baḥrayn, such as Zikrawayh b. Mihrawayh and Abū Saʿīd al-Jannābī. A number of different taxes were levied on the Qarmaṭīs of ʿIrāq, including a fifth of the individual's income to be saved for the expected Qā'im. In 277/890–891, Ḥamdān founded a fortified *dār al-hijra*, an abode of emigration and congregation, near Kūfa for the Qarmaṭīs. The Qarmaṭī movement, however, continued to escape the notice of the ʿAbbāsids, who had not re-established effective control over southern ʿIrāq since the Zanj revolt. It was only in 278/891–892, mentioned by al-Ṭabarī as the year in which the Qarmaṭīs of the Sawād intensified their activity, that the Baghdād officials began to realize the danger of the new movement, on the basis of some reports coming from Kūfa.[128] But no immediate action was taken against the Qarmaṭīs, who staged their first protest in 284/897. However, the energetic caliph al-Muʿtaḍid (279–289/892–902) did not permit any Qarmaṭī unrest to succeed in ʿIrāq, and he repressed the three revolts which were attempted during 287–289/900–902. The doctrine preached by Ḥamdān and ʿAbdān must have been that ascribed to the Qarmaṭīs by al-Nawbakhtī and al-Qummī, and confirmed by the Ibn Rizām-Akhū Muḥsin account. There is no indication that at the time the beliefs of the Qarmaṭīs of ʿIrāq differed in any significant respect from those held by the rest of the Qarmaṭīs (Ismāʿīlīs). It is interesting to note that Ḥamdān and ʿAbdān are not mentioned in any of the early Ismāʿīlī sources, which may be attributed to their eventual rift with the central leadership.

The Ismāʿīlī *daʿwa* was started in other regions, besides ʿIrāq, around the 260s/870s. In southern Persia, the mission was apparently under the supervision of the Qarmaṭī leaders of ʿIrāq. Abū Saʿīd al-Ḥasan b. Bahrām al-Jannābī, born at Jannāba on the coast of Fārs and trained by ʿAbdān, was initially active there with much success.[129] And in Fārs proper, ʿAbdān's brother al-Ma'mūn was appointed as a *dāʿī*, and the Ismāʿīlīs of that region were reportedly called al-Ma'mūniyya after him.[130] The *daʿwa* in Yaman, which has remained an important Ismāʿīlī stronghold over the last eleven centuries, was from its inception in close contact with the central leadership of the movement. The recruitment and despatch of two famous *dāʿīs* to this southwestern corner of the Arabian peninsula in 266/879–880, to start the mission there, is fully narrated by al-Qāḍī al-Nuʿmān.[131] These *dāʿīs* were ʿAlī b. al-Faḍl, a Shīʿī from Yaman who had been converted to Ismāʿīlism while on pilgrimage to the tomb of the Imām al-Ḥusayn in Karbalā'; and Abu'l-Qāsim al-Ḥasan b. Faraj (or Faraḥ) b. Ḥawshab al-Kūfī, known as Manṣūr al-Yaman, who came from a prominent Imāmī Shīʿī family. Ibn al-Faḍl and Ibn Ḥawshab who were to collaborate closely for some time, reached Yaman in 268/881, and, as a result of their initial success, preached their cause publicly as early as 270/883. Ibn Ḥawshab launched his activities from ʿAdan Lāʿa near the Jabal Maswar, where he built a *dār al-hijra*. Ibn al-Faḍl first established himself at Janad and, like his companion, founded a place of refuge. From these mountainous strongholds, the Yamanī Ismāʿīlīs penetrated into the surrounding areas, a strategy fully utilized by the later Nizārī Ismāʿīlīs of Persia and Syria. The mission in Yaman won strong tribal support and met with astonishing success. By 293/905–906, when Ibn al-Faḍl occupied Ṣanʿā', almost all of Yaman had been brought under the control of the Ismāʿīlīs. Later, however, the Ismāʿīlīs were obliged to abandon the greater part of their conquests under pressures from the local Zaydī Imāms who had established a state in northern Yaman in 280/893. Yaman also served as an important base for the extension of the *daʿwa* to adjoining areas, such as Yamāma, as well as to remote lands. In 270/883, Ibn Ḥawshab sent his nephew al-Haytham as a *dāʿī* to Sind, from where the *daʿwa* spread to other parts of the Indian subcontinent;[132] and, as we shall see, another *dāʿī* later went from Yaman to the Maghrib, where he prepared the ground for Fāṭimid rule.

In the meantime, the *daʿwa* had appeared in eastern Arabia in 281/894, or perhaps even earlier in 273/886. After his initial career in southern Persia, Abū Saʿīd al-Jannābī was sent by Ḥamdān to Baḥrayn, entrusted with the mission there.[133] This is reported by the majority of the sources, which also add that Abū Saʿīd had been preceded by another *dāʿī*, a certain Abū Zakariyyā' al-Ṭamāmī (or al-Ẓamāmī), who may have been despatched by Ibn Ḥawshab. Abū Saʿīd, who in time disposed of Abū Zakariyyā', married the daughter of al-Ḥasan b. Sanbar, the head of a prominent local family, and rapidly won converts from amongst the bedouins and the Persians residing there. By 286/899, with the important support of the Rabīʿī tribe of the ʿAbd al-Qafs, Abū Saʿīd had brought under submission a large part of Baḥrayn and had also taken Qaṭīf, on the coastal region of eastern Arabia, causing considerable alarm in Baṣra.[134] In 287/900, the Qarmaṭīs of Baḥrayn were in control of the suburbs of Hajar, the ancient capital of Baḥrayn and seat of the ʿAbbāsid governor. The caliph al-Muʿtaḍid sent an army of 2,000 men, joined by a large number of volunteers, against them; but the ʿAbbāsid force was utterly defeated. Around 290/903, Hajar was finally subdued after a long siege. Abū Saʿīd now established his headquarters at al-Aḥsā' (al-Ḥasā), which became the capital of the Qarmaṭī state of Baḥrayn in 314/926 after Abū Saʿīd's second successor had built a fortress in the locality. Later, the Qarāmiṭa of Baḥrayn extended their control to the adjoining regions, including Yamāma and ʿUmān.

Abū Saʿīd had in effect founded a prospering state which lasted for almost two centuries, and was a menace not only to the Sunnī ʿAbbāsids, but also to the Fāṭimids. Although the *daʿwa* propagated by Abū Saʿīd did not openly contain any specific social programme, nevertheless communal and egalitarian principles seem to have played an important role in the organization of the Qarmaṭī state of Baḥrayn, especially in terms of the ownership of property, cultivation of agricultural land, collection of taxes, distribution of public expenditures, and various types of state assistance to the underprivileged. In governing the affairs of the community, too, Abū Saʿīd and his successors conferred in major decisions with a council known as al-ʿIqdāniyya, comprised of some high-ranking officials and the representatives of the influential families. The state concern for the welfare of the Qarmaṭīs of Baḥrayn, and the particular order established there, evoked the admiration of many a keen observer like Ibn Ḥawqal, and later Nāṣir-i Khusraw, who visited al-Aḥsā' in 443/1051 when the local Qarāmiṭa were still called Abū Saʿīdīs after their initial leader.[135]

Ismāʿīlism spread also in many parts of west-central and northwest Persia, the region called al-Jibāl by the Arabs; like Rayy, Qumm, Kāshān and Hamadān. It was shortly after 260 A.H., when the Qarmaṭī leaders of ʿIrāq were at the beginning of their activities, that the central leaders of the movement despatched *dāʿīs* to the Jibāl; and later the *daʿwa* was extended to Khurāsān and Transoxiana. The most detailed account of this phase of the early *daʿwa*, containing the names of the chief *dāʿīs* until the opening decades of the 4th/10th century, is related by Niẓām al-Mulk, the famous Saljūqid *wazīr* who was assassinated by the Persian Nizārīs in 485/1092.[136] The account of Niẓām al-Mulk, who was an outspoken enemy of the Ismāʿīlīs and apparently had access to the earlier works of Ibn Rizām and Akhū Muḥsin, returns in several other sources utilizing the same anti-Ismāʿīlī authorities.[137]

In the area of Rayy, which served as the headquarters of the Ismāʿīlī mission in the Jibāl, the *daʿwa* was started by a certain Khalaf al-Ḥallāj, after whom the Ismāʿīlīs of Rayy became also known as the Khalafiyya. He established himself in the village of Kulayn (Kulīn), in the district of Pashāpūya (the present Fashāfūya to the south of Tehran), and began to preach secretly in the name of the Qā'im Muḥammad b. Ismāʿīl. Khalaf had barely commenced his activity when he was discovered. Subsequently, he was forced to go into hiding in Rayy, where he died. He was succeeded by his son Aḥmad and then, by the latter's chief disciple Ghiyāth, a native of Kulayn. Ghiyāth, who was well versed in *ḥadīth* and Arabic literature and wrote a book of religious terms entitled *Kitāb al-bayān*,[138] held disputations with the local Sunnīs and won disciples in the cities of Qumm and Kāshān. Eventually, one of the Sunnī jurists, al-Zaʿfarānī, incited the people of Rayy against him and the Ismāʿīlīs, forcing Ghiyāth to flee to Khurāsān. In Marw al-Rūdh, he met and converted the *amīr* al-Ḥusayn b. ʿAlī al-Marwazī (or al-Marwarrūdhī). Many of the inhabitants of the surrounding districts of Ṭāliqān, Maymana, Harāt, Gharjistān and Ghūr, under the influence of this powerful *amīr* who later became a *dāʿī* himself, also adopted Ismāʿīlism. Ghiyāth later returned to Rayy and appointed as his deputy a learned man from the district of Pashāpūya, Abū Ḥātim Aḥmad b. Ḥamdān al-Rāzī, the future chief *dāʿī* of

Rayy and one of the most important early Ismāʿīlī authorities.[139] Ghiyāth disappeared under mysterious circumstances and was succeeded by Abū Jaʿfar-i Kabīr, a descendant of Khalaf. The latter became afflicted with melancholy and was ousted by Abū Ḥātim who now became the fifth chief *dāʿī* of Rayy and the leader of the *daʿwa* in the Jibāl.

Abū Ḥātim greatly expanded the *daʿwa* activities upon assuming office during the first decade of the 4th century/912–923, sending numerous *dāʿīs* to Iṣfahān, Ādharbayjān, Ṭabaristān and Gurgān. He also succeeded in converting the *amīr* Aḥmad b. ʿAlī, who governed Rayy during 307–311/919–924. Around 313/925, after the conquest of Rayy by the Sunnī Sāmānids, Abū Ḥātim went to Ṭabaristān, the mountainous region south of the Caspian Sea and a sanctuary for numerous ʿAlids who had fled the ʿAbbāsids. There, he sided with Asfār b. Shirawahy (d. 319/931), a Daylamī *condottiere* who soon became for a short period the master of Ṭabaristān, Rayy, Gurgān, etc. against the local Zaydī Imām al-Ḥasan b. al-Qāsim, known as al-Dāʿī al-Ṣaghīr.[140] In 316/928, Asfār had this imām killed while seizing many other ʿAlids and sending them to the court of the Sāmānid *amīr* Naṣr II, to whom Asfār had declared his allegiance. Abū Ḥātim acquired many converts in Daylam and Gīlān, including Asfār and his lieutenant Mardāwīj b. Ziyār (d. 323/935), who later rebelled against Asfār and founded the Ziyārid dynasty of northern Persia, with his capital at Rayy. According to the *dāʿī* al-Kirmānī, the famous disputation between Abū Ḥātim and the physician-philosopher Abū Bakr Muḥammad b. Zakariyyāʾ al-Rāzī (Latin, Rhazes) took place in Mardāwīj's presence.[141] Mardāwīj at first supported Abū Ḥātim,[142] but soon afterwards he adopted an anti-Ismāʿīlī policy in the region under his control, perhaps because Abū Ḥātim's predicted date for the emergence of the Mahdī had proved wrong. Consequently, Abū Ḥātim, who had meanwhile returned to Rayy, was obliged to flee to Ādharbayjān where he sought refuge with a local ruler called Mufliḥ. After Abū Ḥātim's death in 322/934, the Ismāʿīlīs of the Jibāl were thrown into disorder, and their leadership eventually passed to two persons, namely, ʿAbd al-Malik al-Kawkabī who resided in Girdkūh, the future Nizārī stronghold, and a certain Isḥāq staying in Rayy; the latter may perhaps be one and the same person as the famous *dāʿī* Abū Yaʿqūb Isḥāq b. Aḥmad al-Sijistānī.

The *daʿwa* was officially taken to Khurāsān, around the last decade of the 3rd century/903–913, by Abū ʿAbd Allāh al-Khādim; while Ghiyāth, as noted, had earlier introduced Ismāʿīlism to that province on his own initiative. It was probably also at that time that Aḥmad b. al-Kayyāl, originally a *dāʿī*, seceded from the Ismāʿīlī movement and claimed the imāmate for himself. This enigmatic Shīʿī gnostic, wrongly identified by some authorities as one of the 'hidden imāms' of the Ismāʿīlīs, later gained the favour of the Sāmānid court during the rule of Naṣr II (301–331/914–943), and acquired a significant following in Transoxiana.[143] In any event, al-Khādim established himself in Nīshāpūr as the first chief *dāʿī* of Khurāsān. He was succeeded around the year 307/919, by Abū Saʿīd al-Shaʿrānī, who was despatched by ʿUbayd Allāh al-Mahdī. This *dāʿī* managed to convert several notable military men of the province. The next head of the *daʿwa* in northeastern Persia and the adjoining region was the already-mentioned al-Ḥusayn b. ʿAlī al-Marwazī who had been converted by Ghiyāth. It was during his time that the provincial seat of the *daʿwa* was transferred from Nīshāpūr to Marw al-Rūdh. Al-Ḥusayn al-Marwazī is well-known in the annals of the Sāmānid dynasty.[144] During the rule of Aḥmad b. Ismāʿīl (295–301/907–914), he commanded the Sāmānid forces in Sīstān (Arabic, Sijistān). Later, he rebelled at Harāt against Aḥmad's son and successor Naṣr II, and was defeated in 306/918. After being pardoned and spending some time at the Sāmānid court, he returned to Khurāsān, and subsequently became designated as the chief Ismāʿīlī *dāʿī* there.

On his deathbed, al-Ḥusayn al-Marwazī appointed as his successor Muḥammad b. Aḥmad al-Nasafī (or al-Nakhshabī), a brilliant philosopher who came from the village of Bazda in the vicinity of the Central Asian town of Nakhshab (Arabicized into Nasaf).[145] This *dāʿī*, who is generally credited with introducing a form of Neoplatonism into Ismāʿīlī thought, soon set out for Transoxiana, where he had been advised to go by his predecessor in order to convert the dignitaries of the Sāmānid court at Bukhārā. He left a certain Ibn Sawāda, an Ismāʿīlī refugee from Rayy, as his deputy in Marw al-Rūdh. After a short and fruitless initial stay in Bukhārā, al-Nasafī retreated to his native Nakhshab from where he had more success in penetrating the inner circles of the Sāmānid capital. He converted several confidants of the Sāmānid *amīr*, including his private secretary Abū Ashʿath. Al-Nasafī then moved to Bukhārā, and, with the help of his influential converts at the court, managed to win over the young *amīr* Naṣr II and his *wazīr*. As a result, the Ismāʿīlī *dāʿī* acquired a particular position of influence in the Sāmānid capital and began to preach openly. At the same time, he extended the *daʿwa* to Sīstān through one of his subordinate *dāʿīs*. These developments displeased the Sunnī religious leaders of the state and their military allies, the Turkish guards of the

Sāmānid rulers. They conspired and finally deposed Naṣr II, under whose son and successor, Nūḥ I (331–343/943–954), the Ismāʿīlīs of Khurāsān and Transoxiana were severely persecuted. Al-Nasafī and his chief associates were executed at Bukhārā in 332/943, soon after the accession of the *amīr* Nūḥ I. But the *daʿwa* in Khurāsān outlived this catastrophe and was later resumed under al-Nasafī's son Masʿūd, nicknamed Dihqān, and other *dāʿīs*, notably Abū Yaʿqūb al-Sijistānī who may also have had the mission in Rayy under his control.[146]

It is worthwhile to digress briefly now and consider the social character of early Ismāʿīlism and the composition of its following. The Muslim Near East experienced important economic transformations during the first two centuries of ʿAbbāsid rule. In particular, there was significant expansion of activity in the fields of industry, crafts and trade, and urban centres were growing very rapidly. There were also changes in the organization of the factors of production and in economic relationships prevalent in Muslim society. All these developments brought about or accompanied important social changes which subjected the ʿAbbāsid empire to new strains and grievances. The Arab tribal aristocracy of the Umayyad times was now replaced by a ruling class composed of merchants, landowners, professional military men, administrators, religious leaders and men of learning. The garrison towns had been transformed from simple military encampments in the conquered territories to urban centres and vital market places where all types of exchange took place. The emancipation of the *mawālī* had finally removed the distinction between the Arab and non-Arab Muslims; a distinction that in earlier times had given rise to a vocal malcontented social class, providing a ready recruiting ground for revolutionary Shīʿism.

In this new and more complex socio-economic setting, there appeared new conflicts of interest. In broad terms, the city had now become sharply delineated from the open country, and the interests of the landless peasantry and the bedouin tribesmen had become distinguishable from those of the prospering urban classes, which derived attractive incomes from their properties and activities. The various distressed groups, along with the common people, were naturally attractable to any movement opposed to the established order. Indeed, there were some minor peasant revolts and anti-regime movements in Persia and ʿIrāq; while the appearance of various local dynasties had signalled the early political disintegration of the caliphate. The first serious sign of unrest came with the revolt of the Zanj, the black slaves who were employed on the large estates near Baṣra for the drainage of the salt marshes. But it was revolutionary Shīʿism, and particularly Ismāʿīlism, that held the greatest appeal for the discontented, both amongst the Arabs and non-Arabs. The message of the Ismāʿīlī movement of the 3rd/9th century, which centred on the expectation of the imminent emergence of the Qā'im, who would establish the rule of justice in the world, was most promising to the underprivileged people of diverse backgrounds. Therefore, as soon as the Ismāʿīlī *daʿwa* had become sufficiently organized, it attracted an ever-increasing number of adherents through the efforts of its able propagandists. In sum, as some Sunnī authorities later observed,[147] the Ismāʿīlī movement from the very beginning paid particular attention to social grievances and inequities, and, as such, it acquired the character of a movement of social protest, posing a serious threat to the developing ʿAbbāsid order.

The Ismāʿīlī *dāʿīs*, as noted, were sent to many regions, and they appealed to different social strata. Their initial success, though, was greatest in the less urbanized milieus that were removed from the vital administrative centres of the caliphate; and, socially speaking, the early Ismāʿīlī movement took the form of protest against the oppressive rule of the ʿAbbāsids, the privileged urban classes and the centralized administration.[148] It cannot be denied that the early Ismāʿīlīs (Qarmaṭīs) also had some partisans in the towns, especially among the upper strata; but, as in the case of the Zanj, the urban proletariat and artisans did not join them, probably because they did not see their interests championed by the Ismāʿīlī *dāʿīs*. In short, early Ismāʿīlism seems to have mainly addressed itself to, and relied upon the support of, the peasants and the bedouins, with the result that one does not find real urban penetration of the movement until later times. There is, however, a hypothesis expounded chiefly by Massignon suggesting that the Ismāʿīlīs were responsible for the creation of the professional corporations or the so-called Islamic guilds (singular, *ṣinf*), in Muslim cities during early mediaeval times, in order to mobilize the support of the urban working classes and the artisan groups against the regime.[149] Recent research does not substantiate the alleged Ismāʿīlī origin of the guilds in the Near East. It has, furthermore, become evident that the Islamic guilds, which were different from their European counterparts, did not exist in the strict sense of the term prior to the later Middle Ages, while during the earlier centuries any such loose associations that may have existed were instruments of state control.[150]

It should be added that the social composition of the Ismāʿīlī following also varied from region to region, despite the fact that early Ismāʿīlism was primarily concentrated in non-urban milieus. In ʿIrāq, the *daʿwa* appealed mainly to the rural inhabitants of the Sawād of Kūfa and, to some extent, to the nearby bedouin tribesmen. It was in this semi-sedentary, semi-bedouin milieu that Ismāʿīlism established a simple socio-economic system and witnessed its initial success. In Baḥrayn and Syria, the bedouin tribes provided the backbone of the movement. In Yaman, Ismāʿīlism was supported by the tribesmen of the mountainous regions; later in North Africa, the mission was based on the Kutāma Berbers. In Persia, the *daʿwa* originally aimed at converting the rural population, and the first *dāʿīs* in the Jibāl concentrated on the villagers around Rayy. But after the early realization of the movement's failure to acquire a large popular following that could be led in open revolt against the authorities, as had been the case in the Arab lands, a new policy was adopted for the mission in Persia. According to this policy, implemented especially in Khurāsān and Transoxiana, the *dāʿīs* directed their efforts towards the ruling classes. It was in line with this that the *amīr* al-Ḥusayn al-Marwazī, himself belonging to aristocracy, was selected to head the *daʿwa* in northeastern Persia. However, in spite of winning over many dignitaries, the new policy did not lead to any lasting political success and the movement failed to gain any of the eastern provinces through the conversion of their rulers. The only eastern region where the early *daʿwa* eventually succeeded in establishing itself for a few decades was Sind. There, the Ismāʿīlīs, recognizing Fāṭimid suzerainty, won over the local ruler and made the city of Multān their capital, but their rule was soon brought to an end in 401/1010–1011, when Maḥmūd of Ghazna invaded Multān and massacred many Ismāʿīlīs.[151]

Meanwhile, a major schism had occurred in the Ismāʿīlī movement. This is reported in detail by Akhū Muḥsin,[152] who had probably derived his information from Ibn Rizām. The main points of this anti-Ismāʿīlī account are corroborated by Ibn Ḥawqal,[153] the famous geographer and traveller of the second half of the 4th/10th century who had strong sympathies with the Fāṭimids, if indeed he was not an Ismāʿīlī himself. Ḥamdān Qarmaṭ, as noted, maintained correspondence with the Ismāʿīlī headquarters. In 286/899, not long after ʿUbayd Allāh (ʿAbd Allāh) had succeeded to the central leadership, Ḥamdān noticed a change of tone in the written instructions sent to him from Salamiyya, suggesting certain doctrinal changes. Consequently, he despatched ʿAbdān to the central headquarters in order to investigate the reason behind the new instructions. It was only at Salamiyya that ʿAbdān learned that ʿUbayd Allāh had succeeded to the leadership, following the death of the previous chief of the sect. Upon returning from his fact-finding mission, which included an interview with ʿUbayd Allāh, ʿAbdān reported that instead of recognizing the Mahdīship of the hidden Muḥammad b. Ismāʿīl, on whose behalf the *daʿwa* had been so far conducted, the new leader now claimed the imāmate for himself.

Having thus become convinced of ʿUbayd Allāh's drastic deviations from the original doctrine of the sect, the Qarmaṭī leaders of ʿIrāq, who may already have drifted away slightly from the Ismāʿīlī headquarters, renounced their allegiance to the central leadership. Thereupon, Ḥamdān assembled his *dāʿīs*, and, after informing them of his discovery, ordered them to suspend the *daʿwa* in their respective districts. Soon afterwards, Ḥamdān went to Kalwādhā from where he disappeared and was never heard of again;[154] ʿAbdān was murdered at the instigation of Zikrawayh b. Mihrawayh, a *dāʿī* of western ʿIrāq. All this happened in the year 286 A.H. It may be added that Zikrawayh had conspired against the local Qarmaṭī leaders in collaboration with some of his subordinates, who had remained loyal to the headquarters, and one of ʿUbayd Allāh's relatives, perhaps on orders from Salamiyya. These reprisals, however, did not prevent the numerous followers of Ḥamdān and ʿAbdān from threatening to take their own revenge on Zikrawayh, now appointed the chief *dāʿī* in ʿIrāq. As a result, Zikrawayh was forced into hiding for some time; and, as we shall see, he soon revealed his own disloyalty towards the central leadership.

The reform introduced by ʿUbayd Allāh, which brought about the apostasy of Ḥamdān and ʿAbdān, concerned the imāmate. As noted, according to the Ibn Rizām-Akhū Muḥsin account, confirmed by al-Nawbakhtī and al-Qummī, the early Ismāʿīlīs, or at least by their overwhelming majority, originally recognized only seven imāms, the last one being Muḥammad b. Ismāʿīl, the expected Qā'im and the seventh *nāṭiq*. This is also attested by the few extant pre-Fāṭimid Ismāʿīlī sources. But in 286/899, ʿUbayd Allāh had felt secure enough to make a public claim to the imāmate for himself and his ancestors who had actually led the movement after Muḥammad b. Ismāʿīl. In order to fully understand this important reform, it is necessary to investigate the nature of the authority assumed by these central leaders up to that time; especially since the original Ismāʿīlī belief in the Mahdīship of Muḥammad b. Ismāʿīl had left no place for any further imāms. On the basis of certain allusions found in the early Ismāʿīlī sources, it seems that the central leaders of the sect, before ʿUbayd Allāh's reform, assumed the rank of the *ḥujja* for themselves.[155] It was through the *ḥujja* that one could establish contact with the exalted *ʿayn*, namely the imām; and the imām referred to the hidden Mahdī. In other words, the leaders of the movement at first apparently acted as the *ḥujja*s of the hidden Muḥammad b. Ismāʿīl and summoned people to obey him. By his reform, ʿUbayd Allāh had in effect openly elevated himself and his predecessors from the *ḥujja*s of the expected Qā'im to actual imāms. This, of course, also implied the denial of the Mahdīship of Muḥammad b. Ismāʿīl.

The term *ḥujja*, which appears in the Qur'ān, means proof or testimony; it also means argument. Amongst the Shīʿīs, the term has been used in different senses. Initially, it meant the 'proof' of God's presence or will, and as such, referred to that person who at any given time served as evidence for mankind, of God's will. It was in this sense that the application of the term was systematized by the Twelver Shīʿīs to designate the category of prophets and imāms and, after the Prophet Muḥammad, more particularly of the imāms without whom the world could never exist. The Imāmiyya had indeed come to use *al-ḥujja* as the equivalent of *al-imām*, as best reflected in the adoption of the term for the heading of the section on the imāmate in al-Kulaynī's *al-Kāfī*.

The original Shīʿī application of the term *ḥujja*, going back to the time of the Imām al-Ṣādiq, was retained by the pre-Fāṭimid Ismāʿīlīs who held that in every era (*ʿaṣr*) there is a *ḥujja* of God, whether he be a prophet (*nabī*), a messenger-prophet (*rasūl*), or an imām.[156] They also used *ḥujja* in reference to a dignitary in their religious hierarchy (*ḥudūd al-dīn*), notably one through whom the inaccessible hidden Mahdī could become accessible to his adherents.[157] As a rank in the early *daʿwa* organization, the *ḥujja* came directly after the imām and had a special significance during the *dawr al-satr*. If the world could at no time exist without a 'proof' of God, it would follow that during the time of the imām's concealment his representative would have to manifest God's true will. In other words, during his concealment, the Qā'im Muḥammad b. Ismāʿīl would have to be represented by his *ḥujja*. It is in line with this usage that al-Shahrastānī attributes to the Ismāʿīlīs the tenet holding that when the imām is visible, his *ḥujja* may be hidden, and when the imām is concealed, his *ḥujja* and *dāʿī*s must be visible.[158] The early Ismāʿīlīs used the term *ḥujja* in a third sense, namely as the designated successor of the *nāṭiq* (or the imām), whilst they were both alive. This is why they referred to ʿAlī b. Abī Ṭālib as Muḥammad's *ḥujja*.[159] In this sense, the imām is at first a *ḥujja* prior to becoming the imām, and the *ḥujja* becomes an imām after his imām.[160] It is interesting to note that the *Kitāb al-kashf* allows for several *ḥujjas* by specifying that only the 'greatest *ḥujja*' (*al-ḥujja al-kubrā*) succeeds to the imāmate after the imām of his time.[161] Our Imāmī heresiographers, too, mention twelve *ḥujjas*, one for each of the twelve regions (*jazā'ir*) into which the *daʿwa* territory was, in theory, divided.[162] But this usage of the term in connection with the *daʿwa* hierarchy attained its full development under the Fāṭimids. During the earlier period, it seems that in the absence of the imām, the *ḥujja* was his full representative in the Ismāʿīlī community. This also explains why ʿUbayd Allāh's open claim to the imāmate did not meet with more resistance on the part of the sectarians. After all, the bulk of the early Ismāʿīlīs (Qarmaṭīs) had already acknowledged ʿUbayd Allāh as the *ḥujja* of the expected Qā'im and as such, he was entitled to the highest religious authority.

Other aspects of ʿUbayd Allāh's doctrinal reform are revealed in his letter to the Ismāʿīlīs of Yaman. In this document, the Ismāʿīlī leader claims descent from ʿAbd Allāh b. Jaʿfar, and explains how the 'misunderstanding' concerning the Mahdīship of Muḥammad b. Ismāʿīl had come about. According to him, the name Muḥammad b. Ismāʿīl referred to all the true imāms in the progeny of ʿAbd Allāh who had assumed the name Ismāʿīl and whose successors had assumed the name Muḥammad. Consequently, the Mahdīship of Muḥammad b. Ismāʿīl, instead of referring to a certain grandson of the Imām al-Ṣādiq, now acquired a collective meaning and referred to every imām after ʿAbd Allāh b. Jaʿfar, until the advent of the Mahdī, the *Ṣāḥib al-Zamān*.[163] In other words, ʿUbayd Allāh denied both the imāmate and the Mahdīship of the particular ʿAlid who had hitherto been regarded as the expected Qā'im by the Ismāʿīlīs (Qarmaṭīs); because, according to his explanation, all the legitimate imāms after ʿAbd Allāh b. Jaʿfar had adopted the name Muḥammad b. Ismāʿīl as a code-name in addition to other pseudonyms whilst assuming the rank of *ḥujja*, for the sake of *taqiyya*. In support of his new doctrine, ʿUbayd Allāh attributed a tradition to the Imām al-Ṣādiq, affirming that the family of the Prophet was to produce more than one Mahdī.[164] These are basically the same points gathered by ʿAbdān in Salamiyya, as described with certain variations by Akhū Muḥsin.

ʿUbayd Allāh's ideas on Mahdīship required modifications of the function of the Mahdī, if the new doctrine was to be adapted to actual realities; especially because the 'order' traditionally expected upon the advent of the Mahdī had not yet materialized. Consequently, the task of the Mahdī was now redefined to essentially encompass the defence of the

Sharīʿa by means of the sword, rather than abrogating the sacred law of Islam and establishing the rule of justice throughout the world.[165] The new ideas concerning the Mahdī and his function were later corroborated by al-Qāḍī al-Nuʿmān, who entered into the service of the first Fāṭimid caliph in 313/925, in his collection of traditions called the *Sharḥ al-akhbār*.[166] Finally, it may be added that by adopting the title of al-Mahdī on becoming the first Fāṭimid caliph, ʿUbayd Allah (ʿAbd Allāh) may have initially aspired to the 'modified' position of the awaited Mahdī. Soon, however, he designated his young son Muḥammad as his successor, and for the role of *al-Imām al-Muntaẓar* and the *Ṣāḥib al-Zamān*,[167] giving him the title al-Qā'im. The significance of this nomination becomes more apparent if it is recalled that ʿUbayd Allāh's son in fact bore the name of the Prophet, Abu'l-Qāsim Muḥammad b. ʿAbd Allāh, the name required by the old Shīʿī traditions and prophecies for the would-be Mahdī from amongst the Ahl al-Bayt. The eschatological importance of this designation is clearly alluded to in some poems composed by the Qāḍī al-Nuʿmān, in which the qualities and deeds of the Mahdī are attributed to the then reigning second Fāṭimid caliph.[168] These, then, were the changes introduced by ʿUbayd Allāh into the doctrine of the imāmate upheld hitherto by the majority of the early Ismāʿīlīs. It should, however, be added that a section of the community had from the beginning traced the imāmate in the progeny of Muḥammad b. Ismāʿīl; and, thus, for this group ʿUbayd Allāh's open claims to the imāmate for himself and his ancestors did not represent doctrinal changes.

The doctrinal reform of ʿUbayd Allāh and the consequent revolt of Ḥamdān and ʿAbdān split the Ismāʿīlī movement into two factions in 286 A.H. On the one side, there were those who accepted the reform, later incorporated into the official Fāṭimid doctrine of the imāmate according to which there was a visible imām at the head of the Ismāʿīlī community. These Ismāʿīlīs maintained continuity in the imāmate and accepted ʿUbayd Allāh's explanation that the Ismāʿīlī Imāmate had been handed down amongst the direct descendants of Jaʿfar al-Ṣādiq. In contrast, the dissident Ismāʿīlīs who lacked united leadership, refusing to recognize ʿUbayd Allāh's claim to the imāmate, retained their original doctrine and expected the return of the hidden Qā'im, Muḥammad b. Ismāʿīl. And in time, some of the leaders of the dissident communities claimed the Mahdīship for themselves or others. Needless to recall that in such instances, in line with the earlier ideas, the Mahdī as the seventh *nāṭiq* was expected to abrogate the Sharīʿa, ending the era of Islam and initiating the final era of the world and the *qiyāma*. Henceforth, the term Qarāmiṭa came to be generally applied to those sectarians who did not acknowledge the Fāṭimid caliphs as imāms, although it was sometimes used in a derogatory sense also in reference to those Ismāʿīlīs supporting the imāmate of the Fāṭimids.

The available evidence on the reaction of the various Ismāʿīlī groups to the schism in the movement can be summed up as follows. The Qarmaṭīs of ʿIrāq were left in a state of confusion and doctrinal crisis following the demise of Ḥamdān and ʿAbdān. Soon, however, ʿĪsā b. Mūsā, a nephew of ʿAbdān, rose to a leading position among them and continued the *daʿwa* in the name of Muḥammad b. Ismāʿīl. These sectarians survived in southern ʿIrāq, with some support in Baghdād, through the first quarter of the 4th/10th century and on into later times.[169] ʿĪsā and other Qarmaṭī *dāʿīs* of ʿIrāq, like the brothers Abū Muslim and Abū Bakr b. Ḥammād in Mawṣil, apparently ascribed their own writings to ʿAbdān, who had continued to be recognized as their authoritative teacher. In doing so, they were perhaps motivated by a desire to stress their doctrinal continuity, besides wanting to attribute a high degree of learning to their fallen teacher. Some of the works attributed to ʿAbdān apparently came to be esteemed also by the Fāṭimid Ismāʿīlīs; and even such a loyal supporter of the Fāṭimids as the Qāḍī al-Nuʿmān did not find it objectionable to quote him.[170]

In the case of Baḥrayn, Ibn Ḥawqal has preserved a very valuable piece of information revealing that Abū Saʿīd al-Jannābī sided with Ḥamdān and ʿAbdān against the central leadership,[171] killing the *dāʿī* Abū Zakariyyāʾ who had remained loyal to ʿUbayd Allāh (ʿAbd Allāh). Abū Saʿīd then claimed to represent the awaited Mahdī. For Abū Saʿīd, who established his rule over Baḥrayn in the same eventful year 286 A.H., the schism may actually have provided a favourable opportunity to make himself completely independent. He had, indeed, succeeded in founding an independent state when he was murdered by a slave in 301/913–914. He was followed by his sons Abu'l-Qāsim Saʿīd (301–311/913–923) and Abū Ṭāhir Sulaymān (d. 332/943–944). Under the latter, the Qarmaṭīs of Baḥrayn, reflecting a view then prevalent amongst the Qarmaṭī *dāʿīs*, were at the time predicting the advent of the Mahdī on the basis of certain astrological calculations for the year 316/928; an event which would end the era of Islam and usher in the seventh, final era of history. In 319/931, they accepted a young Persian as the Mahdī, to whom Abū Ṭāhir turned over the rule. The early and disastrous end of this affair, however, weakened the doctrinal vigour of the Qarmaṭīs of Baḥrayn and their influence over the dissident Ismāʿīlīs of ʿIrāq and Persia. We shall have more to say on the Qarmaṭīs of Baḥrayn; here it suffices to note that their state survived until 470/1077–1078, after they had brought about a political rapprochement with the Fāṭimids.

In western Persia and the Jibāl, too, some Ismāʿīlīs joined the dissident faction. Circumstantial evidence indicates that the Ismāʿīlī community in the area of Rayy repudiated the claims of ʿUbayd Allāh (ʿAbd Allāh) and continued to expect the reappearance of Muḥammad b. Ismāʿīl. It seems that the *dāʿīs* there had close contacts with the Qarmaṭī leaders of ʿIrāq and Baḥrayn, and sided with the dissenters after the schism. Abū Ḥātim al-Rāzī, for instance, corresponded with Abū Ṭāhir and may even have claimed to be the lieutenant of the hidden imām. Later, the *dāʿīs* of Rayy converted some members of the Musāfirid dynasty of Daylam and Ādharbayjān, notably Marzubān b. Muḥammad (330–346/941–957) and his brother Wahsūdān (330–355/941–966).[172] It is interesting to note that in line with the views of the dissident Ismāʿīlīs, these Musāfirid rulers acknowledged the Mahdīship of Muḥammad b. Ismāʿīl, rather than the imāmate of the Fāṭimid caliphs. This is clearly attested to by the inscriptions on the coins of Wahsūdān b. Muḥammad, minted in 343/954–955.[173] In Khurāsān, the Ismāʿīlīs generally maintained their allegiance to ʿUbayd Allāh, who had appointed some of the earliest *dāʿīs* of that region. The dissident view, however, was also present there. It will be recalled that it had been Ghiyāth, the chief *dāʿī* of Rayy upholding the Mahdīship of Muḥammad b. Ismāʿīl, who had introduced Ismāʿīlism to Khurāsān. Moreover, Ghiyāth had also converted al-Ḥusayn al-Marwazī, who later spread Ismāʿīlism in the districts under his influence. It is likely, therefore, that both wings of Ismāʿīlism – Fāṭimid and dissident Qarmaṭī – were strongly represented in northeastern Persia and Transoxiana. On balance, however, the influence of the Fāṭimids in the eastern communities remained stifled until around the middle of the 4th/10th century, when the caliph al-Muʿizz was able to launch with some success an intensive campaign to regain the allegiance of the schismatic eastern Ismāʿīlīs.

The Ismāʿīlī community in Yaman at first remained completely loyal to ʿUbayd Allāh, supporting his imāmate. By 291 A.H., however, Ibn al-Faḍl seems to have manifested signs of disloyalty towards ʿUbayd Allāh al-Mahdī. In Muḥarram 299/August 911, after reoccupying Ṣanʿāʾ, Ibn al-Faḍl publicly renounced his allegiance to ʿUbayd Allāh, abolished the Sharīʿa, and himself claimed to be the Mahdī. Subsequently, he endeavoured unsuccessfully to coerce the collaboration of Ibn Ḥawshab (d. 302/914), the senior *dāʿī* who had remained loyal. After Ibn al-Faḍl's death in 303/915, his movement disintegrated rapidly. Asʿad b. Abī Yaʿfur of the local Yaʿfurid dynasty, who had acted as Ibn al-Faḍl's deputy in Ṣanʿāʾ and had recognized the latter's suzerainty over a part of Yaman, now revolted against the deceased *dāʿī*'s son and successor al-Fa'fā' (or al-Ghāfā'). In 304/917, he captured Mudhaykhira, the former residence of Ibn al-Faḍl and the seat of his movement, killing al-Fa'fā' and many of the dissenting Qarmaṭīs and ending their movement in Yaman. Finally, the *dāʿīs* in the Maghrib, having had close ties with Ibn Ḥawshab, also chose the loyalist camp and made it possible for ʿUbayd Allāh (ʿAbd Allāh) to select their territory for the seat of the Fāṭimid Caliphate.

Zikrawayh b. Mihrawayh, who had gone into hiding after the events of the year 286 A.H., soon showed his own rebellious intentions by organizing the Qarmaṭī revolts of ʿIrāq and Syria during 289–294/902–907.[174] He could not launch his scheme effectively during the reign of the caliph al-Muʿtaḍid, who severely repressed all the Qarmaṭī revolts taking place in ʿIrāq. But on the accession of the next caliph, al-Muktafī (289–295/902–908), Zikrawayh intensified his activities by appealing to the Kalb bedouin tribesmen who lived in the Samāwa desert and transported goods along the trade route between Kūfa and Damascus. In 289/902, he sent one of his sons, al-Ḥusayn (or al-Ḥasan), to the Syrian desert in order to convert the Banū Kalb. Rapid success was gained in winning the support of the Banu'l-ʿUlayṣ and some of the Banu'l-Aṣbagh, clans of the Kalb, who adopted the name al-Fāṭimiyyūn, later utilized by ʿUbayd Allāh. Al-Ḥusayn, who had become known as the *Ṣāḥib al-Shāma* as well as the *Ṣāḥib al-Khāl*, was soon joined by his brother Yaḥya (called the *Ṣāḥib al-Nāqa* and also *Shaykh*). Yaḥyā assumed the leadership of the newly converted bedouins and claimed to be a descendant of Muḥammad b. Ismāʿīl. Yaḥyā's success in Syria was, however, short-lived; he was killed in 290/903 during a lengthy siege of Damascus, then held by the Ṭūlūnids (254–292/868–905), the first local dynasty of Egypt and Syria to acquire autonomy from the ʿAbbāsids. Subsequently, the *Ṣāḥib al-Shāma* succeeded to the leadership. He, too, claimed descent from Muḥammad b. Ismāʿīl, while assuming the titles *Amīr al-Muʾminīn* and al-Mahdī; he made his authority felt in Syria by occupying several towns. Being aware of the hostile intentions of Zikrawayh and his sons, ʿUbayd Allāh had already left Salamiyya before the Qarmaṭīs entered it in 290/903. The *Ṣāḥib al-Shāma* ordered a general massacre of the inhabitants of Salamiyya, also approving the destruction of ʿUbayd Allāh's residence and the killing of the members of his family and household who had been left behind. In

291/903, a severe defeat was inflicted on the Qarmaṭīs near Salamiyya, by an ʿAbbāsid army. The *Ṣāḥib al-Shāma* was captured and taken before the caliph al-Muktafī, who had him executed.

Subsequently, Abu'l-Faḍl, another of Zikrawayh's sons, endeavoured in vain to revive the Qarmaṭī movement in Syria. However, Zikrawayh continued to maintain his aspirations, and in 293/906, he sent a *dāʿī*, Abū Ghānim Naṣr, to lead his Kalb followers. They attacked several towns, including Damascus, pillaging everywhere. In the same year, the ʿAbbāsid armies effectively took the field against these Qarmaṭīs, and as a result, the opportunistic Kalb betrayed and killed Abū Ghānim in order to gain amnesty from the caliph. Zikrawayh now sent another *dāʿī*, al-Qāsim b. Aḥmad, to his Syrian supporters, informing them of his imminent personal appearance. They were apparently also told to migrate secretly to southern ʿIrāq. Soon afterwards, the Syrian tribesmen, joined by Zikrawayh's followers in the area of the Sawād, made a surprise attack on Kūfa but were driven out quickly. Thereupon, the Qarmaṭīs withdrew to the vicinity of Qādisiyya, where they were met in Dhu'l-Ḥijja 293/October 906 by Zikrawayh, who had finally come forth from his hiding place. The Qarmaṭīs repelled an ʿAbbāsid army sent after them and then began to pillage the caravans of the Persian pilgrims returning from Mecca, massacring a large number of them. Zikrawayh and his supporters continued their activities until 294/907, when they were defeated in battle by an ʿAbbāsid force. Zikrawayh was wounded, and died in captivity a few days later; many of his followers were killed at the same time, bringing about an end to the Syro-Mesopotamian Qarmaṭī revolts. Several major factors contributed to Zikrawayh's inability to establish a Qarmaṭī state in ʿIrāq and Syria, like the one founded in Baḥrayn. Not only did he simultaneously engage in hostilities towards the Sunnīs as well as all other Ismāʿīlī Shīʿī groups, he also limited his base of support to the unreliable bedouins from amongst the Banū Kalb, who were more interested in booties than in any ideological issues. In fact, Zikrawayh's followers aroused the enmity of both the townspeople and the peasantry. Furthermore, the area of their activity was too close to the central administration of the caliphate, as in the case of all the defeated Shīʿī revolts of the Umayyad times. On the other hand, the unrest created by the Qarmaṭīs, and the failure of the Ṭūlūnids to control the situation, made it possible for the ʿAbbāsids to re-establish their rule over Egypt and Syria.

Some of the surviving supporters of Zikrawayh in the Sawād of Kūfa denied his death and awaited his return. In 295/907–908, a certain Abū

Ḥātim al-Zuṭṭī was active as a *dāʿī* among these Qarmaṭīs.[175] He prohibited the consumption of certain vegetables and the slaughtering of animals, whence his followers were called the Baqliyya, a name subsequently applied to all the Qarmaṭīs of southern ʿIrāq, who for the most part had retained their belief in the Mahdīship of Muḥammad b. Ismāʿīl. It seems that the Baqliyya, also called the Būrāniyya, were soon joined by the former adherents of Ḥamdān and ʿAbdān. This Qarmaṭī coalition survived for some time in southern ʿIrāq, under leaders like ʿĪsā b. Mūsā and Masʿūd b. Ḥurayth. In 312/925, we hear of these sectarians rallying to the side of a man who pretended to be the expected Mahdī; they were defeated and dispersed by the ʿAbbāsids. Later in 316/928, the Qarāmiṭa (Baqliyya) revolted again in the Sawād, at which time ʿĪsā b. Mūsā was captured by the ʿAbbāsids; but in 320/932, he escaped from prison and resumed his missionary activity. Finally, a section of the Baqliyya, comprised mainly of Persians, joined the forces of Abū Ṭāhir al-Jannābī and went to Baḥrayn, where they became known as the Ajamiyyūn.

In the meantime, ʿUbayd Allāh had fled from Salamiyya in 289/902, shortly before the Qarmaṭī invasion of that town. He had embarked on the fateful journey that was to take him to North Africa, where he was to establish the Fāṭimid dynasty.[176] Prior knowledge of the malevolent designs of Zikrawayh and his sons, and of the intentions of a new ʿAbbāsid governor to arrest the Ismāʿīlī leader, have been mentioned as the main reasons for ʿUbayd Allāh's hurried flight from Syria. Accompanied by his young son Abu'l-Qāsim Muḥammad, the chief *dāʿī* Fīrūz, his chamberlain Jaʿfar, and a few other trusted associates, ʿUbayd Allāh went to Ramla in Palestine, where he stayed for some time. It was there that he received the news of the atrocities committed by the Qarmaṭīs against the inhabitants of Salamiyya and his relatives. Subsequently, he continued his journey and arrived in Egypt, probably in 291/903–904. There, he was met by the *dāʿī* Abū ʿAlī who had been preaching Ismāʿīlism on his instructions for some time. In Egypt, Fīrūz soon deserted the imām and fled to Yaman, where he instigated a revolt against ʿUbayd Allāh. This revolt, which received the support of Ibn al-Faḍl, was opposed by the loyal Ibn Ḥawshab. ʿUbayd Allāh could not stay long in Egypt, as the ʿAbbāsids had resumed their chase. The Ismāʿīlī leader now decided to proceed to the Maghrib, where his *dāʿī* Abū ʿAbd Allāh had already achieved considerable success amongst the Kutāma Berbers, instead of going to Yaman as expected by his entourage all along. This turned out to be a very wise decision, since in Yaman he would have risked ʿAbbāsid confrontation and the menace of the rebellious Qarmaṭīs. He set off on his westward journey and first went to Tripoli. But unable to join Abū ʿAbd Allāh at once in the Kutāma country, he proceeded to Sijilmāsa in eastern Morocco, the capital of the small Midrārid state of Tāfilālt in the extreme Maghrib, then ruled by the Khārijī Alīsaʿ b. Midrār. By 292/905, he was settled in Sijilmāsa, from where he sent Abu'l-ʿAbbās Muḥammad, the brother of Abū ʿAbd Allāh, to inform the latter of his whereabouts and plans. But Abu'l-ʿAbbās was intercepted and detained in Qayrawān by the Aghlabids, who were a local dynasty which ruled in the name of the ʿAbbāsids over Ifrīqiya, the eastern part of the Maghrib, from 184/800 to 296/909. Meanwhile in Sijilmāsa, due to the pressures of the ʿAbbāsids, ʿUbayd Allāh was soon put under house arrest, if not actually imprisoned, by the Midrārid *amīr*. He was to remain so until his rescue by Abū ʿAbd Allāh.

Abū ʿAbd Allāh al-Ḥusayn b. Aḥmad, known as al-Shīʿī, a native of Ṣanʿāʾ, had joined the Ismāʿīlī movement in southern ʿIrāq. He had then spent some time in Yaman working with Ibn Ḥawshab. In 279/892, while making the pilgrimage, he met some Kutāma pilgrims in Mecca and, on Ibn Ḥawshab's instructions, accompanied them to their native land in the Maghrib, where he arrived in 280/893. It seems that the Kutāma had been introduced to Shīʿism by two *dāʿī*s sent there in the time of the Imām al-Ṣādiq. Abū ʿAbd Allāh first established himself in Īkjān, in the mountainous region north of Saṭīf, and began to propagate Ismāʿīlism in the name of the Mahdī among the Kutāma tribesmen of the Lesser Kabylia in present-day Algeria. Aside from capitalizing on Shīʿī inclinations of the Kutāma Berbers, the success of the *daʿwa* was hastened by the fact that the Aghlabids exercised no effective control over that part of the Maghrib. Later, Abū ʿAbd Allāh transferred his headquarters to Tāzrūt and founded a *dār al-hijra* for the Kutāma converts, as earlier *dāʿī*s had done in ʿIrāq and Yaman.

After establishing his authority over the Kutāma, and reorganizing them into seven groups, each one led by a trustworthy chief, Abū ʿAbd Allāh commenced the second phase of his mission, the quest for the conquest of Ifrīqiya and the overthrow of the Sunnī Aghlabids. In 289/902, he easily overtook Mīla and then withstood the attacks of two Aghlabid expeditions. He launched his own offensive in 293/906, against Saṭīf, Ṭubna, Billizma and other towns in the western territory of the Aghlabids. In 296/909, he seized Qafṣa and Qasṭīliya, and began to threaten Qayrawān itself with the full support of the Kutāma. The fall of al-Urbus (Laribus), the key of Ifrīqiya, in the same year, led the last

Aghlabid *amīr* Ziyādat Allāh III (290–296/903–909) to despair; he abandoned the royal city of Raqqāda which had been built on the outskirts of the Aghlabid capital of Qayrawān, shortly before it was entered by Abū ʿAbd Allāh in Rajab 296/March 909. Having consolidated his position in Ifrīqiya, and leaving his brother Abu'l-ʿAbbās behind as his lieutenant, Abū ʿAbd Allāh marched at the head of his Kutāma warriors towards Sijilmāsa, to hand over the reins of power to his master, whom he still had not seen. On his way, he brought about the downfall of another dynasty, the Khārijī Rustamids, who had ruled since 160/777 over a small principality in western Algeria from Tāhart, the headquarters of the Ibāḍī Khārijīs of North Africa. In Sijilmāsa, ʿUbayd Allāh was speedily liberated and presented to his *dāʿīs* and Kutāma followers; he also presided over certain ceremonies which suggest his preliminary investiture as caliph. Soon afterwards, in Rabīʿ II 297/January 910, ʿUbayd Allāh (ʿAbd Allāh) made his triumphant entry into Raqqāda where he was publicly proclaimed as caliph, receiving the homage of all the notables of Ifrīqiya. He became the first Fāṭimid caliph, taking the titles of *al-Mahdī bi'llāh* and *Amīr al-Mu'minīn*. The new caliphate, or anti-caliphate, was appropriately named al-Fāṭimiyyūn, after the Prophet's daughter Fāṭima whom ʿUbayd Allāh al-Mahdī and his successors claimed as ancestress.

The success of the Ismāʿīlī *daʿwa* was thus crowned, less than twenty years after its inauguration in North Africa, by the establishment of the Fāṭimid Caliphate in Ifrīqiya (modern-day Tunisia), in the very heart of Mālikī Sunnī territory. The aspirations entertained by the Shīʿīs, for two and a half centuries, had finally become a reality in this distant land. For the Ismāʿīlīs in particular, this represented a great victory, since it was their imām who was installed to the new Shīʿī caliphate, which was to control important parts of the Muslim world for more than two centuries. With this event, the period of concealment (*dawr al-satr*) and of the 'hidden imāms' in the history of early Ismāʿīlism, had also come to an end, being followed by the period of unveiling or manifestation (*dawr al-kashf*), when the Ismāʿīlī Imām appeared publicly at the head of his community.

We have already discussed certain aspects of the doctrines expounded by the pre-Fāṭimid Ismāʿīlīs. With the dearth of contemporary Ismāʿīlī sources, these doctrines can be derived in their main outlines from later Ismāʿīlī texts and from the writings of anti-Ismāʿīlī polemists. In the early Ismāʿīlī religious system, which was apparently fairly well-developed by the time of ʿUbayd Allāh's accession to power and which was subsequently maintained with some modifications by the Fāṭimid Ismāʿīlīs, a fundamental distinction was made between the exoteric (*ẓāhir*) and the esoteric (*bāṭin*) aspects and dimensions of the sacred scriptures and ritual prescriptions of Islam, between the outward and the inward meanings of the Qur'ān and the Sharīʿa. It was held that every appearance implied an inner, true reality (*ḥaqīqa*). Accordingly, the revealed scriptures and the laws laid down in them had their apparent or literal meaning, the *ẓāhir*, which was contrasted to the *bāṭin*, containing their hidden and true meaning. The *ẓāhir* would undergo changes or abrogations with every law-announcing prophet initiating a new era. The *bāṭin*, by contrast, embodying the truths or the so-called *ḥaqā'iq*, would remain immutable and eternal. For the Ismāʿīliyya, the *ḥaqā'iq* in effect formed a gnostic system, representing an esoteric world of hidden spiritual reality. Before the coming of the Qā'im, this *bāṭinī* world could be accessible only to the elite (*khawāṣṣ*), those initiated into the sect upon taking an oath of secrecy, as distinct from the ordinary masses (*ʿawāmm*) who were merely capable of perceiving the *ẓāhir*, the outward world. The initiation, known as *balāgh*, seems to have been gradual, involving also the payment of dues. The *Kitāb al-ʿālim wa'l-ghulām*, for instance, contains some valuable details of this process of initiation; and the gradualism in question is also described in the Ibn Rizām–Akhū Muḥsin account. But there is no evidence of a strictly fixed number of degrees, seven or nine, as reported by anti-Ismāʿīlī sources. Indeed, very little is known about this initiation and the actual *daʿwa* organization of early Ismāʿīlism. In the broadest terms, it seems that the Qā'im Muḥammad b. Ismāʿīl was represented, during his concealment, by twelve *ḥujja*s. And beneath the *ḥujja*s, a hierarchy of *dāʿī*s performed the various tasks of initiation and instruction.

By exalting the *bāṭin* and the *ḥaqā'iq* contained therein, the early Ismāʿīlīs soon came to be regarded as the most representative Shīʿī group espousing esotericism and gnosticism in Islam, the foremost amongst the Bāṭiniyya. Herein lies also the secret of the special role of the imām and of the religious hierarchy or *ḥudūd* in Ismāʿīlism. The early Ismāʿīlīs held that while the religious laws were announced by the prophets, it was the function of the imāms or the prophets' *awṣiyā'* (singular, *waṣī*), to interpret and explain their true meaning to the worthy few, those who were initiated and acknowledged the imāms. The unchangeable truths contained in the *bāṭin* were the exclusive prerogative of the divinely guided, sinless and infallible Ismāʿīlī Imām, and the hierarchy of teachers installed by him. These truths, furthermore, could not be revealed to anyone except on formal and gradual initiation. Hence, the need for a hierarchy of religious dignitaries or intermediaries between the imām, as the supreme head of the *daʿwa* organization, and the proselyte or the ordinary initiate. In this context, the Ismāʿīlīs reinterpreted the Shīʿī principle of *taqiyya* to imply the obligation of the sectarians not to reveal the *bāṭin* to any unauthorized person, apart from their duty to dissimulate when facing the danger of persecution.

The truths behind the revealed scriptures and laws could be made apparent through the so-called *ta'wīl*, viz., symbolical, allegorical or esoteric interpretation which came to be the hallmark of Ismāʿīlism.[177] The *ta'wīl*, literally meaning to lead back to the origin or to educe the *bāṭin* from the *ẓāhir*, may be distinguished from *tafsīr*, to explain and comment upon the apparent meaning of the sacred texts, and from *tanzīl*, which refers to the revelation of the religious scriptures through angelic intermediaries. The *ta'wīl* practised by the early Ismāʿīlīs was often of a cabalistic form, relying on the mystical properties and symbolism of letters and numbers. Although similar processes of interpretation and of spiritual exegesis had existed in the earlier Judaeo-Christian traditions and among the Gnostics, the immediate origins of the Ismāʿīlī *ta'wīl* are Islamic and may be traced especially to the Shīʿī circles of the 2nd/8th century. The purpose of the *bāṭinī ta'wīl*, utilized extensively by the Ismāʿīliyya, was to manifest the hidden so as to unveil the true spiritual reality. It represented a journey from the *ẓāhir* or the exoteric appearance, to the original ideas hidden in the *bāṭin*, causing the letter to regress to its true meaning, to the esoteric truths (*ḥaqā'iq*) which were later identified with Ismāʿīlī philosophy or theosophy. In short, the passage from *ẓāhir* to *bāṭin*, from *sharīʿa* to *ḥaqīqa*, or from *tanzīl* to *ta'wīl*, entailed the passage from the appearance to the true reality, from the letters of the revelation to the inner message behind them, and from the symbol to the symbolized. It corresponded to a passage from the world of phenomenon to the world of noumenon. The initiation into the *ḥaqā'iq*, attained through the *ta'wīl* or *ta'wīl al-bāṭin*, indeed led to a spiritual rebirth for the Ismāʿīlīs. The *ta'wīl*, translated also as spiritual hermeneutics or hermeneutic exegesis, supplemented the Qur'ānic world view with a more elaborate view which rapidly developed into an intellectual system. The early Ismāʿīlīs thus laid the foundations of their later religious system as well as their intellectual sciences, according to which the sectarians would progress from the *ẓāhir* sciences of the Sharīʿa, history, etc., to the *bāṭin* sciences, comprised of the *ta'wīl*, a means-science, leading to the *ḥaqā'iq*, an ends-science, the final goal of human attainment.

The *ḥaqāʾiq*, as noted above, formed a gnostic system for the early Ismāʿīlīs. The two main components of this gnostic system were a cyclical interpretation of hierohistory and a cosmology. On the basis of the state of knowledge available to them, the early Ismāʿīlīs developed their particular conceptions of time and eternity which were closely related to their views on history and prophetology. Their eclectic temporal vision reflected Greek, Judaeo-Christian and Gnostic influences as well as the eschatological ideas of the earlier Shīʿīs and the Qurʾānic view on the evolution of man. They conceived of time as a progression of successive cycles, with a beginning and an end.[178] As a result of their particular (semi-cyclical and semi-linear) conception of time, the Ismāʿīlīs worked out a cyclical and ultimately teleological view of history, or rather religious history, in terms of the eras of different prophets recognized by the Qurʾān. This view was combined with their doctrine of the imāmate which, in its fundamental framework, had been inherited from the Imāmiyya.

Accordingly, the early Ismāʿīlīs believed that the hierohistory of mankind is consummated in seven eras of various durations, each one inaugurated by a speaker-prophet or enunciator (*nāṭiq*) of a revealed message, which in its exoteric aspect contains a religious law (*sharīʿa*).[179] In the first six eras of human history, the *nāṭiq*s (or *nuṭaqāʾ*), also known as the *ūlu'l-ʿazm* or the prophets 'with resolution', had been Ādam, Nūḥ (Noah), Ibrāhīm (Abraham), Mūsā (Moses), ʿĪsā (Jesus) and Muḥammad. It may be recalled that, according to al-Nawbakhtī and al-Qummī, the Qarmaṭīs had originally included ʿAlī instead of Ādam in their list of law-announcing prophets, which represented an extremist viewpoint. The subsequent substitution of Adam for ʿAlī as one of the *nāṭiq*s, and the change of ʿAlī's rank from prophet to that of Muḥammad's successor, may thus indicate a less radical position. The early Ismāʿīlīs further maintained, probably by projecting their current ideas into the past, that each of the first six *nāṭiq*s was succeeded by a spiritual legatee or executor (*waṣī*), also called a foundation (*asās*) or silent one (*ṣāmit*), who interpreted the inner, esoteric (*bāṭin*) meaning of the revealed messages to the elite. In the first six eras, Shīth (Seth), Sām (Shem), Ismāʿīl (Ishmael), Hārūn (Aaron) or Yūshaʿ (Joshua), Shamʿūn al-Ṣafāʾ (Simon Peter), and ʿAlī had been such legatees. Each *waṣī*, *asās*, or *ṣāmit* was, in turn, followed by seven imāms called *atimmāʾ* (singular, *mutimm*, completer),[180] who guarded the true meaning of the scriptures and the laws in both their *ẓāhir* and *bāṭin* aspects. In every prophetic era, the seventh imām would rise in rank to become the *nāṭiq* of the following era, abrogating the *sharīʿa* of the previous *nāṭiq* and promulgating a new one. This pattern would change only in the seventh, final era of history.

The seventh imām of the sixth era, the era of the Prophet Muḥammad, was Muḥammad b. Ismāʿīl who had gone into concealment. On his parousia, he would become the seventh *nāṭiq*, and the Qā'im or Mahdī, ruling over the final eschatological era. Only he would unite in himself the ranks of *nāṭiq* and *asās*, being also the last of the imāms. Muḥammad b. Ismāʿīl would abrogate the sacred law of Islam and initiate the final era of the world. He was not to announce a new religious law, however. Instead, he would fully reveal the esoteric truths concealed behind all the preceding messages; truths which had so far been revealed imperfectly and only to the elite of humanity. In the final era, before the end of the world, the *ḥaqā'iq* would thus be fully known, free from all their symbolism, and an age of pure spiritual knowledge would be ushered in. In this messianic age, there would be no need for religious laws. Muḥammad b. Ismāʿīl would rule the world in justice and then end the physical world, sitting in judgement over mankind. He would be the *Qā'im al-qiyāma*, the Imām of the Resurrection; and his era would mark the end of time and human history.

In order to reconcile a seemingly eternal universe with a limited number of cycles and with the partial temporality of man, later Ismāʿīlīs allowed for a greater, endless, series of cycles. On the basis of astronomical and astrological speculations, they conceived of a grand cycle (*al-kawr al-aʿẓam*), composed of numerous cycles, each divided into seven periods, the whole to be concluded by the Grand Resurrection. Furthermore, the cycles of time were held to progress through the epochs of concealment (*satr*), when appearance and true reality are essentially different, and epochs of epiphany or revelation (*kashf*), when truth is manifest and there is no need for external law. ʿUbayd Allāh (ʿAbd Allāh) al-Mahdī and his successor Fāṭimid caliphs, because of their open claims to the imāmate, modified the earlier doctrine of the Ismāʿīlīs concerning the position of Muḥammad b. Ismāʿīl as the Qā'im and the final imām. The Fāṭimid Ismāʿīlīs allowed for more than one heptad of imāms during the era of the Prophet Muḥammad, removing the expectations connected with the coming of the Qā'im further into the future.[181] A major result of these doctrinal adjustments was the loss of the eschatological significance of the seventh imām and of that vital sense of messianic anticipation which played such a crucial role in giving early Ismāʿīlism its popular appeal and success.

The cosmology of the pre-Fāṭimid Ismāʿīlīs can be reconstructed only from the fragmentary evidence preserved in some later Ismāʿīlī texts, notably in works by Abū Ḥātim al-Rāzī and Abū Yaʿqub al-Sijistānī,[182] and in a *Risāla* by Abū ʿĪsā al-Murshid,[183] a Fāṭimid *dāʿī* of the time of al-Muʿizz. There are also those precious contemporary references by some Yamanī Zaydī authors.[184] According to this evidence, fully examined by Stern and Halm,[185] there was a crude myth at the very basis of the earliest Ismāʿīlī cosmology. More specifically, various motif complexes were combined into a mythological cosmogony, describing the creation of the universe and the analogies between the celestial and the terrestrial worlds. The early Ismāʿīliyya held that the universe was created by God's fiat *kun*, 'be', reflected as the Qur'ānic creative imperative. From this divine fiat, consisting of the two letters *Kāf* and *Nūn*, there arose through duplication the words *kūnī* and *qadar*, the two original principles; the former was the female principle, and the latter the male. *Kūnī* was formed first, out of *kun*, and then God commanded *kūnī*, a demiurge endowed with creative powers, to create *qadar*, predestination. By creating *qadar*, *kūnī* had also created the seven *karūbiyyūn*, corresponding to the Cherubim of the Judaeo-Christian angelology. The primal pair *kūnī-qadar* thus produced a heptad of letters, KUNI-QDR, called the 'higher letters' (*al-ḥurūf al-ʿulwiyya*), which were utilized in different ways. In this gnostic cosmological system, the myth of the letters had an extremely important function; it provided a ready explanation for the genesis of the universe. The letters produced the names or the words that were, in effect, identical with the things created. Clearly, what we have here may be referred to as a cabalistic mythological cosmogony.

The original pair *kūnī-qadar*, which were wrongly thought by our Zaydī sources to have been the 'gods' of the early Ismāʿīlīs (Qarmaṭīs), were indeed closely associated with the formation of the letters and the higher and lower worlds, and with the prophetic eras. The seven 'higher letters' of *kūnī-qadar* were interpreted as the archetypes of the seven *nāṭiq*s and their revealed messages; each letter standing for one of the speaker-prophets, beginning with K for Ādam and ending with R for al-Qā'im. These primal letters produced the remaining letters of the Arabic alphabet, presumably in heptads, and the elements from which the higher and the physical worlds were built. The two original principles produced three hypostases.

Kūnī ordered *qadar* to create, from his three letters, the triad of the spiritual beings (*rūḥāniyyūn*) or hypostases called *jadd*, *fatḥ* and *khayāl*,[186] identified with the archangels Jibrā'īl (Gabriel), Mīkā'īl (Michael) and Isrāfīl (Seraphiel), which mediated between the spiritual world and men in the physical world. They would also act as intermediaries between God and the *nāṭiq*s in every prophetic era. These hypostases provided important links between the cosmological doctrine of the early Ismāʿīlīs and their ideas on hierohistory and prophetology. *Kūnī* and *qadar*, together with *jadd*, *fatḥ* and *khayāl* formed a pentad that along with the seven *karūbiyyūn* and other created spiritual ranks (*ḥudūd rūḥāniyya*) constituted the higher world existing between God and the cosmos; gnostically speaking, this was the spiritual world or the pleroma. There was correspondence between the higher, spiritual world and the lower, physical world created through the mediation of *kūnī* and *qadar*, with the ranks of religious teaching (*daʿwa*) hierarchy corresponding closely to the ranks of the higher world. The air called 'the throne' (*ʿarsh*), the water called 'the chair' (*kursī*), the seven skies, the earth, and the seven seas, etc., were all formed from the four letters of the original female principle. In al-Murshid's version of the myth, the male principle *qadar*, which is subordinated to *kūnī*, has the character of a heavenly Adam or *anthropos*. Other Ismāʿīlī authorities, notably al-Sijistānī, also present traces of a motif indicating the fall of this cosmic man; Adam-*qadar* disobeyed God and was therefore banished from paradise to the terrestrial world.

All these motifs, and several more, are the components of the *kūnī-qadar* gnostic synthetic myth, representing the cosmological system of the early Ismāʿīlīs. This cosmology had a soteriological purpose; it aimed towards man's salvation and the knowledge or gnosis of his true origin, in order that he might be reintegrated into his cosmic being. As Halm has shown,[187] the main features of the early Ismāʿīlī cosmological system, such as hypostatization of God's will (*irāda*) and the word (*kalima* or logos), primal female-male pair, pentad of the pleroma, heavenly *anthropos*, and the prophetic eras, are traceable to diverse sources. There are doubtless some Judaeo-Christian influences. More significantly, there are strong parallelisms between this Ismāʿīlī system and the Samaritan Gnosis of Simon Magus, in whose central mythologumenon there is a female hypostasis (*Ennoia* or *Sophia*) causing the creation of the universe, and the related 'Ophite' and 'Barbelo-Gnostic' systems that have been classified under the label of 'Syrian-Jewish' types of Gnosticism.[188] There are also close affinities between the pre-Fāṭimid Ismāʿīlī cosmology and the religious concepts of the Mandaeans, an enigmatic sect probably belonging to the same category of Gnosticism. However, none of these earlier systems seem to have served as a direct prototype of the early Ismāʿīlī gnostic system of cosmology. The latter is an original model which developed on its own in an Islamic milieu, relying on Qur'ānic terminology and Shīʿī doctrines, while apparently drawing on the overall pattern of an earlier Simonian type of Gnosticism. The Ismāʿīliyya did appear and remain as a Shīʿī sect, whose revolutionary and messianic propaganda was conducted for a Fāṭimid Imām from the Ahl al-Bayt. As such, the doctrines of the early Ismāʿīlīs were mainly of the Islamic provenance, though they also borrowed, directly or indirectly through the Shīʿī Ghulāt, from some earlier non-Islamic traditions.

4

Fāṭimid Ismāʿīlism

Fāṭimid Ismāʿīlism, the subject of this chapter, covers the period from the establishment of the Fāṭimid Caliphate in 297/909 until the death of the eighth Fāṭimid caliph al-Mustanṣir in 487/1094 and the ensuing major schism in the Ismāʿīlī movement. During this so-called 'classical' Fāṭimid period, lasting some 185 years, Ismāʿīlism remained the state religion of a powerful empire centred first in Ifrīqiya (Tunisia), and after 362/973, in Egypt. The Fāṭimid caliphs were acknowledged as the rightful imāms by the main body of the Ismāʿīliyya not only in their own dominions but also in many other Muslim lands. This represented the 'golden age' of Ismāʿīlism, during which the Ismāʿīlīs achieved a prosperous state of their own and Ismāʿīlī thought and literature reached their summit, as attested by numerous treatises produced by the Ismāʿīlī *dāʿī*s and authors of the period, notably Abū Ḥātim al-Rāzī, Muḥammad b. Aḥmad al-Nasafī, Abū Ḥanīfa al-Nuʿmān b. Muḥammad, better known as al-Qāḍī al-Nuʿmān, Abū Yaʿqūb al-Sijistānī, Ḥamīd al-Dīn al-Kirmānī, al-Mu'ayyad fi'l-Dīn al-Shīrāzī, and Nāṣir-i Khusraw. At the same time, the Fāṭimids, after consolidating their position, began to pay considerable attention to cultural and economic activities as well as Islamic sciences in general. From their initial base in Ifrīqiya, the Fāṭimid rulers soon expanded their territorial domain in the western half of the Muslim world, culminating in their conquest of Egypt. Later, they extended their religio-political influence eastwards as far as Transoxiana and India. At its peak, the Fāṭimid empire, at least for a short period, included North Africa, Sicily, Egypt, the Red Sea coast of Africa, Yaman, the Ḥijāz with the holy cities of Mecca and Medina, Syria, and Palestine. But the Fāṭimids never succeeded in conquering the eastern lands of the Muslim world beyond Syria, as they failed to overthrow the ʿAbbāsids and the latter's Buwayhid and Saljūqid overlords. Consequently, they failed to establish the Ismāʿīlī

Shīʿī creed throughout the world of Islam, hence not realizing their all-important objective of uniting the Muslims under a Shīʿī caliphate headed by the Fāṭimid caliph-imām. Nevertheless, the Fāṭimids made important contributions to Islamic civilization, and it is in recognition of these contributions that L. Massignon has designated the 4th/10th century as the 'Ismāʿīlī century' of Islam.[1]

The Fāṭimid period is one of the best documented periods in Islamic history. Many mediaeval Muslim historians and chroniclers have written about the Fāṭimids, and there are numerous non-literary sources of information on this dynasty. In the latter category, Fāṭimid monuments and works of art have already been thoroughly studied, and scholarly investigations of numismatic, epigraphic and other types of existing evidence related to them have been made. There are also valuable archival documents from Fāṭimid Egypt; documents which are rarely available in connection with other Islamic dynasties and periods in the Middle Ages. Furthermore, the extant Ismāʿīlī literature of the period, recovered in recent decades, illuminates various aspects of the doctrines held by the Fāṭimid Ismāʿīlīs, enabling us to grasp the nature of their intellectual achievement. Due to this relative abundance of evidence, examined extensively by modern Islamists as well as specialists in Ismāʿīlī studies, Fāṭimid Ismāʿīlism has now become the best known major phase in the development of Ismāʿīlism.

Taking a closer look at the nature of the historical evidence available on the Fāṭimids, it is to be noted that with the collapse of the Fāṭimid Caliphate in 567/1171 and the return of Egypt to the Sunnī fold during the subsequent Ayyūbid and Mamlūk periods, the Fāṭimid libraries were effectively destroyed and the sectarian literature of the Fāṭimid Ismāʿīlīs was severely repressed. Henceforth, whatever was salvaged of various types of Ismāʿīlī works came to be preserved secretly and in private collections. As a result, the mediaeval accounts of Fāṭimid history and doctrines come almost exclusively from the pens of Sunnī historians who, as a rule, were hostile towards the Fāṭimids and their Shīʿī ideals. As an example, these writers, with the chief exceptions of Ibn Khaldūn and al-Maqrīzī, categorically reject the claims of the Fāṭimid caliphs to an ʿAlid descent, many of them referring to the members of this dynasty as ʿUbaydids rather than Fāṭimids. It may be recalled that most such anti-Fāṭimid positions had probably originated with Ibn Rizām, who had aimed at discrediting the entire Ismāʿīlī movement. Thus, numerous distortions and negative biases are contained in the narratives of the Sunnī historians and chroniclers who inevitably provide our main sources of information on Fāṭimid history and on the dynasty's political achievements. The Fāṭimid Ismāʿīlī theologians, in line with the characteristic outlook and priorities of the Ismāʿīlīs in general, were not keen on historiography. Consequently, the Ismāʿīlī texts from the Fāṭimid period are surprisingly poor in historical detail; while none of the official Fāṭimid chronicles, compiled at various times, have survived. The only Ismāʿīlī account of Fāṭimid history, aside from al-Qāḍī al-Nuʿmān's *Iftitāḥ al-daʿwa*, explaining the background to the establishment of the dynasty, is contained in the last three volumes of the *ʿUyūn al-akhbār* of the Yamanī *dāʿī* Idrīs ʿImād al-Dīn, which draws on earlier works and was completed some three centuries after the fall of the dynasty.

Considering in more detail the Fāṭimid historiography produced by non-Ismāʿīlīs, it is known that many Arab historians flourished in Fāṭimid Egypt after the dynasty had assured its existence following its turbulent North African phase. But with the exception of a few fragments, the works of these contemporary authors, who wrote local histories of Egypt or dynastic chronicles of the Fāṭimids, have not survived directly. The evidence recorded by them is, however, often preserved and utilized by later authorities, especially al-Maqrīzī. Ibn Zūlāq (d. 386/996) is one of the earliest writers amongst such contemporary Egyptian historians whose works have been completely lost; apparently he wrote among other things an independent book on the reign of the Fāṭimid caliph al-Muʿizz.[2] The tradition of local historiography in Fāṭimid Egypt was continued by al-Musabbiḥī (d. 420/1029), a high official after 398/1007–1008 in the service of the Fāṭimids, and who may have been an Ismāʿīlī himself. He produced a major history of Egypt and the Fāṭimids, covering the period from 365/975 to 415/1025. Only a small portion (volume forty) of al-Musabbiḥī's vast history, relating to the years 414–415 A.H., has survived in a unique manuscript preserved at the Escorial Library, Madrid.[3] Another historian was Muḥammad b. Salāma al-Quḍāʿī (d. 454/1062), a learned judge and a trusted Sunnī in the service of the Fāṭimid caliphs, notably al-Mustanṣir. Al-Quḍāʿī's works are not extant, but al-Maqrīzī and other later sources have utilized his history of the Fāṭimids. The only surviving contemporary account of the Fāṭimids is contained in the history of al-Anṭākī (d. 458/1066), an Arab Christian who spent the earlier part of his life in Egypt and then, during the caliphate of al-Ḥākim, migrated to the Byzantine city of Antioch in Syria where he composed his history of the ʿAbbāsid, Fāṭimid, and Byzantine empires, covering the period 326/937 to around 425/1033.[4]

Amongst the later Egyptian historians, who were for the most part also civil servants in Fāṭimid administration, mention should be made of ʿAlī b. Munjib, better known as Ibn al-Ṣayrafī; a prolific, versatile writer who worked in the *dīwān al-inshāʾ* or chancery of the Fāṭimids in Cairo from 495/1101 until his death in 542/1147. A historical work by Ibn al-Ṣayrafī, apparently an abridgement and continuation of an earlier Fāṭimid chronicle, has not survived, but two other works dealing with different aspects of Fāṭimid institutions have been preserved and published.[5] Amongst later relevant regional and dynastic histories produced during the 7th/13th century, reference may be made to the already-noted short history of the ʿUbaydids (Fāṭimids), the *Akhbār mulūk Banī ʿUbayd*, written in 617/1220 by Ibn Ḥammād (Ḥamādu), a Berber *qāḍī* and historian who died in 628/1231. There is also Ibn al-Ṭuwayr (d. 617/1220), a high-ranking official of the later Fāṭimids who wrote a history of the Fāṭimid and Ayyūbid dynasties which is lost, but on which al-Qalqashandī, al-Maqrīzī, and Ibn Taghrībirdī drew extensively for their knowledge of the last Fāṭimids and their institutions. Ibn Abī Ṭayyiʾ (d. ca. 630/1232–1233), a native of Aleppo and the only Shīʿī historian of the period, is another important source of historical information on the later Fāṭimids. His universal and Egyptian histories, also lost, have been quoted frequently by later historians, notably Ibn al-Furāt. The Egyptian Ibn Ẓāfir (d. 613/1216), who was a secretary in the chancery of the early Ayyūbids, wrote several works, including a universal history classified according to dynasties. The most important part of Ibn Ẓāfir's history concerns the Fāṭimids, and has recently been published for the first time.[6] But the most extensive history of Fāṭimid Egypt, produced in the second half of the 7th/13th century under the early Mamlūks, belongs to Tāj al-Dīn Muḥammad b. ʿAlī b. Yūsuf b. Jalab Rāghib, better known as Ibn Muyassar (d. 677/1278). Unfortunately, his *Akhbār Miṣr*, which may be considered a concise continuation of al-Musabbiḥī's chronicle, has survived in an incomplete form, covering the events of the Fāṭimid Caliphate during the period 439–553/1047–1158, with two fragments on the years 362–365 and 381–387 A.H. This work, based on the lost histories of al-Muḥannak (d. 549/1154) and Ibn al-Maʾmūn al-Baṭāʾiḥī (d. 588/1192), is preserved in a unique and incomplete manuscript held at the Bibliothèque Nationale, Paris, and which derives from a copy made by al-Maqrīzī in 814/1411.[7]

During the later Mamlūk period, the Fāṭimids were treated in certain regional chronicles, and in several universal histories written by Egyptian authors. Ibn ʿIdhārī, a Maghribī historian who died after 712/1312, included an account of the early Fāṭimids in his chronicle of Ifrīqiya, *al-Bayān al-mughrib*. Ibn al-Dawādārī, an Egyptian historian and a Mamlūk officer, wrote an extensive universal history, *Kanz al-durar*, of which the sixth part is devoted to the Fāṭimid dynasty, and which preserves valuable extracts from Akhū Muḥsin, Ibn Zūlāq and other earlier sources whose works have not survived. Ibn al-Furāt (d. 807/1405), another Egyptian historian, attempted to write a universal history, of which only the part covering the years after 500/1106 was completed. This work, surviving in fragments, is important for later Fāṭimid history as it utilizes a wide range of contemporary sources, many of which, like the chronicles of Ibn al-Ṭuwayr and Ibn Abī Ṭayyi', have been lost. The relevant section of Ibn al-Furāt's history concerning the Fāṭimids still remains unpublished. Then there are the three celebrated Egyptian authors of the late Mamlūk period, al-Qalqashandī, Ibn Taghrībirdī, and al-Maqrīzī. Aḥmad b. ʿAlī al-Qalqashandī (d. 821/1418), a secretary in the Mamlūk chancery in Cairo and the author of numerous works, is best known for his secretarial manual, *Ṣubḥ al-aʿshā*, completed in 814/1412. A large number of original documents are preserved in this work, published in fourteen volumes. Amongst such documents, those pertaining to the Fāṭimid and subsequent periods of Egyptian history are of particular significance. Abu'l-Maḥāsin Yūsuf b. Taghrībirdī (d. 874/1470) wrote a detailed history of Egypt from 20/641 to his own times, which includes a full account of Fāṭimid Egypt.[8] But it was left to the dean of the mediaeval Egyptian historians, Taqī al-Dīn Aḥmad b. ʿAlī al-Maqrīzī (d. 845/1442), to produce the most extensive account of the Fāṭimids, in both his *Ittiʿāẓ* and *al-Khiṭaṭ*, utilizing many early and contemporary sources.[9] It may also be added that although he was a Sunnī, al-Maqrīzī was favourably disposed towards the Fāṭimids. The tradition of local historiography in Egypt attained its peak in the works of al-Maqrīzī and Ibn Taghrībirdī, though historical writings on Egypt and the Fāṭimid period were continued by later historians like al-Suyūṭī (d. 911/1505) and Ibn Iyās (d. ca. 930/1524).[10]

Much valuable information on the Fāṭimids is also contained in the famous universal histories of the Muslim authors. For almost two centuries after al-Ṭabarī, the semi-official continuation of his *Ta'rīkh* was maintained. Al-Ṭabarī's *Ta'rīkh* was initially continued to the year 320/932, by ʿArīb b. Saʿd, the Andalusian historian and poet who held various official posts in the administration of the Spanish Umayyads. More significantly, its continuation became the collective work of Thābit b. Sinān (d. 365/

976) and some of the latter's relatives, all belonging to a learned family of Sabaean scholars and secretaries who had left their native city of Ḥarrān in northern Mesopotamia to settle in Baghdād. Thābit continued the narrative up to the year 362/973; and the history was in turn continued by his nephew Hilāl b. al-Muḥassin al-Ṣābi' (d. 448/1056), the first member of his family to embrace Islam. The universal history of Thābit b. Sinān seems to be almost completely lost, while that of Hilāl, which went down to the year 447/1055, survives only in a short fragment covering the period 389–393/999–1003. Hilāl al-Ṣābi' lived in Baghdād when the reigning ʿAbbāsid caliph al-Qādir was conducting his anti-Fāṭimid campaign, which culminated in the famous Baghdād manifesto denouncing the ʿAlid ancestry of the Fāṭimid caliphs; and Hilāl seems to have fully endorsed this hostile ʿAbbāsid view. Many later historians, such as Ibn al-Qalānisī (d. 555/1160), who wrote on the Fāṭimids and their activities in Syria, were directly or indirectly influenced by Hilāl's unfavourable account of the Fāṭimids. Hilāl's history was, in due course, continued down to 479/1086 by his son Ghars al-Niʿma Muḥammad (d. 480/1087), of whose work nothing has been recovered save some extracts, including a section on Fāṭimid Egypt, which are preserved in Sibṭ Ibn al-Jawzī's universal history. Thābit and Hilāl too, are quoted in later universal histories, such as *al-Muntaẓam* of Ibn al-Jawzī (d. 597/1200) and the *Mir'āt al-zamān* of the latter's grandson Yūsuf b. Qizughlu, known as Sibṭ (d. 654/1256). The most important universal history produced in this early period after al-Ṭabarī, however, is the *Tajārib al-umam* of Miskawayh (d. 421/1030), the famous historian, philosopher and physician, with its continuation by the *wazīr* Abū Shujāʿ al-Rūdhrāwarī (d. 488/1095);[11] they both also made extensive use of the histories of Thābit and Hilāl. The tradition of writing continuations to al-Ṭabarī found its culmination in Ibn al-Athīr (d. 630/1233), one of the greatest chroniclers of the Muslim world and the author of a vast general history down to the year 628/1231, which is rich in information on the Fāṭimids.[12] Ibn al-Athīr's history, representing the peak of Muslim annalistic historiography, was supplemented by the universal histories of the already-noted Sibṭ Ibn al-Jawzī, al-Yūnīnī (d. 726/1325–1326); al-Nuwayrī (d. 732/1332); the Syrian prince and historian of the Ayyūbid family Abu'l-Fidā (d. 732/1331); al-Dhahabī (d. ca. 748/1348); Ibn Kathīr (d. 774/1373); the celebrated Tunisian historian, sociologist and philosopher Ibn Khaldūn (d. 808/1406); and al-ʿAynī (d. 855/1451), amongst others.[13]

Aside from historical sources, there exist valuable archival documents concerning the Fāṭimids. In fact, Fāṭimid Egypt is one of the rare periods in the annals of the Islamic Middle Ages from which such materials have survived.[14] In Fāṭimid times, the official documents were issued mainly through the *dīwān al-inshāʾ*, the chancery of state, and their originals were preserved there or in other Fāṭimid archives. Subsequently, these documents, such as decrees, or epistles (singular, *manshūr* or *sijill*), letters of various kinds, diplomas, treaties, etc., came to be scattered in different isolated locations, since no Fāṭimid archives outlived the fall of the dynasty. It is unfortunate that no Islamic archives of the mediaeval times have survived, the only exception being the Ottoman archives. But the texts of some of the Fāṭimid documents have been preserved in certain chronicles, notably in those of al-Maqrīzī and Ibn Taghrībirdī, and in other literary sources, especially in manuals for secretaries. The most impressive example of the latter category is undoubtedly al-Qalqashandī's *Ṣubḥ al-aʿshā*, which is of encyclopaedic dimensions and which remains an indispensable source for the study of Fāṭimid documents and institutions.[15] Then there are those documents from the Fāṭimid period found amongst the famous Geniza collection of papers. The Geniza (a Hebrew term meaning a repository of discarded writings), or Cairo Geniza, refers to the lumber-chamber of an old synagogue in Fusṭāṭ (Old Cairo), where documents of all kinds were deposited and preserved from the 4th/10th century onwards. When the synagogue was renovated in 1890, the great treasure of papers and manuscripts hidden in its Geniza was recovered and dispersed to many public and private libraries throughout the world. In 1897, Solomon Schechter of Cambridge University transferred all of the still-available Geniza records to the Cambridge University Library, where it forms the famous Taylor-Schechter Collection.[16] For Islamic studies, it is mainly the Geniza's documentary material, consisting of thousands of letters, contracts, petitions, etc., concerning the Jewish and non-Jewish communities of the Muslim world, which is of particular interest. Most of these documents, written in Arabic or more commonly in Judaeo-Arabic (Arabic language written in Hebrew characters), date from the Fāṭimid and Ayyūbid periods. Purely Muslim materials from the chancery of the Fāṭimids are also found amongst the Geniza papers; documents which apparently had been taken into the Geniza by Jewish clerks employed in the chancery.[17] The Geniza documents, particularly their Arabic items, provide an invaluable source of information for the economic, social, and cultural history of mediaeval Egypt, especially during the Fāṭimid times.

Finally, mention should be made of a small but unique corpus of eight decrees issued by the Fāṭimid chancery to the monastery of St Catherine in Mount Sinai. These documents, dating from the last phase of Fāṭimid rule, have been preserved over the centuries in the archives of the monastery and in its Cairo and Istanbul branches. Two other extant Fāṭimid decrees of a similar nature, dating from 415/1024, had been originally issued by the Fāṭimid al-Ẓāhir to the Coptic monks and the Karaite Jewish community in Cairo. These documents, which are administrative decrees set forth by the Fāṭimids in response to petitions from non-Muslim communities, shed valuable light on Fāṭimid diplomatic and chancery practice.[18]

In modern times, Ferdinand Wüstenfeld (1808–1899) was the first European orientalist to have written, in 1880–1881, an independent history of the Fāṭimid Caliphate, drawing on a number of Arabic chronicles. Until the 1930's, only one other book in the West, written by the late British scholar O'Leary, had come to be devoted entirely to the history of the Fāṭimids.[19] With modern progress in Ismāʿīlī studies, however, the Fāṭimids too began to receive the fresh attention of the Islamists and specialists who now felt a need for re-writing their history. As a result, there appeared an upsurge of short studies and articles treating various aspects of Fāṭimid history and achievements. Attempts were also made to produce more comprehensive histories of the Fāṭimid dynasty. The late Zāhid ʿAlī of Niẓām College, Hyderabad, belonging to that small group of Indian Ismāʿīlīs who together with W. Ivanow played a decisive role in initiating modern progress in Ismāʿīlī studies, published in 1948 his history of the Fāṭimids. This work, still available only in the Urdu language, utilized for the first time a number of Ismāʿīlī sources; and it remains a valuable secondary source on the subject. Later, Abbas Hamdani, another modern Ismāʿīlī scholar belonging to an eminent Indian Ismāʿīlī family, produced a succinct account of the Fāṭimids in the English language.[20] Professor Hamdani, too, has had access to an important collection of Ismāʿīlī manuscripts preserved in his family for several generations. Meanwhile, Muḥammad Kāmil Ḥusayn of Cairo University (formerly the University of Fu'ād I) had started to edit and make available to scholars a number of Fāṭimid Ismāʿīlī texts in his well-known series of publications entitled Silsilat Makhṭūṭāt al-Fāṭimiyyīn. Other Egyptian scholars, teaching the history and civilization of mediaeval Egypt at various universities in their country, also began to publish important studies on the Fāṭimids, including a number of monographs on different Fāṭimid caliphs.[21] With these developments, an increasing number of students, both Ismāʿīlī and non-Ismāʿīlī, now selected topics related to Fāṭimid Ismāʿīlism for their doctoral dissertations in European and American universities and in some Eastern institutions.[22] At the same time, Western scholars continued to make contributions of their own to the study of the Fāṭimids. The late Professor Marius Canard, who for more than thirty years until his retirement in 1961 taught at the University of Algiers, was undoubtedly the doyen of this group of Westerners. He has written a number of major articles on the Fāṭimids, summing up the current state of research on the subject in his long article in the new edition of the *Encyclopaedia of Islam*.[23] The close co-operation between the Eastern and Western specialists in Fāṭimid Ismāʿīlī studies is well attested to by the papers presented at an international conference held in 1969 in Cairo to commemorate the millenary of that city.[24]

Fāṭimid history during its 'classical' period is normally divided into two phases. The initial phase, commonly designated as the North African phase, lasted just over sixty years from the establishment of Fāṭimid rule in Ifrīqiya in 297/909 to the Fāṭimid conquest of Egypt in 358/969 and the transference of the dynasty's seat of power there in 362/973; during which time the Fāṭimids were chiefly occupied with laying the foundations of their caliphate and assuring their existence. In the second phase, covering a period of some 120 years from 362/973 until the death of the caliph al-Mustanṣir in 487/1094, the Fāṭimid Caliphate, now centred in Egypt and enjoying stability, reached and then passed its peak of glory and territorial expansion, which was subsequently followed by the rapid decline and fall of the dynasty.

The first three Fāṭimid caliphs, ʿUbayd Allāh (ʿAbd Allāh) al-Mahdī bi'llāh (297–322/909–934), Abu'l-Qāsim Muḥammad al-Qā'im bi-Amr Allāh (322–334/934–946) and Abū Ṭāhir Ismāʿīl al-Manṣūr bi'llāh (334–341/946–953), who reigned entirely from Ifrīqiya, encountered numerous internal and external difficulties while they were consolidating their power and position in that remote region of the Muslim world.[25] Not only did they face internal dissent and the continued enmity of the ʿAbbāsids, the Umayyads of Spain, the Byzantines, and the Qarmaṭīs of Baḥrayn, but they also soon came to confront the hostility of various Sunnī and Khārijī dynasties and Berber tribes of the Maghrib, in their more immediate surroundings.

The Fāṭimids, like the ʿAbbāsids before them, came to face a serious internal conflict soon after their victory. This conflict, threatening the very existence of the newly founded Shīʿī dynasty, had its roots in the incompatibility between the ideas and expectations of those *dāʿīs* who had played a vital role in bringing the Fāṭimids to power on the one hand, and the needs of the state and the responsibilities of sound government on the other. The establishment of Fāṭimid rule required some modifications in the revolutionary objectives and policies of the Fāṭimid Ismāʿīlī *daʿwa*. Now that the Ismāʿīlī Imām had become a caliph, the *daʿwa* could no longer address itself primarily to the overthrow of the ʿAbbāsids, as it had done during the 3rd/9th century. It was also obliged to defend and uphold the claims of the Fāṭimids within the world of Islam. In the words of Ḥusayn F. al-Hamdānī, with the establishment of the Fāṭimid state, the Ismāʿīlī movement was obliged to adopt 'a graver and more conservative attitude towards the then existing institutions of Islam'.[26] This changed attitude found its expression also in the Fāṭimid Ismāʿīlī literature, displaying a tendency away from the earlier revolutionary principles of the movement. At any rate, almost immediately after al-Mahdī's accession, serious disagreements developed between the caliph and his chief lieutenant the *dāʿī* Abū ʿAbd Allāh al-Shīʿī. The *dāʿī* evidently had ideas of his own regarding the policies of the state, including taxation measures to be employed; he also resented the new limits put on his authority. Under these circumstances, Abū ʿAbd Allāh, who was extremely popular amongst the Kutāma, had begun to agitate against his master. But al-Mahdī, knowing that the *dāʿī* could easily incite the Berbers against him, moved swiftly. In 298/911, both Abū ʿAbd Allāh and his brother Abu'l-ʿAbbās were murdered on his secret orders, reminiscent of Abū Muslim's fate. The demise of Abū ʿAbd Allāh outraged the Kutāma Berbers, some of whom now rose in open revolt. However, al-Mahdī repressed this revolt speedily, before it could become more widespread.[27]

In North Africa, the Fāṭimids had to struggle against Sunnism, mainly in its Mālikī form, and more importantly, against Khārijism, the predominant religion of the Berbers. The existence of old rivalries in the Maghrib among the various Berber tribal groups, especially between the Zanāta and the Ṣanhāja, which was continuously exploited by the Umayyads of Spain, was another source of trouble for the early Fāṭimids. The Zanāta, who adhered mainly to Ibāḍī Khārijism and who, out of their hatred for the Fāṭimids, often placed themselves under the patronage of the Umayyads, were to be found in the western and furthest Maghrib, while the Ṣanhāja (or Ṣinhāja), who included the Kutāma, were concentrated in the central and eastern regions of the Maghrib.[28] The Kutāma Berbers, it will be recalled, had been converted to Ismāʿīlism and now provided the backbone of the Fāṭimid armies. After disposing of Abū ʿAbd Allāh, the caliph al-Mahdī had to deal with the revolts of the Zanāta, while in the west of his realm he was confronted by the Idrīsids of Fās (Fez), the first ʿAlid dynasty of the Maghrib founded in 172/789.

The Rustamids of Tāhart, a Khārijī dynasty brought to power with the help of the Zanāta, had been overthrown in 296/909 by the Kutāma fighters of the *dāʿī* Abū ʿAbd Allāh. But Tāhart had continued to serve as the rallying point of the Ibāḍī Khārijī Berbers, and soon the Zanāta of western Maghrib revolted against the Fāṭimids. In 299/911, this revolt was subdued and Tāhart retaken, by Maṣāla b. Ḥabūs, who then subjugated the Idrīsids of Morocco in 305/917. The Idrīsid ruler Yaḥyā IV was, however, permitted to retain the governorship of Fās and its province, under the condition that he recognize the sovereignty of the Fāṭimid al-Mahdī. The remainder of the Idrīsid territories was given to Mūsā b. Abi'l-ʿĀfiya, a Miknāsa Berber chief and Maṣāla's cousin. In 307/919–920, Maṣāla was obliged to return to the Idrīsid territories, and this time he deposed Yaḥyā IV, also taking possession of Fās. Subsequently, the Fāṭimid general proceeded to Sijilmāsa, which he took in 309/921. After Maṣāla's death in 312/924, his lieutenant Ibn Abi'l-ʿĀfiya became the sole ruler of western Maghrib as far as Sabta (Ceuta). However, he eventually defected from the Fāṭimid camp, and, in 320/932, transferred his allegiance to the celebrated Spanish Umayyad ʿAbd al-Raḥmān III (300–350/912–961) who, as part of his anti-Fāṭimid campaign, had seized Sabta during the previous year. It was only in the initial year of the second Fāṭimid caliph's reign that a Fāṭimid army, under the command of Mayṣūr, succeeded in defeating Ibn Abi'l-ʿĀfiya and in re-establishing Fāṭimid authority over western Maghrib. As a result, the Umayyads of Cordova became obliged to abandon, at least temporarily, their expansionist policies in North Africa, where they had the support of the Zanāta.[29]

From the beginning of their rule, the Fāṭimids aspired to establish their hegemony over the entire Muslim world. Their more immediate objective, however, was to overthrow the ʿAbbāsids, who were their most obvious adversary. As a first step toward their campaign against the ʿAbbāsids, which was to culminate in the extension of their rule over the entire Muslim East, they addressed themselves to conquering the Egyptian province of the ʿAbbāsid Caliphate. They attacked Egypt twice in al-Mahdī's reign, during 301–302/913–915 and 307–309/919–921, led by the caliph's son and future successor Abu'l-Qāsim Muḥammad. Both invasions, however, ended in failure, with only Barqa remaining in Fāṭimid hands. Meanwhile, in order to have better access to the Mediterranean and eastern lands, al-Mahdī had founded the town of Mahdiyya on the east coast of Ifrīqiya to where, in 308/921, he transferred his capital from Qayrawān. Later, the Fāṭimid capital in Ifrīqiya was moved to Muḥammadiyya and then to Manṣūriyya, towns founded by and named after al-Mahdī's next two successors. Mahdiyya was equipped with an impressive shipyard which soon enabled the Fāṭimids to possess a powerful fleet. This fleet was badly damaged in the second Fāṭimid invasion of Egypt, mainly due to the inexperience of its pilots. It did not take long, however, for the Fāṭimid warships to engage in numerous far-reaching battles and raids throughout the Mediterranean. After his accession, al-Qā'im launched a third expedition against Egypt in 323/935, again without success. The founder of the Ikhshīdid dynasty, Muḥammad b. Ṭughj al-Ikhshīd (323–334/935–946), who was appointed to the governorship of Egypt by the ʿAbbāsids, repelled this attack, forcing the Fāṭimid troops to withdraw to Barqa. Ibn Ṭughj and his able general Kāfūr, who became the real authority behind the later Ikhshīdids, managed to delay the Fāṭimid conquest of Egypt for more than three decades. The military operations of the Fāṭimids in Egypt were accompanied by their Ismāʿīlī propaganda there. This propaganda, conducted by numerous *dāʿī*s and secret agents, was addressed both to the soldiery and the civilian populace, including the non-Muslims of that ʿAbbāsid province. On several occasions, the Egyptian authorities succeeded in arresting and punishing some of these Fāṭimid propagandists and their local collaborators; but the Fāṭimids were not deterred from continuing their campaign.[30]

As successors to the Aghlabids, the Fāṭimids had inherited the island of Sicily (Ṣiqilliyya), separated from Italy by the narrow strait of Messina. The Aghlabids had seized Sicily from the Byzantines in a gradual conquest that was completed by 264/878. Byzantium, however, had continued to have possessions in Calabria, in neighbouring southern Italy. As a result of numerous raids, conquests and migrations, Sicily had come to be inhabited by a mixture of races with different religious beliefs. There were, for instance, Lombards, Greeks, Arabs and Berbers who adhered to Christianity, Islam and Judaism. This heterogeneity was a source of constant friction in the island. Under the Aghlabids, Sicily was governed by an *amīr* residing in Palermo, and this tradition was upheld by the Fāṭimids. The first Fāṭimid governor of Sicily was Ibn Abi'l-Fawāris, a former *amīr* of the island who had championed the Fāṭimid cause there.

Soon afterwards in 297/910, he was replaced by al-Ḥasan b. Aḥmad, better known as Ibn Abī Khinzīr, a more trustworthy individual and a former Fāṭimid police-chief of Qayrawān. In 299/912, the Arabs and the Berbers revolted against Ibn Abī Khinzīr, in Palermo and Girgenti, also rejecting his successor, ʿAlī b. ʿUmar al-Balawī, sent by al-Mahdī. The Sicilians now chose a governor of their own, Ibn Qurhub, a rich nobleman associated with the Aghlabid family. Ibn Qurhub declared himself to be in support of the ʿAbbāsid caliph al-Muqtadir (295–320/908–932), and during the short span of his rule, representing virtual independence for Sicily, there was an influx of Mālikī Sunnīs to the island, refugees who feared the persecution of the new Shīʿī masters of Ifrīqiya. Later, the Berbers of Girgenti, joined by the inhabitants of other parts of Sicily, revolted against Ibn Qurhub and, in 304/916, delivered him to al-Mahdī, who had him executed. After this short interval, Sicily again reverted to the Fāṭimid domain, though periodical troubles continued to erupt on the island.

In 336/948, the Fāṭimid al-Manṣūr appointed al-Ḥasan b. ʿAlī al-Kalbī, of the influential Maghribī Kalbid family of the Banū Abi'l-Ḥusayn, as governor of Sicily, in order to subdue the recurrent anti-Fāṭimid activities there. This appointment led to the foundation of the semi-independent dynasty of the Kalbids, which ruled over Sicily for almost a century on behalf of the Fāṭimids.[31] By the middle of the 5th/11th century, civil wars and Byzantine interventions had paved the way for the downfall of the Kalbids and the gradual reduction of Sicily by the Normans. The Kalbid period, it may be noted, was one of the most prosperous periods in the history of Muslim Sicily. The island developed vital trade relations with Ifrīqiya, while Palermo, with its numerous mosques, became a flourishing centre of traditional Islamic sciences. Fāṭimid Sicily also played an important part in the transmission of Islamic culture into Europe. It is interesting to note, however, that the Fāṭimid *daʿwa* does not seem to have penetrated into Sicily. The Kalbid *amīr*s and the ruling circles associated with them in view of their recognition of Fāṭimid suzerainty, probably adhered to Fāṭimid Ismāʿīlism, at least outwardly. But there is no evidence of the Fāṭimid *dāʿī*s trying to win converts in the island, whose Muslims continued to be mainly Mālikī Sunnīs. There were, however, some Ismāʿīlīs, mainly refugees, amongst the Sicilian masses. The bulk of them had fled from Ifrīqiya to avoid persecution by the Sunnīs, in the aftermath of the departure of the Fāṭimids to Egypt.

The early Fāṭimids used Sicily as a base for launching raids against the coastal towns of Italy and France as well as the islands of the western

Mediterranean. At the same time, they continued to be engaged in war and diplomacy with the Byzantines, who held possessions in eastern Sicily and southern Italy and occasionally benefited from the alliance of the Umayyads.[32] During al-Mahdī's reign, the Fāṭimid forces raided the coast of Lombardy and Calabria, forcing the Byzantines to pay an annual tribute. They also carried further naval assaults against the territories of Salerno and Naples. Later in 322/934, the caliph al-Qā'im sent a fleet of twenty vessels from Mahdiyya to Italy; this expedition sacked Genoa in the following year, returning to Ifrīqiya with much booty. Fāṭimid fleets also attacked the southern coast of France, and temporarily occupied the islands of Sardinia and Corsica. Following several minor entanglements, in 345/956–957 they inflicted a major defeat on the Byzantines in Italy, obliging the emperor Constantine VII (913–959) to send tributes and a peace-negotiating embassy to the Fāṭimid al-Muʿizz in 346/957–958. In 351/962, the second Kalbid governor of Sicily, Aḥmad b. al-Ḥasan, while consolidating his position, staged war against the eastern part of the island, where several Christian towns had survived in a state of semi-independence under Byzantine protection. In the same year, the Kalbids captured Taormina, which had resisted Muslim rule, renaming it Muʿizziyya, after the reigning Fāṭimid caliph. The early Kalbids continued to have periodic clashes with Byzantium whilst they were often asked to intercede in the struggles between the various small states of southern Italy. In 354/964, following the accession of the emperor Nicephorus II Phocas (963–969), who had refused to pay the customary tribute to the Fāṭimids and had also renewed the hostilities in Sicily, the Byzantines were severely defeated on land and sea by the joint Fāṭimid-Kalbid forces. Rametta, the last Sicilian possession of Byzantium, was now seized by the Muslims. According to the terms of a peace treaty signed in 356/967 between the Fāṭimids and the Byzantines, the Muslims acquired the right to exact *jizya* from the Christian inhabitants of Sicily. This defeat of the Byzantines, who had menaced the Muslims of the Near East, was indeed celebrated throughout the Islamic world. But subsequently the Fāṭimids did not find it objectionable to collaborate with Byzantium against a common enemy, the German emperor Otto I (d. 973) who was then establishing his authority in southern Italy. At any rate, after a decade of peace, the relations between the Fāṭimid and the Byzantine empires once again became marked by sporadic conflicts, accompanied by frequent Kalbid raids into Calabria and Apulia, a situation lasting until the downfall of the Kalbid state in Sicily.

Having laid a solid foundation for Fāṭimid rule in North Africa, from Morocco to the borders of Egypt, ʿUbayd Allāh (ʿAbd Allāh) al-Mahdī died in Rabīʿ I 322/March 934, after a caliphate of twenty-five years and an imāmate of some thirty-five years. He was succeeded by his son Abu'l-Qāsim Muḥammad, who had accompanied him from Salamiyya to the Maghrib, and had already participated in the affairs of the state and in numerous military campaigns before ascending to the throne as al-Qā'im bi-Amr Allāh. The second Fāṭimid caliph-imām continued his father's policies of expansion and consolidation; but he was more severe with his subjects, imposing heavy taxes on them to finance his diverse expeditions. It was towards the end of al-Qā'im's reign that the protracted rebellion of the Khārijī Berbers, led by Abū Yazīd, broke out. This revolt, which capitalized on the economic grievances of the Berbers as well as on the Zanāta–Ṣanhāja, Sunnī–Shīʿī and Khārijī–Shīʿī rivalries in the Fāṭimid dominions, almost succeeded in overthrowing the new dynasty.

Abū Yazīd Makhlad b. Kaydād, who traced his tribal origins to the Banū Īfran, the most important branch of the Zanāta, had studied and adopted the teachings of Nukkārī Ibāḍism, one of the main sub-sects of the Ibāḍiyya. The latter, together with the Ṣufriyya, formed the moderate wing of Khārijism. In due time, Abū Yazīd was in fact elected the imām and '*shaykh* of the true believers' by the Nukkārīs of the Maghrib, in succession to Abū ʿAmmār al-Aʿmā, who had taught him the doctrines of the sect. Abū Yazīd was, however, more interested in acquiring political power, thus not finding it difficult to depart from the accepted doctrines of the Ibāḍīs. He authorized *istiʿrāḍ* for instance, the religio-political assassination of adversaries along with their women and children, following the practice of the Azraqīs and other extremist Khārijīs. After spending some time in Tāhart as a schoolmaster, Abū Yazīd returned to Qasṭīliya in southern Ifrīqiya where he had been raised, and started his anti-Fāṭimid agitation in 316/928. He soon acquired a large following among the Ibāḍī Zanāta Berbers of the Awrās and elsewhere, and it was in recognition of his increasing popularity that the imāmate of the Nukkārīs also came to be ceded to him.

With the Berbers moving quickly to his side, Abū Yazīd launched his revolt against the Fāṭimids in 332/943–944. He swiftly conquered almost all of southern Ifrīqiya, seizing Qayrawān in Ṣafar 333/October 944. The inhabitants of Qayrawān, the stronghold of Mālikī Sunnism in North Africa, initially co-operated with the Khārijī rebels. The rebels had promised to relieve them of the rule of the Shīʿī Fāṭimids and the exactions of their Kutāma supporters, who had monopolized most of the privileged positions in the state.[33] Being subjected to the devastation and the pillaging of the Khārijī Berbers, however, the Qayrawānīs soon came to submit themselves once again to the Fāṭimids. In the meantime, al-Qā'im had adopted a purely defensive strategy in dealing with Abū Yazīd, and had split his troops into three groups in order to check the onslaught of the rebels. Abū Yazīd easily defeated the divided Fāṭimid forces, including the group stationed between Qayrawān and Mahdiyya under the command of Mayṣūr, who was killed in battle. Subsequently in Jumādā I 333/January 945, the rebels began their siege of Mahdiyya, where al-Qā'im was now staying. But Mahdiyya put up a vigorous resistance for almost a year, repelling Abū Yazīd's repeated attempts to storm the capital and mounting its own counteroffensive, aided by the new reinforcements sent by Zīrī b. Manād, the *amīr* of the Ṣanhāja. At the same time, many of Abū Yazīd's Berber contingents, having become tired of the prolonged hostilities, had started to desert their leader, who had further irritated his followers by his newly-adopted luxurious manner of living. Consequently, Abū Yazīd was obliged to withdraw to Qayrawān, where he quickly returned to his former simple habits, such as riding a donkey, hence his nickname *ṣāḥib al-ḥimār*. He soon regained his popularity amongst the Khārijī Berbers, and once again heavy fighting broke out between the rebels and the Fāṭimid forces around Tunis and elsewhere in Ifrīqiya. But when al-Qā'im died in Mahdiyya in Shawwāl 334/May 946, after a reign of twelve years, the tide of events had already begun to turn against Abū Yazīd.

Al-Qā'im's son and successor Ismāʿīl, who adopted the title of al-Manṣūr bi'llāh, was the first Fāṭimid caliph born in Ifrīqiya. He came to power in the midst of Abū Yazīd's revolt, and, like his father, kept his predecessor's death secret for awhile. He immediately shifted to an offensive strategy towards the rebels, spending many months chasing them. Soon after his accession, al-Manṣūr defeated the rebels at Sūsa, besieged by them for some time, forcing Abū Yazīd to retreat once again towards Qayrawān, whose inhabitants had now turned against him. Consequently, Abū Yazīd's attempts to seize the city proved futile and, in Muḥarram 335/August 946, he withdrew westward in the direction of the Zāb. Al-Manṣūr, who meanwhile had been well-received in Qayrawān, personally conducted a close chase, defeating Abū Yazīd near Ṭubna and then around Masīla. In Muḥarram 336/August 947, al-Manṣūr, assisted by his general Zīrī b. Manād, inflicted a final defeat on the Khārijī Berbers in the mountains of Kiyāna, where the rebels had entrenched themselves in a fortress overlooking what was to become known as Qalʿat Banī Ḥammād. Abū Yazīd himself was captured and died of his wounds a few days later. His son Faḍl continued the revolt in the Awrās and elsewhere for a few more months until he, too, was defeated and killed. Other sons of Abū Yazīd found refuge at the court of the Umayyad ʿAbd al-Raḥmān III, who in response to Abū Yazīd's request, had at one time allied himself with the Khārijī rebels against their common enemy.[34] Having reasserted the Fāṭimid domination in North Africa and Sicily, al-Manṣūr died in Shawwāl 341/March 953, after a short caliphate and imāmate of about seven years. He was succeeded by his eldest son Abū Tamīm Maʿadd al-Muʿizz li-Dīn Allāh.

We shall now consider the situation of the Qarmaṭīs of Baḥrayn and other dissident eastern Ismāʿīlīs, who had awaited the appearance of Muḥammad b. Ismāʿīl as the Mahdī and the initiator of the final era of history, after the establishment of the Fāṭimid Caliphate. According to al-Ṭabarī and the majority of the later Muslim chroniclers, Abū Saʿīd al-Jannābī, the founder of the Qarmaṭī state of Baḥrayn, was murdered in 301/913–914.[35] He was succeeded by the eldest of his seven sons, Abu'l-Qāsim Saʿīd. The latter was apparently forced out of power in 311/923, or possibly even earlier, by his younger brother Abū Ṭāhir Sulaymān. This sequence of succession may have been in accordance with Abū Saʿīd's own instructions and last testament. At any rate, during the rule of Saʿīd, who lacked energy and authority, the Qarmaṭīs refrained from any outside activity, also maintaining good relations with the ʿAbbāsid regime. During this quiescent period, the Qarmaṭīs were in fact engaged in extensive negotiations with the famous ʿAbbāsid vizier (Arabic, *wazīr*) ʿAlī b. ʿĪsā (d. 334/946), on the latter's peace initiative. In 301 A.H., soon after assuming his high office, and again in 303/915–916, ʿAlī despatched embassies to the Qarmaṭīs, and before being dismissed from the vizierate in 304/917, he had granted some privileges to them, such as access to the important port of Sīrāf on the northern shore of the Persian Gulf. These contacts, coinciding with the Qarmaṭīs' inactivity, gave the vizier's enemies, especially his chief rival and successor the Shīʿī Ibn al-Furāt (d. 312/924), a pretext for accusing him of being in complicity with the Qarmaṭīs. It may be noted in passing that ʿAlī b. ʿĪsā, who subsequently assumed the vizierate several more times, was the person responsible for organizing the ʿAbbāsid military forces that repelled the first two Fāṭimid invasions of Egypt. He is also the same vizier who, in 301 A.H., interrogated the celebrated mystic-theologian al-Ḥusayn b. Manṣūr al-

Ḥallāj, but declined to bring him to trial. Al-Ḥallāj, who had acquired great influence over many people, including some members of the ʿAbbāsid family, had aroused the jealousy of certain officials who accused him of being a Qarmaṭī agent. Deliberate misinterpretations of al-Ḥallāj's symbolic exegeses and of his missionary-like wanderings in remote lands were cited as sufficient evidence by his enemies, led by Ibn al-Furāt, for persecuting this enigmatic personality who claimed a mystical union with God and whose devoted disciples later founded a number of Ḥallājī sects and Ṣūfī orders. After being imprisoned for several years, al-Ḥallāj's trial finally opened in 308/921. Amidst much intrigue, al-Ḥallāj was eventually condemned to death. He was tortured, crucified and then brutally dismembered before a large crowd at Baghdād in 309/922.[36] Ibn ʿĪsā's leniency with the martyred mystic was mentioned as another proof of his favourable disposition towards the Qarmaṭīs.

The Qarmaṭīs ended their temporarily peaceful relations with the ʿAbbāsids in 311/923. It was in that year that under the command of the young Abū Ṭāhir Sulaymān, they entered Baṣra at night by surprise and pillaged the town for more than two weeks before returning to Hajar. Shortly afterwards, the Qarmaṭīs attacked and looted the pilgrims returning from Mecca, murdering a large number of them and taking many prisoners, including the famous Arab lexicographer al-Azharī (d. 370/980), who spent two years in Baḥrayn. These activities marked the beginning of a decade of devastating raids into ʿIrāq, interspersed with attacks on the pilgrim caravans, which greatly enriched the treasury of the Qarmaṭī state. In 312/925, following the ʿAbbāsids' refusal to cede Baṣra, Ahwāz and other territories to Abū Ṭāhir, the Qarmaṭīs sacked and pillaged Kūfa. During the year 314 A.H., when Abū Ṭāhir was busy with the fortification of al-Aḥsāʾ, the ʿAbbāsid caliph al-Muqtadir recalled to ʿIrāq Yūsuf b. Abi'l-Sāj, the hereditary *amīr* of Ādharbayjān and Armenia, in order to have the Qarmaṭī menace checked. However, Abū Ṭāhir again sacked Kūfa in 315/927, and then defeated a much larger ʿAbbāsid army commanded by Ibn Abi'l-Sāj, who himself was captured and later killed. Subsequently, Abū Ṭāhir advanced up the Euphrates, seized al-Anbār and came close to taking Baghdād, before being stopped by the eunuch Mu'nis al-Khādim (d. 321/933), the all-powerful ʿAbbāsid commander-in-chief (*amīr al-umarāʾ*) who had earlier fought the Fāṭimids in their Egyptian expeditions. This campaign, lasting for almost two years, encouraged the Qarmaṭīs of southern ʿIrāq, who were concentrated in the Sawād of Kūfa and who had close ties with their co-religionists in Baḥrayn, to launch rebellious activities of their own. The ʿIrāqī Qarmaṭīs, also known as the Baqliyya, under the leadership of ʿĪsā b. Mūsā and other *dāʿīs*, and joined by the tribesmen of the Banū Rifāʿa, Dhuhl and ʿIjl, rose in revolt in the area of Wāsiṭ and Kūfa in 316/928–929. After initial successes, however, they were subdued by the ʿAbbāsid general Hārūn b. Gharīb. Abū Ṭāhir, like other Qarmaṭī *dāʿīs* and leaders, was at that time predicting the advent of the Mahdī after the conjunction of Jupiter and Saturn in the year 316/928, an occurrence which was expected to end the era of Islam and initiate the seventh, final era. Abū Ṭāhir had indeed intensified his attacks as the expected date approached. Abū Ṭāhir eventually returned to Baḥrayn at the beginning of 317 A.H., having already completed the construction of a fortified *dār al-hijra* near al-Aḥsāʾ and taking with him many of the retreating Qarmaṭīs of southern ʿIrāq, the successors to the earlier Persian *mawālī* who were to become designated as the Ajamiyyūn.

The ravaging activities of Abū Ṭāhir culminated in his attack on Mecca, where he arrived in Dhu'l-Ḥijja 317/January 930, during the pilgrimage season. For several days the Qarmaṭīs massacred the pilgrims and the inhabitants of Mecca, committed innumerable plunderous and desecrating acts in the great mosque and other sacred places, and, finally, dislodged and carried away the Black Stone (*al-ḥajar al-aswad*) of the Kaʿba to their new capital, al-Aḥsāʾ, presumably to symbolize the end of the era of Islam. The sacrilege of the Qarmaṭīs at Mecca shocked the Muslim world, and most sources relate that soon afterwards, the Fāṭimid caliph al-Mahdī sent a letter to Abū Ṭāhir, reprehending him severely for his conduct and requesting him to return the Black Stone. Abū Ṭāhir rejected this however, along with similar requests put to him by the ʿAbbāsids. Having conquered ʿUmān in 318 A.H., he now became the undisputed master of Arabia and the terror of all nearby rulers. Abū Ṭāhir was finally in a position to attempt the conquest of ʿIrāq; and in 319 A.H., he led the Qarmaṭīs as far as Kūfa. But after 25 days of plundering the town, he decided to return to Baḥrayn, alarmed possibly by the internal troubles that were developing in the Qarmaṭī state. At any rate, Abū Ṭāhir, who had been expecting the emergence of the Mahdī since the year 316 A.H., turned over the rule to a young Persian from Iṣfahān, whose name may have been Zakarī or Zakariyyāʾ, in Ramaḍān 319/September–October 931. Abū Ṭāhir had in effect recognized the Mahdī in this Iṣfahānī who had arrived in Baḥrayn a few years earlier and who had rapidly acquired a position of influence amongst the ruling circles there. This, however, proved to be a disastrous decision for the Qarmaṭī movement, and events now took a different course from what had been predicted by the Qarmaṭīs for the advent of the Mahdī. The date had been evidently chosen to coincide with the passing of 1,500 years after Zoroaster (equalling the end of the year 1242 of the era of Alexander) for which prophecies attributed to Zoroaster and Jāmāsp predicted the restoration of the reign of the Zoroastrians or Magians (Arabic, al-Majūs). The Iṣfahānī, who is reported to have been a Zoroastrian, claimed descent from the Persian kings and manifested anti-Arab and antinomian sentiments. He also instituted a number of strange ceremonies, such as the cursing of Muḥammad and all other prophets, the burning of religious books, and the worship of fire, instead of initiating the circumstances prophesied for the advent of the expected Mahdī and ending the era of Islam. Furthermore, he started to execute the notable Qarmaṭīs of Baḥrayn, including some tribal chiefs and even the relatives of Abū Ṭāhir himself. As a result, after waiting some eighty days and now fearing for his own life, Abū Ṭāhir was obliged to admit that the young Persian was an imposter, and had him killed. It is interesting to note that a few years later, the ʿAbbāsid caliph al-Rāḍī (322–329/934–940) executed Isfandiyār b. Ādharbād, the chief priest (*mubid*) of the Zoroastrians, for his alleged complicity with Abū Ṭāhir.

The obscure episode of the false Mahdī seriously demoralized the Qarmaṭīs of Baḥrayn, and weakened their influence over other dissident Ismāʿīlī groups in the east. Many Qarmaṭīs, especially from amongst the Ajamiyyūn and the Arab tribal chiefs, left Baḥrayn to serve during the following decades in the armies of various anti-Qarmaṭī rulers, including the ʿAbbāsids and the Shīʿī Buwayhids (Būyids). The Buwayhids took possession of Baghdād in 334/946 and became the real patrons of the ʿAbbāsid realm for more than a century. The leading Qarmaṭī *dāʿīs* of ʿIrāq, including ʿĪsā b. Mūsā who had remained in Baghdād following his escape from an ʿAbbāsid prison, also severed their ties with Abū Ṭāhir and began to oppose him. The Qarmaṭī *dāʿīs* of ʿIrāq continued to propagate the Mahdīship of Muḥammad b. Ismāʿīl, while devoting the greater part of their efforts to producing treatises which they often attributed to ʿAbdān. In the meantime, after repudiating the false Mahdī, the Qarmaṭīs of Baḥrayn had reverted to their former beliefs and claimed to be acting on the orders of the hidden Mahdī. Abū Ṭāhir himself had not remained idle. After a brief respite, he had again started to plunder the pilgrim caravans and to carry out raids into ʿIrāq and southern Persia. In 322/934, Muḥammad b. Yaʿqūb, the caliph al-Rāḍī's chamberlain, negotiated in vain with Abū Ṭāhir for the restoration of the Black Stone and the Qarmaṭīs' guarantee of safe passage for the pilgrims. In 327/938–939, an agreement was finally concluded between Abū Ṭāhir and the ʿAbbāsid government, due mainly to the efforts of ʿUmar b. Yaḥyā, a Kūfan ʿAlid and a personal friend of the Qarmaṭī leader. Abū Ṭāhir now accepted to protect the pilgrims in return for an annual tribute from the ʿAbbāsid treasury and a specified sum from the pilgrims themselves. The Qarmaṭīs had thus once again adopted a peaceful policy towards the ʿAbbāsids when Abū Ṭāhir died in 332/944, the same year in which the Khārijī Abū Yazīd started his anti-Fāṭimid revolt. Subsequently, the Qarmaṭī state of Baḥrayn was for some time ruled jointly by Abū Ṭāhir's surviving brothers, including Abu'l-Qāsim Saʿīd (d. 361/972), Abū Manṣūr Aḥmad and Abu'l-ʿAbbās al-Faḍl; while Abū Ṭāhir's sons, notably Sābūr, the eldest, enjoyed much esteem in the state and with the council of the ʿIqdāniyya. The Qarmaṭīs, who had continued to honour their peace treaty with the ʿAbbāsids, voluntarily returned the Black Stone in 339/950–951, for a large sum of money paid by the ʿAbbāsids, and not, as held by some authorities, in response to the Fāṭimid al-Manṣūr's request. One of the most distinguished Qarmaṭīs of Baḥrayn, Abū Muḥammad Sanbar, the son of al-Ḥasan b. Sanbar and the brother-in-law of Abū Saʿīd al-Jannābī, the most influential individual on Abū Ṭāhir's council of viziers, accompanied the Black Stone first to Kūfa, where it was displayed in the great mosque, and then to Mecca, where it was reinstalled in the Kaʿba after an absence of almost twenty-two years. The chroniclers do not relate any further activity on the part of the Qarmaṭīs of Baḥrayn for more than one decade.

Much has been written in modern times concerning the relations between the Qarmaṭīs and the Fāṭimid Ismāʿīlīs. De Goeje was the first orientalist to deal with this issue in some detail, and he arrived at the important conclusion that Abū Ṭāhir, in all his important undertakings, acted on the direct orders of the Fāṭimid ʿUbayd Allāh al-Mahdī, who could not publicly acknowledge his secret alliance with the disreputable Qarmaṭīs of Baḥrayn. He further held that with minor fluctuations, the Qarmaṭīs maintained their close co-operation with the Fāṭimid Ismāʿīlīs until the Fāṭimid conquest of Egypt, at which time they broke openly with the Fāṭimids. Subsequently, this view was to be endorsed by others, notably Louis Massignon, Ḥasan I. Ḥasan and Ṭāhā A. Sharaf. More recent scholarship, however, does not attest to the existence of close relations between the Qarmaṭīs and the Fāṭimid Ismāʿīlīs during the first half of the 4th/10th century. To a great extent, the difficulty of determining the precise nature of the relationship between the Qarmaṭīs and the

Fāṭimids has stemmed from the unfortunate fact that we possess little reliable information on the creed of the Qarmaṭīs, who were extremely secretive about their doctrines and whose literature has perished almost completely. The Sunnī writers, who provide our main sources of information on the Qarmaṭīs, generally fail to distinguish between the different groups of the early Ismāʿīlīs, treating all of them as belonging to one and the same heretical Shīʿī Bāṭinī movement. But in the light of what is known about the beliefs of the Qarmaṭīs, modern scholarship has taken cognizance of the fundamental differences between Qarmaṭism and Fāṭimid Ismāʿīlism. It is known that the Qarmaṭīs of Baḥrayn, from the outset of their history, anticipated the return of the Qā'im Muḥammad b. Ismāʿīl, as reported in the earliest chronicles and in the accounts of Ibn Rizām, who, in 329/940, was the head of the *maẓālim* or the tribunal for the investigation of complaints in Baghdād, and Akhū Muḥsin. These reports clearly show that the imminent anticipation of the Mahdī played a dominant part in the creed of the Qarmaṭīs, and that this anticipation was not fulfilled by the appearance of the Fāṭimids in North Africa. In other words, the Qarmaṭīs of Baḥrayn and other areas did not acknowledge the imāmate of the Fāṭimid caliphs, nor did they recognize their expected Mahdī in ʿUbayd Allāh al-Mahdī or his successors. This is why they were so readily drawn into the catastrophic affair of the false Mahdī during the reign of the first Fāṭimid caliph. However, as the Fāṭimids and the Qarmaṭīs of Baḥrayn shared a common hostility towards the Sunnī ʿAbbāsids, it may appear that at times they acted in unison. But there is no solid evidence to support the view that the Qarmaṭīs were in the service of the early Fāṭimids and that the two acted on the basis of a joint strategy.[37]

During the first decade of the 4th century/912–923, when ʿUbayd Allāh al-Mahdī was establishing his authority in North Africa and the Qarmaṭīs of Baḥrayn and ʿIrāq were quiescent, dissident Ismāʿīlism had begun to spread in Persia. The *dāʿī* Abū Ḥātim al-Rāzī, who corresponded with Abū Ṭāhir al-Jannābī, and like the latter was expecting the appearance of the Mahdī, succeeded in extending the *daʿwa* from his seat in Rayy to Ādharbayjān and Daylam, which at the time referred to a number of Caspian provinces, including Daylam proper (Daylamān), Gīlān, Ṭabaristān (Māzandarān) and Gurgān. Abū Ḥātim was particularly successful in converting a number of rulers in the region. We have already noted Aḥmad b. ʿAlī, the governor of Rayy, Asfār b. Shirawayh, a Daylamī *amīr*, and Mardāwīj, the founder of the Ziyārid dynasty. The Persian *daʿwa* also succeeded in attracting Mahdī b. Khusraw Fīrūz

(Fīrūzān), known as Siyāhchashm. He was one of the Justānid rulers of Daylam who, like his predecessors, had his seat at Alamūt, the same locality in the highlands of Daylamān that about two centuries later was to become the headquarters of the Persian Nizārī Ismāʿīlīs. The obscure dynasty of the Justānids (Jastānids) of Daylam was apparently founded towards the end of the 2nd/8th century, and one of its members, Wahsūdān b. Marzubān (d. ca. 251/865), is reported to have built the fortress of Alamūt around 246/860. Until the accession of Siyāhchashm, the Justānids normally supported the ʿAlid rulers of Ṭabaristān, notably al-Ḥasan b. Zayd (d. 270/884) and his brother Muḥammad b. Zayd (d. 287/900), and later al-Ḥasan b. ʿAlī al-Uṭrūsh (d. 304/917), who led the cause of Zaydī Shīʿism in the Caspian region. Justān II b. Wahsūdān was murdered during the last decade of the 3rd century/903–912, after a reign of some forty years, by his brother ʿAlī. Soon afterwards, the latter entered the service of the ʿAbbāsids, becoming a financial agent in Iṣfahān in 300/912 and then the governor of Rayy in 307/919. ʿAlī b. Wahsūdān was killed in 307 A.H. by Muḥammad b. Musāfir, Justān II's son-in-law and founder of the Musāfirid (also called Sallārid, Sālārid or Langarid) dynasty, which ruled from the fortress of Shamīrān in Ṭārum (Arabic, Ṭarm), the region along the middle course of the Safīdrūd before its confluence with the Shāhrūd. Khusraw Fīrūz b. Wahsūdān, another brother of ʿAlī, who had meanwhile ruled from the dynasty's traditional seat in the Rūdbār of Alamūt situated in a side valley of the Shāhrūd basin, now marched against Ibn Musāfir to avenge his murdered brother, but he was killed in battle. Khusraw Fīrūz was succeeded in Alamūt by his son Mahdī (Siyāhchashm) who apparently was the first Justānid to have embraced Ismāʿīlism. After being defeated by Ibn Musāfir, Siyāhchashm sought refuge in 316/928 with Asfār b. Shirawayh who, aspiring to possess Alamūt, had his co-religionist killed.[38] With the demise of Siyāhchashm, the Justānid dynasty began to disintegrate, their local position being now eclipsed by the rise of the Musāfirids.

Qarmaṭī Ismāʿīlism continued to be preached in northwestern Persia for some time under the Daylamī Musāfirids. In 330/941–942, Muḥammad b. Musāfir, who had constructed the castle of Shamīrān with much splendour, was deposed and imprisoned by his sons, Marzubān and Wahsūdān. Both of these Musāfirids adhered to Ismāʿīlism. While Wahsūdān remained at Shamīrān and governed his ancestral territories in Ṭārum, under the overall authority of his brother, Marzubān b. Muḥammad soon conquered Ādharbayjān and began to rule over the expanding

Musāfirid domains from his own seat at Ardabīl. It may be noted that after the governorships of the Sājids Yūsuf b. Abi'l-Sāj and his nephew Abu'l-Musāfir (d. 317/929), Ādharbayjān had become the scene of rivalries among various independent local rulers, including one of Ibn Abi'l-Sāj's officers named Mufliḥ. The latter, who remained in power at least until 323/935, is the same ruler who gave protection to the *dāʿī* Abū Ḥātim and who may have become an Ismāʿīlī himself. At any rate, by 326/937–938, the Khārijī Daysam b. Ibrāhīm al-Kurdī had gained control of the province. In 330/941–942, there appeared a rupture between Daysam and his vizier Abu'l-Qāsim ʿAlī b. Jaʿfar, initially a Sājid financial administrator who, according to Miskawayh, had also been active as a Bāṭinī (Ismāʿīlī) *dāʿī* in Ādharbayjān. Abu'l-Qāsim now fled to Ṭārum and entered the service of Marzubān b. Muḥammad, soon encouraging his new master to invade Ādharbayjān. Marzubān, who after conquering Ādharbayjān in 330 A.H. extended his rule northwards into Transcaucasia as far as Darband, appointed Abu'l-Qāsim as his vizier and, being an Ismāʿīlī himself, allowed him to advocate Ismāʿīlism openly in the Musāfirid dominions. Abu'l-Qāsim, who had previously converted a number of Daylamī notables and army officers in the entourage of Daysam, now became even more successful in his missionary activity. Ibn Ḥawqal, who visited Ādharbayjān around 344/955–956, reports the existence of many Ismāʿīlīs there.[39] Ismāʿīlism flourished also in Daylam under Wahsūdān b. Musāfir, whose rule lasted until around 355/966. Numismatic evidence dating from the year 343/954–955 indicates that Wahsūdān and his more authoritative brother Marzubān (d. 346/957) adhered to the Qarmaṭī form of Ismāʿīlism, recognizing the Mahdīship of Muḥammad b. Ismāʿīl rather than the imāmate of the reigning Fāṭimid, al-Muʿizz. The Musāfirids eventually withdrew to Ṭārum and survived for some time under Saljūqid suzerainty. Their dynasty was finally overthrown by the Persian Nizārī Ismāʿīlīs, who came to occupy Shamīrān and other mountainous fortresses of the region.[40]

In Khurāsān and Transoxiana too, the dissident Ismāʿīlī view persisted after the advent of the Fāṭimids. The *dāʿī* al-Nasafī reaffirmed the imāmate of Muḥammad b. Ismāʿīl, who was to reappear as the Mahdī, in his *Kitāb al-maḥṣūl*, which also introduced a type of Neoplatonic philosophy into Ismāʿīlī thought. It seems that *al-Maḥṣūl* soon gained widespread acceptance within the various Qarmaṭī circles; and, in fact, it played an important part, prior to the episode of the false Mahdī, in unifying the ideas of the dissident eastern Ismāʿīlīs, who lacked central leadership. As

Madelung has noted, it may be assumed that Abū Ḥātim, who like other *dāʿī*s must have been shocked by the events in Baḥrayn, probably wrote his *al-Iṣlāḥ* to correct the erroneous statements of *al-Maḥṣūl*, after the episode of the false Mahdī and as a partial censure of that event and its accompanying manifestations of libertinism.[41] This also explains why *al-Iṣlāḥ* pays particular attention to criticizing the antinomian aspects of *al-Maḥṣūl*. The *Iṣlāḥ* was, in turn, attacked in the non-extant *Kitāb al-nuṣra*, written by al-Nasafī's successor Abū Yaʿqūb al-Sijistānī, who initially defended most of al-Nasafī's views.

Abū Yaʿqūb Isḥāq b. Aḥmad al-Sijistānī (al-Sijzī), curiously nicknamed 'Cottonseed' (Persian, *panba-dāna*, or its Arabic equivalent, *khayshafūj*) who at the time of the writing of the *Nuṣra* did not acknowledge the imāmate of the Fāṭimids, is one of the most eminent early Ismāʿīlī thinkers and *dāʿī*s of Persia.[42] He was particularly influenced by Neoplatonism, and continued the philosophical trend started by al-Nasafī. Having been a prolific writer, al-Sijistānī's contributions to various theological and cosmological doctrines in Ismāʿīlism may be traced through his numerous extant works. It may be added that later in his life, sometime after the accession of the Fāṭimid al-Muʿizz, al-Sijistānī was won over by the Fāṭimids and many of his views became acceptable to the Fāṭimid *daʿwa*. The philosophico-theological system expounded by al-Nasafī and al-Sijistānī, and the general ideas current among the Ismāʿīlī circles of Persia during the 4th/10th century, are also reflected in a long poem (*qaṣīda*) by al-Sijistānī's contemporary Abu'l-Haytham Aḥmad b. al-Ḥasan al-Jurjānī, an obscure Ismāʿīlī philosopher-poet from Gurgān; also, in a commentary to this poem by Muḥammad b. Surkh al-Nīshāpūrī, an Ismāʿīlī disciple of Abu'l-Haytham who had studied under him for nine years.[43]

Few details are known about the life of al-Sijistānī who, contrary to an earlier widely-held opinion, was not executed by the Sāmānids in 332/943 together with al-Nasafī.[44] In fact, he succeeded al-Nasafī as the *dāʿī* of Khurāsān and became prominent also in Sīstān (Arabic, Sijistān), possibly his original base of operation. He may have combined these posts with that of the chief *dāʿī* of Rayy, in which case he may perhaps be identified with the *dāʿī* Abū Yaʿqūb who, residing in Rayy, had succeeded Abū Ḥātim after 322/934 and who is reported by Ibn al-Nadīm to have also had the *daʿwa* in northern ʿIrāq (al-Jazīra) and the adjacent regions under his control.[45] According to the well-informed Ibn al-Nadīm, the brothers Abū Muslim and Abū Bakr b. Ḥammād in Mawṣil and Ibn Nafīs in Baghdād, amongst other high ranking *dāʿī*s of northern ʿIrāq, were subordinate to the same Abū Yaʿqūb, referred to as the deputy (*khalīfa*) of the imām. Al-Sijistānī's date of death is also unknown. According to Rashīd al-Dīn and other sources, he was executed by the Ṣaffārid Khalaf b. Aḥmad who governed Khurāsān from 353/964 to 393/1003,[46] when he was overthrown by Maḥmūd of Ghazna. Internal evidence contained in al-Sijistānī's *Kitāb al-iftikhār* indicates that this work was composed around 361/971.[47] It is, therefore, safe to assume that al-Sijistānī died not too long after the year 361 A.H., and, less probably, perhaps soon after the accession of the Fāṭimid al-Ḥākim in 386/996, another date deducible from two of his other works. At any rate, it is an established fact that, during the early Fāṭimid period, the *dāʿīs* of the Jibāl maintained close contacts with those in ʿIrāq and with the Qarmaṭīs of eastern Arabia, all belonging to the dissident wing of Ismāʿīlism and predicting the imminent return of Muḥammad b. Ismāʿīl. Meanwhile, Qarmaṭī Ismāʿīlism had persisted elsewhere in Persia as well as in other regions of the Muslim East.

Resuming our history of Fāṭimid rule in North Africa, it must be emphasized that only under the fourth Fāṭimid caliph, al-Muʿizz li-Dīn Allāh (341–365/953–975), did the Fāṭimid Caliphate at last find the peace and internal security required for pursuing an effective policy of conquest and territorial expansion.[48] Al-Muʿizz was an excellent planner, an efficient organizer and a statesman amply talented in diplomacy. It was due to these skills of the young caliph and the outstanding military competence of his general, Jawhar, that he soon succeeded in subduing the entire Maghrib as a prelude to implementing his own eastern policy. After gaining some initial victories in the Awrās, and against the Umayyad ʿAbd al-Raḥmān III and the Byzantines, al-Muʿizz next turned his attention to organizing a major military operation to re-establish Fāṭimid authority in the central and extreme Maghrib. He entrusted the command of this campaign to his general Jawhar b. ʿAbd Allāh, a freedman of the Fāṭimids and possibly of Slav origin, who carried various epithets such as al-Ṣaqlabī (the Slav), al-Ṣiqillī (the Sicilian) and al-Rūmī (the Greek), and who had risen in rank to become secretary to the caliphs al-Manṣūr and al-Muʿizz, and then the latter's chief general (*al-qāʾid*).[49] In 347/958, Jawhar led the Fāṭimid forces westwards and defeated, near Ṭāhart, a large army of the Zanāta Berbers commanded by Yaʿlā b. Muḥammad, the chief of the Sunnī Banū Īfran and an ally of the Umayyads of Spain who had rebelled against the Fāṭimids. Yaʿlā, who had come to control the central Maghrib from Ṭāhart to Tangier, was killed in battle. With this defeat, the Īfranid domination of this part of the Maghrib was also brought to an end, at least temporarily. Subsequently, Jawhar invaded the principality of Sijilmāsa, then still ruled by the Banū Midrār, and killed its *amīr*, Muḥammad b. al-Fatḥ. After spending a year in that region of eastern Morocco, Jawhar marched against Fās, and in 349/960, beseiged this important Umayyad stronghold in al-Maghrib al-Aqṣā. He seized the city after a few weeks, mainly due to the bravery of Zīrī b. Manād al-Ṣanhājī, and took prisoner its Umayyad governor. This victory brought all of the far-western Maghrib, with the main exception of Sabta, under Fāṭimid authority, which for a brief period now extended westwards as far as the Atlantic. Even the last of the Idrīsids of Rīf, al-Ḥasan b. Jannūn (d. 375/985), who from the city of Baṣra ruled over a small state in Morocco under Umayyad patronage, now pledged allegiance to the Fāṭimids.

In his North African campaign, Jawhar was assisted, as noted, by Zīrī b. Manād, the chief of the main tribe of the Ṣanhāja. Zīrī who had earlier fought on the side of the Fāṭimids against Abū Yazīd, had become a fervent Ismāʿīlī Shīʿī, defending the cause of the Fāṭimids. In recognition of his services, Zīrī had been given permission by the caliph al-Qāʾim to found and fortify the town of Ashīr in the central Maghrib, on the western borders of the Ṣanhāja territory. He had thus acquired a prestigious semi-autonomous status, ruling from Ashīr over a large area inhabited by the Ṣanhāja tribesmen and always ready to defend the Fāṭimids against the Zanāta and other enemies. As we shall see, Zīrī's son, Buluggīn (Arabic, Buluqqīn), was later entrusted by al-Muʿizz with the governorship of Ifrīqiya, where he founded the Zīrid dynasty.[50] The early Fāṭimids also received the support of the Banū Ḥamdūn, a distinguished family of Yamanī Arabs who had settled in Spain and who had moved, before the end of the 3rd/9th century, to North Africa. ʿAlī b. Ḥamdūn al-Andalusī had accompanied ʿUbayd Allāh al-Mahdī from Sijilmāsa to Raqqāda and had later come to govern the Zāb for the Fāṭimid al-Qāʾim. He had personally supervised the construction of the city of Masīla, which became his capital. According to Ibn Khaldūn, ʿAlī b. Ḥamdūn was killed in 334/945–946 while fighting Abū Yazīd's son. He was succeeded by his son Jaʿfar who also fought against the Khārijī rebels and was in due course reaffirmed as the governor of the Zāb by the caliph al-Manṣūr. Jaʿfar held court, together with his brother Yaḥyā, at Masīla, where he patronized numerous poets and men of learning. Both Jaʿfar and Yaḥyā b. ʿAlī also participated actively in Jawhar's North African campaign.[51]

There existed, however, a bitter rivalry between the Zīrids of Ashīr and the Banū Ḥamdūn of Masīla, both families earnestly competing for the favour of their mutual Fāṭimid overlord. Zīrī b. Manād had gradually managed to acquire the more advantageous position in this contest. His position was particularly enhanced by the incorporation of Tāhart and its dependencies into his domain, while he had also extended his influence to the vicinity of Masīla. As a result of such humiliations, and also envisaging more important roles for himself in the broader context of the Zanāta–Ṣanhāja rivalry, in 360/971 Jaʿfar b. ʿAlī transferred his allegiance to the Umayyad al-Ḥakam II (350–366/961–976) and started a rebellion against the Fāṭimids with the help of the Zanāta. In the same year, Zīrī who had continued to remain loyal to the Fāṭimids, led a Ṣanhāja force against the rebels, but fell in battle, and his head was carried by Yaḥyā b. ʿAlī to the Umayyad court. Soon afterwards, Buluggīn b. Zīrī, the new *amīr* of the Ṣanhāja, defeated the Zanāta Berbers under Jaʿfar's command and also took possession of Masīla and the Zāb. Jaʿfar b. ʿAlī, feeling insecure amongst the Zanāta, who desired to possess his treasures, was now obliged to flee to Cordova. He rendered many valuable services to his new masters, and from 365/975–976, he governed a part of the central Maghrib for the Umayyads while exercising authority on the chiefs of the Banū Īfran, the Maghrāwa, the Miknāsa and other branches of the Zanāta in that region. Jaʿfar was eventually killed in 372/982–983 on the orders of al-Manṣūr Muḥammad b. Abī ʿĀmir (d. 392/1002), the influential chamberlain (*ḥājib*) of the youthful Umayyad caliph al-Hishām II (366–399/976–1009) and the effective ruler of al-Andalus for several decades. Yaḥyā b. ʿAlī, too, served the Umayyads in North Africa, but later returned to the service of the Fāṭimids in Egypt, where he died in the reign of al-Ḥākim.

In the meantime, after pacifying the Maghrib, al-Muʿizz had started making detailed preparations for the conquest of Egypt, a vital Fāṭimid goal which the first two caliphs of Ifrīqiya had failed to achieve. The preparations took some ten years of meticulous work, while al-Muʿizz awaited the opportune moment to launch his invasion. The military base of the Fāṭimid regime was widened to include Berbers from tribes other than the Kutāma, in addition to incorporating Sicilians, Greeks and other non-Berber elements into the Fāṭimid armies. More significantly, al-Muʿizz could now count on the Ṣanhāja for the defence of the Maghrib during major Fāṭimid operations in the east. At the same time, the Fāṭimid *daʿwa* was intensified in Egypt through the activities of Abū Jaʿfar b. Naṣr, Abū ʿĪsā ʿAbd al-ʿAzīz b. Aḥmad, and other *dāʿīs*, as well as many secret agents who advocated the cause of the Fāṭimids and undermined the Ikhshīdids. They also attempted to win over the high military officials and other influential persons of the Ikhshīdid regime, and approached in vain even Kāfūr himself.[52] However, although the Egyptian Muslims respected the numerous ʿAlids living amongst them, Shīʿism had never established roots in Egypt, especially in terms of winning the support of the masses.[53] This state of affairs continued to exist even after the introduction of Ismāʿīlī Shīʿism as the state religion of the country, under the Fāṭimids. In due time, the route of the Fāṭimid expedition to Egypt was carefully chartered while the financial and manpower requirements of the campaign were being determined. Al-Muʿizz had no hesitation in selecting Jawhar to lead the expedition, as this ablest of all the Fāṭimid generals had already proved himself by his shining victories in the Maghrib. Meanwhile, the internal situation of Egypt was rapidly deteriorating due to famine and numerous economic difficulties, natural calamities, and dynastic instability; causing political and civil disorders. In spite of this, Kāfūr, the effective ruler of Egypt for twenty-two years after al-Ikhshīd, had succeeded in averting the Fāṭimid conquest of Egypt. But on Kāfūr's death in 357/968 and the accession to leadership of a weak grandson of al-Ikhsīd, Aḥmad b. ʿAlī (357–358/968–969), the internal disorders soon turned into chaos, aggravated by mutinies in the army. The days of the Ikhshīdid regime were clearly numbered now. And this was fully reported to al-Muʿizz by the famous Ibn Killis, who had sought refuge with the Fāṭimids after Kāfūr's death. Ibn Killis, originally a Jew who had embraced Islam after entering the service of Kāfūr as a fiscal administrator and who may have been won over by the Fāṭimids while still in Egypt, encouraged al-Muʿizz to speed up his conquest. Ibn Killis later accompanied al-Muʿizz to Egypt, where he was to become the first Fāṭimid *wazīr*.

In Rabīʿ I 358/February 969, Jawhar led the Fāṭimid expedition out of Qayrawān after an elaborate ceremonial send-off attended by al-Muʿizz, who, as a reflection of high honour, gave Jawhar his royal garments and ordered all the governors along the way to Egypt to dismount when greeting the general. Jawhar, encountering token resistance near Jīza, entered Fusṭāṭ, the capital of Ikhshīdid Egypt, four months later in Shaʿbān 358/July 969. He behaved diplomatically and leniently towards the Egyptians, declaring a general amnesty and assuring the people of the safety of their lives and property, through a public proclamation. He ordered the name of the reigning ʿAbbāsid caliph, al-Muṭīʿ (334–363/946–974), to be dropped from the *khuṭba* in the Friday sermons, but tolerated religious freedom and introduced the Shīʿī modes of prayer only gradually. Doubtless, he was fully aware of the minoritarian position of the Shīʿīs in Egypt, where the Sunnīs following the Shāfiʿī *madhhab* and the Christians represented the majority. Nevertheless, Egypt was henceforth ruled by an Ismāʿīlī Shīʿī dynasty. Jawhar camped his large army to the north of Fusṭāṭ and immediately proceeded to build a new city there, the future Fāṭimid capital Cairo (al-Qāhira). He also marked the site of the royal palace there, destined for al-Muʿizz and his successors, in accordance with the plans drawn up by the Fāṭimid caliph himself.[54] Soon afterwards, in Jumādā I 359/April 970, Jawhar laid the foundaions of al-Azhar. The original structure of this famous mosque was completed two years later. In 378/988–989, al-Azhar also became a university, the first in the world; it has remained the principal institution of religious learning in the Muslim world. Under the Fāṭimids, al-Azhar played a crucial role also in the dissemination of Ismāʿīlī doctrines, with numerous Ismāʿīlī scholars, jurists and students constantly participating in its seminars. This explains why al-Azhar suffered the hostility of the Sunnī Ayyūbids after the fall of the Fāṭimid dynasty.

The Fāṭimid conquest of Egypt was glorified in the poems of Muḥammad b. Hānī' al-Andalusī, the first great poet of the Maghrib and an ardent Ismāʿīlī.[55] Ibn Hānī' in fact repeats, in a number of panegyrical verses, that not only all of the Muslim world but the entire world belongs legitimately to the Fāṭimid al-Muʿizz. Ibn Hānī' was born in Seville (Ishbīliya), and his father, also a poet, was apparently one of the Fāṭimid missionaries in Muslim Spain. Eventually, Ibn Hānī' too was suspected of pro-Fāṭimid activities and had to flee to the Maghrib from the persecution of the Umayyad ʿAbd al-Raḥmān III, who was a Mālikī Sunnī. After spending some time at the court of the Banū Ḥamdūn at Masīla, the young Ibn Hānī' in 347/958 joined the Fāṭimids and became the chief court-poet and panegyrist of al-Muʿizz. Defending the claims of the Fāṭimids against those of the Sunnī Umayyad and ʿAbbāsid usurpers, he continued to eulogize the merits of al-Muʿizz and other Fāṭimid Imāms, making known their noble aims.[56] He thus rendered a valuable service to Fāṭimid propaganda through his poetry, which was widely read from Cordova to Baghdād. Ibn Hānī' was murdered under mysterious circumstances in 362/973, perhaps by Umayyad or ʿAbbāsid agents, whilst on his way from Ifrīqiya to Egypt.

Having settled in his new quarters, Jawhar became the governor of Egypt for four years, until the arrival of al-Muʿizz. During this period, he assigned high priority to alleviating the problem of famine, improving the country's finances and reforming its existing administrative set-up. His preference was to utilize the Kutāma and other Maghribīs who had accompanied him rather than the Egyptians, especially for the more important government positions. Jawhar also endeavoured to extend Fāṭimid rule beyond Egypt, particularly to the areas previously under Ikhshīdid domination. In 359/969–970, Mecca and Medina submitted readily to the Fāṭimid al-Muʿizz, who had given the local *amīrs* of the two holy cities monetary inducement to ensure their new allegiance. Apart from occasional interruptions, Fāṭimid suzerainty over the Ḥijāz lasted until the fall of the dynasty.[57] It was much more difficult for the Fāṭimids to establish a firm foothold in Syria, hitherto under Ikhshīdid rule, with the Ḥamdānids controlling the northern parts from their seat at Aleppo. The main obstacle to a speedy Fāṭimid victory in Syria was provided by the Qarmaṭīs of Baḥrayn, whose hostility towards the Fāṭimids broke into open warfare following the Fāṭimid conquest of Egypt. The Qarmaṭīs had already cultivated friendly relations with the Ikhshīdids and the Ḥamdānids, besides being ready to receive the help of the ʿAbbāsids and the Buwayhids against the Fāṭimids.

It may be noted that at the time, the Qarmaṭī state was still being ruled jointly by Abū Ṭāhir's brothers. Abū Ṭāhir's eldest son Sābūr (Shāpūr), who aspired to a ruling position and the command of the army, rebelled in vain against his uncles in 358/969; he was captured and executed in the same year. But the ruling sons of Abū Saʿīd al-Jannābī themselves did not survive much longer. Abū Manṣūr Aḥmad died in 359/970, probably of poisoning, and his eldest brother Abu'l-Qāsim Saʿīd died two years later. By 361/972, there remained of Abū Ṭāhir's brothers only Abū Yaʿqūb Yūsuf, who retained a position of pre-eminence in the Qarmaṭī state. Henceforth, the grandsons of Abū Saʿīd were also admitted to the ruling council. After the death of Abū Yaʿqūb in 366/977, the Qarmaṭī state came to be ruled jointly by six of Abū Saʿīd's grandsons, known as *al-sāda al-ruʾasāʾ*.[58] Meanwhile, al-Ḥasan al-Aʿṣam, the son of Abū Manṣūr Aḥmad and a nephew of Abū Ṭāhir, had become the commander of the Qarmaṭī forces. He was usually selected for leading the Qarmaṭīs in their military campaigns outside of Baḥrayn, including their entanglements with the Fāṭimids.

In 357/968, al-Aʿṣam, at the head of the Qarmaṭī army, had taken Damascus after defeating al-Ḥasan b. ʿUbayd Allāh b. Ṭughj, the Ikhshīdid governor of Syria. The Qarmaṭīs had then plundered Ramla and received a substantial tribute from its inhabitants before returning to

Baḥrayn. Three months after the Fāṭimid conquest of Egypt, a Qarmaṭī force, under al-Aʿṣam's cousins, again attacked and defeated the Ikhshīdid al-Ḥasan. The latter, however, managed to have the Qarmaṭīs sign a peace treaty, according to which he was to pay them an annual tribute. Subsequently, the Qarmaṭīs, who never remained in their conquered lands, as they were mainly concerned with augmenting the resources of their treasury, returned to Baḥrayn, leaving behind a small detachment. Soon afterwards, at the beginning of 359/970, a large Fāṭimid army commanded by Jaʿfar b. Falāḥ, sent to conquer Syria, defeated the joint Qarmaṭī and Ikhshīdid forces near Ramla; the Ikhshīdid al-Ḥasan was taken prisoner. The Fāṭimid conquest of Syria, however, meant the loss of the tribute paid previously by the Ikhshīdids to the Qarmaṭīs of Baḥrayn; and this is cited as the main reason for the Qarmaṭī invasion of Syria in the following year. In 360/971, al-Aʿṣam, aided by the Buwayhid ʿIzz al-Dawla Bakhtiyār (356–367/967–978) and the Ḥamdānid Abū Taghlib of Mawṣil, seized Damascus and Ramla, having defeated the Fāṭimids and killed Jaʿfar b. Falāḥ in battle. Al-Aʿṣam, who had also allied himself with the ʿAbbāsids, now proclaimed the suzerainty of the caliphs of Baghdād in these domains and had the Fāṭimid al-Muʿizz cursed in the mosques. Being encouraged by his victories, al-Aʿṣam marched towards Fāṭimid Egypt and advanced to the gates of Cairo, but due to the defection of some of his allies who were bribed by the Fāṭimids, Jawhar's resistance, and internal problems in Baḥrayn, he was obliged to retreat to al-Aḥsā' in Rabīʿ I 361/December 971, with Damascus still remaining in Qarmaṭī hands.

Meanwhile, al-Muʿizz had finished preparations for transferring the seat of the Fāṭimid Caliphate from Ifrīqiya to Egypt. Before embarking on his historic journey in Shawwāl 361/August 972, al-Muʿizz appointed Buluggīn b. Zīrī as his governor of Ifrīqiya, giving him the honorific name Abu'l-Futūḥ Yūsuf. This was a well-deserved reward for the *amīr* of the Ṣanhāja, who, following the precedent set by his father, had faithfully defended the Fāṭimids against the Zanāta and other enemies in North Africa. Buluggīn was in effect vested with the governorship of all the Fāṭimid dominions in the west, except for Kalbid Sicily and for Tripoli, which was placed under the care of the Kutāma Berbers. Thereupon, Buluggīn moved from Ashīr to Qayrawān, where he was to found the Zīrid dynasty (361–543/972–1148). Al-Muʿizz entered Cairo in Ramaḍān 362/June 973, accompanied by his four sons and relatives, most of the Ismāʿīlī notables and *dāʿīs*, including al-Qāḍī al-Nuʿmān who died in the following year, and many Kutāma tribesmen. He had also brought along his treasures and the coffins of his predecessors. This migration marked the termination of the North African phase of the Fāṭimid dynasty.

Akhū Muḥsin, writing shortly after 372/982, has preserved for us the text of a threatening letter sent by al-Muʿizz after his arrival in Cairo, to al-Ḥasan al-Aʿṣam, reproaching him for having deviated from the creed of his forefathers.[59] As Madelung has explained,[60] al-Muʿizz had tried cleverly, but in vain, to convince al-Aʿṣam that Abū Saʿīd and Abū Ṭāhir had been loyal supporters of the Fāṭimids. Al-Aʿṣam made this letter public and denounced the Fāṭimids; as for his response, which he said he would deliver soon, he invaded Egypt in 363/974 for the second time. Al-Aʿṣam besieged Cairo, but betrayed by his ally Ḥassān b. Jarrāḥ, who was commanding the Jarrāḥids of Palestine, he was defeated by the Fāṭimids and retreated to Baḥrayn. Subsequently, the Fāṭimids reoccupied Damascus and al-Muʿizz concluded a peace treaty with the Qarmaṭīs, who successfully demanded to receive the tribute formerly paid to them by the Ikhshīdids.[61] However, soon afterwards, in 364/975, Damascus was seized by the Turk Alftakīn (Alptekin), a former Buwayhid officer in Baghdād. Death prevented al-Muʿizz from expelling Alftakīn from Damascus, where the ambitious rebel had proclaimed the sovereignty of the ʿAbbāsids.

The rule of al-Muʿizz in Egypt lasted just over two years. He had dismissed Jawhar shortly after arriving in Cairo and had entrusted the shrewd Ibn Killis with the task of reorganizing Egypt's financial system. The caliph himself had been mainly preoccupied in Egypt with repelling the menace of the Qarmaṭīs. Having considerably enhanced the power and fortune of his dynasty, and the territorial extent of the Fāṭimid empire, al-Muʿizz li-Dīn Allāh died in Rabīʿ II 365/December 975, at the young age of forty-four and after an imāmate and caliphate of twenty-two years.

Al-Muʿizz was the first of the Fāṭimids who seriously endeavoured to gain the support of the dissident eastern Ismāʿīlīs and to re-establish ideological unity of the Ismāʿīlī movement. He was apparently motivated not only by a desire to utilize the dissident Ismāʿīlīs in the service of his eastward drive to conquer the ʿAbbāsid lands, but also because he was apprehensive of the dangerous influence of the Qarmaṭī ideas on his own followers in the east, the Fāṭimid Ismāʿīlīs, who lived outside the dominions of the Fāṭimid empire. In contrast to his predecessors, who were entirely preoccupied with consolidating their positions, al-Muʿizz could also concern himself with doctrinal issues. As we have noted, he received emissaries from Sind and other remote Fāṭimid Ismāʿīlī communities, and discussed matters of doctrinal importance with them, being particularly alert to rectify their dogmatic misgivings and errors. It has now become evident, through the access to Ismāʿīlī sources, that al-Muʿizz in fact revised the Fāṭimid Ismāʿīlī teachings and accommodated some of the beliefs of the dissident Ismāʿīlīs. The reform of al-Muʿizz implied a partial return to the doctrine of the imāmate held by the majority of the early Ismāʿīlīs.[62] This reform found expression in the works of al-Qāḍī al-Nuʿmān and Jaʿfar b. Manṣūr al-Yaman, the foremost Ismāʿīlī authors of the time, and in certain writings attributed to the Fāṭimid caliph-imām himself.

As noted, ʿUbayd Allāh (ʿAbd Allāh) al-Mahdī had denied the Mahdīship of Muḥammad b. Ismāʿīl by openly claiming the imāmate of the Ismāʿīliyya for himself and his ancestors. The continuity in the imāmate thus propounded by ʿUbayd Allāh, was subsequently corroborated by al-Qāḍī al-Nuʿmān, who explicitly allowed for more than one heptad of imāms in the sixth era of hierohistory, the era of the Prophet Muḥammad.[63] But later, in a treatise written perhaps not too long before his death, al-Nuʿmān came to present a different picture of the Fāṭimid doctrine; one which now incorporated the doctrinal reform of al-Muʿizz, who apparently read al-Nuʿmān's writings with much scrutiny. This treatise seems to have been composed in response to questions put to the learned Qāḍī by an envoy, sent probably by one of the eastern Fāṭimid Ismāʿīlī communities. The questions and al-Nuʿmān's replies are chiefly concerned with the Qā'im and his manifestation. In this work, after reviewing the various Shīʿī ideas hitherto expressed about the Qā'im,[64] al-Nuʿmān explains that the Qā'im essentially has three degrees (*ḥudūd*): the degree in the corporeal world, the degree of resurrection in the spiritual world, and finally, the degree of reckoning (the last judgement). More specifically, he mentions two corporeal degrees for the Qā'im, namely, the degree of speaker-prophet (*nāṭiq*) and that of the rightly-guided deputies or lieutenants (*al-khulafāʾ al-rāshidūn*).

According to al-Nuʿmān, the Qā'im first appeared at the end of the sixth era of history, as the seventh imām of the era of Islam. He had thus attained his first corporeal degree in the person of Muḥammad b. Ismāʿīl, as the seventh *nāṭiq* who had not announced a new *sharīʿa*. However, since the Qā'im had appeared at the time of complete concealment (*satr*), his revelation, too, which consisted of the interpretation of the inner meaning of the religious laws, had remained concealed.[65] This is why the Qā'im appointed deputies (*khulafāʾ*) for himself, in whom he attained his second corporeal degree. It is through these deputies that the Qā'im will reveal the inner meaning of the laws and carry out the deeds prophesied for him; because Muḥammad b. Ismāʿīl will not return. Initially, the deputies were hidden, but starting with ʿUbayd Allāh, they became manifest during the era of unveiling (*dawr al-kashf*); they will continue to rule until the end of the corporeal world, the last of them being the *ḥujja* of the Qā'im. Thereafter, the Qā'im will attain a new degree, appearing in the era of the spiritual world of stars (*dawr al-jirm*) and passing judgement on mankind, before finally ascending to unite with the universal soul.[66] However, this system suffered from an internal anomaly. On the one hand, al-Nuʿmān is extremely careful to emphasize that none of the religious duties specified by the Qur'ān and the Sharīʿa will be dispensed with prior to the Day of Judgement, which meant that the era of Muḥammad and Islam would continue until that time. Yet, according to him, the seventh *dawr*, the eschatological era of the Qā'im–Mahdī, had already begun; since the Qā'im had appeared in the person of Muḥammad b. Ismāʿīl and then in his *khulafā'*, the Fāṭimids. The latter were to disclose his mission by elucidating the hidden meaning of all the previous laws, including the sacred law of Islam.

Similar ideas are found in the writings of al-Muʿizz himself; in *al-Munājāt* ascribed to him by the Syrian Ismāʿīlīs,[67] in his *Seven-Day Prayers*,[68] and elsewhere.[69] Al-Muʿizz, too, speaks of the seven eras of the speaker-prophets and mentions the Qā'im, often referred to as *al-Qā'im bi'l-ḥaqq al-nāṭiq bi'l-ṣidq*, as the seventh *nāṭiq* and the seventh imām of the era of Muḥammad. He does not mention Muḥammad b. Ismāʿīl by name, but he refers to Ismāʿīl b. Jaʿfar as the sixth imām of the era of Muḥammad while counting the Qā'im as the seventh imām and the eighth successor after ʿAlī b. Abī Ṭālib. Clearly then, by the Qā'im he intends to refer to Muḥammad b. Ismāʿīl. The Qā'im, according to al-Muʿizz and al-Nuʿmān, does not announce a new *sharīʿa*, but merely reveals the inner meaning of the previous laws. Al-Muʿizz also speaks of the *khulafā'* who act righteously and represent the doctrine and the deeds of the Qā'im. He further adds that there is no Qā'im and Lord of the Time (*Ṣāḥib al-Zamān*) besides the imām of the time, who interprets the inner meaning of the laws.[70] In other words, al-Muʿizz denies the corporeal return of Muḥammad b. Ismāʿīl as the Qā'im because the Fāṭimids, as his deputies, had already fully assumed his functions.

The doctrinal reform of al-Muʿizz is also reflected in the latest works of

Jaʿfar b. Manṣūr al-Yaman. In his *al-Shawāhid wa'l-bayān* and his *Ta'wīl al-zakāt*, completed in the final years of al-Muʿizz (both of which are still in manuscript form),[71] Jaʿfar discusses the eras of the seven *nāṭiqs*; the seventh one being that of the Qā'im Muḥammad b. Ismāʿīl and of his *khulafā'*. It is interesting to note that Jaʿfar gives great importance to the Qā'im, the revealer of all laws, and his lieutenants, in contradistinction to the ordinary *nāṭiqs*. Very little is known about the life of Jaʿfar, the son of the famous Yamanī *dāʿī* Ibn Ḥawshab (Manṣūr al-Yaman). After the death of Ibn Ḥawshab, when ʿUbayd Allāh al-Mahdī appointed ʿAbd Allāh b. ʿAbbās al-Shāwirī as head of the Ismāʿīlī *daʿwa* in Yaman, Jaʿfar alone amongst his brothers remained loyal to the Fāṭimids. His elder brother Ḥasan (or Abu'l-Ḥasan), who had expected to succeed his father, defected from the *daʿwa* and had the *dāʿī* al-Shāwirī assassinated. It was under these circumstances that Jaʿfar, as a partisan of the Fāṭimids, migrated to North Africa and joined the court of the second Fāṭimid caliph al-Qā'im at Mahdiyya. In 335/947, under al-Manṣūr, he fought against Abū Yazīd. In fact, Jaʿfar has celebrated the various Fāṭimid victories over the Khārijī rebels in several poems.[72] Subsequently, he rose to literary prominence and became one of the leading representatives of the Ismāʿīlī *ta'wīl* under al-Muʿizz, who held Jaʿfar in high esteem and is also reported to have helped him financially.[73] In Ifrīqiya, Jaʿfar evidently did not hold any public office and devoted his time entirely to writing; but Idrīs relates that he rose to a high rank in the *daʿwa*, even superior to that of his contemporary al-Qāḍī al-Nuʿmān, under al-Muʿizz. Jaʿfar b. Manṣūr al-Yaman died at an unknown date, not too long after al-Muʿizz.[74]

In sum, through his reform, al-Muʿizz introduced important changes into the doctrine of the imāmate held by the Fāṭimid Ismāʿīlīs. He acknowledged the imāmates of Ismāʿīl b. Jaʿfar and his son Muḥammad, to whom he traced his genealogy, instead of the imāmate of ʿAbd Allāh b. Jaʿfar, named by ʿUbayd Allāh, in his letter, as the progenitor of the Fāṭimids. He again attributed to Muḥammad b. Ismāʿīl, as the seventh imām of the era of Islam, the rank of the Qā'im and the *nāṭiq* of the final era, but with a different interpretation compared to that held by the pre-Fāṭimid Ismāʿīlīs. Since the Qā'im Muḥammad b. Ismāʿīl had appeared in the time of complete concealment, his functions were to be undertaken by his deputies or *khulafā'*, the Fāṭimid Ismāʿīlī Imāms, who were his descendants. Al-Muʿizz also permitted the incorporation of Neoplatonism, more specifically an Ismāʿīlī Neoplatonic cosmology, into Fāṭimid thought. As a result, the works of the early representatives of this cosmology who ranked amongst the dissident Ismāʿīlīs came to be studied by the Fāṭimid *dāʿīs* and authors.

The efforts of al-Muʿizz to gain the allegiance of the dissident Ismāʿīlīs were partially successful. He won over the *dāʿī* al-Sijistānī, who endorsed the imāmate of the Fāṭimids in the works he wrote after the accession of al-Muʿizz. Consequently, the Ismāʿīlīs of Khurāsān, as well as of Sīstān and Makrān, to a great extent came to support the Fāṭimid cause. Al-Muʿizz also succeeded in establishing a Fāṭimid foothold in Sind, in northern India. As noted previously, around the year 347/958, a Fāṭimid vassal state was founded in Sind, with its seat at Multān, serving as the *dār al-hijra* for the Ismāʿīlīs of that state, through the efforts of a Fāṭimid *dāʿī* who had converted the local ruler. But the *dāʿī* in question evidently also manifested some dissident Ismāʿīlī tendencies, and while al-Muʿizz was contemplating his removal, he was killed in a riding incident. He was succeeded around 354/965 by the *dāʿī* Ḥalam (or Jalam) b. Shaybān, who was completely loyal to the Fāṭimids. The sovereignty of al-Muʿizz was now openly proclaimed in Multān, where the *khuṭba* was read in the name of the Fāṭimid caliphs, instead of their ʿAbbāsid rivals. This Ismāʿīlī state survived until 396/1005–1006, when Maḥmūd of Ghazna invaded Multān and made its last Ismāʿīlī ruler, Abu'l-Futūḥ Dā'ūd b. Naṣr, a tributary. A few years later, in 401/1010–1011, Multān was actually annexed to the Ghaznawid dominions; Abu'l-Futūḥ was taken prisoner and the Ismāʿīlīs of Multān and its surrounding areas were ruthlessly massacred.[75] Another local ruler in Sind, belonging to the Ḥabbārid dynasty ruling from Manṣūra, was later converted to Fāṭimid Ismāʿīlism around 401 A.H.; he apparently made Ismāʿīlism the official religion of his state. Soon afterwards, this Ismāʿīlī ruler too, perhaps called Khafīf, was overthrown by Maḥmūd, who invaded Manṣūra in 416/1025.[76] Despite these setbacks and the continued hostilities of the Sunnī Ghaznawids, Fāṭimid Ismāʿīlism survived in Sind and later became the creed of the Sūmras, who revolted against the Ghaznawids in 443/1051 and established their independent dynasty, ruling from Thatta for almost three centuries.[77] However, Qarmaṭī Ismāʿīlism persisted in some parts of Persia, notably in Daylam and Ādharbayjān, as well as in southern ʿIrāq, even though the Fāṭimids had now endeavoured to restore the name of ʿAbdān and permitted the study of his works. Above all, al-Muʿizz failed in the case of the Qarmaṭīs of eastern Arabia, with whose co-operation he might well have realized his dream of conquering Baghdād and supplanting the ʿAbbāsids.

Al-Muʿizz was succeeded by his third son Abū Manṣūr Nizār, who adopted the regal title of al-ʿAzīz biʾllāh and became the first Fāṭimid caliph to begin his rule in Egypt.[78] He had been designated as the heir apparent or *walī al-ʿahd* only about a year earlier, after the death of his elder brother ʿAbd Allāh in 364/975. Al-Muʿizz had originally nominated his second son ʿAbd Allāh as his successor, in preference to his eldest son Tamīm, since the latter had been suspected of cooperating with those Fāṭimids intriguing against al-Muʿizz. Several documents preserved in Jawdhar's *Sīra*, compiled in the time of al-ʿAzīz, in fact reveal the existence of certain hitherto unknown discords within the inner circles of the Fāṭimid family during the reigns of al-Manṣūr and al-Muʿizz.[79] According to these documents, some of the sons of the first two Fāṭimid caliphs, from amongst al-Manṣūr's uncles and brothers, apparently disagreed strongly with certain policies pursued by al-Manṣūr and his successor, becoming involved in activities against their ruling relatives. The *amīr* Tamīm, born in 337/948–949, had close relations with some of these discordant Fāṭimids, and evidently maintained secret correspondence with them, a fact which was brought to the attention of his father. It was probably due to these contacts, as well as his reportedly libertine manner of living, that Tamīm was passed over as the first in line for succession, in favour of his younger brother ʿAbd Allāh.[80] Around the year 357 A.H., al-Muʿizz designated ʿAbd Allāh as the heir apparent to the Fāṭimid Caliphate and successor to the Ismāʿīlī Imāmate. This nomination, which later surprised many courtiers and members of the Fāṭimid family, was at first divulged by the caliph only to the highly trusted Jawdhar (d. 363/973–974). Jawdhar, in turn, kept this secret for seven months, according to his master's instructions and reminiscent of an earlier precedent set by the caliph al-Qāʾim.[81] After ʿAbd Allāh's death, al-Muʿizz, acting contrary to the beliefs of some of the earliest Ismāʿīlīs (the Mubārakiyya), who had maintained that the imāmate could no longer be transferred between brothers after al-Ḥasan and al-Ḥusayn b. ʿAlī, designated another son, Nizār, as his successor. On this occasion, Tamīm was passed over a second time, now in favour of a yet younger brother seven years his junior. Tamīm had meanwhile shunned political activity, and, unlike ʿAbd Allāh and Nizār, had not participated in any expeditions against the Qarmaṭīs. Instead, he had devoted himself to literary activities and had acquired a reputation as a poet. Tamīm b. al-Muʿizz died at an early age in Cairo, in 374 or 5/984–986.[82]

The consolidation and extension of Fāṭimid power in Syria, at the expense of the ʿAbbāsids and the Byzantines, became the primary objective of al-ʿAzīz in the field of territorial expansion and foreign policy. In 365/976, immediately after his accession, al-ʿAzīz despatched a Fāṭimid army to Syria under the veteran Jawhar, to retake Damascus from Alftakīn, who had allied himself with the Qarmaṭīs. But upon the arrival of new Qarmaṭī forces led by al-Aʿṣam, Jawhar was obliged to retreat to Ramla and then to ʿAsqalān, where he was besieged for nearly seventeen months. During this period, al-Aʿṣam died at Ramla in 366/977, and his cousin Jaʿfar succeeded him as the commander of the Qarmaṭīs. Jawhar was eventually permitted in 367 A.H., under humiliating conditions, to return to Egypt, where he led a quiet life until his death in 381/992. Meanwhile, al-ʿAzīz himself had taken the field and defeated Alftakīn and the Qarmaṭīs near Ramla in 368/978. Alftakīn was taken captive, and the Qarmaṭīs agreed to a peace, again on the condition of receiving a sizeable tribute. Henceforth, the Qarmaṭīs of Baḥrayn were rapidly reduced to a local power. Al-ʿAzīz treated Alftakīn generously, taking him and his Turks into his service; but Alftakīn soon became a victim of the jealousy and hatred of the all-powerful Ibn Killis and was poisoned at his instigation in 372/982. In spite of the victory of al-ʿAzīz in Syria, Damascus remained only nominally in Fāṭimid hands for some time. Shortly afterwards, it was seized by Qassām, one of Alftakīn's former assistants. A Fāṭimid army under al-Faḍl b. Ṣāliḥ failed to defeat Qassām and withdrew to Palestine. There, a series of negotiations took place between the Fāṭimid general and the Ḥamdānid Abū Taghlib who, having been driven out of Mawṣil by the Buwayhid ʿAḍud al-Dawla (367–372/978–983) and having subsequently failed to take Damascus, now aspired to obtain the governorship of that city from al-ʿAzīz.[83] Abū Taghlib promised to help al-Faḍl in his renewed attempt to conquer Damascus. But the Fāṭimid general had already allied himself with the Jarrāḥid Mufarrij b. Daghfal, the master of Palestine who now competed with Abū Taghlib for the favour of al-ʿAzīz. The co-operation between Mufarrij, who captured and killed Abū Taghlib in 369/979, and the vacillating Fāṭimid general al-Faḍl, also proved to be short-lived. Soon, Mufarrij joined Qassām, who had meanwhile continued to resist the Fāṭimids; but the two rebels were finally defeated in 372–373/982–983 by Baltakīn, a Turkish general in the service of the Fāṭimids. Mufarrij fled to Antioch, seeking refuge with the Byzantines, while Qassām was sent to Cairo. It may be noted that al-ʿAzīz was the first Fāṭimid to employ the services of the Turks in the Fāṭimid armies, to the strong disapproval of his Berber officers; a practice that later led to serious consequences for the Fāṭimids.

Al-ʿAzīz also aimed to expand into northern Syria; and in the pursuit of this objective, he capitalized on the enmity existing between the Ḥamdānid *amīr* of Aleppo, Saʿd al-Dawla (356–381/967–991), and the latter's rebellious governor of Ḥimṣ, Bakjūr, who encouraged the Fāṭimid caliph in his conquest of Aleppo. In 373/983, Bakjūr besieged Aleppo with the help of al-ʿAzīz, but soon became obliged to lift the siege and flee, on the approach of a Byzantine army sent to aid the Ḥamdānids. Nevertheless, al-ʿAzīz kept his promise and gave Bakjūr the governorship of Damascus. In 376/986, Saʿd al-Dawla, weary of the declining power of the Buwayhids in the region, nominally acknowledged the sovereignty of the Fāṭimids. In spite of this, al-ʿAzīz did not abandon his plan to possess Aleppo. A few years later, Bakjūr, who had meanwhile been expelled from Damascus in 378/988 due to the intrigues of Ibn Killis, again easily persuaded the Fāṭimid caliph to entrust him with the command of a new expedition against the Ḥamdānids of northern Syria. Receiving insufficient aid from the local Fāṭimid forces, he was defeated and killed in 381/991 by Saʿd al-Dawla, who was assisted effectively by the Byzantines. Following this victory, Saʿd al-Dawla seriously contemplated the invasion of the Fāṭimid possessions in Syria, when he died in 381 A.H. From 382/992 until his own death four years later, al-ʿAzīz made better organized attempts to conquer Aleppo but without any results, owing to the vital assistance extended by Byzantium to Saʿd al-Dawla's son and successor Saʿīd al-Dawla (381–392/991–1002). On one occasion in 385/995, when Aleppo had been besieged for several months by Fāṭimid forces under the Turk Mangūtakīn, the governor of Damascus, the Byzantine emperor Basil II (976–1025) personally rushed to the scene and saved the city from falling into Fāṭimid hands.

The foreign policy of al-ʿAzīz was not very active outside of Syria; and in Syria, as noted, he acquired Damascus but failed in his conquest of the Ḥamdānid amīrate of Aleppo, a Byzantine tributary. He did, however, manage to obtain favourable terms in a treaty with the emperor Basil II, who now removed the Byzantine commercial restrictions against the Fāṭimids. Al-ʿAzīz avoided direct confrontation with the Sunnī ʿAbbāsids and the Shīʿī Buwayhids in ʿIrāq, but tried in vain through diplomatic negotiations to have ʿAḍud al-Dawla recognize the sovereignty of the Fāṭimids. In the case of the Qarmaṭīs of Baḥrayn, al-ʿAzīz received their nominal and interrupted allegiance, mainly by paying them large annual tributes. Finally, in North Africa, al-ʿAzīz confirmed Buluggīn in his position, but under the latter's son and successor al-Manṣūr (373–386/984–996), who fought the Kutāma, the Zīrids had already begun to detach themselves from the Fāṭimid Caliphate. At any event, it was towards the end of the reign of al-ʿAzīz that the Fāṭimid empire attained, at least nominally, its greatest extent, with the Fāṭimid sovereignty being recognized from the Atlantic and the western Mediterranean to the Red Sea, the Ḥijāz, Yaman, Syria and Palestine. The *khuṭba* was read in the name of al-ʿAzīz also in Multān, and, for a short while in 382/992, even in Mawṣil, then ruled by the ʿUqaylid Abu'l-Dawādh Muḥammad (382–386/992–996), the *amīr* of the Banū ʿUqayl who had seized the region from the last Ḥamdānids of Mawṣil. At the same time, the Fāṭimid *dāʿīs* had continued to be active in many eastern regions beyond the frontiers of the Fāṭimid empire, notably in various parts of Persia.[84]

Most sources name al-ʿAzīz as the best and wisest of all the Fāṭimid caliphs of Egypt. Besides being an excellent administrator, he knew how to utilize the services of capable men, without much regard for their religious beliefs. In regulating the affairs of the state, al-ʿAzīz was greatly helped by Abu'l-Faraj Yaʿqūb b. Yūsuf b. Killis, who had continued to serve him in various financial and administrative capacities after the death of al-Muʿizz.[85] In 367/977, al-ʿAzīz made Ibn Killis his vizier, and in 368/978, the caliph conferred on him the title of *al-wazīr al-ajall* (the illustrious vizier). Ibn Killis thus became the first vizier of the Fāṭimid dynasty and retained that position, except for two temporary dismissals, for over twelve years until his death. He was also highly instrumental in giving Egypt an extended period of economic prosperity. Al-ʿAzīz repeatedly failed to listen to the advice of his vizier against invading Aleppo. Nevertheless, the Fāṭimid success in Syria owed much to Ibn Killis, through whose policies the complicated situation in Syria resulting from the conflicting activities of Qassām, the Ḥamdānids and the Jarrāḥids was finally brought under control. Ibn Killis was also noted for his patronage of scholars, jurists and poets, according pensions to such men in his own entourage. He himself was an expert in Ismāʿīlī jurisprudence, which had meanwhile been developed by al-Qāḍī al-Nuʿmān; he composed a legal treatise, known as *al-Risāla al-wazīriyya*, based on the pronouncements of al-Muʿizz and al-ʿAzīz. This was indeed a remarkable achievement for someone who had converted to Islam from Judaism. The credit for utilizing al-Azhar as a university also belongs to Ibn Killis who, moreover, supervised the construction of what later became known as the mosque of al-Ḥākim. Al-ʿAzīz found it difficult to replace this outstanding vizier, who died in 380/991, with a suitable successor. Ibn Killis was followed in rapid succession by six viziers in as many years, during the remainder of the caliphate of al-ʿAzīz, the last of whom was a Coptic Christian, ʿĪsā b. Nasṭūrus (385–386/995–996).[86] The latter was the first of the several Christians to occupy the vizierate under the Fāṭimids. Al-ʿAzīz also appointed the Jews to high positions, though never to the vizierate; probably under the influence of Ibn Killis who had maintained friendly relations with the Jewish community after his own conversion. In this respect, mention may be made of Manashshā (Manasseh) b. Ibrāhīm, a close associate of Ibn Killis, who was given important posts in Fāṭimid Syria.

The unusual policy of assigning numerous high administrative posts to Christians and Jews in a Shīʿī Muslim state was basically in line with the religious toleration practised by the Fāṭimids. But al-ʿAzīz went further than his predecessors and set remarkable precedents in this area, probably being also encouraged by his Christian wife, perhaps the mother of his only surviving son and successor. It was in fact through the recommendations of al-ʿAzīz that his two brothers-in-law, Orestes and Arsenius, became respectively the Melkite patriarch of Jerusalem and the metropolitan of Cairo in 375/986. Moreover, the caliph behaved rather favourably, despite Muslim opposition, towards the Coptic patriarch Ephraim, allowing him to rebuild the church of St Mercurius near Fusṭāṭ. The Christians in particular enjoyed a large degree of religious freedom and participation in government under al-ʿAzīz, as attested by the appointment of Ibn Nasṭūrus to the vizierate and the caliph's open disposition to religious disputations between Severus, the bishop of Ashmūnayn, and *al-qāḍī* Ibn al-Nuʿmān, the Fāṭimid chief jurist. The tolerant religious policy of al-ʿAzīz towards the *ahl al-dhimma* led to growing discontent amongst the predominantly Sunnī Egyptian Muslims, who later reacted by plundering several churches and murdering a number of Christians in 386/996, after the death of al-ʿAzīz. Al-ʿAzīz himself was a devout Shīʿī who greatly encouraged the observance of the mourning ceremonies of *ʿĀshūrāʾ*, commemorating the martyrdom of the Imām al-Ḥusayn at Karbalāʾ some three centuries earlier, and the Shīʿī feast of *al-Ghadīr*, celebrating the investiture of ʿAlī b. Abī Ṭālib at Ghadīr Khumm. Both ceremonies had been introduced to Fāṭimid Egypt under al-Muʿizz.[87] These Shīʿī ceremonies were actually inaugurated at Baghdād in 352–353/

963–964, in the time of the Buwayhid Muʿizz al-Dawla (334–356/945–967), under whose successors Twelver Shīʿī thought and practices started to be systematically developed. The Buwayhids, who originally adhered to Zaydī Shīʿism, also embellished the ʿAlid shrines of ʿIrāq.

Al-ʿAzīz bi'llāh had personally set out to lead the Fāṭimid armies, in yet another expedition against the joint forces of the Ḥamdānids of Aleppo and the Byzantines, when he suddenly fell ill and died at Bilbays, the first stop on his route to Syria, in Ramaḍān 386/October 996. His reign had lasted nearly twenty-one years. He was succeeded by his son Abū ʿAlī al-Manṣūr, with the *laqab* (honorific title) of al-Ḥākim bi-Amr Allāh, who was then about eleven years of age. He had been designated as *walī al-ʿahd* in 383/993, following the death of his elder and only brother Muḥammad. Al-Ḥākim, the most controversial member of his dynasty and the first Fāṭimid ruler to have been born in Egypt, received the *bayʿa* as caliph in Bilbays, to where he had accompanied his father immediately on the latter's death. He made his entry into Cairo on the following day.[88]

Al-Ḥākim faced many problems during his relatively long caliphate. Initially, the struggle between the so-called al-Maghāriba, the western faction of the army consisting of the Berbers, and al-Mashāriqa, the eastern faction comprised mainly of Turkish and Daylamī troops, overshadowed other difficulties. It will be recalled that it was al-ʿAzīz who had encouraged the employment of Turks, along with other non-Berber groups, in his forces. This policy had been adopted in order to facilitate the Fāṭimid conquest of the eastern lands, since the Turks were skilful fighters in addition to having had the valuable experience of serving in the ʿAbbāsid armies. Furthermore, al-ʿAzīz may also have aimed at undermining the monopolistic military position of the Berbers, comprised mainly of the Kutāma tribesmen, in the Fāṭimid state. To the discontent of the Berbers, the Turks had rapidly come to occupy the most important posts in the Fāṭimid armies, giving rise to serious rivalry and animosity between the two main factions of the Fāṭimid armies; the Berbers, who had traditionally provided the backbone of the Fāṭimid troops, and the newly recruited easterners, led by the Turks. This rivalry reached the point of open warfare during the early years of al-Ḥākim's rule.

The death of al-ʿAzīz had provided a suitable opportunity for the Berbers to reassert themselves. Now, the Kutāma demanded that the leadership of the government be entrusted to their chief, al-Ḥasan b. ʿAmmār. The youthful caliph capitulated and appointed Ibn ʿAmmār as his *wāsiṭa*, the highest administrator acting as the intermediary between the caliph and his officials and subjects, a ministerial position without the specific office or title of vizier. This position, known as *wasāṭa*, henceforth became rather common under the Fāṭimids. Ibn ʿAmmār thus replaced Ibn Nasṭūrus, who was executed soon afterwards. As expected, Ibn ʿAmmār began to improve the relative position of the Berbers in the army, at the expense of al-Mashāriqa. His policies soon alarmed Barjawān, the tutor and guardian of al-Ḥākim since before the latter's accession. Being a highly ambitious person, Barjawān envisaged becoming the caliph's chief official. To this end, he sought the support of al-Mashāriqa, and, in particular, made an alliance with Mangūtakīn, the governor of Damascus, who was induced to march towards Egypt at the head of his forces. However, Mangūtakīn, abandoned along the way by his ever unreliable ally the Jarrāḥid Mufarrij, was defeated near ʿAsqalān by Ibn ʿAmmār's forces, which were commanded by Sulaymān b. Jaʿfar b. Fallāḥ. The Berber Sulaymān now became the new governor of Damascus, and soon committed the serious error of dismissing Jaysh b. Ṣamṣām, a powerful Kutāma chief, from the governorship of Tripoli, replacing him with his own brother ʿAlī. Shortly afterwards, Barjawān allied himself with the dissatisfied Jaysh, who had the support of a number of other Berber chiefs, and challenged Ibn ʿAmmār's authority. This time, Ibn ʿAmmār, failing to check the street riots in Cairo which culminated in open revolt, was defeated and forced into hiding. Barjawān now seized power as *wāsiṭa*, in Ramaḍān 387/October 997, and became the effective ruler of the Fāṭimid state for four years.[89] He dealt leniently with the defeated Berbers and even pardoned Ibn ʿAmmār who was, however, executed later. But the loss of the position of the Berbers in the army proved to be irreversible.

Barjawān, a eunuch slave of uncertain origins, governed competently with the help of his able secretary, the Christian Fahd b. Ibrāhīm. He also attempted to reconcile the differences between al-Maghāriba and al-Mashāriqa. But he dealt harshly with the disorders in Syria, where he had sent Jaysh b. Ṣamṣām as his governor. At Tyre, Jaysh repressed the rebellion of a certain Arab adventurer, ʿAllāqa, who was supported by a Byzantine fleet; Jaysh also subdued Mufarrij. Jaysh then restored order to Damascus and defeated the Byzantines at Afāmiya in northern Syria. Following these victories, peace negotiations commenced between the Fāṭimids and the Byzantines, at the initiative of the emperor Basil II, resulting in a ten-year truce beginning in 391/1001. However, Barjawān was not so successful with his policies in the Maghrib. He did repress the disturbances at Barqa, but acted unwisely in engaging the Fāṭimid troops in battle for the first time against the Ṣanhāja Berbers serving the third Zīrid, Bādīs b. al-Manṣūr (386–406/996–1016), over the control of Tripoli. This conflict undermined the position of the Fāṭimids in the Maghrib, further weakening the loyalty of the Zīrids towards them. It was under Bādīs that the control of the western parts of the Zīrid dominions, in the central Maghrib, was given to Ḥammād b. Buluggīn b. Zīrī (405–419/1015–1028), the progenitor of the Banū Ḥammād branch of the Zīrid family. The latter, in effect, became the founder of the Ḥammādid dynasty of the Maghrib, ruling from their newly constructed capital at Qalʿat Banī Ḥammād, northeast of Masīla,[90] while the Zīrids continued to rule over Ifrīqiya proper from Qayrawān. Both dynasties were extinguished in the third quarter of the 6th/12th century, their territories passing to the Almohads (al-Muwaḥḥidūn).

In the meantime, al-Ḥākim had developed a deep hatred for Barjawān, who had been severe and disciplinarian with the caliph, limiting his authority and restricting him to the palace. Al-Ḥākim had Barjawān killed in 390/1000, with the encouragement and collaboration of another eunuch slave Raydān. Henceforth, al-Ḥākim became the real ruler of the Fāṭimid state. Starting with al-Ḥusayn b. Jawhar, who succeeded Barjawān, al-Ḥākim limited both the spheres of authority and the terms of office of his *wazīr*s and *wāsiṭa*s, of whom there were more than fifteen during the last twenty years of his caliphate. Al-Ḥākim issued an endless series of the most extraordinary decrees, which were often abolished or reversed at later dates. His changing moods and eccentricities have given rise to many different descriptions of his character, even causing some to regard al-Ḥākim as a person of unbalanced character. However, some sources regard him as a wise and tactful leader, and have praises for al-Ḥākim's patronage of the arts and sciences. Al-Ḥākim also maintained a keen interest in the *daʿwa* organization and activities, paying special attention to the education of the Fāṭimid *dāʿī*s.

One of the distinguishing features of al-Ḥākim's reign was the adoption of persecutory measures against Christians and Jews. His anti-*dhimmī* policy, which took definite shape by 395/1004, was doubtless partially motivated by the caliph's desire to enhance his popularity amongst the Muslims of Egypt, who had become increasingly antagonistic towards the *dhimmī*s under al-ʿAzīz. Furthermore, by directing his anti-Christian measures mainly against the Melkites, he may have wished to win the support of the Copts, who comprised the Christian majority in Egypt. At any event, al-Ḥākim imposed numerous restrictions on Christians and

Jews, who were also obliged to observe Islamic law. A large number of churches and monasteries were demolished; others were converted to mosques, while their properties and revenues were confiscated. Only the monastery of Mt Sinai was spared. In 400/1009, al-Ḥākim even ordered the destruction of the church of the Holy Sepulchre at Jerusalem,[91] an act which greatly anguished the Christians throughout the world and brought to an end the Fāṭimid-Byzantine truce. In 406/1015–1016, the emperor Basil II issued an edict forbidding commercial relations between Byzantium and the Fāṭimid Caliphate, initiating a declining trend in Fāṭimid trade with Europe. On the other hand, in 404/1013, al-Ḥākim allowed those Christians and Jews who had been obliged to embrace Islam to revert to their original faiths or to emigrate to Byzantine territories. Still later, he restored some of the churches and adopted a more tolerant attitude towards the Christians and their religious practices. In the meantime, al-Ḥākim had maintained his anti-Sunnī measures, although at times he intensified them and then had them temporarily revoked. For instance, his order for the denouncement of Abū Bakr, his two successors and others amongst the Ṣaḥāba, issued in 395 A.H. and according to which the relevant maledictions were inscribed on the walls of the mosques, was repealed after two years, only to be reintroduced in 403/1013.

One of al-Ḥākim's most important acts was the foundation of the Dār al-Ḥikma (House of Wisdom), sometimes also called the Dār al-ʿIlm, which was set up in 395/1005 in a section of the Fāṭimid palace in Cairo.[92] This institute of learning, with its fine library, which served as a meeting place for traditionists, jurists, astronomers and others, was utilized for the propagation of Shīʿī doctrines in general and Fāṭimid Ismāʿīlism in particular. Being directed by the *dāʿī al-duʿāt*, the chief *dāʿī*, the Dār al-Ḥikma was in fact closely associated with the Fāṭimid *daʿwa* activities; and it remained operational, with the exception of a few decades, to the end of the Fāṭimid dynasty. Fāṭimid Ismāʿīlī doctrines, called *ḥikma* since the time of the caliph al-Muʿizz, were instructed at the lecture halls of this institute where *dāʿīs* were also trained. Al-Ḥākim often attended the lectures at the Dār al-Ḥikma, some of which were reserved only for Ismāʿīlīs. Some Sunnī jurists, too, were permitted to teach at the Dār al-Ḥikma. In 400 A.H., al-Ḥākim apparently founded a separate Sunnī institute of learning at Fusṭāṭ, under two Mālikī scholars;[93] this institute was however closed down three years later. Amidst his religious policies, al-Ḥākim concerned himself with the moral standards of his subjects and issued many edicts of an ethico-social nature. He was also prepared to mete out severe punishments. A long list of *wazīrs*, *wāsiṭas*, commanders and other dignitaries, starting with Barjawān, lost their lives at his order, including Fahd b. Ibrāhīm, ʿAlī b. al-Ḥusayn al-Maghribī, Ṣāliḥ b. ʿAlī, Manṣūr b. ʿAbdūn, al-Faḍl b. Ṣāliḥ, al-Ḥusayn b. Jawhar, al-Ḥusayn b. Ẓāhir al-Wazzān, and al-Faḍl b. Jaʿfar b. al-Furāt; in addition to a number of his concubines and numerous ordinary prisoners. Of the five persons who held the post of chief *dāʿī* under al-Ḥākim, al-Ḥusayn b. ʿAlī b. al-Nuʿmān, and his cousin ʿAbd al-ʿAzīz b. Muḥammad b. al-Nuʿmān as well as Mālik b. Saʿīd, all three prominent personalities who simultaneously held the prestigious office of *qāḍī al-quḍāt*, or chief *qāḍī*, were executed.

There occurred several disturbances and open revolts during al-Ḥākim's caliphate. The most serious of these revolts, lasting about two years, was that of Abū Rakwa Walīd b. Hishām, who claimed to be related to the Umayyads of Spain. He started his revolt in 395/1004 in the region of Barqa (Cyrenaica), receiving support from the Zanāta Berbers and the Arab tribe of the Banū Qurra. Abū Rakwa defeated the Fāṭimid forces sent against him and seized Barqa at the end of 395/1005. About a year after this victory, Abū Rakwa left Barqa on the verge of famine and plague and besieged Alexandria for several months. Subsequently, he proceeded as far as Fayyūm, where the rebels were eventually defeated by Fāṭimid troops under the command of al-Faḍl b. Ṣāliḥ. Abū Rakwa, who had sought refuge in Nubia, was delivered to the Fāṭimids; he was executed in Cairo in 397/1007. It was during this revolt that al-Ḥākim decided to adopt more liberal policies, also revising his anti-Sunnī measures.

The Jarrāḥids of Palestine led another important rebellion against al-Ḥākim. The ambitious Mufarrij b. Daghfal, who had helped the Fāṭimids against Abū Rakwa, but was always ready to change sides and desired a semi-independent state of his own, revolted openly in 402/1011–1012. He ambushed and killed the new Fāṭimid governor of Damascus, the Turk Yārūkh, and then occupied Ramla, the main city of southern Palestine. In 403/1012, Mufarrij, assisted by his three sons, took the further significant step of proclaiming an anti-caliph in the person of the *sharīf* of Mecca, the ʿAlid al-Ḥasan b. Jaʿfar, known as Abu'l-Futūḥ. The latter was acknowledged as such in the Ḥijāz and Palestine, where the *khuṭba* came to be read in his name. However, the victory of the Jarrāḥids lasted just over two years, during which time Mufarrij attempted to win the favour of the Byzantine emperor and the Christians of Jerusalem by the partial restoration of the church of the Holy Sepulchre. Al-Ḥākim succeeded in persuading the Jarrāḥids to abandon the anti-caliph, whom they had set up at

Ramla. Abu'l-Futūḥ now chose to return to Mecca, where he was pardoned by al-Ḥākim. He was reappointed as the *sharīf* of Mecca by the Fāṭimid caliph.[94] But the Jarrāḥids continued to retain their mastery of Palestine, where they menaced the inhabitants and raided the pilgrim caravans going from Egypt to the Ḥijāz. In 404/1013, al-Ḥākim decided to deal with the Jarrāḥids more effectively and sent a large army against them. At the same time, Mufarrij died suddenly, perhaps having been poisoned. Thereupon, two of Mufarrij's sons, ʿAlī and Maḥmūd, surrendered, while the third, Ḥassān, later succeeded in obtaining al-Ḥākim's pardon. Ḥassān b. Mufarrij, who was permitted to regain his father's lands in Palestine and who now became the dominant figure of the Jarrāḥid family, remained loyal to the Fāṭimids throughout the rest of al-Ḥākim's reign.[95]

In North Africa, al-Ḥākim did not lose any important territory. However, during the last years of his caliphate, the Ismāʿīlīs began to be severely persecuted in Ifrīqiya. Ismāʿīlism had never deeply penetrated the masses there, including the region's Berber tribesmen; and only small urban groups, in addition to the Kutāma and other Ṣanhāja Berbers, had been won over by the Fāṭimid *daʿwa*. With the transfer of the seat of the Fāṭimid Caliphate to Cairo, large numbers of the Kutāma tribesmen and leading *dāʿīs* had migrated to Egypt, leaving behind in Ifrīqiya the superficially converted Ṣanhāja to defend Ismāʿīlism in an overwhelmingly Sunnī state. This state was ruled by the Zīrids, who were rapidly losing their own allegiance towards the Fāṭimids. Consequently, the conditions had soon become opportune for the anti-Shīʿī sentiments of the Sunnī inhabitants of Ifrīqiya. In 407/1016–1017, following the accession of the Zīrid al-Muʿizz b. Bādīs (406–454/1016–1062), the Ismāʿīlīs of Qayrawān, Mahdiyya, Tunis, Tripoli, and other towns, were attacked and massacred by the Sunnīs of Ifrīqiya, under the leadership of their Mālikī jurists and scholars, and with the connivance of the government. These persecutions and popular riots against the Ismāʿīlīs continued, and the Ismāʿīlī communities of Ifrīqiya were practically extinguished by the time the Zīrid al-Muʿizz transferred his allegiance to the ʿAbbāsids a few decades later.[96]

On the other hand, al-Ḥākim was successful in Syria and finally managed to extend Fāṭimid authority to the amīrate of Aleppo, which had begun to decline after the assassination in 392/1002 of the Ḥamdānid Saʿīd al-Dawla on the orders of his minister Lu'lu'. After this event, Lu'lu' became the effective ruler in Aleppo, though initially he acted as regent for

Saʿīd al-Dawla's two sons, who were later exiled to Cairo in 394/1003–1004. Lu'lu' died in 399/1008–1009 and was succeeded by his son Manṣūr, who received investiture from the caliph al-Ḥākim and in effect became a Fāṭimid vassal. Al-Ḥākim supported Manṣūr against Abu'l-Hayjā', a son of Saʿīd al-Dawla, who unsuccessfully endeavoured, with the help of the Byzantines, to restore Ḥamdānid rule to Aleppo. In 406/1015–1016, Manṣūr was defeated by the chief of the Banū Kilāb, Ṣāliḥ b. Mirdās, and took refuge with the Byzantines. Soon afterwards, the Fāṭimid troops occupied Aleppo, and the first Fāṭimid governor, Fātik, entered the city in 407/1017. But in 414/1023, Aleppo again fell to Ṣāliḥ b. Mirdās, whose descendants, the Mirdāsids, continued to rule (with the exception of brief periods) over northern Syria until 472/1079, when they were overthrown by the ʿUqaylids. With some occasional periods of conflict, the Mirdāsids acknowledged the nominal suzerainty of the Fāṭimids.

By the time of al-Ḥākim, the Fāṭimids had come to realize the difficulty of achieving a speedy conquest of the Muslim East. In effect, a stalemate had developed between the Fāṭimid and the Buwayhid regimes. Nonetheless, whilst more concerned now with a lasting settlement in Egypt, the Fāṭimids still aimed at penetrating the eastern lands of the Muslim world through their *daʿwa* activities. As a result, the Fāṭimid *daʿwa* was greatly expanded under al-Ḥākim, who concerned himself with the *daʿwa* organization and the training of the *dāʿīs*. The Fāṭimid *dāʿīs*, who were carefully selected and trained at the Dār al-Ḥikma and elsewhere in Cairo, were despatched to various regions in the Muslim world, both inside and outside the Fāṭimid empire. Within the Fāṭimid dominions, numerous *dāʿīs*, such as Abu'l-Fawāris (d. ca. 413/1022), who wrote a valuable treatise on the doctrine of the imāmate,[97] worked in Syria where they eventually won many converts amongst the Sunnī population. In Egypt itself, the *dāʿīs* operated in rural and urban areas, and large numbers of Egyptians gathered at the Dār al-Ḥikma to listen to different lectures on Shīʿism. More significantly, the *daʿwa* now became particularly active outside the Fāṭimid empire, in the eastern provinces of the Muslim world, and above all in ʿIrāq and Persia. A large number of *dāʿīs* were assigned to those territories, where they addressed their propaganda to various social strata. In ʿIrāq, the seat of the ʿAbbāsid Caliphate, the *dāʿīs* seem to have particularly concentrated their efforts on local rulers and influential Arab tribal chiefs, with whose support they aimed to bring about the downfall of the ʿAbbāsids.

Foremost amongst the Fāṭimid *dāʿīs* operating in the Muslim East during the reign of al-Ḥākim, was Ḥamīd al-Dīn Aḥmad b. ʿAbd Allāh al-Kirmānī, an eminent Ismāʿīlī philosopher, and, perhaps, the most learned and talented Ismāʿīlī theologian and author of the Fāṭimid period.[98] As in the case of other prominent *dāʿīs* who observed strict secrecy in their affairs, few details are known about al-Kirmānī's life and activities. A prolific writer, he was of Persian origin and was probably born in Kirmān, later maintaining his contacts with the Ismāʿīlī community in that region. As noted, he addressed one of his treatises to a subordinate *dāʿī* in Jīruft, situated in Kirmān. Al-Kirmānī seems to have spent the greater part of his life as a Fāṭimid *dāʿī* in ʿIrāq, having been particularly active in Baghdād and Baṣra. The honorific title *ḥujjat al-ʿIrāqayn*, meaning the chief *dāʿī* of both ʿIrāqs (al-ʿIrāq al-ʿArabī and al-ʿIrāq al-ʿAjamī), which is often added to his name and which may be of a late origin, implies that he was also active in the northwestern and west-central parts of Persia known as the ʿIrāq-i ʿAjam. In the early years of the 5th/11th century, he was summoned to Cairo and intervened in the controversy that had developed amongst the Fāṭimid *dāʿīs*, concerning the nature of the imāmate. More specifically, he now argued against those extremist *dāʿīs* who had begun to preach the divinity of al-Ḥākim. Thereafter, he apparently returned to ʿIrāq, where he completed his last and principal work, *Rāḥat al-ʿaql* (*Peace of the Mind*) in 411/1020–1021, and where he died soon afterwards. In this work, which is the earliest attempt at a systematic exposition of Fāṭimid Ismāʿīlī philosophy, al-Kirmānī, well-acquainted with the Judaeo-Christian sacred scriptures and Hebrew and Syriac languages,[99] introduces many new ideas, including a new cosmological system, showing the influence of the earlier Greek and Muslim philosophers.

The activities of al-Kirmānī and other Fāṭimid *dāʿīs* soon bore fruit, especially in Baghdād and elsewhere in ʿIrāq where the Shīʿīs, being pressured by the ʿAbbāsids who were now acquiring a greater degree of independence from the Buwayhids, were more readily attracted to Fāṭimid Ismāʿīlism. In 401/1010–1011, Qirwāsh b. al-Muqallad (391–442/1001–1050), the ʿUqaylid ruler of Mawṣil, Kūfa, Madāʾin and some other towns, whose family adhered to Shīʿism and whose uncle Muḥammad had earlier rallied to the side of al-ʿAzīz, acknowledged the suzerainty of the Fāṭimids and had the *khuṭba* read in the name of al-Ḥākim. In the same year, ʿAlī al-Asadī, chief of the Banū Asad, declared his loyalty to al-Ḥākim in Ḥilla and other districts under his control. Being alarmed by the success of the Fāṭimid *daʿwa* within his territories, and indeed at the very doorsteps of Baghdād, the ʿAbbāsid caliph al-Qādir (381–422/991–1031) decided to take retaliatory measures. Still in 401 A.H., he obliged Qirwāsh, by threatening to use military force against him, to transfer his allegiance back to the ʿAbbāsids. And in 402/1011, he launched his own carefully planned anti-Fāṭimid propaganda campaign. It was in that year that al-Qādir sponsored the already-noted Baghdād manifesto to discredit the Fāṭimids. He assembled a number of Sunnī and Shīʿī scholars at his court in Baghdād, amongst them some prominent ʿAlids such as the celebrated Imāmī theologians al-Sharīf al-Rāḍī (d. 406/1015) and his brother al-Sharīf al-Murtaḍā (d. 436/1044–1045), who also acted as intermediaries between the ʿAbbāsids and the Buwayhids. He commanded them to declare in a written statement that al-Ḥākim and his predecessors were imposters with no genuine Fāṭimid ancestry. This manifesto was read in mosques throughout the ʿAbbāsid empire, to the deep annoyance of al-Ḥākim. In addition, al-Qādir commissioned several theologians, including the Muʿtazilī ʿAlī b. Saʿīd al-Iṣṭakhrī (d. 404/1013–1014), to write treatises condemning the Fāṭimids and their doctrines.

The Fāṭimid *daʿwa* continued in the east, and it is reported that al-Ḥākim even attempted in 403/1012–1013, though without results, to obtain the allegiance of Maḥmūd of Ghazna who had two years earlier massacred the Ismāʿīlīs of Multān.[100] Most of the Qarmaṭī Ismāʿīlī communities outside of Baḥrayn soon either embraced Fāṭimid Ismāʿīlism or disintegrated. Meanwhile, the power of the Qarmaṭīs of Baḥrayn had been rapidly declining. In 375/985, the Buwayhids inflicted two heavy defeats on the Qarmaṭīs, who had endeavoured to re-establish their hold over southern ʿIrāq by occupying Kūfa. And in 378/988, they suffered another humiliating defeat at the hands of al-Aṣfar, chief of the Banu'l-Muntafiq, who then besieged al-Aḥsā' and pillaged Qaṭīf. Henceforth, the Qarmaṭīs lost the privilege of taxing the pilgrim caravans to al-Aṣfar and other tribal chiefs of the region. Subsequently in 382/992, the Qarmaṭīs of Baḥrayn renewed their nominal political allegiance to the Fāṭimid al-ʿAzīz, probably in exchange for the resumption of the Fāṭimid annual tribute which had been discontinued after al-Aṣfar's victory in 378 A.H. However, they continued to adhere to their own dissident form of Ismāʿīlism and avoided any doctrinal rapprochement with the Fāṭimid Ismāʿīlīs. In al-Ḥākim's time, the relations between the Qarmaṭīs of Baḥrayn and the Fāṭimids were evidently hostile, though no specific details are available. By this time, the Qarmaṭīs of Baḥrayn had indeed become a local power and not much is known about their history and subsequent relations with the Fāṭimids.

In the meantime, al-Ḥākim had developed a strong inclination towards asceticism. In 403/1012–1013, he forbade his subjects from prostrating before him; he also dressed simply and rode on a donkey. In 404/1013, he made yet another unprecedented decision in appointing ʿAbd al-Raḥīm b. Ilyās b. Aḥmad, a great-grandson of ʿUbayd Allāh al-Mahdī, as his *walī al-ʿahd*, to the exclusion of his own son ʿAlī.[101] Thereupon, al-Ḥākim delegated all the affairs of state, at least for some time, to his heir apparent, who attended the official ceremonies and later also became the governor of Damascus. In the final years of al-Ḥākim's reign, there occurred an open division amongst the Fāṭimid *dāʿī*s in Egypt, which led to the genesis of what was to become known as the Druze religion. This religion, though originally derived from Fāṭimid Ismāʿīlism, came to represent so many doctrinal innovations as to be considered to fall beyond the confines of Ismāʿīlism or even Shīʿī Islam. We shall, therefore, consider only the highlights of the origins of the Druzes (Arabic, Durūz or Drūz; singular, Durzī).[102]

Al-Ḥākim's imāmate had witnessed the formation and circulation of certain extremist ideas amongst some Fāṭimid *dāʿī*s, regarding the powers and attributes of this Fāṭimid caliph. These ideas found their roots in the eschatological expectations of the Ismāʿīlīs and, more importantly, in the speculations of the Shīʿī Ghulāt of the earlier times, especially the Khaṭṭābiyya. The earliest expressions of such extremist ideas regarding al-Ḥākim and the identity of their proponents are shrouded in obscurity. It seems however, that a certain al-Ḥasan b. Ḥaydara al-Akhram may have been the first *dāʿī* who began to organize early in 408/1017 (the opening year of the Druze era) a movement for the purpose of proclaiming the divinity of al-Ḥākim. The Fāṭimid *daʿwa*, in line with the basic tenets of the doctrine of the imāmate, recognized al-Ḥākim as the divinely appointed, sinless and infallible leader of mankind as well as the true guardian of Islam and the authoritative interpreter of the inner meaning of the Islamic revelation. But on the basis of their beliefs, the Fāṭimid Ismāʿīlīs could not acknowledge him or any other Fāṭimid caliph-imām as a divine being. Consequently, the official *daʿwa* organization was categorically opposed to this new movement that was gaining a growing number of adherents amongst the Egyptian Ismāʿīlīs. Soon afterwards, al-Akhram, who had been attempting to win over prominent officials by sending them letters, was assassinated in Ramaḍān 408/January–February 1018, while riding in the retinue of al-Ḥākim.

With al-Akhram's death, the propaganda of the new movement was suspended until Muḥarram 410/May 1019, when it was resumed under the leadership of Ḥamza b. ʿAlī b. Aḥmad, a former associate of al-Akhram and of Persian origins. Ḥamza established his headquarters at the mosque of Raydān, outside the walls of Cairo, where he began to preach the new doctrine. Soon, Ḥamza came to confront a prominent rival in the person of the *dāʿī* Muḥammad b. Ismāʿīl al-Darazī (or al-Darzī), also known as Nashtakīn, a Turk from Bukhārā. Although he may initially have been one of Ḥamza's disciples, he now acted independently, competing with Ḥamza for winning the movement's leadership. Al-Darazī, after whom the movement later became designated as al-Daraziyya and al-Durziyya in addition to being called al-Ḥākimiyya, attracted many of Ḥamza's followers and was in fact the first to declare publicly al-Ḥākim's divinity. This occasioned several riots in protest of the new preaching, and the ensuing unrest was aggravated when, in 410/1019, Ḥamza sent a delegation to the Fāṭimid *qāḍī al-quḍāt* demanding his conversion. Now the Turkish troops of al-Ḥākim turned against the movement, killing a number of al-Darazī's followers, while the latter managed to take refuge at the palace. It was under these circumstances that al-Darazī vanished mysteriously in 410 A.H.; he was probably killed on the orders of al-Ḥākim. Subsequently, the Fāṭimid troops besieged Ḥamza and a number of his disciples in the Raydān mosque. But Ḥamza succeeded in going into hiding, and by Rabīʿ II 410/August 1019 he had regained al-Ḥākim's favour. Ḥamza now gave the Ḥākim cult its definitive theological form and developed a strong *daʿwa* organization for the propagation of the new doctrine, under his own overall leadership. He was assisted by a number of *dāʿīs* and disciples, notably Abū Ibrāhīm Ismāʿīl b. Muḥammad al-Tamīmī, Abū ʿAbd Allāh Muḥammad b. al-Wahb al-Qurashī, Abu'l-Khayr Salāma b. ʿAbd al-Wahhāb al-Sāmurrī, and Abu'l-Ḥasan ʿAlī b. Aḥmad al-Ṭāʾī, also known as Bahāʾ al-Dīn al-Muqtanā. The Druze movement was indeed the cause of much of the unrest that occurred during the closing years of al-Ḥākim's caliphate. It was also in relation to this movement that al-Ḥākim, at the end of 410 A.H., ordered his black troops to plunder and burn Fusṭāṭ, where, following the proclamation of al-Ḥākim's divinity, certain circles had accused the Fāṭimid caliph of having abandoned Islam.

Meanwhile, the leaders of the official Fāṭimid *daʿwa* had launched a campaign of their own against the new doctrine. They declared that al-Ḥākim had never supported the extremist ideas propagated by the dissident *dāʿīs*, circulating special decrees and documents to this effect. As part of the Fāṭimid attack on the Ḥākim cult, al-Kirmānī, the most distinguished *dāʿī* of the time, who had already elaborated the official view on the doctrine of the imāmate in a special treatise,[103] was summoned to Cairo probably at the request of Khattigīn al-Ḍayf, the last chief *dāʿī* under al-Ḥākim and a former governor of Damascus. In Egypt, he produced several works in refutation of various aspects of the new doctrine. In 405–406/1014–1015, al-Kirmānī wrote a *risāla* on imāmate in general and on al-Ḥākim's imāmate in particular, upholding that al-Ḥākim was the sole legitimate imām of the time who, like his predecessors, was divinely appointed though not divine himself.[104] In another *risāla* known as *al-Wāʿiẓa*,[105] composed in 408/1017 as a reply to a pamphlet by al-Akhram, al-Kirmānī rejects the claim of al-Ḥākim's divinity (*ulūhiyya*) and accuses the dissenters of *ghuluww* and *kufr*. Recognizing that the Druze heresy was essentially rooted in the hopes for the advent of the Qā'im with its antinomian implications raised by earlier Ismāʿīlī teaching, al-Kirmānī refuted them strongly. He repudiated the ideas that the resurrection (*qiyāma*) had occurred with the appearance of al-Ḥākim and that the era of Islam had ended. The era of Islam and the validity of its Sharīʿa would, indeed, continue under al-Ḥākim's numerous prospective successors as imāms. He also discusses other issues concerning God, imām, etc., raised by al-Akhram, who, according to al-Kirmānī, had propagated his false ideas against the wishes of al-Ḥākim. Another of al-Kirmānī's works, produced after 407 A.H. and discussing the subject of divine unity (*al-tawḥīd*),[106] also had direct bearings on the controversy.

Al-Kirmānī's writings, which were widely circulated, were to some extent successful in checking the spread of extremism in the inner circles of the *daʿwa* organization, and influencing many dissident *dāʿī*s to return to the fold of Fāṭimid Ismāʿīlism. Nevertheless, the new doctrine expounded by al-Akhram, al-Darazī and Ḥamza continued to spread. With al-Ḥākim's disappearance in 411/1021, Ḥamza and several of his chief assistants went into hiding, while the adherents of the Ḥākim cult became subject to severe persecutions during the first years under al-Ḥākim's successor. In this period, when all activities for the new doctrine had been suspended, the leadership of the Druze movement was entrusted to al-Muqtanā who was apparently in contact with Ḥamza. It is not known when or how Ḥamza died, but his return was still expected in 430/1038 by al-Muqtanā, who had resumed the open activities of the movement in 418/1027. Meanwhile, the Ḥākim cult had been fading in Egypt, from where al-Muqtanā had sent letters to various regions. The movement acquired its greatest success in Syria, where a number of Druze *dāʿīs* had been active. In fact, the new doctrine seems to have provided the ideology for a wave of peasant revolts in Syria, the permanent home of the Durūz.

By 425/1034, al-Muqtanā had won many new converts in the eastern Ismāʿīlī communities and as far as Multān,[107] where the Ismāʿīlīs had survived the persecutions of the Ghaznawids. Soon, al-Muqtanā's leadership was challenged by several of his subordinates, notably a certain Ibn al-Kurdī, and Sukayn who was the leading Druze *dāʿī* in Syria. Thus, the movement lost much of its earlier vigour and proselytizing success. Al-Muqtanā withdrew from his adherents after 429/1037, though he continued to send out letters until 435/1043, when the active call of the movement also ended. Henceforth, the Druzes became a closed community, permitting neither conversion nor apostasy. The extant letters of al-Muqtanā, together with those written by Ḥamza and Ismāʿīl b. Muḥammad al-Tamīmī, have been collected into a canon which has served as the sacred scripture of the Druzes. This canon, arranged in six books, is designated as the *Rasāʾil al-Ḥikma* (*The Books of Wisdom*), also called *al-Ḥikma al-Sharīfa*. The Druzes, who are still awaiting the reappearance of al-Ḥākim and Ḥamza, guard their sacred literature and doctrines most secretly. Today, there are some 300,000 Druzes in the Middle East, mainly in Syria, especially in the Ḥawrān mountainous region, as well as in Lebanon and Israel. Smaller Druze communities of Syrian origins are settled in the Americas, Australia and West Africa.

The doctrines of the Druzes, who call themselves Muwaḥḥidūn, 'unitarians', signifying their emphasis on God's unity (*al-tawḥīd*), were based on the eschatological expectations of the Ismāʿīlīs and the special type of Neoplatonism which had come to be adopted as the basis of the cosmological doctrine of the Fāṭimid Ismāʿīlīs. The founders of the Druze religion were, moreover, greatly influenced by certain beliefs, notably the belief regarding the incarnation or *ḥulūl* of the divine essence in human bodies, held by the Shīʿī Ghulāt of earlier times, especially the Khaṭṭābiyya who believed in the divinity of the imāms. Under such influences, Ḥamza and his chief associates had come to believe in the periodical manifestations of the divine spirit in human form. And in their time, the ultimate One, the Godhead, who had created the universal intellect or intelligence (*al-ʿaql al-kullī*), the first cosmic emanation or principle, and who was himself beyond name or rank, was embodied in the person of al-Ḥākim. In other words, al-Ḥākim was the last *maqām*, or locus, of the Creator, and it was only in recognition of al-Ḥākim that men could purify themselves. On the other hand, Ḥamza had now become the imām, the human guide of the believers and the embodiment of the *ʿaql al-kullī*. However, the imām's function no longer included *taʾwīl*, since the time had arrived for the removal of the distinction between the exoteric and esoteric dimensions of religion. Henceforth, the imām was to help the believers to realize themselves by recognizing the unity of God through al-Ḥākim. Ḥamza also expected al-Ḥākim to initiate the final era of the sacred history, abrogating all the previous religious laws, including the Sharīʿa of Islam and its Ismāʿīlī interpretation. In effect, Ḥamza's teaching represented a new religion superseding all the previous religions, and falling outside of Ismāʿīlism. This religion laid a special emphasis on the immediate presence of the One at the expense of the subordinate emanations in the universe that were ultimately caused by the One. What mattered above all else was the worshipping of the One, revealed clearly in al-Ḥākim. This is why the Druzes refer to their religion as the *dīn al-tawḥīd*.

On the basis of the Druze emanational doctrine of cosmology, Ḥamza assigned cosmic ranks, derived from corresponding cosmic emanations, to prominent members of his *daʿwa* organization. There were five such ranks, called *al-ḥudūd*. Besides the universal intellect (*al-ʿaql al-kullī*) embodied in Ḥamza himself, there were the universal soul (*al-nafs al-kulliyya*); the word (*al-kalima*); the right wing (*al-janāḥ al-ayman*) also called the preceder (*al-sābiq*); and the left wing (*al-janāḥ al-aysar*) also called the follower (*al-tālī*). The last four ranks were held, respectively, by Ismāʿīl b. Muḥammad al-Tamīmī, Muḥammad b. al-Wahb al-Qurashī, Salāma b. ʿAbd al-Wahhāb al-Sāmurrī, and Bahāʾ al-Dīn al-Muqtanā.[108] In Druze terminology, these *ḥudūd* are the five highest ministers, or disciples, of al-Ḥākim, embodying the five highest cosmic emanations or principles. Below them, there were three other ranks; namely, *dāʿī*, *maʾdhūn*, and *mukāsir* (or *naqīb*), in charge of the various aspects of propagating the new faith, corresponding to the cosmic principles *jadd*, *fatḥ* and *khayāl*. Subordinated to all these ranks were the common believers. From the time of al-Muqtanā's withdrawal, Ḥamza's hierarchical propaganda organization, including its *dāʿīs* and lower dignitaries, gradually fell into disuse, and the Druze canon came to serve in place of the absent *ḥudūd*. Since then, while the Druzes have been expecting the return of al-Ḥākim and Ḥamza, a much simpler religious organization has taken shape amongst the Druzes of the Middle East. The members of the Druze community have been divided into the *ʿuqqāl* (singular, *ʿāqil*), 'sages', who are initiated into the truths of the faith, and the *juhhāl* (singular, *jāhil*), 'ignorant persons', the majority of the uninitiated members, who are not permitted to read the more secret Druze writings. Any adult Druze may be initiated after considerable preparation and trial; subsequently, he is obliged to live a strictly religious life. The more learned amongst the *ʿuqqāl* are given special authorities in the community as *shaykhs*. They spend much time copying the epistles contained in the Druze canon, offering spiritual guidance to the *juhhāl* and presiding over various communal ceremonies and functions. The Druzes, who possess elaborate doctrines of cosmology and eschatology, believe in metempsychosis or *tanāsukh*. According to them, there are a fixed number of souls in existence and all souls are reincarnated immediately after death in other human bodies. Ḥamza attacked the Nuṣayrī doctrine that the soul of a sinful person may enter the body of lower animals. In the end, when al-Ḥākim and Ḥamza reappear to establish justice in the world, the best amongst the Druzes will be nearest to al-Ḥākim.

Al-Ḥākim's asceticism increased in the closing years of his reign, when he took to nocturnal walks in the streets of Cairo and Fusṭāṭ as well as long solitary excursions in the countryside, especially on the Muqaṭṭam hills outside of Cairo. Al-Ḥākim's end was as enigmatic as his life. On 27 Shawwāl 411/13 February 1021, he left for one of his usual outings to the Muqaṭṭam hills and never returned. A futile search was conducted for the 36 year-old caliph; a few days later his riding donkey and his clothes, pierced by dagger cuts, were found. His body was never recovered, and subsequently several stories came into circulation regarding the incident. According to one plausible version, al-Ḥākim was assassinated on the orders of his scheming sister, Sitt al-Mulk, whose own life had been threatened by the caliph. A Kutāma chief, Ibn Dawwās, had apparently collaborated with her. According to another version, he was killed and his body was carefully hidden at the instigation of Ḥamza, so as to enable the Druze leaders to capitalize on the caliph's mysterious disappearance for their own religious purposes. In fact, the Druzes did interpret al-Ḥākim's disappearance as a voluntary retreat initiating his *ghayba*. His caliphate and imāmate had lasted just over twenty-four years.

About forty days after al-Ḥākim's disappearance, Sitt al-Mulk had al-Ḥākim's only son Abu'l-Ḥasan ʿAlī, then only sixteen years old, proclaimed as imām and caliph with the *laqab* of al-Ẓāhir li-Iʿzāz Dīn Allāh.[109] The shrewd Sitt al-Mulk became regent. It may be added that henceforth the Fāṭimid throne always fell to children or youths; while regents, viziers or generals held the actual reign of power for extended periods. Sitt al-

Mulk, who is given various other names by the chroniclers, ruled efficiently for more than three years until her death in 415/1024. At the beginning of her regency, she managed to have ʿAbd al-Raḥīm, al-Ḥākim's heir designate who had meanwhile revolted in Damascus, arrested and brought to Cairo, where he was imprisoned and murdered shortly before Sitt al-Mulk's own death. She also publicly denounced Ibn Dawwās as al-Ḥākim's murderer and had him killed. After Sitt al-Mulk, who had brought order and stability to the state and had re-opened negotiations with Byzantium, real political authority came to be vested in al-Ẓāhir's *wāsiṭa*, and later *wazīr*, ʿAlī b. Aḥmad al-Jarjarāʾī, whose hands had been cut off on al-Ḥākim's orders. Al-Jarjarāʾī ruled with the help of other notables of the state without the participation of the young caliph. In 415/1024, Egypt suffered a severe famine, which lasted for several years and led to an economic crisis and riots in Cairo and elsewhere. In 416/1025, the Fāṭimid regime began once again to persecute the Sunnīs, culminating in the expulsion of all the Mālikī *faqīh*s from Egypt. In 423/1032, partial agreement was reached between the Fāṭimid and the Byzantine empires, permitting the Byzantine emperor to reconstruct the ruined church of the Holy Sepulchre in Jerusalem. Meanwhile, the *daʿwa* had continued to be active in many regions. In particular, the Fāṭimid *dāʿī*s had won many converts in ʿIrāq, having taken advantage of the disturbances created by the Turkish soldiery during the reign of the Buwayhid Jalāl al-Dawla (416–435/1025–1044).

Fāṭimid control of Syria was seriously threatened during the caliphate of al-Ẓāhir by the alliance between the Jarrāḥids of Palestine, the Kalbīs of central Syria and the Kilābīs of northern Syria. In 415/1024–1025, the Jarrāḥid Ḥassān b. Mufarrij renewed a pact of cooperation with the Kalbid Sinān b. Sulaymān and the Kilābid Ṣāliḥ b. Mirdās, who had already seized Aleppo from the lieutenant of the Fāṭimids in the previous year. According to this pact, Damascus was allotted to Sinān, Aleppo to Ṣāliḥ and Palestine to the ambitious Ḥassān. These allies defeated the Fāṭimid forces at ʿAsqalān. After Sinān's death, however, the Kalbīs rallied to the side of the Fāṭimids, enabling the Fāṭimid general Anūshtigin al-Duzbarī to defeat the joint forces of Ḥassān and Ṣāliḥ at al-Uqḥuwāna in Palestine in 420/1029, and to reoccupy Damascus. Ṣāliḥ b. Mirdās was killed in battle, and Ḥassān, together with his Ṭayy tribesmen, took refuge in Byzantine territory. Due to the efforts of Anūshtigin, who seized Aleppo from the Mirdāsids in 429/1038, Fāṭimid domination was re-established in Syria and then extended to the neighbouring areas as far as Ḥarrān, Sarūj and

Raqqa. The seventh Fāṭimid caliph al-Ẓāhir died of plague in his early thirties in Shaʿbān 427/June 1036, after an imāmate and caliphate of fifteen years.

Al-Ẓāhir was succeeded by his seven year-old son, Abū Tamīm Maʿadd, who adopted the *laqab* of al-Mustanṣir bi'llāh. He had been designated as *walī al-ʿahd* since the age of eight months, in 421/1030.[110] Al-Mustanṣir's caliphate, lasting almost sixty lunar years (427–487/1036–1094), was the longest of his dynasty. His caliphate also marked the closing phase of the classical Fāṭimid period; while it witnessed numerous vicissitudes, the overall fortune of the Fāṭimid empire had now clearly begun its irreversible decline.

During the first nine years of al-Mustanṣir's reign, real political authority remained in the hands of al-Jarjarā'ī, who had retained the vizierate, while al-Mustanṣir's mother, a Sūdānī, had started her regency and continually intrigued behind the scenes. On al-Jarjarā'ī's death in 436/1044, all power was seized and maintained for a long period by the queen mother who had kept her close relations with Abū Saʿd al-Tustarī, a Jewish merchant who had originally brought her to Egypt. Under the influence of Abū Saʿd, she now appointed a renegade Jew, Ṣadaqa b. Yūsuf, to the vizierate. Meanwhile, the racial rivalries in the Fāṭimid army had started to provide a major cause of unrest in Egypt, often leading to open rioting and factional fighting. Berbers, Turks, Daylamīs and Arabs, all undisciplined and hateful of one another, usually joined forces however, in their common opposition to the black regiments. The latter consisted of large numbers of Sūdānī slaves purchased for the army with the active encouragement of the queen mother. The persistent intrigues of the Fāṭimid court added their own share to this chaotic milieu. Both Abū Saʿd, who had held the reins of power with the queen mother, and the vizier Ṣadaqa, fell victim to the rivalries within the inner circles of the court. In 439/1047, Ṣadaqa, in conspiracy with the Turkish guards, had Abū Saʿd murdered; the queen mother then retaliated by arranging Ṣadaqa's own assassination in the following year. It was against this background that inept viziers replaced one another, while the overall situation of Egypt deteriorated. In 442/1050, as an exception to the rule, the vizierate was entrusted to a capable person, the *qāḍī* Abū Muḥammad al-Ḥasan b. ʿAlī al-Yāzūrī, who held that office for eight years and restored some order to the state. With the execution of al-Yāzūrī in 450/1058, the factional fights and internal disorders erupted in an intensified manner. Al-Yāzūrī was followed, in rapid succession, by numerous ineffective viziers, while the Fāṭimid state was undergoing a period of decline, accompanied by the breakdown of the civil administration, chaos in the army and the exhaustion of the public treasury.

Matters came to a head in 454/1062, when open warfare broke out near Cairo, between the Turks, aided by the Berbers, and the black troops. The Sūdānīs were finally defeated in 459/1067, after which they were driven to the region of the Ṣaʿīd. The victorious commander of the Turks, Nāṣir al-Dawla, a descendant of the Ḥamdānids and a former governor of Damascus, now became the effective authority in Egypt. He easily wrested all power from al-Mustanṣir and even rebelled against the helpless Fāṭimid caliph. In 462/1070, Nāṣir al-Dawla had the *khuṭba* pronounced in the name of the ʿAbbāsid caliph al-Qā'im (422–467/1031–1075) in Alexandria and elsewhere in lower Egypt. In the meantime, Egypt was also going through a serious economic crisis, marked by shortage of food and famine which were due to the low level of the Nile during seven consecutive years, from 457/1065 to 464/1072, as well as to the constant plundering and ravaging of the land by Turkish troops, all resulting in the total disruption of the country's agriculture. During these years, Egypt had become prey to the utmost misery.[111] People were reduced to eating dogs, cats, and even human flesh, giving way to all sorts of atrocities, crimes and epidemics. Al-Mustanṣir was forced to sell his treasures in order to meet the insatiable demands of Nāṣir al-Dawla and his Turks. The Fāṭimid palaces, too, were looted by the Turkish guards, who also caused the most regrettable destruction of the Fāṭimid libraries at Cairo in 461/1068–1069.[112] Fusṭāṭ was twice pillaged and burned on Nāṣir al-Dawla's orders. During these desperate years, disturbances and rioting, caused by famine, disease and the tyranny of Nāṣir al-Dawla, became widespread and eventually led to the complete breakdown of law and order. A growing portion of the population, including the caliph's own family, were now obliged to seek refuge outside of Egypt, mainly in Syria and ʿIrāq; and various stories are related of the extreme destitution to which al-Mustanṣir himself was reduced, in his royal quarters in Cairo.

It was under such circumstances that fighting broke out even amongst the Turks themselves, leading to the assassination of Nāṣir al-Dawla by the commander of a rival Turkish faction in 465/1073. In the same year, the seven-year famine was greatly alleviated as a result of a good harvest. Al-Mustanṣir was now finally roused to action and secretly appealed for help from an Armenian general in Syria, Badr al-Jamālī, the governor of ʿAkkā (Acre). Badr was initially a slave of the Syrian *amīr* Jamāl al-Dawla, whence his name al-Jamālī; but he rapidly rose in rank and twice became the Fāṭimid governor of Damascus in 455/1063 and in 458/1066.[113] Badr accepted the caliph's summon on the condition of taking his Armenian troops with him. He arrived in Cairo in Jumādā I 466/January 1074, and, with intrigue, immediately succeeded in killing all the rebellious Turkish leaders who had not suspected the general's mission. Having thus saved al-Mustanṣir and the Fāṭimid Caliphate from definite downfall, Badr speedily restored order in various parts of Egypt. Badr al-Jamālī acquired the highest positions of the Fāṭimid state, being also the first person to be designated as the 'Vizier of the Pen and of the Sword' (*wazīr al-sayf wa'l-qalam*), with full delegated powers. He became not only the commander of the armies, *amīr al-juyūsh*, his best-known title, but also the head of the civil, judicial and even religious administrations. His titles, besides *wazīr*, thus included those of *qāḍī al-quḍāt* and *dāʿī al-duʿāt*. Indeed, it was primarily due to his efforts that Egypt came to enjoy peace and relative prosperity during the remaining twenty years of al-Mustanṣir's caliphate.

Territorially, the overall extent of the Fāṭimid empire began to decline during al-Mustanṣir's reign. With Anūshtigin's seizure of Aleppo in 429/1038, the Fāṭimids had reached the zenith of their power in Syria. Thereafter, their domination of Syria and Palestine was quickly brought to an end. In 433/1041, Palestine was once more in revolt under the Jarrāḥid Ḥassān, and in the same year Aleppo fell again to a Mirdāsid, Thimāl b. Mirdās. The Fāṭimids attempted in vain to regain Aleppo during 440–441/1048–1049, and although Thimāl submitted temporarily to al-Mustanṣir in 449/1057, northern Syria was irrevocably lost to the Fāṭimids in 452/1060. The Mirdāsids, who had often accorded only nominal allegiance to the Fāṭimids, transferred their *bayʿa* to the ʿAbbāsids and their new Saljūqid overlords in 462/1070, in spite of the disapproval of their subjects, who for the most part had adhered to Shīʿism. The Fāṭimids, like many other Muslim dynasties, now faced the growing menace of the Saljūq Turks who were rapidly advancing from the east and laying the foundations of a powerful new empire.

The Saljūqids, as a family of chieftains, had led the Oghuz (Arabic, Ghuzz) Turks, during the early decades of the 5th/11th century, westwards from Khwārazm and Transoxiana. The Saljūq leader Ṭughril, who had defeated the Ghaznawids and proclaimed himself sultan at Nīshāpūr in 429/1038, soon conquered the greater part of Persia, and then crossed into ʿIrāq. The Saljūqids regarded themselves as the champions of Sunnī Islam, which gave them a suitable pretext for wanting to free the ʿAbbāsids from the tutelage of the Shīʿī Buwayhids, and to rid the Muslim world of the Fāṭimids. At any event, Ṭughril entered Baghdād in Ramaḍān 447/December 1055, and soon after extinguished the rule of the Buwayhids of ʿIrāq by deposing and imprisoning the last member of the dynasty, al-Malik al-Raḥīm Khusraw Fīrūz (440–447/1048–1055). The ʿAbbāsid caliph al-Qā'im now confirmed Ṭughril's title of *sulṭān*, and the Saljūqid announced his intention of sending expeditions against the Shīʿī Fāṭimids in Syria and Egypt. However, dissent within the Saljūqid camp and the pro-Fāṭimid activities of al-Basāsīrī in ʿIrāq prevented the founder of the Saljūqid sultanate from carrying out his design against the Fāṭimids, whose cause achieved an unprecedented, though brief success in ʿIrāq.

Abu'l-Ḥārith Arslān al-Basāsīrī, originally a Turkish slave, had become a chief military figure in ʿIrāq during the final decade of Buwayhid rule there. Al-Malik al-Raḥīm's seven-year reign at Baghdād was marked by continuous violence and rioting due to the lack of discipline of the Turkish troops, the Sunnī–Shīʿī contest, and the troubles caused by various Buwayhid and ʿUqaylid pretenders as well as local Arab tribesmen. In this turbulent situation, Baṣra and other towns were temporarily seized by the rebellious Turkish general al-Basāsīrī, who had a powerful adversary at Baghdād in the person of the ʿAbbāsid vizier Ibn al-Muslima. The latter, who had secretly established an alliance with Ṭughril and who, like the ʿAbbāsid caliph, had accepted the Saljūqids' arrival in Baghdād, accused al-Basāsīrī of being in league with the Fāṭimids. Al-Basāsīrī, who had Shīʿī leanings and had been obliged to leave Baghdād before the arrival of the Saljūqids, now appealed to al-Mustanṣir for support to conquer Baghdād in his name. In the meantime, riots had broken out in the ʿAbbāsid capital, in protest of the ravages of Ṭughril's troops. It has now become known that the celebrated Fāṭimid *dāʿī* al-Mu'ayyad al-Shīrāzī had a major part in creating these anti-Saljūqid disorders and in directing al-Basāsīrī's moves. In 448/1056–1057, Fāṭimid propaganda, accompanied by military measures under the overall direction of al-Mu'ayyad, was intensified. Benefiting also from the excesses of the Turkomans, it met with success in Mawṣil, Wāsiṭ, and Kūfa, where the *khuṭba* was read in al-Mustanṣir's name. After receiving a substantial gift of money and arms from Cairo, delivered to al-Basāsīrī at Raḥba by al-Mu'ayyad, and aided by his brother-in-law, the Mazyadid ruler Dubays (408–474/1018–1081), and by numerous Arab tribesmen, al-Basāsīrī inflicted a heavy defeat on the Saljūqids in the region of Sinjār in 448/1057. After this defeat the Fāṭimids were again acknowledged by the ʿUqaylids of Mawṣil. Soon afterwards,

Ṭughril took Mawṣil but was prevented from adopting further measures against al-Basāsīrī due to the revolt of his own half-brother, Ibrāhīm Īnāl, who aspired to seize the Saljūqid sultanate for himself with the assistance of al-Basāsīrī and the Fāṭimids.

The departure of Ṭughril for western Persia to subdue Īnāl, provided a suitable opportunity for al-Basāsīrī to expand his activities. Shortly afterwards, in Dhu'l-Qaʿda 450/December 1058, al-Basāsīrī easily managed to enter Baghdād, accompanied by the ʿUqaylid Quraysh (443–453/1052–1061). Now the Shīʿī form of *adhān* or call to prayer was instituted in Baghdād, where the *khuṭba* was also pronounced in the name of the Fāṭimid al-Mustanṣir. Al-Basāsīrī, drawing popular support from both Sunnīs and Shīʿīs who had been united in their hatred of the Saljūqid soldiery, then attacked the ʿAbbāsid palace. He agreed, however, to leave al-Qā'im in the protection of the ʿUqaylid Quraysh, to the great disappointment of al-Mustanṣir, who had expected to receive the ʿAbbāsid captive in Cairo. But al-Basāsīrī did send the ʿAbbāsid caliphal insignia to the Fāṭimid capital. Subsequently, al-Basāsīrī took possession of Wāsiṭ and Baṣra, while failing to gain Khūzistān for the Fāṭimids. At any rate, al-Basāsīrī had already been abandoned by Cairo when he was at the height of his power, and his success was thus bound to be short-lived. The Fāṭimid vizier Ibn al-Maghribī, who had succeeded al-Yāzūrī, now refused to extend any further help to al-Basāsīrī. Meanwhile, Ṭughril had repressed Īnāl's revolt and was preparing to return to Baghdād. He proposed to leave al-Basāsīrī in Baghdād, provided he would renounce his Fāṭimid allegiance and restore al-Qā'im to the throne. Al-Basāsīrī rejected this offer and left Baghdād in Dhu'l-Qaʿda 451/December 1059. A few days later, Ṭughril entered Baghdād and was met by the freed ʿAbbāsid caliph. Al-Basāsīrī was pursued and killed shortly afterwards near Kūfa by the Saljūqs, who also carried out an intensive persecution of the ʿIrāqī Shīʿīs. Thus ended the Fāṭimid ambitions in ʿIrāq and the episode of al-Basāsīrī, who for a year had gained the acknowledgement of Fāṭimid suzerainty at the ʿAbbāsid capital.[114]

The Saljūqid empire was consolidated in the reigns of Ṭughril's nephew and successor Alp Arslān (455–465/1063–1073) and the latter's son Malikshāh (465–485/1073–1092), who both depended greatly on the organizational talent of their illustrious Persian vizier Niẓām al-Mulk. At the same time, the Saljūqids had continued to expand their territories, never abandoning their dream of marching on to Egypt and overthrowing the Shīʿī dynasty of the Fāṭimids. Fāṭimid Egypt was now in complete disorder, and the rivalries between the Berber and Turkish troops had brought unrest to Syria. As a result, the Fāṭimid governors of Damascus could not exert their authority effectively, nor could they check the Turkoman bands who had appeared in Syria as early as 447/1055. Even Badr al-Jamālī's efforts to enforce Fāṭimid sovereignty in Damascus during the years 455–456/1063–1064 and 458–460/1066–1068 had proved futile. Under these desperate circumstances, the Fāṭimids, according to prevalent custom, hired the services of a Turkoman chieftain, Atsiz b. Uvak, to subdue the rebellious Arab tribes of Palestine. But Atsiz himself revolted against the Fāṭimids and occupied Jerusalem in 463/1071. Later, after Badr's departure for Egypt, Atsiz, who was now carving out a principality in Palestine and Syria, seized Damascus in 468/1076. All subsequent attempts by Badr to regain Damascus proved futile and Syria remained lost to the Fāṭimids. In 469/1077, Atsiz attacked Cairo itself, but was defeated and driven back by Badr. When threatened by a Fāṭimid expedition, Atsiz appealed to Malikshāh, who responded by despatching his brother Tutush to Syria. In 471/1078–1079, Damascus, having been surrendered by Atsiz to Tutush, became the capital of the new Saljūqid principality of Syria and Palestine. By the end of al-Mustanṣir's rule, of the former Fāṭimid possessions in Syria and Palestine, only ʿAsqalān and a few coastal towns, like Acre and Tyre, still remained in Fāṭimid hands. In the meantime, relations had stayed friendly between the Byzantines and Fāṭimids, following the signing in 429/1038 of a thirty-year peace treaty which also permitted the Byzantines to rebuild the church of the Holy Sepulchre. In particular, the emperor Constantine IX Monomachus (1042–1055) maintained excellent relations with al-Mustanṣir and supplied Egypt with wheat after the famine of 446/1054. Subsequently, when the Fāṭimids refused to co-operate with Byzantium against the Saljūqs, relations cooled somewhat between the two empires, to be later ameliorated by the exchange of several embassies, including one in 461/1069 during the reign of Romanus IV Diogenes (1068–1071).

The success of the Saljūqids also affected the position and influence of the Fāṭimids in certain parts of Arabia. In 462/1069–1070, the *sharīf* of Mecca informed Alp Arslān that henceforth the *khuṭba* in Mecca would be read for the ʿAbbāsid caliph and the Saljūqid sultan, and no longer for the Fāṭimids. Furthermore, he abolished the Shīʿī *adhān*. The *sharīf* was rewarded by a generous pension from the Saljūqids. After a brief return to Fāṭimid allegiance during 467–473/1074–1081, the holy cities of the Ḥijāz passed permanently out of Fāṭimid control. On the other hand, the

Fāṭimid Ismāʿīlī cause achieved a new success in Yaman during the reign of al-Mustanṣir, through the efforts of the Ismāʿīlī dynasty of the Ṣulayḥids.[115]

In Yaman, with the death of the *dāʿī* Ibn Ḥawshab, who was a fervent supporter of ʿUbayd Allāh al-Mahdī, and with the extinction of the Ismāʿīlī state he had founded, Ismāʿīlism had come to face a major religio-political setback. Nevertheless, the Ismāʿīlī *daʿwa* had continued to be active in Yaman throughout the 4th/10th century, though in a dormant form, receiving the secret allegiance of several Yamanī tribes, especially some of the Banū Hamdān. For this obscure period of more than one century, lasting until the early years of al-Mustanṣir's caliphate, only the names of the successive Yamanī *dāʿīs*, starting with ʿAbd Allāh b. ʿAbbās who succeeded Ibn Ḥawshab, have been preserved.[116] At the time, amidst continuous tribal strife, Yaman was ruled by several independent dynasties, notably, the Ziyādids (204–412/819–1021), with their capital at Zabīd in the region of Tihāma; the Yaʿfurids (247–387/861–997) who established themselves at Ṣanʿāʾ and Janad; and the Najāḥids, who were originally the Abyssinian slaves of the Ziyādids but eventually succeeded the latter in 412/1021, ruling intermittently over Zabīd until 554/1159, while the Zaydī Imāms held Ṣaʿda in northern Yaman. During this period, around 377/987, the *daʿwa* had succeeded in gaining the allegiance of only one Yamanī ruler, ʿAbd Allāh b. Qaḥṭān, the last Yaʿfurid *amīr*. By the time of the Fāṭimid al-Ẓāhir, the headship of the Yamanī *daʿwa* had come to be vested in a certain *dāʿī* Sulaymān b. ʿAbd Allāh al-Zawāḥī, a very learned and influential man living in the mountainous region of Ḥarāz. Sulaymān chose as his successor ʿAlī b. Muḥammad al-Ṣulayḥī, the son of the *qāḍī* of Ḥarāz, who was also an important Hamdānī chieftain. ʿAlī, who in time came to lead pilgrim caravans to Mecca, had studied Ismāʿīlism under Sulaymān and had eventually become the *dāʿī*'s assistant.

In 429/1038, the *dāʿī* ʿAlī b. Muḥammad al-Ṣulayḥī, who had already established contacts with the *daʿwa* headquarters in Cairo, rose in Masār, a mountainous locality in Ḥarāz, where he constructed fortifications.[117] This marked the foundation of the Ṣulayḥid dynasty, which ruled over Yaman as vassals of the Fāṭimids for almost one century, until 532/1138. Receiving much support from the Hamdānī, Ḥimyarī, and other Yamanī tribes, ʿAlī started on a career of conquest, everywhere instituting the Fāṭimid Ismāʿīlī *khuṭba*. In 452/1060, he seized Zabīd, killing its ruler al-Najāḥ, founder of the Najāḥid dynasty, who had earlier incited the Zaydīs of Ṣaʿda against him. ʿAlī appointed his brother-in-law, Asʿad b. Shihāb, to the governorship of Zabīd and its dependencies in Tihāma, and then proceeded to expel the Zaydīs from Ṣanʿā', which became his own capital. In 454/1062, he conquered ʿAdan, but the Banū Maʿn were permitted to continue for some time as rulers there, though now as tributaries of the Ṣulayḥids. In 476/1083, the Ṣulayḥids conferred ʿAdan's governorship on two Hamdānī brothers, al-ʿAbbās and al-Masʿūd b. al-Karam (or al-Mukarram), who founded the Ismāʿīlī dynasty of the Zurayʿids (476–569/1083–1173). By 455/1063, ʿAlī had subjugated all of Yaman, while his influence extended from Mecca to Ḥaḍramawt. ʿAlī, who desired to meet al-Mustanṣir, in 454/1062 sent Lamak b. Mālik al-Ḥammādī, the chief *qāḍī* of Yaman, to Cairo to discuss his prospective visit.[118] Lamak remained in Cairo for five years and eventually had an audience with al-Mustanṣir. During those years, Lamak stayed at the Dār al-ʿIlm with the chief *dāʿī* al-Mu'ayyad, who furthered his religious knowledge and also acquainted him with the intricacies of Fāṭimid Ismāʿīlism. The Egyptian mission of the *dāʿī* Lamak, who upon returning to Yaman became one of the main Ismāʿīlī leaders and the executive head of the *daʿwa* there, and his friendly relationship with al-Mu'ayyad, served to bring Yaman yet closer to the headquarters of the Fāṭimid *daʿwa*. The exceptionally close ties between the Ṣulayḥids and the Fāṭimids are well attested to by numerous letters sent by the Fāṭimid chancery to the Ṣulayḥid ʿAlī and his successors, being mostly issued on the orders of al-Mustanṣir.[119]

The Ṣulayḥid ʿAlī, who never succeeded in going to Egypt, had set out on a pilgrimage to Mecca when he and a number of his relatives were murdered in 459/1067,[120] in a surprise attack by the sons of al-Najāḥ in revenge for their father. ʿAlī b. Muhammad al-Ṣulayḥī was succeeded by his son al-Mukarram Aḥmad (d. 477/1084) and then by other Ṣulayḥids. However, from the latter part of al-Mukarram's rule, during which time much of northern Yaman was lost to the Zaydī Qāsimī *amīr*s, effective authority in the Ṣulayḥid state through which Fāṭimid sovereignty came to be extended to other parts of Arabia like ʿUmān and Baḥrayn, was exercised by al-Mukarram's consort, al-Sayyida Ḥurra bint Aḥmad al-Ṣulayḥī. Generally known as al-Malika al-Sayyida, she was a capable queen and a most remarkable personality. She maintained close relations with al-Mustanṣir and his next two successors in the Fāṭimid dynasty during her long rule. Upon her death in 532/1138, marking the effective end of the Ṣulayḥid dynasty, Yaman became subjected to the authority of local dynasties, including the Ismāʿīlī Zurayʿids of ʿAdan and the Ismāʿīlī

Hamdānids of Ṣanʿāʾ, who were overthrown in 569/1173 by the Sunnī Ayyūbids, the new masters of Egypt, Syria and Yaman.

The Ṣulayḥids played a crucial part in the renewed efforts of the Fāṭimids to spread Ismāʿīlism on the Indian subcontinent. As noted, Maḥmūd of Ghazna persecuted the Ismāʿīlīs of Sind and destroyed their state at Multān. However, Ismāʿīlism managed to survive, in a greatly reduced and inactive form, in the Indus valley. Soon afterwards, the Druze leaders acquired followers from amongst the surviving Ismāʿīlīs of Sind who no longer had any direct contacts with the Fāṭimid *daʿwa*. And the Ghaznawids, fearing the revival of Ismāʿīlī activity in Sind and other eastern territories under their control, in 423/1032 tried and executed Ḥasanak, Maḥmūd's last vizier, who had earlier accepted a robe of honour from the Fāṭimid al-Ẓāhir, on charges of being a Qarmaṭī (Ismāʿīlī).[121] But now, in the reign of al-Mustanṣir, a new Ismāʿīlī community was founded in Gujarāt, in western India, by the *dāʿīs* sent from Yaman. According to the traditional accounts of the origins of this community,[122] it was in 460/1067–1068 that a *dāʿī* named ʿAbd Allāh arrived in Khāmbāyat (Khambhāt), modern Cambay, in Gujarāt, where he started the *daʿwa* and soon won many converts, including the local rulers. ʿAbd Allāh had been sent from Yaman by Lamak b. Mālik, who had then recently returned to Yaman from his long visit to Egypt, most probably on the instructions of the chief *dāʿī* al-Muʾayyad. The Ṣulayḥids evidently supervised the selection and despatch of *dāʿīs* to western India, with the knowledge and approval of al-Mustanṣir himself. There are extant Fāṭimid documents indicating that the Ṣulayḥid al-Mukarram, for instance, sent a certain *dāʿī* Marzubān b. Isḥāq to India in 476/1083; while in 481/1088, the latter's eldest son Aḥmad was selected to head the *daʿwa* in India after his father's death and upon the recommendation of the Ṣulayḥid queen al-Sayyida, who was officially put in charge of the affairs of the Indian *daʿwa*.[123]

The *daʿwa* in western India maintained its close ties with Yaman; and the Ismāʿīlī community founded in the second half of the 5th/11th century in Gujarāt in fact evolved into the modern Ṭayyibī Bohra community. It may also be added that the revitalization of the Fāṭimid *daʿwa* in Yaman and India may have been directly related to the Fāṭimids' new interest in trading with India, and in diverting the Near Eastern trade with Asia away from the Persian Gulf route, favourable to the ʿAbbāsids, to the Red Sea. As a result, the Fāṭimids had become concerned with developing and channelling any existing and prospective mercantile trade through an old route passing through the port of ʿAydhāb, on the African coast of the Red

Sea, to Yaman and ʿAdan, from where merchant ships sailed to various harbours on the west coast of India. In mediaeval times, Cambay was one of the most important of these Indian ports, having also close commercial ties with Yaman. It is, therefore, quite likely that the extension of the Fāṭimid *daʿwa* in Yaman and Gujarāt, in al-Mustanṣir's time, occurred in connection with the development of the new Fāṭimid commercial interests and policies, which necessitated the utilization of Yaman as a safe base along the Red Sea trade route to India.[124]

In North Africa, the Fāṭimid dominions were practically reduced to only Egypt itself. About the year 440/1048, the fourth Zīrid ruler al-Muʿizz b. Bādīs, who had already persecuted the Shīʿīs of Ifrīqiya, formally renounced the suzerainty of the Fāṭimids and placed himself under that of the ʿAbbāsids. As a result of this complete rupture with Cairo, the *khuṭba* came to be read in the name of the ʿAbbāsid caliph in Zīrid territories. The Mālikī *ʿulamāʾ* of Qayrawān, in order to satisfy the predominantly Sunnī public opinion of Ifrīqiya, had thus succeeded in replacing Shīʿism with Sunnism as the official creed of the Zīrid state. Though al-Muʿizz later in 446/1054–1055 returned briefly to the allegiance of the Fāṭimids, as did his successor Tamīm b. al-Muʿizz (454–501/1062–1108) during the early years of his own reign, the Fāṭimids had now permanently lost Ifrīqiya, their oldest dominion in North Africa. Soon, various independent principalities sprang up in the further Maghrib, in territories dependent on Ifrīqiya. According to traditional accounts of these developments, the Fāṭimid vizier al-Yāzūrī convinced al-Mustanṣir, who lacked sufficient military power, that he should punish the disloyal Zīrid al-Muʿizz by encouraging a number of bedouin tribes, based close to the Nile valley, to migrate towards Ifrīqiya. By this measure, the Fāṭimid caliph would rid himself of these troublesome Arab tribesmen, while at the same time taking vengeance on the Zīrids. The bedouins, led by the Banū Hilāl and Banū Sulaym, captured Barqa and then penetrated Ifrīqiya proper. Defeating the Zīrids decisively in 443/1051–1052, they plundered the countryside and towns ruthlessly. These bedouins, supplemented by new arrivals, gradually spread through North Africa in what was to become known as the Hilālī invasion.[125]

By 449/1057, the Zīrid al-Muʿizz was obliged to abandon his capital, Qayrawān, and to seek refuge in Mahdiyya, then governed by his son Tamīm, while the Zīrid domains were breaking up into different principalities. When al-Muʿizz repudiated al-Mustanṣir, his cousin al-Qāʾid b. Ḥammād (419–446/1028–1054), the second Ḥammādid ruler, also temporarily cast off Fāṭimid suzerainty. Soon afterwards, the Ḥammādids, who were equally hard pressed by the westward migrating Arab bedouins, returned to Fāṭimid allegiance. But the last Ḥammādid, Yaḥyā b. al-ʿAzīz, before surrendering in 547/1152 to the Almohads, had already renounced the Fāṭimids in 543/1148. A few years later, the Zīrid territories, limited to the coastline of Ifrīqiya, also passed into the hands of the Almohads. The later Zīrids are mainly known for their maritime activity and corsair raids, though they failed to take command of the Mediterranean from the Normans of Sicily. The last Zīrid, al-Ḥasan b. ʿAlī, was driven out of Mahdiyya in 543/1148 by Roger II, king of Sicily. He had tried in vain to pay homage to the Fāṭimid caliph so that the latter would intervene on his behalf with the Normans. He was, however, reinstated in Mahdiyya by ʿAbd al-Mu'min (524–558/1130–1163), the founder of the Almohad dynasty, who himself some eight years later exiled al-Ḥasan permanently. Sicily, in the meantime, whose Kalbid *amīrs* had recognized the nominal suzerainty of the Fāṭimids, had been conquered by the Normans. The Fāṭimids had long since lost their interest in Sicily and did not find it difficult to cultivate friendly relations with Norman Sicily.[126] With the Norman conquest of Sicily in 463/1070–1071, Barqa had become the western limit of the Fāṭimid state under al-Mustanṣir.

The Fāṭimid *daʿwa* activities reached their peak in al-Mustanṣir's time. The *daʿwa* organization, which had acquired a definite shape under al-Ḥākim, was expanded during al-Mustanṣir's long imāmate. Many *dāʿīs* now operated not only inside Egypt and other Fāṭimid dominions but also outside of the Fāṭimid empire. The *daʿwa* was particularly active in ʿIrāq and in various parts of Persia, notably, Fārs, Iṣfahān, Rayy, where Ḥasan-i Ṣabbāḥ the future leader of the Nizārī Ismāʿīlīs was converted, and Khurāsān. The Ismāʿīlī *daʿwa* had continued to exist in a subdued form also in Transoxiana, where Ismāʿīlism maintained secret followers under the last Sāmānids and in subsequent decades. Amongst its adherents, there ranked the father and brother of Ibn Sīnā (Latin, Avicenna), the celebrated philosopher-physician who was born near Bukhārā in 370/980 and died in Hamadān in 428/1037. Ibn Sīnā himself became acquainted with the tenets of Ismāʿīlism at an early age through the scholarly discussions held at the house of his father, ʿAbd Allāh, a Sāmānid official; and he perused the *Epistles* of the Ikhwān al-Ṣafā', though he did not adhere to Ismāʿīlism, into which he was born.[127] After the Sāmānids, the *daʿwa* seems to have met with greater success in Central Asia. In 436/1044–1045, a large number of Ismāʿīlīs, who had been converted by Fāṭimid *dāʿīs* and who recognized the imāmate of al-Mustanṣir, were massacred in Bukhārā and elsewhere in Transoxiana on the orders of the local Qarakhānid ruler Bughrā Khān. But Ismāʿīlism survived in that region, and later in 488/1095, Aḥmad b. Khiḍr, another Qarakhānid who ruled over Bukhārā, Samarqand and western Farghāna, was accused by the local Sunnī *ʿulamāʾ* of having embraced Ismāʿīlism, and was executed.[128] Later, we shall have more to say about the Fāṭimid *daʿwa* of the time in Persia. It is a fact, however, that during al-Mustanṣir's reign, the Fāṭimid *dāʿīs*, under the central direction of Cairo, succeeded in spreading Fāṭimid Ismāʿīlism in many regions of the Islamic world, and in gaining the recognition of their numerous converts for al-Mustanṣir as the rightful imām of the time and the caliph of the entire Muslim world. It was also due to the efforts of the *daʿwa* that the suzerainty of the Fāṭimids came to be established in Ṣulayḥid Yaman, and Ismāʿīlism was introduced to an important area like western India.

The most prominent Fāṭimid *dāʿī* of al-Mustanṣir's time was al-Mu'ayyad fi'l-Dīn Abū Naṣr Hibat Allāh b. Abī ʿImrān Mūsā b. Dā'ūd al-Shīrāzī, who was also a prolific writer, a poet, as well as a political organizer and a military strategist.[129] He was born around 390/1000 in Shīrāz, where his father, coming from a Daylamī Ismāʿīlī family, was himself a *dāʿī* with some influence in the Buwayhid circles of Fārs. Al-Mu'ayyad probably succeeded his father as the chief *dāʿī* of Fārs, and in 429/1037–1038, entered the service of the Buwayhid Abū Kālījār al-Marzubān (415–440/1024–1048), who ruled over various provinces from his capital at Shīrāz. The subsequent decades in al-Mu'ayyad's life are well documented in his autobiography, *al-Sīra*, which covers the period 429–451 A.H. He soon succeeded in converting Abū Kālījār and many of his Daylamī troops to Fāṭimid Ismāʿīlism and also held disputations with Sunnī theologians and Zaydī ʿAlids at Abū Kālījār's request. The *dāʿī*'s growing influence with the Buwayhid *amīr* and the people of Fārs, however, resulted in court intrigues and Sunnī reactions against him. In particular, the ʿAbbāsids insisted on his exile from Persia. Eventually, al-Mu'ayyad was obliged to migrate from Shīrāz in early 438/1046. After an eventful journey that took him through Jannāba, Ahwāz, Kūfa and Mawṣil, he arrived in Cairo early in 439/1047 and immediately proceeded to visit the chief *dāʿī* al-Qāsim b. ʿAbd al-ʿAzīz b. Muḥammad b. al-Nuʿmān, a great-grandson of al-Qāḍī al-Nuʿmān. He had his first audience with al-Mustanṣir a few months later in Shaʿbān 439/February 1048. Henceforth, al-Mu'ayyad had easy access to the Fāṭimid caliph-imām and came to participate actively in the affairs of the Fāṭimid state. He established close relations also with the vizier al-Yāzūrī who, in 440/1048, entrusted the Persian *dāʿī* with a section of the Fāṭimid *dār al-inshāʾ*.

Subsequently, al-Mu'ayyad played a leading role as an intermediary between the Fāṭimids and al-Basāsīrī in the latter's activities against the Saljūqids. In 447/1055, he was sent by al-Mustanṣir and al-Yāzūrī to Syria and ʿIrāq. For more than a year, he delved into extensive negotiations and exchanged numerous letters with al-Basāsīrī as well as the Mirdāsid Thimāl, the Mazyadid Dubays and the ʿUqaylid Quraysh, amongst other local *amīr*s who for the most part adhered to Shīʿism, for the purpose of winning over or maintaining their allegiance to the Fāṭimid cause. It was also in pursuit of this general policy that al-Mu'ayyad attacked Ibn al-Muslima for having destroyed in 443/1051 the tomb of Mūsā al-Kāẓim, the seventh imām of the Twelver Shīʿīs.[130] These important dealings, which included the planning of most of al-Basāsīrī's moves and alliances, are fully described in al-Mu'ayyad's autobiography, which has revealed to modern researchers the *dāʿī*'s hitherto unknown crucial part in the al-Basāsīrī incident. Al-Mu'ayyad returned to Cairo in 449/1058, shortly before al-Basāsīrī finally seized Baghdād, and had the *khuṭba* read there in the name of al-Mustanṣir.[131]

In 450/1058, al-Mu'ayyad was appointed *dāʿī al-duʿāt*, and with the exception of a brief period in 453/1061, when he was exiled to Syria by the vizier Ibn Mudabbir, he held that post until about two months before his death, at which time he was succeeded by Badr al-Jamālī. From 454/1062, al-Mu'ayyad was also the head of the Dār al-ʿIlm, which became his residence. It was from here that al-Mu'ayyad directed the affairs of the Fāṭimid *daʿwa*, being in constant contact with the *dāʿī*s in many lands and paying special attention to Yaman and India. As noted, the Yamanī *dāʿī* Lamak stayed several years with al-Mu'ayyad who is considered the spiritual father of the Yamanī *daʿwa*. He also regularly delivered lectures at the Dār al-ʿIlm, where *dāʿī*s had continued to be trained since al-Ḥākim's time. It is possible that most of his so-called *Majālis*, the *dāʿī*'s magnum opus, were composed for these lectures. The *Majālis* of al-Mu'ayyad, arranged in eight volumes of one-hundred assemblies or lectures each, deal with various theological and philosophical questions and represent the high watermark of Fāṭimid Ismāʿīlī thought.[132] They also contain al-Mu'ayyad's famous correspondence with the blind Syrian poet-philosopher and ascetic Abu'l-ʿAlāʾ al-Maʿarrī (d. 449/1057) on the subject of vegetarianism,[133] and his refutation of Ibn al-Rāwandī's Muʿtazilī ideas as expressed in the latter's *Kitāb al-zumurrudh*.[134] Al-Mu'ayyad died in 470/

1078 in Cairo and was buried in the Dār al-ʿIlm, where he had lived and worked. Al-Mustanṣir himself led the funeral rites for this distinguished *dāʿī* who for almost two decades had directed the Fāṭimid *daʿwa*, and with whose foresight the Fāṭimids had come to realize, even though briefly, their perennial objective of having the Fāṭimid *khuṭba* pronounced in the ʿAbbāsid capital.

Another prominent Ismāʿīlī dignitary of al-Mustanṣir's time was Abū Muʿīn Nāṣir b. Khusraw b. Ḥārith al-Qubādiyānī, better known as Nāṣir-i Khusraw. He was a *dāʿī*, a philosopher, a traveller, as well as a renowned poet who in fact ranks amongst the greatest of the Persian poets. Much has been written by orientalists and scholars of Persian literature about this multi-faceted personality; even though major portions of his life still remain shrouded in mystery. There are also numerous legends surrounding Nāṣir-i Khusraw, in addition to a spurious autobiography attributed to him, which has been circulating for several centuries amongst Ismāʿīlīs and non-Ismāʿīlīs.[135] However, Nāṣir's extant works, all of which are written in Persian, especially his *Safar-nāma* and *Dīwān* of poems, in which he eulogizes the Imām al-Mustanṣir, al-Qāḍī al-Nuʿmān and the *dāʿī* al-Mu'ayyad, do provide valuable details on his life and ideas.[136] And yet, most of these writings were subject to censorship and mutilation at the hands of hostile Sunnī scribes so as to delete their Ismāʿīlī features.[137] The available information on Nāṣir's biography can be summed up as follows.[138] According to his own statement,[139] Nāṣir-i Khusraw was born in 394/1004 in Qubādiyān, a district of Balkh, which at the time as part of the province of Marw was attached to Khurāsān. He belonged to a family of government officials and landowners, and apparently, he entered government service as a scribe early in life, and later became a financial administrator in Marw. During his youth, of which few details are known, Nāṣir evidently led a life of pleasure, having access to the Ghaznawid court at Balkh, before Khurāsān became a Saljūqid dominion in 431/1040.

When he was about forty-two years old, Nāṣir experienced a drastic spiritual upheaval which completely changed the future course of his life. As a result of this experience, which he describes symbolically in terms of a dream[140] and in a confession versified in a lengthy *qaṣīda* addressed to the *dāʿī* al-Mu'ayyad,[141] Nāṣir renounced all bodily pleasures, and tendered his resignation from his administrative post at Marw. At the time, Marw was ruled by the Saljūqid Chaghrī Beg, Ṭughril's brother, in the service of whose vizier a brother of Nāṣir-i Khusraw, Abu'l-Fatḥ, held a prominent position for a long time. Nāṣir decided in Jumādā II 437/December 1045 to set off on a long journey for the apparent reason of making the pilgrimage to Mecca. Soon afterwards in Shaʿbān 437/March 1046, accompanied by one of his two brothers Abū Saʿīd, and an Indian servant, he began his famous journey, which was to last for almost seven years. Travelling through Persia, where he spent a few days at the fortress of Shamīrān, Asia Minor, as well as through Syria and Palestine, he made his first of several pilgrimages to Mecca before entering Cairo in Ṣafar 439/August 1047, the same year in which al-Mu'ayyad arrived there. Nāṣir stayed in Cairo for about three years, until Dhu'l-Ḥijja 441/May 1050, during which time he saw al-Mustanṣir, and most probably also established a close relationship with al-Mu'ayyad al-Shīrāzī. It was in Cairo that, after receiving proper instructions, Nāṣir was given a high rank in the *daʿwa* organization. Despite the opinion of earlier scholars, it is almost certain, as Ivanow and Corbin have argued, that Nāṣir-i Khusraw had already been converted to Ismāʿīlism, probably from Twelver Shīʿism, prior to his departure for Egypt. It seems that his journey was primarily motivated by his connection with Ismāʿīlism, as Ḥasan-i Ṣabbāḥ was to be sent to Fāṭimid Egypt a few decades later, rather than for making the pilgrimage which was mentioned as a pretext, allowing Nāṣir to receive the required training as a *dāʿī* at the headquarters of the Fāṭimid *daʿwa*. In his *Safar-nāma*, Nāṣir describes in vivid detail the splendour of the Fāṭimid capital, with its royal palaces, gates, gardens and shops, as well as the wealth of Egypt, even though the country was then undergoing difficult times.[142]

Returning through the Ḥijāz, Yamāma, Baḥrayn, southern ʿIrāq, and Persia, Nāṣir-i Khusraw was back in Balkh in Jumādā II 444/October 1052, a date marking the beginning of the most obscure phase of his life. He immediately began to propagate Ismāʿīlism as a Fāṭimid *dāʿī*, or, according to himself,[143] as the *ḥujja* of Khurāsān. Nāṣir established his headquarters at Balkh, from where he extended his *daʿwa* activities to Nīshāpūr and other cities of Khurāsān. However, his success soon aroused the enmity of the Sunnī *ʿulamā'* who enjoyed the support of the region's Saljūqid rulers. It was also during this period, not too long after returning from Cairo, that Nāṣir went to Ṭabaristān (Māzandarān), to preach the cause of the Fāṭimids in the Caspian provinces, a region already penetrated by Shīʿism. According to the testimony of his contemporary Abu'l-Maʿālī, who completed his well-known work on religions in 485/1092 and who is the earliest authority referring to our *dāʿī*, Nāṣir succeeded in winning many converts in Ṭabaristān, and possibly in other Caspian regions.[144] Subsequently, Nāṣir returned to Balkh, where he became subjected to yet more severe Sunnī persecutions. He was accused of being irreligious (Persian, *bad-dīn*), a heretic (*mulḥid*), a Qarmaṭī and a Rāfiḍī.[145] His house was plundered and destroyed, and there was even an attempt on his life, forcing Nāṣir to flee from his home.[146] Under obscure circumstances, he took refuge in the valley of Yumgān, a mountainous district in the upper Oxus, irrigated by a tributary of the Āmū Daryā called the Kokcha. Yumgān was then one of the territories of an autonomous *amīr* of Badakhshān, ʿAlī b. al-Asad, an Ismāʿīlī who had close relations with Nāṣir. Doubtless, Nāṣir's flight to Yumgān, where he was to spend the rest of his life, took place before 453/1061, the year in which he completed his philosophical treatise *Zād al-musāfirīn* whilst in exile.[147]

It was in Yumgān, the permanent abode of his exile for more than fifteen years,[148] that Nāṣir-i Khusraw produced most of his poetry and prose, including the *Kitāb jāmiʿ al-ḥikmatayn* (*Book Joining the Two Wisdoms*), his latest known work which was completed in 462/1070 at the request of his Ismāʿīlī friend and protector, the *amīr* ʿAlī b. al-Asad.[149] There, he also continued to propagate Ismāʿīlism, while maintaining correspondence with the *dāʿī al-duʿāt* al-Mu'ayyad and the headquarters of the Fāṭimid *daʿwa* in Cairo. According to the local tradition of the present-day Ismāʿīlīs of Badakhshān, who refer to our Persian *dāʿī* as the Shāh Sayyid Nāṣir and who still revere him and preserve some of his genuine and spurious works, it was Nāṣir-i Khusraw who introduced Ismāʿīlism into Badakhshān, a region that subsequently became a stronghold of the Nizārī Ismāʿīlīs and a repository of their literature. The present-day Ṭayyibī Ismāʿīlīs of India, who do not preserve Nāṣir's works in their collections of manuscripts, regard him as a Nizārī Ismāʿīlī, perhaps because he wrote entirely in the Persian language. In many of his odes, Nāṣir-i Khusraw laments his exile and solitude at Yumgān, often calling it his prison, and makes frequent references to the fanatics who drove him from his home and family, reminiscing his earlier happy days in Khurāsān.[150] Nāṣir lived to be at least seventy;[151] he died in Yumgān, at an unknown date after 465/1072–1073, the latest year mentioned in most sources being 481/1088–1089.[152] Nāṣir's tomb, situated on a hillock, is still to be found in Yumgān, in the present-day village of Ḥaḍrat-i Sayyid (or Ḥaḍrat-i Saʿīd) and not too far from Jarm, now in Afghanistan;[153] an epigraph attests to the renovation of the modest mausoleum in 1109/1697. The local inhabitants, who guard the mausoleum as a shrine and claim to be *sayyid*s and descendants of Nāṣir-i Khusraw, are, strangely enough, zealous Sunnīs who strictly discourage visits of the Ismāʿīlīs of Badakhshān and elsewhere to the site. They also maintain that their ancestor Nāṣir was a Ṣūfī *pīr*, and a Sunnī like themselves, with no connections whatsoever with Ismāʿīlism.

The Fāṭimid doctrine of the imāmate during al-Mustanṣir's time was essentially that developed earlier under al-Muʿizz.[154] In the meantime, as noted, a group of extremist *dāʿīs* had proclaimed the divinity of al-Ḥākim; a view that had been officially repudiated especially by the *dāʿī* al-Kirmānī who had argued for the continuity of the imāmate.[155] Al-Kirmānī had, in fact, propounded that the imāmate would continue in the era of Muḥammad until the Day of Judgement; while he essentially endorsed the doctrine propounded by al-Muʿizz, Jaʿfar b. Manṣūr al-Yaman and other earlier Fāṭimid authorities. By the time of al-Mustanṣir, the Fāṭimid Ismāʿīlīs had come to allow for further heptads of imāms after Muḥammad b. Ismāʿīl. Al-Mu'ayyad speaks of the imāms in the progeny of ʿAlī b. Abī Ṭālib throughout his lectures, but without specifying their number. He also refers to the seven eras of history, the seventh one being that of the *Qāʾim al-qiyāma* on whose future appearance the era of the imāms ends and mankind is judged.[156] Muḥammad b. ʿAlī al-Ṣūrī, a Fāṭimid *dāʿī* in Syria who died around 487/1094, enumerates the imāms of the era of Islam in a long poem.[157] According to him, the seventh heptad of imāms in the era of Muḥammad is the most eminent one, because it precedes the coming of the Qā'im.[158] Making a distinction between the functions of the Mahdī and the Qā'im, he further states that the former had appeared in the person of Muḥammad b. Ismāʿīl, who became spiritual after having been corporeal. In sum, al-Ṣūrī held that the Mahdī had already appeared while the Qā'im, who would be a descendant of al-Mustanṣir, was still the awaited one. Meanwhile, the imāms and their gates (*bābs*) would continue to exist in the intervening period, summoning the people to obey the two eschatological personalities.[159]

Al-Ṣūrī's account clearly reveals the adjustment of the earlier doctrine to the realities faced by the Fāṭimid Ismāʿīlīs after the termination of the second heptad of imāms, and similarly to the adjustments made in the time of al-Muʿizz, the fourteenth imām. However, the belief in the advent of the Qā'im had persisted in the Fāṭimid Ismāʿīlī community. It was due to this basic orientation that authors like al-Ṣūrī could not resist the temptation of making more concrete predictions. Such tendencies are also distinctly embodied in *al-Majālis al-Mustanṣiriyya*, a collection of lectures by al-Mālījī, one of the chief *qāḍīs* in al-Mustanṣir's imāmate.[160] According to this source, the heptads of imāms will succeed one another until the arrival of the Qā'im of the Resurrection, whose *ḥujja* will be the seventh imām contiguous to his era; and the Qā'im himself will be the eighth amongst the imāms of that era and the seventh of the *nāṭiqs*.[161] Al-Mālījī does not, however, fail to add that the imām of his own time, al-Mustanṣir, was in fact the eighth imām and the eighth of the *khulafā'*, implying that he might be the one to fulfil the functions of the Qā'im, if the time for the latter's arrival came.[162] Yet, through a special esoteric interpretation of the resurrection, this Fāṭimid author attempts to explain that his ideas on the Qā'im, who may appear imminently, do not represent any denial of the Day of Judgement in the remote future.[163]

Similar views, reflecting the influences of Jaʿfar b. Manṣūr al-Yaman and other earlier Fāṭimid authors, are contained in Nāṣir-i Khusraw's *Wajh-i dīn*, a masterpiece of the *bāṭinī ta'wīl* and still one of the basic books of the Ismāʿīlīs of the upper Oxus region. Nāṣir, too, speaks of the continuity in the imāmate,[164] while constantly referring to the concept of the seven imāms,[165] or the seven imāms after the Prophet Muḥammad,[166] without further explanation. He does, however, specify that the seventh imām will be the Qā'im (or the *Qā'im-i qiyāmat*), possessing the rank (*martabat*) of Resurrection (*qiyāmat*).[167] According to him, the Prophet Muḥammad, who was the sixth *nāṭiq* after Ādam, Nūḥ, Ibrāhīm, Mūsā and ʿĪsā,[168] will be followed by six imāms whose completion lies in the appearance of the Qā'im, the seventh imām in the series and the seventh *nāṭiq* who, instead of promulgating a new *sharīʿa*, will pass final judgement over humanity under divine guidance. Moreover, Nāṣir distinguishes between a grand cycle (*dawr-i mihīn*), referring to the period of the seven *nāṭiqs*, and a small cycle (*dawr-i kihīn*), coinciding with the latter part of the grand cycle and referring to the era of Muḥammad and thereafter.[169] According to him,[170] the era in which we find ourselves is itself comprised of two parts, namely, that of the imāms and that of the *khalqān* (literally, created beings),[171] which is the period of Resurrection. Both parts go back to spiritual principles. Doubtless, Nāṣir-i Khusraw conformed to what may be regarded as the official Fāṭimid doctrine of his time, thinking of the advent of the Qā'im, the seventh imām and the master of the final era, as a future event.[172] But he does not venture to make any more specific predictions regarding the Qā'im's arrival, nor does he seem to attach any particular significance to the actual number of imāms or their heptads. Indeed, as W. Madelung has remarked,[173] Nāṣir's exposition, with its rich symbolism, though lacking in references to historical events and to the names of the imāms, was not meant to apply to the temporal reality as he might have perceived that reality. The account in the *Wajh-i dīn* should, in other words, be taken symbolically. Nāṣir simply and masterfully applies his esoteric exegesis to the system of ideas, concepts, doctrines and methods of interpretation propounded in the Fāṭimid works of an earlier period, works that the exile in Yumgān took as representation of the ideally valid and sacred truth.

The success of the Fāṭimid *daʿwa* in the eastern Islamic lands, especially ʿIrāq and Persia, brought about the hostile reaction of the Sunnī ʿAbbāsids and Saljūqids, as well as that of various local rulers as far as Transoxiana. Several instances of such reactions have already been noted; and in 444/1052, yet another anti-Fāṭimid document was sponsored by the ʿAbbāsid caliph al-Qā'im at Baghdād. This document, to which a number of jurists and ʿAlids subscribed, again aimed at discrediting the claim of the Fāṭimids to an ʿAlid descent.[174] Later, when Ismāʿīlism was spreading rapidly in Persia, the Ismāʿīlīs found a stout enemy in the person of Niẓām al-Mulk, the virtual ruler of the Saljūqid dominions for more than two decades until his assassination in 485/1092 by the Persian Ismāʿīlīs, who were already under the leadership of Ḥasan-i Ṣabbāḥ. Niẓām al-Mulk devoted a long section in his *Siyāsat-nāma* to the denunciation of the Ismāʿīlīs, reflecting his anxiety over their growing importance in Persia. Meanwhile, the ʿAbbāsids had continued to encourage the production of polemical works against the Ismāʿīliyya, or the Bāṭiniyya, as they were more generally designated. The most famous of such works was written by Abū Ḥāmid Muḥammad al-Ghazālī (d. 505/1111), the celebrated Sunnī theologian, jurist, philosopher and mystic. Al-Ghazālī, who had attracted the attention of Niẓām al-Mulk, was appointed by the latter in 484/1091 to a teaching position at the Niẓāmiyya Madrasa in Baghdād, one of the several so-named colleges founded by the Saljūqid vizier; he maintained that post for four years. It was at Baghdād that al-Ghazālī was commissioned by the young ʿAbbāsid caliph al-Mustaẓhir (487–512/1094–1118) to write a treatise in refutation of the Bāṭinīs. This work, which became simply known as *al-Mustaẓhirī*, was written shortly before al-Ghazālī left Baghdād at the end of 488/1095.[175] Subsequently, al-Ghazālī wrote several shorter works against the Ismāʿīlīs.[176] It is interesting to note that a detailed refutation, entitled *Dāmigh al-bāṭil*, of al-Ghazālī's *al-Mustaẓhirī* was later produced in Yaman by the fifth Mustaʿlī-Ṭayyibī *dāʿī*, who died in 612/1215.[177]

In the meantime, the Qarmaṭī state of Baḥrayn had been collapsing rapidly after Nāṣir-i Khusraw's visit to al-Aḥsā' in 443/1051. It may be recalled that Nāṣir had found the state still ruled by a council of six descendants of Abū Saʿīd, assisted by six viziers, from the progeny of Ibn Sanbar. He also noted that the Friday prayers and other Muslim rites such as fasting were not observed at al-Aḥsā', where all mosques had been closed, though a mosque had been built there by a Persian merchant.[178] All this, in a sense, reflected perhaps a second attempt, after the failure of the episode of the Persian Mahdī, to set up a new order in Baḥrayn, though the Qarmaṭīs there by the time of Nāṣir-i Khusraw evidently still believed themselves to be in the era of the Prophet Muḥammad. The troubles that initiated the downfall of the Qarmaṭī state started in the large island of Uwāl (now called al-Baḥrayn) which had hitherto provided an important source of revenue for the state, on account of the customs charges levied on all the ships passing through the Persian Gulf. Around 450/1058, a certain Abu'l-Bahlūl al-ʿAwwām of the tribe of ʿAbd al-Qays, aided by his brother Abu'l-Walīd Muslim, both Sunnīs, revolted against the Qarmaṭī governor of Uwāl and required that the *khuṭba* be read in the name of the ʿAbbāsid al-Qā'im throughout the island. Uwāl was permanently lost to the Qarmaṭīs when, around 459/1066–1067, the rebels defeated a Qarmaṭī fleet sent after them. Soon afterwards, Qaṭīf was taken from the Qarmaṭīs by another local rebel, Yaḥyā b. ʿAbbās, who had taken advantage of the insurrection in Uwāl to assert his own claims and who later seized that island from Abu'l-Bahlūl. More importantly, the Qarmaṭīs were now threatened by ʿAbd Allāh b. ʿAlī al-ʿUyūnī, a powerful local chief of the Banū Murra b. ʿĀmir of ʿAbd al-Qays residing in the province of al-Aḥsā', who rose against them in 462/1069–1070. He defeated the Qarmaṭīs and then besieged the town of al-Aḥsā' for seven years. Meanwhile, ʿAbd Allāh had successfully negotiated with Baghdād for receiving military help from the ʿAbbāsids and the Saljūqids. Assisted by a force of Turkoman horsemen sent from ʿIrāq, he managed to take al-Aḥsā' in 469/1076. ʿAbd Allāh al-ʿUyūnī decisively defeated the Qarmaṭīs and their tribal allies, especially the Banū ʿĀmir b. Rabīʿa of ʿUqal, in 470/1077; putting a definite end to the Qarmaṭī state of Baḥrayn and founding the new local dynasty of the ʿUyūnids in eastern Arabia.[179] ʿAbd Allāh, who had difficulties of his own with the Saljūqids, had shortly earlier acknowledged the suzerainty of the Fāṭimid al-Mustanṣir. The latter had evidently placed the ʿUyānid ruler under the protection of the Ṣulayḥids in Rabīʿ II 469/November 1076.[180] By that time, the remaining Qarmaṭī communities elsewhere, comprised of the dissident Ismāʿīlīs who had continued to expect the return of Muḥammad b. Ismāʿīl, had been by and large won over to the side of Fāṭimid Ismāʿīlism.

Returning to the domestic scene in Fāṭimid Egypt, it may be recalled that Badr al-Jamālī had managed to restore order to the country's administration and finances, after having crushed various rebellious factions, during his long vizierate of some twenty years. The Fāṭimid Caliphate was in effect saved by Badr who became the real master of the state during the final two decades of al-Mustanṣir's reign. The *amīr al-juyūsh* Badr al-Jamālī, also known as Badr al-Mustanṣirī, died at an advanced age in Rabīʿ I 487/March–April 1094, after he had already arranged for his son al-Afḍal to succeed him in office. The military saw to it that the Fāṭimid caliph duly acted according to Badr's wishes. A few months later in Dhu'l-Ḥijja 487/December 1094, Abū Tamīm Maʿadd al-Mustanṣir bi'llāh, the eighth Fāṭimid caliph and the eighteenth imām of the Fāṭimid Ismāʿīlīs, died in Cairo, after a reign of some sixty years during which the Fāṭimid Caliphate was well embarked on its way to collapse. Al-Mustanṣir's death also marked the end of the 'classical' Fāṭimid period. As we shall see later, the dispute over al-Mustanṣir's succession, which was the greatest internal crisis of the Fāṭimid dynasty and revolved around the claims of al-Mustanṣir's sons Nizār and al-Mustaʿlī, caused a major split in Fāṭimid Ismāʿīlism. This schism, as a result of which the Fāṭimid Ismāʿīlīs became divided into two rival wings, the Mustaʿlawiyya or Mustaʿliyya (Mustaʿlians) and the Nizāriyya, proved to have a drastic and lasting consequence for the future course of the Ismāʿīlī movement.

In the remainder of this chapter we shall discuss certain issues related to the organizations of the state and the Ismāʿīlī *daʿwa* under the Fāṭimids as well as some aspects of the doctrines propounded by the Fāṭimid Ismāʿīlīs. In the Fāṭimid Caliphate, especially until al-Mustanṣir, every caliph who was also the imām of the Fāṭimid Ismāʿīlīs, was selected through the *naṣṣ* of his predecessor. This designation, as noted, could be made public or could be divulged to only a few trusted persons for as long as deemed necessary. The succession of the Fāṭimid caliph-imāms was, furthermore, normally governed by the rule of the primogeniture. Starting with al-Ḥākim, however, the Fāṭimid sovereign was usually a minor at the time of his accession to the throne, and, therefore, often a regent or a vizier held the real reins of power in the state. From 466/1074, when Badr al-Jamālī arrived in Egypt and became the all-powerful vizier, the authority of the caliph-imām was reduced drastically and the Fāṭimid rulers became in effect mere figureheads and puppets in the hands of their viziers, henceforth the real masters of the Fāṭimid state.

Indeed, the institution of the vizierate acquired an increasing importance throughout the history of the Fāṭimid dynasty.[181] During their North African phase, the Fāṭimid caliph-imāms also acted as the supreme heads of the government administration and commanders of the armed forces. As such, they personally regulated the affairs of the state and made the major decisions like other autocratic Muslim rulers of the period. The early Fāṭimids did consult with certain trusted individuals, and, at least from the reign of al-Qā'im, a few dignitaries in the Fāṭimid state, like Jawdhar, gradually came to discharge some of the functions of a chief minister. But the actual title of *wazīr* was not given to any high official whilst the Fāṭimids still ruled from Ifrīqiya. Ibn Killis, the organizer of the public administration and finances of the first two Fāṭimids in Egypt, was the first to have received the title under al-ʿAzīz. Until Badr al-Jamālī, the Fāṭimid viziers, whether they carried various forms of the title *wazīr* or were less pretentiously called by the title of *wāsiṭa*, were simply regarded as high agents for the execution of the sovereign's orders. They were intermediaries without any effective authority of their own, corresponding to what the Sunnī jurist and theoretician al-Māwardī (d. 450/1058) designated as *wazīr al-tanfīdh*, or vizier with executive powers only. These viziers were generally selected from amongst civilians, or the so-called men of the pen (*arbāb al-aqlām*); consequently, they were known as 'Viziers of the Pen'. From Badr al-Jamālī onwards, the Fāṭimid vizier obtained full powers from his sovereign and became what in al-Māwardī's terminology is called *wazīr al-tafwīḍ*, or vizier with delegated powers.[182] As this latter type of vizier, acting independently, was normally of military status, he was called 'Vizier of the Pen and of the Sword', or simply 'Vizier of the Sword' (*wazīr al-sayf*). He was not only the commander of the armies (*amīr al-juyūsh*) and the effective head of the civil bureaucracy, but often also the head of the religious hierarchy. A distinguishing feature of the Fāṭimid vizierate, whose occupants were changed frequently, is that several viziers were Christians, serving sovereigns who regarded themselves as the rightful leaders of Muslims throughout the world. In later Fāṭimid times, this position came to be held by yet other Christians, notably the Armenian general Bahrām (d. 535/1140), who was 'Vizier of the Sword' during 529–531/1135–1137 and also bore the title of Sayf al-Islām.[183]

The organization of the Fāṭimid state remained simple during its North

African phase, although al-Mahdī and his three successors developed their own ceremonials and institutions.[184] During that period, when the caliph himself assumed all the major responsibilities, the highly centralized administration known as *al-khidma*, normally situated at the caliphal palace (*dār al-mulk*) in Fāṭimid capitals in Ifrīqiya, required only a few offices for the discharge of different administrative, financial and military tasks. But from the very beginning of the Egyptian phase, the organizational structure of administration and finance introduced by Jawhar and Ibn Killis, with the assistance of ʿUslūj b. al-Ḥasan, provided the basis for a complex system of institutions.[185] These institutions, most of which were derived from those adopted or developed by the ʿAbbāsids, became progressively more elaborate or even modified. The Fāṭimid system of administration in Egypt continued to remain strongly centralized, with the caliph and his vizier at its head; while the provincial organs of the government were subjected to the strict control of the central authorities in Cairo. The central administration of the Fāṭimids, as in the case of the ʿAbbāsids, was carried on through the *dīwān* system; and the various *dīwān*s (ministries, departments or offices) were at times situated at the residence of the caliph or his vizier. Apparently the first central organ in Fāṭimid Egypt, in which the entire government machinery seems to have been concentrated and which at some unknown date split into a number of departments, was the *dīwān al-majālis*. Al-Qalqashandī and al-Maqrīzī discuss three main *dīwān*s through which operated the Fāṭimid central administration in Egypt. These *dīwān*s, each of which was in turn divided into a number of offices also called *dīwān*s, were the *dīwān al-inshā'* or *al-rasā'il*, the chancery of state, entrusted with issuing and handling the various types of official documents including the caliphal decrees and letters; the *dīwān al-jaysh wa'l-rawātib*, the department of the army and salaries; and finally, the *dīwān al-amwāl*, the department of finance. The officials of the Fāṭimid state, both civil (*arbāb al-aqlām*) and military (*arbāb al-suyūf*), in all the administrative, financial, military, judicial and religious organs, were organized in terms of strict hierarchies, marked by differences in rank, insignia, remuneration, and places occupied in official ceremonies.

The *daʿwa* activity on behalf of the Fāṭimid Imāms did not cease upon the foundation of the Fāṭimid dynasty in North Africa. The missionary activity of the Fāṭimids, in contradistinction to that of the ʿAbbāsids in the aftermath of their own victory, continued and became even more organized and extensive, especially following the transference of the

Fāṭimid headquarters to Cairo. This was presumably because the Fāṭimids never abandoned the hope of establishing their rule over the entire Muslim world. Consequently, the Fāṭimid *daʿwa* persistently aimed at convincing the Muslims everywhere that the Fāṭimid Ismāʿīlī Imām, divinely inspired and in possession of special *ʿilm* and the secret allegorical interpretation of the religious prescriptions, was the sole rightful leader of mankind; and that all other dynasties, including those Shīʿī ones descended from ʿAlī b. Abī Ṭālib, had been usurpers. This also explains why the Fāṭimid Ismāʿīlīs referred to their missionary activities as *al-daʿwa al-hādiya*, or the rightly-guiding summons to mankind to follow the Fāṭimid Imām. At any event, Fāṭimid Ismāʿīlism had now become the state religion of an empire, in parts of which some of its doctrines were preached freely. At the same time, the *daʿwa* had been maintained in clandestine form in regions outside the Fāṭimid domain, as the direct continuation of the Ismāʿīlī *daʿwa* of the second half of the 3rd/9th century. By the time of al-Mustanṣir, the Fāṭimids had progressively come to command the religious loyalty of numerous local Ismāʿīlī communities in many parts beyond the borders of their empire; although Ismāʿīlism had never become the majoritarian religion even within the Fāṭimid dominions.

The organization and evolution of the Fāṭimid *daʿwa*, as well as the scope of the functions of various actual or potential ranks (*ḥudūd*) within the organization, are amongst the most obscure aspects of Fāṭimid Ismāʿīlism.[186] Information is particularly meagre concerning the nature of the *daʿwa* organization in non-Fāṭimid regions where, fearing persecution, the *dāʿīs* were continuously obliged to observe secrecy in their activities. Understandably, the Ismāʿīlī literature of the period also maintains silence on the subject. In regions ruled by the Fāṭimids, Ismāʿīlism, enjoying the protection of the state, became the official *madhhab* and its legal doctrines were applied freely by the judiciary. Consequently, the chief *qāḍī*, who headed the judiciary, was normally selected from amongst the Ismāʿīlīs. It is interesting to note that the Fāṭimid chief *qāḍī*, or *qāḍī al-quḍāt*, often also acted as the administrative head of the *daʿwa* and was thus simultaneously the chief *dāʿī*. In Egypt, at least, doctrinal propaganda aiming at increasing the number of Ismāʿīlī adepts, was conducted openly and was accompanied by education and instruction (*taʿlīm*) in various Ismāʿīlī sciences. These lectures, or *majālis*, delivered chiefly in Cairo by Ismāʿīlī theologians and jurists, provided the main occasion for the Ismāʿīlīs of the Fāṭimid capital and its vicinity to assert themselves as a community. Al-Maqrīzī, quoting al-Musabbiḥī and Ibn al-Ṭuwayr, relates valuable details on these lectures and on incidents occurring due to overcrowding in the course of their attendance.[187] In 365/975, ʿAlī b. al-Nuʿmān lectured at al-Azhar to vast audiences, from a legal text composed by his father al-Qāḍī al-Nuʿmān.[188] The vizier Ibn Killis delivered weekly lectures in his residence on Ismāʿīlī jurisprudence, using also a text written by himself. In 385/995, Muḥammad b. al-Nuʿmān, ʿAlī's brother, lectured to large numbers gathered at the Fāṭimid palace on the sciences of the Ahl al-Bayt, in accordance with the custom set by his father in the Maghrib and maintained by him and his elder brother in Egypt. In 394/1004, ʿAbd al-ʿAzīz b. Muḥammad b. al-Nuʿmān, after becoming the chief *qāḍī*, delivered lectures in the palace and also at al-Azhar, drawing especially on one of his grandfather's treatises.[189] Besides these public sessions related mainly to law, there were other types of sessions in Cairo; the so-called *daʿwa* sessions, which had come to be more elaborately organized and specifically designed for the *daʿwa* purposes and for the exclusive benefit of the Ismāʿīlīs.

The *daʿwa* sessions (*majālis al-daʿwa*), initiated in al-Ḥākim's reign under the direction of the chief *dāʿī*, were arranged in terms of systematic courses on different subjects. In due time, these courses came to be compiled in written form, often with a formal division into lectures or *majālis*. The sessions on Ismāʿīlī doctrines, being particularly devoted to theology and theosophy, became known as the *majālis al-ḥikma*. By the end of the 4th/10th century, regular sessions were conducted for the reading of the *majālis* by the chief *dāʿī*, at the Dār al-Ḥikma and elsewhere, and of which several collections had been compiled by that time. The *majālis*, normally composed by or for the chief *dāʿī*, reached their culmination in the collection of al-Mu'ayyad al-Shīrāzī, some of which were originally read out, from 441/1049 onwards, in the *majālis al-ḥikma* by the chief *qāḍī* and chief *dāʿī* al-Yāzūrī, who in 442 A.H. also became al-Mustanṣir's vizier. There were separate meetings for men, held at the great hall (*al-īwān al-kabīr*) of the palace, and for women, held in other quarters of the palace or at al-Azhar. These sessions were arranged according to the degree of learning of the adepts. The fixed monetary contributions of the individual Ismāʿīlīs, known as *najwā*, were apparently collected during the *majālis al-ḥikma*, and the lists of the contributors were kept by a special secretary (*kātib al-daʿwa*) appointed by the chief *dāʿī*. Wealthy Ismāʿīlīs, according to al-Maqrīzī, made substantial voluntary donations, over and above the sums required of all adepts. The meetings of the *majālis al-ḥikma* were often utilized by the chief *dāʿī* also for the purpose of administering a special oath (*ʿahd*) to the new Ismāʿīlī converts. Other categories of courses, open also to non-Ismāʿīlīs, were designed for senior officials, palace personnel and the common people.

The chief *dāʿī* was evidently responsible for appointing the provincial *dāʿīs* within the Fāṭimid empire. These subordinate *dāʿīs*, acting as lieutenants of the chief *dāʿī* and representatives of *al-daʿwa al-hādiya*, were stationed in several cities of Egypt as well as in the main towns of the Fāṭimid provinces, such as Damascus, Tyre, Acre, Ramla, and ʿAsqalān. The Fāṭimid *dāʿīs* were also active in some rural districts of Syria, notably in the Jabal al-Summāq, southwest of Aleppo.[190] The chief *dāʿī* seems to have played a major part also in selecting the *dāʿīs* of the non-Fāṭimid provinces. Not much more is available on the functions of the chief *dāʿī*, who had his headquarters in Cairo and who in the Fāṭimid ceremonial, ranked second after the chief *qāḍī*, if both posts were not held by the same person.[191] Even the title of *dāʿī al-duʿāt*, used frequently in non-Ismāʿīlī sources, rarely appears in Ismāʿīlī texts. In those Fāṭimid Ismāʿīlī sources which refer to different ranks in the *daʿwa*, the term *bāb* (sometimes *bāb al-abwāb*) is reserved for the administrative head of the *daʿwa*, the dignitary immediately after the imām. Thus, in Ismāʿīlī religious terminology, the rank of *bāb* was used as the exact equivalent of the official term *dāʿī al-duʿāt*. For instance, al-Muʾayyad al-Shīrāzī is called the *bāb* of al-Mustanṣir by the *dāʿī* Idrīs and many other Ismāʿīlī writers,[192] while he is named as *dāʿī al-duʿāt* by the Sunnī historians.[193] Ḥamīd al-Dīn al-Kirmānī makes various allusions to the position and importance of the *bāb*, and his closeness to the imām.[194] Other Ismāʿīlī sources also emphasize that under the Fāṭimids in Egypt the *bāb* was the first person to receive the imām's teachings; and as such, he was the imām's mouthpiece. Without mentioning particular details, the Ismāʿīlī literature conveys the impression that the *bāb*, who naturally had to be a highly qualified and pious Ismāʿīlī dignitary, was responsible for the overall administration and certain policies of the *daʿwa*; and in the discharge of his functions he was closely supervised by the imām and assisted by a number of subordinate *dāʿīs*.

The Ismāʿīlī authors make differing and occasional allusions to the seemingly elaborate organizational structure of the *daʿwa*, designated as the *ḥudūd al-dīn* or the *marātib al-daʿwa*. Although no details are available on the *daʿwa* organization during the Fāṭimid period, it is certain that this organization developed over time and attained a definite shape during al-Ḥākim's reign; whilst the *daʿwa* hierarchy became finally fixed by the time of the chief *dāʿī* al-Muʾayyad. At the same time, the *daʿwa* terminology experienced an evolution of its own. During the early Fāṭimid period, differing names were used for the *daʿwa* positions by the Persian and Yamanī Ismāʿīlī authors, such as Abū Ḥātim al-Rāzī and Jaʿfar b. Manṣūr al-Yaman. But some of the earlier designations had already fallen into disuse by al-Mustanṣir's time. It is also important to note that the hierarchy traceable in the Fāṭimid texts seems to have had reference to an idealistic or utopian situation, when the Ismāʿīlī Imām would rule the entire world, and not to any actual *ḥudūd* existing at any given time. In other words, it is certain that the diverse *daʿwa* ranks mentioned by these sources were not actually filled by incumbents at all times; and some of them were never filled at all.

The Fāṭimid *daʿwa* was organized hierarchically, in line with the particular importance accorded to hierarchism in Fāṭimid Ismāʿīlī thought. Indeed, there was a close analogy between the terrestrial hierarchy of the Fāṭimid *daʿwa*, with its highest ranks of *nāṭiq*, *waṣī* (*asās*) and imām, and the celestial or cosmological hierarchy developed in Fāṭimid thought. There are diverse partial accounts of the *daʿwa* ranks or *ḥudūd* after the imām and his *bāb*. All Ismāʿīlī authors agree that the world, presumably the non-Fāṭimid part of it, was divided into twelve *jazāʾir* (singular, *jazīra*; literally, island), for *daʿwa* purposes; each *jazīra* representing a separate and somewhat independent region or diocese for the penetration of the *daʿwa*. Research for this book located the list of these twelve *daʿwa* regions, commonly referred to as the 'islands of the earth' (*jazāʾir al-arḍ*), in only one Fāṭimid source, namely, an esoteric work by al-Qāḍī al-Nuʿmān dating to the 4th/10th century. According to this source,[195] the twelve *jazāʾir* in the author's time were: al-ʿArab (Arabs), al-Rūm (Byzantines), al-Ṣaqāliba (Slavs), al-Nūb (Nubians), al-Khazar (Khazars), al-Hind (India), al-Sind (Sind), al-Zanj (Negroes), al-Ḥabash (Abyssinians), al-Ṣīn (Chinese), al-Daylam (Daylam, probably for Persians), and al-Barbar (Berbers). These regions were apparently delineated on the basis of a combination of geographic, ethnographic and linguistic considerations. The same list, with one variation, al-Turk (Turks) for al-Nūb, and obviously derived from al-Nuʿmān or another source belonging to the same period, is enumerated in a work written in the 6th/12th century by the Yamanī Ismāʿīlī author ʿAlī b. al-Ḥusayn al-Qurashī (d. 554/1159).[196] It is interesting to note that Khurāsān, of which Nāṣir-i Khusraw claimed to be the *ḥujja* in the second half of the 5th/11th century, does not appear as a *jazīra* in al-Nuʿmān's list. However, al-Nuʿmān's well-informed and possibly Ismāʿīlī contemporary, Ibn Ḥawqal, who himself travelled through eastern Persia and

Transoxiana around 358/969, mentions Khurāsān as a *jazīra* of the Fāṭimid *daʿwa* (*daʿwat ahl al-Maghrib*), further adding that the Ismāʿīlī Balūchīs of eastern Persia belonged to that *jazīra*.[197] It is also possible that Khurāsān may have been included in the *jazīra* of Hind. Each *jazīra* was placed under the charge of a high ranking missionary called *ḥujja*; also called *naqīb*, *lāḥiq* or *yad* by the Ismāʿīlī authors of the early Fāṭimid period. The *ḥujja* was the chief local *dāʿī* and the highest representative of the *daʿwa* in the region under his jurisdiction. Amongst the twelve *ḥujjas* serving the imām, four occupied special positions, comparable to the positions of the four sacred months amongst the twelve months of the year.[198]

The *bāb* and the twelve *ḥujjas* were followed, in the *daʿwa* hierarchy, by a number of *dāʿīs* of varying ranks operating in every *jazīra*.[199] Sources distinguish three categories of such *dāʿīs*, who in the descending order of importance are: *dāʿī al-balāgh*, *al-dāʿī al-muṭlaq* and *al-dāʿī al-mahdūd* (or *al-maḥṣūr*). It is not clear what the specific functions of these *dāʿīs* were, although the third was apparently the chief assistant of the *dāʿī al-muṭlaq*, who became the chief functionary of the *daʿwa*, acting with absolute authority in the absence of the region's *ḥujja* and *dāʿī al-balāgh*. And the latter seems to have served as the liaison between the central *daʿwa* headquarters in the Fāṭimid capital and the local headquarters of a *jazīra*. Finally, there was the rank of the assistant to the *dāʿī*, entitled *al-maʾdhūn*, the licentiate. At least two categories of this *ḥadd* in the hierarchy have been mentioned, namely, *al-maʾdhūn al-muṭlaq*, sometimes simply called *al-maʾdhūn*, and *al-maʾdhūn al-maḥdūd* (or *al-maḥṣūr*), eventually designated as *al-mukāsir*. The *maʾdhūn al-muṭlaq*, or the chief licentiate, who often became a *dāʿī* himself, was authorized to administer the oath of initiation (*ʿahd* or *mīthāq*), and to explain the various regulations of the *daʿwa* to the initiates. The *mukāsir* (literally, persuader), who had limited authority, was mainly responsible for attracting converts. At the bottom of the *daʿwa*, and not as a rank in its hierarchy, there was the ordinary initiate called *al-mustajīb* (literally, respondent). Sometimes two grades of ordinary Ismāʿīlīs were distinguished, namely, *muʾmin al-balāgh* or simply *al-muʾmin*, the initiated major member of the community; and *al-mustajīb*, the neophyte or the candidate for initiation. At any event, the initiated members of the community, now belonging to *ahl al-daʿwa*, represented the elite, as compared to the non-Ismāʿīlī Muslims, called *ʿāmmat al-Muslimīn*. These *daʿwa* ranks, numbering to seven from the *bāb* to the *mukāsir*, together with their main functions and corresponding celestial *ḥudūd*, are enumerated fully by the *dāʿī* al-Kirmānī who synthesized the differing ideas of his predecessors.[200] Al-Kirmānī's schema of the *daʿwa* hierarchy, the most elaborate of its kind, endured at least theoretically; providing especially the basis of the hierarchy which was later espoused by the Ṭayyibī *daʿwa*.[201]

The word *dāʿī*, meaning 'he who summons', was used by several Muslim groups to designate their religio-political propagandists. It was utilized by the early Muʿtazila, but soon became particularly identified with certain Shīʿī groups. The designation was adopted by the ʿAbbāsid *daʿwa* in Khurāsān and also by the Zaydiyya and some of the Shīʿī Ghulāt, notably the Khaṭṭābiyya. The term, however, acquired its greatest application in connection with the Ismāʿīliyya, although the Persian Ismāʿīlī authors of the early Fāṭimid period sometimes used other designations such as *al-janāḥ* (plural, *al-ajniḥa*) for *al-dāʿī*.[202] Notwithstanding this lack of uniformity in nomenclature and the existence of different grades of *dāʿīs* during any particular epoch, the term *al-dāʿī* came to be applied generically from early on by the Ismāʿīlīs. It was used in reference to any authorized representative of their *daʿwa*, a propagandist responsible for spreading the Ismāʿīlī religion and for winning suitable followers for the Ismāʿīlī Imām, or the awaited Mahdī-Qā'im of the Ismāʿīliyya. During the Fāṭimid period, the *dāʿī* was moreover the unofficial agent of the Fāṭimid state operating secretly in many non-Fāṭimid territories, where the *daʿwa* aimed to establish the rule of the Fāṭimid caliph-imām.

In spite of its unique importance to the Ismāʿīlīs, almost nothing seems to have been written by them on the subject of the *dāʿī* and his functions. Al-Qāḍī al-Nuʿmān, the most prolific Fāṭimid author, devoted only a short chapter in one of his books, which was on the etiquette to be observed towards the imām, to explaining the virtues of an ideal *dāʿī*.[203] A more detailed though general discussion of the qualifications and attributes of a Fāṭimid *dāʿī* is contained in what is evidently the only independent Ismāʿīlī treatise on the subject, written towards the end of the 4th/10th century by al-Nuʿmān's younger contemporary Aḥmad b. Ibrāhīm al-Nīsābūrī. This treatise has not survived directly, but it is quoted almost completely in some later Ismāʿīlī works.[204] Ismāʿīlism never aimed at mass proselytization, and al-Nuʿmān emphasizes that the *dāʿī* should personally know the individual initiates. The learned jurist also states that the *dāʿī* must be exemplary in his own behaviour and use sound and timely judgement in disciplining the erring members of his local community. According to al-Nīsābūrī's fuller account, a *dāʿī* could be appointed only by the imām's permission (*idhn*); and, having been despatched to a certain locality, he would then operate independently of the central headquarters, receiving general guidance from the imām and the central authorities.

Under such circumstances, only those candidates who possessed the highest necessary educational qualifications combined with the proper moral and intellectual attributes would become *dāʿīs*. In addition to having good organizing abilities, the *dāʿī* was also expected to be sufficiently familiar with the teachings of different non-Muslim religions and Islamic sects, whilst knowing the local language and customs of the province in which he was to operate. Many of the Fāṭimid *dāʿīs*, as noted, were highly trained in various specialized institutions of Cairo and elsewhere, such as the Dār al-Ḥikma and al-Azhar, prior to being sent to the field. And the high degree of learning attained by the Fāṭimid *dāʿīs*, many of whom were outstanding thinkers and scholars, is attested by the fact that the bulk of Ismāʿīlī literature surviving from the Fāṭimid period was written by these *dāʿīs*, who were well-versed in theology, philosophy and other fields of learning. The *dāʿī* was also responsible for the training of his *maʾdhūns*, and for supervising the education of the *mustajībs*. Al-Nīsābūrī also reminds us that in case a *dāʿī* felt unable to fulfil his duties properly, he was not to hesitate in informing the imām and in resigning from his post. The overall picture that emerges from these sketchy accounts, as well as from the existing evidence on the relationships between the Fāṭimids and their provincial missions, notably those in Yaman and Sind, is that the provincial *dāʿīs* normally enjoyed a great deal of independence in their activities, once appointed. There was, nevertheless, a good deal of contact and correspondence between the local *daʿwa* in any region and the central administration of the *daʿwa* in the Fāṭimid capital; between the *ḥujja* and the lesser provincial *dāʿīs*, on the one hand, and the imām and his *bāb* (*dāʿī al-duʿāt*), on the other.

Like so many other aspects of the *daʿwa*, almost nothing is known about the methods used by the Fāṭimid *dāʿīs* for winning and educating new converts. Doubtless, different procedures were adopted for peoples of different religions and socio-ethnic backgrounds. Addressing themselves to one *mustajīb* at a time, the *dāʿīs* treated each case individually with due consideration to the respondent's particular status. However, many Sunnī sources, deriving their information chiefly from the anti-Ismāʿīlī accounts of Ibn Rizām and Akhū Muḥsin, speak of a system of seven or nine degrees of initiation into Ismāʿīlism.[205] Other anti-Fāṭimid sources discuss yet another type of graded system, giving a different name to each stage in the process of detaching the respondent from his previous religion and leading him towards heresy and unbelief.[206] There is no evidence of such fixed graded systems in Ismāʿīlī literature, though a certain amount of gradualism must surely have been unavoidable in the initiation and education of the converts. Al-Nīsābūrī, for instance, relates that the *dāʿī*s were expected to educate the *mustajīb*s in a gradual manner, not revealing too much at a time so as not to confound them. Gradualism, from simpler and exoteric sciences to more complex esoteric ones, was also observed in the organization of lectures for the ordinary Ismāʿīlīs and the training courses for the *dāʿī*s themselves, at various institutions in Cairo.

The Fāṭimid Ismāʿīlīs maintained the basic doctrinal framework developed by the early Ismāʿīlīs, but they gradually modified certain of its aspects. In particular, they retained the fundamental distinction between the exoteric and the esoteric aspects of religion, and the earlier cyclical prophetic view of history, while introducing drastic changes into the pre-Fāṭimid cosmology. However, in contrast to the early Ismāʿīlīs, who tended to emphasize the significance of the *bāṭin*, they now insisted on the equal importance of the *ẓāhir* and the *bāṭin*. Both were considered as complementary dimensions of religion, and consequently, the Fāṭimid *daʿwa* adopted the position of opposing the antinomian tendencies of the more radical Ismāʿīlī circles. These tendencies, such as those manifested by the *dāʿī*s who organized the Druze movement or those espoused by the Qarmaṭīs or even by the dissident Ismāʿīlīs within the Fāṭimid camp, were generally rooted in enthusiasm for the *bāṭin*. There are numerous references in almost every work of the Fāṭimid Ismāʿīlī literature for the necessity of preserving a careful balance between the *ẓāhir* and the *bāṭin*, emphasizing that one could not meaningfully exist without the other.[207] The *ta'wīl* or esoteric exegesis, required for deriving the truths hidden in the *bāṭin*, thus retained its importance in Fāṭimid Ismāʿīlī thought. The *ta'wīl* was the exclusive prerogative of the divinely-guided, infallible Fāṭimid Imām who could convey such knowledge of the inner meaning behind the religious prescriptions, to the lower members of the *daʿwa* hierarchy. In the absence of the Qā'im, the *ḥaqā'iq* could be conveyed to the elite of mankind, the Ismāʿīlī community or the *ahl al-daʿwa*, only by the Fāṭimid Ismāʿīlī Imām and the hierarchy of dignitaries serving him, especially the twelve *ḥujja*s and the lesser *dāʿī*s.

The Fāṭimid Ismāʿīlīs elaborated and expounded their doctrines in what were to become known as the classical works of Ismāʿīlī literature. In line with the basic structure of their religious thought, they paid attention to both the *ʿilm al-ẓāhir* and the *ʿilm al-bāṭin*, exoteric and esoteric knowledge, which found expression in numerous works ranging from the legal treatises of al-Qāḍī al-Nuʿmān to the more complex theological and philosophical writings of other outstanding authors of the period.[208] The works on the *ẓāhir* of religion, propounding the exoteric doctrines, consisted mainly of those on jurisprudence (*fiqh*) and related subjects dealing with the exoteric aspects of the Sharīʿa and the ritual prescriptions of Islam. Historical works, as noted, were rather rare amongst the Ismāʿīlīs. Writings on *tafsīr*, the external philological exegeses and commentaries used for explaining the apparent meaning of the Qur'ānic passages and so important amongst the Sunnīs and the Twelver Shīʿīs, are also absent from the Fāṭimid literature. For the Fāṭimid Ismāʿīlīs, the living imām was the repository of true knowledge and the sole authoritative interpreter of the literal and hidden meaning of the sacred texts. Therefore, they had no need for a *ẓāhirī* science of *tafsīr* apart from what the imām would explain about the Qur'ān, with or without resorting to *ta'wīl*. This is why the Ismāʿīlīs often referred to their imām as the speaking Qur'ān (*al-Qur'ān al-nāṭiq*), in contrast to the actual text of the 'sacred book' which was regarded as the silent Qur'ān (*al-Qur'ān al-ṣāmit*).[209] For similar reasons, the Ismāʿīlīs produced few works on *ḥadīth*, since in that respect, too, the imām would provide the necessary guidance and criteria for the community. The Fāṭimid Ismāʿīlīs did, however, accept those traditions related from the Prophet which had been handed down or sanctioned by their imāms, in conjunction with those traditions related from their recognized imāms, including especially the Imām al-Ṣādiq. Most such traditions were compiled by al-Qāḍī al-Nuʿmān, mainly in his *Daʿā'im al-Islām* and *Sharḥ al-akhbār*.

In the area of the *bāṭinī* sciences, which account for the bulk of the writings produced during the Fāṭimid period, the Fāṭimid Ismāʿīlīs made their greatest contributions to Shīʿī gnosis and Islamic philosophy. It was in expounding the esoteric doctrines of the sect, which constitute the essence of the Ismāʿīlī gnosis, that the highly educated *dāʿīs* produced their elaborate treatises on *ta'wīl* and *ḥaqā'iq*. It was also in connection with developing their theological, philosophical and metaphysical theories that the eminent Ismāʿīlī authors of the classical Fāṭimid period showed their originality of thought, mastery of pre-Islamic religions and Judaeo-Christian scriptures, as well as their profound knowledge of the Hellenistic and Islamic philosophies.

Fāṭimid Ismāʿīlism retained the early Ismāʿīlī views of cyclical hiero-history and prophetology, which conceived of seven eras, each inaugurated by a *nāṭiq*. However, due to the Fāṭimid claims to the imāmate, the early Ismāʿīlī doctrine of the imāmate now required modifications. These modifications necessitated adjustments in the earlier views concerning the duration of the sixth era, the era of the Prophet Muḥammad, the number and functions of the imāms during that era, and the identity and attributes of the Qā'im. We have already discussed these modifications, starting with the reform of ʿUbayd Allāh, who openly claimed the imāmate and denied the Mahdīship of Muḥammad b. Ismāʿīl, causing a split in the movement. By the time of al-Muʿizz, Ismāʿīl b. Jaʿfar and his son Muḥammad were openly recognized as imāms and progenitors of the Fāṭimids. But the earlier doctrine of the imāmate was revised in respect to the role of Muḥammad b. Ismāʿīl as the seventh and final imām of the era of Islam, allowing for more than one heptad of imāms in that era, in contradistinction to the situation in the first five eras. In addition, the Fāṭimid Imāms, succeeding one another in the second heptad, had come to be viewed as the deputies (*khulafā'*) of the Qā'im Muḥammad b. Ismāʿīl, discharging some of the latter's functions. As Fāṭimid rule continued and the eschatological expectations regarding the Qā'im were not fulfilled, further heptads of imāms were permitted in the era of Islam, whose duration was now continuously extended. This postponed the awaited emergence of the Qā'im, who was to initiate the final era of history, still further into the future. By the time of al-Mustanṣir, the Fāṭimid Ismāʿīlīs had come to accept even a spiritual interpretation in respect to the Qā'im's parousia, while in general they had allowed for him to be a person, from the progeny of the Fāṭimids, other than Muḥammad b. Ismāʿīl, who was no longer expected to reappear corporeally.

Before discussing the cosmology of the Fāṭimid Ismāʿīlīs, it is necessary to refer to an important school of thought developed by some eminent *dāʿīs* of Persia and Transoxiana during the earliest decades of the Fāṭimid period. The protagonists of this so-called Persian school of dissident Ismāʿīlism were Muḥammad b. Aḥmad al-Nasafī, Abū Ḥātim al-Rāzī and Abū Yaʿqūb al-Sijistānī. When the Fāṭimids were still preoccupied with establishing the roots of their power in North Africa and not as concerned with doctrinal issues, the above-mentioned *dāʿīs*, all belonging to the dissident eastern Ismāʿīlīs who had not accepted the imāmate of ʿUbayd Allāh (ʿAbd Allāh), were deeply involved in philosophical speculations, propounding their own views on the imāmate, prophecy, metaphysics and cosmology. These *dāʿīs* in fact acted as the main links, in the doctrinal domain, between the early Ismāʿīlīs and the Fāṭimid Ismāʿīlīs. Many of the ideas first elaborated by al-Nasafī and Abū Ḥātim who had already become prominent in the pre-Fāṭimid period and who unlike al-Sijistānī never rallied to the side of the Fāṭimids, were later incorporated into Fāṭimid doctrines during the reign of al-Muʿizz. Without unified leadership, however, these dissident *dāʿīs*, and the communities directed by them, diverged in respect to various doctrinal matters. In fact, they became engaged in a scholarly dispute that lasted for some time during the 4th/10th century.[210] Subsequently, the *dāʿī* al-Kirmānī took it upon himself to act as an arbiter in this famous controversy in his *Kitāb al-riyāḍ* (*Book of the Meadows*).[211]

Al-Nasafī, the leading philosopher amongst the early Ismāʿīlīs, was evidently also the first eastern *dāʿī* to propagate his ideas in writing. He produced a major work, *Kitāb al-maḥṣūl* (*Book of the Yield*), summarizing his views, shortly before the establishment of the Fāṭimid Caliphate or during the earlier years of ʿUbayd Allāh's reign. The first half of *al-Maḥṣūl* apparently contained the exposition of a type of Neoplatonic metaphysical system which al-Nasafī himself introduced into Ismāʿīlism, while the second half of the book dealt with the seven eras of prophecy in human history. *Al-Maḥṣūl*'s rapid popularity amongst the dissident Ismāʿīlīs, who at the time had only a few works at their disposal, prompted Abū Ḥātim to devote an entire work, entitled *Kitāb al-iṣlāḥ* (*Book of the Correction*), to its criticism. Abū Ḥātim seems to have been particularly concerned with correcting the antinomian tendencies expressed by al-Nasafī. Unfortunately, *al-Maḥṣūl*, an important work of Ismāʿīlism, has not survived and our knowledge of it is limited to the quotations and references in *al-Iṣlāḥ*, *al-Riyāḍ* and a few other works. Abū Ḥātim's *al-Iṣlāḥ*, which is still unpublished and in manuscript form[212] evoked a reaction from al-Nasafī's successor and disciple al-Sijistānī, who wrote a special work called *Kitāb al-nuṣra* (*Book of the Support*) to defend his master's views against the attacks of Abū Ḥātim. *Al-Nuṣra*, which was composed before al-Sijistānī was won over to the Fāṭimid camp, has also been lost; but it is quoted extensively, along with *al-Iṣlāḥ*, in *al-Riyāḍ*, which in general vindicates the views of Abū Ḥātim. Al-Kirmānī reviewed the controversy from the official viewpoint of the Fāṭimid *daʿwa* which, by the time of al-Muʿizz, had already rehabilitated Abū Ḥātim,[213] and went even further than the latter in his affirmation of the indispensability of the law. Later, the antinomian tendencies of al-Nasafī and al-

Sijistānī were also attacked by Nāṣir-i Khusraw, who, like al-Kirmānī, reflected the position of the Fāṭimid headquarters.[214] These developments may explain why *al-Iṣlāḥ* remains at least partially extant, while both *al-Maḥṣūl* and *al-Nuṣra*, treated by the Fāṭimids as unorthodox and unworthy of being copied, failed to survive.

Al-Nasafī and Abū Ḥātim both envisaged hierohistory in terms of the Ismāʿīlī scheme of the seven eras, marked by the appearance of the speaker-prophets, announcing new *sharīʿa*s and religions, though they disagreed on some of the details.[215] According to al-Nasafī, the first of the seven *nāṭiq*s (*nuṭaqāʾ*), Adam, promulgated no law; he taught the doctrine of the unity of God, *al-tawḥīd*, without prescribing any action (*ʿamal*) or religious duties. In any event, in the first era, there were no other human beings besides Adam, so no *sharīʿa* was actually required. Consequently, the first law-announcing *nāṭiq* was Noah, at the beginning of whose era other beings had also appeared; and a religious law was now needed. Similarly, the seventh *nāṭiq*, the Qā'im Muḥammad b. Ismāʿīl, would not announce any law, since his function was to reveal the inner meaning of all the previous laws and to re-establish the original lawless state that had existed in Adam's era. Meanwhile, Muḥammad b. Ismāʿīl had disappeared like the fifth *nāṭiq* Jesus, but he would soon return. Apparently, al-Nasafī also maintained that the era of Islam had ended with the first coming of Muḥammad b. Ismāʿīl. In other words, the seventh, lawless *dawr* had already started; and in that era, by contrast to the previous six eras, there were no longer any imāms, but only the *lawāḥiq* (*lāḥiq*s) of the twelve *jazāʾir* of the earth. Herein lay antinomian tendencies which met with the strong disapproval of Abū Ḥātim, who held that all esoteric truth inevitably requires an exoteric revealed law.

Abū Ḥātim countered al-Nasafī's views with detailed arguments that Adam did in fact announce a law, though for him too, Adam could not be classified amongst the *ūlu'l-ʿazm* prophets, since he had not abolished the law of any previous *nāṭiq*. In similar manner, the seventh *nāṭiq*, who himself brings no law, does not abrogate the religious law of Islam; he merely manifests its hidden meaning. Abū Ḥātim, however, holds that there will be no *ʿamal* in the seventh era. In order to avoid the conclusion reached by al-Nasafī that the seventh, lawless era had already begun with the first coming of Muḥammad b. Ismāʿīl, Abū Ḥātim introduced the concept of the interim period. This was a period marked by the absence of imāms, and occurring at the end of each prophetic era, between the disappearance of the seventh imām of that era and the coming of the *nāṭiq* of the following era. During this period of interregnum, or *dawr al-fatra*, the twelve *lawāḥiq* assume command, with one acting as the deputy (*khalīfa*) of the absent seventh imām and as such possessing the right of authoritative arbitration amongst the *lawāḥiq*. It may be added that this is also the earliest usage of the term *khalīfa* by an Ismāʿīlī author. According to Abū Ḥātim, an interim or *fatra* of this nature had occurred after the disappearance of Muḥammad b. Ismāʿīl, implying that the sixth era, the era of Islam, had not yet expired. More specifically, Abū Ḥātim argues that the seventh *nāṭiq* Muḥammad b. Ismāʿīl has three degrees, namely, that of the seventh imām, like the final *mutimm* of the preceding eras, that of absence and that of appearance. Abū Ḥātim also fails to see any comparison between the absence of the seventh *nāṭiq* and the disappearance of the fifth *nāṭiq*, Jesus, since the latter's mission had been completed on his departure from this world, while the cause of Muḥammad b. Ismāʿīl was not concluded upon his disappearance. Indeed, the seventh *nāṭiq* is to reappear, at which time he will attain his final degree. Abū Ḥātim further holds that while the imāms in each era are the descendants of the *nāṭiq* and the *asās* of that era, the ranks of *lāḥiq*, and therefore, *khalīfa*, are exclusively reserved for the rest of mankind. In view of the facts that even after the accession of the Fāṭimids, Abū Ḥātim preached the imminent return of the Qā'im and also maintained his close relations with the Qarmaṭīs of ʿIrāq and Baḥrayn, it can be inferred that the chief *dāʿī* of Rayy did not recognize ʿUbayd Allāh al-Mahdī either as an imām or as the awaited Qā'im. There is in fact reason to assume that Abū Ḥātim regarded himself as the *khalīfa* of the absent imām.

Al-Nasafī and Abū Ḥātim also devoted much energy and imagination to accommodating some other prevalent religions, notably those of the Zoroastrians (Arabic, al-Majūs) and the Ṣābi'a or Sabaeans mentioned in the Qur'ān, within their scheme of the seven prophetic periods, assigning these religions to specific periods and *nāṭiqs*. The Sabaeans, who in the Islamic period have been identified with both the Mandaeans of southern ʿIrāq and the pagan community of Ḥarrān in Mesopotamia, were assigned by al-Nasafī to the era of the fifth *nāṭiq*, Jesus. Their doctrines, therefore, were considered to have been derived essentially from Christianity. Abū Ḥātim concurs with al-Nasafī in attributing the religion of the Sabaeans to the era of Jesus, adding that this religion was originally founded by a *lāḥiq* of that period who was not himself a *nāṭiq* and who did not promulgate any new laws in his book, called *al-Zabūr*. However, as al-Sijistānī also argued later on, the original doctrine of the founder of the Sabaean religion was corrupted during the interregnum of the fifth era by adversaries such as Mānī, Bardesanes (Ibn Dayṣān) and Marcion, who misinterpreted the doctrine. On the other hand, Abū Ḥātim objects to al-Nasafī's assignment of Zoroastrianism to the period of the third *nāṭiq*, Abraham. Al-Sijistānī, as in other cases, supported al-Nasafī's view in this respect, considering Zoroaster as a missionary of Abraham.[216] According to Abū Ḥātim, the Zoroastrians belonged to the period of the fourth *nāṭiq*, Moses; and Zoroaster (Zardusht) was one of the *lāḥiq*s of that period, receiving his investiture during that era's interregnum. But Zoroaster's original doctrine was also corrupted by adversaries such as Mazdak.[217]

Abū Yaʿqūb al-Sijistānī defended al-Nasafī's position against the criticisms of Abū Ḥātim. He, too, believed that Adam had brought no law, and his historical scheme is identical with that of al-Nasafī.[218] Between any two *nāṭiq*s, he explains, there are seven imāms, the last one becoming the speaker-prophet of the following era. But there are no more imāms in the final era after the Qā'im, when the period of the *lawāḥiq* and *khulafā'* who follow him begins in the world.[219] For al-Sijistānī too, the era of Islam had ended with the coming of the Qā'im Muḥammad b. Ismāʿīl. In due time, al-Sijistānī modified some of his more radical, and antinomian views.[220] For instance, in his *Kitāb ithbāt al-nubūwāt*, he states that he does not belong to those who follow the path of *ta'wīl* without paying attention to the religious commandments.[221] He also restricts religious obligations which can be abolished by the Qā'im to only some of what he calls the *waṣfī* regulations, including the ritual prescriptions like prayer and pilgrimage, as compared to the *ʿaqlī* or rational regulations like the prohibitions on murder and theft, which can never be abandoned.[222] He adds that neither the Qā'im nor his deputies will cancel the religious commandments all at once. In fact, interestingly enough, al-Sijistānī concludes this discussion by stating that the commandments in question will be cancelled gradually by the community (*umma*), so that nothing will remain of them by the time of the Qā'im's emergence (*ẓuhūr*).[223] Contrary to the view of Abū Ḥātim, al-Sijistānī explains that the imāmate and the function of the deputies (*khulafā'*) of the Qā'im will belong until the day of resurrection to the progeny of Muḥammad, the Seal of the Prophets. And more significantly, contrary to the view expressed earlier in his own *Kitāb al-nuṣra*, he now designates these deputies, who carry out the deeds of the Qā'im, as imāms.[224] In these statements, al-Sijistānī has clearly approached the reformed doctrine of al-Muʿizz, to the extent that one could have been directly derived from the other. Al-Sijistānī doubtless recognized the imāmate of the Fāṭimids at least since the time he composed his *Ithbāt al-nubūwāt*. Finally, the already-mentioned anti-Ismāʿīlī work entitled the *Kitāb al-siyāsa*, quoted by Akhū Muḥsin and often baselessly attributed to one of the first two Fāṭimid caliphs, may be dated to the period of al-Muʿizz, since, in a distorted manner, it reflects details of the doctrine expounded at the time.[225]

As noted, the first part of al-Nasafī's *Kitāb al-maḥṣūl* was devoted to the exposition of a type of Neoplatonic metaphysical system, containing particularly a new Ismāʿīlī cosmological doctrine and representing the earliest instance of harmonization between Neoplatonism and Ismāʿīlism. Neoplatonism, continuing the tradition of Greek philosophy, especially that maintained by the Platonist school, had been founded in the third century A.D. by Plotinus (d. 270 A.D.). After Plotinus, known to Muslims as al-Shaykh al-Yūnānī, Plotinian philosophy was further developed by a number of his disciples, notably Porphyry (d. ca. 300 A.D.) and the latter's student Iamblichus (d. ca. 330 A.D.). Neoplatonism received its major systematization by the philosopher Proclus (d. 485 A.D.), of the famous Platonic Academy of Athens. It was during the 3rd/9th century, in the course of translating the philosophical texts of the various Greek masters, that the Muslims became familiar with the writings of the Neoplatonists and adopted some of their ideas. Al-Kindī, the founder of Islamic philosophy who died around 252/866, was already influenced by the Neoplatonic school of philosophy. The nascent tradition of Islamic Neoplatonism soon found its full development in the works of the foremost Muslim philosophers al-Fārābī (d. 339/950) and Ibn Sīnā (d. 428/1037). The Ismāʿīlī authors of the Persian school, being in close touch with Khurāsān, an important region for the development of Islamic philosophy from the earliest decades of the 4th/10th century, evidently had access to some Neoplatonic sources in Arabic translation. Included were some pseudo-Aristotelian Neoplatonic treatises, such as a version of what in Arabic was known as the *Theology of Aristotle*, containing excerpts from Plotinus' *Enneads*, and the so-called *Liber de causis* (*Kitāb al-īḍāḥ fi'l-khayr al-maḥḍ*), another pseudo-Aristotelian work based on Proclus' *Elements of Theology*.[226] As al-Sijistānī mentions himself,[227] he seems to have been further acquainted with a Neoplatonic pseudoepigraphon ascribed to Empedocles (Arabic, Anbāduqlīs). Al-Nasafī, Abū Ḥātim and, later, al-Sijistānī, who were elaborating their own metaphysical systems during the first half of the 4th/10th century, became greatly influenced by Neoplatonism, especially by its concept of the unknowable God, its theory of emanation, and its hierarchic chain of being. In their cosmologies, which represented a drastic change over the theory of creation of the early Ismāʿīlīs, the authors of the Persian Ismāʿīlī school did not, however, adopt every dogma of the Neoplatonic school, since they had to integrate these borrowed ideas into an Islamic perspective. As a result, our eastern Ismāʿīlī theologians developed their own unique brand of metaphysics, cosmology and spiritual anthropology.

The *dāʿī* al-Nasafī, as pointed out by Samuel Stern,[228] was probably the founder of Ismāʿīlī philosophy, having been the earliest Ismāʿīlī thinker to introduce Neoplatonism, or more precisely, a type of the nascent Islamic Neoplatonism, into Ismāʿīlī thought. Al-Nasafī's new metaphysical and cosmological doctrines of Neoplatonic origins laid the foundation for the systems developed by Abū Ḥātim, and more importantly, by al-Sijistānī. The new Ismāʿīlī Neoplatonic cosmology, some details of which aroused controversy amongst the three authors of the Persian school, became the prevalent doctrine of the eastern Ismāʿīlī communities during the 4th/10th and the 5th/11th centuries. Later, it came to be adopted by the central headquarters of the Fāṭimid *daʿwa* during the reign of al-Muʿizz, replacing the original cosmology of the Ismāʿīliyya. The outline of al-Nasafī's ideas on this Neoplatonic cosmology introduced to the Ismāʿīlī circles of Persia by himself, may be reconstructed from the fragments of *al-Maḥṣūl* preserved in Abū Ḥātim's *al-Iṣlāḥ* and in al-Kirmānī's *al-Riyāḍ*;[229] also, in a polemical treatise written in refutation of Ismāʿīlism by the Zaydī-Muʿtazilī al-Bustī (d. ca. 420/1029), now extant in a unique manuscript at the Ambrosiana Library in Milan.[230] Abū Ḥātim, in his *al-Iṣlāḥ*, shared the main Neoplatonic propositions of al-Nasafī regarding creation, though disagreeing on some minor details. It is, however, mainly due to al-Sijistānī, an original thinker who further developed al-Nasafī's ideas in several preserved works,[231] that we owe our understanding of the Ismāʿīlī Neoplatonic cosmology formulated during the early decades of the Fāṭimid period.[232]

In this cosmology, God is described as absolutely transcendent, beyond comprehension and any attributes, and completely unknowable. Transcending being and non-being, God could not be comprehended or described by reason. This conception of God most closely resembled the ineffable Neoplatonic god, often referred to by Plotinus as the One or the Good, who was beyond the reach of thought, reason or language. At the same time, it was in close agreement with the fundamental Islamic principle of *al-tawḥīd*, affirming the absolute unity of God. The basic tenet of Neoplatonism could thus find ready acceptance in Ismāʿīlī theology, which adhered to strict monotheism and at its core was revelational rather than rational. This is why al-Sijistānī stresses that the worshipping of the unknowable God and the upholding of *al-tawḥīd* would require, via double negation, the denial of both *tashbīh*, or anthropomorphism, and the most radical anti-anthropomorphist doctrines such as those held by the rationalist Muʿtazila; since the advocation of the latter doctrines would mean committing *taʿṭīl*, or the denudation of the divine essence.[233] It was indeed in the revelational basis of the Neoplatonic conception of the One that al-Nasafī and the Persian school of Ismāʿīlism recognized an essential affinity to their own theology. This also explains why the Neoplatonic Ismāʿīlī theologians found it unnecessary to offer a proof of God, who is beyond reason and being.

The Ismāʿīlīs did, however, introduce some major changes in the next stage of the emanational cosmological doctrine they had borrowed from the Neoplatonists, harmonizing it with their Islamic beliefs and the Qur'ānic view of creation. Instead of having the intellect, called *nous* by the Neoplatonists, emanate directly and involuntarily from the source of being, the One, as with Plotinus and his school, they now held that God originated (*abdaʿa*) intellect (*al-ʿaql*) through his divine command or volition (*al-amr*), or word (*al-kalima*). This represented an act of primordial, extra-temporal origination or innovation (*ibdāʿ*),[234] signifying creation *ex nihilo*. Hence, God could be called the originator or *al-mubdiʿ*. The *ʿaql* is the first originated being (*al-mubdaʿ al-awwal*), also called simply as the first (*al-awwal*) and the preceder (*al-sābiq*), since the *amr* or logos is united with it in existence. The intellect is eternal, motionless and perfect, both potentially and actually.[235] It corresponds to the number one, and, in keeping with the Neoplatonic tradition, it is called the source of all light.[236] From the intellect proceeds through emanation, the soul (*al-nafs*), or the universal soul (*al-nafs al-kulliyya*), also referred to as the second (*al-thānī*) and the follower (*al-tālī*), corresponding to the psyche of the Neoplatonists. In this cosmological doctrine, intellect and soul are also combined together as the two roots or principles (*al-aṣlān*), the original dyad of the pleroma. The *nafs*, the second hypostasis, is much more complex than the *ʿaql*; it is imperfect and belongs to a different plane of existence.[237] The soul is also definitely subservient to the intellect. The Ismāʿīlīs continued the emanational chain of their cosmology beyond the simple triad of the One, intellect, and soul described by Plotinus, though according to them God had created everything in the spiritual and physical worlds all at once (*dafʿatan wāḥidatan*).[238] The various parts of the universe, however, became only gradually manifested through the process of causation and emanation, referred to as *inbiʿāth*, proceeding from the *ʿaql* in accordance with the divine resolution or predestination (*taqdīr*).

The imperfection (*naqṣ*) of the soul expresses itself in movement; and movement is a symptom of defect, just as tranquillity reflects perfection.[239] For Plotinus as for Plato, the essential characteristic of the soul is movement; and it is the soul's movement which causes all other movements. It is interesting to note that for al-Sijistānī, as for Plotinus, time is the measure of motion, resulting from the soul's activity. The soul's defect also accounts for its descent into the depths of the physical world, which owes its existence to this very defect. From the soul, which is the source of matter and form,[240] proceed the seven spheres (*al-aflāk*) with their stars; and the heavenly bodies move with the soul's movement. Then the four elemental qualities or simple elements (*al-mufradāt*), namely, heat, cold, humidity and dryness, are produced. The simple elements are mixed, through the revolution of the spheres, to form the composite elements (*al-murakkabāt*), such as earth, water, air and ether (fire). The composite substances then mingle to produce the plants with the vegetative soul (*al-nafs al-nāmiya*), from which the animals with the sensitive soul (*al-nafs al-ḥissiyya*) originate.[241] From the latter, man with his rational soul (*al-nafs al-nāṭiqa*) comes forth. In order to relate more closely this Ismāʿīlī Neoplatonic cosmology to Islamic tradition, some of the concepts of the spiritual world contained in it were identified with Qur'ānic terms. Thus the *ʿaql* was identified with the pen (*qalam*) and the throne (*ʿarsh*), while the *nafs* was equated with the tablet (*lawḥ*) and the chair or pedestal (*kursī*),[242] always reflecting the subservience of soul to intellect. At the same time, much emphasis was given to analogies between the spiritual, celestial world and the physical, terrestrial world on the one hand, and between man as the microcosm and the physical universe as the macrocosm, on the other. This cosmology, as refined by al-Sijistānī, came to be officially accepted by the Fāṭimid *daʿwa* sometime towards the latter part of the reign of al-Muʿizz, with the caliph-imām's approval and as part of his measures designed to win the allegiance of the dissident eastern Ismāʿīlīs.

Certain conceptions of the earlier Ismāʿīlī cosmology continued however to be retained in the Neoplatonic cosmology that superseded and partly replaced it, though the original character and function of the older elements are unrecognizable in their new context. The *amr* or *kalima*, as the creative command of the new doctrine, may be equated with the *kun* of the earlier doctrine; while the terms *kūnī*, *qadar*, *jadd*, *fatḥ* and *khayāl*, preserved by the authors of the Persian school, now came to lose their original significance. For al-Nasafī, the pair KŪNĪ-QDR represent the letters of the seven days of the week. Al-Sijistānī regards them as the seven upper or divine letters through which the spiritual forms come into being.[243] Abū Ḥātim applies Neoplatonic emanationalism to the cosmological pair of the early Ismāʿīliyya, holding that the three letters QDR are issued from the first three letters of the word *kūnī*. In a general sense, *kūnī* and *qadar* now became synonymous for intellect and soul of the new doctrine. Thus, *kūnī* came to be identified with the first, the preceder, and *al-ʿaql*; and *qadar* was equated with the second, the follower, and *al-nafs*. This identification is also attested by a Yamanī Zaydī historian of the 6th/12th century, Musallam b. Muḥammad al-Laḥjī, who comments on some earlier Zaydī references to the doctrines of the Yamanī Ismāʿīlīs. In one of his commentaries on a reference made to *kūnī-qadar* by ʿAbd Allāh b. ʿUmar al-Hamdānī, a Yamanī author of the beginning of the 4th/10th century who wrote a biography of the Zaydī Imām al-Nāṣir Aḥmad b. Yaḥyā (d. 322/934), al-Laḥjī states that 'they now say of the one they formerly called *kūnī, al-sābiq*, and of the one they used to call *qadar, al-tālī*. . . . and of the preceder and the follower they also say the first two principles (*al-aṣlān al-awwalān*), saying the two ar *alʿaql* and *al-nafs*, from which *al-jadd*, *al-fatḥ* and *al-khayāl* are issued like emanations (*inbiʿāthāt*)'.[244] It may be noted that the original female-male sequence of the primal pair was now reversed, and *qadar* in effect came to precede *kūnī*. The priority of the feminine hypostasis, *kūnī*, that assumed the more preferred place in the older doctrine, was lost in Ismāʿīlī Neoplatonism. The *ʿaql*, occupying the first place in the new doctrine, was masculine and perfect, while the feminine hypostasis, *al-nafs*, now descended to second place and became characterized by imperfection and unrest.

The three spiritual beings *jadd*, *fatḥ* and *khayāl*, preserved from the earlier cosmology, now acquired the function of acting as intermediaries between the terrestrial *daʿwa* hierarchy and intellect and soul, whilst retaining their previous role of rendering the cognition of the upper world feasible for mankind.[245] As in the case of the earlier doctrine, they are also the special graces which bestow certain gifts upon the speaker-prophets of sacred human history, bringing the benefits of intellect and soul directly to the *nuṭaqāʾ*. For al-Sijistānī, the pentad consisting of the *aṣlān* (intellect and soul), *jadd*, *fatḥ* and *khayāl*, in fact, comprise the spiritual *ḥudūd* which together with the five ranks of the terrestrial *daʿwa* (*nāṭiq*, *asās*, *imām*, *lāḥiq* and *janāḥ*) make up what Paul Walker has designated as the normative or moral hierarchy, which is of specifically Ismāʿīlī provenance.[246] Al-Sijistānī harmonizes this hierarchy of the intelligible reality, in a highly intricate fashion, with the hierarchical order derived from Neoplatonism, viz., intellect, soul, the spheres and the lower natural orders, God being at the head of both hierarchies.

The authors of the Persian school also propounded a doctrine of eschatology and salvation as part of their cosmology. The Ismāʿīlī Neoplatonic cosmology, like its predecessor, implied a soteriological purpose from the outset, though salvation is not discussed explicitly in the extant fragments of al-Nasafī's *al-Maḥṣūl*. This doctrine of salvation, as especially elaborated by al-Sijistānī, bears a close affinity to Plotinus' ideas on the mystical union between man and the One; a union that according to the ancient Neoplatonists was the supreme goal of all human endeavour. More generally, it draws heavily on various Neoplatonic and gnostic ideas, and is closely related to al-Sijistānī's doctrine of the soul and the Ismāʿīlī cyclical view of history. The actually imperfect soul, as noted, moves in search of the benefits (*fawāʾid*) of the intellect, because it is only through the intellect that it can come to rest. And man is called upon to assist in the perfection of the soul, since each human soul, according to al-Sijistānī,[247] is a part of the universal soul, just as Abū Ḥātim believed that the human soul is a trace (*athar*) of the higher soul. In Abū Ḥātim's system, however, the intellect and the soul are equally perfect; while for al-Nasafī and al-Sijistānī it is through human souls that the actually defective universal soul can realize its perfection in potentiality. This idea is particularly reminiscent of the theologoumenon of the members characterizing various aspects of Manichaeism. The pivotal idea of Neoplatonic cosmology and Ismāʿīlī soteriology, as expounded by al-Nasafī's school, is that it is only through the perfection of individual human souls that perfection may be restored to the pleroma. Consequently, history becomes the record of the soul's quest for perfection, and also the record of human achievement. In this historical process, marked by different prophetic eras, man seeks the benefits of the intellect in order that the collectivity of human souls may one day rise to intellectual eternity, and thereby, to salvation. The prophets and other members of the terrestrial *daʿwa* hierarchy are charged with conveying the benefits emanating from the intellect to mankind. Indeed, man is saved because of the truth that he receives from the prophets and their successors; and since true knowledge is eternal, that part of man which possesses this knowledge also becomes eternal. It is, therefore, essential for man to understand the nature of the specific prophetic era in which he lives, because it is from the *nāṭiq* of his own time that the blessings of the intellect may be acquired. Nonetheless, the cognition that causes the perfection of the universal soul and the salvation of man comes ultimately from the Qā'im, the last *nāṭiq* who initiates the final era of absolute true knowledge.[248] When the Qā'im has attained the rank that God has intended for him, there steps forth among the forms, viz., the individual human souls, those having the power to attain the benefits of the intellect. The advent of the Qā'im, initiating the final stage of history, will thus bring with it the definite separation between the redeemed and the unredeemed.

The Fāṭimid Ismāʿīlī headquarters in Ifrīqiya did not participate in the development of the Neoplatonic cosmology initiated by the Persian school. The original mythological cosmogony had continued to be adhered to by Fāṭimid Ismāʿīlism until the latter part of the imāmate of al-Muʿizz, as attested, for instance, by Abū ʿĪsā's *Risāla*. It was al-Muʿizz who authorized the adoption of the new cosmological system by the Fāṭimid *daʿwa*. The first tangible influence of Ismāʿīlī Neoplatonism on Fāṭimid thought is detectable in *al-Risāla al-mudhhiba* attributed to al-Qāḍī al-Nuʿmān, in which the original Ismāʿīlī pentad of the pleroma is revised to include *al-ʿaql*, *al-nafs*, *al-jadd*, *al-fatḥ* and *al-khayāl*,[249] corresponding to al-Sijistānī's spiritual *ḥudūd* as part of his normative order of the universe. Henceforth, this Ismāʿīlī Neoplatonic cosmology came to be generally advocated in its essentials by Fāṭimid authors, including Nāṣir-i Khusraw, who refined and elaborated various aspects of it in his own metaphysical system.[250]

A somewhat different cosmological system was propounded by the *dāʿī* al-Kirmānī in his *Rāḥat al-ʿaql*, a summa of Ismāʿīlī philosophy written for the well-prepared adepts. The *Rāḥat al-ʿaql*, composed in 411 A.H.,[251] reveals the depth of al-Kirmānī's knowledge of Aristotelian and Neoplatonic philosophies, al-Kindī's thought, as well as the metaphysical systems of later Muslim philosophers (*falāsifa*) such as al-Fārābī and Ibn Sīnā. Above all, al-Kirmānī's synthetic cosmology, which is a modification of the earlier Ismāʿīlī Neoplatonic cosmology, reflects the influence of Ibn Sīnā's metaphysics. Thus, instead of the previous dyad, intellect-soul, al-Kirmānī's system is comprised of ten intellects, or archangelical hypostases, in the spiritual world, each celestial *ḥadd* being the immediate cause of the following one.[252] The celestial hierarchy of the ten *ḥudūd* is, more specifically, divided into two distinct sub-groups, a triad and a heptad. In this system, the intellect of the previous cosmology becomes the first intellect (*al-ʿaql al-awwal*), while the soul is replaced by the second intellect (*al-ʿaql al-thānī*), also called the first emanation (*al-munbaʿith al-awwal*), proceeding from the higher relation (*al-nisba al-ashraf*) of the first intellect. The third intellect, or the second emanation (*al-munbaʿith al-thānī*), which proceeds from the lower relation (*al-nisba al-adwan*) of the first intellect, is equated with matter (*al-hayūlā*) and form (*al-ṣūra*);[253] it is also the first potential being.

From the primordial dyad, consisting of the first and second intellects, proceed seven further intellects, equated with the seven Cherubim, designated also as the seven divine words. The tenth intellect, also called the active intellect (*al-ʿaql al-faʿʿāl*), governs the physical world as a demiurge. The structure of the physical world and the terrestrial *daʿwa* hierarchy were similarly modified by al-Kirmānī, in close analogy with the hierarchy of the celestial world. Indeed, he emphasizes a close correspondence between the celestial and the terrestrial hierarchies and the comparable functions of the various *ḥudūd* in the two orders. While al-Nasafī, Abū Ḥātim and al-Sijistānī endeavoured to harmonize the earlier ideas with Neoplatonism, the traditional ideas and concepts are almost completely absent from al-Kirmānī's cosmology. The *Rāḥat al-ʿaql* devotes merely a chapter to the so-called seven upper letters (*al-ḥurūf al-ʿulwiyya*);[254] while *kūnī* and *qadar* are mentioned apparently only once by al-Kirmānī, in a rather incidental manner, and as names occurring in the works of earlier authorities.[255] Clearly, the old primal pair *kūnī-qadar* could no longer be assigned a function in al-Kirmānī's doctrine, in which Ismāʿīlī Neoplatonism prevailed thoroughly. Al-Kirmānī's cosmology was not adopted by the Fāṭimids; but, with some modifications, it later came to be utilized by the Ṭayyibī *daʿwa* in Yaman, completely replacing the older Fāṭimid system based on the works of al-Nasafī, al-Sijistānī and Abū Ḥātim.

Besides the Persian school, there was another trend in Ismāʿīlism in the 4th/10th century that came greatly under the influence of Neoplatonism. This trend is manifested in the *Rasāʾil Ikhwān al-Ṣafāʾ*, the *Epistles of the Brethren of Purity*, also translated as the *Epistles of the Sincere Brethren*.[256] Much controversy has surrounded the authorship and the date of composition of these famous *Epistles*, whose Ismāʿīlī origin was already recognized in 1898 by Paul Casanova, long before the modern recovery of Ismāʿīlī literature. There are various anachronistic accounts attributing the authorship of the *Epistles* to different Shīʿī Imāms; while the *dāʿī* Idrīs, reflecting the official view of the Ṭayyibī *daʿwa* in Yaman, has a detailed account in which he ascribes the *Epistles* to the Imām Aḥmad b. ʿAbd Allāh, the grandson of Muḥammad b. Ismāʿīl and one of the hidden imāms of the early Ismāʿīlīs.[257] However, some reliable contemporary authorities from the 4th/10th century, notably the philosopher Abū Ḥayyān al-Tawḥīdī (d. 414/1023), name certain men of letters and secretaries of Buwayhid ʿIrāq, affiliated with the Ismāʿīlī movement and residents of Baṣra, as belonging to the group that composed the otherwise anonymous *Epistles*. Amongst such authors, and in reply to certain questions raised around 373/983 by his patron Ibn Saʿdān, who was the vizier of the Buwayhid Ṣamṣām al-Dawla, Abū Ḥayyān names Abū Sulaymān Muḥammad b. Maʿshar al-Bustī, also known as al-Maqdisī, Abu'l-Ḥasan ʿAlī b. Hārūn al-Zanjānī, Abū Aḥmad al-Nahrajūrī, and al-ʿAwfī. Furthermore, these four persons were somehow associated with the Ismāʿīlī movement; and it seems that al-Zanjānī, a *qāḍī* and an acquaintance of Abū Ḥayyān, was the leader of the group. Abū Ḥayyān's important statements, later reproduced by Ibn al-Qifṭī (d. 646/1248), are essentially corroborated by another contemporary source ʿAbd al-Jabbār b. Aḥmad al-Hamadhānī (d. 415/1025), the famous Muʿtazilī theologian and chief *qāḍī* of Rayy. In his own list, ʿAbd al-Jabbār omits al-Maqdisī but adds the names of Ibn Abi'l-Baghl, a certain astrologer, and the chancery secretary Zayd b. Rifāʿa who, also according to Abū Ḥayyān, was a close friend of the group.[258] On the basis of this evidence, most specialists are now agreed that the *Epistles* were secretly produced in Baṣra by a coterie of secretaries and scholars affiliated with Ismāʿīlism, in the middle of the 4th/10th century, around the time of the Fāṭimid conquest of Egypt.[259]

The small group that composed the *Rasāʾil* did not represent the official view of the Fāṭimid *daʿwa* and evidently did not even adhere to Fāṭimid Ismāʿīlism. As Samuel Stern has argued, it may well be that the Ismāʿīlī authors of the *Epistles* were motivated in their encyclopaedic undertaking by a desire to reunite the non-Fāṭimid Ismāʿīlīs, including the Qarmaṭīs of Baḥrayn and the dissident eastern Ismāʿīlī communities, on a common and idealized doctrinal ground. The authors adopted a type of Ismāʿīlī Neoplatonism, on the basis of which they elaborated their emanational cosmological doctrine, conceiving of a hierarchy of being in nine stages.[260] They also espoused a liberal and highly enlightened attitude towards religion and the wide range of subjects discussed. Written in Baṣra at a time when southern ʿIrāq was under the virtual domination of the Qarmaṭīs of Baḥrayn, the *Epistles* probably also had the tacit approval, if not the active encouragement of the Qarmaṭīs. The Ikhwān al-Ṣafā' do, in fact, place their teaching under the auspices of the hidden seventh imām of the Ismāʿīliyya, the same Muḥammad b. Ismāʿīl whose emergence was at the time expected by the Qarmaṭīs of Baḥrayn and all other dissident Ismāʿīlīs.[261] In other words, the authors did not recognize the imāmate of the Fāṭimids; nor did they find it necessary to mention the early Fāṭimid caliph-imāms and their ancestors. More recently, Abbas Hamdani has pointed out the weaknesses of al-Tawḥīdī's assertions. On the basis of detailed studies, he has argued that the *Epistles* were compiled by a group of pre-Fāṭimid Ismāʿīlī *dāʿīs*, who worked in collaboration with non-Ismāʿīlī colleagues, between the years 260/873 and 297/909, and that the references and verses of later chronology in the *Epistles* represent subsequent editorial interpolations.

The *Epistles* did not have any influence on contemporary Ismāʿīlism, including the doctrines propagated by the Fāṭimid Ismāʿīlīs; and they are not referred to by the authors of the classical Fāṭimid period. It was only about two centuries after their composition that the *Epistles* began to acquire an important place in the literature of the Ṭayyibī Ismāʿīlī *daʿwa*. Evidently, it was the *dāʿī* Ibrāhīm b. al-Ḥusayn al-Ḥāmidī (d. 557/1162) who first introduced the *Rasāʾil* into the literature of the Ṭayyibī community in Yaman.[262] Henceforth, the *Epistles* came to be widely studied and commented upon by the Yamanī *dāʿīs*, and later, also by their Indian successors in the Dāʾūdī Bohra community.

The *Rasāʾil Ikhwān al-Ṣafāʾ*, numbering fifty-two epistles, are divided into four books or sections, dealing with mathematical sciences (geometry, astronomy, music, logic, etc.), bodily and natural sciences, psychical and intellectual sciences (cosmology, eschatology, etc.), and theological sciences. Connected with these *Epistles*, which treat nearly all the sciences known at the time, there is a separate concluding summary of the Ikhwān's corpus, known as *al-Risāla al-jāmiʿa*. The latter work, wrongly attributed to Maslama al-Majrīṭī (d. ca. 398/1007) and of which there exists a further condensation, was evidently intended for the more advanced adepts.[263] The authors of the *Epistles*, who practised tolerance and eclecticism, thought it quite legitimate to adopt all 'the science and wisdoms' of the ancient philosophers in producing their own synthesis of the knowledge of the time. They drew on a wide variety of pre-Islamic sources and traditions, which they combined with Islamic teachings, especially as upheld by the Shīʿīs belonging to the Ismāʿīlī movement. There are, for instance, traces of early Babylonian astrology, and many elements of Judaeo-Christian, Iranian, and Indian origins.[264] Above all, the *Epistles* reflect the influences of diverse schools of Hellenistic wisdom. Characterized by a type of numerical symbolism in a Pythagorean manner, the *Epistles* are permeated throughout with Hermetic, Platonic, Aristotelian, Neopythagorean, and especially Neoplatonic ideas and doctrines. However, Neoplatonism, with its distinctive doctrine of emanation and hierarchism, is the dominant influence of Greek philosophy on the Ikhwān al-Ṣafā', who in an original and enlightened fashion attempted to harmonize religion and philosophy for the ultimate purpose of guiding man to purify his soul and achieve salvation.[265]

The Ismāʿīlī system of *fiqh* or jurisprudence also came to be founded and elaborated during the classical Fāṭimid period, especially under the early Fāṭimids, chiefly by Abū Ḥanīfa al-Nuʿmān b. Muḥammad b. Manṣūr b. Aḥmad b. Ḥayyūn al-Tamīmī al-Maghribī, better known as al-Qāḍī al-Nuʿmān.[266] Destined to become the greatest Ismāʿīlī jurist of all time, al-Nuʿmān came from a learned family of Mālikī Sunnīs in Qayrawān. There is much controversy surrounding the religious background of al-Qāḍī al-Nuʿmān, but it seems certain that his father had already embraced Ismāʿīlism before the year 311/923 and that al-Nuʿmān himself was converted early in life, following his initial training as a Mālikī *faqīh*. Some Imāmī Shīʿī authorities have maintained throughout the centuries that al-Nuʿmān was one of their co-religionists, although the early Imāmī bio-bibliographers like al-Kashshī, al-Najāshī and al-Ṭūsī do not refer to him at all. Ibn Shahrāshūb (d. 588/1192) is evidently the earliest Twelver Shīʿī authority to mention al-Nuʿmān and some of his works, whilst explicitly asserting that the Qāḍī was not an Imāmī.[267] This assertion implies that some Imāmī (Twelver) circles did consider al-Nuʿmān as one of their own. Nūr Allāh al-Shūshtarī, the renowned Persian Twelver jurist who migrated to India and was later executed there in 1019/1610 on the order of the Mughal emperor Jahāngīr, was probably the first Imāmī scholar who, quoting Ibn Khallikān, stated that al-Nuʿmān was originally a Mālikī Sunnī, and then, an Imāmī.[268] In his view, al-Shūshtarī was followed by other Imāmī divines like al-Ḥurr al-ʿĀmilī (d. 1104/1693), al-Majlisī (d. 1110/1699), Baḥr al-ʿUlūm, better known as Sayyid al-Ṭā'ifa (d. 1212/1797), and Mīrzā Ḥusayn al-Nūrī (d. 1320/1902).[269] Āghā Buzurg al-Ṭihrānī (d. 1389/1970), a contemporary Imāmī scholar who produced a valuable encyclopaedia of Shīʿī works and who was acquainted with the writings of W. Ivanow, also maintained that al-Nuʿmān was an Imāmī.[270] All these authorities evidently rely solely on Ibn Khallikān who may have used the term Imāmī in reference to both the Ithnāʿashariyya and the Ismāʿīliyya. There have also been those Imāmī scholars like al-Khwānsārī (d. 1313/1895) who, in line with Ibn Shahrāshūb, have denied that al-Nuʿmān was ever an Ithnāʿasharī Shīʿī.[271] For the Ismāʿīlī authorities, such as the *dāʿī* Idrīs, the question of the original *madhhab* of a prominent Ismāʿīlī figure so closely associated with several of their imāms, is an irrelevant one; they simply do not discuss the matter. Having been a contemporary of some of the most renowned early Imāmī authorities, like al-Kulaynī and Ibn Bābawayh, al-Nuʿmān's works are indeed amongst the earliest Shīʿī contributions to *ḥadīth* and *fiqh*; and this may explain his high esteem by the Twelver Shīʿīs of different generations.

The Qāḍī al-Nuʿmān, born around 290/903, entered the service of ʿUbayd Allāh al-Mahdī in 313/925. He served the first four Fāṭimid caliphs in various capacities, such as the keeper of the palace library and the *qāḍī* of Tripoli and Manṣūriyya. His growing position and importance reached its zenith under al-Muʿizz, when he became the highest judicial functionary of the Fāṭimid state. He accompanied al-Muʿizz to Egypt and died in Cairo in Jumādā II 363/March 974, having faithfully served the Fāṭimid dynasty for almost fifty years. Al-Nuʿmān's funeral prayer was personally led by al-Muʿizz. Al-Nuʿmān was a prolific writer, with more than forty treatises to his credit. He appears to have devoted the greater part of his life to the composition of his numerous works on law as well as on many other subjects, including history, *ta'wīl* and *ḥaqā'iq*. He evidently consulted his contemporary caliph-imāms on whatever he wrote; and it is primarily due to this Ismāʿīlī tradition, related by Idrīs, that al-Nuʿmān has been accorded such a high position of respect and authority amongst the Ismāʿīlīs. One of al-Nuʿmān's principal works on *fiqh*, the *Daʿā'im al-Islām* (*The Pillars of Islam*), was in fact composed at the request of al-Muʿizz, who supervised its writing very closely. The *Daʿā'im*, which is the main source for the study of Fāṭimid Ismāʿīlī law, became the official Fāṭimid *corpus juris* from the time of al-Muʿizz, and it still remains the chief legal text for the Ṭayyibī Ismāʿīlīs, including the Ismāʿīlī Bohras of India. The *Daʿā'im* is divided into two volumes, the first one dealing with *ʿibādāt*, acts of devotion and religious duties, consisting of the seven pillars of Islam according to the Ismāʿīlīs, namely *walāya* (devotion to imāms), *ṭahāra* (ritual purity), *ṣalāt* (prayer) including *janā'iz* (funeral rites), *zakāt* (alms), *ṣawm* (fasting), *ḥajj* (pilgrimage to Mecca), and *jihād* (holy war). The Fāṭimid Ismāʿīlīs, as Shīʿīs, had thus added *walāya* and *ṭahāra* to the five pillars recognized by the Sunnīs. The second volume of the *Daʿā'im* deals with *muʿāmalāt*, or worldly affairs, such as food, drinks, clothing, wills, inheritance, marriage and divorce.

Al-Nuʿmān was the founder of a distinguished family of *qāḍīs* in the Fāṭimid state. His son Abu'l-Ḥusayn ʿAlī (d. 374/984), the chief jurist under al-ʿAzīz for nine years, was in fact the first person to bear the official title of *qāḍī al-quḍāt* under the Fāṭimids. ʿAlī was succeeded as chief *qāḍī* by his younger brother Abū ʿAbd Allāh Muḥammad (d. 389/999). Subsequently, that highest judicial office came to be held successively by two of al-Nuʿmān's grandsons, Abū ʿAbd Allāh al-Ḥusayn b. ʿAlī (d. 395/1004), and Abu'l-Qāsim ʿAbd al-ʿAzīz b. Muḥammad (d. 401/1011), who also became Jawhar's son-in-law. Al-Nuʿmān's great-grandson, Abū Muḥammad al-Qāsim b. ʿAbd al-ʿAzīz, was the last member of the family to hold the position of chief *qāḍī*. He was finally dismissed, after several terms in office, in 441/1049 and was succeeded by al-Yāzūrī, the first to unite in his person the offices of *wazīr* and *qāḍī al-quḍāt*.

In comparison with the four Sunnī schools of law, namely the Ḥanafī, Mālikī, Shāfiʿī and Ḥanbalī, as well as the Ithnāʿasharī *madhhab*, the legal literaure of the Fāṭimid Ismāʿīlīs is extremely meagre. The Ismāʿīlī system of *fiqh* is almost exclusively the work of al-Qāḍī al-Nuʿmān, as few other Ismāʿīlī jurists, during or after the Fāṭimid period, concerned themselves with producing legal compendia. It is therefore not surprising that until recently, it was generally unknown outside of Ismāʿīlī circles that Ismāʿīlism has had its own separate school of jurisprudence; a distinct Shīʿī *madhhab* developed in the 4th/10th century after the appearance of the authentic legal literature of the Imāmī (Twelver) Shīʿīs. In modern times, it has been mainly due to the efforts of Asaf A. A. Fyzee, the foremost contemporary authority on Ismāʿīlī law, that the students of Islamic law and researchers in Ismāʿīlī studies have become acquainted with this Shīʿī school of *fiqh*.[272] Ismāʿīlī Shīʿī jurisprudence, as it has come down to us, is chiefly propounded in al-Nuʿmān's writings. Al-Nuʿmān's works, more of which seem to have been extant at the time of the *dāʿī* Idrīs, have been preserved by the Yamanī and, later, by the Indian Ismāʿīlīs belonging to the Ṭayyibī *daʿwa*, notably the Dā'ūdī Bohras.

Fāṭimid Ismāʿīlī law, which in general agrees with Imāmī law, represents a blending of Shīʿī beliefs, especially as embodied in the doctrine of the imāmate, with the legal concepts of the Muslims. The Ismāʿīlīs, like all other Muslims, did accept the Qur'ān and the *sunna* of the Prophet as the principal sources of law. However, in line with the Imāmīs, the Fāṭimid Ismāʿīlīs departed from the norms of the Sunnī schools in acknowledging only those Prophetic traditions which were reported by their imāms from the Ahl al-Bayt. In addition, they also accepted traditions from the imāms recognized by them. The traditions related by al-Qāḍī al-Nuʿmān are from the Prophet, ʿAlī b. Abī Ṭālib and the latter's five successor imāms, with the majority from the Imāms al-Bāqir and al-Ṣādiq. It is interesting to note that al-Nuʿmān does not normally quote any *ḥadīth*s from the Ismāʿīlī Imāms after Jaʿfar al-Ṣādiq, the fountainhead of Ismāʿīlī *fiqh*. In the case of the Prophetic traditions, the *isnād*s or chains of transmission, aside from having an Ismāʿīlī Imām, are dropped in all Fāṭimid legal literature, implying that when an imām relates a *ḥadīth* from the Prophet, no further authority is necessary. Al-Nuʿmān totally ignores the *ḥadīth*s of the Twelver Shīʿī Imāms after al-Ṣādiq, beginning with Mūsā al-Kāẓim, who are not recognized by the Ismāʿīliyya. Those Imāmī scholars who regard al-Nuʿmān as a co-religionist attribute this to his observance of *taqiyya* in fear of the Fāṭimids. At any event, this is one of the main differences between the *ḥadīth*s used by al-Nuʿmān and those included in the four major Imāmī compendia of traditions, compiled by al-Kulaynī, Ibn Bābawayh and Shaykh al-Ṭāʾifa al-Ṭūsī. On the other hand, al-Nuʿmān quotes opinions of the ʿAlids not recognized as imāms by the Ismāʿīlīs or the Imāmīs, relying on Zaydī transmission.

The fundamental difference between the Shīʿī, Ismāʿīlī or otherwise, and the Sunnī systems of *fiqh*, however, centres around the doctrine of the imāmate. For the Shīʿīs, the imām is the final authority for interpreting the ordinances of God, and, after the Prophet, the sole repository of the rules of human conduct and worship. For the Ismāʿīlīs in particular, he also interprets the all-important inner meaning of the Qurʾān and the Sharīʿa. Therefore, for the Fāṭimid Ismāʿīlīs, the authority of the divinely-guided and infallible imām became the third and most decisive foundation of law, after the Qurʾān and the *sunna*. They did not accept *ijmāʿ* or consensus of opinion, and *qiyās* or analogical deduction, which are the third and fourth bases of Islamic law accepted by the Sunnīs. The Fāṭimid Ismāʿīlīs also rejected all other supplementary roots of law which are substitutes for *qiyās*, such as *istiḥsān*, *istiṣlāḥ* and *istidlāl*.

The Imāmīs, too, rejected *qiyās* and its substitutes, while they later subscribed to a type of *ijmāʿ*, and *ʿaql*, reason or systematic reasoning in law.[273] For the Imāmīs, or rather for the adherents of the predominant Uṣūlī school of Twelver Shīʿī law, the *fuqahāʾ*, who are qualified to form legal judgements and who are present at all times as the agents of their hidden twelfth imām, are the recognized interpreters of the law. These powerful religious lawyers are known as *mujtahids*, practising *ijtihād* in their legal reasoning and judgement. Every ordinary Imāmī (Twelver) believer is expected to follow a *mujtahid* of his choice, thus becoming a *muqallid*, or imitator, practising *taqlīd*. It may be noted, however, that in the Fāṭimid age and earlier, the Imāmīs had not yet accepted *ijtihād*, which in later times continued to be rejected by the Akhbārī school of Twelver Shīʿī law. The Fāṭimid Ismāʿīlīs, with their imām ruling at the head of the community, never recognized any kind of *ijtihād* and *taqlīd*. In other words, Fāṭimid law rejected adjudication or legal interpretation from sources other than the imāms. Al-Nuʿmān, in a work composed after 343/954 on the principles of the law (*uṣūl al-fiqh*), in conjunction with most of the Imāmī scholars of his time, clearly recognizes the Qurʾān, the *sunna* of the Prophet and the dictum or teachings of the imāms (*qawl al-aʾimma*) as the only authoritative sources of law.[274] The Shīʿī Imāms not only enforce the Sharīʿa like the Sunnī caliphs, but also interpret it. This may be considered the major point of difference between the Shīʿī and Sunnī concepts of law. Regarding the specific application of the law, however, the Fāṭimid Ismāʿīlīs, like other Muslims, had courts presided over by trained *qāḍīs* who dealt in legal judgements and issued specific decisions. There are some minor points of difference between the Fāṭimid Ismāʿīlī and the Imāmī schools of law, especially regarding the questions of inheritance and marriage; while some of the specific legal doctrines of the Ismāʿīlīs represent a compromise between those of the Imāmīs and the Zaydīs. For instance, the Ismāʿīlīs, similarly to the Sunnīs and Zaydīs, do not permit *mutʿa*, or temporary marriage for a stipulated period, which is practised by the Twelver Shīʿīs. In this connection, it is interesting to note that al-Nuʿmān based his rejection of *mutʿa* on a Zaydī, rather than any Sunnī, tradition. In Fāṭimid law, *mutʿa* is equivalent to *zināʾ* or unlawful intercourse. In religious rituals, too, there are certain differences between the practices of the Ismāʿīlī and the Imāmī Shīʿīs.[275]

Such were the achievements of the Ismāʿīlīs during the classical Fāṭimid period.[276] The advent of the Fāṭimid dynasty and state in North Africa marked the transformation of a revolutionary Shīʿī movement into a major Islamic empire, initiating at the same time the 'golden age' of Ismāʿīlism. The Fāṭimid caliph was not only the ruler of a vast and prosperous state; he was also the Ismāʿīlī Imām, belonging to the Ahl al-Bayt and descending from the Prophet through Fāṭima. As such, he was the spiritual leader of the Fāṭimid Ismāʿīlīs, comprising the main body of the Ismāʿīliyya, wherever they were to be found. The Ismāʿīlī message did have considerable appeal to different social groups outside the Fāṭimid dominions, penetrated by the secret and hierarchical Fāṭimid *daʿwa* organization, which promised to relieve Muslims from the oppressive rule of the Sunnī ʿAbbāsids and other usurping dynasties. It was in the pursuit of these ideals that the Fāṭimid *dāʿīs* disseminated the message of Ismāʿīlism in many lands, including especially the ʿAbbāsid provinces in the Muslim East. The Fāṭimid triumph was, however, incomplete. The Fāṭimids failed to unite all the Muslims under their own Fāṭimid ʿAlid Imāmate, as they also failed in their policy of eastern conquest. They did, however, succeed in encouraging intensive literary and intellectual activity in Fāṭimid Egypt, also turning their capital, Cairo, into a flourishing centre of commerce, arts and sciences, which rivalled Baghdād in the 5th/11th century. During that crucial century of Islamic history, the Fāṭimid dynasty, at least until the consolidation of Saljūqid power, represented the major political and cultural force of the Muslim world.

The Fāṭimids greatly expanded their territorial possessions, and despite periodical disturbances and crises, Fāṭimid Egypt in general enjoyed economic prosperity. This was primarily due to the capability and stability of Fāṭimid administrative and financial organizations, and substantial revenues earned from expanding trade and economic activities. The doctrines of the Fāṭimid Ismāʿīlīs, as elaborated by gifted theologians and *dāʿīs*, represent a high level of intellectual accomplishment. In their treatises, not only theology but complex metaphysical and philosophical doctrines, drawing on Hellenistic and other traditions, are discussed in an Islamic perspective. The Fāṭimids were also noteworthy in terms of their patronage of artistic activities. There exists considerable evidence of Fāṭimid art, displaying originality as well as the influences of various older artistic traditions. The Fāṭimid mosques, mausoleums and other architectural remains have been thoroughly studied by Keppel A. C. Creswell (1879–1974), the leading modern authority on the Fāṭimid monuments.[277] The Fāṭimids also encouraged artistic endeavours in other areas, like textiles, woodwork, ceramics, glass and mural painting.[278] Scholars generally agree that the successes of the Fāṭimids were in large measure due to the remarkable ethnic and religious tolerance of the dynasty and the administrative stability of the Fāṭimid state. The Shīʿī Fāṭimids did, indeed, have a special talent for utilizing the services of capable individuals and groups, regardless of their race or creed.

As the official religion of an empire, Fāṭimid Ismāʿīlism maintained its unity for close to two centuries, although it witnessed periodical internal dissensions of minor importance. The main body of the Ismāʿīlīs, both inside and outside the Fāṭimid dominion, did on the whole remain faithful to the Fāṭimid caliph-imām, who had failed to win over the Sunnī majority of the Muslim world. It was in this religio-political setting that the challenge of strong enemies, like the Saljūqs, and factional strife from within set the Fāṭimid Caliphate on a course of decline and eventual collapse; a course that had irretrievable consequences for the Ismāʿīlī movement. By the time of al-Mustanṣir's death in 487/1094, which confronted Fāṭimid Ismāʿīlism with its most catastrophic internal conflict and caused a major schism in Ismāʿīlism, the Fāṭimids still had another seventy-seven years to rule, but the dynasty had already passed its peak of accomplishment and glory. The days of Ismāʿīlism as the official religion of an empire were almost terminated. By that time, the Fāṭimids had abandoned their hopes of universal leadership in Islam, and yet, their intellectual achievements and contributions had already forever enriched Islamic thought and culture.

5

Mustaʿlian Ismāʿīlism

In this chapter we shall trace the development of the Mustaʿliyya (or Mustaʿlawiyya) sub-sect of Ismāʿīlism, from its origins in 487/1094 to the present. Until the year 524/1130, the Mustaʿlian Ismāʿīlīs of Egypt, Syria, Yaman and elsewhere, constituted a unified group, as distinct from the Nizāriyya. By then, the Mustaʿlians had recognized two more imāms in the persons of al-Mustanṣir's son and grandson, al-Mustaʿlī and al-Āmir. However, the confusing events following al-Āmir's death in 524/1130 and the claims of al-Ḥāfiẓ, al-Āmir's cousin and successor in the Fāṭimid state, to the imāmate, led to a new split in the Mustaʿlian community, subdividing it into the Ḥāfiẓiyya and the Ṭayyibiyya. Both of these branches of Mustaʿlian Ismāʿīlism will be discussed in the present chapter.

The Ḥāfiẓiyya, also known as the Majīdiyya, accepted al-Ḥāfiẓ and the later Fāṭimid caliphs as their imāms after al-Āmir. The Ḥāfiẓī cause, officially endorsed by the Fāṭimid *daʿwa* in Cairo, found the bulk of its supporters in Egypt and Syria. It received support also in Yaman, where the local dynasties of the Zurayʿids of ʿAdan and some of the Hamdānids of Ṣanʿāʾ adhered to the Ḥāfiẓī *daʿwa*. The Ḥāfiẓiyya, however, did not survive long after the fall of the Fāṭimid dynasty in 567/1171.

The Ṭayyibiyya, initially known as the Āmiriyya, recognized al-Āmir's infant son, al-Ṭayyib, as their imām after al-Āmir; rejecting the claims of al-Ḥāfiẓ, and his successors on the Fāṭimid throne, to the imāmate. The Ṭayyibī cause was at first supported by a minority of the Mustaʿlian Ismāʿīlīs of Egypt and Syria as well as by many of the Ismāʿīlīs of Yaman, where the Ṣulayḥids officially upheld the rights of al-Ṭayyib. Soon afterwards, with the establishment of the independent Ṭayyibī *daʿwa* headed by a *dāʿī muṭlaq*, Yaman became the main stronghold of the Ṭayyibiyya. The Ṭayyibī *dāʿī*s, in time, succeeded in winning a considerable number of adherents in western India, amongst the Bohras of Gujarāt and elsewhere, some of whom had earlier embraced Ismāʿīlism.

The Ṭayyibīs, who closely maintained the traditions of the Fāṭimid Ismāʿīlīs in the doctrinal domain, divide their history of the Islamic era into succeeding periods of concealment (*satr*) and manifestation (*kashf* or *ẓuhūr*), during which the imāms are, or are not, concealed from the public eye. The first period of *satr*, coinciding with the period of early Ismāʿīlism, came to an end with the appearance of ʿUbayd Allāh (ʿAbd Allāh) al-Mahdī in North Africa. This was followed by a period of *ẓuhūr*, continuing until the concealment of the twenty-first Ṭayyibī Imām, al-Ṭayyib, soon after al-Āmir's death. The concealment of al-Ṭayyib initiated another period of *satr* in the history of Ṭayyibī Ismāʿīlism, continuing to the present time. During the current *satr*, al-Ṭayyib, the last visible Ṭayyibī Imām, and his successors from amongst his descendants, have chosen to remain hidden (*mastūr*) from the eyes of their followers. According to the Ṭayyibīs, the present period of *satr* will continue until the appearance of an imām from the progeny of al-Ṭayyib; that imām may be the Qā'im of the present cycle in the history of mankind. At any rate, a few years after the death of al-Āmir, the headquarters of Ṭayyibī Ismāʿīlism were established in Yaman, where the Ṭayyibī *daʿwa* developed under the overall leadership of a powerful *dāʿī*, called *al-dāʿī al-muṭlaq*, who in the absence of the imāms looked after the affairs of the *daʿwa* and the community.

The current period of *satr* in Ṭayyibī Ismāʿīlism is, in turn, divided into a Yamanī period, extending from 526/1132 to around 999/1591, when the Ṭayyibīs were split into the Dā'ūdī and Sulaymānī factions; and an Indian period, covering essentially the history of the Dā'ūdī *daʿwa* during the last four centuries. During the Yamanī period, the Ṭayyibīs maintained their unity in Yaman and also succeeded in winning an increasing number of adherents in western India. By the end of the 10th/16th century, when the Dā'ūdī-Sulaymānī schism occurred, the Indian Ṭayyibīs by far surpassed their Yamanī co-religionists in terms of numbers and financial contributions to the *daʿwa* treasury. In a sense, the Indian Ṭayyibīs had by then become ready to exert their independence from Yaman, where the Ṭayyibī *dāʿīs* had resided for more than four centuries. Under these circumstances, the Indian Ṭayyibīs lent their support mainly to the Dā'ūdī *daʿwa*, while the Yamanī Ṭayyibīs became the chief followers of the Sulaymānī *daʿwa*. There were essentially no doctrinal differences between the two groups, who, henceforth, followed separate lines of *dāʿīs*. During the Indian period, the majoritarian Indian Ṭayyibī community, represented by the Dā'ūdī Bohras, prospered as a trading community and developed rather freely, though it also experienced periods of severe persecution and internal dissent.

The non-Ismāʿīlī historical sources, on al-Mustaʿlī and the later Fāṭimids, relevant to the study of the opening phase of Mustaʿlian Ismāʿīlism, have already been reviewed at the beginning of the previous chapter. For the earliest period, much valuable information is contained, especially, in the *Dhayl ta'rīkh Dimashq* of Ibn al-Qalānisī and in the histories of Ibn Ẓāfir, Ibn Muyassar, Ibn Taghrībirdī and al-Maqrīzī, who, in the final portion of his *Ittiʿāẓ al-ḥunafā'*, continues the history of the Fāṭimids to the fall of the dynasty. The general Muslim histories, notably that of Ibn al-Athīr, are also relevant here. The literary sources for the history of the Yamanī phase of the Ṭayyibī *daʿwa*, essentially a history of the activities of the various Mustaʿlī-Ṭayyibī *dāʿīs* and their relations with the Zaydīs and other local dynasties of Yaman, have been fully discussed by Ayman F. Sayyid in the relevant sections of his bio-bibliographical survey of the sources on the Islamic period in Yaman.[1] For the earliest period in the history of the Ṭayyibīs and Ḥāfiẓīs in Yaman, our chief authority is the already-cited *Ta'rīkh al-Yaman* by Najm al-Dīn ʿUmāra b. ʿAlī al-Ḥakamī, the Yamanī historian and poet who emigrated to Egypt and was executed in Cairo in 569/1174, on charges of plotting to restore the Fāṭimids to power.[2] Ismāʿīlī historical writings on the earliest Mustaʿlians, the Ḥāfiẓīs and the Ṭayyibīs of Yaman, are, as expected, rather meagre. No Ḥāfiẓī sources have survived, and our chief Ismāʿīlī authority on the Yamanī Ṭayyibīs is again the *dāʿī* Idrīs who as the head of the Ṭayyibī *daʿwa* in the 9th/15th century, was well-informed about the details of the movement in Yaman.[3] Idrīs also has extensive quotations from earlier Ismāʿīlī sources, many of which have not survived.

Idrīs ʿImād al-Dīn b. al-Ḥasan came from the prominent al-Walīd family of Quraysh in Yaman, who led the Ṭayyibī *daʿwa* for more than three centuries. He succeeded his uncle as the nineteenth *dāʿī muṭlaq* of the Ṭayyibīs in 832/1428. Idrīs was also a warrior and fought several battles against the Zaydīs; he died in 872/1468. Idrīs was the most celebrated historian of the Ismāʿīlī movement, producing three extensive historical works. In the final, seventh volume of his *ʿUyūn al-akhbār* (*The Choice Stories*), still in manuscript form, he relates valuable details on the Ṣulayḥids, the reigns of al-Mustaʿlī and al-Āmir, and the opening phase of the Ṭayyibī *daʿwa* in Yaman. It also contains important details on various Yamanī *dāʿīs*. His second work, a two-volume history entitled the *Nuzhat al-afkār*, deals with the history of Ismāʿīlism in Yaman, especially after the fall of the Ṣulayḥid dynasty, carrying the narrative to the year 853/1449. This provides the most complete and accurate history of the *daʿwa* in Yaman during the post-Ṣulayḥid period. Idrīs took special interest in the Ismāʿīlī *daʿwa* in India, and has references to this *daʿwa* and to relations between the Ismāʿīlī communities of Yaman and India in his *Nuzhat al-afkār*. Thirdly, in his *Rawḍat al-akhbār*, which is a continuation of the preceding work, Idrīs adds the events of his own time, from 853/1449 to 870/1465. The histories of Idrīs shed valuable light on issues, events and personalities not discussed elsewhere. As such, they are indispensable for understanding the mediaeval history of the Ṭayyibī Ismāʿīlī movement in Yaman. Unfortunately, the latter two works remain unpublished, and manuscript copies of them cannot be easily obtained. It may be added that the tradition of writing compendia of Ismāʿīlī works in Yaman attained its peak in the *Zahr al-maʿānī* of the *dāʿī* Idrīs. Other Ṭayyibī authors and *dāʿīs* have also written important Ismāʿīlī chrestomathies which, however, rarely contain historical details.

The history of the Indian phase of Ṭayyibī Ismāʿīlism, too, is essentially comprised of the history of the activities of different *dāʿīs*, in addition to the accounts of the occasional disputes and minor schisms in the community stemming from conflicting claims to the headship of the Ismāʿīlī Bohras. A number of Dāʾūdī *dāʿīs* and authors have produced historical works, mostly in Arabic, on the Mustaʿlī-Ṭayyibī *daʿwa* in India. In more recent times, some of these works have appeared in a form of Arabicized Gujarātī written in Arabic script, the official language of the Dāʾūdī Bohras, so as to reach a wider public. The bulk of the Ismāʿīlī sources produced in India, however, intermix legend and reality, being concerned chiefly with defending or refuting certain claims to the position of *dāʿī muṭlaq*. As a result, the history of the Ṭayyibī *daʿwa* in India, especially during the earlier centuries, continues to be shrouded in mystery. Amongst the few accurate Ismāʿīlī histories produced in India, mention may be made of the *Muntazaʿ al-akhbār*, in two volumes, written in Arabic by Quṭb al-Dīn Sulaymānjī Burhānpūrī (d. 1241/1826), a Dāʾūdī Bohra author. The second volume of this still unpublished work covers the history of the Ṭayyibīs and their *dāʿīs* until the year 1240/1824. Another noteworthy history of Ismāʿīlism in India is the *Mawsim-i bahār* of Miyān Ṣāḥib Muḥammad ʿAlī Rāmpūrī, an agent of the Dāʾūdī *daʿwa* organization who died in 1315 or 1316/1897–1899.[4] This work, in Gujarātī and written in Arabic script, draws on the *Muntazaʿ al-akhbār* and a number of earlier sources, some of which have not survived. The first two volumes of the *Mawsim-i bahār* deal with the history of the prophets and the Ismāʿīlī Imāms until al-Ṭayyib. The third volume, completed in 1299/1882 and lithographed soon after, contains the history of the Ismāʿīlī *daʿwa* in India from its origins in Gujarāt until the author's time, covering the lives of the Ṭayyibī *dāʿīs* in Yaman and the Dā'ūdī *dāʿīs* residing in India.

In modern times, a number of Dā'ūdīs, who greatly outnumber the Sulaymānīs, have written on various aspects of their community. However, historical studies of any value have remained few in number. In the early decades of this century, Mullā ʿAbd al-Ḥusayn, a Dā'ūdī functionary, produced one of the most popular books in the English language on the Ṭayyibī *daʿwa* in India.[5] The late Zāhid ʿAlī, a learned Dā'ūdī Bohra, has produced the fullest contemporary account of the doctrines of the Ṭayyibīs in his already-cited *Hamārē Ismāʿīlī madhhab*, written in Urdu; he presents the earlier history of the Mustaʿlians and a summary of their beliefs in the second volume of his *Ta'rīkh-i Fāṭimiyyīn*. Several members of the distinguished al-Hamdānī family of Sūrat, descendants of Muḥammad ʿAlī b. Fayḍ Allāh al-Yaʿburī al-Hamdānī (d. 1315/1898), a prominent Dā'ūdī scholar and author, have written on Mustaʿlī-Ṭayyibī Ismāʿīlism and on the Ṭayyibī *daʿwa* in India. Muḥammad ʿAlī al-Hamdānī's grandson, al-Ḥusayn b. Fayḍ Allāh al-Hamdānī, was amongst the pioneers of modern Ismāʿīlī studies, drawing on the valuable collection of the Ismāʿīlī manuscripts preserved in his family. The latter's son, Abbas Hamdani, is currently making noteworthy contributions to Ismāʿīlī studies. Western orientalists and Ismāʿīlī specialists have not so far produced major works on Mustaʿlian Ismāʿīlism, particularly on the history of the Ṭayyibī *daʿwa* in India, owing mainly to the scarcity of reliable sources; the main exception being the survey of John Hollister in his book *The Shīʿa of India*.

The Indian Ismāʿīlīs have also rendered a unique service to Ismāʿīlism by preserving a good portion of the literary heritage of the Ismāʿīlīs, including the classical works of the Fāṭimid period and the treatises written by the Yamanī Ṭayyibīs. These Ismāʿīlī manuscripts, collectively designated as *al-khizāna al-maknūna*, the guarded treasure, were transferred, especially after the 10th/16th century, from Yaman to India, where they continued to be copied by the better educated Ismāʿīlī Bohras of Gujarāt and elsewhere. At present, there are major libraries of such manuscripts at

Sūrat, Bombay, and Baroda, the seats of the Dā'ūdī and the Sulaymānī *daʿwa*s in India. Most Bohras have had their own small collections of manuscripts, many of which have been incorporated into the Ismāʿīlī library at Sūrat. The *dāʿī muṭlaq* of the Dā'ūdī Bohras has instituted very strict rules regarding the use of the vast collections of the library at Sūrat; fortunately however some learned Ismāʿīlī Bohras have come to permit Ismāʿīlī scholars and researchers access to their private collections.

After the death of the Fāṭimid al-Mustanṣir in Dhu'l-Ḥijja 487/December 1094, a major schism occurred in the Ismāʿīlī movement concerning the succession to the imāmate. Al-Mustanṣir had already designated his eldest son Abū Manṣūr Nizār as his successor. Nizār, who had received al-Mustanṣir's *naṣṣ* and was thus expected to succeed to the imāmate, was about fifty years-old at the time of his father's death. However, Abu'l-Qāsim Shāhanshāh, better known by his vizieral title of al-Afḍal, who a few months earlier had succeeded his own father Badr al-Jamālī as the all-powerful vizier and commander-in-chief of the Fāṭimid state, had other plans. Aiming to retain the state reins in his own hands, al-Afḍal favoured the candidacy of al-Mustanṣir's youngest son Abu'l-Qāsim Aḥmad, who would be entirely dependent upon him. At the time, Aḥmad was about twenty years-old and already married to al-Afḍal's sister. Al-Afḍal moved swiftly and, on the day after al-Mustanṣir's death, placed Aḥmad on the Fāṭimid throne with the title of al-Mustaʿlī bi'llāh. He quickly obtained for al-Mustaʿlī the allegiance of the notables of the Fāṭimid court and the leaders of the Ismāʿīlī *daʿwa* at Cairo. There are conflicting accounts of this important event in the history of Ismāʿīlism. Later, the Mustaʿlian Ismāʿīlīs circulated different versions of the dubious circumstances under which, according to them, al-Mustanṣir had allegedly nominated al-Mustaʿlī as his heir apparent, including also a deathbed *naṣṣ*. But it cannot be denied that Nizār's succession rights were never revoked by al-Mustanṣir, and al-Afḍal secured al-Mustaʿlī's accession in what amounted to a palace *coup d'état*.

The dispossessed Nizār hurriedly fled to Alexandria in the company of his half-brother ʿAbd Allāh and a few followers, where he rose in revolt early in 488/1095. In Alexandria, the centre of military factions suppressed by Badr al-Jamālī, Nizār was assisted by the city's governor, the Turk Nāṣir al-Dawla Aftakīn, who aspired to replace al-Afḍal, and its Ismāʿīlī *qāḍī*, Ibn ʿAmmār. He also received much local support, especially from the Arab inhabitants of the area. Soon, Nizār received the oath of allegiance of the Alexandrians, and adopted the caliphal title of al-Muṣṭafā li-Dīn Allāh. The revolt was initially successful, Nizār easily managing to repel al-Afḍal's forces and advancing to the vicinity of Cairo. Nevertheless, towards the end of 488 A.H., the alarmed Fāṭimid vizier effectively besieged Alexandria and forced Nizār to surrender. Nizār was taken to Cairo where he was imprisoned and then immured on al-Mustaʿlī's orders; all of these events taking place during the year 488 A.H.[6]

The fate of Nizār and the strife over the succession to the Fāṭimid caliph-imām al-Mustanṣir left a decisive mark on the history of the Ismāʿīlī movement. By choosing al-Mustaʿlī, al-Afḍal had split the Fāṭimid Ismāʿīlīs into two rival factions which were duly to become bitter enemies. The ambitious al-Afḍal had in effect alienated almost all of the Ismāʿīlī communities of the Muslim East. The imāmate of al-Mustaʿlī came to be recognized by most Ismāʿīlīs in Egypt, many in Syria, and by the whole Ismāʿīlī community in Yaman and that in western India dependent on it. These Ismāʿīlīs now accepted al-Mustaʿlī as their nineteenth imām. On the other hand, the Persian Ismāʿīlīs, under the leadership of Ḥasan-i Ṣabbāḥ and defending al-Mustanṣir's original *naṣṣ*, upheld Nizār's right to the imāmate and refused to acknowledge the ninth Fāṭimid caliph al-Mustaʿlī as their next imām. As part of the Saljūq realm, they and many other eastern Ismāʿīlīs, permanently broke off their relations with the headquarters of the Fāṭimid *daʿwa* in Cairo. Nizār also had partisans within the Fāṭimid territories. In Egypt, they were quickly suppressed, but in Syria, now beyond Fāṭimid control, Nizār's followers became organized by emissaries despatched from Persia. The two factions of the Ismāʿīlī movement henceforth became known as the Mustaʿliyya or Mustaʿlawiyya, and the Nizāriyya, depending on whether they recognized al-Mustaʿlī or Nizār as the rightful imām after al-Mustanṣir. Subsequently, the movement of the Nizārīs, who launched an open revolt against the Saljūqs and who from the beginning were very active also in the doctrinal domain, became designated as *al-daʿwa al-jadīda*, the new preaching, in contradistinction to *al-daʿwa al-qadīma*, the old preaching of the Fāṭimid Ismāʿīlīs maintained by the Mustaʿlians.[7] In modern times, the Nizārīs and the Mustaʿlians, or more specifically the Ṭayyibīs, have also become respectively designated as the Eastern and the Western Ismāʿīlīs.[8]

Al-Mustaʿlī remained a puppet in the hands of al-Afḍal during his short reign (487–495/1094–1101).[9] Al-Afḍal, continuing his father's policies, maintained order and relative prosperity in Egypt. He was also initially successful in Syria, regaining Tyre from a disloyal governor in 490/1097 and recapturing Jerusalem in the following year from the Turkish

Artuqids, Sukmān and Īlghāzī, who had established themselves in Palestine. Close relations had continued between Fāṭimid Egypt and Ṣulayḥid Yaman, now still ruled by al-Malika al-Sayyida, who had recognized al-Musta'lī as the legitimate imām after al-Mustanṣir and who managed the affairs of the Ismā'īlī *da'wa* in Yaman with the help of the *dā'ī* Yaḥyā b. Lamak al-Ḥammādī (d. 520/1126).[10] Yaḥyā had succeeded his father in the headship of the Yamanī *da'wa* shortly before the year 491/1098. Now, however, the Fāṭimids and all Muslims of the Near East faced a new danger from the Crusaders, who had appeared in northern Syria in 490 A.H. to liberate the Holy Land of Christendom. Al-Afḍal had immediately opened negotiations with the Crusaders and had exchanged embassies with them, seeking their aid against the Turkish *amīrs* of Syria. Nonetheless, it seems that he had underestimated the threat of the Crusaders, being taken by complete surprise when the invading Franks moved towards their primary target of Jerusalem. The Crusaders seized Jerusalem easily after defeating the Fāṭimid army, led by al-Afḍal, near 'Asqalān in 492/1099. By 494/1100–1101, they had established themselves firmly in Palestine, having taken Ḥayfā, Arsūf and Qayṣariyya (Caesarea). Al-Afḍal's continued attempts to deal more effectively with them proved futile. It was in the midst of the Fāṭimid entanglements with the Franks that al-Musta'lī died in Ṣafar 495/December 1101. Al-Afḍal now proclaimed al-Musta'lī's five year-old son Abū 'Alī al-Manṣūr as the new Fāṭimid caliph with the *laqab* of al-Āmir bi-Aḥkām Allāh.[11]

During the first twenty years of al-Āmir's caliphate (495–524/1101–1130), al-Afḍal remained the effective master of the Fāṭimid state, and ruled efficiently. Externally, he concerned himself mainly with the Crusaders, and organized numerous expeditions against them. In one of the more successful campaigns led by al-Afḍal's son Sharaf al-Ma'ālī, the Fāṭimids defeated the Franks in 496/1103 and took Ramla. Nevertheless, the greater part of Palestine and the towns on the Syrian coast fell into the hands of the Crusaders. In 497/1103, 'Akkā (Acre) was surrendered by its Fāṭimid commander, and then, in rapid succession, Ṭarablus (Tripoli) and Ṣaydā (Sidon) were lost to the Franks during 502–504/1109–1111. By 518/1124, when Ṣūr (Tyre) fell, only 'Asqalān remained of the former Fāṭimid possessions in the Levant. Egypt itself was invaded in 511/1117 by Baldwin I (1100–1118), king of the Latin state of Jerusalem and one of the original leaders of the First Crusade, who took Faramā and then advanced to Tinnīs. However, the Crusaders were compelled to retreat from Egypt due to Baldwin's fatal illness. After being the unchallenged ruler of

Fāṭimid Egypt for some twenty-seven years, al-Afḍal was assassinated in 515/1121. His assassination seems to have been plotted by al-Āmir, who had become weary of his vizier's tutelage and restrictions. As related in some sources and claimed by the Nizārīs themselves, it is possible that the assassination was planned by the Nizārīs, who deeply despised al-Afḍal. Be it as it may, al-Āmir immediately ordered the confiscation of the murdered vizier's substantial properties and renowned treasures.[12]

After al-Afḍal, al-Āmir appointed al-Ma'mūn al-Baṭā'iḥī to the vizierate. Al-Ma'mūn, implicated in the murder of his patron al-Afḍal, re-opened the Dār al-Ḥikma, which had been closed by al-Afḍal towards the end of the 5th/11th century. Al-Ma'mūn soon fell from al-Āmir's favour and was imprisoned in 519/1125; three years later, he was crucified with his brothers on charges of plotting against the caliph.[13] Al-Āmir did not appoint any viziers after al-Ma'mūn, preferring to run the affairs of the state personally. Financial matters, however, were placed under the charge of a Christian monk, Abū Najāḥ b. Qannā', who was soon afterwards dismissed and flogged to death in 523/1129. Al-Āmir was becoming rapidly detested by his subjects due to his cruel acts, when he, too, was killed. The tenth Fāṭimid caliph and the twentieth imām of the Mustaʿlian Ismāʿīlīs was assassinated by a group of Nizārī *fidā'īs* in Dhu'l-Qaʿda 524/October 1130. He had reigned for almost twenty-nine years, longer than any other Fāṭimid caliph-imām except for his grandfather al-Mustanṣir.

As we shall see, it was in al-Āmir's time that the Nizārī Ismāʿīlīs consolidated their power in Persia and Syria, under the leadership of Ḥasan-i Ṣabbāḥ (d. 518/1124), who resided at the mountain castle of Alamūt. Although the Nizārīs never made any major attempts to penetrate Egypt after the Nizārī-Mustaʿlī schism, it seems that their cause continued for some time to have supporters in Fāṭimid Egypt, finding expression also in occasional plots. The Nizārīs were allegedly involved in al-Afḍal's assassination; and al-Afḍal's successor al-Ma'mūn had to take extensive precautionary measures to prevent the infiltration of the Nizārī agents into Egypt.[14] Some of these agents, carrying material aid as well, were reportedly being sent directly from Alamūt. Nonetheless, the Nizārīs succeeded in killing al-Āmir. The vizier al-Ma'mūn, who himself feared the Nizārīs, also found it necessary to arrange for a public assembly in order to publicize the rights of al-Mustaʿlī and al-Āmir to the imāmate and to refute the claims of Nizār and his partisans. This meeting, convened at the great hall of the palace, was attended by numerous Fāṭimid princes and high state dignitaries. Amongst those present were Walī al-Dawla Abu'l-Barakāt b. ʿAbd al-Ḥaqīq, the chief *dāʿī*, Abū Muḥammad b. Ādam, the head of the Dār al-ʿIlm in Cairo, Abu'l-Thurayyā b. Mukhtār and Abu'l-Fakhr, the foremost Ismāʿīlī jurists, and Ibn ʿUqayl, the chief *qāḍī*. Ibn Muyassar has preserved a detailed account of this event, which took place in 516/1122.[15] It is possible that Ibn Muyassar derived his account from a near contemporary Egyptian annalist, Ibn al-Ma'mūn (d. 588/1192), the son of the Fāṭimid vizier who had organized the assembly.

In the course of this meeting, various circumstances and episodes were mentioned according to which al-Mustanṣir had supposedly expressed his preference for al-Mustaʿlī over Nizār. Most significantly, Nizār's full-sister, seated behind a screen in an adjoining chamber, testified that al-Mustanṣir, on his deathbed, had designated al-Mustaʿlī as his successor, divulging this *naṣṣ* to his own sister (Nizār's aunt). At the end of the meeting, al-Ma'mūn ordered Ibn al-Ṣayrafī (d. 542/1147), then an important secretary (*kātib*) at the Fāṭimid chancery, to draw up an epistle (*sijill*) to be read from the pulpits of the mosques throughout Egypt. This epistle, or perhaps what may be a longer version of it produced later, has been preserved under the title of *al-Hidāya al-Āmiriyya*.[16] Written about twenty-eight years after the Nizārī–Mustaʿlī schism, it is the earliest official refutation of Nizār's claims to the imāmate. The *Hidāya* admits that al-Mustanṣir had originally nominated Nizār as his heir apparent.[17] But it also argues, in violation of the beliefs of the earlier Ismāʿīlīs, that this original *naṣṣ* was subsequently revoked in favour of al-Mustaʿlī, repeatedly referring to al-Mustanṣir's deathbed *naṣṣ*.[18] The *Hidāya* also gives prominence to the testimony of Nizār's sister, who, during the assembly of Shawwāl 516 A.H., had defended the legitimacy of the Mustaʿlian line of imāms. The *Hidāya* was also circulated in Syria, where it caused an uproar amongst the Nizārīs of Damascus. One of the Syrian Nizārīs forwarded al-Āmir's epistle to his chief, who wrote a refutation of it. This Nizārī refutation was, in due course, read at a meeting of the Mustaʿlians in Damascus. A Mustaʿlian *dāʿī* from Damascus then wrote to al-Āmir asking him for further guidance on the matter. Soon afterwards, al-Āmir sent a reply to his Syrian *dāʿī* in the form of an additional epistle, refuting the Nizārī refutation of the *Hidāya*.[19]

After the assassination of al-Āmir on 2 Dhu'l-Qaʿda 524 A.H., the Fāṭimid Caliphate embarked on its rapid decline, with numerous periods of crisis, whilst a new schism developed amongst the Mustaʿlian Ismāʿīlīs. It may be noted in passing that Idrīs, in his *ʿUyūn al-akhbār*, in line with the

Mustaʿlī–Ṭayyibī tradition in general, and for some inexplicable reason, mentions the year 526 A.H. as the year of al-Āmir's death. The Ṭayyibīs hold that a son, named al-Ṭayyib, had been born to al-Āmir a few months before his death. This Ṭayyibī tradition is supported especially by an epistle of al-Āmir sent to the Ṣulayḥid queen of Yaman, al-Malika al-Sayyida, announcing the birth of Abu'l-Qāsim al-Ṭayyib in Rabīʿ II 524 A.H.[20] The historical reality of al-Ṭayyib is also attested by Ibn Muyassar,[21] probably on the authority of the lost chronicle of al-Muḥannak (d. 549/1154), and by other histories written during the 6th/12th century.[22] Al-Ṭayyib was immediately designated as al-Āmir's heir, and the occasion was celebrated by a fortnight of public festivities in Cairo and Fusṭāṭ. After al-Āmir, who had acted as his own vizier during the last years of his caliphate, power was immediately assumed by his cousin, Abu'l-Maymūn ʿAbd al-Majīd, the eldest member of the Fāṭimid family and the son of Abu'l-Qāsim Muḥammad b. al-Mustanṣir. More specifically, Hazārmard (Hizabr al-Mulūk) and Barghash, two favourites of al-Āmir, now came to hold the reins of power in the Fāṭimid state, whilst placing ʿAbd al-Majīd as nominal ruler. ʿAbd al-Majīd ruled officially as regent, pending the expected delivery of al-Āmir's pregnant wife.[23] Hazārmard himself assumed the vizierate, and Yānis, an Armenian general in the service of the Fāṭimids, became the commander-in-chief and the regent's chamberlain. ʿAbd al-Majīd somehow managed to conceal the existence of al-Ṭayyib, born a few months earlier, and nothing more is known of his fate.[24]

The regency of ʿAbd al-Majīd and the vizierate of Hazārmard proved to be brief. Abū ʿAlī Aḥmad, nicknamed Kutayfāt, the son of al-Afḍal b. Badr al-Jamālī, was raised to the vizierate by the army about two weeks after al-Āmir's death. Hazārmard was executed, but ʿAbd al-Majīd continued a while longer as regent (*walī ʿahd al-Muslimīn*) with Abū ʿAlī Kutayfāt as his vizier. This temporary arrangement is confirmed by an epistle issued in Dhu'l-Qaʿda 524 A.H. by the Fāṭimid chancery to the monastery of St Catherine in Mount Sinai.[25] Soon afterwards, probably when the expectation of the birth of a male heir to al-Āmir had proved false, Kutayfāt made radical changes which affected the very foundations of the Fāṭimid regime. ʿAbd al-Majīd was overthrown and imprisoned by Kutayfāt, who now declared the Fāṭimid dynasty deposed and proclaimed the sovereignty of the twelfth imām of the Twelver Shīʿīs, the Imām al-Mahdī whose reappearance had been expected since 260 A.H. As a result of this ingenious religio-political solution to the succession problem created by the absence of a direct heir to the Fāṭimid throne and the imāmate, Kutayfāt, an Imāmī Shīʿī himself, acquired a unique position of power, ruling as a dictator responsible to no one either in theory or in practice. Kutayfāt issued coins in Egypt during 525 and 526 A.H., bearing the names of 'al-Imām Muḥammad Abu'l-Qāsim al-Muntaẓar li-Amr Allāh', and 'al-Imām al-Mahdī al-Qā'im bi-Amr Allāh', in some of which he himself is named as the hidden imām's representative (*nā'ib*) and deputy (*khalīfa*).[26] These developments of course, meant the adoption of Imāmī Shīʿism, instead of Ismāʿīlism, as the state religion of the Fāṭimid state. Nonetheless, Abū ʿAlī Kutayfāt, who came to adopt his father's title of al-Afḍal, allowed the Ismāʿīlīs and other non-Twelver communities some consideration. Kutayfāt's policies, however, created much resentment amongst the Ismāʿīlīs and the supporters of the Fāṭimid dynasty in Egypt who plotted against him, cutting down the period of his rule to just about a year. On 16 Muḥarram 526/8 December 1131, Kutayfāt was overthrown and killed in yet another *coup d'état*, organized by the dissatisfied Ismāʿīlī elements and the Kutāma faction of the army, led by Yānis. ʿAbd al-Majīd was released from prison and restored to power. This event came to be commemorated annually by the so-called feast of victory (*ʿīd al-naṣr*) held on that day, until the end of the Fāṭimid dynasty.[27]

At first, ʿAbd al-Majīd ruled once again as regent, with Yānis assuming the vizierate. But three months later, in Rabīʿ II 526/February 1132, he was proclaimed caliph and imām with the title of al-Ḥāfiẓ li-Dīn Allāh.[28] And Ismāʿīlism was reinstated as the state religion of Fāṭimid Egypt. Al-Ḥāfiẓ became the first Fāṭimid caliph-imām whose father had not reigned before him; clearly, his irregular succession required specific justifications. Thus, a *sijill* was issued on the occasion of his proclamation as caliph-imām, containing various explanations for his legitimacy. Above all, this epistle, preserved by al-Qalqashandī,[29] centred around the idea that al-Āmir, the previous imām, had personally transmitted the caliphate and the imāmate to his cousin ʿAbd al-Majīd, just as the Prophet had designated his cousin ʿAlī as his successor at Ghadīr Khumm. It also referred to the nomination of ʿAbd al-Raḥīm b. Ilyās, al-Ḥākim's cousin, as heir apparent. Yet, it did not mention the uncertainties of the initial interregnum of al-Ḥāfiẓ and the obscurities of his regencies, nor did it make any reference to al-Ṭayyib and to al-Āmir's posthumous child. This important document, claiming legitimacy for the imāmate of al-Ḥāfiẓ on the basis of an alleged *naṣṣ* derived from al-Āmir, provided the foundation on which Fāṭimid rule continued for another four decades. It also provided justification for the claims of the later Fāṭimids to the imāmate of a section of the Mustaʿlian Ismāʿīlī community. The expressions *al-dawla al-Ḥāfiẓiyya* and *al-imāma al-Ḥāfiẓiyya* henceforth occur frequently in documents issued by the Fāṭimid chancery.[30]

The proclamation of al-Ḥāfiẓ as caliph-imām caused the first important schism in the Mustaʿlian community, further weakening the Ismāʿīlī movement. The claims of al-Ḥāfiẓ to the imāmate, though he was not a direct descendant of the previous imām, were supported by the official *daʿwa* organization in Egypt and by the majority of the Mustaʿlian Ismāʿīlīs in both Egypt and Syria. These Mustaʿlians, recognizing al-Ḥāfiẓ and the later Fāṭimids as their rightful imāms, became known as al-Ḥāfiẓiyya or al-Majīdiyya. However, some Mustaʿlian groups in Egypt and Syria, as well as many in Yaman, acknowledged the rights of al-Ṭayyib to the imāmate, accepting him as al-Āmir's successor and rejecting the claims of al-Ḥāfiẓ. These Mustaʿlians were initially known as the Āmiriyya, but later, after the establishment of the independent Ṭayyibī *daʿwa* in Yaman, became designated as the Ṭayyibiyya. Ḥāfiẓī Ismāʿīlism, as we shall see, also found support in Yaman for some time. However, Yaman was to become, for several centuries, the chief stronghold of Ṭayyibī Ismāʿīlism. Thus, by 526/1132, the unified Fāṭimid Ismāʿīlī movement of al-Mustanṣir's time had become split into the rival Nizārī, Ḥāfiẓī and Ṭayyibī factions. While the Nizārīs had by then founded an independent state in Persia and Syria, and the Ṭayyibīs were taking advantage of the mountainous districts of Yaman to consolidate their own position, the days of Ḥāfiẓī Ismāʿīlism, now the official creed of the Fāṭimid state, were already numbered.

Since Badr al-Jamālī's time, the viziers had become the real masters of the Fāṭimid empire. But al-Ḥāfiẓ, the only caliph amongst the later Fāṭimids who was a grown man at the time of his accession, paid special attention to the activities of his viziers. It may be added that from the reign of al-Ḥāfiẓ onwards, the Fāṭimid viziers, or more precisely 'Viziers of the Sword', also competed with the claimants to the vizierate in gaining the loyalties of the various factions of the army, resulting in continuous military rivalries and disturbances in Egypt. Having become fearful of the growing influence of his Armenian vizier Yānis, who had given his name to a private regiment, al-Yānisiyya, al-Ḥāfiẓ had him killed towards the end of 526/1132; the vizierate of Yānis having endured less than a year. After ruling without a vizier for some time, in 528/1133–1134 al-Ḥāfiẓ entrusted the duties of the vizierate to his eldest son Sulaymān, who had that year been designated as heir apparent. When Sulaymān died two months later, al-Ḥāfiẓ named another of his sons, Ḥaydara, as heir, also charging him with the functions of the vizierate.[31] Ḥasan, a third son of al-Ḥāfiẓ, driven by jealousy, successfully plotted against his father and Ḥaydara, seizing power as vizier and killing several army leaders. Irritated by Ḥasan's behaviour, the army now revolted and demanded his head. Al-Ḥāfiẓ was obliged to comply, and had Ḥasan poisoned by his physician. To deal with the deteriorating situation, Ḥasan had previously appealed for aid to Bahrām, an Armenian general who served the Fāṭimids and was at the time the governor of al-Gharbiyya, a province in lower Egypt. When Bahrām entered Cairo with his Armenian troops, Ḥasan had already been killed. Nonetheless, al-Ḥāfiẓ could not ignore Bahrām's presence in the capital and the Armenian general was appointed to the vizierate in Jumādā II 529/March 1135.

The pro-Armenian policies of Bahrām, who encouraged the immigration of his co-religionists to Egypt and gave them important posts, angered the Muslim populace and soon provoked a military revolt led by Riḍwān b. Walakhshī, the new governor of al-Gharbiyya. Abandoned by the Muslim troops in the Fāṭimid army, Bahrām was forced out of office in Jumādā I 531/February 1137, when he fled to upper Egypt to seek the assistance of his brother Vasak, the governor of Qūṣ. But Vasak had been killed by the Muslims, and Bahrām now had to face an army sent after him by Riḍwān, who had meanwhile succeeded to the vizierate. Bahrām was saved through the intervention of Roger II, king of Sicily. Granted safe-conduct by al-Ḥāfiẓ, he was allowed to retire to a monastery. Riḍwān, himself a Sunnī, now began to persecute the Christians. Soon, he came to exercise full authority and took the title of *al-malik*, or king, a title which later passed to other Fāṭimid viziers and then to all members of the Ayyūbid dynasty. Al-Ḥāfiẓ, threatened and displeased by the growing influence of his vizier, removed Riḍwān from office in 533/1139; he was later killed in 542/1147 while attempting to overthrow the caliph. The caliph recalled Bahrām to Cairo, entrusting the vizierate to him without officially appointing him to the post. Bahrām died in the Fāṭimid palace in 535/1140, and al-Ḥāfiẓ personally took part in the funeral procession of his faithful Armenian servant.[32] Subsequently, Ibn Maṣāl held the vizierate for some time during the latter part of the caliphate of al-Ḥāfiẓ.[33] Al-Ḥāfiẓ, the eleventh Fāṭimid caliph and the twenty-first imām of the Ḥāfiẓī Ismāʿīlīs, died in Jumādā II 544/October 1149, after a reign of almost eighteen years beset by numerous revolts and disturbances.

Like al-Ḥāfiẓ, the last three Fāṭimid caliphs, al-Ẓāfir (544–549/1149–

1154), al-Fā'iz (549–555/1154–1160), and al-ʿĀḍid (555–567/1160–1171), were also recognized as the imāms of the Ḥāfiẓiyya. These caliph-imāms who died in their youth were, however, no more than puppets in the hands of their viziers.[34]

Al-Ḥāfiẓ was succeeded by his seventeen year-old son Abū Manṣūr Ismāʿīl, who adopted the title of al-Ẓāfir bi-Amr Allāh. Al-Ẓāfir, strongly inclined to a life of pleasure, chose Ibn Maṣāl as his vizier; this being the last time a vizier was appointed by a Fāṭimid caliph. During his few months in office, Ibn Maṣāl checked the quarrels that raged between the Blacks and the Rayḥānīs in the army, restoring relative order to the country. Soon afterwards, al-ʿĀdil b. al-Salār, the governor of Alexandria, revolted and marched on Cairo at the head of his troops. He defeated and killed Ibn Maṣāl in Shawwāl 544/February 1150, forcing al-Ẓāfir to nominate him as vizier with the title al-Malik al-ʿĀdil. Ibn al-Salār, who in 545/1150 fruitlessly sought an alliance with the Zangid ruler of Aleppo, Nūr al-Dīn (541–569/1146–1174), against the Franks, and who also engaged the Fāṭimid fleet against the Frankish ports of Syria, was murdered in Muḥarram 548/April 1153.[35] The assassination plot, approved by the caliph, had been conceived by Ibn al-Salār's step-son, ʿAbbās, and carried out by the latter's son Naṣr, a favourite of al-Ẓāfir. Thereupon, ʿAbbās, who was commander of the garrison of ʿAsqalān, the last Fāṭimid foothold in Syria, returned to Cairo and seized the vizierate.[36] ʿAsqalān was lost to the Franks shortly afterwards in Jumādā I 548/August 1153. ʿAbbās, rapidly becoming convinced that the caliph was conspiring against him, resolved to move first, with the aid of his son. Accordingly, Naṣr, luring al-Ẓāfir to his house, killed him in Muḥarram 549/April 1154.

ʿAbbās, continuing as vizier, then placed al-Ẓāfir's five year-old son ʿĪsā on the Fāṭimid throne, giving him the title of al-Fā'iz bi-Naṣr Allāh. ʿAbbās also charged two of al-Ẓāfir's brothers with the murder of the caliph and had them executed. These events terrified the members of the Fāṭimid family, and they appealed for help to Ṭalā'iʿ b. Ruzzīk, the Armenian governor of Usyūṭ (Asyūṭ) in upper Egypt. As Ibn Ruzzīk approached Cairo, ʿAbbās and Naṣr fled to Syria, where the Franks, warned in advance, awaited them. ʿAbbās was killed in Rabīʿ I 549/June 1154, whilst Naṣr was delivered to the Fāṭimids and executed the following year. Meanwhile, Ibn Ruzzīk had succeeded ʿAbbās to the vizierate in 549/1154, and became the absolute master of Egypt, a position he maintained throughout the reign of al-Fā'iz. Ibn Ruzzīk, too, carried some military operations against the Crusaders, gaining victories at Ghazza and al-Khalīl (Hebron), in southern Palestine, in 553/1158. But he failed in his endeavours to secure an alliance with Nūr al-Dīn, which would have effectively protected Egypt against the Crusaders. The sickly and helpless al-Fā'iz died in an epileptic seizure in Rajab 555/July 1160 at the age of eleven, after a nominal reign of some six years spent in virtual captivity.

Al-Ṣāliḥ Ṭalā'iʿ b. Ruzzīk now placed Abū Muḥammad ʿAbd Allāh b. Yūsuf, the grandson of al-Ḥāfiẓ and a cousin of al-Fā'iz, on the Fāṭimid throne with the *laqab* of al-ʿĀḍid li-Dīn Allāh. Al-ʿĀḍid's father Yūsuf had been one of the Fāṭimid princes charged with al-Ẓāfir's murder and executed on the orders of ʿAbbās. Al-ʿĀḍid, destined to be the last Fāṭimid caliph, was only nine years-old at the time of his accession. Ibn Ruzzīk continued to act as the effective ruler of the state, and he further enhanced his position by having his daughter married to the caliph. He was assassinated in Ramaḍān 556/September 1161, evidently at the instigation of one of al-ʿĀḍid's aunts. The caliph was obliged to confer the vizierate on Ruzzīk, the son of the murdered vizier, who soon afterwards met a similar fate.[37] Ruzzīk was killed by Shāwar, the governor of upper Egypt who had revolted and entered Cairo to assume the vizierate in Muḥarram 558/January 1163. Shāwar's own vizierate, however, did not last more than nine months. In Ramaḍān 558/August 1163, he was driven out of Cairo by Ḍirghām, an able Fāṭimid officer who had distinguished himself by defeating the Franks at Ghazza in 553/1158. Now there followed a fateful struggle between Shāwar and his successor Ḍirghām, not only influencing the relations of Egypt with the Crusaders and Nūr al-Dīn, but also bringing about the circumstances that led to the downfall of the Fāṭimid dynasty.[38]

Shāwar had succeeded in taking refuge at the Zangid court in Syria, where he sought the help of Nūr al-Dīn for regaining the Fāṭimid vizierate. After some hesitation, Nūr al-Dīn agreed to assist Shāwar, encouraged perhaps by the fact that Amalric I (1163–1174), the new Frankish king of Jerusalem, was then seriously considering his own conquest of Egypt.[39] The Franks had already, in 556/1161, entered Egypt and forced Ibn Ruzzīk to pay them an annual tribute. The following year, another Frankish invasion of Egypt had proved abortive due to the deliberate flooding of the Nile by the Fāṭimids. At any event, towards the end of 559/1163, the advance guards of Amalric had entered Egypt, obliging Ḍirghām to resume the payment of the tribute previously promised to the Franks. It was under these circumstances that Nūr al-Dīn sent Shāwar back to Egypt with a force commanded by Asad al-Dīn

Shīrkūh, an *amīr* of Kurdish origins who along with his brother Ayyūb had entered the service of the Zangids. On this expedition, Shīrkūh took along his nephew Ṣalāḥ al-Dīn (Saladin), the son of Ayyūb and the future founder of the Ayyūbid dynasty. After several battles, Ḍirghām was defeated and killed in Ramaḍān 559/August 1164; Shāwar was restored to the vizierate.

Shāwar's second term as vizier lasted about five years, a most confusing period in the closing years of Fāṭimid history, marked by several more Frankish and Zangid invasions of Egypt, and by Shāwar's vacillating alliances with Amalric I and Nūr al-Dīn, whose forces fought numerous battles on Egyptian soil. It was also in 562/1167 that Amalric I despatched an embassy, headed by Hugh of Caesarea, to al-ʿĀḍid, and successfully demanded a substantial tribute. Even in these final days of the dynasty, the Christian knights were amazed by the splendour and ceremony of the Fāṭimid court.[40] In 564/1168, Nūr al-Dīn, now completely distrustful of Shāwar, who had failed to honour his commitments to the Zangid ruler, sent his third expeditionary force to Egypt, again under the command of Shīrkūh, and accompanied by Saladin. Nominally, the expedition had been undertaken in response to the appeals of Shāwar and al-ʿAḍid, who had become weary of the Frankish occupation of Egypt. But in effect, Nūr al-Dīn now entertained designs of his own for the Fāṭimid territories. Shīrkūh, having caused the withdrawal of Amalric's troops from Egypt, entered Cairo triumphantly, now also resolving to eliminate Shāwar. Saladin arrested Shāwar and had him killed, with al-ʿĀḍid's consent, in Rabīʿ II 564/January 1169. Thereupon, al-ʿĀḍid was obliged to appoint Shīrkūh to the vizierate, giving him the title of al-Malik al-Manṣūr. When Shīrkūh suddenly died two months later in Jumādā II 564/March 1169, he was succeeded by Saladin, the last of the Fāṭimid viziers.[41]

Ṣalāḥ al-Dīn Yūsuf b. Ayyūb (d. 589/1193), who received his formal investiture to the vizierate with the *laqab* of al-Malik al-Nāṣir from al-ʿĀḍid, and became known as Saladin in the European chronicles of the Crusades, was generally referred to by the title of *sulṭān*. He rapidly began to consolidate his position and prepare the ground for ending Fāṭimid rule, an objective persistently sought by his master Nūr al-Dīn, a fervent Sunnī favoured by the ʿAbbāsids. Saladin immediately embarked on the task of building his own loyal military force and destroying the Fāṭimid army. In particular, he dealt effectively and ruthlessly with the mutinous black troops in Egypt, an important contingent of the Fāṭimid army, burning down their quarters and routing their remnants in upper Egypt. He systematically appointed Syrians to key administrative positions at the expense of Egyptians. At the same time, Saladin gradually adopted anti-Ismāʿīlī policies, including the elimination of the Shīʿī form of *adhān* and the closing of the sessions of Ismāʿīlī lectures at al-Azhar and elsewhere in Cairo. He also appointed a Sunnī to the position of chief *qāḍī*, who removed the Ismāʿīlī jurists of Egypt and replaced them with Sunnī ones. About two and a half-years after his accession to the vizierate, Saladin felt sufficiently secure to take the final step in uprooting the Fāṭimid dynasty.

Saladin formally put an end to Fāṭimid rule when, in Muḥarram 567/September 1171, he had the *khuṭba* read in Cairo in the name of the reigning ʿAbbāsid caliph al-Mustaḍīʾ (566–575/1170–1180), thus proclaiming ʿAbbāsid suzerainty in Egypt. A Shāfiʿī theologian, Najm al-Dīn al-Khabūshānī, carried out this act, reciting the misdeeds of the Fāṭimids, who were characterized as infidels. After two centuries, Ismāʿīlism was abandoned as the state religion of Egypt, the sole remnant of the former Fāṭimid empire. Egypt returned to the fold of Sunnism amidst the complete apathy of the populace. A few days after, the helpless al-ʿĀḍid, the fourteenth and the last of the Fāṭimid caliphs, and the twenty-fourth imām of the Ḥāfiẓī Ismāʿīlīs, died following a brief illness. He was barely twenty-one years old. The Fāṭimid Caliphate, established in 297/909 and embodying perhaps the greatest religio-political and cultural success of Shīʿī Islam, had thus come to a close after 262 years. Saladin, who acquired his independence on Nūr al-Dīn's death in 569/1174, succeeded in founding the Ayyūbid dynasty, which was to rule over Egypt, Syria, Yaman and other parts of the Near East.

On al-ʿĀḍid's death, the numerous members of the Fāṭimid family were permanently placed in honourable captivity in sections of the Fāṭimid palace and in other isolated quarters. The immense treasures of the deposed dynasty were divided between Saladin's officers and Nūr al-Dīn. Saladin also caused the destruction of the renowned Fāṭimid libraries at Cairo, including the collections of the Dār al-Ḥikma. At the same time, Saladin started to persecute the Egyptian Ismāʿīlīs, who for the most part were Ḥāfiẓī Mustaʿlians. The Ḥāfiẓī *daʿwa*, which had now lost official support in Egypt, did not survive long after the fall of the Fāṭimid dynasty. It may be noted that during the reigns of the last four Fāṭimid caliphs, recognized as the imāms of the Ḥāfiẓiyya, the Ismāʿīlī traditions of the earlier times had been maintained. These included the appointment of chief *dāʿīs* as administrative heads of the *daʿwa*, starting with Sirāj al-Dīn Najm b. Jaʿfar (d. 528/1134), who became chief *dāʿī* and chief *qāḍī* in 526/

1132, and ending with Ibn ʿAbd al-Qawī and his relatives, who held that office during the final years of the dynasty.[42] It may also be assumed that the Ḥāfiẓī theologians of this period engaged in literary activities. However, as the Ḥāfiẓiyya were to disappear soon afterwards, no Ḥāfiẓī texts analogous to the mediaeval works of the Ṭayyibīs and Nizārīs, preserved by the adherents of these branches of Ismāʿīlism, have survived to the present times.[43]

In the immediate aftermath of the collapse of the Fāṭimid dynasty, the Ismāʿīlīs of Egypt, fleeing from the persecutions of the country's new Sunnī Ayyūbid masters, went into hiding. Many took refuge in upper Egypt, where they continued to agitate against Saladin. And for some time thereafter, the direct descendants of al-Ḥāfiẓ, as well as a few false Fāṭimid pretenders, claimed the imāmate of the Ḥāfiẓīs. Some of them also led revolts which always received limited support in Egypt.[44] Al-ʿĀḍid had appointed his eldest son, Dā'ūd, as his heir apparent. After al-ʿĀḍid, the Ḥāfiẓīs recognized Dā'ūd, with the title of al-Ḥāmid li'llāh, as their next imām. He, like other members of the Fāṭimid family, was detained as a prisoner by the Ayyūbids. In 569/1174, a major conspiracy for overthrowing Saladin and restoring Fāṭimid rule was discovered in Cairo.[45] The chief conspirators, who had also sought the help of Amalric I and the Franks, included the famous Yamanī poet-historian ʿUmāra, a former chief *dāʿī*, several Ismāʿīlī jurists and Fāṭimid commanders, some descendants of the viziers Ibn Ruzzīk and Shāwar, and even some of Saladin's own officers. ʿUmāra and certain of his collaborators were executed on Saladin's orders, while many of the supporters of the fallen dynasty were killed or exiled to upper Egypt, henceforth the main area of pro-Fāṭimid activity. During 569–570/1173–1175, a pro-Fāṭimid revolt led by the general Kanz al-Dawla, and with the participation of the Egyptian Ismāʿīlīs, was suppressed in upper Egypt by al-Malik al-ʿĀdil, Saladin's brother and future successor.[46] In 572/1176–1177, a pretender, falsely claiming to be Dā'ūd b. al-ʿĀḍid, led another pro-Fāṭimid revolt in the town of Qifṭ.[47] Saladin had to send an army, commanded by al-Malik al- ʿĀdil, to deal with the revolt, in which many participated. Some three thousand inhabitants of Qifṭ were killed before the revolt was ended. It may be noted at this juncture that while the Ḥāfiẓiyya and the pro-Fāṭimid elements were thus being annihilated in Egypt, the Nizāriyya had developed into a significant political force in Syria, where, under the leadership of the celebrated Rāshid al-Dīn Sinān, they had to be reckoned with in various local alliances and rivalries, as we shall see later. It was also at this time that the Syrian Nizārīs struggled against Nūr al-Dīn and the Ayyūbids, making two unsuccessful attempts on Saladin's life during 570–571/1175–1176, when he was conducting military campaigns in Syria.

A few more revolts of little significance, led by Fāṭimid pretenders or Ismāʿīlīs, occurred during the final decades of the 6th/12th century,[48] during which time the Ayyūbid regime had become well entrenched in Egypt under Saladin, who left various parts of his empire to different members of his family. The real Dā'ūd b. al-ʿĀḍid died as a prisoner in Cairo in 604/1207–1208, during the reign of the fourth Ayyūbid sultan al-Malik al-ʿĀdil I (596–615/1200–1218). In this same year Dā'ūd and other surviving Fāṭimid prisoners were collectively transferred to a new location in the citadel of Cairo.[49] The Ḥāfiẓīs of Egypt asked and received permission from the Ayyūbids to mourn Dā'ūd publicly in Cairo. The Ayyūbids used the occasion to arrest the Ḥāfiẓī leaders and confiscate their properties. After Dā'ūd, his son Sulaymān, surnamed Badr al-Dīn and conceived secretly in prison, seems to have been generally acknowledged as the imām of the Ḥāfiẓiyya. Sulaymān too, died in his Cairo prison in 645/1248.[50] Evidently, Sulaymān left no progeny, although some of his partisans held that he had a son who was kept in hiding. A number of Fāṭimids from amongst the descendants of al-ʿĀḍid, including two of his grandsons, Abu'l-Qāsim ʿImād al-Dīn and ʿAbd al-Wahhāb Badr al-Dīn, were still alive in 660/1262, during the early decades of the Mamlūk dynasty established in 648/1250 by the Turkish slave troops in Egypt. According to al-Maqrīzī, the Fāṭimid prisoners were finally released in 671/1272–1273.[51] Still later, in 697/1298, a Fāṭimid pretender, claiming to be Dā'ūd b. Sulaymān b. Dā'ūd b. al-ʿĀḍid, appeared in upper Egypt where the remnants of the Ḥāfiẓiyya had clandestinely survived. The Ḥāfiẓiyya had disintegrated almost completely in Egypt by the end of the 7th/13th century. Indeed, by about a century after the fall of the Fāṭimid dynasty, Ismāʿīlism too had disappeared from the land of Egypt. Henceforth, only a few isolated Ismāʿīlī communities, probably Ḥāfiẓī, continued to exist for a while longer in some villages in upper Egypt, such as the one reported to have existed around 727/1327 in the village of ʿUṣfūn.[52] By the end of the 6th/12th century, Ḥāfiẓī Ismāʿīlism had disappeared also in Syria, although an isolated Ḥāfiẓī community is mentioned there in the Baqīʿa mountains near Ṣafad during the early decades of the 8th/14th century.

The Ḥāfiẓī *daʿwa*, as noted, had found support also in Yaman. In fact, the

Zurayʿids of ʿAdan and some of the Hamdānids of Ṣanʿāʾ adhered to Ḥāfiẓī Ismāʿīlism until the Ayyūbid conquest of Yaman. And significant numbers in the territories of these local Yamanī dynasties, as well as in the region of Ḥarāz, later the stronghold of Ṭayyibī Ismāʿīlism, had rallied to the side of the Ḥāfiẓī *daʿwa*, in preference to the Ṭayyibī *daʿwa* which after the collapse of the Ṣulayḥid dynasty in 532/1138 did not have the support of any of the ruling dynasties of Yaman.

The main source for the history of the Zurayʿids is ʿUmāra, who had close relations with several members of the dynasty.[53] ʿUmāra, a zealous partisan of the Fāṭimids, wrote his history of Yaman in the year 563/1167–1168, at the request of al-Qāḍī al-Fāḍil, at the time chief secretary to the caliph al-ʿĀḍid and subsequently a close companion of Saladin. Later south Arabian historians, like al-Khazrajī (d. 812/1410),[54] add very little to ʿUmāra's account of the Zurayʿid dynasty. The Zurayʿids, who belonged to the Yām branch of the Banū Hamdān, had come to prominence during the reigns of the early Ṣulayḥids. In recognition of their services to the Ṣulayḥids and to the cause of the Fāṭimid *daʿwa* in Yaman, the second Ṣulayḥid ruler al-Mukarram Aḥmad (459–477/1067–1084) conferred in 476/1083 the governorship of ʿAdan and its surrounding regions on the brothers al-ʿAbbās and al-Masʿūd b. al-Karam (al-Mukarram). They ruled jointly and founded the Ismāʿīlī dynasty of the Zurayʿids of ʿAdan. The generally accepted name of the house, the Banū Zurayʿ or Zurayʿiyya, was derived from the name of a subsequent ruler, Zurayʿ b. al-ʿAbbās. Al-ʿAbbās was given the hinterland of ʿAdan, ruling from the Ḥiṣn al-Taʿkar, while al-Masʿūd received the port and the coastline of ʿAdan, establishing his residence at the fortress of al-Khaḍrāʾ. The joint system of government, with constant rivalry between the two branches of the Zurayʿid family, continued for some time. Since ʿAdan formed part of the dowry of the queen al-Sayyida, who soon became the real authority in the Ṣulayḥid state, the Zurayʿids were to pay her direct allegiance and a portion of their revenues. Disagreements and conflicts over the actual size of the annual tribute payable to al-Malika al-Sayyida proved to be a constant theme in Ṣulayḥid-Zurayʿid relations, contributing to the eventual estrangement of the Zurayʿids from their Ṣulayḥid overlords.

In 480/1087, when al-Sayyida sent her general and chief advisor al-Mufaḍḍal b. Abiʾl-Barakāt to Zabīd to fight the Najāḥids, the Zurayʿid rulers al-Masʿūd and Zurayʿ, who had succeeded his father al-ʿAbbās in 477/1084, fought on the side of the Ṣulayḥids and lost their lives in that campaign. However, the Zurayʿids themselves periodically attempted in vain to win their independence from the Ṣulayḥids, although they did succeed in gradually reducing the tribute they paid to them. On one occasion, after 484/1091, al-Mufaḍḍal had to be despatched with a large army to ʿAdan so as to force the renewed submission of the Zurayʿid rulers, Abu'l-Suʿūd b. Zurayʿ and Abu'l-Ghārāt b. al-Masʿūd. After the death of al-Mufaḍḍal in 504/1110, al-Sayyida sent a cousin of al-Mufaḍḍal, Asʿad, against the Zurayʿids who had rebelled anew, refusing to pay the customary tribute. It was Saba' b. Abu'l-Suʿūd, the grandson of Zurayʿ, who united the port and the interior of ʿAdan under his own rule. With sufficient tribal support and after prolonged warfare during 531–532/1136–1138, he finally defeated ʿAlī b. Abu'l-Ghārāt, thus permanently ending the rule of the Masʿūdid branch of the family. Saba' died in 533/1138–1139, a few months after he had become the sole Zurayʿid ruler.

Towards the end of his life, Saba' had started to exert his independence from al-Malika al-Sayyida, taking over various fortresses in the southern highlands of Yaman which belonged to the Ṣulayḥids. Saba' also enriched the Zurayʿid treasury by prospering from the flourishing trade between Fāṭimid Egypt and India, which passed through the Red Sea and the port of ʿAdan. When al-Ḥāfiẓ claimed the imāmate in 526/1132, a bitter fight undoubtedly ensued at the court of the Ṣulayḥids and throughout the Mustaʿlian Ismāʿīlī community in Yaman. As a result, the Yamanī Ismāʿīlīs, always closely connected with the headquarters of the Fāṭimid *daʿwa* in Egypt, became split into two factions. The Ṣulayḥid queen championed the cause of al-Ṭayyib and became the official leader of the Ṭayyibī faction in Yaman. On the other hand, the Zurayʿids became the leaders of the Ḥāfiẓī (Majīdī) party, recognizing ʿAbd al-Majīd al-Ḥāfiẓ as their new imām after al-Āmir. It was probably immediately after the Ḥāfiẓī–Ṭayyibī schism that the Zurayʿid Saba', under obscure circumstances, allied himself to al-Ḥāfiẓ and assumed the title of *dāʿī* on behalf of the Ḥāfiẓī *daʿwa* in Yaman.

It seems that the successors of Saba' became officially designated as *dāʿīs* by the headquarters of the Ḥāfiẓī *daʿwa* at Cairo. Muḥammad b. Saba' was the first Zurayʿid to have become so designated as a *dāʿī* in Yaman. Saba' had been initially succeeded by his son ʿAlī al-Aʿazz, who died a year later in 534/1139. Subsequently, Muḥammad b. Saba', a younger brother of ʿAlī, was placed on the throne by the powerful Bilāl b. Jarīr, who retained the Zurayʿid vizierate from that time until his death around 546/1151.[55] Meanwhile, al-Qāḍī al-Rashīd Aḥmad b. ʿAlī b. al-Zubayr had set off from Cairo in 534/1139–1140 with a charter of investiture issued by al-

Ḥāfiẓ, appointing ʿAlī b. Saba' to the office of the *dāʿī* of the Majīdī *daʿwa* in Yaman. By the time of the Qāḍī al-Rashīd's arrival in Yaman, ʿAlī had died, and, consequently, the dāʿīship was transferred to the next Zurayʿid ruler Muḥammad b. Saba'.[56] Al-Ḥāfiẓ also bestowed several honorific titles on the Zurayʿid vizier Bilāl for his loyalty to the Fāṭimids and the Ḥāfiẓī *daʿwa*. Bilāl, who had married his daughter to Muḥammad b. Saba', was followed in the vizierate by two of his sons. In 547/1152–1153, Muḥammad b. Saba' purchased a number of fortresses and towns from the Ṣulayḥids, whose dynasty had effectively ended with the death of al-Malika al-Sayyida in 532 A.H. These acquisitions included the former Ṣulayḥid capital Dhū Jibla which was chosen by Muḥammad as his own place of residence.

Muḥammad b. Saba' died around 550/1155 and was succeeded by his son ʿImrān, who, like his father, carried the title of *dāʿī*. During ʿImrān's rule, close relations continued to be maintained between the later Fāṭimids and the Zurayʿid state. There are extant coins of this Zurayʿid ruler, minted in ʿAdan in the year 556 A.H., and bearing the name of the Imām al-ʿĀḍid, on one side, and ʿImrān's name on the other.[57] With the death of ʿImrān in 561/1166, the affairs of the Zurayʿid state fell into the hands of the vizier Yāsir b. Bilāl, who ruled on behalf of ʿImrān's three minor sons. By then, the Ḥāfiẓī Ismāʿīlī kingdom of the Zurayʿids included ʿAdan, Abyan, Dumluwa, Taʿizz, and other localities as far north as Naqīl Ṣayd. Zurayʿid rule was brought to an end with the Ayyūbid conquest of south Arabia in 569/1173. Tūrānshāh, Saladin's brother, who led the Ayyūbid armies into Yaman, also conquered ʿAdan and killed Yāsir b. Bilāl. The Ayyūbids re-established Sunnism throughout the former Zurayʿid territories. ʿImrān's sons, Muḥammad, Manṣūr and Abu'l-Suʿūd, continued to stay for a while longer, under the guardianship of Jawhar b. ʿAbd Allāh, at the fortress of Dumluwa, the last Zurayʿid outpost. Eventually in 584/1188, Jawhar sold Dumluwa to the Ayyūbids and left south Arabia for Abyssinia in the company of ʿImrān's sons, the last nominal rulers of the Zurayʿid state.[58]

The Ḥāfiẓī *daʿwa* in Yaman was also supported by at least some of the Hamdānid rulers of Ṣanʿā', who like the Zurayʿids had been Ismāʿīlīs and belonged to the tribal confederation of Hamdān.[59] Ṣanʿā' and its environs were often ruled by the large and influential Banū Hamdān, many of whose clans adhered to Zaydī or Ismāʿīlī Shīʿism. Around 467/1074, when the second Ṣulayḥid al-Mukarram retired to Dhū Jibla and left the affairs of the state to his consort al-Malika al-Sayyida, Ṣanʿā' was placed under the joint governorship of al-Qāḍī 'Imrān b. al-Faḍl and As'ad b. Shihāb, al-Mukarram's uncle. 'Imrān, one of the leaders of the Banū Hamdān from the sub-tribe of Yām, had supported the founder of the Ṣulayḥid dynasty in most of his wars and had also undertaken a mission on his behalf to Cairo in 459/1067, urging al-Mustanṣir to permit the visit of 'Alī b. Muḥammad al-Ṣulayḥī to the Fāṭimid court. Later, 'Imrān, who like the Ṣulayḥids adhered to Fāṭimid Ismā'īlism, became the commander of the Ṣulayḥid army. 'Imrān's governorship of Ṣan'ā', however, did not last very long. For some unknown reason, there soon occurred an estrangement between al-Mukarram and 'Imrān, who was removed from his post. It seems that 'Imrān had been intriguing against the Ṣulayḥids, probably out of his resentment for the authority exercised by al-Sayyida. He had also become envious of the power and position of Lamak b. Mālik al-Ḥammādī in the Ṣulayḥid state. As it turned out, the successors of these two rival *qāḍīs* became leaders of opposing Ismā'īlī factions in Yaman. While Lamak's successors held the dā'īship of the Ṭayyibīs, the descendants of 'Imrān were amongst those Hamdānid rulers supporting the Ḥāfiẓī *da'wa*. The rising fortunes of al-Mufaḍḍal b. Abi'l-Barakāt (d. 504/1110), al-Sayyida's confidant who fought against the Najāḥids and the Zuray'ids, was another factor undermining the loyalty of the Zuray'ids and the Hamdānids towards the Ṣulayḥids. In any case, due to the Ṣulayḥid queen's popularity throughout Yaman, 'Imrān could not oppose her openly. In fact, 'Imrān fought for her in the Ṣulayḥid war against the Najāḥids in 479/1086, and was killed in battle.

In the meantime, different Hamdānī clans had been attempting to acquire their independence from the central authority of the Ṣulayḥids. By 492/1098–1099, they had severed Ṣan'ā' from the Ṣulayḥid state. The city and its surrounding districts now came under the rule of Ḥātim b. al-Ghashīm al-Mughallasī, another Hamdānī leader who founded the first of the three Hamdānid dynasties of Ṣan'ā'. Ḥātim died in 502/1108 and was succeeded by his sons 'Abd Allāh (502–504/1108–1110) and then Ma'n, who came to face serious opposition from within the Banū Hamdān. In 510/1116, Ma'n was formally deposed by the Qāḍī Aḥmad b. 'Imrān b. al-Faḍl, the son of the former Ṣulayḥid governor of Ṣan'ā', who had assumed the leadership of the Hamdānī clans. Hishām b. al-Qubayb, from another Hamdānī family and a Musta'lian Ismā'īlī, was now set up as the new ruler of Ṣan'ā'.[60] Hishām, the founder of the second Hamdānid dynasty, died around 518/1124 and was succeeded by his brother Ḥimās b. al-Qubayb. It was during the reign of Ḥimās that al-Āmir died and al-Ḥāfiẓ claimed the imāmate. Ḥimās became the first Hamdānid ruler to support the cause of al-Ḥāfiẓ in Yaman. He died in 527/1132–1133, shortly after the Ḥāfiẓī–Ṭayyibī schism, and his son Ḥātim took over the Hamdānid state. He, too, adhered to Ḥāfiẓī Ismāʿīlism.

When Ḥātim b. Ḥimās died in 533/1138–1139, soon after al-Sayyida, his sons quarrelled over his succession and tribal dissension arose once again within the Banū Hamdān. It was under these circumstances that the Hamdānī house of ʿImrān, with the approval of the tribal leaders, assumed responsibility for ruling over Ṣanʿāʾ. The control of the Ṣanʿāʾ area thus passed in 533 A.H. into the hands of Ḥamīd al-Dawla Ḥātim b. Aḥmad b. ʿImrān, who founded the third Hamdānid dynasty of Ṣanʿāʾ, the Banū Ḥātim. The heritage lost by ʿImrān was regained by his grandson, who, by 545/1150, held the whole country north of Ṣanʿāʾ with the main exception of Ṣaʿda, the chief Zaydī centre in Yaman. Ḥātim, like the Banu'l-Qubayb, supported the Ḥāfiẓī *daʿwa* in the districts under his rule. Religious differences played their part in continuous entanglements between the Ḥāfiẓī Ḥātim and the Rassid Zaydī Imām al-Mutawakkil Aḥmad b. Sulaymān, who in 532/1137–1138 had proclaimed his leadership of the Yamanī Zaydīs in Ṣaʿda. These conflicts began in 545/1150, when the Zaydīs attacked Ḥātim and temporarily wrested the control of Ṣanʿāʾ from the Hamdānids, and continued until Ḥātim's death in 556/1161.[61] When Ḥātim regained control of Ṣanʿāʾ, he restored the inscription at a mosque in Ṣanʿāʾ containing the names of the Fāṭimid Ismāʿīlī Imāms and which had been erased by the Zaydī Imām al-Mutawakkil Aḥmad (d. 566/1170).[62]

Ḥātim was succeeded by his son ʿAlī, the last ruling member of his dynasty. Sultan ʿAlī b. Ḥātim consolidated his position and expanded his territories northward, gaining temporary control of even Ṣaʿda, and westward as far as Ḥarāz, where significant numbers of Ḥāfiẓī Ismāʿīlīs were then to be found. The Hamdānid ʿAlī b. Ḥātim who led the cause of the Ḥāfiẓī *daʿwa* in the Ṣanʿāʾ region, waged a prolonged war against Ḥātim b. Ibrāhīm al-Ḥāmidī, who in 557/1162 had succeeded as the third *dāʿī muṭlaq* to the headship of the Ṭayyibīs. This also represented the most serious military contest between the Ḥāfiẓī and the Ṭayyibī parties in Yaman. The hostilities lasted for three years, starting in 561 A.H. when the *dāʿī* Ḥātim, with the growing support of a large number of Hamdānī tribesmen, rose against ʿAlī b. Ḥātim and then seized the fortress of Kawkabān near Ṣanʿāʾ.[63] ʿAlī b. Ḥātim retaliated and fought the *dāʿī* Ḥātim, eventually defeating him. Kawkabān was surrendered in 564/1168–1169, and the *dāʿī* retreated to Rayʿān and Luʾluʾa before establishing himself in Ḥarāz. The Hamdānids destroyed much of the territory around Kawkabān and Shibām. Sultan ʿAlī also played a leading role in forming an alliance with his Zurayʿid co-religionists and some Hamdānī tribes against the Khārijī ruler of Zabīd, ʿAbd al-Nabī, son of ʿAlī b. al-Mahdī (d. 554/1159) who had seized Zabīd from the Najāḥids and founded a new dynasty there.[64] ʿAbd al-Nabī, in his own campaign of territorial expansion, had laid siege to ʿAdan, obliging the Zurayʿids to seek military assistance from the Hamdānids, both dynasties being Yāmīs and Ḥāfiẓī Ismāʿīlīs. The Mahdid was defeated in 569/1173, and driven back to Zabīd by the combined forces of the Ismāʿīlī dynasties and their tribal warriors.[65] By that time, the Ayyūbids had already started their penetration of Yaman, which was to result in the collapse of the Zurayʿid, Hamdānid and Mahdid dynasties. Only the Zaydī Imāms ruling from Ṣaʿda escaped the Ayyūbid reduction of south Arabia.

Shortly after ʿAlī b. Ḥātim returned to Ṣanʿāʾ from his campaign against the Mahdids, the Ayyūbids under Tūrānshāh managed to reach the outskirts of the city in 570/1174. ʿAlī fled to the safety of his fortress of Birāsh, while Tūrānshāh temporarily secured Ṣanʿāʾ, abandoned by the Hamdānids. This marked the end of Hamdānid rule, although a number of Hamdānids continued to control various localities around Ṣanʿāʾ for some time longer. ʿAlī b. Ḥātim returned to Ṣanʿāʾ after Tūrānshāh left Yaman for Egypt in 571/1175–1176, and put up a vigorous resistance against the Ayyūbids with the help of his brother Bishr b. Ḥātim and other relatives. It was not until 585/1189 that the second Ayyūbid ruler of Yaman, al-Malik al-ʿAzīz Ṭughtakīn b. Ayyūb (577–593/1181–1197), having settled the affairs in the south, entered Ṣanʿāʾ, then still in the hands of the Ḥāfiẓī Hamdānids. Nonetheless, ʿAlī b. Ḥātim's brothers and other Hamdānids, scattered over a wide area around Ṣanʿāʾ, continued to hold on to a number of fortresses during the Ayyūbid period in Yaman (569–626/1173–1229). ʿAlī b. Ḥātim himself remained in possession of different fortresses until his death in 599/1202–1203. The slow progress made by the Ayyūbids in conquering Ṣanʿāʾ and its environs and in uprooting the Hamdānids is related by Badr al-Dīn Muḥammad b. Ḥātim (d. ca. 700/1300), a Yamanī historian and great-grandson of ʿAlī b. Ḥātim.[66] This also explains why Ḥāfiẓī Ismāʿīlism lingered on for quite some time in Yaman after the Ayyūbid conquest of the country, although with the fall of the Zurayʿid and Hamdānid dynasties, Ḥāfiẓī Ismāʿīlism lost its prominence in Yaman, surviving only in isolated communities and amongst some of the descendants of the Hamdānid rulers of Ṣanʿāʾ. It is interesting to note that by the beginning of the 7th/13th century, the Ḥāfiẓiyya were still important enough in Yaman to warrant the writing of polemical treatises by Ṭayyibīs, refuting the claims of al-Ḥāfiẓ and his successors to the imāmate and defending the legitimacy of the Ṭayyibī *daʿwa*. One of these polemical works against the Majīdī (Ḥāfiẓī) *daʿwa*, and written by the fifth *dāʿī muṭlaq* of the Ṭayyibīs, ʿAlī b. Muḥammad b. al-Walīd (d. 612/1215), is extant and has been published.[67] There is no evidence showing that the Ḥāfiẓī *daʿwa* ever gained a foothold in India. The Indian Mustaʿlian Ismāʿīlīs, who had close ties with the Ṣulayḥid state, seem to have rallied completely to the side of the Ṭayyibī *daʿwa*, upheld by the Ṣulayḥids.

Before starting our discussion of Ṭayyibī Ismāʿīlism in Yaman, it may be noted in passing that the few Ṭayyibī communities of Egypt and Syria, known as the Āmiriyya, which had come into existence following the Ḥāfiẓī–Ṭayyibī schism, remained insignificant and short-lived. By the time Ayyūbid rule was firmly established in Egypt and Ismāʿīlism was replaced there by Sunnism as the state religion, the clandestine Egyptian Ṭayyibīs, who had been subjected to severe persecutions, had disintegrated almost completely.[68] In Syria, too, the history of the Ṭayyibīs was of rather short duration. Ibn Abī Ṭayyi', the Shīʿī chronicler of Aleppo who died around 630 A.H., attests to the presence of some Syrian Ismāʿīlīs belonging to the Āmiriyya party at the end of the 6th/12th century.[69] By the early decades of the 8th/14th century, only an isolated community of the Āmiriyya still evidently existed in Syria, in the Baqīʿa and Zābūd mountains near Ṣafad. It was in Yaman, and then in India, that the Ṭayyibī *daʿwa* was successfully propagated and became permanently established in due time.[70]

As noted, a son named al-Ṭayyib was born a few months before his father al-Āmir, the twentieth imām of the Mustaʿlian Ismāʿīlīs, was murdered in 524/1130. We have already referred to Ibn Muyassar's account and to the epistle, preserved by ʿUmāra and the Ṭayyibīs, in which al-Āmir announces the birth of al-Ṭayyib to al-Malika al-Sayyida. At the time, the aged Ṣulayḥid queen had been supporting for some thirty-six years the rights of al-Mustaʿlī and al-Āmir to the imāmate of the Mustaʿlians. It is not clear what happened to al-Ṭayyib, designated heir apparent on his birth, during the critical weeks following al-Āmir's assassination. For instance, it is not known whether he died in infancy or was disposed of in some manner at the instigation of ʿAbd al-Majīd al-Ḥāfiẓ who had then assumed the regency. A near contemporary Syrian chronicler, who has remained anonymous, insinuates that he was secretly killed on the orders of al-Ḥāfiẓ.[71] Ibn Muyassar merely relates that al-Ḥāfiẓ somehow managed to conceal the existence of al-Ṭayyib. Other non-Ismāʿīlī historians of the period maintain silence on the subject. However, there is a Yamanī Ṭayyibī tradition concerning the fate of al-Ṭayyib, who is counted as the twenty-first imām of the Ṭayyibiyya, and the last one whose name is known to his followers. This tradition, preserved in the seventh volume of the *ʿUyūn al-akhbār* of Idrīs, dates back to Ibrāhīm b. al-Ḥusayn al-Ḥāmidī, the second chief *dāʿī* of the Yamanī Ṭayyibīs, a mature man at the time of the Ḥāfiẓī–Ṭayyibī schism.[72]

According to this tradition, a certain Ibn Madyan was the leader of a small group of *dāʿīs* in the entourage of al-Āmir. The other members of this group, selected from amongst the most eminent and trusted *dāʿīs*, were Ibn Raslān, al-ʿAzīzī, Qawnaṣ (Qūniṣ), and Naslān. Just before his death, al-Āmir placed al-Ṭayyib in the custody of Ibn Madyan, who had been appointed to the position of *bāb* by the caliph-imām. On al-Āmir's death, these *dāʿīs* swore allegiance to al-Ṭayyib; and Ibn Madyan, assisted by his brother-in-law Abū ʿAlī, assumed the headship of the *daʿwa* on behalf of al-Ṭayyib. When Abū ʿAlī Kutayfāt seized power and showed his hostility towards the Fāṭimids, Ibn Madyan and his circle of *dāʿīs*, realizing the impending dangers, decided to conceal the infant imām who had received al-Āmir's *naṣṣ*. However, Ibn Madyan and the other four *dāʿīs* who had been highly devoted to al-Āmir were arrested on Kutayfāt's orders. They were subsequently executed due to their refusal to abjure al-Āmir and al-Ṭayyib. In the meantime, Ibn Madyan's brother-in-law Abū ʿAlī, had managed to go into hiding with al-Ṭayyib. Nothing more was heard of al-Ṭayyib. It is the belief of the Ṭayyibīs that al-Ṭayyib survived[73] and that the imāmate continued in his progeny, being handed down from father to son, generation after generation, during the current period of *satr* initiated by al-Ṭayyib's concealment. It is interesting to note that according to this tradition, the blame for usurpation of al-Ṭayyib's rights is put on Kutayfāt, during whose brief rule, many of the supporters of the Ṭayyibī cause were persecuted in Egypt and Twelver Shīʿism was adopted as the state religion. This tradition thus ignores the fact that the mentioning of al-Ṭayyib's name was suppressed from the very beginning of the regency of ʿAbd al-Majīd al-Ḥāfiẓ.

Meanwhile, the news of al-Ṭayyib's birth had been rejoiced at the Ṣulayḥid court. We learn from the *ʿUyūn al-akhbār* that a certain Sharīf Muḥammad b. Ḥaydara was the Fāṭimid envoy, who, in 524 A.H., carried al-Āmir's epistle regarding the birth of the heir apparent to Yaman.

There also exists the eyewitness report of al-Khaṭṭāb, assistant to the first chief *dāʿī* of the Ṭayyibīs, concerning the circumstances under which this epistle was received by the Ṣulayḥid queen.[74] Soon afterwards, the Yamanī Mustaʿlians were thrown into confusion by the news of the events taking place in rapid succession, in Cairo, viz., al-Āmir's murder, ʿAbd al-Majīd's regency and Kutayfāt's vizierate. Muḥammad b. Ḥaydara, still in Yaman at that time, delivered public sermons deploring the murder of al-Āmir and exalting al-Ṭayyib. These sermons must have taken place soon after al-Āmir's death, since in one of them the Fāṭimid envoy names al-Ṭayyib, ʿAbd al-Majīd and Abū ʿAlī Kutayfāt, as, respectively, imām, regent and vizier.[75] It may be assumed that the crisis faced by the Yamanī Ismāʿīlīs reached its peak in 526 A.H., when ʿAbd al-Majīd claimed the imāmate. Idrīs relates how al-Malika al-Sayyida was astonished when al-Ḥāfiẓ adopted the new title of *Amīr al-Muʾminīn*, instead of the previously used one of *Walī ʿahd al-Muslimīn*, in his official correspondence with the queen.[76] It was probably at that time that the Mustaʿlians of Yaman became split into the Ḥāfiẓī and Ṭayyibī parties. The Zurayʿids of ʿAdan and the Hamdānids of Ṣanʿāʾ led the Ḥāfiẓī *daʿwa*, while the Ṣulayḥid queen championed the cause of the Ṭayyibī *daʿwa*.

It is useful at this juncture to recapitulate the succession of the *dāʿī*s in Ṣulayḥid Yaman. The first Ṣulayḥid ruler, ʿAlī b. Muḥammad al-Ṣulayḥī, was also the head of the Fāṭimid Ismāʿīlī *daʿwa* in Yaman; he combined, in his person, the offices of sultan and chief *dāʿī*.[77] However, when Lamak b. Mālik al-Ḥammādī returned to Yaman from his Egyptian mission in 459/1066–1067, the same year in which ʿAlī b. Muḥammad died, the headships of the *daʿwa* and the state became separated. Lamak was now appointed chief *dāʿī* of Yaman by al-Mustanṣir and became the executive head of the *daʿwa*, while the new Ṣulayḥid ruler al-Mukarram remained only nominally in charge of the *daʿwa*.[78] This arrangement was essentially maintained when al-Mukarram retired to Dhū Jibla in 467/1074–1075, leaving the affairs of the state to his consort al-Malika al-Sayyida. When al-Mukarram died in 477/1084 and was nominally succeeded by his minor son ʿAlī b. Aḥmad and then by others, al-Sayyida continued to hold the real authority in Ṣulayḥid Yaman. Henceforth, she also exercised more control over the affairs of the *daʿwa*, especially since she was officially designated by al-Mustanṣir as the *ḥujja* of Yaman, a higher rank than *dāʿī*, shortly after al-Mukarram's death.[79] The highly respected al-Sayyida lent her support to the Yamanī *daʿwa* organization headed by the *dāʿī* Lamak, who in turn solidly backed the queen. Both upheld the rights of al-Mustaʿlī against those of Nizār, thus permanently separating the destiny of the Yamanī Ismā'īlīs from that of the eastern Nizārī communities.

Lamak b. Mālik, who belonged to the Banū Ḥammād branch of the Hamdān and resided at Dhū Jibla, died shortly before 491/1097–1098 and was succeeded by his son Yaḥyā. Yaḥyā's dā'īship coincided with the reigns of al-Musta'lī and al-Āmir, and it seems that during this period relations deteriorated between the Ṣulayḥid queen and the Fāṭimid state. It was perhaps due to this fact that in 513/1119 Ibn Najīb al-Dawla was despatched by al-Āmir to assist the queen and bring the Ṣulayḥid state under greater administrative control of the Fāṭimids. However, there arose strong differences between al-Sayyida and Ibn Najīb al-Dawla, who as commander of the Ṣulayḥid forces had participated in several battles against the enemies of the Ṣulayḥids. In 519/1125, Ibn Najīb al-Dawla was recalled to Cairo, but on his way was thrown overboard and drowned. Rumours were spread to the effect that he had been conducting propaganda in favour of the Nizārīs. The queen then replaced Ibn Najīb al-Dawla by a member of the Ṣulayḥid family, 'Alī ('Abd Allāh) b. 'Abd Allāh, who became the Ṣulayḥid administrator at Dhū Jibla. It is interesting to note that to 'Umāra, and other non-Ismā'īlī Yamanī historians after him, Ibn Najīb al-Dawla and his successor Ibn 'Abd Allāh wrongly appeared as *dā'īs*.[80] According to the Ṭayyibī tradition and literature on the succession of the early Yamanī *dā'īs*,[81] however, Ibn Najīb al-Dawla and Ibn 'Abd Allāh did not hold any positions in the *da'wa* organization.

At any event, before his death in 520/1126, Yaḥyā b. Lamak, in consultation with al-Malika al-Sayyida, appointed his assistant al-Dhu'ayb b. Mūsā al-Wādi'ī al-Hamdānī as his successor. It was during the earlier years of the latter's dā'īship that the Musta'lian Ismā'īlīs became confronted with the Ḥāfiẓī–Ṭayyibī schism. Al-Dhu'ayb, in line with the position of the Ṣulayḥid queen, recognized the rights of al-Ṭayyib and thus became the first Yamanī chief *dā'ī* to propagate the Ṭayyibī *da'wa*. From 524/1130 until her death in 532/1138, the Ṣulayḥid al-Malika al-Sayyida Ḥurra bint Aḥmad made every effort to consolidate the Ṭayyibī *da'wa*. In her will, she bequeathed her renowned collection of jewellery to al-Imām al-Ṭayyib.[82] Al-Dhu'ayb and other leaders of the established *da'wa* in Yaman collaborated closely with al-Sayyida, who, during her final years, evidently broke relations with the Fāṭimid regime. It was after 526 A.H. that al-Dhu'ayb was declared *al-dā'ī al-muṭlaq*, with full authority to conduct and supervise the *da'wa* activities on behalf of the hidden Imām al-Ṭayyib.[83] This marked the foundation of the independent Ṭayyibī *da'wa* in Yaman under the headship of an absolute *dāʿī*. Al-Dhu'ayb thus became the first in the line of *al-duʿāt al-muṭlaqīn* who have followed one another during the current period of *satr* in the history of the Ṭayyibī Ismāʿīlīs.

Al-Dhu'ayb was at first assisted in the affairs of the *daʿwa* by al-Khaṭṭāb b. al-Ḥasan b. Abi'l-Ḥifāẓ, who belonged to a family of chiefs of al-Ḥajūr, a clan of the Hamdān. Al-Khaṭṭāb himself was the Ḥajūrī chief or sultan and had been converted to Ismāʿīlism by his teacher al-Dhu'ayb. An important Ismāʿīlī author and Yamanī poet, al-Khaṭṭāb was also a brave warrior and fought against the Najāḥids and the Zaydīs on behalf of the Ṣulayḥids.[84] His loyalty to al-Malika al-Sayyida and his military services to the Ismāʿīlī cause were crucial to the success of the Ṭayyibī *daʿwa* in Yaman during its formative years. In his *Ghāyat al-mawālīd*, he uses various arguments in support of al-Sayyida's rank as the *ḥujja* of Yaman, insisting that even a woman can hold the rank, and defends al-Ṭayyib's imāmate.[85] Al-Khaṭṭāb was also involved in a prolonged family feud resulting from the murder of his sister and a bitter rivalry with his elder brother Sulaymān, a non-Ismāʿīlī, over the control of al-Ḥajūr. Al-Khaṭṭāb, who had succeeded in driving away and eventually murdering Sulaymān, was killed in revenge by Sulaymān's sons in 533/1138, shortly after al-Sayyida had died. On al-Khaṭṭāb's death, al-Dhu'ayb appointed Ibrāhīm b. al-Ḥusayn al-Ḥāmidī, belonging to the Ḥāmidī branch of the Banū Hamdān, as his new chief assistant or *ma'dhūn*, the second highest rank in the Ṭayyibī *daʿwa* hierarchy. On al-Dhu'ayb's death in 546/1151, Ibrāhīm succeeded him as the second *dāʿī muṭlaq*.[86] Al-Dhu'ayb, al-Khaṭṭāb and Ibrāhīm al-Ḥāmidī were in effect the earliest Yamanī Ṭayyibī leaders who, under the patronage of al-Malika al-Sayyida, founded and consolidated the Ṭayyibī *daʿwa* in southern Arabia. Al-Sayyida's death also marked the effective end of the Ṣulayḥid dynasty. The last Ṣulayḥid rulers only held on to certain isolated fortresses for a while longer until the 560s/1170s, when the Ḥāfiẓī Zurayʿids came into the possession of the remaining Ṣulayḥid outposts. After al-Malika al-Sayyida, the Ṭayyibī *daʿwa*, unlike the Ḥāfiẓī *daʿwa*, did not receive the support of any Yamanī rulers. Nonetheless, Ṭayyibī Ismāʿīlism began to spread successfully in Yaman under the undisputed leadership of the chief *dāʿī*s al-Dhu'ayb and Ibrāhīm. The Ṭayyibī *daʿwa* had now become independent of both the Fāṭimid regime as well as the Ṣulayḥid state, and this explains why it survived the fall of both dynasties.

Ibrāhīm al-Ḥāmidī resided at Ṣanʿā', where he evidently enjoyed the hospitality of Ḥātim b. Aḥmad, the city's Hamdānid ruler who adhered to

Ḥāfiẓī Ismā'īlism. Ibrāhīm introduced the *Rasā'il Ikhwān al-Ṣafā'* into the literature of the Ṭayyibī community in Yaman, and in his own writings drew extensively on the works of Ḥamīd al-Dīn al-Kirmānī. He formulated a new synthesis in the doctrinal domain, combining al-Kirmānī's cosmological system with mythical elements. His major work, *Kitāb kanz al-walad* (*Book of the Child's Treasure*), provided the basis of the peculiar Ṭayyibī *ḥaqā'iq* system and was used as a model for later Ṭayyibī writings on the subject.[87] After the death of his original *ma'dhūn* 'Alī b. al-Ḥusayn b. al-Walīd in 554/1159, Ibrāhīm appointed his own son Ḥātim as his assistant. Subsequently, the position of *dā'ī muṭlaq* remained in the hands of Ibrāhīm's descendants until 605/1209. Ibrāhīm died in 557/1162, and was succeeded by his son Ḥātim. The third *dā'ī muṭlaq* of the Ṭayyibīs, Ḥātim b. Ibrāhīm al-Ḥāmidī, was a prolific author and poet in addition to being a warrior and a capable organizer.[88] He also achieved great success in spreading Ṭayyibī Ismā'īlism in Yaman during his thirty-seven years as a *dā'ī*. Early in his career, Ḥātim won the support of some of the tribes of Hamdān and Ḥimyar, with whose help he seized the fortress of Kawkabān. The *dā'ī*'s increasing influence, which came to be spread also in Dhimār and Naqīl Banī Sharḥa close to Ṣan'ā', soon aroused the jealousy and apprehension of the Hamdānid ruler of Ṣan'ā', 'Alī b. Ḥātim al-Yāmī. We have already referred to the prolonged hostilities between the *dā'ī* Ḥātim and the Hamdānid ruler, which lasted from 561 to 564 A.H. The *dā'ī* was finally defeated and had to surrender Kawkabān to 'Alī b. Ḥātim. Having realized the futility of large-scale warfare, Ḥātim eventually withdrew to a location called Shi'āf (or Sha'āf) in Ḥarāz, where he converted large numbers to Ṭayyibī Ismā'īlism. According to Idrīs, until the arrival of the *dā'ī* Ḥātim in Ḥarāz, the inhabitants of that mountainous region, with its several towns and fortresses, had adhered mainly to Ḥāfiẓī Ismā'īlism.[89] Subsequently, Ḥātim began to conquer various strongholds in Ḥarāz. In 569/1173, he seized the fortress of Ẓahra, and then reached the famous mountain of Shibām, taking the fortress of Ḥuṭayb on its lower peak which was situated in the country of his chief supporters, the Ya'burīs of the Banū Hamdān. He established his headquarters at Ḥuṭayb, which he fortified. Later, he conquered the higher peak of Shibām and repaired its fortress, which had been constructed by the founder of the Ṣulayḥid dynasty. In his conquests, Ḥātim b. Ibrāhīm was effectively helped by Saba' b. Yūsuf, the chief of the Ya'burīs and the commander of the *dā'ī*'s forces. With the murder of the *amīr* Saba' at the hands of the Banū Ḥakam and the extension of Ayyūbid rule over Yaman, Ḥātim could no longer rely on military power for expanding his influence. Nonetheless, he managed to maintain his control over Ḥarāz and the three main fortresses of the Shibām mountain, namely, Shibām, Jawḥab and Ḥuṭayb.

Ḥātim b. Ibrāhīm continued to use Ḥuṭayb as his headquarters, holding his assemblies and delivering his lectures (*majālis*) in a cave below the fortress. The *dāʿī muṭlaq* of the Ṭayyibīs had now assumed the teaching functions of the Fāṭimid *dāʿī al-duʿāt*. It was also at Ḥuṭayb that Ḥātim received the subordinate Ṭayyibī *dāʿī*s from all over Yaman, of whom there were many, as well as the *dāʿī*s he appointed for Sind and Hind. Ḥātim had, however, stationed his assistant, the learned Muḥammad b. Ṭāhir al-Ḥārithī, in Ṣanʿāʾ, where he aimed to undermine the Hamdānid dynasty and win influential converts. It was Muḥammad b. Ṭāhir, closely associated also with the *dāʿī* Ibrāhīm al-Ḥāmidī, who compiled a valuable chrestomathy of Ismāʿīlī works and composed some poems on the occasion of the fall of the Fāṭimid dynasty, an event greatly rejoiced by the Ṭayyibīs, who regarded al-Ḥāfiẓ and the later Fāṭimids as usurpers and deserving of divine punishment.[90] On Muḥammad b. Ṭāhir's death in 584/1188, Ḥātim chose ʿAlī b. Muḥammad b. al-Walīd as his new *maʾdhūn* at Ṣanʿāʾ. ʿAlī b. Muḥammad, who later became the fifth *dāʿī muṭlaq*, visited Ḥarāz frequently and was entrusted with the education of Ḥātim's son ʿAlī. It was on the recommendation of ʿAlī b. Muḥammad that Ḥātim nominated his own son ʿAlī as his successor. Ḥātim b. Ibrāhīm died in 596/1199 and was buried under the fortress of Ḥuṭayb; his grave is still piously visited by the Ṭayyibīs. ʿAlī b. Ḥātim al-Ḥāmidī succeeded his father as the fourth *dāʿī muṭlaq*, and ʿAlī b. Muḥammad continued as his *maʾdhūn*. As the Yaʿburīs of Ḥarāz now turned against ʿAlī b. Ḥātim and fought amongst themselves, killing their leader Ḥātim b. Sabaʾ b. al-Yaʿburī who supported the Ṭayyibī *daʿwa*, the *dāʿī* was obliged to transfer his headquarters from Ḥarāz to Ṣanʿāʾ. There, he was treated hospitably by the Hamdānids and with no opposition from the Ayyūbids. ʿAlī b. Ḥātim died in 605/1209, bringing to an end the dāʿīship of the Ḥāmidī family.

The aged ʿAlī b. Muḥammad b. Jaʿfar b. Ibrāhīm b. al-Walīd succeeded ʿAlī al-Ḥāmidī as the fifth *dāʿī muṭlaq* of the Ṭayyibīs.[91] He belonged to the prominent Banu'l-Walīd al-Anf family of Quraysh. His great-grandfather Ibrāhīm b. Abī Salama was a supporter of ʿAlī b. Muḥammad al-Ṣulayḥī and a descendant of the Umayyad al-Walīd b. ʿUtba b. Abī Sufyān. He had studied first under his uncle ʿAlī b. al-Ḥusayn, the *maʾdhūn* to the second *dāʿī muṭlaq*, and then under Muḥammad b. Ṭāhir al-Ḥārithī, whom he had succeeded as *maʾdhūn*. He resided at Ṣanʿāʾ and maintained friendly relations with the Hamdānids, also visiting as a guest their fortress of Dhū Marmar. ʿAlī b. Muḥammad, one of the most learned Ṭayyibī *dāʿīs*, produced numerous works which are important for understanding the Ṭayyibī esoteric doctrine.[92] He died at Ṣanʿāʾ in 612/1215, at the age of ninety.

Henceforth, the office of *dāʿī muṭlaq* remained amongst the descendants of ʿAlī b. Muḥammad b. al-Walīd al-Anf al-Qurashī, with only two interruptions in the 7th/13th century, until the death of the twenty-third *dāʿī* in 946/1539. During this period of more than three centuries, Ḥarāz remained the traditional stronghold of the Ṭayyibī *daʿwa*. The *dāʿīs* enjoyed the general protection and sometimes military support of the Hamdānids, who permitted them to reside in Ṣanʿāʾ, and later, during the 8th/14th century, in Dhū Marmar, before the *dāʿīs* transferred their residence to Ḥarāz in the 9th/15th century. In general, the Ṭayyibīs maintained peaceful, even friendly relations with Yaman's Ayyūbid (569–626/1173–1229), Rasūlid (626–858/1229–1454) and Ṭāhirid (858–923/1454–1517) rulers. On the other hand, relations between the Ṭayyibīs and the Zaydīs of Yaman were often marked by bitter enmity and open warfare.

In 612/1215, ʿAlī b. Ḥanẓala b. Abī Sālim al-Maḥfūẓī al-Wādiʿī succeeded to the headship of the Ṭayyibī *daʿwa* as the sixth *dāʿī muṭlaq*.[93] He was from the Banū Hamdān, and the first of the two *dāʿīs* of this period not belonging to the family of al-Walīd. He maintained good relations with the Ayyūbids and Hamdānids, staying at both Ṣanʿāʾ and Dhū Marmar. He sent *dāʿīs* to the Ismāʿīlīs of western India, who had retained their close and subservient ties with the Ṭayyibī *daʿwa* in Yaman. ʿAlī b. Ḥanẓala died in 626/1229 and was followed by Aḥmad b. al-Mubārak b. al-Walīd, who headed the *daʿwa* for about one year during 626–627/1229–1230, and then by the eighth *dāʿī muṭlaq* al-Ḥusayn b. ʿAlī (627–667/1230–1268), the son of the fifth *dāʿī*. Al-Ḥusayn was on particularly good terms with the Rasūlids and succeeded in converting several members of the family of Asad al-Dīn, cousin of the second Rasūlid ruler al-Malik al-Muẓaffar (647–694/1250–1295). He was also an important Ismāʿīlī author and produced several works on the *ḥaqāʾiq*, including the already-noted *al-Mabdaʾ waʾl-maʿād*, dealing with cosmogony and eschatology.[94] Al-Ḥusayn b. ʿAlī was assisted by his son, ʿAlī, who succeeded him as the ninth *dāʿī*. He first resided at Ṣanʿāʾ and then moved to the fortress of ʿArūs, where he was well-received by the Hamdānids. After the Hamdānid repossession of Ṣanʿāʾ, however, the *dāʿī* returned to that city and died there in 682/1284.

ʿAlī b. al-Ḥusayn b. al-Walīd was in due course succeeded by ʿAlī, the son of his *ma'dhūn* al-Ḥusayn b. ʿAlī b. Ḥanẓala (d. 677/1278). The tenth *dāʿī muṭlaq* of the Ṭayyibīs, like his grandfather, did not belong to the Banu'l-Walīd. The *dāʿī* ʿAlī died in 686/1287 in Ṣanʿā', and was succeeded by Ibrāhīm b. al-Ḥusayn b. al-Walīd (686–728/1287–1328), who established his headquarters at the fortress of Af'ida. In 725/1325, Ibrāhīm acquired Kawkabān, where he gathered a force for possible confrontation with the Zaydīs. The eleventh *dāʿī* was followed by Muḥammad b. Ḥātim (728–729/1328–1329), and then by ʿAlī b. Ibrāhīm (729–746/1329–1345), who fought the Zaydīs with the help of some of the Banū Hamdān and seized Dhū Marmar in 733/1332. Subsequently, ʿAbd al-Muṭṭalib b. Muḥammad (746–755/1345–1354) became the fourteenth *dāʿī*, and was in turn followed by ʿAbbās b. Muḥammad (755–779/1354–1378) and ʿAbd Allāh b. ʿAlī (779–809/1378–1407). The latter, supported by the ever loyal Yaʿburīs, fought the Zaydīs in Ḥarāz and then inflicted a heavy defeat on the Zaydī pretender al-Manṣūr ʿAlī b. Ṣalāḥ al-Dīn (793–840/1390–1436). He also succeeded in 794/1392 in reconquering the fortress of Shibām. The seventeenth and the eighteenth *dāʿī*s were al-Ḥasan b. ʿAbd Allāh (d. 821/1418) and his brother ʿAlī b. ʿAbd Allāh b. al-Walīd. It was during the latter's time that the Zaydī al-Manṣūr ʿAlī besieged and captured Dhū Marmar in 829/1426, but allowed the *dāʿī* to move to Ḥarāz with his family, associates, and his collection of Ismāʿīlī books. Henceforth, the *dāʿī*s resided in Ḥarāz during the remainder of the Yamanī period of the *daʿwa*. The Zaydīs now captured several of the Ṭayyibī fortresses, including Af'ida. ʿAlī b. ʿAbd Allāh died in 832/1428 at Shibām and was followed by his nephew Idrīs b. al-Ḥasan, whose father and grandfather had been the seventeenth and sixteenth *dāʿī*s.

The nineteenth *dāʿī muṭlaq* Idrīs, who was the last great Yamanī exponent of the *ḥaqā'iq* and the foremost Ismāʿīlī historian, was born in the fortress of Shibām in 794/1392.[95] He succeeded his uncle as the head of the *daʿwa* in 832/1428. Maintaining the policies of his predecessors, Idrīs allied himself with the Rasūlids of Zabīd and remained hostile towards the Zaydīs of Ṣanʿā' and elsewhere in Yaman. Joined by the Rasūlid al-Malik al-Ẓāhir (831–842/1428–1439), the *dāʿī* engaged in battle against the Zaydī al-Manṣūr ʿAlī. Indeed, he fought constantly with the Zaydīs and regained control of several fortresses. He also enjoyed the support and friendship of the Ṭāhirid brothers ʿAlī and ʿĀmir, who, around 858/1454, seized ʿAdan and Zabīd, replacing the Rasūlids as the masters of lower Yaman. Idrīs took special interest in the affairs of the *daʿwa* in western India, and during his long dāʿīship of some forty years, he contributed to the success of Ṭayyibī Ismāʿīlism in Gujarāt. The *dāʿī* Idrīs died in 872/1468 at Shibām, where he had established his headquarters in 838/1434, and was succeeded by his son al-Ḥasan (872–918/1468–1512), and then by another of his sons al-Ḥusayn (918–933/1512–1527). The latter's son, ʿAlī b. al-Ḥusayn b. Idrīs, led the *daʿwa* as the twenty-second *dāʿī* for only a few months during 933/1527. The twenty-third *dāʿī muṭlaq*, Muḥammad b. al-Ḥasan, the grandson of Idrīs, was the last of the *dāʿī*s from the Banu'l-Walīd al-Anf and also the last Yamanī *dāʿī* to lead the undivided Ṭayyibīs of Yaman and India. When he died in 946/1539, the position of *dāʿī muṭlaq* passed to an Indian from Sidhpūr, Yūsuf b. Sulaymān.

In the doctrinal field, the Ṭayyibīs maintained the Fāṭimid traditions and preserved a good portion of the literature of the Fāṭimid Ismāʿīlīs. Like the latter, the Ṭayyibīs stressed the equal importance of the *ẓāhir* and *bāṭin* dimensions of religion. They also retained the earlier interest of the Ismāʿīlīs in cosmology and cyclical hierohistory, which provided the main components of their esoteric, gnostic *ḥaqāʾiq* system. In their esoteric doctrine, however, they introduced some innovations which gave the Ṭayyibī gnosis its distinctive character. In cosmology, the Yamanī Ṭayyibīs from the beginning adopted al-Kirmānī's system with its ten higher intellects, instead of the earlier Ismāʿīlī Neoplatonic system accepted by the Fāṭimids. But the Ṭayyibīs also modified al-Kirmānī's system by introducing a mythical 'drama in heaven', first elaborated by the second *dāʿī muṭlaq*, Ibrāhīm al-Ḥāmidī, who drew extensively on al-Kirmānī's *Rāḥat al-ʿaql*. This represented the final modification of the Ismāʿīlī Neoplatonic cosmology introduced into Ismāʿīlī thought by the *dāʿī* al-Nasafī. The cosmological doctrine first expounded by Ibrāhīm al-Ḥāmidī, and adopted by later authors, shaped the peculiar Ṭayyibī *ḥaqāʾiq* system, which is a synthesis of many earlier Ismāʿīlī and non-Ismāʿīlī traditions and gnostic doctrines. By astronomical and astrological speculations, the Yamanī Ṭayyibīs also introduced certain innovations into the earlier Ismāʿīlī conception of hierohistory, expressed in terms of the seven prophetic eras. The Ṭayyibīs conceived of countless cycles leading the sacred history of mankind from its origins to the Great Resurrection. The Ṭayyibī *ḥaqāʾiq* find their fullest description in the *Zahr al-maʿānī* of Idrīs ʿImād al-Dīn, an extensive compendium of esoteric doctrines completed in 838/1435.[96] Subsequently, the Ṭayyibīs made few further doctrinal contributions, while they continued to copy the works of the earlier authors.

According to the Ṭayyibī cosmological doctrine, the primordial pleroma or the intelligible world (*ʿālam al-ibdāʿ*) was created all at once, with innumerable spiritual forms (*ṣuwar*) which were all equal to one another in terms of life, power and capacity. This was the state of the so-called first perfection (*al-kamāl al-awwal*). One of these forms of primordial beings, in contemplating itself, became the first to realize that it was originated; it recognized and worshipped the originator (*al-mubdiʿ*). As a result, this particular form was singled out for special distinction, meriting to be called the first originated being (*al-mubdaʿ al-awwal*), or simply the first (*al-awwal*). He also became known as the first intellect (*al-ʿaql al-awwal*), identified with the Qur'ānic term *al-qalam*, or the pen. The first intellect now invited, in what may be called the *daʿwa* in heaven, all the other primordial beings to follow his example by recognizing the originator and his unity or *tawḥīd*. Those responding positively to this call were ranked in descending order according to the swiftness of their response, occupying the *ḥudūd* of the celestial world.

According to the mythical 'drama in heaven', introduced by Ibrāhīm al-Ḥāmidī,[97] the first two emanations from the first intellect, viz., the first emanation (*al-munbaʿith al-awwal*) and the second emanation (*al-munbaʿith al-thānī*), respectively designated as the second intellect and third intellect, were rivals for the second rank (*ḥadd*) in the celestial hierarchy, after the first intellect. It was the second intellect who, by his superior efforts and swifter response, attained that position. But the third intellect, whilst acknowledging the originator, refused to recognize the superior rank of the second intellect, the universal soul, also identified with the Qur'ānic term *al-lawḥ*, the tablet, since he considered himself to be his equal. Thus, the third intellect, the protagonist of the cosmic dramaturgy, fell into a state of negligence and stupor, and, by hesitating to accord due recognition to his preceding archangelical hypostasis, committed the first cosmic sin or error. As punishment for his insubordination, he fell from the third to the tenth rank in the archangelical hierarchy, coming after the other seven intellects who had meanwhile responded to the call of the first intellect. In other words, after awakening from his stupor, the third intellect discovered that he had descended by seven ranks, due to his immobilization that gave rise to a temporal gap or retard (*takhalluf*) in the pleroma, the so-called 'retarded eternity' which may be viewed as the prototype of cyclical time and history based on the number seven. The doubt or hesitation expressed by the third intellect may also be described as the exteriorization of the darkness which had remained hidden within him, a being of light, and which had to be overcome. After repenting, the third intellect became stabilized as the tenth intellect and demiurge (*mudabbir*) of the physical world, an inferior and opaque world. The tenth intellect is also called the celestial or spiritual Adam (*Ādam al-rūḥānī*), the angel corresponding to Christos Angelos and showing certain traits of the Manichaean and Gnostic *anthropos*. As Corbin has explained,[98] his role corresponds even more closely to that of the angel Zervān in Zervānite Zoroastrian myths.

There were other spiritual forms (*ṣuwar*) that, like the third intellect, committed the error of failing to acknowledge the superior rank of the second intellect. The physical world was produced out of these fallen forms, belonging to the circle (*dāʾira*) of the tenth intellect, and out of the darkness generated by their sin. Through their movements, reflecting confusion and doubt, the fallen forms produced length, width, depth, the dimensions of space, matter (*hayūlā*), the spheres (*aflāk*), the elements (*arkān*), etc. In this Ṭayyibī cosmology, characterized by the fall and repentance of one of the archangels in the pleroma, the tenth intellect or the spiritual Adam, who is charged with administering the affairs of the physical world, tries to regain his lost position by calling on other fallen spiritual forms to repent, like himself. This *daʿwa*, corresponding to the *daʿwa* of the first intellect, is indeed the outstanding motif of the Ṭayyibī cosmogony. The primordial universe, which becomes the scene of combat between the posterities of Adam and Iblīs, was created for this soteriological purpose, namely, the redemption of the spiritual Adam and the salvation of the fallen forms which had manifested themselves as darkness and matter. Some of the fallen spiritual forms respond to the appeal of the spiritual Adam. They are the celestial archetypes of the earthly proclaimers of the mystical *daʿwa*, becoming the posterity of the spiritual Adam. On the other hand, various categories of forms belonging to the circle of the tenth intellect persist in their negation and denial. The implacable adversaries constitute, throughout the cycles, the posterity of Iblīs, the devil. The spiritual Adam, helped by his supporters, carries on a combat which finally, after innumerable cycles, will destroy darkness and the progeny of Iblīs.

The earliest representative of the spiritual Adam's *daʿwa* on earth was the first, universal Adam (*Ādam al-awwal al-kullī*), the terrestrial homologue of the first intellect and the epiphanic form or *maẓhar* of the spiritual Adam. He appeared, together with his twenty-seven loyal companions, on the island of Sarandīb (Ceylon), a region of the earth having the best climatic and astronomical conditions. The primordial universal Adam made his appearance at the dawn of the Ṭayyibī mythohistory, at the beginning of the cycle of cycles, and inaugurated the first cycle of epiphany or manifestation (*dawr al-kashf*). He was the first repository of the imāmate, the primordial imām, who as such was *maʿṣūm*, being immunized against all impurity and sin. He instituted the terrestrial *daʿwa* hierarchy, corresponding to the celestial order, and divided the earth into twelve regions (*jazāʾir*), each one placed under the charge of one of his companions who, themselves, had responded to the *daʿwa* of the spiritual Adam. This original cycle lasted for 50,000 years; it was a period of knowledge (*ʿilm*) and not of action (*ʿamal*), an era of true gnosis in which no laws were required. It endured until the approach of the first cycle of concealment (*dawr al-satr*), when the form of Iblīs reappeared, disturbing the preceding state of harmony. The Ṭayyibī mythohistory allows for a great number of such cycles, the original one having been a cycle of manifestation rather than concealment, because the spiritual Adam, the Ṭayyibī figure of the saved-saviour, had defeated his Iblīs. The universal Adam of this doctrine must be distinguished from the 'historical' Adam described in the Bible and the Qur'ān. The latter, who opened the present cycle of concealment, was only a partial Adam (*Ādam al-juzʾī*), like so many others preceding and following him in the partial cycles of history.

At the end of the first cycle, the universal Adam, along with his supporters, rose to the horizon of the tenth intellect and took his place, while the tenth intellect rose by one rank towards his original *ḥadd* in the pleroma. Similarly, the *qāʾim* of every following cycle, which is closed by a resurrection or *qiyāma*, after his passing, rises and takes the place of the tenth. In this manner, the ascension of each *qāʾim al-qiyāma* at the end of every cycle marks the progressive elevation of the spiritual Adam towards the primordial archangelical dyad in the celestial hierarchy in which he originated, and which he lost due to the crisis that befell him in heaven. This process continues throughout the cycles and from *qāʾim* to *qāʾim*, and the spiritual Adam gradually rises in rank and annuls the form of Iblīs which he tears out of himself, until he actually joins the second intellect. This conjunction is the central idea of the Ṭayyibī gnosis. The universal Adam, as noted, in initiating the first cycle also initiated the imāmate; he was the first imām to accomplish the task which henceforth became the work of each imām and *qāʾim* in a partial cycle, and particularly of the final Qā'im. Just as the universal Adam is the first terrestrial manifestation of the spiritual Adam, exemplified in the partial Adams, so the Qā'im (exemplified in the partial *qā'ims*) will be his final manifestation. The *imām–qā'im* of each partial cycle is, thus, the manifestation of an eternal imām who, in the person of the seal of the series, will consummate the aeon, consisting of a vast number of cycles. All the partial *qā'ims* are, in a sense, 'recapitulated' in the last one amongst them, the Qā'im of the Great Resurrection (*qiyāmat al-qiyāmāt*), which consummates the grand cycle (*al-kawr al-a'ẓam*), restoring the Angel Adam to his original position and redeeming humanity.

The original cycle of manifestation, as noted, was followed by a cycle of concealment, initiated by a partial Adam and closed by a partial *qā'im*, and then by another cycle of manifestation, and so on. An unknown number of successive cycles of *kashf* and *satr*, each one composed of seven periods or eras, occurred until the present cycle of *satr*, which was initiated by the 'historical' Adam of the Qur'ān, the first *nāṭiq* of the present age. When this cycle is closed by the seventh *nāṭiq* and the expected *qā'im* of the current cycle, there will begin again another cycle of manifestation, inaugurated by an *Ādam al-juz'ī*, and so on. The countless alternations of these cycles will continue until the parousia of the final Qā'im, proclaiming the final *qiyāma*, the Resurrection of the Resurrections (*qiyāmat al-qiyāmāt*), at the end of the grand cycle. According to some Ṭayyibī calculations, the duration of the grand cycle (*al-kawr al-a'ẓam*) is estimated at 360,000 times 360,000 years, amounting to almost 130 billion years. The consummation of the grand cycle will also mark the end of the Ṭayyibī mythohistory. The final Qā'im is not merely a final legitimate leader of mankind from amongst the descendants of 'Alī and Fāṭima; he is the Lord of the Resurrection and the summit of the eternal imāmate in which the Ismā'īlī vision of the aeon finds its culmination. As Corbin has remarked,[99] this imām, resembling the perfect child (*al-walad al-tāmm*) of the Gnostics, engenders himself in the secret of the cycles of the aeon, and in his eschatological epiphany is expected to be the ultimate 'exegete' of mankind. He is the final manifestation of the spiritual Adam, and a member of his true posterity, which he will lead back to its original celestial archetype.

Ṭayyibī gnosis is indeed rich in eschatological doctrines, which draw heavily on Manichaean ideas. The eschatology of the Ṭayyibīs, closely related to their cosmogony, is expounded in terms of a cosmic process which includes the eschatological fate or *ma'ād* of the individuals. Naturally, different posthumous fates await the believers and unbelievers. A person is categorized as a believer (*mu'min*) if he affirms the unity of God, recognizes and obeys the true imām of his time, and acknowledges the *ḥudūd* of the *daʿwa* hierarchy. These are, in fact, the conditions for man's salvation, although other groups of human beings may also ultimately receive an opportunity for redemption.

At the moment of initiation into the *daʿwa*, the soul of each neophyte (*mustajīb*) is joined by a point of light, which is his spiritual soul. This point stays with the initiate and grows as its possessor advances in knowledge and virtue. On his passing from this world, the point of light, which by then has grown into a form of light (*al-ṣūra al-nūrāniyya*), becomes completely integrated with the believer's soul. The resulting luminous soul leaves the body and rises to join the soul of the holder of the next higher rank (*ḥadd*) in the hierarchy. This ascension toward the superior *ḥadd* is caused by the magnetism of the column of light (*ʿamūd min nūr*, or *al-ʿamūd al-nūrānī*), the summit of which reaches into the pleroma of the archangels and towards which the souls of the believers are drawn. This column of light, which in Ṭayyibī gnosis assumes a two-fold function in eschatolgy and imamology, is one of the characteristic motifs of Manichaeism, where it has an essential, salvational function. The elevation of the soul of each believer from *ḥadd* to *ḥadd* does not, it may be emphasized, imply transmigration (*tanāsukh*), or the reincarnation of human souls in the bodies of other persons or animals, a doctrine rejected by the Ṭayyibīs. Here, the Ṭayyibī authors are in fact referring to the conjunction of souls, and more precisely, the souls of the holders of different ranks in the hierarchy. Each *ḥadd* is the superior spiritual limit of the *ḥadd* immediately below it, viz., its *maḥdūd*. And the relationship between *ḥadd* and *maḥdūd* acquires a particular significance in this eschatological context. Each *ḥadd* becomes an imām for its *maḥdūd*. And the 'quest for the imām' raises each adept, metamorphosing and elevating him from rank to rank, throughout the hierarchy.

The soul of each believer continues to ascend in the hierarchy until it is gathered together with the luminous souls of all other believers. Their collectivity constitutes the temple of light (*haykal nūrānī*), which has the shape of a human being but is purely spiritual. Without any confusion, each individual soul subsists as a member in the coalescence of the souls. This temple of light is the imāmate, representing the *lāhūt* or divinity of the imām, as distinct from his *nāsūt* or humanity. Each imām has his own temple of light or *corpus mysticum*, and as the epiphanic form of the celestial Adam, he is also the terrestrial support of the column of light. On the passing of each imām, he and his temple of light rise into the pleroma.

This holds true also for the imāms of the era of Muḥammad who are recognized by the Ṭayyibī Ismāʿīlīs, including the concealed imāms succeeding al-Ṭayyib. The *qāʾim* of each partial cycle, the last imām of that cycle, has his own *corpus mysticum*, or sublime temple of light (*haykal nūrānī ʿaẓīm*), composed of all the temples of light belonging to that cycle and constituting the form of the *qāʾim* (*al-ṣūra al-qāʾimiyya*), again having a human shape. At the end of each partial cycle, when a resurrection is proclaimed, the *qāʾim* of that cycle rises into the pleroma with his sublime temple of light and takes the place of the tenth intellect. The latter, as noted, ascends by one *ḥadd* in the celestial hierarchy, drawing the entire universe of beings one degree closer to reconquering the 'retarded eternity' and bringing the repentant beings of the cosmos a step closer to redemption and salvation. This celestial ascension, representing the denouement of the 'drama in heaven' that befell the spiritual Adam, and reflecting a symmetrical relationship between the cosmogony and the eschatology of the Ṭayyibīs, is aimed toward the second intellect whose circle is designated as the *ḥaẓīrat al-quds*, the paradise. The process will continue, from cycle to cycle, until the consummation of the grand cycle. At the time of the Great Resurrection, the final Qāʾim will rise and take his own sublime temple of light, the coalescence or *majmaʿ* of all the luminous souls located at the horizon of the tenth intellect, to the second intellect, the universal soul. The error of the third intellect is now completely atoned. The spiritual Adam, the saved-saviour angel of humanity, and his supporters in both the celestial and terrestrial worlds are thus ultimately redeemed. Once more, there is only the harmonious world of the *ibdāʿ*.

The unbelievers, designated as the adversaries (*mukhālifūn*) of the people of truth (*ahl al-ḥaqq*), cannot emancipate themselves from matter so as to obtain salvation. Their souls, representing the form of darkness (*al-ṣūra al-ẓulmāniyya*) and being inseparable from their bodies, stay with their corpses when they die. In time, the bodies of the unbelievers decompose in the earth and join the elements. After several mutations, they are transformed into various substances and creatures in descending order. Depending on the nature and seriousness of their sins, they may eventually rise again through the ascending forms of life, culminating in the human form. As human beings, they may either accept the *daʿwa* and become believers or reject it. Those belonging to the latter category end up in *Sijjīn*, a place for the supreme torment (*al-ʿadhāb al-akbar*) located in the depths of the earth, where they stay throughout the entire duration of the grand cycle.

The Yamanī Ṭayyibīs also inherited the *daʿwa* hierarchy of the Fāṭimids, especially as described by the *dāʿī* al-Kirmānī. However, since the Ṭayyibī *daʿwa* had to operate under changed realities, some modifications were required in the earlier structure. The organization of the Ṭayyibī *daʿwa*, first explained in Ḥātim b. Ibrāhīm al-Ḥāmidī's *Tuḥfat al-qulūb*, came to be much simpler with fewer ranks (*ḥudūd*) than that under the Fāṭimids. The imām had now gone into concealment, along with his *bāb* and *ḥujja*s, a situation continuing from generation to generation after al-Ṭayyib, the twenty-first imām. Similarly no longer was there any person occupying the position of *dāʿī al-balāgh*, who in earlier times evidently acted as an intermediary between the central headquarters of the Fāṭimid *daʿwa* and the local headquarters of a *jazīra*. In Yaman, Lamak b. Mālik was the only chief dignitary to have borne the designation of *dāʿī al-balāgh*, when al-Malika al-Sayyida was accorded the rank of *ḥujja*. In the absence of these higher ranks of the hierarchy, the administrative head of the Ṭayyibī *daʿwa*, starting with al-Dhu'ayb b. Mūsā, was designated as *dāʿī*, or more precisely as *al-dāʿī al-muṭlaq*. As al-Kirmānī had argued,[100] the holder of every *ḥadd* in the *daʿwa* hierarchy was potentially entitled to the position of the next higher *ḥadd* and as such, a *dāʿī* was potentially in possession of the authority reserved for higher *ḥudūd*. At any rate, the *dāʿī muṭlaq*, as the chief of the *daʿwa*, enjoyed absolute authority in the community. Obedience to the imām, required of all the believers, now meant submission to the *dāʿī muṭlaq*, the concealed imām's highest representative in the Ṭayyibī community. As in the case of the imāms, every *dāʿī muṭlaq* nominated his successor by the rule of the *naṣṣ*.

The *dāʿī muṭlaq* was assisted in the affairs of the *daʿwa* by several subordinate *dāʿī*s, designated as *ma'dhūn* and *mukāsir*.[101] These lower ranks are mentioned for the first time in the *Tuḥfat al-qulūb* as having fixed status in the hierarchy. One or two chief assistants to the *dāʿī muṭlaq* received the designation of *ma'dhūn*. Normally, the *dāʿī* chose the *ma'dhūn* as his successor. The *mukāsir*, who had more limited authority, was now identical with *al-ma'dhūn al-maḥṣūr* and *al-ma'dhūn al-maḥdūd* of the Fāṭimid hierarchy. At the bottom of the hierarchy were the ranks of *mu'min*, the ordinary initiated member of the community, and *mustajīb*, the neophyte or candidate for initiation. The Ṭayyibīs maintained the concern of the Fāṭimid period in the training of the *dāʿī*s and the education of the adepts, though on a much more limited scale. The Yamanī *dāʿī*s were amongst the most learned members of the Ṭayyibī community, and many of them, as thinkers and authors, produced elaborate treatises synthesizing different

Islamic and non-Islamic traditions. In principle, the Ṭayyibī *daʿwa* in Yaman seems to have functioned similarly to the Fāṭimid *daʿwa* in terms of its initiation procedures, secrecy, teaching, as well as the gradual training of the adepts and the members of the hierarchy, though few specific details are available. There is no evidence showing that the Ṭayyibī *daʿwa* was active in any region outside of Yaman and India. The Indian *daʿwa* continued to be under the strict supervision of the Ṭayyibī *dāʿīs* and headquarters in Yaman until the middle of the 10th/16th century, when the headquarters were transferred to Gujarāt. Until then, the head of the Indian *daʿwa*, locally known as *wālī*, was regularly selected by the *dāʿī muṭlaq* residing in Yaman. The *wālī* had a hierarchy of assistants of his own, about which few details are available until more recent times, but which essentially seems to have been the replica of the pattern utilized in Yaman. The Ṭayyibī *daʿwa* operated with such an organization until the Ṭayyibīs of Yaman and India became split into Dā'ūdīs and Sulaymānīs, with their separate *dāʿīs*, headquarters and organizations.

In the meantime, the Ismāʿīlī community in western India had grown steadily since the arrival of the first Ismāʿīlī *dāʿī* in Gujarāt in 460/1067–1068. The Ismāʿīlīs of Gujarāt, who were mainly of Hindu descent, had become known as Bohrās (Bohorās). According to the usual etymological explanation, the name *bohrā* (*bohorā*) is derived from the Gujarātī term *vohōrvū* (*vyavahār*), meaning 'to trade'. The term was applied to the Ismāʿīlīs of Gujarāt probably because they were originally a trading community; trade having also been the occupation of the earliest Gujarātī converts to Islam. According to another explanation, the Bohras were so designated because they had been converted to Ismāʿīlism from the Hindu Vohra caste. At any rate, the first Ismāʿīlī *dāʿī*, ʿAbd Allāh, had been despatched, as noted, from Yaman to Cambay, where he succeeded in firmly establising the *daʿwa*. According to the Ismāʿīlī Bohra traditions or *riwāyāt*,[102] ʿAbd Allāh eventually converted Siddharāja Jayasingha (487–527/1094–1133), the Rājpūt Hindu king of Gujarāt who had his capital at Anhalwāra (modern Pātan), and his two ministers, the brothers Bhārmal and Tārmal, along with a large portion of the local populace. According to these traditions, after ʿAbd Allāh, it was Yaʿqūb, the son of Bhārmal, who became the head of the *daʿwa* in India. He sent his cousin Fakhr al-Dīn, the son of Tārmal, to propagate Ismāʿīlism in western Rajasthan, where he was murdered. The tomb of Fakhr al-Dīn, who is considered the first Indian Ismāʿīlī martyr, is located at Galiakot, and is one of the most venerated Bohra shrines.[103] Yaʿqūb was succeeded by his son Isḥāq and then by his grandson ʿAlī b. Isḥāq. Subsequently, the wālīship of the *daʿwa* in India passed to Pīr Ḥasan, a descendant of the *dāʿī* ʿAbd Allāh. Ḥasan was killed while conducting missionary activity and his grave is still located near Hārij. Pīr Ḥasan was succeeded by his grandson Ādam b. Sulaymān, whose descendants occupied the wālīship for several generations.[104]

The Ismāʿīlī community in Gujarāt had maintained close religious ties with Yaman, and like the Ṣulayḥids, upheld the rights of al-Mustaʿlī and al-Āmir to the imāmate. Similarly, in the Ḥāfiẓī–Ṭayyibī conflict, the Mustaʿlians of Gujarāt sided with al-Malika al-Sayyida and the established *daʿwa* organization in Yaman, in supporting the Ṭayyibī cause. After the collapse of the Ṣulayḥid state, the Ṭayyibīs of India were closely supervised by the *dāʿī muṭlaq* in Yaman, who selected the successive heads of the Indian community and received regular Bohra delegations from Gujarāt. Under these circumstances, the Ṭayyibī community in Gujarāt grew appreciably, and large numbers of Hindus embraced Ṭayyibī Ismāʿīlism, especially in Cambay, Pātan, Sidhpūr and later, in Aḥmadābād, where the headquarters of the Indian *daʿwa* were established.

The Ṭayyibīs of Gujarāt and their *dāʿīs* were not persecuted by the local Hindu rulers, who did not feel endangered by their activities. The Ṭayyibī community thus developed without any hindrance until the Muslim conquest of Gujarāt in 697/1298, when the *daʿwa* activities became somewhat scrutinized by the region's Muslim governors, who recognized the suzerainty of the Sultans of Delhi, belonging to the Khaljī and Tughluqid dynasties. The situation of the Indian Ṭayyibīs deteriorated further with the invasion of Gujarāt by Ẓafar Khān Muẓaffar in 793/1391. Ẓafar Khān, who had been sent out by the Tughluqid Muḥammad Shāh III (792–795/1390–1393), established the independent sultanate of Gujarāt in 810/1407, which lasted until 991/1583 when Gujarāt was annexed to the Mughal empire, then ruled by Akbar. Ẓafar Khān favoured the propagation of Sunnism, his own newly-acquired religion. Being apprehensive of the success of Ismāʿīlism, he became the first ruler of Gujarāt to suppress Shīʿism in his domains. It was, however, under Ẓafar Khān's son and successor, Aḥmad I (814–846/1411–1442), that Ismāʿīlīs began to be severely persecuted. During the reign of Aḥmad I, who founded his capital at Aḥmadābād in 814/1411, the Ṭayyibīs observed *taqiyya* very strictly, adhering outwardly to many of the Sunnī formalities. It was during his oppressive rule that many Ismāʿīlīs were obliged to convert to

Sunnism, while an important schism in the Ismā'īlī Bohra community, the first of its kind, divided the community and caused even greater numbers to join Sunnī Islam. This schism resulted from an estrangement arising between a *wālī* and a certain charismatic Bohra by the name of Ja'far.

In the time of the eighteenth *dā'ī muṭlaq*, 'Alī b. 'Abd Allāh (821–832/1418–1428), the wālīship in India passed to Ḥasan b. Ādam b. Sulaymān, who founded a *madrasa* at Aḥmadābād for religious sciences. A certain Ja'far, from Pātan, was one of the many Bohra students attending the *wālī*'s school. Later, Ja'far decided to proceed to Yaman to study under the *dā'ī* himself, without the *wālī*'s permission. In the *wālī*'s judgement, Ja'far had not yet completed his courses of study in Gujarāt; hence, he was not adequately prepared for benefiting from the more advanced courses offered in Yaman. However, Ja'far went to Yaman despite the *wālī*, and won the confidence of the *dā'ī muṭlaq*. He studied in Yaman for two years. On his return to Gujarāt, Ja'far was asked by the Ṭayyibīs of Cambay and elsewhere to lead them in prayers. When pressed sufficiently, Ja'far complied, although he did not have the *wālī*'s required authorization. These developments further aggravated the *wālī*, who, in due course, reprimanded Ja'far at Aḥmadābād for his unorthodox conduct. A deep rupture had now occurred between the *wālī* and the defiant Ja'far who proceeded to Pātan, where he declared himself a Sunnī and began an intensive campaign against the *wālī* and the Ṭayyibī *da'wa* in Gujarāt. He met with immediate success as many Bohras in Pātan, and its surrounding villages responded positively to his call and left the fold of Ismā'īlī Shī'ism. In his anti-Ismā'īlī campaign, Ja'far had the active support of Aḥmad Shāh and his son Muḥammad, who at the time deputized for his father in Aḥmadābād. On the other hand, the attempts of the *dā'ī muṭlaq* to resolve this serious internal conflict in the Bohra community, and his insistence that the *wālī* should reconcile his differences with Ja'far, proved futile. An increasing number of Bohras followed Ja'far's example and embraced Sunnism, doubtless having also been fearful of the persecutions of the sultan. According to some accounts,[105] more than half of the entire Bohra community seceded, and became known as Ja'farī Bohras. The secessionist Sunnī Bohras were also designated as the *jamā'at-i kalān*, the large community, in contrast to the *jamā'at-i khurd*, or the small community, an appellation reserved for the loyal Ṭayyibī Ismā'īlī Bohras.[106] These events gave further encouragement to the sultan Aḥmad's persecution of the Ismā'īlīs. The *wālī* himself had to go into hiding and his deputy in Pātan and future successor, Rāja, was obliged to seek refuge in Morbi around

840/1436. The harassment of the Ismāʿīlī Bohras continued until Jaʿfar's assassination in 845/1441.

The Ṭayyibī Bohras continued to be persecuted in the sultanate of Gujarāt. Mullā Rāja Jamāl al-Dīn b. Ḥasan, who succeeded his father as *wālī*, was a learned man who endeavoured to consolidate the position of the Ṭayyibīs in Gujarāt. He became very popular amongst the Ṭayyibī Bohras, and, according to their traditions, he was the only *ʿālim* in India who successfully carried disputations with a Shīʿī envoy sent from the Ṣafawid court in Persia. Rāja's reputation, however, angered the sultan of Gujarāt, Muẓaffar II (917–932/1511–1526), who had the *wālī* executed in 924/1518.[107] Meanwhile, the disruptive work of Jaʿfar was pursued by another Sunnī missionary, Aḥmad Jaʿfar Shīrāzī, who caused a deeper rift between the Ṭayyibī and Sunnī Bohras. Aḥmad Jaʿfar arrived in Gujarāt from Sind and soon won the favour of Maḥmūd I Begra (862–917/1458–1511) and his successor Muẓaffar II. Until then, intermarriages had occurred frequently between the Ṭayyibī and Sunnī Bohras, whilst the social identity and homogeneity of the Bohra community had not been drastically affected by the earlier religious schism. But Aḥmad Jaʿfar now persuaded the Sunnī Bohras to sever all ties with the Ṭayyibī Shīʿīs of their community. Henceforth, the two Bohra factions became distinctively and permanently separated from one another, developing different socio-religious identities. The Ṭayyibī Bohras were also severely persecuted in the reign of Maḥmūd III (943–961/1537–1554). It was only after the establishment of Mughal rule that the Ṭayyibī Bohras began to enjoy a certain degree of religious freedom, abandoning *taqiyya* and praying publicly in their mosques.

As noted, taking advantage of the close ties existing between the Ṭayyibī Bohras and their central *daʿwa* headquarters, promising Indian Ṭayyibīs were often sent to Yaman to further their education. It was according to this custom that Jaʿfar, the future Sunnī dissident, travelled to Yaman during the first half of the 9th/15th century. Subsequently, several prominent Ṭayyibī Bohras distinguished themselves by advancing their religious learning in Yaman. Ḥasan b. Nūḥ al-Bharūchī (d. 939/1533), the famous Ṭayyibī author born in Cambay, made the journey to Yaman around 904/1498 and became a student of al-Ḥasan b. Idrīs, the twentieth *dāʿī*.[108] The courses of study pursued by him are described in the introduction to his *Kitāb al-azhār*, a seven-volume chrestomathy of Ismāʿīlī literature. He was closely associated also with ʿAlī b. al-Ḥusayn b. Idrīs and Muḥammad b. al-Ḥasan b. Idrīs, who later became the twenty-second and twenty-third *dā'īs*. Yūsuf b. Sulaymān, who succeeded to the headship of the Ṭayyibīs, was another Bohra selected by the *wālī* to further his studies in Yaman. Yūsuf arrived in Yaman while still in his youth and first studied under al-Bharūchī. Yūsuf's learning soon attracted the attention of the twenty-third *dā'ī*, who nominated him as his successor.[109] Yūsuf thus became the first Indian to head the Ṭayyibī *da'wa* as the twenty-fourth *dā'ī muṭlaq*. When the twenty-third *dā'ī* died in 946/1539, his successor Yūsuf was in Sidhpūr, and it was from Gujarāt that he conducted the affairs of the *da'wa* for a few years, before settling down in Yaman. When Yūsuf died in 974/1567, the central headquarters of the Ṭayyibī *da'wa* were transferred from Yaman to Gujarāt by his Indian successor, Jalāl b. Ḥasan. The twenty-fifth head of the Ṭayyibīs, who had now established his residence at Aḥmadābād, appointed a deputy for the administration of the Yamanī community. By that time, the Ṭayyibīs of India had grown to such an extent, despite persecutions and mass conversions to Sunnism, so as to overshadow the original community in Yaman. Clearly, the larger share of the religious income of the *dā'ī* was now contributed by the Indian Ṭayyibīs. The Yamanī Ṭayyibīs, meanwhile, had been experiencing difficulties of their own, in the aftermath of the Ottoman occupation of Yaman, which had started in 923/1517. This was at a time when the Banu'l-Anf were practically annihilated in the 10th/16th century by the Zaydī Imām al-Muṭahhar b. Sharaf al-Dīn, who was extremely hostile towards the Ismā'īlīs of Yaman. The transference of the *da'wa* headquarters to India was therefore in recognition of these realities. It marked the definite end of the Yamanī phase of Ṭayyibī Ismā'īlism.

Jalāl b. Ḥasan died in 975/1567, after a dā'īship of only a few months. His son, Amīnjī b. Jalāl (d. 1010/1602), was an eminent Ismā'īlī jurist who attained high ranks in the Dā'ūdī *da'wa*.[110] The Ṭayyibī Bohras still regard him as a great authority on legal matters after al-Qāḍī al-Nu'mān, whose *Da'ā'im al-Islām* was used from the beginning by the Ṭayyibīs as their most authoritative compendium on *fiqh*. Jalāl b. Ḥasan was succeeded by Dā'ūd b. 'Ajabshāh, whose dā'īship coincided with the closing years of the sultanate of Gujarāt. In his time, the Ṭayyibī Bohras were subjected to a new wave of persecutions spurred by the activities of Muḥammad Ṭāhir, a Sunnī propagandist and leader of the Ja'farī Bohras, who was assassinated by a Ṭayyibī in 986/1578. Muḥammad Ṭāhir also briefly received the support of the Mughal emperor Akbar the Great (963–1014/1556–1605), who conquered Gujarāt in 980/1573. Akbar's deputy at Aḥmadābād, too, adopted anti-Shī'ī policies. Dā'ūd b. 'Ajabshāh was obliged to go to Āgra and personally present the grievances of his community to Akbar, who enjoyed a reputation for religious tolerance. Before leaving Aḥmadābād in 981/1573, the *dāʿī* appointed Dā'ūd b. Quṭbshāh as his deputy in Gujarāt, an appointment later cited by the Dā'ūdīs in their argument against the Sulaymānīs. The *dāʿī* was well-received by the Mughal emperor, who ordered his officals in Gujarāt to accord religious freedom to the Ṭayyibīs. Henceforth, it was no longer necessary for the Ṭayyibī Bohras to observe *taqiyya*. Dā'ūd b. ʿAjabshāh now launched a programme of revitalizing the community, reinstating the Ṭayyibī practices of worship which had been set aside for a long time in Gujarāt. In 986/1578, he was also able to reprimand Muẓaffar III, the last sultan of Gujarāt, who was then visiting Kapadwanj whilst fleeing from the Mughals, for his anti-Ismāʿīlī policies. When Dā'ūd b. ʿAjabshāh, the twenty-sixth *dāʿī muṭlaq*, died in 999/1591, or in 997/1589 according to the Sulaymānī Ṭayyibīs, his succession was disputed, causing a schism in the Ṭayyibī community.

Dā'ūd b. ʿAjabshāh was succeeded in India by Dā'ūd Burhān al-Dīn b. Quṭbshāh, and the Yamanī Ṭayyibīs were duly informed of this event. However, four years later, Sulaymān b. Ḥasan al-Hindī, the grandson of the twenty-fourth *dāʿī muṭlaq* and the deputy of Dā'ūd b. ʿAjabshāh in Yaman, claimed the succession for himself and returned to India to establish that claim. Sulaymān produced a document, still extant, showing that he had been the beneficiary of the *naṣṣ* of the twenty-sixth *dāʿī*. According to certain Ṭayyibī groups, this document had been forged with the help of some of the relatives of the deceased *dāʿī*, who had been implicated in financial misconduct. Matters became further complicated due to an inheritance suit filed in Mughal courts by Ibrāhīm b. Dā'ūd b. ʿAjabshāh against Dā'ūd b. Quṭbshāh. The heated succession dispute was brought before the emperor Akbar at Lahore in 1005/1597. To investigate the matter, Akbar appointed a special tribunal consisting of Abu'l-Faḍl ʿAllāmī, his biographer and secretary; Ḥakīm ʿAlī Gīlānī, his Persian Shīʿī physician; and the governor of Gujarāt. The tribunal decided in favour of Dā'ūd b. Quṭbshāh, but the dispute, having essentially an Indian versus Yamanī characteristic, was not resolved definitely and led to a schism in the Ṭayyibī community.[111] The great majority of the Ṭayyibī Bohras, comprising the bulk of the Ṭayyibī Ismāʿīlīs, acknowledged Dā'ūd Burhān al-Dīn as their twenty-seventh *dāʿī muṭlaq*; henceforth they became known as Dā'ūdīs. An insignificant number of Yamanī Ṭayyibīs, too, rallied to the side of the Dā'ūdī cause. On the other hand, a minority, consisting of the bulk of the Yamanī Ṭayyibīs and a small group of the

Ṭayyibī Bohras, upheld the succession rights of Sulaymān b. Ḥasan. These Ṭayyibīs, designated as Sulaymānīs, accepted Sulaymān b. Ḥasan as their twenty-seventh *dā'ī*. Henceforth, the Dā'ūdīs and the Sulaymānīs followed different lines of *dā'īs*.[112] The Dā'ūdī *dā'ī muṭlaq* continued to reside in India, while the head of the Sulaymānī *da'wa* established his headquarters in Yaman.

Dā'ūd Burhān al-Dīn, who had managed to win the support of the majority of the Indian Ṭayyibīs, continued to have his headquarters at Aḥmadābād. He was not troubled during the remaining years of Akbar's reign. He also established friendly relations with Qulīj Khān, the Mughal governor of Gujarāt under Akbar's son and successor Jahāngīr (1014–1037/1605–1627), who, at the instigation of the Sunnī *'ulamā'*, ordered the execution of the Imāmī scholar Nūr Allāh al-Shūshtarī. Dā'ūd died in 1021/1612; his tomb and that of his rival, Sulaymān b. Ḥasan, who died in 1005/1597, are still visited at Aḥmadābād by the Dā'ūdīs and Sulaymānīs. Dā'ūd Burhān al-Dīn was succeeded by his chief lieutenant, Shaykh Ādam Ṣafī al-Dīn. On the latter's death in 1030/1621, 'Abd al-Ṭayyib Zakī al-Dīn, the son of the twenty-seventh *dā'ī*, became the twenty-ninth *dā'ī muṭlaq* of the Dā'ūdīs. Soon afterwards, his authority was challenged by 'Alī b. Ibrāhīm, the grandson of the twenty-eighth *dā'ī*, Ādam. 'Alī, supported by his paternal uncles and some others, claimed the succession for himself and carried his protest to the court of Jahāngīr. The Mughal emperor decided in favour of the incumbent *dā'ī* and had 'Alī reconcile his differences with the *dā'ī* in his presence at Lahore. After both parties returned to Aḥmadābād, however, 'Alī once again refused to acknowledge the *dā'ī*'s leadership and seceded, with his followers, from the Dā'ūdī Bohra community. 'Alī had in fact founded, in 1034/1624–1625, a new Ṭayyibī Bohra sub-sect called 'Aliyya, after his own name.[113] 'Alī b. Ibrāhīm (d. 1046/1637) thus became the twenty-ninth *dā'ī* of the 'Aliyya, who have followed their own line of *dā'īs*.[114] 'Alī was succeeded by one of his uncles, Zakī al-Dīn Ṭayyib b. Shaykh Ādam (d. 1047/1638). Since the time of the thirty-second *dā'ī*, Ḍiyā' al-Dīn Jiwābhā'ī b. Nūḥ (d. 1130/1718), the headquarters of the 'Aliyya have remained at Baroda in Gujarāt. At present, the 'Aliyya are a small community confined essentially to Baroda, and their present *dā'ī*, the forty-fourth in the series, Ṭayyib Ḍiyā' al-Dīn b. Yūsuf Nūr al-Dīn, succeeded to office in 1394/1974. The 'Aliyya do not intermarry with the orthodox Dā'ūdī Bohras, and evidently have produced no particular sectarian literature. In the time of their thirty-seventh *dā'ī*, Shams al-Dīn 'Alī (1189–1248/1775–1832), a small group of dissenters broke away from the ʿAliyya community in 1204/1789. The dissenters, who were excommunicated by the *dāʿī*, preached that the era of Islam had ended. They also held some Hindu doctrines, especially the sinfulness of eating the flesh of animals, which won them the name of Nāgoshiyya. The vegetarian Nāgoshias, who like their parent sub-sect of the ʿAliyya subsisted on the fringe of the Dā'ūdī community in Baroda, are now practically extinct.

Meanwhile, the Dā'ūdī Bohra community had grown and prospered under the successive *dāʿīs*, who were for the most part allowed religious freedom by the Mughal emperors and their governors or *ṣūbadārs* in Gujarāt. Violating the religious policies of his dynasty, Awrangzīb was the only Mughal to launch a major wave of persecutions against the Ismāʿīlīs, both during his governorship of Gujarāt and after ascending to the Mughal throne in 1068/1658. The twenty-ninth Dā'ūdī *dāʿī*, ʿAbd al-Ṭayyib, was succeeded by ʿAlī Shams al-Dīn (1041–1042/1631–1632), a descendant of Idrīs ʿImād al-Dīn and the first Yamanī to head the Dā'ūdīs. ʿAlī's father, al-Ḥasan, had been appointed the deputy of the *dāʿī muṭlaq* in Yaman by Dā'ūd Burhān al-Dīn, a position he retained until after the succession of his own son to the dāʿīship. The tenure of the thirty-second *dāʿī*, Quṭbkhān Quṭb al-Dīn (1054–1056/1644–1646), coincided with Awrangzīb's brief governorship of Gujarāt, when the Dā'ūdīs were persecuted. Awrangzīb, who himself did not exercise religious toleration, had come also under the influence of ʿAbd al-Qawī, his mentor and close adviser, who was strongly anti-Shīʿī. Upon his arrival in Aḥmadābād in 1055/1645, Awrangzīb started a campaign against the Ismāʿīlīs. The *dāʿī* Quṭbkhān and his close associates were arrested and imprisoned. The Ismāʿīlī Bohras, accused of heresy, were now pressured into embracing Sunnism and their mosques were placed in the hands of Sunnī administrators. Many Dā'ūdīs converted to Sunnism or fled from Aḥmadābād in fear of persecution, and the community once again resorted to *taqiyya*. These persecutory measures culminated in the trial of the *dāʿī* Quṭbkhān in a Sunnī court and in his execution in 1056/1646 on Awrangzīb's orders.[115]

Soon after, Awrangzīb left Aḥmadābād, handing the governorship of Gujarāt to Shāyasta Khān, who was tolerant towards the Bohras and allowed them religious freedom. Awrangzīb, now engaged in his military campaigns, took along with him Quṭbkhān's successor as the thirty-third *dāʿī*, Pīrkhān Shujāʿ al-Dīn (1056–1065/1646–1655), and the latter's chief deputies. Pīrkhān accompanied Awrangzīb as a prisoner to Deccan and elsewhere, but he was later released and permitted to return to

Aḥmadābād. The Ismāʿīlīs were once again persecuted by Ghayrat Khān, who arrived in Gujarāt in 1058/1648 as Dārā Shukōh's deputy there. He also kept Pīrkhān in prison for some time, freeing him only on the orders of Shāh Jahān (1037–1068/1628–1657). In Pīrkhān's time, another split which proved to be of temporary duration occurred in the Dā'ūdī Bohra community. The original protagonist of this split was a certain Bohra named Aḥmad, a trusted associate of Pīrkhān who had mishandled his mission to Āgra for obtaining the Mughal emperor's intercession on behalf of the imprisoned *dāʿī*. Angered by Pīrkhān's refusal to reconcile with him, Aḥmad started an anti-*dāʿī* campaign, and preached certain ideas which were to have important consequences later on. Aḥmad adopted the view that the *dāʿī*, due to his erroneous judgement, had disqualified himself from office and that he should have been replaced by his *ma'dhūn*. Aḥmad was now in effect expounding a new doctrine, holding that in the period of *satr*, when the concealed imām cannot rectify the errors of his *dāʿīs*, the *dāʿī muṭlaq* is to be *ka'l-maʿṣūm*, nearly possessing sinlessness and infallibility. Aḥmad and his followers, failing to win the support of Pīrkhān's *ma'dhūn* and future successor Ismāʿīl, seceded from the Dā'ūdī community and became known as the Hujūmiyya.[116] Initially, Aḥmad gained some success and even managed to have Pīrkhān imprisoned in 1064/1654 by the new governor of Gujarāt, Shāh Jahān's youngest son Murād Bakhsh. However, the Hujūmiyya did not survive long.

Ismāʿīl Badr al-Dīn b. Mullā Rāj (1065–1085/1655–1674), who succeeded Pīrkhān as the thirty-fourth *dāʿī*, was the first Rājpūt *dāʿī* of the Dā'ūdīs, tracing his ancestry to Bhārmal and Rāja, the *wālī*'s deputy in Pātan at the time of Jaʿfar's secessionist activities. Ismāʿīl transferred the headquarters of the *daʿwa* (or *daʿwat*, as pronounced by the Dā'ūdīs themselves) from Aḥmadābād to Jāmnagar. It was during the dāʿīship of Ismāʿīl's son and successor, ʿAbd al-Ṭayyib Zakī al-Dīn (1085–1110/1674–1699), that the Ismāʿīlī Bohras experienced the renewed persecutions of Awrangzīb (1068–1118/1658–1707), who had meanwhile installed himself as the Mughal emperor of India. The new sectarian troubles began around 1091/1680, when the Dā'ūdī *dāʿī* held a large public assembly in Aḥmadābād, where he intended to reside, for announcing his *naṣṣ* in favour of his son Mūsā. The governor of Gujarāt, apprehensive of the increasing influence of the Dā'ūdīs, ordered the arrest of the *dāʿī* in 1093/1682. But ʿAbd al-Ṭayyib fled to Jamnagar and the officials contented themselves with seizing a number of prominent Dā'ūdīs of Aḥmadābād who were sent to Awrangzīb. The *dāʿī* himself was forced to go into hiding in Khambhlia and elsewhere. Under the new persecutions, the religious rituals and practices of the Indian Ṭayyibīs, including their pilgrimages to various shrines and the mourning ceremonies for the martyrdom of the Imām al-Ḥusayn b. ʿAlī during the month of Muḥarram, were banned. The regular Ṭayyibī religious ceremonies, such as the daily prayers, were to be performed by Sunnī functionaries, who also became the custodians of the sectarian mosques. The Ismāʿīlī Bohras were subjected to heavy punitive taxes and other monetary exactions. At the same time, Sunnī instructors were appointed for teaching the doctrines of Sunnī Islam to the Ismāʿīlīs. Periodical reports on this official educational programme were to be forwarded to Awrangzīb. These persecutions, necessitating the strict observance of *taqiyya*, continued during the dāʿīship of ʿAbd al-Ṭayyib's son and successor, Mūsā Kalīm al-Dīn (1110–1122/1699–1710), whose tenure coincided with the final years of the ʿĀlamgīrī era. As late as 1116/1704, yet more leading Bohras working on behalf of the Dā'ūdī *daʿwa* were seized with their books and sent to the Mughal emperor.[117]

With Awrangzīb's death in 1118/1707 and the subsequent decline of the Mughal empire, the Ismāʿīlī Bohra community was in general permitted to develop freely. As a trading and wealthy community, however, the Ismāʿīlī Bohras continued to attract the attention of various petty rulers of India, who often exacted irregular payments from them. The *dāʿī* Mūsā Kalīm al-Dīn's son and designated successor, Nūr Muḥammad, was imprisoned for unknown reasons by the ruler of Jāmnagar, which was at the time the seat of the Dā'ūdī *daʿwa*. He was released after the payment of a large ransom by the *dāʿī*, reflecting an often utilized form of exaction applied to the Dā'ūdīs. Nūr Muḥammad Nūr al-Dīn b. Mūsā, the thirty-seventh *dāʿī*, died in Mandvi, Cutch, and was succeeded by his cousin and brother-in-law Ismāʿīl Badr al-Dīn b. Shaykh Ādam Ṣafī al-Dīn (1130–1150/1718–1737). The Dā'ūdīs were required by him to attend the mourning assemblies held during the early days of Muḥarram, and to read verses from the Qur'ān after their morning prayers. It was also in Ismāʿīl's time that the dissenting Hujūmiyya returned to the fold of the Dā'ūdī *daʿwa*. Ibrāhīm Wajīh al-Dīn's accession to the headship of the Dā'ūdīs as the thirty-ninth *dāʿī* in 1150/1737 marks a shift in the family line of *dāʿīs*. Ibrāhīm's father, ʿAbd al-Qādir Ḥakīm al-Dīn (d. 1142/1730), was an influential and learned Bohra from Mālwā in central India, who had risen to the rank of *ma'dhūn* of the thirty-eighth *dāʿī*. Ibrāhīm Wajīh al-Dīn transferred the headquarters of the *daʿwa* to Ujjain, where he died in 1168/

1754. At the time, Burhānpūr had become another important Dā'ūdī centre outside of Gujarāt.

During the dā'īship of Ibrāhīm's son and successor, Hibat Allāh al-Mu'ayyad fi'l-Dīn (1168–1193/1754–1779), coinciding with the early phase of the British subjugation of India, another insignificant dissident movement occurred in the Dā'ūdī community. The leaders of this new anti-*dā'ī* movement were Ismā'īl b. 'Abd al-Rasūl al-Majdū', the author of the famous Ismā'īlī bibliographical work, *Fihrist al-kutub*, and his son Hibat Allāh. Ismā'īl who had studied under Luqmānjī b. Ḥabīb (d. 1173/1760), a renowned Dā'ūdī scholar, and Hibat Allāh had distinguished themselves as Ismā'īlī scholars and aspired to the leadership of the community. In 1175/1761, Hibat Allāh claimed to have established direct contact with the concealed Ṭayyibī Imām through his *dā'ī al-balāgh*, 'Abd Allāh b. Ḥārith. He further claimed to have been appointed by the hidden imām to the position of *al-ḥujja al-laylī*, a rank superior to that of *dā'ī muṭlaq*. By these claims, which were supported by Ismā'īl, Hibat Allāh evidently expected the reigning *dā'ī* to yield his position to him. Hibat Allāh acquired some followers in Ujjain and elsewhere, who became known as Hiptias (Hibtias) after his name.[118]

The *dā'ī* attempted in vain to persuade the new dissenters to abandon their propaganda. They were attacked and chased out of Ujjain, their initial seat, by angered orthodox Dā'ūdīs. Ismā'īl managed to escape unharmed but Hibat Allāh was seized and his nose was amputated as a mark of disgrace, before he was permitted to leave Ujjain. The derogatory nickname al-Majdū', meaning a person whose nose is cut off, was later given to Hibat Allāh's father, Ismā'īl, who died in 1183 or 4/1769–1770 in Ujjain. Hibat Allāh conducted his campaign in various towns, but he failed to acquire any significant following. The *dā'ī muṭlaq* himself travelled widely throughout the community, countering the propaganda of the Hiptias. Today, the Hiptias are almost extinct, except for a few families in Ujjain, where the survivors of this minor Ṭayyibī sub-sect live in isolation from the orthodox Dā'ūdīs. In his travels, the *dā'ī* also spent a few years in Sūrat, then rapidly becoming another important Dā'ūdī town in India. The fortieth *dā'ī*, who had statesmanship qualities, averted the occurrence of what could have been a major schism in the Dā'ūdī community. He also maintained cordial relations with the Mughal emperor of his time, Shāh 'Ālam II, who appointed him the *qāḍī* of Ujjain, and with other petty rulers as well as with the British, who by then controlled parts of Gujarāt. The *dāʿī* Hibat Allāh died in 1193/1779 at Ujjain. He was succeeded by his son-in-law ʿAbd al-Ṭayyib Zakī al-Dīn b. Ismāʿīl Badr al-Dīn (1193–1200/1779–1785), marking the reversion of the dāʿīship to the Rājpūt dynasty and the abandonment of Ujjain as the headquarters of the Dāʾūdī *daʿwa*. ʿAbd al-Ṭayyib, who was very strict in enforcing the Dāʾūdī Bohra prohibitions against the use of tobacco and liquor, spent most of his time in Gujarāt and died in Burhānpūr.

The forty-second *dāʿī*, Yūsuf Najm al-Dīn b. ʿAbd al-Ṭayyib Zakī al-Dīn (1200–1213/1785–1798), transferred the headquarters of the *daʿwa* to Sūrat, then controlled by the British and as such a safe refuge for the Ismāʿīlīs. Yūsuf Najm al-Dīn's brother and successor, ʿAbd ʿAlī Sayf al-Dīn (1213–1232/1798–1817), founded the famous seminary at Sūrat, known as the Sayfī Dars, for the training of the Dāʾūdī functionaries and for imparting higher religious education to the members of the community. The tenure of the forty-third *dāʿī* coincided with the consolidation of British rule in India and the virtual termination of persecutions against the Ismāʿīlī Bohras and Khojas. However, occasional internal strife and factionalism, often due to succession or financial disputes, as well as conflicts with other Muslim groups and Hindus, continued to mark the subsequent history of the Dāʾūdīs of India.

The forty-sixth *dāʿī*, Muḥammad Badr al-Dīn b. ʿAbd ʿAlī Sayf al-Dīn (1252–1256/1837–1840), was the last of the *dāʿīs* belonging to the Rājpūts of Gujarāt. He died suddenly in 1256/1840, without having pronounced the so-called *naṣṣ al-jalī*, the public designation of a successor, thus causing a heated succession controversy in the community which has continued to the present.[119] Under the circumstances, the Dāʾūdī *ʿulamāʾ* did not divulge the matter to the public, and four of the most prominent *ʿulamāʾ*, led by ʿAbd-i ʿAlī ʿImād al-Dīn (d. 1271/1854), nominated ʿAbd al-Qādir Najm al-Dīn for administering the affairs of the *daʿwa*. ʿAbd al-Qādir, who at the time held the rank of *mukāsir*, was the son of the forty-fifth *dāʿī*, Ṭayyib Zayn al-Dīn b. Shaykh Jīwanjī Awrangābādī (1236–1252/1821–1837). Shaykh Jīwanjī, it may be noted, is the ancestor of the most recent family of the Dāʾūdī *dāʿīs*, initiated by the forty-fourth *dāʿī* and continuing to the present fifty-second *dāʿī* with the exception of the forty-sixth *dāʿī*. According to the agreement reached between the *ʿulamāʾ* and ʿAbd al-Qādir, the latter was to become *al-nāẓim*, an adjuster or caretaker for administrative purposes only, without laying any claim to the spiritual position of *al-dāʿī al-muṭlaq*. At any rate, the Dāʾūdīs now recognized ʿAbd al-Qādir as their new head while certain learned circles continued to debate his accession and doubted his legitimacy.

Some of the *ʿulamāʾ*, greatly disturbed by the suspension of the *naṣṣ* (*inqiṭāʿ al-naṣṣ*) and the regular succession of the *dāʿīs*, even began to expect the imminent emergence of the imām. As a result, in 1293/1876, five renowned Dāʾūdī *ʿulamāʾ*, including Muḥammad ʿAlī b. Fayḍ Allāh al-Hamdānī (d. 1315/1898), left India for Arabia on a search for the imām. The group visited many localities in the Ḥijāz and elsewhere, and also ran into difficulties with the Ottoman authorities who suspected the Ismāʿīlī Bohras as spies. In 1295/1878, the leading Dāʾūdī scholars, headed by Ibrāhīmbhāʾī Ṣafī al-Dīn b. ʿAbd-i ʿAlī ʿImād al-Dīn (d. 1315/1897), set up a consultative council in Sūrat, known as *ḥilf al-faḍāʾil*, to guide the community in religious matters in accordance with the Sharīʿa, especially since religious education in the meantime had been discontinued at the Sayfī Dars. The council proved to be short-lived and various Dāʾūdī circles remained perturbed by the controversy surrounding the dāʿīship of ʿAbd al-Qādir Najm al-Dīn.

Appearing as early as 1264/1847–1848, the circulation of the so-called Imāmī letters, with their mysterious content and threatening tone, indeed indicated the existence of growing opposition in the community to ʿAbd al-Qādir Najm al-Dīn's leadership and policies. Meanwhile, after being securely established, ʿAbd al-Qādir had assumed the title of *dāʿī muṭlaq*. He had also adopted a policy of weakening the position of the *ʿulamāʾ* who were opposed to him. For instance, he appointed numerous members of his own family to the ranks of the *daʿwa* hierarchy. And the status of *shaykh* (plural, *mashāyikh*), hitherto bestowed on Dāʾūdīs in recognition of their learning and piety, was now given to unworthy persons in the community. These developments had, in turn, adverse effects on the financial situation of the *daʿwa*, further aggravating the fears of the discontented Dāʾūdīs. Financial difficulties were accentuated by the fact that ʿAbd al-Qādir's relatives, made responsible for collecting the religious dues of the Dāʾūdīs in many regions, including the prosperous Bohra community of Bombay, often kept the funds for themselves.

ʿAbd al-Qādir survived various vicissitudes during his long dāʿīship of nearly forty-five years, but at the cost of causing irrevocable damage to the office of *dāʿī muṭlaq*. He also laid the ground for the grievances which later led to more active dissent in the Dāʾūdī Bohra community. The events of this tumultuous period were subsequently brought out during the court hearings related to two well-known Bohra civil suits filed in British India, viz., the Chandabhai Gulla case of 1917 and the Burhanpur Durgah case of 1925. ʿAbd al-Qādir Najm al-Dīn died in 1302/1885 and was succeeded by his brother ʿAbd al-Ḥusayn Ḥusām al-Dīn (1302–1308/1885–1891), who devoted his brief dāʿīship mainly to campaigning against the superstitious beliefs and practices of the Dā'ūdī Bohras, often reflecting Hindu influences.

The forty-eighth *dāʿī* was succeeded by his nephew Muḥammad Burhān al-Dīn b. ʿAbd al-Qādir Najm al-Dīn (1308–1323/1891–1906). The latter succumbed to the Dā'ūdī opposition circles and admitted in a written document, issued in 1309/1891, that he and his two predecessors were merely *nāẓim*s or caretakers of the community and not *dāʿī*s, since the forty-sixth *dāʿī muṭlaq* had died without appointing a successor.[120] Overt dissension now broke out in the community, and Muḥammad's leadership was contested even by his own brother ʿAbd Allāh, whilst financial difficulties continued to beset the *daʿwa*. At the same time another split occurred in the Dā'ūdī Bohra community. In 1315/1897, a talented young Dā'ūdī called ʿAbd al-Ḥusayn Jīwājī, originally a petty merchant in Bombay, came to Nagpur, claiming that he was in direct communication with the hidden imām and that he had been appointed his *ḥujja*. At first he gained some supporters, including some Dā'ūdī *ʿulamā'*, who came to be known as the Mahdībāghwālās, or the Mahdībāgh party, named after their place of residence in Nagpur.[121] The *ʿulamā'*, however, soon became disillusioned with ʿAbd al-Ḥusayn, who had also attracted some wealthy and enterprising Bohra merchants, and left the new Dā'ūdī sub-sect. ʿAbd al-Ḥusayn, popularly known as Malak Ṣāḥib, designated as his successor one Ghulām Ḥusayn (Khan Bahadur H. H. Malik), who became the head of the Mahdībāgh colony at Nagpur in 1321/1903. In 1341/1922, Ibrāhīm Riḍā Ṣāḥib took over the leadership of this group; he was then followed by Ḥasan Nūrānī, who succeeded to that non-hereditary position in 1376/1956.

The Mahdībāghwālās, continuing to live in their settlement in Nagpur, never acquired any significance and were refuted in several treatises written by prominent Dā'ūdīs.[122] A small group of the Mahdībāghwālās, believing that the *dawr al-kashf* had commenced and that it was no longer necessary to observe the prescriptions of the Sharīʿa, gave up praying and fasting in the month of Ramaḍān, along with other Muslim rituals and obligations; they became known as the Dā'ūdī Atbāʿ-i Malak Vakīl, or Artāliswālās.

ʿAbd Allāh Badr al-Dīn b. ʿAbd al-Ḥusayn Ḥusām al-Dīn (1323–1333/1906–1915) succeeded his cousin Muḥammad Burhān al-Dīn as the fiftieth *dāʿī* of the Dā'ūdīs. During his short term in office, he introduced some changes designed to improve the functioning of the *daʿwa* and its regional machinery in India. He was, however, opposed to the dissemination of Western-style secular education among the Dā'ūdīs, which at the time was the foremost desideratum of the reform-oriented members of the community. It was also during ʿAbd Allāh Badr al-Dīn's dāʿīship that serious troubles broke out between the Ismāʿīlī Bohras and other Muslim groups, leading to serious riots in Bhopal. A new era in the modern history of the Dā'ūdī Bohras began with the fifty-first *dāʿī*, Ṭāhir Sayf al-Dīn b. Muḥammad Burhān al-Dīn (1333–1385/1915–1965), who headed the community for fifty years, longer than any of his predecessors. Henceforth, the Dā'ūdīs became strongly polarized between the *dāʿī* and his supporters on the one side, and the opposition comprised of reformist groups on the other. From early on, Ṭāhir Sayf al-Dīn strove to acquire a firm hold over the community by assuming the title of *dāʿī muṭlaq* and making unprecedented claims to sinlessness and infallibility, while pursuing specific policies designed to ensure the unquestioning submission of the Dā'ūdīs to his authority in both religious and secular matters. The *dāʿī*, maintaining the policies of his grandfather ʿAbd al-Qādir Najm al-Dīn, appointed his own family members to the high positions in the *daʿwa* organization. He undermined the status of the *ʿulamā'* and took into control all the communal and endowed properties, the so-called *awqāf*. The opposition, initially emphasizing secular education, in time came to campaign for social change and individual rights, democratization of the local institutions belonging to the *daʿwa*, and financial accountability of the funds collected from the Dā'ūdīs. During the 1950s and 1960s, more reformist groups were formed which soon joined forces with the old opposition in the community, establishing a united front under the name of Pragati Mandal (Progressive Group).[123] So far, the reformist movement has had its greatest appeal amongst the elite of the community. The majority of the Dā'ūdī Bohras, traditional in their ways and outlook, continue to be apathetic and submissive to their *dāʿī*. In no small measure, the Dā'ūdī reformist efforts have been undermined by the effective use of excommunication and the ordering of social boycotts, amongst other punitive measures, exercised by the *dāʿī*. The present *dāʿī muṭlaq* of the Dā'ūdīs, the fifty-second in the series, is Muḥammad Burhān al-Dīn b. Ṭāhir Sayf al-Dīn, who succeeded his father in 1385/1965. In his time, the Dā'ūdīs of East Africa, too, have raised questions regarding his authority.

No accurate information is available on the number of the Dā'ūdī Bohras, since the government of India does not publish separate census figures for various Muslim groups in the country. According to the population census of 1931, the Bohras of different religious persuasions, including the Ismāʿīlīs as well as those Sunnīs, Hindus and Jayns who reported themselves as Bohras, numbered to about 210,000 persons in India. On the basis of some recent estimates, accounting also for natural annual increases, the total Dā'ūdī population of the world is currently placed at around 500,000 persons, of which four-fifths reside in India.[124] More than half of the Indian Dā'ūdī Bohras live in Gujarāt, while the remainder are located mainly in Bombay and central India. The major urban centres of the Dā'ūdīs of India are Bombay, Dohad, Udaipur, Ujjain, Sūrat, Aḥmadābād, Sidhpūr, and other cities in Gujarāt, Madhya Pradesh and Maharashtra. Outside of India, the largest number of Dā'ūdīs are to be found in Pakistan, where there are about 30,000 Dā'ūdī Bohras residing chiefly in Karachi. In Yaman, the Dā'ūdīs represent a small community, perhaps not exceeding 5,000 persons living in the Ḥarāz region, especially amongst the Banū Muqātil and on the Jabal Ṣaʿfān. Small trading communities of the Dā'ūdī Bohras are also settled in Ceylon (Sri Lanka), in various parts of the Far East, and along the southern shores of the Persian Gulf; while a few hundred have immigrated to Europe and America in recent decades. The largest Dā'ūdī Bohra settlement outside of India after Pakistan, however, is located in East Africa, where some 20,000 Dā'ūdīs currently live in Tanzania (incorporating since 1964 the island of Zanzibar and the former territory of Tanganyika on the mainland), Kenya and Uganda. The Ismāʿīlīs of East Africa have been increasingly obliged to immigrate to the West, due to the repressive policies of some of the local governments.

The Dā'ūdī Bohras, along with the Nizārī Khojas, were amongst the earliest Asian immigrants to East Africa. The permanent settlement of the Ismāʿīlī Bohras and Khojas in East Africa was greatly encouraged during the early decades of the nineteenth century by the ʿUmānī sultan Sayyid Saʿīd (1220–1273/1806–1856), belonging to the Ibāḍī Bū Saʿīd dynasty of ʿUmān and Zanzibar. Sultan Saʿīd was interested in foreign trade, and, benefiting from British protection, he managed to extend and consolidate his African dominions into a commercial empire. In the pursuit of his policies, Saʿīd encouraged the immigration of Indian traders, who were accorded religious freedom, to Zanzibar. After the Khojas, the Bohras, coming mainly from the districts of Cutch and Kathiawar in Gujarāt, constituted the largest group of Indian immigrants in Zanzibar. The movement to East Africa of the Indian Ismāʿīlīs, engaged in trade, was intensified after 1840, when Saʿīd transferred his capital from Muscat to

Zanzibar. Subsequently, the Indian Ismāʿīlīs moved from Zanzibar to the growing urban areas on the east coast of Africa, notably Mombasa, Tanga and Dar-es-Salaam, where they acted as commercial agents for firms in Zanzibar or became petty merchants and shopkeepers. Further penetration of the Indian Ismāʿīlī settlers into the interior of East Africa followed the establishment of British and German rule in the region. Both of these European colonial powers were in need of the commercial skills and connections of the Bohras and Khojas in the territories under their rule. By the early decades of the twentieth century, however, the immigration of the Indian Ismāʿīlīs to East Africa had practically come to an end; only a few Bohra families have gone there since 1918. From the beginning, the Bohras of each town in Africa have lived in their own separate quarters, while maintaining their religious practices and social customs. Almost all of the Ismāʿīlī Bohras of East Africa belong to the Dāʾūdī faction, with virtually no Sulaymānīs amongst them.[125]

The organization of the Dāʾūdī *daʿwa* has been based on the pattern developed during the Yamanī phase of Ṭayyibī Ismāʿīlism.[126] The Dāʾūdīs are headed by a *dāʿī muṭlaq*, who is in fact a substitute for the concealed imām. The *dāʿī*, appointed by the *naṣṣ* of his predecessor, is considered to be *maʿṣūm*, sinless and infallible, and in possession of the required religious knowledge or *ʿilm*. With absolute authority over every aspect of the community, the *dāʿī* is the supreme head of the *daʿwa* organization and governs autocratically with the help of his personally chosen assistants. The *dāʿī muṭlaq* is commonly known as the Mullājī Ṣāḥib or Sayyidnā Ṣāḥib. Since the early decades of the twentieth century, he has resided in Bombay, although the headquarters of the Dāʾūdī *daʿwa*, known as the Ḍeorḥī, have continued to be located in Sūrat. In both places, there are good collections of Ismāʿīlī manuscripts, under the direct supervision of the *dāʿī* himself. The private manuscript collections of deceased Dāʾūdīs are normally confiscated for these officially administered libraries, especially the one at Sūrat. Unfortunately, it is almost impossible for researchers to obtain access to these treasures of Ismāʿīlī literature.

The next lower ranks in the Dāʾūdī *daʿwa* hierarchy are those of *maʾdhūn* and *mukāsir*. The *dāʿī* appoints one *maʾdhūn* who acts as his chief assistant. The *maʾdhūn* is normally chosen from amongst the close relatives of the *dāʿī* and succeeds to the dāʿīship. The *dāʿī* also nominates one *mukāsir*, again usually a relative. The *mukāsir* assists the *maʾdhūn* and sees to the lesser details and the more routine administrative affairs of the *daʿwa*. Next, there are the *mashāyikh* (singular, *shaykh*), also known as *ḥudūd*, who are normally eighteen in number. The *mashāyikh* are of varying ranks but all of them are addressed as Bhā'ī Ṣāḥib, the reverend brother. Each *dāʿī* selects his own *mashāyikh* from amongst the Dā'ūdīs most learned in Ismāʿīlī doctrine and in Arabic. The *mashāyikh*, who are trained at the Sayfī Dars, officiate in the larger Dā'ūdī centres, also announcing the orders of the *dāʿī*.

Next in the *daʿwa* hierarchy comes the *ʿāmil* or agent, who is the head of any local Dā'ūdī congregation or *jamāʿat*. Addressed as Bhā'ī Ṣāḥib or Miyān Ṣāḥib, the *ʿāmil* is sent by the *dāʿī* to every Dā'ūdī community whose population exceeds fifty families. The main duty of the *ʿāmil* is to lead the community under his charge in prayers and to perform the various religious ceremonies, including marriage, funeral rites, and circumcision (*khaṭna*). Being the local representative of the *dāʿī*, no religious or communal ceremony is valid without his permission; and for every ceremony that the *ʿāmil* performs, he receives a fee out of which the greater share is sent to the *dāʿī*'s treasury, while the rest is retained by him. The *ʿāmil* is also responsible for collecting the various religious dues and offerings for the *dāʿī*. He is usually appointed for a period of five years, and his tenure is seldom renewed; while the *dāʿī* favours the inter-communal transfers of his *ʿāmil*s. These policies are aimed at preventing the *ʿāmil*s from developing privileged positions in any particular community, which would enable them to misappropriate local funds. In important Dā'ūdī cities like Bombay and Karachi, the *ʿāmil*s are likely to be the *dāʿī*'s relatives or highly trusted individuals. In East Africa, the earliest *ʿāmil*s were despatched around the turn of the last century from Gujarāt to Zanzibar and Mombasa. At present, there are two Bhā'ī Ṣāḥibs in East Africa. One acts as the head *ʿāmil* of East Africa, with his headquarters at Mombasa; and the second is the *ʿāmil* of the Dā'ūdī Bohra congregation at Nairobi. Furthermore, unlike other areas, the *ʿāmil*s of East Africa often hold their positions for long periods, sometimes exceeding two decades. The lowest rank in the Dā'ūdī *daʿwa* organization is that of *mullā*, who is usually appointed by the *dāʿī* from amongst the qualified members of the community where he is to serve. The Dā'ūdī *mullā*s are numerous, and in the larger towns there is also the position of *wālī mullā*, who leads the communal prayers in the absence of the *ʿāmil*. The *ʿāmil*s may delegate some of their functions to the *mullā*s, who normally have some knowledge of Arabic and Ismāʿīlī rituals and who are employed as instructors at the elementary schools or *madrasa*s for the Bohra children.

Every Dā'ūdī on attaining the age of fifteen takes an oath of allegiance or *mīthāq*, also known as the *ʿahd al-awliyāʾ*, pledging loyalty to the Ṭayyibī Ismāʿīlī Imāms and the Dāʾūdī *dāʿīs*. Thereupon, he is officially initiated into the community as a believer (*muʾmin*). The same covenant is renewed annually by every adult Dāʾūdī on the 18th of Dhuʾl-Ḥijja, celebrated by the Dāʾūdīs like other Shīʿīs as the *ʿīd Ghadīr Khumm*, which is a day of fasting for the Dāʾūdīs. The *mīthāq*, reminiscent of a custom adopted in Fāṭimid times, is administered by the *ʿāmil* of every congregation, and its present text, introduced in recent times, includes a promise of unconditional obedience to the *dāʿī muṭlaq*.[127] The Dāʾūdīs pay a number of dues to the *dāʿī muṭlaq*:[128] these include the annual *khums*, also payable by other Shīʿīs, and *zakāt*; as well as special occasional dues like *ḥaqq al-nafs*, levied on the relatives of a deceased Dāʾūdī, and *salām*, a voluntary but customary offering to the *dāʿī*. These dues, representing substantial annual payments to the *dāʿī*'s central treasury, are regularly collected on a local basis by the *ʿāmils*, normally once a year during the month of Ramaḍān. Sometimes, the collections are made by a special envoy of the *dāʿī*, referred to as the *ṣāḥib al-daʿwa*.

Amongst their more important religious practices, the Dāʾūdīs make the *ḥajj* pilgrimage to Mecca and pay equal attention to visiting the shrines of the Imāms ʿAlī b. Abī Ṭālib and al-Ḥusayn b. ʿAlī, at Najaf and Karbalāʾ. They also hold elaborate mourning sessions, or *majālis*, during the first ten days of the month of Muḥarram, commemorating the martyrdom of the Imām al-Ḥusayn. The Dāʾūdīs pray three times a day, at dawn, mid-day and just after sunset, in their separate mosques, found in every Dāʾūdī community. The names of their twenty-one revealed imāms are repeated at the end of every prayer. The Dāʾūdīs do not participate in special communal prayers on Fridays or on religious festivals as do the Twelver Shīʿīs, and they do not recite the sermon or *khuṭba* reserved for those occasions. According to a Ṭayyibī belief developed in Yaman, such sermons could be pronounced only under a manifest imām. As a result, there are no *minbar*s or pulpits in the Dāʾūdī mosques. The Dāʾūdī Bohras also have their *jamāʿat-khāna*s or assembly halls, reserved for communal and religious gatherings and ceremonies. They are managed by the committees of the leading Bohras, appointed by the *ʿāmil* of each community. The Dāʾūdī Bohras use a form of Gujarātī language, permeated with Arabic words, and write in the Arabic script. They have retained many Hindu customs in their marriage ceremonies and other rituals. Disputes in the Dāʾūdī communities are resolved by the *ʿāmil*s or referred to the *dāʿī* in Bombay. In such cases, the *dāʿī*'s decisions are binding on all parties. In legal disputes relating to the Ismāʿīlī Bohras, the Indian courts now apply the Islamic law, especially as enunciated in al-Qāḍī al-Nuʿmān's *Daʿāʾim al-Islām*, the chief legal compendium of the Dāʾūdī and Sulaymānī Ṭayyibīs throughout the world. The Ismāʿīlī Bohras have their own version of the Islamic lunar calendar, developed in Fāṭimid times, which is based on astronomical calculations for determining the beginning of the months. This calendar is therefore fixed, and as such it may differ from the usual Muslim dating based on the sighting of the new moon by one or two days. A general feature of the Dāʾūdī Bohra communities in India and elsewhere is their strong inclination towards seclusion. Although such isolationist tendencies are diminishing, the Dāʾūdīs still keep their books secret, indulge in limited contact with outsiders, and refrain from intermarrying with Hindus or with other Muslim groups. These customs, along with the fact that the Dāʾūdī *daʿwa* no longer attempts to win new converts, have combined to limit the total size of the Dāʾūdī population of the world.[129]

In Yaman, meanwhile, the unified Ṭayyibī *daʿwa* had been succeeded mainly by the Sulaymānī *daʿwa*, which had few adherents in India. As noted, the twenty-seventh *dāʿī muṭlaq* of the Sulaymānīs, Sulaymān b. Ḥasan, was an Indian who had originally been sent to Yaman as the deputy of Dāʾūd b. ʿAjabshāh, the last Ṭayyibī *dāʿī* recognized by both the Dāʾūdīs and the Sulaymānīs. Subsequently, Sulaymān went to India to establish his claims to the dāʿīship of the Ṭayyibīs, then consisting chiefly of the Ṭayyibī Bohras. Failing to win much support amongst the Bohras, who had already acknowledged Dāʾūd b. Quṭbshāh as their new *dāʿī*, Sulaymān b. Ḥasan died at Aḥmadābād in 1005/1597, during the earliest years of the Dāʾūdī–Sulaymānī dispute. This dispute, it may be recalled, also represented a conflict of interests of the majoritarian Indian and the minoritarian Yamanī wings of Ṭayyibī Ismāʿīlism. At any rate, while the Ṭayyibī Bohras rallied to the side of Dāʾūd b. Quṭbshāh and his successors, the Yamanī Ṭayyibīs mainly supported the claims of Sulaymān b. Ḥasan, who initiated a separate line of Sulaymānī *dāʿī*s. Sulaymān b. Ḥasan was succeeded by his minor son, Jaʿfar b. Sulaymān (1005–1050/1597–1640), who was one of the four Indian *dāʿī*s of the Sulaymānīs, along with his father, his successor, and the forty-sixth *dāʿī*. Henceforth, the Sulaymānī *dāʿī*s established their headquarters in Yaman, where the great bulk of the Sulaymānīs lived. During the youth of Jaʿfar b. Sulaymān, Ṣafī al-Dīn Muḥammad b. al-Fahd (d. 1042/1633), belonging to the influential Makramī family of the Yamanī Ismāʿīlī tribe of Yām, ran the affairs of the

Sulaymānī *daʿwa* as the *mustawdaʿ* or acting *dāʿī*. Muḥammad b. al-Fahd al-Makramī was also one of the foremost Sulaymānī authors who, in line with the main characteristic of the Sulaymānī literature, wrote several works in refutation of the claims of Dā'ūd b. Quṭbshāh and the Dā'ūdīs.[130] With the death of the twenty-ninth *dāʿī*, ʿAlī b. Sulaymān (1050–1088/1640–1677), the dāʿīship of the Sulaymānīs passed to Ibrāhīm b. Muḥammad b. al-Fahd al-Makramī (1088–1094/1677–1683), and that hereditary position has remained since 1088/1677 in the same Makramī family, with only a few interruptions. The Sulaymānī *dāʿīs* followed one another in Yaman, by the rule of the *naṣṣ*, without any succession disputes. Consequently, there have been no schisms in the Sulaymānī community. The Makramī *dāʿīs* established their headquarters in Najrān in northeastern Yaman. Supported by the Banū Yām, who, like the bulk of the Yamanī Ismāʿīlīs, had sided with Sulaymān b. Ḥasan and the Sulaymānī cause, the Makramī *dāʿīs* ruled Najrān, usually from Badr, independently.

The Makramī Sulaymānī *dāʿīs* had frequent conflicts with the local Zaydī Imāms, who belonged to the Qāsimī line of al-Qāsim al-Manṣūr (d. 1029/1620), who had expelled the Ottoman Turks from Yaman in 1045/1635. In the earliest decades of the long dāʿīship of Hibat Allāh b. Ibrāhīm al-Makramī (1109–1160/1697–1747), however, the Zaydī Imām al-Manṣūr b. al-Mutawakkil granted the *dāʿī* control over Ḥarāz, in return for the *dāʿī*'s earlier support of al-Manṣūr against rebels in his family. Subsequently, the Makramīs resisted all attempts of the Zaydīs to expel them from that region. In the middle of the 12th/18th century, the Banū Yām, led by the Makramī *dāʿīs*, penetrated into the Mikhlāf al-Sulaymānī (Ḥaly), adjoining the Red Sea, a region then under the control of the *amīrs* of the Āl Khayrāt. Later, the thirty-third *dāʿī*, Ismāʿīl b. Hibat Allāh (1160–1184/1747–1770), conquered Ḥaḍramawt in 1170/1756–1757. Subsequently, however, the Makramī dynasty of the Sulaymānī *dāʿīs* endeavoured in vain to fight the rising power of the Saʿūdī family of central Arabia. In the middle of the 12th/18th century, a new era had commenced in Arabia with the spread of the Wahhābiyya, a religious and reformist movement founded by Muḥammad b. ʿAbd al-Wahhāb (d. 1206/1792), a Ḥanbalī Sunnī theologian from Najd who was also very hostile towards Shīʿism. Ibn ʿAbd al-Wahhāb acquired powerful protectors in Muḥammad b. Saʿūd (d. 1179/1765), the *amīr* of Dirʿiyya near Riyāḍ, and the Āl Saʿūd. In 1157/1744, Ibn Saʿūd and Ibn ʿAbd al-Wahhāb concluded a basic alliance, marking the effective beginning of the Wahhābī state in central Arabia. By 1202/1788, all of Najd had been conquered by Ibn Saʿūd's son and successor, ʿAbd al-ʿAzīz (1179–1215/1765–1801), who had repelled three expeditions sent against him by the Sulaymānīs. The Saʿūdīs soon expanded their territories in the Ḥijāz and in southern Arabia, alarming the Ottoman Turks into taking military action against them. It was in the aftermath of these events that the Ottomans, led by Aḥmad Mukhtār Pasha, occupied Yaman anew in 1288/1871, significantly curtailing the power of both the Qāsimī Zaydī Imāms and the Makramī Sulaymānī *dāʿīs*. The Makramīs were in fact expelled from Ḥarāz in 1289/1872 by the general Mukhtār Pasha, who destroyed their fortress at ʿAttāra and killed the forty-first *dāʿī*, al-Ḥasan b. Ismāʿīl Āl Shibām al-Makramī (1262–1289/1846–1872). At the same time, the Banū Yām were coerced into accepting a peace settlement, and the *dāʿīs*, now divested of their fighting capability, retired quietly to Najrān. This marked the end of the political significance of the Makramī dynasty of Sulaymānī *dāʿīs* and their followers in Yaman.

Subsequently, the Sulaymānī *dāʿīs* and their community in Yaman had to withstand the hostilities of the Zaydī Imāms and the puritanic Saʿūdīs of central Arabia. In the twentieth century, the Saʿūdīs rose to prominence under ʿAbd al-ʿAzīz II (1319–1373/1902–1953), who, after becoming the ruler of the Ḥijāz and Najd, proclaimed himself the king of Saudi Arabia in 1351/1932. In 1353/1934, ʿAbd al-ʿAzīz went into war with Yaman over a boundary conflict, and easily defeated the Zaydī Imām al-Mutawakkil Yaḥyā (1322–1367/1904–1948). As a result of the ensuing truce and treaty for the demarcation of the boundaries, Najrān, the seat of the Makramīs, was apportioned to Saudi Arabia. During these eventful years, the reigning forty-fifth *dāʿī*, ʿAlī b. Muḥsin (1331–1355/1913–1936), handled his disputes with Malik Ibn Saʿūd and Imām Yaḥyā with great tact and diplomacy. The forty-seventh *dāʿī*, Sharaf al-Dīn al-Ḥusayn b. Aḥmad al-Makramī (1357–1358/1938–1939), too, attempted to protect the Yamanī Sulaymānīs in those difficult times, but he was obliged to spend his short term in office in Saudi Arabia; he died at Ṭāʾif. Under these turbulent circumstances, the forty-sixth Sulaymānī *dāʿī*, al-Ḥājj Ghulām Ḥusayn (1355–1357/1936–1938), another Indian to occupy that office, chose to stay in India. Ghulām Ḥusayn had visited Yaman in 1303/1885–1886, and in 1327/1909 he was selected by the forty-fourth *dāʿī* ʿAlī b. Hibat Allāh (1323–1331/1905–1913) to head the Sulaymānī Bohras. He was designated in 1333/1915, by the forty-fifth *dāʿī*, to succeed to the dāʿīship. Ghulām Ḥusayn, who lived and died near Bombay, was a religious scholar and the author of numerous works in Arabic and Urdu, including an abridgement of al-Kirmānī's *Rāḥat al-ʿaql*. He also introduced al-Nuʿmān's *Daʿāʾim al-*

Islām to the general Indian Ismāʿīlī public in an abridged form, in his *Sharḥ al-masāʾil*, written in both Arabic and Urdu.[131] The complete text of the *Daʿāʾim*, utilized by the Sulaymānī and Dāʾūdī Ṭayyibīs, was edited by the late Asaf A. A. Fyzee (Āṣaf b. ʿAlī Aṣghar Fayḍī), the foremost modern Sulaymānī scholar and the leading contemporary expert on Ismāʿīlī jurisprudence. After Ḥusām al-Dīn al-Ḥājj Ghulām Ḥusayn, the dāʿīship of the Sulaymānīs reverted to the Makramī family. The present *dāʿī*, the forty-ninth in the series, is al-Sharafī al-Ḥusayn b. al-Ḥasan al-Makramī, who succeeded to office in 1396/1976.

The total number of Yamanī Sulaymānīs may currently be placed around 50,000–70,000 persons,[132] living mainly in the northern districts of Yaman and on the northern border region between Yaman and Saudi Arabia. Besides the Banū Yām of Najrān, the Sulaymānīs are found in Ḥarāz, amongst the inhabitants of the Jabal Maghāriba and in Hawzan, Lahāb and ʿAttāra, as well as in the district of Hamdān and in the vicinity of Yarīm. In Yaman, the Sulaymānīs live in isolation from the Zaydīs and evidently also from the less significant Dāʾūdīs. By the early decades of the twentieth century, the Sulaymānīs of India were still fewer than a thousand persons.[133] At present, there are only a few thousand Sulaymānī Bohras living mainly in Bombay, Baroda, Aḥmadābād, and Ḥaydarābād in the Deccan. There are also some Sulaymānīs in Pakistan.

The Sulaymānī *daʿwa* essentially continued the traditions of the post-Fāṭimid Yamanī Ṭayyibīs. The religious organization of the Sulaymānīs maintained the simplicity of the *daʿwa* organization developed during the Yamanī phase of Ṭayyibī Ismāʿīlism, in contrast to the more elaborate Dāʾūdī *daʿwa* in India. In addition, being a small community distributed over a relatively small area, the needs of the Yamanī Sulaymānīs could be adequately served by a simple *daʿwa* organization. The Sulaymānī *dāʿī muṭlaq* personally sees to the major problems of his followers, being helped by his assistants who occupy the ranks of *maʾdhūn* and *mukāsir*. He also has a few representatives, *ʿāmil*s, in the more important Sulaymānī districts of Yaman. The Sulaymānī *dāʿīs*, unlike those of the Dāʾūdīs, do not use honorific titles, being simply addressed by the designation of Sayyidnā. In the nomenclature of the Sulaymānī *daʿwa*, the *dāʿī muṭlaq* has three *jazāʾir*, or *daʿwa* regions, under him, viz., Yaman, Hind (India) and Sind (Pakistan). The *dāʿī* himself resides in Yaman, where he is known as the *dāʿī qabāʾil Yām*. In India, where he is referred to as Sayyidnā Ṣāḥib, the *dāʿī* has his chief representative or agent, known as the *manṣūb*. The *manṣūb* resides at Baroda, the headquarters of the Sulaymānī *daʿwa* in the Indian subcontinent, where there is a Sulaymānī library of Ismāʿīlī manuscripts. The *manṣūb* in India also supervises the affairs of the Sulaymānīs of Pakistan. Sometimes, as in recent decades, the *dāʿī* simultaneously has two *manṣūb*s in India, residing in Baroda and Ḥaydarābād. A person selected by the *dāʿī* for the position of *manṣūb* is known as *al-manṣūb al-muṭlaq*, while on actually assuming his post he is called *al-manṣūb al-mustaqill* (or *al-munfarid*). There is no rank of *shaykh* in the Sulaymānī *daʿwa* hierarchy in India. The *manṣūb*s are chiefly assisted by a number of *ʿāmil*s who are generally *mullā*s residing in different Sulaymānī Bohra communities. These lesser functionaries conduct the communal prayers, perform religious ceremonies, and collect the dues for the *dāʿī* in Yaman.

In India, the official language of the Sulaymānī *daʿwa* is Urdu, the language commonly used by the majority of the Indian Muslims. The Sulaymānī Bohras deliver their sermons in Urdu. On the other hand, Arabic is used in the correspondence between the Sulaymānī Bohras and their *dāʿī* in Yaman. The official letters of the *dāʿī muṭlaq* are publicly read and translated for the Indian Sulaymānīs by the *manṣūb*; such letters of the *dāʿī* are called *musharrifāt*. The Sulaymānīs, too, are particular in secretly guarding their books. The Ismāʿīlī literature produced in the pre-Fāṭimid and Fāṭimid periods and by the Mustaʿlī-Ṭayyibī Ismāʿīlīs up to the Dā'ūdī–Sulaymānī schism is accepted by both of these main factions of Ṭayyibī Ismāʿīlism. Subsequent to the schism, the Dā'ūdīs and the Sulaymānīs produced their own separate literatures, devoted mainly to polemical issues and claims or counterclaims of various *dāʿī*s. The Dā'ūdīs and the Sulaymānīs, adhering to the same Mustaʿlī-Ṭayyibī heritage and religious beliefs, disagree primarily in respect to their line of *dāʿī*s. There are few differences between the customs of the two groups, in particular setting apart the Yamanī Sulaymānīs of Arab origins from the Dā'ūdī Bohras who have been influenced by many Hindu traditions; within India, increasing differences have separated the Dā'ūdīs from the Sulaymānīs, who are following their own distinctive paths of socio-religious development.

In Yaman, the Sulaymānī community has enjoyed a great degree of cohesion, partly inspired by the fact that the Sulaymānī *daʿwa* was the direct continuation of the post-Fāṭimid Ṭayyibī *daʿwa* and partly necessitated by the local environment of the Sulaymānīs, which was often under the control of their Zaydī and other opponents. Under these circumstances, the Yamanī Sulaymānīs lent full support to their Makramī *dāʿī*s, consolidating themselves into an effective fighting force and avoiding schisms and internal strifes. In India, the small and scattered Sulaymānī Bohra community, as in the case of other Ismāʿīlīs, has been subjected to frequent persecutions, often resulting in the mass conversions of the Ismāʿīlī sectarians to Sunnism. The Sulaymānī Bohras have also encountered the hostility of the much larger Dā'ūdī community of India. On the other hand, similar to their Yamanī co-religionists, the Indian Sulaymānīs have not experienced any internal conflicts. Under these realities, the Sulaymānī Bohras have been increasingly inclined to cultivating friendly relations with other Muslim groups; relations that would lessen their social difficulties as one of the smallest Muslim groups of India. This explains why in the course of time the Sulaymānī Bohras, in contrast to the Dā'ūdīs, have developed closer affinities to other Muslims in terms of language, dress and behaviour. Not only have the Sulaymānī Bohras adopted Urdu instead of the special Gujarātī language used by the Dā'ūdī Bohras, but they have also abandoned the Gujarātī Bohra dress and turban and intermarry with Sunnī Muslims. Nor are the Sulaymānīs under the strict central control of their *dāʿī* and his *manṣūb*s. The Sulaymānī Bohras have been allowed a much greater degree of freedom than the Dā'ūdīs, and they have readily resorted to the Qāḍī courts of India. In sum, the Sulaymānī Bohras have come to represent a progressive group, approving of social change and encouraging modern secular education and the attainment of specialized training at the higher occidental institutions. It is not surprising, therefore, that the small Sulaymānī Bohra community has produced, proportionately speaking, a significant number of prominent men, including India's first Muslim barrister. In particular, numerous members of the Tyabji family of Bombay have distinguished themselves in legal careers and in other professions, while the ladies of the same Sulaymānī Bohra family were amongst the earliest Indian Muslims to publicly defy the *pardah* (Persian, *chādur*), or the special veil still worn by women in many regions of the Islamic world.[134]

6

Nizārī Ismāʿīlism of the Alamūt period

In this chapter we shall discuss the initial phase in the development of Nizārī Ismāʿīlism, the so-called Alamūt period from around 483/1090, the year marking the effective foundation of what was to become the Nizārī Ismāʿīlī state of Persia and Syria, to the downfall of that state in Persia in 654/1256. During this period of some 166 years, under the initial leadership of the redoubtable Ḥasan-i Ṣabbāḥ, the Nizāriyya succeeded in maintaining an independent state of their own in the midst of a hostile Sunnī environment controlled mainly by the Saljūq Turks. During al-Mustanṣir's succession dispute in 487/1094, Ḥasan-i Ṣabbāḥ and the Persian Ismāʿīlīs, who had shortly earlier launched their anti-Saljūq revolt, upheld the rights of Nizār to the imāmate. Henceforth, becoming known as the Nizāriyya, the Persian and some other eastern Ismāʿīlī communities severed their relations with the Fāṭimid Caliphate and the Mustaʿliyya, the other major branch of the Ismāʿīlī movement of the time.

The Nizārī state, with its seat mainly at the mountain fortress of Alamūt in Daylamān in northern Persia, was widely scattered territorially, stretching from Syria to eastern Persia and controlling numerous fortresses with their surrounding lands and villages, as well as a few towns. This independent state retained its cohesion in the face of various upheavals and the persistent enmity of the majority of the Muslim society, which never ceased its endeavours to uproot the Shīʿī Nizārīs and the dynasty ruling over their state. The Nizārī state of Persia, having eventually weakened internally as a result of prolonged struggles against formidable adversaries and lacking in capable leadership, collapsed under the onslaught of the all-conquering Mongols. The destruction of the Persian Nizārī state in 654/1256 had indeed been one of the primary objectives of Hülegü's Mongol armies invading Persia. Soon afterwards, the Syrian Nizārīs, who had developed somewhat independently of Alamūt though maintaining a subservient position to the parent sect in Persia, were completely subdued by the Mamlūk sultan Baybars I. By 671/1273, Baybars had seized all the fortresses of the Syrian Nizārīs, who themselves were permitted to survive as a semi-autonomous community. Subsequently, the Nizārīs never succeeded in regaining their earlier political prominence; but they managed to survive clandestinely and as scattered communities in many parts of the Muslim world, often in the guise of Ṣūfism.

The Nizārī movement was from the very beginning associated with certain doctrinal developments, subsequently designated as the new preaching or *al-daʿwa al-jadīda*, which was to set the Nizāriyya apart also doctrinally from the Mustaʿliyya, who essentially maintained the old preaching, or the so-called *al-daʿwa al-qadīma*, of Fāṭimid Ismāʿīlism, the common heritage of both branches of the movement. Soon, the Nizārīs also came to have an imām present at the head of their community; an imām who interpreted the Sharīʿa and guided his followers as he deemed necessary. In sum, by contrast to the Mustaʿliyya, or more precisely the Ṭayyibiyya, not only did the Nizāriyya acquire political prominence but they also developed and interpreted their doctrines in the face of changing circumstances. The Persian Nizārīs, who used the Persian language in their religious works, did not develop any special interest in copying and studying the classical works of the Ismāʿīlī literature produced during the Fāṭimid period. On the other hand, the Syrian Nizārīs, who followed a somewhat different religio-political path and produced their own literature in Arabic, preserved some of the Fāṭimid Ismāʿīlī treatises, also retaining certain traditions of the Fāṭimid period. It should also be mentioned that the Persian Nizārīs of the later Alamūt period played an active role in the cultural life of the time, acting as hosts to a number of celebrated Muslim scholars and developing significant libraries, notably the chief Nizārī library at Alamūt.

The study of Nizārī Ismāʿīlism during the Alamūt period presents research difficulties of its own, resulting from the loss of the bulk of the Nizārī literature of that period and the general hostility of the non-Ismāʿīlī literary sources on the subject. Living under adverse conditions and often being involved in long-drawn military entanglements, the Persian Nizārīs evidently did not produce any voluminous religious literature during the Alamūt period.[1] The bulk of what they did produce did not survive the fall of their state, which resulted in the massacre of the Nizārīs and the burning of the famous library at Alamūt. Less noteworthy collections of manuscripts held at other Nizārī castles, too, did not escape the rage of the Mongols. Indeed, only a handful of Nizārī doctrinal works have survived directly from that period, including an anonymous treatise, the *Haft bāb-i Bābā Sayyidnā*, written around 596/1199–1200, and a few Ismāʿīlī works produced during the final decades of the Alamūt period and attributed to Naṣīr al-Dīn al-Ṭūsī (d. 672/1274). Also, excerpts from some non-extant Nizārī works, such as Ḥasan-i Ṣabbāḥ's autobiography and doctrinal writings as well as the epistles (*fuṣūl*) of the lords of Alamūt, are preserved by al-Shahrastānī as well as in some post-Alamūt Nizārī treatises and in a few Persian historical sources. This extant Nizārī literature, despite its meagreness and fragmentary nature, does shed valuable light on important aspects of the doctrines propounded by the Persian Nizārīs. Evidently, the Persian Nizārīs also maintained chronicles at Alamūt and other fortresses. These chronicles, recording the detailed history of the Persian Nizārī state, have not survived, but some later Persian historians fortunately found access to them. The accounts of these historians, as we shall see, provide our chief sources on the history of the Persian Nizārīs of the Alamūt period. During the post-Alamūt period, the various Nizārī communities, notably those of Persia, Syria, Badakhshān and India, developed independently of one another; but none of these communities ever produced any reliable and continuous account of Nizārī Ismāʿīlism of the Alamūt period.

The non-literary sources on the Nizārīs of Persia are rather insignificant. The Mongols demolished most of the Nizārī castles in Persia, which may have provided valuable archaeological evidence on various aspects of the Nizārī history and intellectual achievement. At any event, the remains of the main Persian Nizārī fortresses, whose exact locations have now been identified, and their vicinities, have not been subjected to systematic archaeological study and excavation in modern times. Furthermore, the Nizārī mausoleums, which evidently existed in the Alamūt area, have been destroyed. Indeed, no Persian epigraphic evidence remains from that period, while only a few Nizārī coins, known to have been minted at Alamūt and elsewhere, have been recovered. In sum, the limited non-literary evidence has not significantly augmented our knowledge of the Persian Nizārīs of the Alamūt period, though the ruins of the rock fortresses have provided valuable details on the ingenious methods adopted by the Persian Nizārī community, notably those underlying their water supply systems, for coping with highly difficult living conditions, and which manifested their formidable, striving spirit.[2]

The celebrated Persian historians of the Īlkhānid period (654–756/1256–1355) are our chief authorities for the history of the Nizārī state in Persia. Amongst these Persian Sunnī historians, ʿAlāʾ al-Dīn ʿAṭā-Malik b. Muḥammad Juwaynī is the earliest historian of the Mongol invasions. Juwaynī entered the service of the Mongols in his youth, and later, upon the arrival of Hülegü in Khurāsān early in 654/1256, he joined the entourage of Hülegü and accompanied the Mongol conqueror on his military campaigns against the Nizārīs. Juwaynī was with the Mongols when they converged on Alamūt and other Nizārī castles in Daylam later in 654 A.H. Having taken part in the peace negotiations between Hülegü and Rukn al-Dīn Khurshāh, it was Juwaynī who drew up the actual terms of surrender of the last Nizārī ruler in Persia. He was also responsible for writing the *Fatḥ-nāma*, or proclamation of victory, declaring the final defeat of the Nizārīs. Having personally witnessed many of the events marking the downfall of the Persian Nizārīs, Juwaynī relates how, with Hülegü's permission, he examined the Ismāʿīlī library at Alamūt, founded in Ḥasan-i Ṣabbāḥ's time, wherefrom he selected many 'choice books', while consigning to the flames those which, according to him, related to the heresy and error of the Nizārīs. Of the latter category, however, he fortunately preserved a work known as the *Sargudhasht-i Sayyidnā*, containing Ḥasan-i Ṣabbāḥ's biography, which he quotes extensively. Juwaynī, who began writing his history of the Mongols around 650/1252 and stopped working on it in 658/1260, composed his account of the Ismāʿīlīs soon after the fall of Alamūt, adding it to the end of the third and final volume of his history. This account is a detailed history of Ḥasan-i Ṣabbāḥ and his seven successors as rulers of the Nizārī state, based on the Nizārī chronicles and other texts and records which Juwaynī found at Alamūt and elsewhere, and which have not survived. Juwaynī's account of the Persian Nizārīs is preceded by sections relating to the earlier history of the Ismāʿīlīs and the Fāṭimid caliph-imāms, a pattern adopted by later Persian historians. Subsequent to the collapse of the Nizārī state, Juwaynī accompanied Hülegü to Baghdād, where the Mongols had proceeded to overthrow the ʿAbbāsid Caliphate. In 657/1259, Hülegü appointed Juwaynī to the governorship of Baghdād and its dependencies; a post Juwaynī maintained for more than twenty years, with the exception of a brief period of dismissal and imprisonment, until his death in 681/1283. The renowned Persian scholar Mīrzā Muḥammad Qazvīnī (1877–1949) undertook, for the E. J. W. Gibb Memorial Series, the monumental edition of the Persian text of Juwaynī's *Taʾrīkh-i jahān-gushāy*, and the late

Professor John Andrew Boyle (1916–1978), a leading authority on the history of the Mongols and its sources, produced an English translation of this work, the first complete translation in a Western language.[3]

The second of our chief Persian authorities on the Nizārīs is the slightly later famous historian, physician and statesman, Rashīd al-Dīn Faḍl Allāh, often referred to by his contemporaries as Rashīd al-Dīn Ṭabīb. Being of Jewish origin, Rashīd al-Dīn converted to Islam and rose in the service of the Mongol Īlkhāns of Persia to the rank of vizier, a position he held for almost twenty years until his execution in 718/1318. In 694/1295, the Īlkhān Ghāzān (694–703/1295–1304) commissioned Rashīd al-Dīn, initially his personal physician and later his vizier, to compile a detailed history of the Mongols. It was at the request of Ghāzān's brother and successor Öljeytü (703–716/1304–1316) that Rashīd al-Dīn subsequently added to his already voluminous work the histories of all the important Eurasian peoples with whom the Mongols had come into contact during their conquests. Thus, on its completion in 710/1310, Rashīd al-Dīn's vast *Jāmiʿ al-tawārīkh* (*Collection of Histories*) had acquired the form in which we know it today, with the distinction of being the very first history of the world written in any language. Rashīd al-Dīn's section on the Ismāʿīlīs, Nizārī and pre-Nizārī, is contained in the second volume of the *Jāmiʿ al-tawārīkh*, the volume which is in fact the first universal history. This Ismāʿīlī section, more detailed than Juwaynī's account, is now available in print.[4]

In writing his own history of the Ismāʿīlīs, Rashīd al-Dīn undoubtedly made use of Juwaynī's work, which he quotes verbatim at some points. In addition, Rashīd al-Dīn seems to have had direct access to the Ismāʿīlī sources available to his predecessor, along with some other sectarian items which he names, whilst also making greater independent use of the Sunnī sources existing in his time. As a result, Rashīd al-Dīn's account of the Ismāʿīlīs is significantly fuller than Juwaynī's. Omitting very little which is found in Juwaynī except the curses, Rashīd al-Dīn quotes more extensively from the Nizārī chronicles and preserves many details ignored by his predecessor. Furthermore, Rashīd al-Dīn, who displays a sense of objectivity not found in other Sunnī historians writing about the Ismāʿīlīs, seems to have utilized his Nizārī texts in the form he had found them. By contrast, Juwaynī wrote with a distinctly anti-Ismāʿīlī bias, often manifesting itself in outright condemnation of the sectarians, a position not incomprehensible for a Sunnī historian aiming to please a master who had almost exterminated the Nizārī Ismāʿīlīs of Persia. Rashīd al-Dīn's closer and fuller treatment of the Ismāʿīlī sources, in contrast to Juwaynī, has continued to puzzle some scholars, since Juwaynī ordered the destruction of the library at Alamūt which he alone apparently utilized for his history. It has also been suggested that perhaps Rashīd al-Dīn used an earlier, fuller draft of Juwaynī's history, which is no longer extant. It is more reasonable to assume, however, that Rashīd al-Dīn found direct access to some of the Ismāʿīlī books which originally belonged to the collections held at fortresses other than Alamūt, or which were possessed by individual Nizārīs; books which had somehow survived the Mongol debacle. It is also possible, as it was one of the methods adopted in compiling the *Jāmiʿ al-tawārīkh*, that Rashīd al-Dīn had personal contact with some Nizārīs who possessed such manuscripts. In this connection, it is interesting to note that Rashīd al-Dīn's grandfather, Muwaffaq al-Dawla ʿAlī, had been at Alamūt for some time as a guest when that fortress surrendered to Hülegü. It is, therefore, not unlikely that Muwaffaq al-Dawla, who was received into Hülegü's service, might have come into the possession of some Ismāʿīlī books, in addition to developing friendly relations with the Nizārīs.

Chronologically, our third major authority on the Nizārīs from amongst the Persian historians of the Mongol period, is Jamāl al-Dīn Abu'l-Qāsim ʿAbd Allāh b. ʿAlī Kāshānī (al-Qāshānī), a relatively unknown chronicler belonging to the Abū Ṭāhir family of leading potters from Kāshān. Few details are known about the life of this Persian Shīʿī historian who also held official posts in Īlkhānid administration. Having served Öljeytü, Kāshānī worked as a secretary in the court of Öljeytü's son and successor Abū Saʿīd (717–736/1317–1335), the last effective member of his dynasty who ordered the execution of Rashīd al-Dīn. It is known that he was associated with Rashīd al-Dīn and most probably worked, under his supervision, on parts of the *Jāmiʿ al-tawārīkh*. Kāshānī claims that he himself was the real author of that work.[5] He died around 738/1337–1338. Kāshānī produced a chronicle of Öljeytü's reign and a general history of the Muslim world to the fall of the ʿAbbāsid Caliphate, entitled the *Zubdat al-tawārīkh*. The latter history, dedicated to Öljeytü and still unpublished, contains a section on the Ismāʿīlīs, following the model of Juwaynī and Rashīd al-Dīn. Kāshānī's history of the Ismāʿīlīs is very similar to Rashīd al-Dīn's account and is probably related to it, especially considering the fact that Kāshānī participated in the compilation of the *Jāmiʿ al-tawārīkh*.[6] The two versions, however, differ at some points, and Kāshānī mentions details missing in both Juwaynī and Rashīd al-Dīn.

Later Persian historians produced summary accounts of Ḥasan-i Ṣabbāḥ and his successors at Alamūt, based mainly on Juwaynī and Rashīd al-Dīn, but also occasionally drawing on sources of legendary origins. Amongst such later Persian authors writing general histories, with a separate section devoted to the Ismāʿīlīs, the earliest and perhaps the most famous one is Ḥamd Allāh Mustawfī Qazwīnī. He was appointed financial director of his native town of Qazwīn and of several neighbouring districts by the vizier Rashīd al-Dīn, his master and patron who encouraged his historical studies. Ḥamd Allāh used Juwaynī, Kāshānī, and especially Rashīd al-Dīn, amongst other authorities mentioned by him, in compiling his *Taʾrīkh-i guzīda*, a general history of Islam and the Islamic dynasties of Persia.[7] This work, completed in 730/1330, was dedicated to Ghiyāth al-Dīn Muḥammad, the son and successor of Rashīd al-Dīn. Ḥamd Allāh died after 740/1339–1340, the year in which he composed, at least partially, his *Nuzhat al-qulūb*, a manual of cosmography and geography. Ḥamd Allāh's contemporary al-Shabānkāraʾī also included a short and hostile account of Ḥasan-i Ṣabbāḥ and his successors in his *Majmaʿ al-ansāb*, a concise general history.[8] This work, too, originally completed in 736/1335–1336, was dedicated to the vizier Ghiyāth al-Dīn Muḥammad. Upon the vizier's death and the pillaging of his house in 736 A.H., however, this history was lost and the author, also a panegyrist at the court of Abū Saʿīd, rewrote it in 743/1342–1343.

Amongst later Persian chroniclers writing on the Ismāʿīlīs, a special place is occupied by ʿAbd Allāh b. Luṭf Allāh b. ʿAbd al-Rashīd al-Bihdādīnī, better known under his *laqab* of Ḥāfiẓ Abrū (d. 833/1430). This Sunnī historian of the Tīmūrid period, who joined the suite of Tīmūr and became the court historian of Tīmūr's son and successor Shāhrukh (807–850/1405–1447), produced several historical and geographical works, based mainly on earlier authorities. In 826/1423, at the request of Bāysunghur (d. 837/1433), Shāhrukh's son and a noteworthy patron of the arts, Ḥāfiẓ Abrū began to compile a vast universal history, the *Majmaʿ al-tawārīkh*, in four volumes or *arbāʿ*. In the third volume of his *Majmaʿ al-tawārīkh*, Ḥāfiẓ Abrū devotes an extensive section to the Fāṭimid caliphs and the history of the Persian Nizārī state, following closely, with certain omissions, the account of Rashīd al-Dīn. Ḥāfiẓ Abrū's account of the Ismāʿīlīs was recently published for the first time.[9] Amongst subsequent Persian chroniclers who produced relatively detailed accounts of the Fāṭimids and the Persian Nizārī rulers, though still less detailed than that of Ḥāfiẓ Abrū, one of the more noteworthy ones, whose general history has been published in numerous extracts in Europe since the earlier decades of the last century, is Muḥammad b. Khwāndshāh, known as Mīrkhwānd (d. 903/1498).[10] The latter's grandson, Ghiyāth al-Dīn b. Humām al-Dīn Muḥammad, surnamed Khwānd Amīr (d. 942/1535–1536), also included a section on the Ismāʿīlīs in his own general history, completed in 930/1524.[11] The Fāṭimids and the Nizārī rulers of Alamūt continued to be treated, to various extents, in the general Persian histories of subsequent times.[12] It should be noted that when discussing the Nizārīs, these Persian historians concern themselves almost exclusively with the history of the Nizārī state in Persia, making only minor references to the Syrian Nizārīs.

There are other historical sources on the Persian Nizārīs of the Alamūt period. Numerous relevant details are contained in the contemporary and near contemporary chronicles of the Saljūqid empire. The earliest Saljūq history with references to the Nizārīs, is the already-noted *Nuṣrat al-fatra*, written in 579/1183 by ʿImād al-Dīn Muḥammad al-Kātib al-Iṣfahānī (d. 597/1201), now extant only in an abridgement, the *Zubdat al-nuṣra*, compiled in 623/1226 by al-Bundārī. There are, too, the *Saljūq-nāma* of Ẓahīr al-Dīn Nīshāpūrī, composed around 580/1184 and used by most of the later chroniclers; a work written around 622/1225 and ascribed to Ṣadr al-Din ʿAlī al-Ḥusaynī;[13] and especially Najm al-Dīn Muḥammad b. ʿAlī al-Rāwandī's *Rāḥat al-ṣudūr*, an important history of the Great Saljūqs completed in 603/1206–1207 and containing many references to the Persian Nizārīs. The mediaeval local histories of the Caspian provinces, starting with Ibn Isfandiyār's *Taʾrīkh-i Ṭabaristān*, written at least partly in 613/1216–1217, provide another category of historical sources on the Nizārīs of northern Persia during the Alamūt and early post-Alamūt periods. Finally, the Persian Nizārīs are treated in many of the general histories of the Arab authors, amongst which the most comprehensive one is *al-Kāmil* of Ibn al-Athīr (d. 630/1233). This chronicle contains much relevant information on the Persian and Syrian Nizārīs, including a short biography of Ḥasan-i Ṣabbāḥ which is independent of the *Sargudhasht-i Sayyidnā*.

The different sources of information on the Syrian Nizārīs have been fully discussed by Bernard Lewis.[14] The Nizārīs of Syria produced their own religious literature in Arabic, during the earliest centuries of their history; and, in contradistinction to the Persian Nizārīs, they also preserved many of the Fāṭimid treatises, including some of the works of al-Qāḍī al-Nuʿmān and Jaʿfar b. Manṣūr al-Yaman. The Persian Nizārī works of the Alamūt period were evidently not translated into Arabic in Syria, and similarly, the sectarian literature originating in Syria was not rendered into Persian. Furthermore, there is no evidence that the Syrian Nizārīs kept chronicles similar to those maintained by their Persian co-religionists, and which were cited by Juwaynī, Rashīd al-Dīn and Kāshānī. Most of what the Syrian Nizārī authors produced independently of the Persian sources, however, has not survived, even though the Nizārīs in Syria were spared the Mongol catastrophe. The literature of the Syrian Nizārīs has been destroyed throughout the centuries in constant entanglements with neighbouring communities, especially the Nuṣayrīs. Amongst the few surviving Nizārī works of Syrian provenance,[15] a significant place is occupied by the anecdotal and legendary biography of Rāshid al-Dīn Sinān, the most famous leader of the Syrian Nizārīs. The surviving archaeological evidence and especially the epigraphic inscriptions of the Syrian Nizārīs at Maṣyāf and elsewhere in the Jabal Bahrā' have also yielded some valuable historical information.[16]

The main literary sources on the history of the Syrian Nizārīs, from the arrival of the first emissaries of Alamūt in Aleppo around the earliest years of the twelfth century A.D. until the complete subjugation of the Nizārī fortresses by the Mamlūks in 671/1273, are the regional histories of Syria and the general Arabic chronicles.[17] Unfortunately however, many of the relevant regional histories have not survived directly or still remain unpublished; only a few have been critically edited. Amongst such authorities whose works are extant, the chief ones are Ibn al-Qalānisī, utilized by most later chroniclers; Kamāl al-Dīn b. al-ʿAdīm (d. 660/1262),[18] the historian of Aleppo; Ibn al-Athīr, who uses several sources no longer extant; and Ibn al-Jawzī's grandson known as Sibṭ Ibn al-Jawzī.[19] There are also some works by lesser-known historians such as Muḥammad b. ʿAlī al-Tanūkhī, known as al-ʿAẓīmī (d. after 556/1161),[20] chronicler of Aleppo, as well as the anonymous *Bustān al-jāmiʿ*, written in the 6th/12th century.[21] Ibn al-ʿAdīm is a valuable source for the biography of Rāshid al-Dīn Sinān, who led the Syrian Nizārīs to the zenith of their power during 557–588/1162–1192.[22] For this period, Ibn Shaddād (d. 632/1235), the biographer of Saladin, is another important primary authority. For the subsequent period, until the accession of Baybars I in 658/1260, aside from Ibn al-ʿAdīm, Ibn al-Athīr and Sibṭ Ibn al-Jawzī, other authorities are Abū Shāma (d. 665/1267) and Ibn Wāṣil (d. 697/1298). Needless to add that these Sunnī historians, writing mainly during the Ayyūbid and Mamlūk periods in Syria, are generally hostile towards the Ismāʿīlīs. The Syrian Nizārīs are also treated in some biographical works, memoirs and travel accounts, amongst other types of non-historical sources. In addition, most of the occidental chroniclers of the Crusaders make some reference to the Syrian Nizārīs. Amongst such writers, William of Tyre was the earliest to have produced a general account of the Syrian Nizārīs, setting the pattern for later descriptions by Europeans.

We have already traced the main steps in the development of Nizārī studies in modern times. As noted, the Westerners had first come into contact with the Nizārī branch of the Ismāʿīlī sect in Syria, through the Crusaders and their occidental chroniclers. Consequently, Western scholars for centuries concentrated their Ismāʿīlī studies on the Nizārīs, under the name of Assassins, reflecting the hostile point of view of the Crusaders and the Sunnī chroniclers. In the early decades of the nineteenth century, de Sacy and Quatremère produced their more scholarly studies of the Nizārīs, using for the first time a large number of Muslim histories, while von Hammer was the first European to devote an entire book, published originally in German in 1818, to the history of the Nizārī state in Persia. This book, displaying obvious hostilities towards the Nizārīs, who are portrayed as a diabolical 'order of assassins', served as the generally accepted interpretation of the Nizārīs until a few decades ago. Meanwhile, the ground was being prepared for more objective studies. Defrémery collected a large number of scattered passages on the Nizārīs, which provided the basis for his two articles on the Nizārīs of Syria and Persia, published during 1854–1860, and in which he summed up the state of knowledge then available to European orientalists. At the same time, some Nizārī texts in Arabic, recovered in Syria, were becoming available to orientalists, mainly through the efforts of Guyard. Soon, more Nizārī texts, written in Persian and preserved by the Central Asian Ismāʿīlīs, were obtained and studied by Russian scholars. However, the distorted image of the Nizārīs, representing the earlier hostile and legendary impressions, was maintained until the commencement of the modern progress in Ismāʿīlī studies in the 1930s.

This progress, made possible by the recovery and study of numerous Ismāʿīlī manuscripts and the publication of an ever increasing number of Muslim chronicles, also affected the Nizārīs. By contrast to the earlier interest of the scholars in the Nizārīs, modern progress in Ismāʿīlī studies came to be centred mainly on Fāṭimid Ismāʿīlism, since by far the greatest number of the Ismāʿīlī texts recovered belong to the Fāṭimid period. Nevertheless, Nizārī studies, too, have been revolutionized. As a result of the recovery and study of the meagre Nizārī literature dating from the Alamūt period and the post-Alamūt works quoting earlier texts, as well as the evidence preserved by the Persian and Arabic chronicles, we now possess a much better knowledge of the history and doctrines of the Nizārīs during the Alamūt period. More than anyone else, W. Ivanow has been responsible for the re-evaluation of the Nizārīs and our understanding of Nizārī Ismāʿīlism of the Alamūt period. Although his interpretations are sometimes arbitrary and his translations suffer from a certain degree of freeness, Ivanow spent a lifetime acquiring, editing and analyzing the extant literature of the Nizārīs, and as such, he is undoubtedly the founder of modern Nizārī studies. Most of the Nizārī texts edited and translated by Ivanow appeared, as previously noted, in the series of publications put out during 1946–1963 by the Ismaili Society in Bombay. This valuable series was not resumed after Ivanow's death. Besides Ivanow, very few modern Islamists and Ismāʿīlī specialists have produced any major work on the Nizārīs. The chief contributor was the late Marshall G. S. Hodgson, who, using Ivanow's works and a host of Ismāʿīlī and non-Ismāʿīlī primary sources, wrote what has remained the standard book on the history and doctrines of the Persian Nizārīs during the Alamūt period, with a shorter treatment of the Syrian Nizārīs.[23] Subsequently, Lewis, known particularly for his studies of the Syrian Nizārīs, and Filippani-Ronconi produced less detailed monographs on the Nizārīs,[24] while Corbin studied some aspects of the Nizārī doctrines. The modern Nizārī community, scattered in many regions including the upper Oxus, India, Pakistan, Afghanistan, Iran, Syria, Lebanon, East Africa, and several countries in the West has not shown too much interest in investigating its history during the Alamūt period; only ʿĀrif Tāmir and the late Muṣṭafā Ghālib, prominent Nizārīs from Syria, have produced some studies related to the Nizārīs of the Alamūt period, in addition to having edited numerous Ismāʿīlī texts. More recently, a number of Nizārī Khojas of India and elsewhere have produced studies dealing with the history of post-Alamūt Indian Nizārism and the various aspects of the modern Nizārī communities of India, Pakistan and East Africa, which do not extend their coverage to the non-Indian Nizārī communities of the Alamūt period.

The Nizārī state in Persia was ruled by Ḥasan-i Ṣabbāḥ and his seven successors, who are commonly referred to as the lords (Persian singular, *khudāwand*) of Alamūt. On the basis of their reigns, as well as their ideologies and policies towards the outside world, the history of Nizārī Ismāʿīlism during the Alamūt period may be subdivided into three main phases.[25] During the initial phase, stretching from the foundation of the Nizārī state in 483/1090 to the end of the rule of Ḥasan-i Ṣabbāḥ's second successor in 557/1162, the Nizārīs succeeded in establishing and consolidating their independent state, after having failed in their initial revolt against the Saljūqs. In the second phase (557–607/1162–1210), coinciding with the reigns of the fourth and fifth lords of Alamūt who claimed the imāmate of the Nizārīs, the Nizārī community symbolically turned to the realm of the Resurrection (*qiyāma*), which also represented a spiritual rejection of the outside world. In the third and final phase (607–654/1210–1256), concurrent with the rules of the last three lords of Alamūt, the Nizārīs, while partially retaining their inwardness and their ideal of the *qiyāma*, attempted a rapprochement with the Sunnī world, and at the same time revived their political aspirations; these endeavours were, however, terminated by the invading Mongols, who destroyed the Nizārī state in Persia.

By the final decades of al-Mustanṣir's imāmate, the Ismāʿīlīs of Persia and elsewhere in the Muslim East had by and large rallied to the side of the Fāṭimid *daʿwa*, centrally directed from Cairo. The success of Fāṭimid Ismāʿīlism in the eastern lands had come about as a result of the activities of numerous Fāṭimid *dāʿīs* operating in those regions over a long period, while at the same time dissident Ismāʿīlism had rapidly begun to lose its appeal due to the declining fortunes of the Qarmaṭīs of Baḥrayn and southern ʿIrāq. Even though the Fāṭimid Caliphate was now beset by numerous difficulties, the Fāṭimid *daʿwa* had not ceased in Persia, as the ardently Sunnī Saljūqs replaced various local dynasties there in Buwayhid times. In fact, the Ismāʿīlī movement had continued to be strong in Persia, where a growing number of converts in different towns as well as amongst the soldiery and the inhabitants of the northern highlands supported the Fāṭimid Ismāʿīlī *daʿwa* and acknowledged al-Mustanṣir as the sole rightful imām of the time. Few details are available on the specific ideas preached at the time in Persia and the adjacent regions by the Fāṭimid *dāʿīs*, who maintained their close contacts with the *daʿwa* headquarters in Cairo. It seems that the *dāʿīs* emphasized existing social injustices while also capitalizing, in a general sense, on the dislike of the Persians for their new Turkish rulers.

The eastern Ismāʿīlīs were not unaware of the declining power of the Fāṭimid Caliphate, and consequently they did not expect to rely on the continued central leadership of the *daʿwa* headquarters in Cairo, although they were not ready to assert their independence from the Fāṭimid regime until after al-Mustanṣir's death. At any rate, for some time prior to the Nizārī–Mustaʿlī schism, the Persian Ismāʿīlīs in the Saljūq territories seem to have owned the authority of a single chief *dāʿī* who had his headquarters at Iṣfahān, the main Saljūq capital. At least by the early 460s/1070s, the *dāʿī* at Iṣfahān was ʿAbd al-Malik b. ʿAṭṭāsh, who headed the Ismāʿīlī movement throughout the central and western regions of Persia, from Kirmān to Ādharbayjān. He may have been responsible for the *daʿwa* activities in some other regions as well; it is not known with certainty, however, whether he provided overall supervision for the *dāʿīs* operating in Khurāsān, Quhistān (Persian, Kūhistān), and ʿIrāq. Ibn ʿAṭṭāsh himself evidently received his general instructions from Cairo; the *dāʿī al-duʿāt* then having been Badr al-Jamālī, who had succeeded to that position in 470/1078 after al-Mu'ayyad al-Shīrāzī. Few details are known about Ibn ʿAṭṭāsh, a learned man who seems to have been respected for his scholarship even in the Sunnī circles. As the *dāʿī* at Iṣfahān, he came to be behind the renewed Ismāʿīlī activities in many parts of the Saljūq dominions; and, significantly enough, he was also responsible for launching the career of Ḥasan-i Ṣabbāḥ in the service of the Ismāʿīlī movement.[26]

On Ḥasan-i Ṣabbāḥ, as noted, we have fragments of an Ismāʿīlī biography, preserved by later Persian historians, the first part of which seems to have been based on his autobiography. According to these quotations from the *Sargudhasht-i Sayyidnā*,[27] Ḥasan was born at Qumm into an Imāmī Shīʿī family. His father, ʿAlī b. Muḥammad b. Jaʿfar b. al-Ḥusayn b. Muḥammad b. al-Ṣabbāḥ al-Ḥimyarī, a Kūfan Arab claiming Yamanī origins, had migrated from the Sawād of Kūfa to the traditionally Shīʿī town of Qumm in Persia. Subsequently, the Ṣabbāḥ family had moved to the nearby city of Rayy, where the youthful Ḥasan received his early religious education as a Twelver Shīʿī. It was at Rayy, a centre of Ismāʿīlī activity, that, soon after the age of seventeen, Ḥasan was introduced to Ismāʿīlī doctrines by a certain Amīra Ḍarrāb, one of the several local Ismāʿīlī propagandists. Until then, Ḥasan had thought of Ismāʿīlism as heretical philosophy, not deserving serious consideration. However, on reading some Ismāʿīlī books and receiving gradual instructions from Amīra Ḍarrāb and other Ismāʿīlī propagandists at Rayy, Ḥasan became convinced of the legitimacy of the imāmate of Ismāʿīl b. Jaʿfar and his successors and was won over by the Fāṭimid Ismāʿīlī *daʿwa*. Thus, he embraced Ismāʿīlism and took the oath of allegiance (*ʿahd*) to al-Mustanṣir, whom he had now come to regard as the rightful imām of the time. In Ramaḍān 464/May–June 1072, the initiated Ḥasan was brought to the attention of the *dāʿī* Ibn ʿAṭṭāsh, who was then visiting Rayy. Ibn ʿAṭṭāsh approved of Ḥasan and evidently recognized his capabilities, appointing him to a post in the *daʿwa* organization. At the same time, Ibn ʿAṭṭāsh urged Ḥasan to proceed to Cairo, probably to further his training as Nāṣir-i Khusraw had done three decades earlier. A few years had to pass, however, before Ḥasan could embark on his journey to the Fāṭimid *daʿwa* headquarters.

The *Sargudhasht-i Sayyidnā* also contained a colourful legend about a schoolfellow vow exchanged by Ḥasan-i Ṣabbāḥ, Niẓām al-Mulk, and ʿUmar Khayyām. This tale was first quoted by Rashīd al-Dīn and then repeated by several later Persian historians.[28] In modern times, the tale has been introduced into the West by Edward FitzGerald (1809–1883) in the introduction to his English rendition of Khayyām's quatrains.[29] It should be added, however, that FitzGerald derived the tale from Mirkhwānd, who had recounted a different version of it based on a spurious work, the *Waṣāyā*, attributed to Niẓām al-Mulk.[30] According to this so-called tale of the three schoolfellows, Ḥasan-i Ṣabbāḥ, Niẓām al-Mulk, and the astronomer-poet ʿUmar Khayyām had been in their youth students of the same master at Nīshāpūr. They made a pact that whichever of them rose to a high position first would help the other two. In due time, Niẓām al-Mulk succeeded to the vizierate in the Saljūq empire, and his schoolfellows now came forth with their claims. Niẓām al-Mulk offered them provincial governorships, which they both refused for different reasons. Khayyām, not desiring public office, contented himself with receiving a regular stipend from the vizier. But the ambitious Ḥasan-i Ṣabbāḥ sought a higher post at the Saljūq court. Ḥasan's wish was granted, and soon he became a serious rival to Niẓām al-Mulk. Consequently, Niẓām al-Mulk plotted against Ḥasan and eventually succeeded in disgracing him before the sultan. Ḥasan was obliged to flee to Rayy and then to Egypt, while contemplating to take his revenge. Suffice it to say that on the account of the age discrepancies of its protagonists, who were also raised in different towns in their youth, most modern scholars have dismissed this tale as a fable.

At any rate, in 467/1074–1075 Ḥasan moved from Rayy to Iṣfahān, the *daʿwa* headquarters in Persia. Subsequently in 469/1076–1077, when al-Mu'ayyad was still the chief *dāʿī* at Cairo, Ḥasan-i Ṣabbāḥ finally set off from Iṣfahān for Egypt with Ibn ʿAṭṭāsh's permission and help. First he travelled north to Ādharbayjān and thence to Mayyāfāriqīn. There, he held religious disputations, refuting the authority of the Sunnī *ʿulamā'* and asserting the exclusive right of the imām to interpret religion. He was expelled by the town's Sunnī *qāḍī*. Ḥasan then proceeded to Mawṣil and

Damascus. In Syria, he found that the land route to Egypt was blocked by the military operations of Atsiz, who had revolted against the Fāṭimids. Ḥasan was, therefore, obliged to turn to the coast, and, travelling through Beirut, Sidon, Tyre, Acre and Caesarea, he sailed to Egypt. He arrived in Cairo in Ṣafar 471/August 1078, and was greeted by high Fāṭimid dignitaries. Almost nothing is known about Ḥasan's experiences in Fāṭimid Egypt, where he stayed for about three years, first in Cairo and then in Alexandria. He did not, however, see al-Mustanṣir. According to later Nizārī sources used by Juwaynī and Rashīd al-Dīn, whilst in Egypt, Ḥasan incurred the jealousy of the all-powerful vizier Badr al-Jamālī, because of his support for Nizār. According to another anachronistic detail of the later sources, cited also by Ibn al-Athīr, al-Mustanṣir personally revealed to Ḥasan that his successor would be Nizār.[31] At any event, eventually Ḥasan seems to have been banished from Egypt to North Africa, but the ship on which he was travelling was wrecked and he was saved and taken to Syria. On the return journey, Ḥasan travelled through Aleppo, Baghdād and Khūzistān, and finally arrived in Iṣfahān in Dhu'l-Ḥijja 473/June 1081.[32]

During the next nine years, Ḥasan-i Ṣabbāḥ travelled extensively in Persia in the service of the *daʿwa*, as related in the fragments of his biography.[33] Initially, he went to Kirmān and Yazd, where he preached Ismāʿīlism for a while. Then, he spent three months in Khūzistān before going to Dāmghān, where he stayed for three years. Gradually Ḥasan had come to realize the difficulties of achieving success in the central and western parts of the country, the centres of Saljūq power. He was now concentrating his attention on the Caspian provinces and the northern highlands of Persia, the general region of Daylam which had traditionally been a safe refuge for the ʿAlids. Daylam, a stronghold of Zaydī Shīʿism, was not only out of the reach of the Saljūqs, but it had also been penetrated by the Ismāʿīlī *daʿwa*. Ḥasan, who had realized that the Persian Ismāʿīlīs could not rely on the Egyptians in their own struggle against the Saljūqs, was then already planning a major revolt and searching for a suitable site to establish his headquarters. At the time, the *daʿwa* in Persia was still under the overall direction of ʿAbd al-Malik b. ʿAṭṭāsh. By around 480/1087–1088, Ḥasan seems to have chosen the remote and inaccessible castle of Alamūt in Daylamān as the best possible stronghold for his revolt. From his initial base at Dāmghān, and then from Shahriyārkūh in Māzandarān, he despatched a number of *dāʿīs*, including Ismāʿīl Qazwīnī, Muḥammad Jamāl Rāzī and Kiyā Abu'l-Qāsim Lārījānī, to various districts around

Alamūt to convert the local inhabitants. Ḥasan, who was eventually appointed *dāʿī* of Daylam, was indeed now reinvigorating the Ismāʿīlī cause in Persia, and his activities did not escape the attention of Niẓām al-Mulk who ordered Abū Muslim, the governor of Rayy and his son-in-law, to arrest him. Abū Muslim, it may be noted, was later assassinated in 488/1095 by a Persian Ismāʿīlī. At any rate, Ḥasan managed to remain in hiding, and, having carefully planned the seizure of Alamūt, he proceeded in due time to Daylamān. Choosing a mountainous route to avoid the authorities at Rayy, he first spent some time at Qazwīn.

At the time of Ḥasan's arrival in Qazwīn, the castle of Alamūt was in the hands of a certain Ḥusaynid ʿAlid called Mahdī, who held it from the sultan Malikshāh. He was a descendant of al-Ḥasan b. ʿAlī al-Uṭrūsh (d. 304/917), one of the ʿAlid rulers of Ṭabaristān and a Zaydī Imām better known under the name of al-Nāṣir li'l-Ḥaqq, who founded the separate Zaydī community of the Nāṣiriyya in the Caspian region.[34] Some of the soldiers under Mahdī's command had already been secretly converted to Ismāʿīlism by Ḥasan's emissaries, notably Ḥusayn Qā'inī; and Mahdī, aiming to dispose of the converts in his garrison, pretended to have accepted the *daʿwa*. From Qazwīn, Ḥasan sent yet another *dāʿī* to Alamūt, who won more converts. Ḥasan also infiltrated the Alamūt area with Ismāʿīlīs from elsewhere. These final preparations were completed by the early months of the year 483 A.H., and thereupon, Ḥasan moved closer to his target, going to Ashkawar and then Anjirūd, adjacent to Alamūt. On the eve of Wednesday the 6th of Rajab 483/4th of September 1090, Ḥasan secretly entered the castle of Alamūt. He lived there for awhile in disguise, calling himself Dihkhudā. In due time, Mahdī learnt of Ḥasan's identity in the castle, realizing that he had been tricked. The bulk of Alamūt's garrison and many of the inhabitants of the surrounding districts had embraced Ismāʿīlism, rendering Mahdī powerless to defend his position. Ḥasan permitted Mahdī to leave peacefully and, according to our Persian chroniclers, gave him a draft for 3,000 gold dinars as the price of the castle. The draft, drawn on the *ra'īs* Muẓaffar, the future governor of Girdkūh and Dāmghān and a secret convert to Ismāʿīlism, was honoured in due time, to Mahdī's astonishment.[35]

The seizure of Alamūt in 483/1090, marking the effective foundation of what was to become the Nizārī state, initiated a new phase in the activities of the Persian Ismāʿīlīs who had hitherto operated clandestinely. Henceforth, the *daʿwa* in Persia adopted a new policy of open revolt aimed at the heart of the Saljūq regime, and the capture of Alamūt represented the first blow in that Ismāʿīlī revolt. The fortress of Alamūt in Daylamān was situated about thirty-five kilometres northeast of Qazwīn in the region of Rūdbār, named after the river Shāhrūd flowing through it. The region, as noted earlier, was the traditional seat of the Justānid rulers of Daylam, one of whom is said to have constructed the castle of Alamūt in 246/860. Subsequently, the area came under the influence of the Musāfirids and the castle was held for some time by the Zaydī ʿAlids until its capture by the Ismāʿīlīs. According to legend, an eagle had indicated the site to a Daylamī ruler whence its name of Alamūt in the Daylamī dialect, derived from *āluh* (eagle) and *āmū(kh)t* (taught).[36] The fortress itself, constructed on the top of a high piercing rock before the massive Hawdigān range in the central Alburz mountains, dominated a fertile valley surrounded by mountains on all sides; at present, the rock of Alamūt is next to the village of Gāzurkhān. Access to the fortress was evidently possible only through a narrow, steep and winding path on the northern face of the Alamūt rock. The fortress was truly impregnable and it was evidently never taken by force. Ḥasan immediately embarked on the task of renovating the castle, which was in great need of repair, improving its fortifications, storage facilities and water supply sources. He also improved and extended the systems of irrigation and cultivation of crops in the Alamūt valley, where many trees were planted.[37]

Once Ḥasan-i Ṣabbāḥ was firmly established at Alamūt, he despatched *dāʿī*s and agents in various directions to spread the *daʿwa*, which after his death came to be called the new preaching (Persian, *daʿwat-i jadīd*). His immediate objectives, however, were to convert the rest of Rūdbār and to gain possession of more castles in the neighbourhood of his headquarters. He exerted every effort to capture, by conversion or assault, the places adjacent to Alamūt or in its vicinity; he took such castles as he could and wherever he found a suitable rock he built a castle upon it. Soon, Ḥasan's headquarters came to be raided by the Saljūq forces under the command of the nearest military lord, a certain *amīr* Yūrun Tāsh, who held the district of Alamūt as his *iqṭāʿ* granted by the Saljūq sultan. He constantly attacked the foot of Alamūt and massacred the Ismāʿīlīs of the area. As the store of provisions was still inadequate in Alamūt, its occupants were reduced to great distress and they suggested abandoning the fortress. Ḥasan, however, persuaded the garrison to continue resisting, claiming to have received a special message from the Imām al-Mustanṣir, who promised them good fortune. For this reason, Alamūt was to be called *baldat al-iqbāl*, or the city of good fortune. Meanwhile, Sanamkūh, near Abhar in the mountains to the west of Qazwīn, was taken by the Ismāʿīlīs; and in 484/1091–1092, Ḥasan sent Ḥusayn Qā'inī, a capable *dāʿī* who had played a prominent role in the capture of Alamūt, to his native Quhistān to spread the *daʿwa* there. Quhistān, a barren region in the south of Khurāsān, was to become another major area of Ismāʿīlī activity in Persia. In both Daylam and Quhistān, the Ismāʿīlī *daʿwa* found suitable ground due to previous Shīʿī traditions. In eastern Persia, the situation was even more favourable. The Quhistānīs were highly discontented with the oppressive, alien rule of a local Saljūq agent. Consequently, the Ismāʿīlī *daʿwa* in Quhistān did not merely unfold in terms of secret conversion of the populace and the capture of the existing castles, but it erupted into what amounted to a popular rising. The *daʿwa* met with immediate success in Quhistān, and in many parts of that region the Ismāʿīlīs, who were placed under the authority of a deputy appointed by Ḥasan, rose in open revolt, seizing control of several main towns in eastern Quhistān, such as Ṭabas, Qā'in, Zūzan and Tūn. In eastern Quhistān, as in Rūdbār, the Ismāʿīlīs had thus succeeded in asserting their local independence from the Saljūqs. The Persian Ismāʿīlīs had now virtually founded an independent territorial state of their own.[38]

Upon realizing that the local Saljūq agents could not check the Ismāʿīlī menace, Malikshāh decided early in 485/1092, probably on the advice of his vizier Niẓām al-Mulk, to send armies against the Ismāʿīlī of Rūdbār and Quhistān. The Rūdbār expedition, led by the *amīr* Arslān Tāsh, reached Alamūt in Jumādā I 485 A.H. At the time, Ḥasan-i Ṣabbāḥ had with him only about seventy men with limited supplies. Besieged by the Saljūq forces, he appealed for help to one of his *dāʿīs*, a certain Dihdār Abū ʿAlī Ardistānī, who resided in Qazwīn and had converted many people there, as well as in Ṭāliqān, Rayy and elsewhere. The *dāʿī* gathered a force of 300 Ismāʿīlīs who threw themselves into Alamūt, bringing the needed supplies. The reinforced Alamūt garrison, supported by some of the local converts in Rūdbār, made a surprise attack one evening at the end of Shaʿban 485/September–October 1092, and routed the army of Arslān Tāsh, forcing the Saljūqs to withdraw from Alamūt. Meanwhile, the Quhistān expedition under Qizil Sāriq, who was supported by extra troops from Khurāsān to the north and from Sīstān to the south, had apparently concentrated its attacks on the Ismāʿīlī castle of Dara, one of the dependencies of Mu'minābād and close to the border of Sīstān.[39] Whilst the Saljūqs were contemplating further plans against Rūdbār, the Ismāʿīlīs achieved their first great success in what was to become one of their important techniques of struggle, the assassination of prominent enemies. The chosen victim was the all-powerful Saljūq vizier Abū ʿAlī al-Ḥasan b. ʿAlī al-Ṭūsī, carrying the honorific title of Niẓām al-Mulk, an ardent enemy of Ḥasan-i Ṣabbāḥ and the Ismāʿīlīs. On 12 Ramaḍān 485/16 October 1092, whilst Niẓām al-Mulk was accompanying Malikshāh to Baghdād, at Ṣaḥna in the district of Nahāwand in western Persia, the vizier was stabbed and killed by an Ismāʿīlī volunteer for the mission.[40] The assassin, a certain Abū Ṭāhir Arrānī, was the first Ismāʿīlī *fidāʾī* (*fidāwī*) or devotee to risk his life in the service of the *daʿwa*.

At any rate, when Malikshāh himself died shortly afterwards in Shawwāl 485/November 1092, the pending Saljūq plans for renewed action against Alamūt were abandoned. At the same time, on receiving the news of the sultan's death, the Quhistān expedition, which had failed to take Dara from the Ismāʿīlīs, dispersed, as the Saljūq forces traditionally owed their allegiance to the person of the ruler. On Malikshāh's death, the Saljūq empire was thrown into civil war and internal confusion, which lasted for more than a decade, marked by disunity among Malikshāh's sons and the constant shifting of alliances among the Saljūq *amīr*s who controlled various provinces in an independent fashion. Now there were rival claimants to the Saljūq sultanate, of whom the most prominent one was Malikshāh's eldest son Barkiyāruq. While Malikshāh's four-year-old son Maḥmūd had immediately been proclaimed as sultan, Barkiyāruq, who initially enjoyed the support of the rival party of the Niẓāmiyya, consisting of the murdered vizier's relatives and partisans, was taken to Rayy where he was placed on the throne. Maḥmūd died in 487/1094, and Barkiyāruq was recognized by the new ʿAbbāsid caliph al-Mustaẓhir in Baghdād, the caliphal arbitration having already become a significant factor in the succession to the Saljūq sultanate. Barkiyāruq's chief rivals came to be his uncle Tutush, who held Syria as his appanage, and his half-brother Muḥammad Tapar. Tutush was soon killed in battle at Rayy in 488/1095, while Barkiyāruq, whose seat of power was in western Persia and ʿIrāq, fought a series of indecisive battles with Muḥammad Tapar, who received much help from his brother Sanjar, the ruler of Khurāsān and Tukhāristān from 490/1097 onwards. On occasions when his fortunes were low, Barkiyāruq, who never enjoyed the reputation of being a strong defender of Sunnism, accepted Ismāʿīlīs in his army. On one such occasion in 493/1100, when he was fighting his brother, Barkiyāruq is said to have received 5,000 Ismāʿīlīs into his army. However, Barkiyāruq eventually purged the Ismāʿīlīs from his forces, and, towards the end of his reign, encouraged the persecution of the Ismāʿīlīs in his territories. Peace was restored to the Saljūq dominion only on Barkiyāruq's death in 498/1105, when Muḥammad Tapar became the undisputed sultan and Sanjar remained at Balkh as his viceroy in the east.

During this period of civil war, when the Saljūq armies were quarrelling among themselves, the Ismāʿīlīs of Persia took advantage of the prevailing disorders to consolidate and extend their position, perhaps finding more sympathy for their message of resistance against the alien and oppressive Turkish rulers. The Ismāʿīlīs already held a number of fortresses in Daylam besides Alamūt, and controlled a group of towns and castles in Quhistān. They now began to seize more fortresses in widely scattered but still relatively inaccessible places. They extended their activities from the western to the central and eastern parts of the Alburz range, taking the fortresses of Manṣūrakūh and probably also Mihrīn (Mihrnigār) to the north of Dāmghān, and Ustūnāwand in the district of Damāwand.[41] Around the same time, the Ismāʿīlīs took possession of one of their most important strongholds, Girdkūh, in the same mediaeval Persian province of Qūmis. The fortress, built on a high rock, some fifteen kilometres northwest of Dāmghān, was situated strategically in the Alburz chain along the main route between western Persia and Khurāsān. The *ra'īs* Mu'ayyad al-Dīn Muẓaffar b. Aḥmad al-Mustawfī, who was well-connected among the Saljūq officers at Iṣfahān and who had been secretly converted to Ismāʿīlism by ʿAbd al-Malik b. ʿAṭṭāsh himself, persuaded his superior the Saljūq *amīr* Amīrdād Ḥabashī to acquire Girdkūh from Barkiyāruq and to install him there as his lieutenant. The sultan granted the request, and Ḥabashī acquired the castle, after forcing its reluctant Saljūq commandant to surrender in 489/1096. Thereupon, Ḥabashī appointed the *ra'īs* Muẓaffar as his lieutenant in Girdkūh. Muẓaffar, who still posed as a loyal Saljūq officer, immediately proceeded to make Girdkūh as self-sufficient as possible. It is reported that he had an extremely deep well dug in the solid rock of Girdkūh without reaching water, but years later, after an earthquake, a spring gushed out in that well. It was near Girdkūh that Muẓaffar, with 5,000 Ismāʿīlīs coming from Quhistān and other places, fought on the side of Ḥabashī and Barkiyāruq against the forces of Sanjar in 493/1100. However the Ismāʿīlīs failed to win the day for Barkiyāruq and Muẓaffar's patron, Ḥabashī, was killed in battle. Nevertheless, Muẓaffar succeeded in transferring Ḥabashī's treasures to Girdkūh, and some time later, having completed the fortification of the castle, openly declared himself an Ismāʿīlī. He stayed in

Girdkūh a long time, taking orders from Ḥasan-i Ṣabbāḥ and rendering valuable service to the Ismāʿīlī cause in Persia. The *raʾīs* Muẓaffar was succeeded in Girdkūh by his son, Sharaf al-Dīn Muḥammad, a learned man who had earlier spent some time in Alamūt.[42]

The Ismāʿīlīs had now also come to direct their attention to a new area in the Zagros range, especially the border region between the provinces of Khūzistān and Fārs in southwestern Persia. The Ismāʿīlī leader in this mountainous area was the *dāʿī* Abū Ḥamza, a shoemaker from Arrajān, who, like Ḥasan-i Ṣabbāḥ, had spent some time in Egypt. He seized at least two fortresses near the town of Arrajān and used them as bases for further Ismāʿīlī activity.[43] The Ismāʿīlī *daʿwa* spread to many towns and non-mountainous regions in the Saljūq empire, often with the temporary support of various Turkish *amīrs*. The Nizārīs achieved particular success in Kirmān, for instance, and even managed to win the local Saljūq ruler Bahāʾ al-Dawla Īrānshāh b. Tūrānshāh (490–494/1097–1101), to their side; but the Sunnī *ʿulamāʾ* of Kirmān soon aroused the townspeople against Īrānshāh and had him deposed and killed.[44] In 488/1095, a Saljūq vizier, al-Balāsānī, who himself adhered to Imāmī Shīʿism, entrusted the town of Takrīt on the Tigris north of Baghdād to an Ismāʿīlī officer, Kayqubād Daylamī. The Ismāʿīlīs held the citadel of Takrīt, one of their few open strongholds, for twelve years; while the vizier who had given it to them was later accused of Ismāʿīlism and lynched by the Saljūq officers.[45]

Meanwhile, in Rūdbār, where the centre of Nizārī Ismāʿīlī power was to be located, the sectarians were rapidly consolidating their position, profiting from the continuing Saljūq quarrels. Ḥasan-i Ṣabbāḥ systematically made Alamūt as impregnable as possible, ready to withstand an indefinite siege, while capturing several other fortresses in Rūdbār, often with the co-operation of the local leaders, who were assisted by the Ismāʿīlīs against domination from Rayy or Qazwīn. In 486/1093, the Ismāʿīlīs took the village of Anjirūd, repelling a force gathered there against them. In the same year, they defeated in Ṭāliqān an army of 10,000, consisting mainly of the Sunnī inhabitants of Rayy, led by Abū Muḥammad Zaʿfarānī, a leading Ḥanafī scholar from Rayy.[46] Soon afterwards, the Ismāʿīlīs of Rūdbār beat off another raid led by the *amīr* Nūshtagīn. With these Ismāʿīlī victories, the local chiefs in Daylam gradually submitted themselves to Ḥasan-i Ṣabbāḥ and received his help in time of need. Ḥasan thus prepared the way for seizing Lamasar, also called Lambasar and Lanbasar, in the Rūdbār district of the upper Shāhrūd, tributary of the Safīdrūd, about forty kilometres northeast of Qazwīn and west of

1 The rock of Alamūt

2 Some fortifications on the rock of Alamūt

3 General view of the rock and castle of Lamasar

4 The castle of Shamīrān

5 The rock of Girdkūh

6 The castle of Mihrīn (Mihrnigār)

Alamūt. Lamasar was then held by a certain Rasāmūj and his relatives, who after submitting to Ḥasan-i Ṣabbāḥ had rebelled and repudiated their agreement with the Ismāʿīlīs, wanting to entrust the castle to the Saljūq *amīr* Nūshtagīn. Ḥasan now sent Kiyā Buzurg-Ummīd along with three other Ismāʿīlī chiefs, Kiyā Abū Jaʿfar, Kiyā Abū ʿAlī and Kiyā Garshāsb, to Lamasar; they assaulted the castle in Dhu'l-Qaʿda 489/November 1096, or in 495/1102 according to Juwaynī. Ḥasan appointed Buzurg-Ummīd as the governor of Lamasar, the largest castle held by the Nizārīs. Using local labour, Buzurg-Ummīd rebuilt Lamasar into a major stronghold, equipping it with ample water resources and cisterns, which are still in existence, and fine buildings and gardens. Lamasar's position guarded the western approaches to Alamūt from the Shāhrūd valley and it considerably enhanced the power of the Ismāʿīlīs in the Rūdbār area. Buzurg-Ummīd stayed at Lamasar, the second most important unit in the network of the Nizārī castles in Daylam, for more than twenty years until he was summoned by Ḥasan-i Ṣabbāḥ to succeed him.[47]

In the meantime, as the Ismāʿīlī revolt was successfully unfolding in Persia, Ismāʿīlism suffered its greatest internal conflict. In 487/1094, the caliph-imām al-Mustanṣir died in Cairo after a long and eventful reign, leaving a disputed succession. The vizier al-Afḍal moved quickly and placed the youthful al-Mustaʿlī on the Fāṭimid throne, depriving his elder brother Nizār of his succession rights. Al-Mustanṣir, as we have seen, had originally designated his eldest son Nizār as heir and had not subsequently revoked his *naṣṣ* for him. Al-Mustaʿlī was acknowledged as his father's successor by the Egyptian Ismāʿīlīs, a good portion of the Syrian Ismāʿīlīs, as well as the Ismāʿīlī communities in Yaman and western India; that is, by those Ismāʿīlīs under the direct influence of the Fāṭimid regime. By contrast, the Ismāʿīlīs of the Saljūq dominions, notably those of Persia and ʿIrāq and a faction of the Syrian Ismāʿīlīs, refused to recognize al-Mustaʿlī's imāmate. Upholding al-Mustanṣir's initial *naṣṣ*, they acknowledged Nizār as their nineteenth imām. The Persian Ismāʿīlīs in particular, who had already revolted against the Saljūqs and had weakened their relations with the Fāṭimid regime, now completely severed their ties with the Fāṭimid Ismāʿīlī *daʿwa* headquarters in Cairo.

These rebel eastern Ismāʿīlīs had now in effect founded the independent Nizārī *daʿwa*. Soon, Ḥasan-i Ṣabbāḥ, who eventually succeeded ʿAbd al-Malik b. ʿAṭṭāsh as the leader of the Ismāʿīlī movement within the Saljūq realm, came to be recognized as the head of the Nizārī *daʿwa*. The Nizārī *daʿwa* seems to have been largely restricted to the Saljūq domains, having succeeded the Fāṭimid *daʿwa* in the Saljūq empire. The farthest eastern regions in the Ismāʿīlī world, notably Ghazna and the Oxus valley, where evidently independent *dāʿīs* like Nāṣir-i Khusraw had been active in al-Mustanṣir's time, remained for a long time outside the sphere of influence of the Nizārī movement. In Syria, both the Nizārī and the Mustaʿlian wings of the movement continued for some time to be present in rivalry with one another. Tutush's son Riḍwān, the Saljūq ruler of Aleppo, briefly accepted the suzerainty of al-Mustaʿlī; and we have evidence, in such works as al-Āmir's epistle *al-Hidāya*, on the disputations between the Nizārīs and the Mustaʿlians of Damascus. However, the Nizārī *daʿwa* soon gained the upper hand in Syria, especially in Aleppo and in the Jazr, a group of towns in northern Syria. By the time of al-Āmir's death, the Syrian Ismāʿīlīs had by and large acknowledged the Nizārī *daʿwa*, and the Mustaʿlian Ismāʿīlīs, who themselves were subsequently subdivided into the Ṭayyibiyya and the Ḥāfiẓiyya, were reduced to insignificance there. In the eastern lands, the more active Nizārī *daʿwa* with its revolutionary ideals had greater success than the conservative Mustaʿlian *daʿwa* of the remote and the then rapidly declining Fāṭimid regime. It managed to win an increasing number of new converts, especially from amongst the various non-Ismāʿīlī Shīʿī groups of Persia, ʿIrāq and Syria.

The eastern Ismāʿīlīs, who after the Nizārī–Mustaʿlī schism became known as the Nizāriyya and who had already drifted away from the Fāṭimid headquarters, also had a doctrinal justification for their breach with Cairo. They adhered to al-Mustanṣir's original *naṣṣ* in Nizār's favour, refusing to accept the claims made on behalf of al-Mustaʿlī, just as the earliest Ismāʿīlīs had supported Ismāʿīl's rights to the imāmate against those of his brothers. The Nizārīs thus argued, perhaps retrospectively, that any subsequent *naṣṣ* of al-Mustanṣir for al-Mustaʿlī, even if it had actually occurred, could not have superseded the imām's first designation for his successor, reminiscent of the doctrinal point established by the earliest Ismāʿīlīs to the effect that the imāmate could no longer be transferred between brothers after the case of al-Ḥasan and al-Ḥusayn b. ʿAlī. The Nizārīs, in fact, later came to recognize al-Ḥasan only as a *mustawdaʿ* or temporary imām, since the imāmate had not continued in his progeny, while considering al-Ḥusayn as the *mustaqarr* imām and counting him as the second imām after ʿAlī in the line of imāms recognized by them.

The Nizārīs soon came to confront a major difficulty, like the Mustaʿlians of a generation later. The Nizārīs had acknowledged Nizār as their true imām after al-Mustanṣir. But a year later, by the end of 488/1095, Nizār's revolt had been crushed in Egypt and he was immured, on al-Mustaʿlī's orders, in a Cairo prison. It is a historical fact that Nizār did have male progeny. Some of these Nizārids even launched unsuccessful revolts against the later Fāṭimids from their base in the Maghrib.[48] However, Nizār does not seem to have designated any of his sons as his successor. As a result, about a year after al-Mustanṣir's death, the Nizārīs were left without an accessible imām as their leader. Doubtless, many Nizārīs must have wondered about the identity of their imām after Nizār. Before long, as related by our Persian historians, many came to hold the belief that a son or grandson of Nizār had been smuggled from Egypt to Alamūt and was kept there secretly; while al-Āmir's epistle *al-Hidāya al-Āmiriyya*, sent to the Mustaʿlians of Syria, ridicules this idea.[49] At any rate, no account seems to have been taken of the presence of any Nizārid in Alamūt during Ḥasan-i Ṣabbāḥ's time. It is also interesting to note in this connection that the Nizārī coins minted during the reign of Muḥammad b. Buzurg-Ummīd (532–557/1138–1162), Ḥasan-i Ṣabbāḥ's second successor, simply mention the name of Nizār himself, blessing his descendants anonymously.[50] It was later that a Nizārid Fāṭimid genealogy was claimed for the lords of Alamūt succeeding Muḥammad b. Buzurg-Ummīd.

At any event, Ḥasan-i Ṣabbāḥ and his next two successors at Alamūt did not name any imāms after Nizār. In the absence of a manifest imām, it seems that Ḥasan-i Ṣabbāḥ, as the supreme head of the Nizārī *daʿwa*, was eventually recognized as the *ḥujja* of the imām. The term *ḥujja*, or proof, had already been used as a high ranking position in the Fāṭimid *daʿwa* organization, while the bulk of the early Ismāʿīlīs had evidently regarded the central leaders of the Ismāʿīlī movement as the *ḥujja*s of the concealed Muḥammad b. Ismāʿīl, who was to reappear as their expected Qā'im. On the basis of this tradition, it was held that in the time of the imām's concealment his *ḥujja* would represent him amongst his followers. In line with this usage, Ḥasan came to be regarded as the imām's full representative and living proof or *ḥujja* in the Nizārī community, acting as the custodian of the Nizārī *daʿwa* until the time of the imām's reappearance, when Ḥasan was expected to identify the imām for the faithful. Indeed, in the earliest extant Nizārī treatise, written around 596 A.H. by an anonymous author, Ḥasan-i Ṣabbāḥ is said to have predicted the imminent coming of the Qā'im while he himself is given the rank of *ḥujja* of the Qā'im.[51] According to Hodgson, it was perhaps due to a misunderstanding of Ḥasan's rank as the *ḥujja* of the inaccessible imām that the outsiders and even some Nizārīs came to believe that Ḥasan had concealed the imām in Alamūt,[52] a belief reflected in later Nizārī traditions. This interpretation of Ḥasan's rank as *ḥujja* was probably adopted when he became the leader of the Ismāʿīlī movement in the Saljūq territories, in succession to Ibn ʿAṭṭāsh, not long after the Nizārī–Mustaʿlī schism.

The Nizārī revolt had certain characteristic features which manifested themselves from the very beginning, giving the revolt its own distinctive pattern and methods of struggle.[53] Many Islamic movements, both Shīʿī and non-Shīʿī, adopted as their model the Prophet's emigration from Mecca to Medina and set up in a similar fashion a *dār al-hijra*, a place of emigration or refuge as headquarters for their campaign from which to return victoriously into the Muslim society at large. For instance, Khurāsān provided such a *dār al-hijra* for the ʿAbbāsids against the Umayyad regime, while the early Ismāʿīlīs had established *dār al-hijra*s of their own, for more limited purposes, in ʿIrāq, Baḥrayn and Yaman. Under the changed circumstances of the Saljūq period, however, the Nizārīs realistically aimed at acquiring a score of *dār al-hijra*s, rather than a single fixed base of operation. Every stronghold which could be seized by local Ismāʿīlī groups now became a *dār al-hijra* for the Ismāʿīlīs of the Saljūq lands. But the multiplicity of such places in effect formed a single coherent society unified in its ultimate purposes and ideology; if one of them was lost to the enemy, its occupants could readily find refuge in another *dār al-hijra*. In this network, each stronghold was at once a defensible place of refuge and headquarters for conducting local operations, serving as nucleus for the armed groups of Ismāʿīlīs who could raid the surrounding lands. The very leadership of the Ismāʿīlī revolt in the Saljūq domains, at least in its initial phase, seems to have been as decentralized as the sites of the revolt. For instance, after Ibn ʿAṭṭāsh's death, the *dāʿī* of Iṣfahān, originally the supreme leader of the Ismāʿīlī movement in the greater part of the Saljūq realm, does not seem to have had any precedence over the *dāʿī* of Daylam. But the *dāʿī*s operating somewhat independently in different regions did co-operate with one another. At any rate, the Nizārī revolt soon acquired its distinctive pattern marked precisely by its co-ordinated decentralization which was very appropriate to the times.

After Malikshāh, there was no longer a single all-powerful Saljūq ruler to be overthrown by a strong army, even if such an army could be mobilized by the Ismāʿīlīs. Even before Malikshāh's death, when the central Saljūq regime was still essentially intact, socio-political power in the Saljūq empire had come to be increasingly localized in the hands of numerous military and religious leaders; leaders who were virtually equal and autonomous as loyal but independent Saljūq vassals. Under these circumstances, when the central Saljūq bureaucracy was decaying and losing control over innumerable areas which had been parcelled out as *iqṭāʿ* assignments to individual *amīr*s and commanders of garrisons, the strategy best suited to the objectives of a rebellious movement had also to be decentralized. The Persian Ismāʿīlīs adopted precisely such a piecemeal strategy in their efforts to subdue the Saljūq domains, locality by locality, stronghold by stronghold, and leader by leader. In the regime of the many *amīr*s, there scarcely existed a major or central target for military conquest by a regularly recruited army as had been the case in the Fāṭimid conquest of Egypt. Consequently, the Nizārī revolt was based on the seizure of a host of strongholds from where a multiplicity of simultaneous risings could be launched throughout the Saljūq realm, so as to overwhelm the existing decentralized socio-political structure from within. These co-ordinated local efforts of the Ismāʿīlīs would ultimately free the whole society from the unjust rule of the Turks and prepare the way for the rule of the Ismāʿīlī Imām, the sole legitimate leader of mankind. There were Ismāʿīlī cells in many towns and localities of the Saljūq empire even prior to the Nizārī–Mustaʿlī schism; these cells often served as nuclei for armed groups which seized key mountain fortresses as *dār al-hijra*s and bases for further operations. In some cases, however, the fortresses were acquired through the submission of their commandants who needed the assistance of the Ismāʿīlīs in their own factional fights. Indeed, if circumstances required, the Ismāʿīlīs openly helped one Saljūq *amīr* against another, always considering the overall benefits of such alliances in the cause of their own revolt.

The same atomization of established power suggested to the Nizārī Ismāʿīlīs the use of an important auxiliary technique for achieving military and political aims, the technique of assassination in connection with which so many anti-Nizārī legends have circulated throughout the centuries. Many earlier Muslim sects, including the Khārijīs and some Shīʿī Ghulāt groups like the Mughīriyya and the Manṣūriyya, had used assassination as a technique in their struggle against religio-political opponents. And at the time of the Nizārī revolt, when authority was distributed locally and on a personal basis, assassination was commonly resorted to by all factions. This method of eliminating individual enemies has continued to be utilized by various Muslim and non-Muslim groups up to the present time. But it was the Nizārīs who assigned to assassination a major political role in their methods of struggle. Initially, it seems that the Nizārīs utilized assassination as an occasional convenience, as did other groups. But soon, with the commencement of their all-out struggle against the much more powerful Saljūqs, they began to make a relatively systematic and open use of it. The Nizārīs did not use assassination, or the threat of it, against all of their enemies; but they did use it often enough so that almost any such attempt was normally attributed to them.

Doubtless, accepting a mission to kill a notorious military or civilian figure normally surrounded by guards, and with very slim chances of surviving, was glorified as heroic by the Nizārīs. The Nizārīs praised the courage and devotion of their *fidāʾīs*, the young self-sacrificing devotees of the sect who offered themselves for such suicidal missions;[54] evidently rolls of honour of their names and assassination missions were kept at Alamūt and other fortresses.[55] The assassination of single prominent individuals who caused the Nizārīs special damage, often served to eliminate bloodshed among many ordinary men on battlefield. Consequently, the Nizārīs presumably saw even a humane justification for their assassinations. The assassinations were performed in as public a setting as possible, since part of the purpose was to intimidate other actual or potential enemies.

Few details are known about the selection and training of the Nizārī *fidāʾīs*. However, contrary to the mediaeval legends fabricated by uninformed writers and the enemies of the sect, there is no evidence that *ḥashīsh* was used in any way for motivating the *fidāʾīs* who displayed an intensive group sentiment and solidarity. It is doubtful whether the *fidāʾīs* formed a special corps at the beginning, although towards the end of the Nizārī state in Persia they probably did.[56] At the time of Niẓām al-Mulk's assassination and probably until much later, all the ordinary Persian Ismāʿīlīs, who referred to one another as *rafīq* (plural, *rafīqān*) or comrade, were presumably ready in principle to perform any task in the cause of the *daʿwa*. But it is safe to assume that some Ismāʿīlīs held themselves in special readiness for such risky missions. At any event, the *fidāʾīs* do not seem to have received special training in languages, etc., as suggested by some occidental chroniclers of the Crusaders and later European authors. At some point in the history of the Nizārī state, the practice allegedly also arose of sending the would-be assassins to insinuate themselves into the households of different dignitaries as servants. These undercover *fidāʾīs* would be in an ideal position to carry out their assassination missions if and when the necessity arose. As noted, the Persian Ismāʿīlīs intervened militarily in non-Ismāʿīlī factional disputes during the initial decades of their open revolt. It seems that from an early date they also used their assassinations for the benefit of their non-Ismāʿīlī allies. The Nizārī assassinations were for the most part aimed at those military or civilian men who had acted against the Nizārī *dār al-hijra*s or had in some way posed serious threats to the success of the Nizārī *daʿwa* and the survival of the community in specific localities.

The assassinations were soon countered by the massacres of the Ismāʿīlīs. The assassination of a Saljūq *amīr* or a Sunnī *qāḍī*, who had initiated action against the Ismāʿīlīs, would often rouse the Sunnī population of a town to gather all those suspected, or accused by private enemies, of being Ismāʿīlīs, and to kill them. Around 486/1093, the people of Iṣfahān, apparently moved by a report that a certain Ismāʿīlī couple had been luring passers-by into their house and torturing them to death, rounded up all the Ismāʿīlī suspects and threw them alive into a large bonfire in the centre of the town.[57] And in 494/1101, Barkiyāruq and Sanjar, who could not tolerate the revolutionary, anti-Saljūq movement of the Persian Nizārīs, came to an agreement for eliminating the Ismāʿīlīs of their respective regions. Sanjar sent the *amīr* Bazghash against the Ismāʿīlīs of Quhistān. This expedition caused much devastation, and three years later, another Saljūq expedition destroyed Ṭabas, killing many Ismāʿīlīs in the region.[58] However, the Ismāʿīlīs of Quhistān maintained their position, and in 498/1104–1105 the Ismāʿīlīs of Turshīz were able to launch attacks as far west as Rayy.[59] At the same time, Barkiyāruq ordered a second massacre of the Ismāʿīlīs of Iṣfahān in 494 A.H. The massacres, in turn, provoked assassinations of their instigators, which led to further massacres. It was under such circumstances that the Nizārīs came to be called by derogatory terms such as *malāḥida*, or heretics, and *ḥashīshiyya*, or smokers of *ḥashīsh*; names indicating strongly anti-Nizārī feelings.

Despite the repressions and massacres, the Nizārī fortunes continued to rise in Persia during the turbulent years of Barkiyāruq's reign, especially after 489/1096. Not only were the Nizārīs seizing strongholds and consolidating their position in Rūdbār, Qūmis and Quhistān, as well as in many other mountainous areas, but they were spreading the *daʿwa* in numerous towns and had begun to intervene directly in Saljūq affairs. Encouraged by their success, the Nizārīs now directed their attention closer to the seat of the Saljūq power, against Iṣfahān. The Ismāʿīlī *dāʿī*s had been at work in Iṣfahān for several decades, and, as noted, ʿAbd al-Malik b. ʿAṭṭāsh, the chief *dāʿī* in western Persia and ʿIrāq, had established his headquarters in that city. Taking advantage of the factional fights amongst the Saljūqs, they now intensified their activities in and around Iṣfahān. In this area, the Nizārīs, under the leadership of Aḥmad Ibn ʿAṭṭāsh, the son of ʿAbd al-Malik, achieved their greatest success by seizing the important fortress of Shāhdiz, situated on a mountain about eight kilometres to the south of Iṣfahān.[60] Aḥmad, who eventually succeeded his father as the *dāʿī* of Iṣfahān, had been secretly propagating Ismāʿīlism in the very centre of the Saljūq sultanate in Persia. According to Saljūqid chroniclers, Aḥmad set himself up as a schoolmaster for the children of the garrison of Shāhdiz, which was composed mostly of Daylamī soldiers with Shīʿī tendencies. Shāhdiz, which was evidently called Dizkūh in earlier times, had been rebuilt by Malikshāh as a key military fortress for guarding the routes to the Saljūq capital. Aḥmad gradually converted the Shāhdiz garrison, and by 494/1100, gained possession of the fortress. It is reported that Aḥmad, who had set up a mission house (*daʿwat-khāna*) near Iṣfahān, managed to convert some 30,000 people in the Iṣfahān area. Be that as it may, the Nizārīs soon began to collect taxes in districts around Shāhdiz, to the detriment of the Saljūq treasury. The capture of Shāhdiz was indeed a serious blow to the power and prestige of the Saljūqs. The Nizārīs seized a second fortress, Khānlanjān (Khālanjān), about thirty kilometres south of Iṣfahān. According to some unreliable reports, the *dāʿī* ʿAbd al-Malik himself had by now left Iṣfahān for Alamūt, where he spent his final years under Ḥasan-i Ṣabbāḥ's protection. There are no reliable details on the final phase of this *dāʿī*'s career, but it is safe to assume that by 494 A.H. he was no longer active in Iṣfahān, having been succeeded in a much more limited capacity by his son Aḥmad.

With the capture of Shāhdiz, which was fortified like other Nizārī castles, the Nizārīs became bolder in their ventures. The *daʿwa* was now successfully infiltrating Barkiyāruq's own court and armies. So large was the number of Barkiyāruq's *amīr*s and soldiers converted to Ismāʿīlism that, according to Ibn al-Athīr, some Saljūq officers asked the sultan for permission to appear before him in armour, for fear of attack by their own Ismāʿīlī soldiers.[61] Meanwhile, the Saljūq factions opposed to Barkiyāruq were accusing all of the sultan's soldiery of Ismāʿīlism, in addition to blaming Barkiyāruq for the Nizārī attacks on those officers opposing him, although Barkiyāruq's own life had been threatened by *fidāʾī*s. At any event, the growing power of the Nizārīs finally forced Barkiyāruq to move against them. Under such circumstances, Barkiyāruq in western Persia and Sanjar in Khurāsān agreed in 494/1101 to take combined action against the Nizārīs, who were now posing a serious threat to Saljūqid power in general. Accordingly, Barkiyāruq sanctioned the massacres of Nizārīs in Iṣfahān and Baghdād, as well as many of the Saljūq officers suspected of conversion, while Sanjar had many Nizārīs killed or enslaved in Quhistān. Nevertheless, the Nizārīs did not lose any of their castles to the Saljūqs and managed to retain their overall position in Persia. The Nizārī revolt, despite occasional setbacks, was still continuing when Barkiyāruq died in 498/1105 and was succeeded by Muḥammad Tapar.

It was during the opening years of the twelfth century A.D., or a few years earlier, that the Persian Nizārīs began to extend their activities to Syria. A number of emissaries from Alamūt began to be despatched to Syria to organize the Syrian Nizārīs and to win new converts. The political fragmentation of Syria at the time as well as the religious traditions of the country were significant factors favouring the spread of the Nizārī *daʿwa* in Syria. The first Turkoman bands, as noted, had entered Syria as early as 447/1055, and the country was subsequently invaded by the regular Saljūq armies. By 471/1078, the whole of Syria, apart from a coastal strip retained by the Fāṭimids, was under Saljūq rule or suzerainty; Tutush, the brother of the Great Sultan Malikshāh, had come to be recognized as the Saljūq overlord of Syria. As in Persia, Saljūq rule in Syria had caused many problems and was resented by the Syrians who were divided amongst themselves and incapable of expelling the alien Turks. With Malikshāh's death and the ensuing factional fights among the Saljūqs, the relative political stability of Syria too was disrupted. Soon after, when Tutush was killed in Persia in 488/1095, political confusion became openly manifest in Syria and Tutush's kingdom was broken into a number of smaller states. Syria now became the scene of rivalry among different Saljūq princes and *amīr*s, each one claiming a part of the country, while various minor local dynasties were at the same time attempting to assert their independence. The political fragmentation of Syria became more pronounced by the appearance of the Crusaders in 490/1097. Starting from Antioch, the Crusaders advanced swiftly along the Syrian coast and settled down in the conquered territories, establishing four Latin states based in Edessa, Antioch, Tripoli and Jerusalem. The Frankish encroachment of Syria naturally added to the apprehensions of the local population, complicating the Saljūq quarrels. In these troubled times, the most important Saljūq rulers of Syria were Tutush's sons Riḍwān (488–507/1095–1113) and Duqāq (488–497/1095–1104), who ruled respectively from Aleppo and Damascus.

The emissaries of Alamūt took advantage of Syria's political disarray and capitalized on the fears and grievances of the local population. The religious background of the country was also favourable to the propagation of the Nizārī *daʿwa*. The Syrians adhered to many religions. Amongst the Syrian Muslims, the Sunnīs were closely rivalled by the Shīʿīs belonging to a variety of sects, including several extremist sects, which provided suitable recruiting ground for the Nizārī *dāʿīs*. There were the extremist Nuṣayrīs and the Druzes, who had earlier broken off from the Fāṭimid Ismāʿīlīs. Amongst the Shīʿīs, there were also the Imāmīs and the Ismāʿīlīs. Indeed, the Syrians had been exposed to Ismāʿīlī doctrines for more than two centuries. Salamiyya, as noted, had served as the headquarters of the central leaders of the Ismāʿīlī movement in the 3rd/9th century. Subsequently, when the Fāṭimids extended their rule to Syria during the second half of the 4th/10th century, Ismāʿīlism was propagated openly there by numerous Fāṭimid *dāʿīs*. After the Nizārī–Mustaʿlī schism, both branches of the Ismāʿīlī movement were represented in Syria. Threatened by the Turks and the Crusaders, and despaired by the collapse of the Fāṭimid regime under al-Mustanṣir's successors, many Sunnīs and Shīʿīs, including both non-Ismāʿīlīs and Mustaʿlians, were now prepared to transfer their allegiance to Nizārī Ismāʿīlism which was increasingly appearing as the more active branch of the movement. The Nizārī movement, also boasting a record of rapid success in Persia, seemed to be the only force offering potential challenge to the alien invaders and rulers of Syria.

From the very beginning, the Persian *dāʿīs*, who were despatched from Alamūt to Syria for organizing the Nizārī *daʿwa* there, used the same methods of struggle as their co-religionists in Persia. They attempted to seize strongholds for use as bases for extending their activities into the surrounding areas. Furthermore, the Syrian Nizārīs resorted to political assassination and co-operated with various local rulers, when such temporary alliances seemed expedient. Despite occasional successes, however, the Nizārīs found their task in Syria much more difficult than it had been in Persia. Almost half a century of continuous effort was needed before the Nizārīs could finally gain control of a group of strongholds in Syria. Three separate periods can be distinguished in the initial struggles of the Nizārī leaders in Syria, who were evidently all Persians sent from Alamūt and who took their orders from Ḥasan-i Ṣabbāḥ and his successors. During the first and second periods, from the earliest years to 507/1113 and then from the latter year to 524/1130, the Nizārīs operated from Aleppo and subsequently from Damascus, with the support of the Saljūq rulers of these rival cities; but they failed to acquire any permanent bases. During the third period, from 524/1130 to around 545/1151, the Nizārīs succeeded in acquiring a number of fortresses in the mountain area known then as the Jabal Bahrā', today called the Jabal Anṣāriyya after its Nuṣayrī population.[62]

The first Nizārī leader in Syria, mentioned by Ibn al-Qalānisī and later sources, was a *dāʿī* known as al-Ḥakīm al-Munajjim, the physician-astrologer. Probably accompanied by a number of subordinate agents sent from Alamūt, he appeared in Aleppo, and, by the very beginning of the twelfth century A.D., managed to find a protector in the city's Saljūq ruler, Riḍwān. Aleppo, in northern Syria, was a suitable location for the initiation of the Nizārī activities. It had an important Shīʿī population, perhaps even outweighing the city's Sunnī inhabitants, and was close to the Shīʿī areas of the Jabal al-Summāq, already penetrated by Ismāʿīlism. Riḍwān, aware of his military weakness against his rival *amīrs* in Syria and seeking new alliances, allowed the free propagation of the Nizārī *daʿwa* in Aleppo; and, significantly, al-Ḥakīm al-Munajjim is reported to have openly joined his entourage. Riḍwān himself may have been a convert, although he lacked religious convictions and was evidently more concerned with political expediency. A few years earlier in 490/1097, he had briefly recognized the suzerainty of al-Mustaʿlī and had pronounced the *khuṭba* for the Fāṭimids.[63] He now permitted the Nizārīs to practise and preach their religion and use Aleppo as a base for further activities, also helping them to construct a *dār al-daʿwa*, or a mission house.[64] Riḍwān's patronage of the Nizārīs soon proved rewarding. In Rajab 496/May 1103, Janāḥ al-Dawla, the independent ruler of Ḥimṣ (Homs) and one of Riḍwān's crucial opponents, was murdered by three Persian *fidā'īs* in the great mosque of Ḥimṣ during the Friday prayers. Most sources agree that this assassination was ordered by al-Ḥakīm al-Munajjim at Riḍwān's instigation.[65] The people of Ḥimṣ were much disturbed by this event, and, interestingly, most of the Turks living there fled to Damascus. Prompt action by Duqāq, the ruler of Damascus, prevented the Franks from seizing Ḥimṣ, and the city was now brought under Damascene control.

Al-Ḥakīm al-Munajjim himself died in 496/1103, a few weeks after Janāḥ al-Dawla, and was succeeded as the leader of the Syrian Nizārīs by another Persian *dāʿī*, Abū Ṭāhir al-Ṣā'igh, the goldsmith. Abū Ṭāhir retained the favour of Riḍwān and attempted to seize strongholds in the areas inhabited by Ismāʿīlī sympathizers, especially around the Jabal al-Summāq to the south of Aleppo. From early on, the Nizārī *dāʿīs* seem to have received local support in Sarmīn and other towns of the Jazr and may even have controlled a few localities in northern Syria. However, the first Nizārī attack was aimed at Afāmiya (Apamea), a fortified outpost of Aleppo. Its Arab ruler, Khalaf b. Mulāʿib, a Shīʿī and probably a Mustaʿlian, had seized the town from Riḍwān in 489/1096 and thereupon had held it for the Fāṭimids. Khalaf, who was evidently unwilling to co-operate with the Nizārīs, had amply demonstrated the suitability of Afāmiya as a base in his successful career of brigandage. Abū Ṭāhir devised a plan for killing Khalaf and seizing the citadel of Afāmiya, counting on the assistance of the local Nizārīs who were then led by a certain Abu'l-Fatḥ, a judge originally from Sarmīn. Khalaf was killed in Jumādā I 499/February 1106 by a group of *fidāʾīs* sent from Aleppo, and Afāmiya readily fell into the hands of the Nizārīs.[66] Soon after, Abū Ṭāhir arrived on the scene to take charge, nominally on behalf of Riḍwān. This attempt to make Afāmiya the first Nizārī stronghold in Syria was short-lived, however. Tancred, the Frankish prince of Antioch who had already occupied the surrounding districts, now besieged Afāmiya, bringing with him as a prisoner a brother of Abu'l-Fatḥ. After lifting his initial siege in return for receiving a tribute from the Nizārīs, Tancred returned and forced Afāmiya to surrender in Muḥarram 500/September 1106. Abu'l-Fatḥ was tortured to death, while Abū Ṭāhir and a number of his associates managed to ransom themselves from captivity and returned to Aleppo. This was probably the first encounter between the Nizārīs and the Crusaders in Syria. In 504/1110, the Nizārīs also lost Kafarlāthā to Tancred, a lesser locality in the Jabal al-Summāq, which had come into their possession sometime earlier.

Abū Ṭāhir, now back in Aleppo, continued with his *daʿwa* activities as well as his search for suitable strongholds; and the association between Riḍwān and the Nizārīs was retained to their mutual benefit. In 505/1111, when Riḍwān decided to close the gates of Aleppo to Mawdūd, the Saljūq *amīr* of Mawṣil, who had come to Syria with an army to fight the Crusaders, armed groups of Nizārīs rallied to Riḍwān's side.[67] Both Riḍwān and the Nizārīs were apprehensive of the presence of this eastern expeditionary force in Syria, as was Ṭughtigīn (d. 522/1128), Duqāq's *atabeg*, or guardian-tutor, who became the effective ruler of Damascus on Duqāq's death in 497/1104 and founded the independent Būrid dynasty. Nevertheless, Riḍwān could not completely disregard the anti-Ismāʿīlī campaigns of Muḥammad Tapar, who had succeeded the more lenient Barkiyāruq; nor could he ignore the increasing unpopularity of the Nizārīs amongst his subjects. Consequently, Riḍwān somewhat retracted from his pro-Nizārī position during his final years. In 505/1111, an unsuccessful attempt on the life of a certain Abū Ḥarb ʿĪsā b. Zayd, a wealthy merchant and a declared enemy of the Ismāʿīlīs from Transoxiana who was then passing through Aleppo, led to a popular outburst against the Nizārīs, which Riḍwān was obliged to condone. Two years later, in 507/1113, Mawdūd was murdered in the great mosque of Damascus.[68] Most sources attribute this assassination to the Nizārīs, although the event is surrounded by some uncertainty. A few authorities suggest that Ṭughtigīn may have had a hand in it.

With Riḍwān's death in Jumādā II 507/December 1113, the Nizārī fortunes began to be definitely reversed in Aleppo. Riḍwān's young son and successor Alp Arslān at first maintained his father's policy towards the Nizārīs and even ceded them a fortress outside Bālis, on the road from Aleppo to Baghdād. But soon afterwards, he authorized a widespread anti-Ismāʿīlī campaign. According to Ibn al-ʿAdīm, Muḥammad Tapar had written to Alp Arslān warning him against the menace of the Nizārīs and insisting on their elimination. At the same time, Ṣāʿid b. Badīʿ, the *ra'īs* of Aleppo and the commander of the militia, had been urging Alp Arslān to take measures against the Nizārīs. Alp Arslān finally agreed and entrusted the task to Ibn Badīʿ.[69] Abū Ṭāhir and other Nizārī leaders, including the *dāʿī* Ismāʿīl, and a brother of al-Ḥakīm al-Munajjim, were arrested and killed. Some two hundred Nizārīs of Aleppo were also killed or imprisoned and their properties were confiscated. Many Nizārīs, however, managed to escape to different areas, some even finding refuge in Frankish territories. Ḥusām al-Dīn b. Dumlāj, the commander of the Nizārī armed groups in Aleppo, fled to Raqqa where he died, and Ibrāhīm al-ʿAjamī who had held the fortress of Bālis, abandoned it and took refuge at the fortress of Shayzar on the Orontes between Afāmiya and Ḥamāt, then held by the Banū Munqidh. By the spring of 507/1114, some one hundred Nizārīs from Aleppo as well as Afāmiya, Sarmīn, Maʿarrat al-Nuʿmān and Maʿarrat Maṣrīn, were at Shayzar and made an unsuccessful attempt to seize the place when its lords had gone out to view the Easter celebrations of the local Christians. On returning to the citadel of Shayzar, the Banū Munqidh, assisted by the townspeople, fought the Nizārīs from tower to tower and eventually killed them all.[70] The sectarians evidently had hoped to use Shayzar as a new base of operations, in the immediate aftermath of their debacle in Aleppo. With these events, the initial period in the activities of the Syrian Nizārīs came to an end. The Nizārīs had hitherto failed to secure a permanent base or any castles in Syria, but, on the positive side, they had made contacts with the local population and had won many converts and sympathizers, especially in the Jabal al-Summāq, the Jazr, and the territory of the Banū ʿUlaym, situated between Shayzar and Sarmīn.

Meanwhile, the ardently Sunnī Muḥammad Tapar had succeeded his brother Barkiyāruq in Persia, while Sanjar remained at Balkh as his viceroy in the East. Muḥammad reigned for some thirteen years, from 498/1105 to 511/1118, as the undisputed sultan, bringing order to the Saljūq empire. Probaby Barkiyāruq and Sanjar had already checked what might have been a Nizārī sweep through the Saljūq dominions in Persia and ʿIrāq. Nonetheless, the Nizārīs had maintained their position in widely scattered territories and posed a continued threat to the Saljūqs, from Syria to eastern Persia as well as in Iṣfahān itself. Therefore, Muḥammad, who had secured sole power in the aftermath of the civil wars of Barkiyāruq's reign, immediately set to work to take action against the Nizārīs. Within two years of his accession, Muḥammad launched a series of campaigns against the Nizārīs, and succeeded in checking their expanding revolt. In 500/1106, he sent an expedition against Takrīt, which the Nizārīs had held for twelve years. The Saljūqs failed to capture Takrīt after besieging it for several months, although the Nizārīs, too, lost the place. In order to prevent the Saljūqs from taking Takrīt, its Nizārī commandant, Kayqubād, surrendered the citadel to the Mazyadid Sayf al-Dawla Ṣadaqa (479–501/1086–1108), an Arab Imāmī Shīʿī ruler who had asserted his independence in central ʿIrāq.[71] At about the same time, Muḥammad had Sanjar again attack the Nizārī strongholds in Quhistān, though no details are available on the results.

Muḥammad's chief anti-Nizārī campaign was, however, against Shāhdiz. The sultan led a large force in person and besieged the fortress in 500/1107.[72] It is noteworthy that the siege and capture of Shāhdiz were delayed by a series of manoeuvres and tactics utilized by Aḥmad Ibn ʿAṭṭāsh, and supported by friends and sympathizers of the Nizārīs within the Saljūq camp. Aḥmad managed to engage the Saljūqs in a series of negotiations, involving the Sunnī *ʿulamāʾ* of Iṣfahān in a long, drawn-out religious disputation. In a message to the sultan, Aḥmad argued that the Nizārīs were true Muslims, believing in God and the Prophet Muḥammad and accepting the prescriptions of the Sharīʿa. They differed from the Sunnīs only concerning the matter of the imāmate, and therefore maintained that the sultan had no legitimate ground for acting against them, especially since the Nizārīs were willing to recognize the sultan's suzerainty and pay him tribute. This message led to a religious debate. It seems that at first most of the sultan's advisers and the Sunnī jurists and scholars were inclined to accept the Nizārī argument; a few, notably Abu'l-Ḥasan ʿAlī b. ʿAbd al-Raḥmān al-Samanjānī, a leading Shāfiʿī divine, stood fast in refuting the Nizārīs, denouncing them as going outside the pale of Islam, and convincing the sultan to reject Aḥmad's request. The debate thus ended and the siege continued. The Nizārīs now bargained for alternative fortresses, but this phase of the negotiations also proved fruitless and ended when a Nizārī *fidāʾī* attacked and wounded one of the sultan's *amīrs*, who had been particularly opposed to the Nizārīs. The sultan once again pressed ahead with his siege of Shāhdiz and the only matter remaining concerned the terms of surrender by the defenders of the great fortress. Finally, the conditions of capitulation were agreed upon. Part of the Shāhdiz garrison was to be given safe-conduct to go to other Nizārī strongholds in Arrajān and Quhistān, while the remainder, holding on to only one wing of the fortress, was to surrender upon receiving the news of the safe arrival of those departed; thereupon, being permitted to go to Alamūt. In due time, the awaited news was received at Shāhdiz, but Aḥmad declined to come down from the fortress. He had evidently decided to fight to the end. He and his small band of Nizārīs, some eighty men in all, fought the Saljūqs and defended themselves even from the last tower remaining in their hands. In the final assault, most of the Nizārīs were killed and a few managed to escape. Aḥmad's wife, decked in jewels, threw herself down from the ramparts, but Aḥmad was captured. He was paraded through the streets of Iṣfahān and then skinned alive. Aḥmad's son was also put to death, and their heads were sent to al-Mustaẓhir at Baghdād. The fortress of Khānlanjān too was apparently destroyed by the Saljūqs during the siege of Shāhdiz. With these defeats, the influence of the Nizārīs disappeared from the Iṣfahān region.

It was probably soon after the fall of Shāhdiz in 500 A.H. that Muḥammad Tapar caused the destruction of the Nizārī fortresses around Arrajān. The mission was carried out by Fakhr al-Dīn Chāwlī (d. 510/1116), the *atabeg* of Fārs; thereafter, little was heard of the Nizārīs who survived in the border region between Fārs and Khūzistān. Ibn al-Balkhī who composed his *Fārs-nāma*, a local history and geographical account of his native province during 498–510 A.H. at Muḥammad Tapar's request, already speaks of the Nizārī occupations of these fortresses in south-western Persia as a past event.[73] Sultan Muḥammad from early on directed his attention also to the main centre of Nizārī power, the Rūdbār area with its numerous castles.[74] Ḥasan-i Ṣabbāḥ, while remaining the *dāʿī* of Daylam, was then acknowledged as the head of the entire Nizārī movement, and Alamūt, his residence, became the central headquarters of the Nizārī *daʿwa*. In 501/1107–1108, or 502/1108–1109, the sultan sent an expedition to Rūdbār under the command of his vizier Ḍiyā' al-Mulk Aḥmad, a son of Niẓām al-Mulk, who was accompanied by the *amīr* Chāwlī (Jāwalī). The expedition fought the Nizārīs for some time and caused much devastation in the area. But the expedition failed to accomplish its primary objective, the reduction of Alamūt, and withdrew from Rūdbār. On that occasion, the sultan had sought in vain the assistance of Ḥusām al-Dawla Shahriyār b. Qārin (466–503/1074–1110), a local Bāwandid ruler in Ṭabaristān and Gīlān, against the Nizārīs of Rūdbār.[75] The Nizārīs later made an unsuccessful attempt in Baghdād to assassinate Aḥmad b. Niẓām al-Mulk, who had led the expedition against Rūdbār.

In 503/1109, the reduction of Alamūt was entrusted to Anūshtagīn Shīrgīr, the governor of Sāwa. Realizing the futility of a direct assault against Alamūt, Shīrgīr decided to undermine the position of the Nizārīs by attrition. For eight consecutive years, he destroyed the crops of Rūdbār, besieged Lamasar and other castles in the area, and engaged in sporadic battles with the Nizārīs. It was during this period, when severe hardship was inflicted on the Nizārīs, that Ḥasan-i Ṣabbāḥ and many others sent their wives and daughters to safer places, such as Girdkūh; a practice followed by the later Nizārīs. Shīrgīr received regular reinforcements from other Saljūq *amīrs*, while the resistance of the hard-pressed Nizārīs had continued to amaze the enemy. Finally, by Dhu'l-Ḥijja 511/April 1118, when Shīrgīr was evidently on the verge of taking Alamūt, whose garrison was near exhaustion, news arrived of Muḥammad Tapar's death. Thereupon the Saljūqs broke camp and left Rūdbār, paying no attention to Shīrgīr's pleas to stay and fight longer. Shīrgīr was obliged to abandon his siege of Alamūt, and lost many men upon retreating. The Nizārīs came into possession of all the food supplies and implements of war left behind by the Saljūq armies. Alamūt was thus saved and the Nizārīs of Rūdbār were rescued from what could have been an irrevocable defeat. According to al-Bundārī, the Saljūq vizier Qiwām al-Dīn al-Dargazīnī, a secret convert to Ismāʿīlism, may have played an important part in preventing the victory of the Saljūqs and in procuring the withdrawal of Shīrgīr's army from Rūdbār.[76] At any event, al-Dargazīnī roused Muḥammad's son and successor in Iṣfahān, Maḥmūd, against Shīrgīr, who was imprisoned and executed soon afterwards.

The death of Muḥammad b. Malikshāh was followed by another period of internal strife in the Saljūq empire, which gave the Nizārīs a respite to recover from the blows inflicted on them during Muḥammad's reign. Sultan Muḥammad was succeeded at Iṣfahān by his son Maḥmūd, who ruled for fourteen years (511–525/1118–1131) over western Persia, and, at least nominally, ʿIrāq. But Maḥmūd, unlike his father, was faced with other claimants to the sultanate. These claimants often sought the support of their *atabegs* or Saljūq *amīrs*, who increasingly came to enjoy local autonomy in different parts of the empire. In time, three other sons of Muḥammad Tapar, viz., Ṭughril II (526–529/1132–1134), Masʿūd (529–547/1134–1152) and Sulaymānshāh (555–556/1160–1161), as well as several of his grandsons, some of whom held power in various parts of the empire during Maḥmūd's reign, succeeded to the sultanate in the west. However, Maḥmūd's uncle Sanjar, who had controlled the eastern provinces since 490/1097, now became generally recognized as the head of the Saljūq family, acquiring the precarious position of supreme sultan among the Saljūq rulers until his death in 552/1157. In this capacity, Sanjar played a decisive role in settling the succession disputes of the later Saljūq sultans. At the beginning of his rule, however, Maḥmūd had to face an invasion of his domains by Sanjar, commanding a large army which included bands of Nizārīs. Sanjar defeated Maḥmūd at Sāwa and then advanced as far as Baghdād. But in the ensuing truce, Sanjar made Maḥmūd his heir, while seizing from him important territories in northern Persia. Sanjar continued to control these territories, including Ṭabaristān and Qūmis, which were already penetrated by the Nizārīs or were adjacent to their strongholds in Daylam. Maḥmūd's brother Ṭughril rebelled and succeeded in taking Gīlān and other districts in northern Persia, in addition to Qazwīn. Dissension in the Saljūq camp encouraged the ʿAbbāsid caliphs to seek an increasing degree of independence at Baghdād during the 6th/12th century, starting with the caliph al-Mustarshid (512–529/1118–1135).

Meanwhile, the Nizārīs had entered a new period in their relations with the Saljūqs, designated by Marshall Hodgson as a period of stalemate.[77] The great Saljūq offensive against the Nizārīs had clearly ended on Muḥammad Tapar's death, and so had the Nizārī open revolt. For almost three decades the Nizārīs had carried out an open revolt in the Saljūq lands, for a while threatening Iṣfahān itself. But they had also sustained severe blows. In particular, their partisans in the cities had been massacred on numerous occasions, and they had lost many of their fortresses in the Alburz and Zagros mountains and around Iṣfahān. The Nizārīs had in effect failed in their revolt against the Saljūqs, and their remaining strongholds, located chiefly in Rūdbār, Qūmis, and Quhistān, could not be used as adequate bases for continuing the revolt as they had done during the first period of their activity in Persia. Doubtless, the Nizārīs did not abandon the ultimate aims of their struggle, and they did maintain their cohesion from eastern Persia to Syria in spite of hardships and defeats. The Nizārī revolt had indeed been successful on a local basis in several scattered territories. But the Nizārī movement was now in need of reorganization and a new effort in the light of the experiences gained hitherto. The Nizārīs were now more concerned with consolidating their position and defending the territories which they controlled, rather than waging war against the Saljūqs. Instead of being merely a revolutionary party, the Nizārī community was now transforming itself into a permanent and independent state, with substantial though scattered territories. This state, with its numerous *dār al-hijra*s which had earlier served as bases for revolutionary activities, was now beginning to take its own special place amongst the small states within the boundaries of the Saljūq empire.

The remaining years of Ḥasan-i Ṣabbāḥ's life, after 511/1118, were essentially peaceful and devoted to consolidating the Nizārī state which he, more than anyone else, had worked to create. Ḥasan, who was now the central leader of the Nizārī community whilst continuing as the *dāʿī* of Daylam, recaptured some of the castles which Shīrgīr had seized in Rūdbār and evidently even intensified the *daʿwa* in many regions like ʿIrāq, Ādharbayjān, Māzandarān, Gīlān and Khurāsān. The sources attribute the Nizārī successes of this period and the subsequent decades, to Sanjar's tolerance towards the Nizārīs. Indeed, Sanjar seems to have sought peaceful relations with the Nizārīs, allegedly procured by a dagger which Ḥasan-i Ṣabbāḥ contrived to have thrust onto the floor beside the sultan's bed. Juwaynī also relates seeing several of Sanjar's *manshūr*s or decrees at the Alamūt library, in which the sultan conciliated the Nizārīs and sought their friendship.[78] Our Persian chroniclers state that Sanjar gave the Nizārīs an annual pension of 3,000–4,000 dinars from the taxes on the lands belonging to them in the region of Qūmis, also allowing them to levy a toll on travellers beneath Girdkūh.[79] It seems that Ḥasan-i Ṣabbāḥ reinvigorated the Nizārī cause in Egypt during his final years, though earlier he had made no serious attempts in that direction. Ḥasan's intensive activities in Fāṭimid Egypt date to around 515/1121, the year of the assassination of al-Afḍal, who had dispossessed Nizār of his rights to the imāmate. According to the Nizārī sources used by our Persian historians, this assassination was carried out by three *fidāʾīs* from Aleppo. On receiving this news at Alamūt, Ḥasan ordered the Nizārīs to celebrate for seven days and nights.[80] Al-Afḍal's successor al-Maʾmūn, as noted, had to adopt security measures against the Nizārī agents and *fidāʾīs* who were then reportedly being sent from Alamūt to Egypt. Many such agents were arrested. Soon after, in 516/1122, the Fāṭimid regime deemed it necessary to hold a public assembly in defence of the rights of al-Mustaʿlī and al-Āmir to the imāmate, as against those of Nizār; an assembly which led to the issuance of the epistle entitled *al-Hidāya al-Āmiriyya*. Ibn Muyassar, who relates these details indicating the apprehension of the Fāṭimids of the Nizārī activities in Egypt and Syria, also mentions that at about the same time, al-Maʾmūn had a long letter issued by the Fāṭimid chancery, in Ibn al-Ṣayrafī's writing, urging Ḥasan-i Ṣabbāḥ in harsh terms to renounce his support of the Nizārī cause and to return to the truth.[81] The Nizārī activities in Egypt, however, do not seem to have continued for long; while relations between the Nizāriyya and the Mustaʿlawiyya, who themselves soon split into the Ḥāfiẓiyya and the Ṭayyibiyya, continued to deteriorate.

Ḥasan-i Ṣabbāḥ fell ill early in the month of Rabīʿ II 518/May 1124. Feeling that his end was near, he made careful arrangements for the future leadership of the Nizārī community. He called for his lieutenant at Lamasar, Kiyā Buzurg-Ummīd, and designated him his successor as *dāʿī* of Daylam and head of the Nizārī community. At the same time, Ḥasan appointed three senior Nizārī personalities to what may be viewed as a council of advisers for assisting Buzurg-Ummīd in conducting the affairs of the Nizārī state and community as well as the *daʿwa* until such time as the imām himself appeared. These advisers were Dihdār Abū ʿAlī Ardistānī, a veteran *dāʿī* who had once rescued Ḥasan from a difficult situation at Alamūt; Ḥasan Ādam Qaṣrānī, and Kiyā Bā Jaʿfar, the commander of the Nizārī forces who died in 519/1125.[82] The *dāʿī* Abū ʿAlī was singled out for the affairs of the *daʿwa*. Ḥasan died at an old age towards the end of Rabīʿ II 518/middle of June 1124.

Ḥasan-i Ṣabbāḥ was indeed a remarkable man. An organizer and a political strategist of unrivalled capability, he was at the same time a thinker and writer who led an ascetic life. Several examples of his asceticism and harshness have been cited by our Persian historians. He was evidently equally strict with friend and foe, and highly uncompromising in his austere and Islamic life style which he imposed on the Nizārī community, especially in Rūdbār. In particular, he insisted on the observance of the Islamic religious duty of *amr bi maʿrūf va nahy az munkar* (commanding the good and prohibiting the evil).[83] During all the years spent at Alamūt, Ḥasan evidently never descended from the castle, and he is said to have left his living quarters only twice to mount the roof-top. During that period, nobody drank wine openly in Alamūt, and the playing of musical instruments was also forbidden. Ḥasan sent his wife and daughters to Girdkūh where they earned a simple life by spinning, never having them return to Alamūt. He also had both his sons, Ustād Ḥusayn and Muḥammad, executed.[84] Muḥammad's guilt was wine-drinking, while Ustād Ḥusayn had been suspected of complicity in the murder of the *dāʿī* Ḥusayn Qā'inī in Quhistān, a suspicion which proved unfounded. A year later, the real instigator of the *dāʿī*'s assassination, a certain ʿAlid called Zayd, was discovered and put to death along with his son, on Ḥasan's orders. This ʿAlid, a resident of Alamūt who aimed to undermine Ḥasan's position, had been successful in secretly conducting propaganda on his own behalf, claiming to have been the *mustawdaʿ* imām. Ḥasan is said to have been learned in philosophy and astronomy and when he was not performing the duties prescribed by the Sharīʿa, he devoted his time to reading, writing and administering the affairs of the Nizārī community. Always remaining the *dāʿī* of Daylam, Ḥasan was, after Nizār's death, regarded as the *ḥujja* of the hidden Nizārī Imām. He founded the Nizārī state in Persia with its subsidiary in Syria, guided the Nizārī community in difficult times, and eventually became the undisputed leader of that community and the Nizārī *daʿwa*. He was highly revered by the Nizārīs, who called him Sayyidnā, or 'our master'. Ḥasan's mausoleum in Rūdbār became a shrine for the Nizārīs, who made regular pilgrimages to the site until it was destroyed by the Mongols.

ʿAbd al-Malik b. ʿAṭṭāsh and Ḥasan-i Ṣabbāḥ, and possibly other Persian Ismāʿīlī *dāʿīs* living during the final decades of the 5th/11th century, were also active intellectually and doubtless produced some doctrinal treatises which have not survived. However, the early Nizārīs, conducting an open revolt in hostile territories and being very concerned with their survival, did not have time for philosophical speculations and highly sophisticated doctrinal arguments. In a sense, their intellectual activities were also closely geared to the more pressing and practical needs of their struggle. In particular, the Nizārīs did not retain the earlier interest in cosmology and some other esoteric doctrines, expounded in the classical works of the Fāṭimid period and central to Ṭayyibī Ismāʿīlī thought. The early Nizārīs, on the other hand, showed a particular interest in the doctrine of the imāmate. From the time of Ḥasan-i Ṣabbāḥ and even during the years preceding their break with the Fāṭimid regime, the Persian Ismāʿīlīs concentrated their doctrinal investigations on the reality of the imām and the imāmate, transcending history and the physical world. Indeed, from early on, the Sunnī observers and other outsiders developed the distinct impression that the Nizārī movement reflected a 'new preaching', which became designated as *al-daʿwa al-jadīda*. The 'new preaching' did not, however, entail the formulation of any set of new doctrines; it was, rather, the reformulation of an old Shīʿī doctrine which already had a long history also amongst the Ismāʿīlīs. This reformulation of the Shīʿī doctrine of *taʿlīm*, or authoritative teaching, was apparently most eloquently expounded by Ḥasan-i Ṣabbāḥ himself, though he was not probably its originator. At any event, in its fully developed form the doctrine is commonly ascribed to Ḥasan, who devoted a theological treatise to it in the Persian language. This treatise, entitled *Fuṣūl-i arbaʿa* (*The Four Chapters*) has not survived. But it was seen and paraphrased by our Persian historians,[85] and quoted extensively by Ḥasan's contemporary Muḥammad b. ʿAbd al-Karīm al-Shahrastānī (d. 548/1153) in his famous heresiographical work produced around 521/1127.[86]

Al-Shahrastānī, who spent most of his life in his native Khurāsān and became an associate of the sultan Sanjar, was widely renowned as an Ashʿarī theologian and noted for his open-minded interest in all religions and philosophies. However, some of his contemporaries believed that he had secretly converted to Ismāʿīlism and worked on behalf of the Nizārī *daʿwa*.[87] The well-informed Naṣīr al-Dīn al-Ṭūsī (d. 672/1274), who himself adhered temporarily to Nizārī Ismāʿīlism, asserts in his spiritual autobiography that al-Shahrastānī was an Ismāʿīlī, calling him *dāʿī al-duʿāt*; al-Ṭūsī furthermore adds that al-Shahrastānī was the teacher of his father's maternal uncle.[88] At any event, several of al-Shahrastānī's extant works bear an Ismāʿīlī imprint and attest that at least during the final decades of his life he espoused Ismāʿīlī terminologies and methods of interpretation.[89] Aside from the *Mafātīḥ al-asrār*, an incomplete Qur'ānic exegesis, and the *Majlis-i maktūb-i Shahrastānī munʿaqid dar Khwārazm*, his crypto-Ismāʿīlī works include *al-Muṣāraʿa*, a refutation of Ibn Sīnā's theological doctrine on the basis of traditional Ismāʿīlī theology.[90] Be it as it may, al-Shahrastānī was interested in ideas propounded by the earliest Nizārīs, and he has preserved for us in Arabic translation an abridgement of Ḥasan-i Ṣabbāḥ's reformulation of the doctrine of *taʿlīm*, the central doctrine of the earliest Nizārīs.

The Shīʿīs had always condemned the Sunnīs for exercising the right to choose for themselves in religious matters, starting with the choice of the Prophet's first successor. The Shīʿīs, by contrast, held that Muslims had no right to rely on their own arbitrary decisions and that they must base their understanding of religious truths and especially law on the teaching (*taʿlīm*) of proper authorities; authorities or true imāms, who, according to the Shīʿa, are designated by divine ordinance and not by human choice or reasoning, as in the case of the Prophet himself. This was essentially the crux of the Shīʿī doctrine of *taʿlīm*, the authoritative teaching in religion, which could be undertaken by authoritative teachers in every age. And for the Shīʿīs, only their divinely appointed and guided ʿAlid Imāms were qualified to perform the functions of such teachers. As explained by al-Shahrastānī, Ḥasan-i Ṣabbāḥ reformulated the Shīʿī doctrine of *taʿlīm* in a series of four propositions, translated by al-Shahrastānī from Persian into Arabic with the title of *al-Fuṣūl al-arbaʿa*. These propositions which took the form of a critique of the traditional statement of the doctrine, in effect aimed to prove that only the Ismāʿīlī Imām fulfilled the role of the authoritative teacher after the Prophet.

In the first proposition, Ḥasan reaffirmed the need of men for an authority or teacher (*muʿallim*) and the inadequacy of reason (*ʿaql*) alone in enabling men to understand religious truths. This proposition also aimed at refuting the position of those, notably the philosophers, who believed in the adequacy of reason and independent human judgement in comprehending the ultimate truth. In the second proposition, Ḥasan argued, in line with the traditional Shīʿī position, that the needed teacher must be authoritative or trustworthy (*ṣādiq*). He stated, in opposition to the position of the Sunnīs, that there must be only one single divinely appointed arbiter, the true imām, in every age. Here, the single authoritative teacher (*muʿallim-i ṣādiq*) of the Shīʿīs is set against the numerous scholars and jurists who are accepted as guides and teachers by the Sunnīs in every age. The third proposition brings out the dilemma faced by the ordinary Shīʿīs themselves; since the identification of the sole authoritative teacher at any time requires the demonstration of his authority, which is possible only on the basis of some further authority whose own authority must be demonstrated, and so on. In the fourth proposition, Ḥasan attempts to solve this dilemma by reformulating the whole question in such a manner as to arrive at the desired result. He held that the authority of the needed teacher could be known not through something beyond itself but through the very nature of knowledge, in which he recognized a dialectical principle. Emphasizing that all true knowledge requires a contrast of two opposites which can be recognized only through one another, Ḥasan then proceeds to apply this dialectical principle to the relationship between the individual person who wishes to know and the authoritative teacher whom he must discover. The individual's reasoning enables him to realize his need for the recognition of an authoritative teacher; but it does not by itself determine who that teacher is, nor does it lead him to the ultimate truth. On the other hand, the claimant to the position of final authority, the imām, need not prove his claims by resorting to any proof beyond himself. But a conjunction of the individual's reasoning and the authoritative teacher solves the dilemma. The individual's reasoning does, as noted, indicate his need for the teaching of an authoritative teacher, the imām. And when reasoning has reached this point, the imām can present himself as satisfying this very need. Accordingly, the true imām does not seek extrinsic proofs for his authority or imāmate, which is proved only by his own existence. Indeed it is through his very existence that the true imām can fulfil the need which only reasoning can demonstrate. For Ḥasan-i Ṣabbāḥ, this imām, who did not need to resort to miracles or refer to his ancestry, was the Ismāʿīlī Imām, whose very being and claims were sufficient proofs of his legitimacy.

The doctrine of *taʿlīm* presented by Ḥasan-i Ṣabbāḥ was both more rigorous and self-sufficient than the traditional Shīʿī view on the subject. In his argumentation, Ḥasan consistently emphasized the role of the imām, with the Prophet having been a link in the logical chain from God to imām. This doctrine, stressing the autonomous teaching authority of each imām in his time, became a powerful ideological tool in the hands of the Nizārī community of the later Alamūt period. Meanwhile, in the absence of an accessible imām, the community authority depended on his *ḥujja*; and Ḥasan himself, as noted, was recognized as that *ḥujja*. The doctrine of *taʿlīm*, as restated by Ḥasan-i Ṣabbāḥ and others, became so central to early Nizārī thought that the followers of the Nizārī *daʿwa* came to be known as the Taʿlīmiyya. The Nizārī doctrine of *taʿlīm* also had a strong impact on the Sunnīs, many of whom had continued to view the Ismāʿīlīs as their arch-enemies. Many Sunnī writers responded to the intellectual challenge posed by this new Ismāʿīlī sub-sect and in particular attacked the doctrine of *taʿlīm*. Al-Ghazālī, as noted, was the foremost and probably the earliest

Sunnī thinker in this group. He wrote several treatises against the Ismāʿīlīs and paid special attention to refuting the doctrine of *taʿlīm* in his *al-Mustaẓhirī* and other treatises.

On Ḥasan-i Ṣabbāḥ's death, Kiyā Buzurg-Ummīd was installed at Alamūt as *dāʿī* of Daylam and head of the Nizārī community and state.[91] The *dāʿī* Abū ʿAlī Ardistānī immediately set off for various Nizārī castles and obtained their allegiance to the new Nizārī leader. Buzurg-Ummīd's leadership was not challenged by any segment of the community, which must have been rather difficult to understand by the quarrelling Saljūqs. Ruling for fourteen years (518–532/1124–1138), Buzurg-Ummīd maintained the policies of his predecessor and succeeded in further strengthening the Nizārī state, despite the renewed Saljūq offensive. He, too, was a capable administrator and military strategist, and was furthermore well-placed in northern Persia as a native of Rūdbār. He was not, however, related by marriage to the local Caspian rulers, as believed by some authorities. It was a sister of Kiyā Buzurg al-Dāʿī ila'l-Ḥaqq b. al-Hādī (d. ca. 551/1156), an ʿAlid Zaydī ruler of Daylamān, and not Buzurg-Ummīd's sister, who was married to Hazārasf b. Fakhr al-Dawla Namāwar, the Bādūspānid ruler of Rustamdār and Rūyān. The latter's son Kaykā'ūs (d. 560/1164–1165), who adhered to Zaydism and ruled for thirty-seven years, was hostile towards the Nizārīs. On the other hand, Hazārasf's grandson, Hazārasf b. Shahrnūsh (d. 586/1190), another Bādūspānid ruler, cultivated very friendly relations with the Nizārīs. Again, it was Kiyā Buzurg, and not Buzurg-Ummīd, who married a daughter of Shāh Ghāzī Rustam b. ʿAlā' al-Dawla ʿAlī, who later became the Bāwandid ruler of Māzandarān and Gīlān (534–558/1140–1163). Shāh Ghāzī became an enemy of the Nizārīs, subsequent to the Nizārī assassination in 537/1142 of his son Girdbāzū, who had been sent to Khurāsān to serve Sanjar; while the Nizārī *fidā'īs* made unsuccessful attempts to murder Shāh Ghāzī himself. At any event, this Bāwandid ruler co-operated with the Saljūqs and fought the Nizārīs on numerous occasions. He attacked Alamūt in vain several times, but eventually succeeded in seizing the castles of Mihrīn and Manṣūrakūh in Qūmis from the Nizārīs. Another of Shāh Ghāzī's daughters was married to Shahrnūsh b. Hazārasf b. Namāwar, the Bādūspānid ruler who reigned contemporaneously with Buzurg-Ummīd. Shahrnūsh seems to have maintained cordial relations with the Nizārīs and Buzurg-Ummīd.[92]

Buzurg-Ummīd was confronted with the enmity of the local *amīrs* from the very beginning of his reign, and in 518/1124 some 700 Nizārīs were massacred in Āmid in Diyār Bakr.[93] In 520/1126, two years after his accession, the Saljūqs launched new attacks against the Nizārī strongholds in both Rūdbār and Quhistān, probably to test the leadership capabilities of Ḥasan-i Ṣabbāḥ's successor. Sultan Sanjar had not sanctioned any anti-Nizārī activity for almost two decades, which may reflect the existence of some sort of a truce agreement between the sultan and the sectarians. However, he had now decided to deal with the Nizārīs, and a large army, commanded by his vizier, was sent against Ṭuraythīth in Quhistān, as well as against Bayhaq and Ṭarz in the district of Nīshāpūr, with orders to kill the Nizārīs of those places and pillage their properties.[94] This expedition despatched from Khurāsān eventually withdrew without accomplishing much. The expedition sent in 520 A.H. by the sultan Maḥmūd to Rūdbār, under the command of Shīrgīr's nephew Aṣīl, was even less successful; it was defeated and driven back by the Nizārīs. A second Saljūq attack in the same year was similarly repelled by the Nizārīs of Rūdbār, who captured one of the enemy's *amīr*s, Ṭamūrṭughān. The latter was kept as a prisoner at Alamūt for some time before being released on Sanjar's request. In spite of these entanglements, the Nizārī position in Rūdbār was actually strengthened during the earliest years of Buzurg-Ummīd's reign. Several fortresses were seized in the area, including Manṣūra and others in Ṭāliqān, while a few castles were built, such as Saʿādatkūh, and most significantly, Maymūndiz, a major stronghold which began to be erected in Rabīʿ I 520/April 1126.[95] In eastern Persia, too, the Nizārīs had continued to be active. In 521/1127, the *fidāʾī*s killed Muʿīn al-Dīn Abū Naṣr Aḥmad, the Saljūq vizier who had convinced Sanjar to take action against the Nizārīs, having himself led the expedition to Quhistān.[96] In 523/1129, the Quhistānī Nizārīs were able to mobilize and send an army to Sīstān.[97]

By Jumādā I 523/May 1129, the sultan Maḥmūd found it expedient to enter into peace negotiations with the Nizārīs, and for this purpose invited Alamūt to send an envoy to Iṣfahān. Buzurg-Ummīd despatched Khwāja Muḥammad Nāṣiḥī Shahrastānī. But the discussions proved abortive as the Nizārī emissary and his colleague were lynched upon leaving the Saljūq court by some of the townspeople. The sultan disclaimed all responsibility, also rejecting Buzurg-Ummīd's demand to punish the murderers. Soon afterwards, the Nizārīs took their own revenge and attacked Qazwīn, killing some 400 persons and taking much booty. This marked the beginning of a long-lasting enmity between the Qazwīnīs and their neighbouring Nizārīs, which often manifested itself in open warfare. Subsequently, Maḥmūd made another unsuccessful raid on the Alamūt district, while an army sent from ʿIrāq against Lamasar failed to accomplish much.[98]

Sultan Maḥmūd died in 525/1131 and his succession was disputed by his brothers and son Dāʾūd, giving the Nizārīs another respite. It was during this period that the Persian Nizārīs directed their attention to the Caspian region, where the Bāwandids of Māzandarān had become their active enemy and the local Zaydīs had hindered the spread of their *daʿwa* in northern Persia. The Nizārīs achieved a great triumph in dealing with Abū Hāshim ʿAlawī, who claimed the imāmate of the Zaydīs in Daylam, and had adherents as far as Khurāsān.[99] Buzurg-Ummīd sent a letter of advice, but Abū Hāshim persisted in accusing the Nizārīs of unbelief and heresy. In Muḥarram 526 A.H., an army was sent from Alamūt to Gīlān against Abū Hāshim, who had gathered a force of his own. The Zaydīs were defeated and Abū Hāshim was captured and brought to Alamūt, where the Nizārīs held disputations with him. According to the Nizārī chronicler of the reign of Buzurg-Ummīd, Abū Hāshim eventually renounced his claim to the imāmate and expressed his willingness to convert to Ismāʿīlism. He was later executed.

During the remaining years of Buzurg-Ummīd's reign, the Persian Nizārīs further consolidated their position and made a few more raids on Qazwīn and more remote areas such as Georgia. At the same time, the Nizārī *dāʿīs* spread the *daʿwa* in different regions while the *fidāʾīs* removed more of the sect's enemies. In addition to the usual Sunnī *qāḍīs* and local officials, the victims now included a Zaydī Imām, the Fāṭimid caliph al-Āmir and an ʿAbbāsid caliph, representing the first successful Ismāʿīlī attempt on the life of the titular head of Sunnī Islam.[100] On Ṭughril b. Muḥammad's death in 529/1134, his brother Masʿūd had succeeded to the Saljūq sultanate in western Persia, Ādharbayjān and ʿIrāq. Sultan Masʿūd ruled relatively unchallenged with Sanjar's support for eighteen years (529–547/1134–1152). From the very beginning of his rule, however, the ʿAbbāsid caliph al-Mustarshid, aiming to assert his independence from the Saljūqs, refused to recognize Masʿūd's authority and declined to name him in the *khuṭba* at Baghdād. As a result, al-Mustarshid and Masʿūd soon engaged in battle near Hamadān. The ʿAbbāsid caliph was defeated and taken as prisoner to Marāgha, where he was treated respectfully by the sultan Masʿūd on Sanjar's request. At Marāgha, a large band of *fidāʾīs* found the opportunity to enter al-Mustarshid's pavilion and stabbed him to death in Dhu'l-Qaʿda 529/August 1135. Al-Mustarshid's death was celebrated at Alamūt for an entire week.[101]

In Syria, meanwhile, the Nizārīs had survived their debacle of 507/1113. During the second period of their initial efforts to establish themselves, the Syrian Nizārīs no longer used Aleppo as the base of their operations; they soon came to concentrate their activities in southern Syria.[102] But even in Aleppo, where they were massacred on Riḍwān's death, the Nizārīs retained some foothold for a while and established friendly relations with Īlghāzī, the Artuqid ruler of Mārdīn and Mayyāfāriqīn who gained possession of Aleppo in 512/1118. In 512 A.H., their enemy Ibn Badīʿ, who was then fleeing Aleppo, was killed together with his two sons by the Nizārī *fidāʾīs*.[103] In 514/1120, the Nizārīs of Aleppo were strong enough to demand a small castle known as Qalʿat al-Sharīf from Īlghāzī. Instead of ceding it or refusing the demand, Īlghāzī had the castle demolished in haste, pretending to have ordered this action earlier. The *qāḍī* Ibn al-Khashshāb, who conducted the demolition and was involved in the massacre of the Nizārīs in Aleppo, was assassinated in 519/1125. The end of Nizārī power in Aleppo, however, came in 517/1124, when Balak, Īlghāzī's nephew and new ruler of the city, arrested the local representative of Bahrām, the chief *dāʿī* of the Syrian Nizārīs, and ordered the expulsion of the Nizārīs, who sold their properties and departed from Aleppo.[104] The following year, the inhabitants of Āmid massacred a large number of the local Nizārīs. It seems that Bahrām had succeeded to the leadership of the Syrian Nizārīs soon after Abū Ṭāhir's execution in 507 A.H. Like his predecessors, Bahrām was a Persian, the nephew of al-Asadābādī, a high Saljūq official who was executed as a Nizārī in Baghdād in 494/1101 on Barkiyāruq's order. Bahrām had subsequently fled from ʿIrāq to Syria, where he became active as a *dāʿī*. Shortly after the massacre of the Nizārīs of Aleppo, Bahrām, now chief *dāʿī*, transferred the centre of the *daʿwa* activities to southern Syria. For a while he lived under different guises and conducted the *daʿwa* secretly in various localities, according to Ibn al-Qalānisī, the contemporary chronicler of Damascus.[105]

By 520/1126, the Syrian Nizārī movement was revived in the south and Bahrām's influence was noteworthy in Damascus and other localities. In the same year, Bahrām had a hand in the murder of Āq Sunqur al-Bursuqī, the governor of Mawṣil and an enemy of the Ismāʿīlīs. Some of the *fidāʾīs* who assassinated al-Bursuqī in the great mosque of Mawṣil had been despatched from Syria.[106] Already in 519 A.H., when Damascus was threatened by the Franks, the Nizārīs were in a position to send armed groups from Ḥimṣ and elsewhere, who according to Ibn al-Qalānisī were noted for their courage, to join the troops of Ṭughtigīn in an unsuccessful attack on the Crusaders.[107] At any rate, Bahrām appeared openly in Damascus in 520/1126, with a letter of recommendation from Īlghāzī. Whilst in Aleppo, Bahrām had established friendly relations with Īlghāzī, who himself had an understanding with Ṭughtigīn. The Turkish *atabeg* of Damascus received Bahrām with honour and gave him official protection, further enhancing the position of the Nizārīs there. At the same time, Bahrām found an influential and reliable ally in Ṭughtigīn's vizier Abū ʿAlī Ṭāhir b. Saʿd al-Mazdaqānī, who was not himself an Ismāʿīlī. In pursuance of the established Nizārī strategy, Bahrām immediately demanded to be given a castle, which he could use as base of operations. In Dhu'l-Qaʿda 520 A.H., Ṭughtigīn ceded the sectarians the frontier fortress of Bāniyās, on the border with the Latin kingdom of Jerusalem, which was then menaced by the Franks.[108] Enjoying the continued support of al-Mazdaqānī, Bahrām was also given a building in Damascus which he used as a mission house and local headquarters. Henceforth, Bahrām preached the Nizārī doctrines openly. He despatched *dāʿīs* in all directions and won an increasing number of converts among both the urban people and the peasantry. Meanwhile, he fortified Bāniyās, his residence, and gathered a large group of followers there. From Bāniyās, the Nizārīs embarked on further military and propagandist activities, attempting to spread their influence in the surrounding country. In their systematic raids, the Nizārīs seem to have captured a number of places. However, their success in southern Syria was to be short-lived.

The Wādī al-Taym, in the region of Ḥāṣbayyā to the north of Bāniyās and on the western side of Mount Hermon, offered favourable opportunities for the spread of the Nizārī *daʿwa*. Inhabited mostly by Druzes, Nuṣayrīs and bedouin tribes, this valley had in fact attracted the attention of Bahrām, who came to be suspected of the murder of Baraq b. Jandal, a local tribal chief. In 522/1128, Bahrām set out from Bāniyās at the head of his Nizārī troops to occupy the Wādī al-Taym. But Ḍaḥḥāk b. Jandal, Baraq's brother and sworn avenger, had already made sufficient preparations to confront the Nizārīs. In a fierce battle, the Nizārīs were defeated and Bahrām was killed; his head and hands were taken to Cairo, where the bearer was generously rewarded.[109] With this defeat and Ṭughtigīn's death earlier in the same year 522 A.H., the Nizārī fortunes began to be reversed in southern Syria. Bahrām was succeeded as chief *dāʿī* in Syria by another

Persian, Ismāʿīl al-ʿAjamī, who stayed at Bāniyās and maintained the policies of his predecessor. Al-Mazdaqānī, who had been retained as vizier by Ṭughtigīn's son and successor Tāj al-Mulūk Būrī (522–526/1128–1132), continued to support Ismāʿīl and the Nizārīs. But Būrī waited for the right opportunity to rid himself of al-Mazdaqānī and the Nizārīs, being spurred on towards these objectives by the prefect of Damascus, Mufarrij b. al-Ḥasan b. al-Ṣūfī, and the city's military governor, Yūsuf b. Fīrūz. Al-Mazdaqānī was murdered in Ramaḍān 523/September 1129, and this was followed by a massacre of the Nizārīs in Damascus, similar to the anti-Nizārī reaction of the Aleppines after the death of Riḍwān. The town militia (*al-aḥdāth*) and the mob, supported by the predominantly Sunnī inhabitants of Damascus, now turned on the Nizārīs, killing more than 6,000 people and pillaging their properties. Their *dār al-daʿwa* was also destroyed and some Nizārīs were crucified on the wall of Damascus, including a freedman called Shādhī al-Khādim, a disciple of Abū Ṭāhir in Aleppo and, according to Ibn al-Qalānisī, the root of all the trouble.[110] Following this massacre, and realizing the untenability of his position at Bāniyās, Ismāʿīl surrendered the fortress to the Franks, who were advancing on Damascus, and fled together with some of his associates to the Frankish territories. The *dāʿī* Ismāʿīl died soon afterwards, at the beginning of 524/1130, in exile among the Franks.

These developments marked another temporary disorganization in the Nizārī *daʿwa* in Syria, bringing to an end the second period in the earliest history of the Syrian Nizārīs. In the meantime, Būrī and his chief officers had taken elaborate precautions against the vengeance of the Nizārīs. Nevertheless, in Jumādā II 525/May 1131, Būrī was struck down by two Persian *fidāʾīs* sent from Alamūt who had disguised themselves as Turkish soldiers.[111] He died of his wounds a year later, but the Nizārīs never recovered their position in Damascus. During the same period, the rivalry between the Syrian Nizārīs and the Mustaʿlians had intensified, necessitating the public assembly of 516/1122 in Cairo in the defence of the rights of al-Mustaʿlī and al-Āmir to the imāmate. The Nizārīs were accused of the murder of their arch-enemy al-Afḍal in 515/1121, while the Fāṭimid regime rejoiced at receiving Bahrām's head in Cairo. The rivalry between the two wings of the Ismāʿīlī movement culminated in the assassination of al-Āmir by the Nizārī *fidāʾīs* in 524/1130, shortly before the attempt on Būrī's life. Henceforth, Ismāʿīlism weakened in Egypt, while the bulk of the Syrian Ismāʿīlīs rapidly rallied to the side of the Nizārī *daʿwa*. In subsequent times, the Nizāriyya continued to represent the most active

Ismāʿīlī wing. There do not seem to have occurred any major confrontations between the Nizārīs, entrenched in their mountain *dār al-hijra*s in Persia and Syria, and the Ḥāfiẓiyya and the Ṭayyibiyya, restricted respectively to Egypt and Yaman.

In contrast to the first two periods, the Syrian Nizārīs succeeded during the third period of their earliest history, lasting some two decades after their debacle of 523/1129 in Damascus, in finally acquiring a number of permanent strongholds. During this period, they directed their efforts to the Jabal Bahrā', a mountainous region between Ḥamāt and the coastline southwest of the Jabal al-Summāq, which was inhabited by Nuṣayrīs and possessed a number of castles suitable as *dār al-hijra*s for the Nizārīs. Few details are known about the Syrian Nizārīs and their *dāʿī*s during this third period, when they transferred their activities out of the cities. It seems that the Nizārīs, including those who had taken refuge in Frankish territories, recovered swiftly from their setback in Damascus. They were soon reorganized under the leadership of Ismāʿīl al-ʿAjamī's successor, Abu'l-Fatḥ, and effectively penetrated the Jabal Bahrā', in the aftermath of the Crusaders' failure to establish themselves there. In 527/1132–1133, the Nizārīs came into possession of their first fortress in the Jabal Bahrā' by purchasing Qadmūs from the Muslim lord of Kahf, Sayf al-Mulk b. ʿAmrūn, who, with the assistance of the Nuṣayrīs, had recovered the place from the Franks the previous year.[112] From Qadmūs, which became one of their chief strongholds and often served as the residence of their leader, the Syrian Nizārīs extended their dominion in the region.[113] Shortly afterwards, Mūsā, another of the Banū ʿAmrūn and the son of Sayf al-Mulk, sold Kahf itself to the Nizārīs, to prevent its falling into the hands of his cousins in the course of a succession dispute. In 531/1136–1137, the Frankish occupants of the fortress of Kharība were driven out by the local Nizārīs, who subsequently regained control of the place after being temporarily dislodged by Ibn Ṣalāḥ, the Zangid governor of Ḥamāt. In 535/1140–1141, the Nizārīs captured Maṣyāf, their most important stronghold in Syria, by killing Sunqur, who held the place on behalf of the Banū Munqidh of Shayzar.[114] Maṣyāf, situated about forty kilometres to the west of Ḥamāt, subsequently became the usual headquarters of the chief *dāʿī* of the Syrian Nizārīs. Around the same time, the Nizārīs captured several other fortresses in the Jabal Bahrā', including Khawābī, Ruṣāfa, Manīqa and Qulayʿa, which became collectively designated as the *qilāʿ al-daʿwa*.[115] As noted, William of Tyre, writing a few decades later,

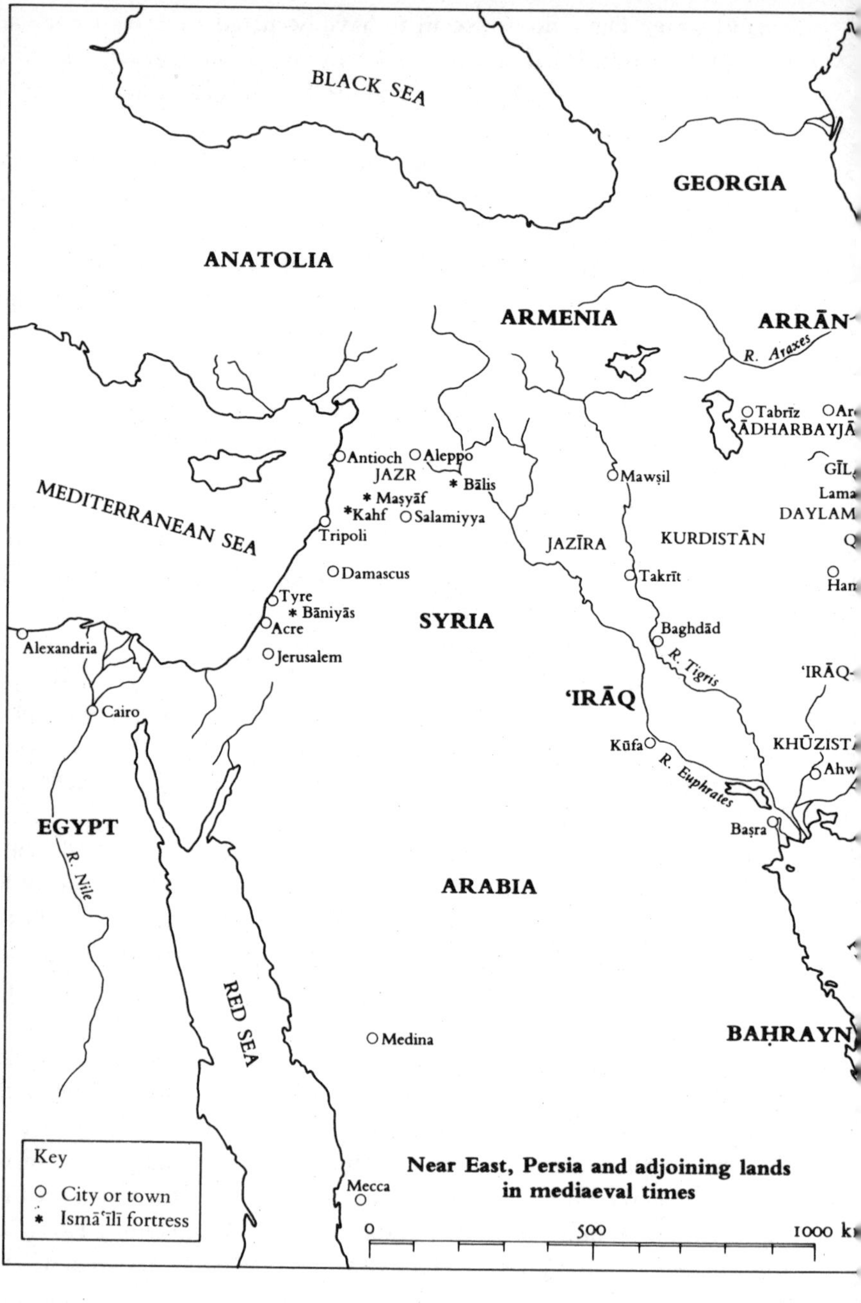

Near East, Persia and adjoining lands in mediaeval times

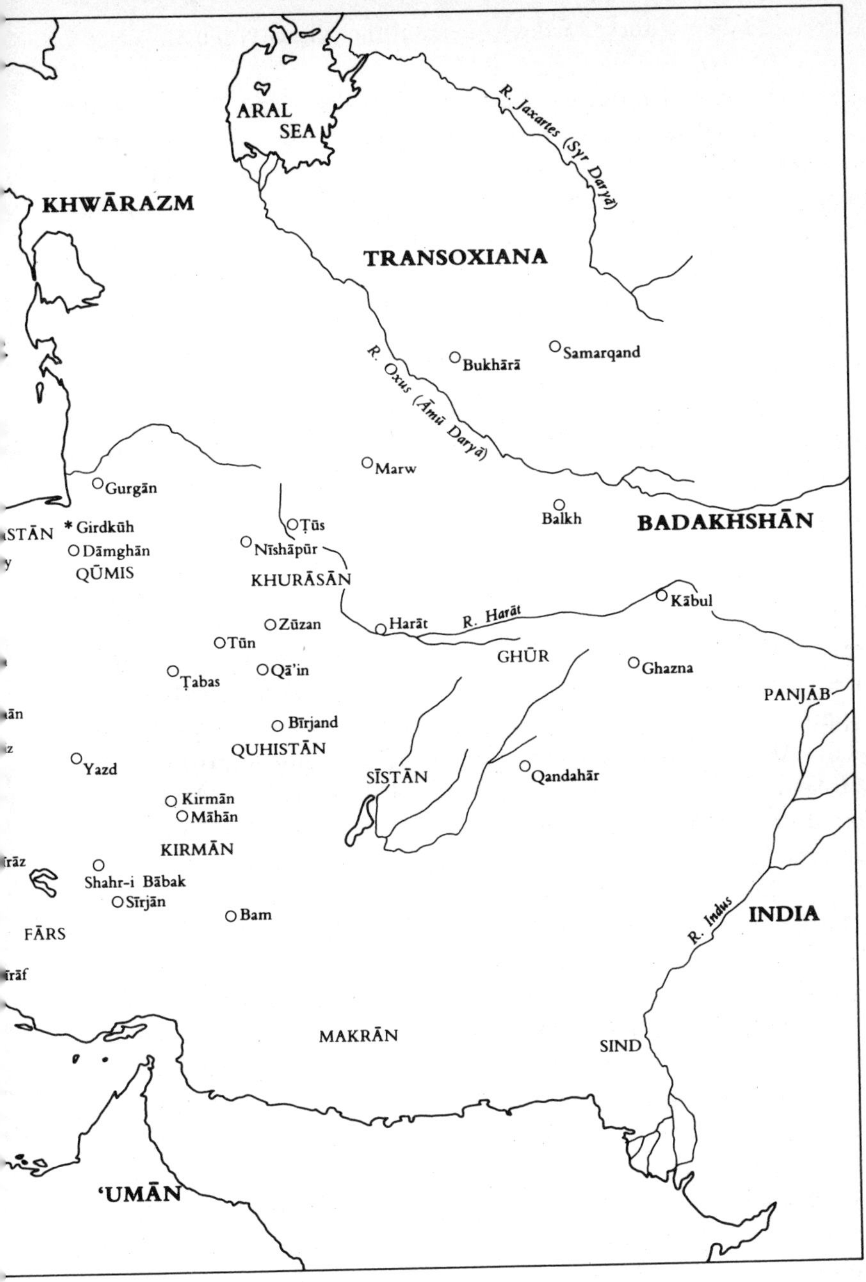
ARAL SEA
R. Jaxartes (Syr Daryā)
KHWĀRAZM
TRANSOXIANA
Bukhārā
Samarqand
R. Oxus (Āmū Daryā)
Marw
Gurgān
Balkh
BADAKHSHĀN
* Girdkūh
Ṭūs
Dāmghān
Nīshāpūr
QŪMIS
KHURĀSĀN
Kābul
R. Harāt
Harāt
Zūzan
Tūn
GHŪR
Ghazna
Ṭabas
Qāʾin
PANJĀB
Bīrjand
QUHISTĀN
Yazd
SĪSTĀN
Qandahār
Kirmān
Māhān
KIRMĀN
Shahr-i Bābak
R. Indus
INDIA
Sīrjān
Bam
FĀRS
MAKRĀN
SIND
ʿUMĀN

puts the number of these castles at ten and the Nizārī population of the region at 60,000.

Indeed, in less than twenty years after their debacle in Damascus, the Syrian Nizārīs had succeeded in establishing a network of mountain fortresses and consolidating their position despite the hostility of the local Sunnī rulers of Syria and the threats posed by the Crusaders, who were active in the adjacent areas belonging to the Latin states of Antioch and Tripoli. As in Persia, however, the Nizārīs of Syria were content as a local power controlling a particular territory and enjoying for some time an independent status. The sources relate only a few scanty details on the relations between the Syrian Nizārīs and the outside world during this period when the sectarians were chiefly preoccupied with consolidating themselves in the Jabal Bahrā'. Doubtless, the Syrian Nizārīs had always been apprehensive of the Turkish rulers of Mawṣil, who were friendly with the Saljūqs and who held a strategic region along the line of communication between the Syrian and Persian centres of the sect. And when Zangī b. Āq Sunqur (521–541/1127–1146), the Saljūq governor of Mawṣil, took Aleppo in 522/1128, the Syrian Nizārīs became even more threatened. In 543/1148, Zangī's son and successor Nūr al-Dīn Maḥmūd (541–569/1146–1174) abolished the Shīʿī forms of prayer hitherto used in Aleppo, which amounted to an open declaration of war on the Ismāʿīlīs and the Aleppine Shīʿīs in general.[116] It is therefore not surprising that in the following year, a contingent of Nizārīs led by a certain ʿAlī b. Wafā' assisted Raymond of Antioch in his campaign against Nūr al-Dīn; ʿAlī b. Wafā' and Raymond were amongst those who perished in the fighting in Ṣafar 544/June 1149 at Inab.[117] Furthermore, only two assassinations by the Syrian Nizārīs are recorded for this period. In 543/1149, two *fidā'īs* murdered Ḍaḥḥāk b. Jandal, the tribal chief of the Wādī al-Taym, who had earlier inflicted a severe defeat on the Nizārīs, killing Bahrām.[118] And in 547/1152, a band of *fidā'īs* attacked and assassinated count Raymond II of Tripoli, together with Ralph of Merle and another knight who at the time were accompanying the count to the gates of Tripoli.[119] The motives behind the assassination of Raymond II, the first Frankish victim of the Nizārīs, were never revealed. But the Christians of Tripoli in a frenzy of revenge, attacked the Syrians, and the Templars raided the Syrian Nizārīs. It was probably from that time that the Syrian Nizārīs were obliged to begin paying an annual tribute to the Templar military order.

By the end of Buzurg-Ummīd's rule, the Nizārīs had clearly established an independent state of their own. The scattered territories of this state consisted primarily of two areas in Persia, namely, Rūdbār and a large tract of Quhistān, as well as the southern part of the Jabal Bahrā' in Syria. The capital of this state, where the Persian head of the Nizārī community resided, was normally at Alamūt, and less frequently at other fortresses of Rūdbār. The Nizārī territory in Quhistān was extensive, though not continuous, and it included several towns and fortresses. The Quhistānī Nizārīs owned the authority of a single chief, sometimes called *muḥtashim*, who was appointed from Alamūt and usually resided in Tūn, Qā'in, or in the castle of Mu'minābād, in the vicinity of Bīrjand. The Nizārīs soon lost their strongholds in eastern Alburz, but they retained two other scattered tracts in Persia. In Qūmis, they held on to Girdkūh and a few other isolated fortresses near Dāmghān. Girdkūh became the last Nizārī stronghold in Persia to surrender to the Mongols. The Persian Nizārīs also held some fortresses in cental Zagros, in the region of Luristān, which they had probably acquired after losing Arrajān and other castles in southern Zagros. In Syria, they controlled the southern Jabal Bahrā' region from their fortresses. Their chief, residing at Maṣyāf or Kahf, was normally appointed from Alamūt. For some time, the Nizārī community included not only those living in the Nizārī territories, but also a significant number of Nizārīs in other Persian and Syrian towns. However, gradually the Nizārīs came to be located chiefly in their own territories, though some sectarians continued to be found in the Jazr district of Syria, and in parts of Quhistān and Sīstān not under Nizārī rule. At the same time, there were non-Ismāʿīlīs, including Sunnīs, Imāmīs, Zaydīs and Nuṣayrīs, living in the areas held by the Nizārīs. The Nizārī state had its own mint and supreme head, who acted as an independent territorial ruler and was generally accepted as such by others. This was clearly demonstrated already in 530/1136 when a certain Saljūq *amīr* Yaranqush (Yarnaqash), dislodged from his *iqṭā*ʿs by the Khwārazmians, took refuge at Alamūt. Although this *amīr* had been an enemy of the Nizārīs, Buzurg-Ummīd declined to deliver him to the Khwārazmshāh, a Saljūq vassal who himself had been friendly with the Nizārīs, declaring that he would not betray a man who had taken asylum with him.

The Nizārī territories were separated from one another by long distances, and yet the Nizārī state maintained a remarkable cohesion and sense of unity both internally and against the outside world, which could not have been enforced by military power or centralization of authority alone. Indeed, each territory enjoyed a certain degree of independence and initiative in conducting its local affairs, while they all shared a common purpose and acted in unison *vis-à-vis* the outside world. The Nizārī groups, differing in their local conditions and problems, nevertheless shared a common heritage and sense of mission. Having acquired its independence from the Fāṭimid regime, the Nizārī community, highly disciplined and dedicated to its purpose, continued to manifest a strong sense of solidarity in maintaining its independence from the surrounding Turkish rulers. Consequently, the most drastic changes of policy initiated at Alamūt were accepted throughout the Nizārī community. Similarly, the Nizārī territories readily acknowledged the supreme leadership of the central head of the sect, while the Quhistānī and Syrian Nizārīs accepted the authority of their local chiefs designated by Alamūt. The tradition of the centralization of authority in the Ismāʿīlī movement and the hierarchism in the *daʿwa* organization were obviously effective antecedents contributing to the cohesion of the Nizārī community, but doubtless the common vision of the community also played an important part. The Nizārīs maintained a strong sense of their mission, and even after failing in their initial revolt against the Saljūqs, they continued to dedicate themselves to preparing the way for the general rule of the Nizārī Ismāʿīlī Imām. As a result, the Nizārī state manifested a stability rarely encountered at the time in similarly situated small principalities of the Muslim world. Most of the lords of Alamūt had long reigns, and there seem to have been no succession disputes in the state, whether the community was led by a *dāʿī*, or later, by an imām. Indeed, the central heads of the Nizārī community continued to enjoy the allegiance of the widely dispersed Nizārī territories for more than one and a half centuries.

The Nizārī community of the Alamūt period, comprised of highlanders and mountain dwellers, villagers, and urban groups living in small towns, maintained a sophisticated outlook and placed a high value on intellectual activities, encouraged by the local sense of initiative in the main Nizārī territories. In Alamūt, Quhistān, and Syria, the Nizārīs established impressive libraries, containing not only religious literature of all sorts, including Ismāʿīlī works, but also scientific tracts and equipments. The Nizārīs seem to have been interested in different branches of learning, and the vitality of their community was reinforced by the continuing arrival of a certain number of outsiders into their centres. Eminent Muslim scholars such as Naṣīr al-Dīn al-Ṭūsī, availed themselves of the Nizārī libraries and patronage of learning; some of them even embraced Ismāʿīlism at least temporarily. In sum, as Hodgson has observed, the vigour and stability of the Nizārī state can only in part be attributed to the specific methods of struggle used by the sectarians or to the genius of the earliest Nizārī leaders in Persia. Doubtless, the Nizārī solidarity under outside pressure, total dedication to their mission, a strong sense of initiative among the local Nizārī groups, and the special appeal of the movement to outstanding individuals in the Muslim society, also played a role.[120]

Kiyā Buzurg-Ummīd died in Jumādā I 532/February 1138, and was buried next to Ḥasan-i Ṣabbāḥ, where his tomb was piously visited. Buzurg-Ummīd was succeeded as *dāʿī* in Alamūt by his son Muḥammad, whom he had designated as heir only three days before his death.[121] Muḥammad b. Buzurg-Ummīd readily received the allegiance of all the Nizārī territories, and henceforth hereditary central leadership became established in the Nizārī state. This was indeed a new feature of the Nizārī community, although the Nizārīs were already familiar with hereditary rule on a local basis in Girdkūh and elsewhere. The enemies of the Nizārīs had evidently counted on some resistance to Muḥammad's leadership, but such hopes soon proved ill-founded as the Nizārīs maintained their solidarity.

At least in the earlier part of Muḥammad's long reign (532–557/1138–1162), the area under the control of Alamūt was extended in Daylamān and Gīlān, where several new fortresses were acquired or constructed. Amongst such mountain castles, the Nizārī chroniclers, notably the *ra'īs* Ḥasan b. Ṣalāḥ Munshī Bīrjandī, quoted by our Persian historians, mention Saʿādatkūh, Mubārakkūh and Fīrūzkūh. These castles were acquired chiefly through the efforts of a Nizārī commander called Kiyā Muḥammad b. ʿAlī Khusraw Fīrūz, who led expeditions from Alamūt and was subsequently appointed as commandant of some of the new fortresses. During these years, the Nizārī raids were sometimes led by Kiyā ʿAlī (d. 538/1144), Muḥammad b. Buzurg-Ummīd's brother. The Nizārīs are also reported to have extended their activities to Georgia (Gurjistān), where they raided and carried on the *daʿwa*. They also made a major effort to penetrate an entirely new region, Ghūr, to the east of Quhistān, in present-day central Afghanistan. It seems that the Nizārī *daʿwa* was established in that region around 550/1155 at the request of the Ghūrid ruler ʿAlā' al-Dīn Ḥusayn Jahānsūz (544–556/1149–1161). But soon after ʿAlā' al-Dīn's death, his son and succesor Sayf al-Dīn Muḥammad (d. 558/1163) massacred the Nizārī *dāʿīs* despatched from Alamūt, as well as their converts in Ghūr.[122] As a territorial power, the Nizārīs were mainly involved in petty quarrels with their immediate neighbours. The Nizārī chroniclers of Muḥammad's reign pay special attention to these local conflicts, especially the continuing series of raids and counter-raids between Rūdbār and Qazwīn, providing details on the number of sheep, cows and other booty taken on each occasion. Although the Nizārīs continued to maintain a strong sense of their mission even during this period of stalemate, the days of the great Nizārī revolt had clearly ended and the vigorous campaigns of the earliest years in Nizārī history had now transformed into petty local entanglements.

In the area of assassination, too, the Persian Nizārīs now made fewer attempts as compared to Ḥasan-i Ṣabbāḥ's time. A total of fourteen assassinations are recorded for Muḥammad b. Buzurg-Ummīd's reign, mostly occurring during his earlier years between 532 and 537 A.H.[123] The first victim of this period was another ʿAbbāsid, al-Mustarshid's son and successor al-Rāshid (529–530/1135–1136). Like his father, al-Rāshid had become involved in Saljūq disputes and, refusing to give allegiance to the Saljūq sultan Masʿūd, he was deposed after a short caliphate in favour of his uncle al-Muqtafī (530–555/1136–1160). Subsequently, al-Rāshid was exiled from ʿIrāq to Persia, where he was killed in Iṣfahān by four Nizārī *fidāʾīs* in Ramaḍān 532/June 1138, a few months after Muḥammad's accession. The Nizārī chroniclers relate, however, that al-Rāshid had set out for Persia to avenge his father. His assassination was countered by the massacre of the Nizārīs by the townspeople of Iṣfahān, while Alamūt rejoiced at al-Rāshid's death with a week of celebrations.[124] Besides al-Rāshid, the most notable victim of this period was the Saljūq sultan Dāʾūd, who had severely persecuted the Nizārīs in Ādharbayjān, then under his rule. He was murdered in Tabrīz, curiously enough by four Syrian *fidāʾīs*, in 538/1143. Amongst other famous victims, the roll of honour kept at Alamūt lists Girdbāzū, the son of the local ruler of Māzandarān, a Georgian ruler, and the *qāḍīs* of Tiflīs, Hamadān, and Quhistān, who had authorized the execution of the Nizārīs.

The Nizārīs of northern Persia were also confronted with two persistent enemies in the persons of Shāh Ghāzī Rustam b. ʿAlāʾ al-Dawla ʿAlī, the Bāwandid ruler of Māzandarān and Gīlān, and ʿAbbās, the Saljūq governor of Rayy. After the assassination of his son Girdbāzū in 537/1142 at the hands of the Nizārīs, Shāh Ghāzī continuously attacked the Nizārīs of Rūdbār, killing large numbers of them and building towers of their heads. Similarly, ʿAbbās, upon hearing in 535/1141 the news of the Nizārī assassination of Jawhar, his master, in Sanjar's camp, massacred the Nizārīs of Rayy and thereafter attacked and killed many Nizārīs in Alamūt and elsewhere. In 541/1146, the Nizārīs were obliged to send an emissary to Sanjar asking for his intervention to end the menace posed by ʿAbbās. A few months later, ʿAbbās was murdered whilst on a visit to Baghdād, on the sultan Masʿūd's order and evidently at Sanjar's request; his head was sent to Alamūt.[125] This was apparently another period of agreement between the Nizārī leaders and Sanjar. However, earlier in 538/1143, the Nizārīs had repelled an attack by Masʿūd's army on Lamasar and other localities in Rūdbār. And later, Sanjar lent his support to the enemies of the Quhistānī Nizārīs. Al-ʿAmīd b. Manṣūr (or Masʿūd), the governor of Ṭuraythīth, had somehow submitted to the Nizārīs of Quhistān, but his son and successor ʿAlā' al-Dīn Maḥmūd attempted to restore Sunnism in the area in 545/1150 and was expelled. He appealed to Sanjar for help, but in the following year a Saljūq army led by the *amīr* Qajaq failed to reinstate Maḥmūd.[126] Shortly afterwards, one of Sanjar's *amīrs*, Muḥammad b. Anaz, probably with his master's approval, began conducting an almost personal series of raids against the Nizārīs of Quhistān, who carried out raids of their own in the region.[127] The anti-Nizārī activities of Ibn Anaz continued for at least six years until 554/1159, even after Sanjar's death in 552/1157.

The stalemate between the Nizārīs and the Saljūqs, and the overall setback in the Nizārī struggle, must have been disappointing to the Nizārī community. By the time of Muḥammad b. Buzurg-Ummīd, many Nizārīs doubtless looked back to the glorious past and the campaigns of Ḥasan-i Ṣabbāḥ's days. At the same time, the Nizārīs had continued to wait since Nizār's death for the open manifestation of their imām, who was to deliver them from injustice. It seems that by the later years of Muḥammad b. Buzurg-Ummīd, a number of young Nizārīs had begun to favour certain radical Ismāʿīlī doctrines of earlier times. These Nizārīs indeed seemed to be highly restive for the parousia of their imām and the coming of the *qiyāma*. At any rate, the young Nizārīs inclined to such ideas found a leader in Muḥammad b. Buzurg-Ummīd's heir apparent Ḥasan, who shared and encouraged their ideals.

According to our Persian historians, Ḥasan, born in 520/1126, developed an early interest in studying the past history and doctrines of the Ismāʿīlī movement. He examined the teachings of Ḥasan-i Ṣabbāḥ. He also read philosophic and Ṣūfī writings. Possessing intellectual qualities and reading widely, Ḥasan became quite learned and acquired many followers in Alamūt. In particular, he became well versed in the Ismāʿīlī *ta'wīl*, and his allegorical interpretations became popular amongst his followers.

Indeed, many of the younger Nizārīs soon began to regard Ḥasan as the imām who had been promised by Ḥasan-i Ṣabbāḥ. Having been endowed with eloquence and a charismatic personality, Ḥasan's popularity increased rapidly in Rūdbār. Already in Muḥammad b. Buzurg-Ummīd's time, many Nizārīs followed and obeyed him as their leader.[128]

Eventually, Muḥammad b. Buzurg-Ummīd, who like his predecessors was rigid in his observance of the Sharīʿa and the conduct of the *daʿwa* on behalf of the imām, was obliged to take drastic action against the radical Nizārīs who followed Ḥasan and believed in his imāmate. On one occasion, he had 250 of them killed in Alamūt and exiled the same number from the castle. From that time till Muḥammad's death, Ḥasan made every effort, orally and in writing, to refute the earlier ideas preached by himself and his partisans. But Ḥasan was merely waiting for the opportune time to propagate his drastic ideas.

Muḥammad b. Buzurg-Ummīd fell ill and died in Rabīʿ I 557/March 1162; he was buried next to Ḥasan-i Ṣabbāḥ, Kiyā Buzurg-Ummīd and Abū ʿAlī Ardistānī. Muḥammad was succeeded by Ḥasan, at the time about thirty-five years old, who had earlier been designated as heir.[129] Ḥasan, who was then considered to be Muḥammad b. Buzurg-Ummīd's son, proceeded cautiously to prepare the way for a religious revolution which was to initiate a new phase in the history of Nizārī Ismāʿīlism. About two and a half years after his accession, he gathered at Alamūt the representatives of the various Nizārī territories, at least those in Persia, to announce his religious revolution. The accounts of this amazing event are preserved by our Persian historians and a few later Nizārī authors.[130]

In Ramaḍān 559 A.H., Ḥasan ordered a pulpit (*minbar*) to be erected, facing towards the west in the public prayer ground at the foot of Alamūt. And four large banners (singular, *ʿalam*) of four colours, white, red, yellow and green, were attached to the four pillars of the pulpit. Then, on 17 Ramaḍān 559/8 August 1164, he ordered the people of his territories, whom he had previously summoned to Alamūt, to assemble there. The Nizārīs from Rūdbār and Daylam were placed in front of the pulpit, those from Khurāsān and Quhistān were stationed on the right side, while the *rafīqs* from central and western parts of Persia stood on the left side of the pulpit. Ḥasan, wearing a white garment and a white turban, came down from the castle about noon and ascended the pulpit. He greeted the assembly and, after sitting down for a moment, rose up and holding his sword, delivered in a loud voice a message which supposedly had been secretly sent to him by the hidden imām who now had new instructions for his followers. The imām of our time, Ḥasan declared, has sent you his blessings and compassion; he has called you his special chosen servants, he has relieved you of the duties and burdens of the Sharīʿa, and has brought you to the *qiyāma*, the Resurrection. Ḥasan then delivered a *khuṭba* in Arabic, claiming that his address represented the exact words of the imām. The jurist Muḥammad Bustī, who knew Arabic, had been placed at the foot of the pulpit to translate this *khuṭba* into Persian for those present. The *khuṭba* named Ḥasan not only as the imām's *dāʿī* and *ḥujja* or proof, like Ḥasan-i Ṣabbāḥ, but also his *khalīfa*, or deputy, with plenary authority, a higher rank yet. The imām also required that his *shīʿa* must obey and follow Ḥasan in all religious and temporal matters, recognize his commands as binding, and deem his word as that of the imām's. After completing his address, Ḥasan descended from the pulpit and performed the two prostrations (*rakʿat*) of the festival prayer (*namāz-i ʿīd*). Then he invited the people to join him at a table which had been prepared for the breaking of their fast. Ḥasan declared that day the Festival of the Resurrection (*ʿīd-i qiyāmat*), and the people feasted and made merry. Henceforth, the 17th of Ramaḍān was celebrated annually as the Festival of the Resurrection by the Nizārīs who rejoiced on that day.

A few weeks later, shortly before the time of the *ḥajj* pilgrimage, a similar ceremony was held at the fortress of Mu'mināābād, to the east of Bīrjand in Quhistān. Ḥasan had sent the *khuṭba*, the epistle and the message which he had delivered at Alamūt, to the *ra'īs* Muẓaffar, his deputy who had headed the Nizārīs of Quhistān since 555/1160, by the hand of a person called Muḥammad Khāqān. These documents, proclaiming the *qiyāma* and indicating the position of Ḥasan, were read out to the representatives of the Quhistānī Nizārīs, in Dhu'l-Qaʿda 559/September–October 1164, by the *ra'īs* Muẓaffar from a special pulpit set up for the occasion. In addition, Muḥammad Khāqān delivered an oral message from Ḥasan. The lord of Alamūt now declared that just as previously al-Mustanṣir had been God's *khalīfa* or representative on earth and Ḥasan-i Ṣabbāḥ had been al-Mustanṣir's *khalīfa*, so now Ḥasan II himself was the *khalīfa* of God on earth and the *ra'īs* Muẓaffar was Ḥasan's *khalīfa* in Quhistān; hence his commands were to be obeyed. At the close of the ceremony, the Nizārī assembly rejoiced at the steps of the pulpit in Mu'minābād. In Syria, too, the *qiyāma* was announced, evidently a while later, and the Syrian Nizārīs likewise celebrated the beginning of a new era.

The public proclamations made at Alamūt and Mu'minābād, in 559/1164, indeed amounted to a religious revolution. Ḥasan II, whom the

Nizārīs called *ʿalā dhikrihi'l-salām* (on his mention be peace), had in effect introduced the doctrine of the *qiyāma*. To the Nizārī inhabitants of Rūdbār, Quhistān, and other territories, Ḥasan had announced the *qiyāma* (Persian, *qiyāmat*), the long-awaited Last Day when mankind would be judged and committed forever to either Paradise (*bihisht*) or Hell (*dūzakh*). Relying heavily on the Ismāʿīlī *ta'wīl*, however, *qiyāma* and *maʿād*, or the end of the world, was interpreted symbolically and spiritually.[131] The Resurrection was interpreted to mean the manifestation of the unveiled truth (*ḥaqīqa*) in the person of the Nizārī Imām. Accordingly, the believers, those who had embraced Nizārī Ismāʿīlism, were now capable of comprehending the truth or spiritual reality, the *bāṭin* of the religious laws, and as such, Paradise was actualized for them in this world. On the other hand, the non-Nizārīs who had refused to acknowledge the Nizārī Imām, were henceforth cast into Hell, which was spiritual non-being. As the person who had brought the *qiyāma*, the Nizārī Imām of the time was also the judge of mankind and the Qā'im of the Resurrection (*Qā'im al-qiyāma*), a rank which in Ismāʿīlī thought was above that of ordinary imāms; and his *daʿwa* was the *daʿwa* of the Resurrection (*daʿwat-i qiyāmat*). As noted, Ḥasan *ʿalā dhikrihi'l-salām* had initially claimed to have been the *khalīfa* of the *Qā'im al-qiyāma*. According to the later Nizārī sources, Ḥasan-i Ṣabbāḥ, designated as the *ḥujja* of the *Qā'im al-qiyāma*, had sounded the first blast of the trumpet that had prepared the way for the *qiyāma*, and Ḥasan *ʿalā dhikrihi'l-salām* sounded the second blast that actually brought the *qiyāma*.[132] According to this interpretation of the Resurrection, all believers could come to know God and the mysteries and realities of creation through the Nizārī Imām, as was appropriate in Paradise. This was indeed the time of the Great Resurrection, or the Resurrection of the Resurrections (*qiyāmat-i qiyāmāt*), towards which all lesser searchings, all the partial consummations of the preceding cycles in the history of mankind had been tending. It was the culmination of the ages.

Our Persian historians relate that in line with the expectations of the earlier Ismāʿīlīs concerning the *qiyāma*, Ḥasan II had also announced the abrogation of the Sharīʿa, which had been vigorously enforced by Ḥasan-i Ṣabbāḥ, Buzurg-Ummīd and Muḥammad b. Buzurg-Ummīd. As a consequence of the Resurrection, and as was fitting in Paradise, the believers could henceforth be relieved of the duties and obligations imposed by the law; for in this world all is action (*ʿamal*) and there is no reckoning (*ḥisāb*), but in the world of the *qiyāma* all is reckoning and there is no action. According to the same sources, this doctrine thus taught that in the era of the Resurrection (*dawr-i qiyāmat*), men were to turn in every sense towards God and abandon the established habits of worship. For instance, instead of praying five times a day, as required by the Sharīʿa, in the time of the Resurrection they would constantly be with God in their hearts, for such is true prayer (*namāz-i ḥaqīqī*). Our sources add that in like manner, the Nizārīs interpreted, through *ta'wīl*, all the other principles of the Sharīʿa and the practices of Islam. According to Rashīd al-Dīn and Kāshānī, it was for their abolition of the Sharīʿa that the Nizārīs became designated as the *malāḥida*, or heretics.[133]

The announcement of the *qiyāma* was in fact a declaration of independence from the larger Muslim society and, at the same time, an admission of failure of the Nizārī struggle to take over that society; for the *qiyāma* declared the outside world irrelevant. The Nizārīs envisaged themselves in spiritual Paradise, while condemning the non-Nizārīs to the Hell of spiritual non-existence. Now the Nizārīs had the opportunity of being collectively introduced to Paradise on earth, which was the knowledge of the unveiled truth; the Nizārī Imām was the epiphany (*maẓhar*) of that unchangeable *ḥaqīqa*. It was in this sense that the Nizārīs reportedly celebrated the end of the religious era (*dawr-i sharīʿat*) and earthly life, represented by the *ẓāhir* of reality. Henceforth, the *bāṭin* of that reality became apparent to the Nizārīs, who were to lead a purely spiritual life. Like the Ṣūfīs, the Nizārīs were now to leave behind all material compromise and rise to the spiritual level of existence. In the year 559/1164 the Nizārī Ismāʿīlīs of the Alamūt period entered the second phase of their history, the phase of the *qiyāma*, which was to last forty-six years until the year 607/1210.

The announcement of the *qiyāma*, as noted, also introduced an important change in the status of the lord of Alamūt. In his initial proclamation at Alamūt, Ḥasan II had declared himself the imām's *dāʿī*, like his predecessors, and *ḥujja*, like Ḥasan-i Ṣabbāḥ, and his *khalīfa*. By the latter term, now used for the first time by a lord of Alamūt, Ḥasan II was claiming a specific position, evidently superior to the ranks of *dāʿī* and *ḥujja*. Our Persian historians explain that Ḥasan II claimed to be the imām's sole vicegerent and deputy (*qā'im maqām va nā'ib-i munfarid*).[134] At Mu'minābād, Ḥasan's position as *khalīfa* was explicitly identified with that of the Fāṭimid caliph al-Mustanṣir, who had been the imām. After the proclamation of the *qiyāma*, Ḥasan, in his epistles (*fuṣūl*) and addresses, apparently hinted that he himself was the imām and the *Qā'im al-qiyāma*, the son of an imām from the progeny of Nizār b. al-Mustanṣir, though in appearance he had been considered to be the son of Muḥammad b. Buzurg-Ummīd.[135] At any rate, it seems that Ḥasan II claimed the imāmate in some sense towards the end of his life.[136]

The account of the doctrine of the *qiyāma* presented in this chapter is based, as noted, on our Persian historians, some Nizārī works of later times, and the standard interpretation of Hodgson, endorsed by Corbin and Madelung, amongst other modern specialists in the field. The declaration of the *qiyāma* and its particular implications for the Nizārīs of the Alamūt period, however, represent a highly controversial episode in the history of Nizārī Ismāʿīlism. Many modern day Nizārīs, indeed, question the truth behind certain aspects of the narratives of this episode. According to them, a fundamental function of the current Nizārī Imām has always been the contextualization of the interpretation of the Sharīʿa and the practice of the faith in his own time. As a result, they are of the opinion that the declaration of the *qiyāma* represented an attempt by the imām to give an interpretation to the Sharīʿa that fitted the times. And the few modern Nizārī scholars who have occasionally referred to the declaration of the *qiyāma* in the Alamūt period, have made statements such as 'the outward performance of ritual elaborated in the *sharīʿah*, or religious law, was not abrogated as is generally thought'.[137] In view of the fact that no contemporary Nizārī sources have survived from the *qiyāma* period, it is very difficult to know precisely how the *qiyāma* was actually perceived by the rank and file of the Nizārī community, who were scattered in remote areas with diverse socio-economic and cultural as well as rural-urban characteristics. Highly valuing the preservation of their identity, the Nizārīs doubtless continued to regard themselves as Shīʿī Muslims, and as such, especially when soon after the declaration of the *qiyāma* the community came to be led by a manifest imām, they did not become a lawless society indulging in libertinism. Indeed, our Persian historians do not report any instances of libertinism in connection with the Persian Nizārī community of the *qiyāma* times. Even Juwaynī, always ready to express his strong anti-Ismāʿīlī sentiments, remained silent on the subject.

In the absence of contemporary reports, we cannot determine the extent to which the observance of different religious commandments came to be affected in the Nizārī community as a result of the declaration of the *qiyāma*. It seems that the community conformed to the new doctrine at least outwardly. Doubtless, many Nizārīs who in general had been used to a strict moral purism founded on the sacred law of Islam, continued to closely obey the commands and prohibitions of the Sharīʿa. According to Juwaynī, some Nizārīs even chose to give up their houses and properties and emigrated from the Nizārī territories, especially going from Quhistān to nearby areas in Khurāsān.[138] Be that as it may, the Nizārī leadership had now stressed the spirituality and the inner meaning of the religious commandments as compared to their routine performance. In other words, the faithful, now once again led directly by an infallible imām, were henceforth expected in the *qiyāma* times to concentrate on the spiritual reality behind the positive law. The salvation of the Nizārīs now depended on their recognition of the true spiritual reality of the Nizārī Imām rather than on blindly observing the rituals specified by the Sharīʿa.

Meanwhile, the Nizārīs had for some time not had any entanglements with the Saljūqs, whose power was rapidly on the decline. But in 560/1165, immediately after the proclamation of the *qiyāma* when the sultan Arslān (556–571/1161–1176) was ruling over western Persia, the Nizārīs, who had then built a new fortress just outside Qazwīn, besieged that town. But they were obliged to retreat when the sultan's forces came to the aid of the Qazwīnīs.[139] Around the same time, the *amīr* Muḥammad b. Anaz raided the Quhistānī Nizārīs, killing many and taking much booty.[140]

A year and a half after the declaration of the Resurrection, on 6 Rabīʿ I 561/9 January 1166, Ḥasan II was stabbed in the castle of Lamasar by a brother-in-law, Ḥasan b. Nāmāwar, who belonged to a local Daylamī branch of the Imāmī Buwayhid family and who opposed Ḥasan II's new policies. Ḥasan *ʿalā dhikrihi'l-salām* died of his wounds and was succeeded by his nineteen-year-old son Muḥammad, who was born in Shawwāl 542/March 1148. Nūr al-Dīn Muḥammad II reigned for forty-four years, longer than any other Khudāwand of Alamūt.[141] Immediately upon his accession, Muḥammad II put to death Ḥasan b. Nāmāwar, together with all his relatives. Muḥammad II, who is said to have been a prolific writer, reaffirmed Ḥasan II's policies and devoted his life to a systematic elaboration of the doctrine of the *qiyāma*. Aside from adopting and sharpening the doctrine of the *qiyāma* to an ongoing life, however, Muḥammad II seems to have altered or modified his father's teachings in two respects. He claimed the imāmate for his father and, therefore, for himself in the fullest sense. He also put the imām, more specifically the present Nizārī Imām, at the very centre of the doctrine of the *qiyāma*.

In accordance with the earliest expectations of the Ismāʿīlīs, the imām had to be present in person at the time of the *qiyāma*; for it was precisely the eschatological role of the culminating imām, the Qā'im, to inaugurate the *qiyāma*. The Nizārīs of the time of the Resurrection thus expected to know the identity of the imām who had ushered in the *qiyāma* for his community. As noted, Ḥasan II had hinted that he was not merely the representative of the imām, but the imām himself. Muḥammad II explicitly claimed that his father had been the imām also by physical descent. According to our Persian historians and the Nizārī tradition, he claimed that Ḥasan II was not the son of Muḥammad b. Buzurg-Ummīd, as it had been previously believed, but the son of a descendant of Nizār who had secretly found refuge in a village near Alamūt. He in effect claimed a Nizārid ʿAlid genealogy for his father and himself. Thus, after a period of some seventy years following Nizār's death, the line of the Nizārī Imāms emerged openly and the Nizārīs henceforth recognized the lords of Alamūt, beginning with Ḥasan II, as their imāms. There were alternative versions of Ḥasan II's Nizārid ancestry, as reported by Juwaynī and other Persian historians.[142] The Nizārīs maintained that in 488/1095, a year after al-Mustanṣir's death, a certain *qāḍī* Abu'l-Ḥasan Ṣaʿīdī went from Egypt to Alamūt, secretly taking with him a grandson of Nizār who was known as al-Muhtadī. The secret was divulged only to Ḥasan-i Ṣabbāḥ, who protected Nizār's grandson, who was living clandestinely at the foot of Alamūt. According to the most widely popular version, a son born to Nizār's grandson or great-grandson, and who subsequently ruled as Ḥasan II, was exchanged with a son born at the same time to Muḥammad b. Buzurg-Ummīd, without the latter's knowledge. According to yet another version, a pregnant wife of Nizār's descendant at Alamūt was given to Muḥammad's care, and, in due course, gave birth to Ḥasan II. On the basis of the genealogy subsequently circulating amongst the Nizārīs, there were three generations between Ḥasan II and Nizār, Ḥasan being represented as the son of al-Qāhir b. al-Muhtadī b. al-Hādī b. Nizār.[143] Once Ḥasan II and his son Muḥammad II were recognized as Nizārids and imāms, the breach with the preceding period of *satr* in early Nizārī Ismāʿīlism, when the imām was hidden from his followers and there were only his *ḥujja*s and *dāʿī*s at Alamūt, was complete. The Nizārī community had now clearly entered the period of the Resurrection, ushered in by the Nizārī Imāms who were at the same time the Qā'ims of the *qiyāma*.

In his elaboration of the doctrine of the *qiyāma*, Muḥammad II assigned a central role to the imām, and more specifically to the present imām.[144] The exaltation of the autonomous teaching authority of the present imām over that of the previous imāms, already taught by Ḥasan-i Ṣabbāḥ, and over that of the prophets, in fact became the outstanding feature of Nizārī thought. The *qiyāma* entailed much more than the psychological independence of the believers from the outside world. It implied a complete personal transformation of the Nizārīs who henceforth were expected to see nothing but the imām, and the manifestation of the divine truth in him. The imām in his eternal essence was defined as the epiphany (*maẓhar*) of the word (*kalima*) or command (*amr*) of God.[145] In Shīʿī thought, the imām had been considered as the *ḥujja* or proof of God. But in the Paradise of the *qiyāma*, the present Nizārī Imām became the manifestation of the divine word or order to create, the cause of the spiritual world. It was essentially through this vision of the imām that men could find themselves in Paradise, and not by being in Rūdbār, Quhistān, or any other particular locality. More specifically, this vision did not consist of merely knowing the identity of the true imām of the time, or of seeing the body of that imām. The imām had to be seen in his spiritual reality, by penetrating the metaphysical and mystical significance of his person. If one saw the imām in his spiritual reality, then all else that one saw and did would follow from that knowledge, enabling one to view the whole world from the imām's viewpoint and no longer from one's personal viewpoint. As a result, one would see only the imām, and not oneself, living a totally spiritual life which was the afterlife expected by the Ismāʿīlīs.[146]

This viewpoint towards the universe, and the imām in particular, would lead the individual to a third level of being, in effect a world of *bāṭin* behind the *bāṭin*, the ultimate reality or *ḥaqīqa*, contrasted to the worlds of the *sharīʿa* and its *bāṭin* as interpreted by the ordinary Ismāʿīlī *ta'wīl*. In the realm of the *ḥaqīqa*, the believers would turn from the world of appearances to the realm of ultimate reality and unchangeable truths. The *qiyāma* was thus identified with *ḥaqīqa*, a realm of spiritual life and awareness in the presence of God. On that level of existence, the believers had only an inward-spiritual life, merging into their idealized roles as expressions of cosmic harmony. In this sense, the *qiyāma* also amounted to a declaration of spiritual maturity, in which the individual acted solely on the basis of his own consciousness which was at one with the rest of existence in the present imām.

The doctrine of the *qiyāma*, drawing on various earlier religious traditions, introduced a further element in the cyclical history of the Ismāʿīlīs in the new figure of the *imām-qā'im*. There had been *imām-qā'im*s also in earlier prophetic eras. In each era, the *imām-qāʾim* was contemporary with that era's prophet but superior to the latter's *waṣī*. According to the series given in the *Haft bāb-i Bābā Sayyidnā*,[147] the *imam-qāʾims* of the eras of Adam, Noah, and Abraham were, respectively, Malik Shūlīm, Malik Yazdāq and Malik al-Salām, who collectively corresponded to the Biblical Melchizedec, the priest who was honoured by Abraham.[148] In the eras of Moses, Jesus, and Muḥammad, the *imām-qāʾims* were Dhu'l-Qarnayn, identified with the Qur'ānic figure Khiḍr who had drunk of the water of life and would live for ever, Maʿadd, and ʿAlī. Muḥammad II now identified the present imām, the imām who was the master of the *qiyāma*, with the figure of the *imām-qāʾim*, and clearly exalted the authority and status of the present imām, independently from the preceding imāms and the prophets. Furthermore, every imām, when seen rightly, was seen to be ʿAlī, who was identified with the Melchizedec-Dhu'l-Qarnayn-Khiḍr *imām-qāʾim* figure; and every believer was again Salmān, the faithful disciple of the Prophet of Islam and one of the earliest followers of ʿAlī. Thus, in the *qiyāma*, the *imām-qāʾim*, the present imām who was identical with ʿAlī, appeared openly in his spiritual reality to the believers, who in their spiritual relationship to him were identical with Salmān.

The small and scattered Nizārī community of the Alamūt period did not have any use for the elaborate *daʿwa* organization developed by the Fāṭimid Ismāʿīlīs. Until the declaration of the *qiyāma* and the emergence of the imāms, a chief *dāʿī*, with the title of the *dāʿī* of Daylam or the *ḥujja* of the imām, provided central leadership from Alamūt for the Nizārīs, who referred to themselves as *rafīqs*, comrades. The chief *dāʿī* apparently selected the local *dāʿīs* of Quhistān and other Nizārī territories. Only the Syrian Nizārīs seem to have occasionally enjoyed a certain degree of independence from Alamūt. The chief *dāʿī* as well as the local *dāʿīs*, who often acted as military commanders, doubtless must have had a hierarchy of assistants or subordinate *dāʿīs*, about whom no particular details are available. At any event, towards the end of the Alamūt period, the less formal *muʿallim* or religious teacher gradually seems to have replaced the *dāʿī*, as the function of teaching the Nizārī tenets to the members of the sect displaced the function of preaching the *daʿwa* to win new converts. But in the period of the *qiyāma*, when the spiritual reality of the *imām-qāʾim* manifested itself openly to the faithful and in accordance with the earlier predictions about the advent of the Qā'im and the event of the Resurrection, the *daʿwa* organization and its hierarchical ranks intervening between the imām and his followers, whatever they may have been, faded away. In the *qiyāma*, we are informed, there remained only three categories of men.

The Nizārī sources define these categories, representing three different levels of being, in terms of the relationship between the individual and the Nizārī Imām.[149] There are the opponents of the imām (*ahl al-taḍādd*), the non-Nizārī bulk of mankind, including both Muslims and non-Muslims. The opponents, or the common people (*ʿāmm*), who exist only on the realm of appearance (*ẓāhir*) and who do not recognize the imām, are spiritually non-existent in the *qiyāma*. They can be ignored. Secondly, there are the ordinary followers of the imām, the so-called people of gradation (*ahl al-tarattub*), representing the elite of mankind (*khāṣṣ*). These ordinary Nizārīs have gone beyond the Sharīʿa and the *ẓāhir* to the *bāṭin*, the inner meaning of religion. Having found only partial truth, however, they still see both the *ẓāhir* and the *bāṭin*. As a result, they still see both themselves and the imām, and as such, they are not fully saved in the *qiyāma*. Finally, there are the people of union (*ahl al-waḥda*), the super-elite (*akhaṣṣ-i khāṣṣ*) amongst the Nizārīs, who see only the imām in his true nature. Discarding all appearances, the people of union have found full (*kullī*) as opposed to partial (*juzʾī*) truth. They have arrived in the realm of *ḥaqīqa*, the *bāṭin* behind the *bāṭin*, and see only the imām in his true spiritual reality. It is the people of union who are truly resurrected and existent in eternal Paradise; they have obtained full salvation in the *qiyāma*. The other two categories should, therefore, strive to attain the state of the people of union.

There are close analogies between the doctrine of the *qiyāma* and certain Ṣūfī ideas and terminologies. The imām was to serve for his followers as a Ṣūfī *shaykh* or *pīr* did for his disciples. By concentrating their attention on him, they could be made to forget their separate selves; and through him, they could come to attain spiritual birth. However, the Nizārī Imām was more than a mere Ṣūfī *pīr*, one amongst the many such guides. He was a single cosmic individual who summed up in his position the entire reality of existence; the perfect microcosm, for whom no lesser *pīr* could be substituted. The cosmic position of the Nizārī Imām, as the representative of the cosmic reality, was also analogous to the Perfect Man (*al-insān al-kāmil*) of the Ṣūfīs, though again such an abstract figure could not offer a full equivalent of the present and visible Nizārī Imām, with whom the Nizārīs shared a joint spiritual experience. There are many other analogies, such as the identification of the *ḥaqīqa* of the Ṣūfī inner experience with the spiritual afterlife of the Nizārīs in the *qiyāma*. Be it as it may, the doctrine of the *qiyāma* laid the ground for the coalescence between Nizārī Ismāʿīlism and Ṣūfism in Persia during the post-Alamūt period.

The doctrine of the *qiyāma* now effectively replaced the doctrine of *taʿlīm* as central in Nizārī thought. But the doctrine of the *qiyāma*, unlike its predecessor, did not have any impact on the outside world. The contemporary Sunnī chroniclers and theologians, fully aware of the earlier Nizārī revolt and the doctrine of *taʿlīm*, do not refer to the teachings of Ḥasan II and Muḥammad II. Ibn al-Athīr, for instance, does not even mention the Nizārī declaration of the *qiyāma* in 559/1164. It was only after the fall of Alamūt, when Nizārī sources became available to outsiders, that the Sunnī writers, beginning with Juwaynī, took notice of the episode of the *qiyāma* in the Nizārī community. Politically, too, the first three decades of Muḥammad II's reign were rather uneventful. Outside of Syria, the Nizārīs of the *qiyāma* times evidently ignored the Sunnī world, and did not launch any major campaign against their enemies. The Nizārīs of Rūdbār did evidently, however, continue with their local raids against Qazwīn and other neighbours, about which our Persian historians do not seem to have found any specific details. During that period, the Persian Nizārīs assassinated only an ʿAbbāsid vizier in Baghdād; and we come across a single case of an outsider taking refuge at Alamūt; he was Ustandār Hazārasf b. Shahrnūsh (560–586/1164–1190), the Bādūspānid ruler of Rustamdār and Rūyān.[150] The latter, unlike his predecessor Kaykā'ūs, cultivated close relations with the Nizārīs of Rūdbār and gave them a number of castles in his territories. Hazārasf eventually ran into difficulties with his superior, Ḥusām al-Dawla Ardashīr (567–602/1172–1206), the Bāwandid Ispahbad of Māzandarān, and took refuge at Alamūt. Subsequently, with the assistance of the Nizārīs, Hazārasf raided his former territories, also killing an ʿAlid who ruled over Daylamān. Hazārasf was eventually captured by Ardashīr and killed in 586/1190. Rashīd al-Dīn and other Persian historians also relate a story about how the Nizārīs persuaded, initially through a *fidāʾī* and then through bribery, the celebrated Sunnī theologian Fakhr al-Dīn Muḥammad b. ʿUmar al-Rāzī (d. 606/1209) to refrain from speaking against them in public.[151]

Meanwhile, the Syrian Nizārīs had entered the second phase of their history, coinciding with the career of their greatest leader Rāshid al-Dīn Sinān.[152] One of the most prominent figures in Nizārī history, Sinān b. Salmān (or Sulaymān) b. Muḥammad Abu'l-Ḥasan al-Baṣrī, known also as Rāshid al-Dīn, was born into a Shīʿī family in ʿAqr al-Sudan, a village near Baṣra on the road to Wāsiṭ.[153] Sinān was brought up in Baṣra, where he became a schoolmaster and was converted to Nizārī Ismāʿīlism. Subsequently, he went to Alamūt and attended school there with Muḥammad b. Buzurg-Ummīd's heir apparent Ḥasan. During his stay at Alamūt, Sinān studied Ismāʿīlism, the doctrines of the philosophers, and the *Epistles* of the Ikhwān al-Ṣafāʾ, amongst other works, and became a close companion of the young Ḥasan II. Soon after his accession to power in 557/1162, Ḥasan II sent Sinān to Syria. Travelling cautiously through Mawṣil, Raqqa and Aleppo, then ruled by Nūr al-Dīn Maḥmūd b. Zangī, Sinān finally arrived at Kahf, one of the major Nizārī fortresses in the Jabal Bahrāʾ. He remained at Kahf for a while, making himself extremely popular with the local Nizārīs, until Shaykh Abū Muḥammad, the head of the Syrian Nizārī *daʿwa*, died in the mountain.[154] The death of Abū Muḥammad, an obscure *dāʿī*, led to a succession dispute which intensified the existing dissension in the Syrian Nizārī community. Abū Muḥammad was succeeded, without the approval of Alamūt, by a certain Khwāja ʿAlī b. Masʿūd, who had the support of a faction of the community. However, another group of the Syrian Nizārīs, led by Abū Manṣūr, the nephew of Abū Muḥammad, and the *raʾīs* Fahd, conspired against Khwāja ʿAlī and had him murdered. Soon after these events, Sinān assumed the leadership of the Syrian *daʿwa* on the orders of Alamūt. Once established, Sinān began to consolidate the position of his community while adopting suitable policies towards the neighbouring Sunnī rulers and the Crusaders who were a constant threat to the Syrian Nizārīs. He rebuilt the fortresses of Ruṣāfa and Khawābī, fortified and constructed other strongholds, and captured the fortress of ʿUllayqa, near the Frankish castle of Marqab held by the Hospitallers.[155] At the same time, while moving among the various Nizārī castles, especially Maṣyāf, Kahf and Qadmūs, Sinān rapidly ended the internal dissensions of the community and reorganized the Nizārīs; paying particular attention to organizing an independent corps of *fidāʾ*īs.

Externally, Sinān, aiming to protect his state from numerous enemies, concentrated his attention on the Sunnī rulers who were extending their hegemony over Syria. Indeed, in his time, Nūr al-Dīn and Saladin, who were at the height of their power and led the Muslim holy war against the Crusaders, were potentially greater enemies than the Franks for the Nizārīs. And Sinān, a shrewd strategist like Ḥasan-i Ṣabbāḥ, recognized these realities and adopted suitable policies in his dealings with the outside world; policies which were revised when needed to reassure the safety and independence of his state. As a result, from early on, Sinān established peaceful relations with the Crusaders, who had been sporadically fighting the Nizārīs for several decades over the possession of various strongholds. The Nizārīs, however, had meanwhile acquired a new Frankish enemy in the Hospitallers, who in 537/1142 had received from the lord of Tripoli the celebrated fortress of Krak des Chevaliers (Ḥiṣn al-Akrād) at the southern end of the Jabal Bahrā'. The Nizārīs continued to have minor entanglements with the Hospitaller and Templar military orders, which owed their allegiance directly to the Pope and often acted independently, whilst paying an annual tribute to the Templars. Subsequently, around 569/1173, Sinān sent an embassy to Amalric I, seeking a formal rapprochement with the kingdom of Jerusalem in the hope of being relieved from the tribute to the Templars. The negotiations were evidently successful as the king of Jerusalem promised the cancellation of the tribute. The Templars naturally disapproved of this Nizārī embassy, and on their return journey Sinān's emissaries were ambushed and killed by a Templar knight, Walter of Mesnil. Amalric took punitive measures against the Templars, but as he himself died soon afterwards in 570/1174, the negotiations between Sinān, known to the Crusaders as the Old Man of the Mountain, and the Franks of Jerusalem proved fruitless. William of Tyre curiously relates that it was at the time of this embassy that the Syrian Nizārīs proposed to collectively embrace Christianity, having asked Amalric to send them Christian teachers.[156] Needless to say that this story can be regarded as purely fictitious.

When Sinān assumed power, Nūr al-Dīn was preoccupied with his policies against the Crusaders and the declining Fāṭimid Caliphate. Nevertheless, relations between Sinān and Nūr al-Dīn remained relatively tense, due to the activities of the Nizārīs in northern Syria. But Nūr al-Dīn, who finally succeeded through Saladin in overthrowing the Fāṭimids in 567/1171, did not attack the Nizārīs, though it is reported that he was planning a major expedition against them just before his death, when he allegedly exchanged an unfriendly correspondence with Sinān.[157] The death of Nūr al-Dīn in 569/1174, the same year in which Amalric I died, finally gave Saladin his opportunity to act as the champion of the Muslim orthodoxy and the leader of the holy war against the Crusaders. As the strongest of the Muslim rulers in the area, Saladin strove towards incorporating Arabia, Syria and ʿIrāq into his nascent Ayyūbid empire. As a result, he now became the most dangerous enemy of the Syrian Nizārīs, while the Zangids of Aleppo and Mawṣil were equally threatened by his expansionary policies. Under the circumstances, the Nizārīs and the Zangids were induced to cultivate friendly relations in fear of their mutual enemy

Saladin, who had entered Damascus in 570/1174.[158] From Damascus Saladin marched northward, and after capturing Ḥimṣ he laid siege to Aleppo. It was at that time that Gümüshtigin, the effective ruler of Aleppo and the regent of Nūr al-Dīn's young son and nominal successor al-Malik al-Ṣāliḥ, sent messengers to Sinān, offering him land and money in return for the assassination of Saladin. The Nizārī chief accepted the offer and despatched *fidāʾīs*, who penetrated Saladin's camp but failed in their attempt to kill him in Jumādā II 570/December 1174–January 1175. In the following year, when Saladin was besieging ʿAzāz, north of Aleppo, the Nizārī *fidāʾīs* failed in their second attempt to assassinate him on 11 Dhu'l-Qaʿda 571/22 May 1176; thanks to his armour, Saladin received only superficial wounds.[159] Shortly after these events, Saladin, in a vengeful move, invaded the Nizārī territory and besieged Maṣyāf. The siege lasted very briefly, and, on the mediation of his maternal uncle Shihāb al-Dīn Maḥmūd b. Takash, the governor of Ḥamāt and a neighbour interested in having good relations with the Nizārīs, Saladin concluded a truce with Sinān and withdrew his forces from the area. Various reasons have been given for Saladin's withdrawal from the Jabal Bahrāʾ.[160] Whether the mediation was invoked by Sinān or Saladin himself, and for whatever reason, hostilities henceforth ceased between the two men, who had evidently arrived at some sort of agreement. Meanwhile, the Syrian Nizārīs had been menaced by the Nubuwwiyya, a local Sunnī order based in ʿIrāq and bent on harassing the Shīʿīs of the region. It is reported that in 570 A.H., 10,000 Nubuwwī horsemen attacked the Nizārīs of Bāb and Buzāʿa, massacring several thousand people and taking much booty. Ibn Jubayr (d. 614/1217), the Andalusian traveller and writer who passed through Syria in 580/1184–1185, places this event at around 572/1176–1177.[161]

The Nizārīs did not engage in any aggressive acts against Saladin following the latter's withdrawal from Maṣyāf. In fact it seems that henceforth Sinān and Saladin acted in collusion. By contrast, relations between Sinān and the Zangids of Aleppo now deteriorated. In 573/1177, the Nizārī *fidāʾīs* assassinated Shihāb al-Dīn b. al-ʿAjamī, the influential vizier of al-Malik al-Ṣāliḥ, in the principal mosque of Aleppo. The vizier had been in serious rivalry with Gümüshtigin, who, according to some sources, had instigated this assassination.[162] Gümüshtigin had allegedly forged his master's signature on a letter to Sinān, asking him to send *fidāʾīs*. At any rate, the opportunity was seized by the enemies of Gümüshtigin, and he was removed from office and tortured to death. In 575/1179–1180, al-Malik al-Ṣāliḥ (d. 577/1181) seized the fortress of Hajīra from the Nizārīs, who protested in vain. Sinān then sent Nizārī agents to Aleppo, where they set fire to several locations in the city's market places.[163]

Sinān, as noted, assumed power in Syria at about the same time as Ḥasan II in Alamūt. The two men had been close companions at Alamūt, where Sinān had probably belonged to that circle of young Nizārīs who supported Ḥasan II's new ideas. When Ḥasan II announced the doctrine of the *qiyāma* in 559/1164 in Alamūt and thereupon sent messengers carrying the tidings to the Nizārīs of other territories, it fell upon Sinān to inaugurate the new dispensation in Syria. Sinān did proclaim the Resurrection in Syria, and the doctrine of the *qiyāma* was introduced there, but the doctrine seems to have had a very limited impact on the Syrian Nizārī community. The Syrian authors of doctrinal works, having little acquaintance with the literature of their Persian co-religionists, evidently maintained the Fāṭimid interest in cosmology and cyclical hierohistory, and did not pay any special attention to the autonomous status of the present imām, independently from his predecessors, which had now come to occupy a central position in the doctrine of the Persian Nizārīs. The Nizārīs of Syria, therefore, unlike those in Persia, do not seem to have explicitly recorded the declaration of the *qiyāma*, and the new doctrine has not been expounded in any of the Syrian Nizārī texts recovered thus far. On the other hand, the event is briefly referred to by the Sunnī historians of Syria, who were unaware of a similar event taking place in Persia and of the accounts of it produced by the Persian historians.[164]

Some time after 559/1164, Sinān did proclaim the *qiyāma*, and held ceremonies similar to those held earlier in Persia. But the doctrine of the *qiyāma* as developed in Persia does not seem to have become the central doctrine of the Syrian Nizārīs in the time of Sinān, who acquired increasing independence from Alamūt during Muḥammad II's reign. Indeed, there are reports that as a result of the growing conflict between Sinān and Muḥammad II, the latter repeatedly sent *fidāʾī*s from Alamūt to kill Sinān.[165] These would-be assassins failed in their mission and Sinān avoided a complete break with Alamūt. At any event, Sinān evidently taught his own version of the doctrine of the *qiyāma*. The specific features of this Syrian version, which never acquired any deep roots in the community, remain rather obscure, since it has not been expounded in any available Ismāʿīlī or non-Ismāʿīlī source. Later Syrian Nizārī writings, like the *Faṣl* of Abū Firās, or the fragment ascribed to Sinān, make only vague references to what may have been Sinān's teaching.[166] But these writings do not explicitly emphasize the status of the current imām and the manifestation of the unveiled truth in him. On the contrary, their emphasis is on self-knowledge and self-discovery as constituting important steps towards knowing God.

Sinān enjoyed unprecedented popularity in the Syrian Nizārī community, which enabled him to drift away from the central headquarters of the movement in Alamūt. But it is not known just what role he claimed for himself. Some sources relate that he was venerated as the imām, at least by some of his followers who were called Sinānīs after him.[167] In the popular Syrian Nizārī literature of later times he is exalted as a saintly hero with a cosmic rank appropriate to the imām himself; a rank much higher than that accorded to any representative of the imām. Indeed, Abū Firās ascribes the glory of Sinān's achievement directly to God, as if he received divine protection and guidance. The Syrian Nizārīs had been exposed to a wider variety of Shīʿī ideas than the Nizārīs of Rūdbār and Quhistān. Sinān probably made his version of the new doctrine bear a distinct Syrian flavour and readily admitted the popular impressions available to Ismāʿīlism. Finally, in the Syrian Nizārī ideas one comes across certain popular Shīʿī motifs absent in the doctrine of the *qiyāma* developed in Persia. For instance, Abū Dharr, one of the original partisans of ʿAlī, has a prominent place in Syrian Nizārī thought; and the Syrian works of later times display belief in some sort of metempsychosis or transmigration of souls, an important doctrine for the Nuṣayrīs and the Druzes. As can be gathered from these popular works of the later Syrian Nizārīs, their ideas on metempsychosis were essentially of a symbolic nature and related mainly to the destiny of those souls whose possessors had gone astray.[168] Such persons would not, however, be reincarnated in the form of animals; but their souls would be punished within the ordinary routine of life, if not rendered non-existent. The Syrian Ismāʿīlīs have been exposed to the doctrines of their Nuṣayrī neighbours through the centuries, and in Sinān's time the two Shīʿī sects had several entanglements in the Jabal Bahrā', while occasionally, some Nuṣayrīs were converted to Nizārī Ismāʿīlism. Doubtless, the Nuṣayrīs provided the chief source for the Syrian Nizārī ideas on metempsychosis.[169]

There are indications that the doctrine of the *qiyāma*, or more specifically its Syrian version, was not fully understood by all the factions of the Syrian community, particularly by the Nizārīs who lived in the Jazr and the Jabal al-Summāq, outside the main strongholds in the Jabal Bahrā'. Ibn al-ʿAdīm for instance reports that in the year 572/1176–1177, when Sinān had not yet reached a settlement with Saladin, a faction of the Nizārīs of the Jabal al-Summāq embarked on a programme of libertinism.[170] These Nizārīs called themselves al-Ṣufāt, the Pure, reflecting Sinān's injunction to his followers to live together in purity and in fraternity. Disclaiming any responsibility for their behaviour, Sinān succeeded in preventing the intervention of the Zangids of Aleppo with whom he had good relations at the time. He personally dealt with the Ṣufāt, who had fortified themselves in the mountains, killing many of them and effectively ending the antinomian activities of his rebellious followers. It should be recalled that the Persian Nizārīs were not accused of similar behaviour and that the community there did not experience any internal dissension comparable to the episode of the Ṣufāt.

In Rabīʿ II 588/April 1192, the Syrian Nizārīs brought off their greatest coup, the assassination in Tyre of the marquis Conrad of Montferrat, the newly-elected Frankish king of Jerusalem and the husband of Amalric I's daughter Isabella. This event, which shocked the Crusaders, is, as noted, reported by most of the occidental chroniclers of the Third Crusade and by many Muslim historians.[171] Most sources agree that the act was carried out by two assassins who had disguised themselves as Christian monks and who had managed to win Conrad's confidence. There is, however, much controversy regarding the instigator of this assassination. Many Muslim sources, as well as some occidental ones, state that its instigator was Richard I, surnamed the Lion Heart (Coeur de Lion), the king of England (1189–1199), who was then in the Holy Land and had an enmity with Conrad. On the other hand, Ibn al-Athīr, who was favourably disposed towards the Zangids and as such disliked Saladin, reports that it was Saladin who commissioned Sinān to murder both Conrad and Richard, in return for a certain sum of money. In a confused account, Abū Firās, too, attributes the initiative to Sinān, who was then evidently not on good terms with the Franks, because he wanted to help his friend Saladin.[172] In any case, when soon afterwards Richard I signed a peace treaty with Saladin, the Nizārī territories were included in the treaty at Saladin's request.

Rāshid al-Dīn Sinān died in 588/1192 or 589/1193, in the castle of Kahf.[173] In the course of some thirty years, Sinān consolidated the Syrian Nizārī state and led his followers to the peak of power and fame. The ablest of the Syrian Nizārī chiefs, he was the only one amongst them to acquire effective independence from Alamūt. He gave the Syrian Nizārīs an independent identity; with their own sphere of influence, a network of strongholds, a hierarchy of *dāʿīs*, and a strong corps of *fidāʾīs*. At the same time, his shrewd strategies and appropriate alliances with the Zangids, the Crusaders, and Saladin, served to ensure the independence of his community in difficult times.

Meanwhile, important political changes had been taking place in Persia and other eastern lands. The Great Saljūq Sultanate had been disintegrating after Sanjar's death in 552/1157, being replaced by a host of more or less independent principalities held mainly by Turkish *amīrs* and generals. At the same time, a new expansionary power with great ambitions, based on Khwārazm, had emerged on the political scene of the East. The region of Khwārazm, on the lower Oxus in Central Asia, had passed a century earlier into the hands of a Turkish dynasty acting as vassals of the Saljūqs. These hereditary rulers adopted the old title of the kings of the region and called themselves the Khwārazmshāhs. Taking advantage of the Saljūqid dissensions after Sanjar, the Khwārazmshāhs asserted their independence and began to expand their dominions. Around 586/1190, the Khwārazmshāh ʿAlāʾ al-Dīn Tekish (567–596/1172–1200) occupied Khurāsān and came to control the bulk of Sanjar's former territories. The decline of the Saljūqs had provided an opportunity also for the ʿAbbāsids to revive their power and prestige; and with the accession of al-Nāṣir (575–622/1180–1225), the caliph at Baghdād became a central figure in eastern Islamic diplomacy and politics. Al-Nāṣir strove to restore the religious unity of Islam, with the ʿAbbāsid caliph as its real, not just titular, head; he also had limited territorial ambitions and wanted to rule over a small caliphal principality in ʿIrāq. These objectives determined the nature of al-Nāṣir's policies and alliances. Al-Nāṣir did not hesitate to ask the assistance of his potential enemy Tekish against the last Saljūq ruler of Persia, Ṭughril III (571–590/1176–1194), thus providing the occasion for the Khwārazmian armies to advance westwards. The Saljūq dynasty came to an end when Tekish defeated Ṭughril III at Rayy in 590/1194. The triumphant Khwārazmshāh was the obvious ruler to fill the vacancy created by the Saljūqs, and in the following year al-Nāṣir invested Tekish with the sultanate of western Persia, Khurāsān, and Turkistān. The Khwārazmians soon came to have an impressive empire of their own, stretching from the borders of India to Anatolia, but this empire was short-lived, and like the Persian Nizārī state, it succumbed to the Mongols.

During the last sixteen years of Muḥammad II's reign, the Persian Nizārīs were once again engaged in petty warfare with their neighbours. The Nizārīs of Rūdbār had entanglements with Māzandarān. Alamūt gave refuge to Bīsutūn, a ruler of Rūyān who had rebelled against the Bāwandid Ḥusām al-Dawla Ardashīr; and later the Nizārīs of Rūdbār spread their influence in Māzandarān, assassinating in the course of their raids Rukn al-Dawla Qārin, the younger brother of the Bāwandid Shams al-Mulūk Shāh Ghāzī Rustam II (602–606/1206–1210).[174] At the same time, the Rūdbārī Nizārīs were confronted with the Khwārazmians, who had replaced the Saljūqs in western Persia and were now expanding into Daylam. Around 602/1205, Miyājiq, a Khwārazmian general, tricked and killed a number of Nizārīs from Alamūt, and thereupon the Khwārazmian troops established themselves as the partisans of the Qazwīnīs, the traditional enemies of the Nizārīs, and made regular raids into Rūdbār.[175] In 590/1194, the Nizārīs of Quhistān had begun to have their own troubles and battles with the rulers of Sīstān. Later, the Ghūrids, under Ghiyāth al-Dīn Muḥammad (558–599/1163–1203), the chief rivals of the Khwārazmians in eastern Persia, attacked and devastated Quhistān, forcing the submission of the Nizārīs there.[176] Ghiyāth al-Dīn's brother, Shihāb al-Dīn, however, conducted further raids of his own against the Quhistānī Nizārīs, who had to ask for Ghiyāth al-Dīn's intervention; he had also attacked the Ismāʿīlīs of Multān in 571/1175. The Ghūrid Shihāb al-Dīn was assassinated in 602/1206; and the Nizārīs claimed responsibility for the act, probably in order to win the favour of the Khwārazmshāh ʿAlā' al-Dīn Muḥammad (596–617/1200–1220).[177] The Nizārīs had, meanwhile, retained their reputation as a body willing to fight the enemies of their allies and to protect refugees fleeing from their common adversaries. Though they were then defending themselves against the Khwārazmians, it is reported that the Nizārīs in 596/1200 murdered Niẓām al-Mulk Masʿūd b. ʿAlī, the vizier of Tekish, allegedly at the request of the Khwārazmshāh.[178] Sometime in the reign of Tekish's successor ʿAlā' al-Dīn Muḥammad, the lord of Zawzan Nuṣrat al-Dīn was accused of Ismāʿīlism and had to take refuge in the Nizārī castles in Quhistān. He was, however, lured back and killed by the new Khwārazmian governor of Zawzan.[179] Meanwhile, the Sunnī rulers had maintained the practice of occasionally massacring the Nizārīs; it is reported, for instance, that in the year 600/1204, a large number of people accused of Ismāʿīlism were killed in lower ʿIrāq.[180]

There are indications that at least some of the Persian Nizārīs were becoming increasingly weary of their isolation from the outside world in the *qiyāma* times. Our Persian historians relate that during the later years of Muḥammad II's reign, a growing breach had occurred between the lord of

Alamūt and his eldest son Ḥasan, born in 562/1166–1167.[181] Ḥasan, who in his childhood had received the *naṣṣ* to succeed his father, had shown signs of dissatisfaction with the doctrine and practices of the *qiyāma*; he evidently desired a rapprochement between the Nizārīs and the larger Sunnī world. Ḥasan had communicated his own ideas secretly to several Sunnī rulers, with whom he desired to have good relations in the future.

Muḥammad II died, possibly of poison, in Rabīʿ I 607/September 1210, and was succeeded by his son Ḥasan III, who, as had become customary by then with the lords of Alamūt, carried the honorific title of Jalāl al-Dīn.[182] As noted, intending to achieve a rapprochement with the Sunnī world, Ḥasan had already prepared the way for his own drastic reform. Our Persian historians relate that upon his accession, Ḥasan publicly repudiated the doctrine of the *qiyāma* and proclaimed his adherence to Sunnī Islam, ordering his followers to observe the Sharīʿa in its Sunnī form. Ḥasan sent messengers to the caliph al-Nāṣir, Muḥammad Khwārazmshāh and the *amīr*s of other lands to notify them of his reform. The Nizārīs of the Alamūt period had now in effect entered the third and final phase of their history, later interpreted as a new period of *satr* or concealment which lasted until the destruction of their state by the Mongols.

During the initial years of his reign, Jalāl al-Dīn Ḥasan did his utmost to convince the Sunnī world that his community had abandoned its previous teaching and practices and that it had now adopted the law in its Sunnī form. He ordered the building of mosques and baths in every Nizārī village, to prove their status as full-fledged centres of normal Muslim life. He invited Sunnī *faqīh*s from ʿIrāq and Khurāsān to instruct his people. The outside world, and especially the caliph at Baghdād, accepted Ḥasan's new orthodoxy; and in Rabīʿ I 608/August 1211, the caliph al-Nāṣir issued a decree confirming Ḥasan's conversion to Sunnī Islam. Ḥasan III became commonly known as the New Muslim (*naw-musalmān*). Ḥasan was thus accepted as an *amīr* amongst other *amīr*s, and his rights to the territories held by the Nizārīs were officially acknowledged by the ʿAbbāsid caliph who showed him all manner of favours. Ḥasan's mother went on the pilgrimage to Mecca in 609/1213 under the patronage of al-Nāṣir, who treated her with the highest honours. The caliph also intervened to persuade the nobility of Gīlān to allow four of their daughters to marry Ḥasan. Among these Gīlānī wives of Ḥasan, there was the sister of Kaykāʾūs b. Shāhanshāh, the hereditary ruler of Kūtum who bore Ḥasan's successor Muḥammad III.[183] The Qazwīnīs, however, remained skeptical for some time regarding the authenticity of Ḥasan's announcements. The

Nizārī leader asked a number of religious scholars and notables of Qazwīn to visit Alamūt, allowing them to inspect its library and burn all books deemed heretical. The Qazwīnīs, too, were finally convinced.

All the Nizārīs in Rūdbār, Qūmis, Quhistān and Syria seem to have accepted Ḥasan's new dispensation without any question. The Syrian Nizārīs, and probably also the Nizārīs in other territories, chose the Shāfiʿī *madhhab*. To the Nizārīs, Ḥasan was undeniably the infallible imām, having received the *naṣṣ* of the previous imām and acting as the leader of the Nizārī community and state. His orders, therefore, were to be obeyed without any hesitation. The Nizārīs evidently regarded Ḥasan's declarations as a reimposition of *taqiyya*, which had been lifted in the *qiyāma*; its reinstatement could now be taken to imply any sort of accommodation to the outside world deemed necessary by the imām. Ḥasan's new policies had obvious political advantages for the Nizārī community and state, which had survived only precariously. The Nizārīs had failed in their revolt, and had subsequently isolated themselves in their strongholds during their spiritual Resurrection. The outside world, however, had continued to be very much in existence, despite the Nizārī declaration of the *qiyāma*. Under the circumstances, many Nizārīs, it would seem, had become disenchanted with their isolation, desiring to have normal relations with other Muslims. Jalāl al-Dīn Ḥasan had in effect boldly accommodated the Nizārīs to the outside world. For the first time, the Nizārī state now became recognized as such by the leading rulers in the Muslim world, which implied territorial security for the Nizārīs, especially in Quhistān and Syria, where their position had been constantly threatened. In Quhistān, the Ghūrid attacks against the Nizārīs came to an end; and in Syria, where the Nizārīs were facing new troubles from the Franks, they received opportune help from the Ayyūbids. The improved relations were naturally beneficial to the Sunnīs as well. For instance, around the end of Ḥasan III's reign, many Sunnīs, including scholars who were fleeing from the invading Mongols in Khurāsān and other eastern regions, found asylum in the Nizārī towns of Quhistān.[184] The Nizārī state also played an effective role in the caliphal alliances of al-Nāṣir.

Indeed, Jalāl al-Dīn Ḥasan's reform was accepted sufficiently by his people to allow him to leave Rūdbār for some time to engage in military operations, as none of his predecessors had done. According to al-Nasawī (d. 647/1249–1250), the secretary and chronicler of Sultan Muḥammad Khwārazmshāh's son and successor Jalāl al-Dīn (617–628/1220–1231), Ḥasan III had at first recognized the suzerainty of the Khwārazmshāh.[185]

However, he soon allied himself with the caliph al-Nāṣir, the chief opponent of the Khwārazmians. As a result of this shift in alliance, Ḥasan developed a close and personal relationship with Muẓaffar al-Dīn Özbeg (607–622/1210–1225), the last Eldigüzid ruler of Arrān and Ādharbayjān and an important ally of al-Nāṣir. When Özbeg decided to deal with Mengli, his lieutenant in ʿIrāq-i ʿAjam who had rebelled and asserted his independence, Ḥasan offered his assistance. It was for this purpose that in 610/1213–1214 Ḥasan, accompanied by his army, departed from Alamūt to Ādharbayjān, where he stayed at Özbeg's court. Özbeg treated him hospitably and paid for the expenses of the Nizārī troops. The caliph played a central role in organizing the military coalition against Mengli, as ʿIrāq-i ʿAjam had been a primary area of contention between al-Nāṣir and Muḥammad Khwārazmshāh. Besides sending his own troops, the caliph persuaded the *amīr*s of ʿIrāq, Syria and elsewhere to participate in the campaign against Mengli. After ample and prolonged preparations, battle was joined in 611/1214–1215 near Hamadān. Mengli was defeated and later executed by Özbeg, who now appointed Ighlamish as his governor in ʿIrāq-i ʿAjam.[186] After the victory, Ighlamish received the bulk of the conquered territories, including Hamadān, Rayy and Iṣfahān, but Jalāl al-Dīn Ḥasan was given Abhar and Zanjān and their environs, which remained in Nizārī hands for a few years.

After an absence of one and a half years, Ḥasan returned to Alamūt and maintained his close relations with al-Nāṣir and Özbeg. When Ighlamish rebelled, no campaign was conducted against him, as in the case of Mengli. At the caliph's request, Ḥasan despatched Nizārī *fidāʾī*s, who assassinated Ighlamish in 614/1217.[187] Later, Ḥasan was quick to recognize the danger of the Mongols, and was evidently the first Muslim ruler to come to terms with them after the Mongol armies had crossed the Oxus. After a reign of eleven years, Jalāl al-Dīn Ḥasan III died of dysentery in Ramaḍān 618/November 1221. But his vizier, who was the tutor of the next imām, accused Ḥasan III's Sunnī wives and sister of having poisoned him. They were all put to death.

Jalāl al-Dīn Ḥasan III was succeeded by his only son ʿAlāʾ al-Dīn Muḥammad III, who was then nine years old.[188] The vizier previously appointed by Ḥasan III continued to be the effective ruler of the Nizārī state for some time and the Nizārī community under Muḥammad III remained officially Sunnī in the eyes of the outside world. Indeed, Ḥasan III's Sunnī policies were never formally renounced at Alamūt, but gradually the enforcement of the Sunnī Sharīʿa was relaxed and the ideas associated with *qiyāma* were revived. After a while, the community once again came to openly regard itself as specifically Nizārī Ismāʿīlī. In Muḥammad III's time, the doctrine of the *qiyāma* introduced by Ḥasan II, the Sunnism of Ḥasan III, and the partial reversion of the community to its earlier practices during Muḥammad III's reign, were explained to the satisfaction of the rank and file of the community. In other words, it was explained that these seemingly contradictory policies were in effect identical in their spiritual reality, since each infallible imām had acted in accordance with the requirements of his own time. In the process, an adjusted doctrine which may be called the doctrine of the *satr*, was formulated to explain the new religious situation of the Nizārī community in line with the actual course of events pursued since the declaration of the *qiyāma* in the year 559/1164. Muḥammad III, who now clearly and openly acted as the imām, does not seem to have made any specific contribution to the Nizārī thought of his time. The doctrine of the *satr* was formulated by others in the community; thinkers who had taken cognizance of the many questions which perturbed the ordinary members of the community.

There were also those outside scholars and theologians who, especially after the Mongol catastrophe, had availed themselves of the learned patronage of the Nizārīs, and played an active part in the intellectual life of the Nizārī community. Amongst such scholars who found asylum in the Nizārī strongholds of Quhistān and Rūdbār, the most prominent was the celebrated astronomer and Shīʿī theologian Naṣīr al-Dīn Abū Jaʿfar Muḥammad b. Muḥammad al-Ṭūsī, a leading Muslim philosopher of his age. Indeed, several of the Nizārī fortresses had become flourishing centres of intellectual activities by the late Alamūt period. There is no evidence suggesting that these outside scholars were detained in the community against their will or that they were forced to embrace Ismāʿīlism during their stay amongst the Nizārīs, although at the time of the Mongol invasion, al-Ṭūsī and a few other similarly situated scholars claimed otherwise. On the contrary, it seems that these learned guests partook of the hospitality of the Nizārīs willingly, and were free, in the time of *satr*, to maintain their previous religious convictions.

There is, nonetheless, much controversy surrounding the Ismāʿīlī affiliations of Naṣīr al-Dīn al-Ṭūsī, who was born into an Imāmī family in Ṭūs, Khurāsān, in 597/1201.[189] In his youth, around the year 624/1227, al-Ṭūsī entered the service of Nāṣir al-Dīn ʿAbd al-Raḥmān b. Abū Manṣūr (d. 655/1257), the *muḥtashim* or head of the Quhistānī Nizārīs, who himself was a learned man. During his long stay at Qā'in and other Nizārī strongholds in Quhistān, al-Ṭūsī developed a close friendship with the *muḥtashim* Nāṣir al-Dīn, to whom he dedicated in 633/1235 his great work on ethics, the *Akhlāq-i Nāṣirī*, which originally contained an Ismāʿīlī preamble. Subsequently, al-Ṭūsī went to Alamūt and enjoyed the patronage of Muḥammad III and his successor, until the collapse of the Nizārī state in 654/1256. After the fall of Alamūt, al-Ṭūsī, claiming to have been a captive amidst the Nizārīs, became a trusted adviser of the Mongol conqueror Hülegü, who built a great observatory for him at Marāgha, Ādharbayjān. Having also served Abaqa, Hülegü's successor in the Īlkhānid dynasty of Persia, al-Ṭūsī died in 672/1274 at Baghdād. He had thus spent almost three decades with the Nizārīs, which was in effect the most productive period of his career. It was during that time that he produced his well-known works, *Akhlāq-i Nāṣirī* and *Akhlāq-i Muḥtashimī*, also written for the same Nizārī dignitary in Quhistān, as well as numerous treatises on astrology, philosophy and theology. The *Rawḍat al-taslīm* (*Meadow of Submission*), his major Ismāʿīlī work, and a few other short treatises bearing an Ismāʿīlī imprint, also date from that period. The Ithnāʿasharī *ʿulamāʾ*, who consider al-Ṭūsī as one of their co-religionists, have persistently denied that he ever embraced Ismāʿīlism, rejecting the authenticity of the Ismāʿīlī treatises ascribed to him; treatises which have been preserved by the Nizārīs. Other Twelver writers, including his modern Persian biographers, believe that al-Ṭūsī, observing *taqiyya* as an Imāmī Shīʿī, was obliged to compose these works for fear of his life during his captivity at the Nizārī strongholds. There is, however, no reason to doubt the authenticity of his spiritual autobiography, the *Sayr va sulūk*, in which al-Ṭūsī narrates how, after his initial dissatisfaction with scholastic theology (*kalām*) and philosophy (*ḥikma*), he came to realize the necessity of following an infallible teacher (*muʿallim*) who would guide reason to its perfection. Hence, he joined the Ismāʿīlīs (*ahl-i taʿlīm*) and recognized their imām.[190] In the same autobiographical account, al-Ṭūsī explains how he had been influenced by the Ismāʿīlī teaching of al-Shahrastānī, the teacher of his father's maternal uncle and teacher.[191] In all probability, then, al-Ṭūsī willingly embraced Nizārī Ismāʿīlism temporarily during the time of his stay within the Persian Nizārī community, but, upon the fall of the Nizārī state, reverted to Twelver Shīʿism and wrote some theological works supporting the Twelver views. At any rate, he contributed significantly to the development of the Nizārī thought of his time, especially to the formulation of the doctrine of the *satr*. It is indeed in his Ismāʿīlī writings, constituting the only extant works from Muḥammad III's period, that we find a detailed exposition of this doctrine.[192] Various aspects of the doctrine of the *satr* are also reflected, in modified forms, in the Nizārī works of the post-Alamūt period.

The doctrine of the *satr* explained Ḥasan III's reform and at the same time reinterpreted the doctrine of the *qiyāma*. It was explained that the *qiyāma* was not necessarily a final event but a transitory condition of life, when the veil of *taqiyya* was lifted so as to make the unveiled truth available to all. The tacit identification between the *sharīʿa* and *taqiyya*, implied in the teaching of Ḥasan *ʿalā dhikrihi'l-salām*, was thus confirmed, and so was the identification between the *qiyāma* and *ḥaqīqa*.[193] Accordingly, the strict imposition of the Sunnī Sharīʿa by Ḥasan III was depicted as a return to *taqiyya*, or precautionary dissimulation of one's true religious belief, and to a new period of *satr* or concealment, when the truth would be once again hidden in the *bāṭin*. The condition of the *qiyāma* could, in principle, be granted or withheld by the current imām to mankind, or to the elite, at any time; consequently, at the will of the imām, human life could alternate between the times of the *qiyāma*, when reality is manifest, and *satr*, when reality is hidden. In this sense, Ḥasan II had introduced a brief period of *qiyāma*, while Ḥasan III had closed that period, initiating a new period of *satr* requiring the observance of *taqiyya*. Such alterations between the periods of *qiyāma* and *satr* could occur, according to the decision of the imāms, because every imām was potentially also a Qā'im; that is, an *imām-qā'im*.[194] Al-Ṭūsī clearly allows for the sequence by stating that the era of each prophet of the *ẓāhir* of the *sharīʿa* is called the period of *satr*; and the period of each *qā'im*, who possesses the truths (*ḥaqā'iq*) of the religious laws (*sharā'iʿ*), is called *qiyāma*.[195] In the current cycle of human history, however, it was still expected, as with the earliest Ismāʿīlīs, that full *qiyāma* would come at the end of the final millennial era after Adam; that is, at the end of the sixth millennium initiated by the sixth law-announcing prophet, Muḥammad. The Prophet Muḥammad himself had introduced an era of *satr*, like the other five law-announcing prophets preceding him in the current cycle of history; but within Muḥammad's millennial era, and in special honour of his greatness, there could be on occasion anticipatory periods of *qiyāma*, each one a foretaste of the *qiyāma* coming at the end of his era, which would initiate the seventh and final millennium of the current cycle in the religious history of mankind. Accordingly, the *qiyāma* proclaimed by Ḥasan II, roughly in the middle of Muḥammad's era, was one of such anticipatory *qiyāmas*; and the remainder of that era were times of *satr* or concealment.[196] In sum, it was explained that in the era of

Muḥammad, periods of *satr* and *qiyāma* could alternate at the discretion of each imām.

Earlier Ismāʿīlīs had used the term *satr* in reference to those periods in their history when the imāms were hidden from the world at large, or even from their followers, as had been the case with the period in early Ismāʿīlism between Muḥammad b. Ismāʿīl and ʿUbayd Allāh al-Mahdī and again with the period of *satr* in Nizārism between Nizār and Ḥasan II. But in the Nizārī teaching of the late Alamūt period the term acquired a different and broader meaning. It now came to mean specifically the concealment of the true spiritual reality of the imām, his reality as the manifestation of the unveiled truth, and not merely the hiddenness of the person of the imām. Accordingly, despite the physical availability of the imām, there could be a period of *satr*. For al-Ṭūsī, writing in Muḥammad III's time, such a period of *satr* had started with the advent of Ḥasan III in 607/1210, even though the imāms were visible and ruling at the head of the community.[197] Indeed, for the Nizārīs of the late Alamūt period, the Fāṭimid period, when the imāms were visible; and the earliest period in their history between Nizār and Ḥasan II, when the imāms were hidden; as well as the post-*qiyāma* period, when the imāms were again visible, were all regarded as times of *satr*.

As we have seen, this doctrine of the *satr* retained, in a more discreet sense, the ideas of the earlier Ismāʿīlīs regarding cyclical hierohistory, while reinterpreting the doctrine of the *qiyāma*. At the same time, it retained in a modified form certain specific features of the *qiyāma* doctrine, including its categorization of mankind in terms of three classes. It allowed for the state of spiritual *waḥda* or union with the imām even in the time of *satr*, which was depicted as the normal condition of mankind due to human weakness. It seems, however, that in the time of *satr* the state of *waḥda* was restricted to a few, though possibly to a single figure, the *ḥujja* of the imām.[198] Therefore, only the *ḥujja*, having achieved spiritual perfection, attained access to unveiled truth and could dispense with *taqiyya*; all other members of the community, even though they acknowledged the Nizārī Imām as the sole legitimate leader of mankind, would have to obey the Sharīʿa, otherwise they would be on the same level as the people of opposition, heretical (*mulḥid*) and irreligious (*bī-dīn*).[199] The position of *ḥujja*, originally occupied in the Nizārī community by Ḥasan-i Ṣabbāḥ, now acquired a new prominence as the sole access to the imām and the truth. This highest position in the *daʿwa* hierarchy, ranking only after the imām, became even more important amongst the Nizārīs of the post-Alamūt period. It is not known however whether the position of *ḥujja* was actually occupied by any persons during the period of Muḥammad III. The ordinary followers of the Nizārī Imām, comprising the entire community with the exception of the *ḥujja* and possibly a few others, were now characterized as the people of gradation (*ahl al-tarattub*). Not possessing the *ḥaqīqa*, they remained on the level of the *bāṭin*, merely understanding the inner meaning of the Sharīʿa but not the imām's ultimate reality. The *ahl al-tarattub* themselves were, however, divided into the strong (*aqwiyāʾ*) and the weak (*ḍuʿafāʾ*) according to their closeness to the truth.[200] The doctrinal system of the Nizārīs of the later Alamūt period in effect enabled the Nizārī community to maintain its identity and spiritual independence under changing circumstances. The Nizārīs had indeed moved closer to the ideas and practices of a Ṣūfī order and in Persia they survived under the mantle of Ṣūfism after the fall of their state.

Politically, too, Muḥammad III's reign was a very active period, not only for the Nizārī state but also for the entire Muslim East, which now experienced a foretaste of the Mongol menace. Muḥammad had come to power in 618/1221, immediately after the first Mongol conquests that destroyed the Khwārazmian empire. The Mongol conquest of Transoxiana was accomplished with incredible speed. By 1219, Chingiz Khan, the mighty ruler of the new Mongol empire, was already leading his armies into the lands of Islam. By 1220, Chingiz Khan had captured Bukhārā and Samarqand, from where he despatched his generals in pursuit of Sultan Muḥammad Khwārazmshāh (d. 617/1220), who was now fleeing across Persia in the aftermath of the collapse of his empire. The Mongols had meanwhile continued their westward advance through Ādharbayjān and the Caucasus. Early in 1221, Chingiz Khan crossed the Oxus and seized Balkh. He then sent his youngest son Toluy to complete the conquest of Khurāsān, a task accomplished with unprecedented thoroughness from which the province never recovered. The Mongols totally devastated Marw and Nīshāpūr, massacring the populations of both cities. They had now acquired a solid foothold in eastern Persia, and the death of Chingiz Khan in 624/1227 brought only a brief respite. It was at that time in the early years of Muḥammad III's reign that an increasing number of refugees, including numerous Sunnī ʿ*ulamāʾ* of Khurāsān, found asylum in the Nizārī towns of Quhistān; since during this initial phase of the Mongol invasion the Nizārī state had proved to be stronger than most other small principalities and because some sort of an entente seems to have existed between the Nizārī leaders and the Mongols. Ḥasan III, as noted, had previously made friendly overtures to the Mongols at the beginning of their westward advance, probably sometime in the autumn of 616/1219; and his secret emissaries had apparently met with Chingiz Khan himself in the spring of 618/1221 at Balkh or Ṭāliqān, informing him of the Nizārī ruler's desire for peace.

At any rate, the Quhistānī Nizārīs, unaffected by the initial Mongol invasions, continued to enjoy their prosperity and stability, and were able to share their good fortune with the refugees who were now pouring into their midst. Indeed, Shihāb al-Dīn, the learned chief of Nizārī Quhistān, was so lavish in his treatment of these refugees that soon the Nizārīs of the area were forwarding complaints to Alamūt about the negative effects of his hospitality on the resources of their treasury. But Shams al-Dīn, the new *muḥtashim* of Quhistān designated by Alamūt, came to be equally admired and respected by the refugees. These events, and the contemporary situation of the Nizārīs in Quhistān are related in detail by Minhāj al-Dīn ʿUthmān b. Sirāj al-Dīn al-Jūzjānī, commonly known as Minhāj-i Sirāj, a Sunnī jurist and the historian of the Ghūrids and the Muʿizzī or Slave dynasty of India, who spent his earlier years in the service of the Ghūrids and visited Quhistān three times between 621 and 623/1224–1226.[201] He knew both Shihāb al-Dīn, for whom he had the highest praises, and Shams al-Dīn, and conducted diplomatic negotiations with the latter *muḥtashim* on behalf of Sīstān.

The arrival of Shams al-Dīn in Quhistān had coincided with the outbreak of new troubles between the Nizārīs and their Sīstānī neighbours. Yamīn al-Dīn Bahrāmshāh, the local *amīr* of Sīstān, had previously fought two wars against the Nizārīs during Ḥasan III's reign, and his nephew had sold them the fortress of Shahanshāh near the town of Nih. Yamīn al-Dīn now wanted the Nizārīs to give up that fortress, threatening to take it by force. Thereupon, Yamīn al-Dīn was assassinated in 618/1221 by four Nizārī *fidāʾīs* despatched from Quhistān. There ensued a series of succession disputes in Sīstān, and the Quhistānī Nizārīs began to interfere directly in the affairs of that province.[202] The Nizārīs supported Rukn al-Dīn against his younger brother Nuṣrat al-Dīn b. Bahrāmshāh, who had been put on the throne by a group of the notables of Sīstān. But soon Rukn al-Dīn assumed power with the assistance of the Nizārīs. At this time, in 619/1222, the Mongols attacked Sīstān, without staying there, and Rukn al-Dīn was killed by one of his slaves. The Sīstānīs then successively raised to the throne Shihāb al-Dīn b. Ḥarb and his brother ʿAlī, to the dissatisfaction of the Nizārīs who again had their own candidate, ʿUthmān. They sought the help of a Khwārazmian general, Bināltigīn (Yināltigīn), who was then in Kirmān, for the enthronement of ʿUthmān. When Bināltigīn arrived in Sīstān in 622/1225, he assumed power in his own name. At this point, Shams al-Dīn, a capable military commander, was already the *muḥtashim* in Quhistān and led the Nizārīs in battle against Bināltigīn, who was defeated in 623/1226. It was after this battle that Bināltigīn sent Jūzjānī as his envoy to conclude a truce with the Nizārī chief of Quhistān. The Nizārī community in Quhistān clearly pursued an independent policy in its local affairs, also developing important trade routes with other regions, which contributed significantly to its economic prosperity.

The Nizārīs had never abandoned their expansionary ambitions, and now in the aftermath of their accord with the caliph at Baghdād and the crumbling of the Khwārazmian empire, they found it possible to extend their territories. At the time, the Nizārīs still maintained their understanding with the Mongols, who may even have been in alliance with them. At any rate, the Mongols then appeared to be a lesser threat to the Nizārī state than the Khwārazmians, who, under Sultan Jalāl al-Dīn, the last of the Khwārazmshāhs, were making a last effort to restore their kingdom in Persia. Around 619/1222, the Nizārīs seized Dāmghān, the town near Girdkūh, and recaptured some fortresses in Qūmis. They also acquired further strongholds in Ṭārum and in the Zagros mountains. At the same time, the Nizārīs seem to have had designs for Rayy, at least through their more traditional method of converting the local populace, for around 619/1222 a group of Nizārī *dāʿīs* were arrested and executed in Rayy on the orders of Muḥammad Khwārazmshāh's son Rukn al-Dīn.[203] The Nizārī territories in Persia thus expanded during the first six years of Muḥammad III's reign. It was during that time, when the false news had spread of Sultan Jalāl al-Dīn's death in 624/1227 in battle against the Mongols at Iṣfahān, that the Syrian Nizārīs boasted to the Saljūq ruler of Rūm (Anatolia) of the imminent seizure of ʿIrāq-i ʿAjam by their Persian comrades.[204]

It is possible that the Nizārī *daʿwa* was also introduced into the Indian subcontinent sometime during the first half of the 7th/13th century, or even earlier. There are no reliable sources on the origins of Nizārism in India, and it is not known whether any of the Indian Ismāʿīlī communities that had come into existence in Fāṭimid times accepted the Nizārī *daʿwa* following the Nizārī–Mustaʿlī schism of 487/1094. For the earliest phase of Nizārī activities in India we have only the traditional accounts of the Indian Nizārīs or Khojas themselves as reflected mainly in the *ginān*s (*gnān*s), the community's indigenous religious literature, written in verse form and recorded in several Indian languages. The *ginān*s, ascribed mostly to various *pīr*s, are often anachronistic and legendary in nature, and as such, are not reliable as historical sources. According to the tradition of the Nizārī Khojas, a certain Satgur Nūr, also called Nūr al-Dīn, was the first Nizārī *dāʿī* sent from Daylamān to Gujarāt.[205] There, in Pātan, he allegedly converted the local ruler Siddharāja, the same Hindu king of Gujarāt who is reported to have embraced Ṭayyibī Ismāʿīlism. Satgur Nūr, the community's tradition adds, soon converted all of Pātan, which became known as Pīrna Pātan, the *pīr*'s city. The dates mentioned for Satgur Nūr's arrival in India vary widely. According to one tradition, he was despatched by the Fāṭimid al-Mustanṣir in order to preach in favour of his son Nizār. According to another version, he started his activities in the time of Ḥasan *ʿalā dhikrihi'l-salām*; while in yet another account he is identified with the early Ismāʿīlī Imām Muḥammad b. Ismāʿīl. Be it as it may, there is no concrete evidence attesting the success of the Nizārī *daʿwa* in Gujarāt during the 7th/13th century, when Ṭayyibī Ismāʿīlism was already well-established in the region.

The Nizārī activities in the Indian subcontinent seem to have been originally concentrated in Sind, where different forms of Ismāʿīlism had persisted in Multān despite periodical persecution of the Shīʿī sectarians. The figure traditionally associated with the commencement of Nizārī activities in Sind is Pīr Shams al-Dīn; although a previous *pīr*, Ṣalāḥ al-Dīn, sometimes named as Shams al-Dīn's father, is also reported to have been sent from Alamūt to India. Shams al-Dīn is an obscure figure surrounded by all sorts of legends while the dates mentioned for his activities cover a long period. In legendary accounts, Shams al-Dīn, whose grave is located in Multān, has been identified with Shams al-Dīn Muḥammad Tabrīzī (d. 645/1247), the spiritual guide of Mawlānā Jalāl al-Dīn Rūmī (d. 672/1273), the celebrated Persian mystic and poet, and also with Shams al-Dīn Muḥammad, the first post-Alamūt Nizārī Imām.[206] It is interesting to note in passing that some sources trace the genealogy of Shams-i Tabrīzī himself to the imāms of the Alamūt period.[207] In some of the *ginān*s attributed to Pīr Shams al-Dīn, Qāsim Shāh, one of the earliest Nizārī Imāms of the post-Alamūt period, is often named as the contemporary imām, thus placing the *pīr*'s activities around the middle of the 8th/14th century. In other *ginān*s he is placed in the 6th/12th century. The opening phase of Nizārī Ismāʿīlism in India is uncertain. It is safe to assume, however, that the Nizārī *daʿwa* initially acquired a strong foothold amongst the Hindus of Sind, rather than Gujarāt, only after the fall of Alamūt, following the activities of the first *dāʿīs* who arrived in Sind towards the end of the Alamūt period.

Meanwhile, Jalāl al-Dīn Khwārazmshāh, who had been defeated in 618/1221 by Chingiz Khan on the banks of the Indus and had subsequently spent three years in India, appeared in Persia, where his brother Ghiyāth al-Dīn had successfully established himself in ʿIrāq-i ʿAjam. Jalāl al-Dīn soon removed Ghiyāth al-Dīn from his position, and in 622/1225, he overthrew Özbeg, the last Eldigüzid ruler of Ādharbayjān, who had been allied with the caliph and Ḥasan III. The Nizārīs who had inherited Ḥasan III's pro-caliphal policy and quarrels with the Khwārazmians, began to feel menaced by Jalāl al-Dīn Khwārazmshāh, who was conducting his desperate campaigns and sporadic battles with the Mongols in many parts of Persia. The relations between Alamūt and Jalāl al-Dīn, during this brief period before the Mongols finally caught up with the last Khwārazmshāh, have been recorded by al-Nasawī. It seems that after some initial hostilities, the Nizārīs were obliged in 624/1227 to accept a peace treaty imposed on them by Jalāl al-Dīn.[208] According to this truce agreement, reached in Ādharbayjān between Badr al-Dīn Aḥmad, the envoy of Alamūt, and Sharaf al-Mulk, Jalāl al-Dīn's vizier, the Nizārīs were allowed to retain Dāmghān in return for the payment of an annual tribute of 30,000 dinars to the Khwārazmian treasury. This agreement was reached soon after Ūrkhān, one of Jalāl al-Dīn's most trusted commanders who held Khurāsān as his *iqṭāʿ*, was assassinated by three Nizārī *fidāʾīs* in Ganja, in revenge for the activities of his lieutenants against the Quhistānī Nizārīs. In the course of the negotiations, Badr al-Dīn boasted that several *fidāʾīs* had been posted in the service of the Khwārazmshāh and his vizier, and summoned five of these agents to prove his claim. On hearing this news, Jalāl al-Dīn ordered Sharaf al-Mulk to burn the *fidāʾīs* alive. The vizier, who had become highly intimidated, tried in vain to change the sultan's mind. The *fidāʾīs* shouted the name of ʿAlāʾ al-Dīn Muḥammad as they were dying, like the *fidāʾīs* who had killed Ūrkhān and were stoned to death by the townspeople of Ganja. Alamūt now sent another envoy, Ṣalāḥ al-Dīn ʿAlī, to Sharaf al-Mulk, demanding 10,000 dinars in recompense for each of the five *fidāʾīs* burned, and threatened his life should he refuse. Thereupon, Sharaf al-Mulk reduced the annual tribute payable by the Nizārīs by 10,000 dinars for a period of five years.

The truce between the Nizārīs and Jalāl al-Dīn, however, did not prove very effective, as Alamūt continued to maintain friendly relations with the caliph and the Mongols, the two main enemies of the Khwārazmians. In 625/1228, Alamūt gave refuge to Özbeg's son, Malik Khāmūsh, and to Jalāl al-Dīn's brother Ghiyāth al-Dīn, who had been dispossessed of their power by the Khwārazmshāh.[209] The Nizārīs helped Ghiyāth al-Dīn, despite the Khwārazmian blockade of Rūdbār, to go to Kirmān. There however he was murdered. Al-Nasawī relates that the Nizārīs had offered at this time to place a group of their *fidā'īs* at the disposal of Jalāl al-Dīn, who refused the offer.[210] In the same year (625/1228), while the Nizārī envoy Badr al-Dīn was travelling east across the Oxus to the Mongol court, Sultan Jalāl al-Dīn ordered the stopping of all caravans in that direction, on the pretence that a Mongol envoy was on his way to Syria in the company of some Ismāʿīlīs. On these orders, Sharaf al-Mulk put to death in Ādharbayjān a westward Syrian Nizārī caravan of seventy merchants.[211] Later, Alamūt sent an emissary to the Khwārazmshāh, successfully demanding retrieval of the goods taken from the massacred caravan. This event took place after the arrival of the news of Ghiyāth al-Dīn's flight from Alamūt, which had enraged Jalāl al-Dīn. It was also at this time that Muḥammad III's vizier, captured in the vicinity of Qazwīn by the *iqṭāʿ* holder of Sāwa, was sent as prisoner to Jalāl al-Dīn, who had him executed.[212] On one occasion during this period, al-Nasawī himself was despatched as Jalāl al-Dīn's envoy to Alamūt, to demand the balance of the tribute that the Nizārīs still owed on Dāmghān and to settle other points of dispute. Al-Nasawī succeeded in meeting with Muḥammad III and his vizier ʿImād al-Dīn, who gave him lavish gifts. Al-Nasawī obtained only a compromise solution; nonetheless, he describes his mission with extreme satisfaction.[213] Relations between the Nizārīs and the Khwārazmians, who had replaced the Saljūqs as Alamūt's foremost enemy, were thus characterized by warfare, assassination and negotiation till Jalāl al-Dīn, the last of the Khwārazmshāhs, was mysteriously murdered by Kurds in 628/1231, following his decisive defeat at the hands of the Mongols.

Beside its quarrel with the Khwārazmians, the Nizārī state had continued to have periodical problems with its neighbours. In particular, relations between Rūdbār and the Caspian provinces seem to have deteriorated in Muḥammad III's time, following the execution of Ḥasan III's Gīlānī wives. The Nizārīs acquired new places in Gīlān and entered Rūyān, effectively aiding the local rebels there against the new Bādūspānid ruler, Fakhr al-Dawla Namāwar b. Bīsutūn, who had succeeded his father shortly before in 620/1223. Fakhr al-Dawla was obliged to leave Rūyān and seek refuge for a while at Jalāl al-Dīn Khwārazmshāh's court.[214] On the other hand, relations between the Rūdbārī Nizārīs and the Qazwīnīs, their perennial enemy, had finally become peaceful. Muḥammad III had evidently developed a close association with a Ṣūfī *shaykh* of Qazwīn, Jamāl al-Dīn Gīlī (d. 651/1253), and sent him an annual grant of 500 gold dinars. Muḥammad is reported to have informed the Qazwīnīs that had it not been for the sake of the *shaykh*, he would have destroyed their town.[215]

With the disappearance of the Khwārazmshāhs, the Nizārīs came to be confronted by the Mongols, who, under Chingiz Khan's son and first successor Ögedei (1229–1241), were making new efforts to conquer all of Persia. The Nizārīs soon lost Dāmghān to the Mongols, who had filled the position vacated by the Khwārazmians. As Muḥammad III had by now decided to resist the Mongols, in 1238 he despatched an embassy, in co-operation with the ʿAbbāsid caliph al-Mustanṣir (623–640/1226–1242), to the kings of France and England to seek an alliance between Muslims and Christians against the Mongols. Matthew Paris, as noted, relates the dealings of this embassy in Europe, particularly at the English court of Henry III. The mission failed however to have any results, since the Christian monarchs of Europe were soon attempting to ally themselves with the Mongols against all Muslims. A few years later, the Nizārīs completely severed their relations with the Mongols when their overtures to the new Great Khan Güyük (1246–1248) were rejected. In 644/1246, on the occasion of the enthronement of Güyük in central Mongolia, ʿAlāʾ al-Dīn Muḥammad, along with the caliph al-Mustaʿṣim (640–656/1242–1258) and many other Muslim rulers, sent a mission under Shihāb al-Dīn and Shams al-Dīn, Nizārī *muḥtashims* in Quhistān, to Mongolia to participate in the celebrations and deliver a memorandum to Güyük. The Nizārī ambassadors were, however, dismissed with contempt by Güyük, who replied to Muḥammad III's memorandum in the harshest terms.[216] Soon after, Güyük prepared to match his words with deeds. He despatched Eligidei to Persia at the head of reinforcements for the Mongol armies already there and instructed him that two out of every ten soldiers in Persia were to be used for reducing the rebellious territories, beginning with those of the Nizārīs.[217] He himself intended to follow after, but his death prevented him from carrying out his operations. Güyük's designs against the Nizārīs were taken up by his cousin and successor to the Khanate, Möngke (1251–1259). The Mongols had already been spurred against the Nizārīs by the Sunnīs at their court, and now more such complaints, including one forwarded by Shams al-Dīn, a chief *qāḍī* of Qazwīn, were brought to Möngke's notice, in addition to the warnings of the Mongol commanders in Persia.[218] At any rate, when Möngke decided to consolidate and complete the Mongol conquest of western Asia, he assigned first priority to the destruction of the Nizārī state in Persia, and of the ʿAbbāsid Caliphate. In 650/1252, Möngke entrusted this mission to his brother Hülegü, who was to lead a major expedition against the two powers that still held out in the Muslim lands. Elaborate preparations were made for this expedition, and Hülegü did not in fact set out on the westward journey from Mongolia until 651/1253; it took more than another two years before Hülegü actually arrived in Persia. As we have noted earlier on the authority of William of Rubruck, who was in Mongolia in 1254, it was during this period that a group of *fidāʾī*s were allegedly despatched to Mongolia to kill Möngke in reprisal for his anti-Nizārī operations.

Meanwhile in Syria, Rāshid al-Dīn Sinān had been succeeded, in 588/1192 or a year later, by a Persian *dāʿī* called Abū Manṣūr b. Muḥammad, or Naṣr al-ʿAjamī.[219] With Sinān's successor the authority of Alamūt over the Syrian Nizārī community was restored fully and remained unshaken until the collapse of the Persian Nizārī state in 654/1256.[220] The names of several chief *dāʿī*s who led the Syrian Nizārīs during this third phase of their history, lasting some sixty-five years, are known to us from the inscriptions at Maṣyāf, Kahf and other strongholds, and from a few Syrian literary sources.[221] Between the years 620/1223–1224 and 656/1258, these *dāʿī*s were Kamāl al-Dīn al-Ḥasan b. Masʿūd, Majd al-Dīn, Sirāj al-Dīn Muẓaffar b. al-Ḥusayn, Tāj al-Dīn Abu'l-Futūḥ b. Muḥammad, and Raḍī al-Dīn Abu'l-Maʿālī. Most of these Syrian leaders are specifically referred to as the delegates of Alamūt, their names appearing after that of the imām in the Syrian inscriptions. Like the community in Quhistān, the Syrian Nizārīs continued during this period to exercise a certain degree of local initiative in dealings with their Muslim and Frankish neighbours. The Syrian Nizārīs had, on the whole, maintained peaceful relations with Saladin's Ayyūbid successors in Syria; but upon Jalāl al-Dīn Ḥasan III's rapprochement with the Sunnīs, even closer relations developed between the two sides. Henceforth, the Nizārīs could count on the Ayyūbids as allies. The Arabic sources place the declaration of Ḥasan III's new policies in the year 608/1211–1212, and add that he sent messengers to Syria and other Nizārī territories, ordering his followers to adopt the Sunnī Sharīʿa and to build mosques.[222] Besides emissaries, the imām evidently despatched a letter to the same effect to Syria.[223] As subjects of Alamūt, the

Syrian Nizārīs apparently carried out these orders; and in view of Ḥasan III's alliance with the ʿAbbāsid caliph al-Nāṣir, their own relations were now markedly improved with the Ayyūbids, especially with al-Malik al-Ẓāhir (582–613/1186–1216), Saladin's son and ruler of Aleppo. Moreover, the Syrian Nizārīs did not attempt to assassinate any local Muslim personality during this period of *satr*, but they continued to have quarrels and dealings with the Franks, who still held the Syrian coast.

In 610/1213, the Syrian *fidāʾīs* killed Raymond, the youthful son of Bohemond IV (1187–1233) of Antioch, in the cathedral of Ṭarṭūs (Tortosa). In 611/1214–1215, Bohemond in an act of vengeance laid siege to the fortress of Khawābī. The Nizārīs appealed to al-Malik al-Ẓāhir for help, and he sent a force to their rescue; when al-Ẓāhir's own troops suffered a setback in the Jabal Bahrāʾ, al-Malik al-ʿĀdil I, the Ayyūbid ruler of Damascus, sent another army compelling the withdrawal of the Franks from Khawābī.[224] The Syrian Nizārīs had meanwhile found a way to exact payments from a number of Muslim and Christian rulers. In 624/1227, Frederick II (1212–1250), the emperor of Germany who went to the Holy Land on his own Crusade, sent envoys to Majd al-Dīn, the Syrian Nizārī chief. The envoys of Frederick, who was also the king of Sicily and the titular king of Jerusalem, had brought gifts worth almost 80,000 dinars, destined eventually for Alamūt. However, explaining that the road to Alamūt was too dangerous due to the activities of the Khwārazmians and others, Majd al-Dīn retained the gifts in Syria.[225] But he did not hesitate to inform the ruler of Aleppo, al-Malik al-ʿAzīz (613–634/1216–1237), about the emperor's friendly overtures, ensuring the Ayyūbids of his continued co-operation with them in case of need.[226] Earlier in the same year of 624 A.H., Majd al-Dīn had sent his own emissaries to the Saljūq ruler of Rūm, ʿAlāʾ al-Dīn Kayqubād I (616–634/1219–1237), demanding that the regular tribute of 2,000 dinars hitherto sent by the sultan to Alamūt should now be diverted to him.[227] The sultan consulted with the lord of Alamūt, who confirmed the request of the Syrian Nizārī chief. Eventually the tribute in question came to be paid to the Syrian community.

However, around the same time, the Hospitallers who had been highly displeased with the dealings between the Nizārīs and Frederick II, demanded tribute from the Nizārīs. The Nizārīs refused by boasting that they themselves were then receiving gifts and payments from Frankish emperors and kings. Thereupon, the Hospitallers attacked the Nizārīs and carried off much booty.[228] By around 625/1228, the Syrian Nizārīs had become tributaries to the Hospitallers as well as to the Templars. There are hints to the effect that the Nizārīs were now actually allied with the Hospitallers; on hearing this news, Pope Gregory IX (1227–1241) wrote a letter in 633/1236 to his representatives in the Holy Land strongly condemning such relations.[229] The last important event in the history of the Syrian Nizārīs of this period relates to the dealings between the sectarian chief and Louis IX, better known as St Louis, the French king who led the Seventh Crusade. These dealings, recorded by Joinville, the king's biographer and secretary, to which we have already referred, occurred soon after the arrival of St Louis in ʿAkkā (Acre) in Ṣafar 648/ May 1250.[230] At the time, the Syrian Nizārīs were most probably still under the leadership of Tāj al-Dīn Abu'l-Futūḥ, whose name is mentioned in an inscription at Maṣyāf dated Dhu'l-Qaʿda 646/February–March 1249. At any rate, Nizārī emissaries came to the French king and asked him either to pay tribute to their chief or at least release the Nizārīs from the tribute which they themselves paid to the Templars and the Hospitallers. On the intervention of Reginald de Vichier and William de Chateauneuf, the grand masters of the Temple and the Hospital, the negotiations between the Old Man of the Mountain and St Louis did not lead to any results. St Louis, himself more interested in establishing friendly relations with the Mongols, did not pay any tribute to the Nizārīs, who continued to pay their own tribute to the Hospitallers and the Templars. But the French king and the Syrian Nizārī chief exchanged gifts. It was in the course of these embassies that the Arabic-speaking friar Yves le Breton met the Old Man of the Mountain and discussed religious doctrines with him in Maṣyāf or another of the Nizārī strongholds in the Jabal Bahrā'.

We shall now resume our account of the final years of the Nizārī state in Persia. Hülegü, as noted, took his time in making detailed preparations to lead the main Mongol expedition across Central Asia to Persia, where he did not arrive before the beginning of 654/1256. But already in Jumādā II 650/August 1252, he had despatched an advance army of 12,000 men from Mongolia, under the command of his famous Nestorian Christian general Ket-Buqa, to join forces with the Mongol garrisons in Persia and attack as many Nizārī strongholds as possible.[231] Ket-Buqa crossed the Oxus in Muḥarram 651/March 1253 and soon afterwards attacked the Nizārī strongholds in Quhistān, capturing several places there. In Rabīʿ I 651/ May 1253, he appeared at the head of some 5,000 men at the foot of Girdkūh, where he erected walls and other siege works around the stronghold. Leaving one of his officers, Büri, in charge of the siege at

Girdkūh, Ket-Buqa next proceeded to attack the castles of Mihrīn, near Girdkūh, and another one in Qaṣrān. which were in Ismāʿīlī hands; while in Jumādā II 651/August 1253, he sent raiding parties into Rūdbār and Ṭārum, where little was accomplished. In Shawwāl 651/December 1253, the besieged garrison of Girdkūh made a daring night attack on the Mongols, killing a hundred of them, including Büri. The siege of Girdkūh however continued, and when cholera decimated the Nizārī garrison and the fortress was on the verge of falling in the summer of 652/1254, Alamūt supplied reinforcements and saved the situation. The strengthened garrison of Girdkūh continued to resist the Mongols for a long time. Meanwhile, Ket-Buqa had returned to Quhistān, where the Mongols pillaged, slaughtered and finally seized, at least temporarily, Tūn and Turshīz, in Jumādā I 651/July 1253. A few months later, the Mongols had captured Mihrīn and some other castles in Qūmis.

The Mongols had now come to exert constant pressure on the Persian Nizārīs, whose situation was further threatened by the imminent arrival of Hülegü. These external pressures seem to have aggravated the internal tensions within the Nizārī leadership, especially those between ʿAlāʾ al-Dīn Muḥammad III and his chief advisers, who evidently wanted to submit to the Mongols. At any rate, Muḥammad III, who is reported to have been afflicted by melancholia, had gradually isolated himself from the Nizārī leaders whilst persisting in defying the Mongols. At the same time, relations between Muḥammad III and his eldest son Rukn al-Dīn Khurshāh (Khwurshāh), who had received the *naṣṣ* in his childhood, were also deteriorating. It was under such circumstances that certain Nizārī leaders eventually began, according to our Persian historians, to formulate a plan against Muḥammad III, aiming to replace him by his designated successor. Accordingly, Khurshāh was to take charge of the affairs of the state and immediately enter into negotiations with the Mongols. Before this plan could be implemented, however, Khurshāh fell ill and was confined to his bed. Soon afterwards, on the last day of Shawwāl 653/1 December 1255, ʿAlāʾ al-Dīn Muḥammad III, who had always been fond of shepherding, was found murdered in a hut, adjoining his sheep-fold, in Shīrkūh near Alamūt. After putting several suspects to death, it was discovered that the murder had been committed by Ḥasan-i Māzandarānī, a favourite and constant companion of Muḥammad III, whom the imām had injured. The secret was divulged to Khurshāh by Ḥasan's wife, a former concubine of Muḥammad III. Ḥasan and several of his children were put to death.

ʿAlāʾ al-Dīn Muḥammad III, who had reigned for thirty-four years, was succeeded by his youthful son Rukn al-Dīn Khurshāh, born around 627/1230.[232] Before entering into any negotiations with the Mongols, the new Nizārī ruler attempted to strengthen his situation with his neighbours and with other Muslim rulers. The Nizārīs first completed a campaign in western Daylam and seized a fortress in Khalkhāl which they had besieged. Then Khurshāh sent messengers to Gīlān and other neighbouring areas to inform their rulers of his father's death and of his own accession, and also attempted to establish better relations with them. At the same time, he ordered all the Nizārīs to follow the Sharīʿa very closely. Soon after his accession, and in order to inform the Mongols of the new policy of the Nizārī leadership, Khurshāh sent an envoy to Yasa'ur Noyan, the Mongol commander stationed at Hamadān, offering his submission. Yasa'ur's reply was to the effect that the Nizārī ruler should present himself in person before Hülegü, whose arrival was now imminent. This was the first of a long series of messages exchanged during the year 654/1256 between the Nizārīs and the Mongols.

Meanwhile, Hülegü had been advancing westward at the head of the main Mongol force at a leisurely pace. Having set out from his *ordu* or encampment in Mongolia in Shaʿbān 651/October 1253, Hülegü arrived at the gates of Samarqand two years later, in Shaʿbān 653/September 1255. After two months, he despatched messengers from his camp at Kish to various Persian rulers informing them of his intention to extirpate the Nizārīs and asking them to render assistance or suffer the consequences. In Dhu'l-Ḥijja 653/January 1256, Hülegü crossed the Oxus and passed the remaining winter months in the meadows of Shafūrqān to the west of Balkh, the area now situated in northern Afghanistan. Hülegü entered Persia through Khurāsān in Rabīʿ I 654/April 1256 and selected the town of Tūn, which had not been effectively reduced by his advance guards under Ket-Buqa, as his first target. But he was prevented from personally supervising the Mongol assault against Tūn, by some obscure incidents that occurred as he was passing in the district of Zāwa and Khwāf on the northeastern border of Quhistān. The task was entrusted to Ket-Buqa and Köke-Ilgei, who, after besieging Tūn for a week, seized the town in the middle of Rabīʿ II 654/May 1256. The Mongols slaughtered all the inhabitants of Tūn except the younger women, according to Juwaynī, or the artisans (*pīshihvarān*), according to Rashīd al-Dīn.[233] The triumphant Mongol generals then joined Hülegü and proceeded towards Ṭūs. It was probably at Ṭūs that Hülegü shortly afterwards received Nāṣir al-Dīn, the last Nizārī *muḥtashim* of Quhistān and Naṣīr al-Dīn al-Ṭūsī's friend and patron. Hülegü had earlier despatched Malik Shams al-Dīn (643–684/1245–1285), the founder of the Kart dynasty of Harāt, on a mission to the *muḥtashim*, who was then residing at the fortress of Sartakht. Shams al-Dīn had succeeded in persuading Nāṣir al-Dīn to present himself before Hülegü, who asked the Nizārī chief why he had not brought down the garrison of the fortress. He replied that his people obeyed only the commands of Khurshāh, their ruler. Hülegü gave the aged Nāṣir al-Dīn a *yarlïgh* (decree) and a *paiza* (tablet of authority), granting him safe-conduct and appointed him to the governorship of the ruined town of Tūn. Nāṣir al-Dīn died in Ṣafar 655 A.H.

Meanwhile in Jumādā I 654/May 1256, after further negotiations of messengers, Khurshāh had sent his brother Shahanshāh with a retinue of dignitaries to announce his submission to the Mongols. They reached Yasa'ur near Qazwīn, and he delegated his own son to accompany the Nizārī mission to Hülegü. On 10 Jumādā I/5 June, Yasa'ur unexpectedly engaged in battle with the Nizārīs around Alamūt. But he withdrew after a short while and subsequently left Rūdbār upon the instructions of Hülegü, who had received the Nizārī mission at Qūchān (Khabūshān). Hülegü's own *elchi*s or ambassadors reached Khurshāh at the end of Jumādā II/July and delivered a *yarlïgh* full of encouragement to the effect that since Khurshāh had sent his brother and had demonstrated his submission and loyalty, the king had forgiven the crimes committed by his father. Khurshāh, who himself had committed no crime, was asked to destroy his castles and come down to pay homage so that the Mongol armies would not devastate his territories. The Nizārī ruler did destroy some castles, but in the case of Alamūt, Maymūndiz and Lamasar, he simply removed a few battlements (*sardīvār*) and turrets (*kungara*). Some of the Mongol ambassadors, accompanied by Khurshāh's envoy Ṣadr al-Dīn, returned to report the situation to Hülegü. Khurshāh now asked for a year's grace before presenting himself. The rest of the *elchi*s had stayed behind in Rūdbār to supervise the demolition of the Nizārī castles. In the beginning of Shaʿbān/September, the Mongol envoys came to Khurshāh with a new message that the Nizārī ruler should immediately present himself before Hülegü, and in his absence a Mongol called Tükel Bahadur would act as *basqaq* or protecting governor in Rūdbār. Khurshāh, who was obviously playing for time, sent his reply through a distinguished embassy headed by his vizier, Shams al-Dīn Gīlakī, and the son of his father's paternal uncle, Sayf al-Dīn Sulṭān Malik b. Kiyā Bū Manṣūr b. Muḥammad II, who accompanied the Mongol ambassadors and reached Hülegü on 17 Shaʿbān/9 September.[234] Khurshāh had again asked for a year's grace and the exemption of Alamūt and Lamasar from the demolition order. He had also instructed his lieutenants in Girdkūh and Quhistān to present themselves before Hülegü in submission, which they did shortly afterwards.

By this time, Hülegü's patience had become exhausted by Khurshāh's delaying tactics in surrendering. In the middle of Shaʿbān 654/September 1256, Hülegü set out from his encampment near Basṭām to launch his assault on the Nizārī castles in Rūdbār. All the Mongol garrisons in ʿIrāq-i ʿAjam were now instructed to prepare for battle. At the same time, the main Mongol force proceeded towards Rūdbār from various directions. The right wing of Hülegü's forces, under Buqa-Temür and Köke-Ilgei, proceeded by way of Māzandarān, and its left wing, under the Chaghatai prince Tegüder and Ket-Buqa, advanced through Khuwār and Simnān. Hülegü himself, with the main army, followed a parallel route passing through Fīrūzkūh, Damāwand and Rayy. Two other Chaghatai princes, Balaghai and Tutar, had meanwhile set out from ʿIrāq-i ʿAjam in the direction of Alamūt. Hülegü halted at Damāwand for a while, and from there sent yet another message to Khurshāh. The Nizārī leader was to come to Damāwand immediately, and were he to be delayed up to five days by his preparations, he was to send his son in advance. Khurshāh did despatch his son, or a youthful brother, on 17 Ramaḍān/8 October. But Hülegü returned the boy on the grounds of his youth, and suggested that if Khurshāh could not come till later, he should send another brother to relieve Shahanshāh. Hülegü was by this time in the general area of Rayy, and messages were constantly exchanged between him and Khurshāh. On 5 Shawwāl/26 October, Khurshāh sent out his brother Shīrānshāh in the company of 300 men, who arrived at Hülegü's camp two days later. At the same time, the vizier Shams al-Dīn Gīlakī had returned from Girdkūh and brought its governor, the *qāḍī* Tāj al-Dīn Mardānshāh, before Hülegü, while Girdkūh itself still held out. Shahanshāh was now sent back to Rūdbār with the message that if Khurshāh destroyed the castle of Maymūndiz and presented himself in person before the king, he would be received with honour; otherwise God alone knew what would befall him. Around this time, Hülegü secretly put to death near Qazwīn many of the Nizārīs who on different occasions had been sent to him.

By this time, the Mongol armies were entering Rūdbār from every side. Having finally decided to seize Maymūndiz, where Khurshāh was staying, Hülegü broke up his camp in Pishkildara on 10 Shawwāl/31 October and advanced towards Rūdbār through Ṭāliqān. On 18 Shawwāl 654/8 November 1256, Hülegü encamped on a hilltop facing Maymūndiz. He made a last appeal to Khurshāh to surrender, but he was told that the Nizārī ruler was absent from Maymūndiz and that nothing could be decided without his permission. Having been greatly impressed by the defences of Maymūndiz, Hülegü consulted with his commanders as to whether they should besiege the castle or turn back and wait until the spring. Most of his advisers favoured withdrawal in view of the onset of the winter and the consequent impossibility of procuring provisions for the troops and fodder for the animals. A few, including Ket-Buqa, insisted on laying siege to the castle immediately, and Hülegü supported their view. The Mongol armies began to prepare for a siege. To provide poles for their mangonels, the Mongols felled the trees which the Nizārīs themselves had planted in former times. When battle was joined, the Nizārīs gained some initial victories, pouring down stones from their own mangonels upon the besiegers. But on the second day of fighting, the Mongols brought into play a Chinese ballista (*kamān-i gāv*) with a range of 2,500 paces. The garrison of Maymūndiz now ceased fighting and asked for truce, which was granted. On the following day, Khurshāh, who had in fact been present at the castle, asked for a *yarlīgh* to grant him safe-conduct. The decree was drawn up by Juwaynī, who then acted as Hülegü's secretary and accompanied his master to the Nizārī castles. Khurshāh was evidently persuaded not to come down from Maymūndiz by some zealous *fidāʾī*s, who, in contradistinction to the foreign scholars present at his court, were strongly against surrendering to the Mongols. Meanwhile, more messages continued to be exchanged. It is clear that all along, Khurshāh had been playing for time in the hope that the snows of winter would come to his aid and render the siege operations of the Mongols impracticable; but the weather remained unseasonably mild in that autumn of 654/1256. On 25 Shawwāl/15 November, the Mongols resumed their bombardment of Maymūndiz on a much larger scale. At last, Khurshāh decided to surrender, being greatly encouraged in this decision by Naṣīr al-Dīn al-Ṭūsī and other outside scholars then staying at Maymūndiz.

Khurshāh first sent down his son and another brother called Īrānshāh with a delegation of notables. Then, on Sunday 29 Shawwāl 654/19 November 1256,[235] he himself descended, surrounded by a group of dignitaries including Naṣīr al-Dīn al-Ṭūsī, Khwāja Aṣīl al-Dīn Zūzanī and the vizier Mu'ayyad al-Dīn. Rukn al-Dīn Khurshāh had reigned for exactly one year, and his surrender marked the close of the Nizārī state of Persia, which had been founded some 166 years earlier with the capture of Alamūt by Ḥasan-i Ṣabbāḥ. On the day following his surrender, Khurshāh brought out all his family, dependants and the other inmates of the castle, also offering the meagre treasures of Maymūndiz as a token of his submission. When the Mongols went up to the castle to commence the work of dismantling its buildings and structures, they were confronted by a group of highly devoted *fidā'īs* whose desperate resistance was broken up only after three days of fierce fighting.

Khurshāh was well received by Hülegü, though he was kept under the surveillance of a Mongol commander. At Hülegü's request, the Nizārī ruler despatched his representatives in the company of Mongol *elchis* to all the Nizārī castles in Rūdbār with orders for their destruction. Some forty castles were thus demolished, after the evacuation of their garrisons. In Rūdbār, only the commanders of Alamūt and Lamasar refused to surrender, perhaps thinking that their imām was acting under duress and was observing a new sort of *taqiyya*. Hülegü himself proceeded to the foot of Alamūt, where Khurshāh tried in vain to persuade that castle's commandant, Muqaddim al-Dīn, to capitulate. Leaving Balaghai behind to besiege Alamūt with a large force, Hülegü now set out for Lamasar. After a few days, the garrison of Alamūt decided to surrender; and Khurshāh, who had accompanied Hülegü to Lamasar, interceded on their behalf with the Mongol conqueror. The inmates of Alamūt were given three days' grace to bring down their belongings, a party of Mongols having first entered the castle to remove its mangonels and gates. Khurshāh himself received permission to visit the castle. On the fourth day, towards the end of Dhu'l-Qaʿda 654/December 1256, the Mongols ascended to the fortress of Alamūt and plundered whatever had been left behind. They also began the tedious work of demolishing Alamūt and setting fire to its buildings and its library. Meanwhile, Juwaynī, who had accompanied Hülegü to the foot of Lamasar, had been allowed to examine the library at Alamūt and to salvage whatever he deemed necessary. He saved the Qur'āns, and a number of choice books, including some Ismāʿīlī works, as well as certain astronomical instruments, before consigning the library to flames. Juwaynī has left a valuable description of the fortress of Alamūt, which he surveyed in connection with his inspection of the library.[236] Juwaynī was greatly impressed by the storage facilities and the food supplies there, as well as the castle's water supply system and fortifications. He describes the difficulties faced by a large group of Mongols who were assigned the task of demolishing the castle.

Hülegü had meanwhile failed to capture Lamasar or to induce its commandant to surrender, despite Khurshāh's intervention. He left Tayir-Buqa to besiege the place with an army of Mongols and Persians. Lamasar held out for another year, before cholera broke out and killed the bulk of the garrison. The few who survived the epidemic were obliged to surrender sometime at the end of 655 A.H.[237] Hülegü left Rūdbār for his main *ordu* near Hamadān in Dhu'l-Ḥijja 654/January 1257. Khurshāh, being still useful to the Mongols, accompanied the Īlkhān, while the imām's family, servants and belongings were sent to Qazwīn. From Hülegü's *ordu*, Khurshāh despatched his emissaries along with Mongol *elchi*s to the Nizārī castles in Syria, instructing them to guard the castles as subjects of the king until such time as Hülegü himself should arrive there; but his instructions were ignored in Syria. Meanwhile, with Khurshāh's co-operation it had become possible for the Mongols to secure the speedy surrender and dismantlement of the Nizārī castles in Ṭārum, Rūdbār, Qūmis, Quhistān and elsewhere, with the major exceptions of Lamasar and Girdkūh. The commandants (singular, *kūtvāl*) and the bulk of the garrisons of these fallen castles were placed under the supervision of different Mongol units and commanders.

Khurshāh continued to be treated respectfully by the Mongols while he was of use to them. But the surrender of the bulk of the Nizārī castles made his presence an embarrassment to Hülegü. Therefore, when he asked to be sent to the court of Möngke, Hülegü readily approved his request. On 1 Rabīʿ I 655/9 March 1257, Khurshāh set out on his fateful journey to Mongolia with nine companions and a group of Mongols led by Bujrai. On the way, when the party arrived at the foot of Girdkūh, Khurshāh tried once again in vain to bring down the castle's garrison, though he may have told them secretly not to surrender. Khurshāh was not evidently treated respectfully by his escorts; and, by the time they reached Bukhārā, Khurshāh had to engage in fist-fighting with his Mongol guards. Möngke refused to see Khurshāh when he finally arrived in Karakorum (Qaraqorum). He was dismissed and reproached by the Great Khan for not having yet dismantled Girdkūh and Lamasar. On the return journey, somewhere along the edge of the Khangai mountains in northwestern Mongolia, the eighth and final lord of Alamūt and his companions were led away from the road and put to the sword by the Mongols. In the meantime, after Khurshāh's departure for Mongolia, there had taken place a general massacre of the Persian Nizārīs who were in Mongol custody. Khurshāh's family and dependants detained at Qazwīn were put to the sword by Qaraqai Bitikchi, while Ötegü-China, the Mongol commander in Khurāsān, summoned the Quhistānī Nizārīs to great gatherings and slaughtered some 12,000 of them. According to Juwaynī, the massacre of the Nizārīs had been carried out in accordance with a decree of Möngke to the effect that none of the Nizārīs should be spared, reflecting an earlier order of Chingiz Khan himself.[238]

As Hodgson has pointed out, it seems that given the spirit of earlier times, when the Nizārīs were enthusiastically fighting the Saljūqs under Ḥasan-i Ṣabbāḥ and his immediate successors, some of the Nizārī fortresses might have been able to resist the Mongol assaults at least long enough to persuade Hülegü to come to some sort of an accommodation with them.[239] Juwaynī, who accompanied the Mongols to Alamūt, Maymūndiz and Lamasar, clearly emphasizes the impregnability and self-sufficiency of the Nizārī fortresses, especially Alamūt, which would have enabled them to withstand Mongol sieges for indefinite periods; he also recalls how Alamūt had earlier successfully resisted the Saljūq armies for over a decade.[240] Rashīd al-Dīn, too, speaks of the good fortune of Möngke and Hülegü in having extirpated the Nizārīs and their castles so quickly.[241] Indeed, as Girdkūh was to demonstrate, at least the key Nizārī fortresses could have held out for long periods on the basis of their own resources. Girdkūh continued to resist its Mongol besiegers, as the last surviving Nizārī outpost in Persia, for thirteen years after the fall of Alamūt. The garrison of Girdkūh finally yielded from want of clothing on 29 Rabīʿ II 669/15 December 1270, during the reign of the Īlkhānid Abaqa, seventeen years after the first investment of the place by Hülegü's advance guards.[242] The Mongols, who had erected permanent structures and dwelling places of their own around Girdkūh (the remains of which together with the stones of their mangonels are still found there), killed the survivors of the garrison on their descent. But the Mongols did not evidently demolish Girdkūh, which they continued to use under the Īlkhānids succeeding Abaqa.[243] In its decision to surrender, the central Nizārī leadership seems to have been greatly influenced by Naṣīr al-Dīn al-Ṭūsī and other outside scholars amongst the Nizārīs; scholars who, having enjoyed the hospitality of the Nizārīs, were now eager to taste the yet larger munificence of the Mongols, which they did upon dissociating themselves from the last lord of Alamūt and entering into the service of the Īlkhānid dynasty of Persia founded by Hülegü (654–663/1256–1265).

The collapse of the Nizārī state in Persia must have disheartened the Syrian Nizārīs, who could no longer count on the support and leadership of Alamūt and the personal guidance of the Nizārī Imām, who was now no longer accessible to his followers. Under the circumstances, the Syrian Nizārīs began to select their leaders locally, sometimes two persons jointly holding the office of their chief *dāʿī*. Deprived of any sort of strong central leadership and threatened by the designs of various powers – especially the Mongols and the Mamlūk dynasty of Egypt – for the invasion of Syria, the Syrian Nizārī community began to experience serious internal dissensions, often manifested in the form of rivalries among the senior *dāʿīs* and independent behaviour of the governors of various fortresses. All of these factors prepared the ground for the eventual submission of the Syrian Nizārīs to al-Malik al-Ẓāhir Rukn al-Dīn Baybars I (658–676/1260–1277), the Baḥrī Mamlūk sultan of Egypt, who soon extended his hegemony over Syria and its different principalities.[244] Meanwhile, having dealt with the Persian Nizārīs, Hülegü had proceeded towards his second major objective, the extinction of the ʿAbbāsid Caliphate. By Ṣafar 656/February 1258, the Mongols seized Baghdād and devastated the ancient capital of the ʿAbbāsids for a whole week. The caliph al-Mustaʿṣim, who had endeavoured in vain to prevent the Mongol cataclysm, was put to death on Hülegü's orders. Hülegü's third campaign was directed against the Ayyūbid states in Syria. In 658/1260, the Mongols seized Aleppo, and soon afterwards Ḥamāt and Damascus surrendered to Hülegü. In Rabīʿ I 658/March 1260, Ket-Buqa, who had been in charge of the advance operations of the Mongols in Syria, made his triumphal entry into Damascus, accompanied by Hetʿum, the king of Little Armenia, and the latter's son-in-law Bohemond VI of Antioch, the allies of the Mongols. It was during the same year, 658/1260, that four of the Nizārī fortresses, including Maṣyāf, were surrendered to the Mongols by their governors.[245] The Mongol success in Syria was, however, short-lived. Hülegü returned to Persia in the summer upon hearing the news of Möngke's death, which in fact had occurred a year earlier in 657/1259, leaving Ket-Buqa in command of his reduced forces in Syria. On 25 Ramaḍān 658/3 September 1260, the Mongols suffered a drastic defeat at ʿAyn Jālūt, in Palestine, at the hands of the Mamlūk armies of Egypt, led by the sultan al-Muẓaffar Quṭuz (657–658/1259–1260). Ket-Buqa was captured and put to death.

The vanguard of the Mamlūk forces was commanded by Baybars, who succeeded Qutuz to the Mamlūk sultanate and thwarted the Mongols in their subsequent attempts to establish themselves in the region. Soon, the Mongols were expelled from all of Syria, where Baybars rapidly emerged as the dominant power. The Nizārīs evidently collaborated with the Mamlūks and other Muslim rulers in repelling the Mongols from Syria, and after the battle of ʿAyn Jālūt recovered the four fortresses which they had earlier lost to them. At the time of the Mongol invasion of Syria, the Syrian Nizārīs were under the leadership of Raḍī al-Dīn Abu'l-Maʿālī, who punished the Nizārī governors who had yielded their castles to the Mongols. According to Ibn Muyassar, Raḍī al-Dīn had become the chief *dāʿī* in Syria in 656/1258, and shortly before succeeding to that office he had gone to Mamlūk Egypt as a Nizārī envoy.[246]

The Syrian Nizārīs now attempted to establish friendly relations with Baybars by sending him embassies and gifts. Baybars, who was then preoccupied with the Mongols and the Franks, reciprocated by granting certain favours to the community. Nonetheless, from early on Baybars capitalized on the weakness and internal dissensions of the Nizārī community and systematically adopted measures which ultimately led to the loss of the political independence of the Syrian Nizārī community. Ibn ʿAbd al-Ẓāhir (d. 692/1293), the biographer of Baybars, reports that already in 659/1261 Baybars granted rights to Nizārī territories to al-Malik al-Manṣūr (642–683/1244–1285), the Ayyūbid prince of Ḥamāt.[247] At the same time, however, the Nizārīs sent an embassy to Baybars and successfully demanded to receive the privileges which they had enjoyed under the Ayyūbids. Baybars, in an attempt to divide the Nizārīs, now appointed the Nizārī envoy, a certain Jamāl al-Dīn Ḥasan b. Thābit, to the headship of the Nizārī community, which was then still held by Raḍī al-Dīn, perhaps conjointly with Najm al-Dīn Ismāʿīl b. al-Shaʿrānī.[248] But the community refused to acknowledge Jamāl al-Dīn, who was put to death. It was about this time that Raḍī al-Dīn died and the aged Najm al-Dīn became the head of the Syrian *daʿwa* in 660/1261–1262. Najm al-Dīn was later assisted by his son Shams al-Dīn and his son-in-law Ṣārim al-Dīn Mubārak, who was Raḍī al-Dīn's son. The Nizārī community had continued to retain possession of eight permanent strongholds; namely, Maṣyāf, Qadmūs, Kahf, Khawābī, Ruṣāfa, Manīqa (Maynaqa), ʿUllayqa and Qulayʿa. Kharība seems to have been lost sometime earlier.[249]

As Baybars continued to consolidate his position in Syria, the Nizārīs found it advisable to periodically renew their friendly overtures to him. In

661/1263, when Baybars was engaged in his campaigns against the Franks, a Nizārī mission under the two sons of the Nizārī chiefs came to the sultan with gifts.[250] The envoys of the *dār al-daʿwa*, probably Shams al-Dīn and Ṣārim al-Dīn, were treated kindly. However, in 664/1265, Baybars felt strong enough to order the collection of taxes and tolls on the gifts sent to the Nizārīs by the various Frankish kings and the ruler of Yaman; gifts which passed through Egypt.[251] Henceforth, the political significance of the Syrian Nizārīs, who were in no position to resist Baybars' encroachments on their sovereignty, declined rapidly. Soon afterwards, the Nizārīs themselves began to pay tribute to Baybars, following the conclusion of a peace treaty in 664/1266 between the Mamlūk sultan and the Hospitallers. According to this treaty, the Hospitallers renounced the tributes which they had hitherto received from the Nizārīs and other Muslim states around Ḥamāt and Ḥimṣ. Furthermore, starting in 665/1267, the Nizārīs became tributaries of Baybars, paying him what they previously sent to the Hospitallers, for which payment Baybars had already reproached them.[252] In effect, the Nizārīs had now placed themselves under the suzerainty of the Mamlūk state, and it did not take long before they lost their nominal independence completely as Baybars maintained his pressure on the community. Indeed, Baybars soon began to appoint and dismiss the heads of the Nizārī community, as the lords of Alamūt had done previously.

In 668/1270, while Baybars was travelling to Ḥiṣn al-Akrād in the vicinity of the Nizārī territory, Najm al-Dīn, unlike other *amīr*s in the area, did not present himself before the sultan to pay homage. Baybars was greatly offended by this chief and reacted by deposing him. When Najm al-Dīn shortly afterwards sent his son-in-law Ṣārim al-Dīn Mubārak, the governor of ʿUllayqa, as an envoy to Baybars, evidently in the hope of receiving a reduction in the Nizārī tribute paid to the Mamlūks, the sultan designated Ṣārim al-Dīn to the headship of the Nizārī community.[253] The sultan now demanded possession of Maṣyāf, which was to be entrusted to one of his own *amīr*s, ʿIzz al-Dīn al-ʿAdīmī. Ṣārim al-Dīn, who was to hold the Nizārī castles as the deputy of Baybars, proceeded to take charge of them in Jumādā II 668/February 1270. His authority was initially contested by Najm al-Dīn, who soon yielded. But Ṣārim al-Dīn, too, angered the sultan by attempting through trickery to take possession of Maṣyāf, in violation of the sultan's instructions. Once inside, he put to death a large number of the residents of Maṣyāf, who, abiding by the sultan's orders, had refused to yield the castle to him. On Baybars' request, al-Malik al-

Manṣūr, the ruler of Ḥamāṭ, dislodged the rebellious Ṣārim al-Dīn from Maṣyāf and sent him as a prisoner to Cairo, where he later died. Baybars reinstated Najm al-Dīn, who had meanwhile apologized to the sultan; his son Shams al-Dīn was kept in Cairo.

In Rajab 669/February 1271, when Baybars was besieging the Frankish castle of Ḥiṣn al-Akrād, two Nizārīs from ʿUllayqa, who allegedy had been sent to kill the sultan, were apprehended. It became known that the *fidāʾī*s had initially visited Bohemond VI, the sultan's enemy, with whose assistance they were to carry out their assassination mission. The discovery of this plot put an end to any existing entente between Baybars and the Nizārī leadership in Syria. Baybars now decided to deal effectively with the sectarians. Shams al-Dīn was arrested on charges of collaborating with the Franks against the sultan. Najm al-Dīn pleaded successfully with Baybars for the release of his son, but he was forced to give up his leadership position and surrendered control of the Nizārī fortresses to the Mamlūks. Najm al-Dīn, then ninety years of age, accompanied Baybars to Cairo, where he died in 672/1274.[254] Shams al-Dīn, who had acted as his father's chief assistant and probably had also held the office of chief *dāʿī* conjointly with him, was allowed to remain temporarily in Syria for settling the affairs of the Nizārī *daʿwa* and castles. However, for a time he tried in vain to organize the Nizārīs against Baybars. The Nizārī castles now began to submit in rapid succession to Baybars, who used military blockades, threats, negotiations, and tempting promises in dealing with them.[255] ʿUllayqa and Ruṣāfa surrendered in Shawwāl 669/May 1271; and by Dhu'l-Qaʿda 671/May 1273, Khawābī, Qulayʿa, Manīqa and Qadmūs had also capitulated. Meanwhile, Shams al-Dīn, discouraged in his efforts to launch a revolt, gave himself up to the Mamlūks and was sent to Cairo. Only the garrison of Kahf mustered some resistance, and with the fall of that fortress in Dhu'l-Ḥijja 671/July 1273 the last independent Nizārī outpost in Syria fell into the hands of the Mamlūks, less than three years after the garrison of Girdkūh had surrendered to the Mongols.

Having acquired complete control of the Nizārī strongholds, Baybars, unlike the Mongols in Persia, tolerated the Nizārīs and did not attempt to exterminate them. The Nizārīs were in fact permitted to remain in their fortresses in the Jabal Bahrāʾ, but only under the strict supervision of Mamlūk lieutenants. Indeed, there are reports that Baybars and his successors employed the services of the Nizārīs against their own enemies.[256] Already prior to the submission of all the Nizārī fortresses, Baybars is alleged to have used the services of the Nizārī *fidāʾī*s against his opponents. Baybars is reported to have threatened the count of Tripoli with assassination in Shaʿbān 669/April 1271, while the murder of Philip of Montford, lord of Tyre, in 1270 and the unsuccessful attempt on the life of prince Edward of England in 1272 are also said to have been instigated by him.[257] Amongst the sources speaking of the use of Nizārī *fidāʾīs* by the early Mamlūks, an elaborate account is related by the celebrated Moorish traveller Ibn Baṭṭūṭa, who passed through Syria for the first time in his travels in 726/1326. He names Manīqa, ʿUllayqa, Qadmūs, Kahf and Maṣyāf as the fortresses which were still in the hands of the Ismāʿīliyya (Fidāwiyya), and then proceeds to give interesting details on the arrangements existing between the *fidāʾīs* and the Mamlūk sultan al-Nāṣir Nāṣir al-Dīn Muḥammad, who reigned intermittently between 693/1294 and 741/1340.[258]

Thus, the Syrian Nizārīs were allowed to exist in a semi-autonomous fashion as loyal subjects of the Mamlūks and their successors. This gave the Syrian Nizārī community the opportunity to maintain its identity, and its traditions and practices, a fate denied to the Persian Nizārīs, who never really recovered from the Mongol catastrophe. But for all practical purposes, the days of Nizārī Ismāʿīlism as the religion of a state and a political power to be reckoned with had already ended before the Mongols and the Mamlūks dealt their decisive blows to the Persian and Syrian branches of the movement. Whatever diminished political significance the Nizārīs had retained precariously during the later Alamūt period was irrevocably lost in the year 654/1256. With the fall of Alamūt, the majestic mountain fortress selected by Ḥasan-i Ṣabbāḥ as the original headquarters of the movement, Nizārī Ismāʿīlism entered a totally different and often obscure phase of its history, surviving merely as a minor Shīʿī Muslim sect without its earlier political significance.

7

Post-Alamūt Nizārī Ismāʿīlism

In this final chapter, we shall trace the development of Nizārī Ismāʿīlism from the fall of Alamūt in 654/1256 to the present time, a period of seven centuries. The first five centuries of this period represent the darkest phase in Nizārī history and constitute the longest obscure period in the history of the Ismāʿīlī movement. Only the main events of this period are currently known to researchers in Nizārī studies. The Nizārīs of Persia, contrary to the declarations of Juwaynī and later historians, did in fact survive the destruction of their state and strongholds at the hands of the Mongols. Despite the Mongol massacres, the Persian Nizārī community was not totally extirpated during 654–655/1256–1257, and significant numbers escaped the Mongol debacle in both Rūdbār and Quhistān. And while Rukn al-Dīn Khurshāh was spending the last few months of his life amongst the Mongols, the Nizārī leadership evidently managed to hide his son and designated successor, Shams al-Dīn Muḥammad, who became the progenitor of the Nizārī Imāms of the post-Alamūt period. The Nizārī Imāmate was thus preserved, and it was soon handed down through two different lines of imāms. For at least two centuries, however, the Nizārīs did not have direct access to their imāms, who were at the time living clandestinely in different parts of Persia. Meanwhile, in order to escape further persecution at the hands of the Īlkhānids, the Tīmūrids and other dynasties ruling over Persia, the highly disorganized and demoralized Persian Nizārīs were once again obliged to observe the strictest form of *taqiyya*. Under such circumstances, when mere survival was the prime concern of the community, the doctrinal background of the Persian Nizārīs enabled them to seek refuge under the mantle of Ṣūfism.

In Syria, as noted, Baybars I subjugated the Nizārī community completely by the year 671/1273. Thereafter, the Syrian Nizārīs, devoid of any political significance and with almost no contact with the Persian Nizārīs, lived in a semi-autonomous manner as the loyal subjects of the Mamlūks and later the Ottomans. Meanwhile, a third Nizārī tradition had come into existence in the upper Oxus region, where Ismāʿīlism had been introduced several centuries earlier. The Ismāʿīlīs of Badakhshān and the surrounding areas evidently acknowledged the Nizārī Imāms sometime before the fall of Alamūt. The Nizārīs of those remote parts remained unaffected by the Mongol invasion of Persia and during the post-Alamūt period developed a somewhat distinctive literary tradition of their own, according particular importance to the works of Nāṣir-i Khusraw. They also preserved the bulk of the extant Nizārī literature of the Alamūt and post-Alamūt periods written in the Persian language. It was in the post-Alamūt period that Nizārism had its greatest success on the Indian subcontinent. The Indian Nizārī community, designated chiefly by the term Khoja, grew steadily under the leadership of its local leaders or *pīrs* until it became the main stronghold of the Nizārī sect. The Nizārī Khojas, too, developed a specific religious tradition, interfacing Islamic and Hindu traditions. The Indian Nizārīs experienced a major schism in the first quarter of the 10th/16th century. When Imām Shāh, one of the community's leaders, died in 919/1513, his son and successor Nar (Nūr) Muḥammad Shāh repudiated the Nizārī Imāms living in Persia and claimed the imāmate for his father and himself. He in effect founded a separate Indian Nizārī sub-sect whose adherents became known as the Imām-Shāhīs or Satpanthīs. This sect was later further subdivided, while different groups continued to split off periodically from the main Nizārī Khoja body.

The widely dispersed Nizārī communities of the post-Alamūt period, differentiated in terms of their language and socio-ethnic characteristics as well as their historical backgrounds, developed independently of one another, each retaining its own particular heritage and religious literature. Having been deprived of any central leadership under the guidance of their imāms, for quite some time after the fall of Alamūt, the Nizārī communities, especially outside of Persia, now came to be led by their own local leaders, *dāʿīs*, *pīrs* or *shaykhs*, who alone could claim access to the Nizārī Imāms living secretly in Persia. In time, these local leaders established their own independent dynasties, which caused occasional schisms in the Nizārī movement. All of these factors have combined to create numerous research problems in post-Alamūt Nizārī studies, especially in view of the fact that very few reliable sources, Nizārī or otherwise, are available on the subject. In fact, it has been only during the last few decades that we have acquired some insights into the main trends in the development of post-Alamūt Nizārism.

As a result of modern progress in Nizārī studies, initiated by Ivanow, we can now distinguish three approximate periods in the history of post-Alamūt Nizārī Ismāʿīlism. The earliest period, covering roughly the first two centuries after the fall of Alamūt, is the most obscure, during which time the Persian Nizārīs attempted in vain to reassert their control over the Rūdbār region. It was also during that initial period that the Persian Nizārīs camouflaged themselves under the cloak of Ṣūfism and that a succession dispute in the family of the imāms split the Nizārī community into two factions, the Muḥammad-Shāhīs and the Qāsim-Shāhīs. The Muḥammad-Shāhī Imāms, who, initially, seemingly had the support of the Nizārī majority in certain regions, emigrated to India during the earlier part of the 10th/16th century, but by the beginning of the 13th/19th century this line of the Nizārī Imāms became discontinued. The Qāsim-Shāhī Imāms, who were gradually acknowledged by the Nizārī majoritarian, emerged in Anjudān, a village in central Persia, at least by the second half of the 9th/15th century. This marks the beginning of the second period in post-Alamūt Nizārism, designated by Ivanow as the Anjudān revival, a renaissance in Nizārī thought and *daʿwa* activity. During this phase, lasting for about two centuries, the Nizārī Imāms of the Qāsim-Shāhī line, who developed close relations with the Niʿmat Allāhī Ṣūfī order in Persia, attempted to extend their control over the outlying Nizārī communities in Syria, Central Asia and India, where great numbers had hitherto acknowledged the Muḥammad-Shāhī Imāms or had come to owe their immediate allegiance to their hereditary dynasty of *pīrs*.

Under the more favourable conditions created by the adoption of Twelver Shīʿism as the state religion in Ṣafawid Persia, the Qāsim-Shāhī Imāms conducted the *daʿwa* activities more openly. The Anjudān period also witnessed a revival in literary activities amongst the Nizārīs of Persia and some adjoining areas, who now produced the first doctrinal treatises after the fall of Alamūt. In the second half of the 12th/18th century, the Qāsim-Shāhī Imāms, who had meanwhile moved from Anjudān to the nearby village of Kahak and thence to Kirmān, began to acquire political prominence in Persia under the Zand and Qājār dynasties. By the middle of the 13th/19th century, when the Nizārī Imām had become known to the outside world as the Āghā Khān and the seat of the Nizārī Imāmate had been transferred to India, the Nizārīs entered the modern phase of their history. This period in Nizārī history has been characterized by the efforts of the Nizārī Imāms, or the Āghā Khāns, to consolidate their leadership over the community and improve the socio-economic conditions of their followers, especially of those living on the Indian subcontinent and on the coast of East Africa.

By contrast to the Ṭayyibīs, the literary output of the Nizārīs has always remained meagre. The difficult conditions under which the Nizārīs have often lived and the generally limited standard of literacy and intellectual accomplishment attained by the community until recent times made it almost impossible for the Nizārīs to produce outstanding theologians and authors comparable to the great Yamanī Ṭayyibī *dāʿīs*. This dearth of education, together with the specific doctrinal trends of the Alamūt period, caused the post-Alamūt Nizārīs, especially outside of Syria, to lose interest in studying the literature of the Fāṭimid Ismāʿīlīs, a literature preserved and utilized mainly by the Ṭayyibī Ismāʿīlīs. Of all the Nizārī communities, only the Syrian Nizārīs have preserved a certain number of the classical Ismāʿīlī treatises of the Fāṭimid period. The few doctrinal treatises written during the post-Alamūt period essentially retain the Nizārī teaching of the late Alamūt period; one does not come across any major or original work in the literature of this period. Furthermore, until more recent times, the post-Alamūt Nizārīs did not show any interest in studying the history of their sect, and consequently did not undertake to compile any historical works. It is, therefore, not surprising that many present-day Nizārīs have continued to remain rather ill-informed about their past heritage and the development of the Ismāʿīlī movement in general. Needless to repeat that the various Nizārī communities of the post-Alamūt period, separated geographically and by language barriers, have developed distinctive literary traditions of their own with little or no contact with one another.

On the basis of a mixture of geographical, linguistic, ethnological, and other criteria, the Nizārī literature of the post-Alamūt period can be classified into four main categories; namely, the Persian, the Central Asian, the Syrian and the Indian sources. The sources produced in Persia, Afghanistan and the upper Oxus region are written entirely in the Persian language, while the Syrian sources are in Arabic. The Nizārīs of the Indian subcontinent, including the Khojas, the Satpanthīs and the adherents of some lesser sub-sects, have utilized various Indian languages and dialects in committing their religious doctrines and traditions to writing. It should also be noted that our discussion of the post-Alamūt Nizārī sources refers mainly to the doctrinal works produced by the followers of the Qāsim-Shāhī Nizārī Imāms. The Muḥammad-Shāhī Nizārīs evidently produced very few works in Syria, the upper Oxus and India, which have not been studied adequately.[1]

The Nizārīs of Persia and the adjacent regions, who use the Persian language in their religious literature, evidently did not produce any doctrinal works during the first two centuries after the fall of Alamūt. From that early post-Alamūt period, we have only the poetical works of Nizārī Quhistānī, a poet and government functionary from Bīrjand who died around 720/1320. He was perhaps the first post-Alamūt Nizārī author to choose the verse and Ṣūfī forms of expression for camouflaging his Ismāʿīlī ideas, a model readily adopted by later Persian Nizārī writers. The revival of Nizārism during the Anjudān period also encouraged the literary activities of the community, and a number of better-educated Nizārīs living in and around Persia now began to produce the first doctrinal works of the post-Alamūt period in the Persian language.[2] The earliest and most noteworthy amongst such authors were Abū Isḥāq Quhistānī, probably a native of the district of Mu'minābād, who flourished during the second half of the 9th/15th century,[3] and Khayrkhwāh-i Harātī, a *dāʿī* and prolific writer with limited poetical talent who died after 960/1553.[4] They were followed by Imām Qulī Khākī Khurāsānī, who died after 1056/1646, and his son ʿAlī Qulī Raqqāmī Khurāsānī (or Dizbādī),[5] amongst others. Khākī and his son, too, living in Dizbād, a village in the mountains between Mashhad and Nīshāpūr, resorted to poetry and Ṣūfī expressions for disguising their Nizārī ideas.

In modern times, a few more doctrinal works have been written in the Persian language by Nizārī authors. These works, produced in Persia, Afghanistan, and even India, marked a new revival in Nizārī literary activities. This new revival, which faded out in the opening decades of the present century, had been encouraged by the efforts of the Āghā Khāns following the transfer of their residence to India, to re-establish their control over the various Nizārī communities, similar to the efforts of the imāms of the Anjudān period. Amongst such modern Nizārī works written in Persian, mention may be made of some short treatises composed by Shihāb al-Dīn Shāh al-Ḥusaynī, the eldest son of Āqā ʿAlī Shāh, the second Āghā Khān.[6] He spent the greater part of his life in Bombay and Poona, and predeceased his father by a few months in 1302/1884 whilst still in his early thirties. In Persia, the most learned Nizārī author of recent times was Muḥammad b. Zayn al-ʿĀbidīn Khurāsānī, who adopted the poetical *takhalluṣ* or pen name of Fidā'ī and was also referred to as Ḥājjī

Ākhūnd by the Persian Nizārīs. He was a descendant of Khākī Khurāsānī and lived in the important Nizārī village of Dizbād near Mashhad, where his relatives are still residing. Fidā'ī travelled to India three times between 1313 and 1324/1896–1906, to see the Nizārī Imām of the time, Sulṭān Muḥammad Shāh, Āghā Khān III, who treated him most kindly and appointed him to an important teaching position in the Persian Nizārī community. He died at Dizbād in 1342/1923 and was buried next to Khākī Khurāsānī; the site was modestly repaired in 1966.

Fidā'ī composed several doctrinal works, including the *Irshād al-sālikīn*, completed in 1317/1900, the *Kashf al-ḥaqā'iq*, written in 1332/1914, the *Kitāb-i dānish-i ahl-i bīnish*, and the *Ḥadīqat al-maʿānī*, a treatise on *fiqh*. Copies of these works were either given or shown to the present writer in Dizbād and Mashhad in the summer of 1985 by Fidā'ī's sole grandson Ṣadr al-Dīn b. Mullā Shams al-Dīn Mīrshāhī; but none of these works have been listed in the Ismāʿīlī bibliographies of Ivanow and Poonawala.[7] Fidā'ī was also a prolific poet and his *Dīwān* of poetry, collected by his descendants, contains about 12,000 verses. Fidā'ī was the only contemporary Persian Nizārī to write a history of Ismāʿīlism, the already-cited *Kitāb-i hidāyat al-mu'minīn al-ṭālibīn*, completed around 1320/1903, probably at the request of Āghā Khān III. Fidā'ī's history, extending from the origins of the Ismāʿīlī movement to the imāms of the post-Alamūt period, and filled with anachronisms and inaccuracies, was revised and updated to around 1328/1910 by Mūsā Khān b. Muḥammad Khān Khurāsānī (d. 1937), whose family had been in the service of the Āghā Khāns. Mūsā Khān himself had been an employee of Shihāb al-Dīn Shāh before entering the service of his younger half-brother Āghā Khān III. He was a poorly educated man with limited knowledge of the Persian language; but he had access to the library of the Āghā Khāns in Bombay and had heard many of the oral traditions of the sect, including those circulating in the imām's own family. The portion added by Mūsā Khān to Fidā'ī's history deals mainly with the lives of the Āghā Khāns and their miraculous deeds; the continuation is particularly noteworthy for reflecting the mentality and some of the beliefs of the nineteenth-century Nizārī Khojas.

As noted, within Persian Nizārī Ismāʿīlism, the Nizārī community in Badakhshān and the adjacent areas in the upper Oxus region has retained a specific literary tradition. This tradition represents several strata of Ismāʿīlī literature, though the Badakhshānī sectarians have been especially attached to Nāṣir-i Khusraw and his works.[8] Consequently, the Nizārīs of Badakhshān have preserved and transmitted the anonymous *Umm al-*

kitāb, the genuine and spurious writings of Nāṣir-i Khusraw, and the Persian Nizārī works of the Alamūt and post-Alamūt periods, including the treatises representing the coalescence of Ismā'īlism with Ṣūfism and many anonymous works whose authorship cannot definitely be attributed to the Nizārīs. The Nizārīs of Badakhshān have played an important part in preserving the Nizārī literature written in the Persian language, which strangely enough has always been a foreign language to them. As noted, a large number of Nizārī manuscripts were recovered during 1959–1963 by a Soviet research expedition sent to the Gorno-Badakhshān region in Tājikistān.[9] These manuscripts, all written in Persian, have been preserved mainly by the Nizārīs of Shughnān in western Pāmīr, whose own native language is a Tājik dialect. During the post-Alamūt period, the Nizārī community in Badakhshān did not produce any noteworthy authors after Sayyid Suhrāb Valī Badakhshānī, who wrote around 856/1452.[10]

The underground existence of the Persian Nizārīs did not attract the attention of the Persian historians of the post-Alamūt period, who did not have any direct contacts with the Nizārī communities and who, like Juwaynī, thought that the Mongols had completely extirpated the sectarians. Only a few Persian chroniclers writing during the first three post-Alamūt centuries, including the historians of the Caspian region, occasionally refer to the Persian Nizārīs. It was after the latter part of the 12th/18th century, when the Nizārī Imāms had acquired political prominence in Persia, that the chroniclers of the Zand and Qājār dynasties began to make frequent references to the Nizārī Imāms and their political activities, especially in the province of Kirmān. Amongst such later chroniclers, mention may be made of Aḥmad 'Alī Khān Vazīrī Kirmānī (d. 1295/1878), Riḍā Qulī Khān Hidāyat (d. 1288/1871), and Muḥammad Taqī Lisān al-Mulk Sipihr (d. 1297/1880).

The Syrian Nizārīs, who adhered almost entirely to the Muḥammad-Shāhī line of the Nizārī Imāms until the 13th/19th century, retained their own literature written in Arabic. During the post-Alamūt period, as in earlier times, the Syrian Nizārīs developed their literature independently of the Persian Nizārīs. The Syrian community preserved many of the Ismā'īlī works of the Fāṭimid period, and consequently, some of the traditions of the Fāṭimid Ismā'īlīs continued to be represented in the Nizārī texts of the Syrian provenance. However, the Syrian community, too, produced a few authors and genuine treatises during the period under survey.[11] The most famous Syrian Nizārī author of this period was the *dā'ī* Abū Firās Shihāb al-Dīn b. al-Qāḍī Naṣr al-Daylamī al-Maynaqī, who died either in 937/1530–1531 or 947/1540–1541.[12] The father of Abū Firās had migrated from Daylam to Syria in 859/1455 and settled down in the fortress of Maynaqa, where Abū Firās was born in 872/1467–1468. The Nizārīs of Syria led an uneventful life under the Ottomans, who mention the sectarians and their *qilāʿ al-daʿwa*, the Nizārī castles west of Ḥamāt, in their land registers of Syria. The Syrian Nizārīs did not attract the attention of the outsiders until the early decades of the nineteenth century, when they were reported to be in conflict with their rulers and their Nuṣayrī neighbours. It was also around that time that the European diplomats, travellers and orientalists began to make references to the Syrian Nizārī community. In modern times, a few Syrian Nizārī scholars, notably ʿĀrif Tāmir, a Muḥammad-Shāhī, and the late Muṣṭafā Ghālib (1923–1981), a Qāsim-Shāhī, have written about the history of their community. Professor Tāmir of Salamiyya has also edited a few of the surviving Syrian Nizārī texts.

The Indian Nizārīs, too, have developed their own distinctive literature, the *ginān*s (*gnān*s), representing the traditions of the Nizārī Khojas and the Imām-Shāhīs.[13] They did not produce any elaborate theological or philosophical treatises nor did they translate the Persian and Arabic texts of other Nizārī communities into their own languages. The word *ginān* is evidently a popularization of *jnāna*, a Sanskrit word generally defined to mean contemplative or meditative knowledge. The authorship of the *ginān*s is attributed chiefly to various *pīr*s whose activities on the Indian subcontinent began as early as the 7th/13th century. The *ginān*s continued to be composed and revised until the early decades of the present century; they amount to a total of about 800 separate compositions of different lengths. Originally, the *ginān*s were transmitted only orally, but in time, starting at least in the first half of the 10th/16th century, they began to be collected and recorded in writing.[14] Āghā Khān II made a special effort to collect the *ginān*s by assigning the task of locating and acquiring the relevant manuscripts to a specific group of his Indian followers. The *ginān*s exist in a number of Indian languages, including Sindhī, Gujarātī, Hindī, Panjābī, and Multānī. The bulk of the recorded corpus of the *ginān* literature has survived in the Khojkī script, one of the earliest forms of written Sindhī. Since the middle of the last century, an increasing number of *ginān*s preserved by the Nizārī Khojas have been published, mainly in Gujarātī script. In the present century, the Imām-Shāhīs too, started to publish the *ginān*s preserved amongst them, which are similar to those recorded by the Nizārī Khojas.[15] The Khojas and the Imām-Shāhīs share the same *ginān*s composed prior to the early decades of the 10th/16th century. Other offshoots of the Nizārī Khojas, like the Mōmnas, preserve a religious literature that is very similar in form to the *ginān*s. The *ginān*s, as noted, are composed in verse form, and are meant to be sung and recited melodically. In some instances, the *ginān* manuscripts specify the melodies or *rāga*s according to which the *ginān*s should be sung.

The *ginān*s mainly contain moral and religious instructions, mystical poems, and legendary histories of the *pīr*s. On the whole, the *ginān* literature is not a reliable source of historical information, since it essentially reflects the community's self-image about its history and mixes reality with legend. Since the last century, a number of Nizārī Khojas and Imām-Shāhīs have produced works dealing with the history and beliefs of the Indian Nizārīs. The earliest of these works were written by the Imām-Shāhīs, such as Qāḍī Raḥmat Allāh b. Ghulām Muṣṭafā's *Manāzil al-aqṭāb*, a history of the Imām-Shāhī sect written in Persian around 1237/1821–1822. The majority of these works are written in Gujarātī and are polemical, reflecting the oral traditions of the specific Nizārī sub-sects of the Indian subcontinent.[16] More recently, a number of Khojas have written books and doctoral theses on various aspects of Nizārism in India, Pakistan and East Africa, especially emphasizing the socio-economic progress of those Nizārī communities in the imāmate of the Āghā Khāns. The Āghā Khāns, who entered the political scene in British India in 1258/1842 and subsequently played an active part in international affairs, have of course been discussed and studied in numerous modern works, including several biographies.

Post-Alamūt Nizārism is one of the least understood phases of the Ismāʿīlī movement; and many aspects of its first five centuries will probably continue to be surrounded by controversy. The research difficulties of studying post-Alamūt Nizārism stem not only from the scarcity of reliable sources but also from the fact that the various Nizārī communities of this obscure period developed independently of one another and produced their own literatures in different languages. Under the circumstances, modern scholars, including the specialists in Ismāʿīlī studies, have not so far produced major studies dealing with this phase of Nizārī Ismāʿīlism. Only Ivanow, the founder of modern Nizārī studies, has made important contributions to this field. He indefatigably acquired, edited and published a number of post-Alamūt Nizārī texts written in Persian and preserved in the upper Oxus region, India, and elsewhere. These texts, published in the Ismaili Society Series, together with several original studies produced by Ivanow, have in fact set the perspective for the study of the history and doctrines of the post-Alamūt Nizārīs, especially in Persia and some adjacent regions. The investigation of post-Alamūt Nizārism in Persia, where the imāms lived until the last century, has to some extent illuminated the history of other Nizārī communities. The various Nizārī communities, however, need to be studied independently. The greatest progress to date has been made in the case of the Nizārī community of the Indian subcontinent, which is not only one of the largest and best organized Nizārī communities of the world but has also produced the majority of contemporary Nizārī scholars and researchers. On the other hand, the post-Alamūt Nizārīs of Syria and the upper Oxus have received very little attention from modern scholars, who have doubtless been aware of the decline in the overall significance of these isolated Nizārī communities. In this chapter we shall present the preliminary and often fragmentary results of modern research in post-Alamūt Nizārism. The writing of a connected history of Nizārism during the post-Alamūt period still requires a more profound understanding of the development of the individual Nizārī communities. Hopefully, the efforts of the Institute of Ismaili Studies, established in 1977 in London under the patronage of H.H. Karīm Āghā Khān IV, will enhance our knowledge of this branch of Ismāʿīlī studies.

The Nizārīs of Persia became completely disorganized and disoriented in the immediate aftermath of the destruction of their state and fortresses in the year 654/1256. Those who survived the Mongol massacres of Rūdbār and Quhistān entered a new phase of their history, living mainly outside their traditional mountain strongholds and strictly observing *taqiyya*. The news of the execution of Rukn al-Dīn Khurshāh in Mongolia in 655/1257 must have dealt another demoralizing blow to the confused and displaced Nizārīs who had been accustomed to having access to their imām or his local representatives. The Nizārī communities of Persia were now deprived of any central leadership which hitherto had been provided by the headquarters of the Nizārī movement at Alamūt. Henceforth the Nizārī communities were to develop on a local basis and independently of one another. In Persia, whilst the garrison of Girdkūh was still holding out against the Mongols and their local allies in the Caspian region, the Nizārīs had come to be located almost entirely in Daylam and Quhistān. The isolated Nizārīs of other areas in Persia either migrated to these regions or were gradually assimilated into the surrounding non-Nizārī communities. At the same time many of the Quhistānī Nizārīs who survived the Mongol massacres migrated to Afghanistan, Sind, Panjāb and other parts of the Indian subcontinent. It seems that the Nizārīs of Rūdbār soon succeeded in reorganizing themselves under some sort of local leadership; and less than two decades after the fall of Alamūt they had acquired a military force that continued to be active for quite some time. The Nizārīs of northern Persia made periodic attempts to reoccupy Alamūt and other key fortresses of Rūdbār which evidently had not been completely demolished, as reported by Juwaynī and reiterated by later Persian historians of the Īlkhānid period. The Mongols themselves had in fact reconstructed Alamūt and Lamasar for their own use. In 674/1275–1276, five years after the fall of Girdkūh, the Rūdbārī Nizārīs were strong enough to recapture Alamūt in a coalition with a descendant of the Khwārazmshāhs. They retained Alamūt for almost one year before they were dislodged by a force sent against them by Hülegü's son and successor in the Īlkhānid dynasty, Abaqa (663–680/1265–1282).[17]

According to Nizārī tradition, in the months following the fall of Alamūt, the Persian Nizārī community managed to hide Rukn al-Dīn Khurshāh's minor son, Shams al-Dīn Muḥammad, who had received the *naṣṣ*. Shams al-Dīn, who succeeded to the imāmate on his father's death in 655/1257, was reportedly taken to Ādharbayjān by some of the Nizārī dignitaries. There, he grew up and lived clandestinely as a tradesman and an embroiderer, whence his nickname of Zardūz. Certain allusions in the still unpublished *Safar-nāma* of Nizārī Quhistānī indeed indicate that Shams al-Dīn Muḥammad, and possibly his next successor, lived in concealment in Ādharbayjān or in southern Caucasus. Ḥakīm Sa'd al-Dīn (or Na'īm al-Dīn) b. Shams al-Dīn (or Jalāl al-Dīn) b. Muḥammad Nizārī Quhistānī was, as noted, a Nizārī poet born in Bīrjand in 645/1247–1248 into a land-owning Ismā'īlī family.[18] Nizārī's father, a poet himself, lost his wealth in the Mongol invasion of Quhistān. After receiving his early education in Bīrjand and Qā'in, Nizārī studied Persian and Arabic literature as well as philosophy, and subsequently served at the court and chancery of Shams al-Dīn Muḥammad I (643–684/1245–1285), the founder of the Kart (or Kurt) dynasty of Harāt, and his successors. Nizārī was in fact obliged to panegyrize the Sunnī Kart rulers in many of his *qaṣīdas*. Both in his official capacity and on his own initiative, Nizārī travelled widely. In Shawwāl 678/February 1280,[19] he set off from Tūn on a long journey to Ādharbayjān, Arrān, Georgia, Armenia and Baku, which lasted for two years (678–679/1280–1281). It was during this journey that Nizārī evidently saw the Imām Shams al-Dīn Muḥammad, named by him as Shams-i Dīn Shāh Nīmrūz ʿAlī and Shāh Shams.[20] Nizārī fell ill in Tabrīz, possibly the place of residence of the imām, and after being helped by some local Nizārīs, whom he calls the Ikhwān al-Ṣafā', he continued on his northward journey in Ṣafar 679/June 1280. Nizārī relates the account of this journey in his versified *Safar-nāma*, written in *mathnawī* form and containing about 1200 verses. He praises the current imām in his poems, and also speaks of the spiritual *qiyāma* and other Ismāʿīlī ideas, resorting extensively to Ṣūfī forms of expression. After returning to Quhistān, Nizārī served for a while longer the Kart rulers who had extended their influence throughout Afghanistan and Khurāsān. However, Nizārī's enemies eventually succeeded in arousing the Karts against him. He was dismissed and his properties confiscated. Disillusioned and impoverished, Nizārī took up agriculture during his final years. He died in Bīrjand in 720/1320–1321, during the reign of Ghiyāth al-Dīn (708–729/1308–1328), who was Shams al-Dīn Muḥammad Kart's grandson. His grave was destroyed when the cemetery of Bīrjand was turned into a park after 1344/1925. In recent years, a new mausoleum has been constructed for Nizārī in his native Bīrjand.

Shams al-Dīn Muḥammad died around 710/1310–1311 in Ādharbayjān, after an imāmate of almost half a century.[21] It was during his long imāmate that the Persian Nizārīs, especially in Rūdbār, reorganized themselves to some extent and temporarily reoccupied Alamūt, while the Syrian Nizārīs became completely subjugated by the Mamlūks. Between Shams al-Dīn's death and the second half of the 9th/15th century, when the Qāsim-Shāhī Nizārī Imāms emerged in Anjudān, there lies an obscure period in the history of Nizārī Ismāʿīlism. Practically nothing is known about the imāms who, according to Nizārī traditions, succeeded one another in Persia during this period of more than one and a half centuries. Only the names of these imāms have been preserved by later Nizārīs. Indeed, the sectarian traditions present an unbroken chain of succession to the Nizārī Imāmate during the post-Alamūt period, although later lists of these imāms differ concerning their names, number and sequence. The official list currently circulating amongst the Qāsim-Shāhī Nizārīs was evidently finalized only during the latter part of the last century.

After Shams al-Dīn Muḥammad, there occurred once again a dispute over the succession to the imāmate, splitting the line of the Nizārī Imāms and their followers into what became known as the Muḥammad-Shāhī and Qāsim-Shāhī branches. The Muḥammad-Shāhī line of imāms, whose most famous figure was Shāh Ṭāhir Dakkanī, was discontinued about two centuries ago; while the Qāsim-Shāhī line has endured to the present day. The Qāsim-Shāhī Imāms, who since the earlier decades of the last century have carried the title of Āghā Khān, an honorific meaning chief master or lord, are now the sole Nizārī Imāms. The origins of this schism, which further weakened the Nizārī movement of the post-Alamūt period, have remained rather obscure, especially since the existing sectarian sources do not discuss the matter in detail. The Qāsim-Shāhī sources, constituting almost all of the extant Nizārī sources, do not refer to this schism at all. The few surviving Muḥammad-Shāhī works, furthermore, merely mention the schism without explaining the circumstances surrounding it. The Muḥammad-Shāhī sources themselves do not agree on the precise date of the succession dispute in the family of the Nizārī Imāms.

According to the oral tradition of the Muḥammad-Shāhīs of Syria, where the bulk of the Nizārī community continued to adhere to the Muḥammad-Shāhī line of imāms until the second half of the last century and where the only remnants of this Nizārī sub-sect are still to be found, the schism occurred on the death of Shams al-Dīn Muḥammad.[22] The succession to Shams al-Dīn, considered the twenty-fifth imām of the Muḥammad-Shāhīs, was disputed by his eldest and youngest sons, namely, ʿAlāʾ al-Dīn Muʾmin Shāh and Qāsim Shāh; a middle son, Kiyā Shāh, did not play any part in the dispute. According to this Syrian tradition, Qāsim Shāh was merely to act as the *ḥujja* of his elder brother, Muʾmin Shāh, who in due course was succeeded by his own son Muḥammad Shāh. The members of this sub-sect in Syria, therefore, more commonly referred to themselves as al-Muʾminiyya or the Muʾminī Nizārīs, in contrast to al-Qāsimiyya, since it was with Muʾmin Shāh rather than his son Muḥammad Shāh that they split off from the Qāsim-Shāhī Nizārīs. On the other hand, according to the *Irshād al-ṭālibīn*, a Muḥammad-Shāhī work written in Badakhshān in 929/1523 by a certain Muḥibb ʿAlī Qunduzī, the schism took place after the imāmate of Muʾmin Shāh, who had succeeded his father, Shams al-Dīn. According to this source, corroborated by the versified *Lamaʿāt al-ṭāhirīn*, the sole extant Muḥammad-Shāhī work produced in India in 1110/1698–1699 by Ghulām ʿAlī b. Muḥammad, Muḥammad Shāh and Qāsim Shāh were in fact brothers, both being the sons of Muʾmin Shāh.[23] And on their father's death, each of the two sons claimed his succession. The issue is further complicated by the fact that the earliest extant Qāsim-Shāhī Nizārī sources also name Muʾmin Shāh as the son and successor of Shams al-Dīn Muḥammad. According to these sources, Muʾmin Shāh was in turn succeeded by his son

Qāsim Shāh.[24] But Mu'min Shāh's name is omitted altogether from the later Qāsim-Shāhī lists of their imāms as well as from the list currently accepted by the Āghā Khān's Nizārī followers. Thus, it is not clear whether Muḥammad Shāh and Qāsim Shāh were the sons of Mu'min Shāh, or whether Mu'min Shāh b. Shams al-Dīn was himself the elder brother of Qāsim Shāh. Be it as it may, Mu'min Shāh b. Shams al-Dīn, who died around 738/1337–1338, was the father of Muḥammad Shāh, who soon after Shams al-Dīn's death led a faction of the Nizārī community in rivalry with his paternal uncle (or brother) Qāsim Shāh. This split in the family of the imāms did subdivide the Nizārīs into two branches. The Muḥammad-Shāhī Imāms, possibly representing the elder of the two lines, initially seem to have acquired a greater number of followers than the Qāsim-Shāhī Imāms. Almost the entire community in Syria as well as large numbers in Persia, especially in Daylam, and in Badakhshān, upheld the Muḥammad-Shāhī cause for some time. In India, where Shāh Ṭāhir and his successors, the final ten imāms of the Muḥammad-Shāhī line, resided, this Nizārī sub-sect had a significant following. By the early Anjudān period, however, an increasing number of Nizārīs began to acknowledge the Qāsim-Shāhī Imāms, who had remained in Persia and who by then were making systematic efforts to extend their influence to the various Nizārī communities.

The Nizārīs had continued to be active in Daylam during the Īlkhānid and Tīmūrid times. In fact, it did not take long after the Mongol conquest of Persia before the various petty local rulers began to assert their authority over different parts of the Caspian region. This situation provided suitable opportunities for renewed Nizārī activities in Daylam. The post-Alamūt Nizārīs of northern Persia had evidently concentrated their efforts in Daylamān proper, the mountainous region to the south of Lāhījān and to the east of Safīdrūd, one of the largest districts of Gīlān. By 770/1368–1360, Daylamān was ruled by Kiyā Sayf al-Dīn Kūshayjī, who resided at Marjikūlī, and was, like his forefathers, a Nizārī Ismāʿīlī.[25] His open advocacy of Nizārism in Daylamān soon aroused the hostile reactions of the neighbouring rulers, especially the Zaydī Sayyid ʿAlī Kiyā, who asked him to abandon the Nizārī creed. As Kiyā Sayf al-Dīn persisted in his religious beliefs, the troops of Gīlān were despatched against him in 779/1377–1378 by Sayyid ʿAlī Kiyā b. Amīr Kiyā Malāṭī, who had become the master of Biyapīsh in eastern Gīlān in 769/1367–1368 and had subsequently, with the help of the Marʿashī Sayyids of Māzandarān, extended his authority over Daylamān, Ashkawar, Kuhdum and as far as Ṭārum and Qazwīn. Sayyid ʿAlī Kiyā had now effectively founded a new local Zaydī dynasty of the Amīr (or Kār) Kiyā'ī Sayyids, also known as the Malāṭī Sayyids, who ruled over Daylamān and adjacent territories from Biyapīsh until 1000/1592 when Gīlān was seized by the Ṣafawids. At any rate, Kiyā Sayf al-Dīn was defeated in battle and killed soon afterwards by Amīr ʿAlī, Sayyid ʿAlī Kiyā's new lieutenant in Daylamān who also began persecuting the local Nizārīs. Some of the Nizārīs of Daylamān, joined by the remaining forces of Sayf al-Dīn and other Kūshayjī *amīr*s who had meanwhile succeeded in murdering Amīr ʿAlī, now moved to Qazwīn from where they began to conduct raids into Daylamān. In 781/1379, Sayyid ʿAlī Kiyā chased these Nizārīs and their Kūshayjī allies out of Qazwīn and retained control of that city for seven years until 788/1386, when he was obliged to surrender Qazwīn, as well as Ṭārum and its castle of Shamīrān, to Tīmūr (771–807/1370–1405), the founder of the Tīmūrid dynasty of Persia and Transoxiana.[26]

In the meantime, a certain Nizārī leader known as Khudāwand Muḥammad, who may perhaps be identified with the Muḥammad-Shāhī Nizārī Imām Muḥammad Shāh b. Mu'min Shāh (d. 807/1404), had appeared in Daylam, where the bulk of the local Nizārīs acknowledged him and his successors as their imāms for some time. With the help of his adherents in Daylamān, Rūdbār of Qazwīn, Pādiz, Kūshayjān and Ashkawar, Khudāwand Muḥammad soon began to play an active part in the local alliances and quarrels of Daylam.[27] In particular, he became involved in serious entanglements with Sayyid ʿAlī Kiyā, the most important ruler of the time in Daylamān and its environs. As Sayyid ʿAlī Kiyā then aimed at subduing Kiyā Malik Hazāraspī of Ashkawar, he promised to give Daylamān to Khudāwand Muḥammad on the condition that he would publicly abjure Nizārī Ismāʿīlism. Doubtless, Sayyid ʿAlī had no objection to utilizing the local influence of this Nizārī leader against his own enemies. Khudāwand Muḥammad accepted this offer and went to Lāhījān to renounce Nizārism in the presence of Sayyid ʿAlī and his circle of jurists. Thereupon, Sayyid ʿAlī had his *fuqahā'* issue a declaration to the effect that Khudāwand Muḥammad had repented and returned to the fold of Islam. Soon afterwards in 776/1374–1375, Kiyā Malik and the forces he had gathered in Daylamān were defeated by the Gīlānī troops of Sayyid ʿAlī led by the latter's brother Sayyid Mahdī Kiyā. Kiyā Malik himself fled to Alamūt. However, Sayyid ʿAlī Kiyā now broke his word and instead of appointing Khudāwand Muḥammad to the governorship of Daylamān, gave Daylamān and Ashkawar to his brother Sayyid Mahdī. As a result,

Khudāwand Muḥammad, too, went to Alamūt and joined Kiyā Malik, who promised to give the fortress of Alamūt to the Nizārī leader if he helped the Hazāraspid ruler to recapture Ashkawar. Khudāwand Muḥammad allied himself with Kiyā Malik against Sayyid ʿAlī Kiyā. He gathered the Nizārīs of Alamūt and Lamasar, and in the company of Kiyā Malik, headed for Ashkawar where Sayyid Mahdī Kiyā was defeated in battle. Sayyid Mahdī was captured and sent as a prisoner to Tabrīz to the court of Sultan Uways (757–776/1356–1374), the Jalāyirid ruler of Ādharbayjān, ʿIrāq and Kurdistān whose dynasty had been one of the successors of the Mongol Īlkhānids in Persia. Kiyā Malik Hazāraspī reinstated himself as ruler of Ashkawar, and gave Alamūt and its environs to Khudāwand Muḥammad.

A year and a half later, Sayyid Mahdī Kiyā was released by the Jalāyirids, on the intercession of Tāj al-Dīn Āmulī, one of the local Hārūnī Zaydī Sayyids of Tīmjān, and was thereupon appointed to the governorship of Rānikūh by his brother Sayyid ʿAlī. Soon after, Sayyid ʿAlī himself led his troops to Ashkawar and defeated the Hazāraspid Kiyā Malik, who fled to Alamūt in the hope of being aided once again by Khudāwand Muḥammad. Being ill received by the Nizārī holder of Alamūt, however, Kiyā Malik sought refuge with Tīmūr, who eventually sent him to reside in Sāwa. Meanwhile, the troops of Sayyid ʿAlī Kiyā had laid siege to the fortress of Alamūt whilst pursuing Kiyā Malik. Sayyid ʿAlī seized the district of Alamūt and soon forced Khudāwand Muḥammad to surrender the castle. Khudāwand Muḥammad was given safe-conduct and sought refuge with Tīmūr, who later sent him to confinement in Sulṭāniyya. Meanwhile, Sayyid ʿAlī had reinstated Sayyid Mahdī as the governor of Ashkawar and had seized Lamasar, which had been held by Kiyā Malik.

After Sayyid ʿAlī Kiyā was defeated and killed at Rasht in 791/1389 by the Nāṣirwands of Lāhījān and other *amīrs* of Gīlān, Kiyā Malik Hazāraspī returned to Daylamān, seizing Alamūt from the Amīr (Kār) Kiyāʾī Sayyids. Soon afterwards, amidst further confusion following the murder of Kiyā Malik by his own grandson and successor Kiyā Jalāl al-Dīn Hazāraspī, Khudāwand Muḥammad reappeared in Daylamān, and with the help of the local Nizārīs, once again seized Alamūt.[28] But he soon surrendered the stronghold to Malik Kayūmarth b. Bīsutūn, one of the Gāwbāra rulers of Rustamdār. During the following years, Alamūt passed into the hands of the rulers of Lāhījān. In 813/1410–1411, Sayyid Raḍī Kiyā (798–829/1395–1426), a son of Sayyid ʿAlī Kiyā and one of the most powerful rulers of Lāhījān, expelled the Hazāraspī and Kūshayjī *amīrs* from Daylamān, also dealing a severe blow to the Nizārīs of that region and killing a few of the descendants of the Nizārī Imām ʿAlāʾ al-Dīn Muḥammad who were still amongst them. The subsequent fate of Khudāwand Muḥammad himself is unknown, but his descendants were still living in Sulṭāniyya during the final decades of the 9th/15th century.[29] Meanwhile, the Nizārīs had continued to be active in some limited manner in Daylam, especially in Daylamān which remained under the suzerainty of the rulers of Biyapīsh until after the advent of the Ṣafawids in 907/1501.[30] One of the latest references to the Nizārīs of Daylam, who retained some local importance by the end of the 10th/16th century, is provided by Mullā Shaykh ʿAlī Gīlānī, who wrote a history of Māzandarān in 1044/1634.[31] In discussing the Banū Iskandar rulers of Kujūr, he states that Sultan Muḥammad b. Jahāngīr, who succeeded his father in 975/1567, was a Nizārī Ismāʿīlī. According to this source, Sultan Muḥammad officially encouraged the spread of Nizārism throughout Rustamdār. He seized Nūr and other localities in Māzandarān and spread his creed as far as Sārī. Sultan Muḥammad died in 998/1589–1590 and was succeeded by his eldest son Jahāngīr, who also adhered to Nizārism. Jahāngīr was obliged to go to the court of the Ṣafawid Shāh ʿAbbās I, following the latter's conquest of Gīlān and other Caspian provinces in 1000/1591–1592. Later, Jahāngīr returned briefly to Rustamdār but he was subsequently captured by the local lieutenant of Shāh ʿAbbās who led a large force against him. Jahāngīr was sent to Qazwīn where he was executed in 1006/1597–1598. By that year, Daylam was completely subdued by Shāh ʿAbbās, who appointed his own governors in various parts of that region. With the establishment of Ṣafawid authority in northern Persia, the Nizārīs, like other local dynasties, lost their influence in Daylam. Only a few isolated Nizārī groups survived a while longer in the Caspian region during the Ṣafawid period, when the fortress of Alamūt was utilized as a state prison, especially for the rebellious members of the Ṣafawid family.

Meanwhile, the Qāsim-Shāhī Imāms, who succeeded one another regularly by the rule of the *naṣṣ*, had been secretly engaged in their own *daʿwa* and reorganization activities, in rivalry with the Muḥammad-Shāhī Imāms. Nothing definite is known about the Qāsim-Shāhī Imāms until the second half of the 9th/15th century when they emerged in Anjudān posing as Ṣūfī *shaykh*s or *pīr*s. All that is available on Shams al-Dīn Muḥammad's first three successors in this line are their names and a few unreliable dates and details preserved in the traditions of the Qāsim-Shāhī Nizārīs.[32] According to these traditions, Qāsim Shāh, the twenty-ninth imām and the eponym of this line, succeeded to the imāmate around 710/1310. As noted, he was either the son or the grandson of Shams al-Dīn Muḥammad, and it was in his time that the Nizārīs became split into two factions. Qāsim Shāh too, apparently lived in Ādharbayjān and devoted his long imāmate of some sixty years mainly to defending the legitimacy of his line. He died around 771/1369–1370 and was succeeded by his son Islām Shāh, also called Aḥmad Shāh. Islām Shāh, a contemporary of Khudāwand Muḥammad and Tīmūr, died in about 829/1425–1426 and was succeeded by Muḥammad b. Islām Shāh. It was evidently Islām Shāh who transferred the residence of the Qāsim-Shāhī Imāms to certain localities around Qumm and Maḥallāt, in central Persia, during the earliest decades of his imāmate of almost fifty-five years. He may indeed have been the first imām of his line to establish a foothold in Anjudān, which shortly afterwards became the permanent residence of the Qāsim-Shāhī Imāms. The Persian chroniclers of Tīmūr's reign do refer to Nizārī activities in Anjudān and mention an interesting expedition led by Tīmūr himself in Rajab 795/May 1393 against the Nizārīs of Anjudān, who evidently belonged to the Qāsim-Shāhī branch and had by then attracted enough attention to warrant this action.[33] Tīmūr was then engaged in his campaigns in Persia, and whilst en route from Iṣfahān to Hamadān and Baghdād, his attention was diverted to the Nizārīs of the Anjudān area where he spent a few days. Tīmūr's soldiers killed many Nizārīs and pillaged their properties. According to Sharaf al-Dīn ʿAlī Yazdī (d. 858/1454), the rebellious Anjudānī Nizārīs had attempted in vain to seek shelter in their special underground tunnels, and most of them lost their lives when they were flooded out by the Tīmūrid troops. It may also be added that a year earlier, at the end of 794/1392, whilst passing through Māzandarān, Tīmūr had put to the sword many of the Nizārīs of that region who probably belonged to the Muḥammad-Shāhī faction.[34] It is with Muḥammad b. Islām Shāh's son and successor Mustanṣir bi'llāh II, who assumed the imāmate around 868/1463–1464, that the Qāsim-Shāhī Imāms became definitely established at Anjudān, initiating the Anjudān revival in post-Alamūt Nizārism.

As noted, the coalescence between Persian Nizārism and Ṣūfism, too, dates to the early post-Alamūt period. The origins and early development of this complex association remain rather obscure in the absence of adequate studies. The subject itself was brought to the attention of modern scholars only a few decades ago, following our better understanding of the development of Ṣūfism in Persia and our access to the post-Alamūt Persian

Nizārī literature. This meagre literature and the traditions of the Persian and Central Asian Ismāʿīlīs attest to the fact that after the fall of Alamūt, Nizārism became increasingly infused in Persia with Ṣūfī teachings and terminology, for which the ground had been prepared during the Alamūt period. At the same time, Ṣūfī *shaykhs* and thinkers who relied on the *bāṭinī ta'wīl* like the Ismāʿīlīs, had begun to use ideas which were more widely ascribed to the Ismāʿīlīs. As a part of this coalescence, the Nizārī Ismāʿīlīs began to adopt Ṣūfī ways of life even externally. Thus, it is said that Shams al-Dīn Muḥammad and his immediate successors in the Qāsim-Shāhī line, lived clandestinely for the most part as Ṣūfī *pīrs*, while their followers adopted the typically Ṣūfī title of *murīd* or disciple.[35] Doubtless, this was done partly for reasons of *taqiyya* which enabled the imāms and their followers to survive anonymously under hostile circumstances. Nonetheless, the adoption of a Ṣūfī exterior by the Nizārīs would not have been readily possible if the two esoteric traditions had not had common grounds. At any rate, due to the close relationship between Persian Nizārism and Ṣūfism, it is often difficult to ascertain whether a certain post-Alamūt Persian treatise was written by a Nizārī author influenced by Ṣūfism, or whether it was produced in Ṣūfī milieus impregnated by Ismāʿīlī ideas. This applies, for instance, to the celebrated Ṣūfī treatise *Gulshan-i rāz* (*The Rose-Garden of Mystery*) and its later commentary by a Nizārī author, providing a clear literary example of the Nizārī–Ṣūfī association.

The versified *Gulshan-i rāz* was composed in 717/1317 by Saʿd al-Dīn Maḥmūd Shabistarī, a relatively obscure Ṣūfī *shaykh* and poet from Ādharbayjān. He was born around 686/1287 in Shabistar near Tabrīz, and died in his youth in 720/1320–1321. Thus, he was a contemporary of Nizārī Quhistānī who was probably the first Nizārī to express his religious ideas in the guise of Ṣūfī expressions and poetry. Maḥmūd Shabistarī produced his *Gulshan-i rāz*, a *mathnawī* containing about one thousand couplets, in reply to a number of questions on the doctrines of the Ṣūfīs propounded by Ḥusaynī Sādāt Amīr (d. after 729/1328), a Ṣūfī master of Harāt. This short summary of symbolic Ṣūfī terminology, one of the earliest of its kind, has remained very popular amongst the Ṣūfī circles. Consequently, many commentaries have been written on the *Gulshan-i rāz*, the most detailed and famous one being that produced by Shams al-Dīn Muḥammad b. Yaḥyā Lāhījī (d. 912/1506–1507), an eminent *shaykh* of the Nūrbakhshī Ṣūfī order.[36] The Nizārī Ismāʿīlīs of Persia and Central Asia, however, consider the *Gulshan-i rāz* as belonging to their own literature, and as such, it has been chosen to be partially commented upon in Persian by at least one Nizārī author. This anonymous Nizārī commentary consists of the *ta'wīl* interpretations of selected passages of Shabistarī's poems. The authorship of this Nizārī commentary may possibly be attributed to Shāh Ṭāhir, the most famous imām of the Muḥammad-Shāhī line, who in fact wrote a work entitled *Sharḥ-i gulshan-i rāz*.[37] Similarly, as a result of their close relationship with Ṣūfism, the Nizārīs have regarded some of the greatest Ṣūfī poets of Persia as their co-religionists, and selections of their works have been preserved by the Nizārīs of the upper Oxus region. In this category, mention may be made of Sanā'ī (d. ca. 535/1140), Farīd al-Dīn ʿAṭṭār (d. ca. 627/1230), and Jalāl al-Dīn Rūmī (d. 672/1273), as well as lesser Ṣūfī personalities such as Qāsim al-Anwār (d. ca. 837/1433).[38] The Nizārīs of the upper Oxus consider ʿAzīz al-Dīn Nasafī, too, as a co-religionist. Nasafī was a celebrated Ṣūfī master and author of Central Asia who later emigrated to Persia and died there around 661/1262–1263. His Ṣūfī treatise entitled the *Zubdat al-ḥaqā'iq* has been preserved in Badakhshān as an Ismāʿīlī work.[39]

It should also be noted that Twelver Shīʿism developed its own rapport with Ṣūfism in Persia during the period stretching from the fall of Alamūt to the rise of the Ṣafawid dynasty. The earliest instance of this non-Nizārī Shīʿī–Ṣūfī coalescence is reflected in the works of Sayyid Ḥaydar Āmulī, the eminent Ithnāʿasharī theologian, theosopher and gnostic (*ʿārif*) from Māzandarān who died after 787/1385. Strongly influenced by the teachings of Ibn al-ʿArabī (d. 638/1240), one of the greatest Ṣūfīs of Islam whom the Nizārīs consider as another of their co-religionists,[40] Ḥaydar Āmulī combined his Shīʿī thought and convictions with the traditions of Ṣūfism, especially as developed in Persia and ʿIrāq. More than anyone else before him, he emphasized the common origins of Shīʿism and Ṣūfism and prepared the ground for the doctrines held by many of the Persian Ṣūfī orders.[41] Thus, according to Āmulī, a Muslim who combines *sharīʿa* with *ḥaqīqa* and *ṭarīqa*, the spiritual path to God followed by the Ṣūfīs, is not only a believer but a believer put to test (*al-mu'min al-mumtaḥan*). Such a gnostic Muslim or Ṣūfī, who is also a true Shīʿī, preserves a careful balance between the *ẓāhir* and the *bāṭin*, equally avoiding the literalist and juridical approaches to Islam as well as the radical and antinomian tendencies of the Ṣūfīs and the extremist Shīʿīs. Ḥaydar Āmulī, who upheld the legitimacy of Ithnāʿasharī Imāmī Shīʿism, denounced the Ismāʿīliyya and the Shīʿī Ghulāt, amongst other Muslim groups, as heretics, because, according to him, they undermined the *ẓāhir* (*sharīʿa*) in favour of the *bāṭin* (*ḥaqīqa*).[42]

It may be noted at this juncture that several Ṣūfī orders, which contributed significantly to the circulation of Shīʿī ideas in pre-Ṣafawid Persia, were founded during the early post-Alamūt period. We shall have more to say on these orders, especially on the Niʿmat Allāhiyya with which the Nizārī Imāms were to develop close relations. At the same time, several extremist movements with Shīʿī tendencies appeared in Persia. In this connection reference should be made in particular to the Ḥurūfī movement, which dates to the second half of the 8th/14th century. This movement, whose doctrines were derived from Persian Ṣūfism and Ismāʿīlism, amongst other traditions, was founded by a certain Faḍl Allāh Astarābādī, who was born in 740/1339–1340 into an Imāmī family and began his early career as a Ṣūfī wanderer. Faḍl Allāh was well-versed in the interpretation of dreams, and, like the Ismāʿīlīs, adhered to a cyclical view of history. He started to preach his own ideas on prophecy and on man around 780/1378, and by 788/1386 he announced that the period of prophecy had been superseded by that of the manifestation of the divinity (*ẓuhūr-i kibriyāʾ*) in man, particularly in Faḍl Allāh himself. Faḍl Allāh acquired numerous disciples and followers amongst the artisan classes and the wandering *darwīsh*es or *qalandar*s in many parts of Persia and adjoining areas. He eventually aroused the apprehension of Tīmūr and his Sunnī jurists, who sentenced him to death at Samarqand. He then sought refuge in the Caucasus with Tīmūr's son Mīrānshāh, who had him executed in 796/1394. The Ḥurūfīs, with their strong cabalistic-gnostic tendencies, adopted the *bāṭinī taʾwīl* and stressed the hidden meaning of the letters (*ḥurūf*), whence the name of the sect. From early on, Ḥurūfism spread to Anatolia due to the initial missionary efforts of ʿAlī al-Aʿlā (d. 822/1419), one of Faḍl Allāh's original disciples and the author of several Ḥurūfī books. In fact, Anatolia soon became the main stronghold of Ḥurūfism, and the Ḥurūfī doctrines were adopted there by several Ṣūfī orders, especially by the Bektāshiyya. Subsequently, the Ḥurūfīs disappeared in Persia, but their doctrines have continued to be upheld by the Bektāshī dervishes of Turkey, who have also preserved the earlier literature of the sect.[43]

Several groups split off from the Ḥurūfiyya, notably the Nuqṭawiyya or Ahl-i Nuqṭa who had close relations with Persian Ṣūfism and Nizārism. The Nuqṭawīs were influenced by the Nizārī doctrines of the Alamūt period, and later apparently opposed the organized Twelver Shīʿism adopted by the Ṣafawids as the official religion of Persia. At least some eminent Nuqṭawīs may even have been crypto-Ismāʿīlīs. The Nuqṭawiyya sect, also called the Pasīkhāniyya and the Maḥmūdiyya, was founded around 800/1397–1398 by Maḥmūd Pasīkhānī (d. 831/1427–1428), one of Faḍl Allāh Astarābādī's disciples in Gīlān. The movement became very popular in Persia, and by the time of the early Ṣafawids, it had numerous followers in the Caspian region and in the cities of Qazwīn, Kāshān, Iṣfahān and Shīrāz. Shāh Ṭahmāsp I (930–984/1524–1576) persecuted the Nuqṭawīs during the final years of his reign, but it was Shāh ʿAbbās I who took severe measures against them in 1002/1593–1594, killing many of the sectarians and their leaders, including Darwīsh Khusraw Qazwīnī, and Mīr Sayyid Aḥmad Kāshī, who was put to the sword in Kāshān by the Ṣafawid king himself.[44] The Nuqṭawī sect evidently disintegrated completely in Persia after the persecutions of Shāh Abbās, while many Nuqṭawīs, including a number of poets, took refuge in India where the sect survived for some time longer. Amongst the prominent Persian Nuqṭawīs who migrated to Mughal India, the most prominent was Mīr Sharīf Āmulī, who rose to high positions in the service of the emperor Akbar.[45] The Nuqṭawīs believed in metempsychosis and, like the Persian Nizārīs of the *qiyāma* times, interpreted the Resurrection, Paradise and Hell spiritually. Evidently they also dispensed with the commandments of the Sharīʿa, which, in the eyes of Shāh ʿAbbās and his militant Twelver *fuqahā*ʾ, amounted to intolerable heresy or *ilḥād*. Qāsim al-Anwār was amongst the well-known Ṣūfī poets suspected of Ḥurūfism. He was expelled from Harāt following an unsuccessful attempt there in 830/1427 on the life of Tīmūr's son and successor Shāhrukh.[46] There was also Abu'l-Qāsim Muḥammad Kūhpāya'ī, better known as Amrī Shīrāzī, a Ṣūfī poet of the Ṣafawid period who served Shāh Ṭahmāsp I for thirty years before falling into disfavour. In 973/1565–1566, Amrī was blinded on charges of heresy. Later in 999/1590–1591, he was executed in Shīrāz as a Nuqṭawī heretic by the order of Shāh ʿAbbās I. The Persian Nizārīs, however, regard Amrī as a co-religionist. Ivanow, who examined Amrī's scattered poems in some Ismāʿīlī anthologies, reports on the poet's eulogies of his contemporary Nizārī Imāms, including Murād Mīrzā. It is possible then that Amrī Shīrāzī may have been a Nizārī, or perhaps a crypto-Nizārī who appeared as a Nuqṭawī.[47]

The Anjudān period in the history of post-Alamūt Nizārism started in the latter part of the 9th/15th century. The thirty-second imām of the Qāsim-Shāhīs, ʿAlī Shāh, better known as Mustanṣir bi'llāh II, is the first Nizārī Imām who is definitely connected with Anjudān. The locality remained the seat of the Qāsim-Shāhī Imāms until the end of the 11th/17th century, a period of two centuries coinciding with the greater part of the

7 The mausoleum of Imām Mustanṣir bi'llāh II (Shāh Qalandar), Anjudān

8 The mausoleum of Imām Mustanṣir bi'llāh III (Shāh Gharīb), Anjudān

9 An epigraph, dated 1036/1627, reproducing the edict of the Ṣafawid Shāh ʿAbbās I addressed to Imām Amīr Khalīl Allāh Anjudānī

Ṣafawid period in Persia. Anjudān, or Anjidān, is situated at the foot of a relatively low rocky range thirty-seven kilometres east of Arāk (former Sulṭānābād) and about the same distance westward from Maḥallāt in central Persia. One of the important villages of the district of Mushkābād in the agriculturally prosperous plain of Farāhān, Anjudān was probably a more populous place when the Nizārī Imāms emerged there. Currently, it has a population of about a thousand persons who are Ithnāʿasharī and Persian-speaking, engaged mainly in orchard cultivation. The Nizārī antiquities of Anjudān, discovered in 1937 by Ivanow, include an old mosque and three mausoleums, containing the tombs of several imāms and their relatives. By the time the author first visited Anjudān in 1976, some of the architectural remains described by Ivanow had already disappeared, having been abandoned in an unrepaired state.[48] It is interesting to note in passing that when Nāṣir al-Dīn Shāh Qājār visited Anjudān in Dhu'l-Qaʿda 1309/June 1892, he did not suspect the locality's past connections with Nizārī Ismāʿīlism.[49]

Mustanṣir bi'llāh II succeeded to the imāmate around 868/1463–1464 and died in 885/1480. The latter date is inscribed on the wooden box (*ṣanduq*) placed on the grave of this imām. The octagonal mausoleum of Mustanṣir bi'llāh, still locally referred to as Shāh Qalandar, is the oldest surviving Nizārī monument in Anjudān. The Nizārī tradition places Mustanṣir's death in 880/1475–1476,[50] which is in close agreement with the date given in his mausoleum, built during the imāmate of his son and successor ʿAbd al-Salām Shāh. But the sectarian tradition erroneously holds that Mustanṣir bi'llāh II and his next few successors resided at Shahr-i Bābak in Kirmān. The grave of ʿAbd al-Salām, who, according to the sectarian tradition, died in 899/1493–1494, has not been discovered; but the mausoleum of his son and successor, ʿAbbās Shāh, who also carried the title of Mustanṣir bi'llāh, is preserved at Anjudān. This imām, the thirty-fourth in the series, was also known as Gharīb Mīrzā and is still referred to as Shāh Gharīb by the Anjudānīs who are unaware of the true identity of the Nizārī dignitaries buried in their village. Taking into account the Fāṭimid caliph-imām and his own grandfather, Gharīb Mīrza was in fact the third Ismāʿīlī Imām to bear the title of al-Mustanṣir bi'llāh. According to the sectarians, he died in 902/1496–1497 after a brief imāmate, corroborated by the date of Muḥarram 904/August 1498 which was inscribed on the wooden box constructed for the grave of Shāh Mustanṣir b. Shāh ʿAbd al-Salām. In recent decades the box was dismantled by intruders; hence, only bits and pieces remain in his mausoleum.

There are, however, five tombstones inset in one of the walls of this octagonal mausoleum, including that of Shāh Khalīl Allāh II, the thirty-ninth imām, who according to his epitaph died in Dhu'l-Ḥijja 1090/January 1680. The chamber adjoining this mausoleum, containing two more graves, including that of a certain Nūr al-Dahr Khalīl Allāh (d. 1082/1671), who may be identified with the thirty-eighth imām, has disappeared. According to the traditional sequence of the Qāsim-Shāhī Nizārī Imāms, the successors of Gharīb Mīrzā (Mustanṣir bi'llāh III), who died in 904/1498, were Abū Dharr ʿAlī (Nūr al-Dīn), Murād Mīrzā, Dhu'l-Faqār ʿAlī (Khalīl Allāh I), Nūr al-Dahr (Nūr al-Dīn) ʿAlī, and Khalīl Allāh II (d. 1090/1680), the last imām to reside in Anjudān.[51]

The Anjudān period marks a revival in the *daʿwa* and literary activities of the Persian Nizārīs. This renaissance of post-Alamūt Nizārism, or more specifically of Qāsim-Shāhī Nizārism, can be traced to the time of the thirty-second Qāsim-Shāhī Imām, Mustanṣir bi'llāh II. The Nizārīs were still obliged, in predominantly Sunnī Persia, to practise *taqiyya* and camouflage their beliefs mainly in the guise of Ṣūfism. Nevertheless, the general religio-political situation of Persia had now become more favourable for the activities of the Nizārīs and some other movements penetrated by Shīʿī ideas. As a result, with the emergence of the imāms in Anjudān around the middle of the 9th/15th century, the Qāsim-Shāhī Nizārī *daʿwa* activities could now be conducted somewhat more openly and with greater intensity. This revival soon led to the spread of Qāsim-Shāhī Nizārism and to the reassertion of the direct control of the imāms of this branch over the various outlying Nizārī communities. The Anjudān revival, however, did not occur abruptly, as may be thought. The ground for the revival had been gradually prepared ever since the fall of Alamūt, especially after the collapse of the Īlkhānid dynasty in the first half of the 8th/14th century. By the middle of the 9th/15th century, at least the imāms of the Qāsim-Shāhī branch of Nizārism, like the leaders of certain other religious groups, were able to take effective advantage of the improved religio-political atmosphere of Persia, an atmosphere characterized by political decentralization and the spread of Shīʿī tendencies and ʿAlid loyalism, especially through certain Ṣūfī *ṭarīqa*s or orders.

Īlkhānid rule, which had been extended to all of Persia, effectively ended with Abū Saʿīd (717–736/1317–1335), the last great ruler of the dynasty. Subsequently, until the advent of the Ṣafawids, Persia became increasingly fragmented, with the exception of certain periods during the reigns of Tīmūr (d. 807/1405), who reunited the Persian lands, and that of his son

Shāhrukh (807–850/1405–1447). During this turbulent period in the history of Persia, in the absence of any strong central authority, different parts of the country were held by local dynasties, including the minor Īlkhānids, the later Tīmūrids, the Jalāyirids, and the Qara Qoyunlu and Aq Qoyunlu dynasties, based on federations of Turkoman tribes.[52] The political fragmentation of Persia doubtless provided more favourable conditions for the activities of various radical movements, most of which were essentially Shīʿī or influenced by Shīʿī ideas. The same political atmosphere was conducive to the rising tide of Shīʿism which was taking place in post-Mongol Persia. Indeed, at times some of the local rulers of Persia who were in constant rivalry with one another openly supported Shīʿism, at least for political reasons. At any rate, the Nizārīs and certain Shīʿī-related movements with millennarian aspirations such as those of the Sarbadārs, the Ḥurūfiyya, the Nuqṭawiyya and the Mushaʿshaʿ, as well as some Ṣūfī organizations, now found a respite in Persia to organize or reorganize themselves during the 8th/14th and 9th/15th centuries, though they were still occasionally persecuted by different local rulers who detected their revolutionary message of opposition to the established order.

Meanwhile, Shīʿī tendencies had been spreading in Persia since the 7th/13th century, rendering the country's religious milieu more favourable for the activities of the Nizārīs and other crypto-Shīʿī or Shīʿī-related extremist movements. These movements normally entertained chiliastic or Mahdist aspirations for the deliverance of the oppressed and the economically under-privileged who rallied in large numbers, especially after Tīmūr's death, in support of the leaders of these movements who often hailed from Shīʿī-Ṣūfī backgrounds. It should be emphasized, however, that instead of the outright propagation of any particular school of Shīʿism, a new form of Shīʿism was now arising in pre-Ṣafawid Persia. Being of a popular type and expressed largely in Ṣūfī forms, this Shīʿism ultimately culminated in Ṣafawid Shīʿism. Hodgson designated this new Shīʿism at 'ṭarīqah Shīʿism', since it was effectuated mainly through certain Ṣūfī orders.[53] It was indeed due to the leaders of the Ṣafawiyya *ṭarīqa*, who eventually ascended to the throne of Persia in the opening decade of the 10th/16th century, that Shīʿism came to be adopted as the state religion of Persia. The Ṣūfī orders in question, most of which were formed in post-Mongol Persia, remained outwardly Sunnī for quite some time after their foundation. They followed one of the Sunnī *madhhab*s, usually the Shāfiʿī school, whilst being particularly devoted to ʿAlī and the Ahl al-Bayt and accepting ʿAlī's spiritual guidance. In time, some of these Ṣūfī *ṭarīqas* came to profess Shīʿism formally. In this atmosphere of religious eclecticism, ʿAlid loyalism, initially espoused by certain Ṣūfī *ṭarīqas* and extremist movements, soon came to be more widespread. As a result, Shīʿī elements began to be superimposed on Sunnī Islam. By the 9th/15th century there appeared a general increase in Shīʿī allegiance throughout Persia, where the bulk of the population still adhered to Sunnism. Professor Cahen has referred to this process as the 'Shīʿitization of Sunnism', as opposed to the conscious propagation of Shīʿism of any specific school, Twelver or otherwise.[54] It was through such a process that the religious outlook of the populace came to be increasingly moulded by this type of *ṭarīqa*-diffused Shīʿī-Sunnī syncretism, preparing Persia for the official adoption of Shīʿism under the Ṣafawids.[55]

Amongst the Ṣūfī orders that played a leading role in bridging the gap between Sunnism and Shīʿism and in spreading Shīʿism in Persia, mention should be made of the Nūrbakhshiyya and the Niʿmat Allāhiyya *ṭarīqas*. Both orders, as well as the Ṣafawiyya, which played the most active and direct political role in establishing a Shīʿī state in Persia, eventually became fully Shīʿī Ṣūfī *ṭarīqas*. The Nūrbakhshī order was founded by Muḥammad b. ʿAbd Allāh, known as Nūrbakhsh. He was born in 795/1393 at Qā'in into an Imāmī Shīʿī family that had migrated from Baḥrayn to Quhistān. In his youth, Nūrbakhsh was initiated into the Kubrawiyya, one of the major Ṣūfī orders of the time in Central Asia and northeastern Persia, founded by Shaykh Najm al-Dīn Kubrā (d. 617/1220). ʿAlā' al-Dawla Simnānī (d. 736/1336), the celebrated Sunnī Ṣūfī and one of the Kubrawī *shaykhs*, had already emphasized the special position of ʿAlī, allowing him primacy amongst the Orthodox Caliphs. But ʿAlid loyalism and Shīʿī ideas were introduced more directly into the Kubrawī order by Isḥāq al-Khuttalānī, a later *shaykh* who was also politically active and unsuccessfully planned a revolt against the Tīmūrids. He was killed, together with some of his associates, around 826/1423 by emissaries of the Tīmūrid Shāhrukh. Al-Khuttalānī appointed Muḥammad Nūrbakhsh as his successor, also designating him as the Mahdī. The majority of the Kubrawīs accepted Nūrbakhsh's leadership as their *quṭb* or *khalīfa* and became known as the Nūrbakhshiyya, while a minority supported a certain ʿAbd Allāh Barzishābādī Mashhadī and later became designated as the Dhahabiyya. Nūrbakhsh professed Shīʿism openly, and in his teachings he aimed at fusing Shīʿism and Sunnism through Ṣūfism, claiming also the Mahdīship for some time. Due to his Shīʿī ideas and the increasing popularity of his Ṣūfī order, Nūrbakhsh was arrested and exiled several times on Shāhrukh's orders. On one such occasion in 840/1436, Nūrbakhsh was forced to repudiate his ideas and claims publicly at Harāt. He died in 869/1464 at Rayy, where he had spent his final years. The Nūrbakhshiyya flourished into the Ṣafawid period, as a fully Shīʿī order under Nūrbakhsh's son and successor, Shāh Qāsim Fayḍbakhsh (d. 917/1511), and other *shaykhs*.[56] Shams al-Dīn Lāhījī, the author of the best-known commentary on the *Gulshan-i rāz* who died in 912 A.H., led a section of the Nūrbakhshiyya from Shīrāz in succession to Nūrbakhsh himself. The eminent Persian Imāmī scholar Nūr Allāh al-Shūshtarī, who emigrated to India where he was executed in 1019/1610, was evidently an initiate of the Nūrbakhshī order. The Nūrbakhshiyya did not stretch far into the Ṣafawid period as an organized Ṣūfī order in Persia, though their mystical tradition continued for a while. On the other hand, the Dhahabī order has survived in Persia as a minor Shīʿī Ṣūfī *ṭarīqa*, with chief centres in Shīrāz and Tehran, to the present time.

The Niʿmat Allāhiyya, too, played a vital role in spreading ʿAlid loyalism and Shīʿī sentiments in pre-Ṣafawid Persia, though the order remained outwardly Sunnī until after the advent of the Ṣafawids. This Ṣūfī order became widespread during the lifetime of its founder, Shāh Niʿmat Allāh Walī, and in the course of the 9th/15th century it acquired numerous initiates in different parts of Persia, including Kirmān, Yazd, Fārs and Khurāsān.[57] At the same time, its influence spread to the Indian subcontinent, where it received the patronage of the Bahmanid rulers of the Deccan. From the 8th/14th century onwards, the term Shāh came to be prefixed or suffixed to the name of many Ṣūfī saints, in combination with ʿAlī or Walī, reflecting ʿAlid loyalism and their recognition of the *wilāya* and spiritual guidance of ʿAlī. Accordingly, Nūr al-Dīn Niʿmat Allāh b. ʿAbd Allāh is commonly referred to as Shāh Niʿmat Allāh Walī. A prolific writer on mystical subjects and also a poet, the eponymous founder of the Niʿmat Allāhī order traced his Fāṭimid ʿAlid genealogy to Muḥammad b. Ismāʿīl b. Jaʿfar al-Ṣādiq, the seventh imām of the Ismāʿīlīs.[58] This is perhaps why Shāh Niʿmat Allāh has been considered as a co-religionist by certain Ismāʿīlī circles, and the Central Asian Nizārīs have preserved some of his works, including a commentary on one of Nāṣir-i Khusraw's *qaṣīdas*.[59] This may also partly explain why the Nizārī Imāms chose this particular order for their Ṣūfī affiliation.

Shāh Niʿmat Allāh was born in Aleppo in 731/1330. His father ʿAbd Allāh was an Arab and his mother came from the Fārs region in Persia.

From early on, he was attracted to Ṣūfism (*taṣawwuf*) and gnosis (*ʿirfān*) and searched for a perfect spiritual master (*murshid-i kāmil*), wandering and serving different Ṣūfī *shaykhs*. He is said to have finally found his spiritual master in ʿAbd Allāh al-Yāfiʿī (d. 768/1367), the founder of the Yāfiʿiyya branch of the Qādirī Ṣūfī order. After spending several years with al-Yāfiʿī in Mecca, Shāh Niʿmat Allāh began to travel extensively, a common practice among the Ṣūfīs during a certain phase in their career. He went to Egypt and then journeyed to Ādharbayjān, where he may have met Qāsim al-Anwār. Subsequently, he wandered to Transoxiana where he settled near Samarqand. Niʿmat Allāh was banished after some time from Transoxiana by Tīmūr. Later at Harāt, he married the granddaughter of Ḥusaynī Sādāt Amīr, who had induced the composition of the *Gulshan-i rāz*; she was to become the mother of the Shāh's only son and successor Khalīl Allāh, born near Kirmān in 775/1374. After Khurāsān, Shāh Niʿmat Allāh went to Kirmān and spent the rest of his years in and around that city. He spent the last twenty-five years of his life mainly in Māhān, about forty kilometres south of Kirmān, where he established the headquarters of the Niʿmat Allāhī *ṭarīqa*. The saint's relations were friendly with Tīmūr's son Shāhrukh, especially after the Tīmūrid conquest of Kirmān in 819/1416. By that time, Shāh Niʿmat Allāh Walī had become quite well-known, having acquired numerous *murīd*s or disciples in different parts of Persia whilst his *ṭarīqa* had extended to India. Aḥmad I Walī (825–839/1422–1436), the Bahmanid ruler of the Deccan who adopted the title of Walī (saint) given to him by Shāh Niʿmat Allāh and who may have converted to Shīʿism around 833/1429, called himself a disciple of this saint. Aḥmad Shāh persistently invited Shāh Niʿmat Allāh to visit him in India. The Ṣūfī master, however, declined the invitations due to his old age and instead sent a grandson, Nūr Allāh, who settled in the Deccan and married one of the Bahmanid ruler's daughters. Shāh Niʿmat Allāh had a Sunnī background, and, in his lifetime, the outward form of his *ṭarīqa* remained Sunnī, though it became increasingly imbued with ʿAlid loyalism. As most Ṣūfīs would attest even today, the inward structure of the Niʿmat Allāhiyya and many other *ṭarīqa*s, being Ṣūfī, remained above the Shīʿī-Sunnī distinctions raised by non-Ṣūfīs. Shāh Niʿmat Allāh, whose most lasting contribution to Ṣūfism was the order he founded, died in 834/1431, a centenarian, in Kirmān. He was buried at Māhān. The original structures of his mausoleum, still piously visited by the Ṣūfīs, were constructed through donations made by Aḥmad Shāh Bahmanī and his successor ʿAlāʾ al-Dīn Aḥmad II (839–862/1436–1458).

Shāh Niʿmat Allāh had designated his sole son Burhān al-Dīn Khalīl Allāh to succeed him as the *quṭb* or pole, a term still used by the Ṣūfīs to describe their spiritual master. After a few years in Māhān and then in Harāt where he was Shāhrukh's guest, Shāh Khalīl Allāh migrated permanently to the Deccan. He rightly expected to benefit from the patronage and devotion of the Bahmanid rulers towards his family and *ṭarīqa*, having probably experienced certain difficulties in Tīmūrid dominions. He left one of his four sons, Shams al-Dīn, in Māhān to take care of the affairs of the Persian Niʿmat Allāhīs, and took with him to the Deccan another two of his sons, Muḥibb al-Dīn Ḥabīb Allāh and Ḥabīb al-Dīn Muḥibb Allāh, who became the third *quṭb* of the order after Khalīl Allāh's death in 860/1456. Shāh Khalīl Allāh's mausoleum near Bīdar became known as Khalīliyya and later other members of the family were buried there. Shāh Ḥabīb al-Dīn, who married one of the daughters of the Bahmanid Aḥmad II, became Shīʿī outwardly. Shāh Niʿmat Allāh's descendants and successors were treated with respect in the Deccan, where the Niʿmat Allāhī *quṭb*s resided for more than three centuries.[60] The *quṭb*s established a *khāniqāh* (Arabic, *zāwiya*) or Ṣūfī centre at Bīdar, which remained the Indian seat of the Niʿmat Allāhī order until the latter part of the 12th/18th century, when the position of *quṭb* had already passed out of Shāh Niʿmat Allāh's family and the order was revived in Persia by emissaries sent from the Deccan. Meanwhile, the Persian wing of the order, increasingly Shīʿī, helped the Ṣafawid Shāh Ismāʿīl to power. Soon after the establishment of Ṣafawid rule, the Niʿmat Allāhiyya declared themselves to be Shīʿīs. Shāh Niʿmat Allāh's descendants in Persia inter-married with the Ṣafawid house and acquired prominence, often being appointed to the governorship of Yazd. The Persian section of the order, with its new headquarters at Taft near Yazd, became probably the most highly organized Persian Ṣūfī *ṭarīqa* in the 10th/16th century; but subsequently it lost its significance mainly due to the adverse policies of the Ṣafawids, a fate shared by other *ṭarīqa*s in Persia. At present, the Niʿmat Allāhī order, with its several branches, is the most widespread Ṣūfī *ṭarīqa* in Persia, having initiates also in Pakistan and other Muslim countries, especially amongst the Twelver Shīʿīs.

Amongst the Ṣūfī orders that contributed to the 'Shīʿitization' of Persia, the most direct part was played by the Ṣafawī *ṭarīqa*, which occupied a unique position also in terms of the political ambitions of its masters.[61] The political success of the Ṣafawiyya eventually culminated in the accession of the Ṣafawī *shaykh* to the throne of Persia. The Ṣafawī *ṭarīqa* was founded by Shaykh Ṣafī al-Dīn (d. 735/1334), an eminent Ṣūfī *shaykh* of the Īlkhānid period and a Sunnī of the Shāfiʿī *madhhab*. It was only after the establishment of the Ṣafawid state that the dynasty claimed an ʿAlid genealogy, tracing Shaykh Ṣafī's ancestry to the seventh imām of the Twelver Shīʿīs, Mūsā al-Kāẓim. The Ṣafawī order, centred in Ardabīl, soon spread throughout Ādharbayjān, eastern Anatolia, Syria and Khurāsān. It is related that Qāsim al-Anwār, too, became an initiate of this order in the time of Shaykh Ṣafī's son and successor Ṣadr al-Dīn (d. 794/1391). Most significantly, the order acquired deep influence over several Turkoman tribes in Ādharbayjān and adjoining areas. With Shaykh Ṣafī's fourth successor, Junayd, the Ṣafawī order was transformed into a militant revolutionary movement with a policy of conquest and domination. The order's *murīd*s amongst the Turkomans were gradually organized into a dedicated fighting force of Ṣūfī soldiers (*ghuzāt-i ṣūfiyya*) and were initially used especially against the surrounding non-Muslim powers. Junayd was also the first Ṣafawī *shaykh* to display Shīʿī sentiments combined with radical religious notions of the type held by the Shīʿī Ghulāt. Junayd fought the Caucasian Christians around Ādharbayjān and lost his life in 864/1460 in one of these battles.

Shaykh Junayd's policies and political ambitions were maintained by his son and successor Ḥaydar, who was killed in the course of one of his military expeditions in 893/1488. Shaykh Ḥaydar was responsible for instructing his followers to adopt the scarlet headgear of twelve gores commemorating the twelve Ithnāʿasharī Imāms, which led to their being designated by the Turkish term Qizil-bāsh (Red-head). Sulṭān ʿAlī, Ḥaydar's son and successor, also fell in battle, in 898/1493. By that time, the Ṣafawī order enjoyed a strong military organization, supported by many loyal adherents and powerful Turkoman tribes which constituted the backbone of the Qizil-bāsh soldiers. Consequently, Ismāʿīl, Sulṭān ʿAlī's youthful brother and successor as the master of the Ṣafawiyya, easily managed to take Ādharbayjān from the Aq Qoyunlu dynasty. Thereupon, in the summer of 906–907/1501, Ismāʿīl entered Tabrīz, the capital of the deposed dynasty, and proclaimed himself Shāh Ismāʿīl, the first ruler of the new Ṣafawid dynasty, which was to last until the second quarter of the 12th/18th century. Shāh Ismāʿīl I brought the whole of Persia under his control during the ensuing decade and thus established the Ṣafawid state in the territories hitherto ruled by different dynasties. Under Ismāʿīl (907–930/1501–1524), Persia became a national state for the first time since the Arab conquest in the first century of Islam. Immediately upon his accession, he proclaimed Twelver Shīʿism as the official religion of the Ṣafawid state, inaugurating a new era for Shīʿism and the activities of the Shīʿī movements and scholars in Persia.

It was under such circumstances, when Shīʿī sentiments were gaining increasing popularity in Persia, that the Anjudān revival of Nizārism commenced around the middle of the 9th/15th century, in the imāmate of Mustanṣir bi'llāh II. The very titles adopted by this Qāsim-Shāhī Imām and his grandson indicate that the Nizārī Imāms now clearly strove to revive the old glories of the Ismāʿīlīs. Despite the improved conditions, however, the imāms and their followers were still obliged to practise *taqiyya* and to utilize the cloak of Ṣūfism. Mustanṣir bi'llāh II, the thirty-second imām whose Ṣūfī name was Shāh Qalandar, may in fact have been the first Qāsim-Shāhī Imām to associate with the Niʿmat Allāhī Ṣūfī order, though concrete evidence is lacking. The formal association of the Qāsim-Shāhī Imāms with the Niʿmat Allāhī *ṭarīqa* began more than two centuries later. But even at the beginning of the Anjudān revival, Nizārism utilized the guise of Ṣūfism, appearing as a Ṣūfī order, one amongst many such orders then existing in Persia. For this purpose, the Nizārīs readily adopted the master-disciple (*murshid-murīd*) terminology and relationship of the Ṣūfīs. To the outsiders, the Nizārī Imāms appeared as Ṣūfī *murshids*, *shaykhs*, *pīrs* or *quṭbs*; they were generally regarded, it seems, also as pious Ḥusaynid Sayyids, descendants of the Prophet through Fāṭima. Similarly, the followers of the imāms posed as their *murīds*, who were guided along the *ṭarīqa* or path to *ḥaqīqa* by a highly revered spiritual master. With Shīʿī ideas and ʿAlid loyalism then spreading in many Ṣūfī orders and religious movements, the veneration of ʿAlī and other early Ḥusaynid Imāms by the Nizārīs did not cause any particular alarm regarding the true identity of the sectarians. In the course of the Anjudān period it became customary for the Qāsim-Shāhī Imāms to adopt Ṣūfī names, like Shāh Qalandar and Shāh Gharīb, often also adding the Ṣūfī terms Shāh and ʿAlī to their names.

It seems that the Qāsim-Shāhī Nizārī Imāms selected Anjudān only after a thorough search for a suitable locality to establish their residence and *daʿwa* headquarters. Anjudān had a central position whilst at the same time it was removed from the seats of the main Sunnī powers then controlling western and eastern parts of Persia, notably the Aq Qoyunlu and the later Tīmūrids who ruled chiefly from Tabrīz and Harāt, respectively. Furthermore, Anjudān was conveniently close to the cities of Qumm and Kāshān, also known as the *dār al-muʾminīn* (abode of the faithful), that were traditional Shīʿī centres in Persia. The Qāsim-Shāhī Nizārī *daʿwa* was now reorganized and reinvigorated from Anjudān, not only to win new converts in remote lands and from amongst those Nizārīs who had hitherto given their allegiance to the rival Muḥammad-Shāhī Imāms, but also to reassert the central authority of the imāms over the various outlying regions, notably India and Central Asia, which had increasingly come under the control of their local dynasties of *pīr*s. During the earliest post-Alamūt centuries when the imāms were deprived of direct contacts with their followers, the different Nizārī communities in Persia and adjoining regions as well as in India, had gradually come under the authority of their local leaders, who were often referred to by the Ṣūfī term *pīr*, the Persian equivalent of *shaykh*. These *pīr*s or chief *dāʿī*s were either appointed by the imāms, who accorded them extensive powers, or were selected locally by the particular Nizārī community. In most communities the position of the local *pīr* had gradually become hereditary, with the result that some dynasties of *pīr*s had become largely independent of the imāms whose precise whereabouts were often unknown to the bulk of their followers. The hereditary *pīr*s had become particularly autonomous in the areas farthest removed from the residence of the imāms; notably Afghanistan, Badakhshān and other localities in Central Asia, as well as the Indian subcontinent. Needless to add that often, the local *pīr*s in charge of these communities had acquired financial independence as well, relying on the religious dues which they collected. It was for these reasons that the imāms of the Anjudān period directed a good part of their revived efforts towards undermining the position of the local *pīr*s, with the objective of replacing them by their own loyal appointees. Mustanṣir bi'llāh II began sending a number of trusted *dāʿī*s to various localities in Khurāsān, Afghanistan, Badakhshān and elsewhere, a policy continued by his successors, who, in addition, seem to have regularly summoned the local *dāʿī*s for consultation and instruction to Persia.[62]

In order to reorganize the *daʿwa* and re-establish their control over different Nizārī communities, the imāms required adequate financial resources and loyal *dāʿī*s who would act as local guides for the sectarians, emphasizing especially their obedience towards the imām of the time. These points are indeed reiterated throughout the *Pandiyāt-i jawānmardī*, the sermons of Mustanṣir bi'llāh II containing the advices (Persian, *pandiyāt*) of this imām to the true believers or *mu'min*s, and to those seeking to attain the exemplary standards of chivalry (Persian, *jawānmardī*).[63] These sermons or religious admonitions were evidently compiled and written down in Persian by an anonymous Nizārī author during the imāmate of Mustanṣir bi'llāh's son and successor, ʿAbd al-Salām Shāh.[64] The Nizārī Khojas, who have preserved Sindhī (Khojkī) and Gujarātī versions of the *Pandiyāt*, maintain that the book was sent to India for their religious guidance. It is possible that this book was subsequently despatched to other Nizārī communities so as to reinforce their allegiance to the Qāsim-Shāhī line of imāms; copies of the Persian version of the *Pandiyāt* are still preserved in the Nizārī manuscript collections of Badakhshān and adjoining regions, including Hunza and Kāshghar in Chinese Turkistān.[65] It is interesting to note that the Nizārīs are referred to in the *Pandiyāt* by Ṣūfī terms such as *ahl-i ḥaqq* and *ahl-i ḥaqīqat*, the people of the truth,[66] whilst the imām himself is designated as *pīr*, *murshid* and *quṭb*.[67] Indeed, the *Pandiyāt* are clearly influenced by Ṣūfī ideas; and the imām's admonitions start with the *sharīʿat-ṭarīqat-ḥaqīqat* classification of the Ṣūfīs, portraying the *ḥaqīqa* as the *bāṭin* of the *sharīʿa* which can be attained through the spiritual path (*ṭarīqa*) followed by the faithful. It is immediately explained, however, that the *ḥaqīqa* essentially consists of recognizing the current imām.[68] The *Pandiyāt* continuously stress the duty of the faithful to recognize and obey the current imām,[69] emphasizing that no sacrifice is great enough for making the *dīdār* journey to see the imām.[70] An equal stress is placed on the obligation of the true believer to pay his religious dues, notably the tithe (Persian, *dah-yik*) amounting to ten per cent of his annual income, to the imām of the time.[71] These admonitions find expression also in the works of Khayrkhwāh-i Harātī, who wrote in the middle of the 10th/16th century, a few decades after Mustanṣir bi'llāh II and ʿAbd al-Salām Shāh.[72] The latter imām himself, following the footsteps of his father, invited the Muḥammad-Shāhī Nizārīs of Badakhshān and Afghanistan to transfer their allegiance to the true line of the imāms, viz., the Qāsim-Shāhī Imāms. This invitation by the thirty-third Qāsim-Shāhī Imām is reflected in at least one extant *farmān* or epistle written in 895/1490.[73]

The Anjudān renaissance in Nizārī Ismāʿīlism also brought about a revival of literary activities amongst the Nizārīs. The earliest fruits of these efforts, which include the first Persian doctrinal treatises produced after the fall of Alamūt, are those written by Abū Isḥāq Quhistānī, a contemporary of Mustanṣir bi'llāh III (Gharīb Mīrzā) b. ʿAbd al-Salām Shāh (d. 904/1498); and Muḥammad Riḍā b. (Khwāja) Sulṭān Ḥusayn Ghūriyānī Harātī, better known as Khayrkhwāh-i Harātī, who flourished a few decades later and died after 960/1553.[74] Khayrkhwāh was a prolific writer and a poet with the pen name (*takhalluṣ*) of Gharībī; he plagiarized

Abū Isḥāq's *Haft bāb* into the *Kalām-i pīr*, attributing it to Nāṣir-i Khusraw. As Ivanow has argued, Khayrkhwāh seems to have introduced certain ideas of his own, especially on the status of the *ḥujja*, into the Nizārī works that passed through his hands. Khayrkhwāh was an ambitious man and according to his own account was appointed, whilst only nineteen years old, by the imām of the time to succeed his father as a local Nizārī *pīr* in his native province of western Afghanistan and possibly some adjoining areas. The writings of Abū Isḥāq and Khayrkhwāh, which constitute the chief Qāsim-Shāhī Persian treatises of the Anjudān period, have been preserved by the Nizārīs of Central Asia and elsewhere.

Khayrkhwāh's works, especially his untitled *Risāla*,[75] are of historical value and shed light on various aspects of the Nizārī communities of his time in Khurāsān and Afghanistan. He also reveals that by the first half of the 10th/16th century, direct contacts had been established between the Qāsim-Shāhī Imāms and their followers in those regions as well as in the Indian subcontinent, from where *dāʿī*s and other Nizārī dignitaries regularly travelled to the headquarters of the *daʿwa* to see the imām. Khayrkhwāh relates how the imām had sent a messenger, Mīr Maḥmūd, summoning his father, Khwāja Sulṭān Ḥusayn, who resided at Harāt, and another Nizārī dignitary called Khwāja Qāsim who lived in Quhistān; the imām evidently intended to designate Khayrkhwāh's father as the *dāʿī* of Khurāsān, Badakhshān and Kābul.[76] Khwāja Sulṭān Ḥusayn was, however, murdered in Khurāsān, whilst heading for Anjudān. Khayrkhwāh himself was then taken in his father's place for the *dīdār* of the imām despite the objection of some members of the community who disapproved of his young age and lack of religious qualifications. Khayrkhwāh does not mention Anjudān by name but from some of the nearby localities mentioned by him, like Maḥallāt,[77] it is clear that he went to Anjudān to see the imām, whose name is not divulged. By Khayrkhwāh's time, the term *pīr* had acquired a wide application and was used in reference to *dāʿī*s of different ranks, the heads of any Nizārī community, as well as to the persons of the imām and his *ḥujja*. Khayrkhwāh vividly describes how different *pīr*s arrived at Anjudān during the fortnight that he spent there, bringing along the religious dues of their congregations and communities. He has interesting details on how carefully the imām checked and appraised these dues and how he punished those who had misappropriated the funds (*ḥaqq-i imām*).[78] Having been assured of the trustworthiness of Khayrkhwāh, the imām appointed him to the dāʿīship of Khurāsān and adjoining lands, a post possibly held by or intended for his father.[79] Khayrkhwāh in fact claims to have been designated as the chief *pīr* (*pīr-i kull*).[80] At any event, he explains how his appointment to such a high rank in the *daʿwa* proved disappointing to those members of his community who regarded themselves as more deserving of the post. Indeed, Khayrkhwāh's autobiographical account attests to the existence of intense rivalry amongst various Nizārī dignitaries or *pīr*s who challenged each other's competency and continuously attempted to win the favour of the imām, who had by then greatly reasserted his authority over the outlying Nizārī communities.[81]

Meanwhile, the advent of the Ṣafawids and the proclamation of Twelver Shīʿism as the state religion of Ṣafawid Persia in 907/1501 promised yet more favourable opportunities for the activities of the Nizārīs and other Shīʿī movements in Persia. The Nizārīs did in fact reduce the intensity of observing *taqiyya* during the initial decades of Ṣafawid rule. At the time, the Muḥammad-Shāhīs were led by Shāh Ṭāhir, their most famous imām; and Nūr al-Dīn Muḥammad, known as Abū Dharr ʿAlī, had succeeded to the imāmate of the Qāsim-Shāhīs.[82] Abū Dharr ʿAlī, who succeeded Gharīb Mīrzā as the thirty-fifth imām of the Qāsim-Shāhī line, was contemporary with Shāh Ismāʿīl I and with Ismāʿīl's son and successor Shāh Ṭahmāsp I; he evidently married a sister or daughter of Ṭahmāsp I. The new optimism of the Nizārīs was short-lived, however, as the Ṣafawids soon adopted a rigorous religious policy which aimed to suppress the popular types of Ṣūfism and the various Shīʿī movements that fell outside the boundaries of Ithnāʿasharism. This policy was directed even against the Qizil-bāsh, who had brought the Ṣafawid dynasty into power. The conversion of Persia to Twelver Shīʿism, mainly at the expense of Sunnism, proceeded rather slowly under Ismāʿīl I and Ṭahmāsp I, who brought into Persia a number of Imāmī theologians and jurists from ʿIrāq and Syria. But from early on, the Ṣafawids persecuted the radical Shīʿī groups and the Ṣūfī orders. Most of the Ṣūfī orders of Persia were in fact extirpated in the reign of Shāh Ismāʿīl, with the major exceptions of the Niʿmat Allāhiyya, Nūrbakhshiyya and Dhahabiyya which gradually lost their importance during the Ṣafawid period.

It seems that the true identity of the Nizārī Imāms and their followers had become somewhat better known after the establishment of Ṣafawid rule, despite their continued use of the *murshid-murīd* Ṣūfī guise. The increased and more overt activities of the Nizārī Ismāʿīlīs soon came to the attention of the earliest Ṣafawid kings and their Twelver *ʿulamāʾ*, who reacted by subjecting the sectarians to renewed persecutions. We have records of two particular instances of such persecutions taking place during the first Ṣafawid century. Shāh Ismāʿīl, as we shall see, eventually issued an order for the execution of Shāh Ṭāhir, who had become rather popular in Kāshān, obliging him to flee to India where the later imāms of the Muḥammad-Shāhī line resided. And Shāh Ṭahmāsp persecuted the Qāsim-Shāhī Nizārīs in the time of their thirty-sixth imām, Murād Mīrzā, the son and successor of Abū Dharr ʿAlī. The *Ta'rīkh-i alfī*, an extensive history of the Muslim world from the death of the Prophet to around the year 1000/1591–1592, which was compiled in India by several authors at the request of the emperor Akbar, refers under the year 982/1574–1575 to the persecution of the Nizārīs of Anjudān in the time of a certain Murād who claimed their imāmate.[83] More details of the same episode, occurring in the reign of Shāh Ṭahmāsp, are recorded under the year 981/1573–1574 by Qāḍī Aḥmad al-Qummī, a contemporary Ṣafawid chronicler who died after 1015/1606.[84] Both sources relate that Murād had numerous followers also in India, who sent him large sums of money from Sind and elsewhere. Murād Mīrzā and his predecessor evidently did not reside permanently at Anjudān, where the headquarters of the Qāsim-Shāhī Nizārī *daʿwa* had been located. Murād Mīrzā was engaged in political activity outside of Anjudān, having acquired supporters in Kāshān and elsewhere in central Persia. Being alarmed by the activities of Murād Mīrzā, early in 981/1573 Shāh Ṭahmāsp ordered Amīr Khān Mūṣilū, the governor of Hamadān, to proceed to the Anjudān area to capture Murād and deal with his followers (*murīdān*). Amīr Khān killed a large number of the Nizārīs of Anjudān and its surroundings and took much booty from them, but Murād Mīrzā himself, who was then staying at a fortress in the district of Kamara around Anjudān, managed to escape. Soon afterwards, he was captured and imprisoned near the royal quarters. In Jumādā II 981/October 1573, Murād Mīrzā escaped from prison with the assistance of Muḥammad Muqīm, a high Ṣafawid official who had come under the influence of the Nizārī Imām. Murād proceeded to the vicinity of Qandahār, receiving help on the way from his followers in Fārs, Makrān and Sind. A few months later, he was recaptured in Afghanistan by Ṣafawid guards. Murād was brought before Shāh Ṭahmāsp, who had him executed along with Muḥammad Muqīm. It is interesting to note that Khayrkhwāh, a contemporary of Ṭahmāsp I as well as Murād Mīrzā and the latter's predecessor, states that one of the Nizārī Imāms of his time went into hiding (*satr*) for seven years, probably making reference to Murād Mīrzā.[85] At any rate, the Persian Nizārīs experienced new difficulties during the reigns of Ismāʿīl I and Ṭahmāsp I; and the graves of Abū Dharr ʿAlī and Murād Mīrzā, who were the Qāsim-Shāhī Imāms from around 904/1498 to 981/1574, have not been discovered at Anjudān.

With the third Ṣafawid ruler, Ismāʿīl II (984–985/1576–1577), who attempted unsuccessfully to re-establish Sunnism during his brief reign, and his elder brother and successor, Muḥammad Khudābanda (985–995/1577–1587), the Ṣafawids came to have their own dynastic disputes and domestic strifes, which almost brought about the downfall of their newly founded empire. The religious movements that had survived the persecutions of the first two Ṣafawid kings now received a respite which was particularly timely for the Nizārīs. Order was restored to the Ṣafawid state only during the reign of Shāh ʿAbbās I (995–1038/1587–1629), who systematically repressed the disruptive Qizil-bāsh tribes. ʿAbbās I, whose long reign marked the golden age of Ṣafawid rule, introduced numerous administrative reforms and patronized the arts. It was also this monarch who transferred the Ṣafawid capital from Qazwīn to Iṣfahān in 1006/1598. Although Shāh ʿAbbās I continued his predecessors' policy of persecuting the Sunnīs, the majority of the Ṣūfī orders and some of the radical Shīʿī movements like the Nuqṭawiyya, he was tolerant towards certain minoritarian organizations and religious sects, including the Nizārīs, who were henceforth not molested by the Ṣafawids.

In the meantime, the Qāsim-Shāhī Imāms after Murād Mīrzā had once again appeared at Anjudān, from where they quietly conducted the affairs of their followers without involving themselves in political activities. The imāms of the later Anjudān period had indeed developed friendly relations with the Ṣafawids. Murād Mīrzā's successor as the thirty-seventh imām, Khalīl Allāh I, who also carried the Ṣūfī name of Dhu'l-Faqār ʿAlī, married a Ṣafawid princess, possibly the sister of Shāh ʿAbbās I. The close relationship existing between this imām and the Ṣafawids is attested by an epigraph, recovered in 1976 at Anjudān by the author, which reproduces the text of a royal edict issued by Shāh ʿAbbās I in Rajab 1036/March–April 1627. According to this edict, addressed to Amīr Khalīl Allāh Anjudānī, the current Qāsim-Shāhī Imām, the Shīʿīs of Anjudān, named as a dependency of the *dār al-mu'minīn* of Qumm, were exempted, like other Shīʿīs around Qumm, from paying certain taxes. It is interesting to note that in this edict the Anjudānī Shīʿīs are regarded as Ithnāʿasharīs, indicating that by that time the Persian Nizārīs had adopted the cover of Twelver Shīʿism, in addition to Ṣūfism, as a form of *taqiyya*.

Dhu'l-Faqār ʿAlī (Khalīl Allāh I) may be identified with Khalīl Allāh, who, according to his tombstone at Anjudān, died at the age of sixty-eight in Ramaḍān 1043/March 1634, seven years after the above-mentioned edict was issued. Imām Khalīl Allāh I's successor, too, carried a Ṣūfī-sounding name, Nūr al-Dahr (Nūr al-Dīn) ʿAlī. This imām, the thirty-eighth in the series, may be identified with Nūr al-Dahr (b.) Khalīl Allāh, who died in Rajab 1082/November 1671 and was buried in Anjudān. The Nizārī poet Khākī Khurāsānī, a contemporary of both of these imāms who died after 1056/1646,[86] repeatedly eulogizes Shāh Dhu'l-Faqār (Khalīl), possibly also named Ḥaydar,[87] and Shāh Nūr al-Dahr b. Dhu'l-Faqār.[88] He also names Anjudān as their place of residence, which he apparently visited himself.[89] Fidā'ī Khurāsānī quotes some poems in praise of Shāh Dhu'l-Faqār by two obscure Nizārī poets of this imām's time, viz., ʿAzīz Allāh Qummī and a certain Niyāzī who was also a *dāʿī*.[90] Khākī refers to his imām's followers and spreading influence in Khurāsān and ʿIrāq-i ʿAjam as well as in Multān and Hind. By the second half of 11th/17th century, the Anjudān revival of the Qāsim-Shāhī *daʿwa* had, indeed, resulted in definite successes. Maḥmūd ʿAlī, a Nizārī poet from Mu'minābād and a contemporary of the Imām Nūr al-Dahr, in a long poem names the Qāsim-Shāhī *dāʿīs*, teachers or *muʿallims*, and lesser functionaries, in numerous localities in Khurāsān, Quhistān, ʿIrāq-i ʿAjam, Kirmān, Afghanistan, Badakhshān, Turkistān and the Indian subcontinent, including Multān, Lahore and Gujarāt. This and other poems of this poet, not listed in the Ismāʿīlī bibliographies of Ivanow and Poonawala, were kindly given to the author by the leaders of the Nizārī community in Khurāsān. Nūr al-Dahr's son and successor, Shāh Khalīl Allāh II, was the last Qāsim-Shāhī Imām to reside at Anjudān. This imām, the thirty-ninth in the series, died in Dhu'l-Ḥijja 1090/January 1680, and his tombstone is still preserved in one of the walls of Gharīb Mīrzā's mausoleum at Anjudān. With Khalīl Allāh II's successor, Shāh Nizār, the seat of the Qāsim-Shāhī *daʿwa* was transferred from Anjudān to the nearby village of Kahak, initiating a new sub-period in the post-Alamūt history of Nizārī Ismāʿīlism.

During the earliest post-Alamūt centuries when the imāms were not in direct contact with the bulk of their followers, different Nizārī communities developed independently of one another and of the headquarters of the *daʿwa*. Each of these communities gradually came to own the authority of a chief *dāʿī* or *pīr*, who was usually selected locally, if not belonging to the hereditary dynasties of such *dāʿīs*. Under these circumstances, the central headquarters of the *daʿwa* represented little more than the places of residence of the imāms, who were then unable to direct the affairs of the outlying Nizārī communities. Matters began to change, however, with the Anjudān renaissance, at least in the Qāsim-Shāhī branch of Nizārī Ismāʿīlism. From the earliest decades of the Anjudān period, the Qāsim-Shāhī *daʿwa* was reorganized not only for reinvigorating the *daʿwa* activities, but also for the connected purposes of asserting the central authority of the imāms over the scattered communities and undermining the position of the local dynasties of *pīrs*. Nonetheless, the *daʿwa* hierarchy of Qāsim-Shāhī Nizārism remained rather simple as compared to the elaborate organization adopted by the Fāṭimid Ismāʿīlīs, also representing further simplification of the organization utilized by the Nizārīs of the Alamūt period.

The Qāsim-Shāhī *daʿwa* hierarchy of the Anjudān period was naturally headed by the manifest imām, who now made every effort to establish direct contact with his followers. As can be gathered from the few Qāsim-Shāhī works preserved from that period, there were five lower ranks, after the imām, in the *daʿwa* organization of this Nizārī sub-sect.[91] The imām was followed by a single *ḥujja*, designated as *ḥujjat-i aʿẓam*, or the great *ḥujja*. Normally residing at the headquarters of the *daʿwa*, like the imām himself, he was the highest religious and administrative officer of the *daʿwa* and the imām's chief assistant. The *ḥujja* was often selected from amongst the close relatives of the imām, persons who were not in the direct line of succession to the imāmate. Next, there was a single category of *dāʿī*, a propagandist at large who was not apparently restricted to any particular region or community. Selected from amongst the better educated Nizārīs, the *dāʿī* was apparently mainly responsible for periodically inspecting the different communities and reporting their conditions to the *daʿwa* headquarters in addition to conveying the directives of the headquarters to the local leaders. Furthermore, the *dāʿī* was in charge of propagating the *daʿwa* in places beyond the jurisdiction of particular Nizārī communities. There were presumably many such *dāʿī*s operating as roaming propagandists and inspectors of the sect, travelling from locality to locality in the service of the Qāsim-Shāhī *daʿwa*. The next lower rank in the hierarchy was that of *muʿallim* or teacher, who was normally in charge of the *daʿwa* activities in a particular community or region. The earlier Ismāʿīlī term *jazīra* (plural, *jazāʾir*) was again utilized during the Anjudān period in reference to the various *daʿwa* regions. The *muʿallims* were appointed by the *ḥujja*, doubtless in consultation with the imām; and by considering only the obedient persons for this position, the imām could assert his control over the remote circles of his followers. Every *muʿallim* was normally assisted by two categories of *ma'dhūn*. The senior one, or *ma'dhūn-i akbar*, was allowed to propagate the doctrines of the sect and to convert anyone on the basis of his own judgement and initiative. But the junior assistant, *ma'dhūn-i aṣghar*, who held the lowest rank in the hierarchy, could perform these tasks only on receiving the *muʿallim*'s permission. The ordinary initiates, as in earlier times, were referred to as *mustajībs*. On acquiring proper qualifications, a *mustajīb*, who as such did not hold a rank in the *daʿwa* hierarchy, could be appointed by the *muʿallim* to the position of *ma'dhūn-i aṣghar*. Appointments to the higher *daʿwa* ranks were made, at least ideally, by the *ḥujja* and the imām, extending the central authority of the *daʿwa* headquarters. It may be noted, however, that not all of the lower *daʿwa* ranks were occupied at all times and in every community, especially in the smaller Nizārī milieus. By the middle of the 10th/16th century, the term *pīr* had come to be generally used in reference to most positions in the *daʿwa* organization, notably in place of the highest ranks of imām, *ḥujja*, *dāʿī* and *muʿallim*. The ordinary members of the sect, the *mustajībs*, were often designated as *murīds*, reflecting the Ṣūfī guise of the *daʿwa* organization. Khayrkhwāh, the chief doctrinal author of the Anjudān period, in particular uses the terms *ḥujja* and *pīr* interchangeably. The term *pīr*, however, rapidly fell into disuse in Persia after the termination of the Anjudān period, while it was retained by the Central Asian Nizārīs until modern times.

The Qāsim-Shāhī Nizārīs of the Anjudān period essentially retained the teaching of the late Alamūt period as reflected in the Ismāʿīlī writings of Naṣīr al-Dīn al-Ṭūsī. But the Ismāʿīlī works of the Fāṭimid age, which had influenced al-Ṭūsī's Ismāʿīlī thought, were apparently no longer available to the post-Alamūt Nizārīs living outside of Syria. Consequently by the time of the Anjudān revival, the Nizārīs had completely lost the earlier interest of the Ismāʿīlīs in cosmology and in speculating about the creation in general, while they made only passing references to cyclical prophetic history.[92] In other words, the post-Alamūt Nizārīs, in contrast to the Ṭayyibīs, were not interested in the *ḥaqā'iq*, which comprised the essence of the esoteric thought of the early and the Fāṭimid Ismāʿīlīs. The Qāsim-Shāhī Nizārīs of the Anjudān period, as noted, retained the doctrine of the *qiyāma* as reinterpreted during the final decades of the Alamūt period. The present imām continued to have a central role in the Nizārī doctrine.[93] Furthermore, the current imām had to be seen in his true spiritual reality as the manifestation of the divine word; and the attainment of that knowledge and vision was the ultimate desideratum of the faithful. In other words, the Nizārīs were expected, through improving their religious knowledge and attaining better recognition of the true essence of the imām, to journey from the physical *ẓāhirī* world to the spiritual world of the *ḥaqīqa*; from merely understanding the apparent meaning of the Sharīʿa to comprehending the unchangeable truths as manifested in the person of the present imām.[94] And those who recognized the true spiritual reality of the imām would thus penetrate the *ẓāhir* of the law.[95]

The role of the *ḥujja*, already stressed by Naṣīr al-Dīn al-Ṭūsī, was further elaborated in the doctrinal works of the Anjudān period, especially by Khayrkhwāh-i Harātī, who claimed the position for himself.[96] The Nizārīs of the later Alamūt period had held that even in the time of *satr* and *taqiyya*, the *ḥaqīqa* and the true essence of the imām could be known at least to a few individuals in the community. The Nizārīs of the Anjudān period definitely reduced this elite group into a single person, the *ḥujja*. They held that the *ḥujja*, like the imām himself, was born to his status, and as such, he too was *maʿṣūm* or sinless and received divine support (*ta'yīd*).[97] The *ḥujja* was, indeed, held to be almost of the same essence as the imām.[98] The *ḥujja*, by the virtue of his miraculous knowledge (*muʿjiz-i ʿilmī*), not available to the holders of the lower *daʿwa* ranks, knew the true essence of the imām and was, thus, the revealer of the spiritual truth for the Nizārīs. He was the sole access to the imām, and it was only through him that the Nizārīs could recognize fully the current imām and attain salvation.[99] The *ḥujja* or chief *pīr*, was the only person, besides the imām himself, who was not bound by the Sharīʿa.[100] Reminiscent of the view of the early Ismāʿīlīs, the doctrine of the Anjudān period also emphasized that the imām and his *ḥujja* could not both be hidden at the same time.[101] The Qāsim-Shāhīs of that period, like the Nizārīs of the *qiyāma* and later times in the Alamūt period, recognized three categories of men, viz., the *ahl-i taḍādd*, *ahl-i tarattub* and *ahl-i waḥdat*.[102] The *ahl-i taḍādd*, consisting of the infidels as well as all the non-Nizārī Muslims, were the opponents of the imām. Seeing only themselves and refusing to acknowledge the rightful Nizārī Imām, they had continued to be spiritually non-existent. The people of gradation, the *ahl-i tarattub*, also called *ahl-i ḥaqq* or *ḥaqīqat*, were the Qāsim-Shāhī Nizārīs who saw both themselves and the imām; they had acquired access to partial truth. The *ahl-i tarattub* were themselves divided into the strong (*qawiyān*) and the weak (*ḍaʿīfān*). The strong group was comprised of the *dāʿīs*, *muʿallims* and *ma'dhūns*, the holders of the *daʿwa* ranks below the *ḥujja*, while the weak group was restricted to the ordinary members of the community, the *mustajībs*. The *qawiyān* recognized the authority of the *ḥujja*, and invited the *mustajībs* to do likewise. Both factions of the *ahl-i tarattub* were expected to concentrate on the inner meaning of the so-called *khalqī* commandments of the Sharīʿa, such as those related to praying, fasting, the *ḥajj* pilgrimage, and so forth, especially when not practising *taqiyya*.[103] Finally, the *ahl-i waḥdat* category consisted of the *ḥujja* alone, who concentrated only on the person of the imām as the manifestation of the divine word and truth. Forgetting his own self completely, the *ḥujja* had truly entered the spiritual realm of the *ḥaqīqa*. The paradisal state made available to the Nizārīs of the Alamūt period by the announcement of the *qiyāma* could now, in the Anjudān period, be enjoyed by a single person, the most trusted associate of the imām.

In the meantime, the Nizārī *daʿwa* had spread successfully on the Indian subcontinent.[104] As noted, the origins and early development of Nizārī Ismāʿīlism in India remain rather obscure due to the absence of reliable sources. The *ginān*s and other sectarian religious writings and traditions are often inaccurate on chronological details and on the sequence of events, frequently mixing legend with reality, especially regarding the earliest centuries of the *daʿwa* activities. According to the sectarian traditions, the *daʿwa* in India was initiated by the emissaries or *pīr*s despatched by the Nizārī Imāms from Persia. These emissaries, who probably began their missionary work during the later Alamūt period, at first concentrated their efforts chiefly in Sind.[105] It may be noted that the available information on the post-Alamūt *daʿwa* activities in India stem solely from the traditions preserved by the followers of the Qāsim-Shāhī line of imāms and the Imām-Shāhīs who split off from the community. Later, we shall refer to the activities of the Muḥammad-Shāhī Imāms, notably Shāh Ṭāhir, who resided in India.

Satgur Nūr, as noted, is reported to have been the earliest *pīr* or guru sent from Persia to India for the propagation of Nizārism, which in India became designated as Satpanth, that is, Sat Panth, the True Path.[106] According to the traditions, Satgur Nūr was mainly active in Pātan, Gujarāt. His shrine is located at Nawsarī near Sūrat, and the tombstone, oddly enough, gives the date as 487/1094. The next important *pīr* is Shams al-Dīn, whose activities centred on Sind. In most of the religious poetry ascribed to him, Qāsim Shāh is named as the imām of his time;[107] Pīr Shams al-Dīn thus seems to have flourished in the first half of the 8th/14th century. He was particularly active in Multān and Uchchh, in Sind; his mausoleum at Multān is locally known as that of Shams-i Tabrīz. The Nizārī community of the Shamsīs, who now acknowledge the Āghā Khān and live as goldsmiths chiefly in Multān and elsewhere in Panjāb, claim to have been converted to Nizārī Ismāʿīlism by Pīr Shams al-Dīn. The work of Shams al-Dīn was continued by his son and grandson, Naṣīr al-Dīn and Shihāb (or Ṣāḥib) al-Dīn. Almost nothing is known about these two *pīrs*, who occupy the twenty-first and twenty-second places on the traditional lists of *pīrs*; it is merely reported that they conducted the *daʿwa* in secret.[108] Pīr Shihāb al-Dīn was, in turn, succeeded by his son Ṣadr al-Dīn. By that time in the post-Alamūt period, the chief Nizārī *pīrs* in India had acquired a certain degree of autonomy and had also established a hereditary dynasty.

Pīr Ṣadr al-Dīn, to whom the largest number of *ginān*s is attributed, played a key role in the propagation and organization of the Nizārī *daʿwa* in India. He is reported to have died sometime between 770/1369 and 819/1416;[109] he was thus contemporary with the Imām Islām Shāh.[110] Ṣadr al-Dīn converted large numbers of Hindus from the Lohana caste and gave them the name of Khōja, derived from the Persian word *khwāja*, meaning lord or master. This name corresponded to the Hindu term *thakur* (or *thakkar*), also meaning master, by which the Lohanas were addressed, since they were regarded as Kshatriyas. The Lohanas and Khojas still use the Hindu designation amongst themselves. Ṣadr al-Dīn is credited with building the first Nizārī *jamāʿat-khāna*, or assembly and prayer hall, in Kotri, Sind. Subsequently, he established two other Nizārī centres in Panjāb and Kashmir and appointed their *mukhi*s or leaders. The term *mukhi* (pronounced *mukī*) is derived from the Sanskrit word *mūkhya*, meaning most important or chief. Ṣadr al-Dīn, thus, laid the foundation of the communal organization of the Indian Nizārīs who henceforth became known mainly as Khojas. In time, he extended the *daʿwa* to Gujarāt and won success amongst the Lohanas and other trading Hindu castes of that region. The centre of Ṣadr al-Dīn's activities, however, remained in Uchchh, from where he now conducted the *daʿwa* somewhat more openly. It may be noted in passing that Sind was at the time ruled by the Sammas, who around 752/1351 had succeeded the Sūmras who adhered to Ismāʿīlism. The later members of the Sūmra dynasty were probably influenced by the Nizārī *daʿwa* in Sind whilst maintaining an independent Ismāʿīlī tradition of their own, but the Sammas soon became Sunnī Muslims.[111] Pīr Ṣadr al-Dīn evidently visited the Imām Islām Shāh in Persia to submit to him the *dassondh* or tithes collected from the Nizārī community of India. Ṣadr al-Dīn's shrine is located near Jetpur, in the vicinity of Uchchh, to the south of Multān. The overseers of this shrine now consider themselves as Twelver Shīʿīs and refer to the *pīr* as Ḥājjī Ṣadr Shāh.

Ṣadr al-Dīn was succeeded as *pīr* by his eldest son Ḥasan Kabīr al-Dīn. According to the well-known hagiographical work written in India by ʿAbd al-Ḥaqq b. Sayf al-Dīn Dihlawī (d. 1052/1642), Kabīr al-Dīn travelled extensively before settling down in Uchchh.[112] He too apparently visited the imām in Persia and converted a large number of Hindus during his pīrship. The death dates mentioned for this *pīr* vary from 853/1449 to 896/1490–1491; but most probably he died around 875/1470–1471, the year mentioned in the yet unpublished *Manāzil al-aqṭāb*, the history of the Imām-Shāhī sect compiled around 1237/1821 in Gujarāt by Qāḍī Raḥmat Allāh b. Ghulām Muṣṭafā.[113] Kabīr al-Dīn's shrine is outside Uchchh and is locally known as Ḥasan Daryā. It is interesting to note that this *pīr* is reported to have been affiliated with the Suhrawardī Ṣūfī order, which was prevalent at the time in the region of Multān. In fact, Pīr Kabīr al-Dīn's name appears in the list of the *shaykh*s of this Ṣūfī *ṭarīqa*.[114] Be it as it may, this indicates that in India, too, close ties had developed in the post-Alamūt period between Nizārism and organized Ṣūfism. On Ḥasan Kabīr al-Dīn's death, the Indian Nizārī community began to experience internal dissensions which eventually led to an important schism. Ḥasan Kabīr al-Dīn is said to have had eighteen sons, but his brother Tāj al-Dīn was appointed as the next *pīr* by the imām. This appointment was opposed by some of the sons of Kabīr al-Dīn, who were at the time also quarrelling amongst themselves. When Tāj al-Dīn returned from a visit to the imām in Persia, where he had gone for delivering the tithes of the Indian Nizārīs, he was accused by his nephews of embezzling a portion of the religious dues. Thereupon, the *pīr* is said either to have died of grief or committed suicide. Tāj al-Dīn, who is not recognized as a *pīr* by the later Imām-Shāhīs, died towards the end of the 9th/15th century, not long after Kabīr al-Dīn. Tāj al-Dīn's grave is located in Jhun in Sind.

After Tāj al-Dīn, Imām al-Dīn ʿAbd al-Raḥīm b. Ḥasan, better known as Imām Shāh, a son of Kabīr al-Dīn and the eponym of the Imām-Shāhī sect, tried in vain to succeed to the leadership of the Nizārī Khojas in Sind.[115] Later, he saw the imām in Persia but was not designated by him to the position of *pīr*.[116] On returning to India, Imām Shāh settled in Gujarāt where he spent the rest of his life and had much success in converting the local Hindus, especially from amongst the agricultural communities, to Nizārī Ismāʿīlism. According to some legendary accounts, he also converted the sultan of Gujarāt, Maḥmūd Begrā (862–917/1458–1511), who gave his daughter in marriage to Imām Shāh's eldest son Nar Muḥammad. Imām Shāh, who according to some unreliable accounts seceded from the Nizārī community and himself became the founder of the Imām-Shāhī sect, is not recognized as a *pīr* by the Nizārī Khojas, who regard him merely as a *sayyid*. He died in 919/1513 in Pīrāna, the town founded by himself near Aḥmadābād, where his shrine is located. Meanwhile, due to continuing conflicts in the family of Pīr Ḥasan Kabīr al-Dīn, the imām had not appointed a new *pīr* after Tāj al-Dīn. Instead, a book of guidance, occupying the twenty-sixth place on the traditional lists of *pīrs*, was sent to the Indian Nizārī community. This book, the already-noted *Pandiyāt-i jawānmardī* containing the religious admonitions of Imām Mustanṣir bi'llāh II, appears to have reached Sind around the middle of the 10th/16th century. At the time, it will be recalled, the Qāsim-Shāhī Imāms were successfully endeavouring to assert their control over the Nizārī communities of India and other remote places. Khayrkhwāh, for instance, refers to the pilgrimages of the Indian *dāʿīs* for seeing the imām at Anjudān, also noting that the Indian Nizārīs by then greatly outnumbered their Persian co-religionists.[117] The *Pandiyāt-i jawānmardī* was in due course translated into Sindhī and Gujarātī and transcribed in Khojkī for the benefit of the Nizārī Khojas.

Meanwhile, Imām Shāh had been succeeded in Gujarāt by his son Nar (Nūr) Muḥammad. Imām Shāh himself had apparently remained loyal to the imāms in Persia, but Nar Muḥammad seceded from the Nizārī *daʿwa* and the Khoja community, founding an independent sect. At an unknown date not long after 919/1513, Nar Muḥammad demanded that the *dassondh* or tithes should henceforth be delivered to him in Gujarāt, instead of being sent through Sind to the imām in Persia. Nar Muḥammad had now in fact claimed the imāmate for himself, and, retrospectively, for his father. The new instructions caused a schism in the Nizārī community of Gujarāt. In particular, Nar Muḥammad's requests and claims were rejected by a certain Kheta, who was the *mukhi* of some 18,000 converted Hindus. But the majority of Nar Muḥammad's followers in Gujarāt sided with him and formed the separate Imām-Shāhī sect, also known as Satpanthī. A minority of Nar Muḥammad's earlier followers, together with other Nizārīs of Gujarāt, remained loyal to the Nizārī Imāms and the main *daʿwa* in India. Nar Muḥammad died in 940/1533–1534, and was buried in his father's mausoleum in Pīrāna. The Imām-Shāhīs later came to deny any connection with Ismāʿīlism, though they continued to acknowledge the line of the Ismāʿīlī Imāms until Islām Shāh, the thirtieth Qāsim-Shāhī Nizārī Imām. They do not, however, recognize some of the Nizārī Imāms, such as Rukn al-Dīn Khurshāh, Muḥammad b. Islām Shāh, and the latter's successors until the schism. They claim that the early *pīrs*, until Ḥasan Kabīr al-Dīn, were in fact Twelver Shīʿīs. They do not recognize Tāj al-Dīn as one of their *pīrs*; and Nar Muḥammad is regarded as their last imām.

After Nar Muḥammad, there occurred several splits in the Imām-Shāhī community due to succession disputes over the position of the *pīr*. Different factions followed different lines of *pīrs* from amongst Nar Muḥammad's descendants. In Awrangzīb's reign, the *sajjāda-nishīn* or leader of the Imām-Shāhī community centred in Pīrāna was a certain Shāhjī Mīrān Shāh. In 1067/1657, he had succeeded his father, Muḥammad Shāh, a descendant of Nar Muḥammad's son Saʿīd Khān, as the *pīr* of the so-called Āṭhṭhiyā branch of the sect. Having heard about the heretical beliefs of Shāhjī, Awrangzīb summoned the aged saint to have his beliefs examined by the Sunnī jurists of his court. Shāhjī was forced to set off for Awrangzīb's court by the local governor of Gujarāt. But Shāhjī died on the way, possibly poisoning himself, near Pīrāna or in Aḥmadābād. Thereupon, Shāhjī's numerous followers, especially from amongst the Matiya Kanbis caste, launched a revolt and seized the fort of Broach.[118] They proclaimed Shāhjī Mīrān's son and successor, Sayyid Muḥammad Shāh (d. ca. 1130/1718), as king of Broach. This rebellion, which occurred around 1100/1688–1689, was eventually suppressed by Awrangzīb. The pīrship of this Imām-Shāhī sub-sect remained in the hands of Shāhjī's direct descendants until Bāqir ʿAlī, the last *pīr* of the Āṭhṭhiyā who died around 1251/1835. Shāhjī Mīrān's wife, Rājī Ṭāhira, founded a separate branch of the Imām-Shāhī sect. The Imām-Shāhīs, through their various branches, have tended to revert towards Hinduism. The adherents of this syncretist sect, who are now mainly located in the rural communities of Gujarāt, Khāndesh and western Madhya Pradesh, near Burhānpūr, consider themselves chiefly as Twelver Shīʿīs or Sunnīs rather than Ismāʿīlīs.

The immediate reaction of the Qāsim-Shāhī *daʿwa* headquarters in Anjudān to the Imām-Shāhī schism in India remains unknown. In the aftermath of the dissensions in the Indian community, culminating in the secession of the Imām-Shāhīs, the imāms did not appoint any new *pīrs* in succession to Tāj al-Dīn. As noted, the *Pandiyāt-i jawānmardī* was sent to India as a book of guidance for the Nizārīs of the subcontinent. Some of the oldest lists of *pīrs* mention after the *Pandiyāt* only one other *pīr* named Dādū. He is said to have been sent by the imām to Sind for the purpose of preventing the conversion of the Nizārī Khojas to Sunnism. Around 1584, however, Dādū was obliged to leave for Navanagar (Jamnagar) in Gujarāt, where he settled down with some of the Sindhī Nizārīs who had fled with him. Subsequently, Dādū moved to Bhuj, where he died in 1593. Dādū played an important role in reorganizing the Indian Nizārī community and in strengthening the ties of that community with the imām and the central *daʿwa* headquarters in Anjudān. Dādū's name is, however, omitted from the later lists of the Indian *pīrs*. With the termination of the line of *pīrs*, the imāms came to be represented locally in India by *wakīls* and *bāwās*. The latter term probably represents the Khojkī pronunciation of the Turkish and Persian word *bābā*, meaning father, and used also as an honorific for older men. Dissatisfied with the dynasty of *pīrs*, the imāms of the Anjudān period now attempted to acquire more direct controls over the Indian Nizārīs. One of the most important duties of the *wakīl* and other local representatives of the imāms was the collection of the religious dues and their proper transference to the central treasury of the *daʿwa* in Persia, located at the imām's place of residence. At the same time, some local families of Sayyids, that is, descendants of Pīr Ḥasan Kabīr al-Dīn, maintained their influence in the Khoja Nizārī community, sometimes holding the position of *wakīl*. Remaining faithful to the imāms in Persia, they also conducted the *daʿwa* on their behalf and performed certain teaching functions in the Khoja community. The Kadiwala Sayyids, who also composed *ginān*s, represent one of the most important families of such Sayyids. They are still active in Sind. Their ancestor, Sayyid Fāḍil Shāh, a descendant of Raḥmat Allāh b. Ḥasan Kabīr al-Dīn, was originally active in the town of Kadi in Cutch around the middle of the 11th/17th century, before the family moved to Sind. In Sind, the family eventually settled around 1780 in Tando Muḥammad Khān, where the Kadiwala Sayyids still reside.

In India, the Nizārī *daʿwa* had, meanwhile, continued in Gujarāt. One group of Gujarātī Nizārīs, who had remained loyal to the imāms and their representatives in India, had come to be known as Mōmnas; a designation derived from the word *muʾmin*. This term has also been used in reference to some of the Imām-Shāhī groups.[119] The Nizārī Mōmnas allege that in time they came to obey the Kadiwala Sayyid Fāḍil Shāh, who collected their tithes and sent them to Persia. Pīr Mashāyikh and Ḥasan Pīr, sons of Sayyid Fāḍil, played important roles amongst the Nizārī Mōmnas of northern Gujarāt. According to the Nizārī Mōmna tradition, Mashāyikh was designated as the local head of the Nizārī *jamāʿat* or community in northern Gujarāt, where he attempted to suppress the Hindu practices of the sectarians. Mashāyikh eventually settled down in Aḥmadābād and asserted his independence from the *daʿwa* headquarters in Anjudān. He kept the tithes collected in the community for himself and also renounced his allegiance to the imām in Persia. Indeed, some sources report that he even converted to Sunnism and visited Awrangzīb in the Deccan. Pīr Mashāyikh is also said to have sided with this Mughal emperor against the Shīʿī rulers of Bījāpūr. Many of Mashāyikh's adherents, who later followed his descendants, converted to Sunnism, while the Nizārī Mōmnas came to support the Kadiwala Sayyids. Pīr Mashāyikh died in 1108/1697 in Aḥmadābād, and his followers later quarrelled as to whether he had been a Sunnī or a Shīʿī, causing further divisions. The matter is obscure, as Mashāyikh's writings reflect both Sunnī and Shīʿī tendencies. Azim Nanji has made the interesting suggestion that Pīr Mashāyikh may in fact have transferred his allegiance to the Muḥammad-Shāhī Nizārī Imāms, who then resided in the Deccan, professing Sunnism for the purpose of *taqiyya*.[120] Pīr Mashāyikh's brother Ḥasan, who was active in Kathiawar, remained loyal to the Nizārī Imām and became the saint of the Nizārī Mōmnas. In addition to his mausoleum in Thanapipli near Jūnāgarh, the Nizārī Khojas and Mōmnas in 1717 constructed a shrine in Ganod, Gujarāt, as a tribute to Ḥasan Pīr. The Mōmnas, now found chiefly in Gujarāt, are sub-divided into various groups adhering to Sunnism, Twelver Shīʿism, Nizārī Shīʿism, and admixtures of these religions.

From early on, the Nizārī *pīr*s who preached the *daʿwa* in India paid special attention to the beliefs and rituals of the Indian communities that were to be converted. They attempted to present the Islamic teachings and Ismāʿīlī doctrines in terms that would be readily comprehensible to Hindu inhabitants of Sind, Gujarāt and other regions of the Indian subcontinent. This approach is clearly reflected in the religious content of the *ginān*s which represent an interfacing of Islamic and Hindu elements. The *pīr*s condemned idol worship but they used Hindu mythology and Hindu motifs to explain certain aspects of their teachings.[121] In particular they expounded within a Hindu framework the doctrine of the imāmate, especially as held by the Nizārīs of the post-*qiyāma* times. This formulation is contained in an important *ginān* entitled *Dasa Avatāra*, which is extant in three separate versions attributed to Pīr Shams al-Dīn, Pīr Ṣadr al-Dīn, and Imām Shāh.[122] The *Dasa Avatāra*, which like many other *ginān*s is no longer in usage, conveys the post-*qiyāma* Nizārī doctrines in the light of the tenets of Vaishnavism, and presents the Nizārī Imām as the awaited saviour on the basis of Vaishnavite ideas concerning the different manifestations of the Hindu deity Vishnu through the ages.

In general, the term *avatāra* in Vaishnavism had come to signify the manifestation of deity, viz., the assumption of different forms, anthropomorphic or otherwise, in which Vishnu descended to earth and lived there until his particular purpose was realized. The number of such *avatāra*s had gradually come to be fixed at ten, whence the name of the *ginān* in question, *Dasa Avatāra*.[123] The ten *avatāra*s were also adjusted in the *ginān*s within the Hindu frame of cyclical time and history. This was accomplished on the basis of the concept of *yuga* or age, expressed in terms of the doctrine of the four *yuga*s of unequal lengths, or a *mahāyuga*, referring to the four cosmic cycles wherein the universe was periodically created and destroyed. The final *yuga*, the present epoch, was called Kali Yuga, an age of evil and darkness associated with the goddess Kali, the Black. The Hindus had awaited the appearance of the tenth *avatāra* who would fight the forces of evil in the Kali Yuga, the current age of darkness. The Nizārī *pīr*s now introduced ʿAlī b. Abī Ṭālib, instead of the standard Hindu figure of Kalki, as the tenth *avatāra* or manifestation of Vishnu. ʿAlī would thus fulfil the eschatological expectations of the Hindu converts to Nizārism by fighting the forces of evil in the Kali Yuga, the final age; he would eventually kill Kalinga, the Iblīs of Hindu mythology. Furthermore, all the imāms succeeding ʿAlī, who were recognized by the Nizārīs, were held to be identical with him in their status and authority. Consequently, each and every Nizārī Imām came to be represented as the tenth *avatāra* of Vishnu. Such explanations were easily comprehensible to the Hindus, who had been converted to Nizārism and were now taught the doctrines of the imāmate and the *qiyāma*, depicting the current imām as the expected saviour. The recognition of the true path (*sat panth*) and imām would liberate the Nizārī Khoja believers from the cycles of rebirth, opening Paradise to them. The Qur'ān was represented as the last of the Vedas, or sacred scriptures whose true interpretation (*ta'wīl*) was known only to the *pīr*s. Indeed, the *ginān*s exalt the religious role of the Nizārī *pīr* or guru, who guides the believers to attain the knowledge (*ginān*) of the imām and the true religion. The traditional Ismāʿīlī cosmology and cyclical hierohistory are not treated in the *ginān*s of the Nizārī Khojas and the Imām-Shāhīs.

The available information on the Muḥammad-Shāhī Nizārī Imāms and their *daʿwa* activities is rather meagre. As noted, the bulk of the Nizārī community in Syria adhered, until the last century, to this line of imāms. There were large numbers of Muḥammad-Shāhīs, at least through the 10th/16th century, in Persia, especially in Daylam, as well as in Afghanistan and the adjacent areas in Badakhshān and the upper Oxus. With the migration of the Muḥammad-Shāhī Imāms to India early in the 10th/16th century, this Nizārī sub-sect acquired followers also on the Indian subcontinent for a few centuries. In the absence of adequate sectarian sources, however, most of the Muḥammad-Shāhī Imāms continue to remain obscure figures, with only their names having been preserved in the sectarian traditions especially as handed down by the Syrian Nizārīs.[124] We have already made references to Muḥammad Shāh b. Mu'min Shāh, the twenty-seventh imām of this line who may be identified with Khudāwand Muḥammad. The latter led his Nizārī followers in Daylam, often from Alamūt, and played an active part in that region's alliances and entanglements until he was exiled to Sulṭāniyya by Tīmūr. Khudāwand Muḥammad's descendants, including perhaps his immediate successors, lived in Sulṭāniyya until the final decades of the 9th/15th century. Meanwhile, Muḥammad Shāh b. Mu'min Shāh had been succeeded by his son Raḍī al-Dīn (d. 838/1434). The latter imām was, in turn, succeeded by Ṭāhir b. Raḍī al-Dīn (d. 868/1463–1464) and Raḍī al-Dīn II b. Ṭāhir, the thirtieth imām of this line and the father of the celebrated Shāh Ṭāhir al-Dakkanī. Imām Raḍī al-Dīn II may perhaps be identified with Shāh Raḍī al-Dīn, the Nizārī leader who early in the 10th/16th century appeared in Badakhshān, a mountainous region situated on the left bank of the upper reaches of the Oxus (Āmū Daryā), or more accurately of the Panj, the source of the Oxus.

The Ismāʿīlīs of the upper Oxus region who remained particularly devoted to Nāṣir-i Khusraw acknowledged the Nizārī *daʿwa* sometime during the later Alamūt period. But the exact date and circumstances of this event are unknown. According to the Ismāʿīlī tradition preserved in Shughnān, a district on the upper Oxus situated on both banks of the Panj and on the western end of the Pāmīr, Nizārism was brought to Badakhshān by two *dāʿīs* sent by the Nizārī Imāms of the Alamūt period.[125] It is related that a certain *dāʿī* called Sayyid Shāh Malang went to Shughnān from Khurāsān and took control of the area by deposing its ruler. Shāh Malang was followed by a second Nizārī *dāʿī*, Sayyid Shāh Khāmūsh, who was a Ḥusaynid ʿAlid tracing his descent to the Imām Mūsā al-Kāẓim. These *dāʿīs* became the founders of the local dynasties of *pīrs* and *mīrs* who ruled over Shughnān and adjacent districts. Meanwhile, Badakhshān in the wider sense escaped the Mongol catastrophe, having remained in the hands of its own local rulers. The region was later annexed to the Tīmūrid empire in the time of Tīmūr's great-grandson Abū Saʿīd (855–873/1451–1469). Still later, at the beginning of the 10th/16th century, Badakhshān was temporarily conquered by the Özbegs. Özbeg rule in Badakhshān was, however, resisted by different local rulers, including a certain Tīmūrid *amīr* called Mīrzā Khān (d. 926/1520). It was under these chaotic circumstances that, in 913/1507–1508, the already-noted Shāh Raḍī al-Dīn, a Nizārī dignitary who had earlier led the Quhistānī Nizārīs and who may be identified with the thirtieth imām of the Muḥammad-Shāhīs, came from Sīstān to Badakhshān. With the help of the local Nizārīs, he established his rule over a large part of Badakhshān. In the midst of the quarrels that soon broke out amongst his supporters, Shāh Raḍī al-Dīn was killed in the spring of 915/1509 and his head was taken to Mīrzā Khān, a local Tīmūrid ruler who resided at the fortress of Ẓafar situated on the left bank of the Kokcha. After defeating another local ruler called Zubayr Rāghī, Mīrzā Khān dealt a severe blow to the Nizārīs of Badakhshān who had then gathered around Shāh Raḍī al-Dīn.

Imām Raḍī al-Dīn II was succeeded by his son Shāh Ṭāhir al-Ḥusaynī al-Dakkanī, the thirty-first and the most famous imām of the Muḥammad-Shāhī line. Shāh Ṭāhir was a learned theologian as well as a poet, a stylist and an accomplished diplomat who rendered valuable services to the Niẓām-Shāhī dynasty of Aḥmadnagar in the Deccan. The most detailed account of this imām is related by Muḥammad Qāsim Hindū Shāh Astarābādī, better known as Firishta, in his well-known work entitled *Gulshan-i Ibrāhīmī*, usually called *Ta'rīkh-i Firishta*, a general history of India completed in 1015/1606–1607.[126] Firishta, who was aware of Shāh Ṭāhir's position as a Nizārī Ismāʿīlī Imām, states that his ancestors had acquired a large following in Persia, where they resided in a locality called Khund (Khwānd) near Qazwīn. In time, Shāh Ṭāhir became the *sajjāda-nishīn* or head of his family and following. He was a highly gifted personality and attained much popularity due to his learning and piety, eclipsing his predecessors. The Ṣafawid Shāh Ismāʿīl, too, heard about Shāh Ṭāhir and became apprehensive of his popularity. But through the intercession of Mīrzā Ḥusayn Iṣfahānī, an influential dignitary at the Ṣafawid court and a supporter of Shāh Ṭāhir, the Nizārī Imām was invited to join other scholars at Shāh Ismāʿīl's court in Sulṭāniyya. However, Shāh Ṭāhir's religious following began to arouse Shāh Ismāʿīl's suspicion. Once again, on the intercession of Mīrzā Ḥusayn Iṣfahānī, who may have been a secret convert to Nizārī Ismāʿīlism of the Muḥammad-Shāhī faction, Shāh Ṭāhir was permitted to settle down in Kāshān. There, Shāh Ṭāhir became a religious teacher (*mudarris*) at the local theological seminary and acquired many students and disciples. It seems that many of Shāh Ṭāhir's followers (*murīdān*) proceeded to Kāshān to attend the lectures of their master. Shāh Ṭāhir's success soon aroused the hostility of the local officials and the Twelver Shīʿī scholars, who forwarded malicious reports to Shāh Ismāʿīl about the Ismāʿīlī teachings of Shāh Ṭāhir. He was also accused of leading the Ismāʿīlīs and other heretical sectarians and of corresponding with foreign rulers.

Shāh Ismāʿīl, who had been waiting for a suitable opportunity to deal with Shāh Ṭāhir, now issued an order for the imām's execution. But Shāh Ṭāhir was warned in time by his friend at the Ṣafawid court, Mīrzā Ḥusayn Iṣfahānī. In 926/1520, the imām fled from Kāshān with his family, barely missing the guards who had been sent after him. He went to Fārs and then sailed to India, landing in Goa. Shāh Ṭāhir immediately proceeded to the court of Ismāʿīl ʿĀdil Shāh (916–941/1510–1534), who ruled from Bījāpūr over one of the five states succeeding the Bahmanid kingdom in the Deccan. Ismāʿīl's father Yūsuf was the first Muslim ruler in India to adopt Shīʿism as the religion of his state. But Ismāʿīl ʿĀdil Shāh himself did not have deep religious convictions and did not pay any particular attention to Shāh Ṭāhir. Disappointed about his reception at Bījāpūr, the imām then decided to make the pilgrimage to Mecca and to the Shīʿī shrines in ʿIrāq before returning to Persia. On his way to the seaport, Shāh Ṭāhir stopped at the fort of Paranda where he came in contact with Khwāja Jahān, the famous vizier of the Bahmanid kings who was then in the service of the Niẓām-Shāhs of Aḥmadnagar, another of the dynasties succeeding the Bahmanids. At Paranda, Shāh Ṭāhir also met Pīr Muḥammad Shirwānī, a Ḥanafī Sunnī scholar of Aḥmadnagar who had been sent by Burhān I Niẓām Shāh (914–961/1508–1554) on some errand to Khwāja Jahān. Pīr Muḥammad was much impressed by Shāh Ṭāhir's scholarship and reported the matter to Burhān Niẓām Shāh, who invited Shāh Ṭāhir to Aḥmadnagar.

In 928/1522, Shāh Ṭāhir arrived in Aḥmadnagar, the capital of the Niẓām-Shāhī state which was to become his permanent abode. Soon Shāh Ṭāhir became the most trusted adviser of Burhān Niẓām Shāh and attained a highly privileged position at his court. At the request of Burhān Niẓām Shāh, Shāh Ṭāhir started delivering weekly lectures on different religious subjects inside the fort of Aḥmadnagar. These sessions, attended by numerous scholars and the ruler himself, spread Shāh Ṭāhir's fame throughout the Deccan. Firishta relates interesting details on Shāh Ṭāhir's miraculous healing of Burhān Niẓām Shāh's young son, ʿAbd al-Qādir, which apparently brought about the conversion of Burhān I from Sunnism to Shīʿism. The sources specify that Burhān Niẓām Shāh adopted Ithnāʿasharī Shīʿism, which, according to all authorities, was the form of Shīʿism propagated from the beginning by Shāh Ṭāhir. The propagation of Twelver Shīʿism by a Nizārī Imām may seem rather strange. One must bear in mind, however, that Shāh Ṭāhir and other Nizārī leaders of the period were obliged to observe *taqiyya* very strictly. It is certain that Shāh Ṭāhir propagated his form of Nizārī Ismāʿīlism in the guise of Twelver Shīʿism, which was more acceptable to the Muslim rulers of India who were interested in cultivating friendly relations with the Twelver Shīʿī Ṣafawid dynasty of Persia. This may explain why he wrote several commentaries on the theological works of the well-known Imāmī scholars. Furthermore, like his rivals in the Qāsim-Shāhī line, Shāh Ṭāhir apparently expressed his Nizārī ideas also in the guise of Ṣūfism, though specific details are lacking on the matter. In this connection, it may be recalled that the authorship of the already-cited Ismāʿīlī commentary on the *Gulshan-i rāz* is sometimes attributed to Shāh Ṭāhir. At any rate, these associations are well reflected in the *Lamaʿāt al-ṭāhirīn*, a versified Muḥammad-Shāhī treatise composed in the Deccan around 1110/1698 by Ghulām ʿAlī b. Muḥammad.[127] In the *Lamaʿāt*, the only Muḥammad-Shāhī work preserved in India, the author clearly camouflages his scattered Nizārī ideas under Ithnāʿasharī and Ṣūfī expressions. He often eulogizes the twelve imāms of the Ithnāʿasharīs whilst also alluding to the imāms of the Muḥammad-Shāhī line.

Shāh Ṭāhir achieved his greatest religious success in the Deccan when Burhān Niẓām Shāh, shortly after his own conversion, proclaimed Twelver Shīʿism as the official religion of the Niẓām-Shāhī state in 944/1537. The ruler of Aḥmadnagar easily succeeded, with Shāh Ṭāhir's advice, in subduing a rebellion led by Pīr Muḥammad Shirwānī against this proclamation. Henceforth, an increasing number of Shīʿī scholars, including Shāh Ṭāhir's own brother Shāh Jaʿfar, gathered at Burhān I's court and received his patronage. The Ṣafawid court in Persia rejoiced at hearing about the official endorsement of Shīʿism in the Niẓām-Shāhī state, and Shāh Ṭahmāsp sent an emissary carrying presents to Burhān Niẓām Shāh. In return, Shāh Ṭāhir's son Ḥaydar was despatched on a goodwill mission from Aḥmadnagar to Persia. Firishta and other authorities relate many details on the diplomatic services rendered by Shāh Ṭāhir to Burhān Niẓām Shāh. This Muḥammad-Shāhī Nizārī Imām participated during more than two decades in many negotiations and mediations on behalf of his patron with the surrounding Muslim rulers in Gujarāt, Bījāpūr, Golconda and Bīdar. After an imāmate of some forty years, Shāh Ṭāhir died at Aḥmadnagar between 952/1545–1546, the year mentioned by the contemporary Ṣafawid prince Sām Mīrzā, and 956/1549, the most probable date recorded by Firishta. His remains were later transferred to Karbalā' and buried in the Imām al-Ḥusayn's shrine. Shāh Ṭāhir was the author of numerous works on theology and jurisprudence, which do not seem to be extant; but many of his poems have been preserved.

Shāh Ṭāhir was succeeded by his eldest son Shāh Ḥaydar, who at the time of his father's death was still at the court of Shāh Ṭahmāsp in Persia. Soon after, he returned to Aḥmadnagar as the *sajjāda-nishīn* of his sect and acquired a respectful position at the court of the Niẓām-Shāhs. Besides Ḥaydar, Shāh Ṭāhir had three other sons, Shāh Rafīʿ al-Dīn Ḥusayn, Shāh Abu'l-Ḥasan and Shāh Abū Ṭālib, who had been born in India. They, too, received honour and respect at the courts of the ʿĀdil-Shāhs and other rulers of the Deccan. The Muḥammad-Shāhī Imāmate was handed down amongst the descendants of Shāh Ḥaydar (d. 994/1586), who continued to live in Aḥmadnagar and later in Awrangābād. According to the traditions of the Syrian Muḥammad-Shāhīs, the successors of Shāh Ḥaydar were Ṣadr al-Dīn Muḥammad (d. 1032/1622); Muʿīn al-Dīn (d. 1054/1644); ʿAṭiyyat Allāh, also known as Khudāybakhsh, who apparently took up residence in Badakhshān and died there in 1074/1663; ʿAzīz Shāh, who died at Awrangābād in 1103/1691; Muʿīn al-Dīn II (d. 1127/1715); Amīr Muḥammad al-Musharraf (d. 1178/1764); Ḥaydar (d. 1201/1786); and Amīr Muḥammad al-Bāqir. The last, counted as the fortieth in the series, was evidently the final Muḥammad-Shāhī Imām.

Amīr Muḥammad al-Bāqir had his last contact with his Syrian followers in Shaʿbān 1210/February 1796.[128] The Syrian Nizārī community had, as noted, continued to generally acknowledge the Muḥammad-Shāhī Imāms; but after searching in vain in India to locate the descendants of Amīr Muḥammad al-Bāqir, in 1304/1887 the majority of the Syrian Muḥammad-Shāhī Nizārīs transferred their allegiance to the Qāsim-Shāhī line, then represented by Āghā Khān III. With the settlement of the Muḥammad-Shāhī Imāms in the Deccan, the religious following of this line disintegrated in Persia in the course of the 10th/16th century. While some Persian Muḥammad-Shāhīs may have joined the Qāsim-Shāhī faction, the majority of the members of this Nizārī sub-sect probably embraced Twelver Shīʿism, the official religion of Ṣafawid Persia. It is interesting to note, however, that the members of the Shāh-Ṭāhirī family, who currently reside in Qumm and some other towns in Persia, claim descent from Shāh Ṭāhir. The Muḥammad-Shāhī Imāms continued to have supporters in Badakhshān and the Kābul area at least through the 11th/17th century. But by the beginning of the 13th/19th century, the Nizārīs of the upper Oxus region and Afghanistan seem to have generally adhered to the Qāsim-Shāhī line. The Nizārī communities of Badakhshān, including those now under Soviet domination, have continued to be led by their local dynasties of *pīrs*. In India, too, the followers of the Muḥammad-Shāhī line gradually disappeared after the 11th/17th century, following the general persecution of the Shīʿīs in the Deccan by Awrangzīb. At present, there do not seem to be any Muḥammad-Shāhīs in India. The only known members of this Nizārī sub-sect are currently located in Syria. The Syrian Muḥammad-Shāhīs have always followed the Shāfiʿī *madhhab* in the legal affairs of their community.

In the meantime, the Qāsim-Shāhī Imāms had succeeded by the end of

10 The restored mausoleum of Imām Shāh Nizār II, Kahak

11 The tombstone of Imām Shāh Nizār II (d. 1134/1722), Kahak

12 A surviving section of the wall encircling Āghā Khān I's residential compound, Maḥallāt

13 General view of the citadel of Bam

14 Ḥasan ʿAlī Shāh, Āghā Khān I

15 Āghā Khān I and (on the right) Āghā Khān II

16 One of Āghā Khān I's granddaughters, Bombay

the 11th/17th century to gain the allegiance of the Nizārī majoritarian. Khalīl Allāh II, the thirty-ninth imām of this line, died in 1090/1680 and was succeeded by his son Shāh Nizār II.[129] By that time, the Qāsim-Shāhī Imāms had developed deep roots in central Persia, in Maḥallāt and other localities around Anjudān. Sometime during the earliest decades of his imāmate and for unknown reasons, Shāh Nizār transferred his residence and the headquarters of the *daʿwa* to Kahak, a village situated about thirty-five kilometres northeast of Anjudān and northwest of Maḥallāt. Anjudān, separated from Kahak by a number of shallow ranges, was now abandoned permanently by the imāms. This marked the termination of the Anjudān period in Nizārism which had lasted about two centuries. Shāh Nizār and his immediate successor lived in Kahak, which was soon abandoned as the residence of the imāms. However, Nizār's later successors maintained roots in Kahak at least by the beginning of the 13th/19th century. Kahak is now an insignificant and isolated village, with an Ithnāʿasharī population of about 500 persons. The locality seems to have enjoyed greater importance in former times as a resting place with a Ṣafawid caravanserai on the road between Qumm and Arāk.

The Qāsim-Shāhī Imāms evidently maintained their affiliation with the Niʿmat Allāhī Ṣūfī order continuously from the time of Mustanṣir bi'llāh II. But the earliest definite evidence of this affiliation can be traced back to Shāh Nizār. He had close connections with this Ṣūfī order, which at the time was not yet revived in Persia, and adopted the *ṭarīqa* name of ʿAṭā' Allāh. This also explains why his followers in certain parts of Kirmān came to be known as ʿAṭā' Allāhīs.[130] These Nizārīs, originally nomadic tribesmen in Khurāsān, were settled down in the district of Sīrjān and elsewhere in Kirmān on Nizār's own initiative. Imām Shāh Nizār II died, according to the inscription of his tombstone, in Dhu'l-Ḥijja 1134/September 1722, shortly before the Afghan invasion of Persia which extended also to Kahak. Sectarian sources place Nizār II's death almost a century earlier, in 1038/1628–1629. His mausoleum is still preserved at the western end of Kahak. The building, which may in fact have been a part of the former residence of the imām, has several chambers, each one containing a few graves. In the compound and in its adjacent garden there are several tombstones with inscriptions in Khojkī Sindhī characters, attesting to the pilgrimage of the Indian Nizārīs who regularly embarked on the long and dangerous journey to see their imām. By that time, close relations had developed between the Nizārī Imāms and their Khoja followers in Sind, Panjāb, Gujarāt and elsewhere in the Indian subcontinent. Nizār's mausoleum was restored, at the cost of destroying its original carved wooden doors and other fixtures, in 1966. A stone platform, discovered in 1937 by Ivanow, which was then situated in the former gardens of Nizār's residence, was no longer in existence when the author visited Kahak in 1976. It has been related that Nizār used to sit on this platform when he received his followers.

Shāh Nizār II was succeeded by his son Sayyid ʿAlī, whose grave is located in the largest chamber of Nizār's mausoleum.[131] Sayyid ʿAlī was, in turn, succeeded by Sayyid Ḥasan ʿAlī, also known as Sayyid Ḥasan Beg, the forty-second imām of this line. It was during Ḥasan ʿAlī's imāmate that Nādir Shāh expelled the Afghan invaders from Persia, and then overthrew the Ṣafawid dynasty and proclaimed himself king, founding the short-lived Afshārid dynasty. Towards the end of Nādir Shāh's reign (1148–1160/1736–1747), Imām Ḥasan ʿAlī moved to Shahr-i Bābak in Kirmān, situated about 180 kilometres southwest of the city of Kirmān, between Rafsanjān and Sīrjān. This decision was apparently mainly motivated by the imām's concern for the safety of the Indian Nizārī pilgrims coming to Persia and the proper flow of the tithes from India to his treasūry. Aḥmad ʿAlī Khān Vazīrī (d. 1295/1878), who wrote a detailed regional history of his native province of Kirmān, relates that in the chaotic conditions of Persia after the downfall of the Ṣafawids, the Indian Nizārīs who regularly travelled to the Anjudān and Maḥallāt areas for seeing their imām and remitting to him their religious dues, were often plundered and killed between Nāʾīn and Yazd by the Bakhtiyārī tribesmen, in addition to being extorted on the route by various officials.[132] Consequently, the imām decided to move to Shahr-i Bābak in southeastern Persia, a location closer to the Persian Gulf ports and the pilgrimage route of his Indian followers. Some Nizārīs already lived in Shahr-i Bābak, and with the imām's arrival there, the town became an important Nizārī centre. With the improved flow of the tithes of the Nizārī Khojas, Imām Ḥasan ʿAlī soon acquired extensive properties in Shahr-i Bābak, also establishing a winter residence in the city of Kirmān. He was, indeed, the first imām of his line to emerge from concealment and obscurity. He became actively involved in the affairs of Kirmān, and was treated with respect by the Afshārid Shāhrukh who ruled the Kirmān province from the time of Nādir Shāh's murder in 1160/1747 until he himself was killed in 1172/1758–1759, at which time Kirmān was annexed to the territories of Karīm Khān Zand, the founder of another short-lived dynasty in Persia. The close association between Ḥasan ʿAlī and Shāhrukh culminated in the marriage between the imām's daughter and the Afshārid governor's son Luṭfʿ Alī Khān.[133] Imām Ḥasan ʿAlī was succeeded by his son Qāsim ʿAlī (Shāh), also known as Sayyid Jaʿfar, about whom no particular details are mentioned in the sources.[134]

Qāsim ʿAlī's son and successor as the forty-fourth imām of his line, Abu'l-Ḥasan ʿAlī (Shāh), also known as Sayyid Abu'l-Ḥasan Kahakī, became the governor of Kirmān during the Zand period (1163–1209/1750–1794).[135] He played an active part in that province's political scene in the turbulent years when the Zand dynasty was being replaced by the Qājār dynasty in Persia. Abu'l-Ḥasan had friendly relations with Karīm Khān Zand (1163–1193/1750–1779), and the latter's governor of Kirmān, Mīrzā Ḥusayn Khān. The Nizārī Imām was treated most respectfully by Mīrzā Ḥusayn Khān, who placed certain towns and districts of Kirmān, such as Sīrjān and Zarand, under his rule. Later, Sayyid Abu'l-Ḥasan advanced to the position of *beglerbegi* or governor of the city of Kirmān. He continued to be popularly referred to by the title of *beglerbegi* even after being appointed by Karīm Khān to the governorship of the province of Kirmān around 1170/1756. It has been reported that Abu'l-Ḥasan received, during his imāmate, an annual sum of 20,000 *tūmān*s in religious dues from his followers in India. This enabled the imām both to acquire further property in Kirmān and spend generously for the benefit of the Kirmānīs, which won him increasing local popularity. Consequently, he was able to continue as the governor of Kirmān when the Zand dynasty disintegrated on Karīm Khān's death in 1193/1779. In fact, the Nizārī Imām henceforth ruled over Kirmān in an independent manner, supporting or opposing various Zand rulers, who in their struggles for the control of Persia were soon confronted by their greatest common enemy, Āghā Muḥammad Khān (1193–1212/1779–1797), the founder of the Qājār dynasty of Persia. In the succession disputes following Karīm Khān Zand's death, Sayyid Abu'l-Ḥasan lent his support to Karīm Khān's brother Ṣādiq Khān (1193–1195/1779–1781), who was assisted by the imām in collecting an army in Kirmān and asserting his authority in Shīrāz, the Zand capital. Ṣādiq Khān reinstated Abu'l-Ḥasan as the Zand governor of Kirmān.

Under the chaotic conditions of the time, Abu'l-Ḥasan soon lost control over certain parts of Kirmān, including Narmāshīr and the citadel of Bam. The border region between Kirmān and Afghanistan, including Narmāshīr, was invaded by the Afghan and Balūchī forces of Aʿẓam Khān, an *amīr* from Qandahār. Later, Aʿẓam Khān was defeated in battle by an army of 7,000 men sent after him by Sayyid Abu'l-Ḥasan. This army was placed under the command of Mīrzā Ṣādiq, Abu'l-Ḥasan's cousin and capable military commander. Subsequently, when Abu'l-Ḥasan was on one of his visits to Shahr-i Bābak, Aʿẓam Khān once again ravaged the various districts of Kirmān from Narmāshīr and led his forces as far as the gates of the city of Kirmān. This time, Abu'l-Ḥasan personally led his own forces from Shahr-i Bābak and defeated Aʿẓam Khān outside Kirmān. The retreating Afghans managed to hold on to Narmāshīr and a few other border localities in Kirmān. Imām Abu'l-Ḥasan's rule was more seriously endangered when Muḥammad Ḥasan Khān Sīstānī, who held Bam independently, encouraged Luṭf ʿAlī Khān (1203–1209/1789–1794) to invade Kirmān. Luṭf ʿAlī Khān, the grandson of Karīm Khān's brother Ṣādiq and an able military commander, was the last of the Zand rulers. His father Jaʿfar Khān (1199–1203/1785–1789) had briefly ruled over certain parts of Persia before him. It was during Jaʿfar Khān's reign that Āghā Muḥammad Khān Qājār made himself master of northern Persia, also seizing Iṣfahān and making Tehran his capital in 1200/1786. Āghā Muḥammad Khān and Luṭf ʿAlī Khān struggled intensely with each other over the throne of Persia, which eventually resulted in the victory of the Qājārs. In Ṣafar 1205/October 1790, Luṭf ʿAlī Khān proceeded to Sīrjān, aiming to capture Shahr-i Bābak, Abu'l-Ḥasan's main stronghold in Kirmān where the imām had numerous adherents amongst the Khurāsānī and ʿAṭā' Allāhī inhabitants of the area. The imām also had a fortified and well-provisioned fortress in Shahr-i Bābak which was then guarded by a large number of armed Nizārīs under the command of Mīrzā Ṣādiq. Being informed in Sīrjān of the difficulty of taking Shahr-i Bābak, Luṭf ʿAlī Khān then proceeded towards the city of Kirmān. In view of the fact that only Shīrāz and other parts of Fārs then remained in the hands of the Zands while Āghā Muḥammad Khān was rapidly extending Qājār rule over Persia, Sayyid Abu'l-Ḥasan prudently refused Luṭf ʿAlī Khān admittance to the city, also refusing to present himself before the Zand ruler. He reinforced the city's defences and prepared to withstand a long siege. Due to adverse weather conditions, Luṭf ʿAlī Khān was eventually obliged to lift his siege of Kirmān and returned to Shīrāz in Jumādā I 1205/January 1791.

In the meantime, the Niʿmat Allāhī Ṣūfī order was revived in Persia by the order's thirty-fourth *quṭb*, Riḍā ʿAlī Shāh Dakkanī (d. 1214/1799), who, like his predecessors, resided in the Deccan. The Persian Niʿmat Allāhīs, isolated from their spiritual master, had persistently asked their *quṭb* in India to send them a trusted representative. Riḍā ʿAlī Shāh, who was the order's *quṭb* for more than fifty years, eventually despatched one of his most important disciples, Maʿṣūm ʿAlī Shāh, to Persia. Maʿṣūm ʿAlī arrived in Shīrāz around 1184/1770, and soon acquired a number of devoted disciples, including Nūr ʿAlī Shāh and a certain young musician called Mīrzā Muḥammad Turbatī, who later became famous under his *ṭarīqa* name of Mushtāq ʿAlī Shāh. After travelling extensively in various parts of Persia and Afghanistan, and suffering persecution at the hands of different Zand rulers and their fanatical *ʿulamāʾ*, Nūr ʿAlī Shāh and Mushtāq ʿAlī Shāh arrived in Māhān in 1200/1785–1786 to be near the shrine of Shāh Niʿmat Allāh. They rapidly acquired a large number of supporters and settled in the city of Kirmān. The arrival of these Ṣūfīs in Kirmān revived the ties between the Niʿmat Allāhī *ṭarīqa* and the Nizārī Imāms.[136] Imām Abu'l-Ḥasan was amongst the numerous notables of Kirmān who supported Nūr ʿAlī and Mushtāq ʿAlī. This imām too had close connections with the Niʿmat Allāhī order, though there is no concrete evidence showing that he was actually initiated into the order. But Abu'l-Ḥasan's cousin Mīrzā Ṣādiq was an initiate of the order; he was trained by Muẓaffar ʿAlī Shāh, a physician and one of the leading members of the order in Kirmān.

The success of the Niʿmat Allāhī Ṣūfīs in Kirmān naturally aroused the envy and enmity of the local Ithnāʿasharī *ʿulamāʾ*, whose efforts to uproot the Ṣūfīs were frustrated by Abu'l-Ḥasan's support for them. Nonetheless, Mullā ʿAbd Allāh, one of the influential *mujtahid*s of Kirmān, persisted in his campaign against the Ṣūfīs. He found a suitable opportunity to act when Imām Abu'l-Ḥasan had left the city of Kirmān to restore order in Shahr-i Bābak and Sīrjān, where the Qashqāʾī and Arab tribesmen were menacing the local populace. At the same time, Nūr ʿAlī Shāh himself, the foremost Niʿmat Allāhī of Kirmān, had gone on pilgrimage to the holy shrines of ʿIrāq. In Ramaḍān 1206/May 1791, when Imām Abu'l-Ḥasan and Nūr ʿAlī Shāh were out of the city, Mullā ʿAbd Allāh, while preaching in the Friday mosque of Kirmān, saw Mushtāq ʿAlī Shāh, who had come to say his prayers. Thereupon, Mullā ʿAbd Allāh incited those present to stone Mushtāq to death as an infidel. Mushtāq ʿAlī Shāh was buried near the same mosque, and his mausoleum, known as Mushtāqiyya, is still preserved and visited regularly by Persian *darwīsh*es. Imām Abu'l-Ḥasan died later in the same year 1206/1792, and was evidently buried in Mushtāq ʿAlī Shāh's mausoleum.[137] A few years later, Maʿṣūm ʿAlī Shāh, Nūr ʿAlī Shāh, and Muẓaffar ʿAlī Shāh were killed at the instigation of other Ithnāʿasharī *mujtahids*, notably Muḥammad ʿAlī Bihbahānī (d. 1216/1801–1802). Imām Abu'l-Ḥasan was succeeded briefly as governor of Kirmān by his cousin Mīrzā Ṣādiq. In 1207/1792, ʿAghā Muḥammad Khān seized Shīrāz and sent his nephew and future successor Fatḥ ʿAlī Khān to conquer Kirmān. Fatḥ ʿAlī Khān replaced Mīrzā Ṣādiq by his own appointee. Subsequently, Luṭf ʿAlī Khān Zand briefly held Kirmān before losing the place permanently to the Qājārs in 1209/1794, when Āghā Muḥammad Khān massacred a large number of Kirmānīs. The local Nizārīs were, however, spared. The Nizārī Sayyids and their families, relatives of the imām, who lived in Shahr-i Bābak, were permitted to move to Kahak, where Āghā Muḥammad Khān gave the imām's family new landed properties in compensation for what had been left behind in Kirmān. A few hundred Nizārī ʿAṭā' Allāhī families of the same locality were settled outside of Kirmān.[138] Luṭf ʿAlī Khān, then a fugitive, was captured at Bam and sent to Āghā Muḥammad Khān who had him blinded and then executed in 1209 A.H. Āghā Muḥammad Khān, crowned as the first Qājār ruler of Persia in 1210/1796, was himself murdered shortly afterwards in 1211/1797.

Abu'l-Ḥasan ʿAlī was succeeded as the imām of the Qāsim-Shāhī Nizārī Ismāʿīlīs by his eldest son Khalīl Allāh ʿAlī, designated also as Shāh Khalīl Allāh III.[139] Soon after his accession in 1206/1792, Shāh Khalīl Allāh transferred the seat of the imāmate from Kirmān to Kahak, where he stayed for about twenty years. Shāh Khalīl Allāh married Bībī Sarkāra, the daughter of Muḥammad Ṣādiq Maḥallātī, who bore the next imām, Āghā Khān I, in 1219/1804 in Kahak. Muḥammad Ṣādiq Maḥallātī, a Nizārī Sayyid who was perhaps a brother of Imām Abu'l-Ḥasan, was a Niʿmat Allāhī Ṣūfī. Initiated by Muẓaffar ʿAlī Shāh (d. 1215/1800), he carried the Ṣūfī name of Ṣidq ʿAlī Shāh. Āghā Khān I's maternal grandfather, who was also a poet, died in 1230/1815, and was buried in Qumm. Ṣidq ʿAlī Shāh's son Muḥammad ʿAlī, better known by his *ṭarīqa* name of ʿIzzat ʿAlī Shāh, was another prominent Niʿmat Allāhī *darwīsh*. This maternal uncle of Āghā Khān I was initiated into the Niʿmat Allāhī *ṭarīqa* by Majdhūb ʿAlī Shāh (d. 1238/1823), the thirty-eighth *quṭb* of the order.[140] Later, ʿIzzat ʿAlī Shāh developed close relations with Zayn al-ʿĀbidīn Shīrwānī (d. 1253/1837), who carried the Ṣūfī name of Mast ʿAlī Shāh and became the chief successor of Majdhūb ʿAlī Shāh as a *quṭb* of the Niʿmat Allāhīs, who were now split into several groups. ʿIzzat ʿAlī Shāh spent the greater part of his life in Maḥallāt, where the influence of the Nizārī Imām was by then extended, and died there around 1245/1829. Although Shāh Khalīl Allāh

III carried a Niʿmat Allāhī Ṣūfī name, he did not have any active interest in Ṣūfism.

In 1230/1815, Shāh Khalīl Allāh moved to Yazd, situated between Iṣfahān and Kirmān on the route to Balūchistān and Sind. Most probably this decision was motivated by the imām's desire to be yet closer to his Indian followers, who continued to make the pilgrimage to see their imām in Persia. It was at Yazd that two years later, in 1232/1817, the Nizārī Imām became a victim of the intrigues of the Ithnāʿasharī *ʿulamā*ʾ and lost his life in the course of a dispute between some of his adherents and the local shopkeepers. The Nizārīs involved, who had used violence to settle their differences with the shopkeepers in the market place, took refuge in Shāh Khalīl Allāh's residence and refused to emerge. A certain Mullā Ḥusayn Yazdī, who as a Twelver resented the spreading influence of the Nizārī Imām, collected a mob and attacked the imām's house. In the ensuing uproar Shāh Khalīl Allāh and several of his followers, including an Indian Khoja, were murdered, and the imām's house was plundered. The Qājār ruler ordered his governor of Yazd, Ḥājjī Zamān Khān, to send Mullā Ḥusayn and his accomplices to Tehran for punishment. Shāh Khalīl Allāh had had good relations with the second Qājār monarch, Fatḥ ʿAlī Shāh (1212–1250/1797–1834), who is groundlessly reported to have secretly embraced Ismāʿīlism.[141] Mullā Ḥusayn was bastinadoed and his beard was plucked out, but no one was executed for the imām's murder. Shāh Khalīl Allāh, the forty-fifth and last of the Qāsim-Shāhī Nizārī Imāms to spend his entire imāmate of some twenty-five years in Persia, was taken for burial to the holy city of Najaf in ʿIrāq, where a mausoleum was constructed for this imām and some of his relatives and descendants.

Shāh Khalīl Allāh III was succeeded by his eldest son Muḥammad Ḥasan, also known as Ḥasan ʿAlī Shāh.[142] On moving to Yazd, Shāh Khalīl Allāh had left his wife, Bībī Sarkāra, and children in Kahak to live on the proceeds of the family holdings in the Maḥallāt area. However, disputes between the local Nizārīs and Īmānī Khān Farāhānī, who was married to one of the imām's daughters Shāh Bībī and who had been placed in charge of the imām's land holdings, left the family unprovided for. Soon, Ḥasan ʿAlī Shāh and his mother settled down in the nearby town of Qumm, where their situation became even worse. Ḥasan ʿAlī Shāh was thirteen when his father was murdered and he became the forty-sixth Nizārī Imām. Soon after, the youthful imām's mother went to the Qājār court in Tehran to seek justice for her husband and her son. Her pleadings were eventually successful. The instigators of Shāh Khalīl Allāh's murder were, as noted, punished after a fashion; and, in addition, Fatḥ ʿAlī Shāh added to the imām's lands in the Maḥallāt area and gave one of his daughters, Sarv-i Jahān Khānum, in marriage to Ḥasan ʿAlī Shāh.[143] At the same time, the Qājār monarch appointed the imām as governor of Qumm and bestowed on him the honorific title of Āghā Khān (less commonly but more correctly, Āqā Khān). Henceforth, Ḥasan ʿAlī Shāh became generally known as Āghā Khān Maḥallātī; and the title of Āghā Khān remained hereditary amongst his successors, the Nizārī Imāms of modern times. Āghā Khān I's mother, who later moved to India, died in Cutch in 1267/1851.

Ḥasan ʿAlī Shāh, Āghā Khān I, led a tranquil life and enjoyed honour and respect at the Qājār court until the death of Fatḥ ʿAlī Shāh in Jumādā II 1250/October 1834. The Āghā Khān had by then acquired a personal military force, which he used to restore order on his way to Tehran to pay homage to Fatḥ ʿAlī Shāh's grandson and successor Muḥammad Shāh (1250–1264/1834–1848). Soon after his accession, Muḥammad Shāh, in consultation with his chief minister Qā'im-maqām-i Farāhānī (d. 1251/1835), appointed the Āghā Khān as governor of Kirmān in 1251/1835.[144] On the occasion of this appointment, Qā'ānī (d. 1270/1854), the greatest panegyrist of the Qājār period and a friend of the Āghā Khān, composed a *qaṣīda* praising the imām's virtues.[145] The province of Kirmān was then in the hands of the rebellious sons of Shujāʿ al-Salṭana, a pretender to the Qājār throne; it was also raided regularly by Afghans and Balūchīs. Āghā Khān I soon succeeded in restoring order in Kirmān without receiving any advance payment from the Qājār treasury. Both Bam and Narmāshīr, held for a long time by rebellious elements, were also reduced to obedience. In pacifying Kirmān, the Āghā Khān was assisted by the local ʿAṭā' Allāhī and Khurāsānī tribesmen who recognized him as their imām. Henceforth, the Āghā Khān's younger brother Abu'l-Ḥasan Khān, known as Sardār (Commander), often acted as the commander of the Āghā Khān's forces.

In time, Āghā Khān I sent an account of his victories to Tehran, but he waited in vain in the expectation of receiving compensatory payments and further royal favours. The Āghā Khān's governorship of Kirmān, despite his services, was short-lived. In 1252/1837, less than two years after his arrival in Kirmān, he was dismissed and recalled to Tehran. He had been replaced as the governor of Kirmān by Fīrūz Mīrzā Nuṣrat al-Dawla, one of the younger brothers of Muḥammad Shāh Qājār. However, Āghā

Khān refused to acknowledge his dismissal and withdrew with his forces to the citadel at Bam. Recalling his brother Sardār Abu'l-Ḥasan Khān from Balūchistān, where he was conducting military campaigns, and his other brother Muḥammad Bāqir Khān from Rāwar, the Āghā Khān prepared to resist the government forces sent against him under the command of Suhrāb Khān. Āghā Khān was besieged at Bam for fourteen months, during which time his brother Muḥammad Bāqir Khān was seriously wounded and taken prisoner. When it had become evident that further resistance would be futile, the Āghā Khān despatched Sardār Abu'l-Ḥasan Khān to Shīrāz, appealing to the governor of Fārs, Farīdūn Mīrzā, to intervene on his behalf and arrange for his safe passage out of Kirmān. On Farīdūn Mīrzā's intercession, the Āghā Khān surrendered and emerged from the citadel at Bam, but he was seized and his possessions were plundered by the government troops.[146] Āghā Khān I and his dependants were then transferred to the city of Kirmān, where they remained captives for eight months. It was during that period that the Nizārī Imām was permitted to receive the religious dues sent to him by the Nizārī deputations coming from Khurāsān, Badakhshān and India.[147] On Muḥammad Shāh's return from his unsuccessful campaign against Harāt, the Āghā Khān was finally allowed to proceed to Tehran towards the end of 1254/1838–1839. He presented his case before the Qājār monarch, who pardoned him on the condition that he retire peacefully to his family lands at Maḥallāt. After a short stay in Qumm, the Āghā Khān did retreat to Maḥallāt, where he had built a large fortified residential compound for his family and numerous dependants and servants.[148]

The Āghā Khān's dismissal from the governorship of Kirmān was probably occasioned by rivalries for the leadership of the Niʿmat Allāhī order in Persia; rivalries that had appeared after the death of Majdhūb ʿAlī Shāh, the thirty-eighth *quṭb* of the order, in 1238/1823. As noted, Ḥājji Zayn al-ʿĀbidīn Shīrwānī, better known by his Ṣūfī name of Mast ʿAlī Shāh, had been recognized as Majdhūb ʿAlī Shāh's successor by the majority of the Niʿmat Allāhīs. According to the Niʿmat Allāhī sources, the Āghā Khān had been actually initiated into their order in his youth and carried the *ṭarīqa* name of ʿAṭā' Allāh Shāh. This alleged initiation, not substantiated by the Nizārī sources, would represent a rather unusual relationship, since it would have required a Nizārī Imām to become a follower of a Ṣūfī master. The Āghā Khān did, however, support the claims of Mast ʿAlī Shāh. The Āghā Khān had once, during Fatḥ ʿAlī Shāh's reign, given refuge in the village of Dawlatābād near Maḥallāt to

Mast ʿAlī Shāh, who had escaped the persecution of the Twelver *ʿulamā*ʾ of Fārs. At the time of Muḥammad Shāh's coronation, Mast ʿAlī Shāh, who had been enjoying the Āghā Khān's hospitality for some time at Maḥallāt, accompanied his Nizārī friend to Tehran. As a reflection of their close friendship, Mast ʿAlī Shāh indeed once boasted to Muḥammad Shāh that 'I have a *murīd* like the Āqā Khān who himself has thousands of *murīd*s in most countries (*bilād*) of the world'.[149] Muḥammad Shāh too, had firm Ṣūfī loyalties. He had been initiated into the Niʿmat Allāhī order, sometime before his accession, probably by Mast ʿAlī Shāh, who later joined the entourage of the Qājār monarch. However, at Muḥammad Shāh's court, Mast ʿAlī Shāh soon came to confront a powerful rival in the person of Ḥājjī Mīrzā Āqāsī, Qāʾim-maqām's successor as chief minister (*ṣadr-i aʿẓam*) who as a Niʿmat Allāhī aspired to the leadership of that order. Muḥammad Shāh soon came under the influence of his chief minister and evidently accepted him as the *quṭb* of the Niʿmat Allāhī order. Consequently, Mast ʿAlī Shāh incurred the disfavour of the monarch and was driven from the court. Since the Āghā Khān had continued to support the claims of his Ṣūfī friend, he aroused the enmity of Mīrzā Āqāsī, who persistently intrigued against him and eventually caused his removal from the governorship of Kirmān.[150]

Ḥājjī Mīrzā Āqāsī's enmity towards the Āghā Khān was aggravated by the imām's refusal to give one of his daughters in marriage to the son of a certain ʿAbd al-Muḥammad Maḥallātī.[151] The latter, a lowborn Maḥallātī initially in the service of the Āghā Khān, had risen to a high position in the service of Mīrzā Āqāsī and supported his master's Ṣūfī claims. At any rate, the Āghā Khān maintained his connections with the Niʿmat Allāhī order even after settling down in India. Āghā Khān I had close relations with Raḥmat ʿAlī Shāh (d. 1278/1861), who became the *quṭb* of one of the branches of the Niʿmat Allāhī order on Mast ʿAlī Shāh's death in 1253/1837. Raḥmat ʿAlī Shāh, too, had spent some time, along with Mast ʿAlī Shāh, at Maḥallāt as a guest of the Āghā Khān. Later in 1298/1881, the Āghā Khān and his sons extended their hospitality in Bombay to Raḥmat ʿAlī Shāh's son, Maʿṣūm ʿAlī Shāh, then on a tour of India. Maʿṣūm ʿAlī Shāh, who produced the celebrated Ṣūfī work entitled the *Ṭarāʾiq al-ḥaqāʾiq*, participated in the first Āghā Khān's burial ceremony in Bombay in Jumādā I 1298/April 1881.[152]

Āghā Khān I lived peacefully at Maḥallāt for about two years following his dismissal from Kirmān and the failure of the first stage of his rebellion. Soon rumours spread that the Āghā Khān was collecting men and material in order to resume his revolt. The Āghā Khān attributed the origin of these rumours to ʿAbd al-Muḥammad Maḥallātī, who in vain had sought the imām's daughter in marriage for his son.[153] Be it as it may, the Āghā Khān was then actually gathering an army of mercenaries in Maḥallāt, comprised of Nizārīs and non-Nizārīs. Early in 1256/1840, Muḥammad Shāh himself went to Dilījān near Maḥallāt, on the pretence of recreation, to verify the truth of the alarming reports about the Āghā Khān's activities. At the time, the imām was away on a hunting trip, but he did send a messenger to Ḥājjī Mīrzā Āqāsī requesting the permission of the monarch to proceed to Mecca for the *ḥajj* pilgrimage. Royal permission was granted, and initially the Āghā Khān's mother and a few relatives were despatched to the *ʿatabāt*, viz., Najaf and other holy cities of ʿIrāq containing the shrines of the Shīʿī Imāms. The Āghā Khān himself left Maḥallāt, ostensibly to proceed to the Ḥijāz, early in Rajab 1256/September 1840. He was accompanied by his brothers, nephews, and a number of other relatives, dependants and many followers.[154]

Before leaving Maḥallāt, the Āghā Khān seems to have equipped himself with letters appointing him to the governorship of Kirmān.[155] At any rate, instead of going to Bandar ʿAbbās on the Persian Gulf for travelling to Arabia, the Āghā Khān headed for Yazd, where he intended to be reinforced by the local Nizārī ʿAṭāʾ Allāhīs. As he approached Yazd, the Āghā Khān sent the city's governor, Bahman Mīrzā Bahāʾ al-Dawla, the documents that reinstated him in the governorship of Kirmān. Accepting the documents as genuine, Bahman Mīrzā offered the Āghā Khān lodging in the city. However, the Āghā Khān declined the invitation, stating that he wanted to visit the Nizārī ʿAṭāʾ Allāhīs living around Yazd. Whilst he was staying in Mahrīz near Yazd, Bahman Mīrzā was informed through the despatches of Ḥājjī Mīrzā Āqāsī of the spuriousness of the Āghā Khān's documents. In the battle that ensued, Bahman Mīrzā was defeated by the Āghā Khān. Several other minor battles were won by the Āghā Khān before he arrived in Shahr-i Bābak, which he intended to use as his base of operations for seizing Kirmān. Shahr-i Bābak, as noted, was a stronghold of ʿAṭāʾ Allāhī and Khurāsānī tribesmen who accepted the Āghā Khān as their imām. At the time, the citadel at Shahr-i Bābak was in the hands of Kuhandil Khān and his associates from Qandahār, who had sought refuge in Persia after the British invasion of Afghanistan. The Afghans had made themselves quite unpopular in the locality, and the Āghā Khān's arrival there coincided with the campaign of a former local governor, Ḥājjī Muḥammad ʿAlī, to dislodge them from the citadel of

Shahr-i Bābak. The Āghā Khān, joined by a large number of ʿAṭā' Allāhīs and Khurāsānīs, participated in the siege of Shahr-i Bābak, forcing the Afghans to surrender.[156]

The Āghā Khān then despatched his brother Muḥammad Bāqir Khān to Sīrjān to secure provisions, and himself retreated to Rūmanī, a village near Shahr-i Bābak. By then, Faḍl ʿAlī Khān Qarabāghī, the governor of Kirmān, had been ordered by Tehran to deal with the Āghā Khān. Accordingly, the *beglerbegi* of Kirmān besieged Muḥammad Bāqir Khān in the fortress of Zaydābād in Sīrjān. The Āghā Khān set out in person at the head of his army to relieve his brother, and succeeded in evacuating him and his troops from Sīrjān. The Āghā Khān then headed towards Fārs and spent the winter months in Mīnāb, near Bandar ʿAbbās. It was at that time that the Āghā Khān acquired two cannons of British provenance, which gave him an effective advantage in subsequent clashes with the government troops.[157]

Soon after Muḥarram 1257/March 1841, the Āghā Khān set out once more in the direction of Kirmān. Sardār Abu'l-Ḥasan Khān was despatched to seize Dashtāb, where he was subsequently joined by the Āghā Khān. It was near Dashtāb that the Āghā Khān defeated a government force of 4,000 men under the command of Isfandiyār Khān, the brother of Faḍl ʿAlī Khān. Isfandiyār Khān himself was killed and many of his men went over to the Āghā Khān, who won a number of further victories against the government troops before resting for a while at Bam. By that time, Faḍl ʿAlī Khān had collected a force of 24,000 men, obliging the Āghā Khān to flee from Bam to Rīgān on the border of Balūchistān. There, a decisive defeat was inflicted on the Āghā Khān, who was greatly outnumbered by the forces of the *beglerbegi* of Kirmān. Thereupon, the Āghā Khān decided to seek refuge either in India or Arabia. As the way to the port of Bandar ʿAbbās was then blocked, the Āghā Khān decided to escape overland, through southern Khurāsān, to Afghanistan. Starting at Rāwar, he traversed the arid Dasht-i Lūt to Sarbīsha, southeast of Bīrjand. Accompanied by his brothers and many soldiers and servants, the Āghā Khān then proceeded eastwards, and, after crossing the border, arrived at Lāsh va Juvayn in Afghanistan in 1257/1841.[158] This marked the end of the Persian period of the Nizārī Ismāʿīlī Imāmate.

Once inside Afghanistan, Āghā Khān Maḥallātī advanced by way of Girishk to Qandahār, the major city of western Afghanistan which had been occupied by an Anglo-Indian army in 1254/1839. Henceforth, a close association developed between the Āghā Khān and the British, who may possibly have encouraged his earlier rebellious activities in Persia in the interest of safeguarding British rule in India. More specifically, it has been contended that the Āghā Khān's revolt in Kirmān played an effective part in preventing the success of the Persian campaign against Harāt conducted during the reign of Muḥammad Shāh Qājār.[159] Be it as it may, the Āghā Khān's association with the British after his arrival in Afghanistan, coinciding with the final years of the period of the so-called First Afghan War, 1838–1842, is openly recorded in his autobiography and elsewhere. From Girishk, the Āghā Khān had sent notices of his impending arrival to Muḥammad Tīmūr, the British-appointed governor of Qandahār, and to Major Henry Rawlinson, the local British political agent. The latter had been in Persia during 1833–1839 and may have made the personal acquaintance of the Āghā Khān at Muḥammad Shāh's coronation ceremonies in Tehran. Rawlinson granted the Āghā Khān a daily stipend of one hundred rupees for the duration of his stay in Qandahār. Soon after his arrival in Qandahār in the summer of 1257/1841,[160] the Āghā Khān wrote to Sir William Macnaghten, the British political agent in Kābul who was later murdered by the Afghans in December 1841, discussing his future plans. He now proposed to seize and govern Harāt on behalf of the British and their puppet, Shāh Shujāʿ al-Mulk, who had been temporarily placed on the throne of Kābul in 1255/1839 in succession to the rebellious Dūst Muḥammad, the founder of Bārakzāy rule in Afghanistan. The proposal was apparently approved, but soon all British designs in Afghanistan were frustrated by the uprising of Dūst Muḥammad's son Muḥammad Akbar Khān, who in January 1842 annihilated the British-Indian garrison on its retreat from Kābul. The uprising extended to Qandahār, and in the ensuing clashes the Āghā Khān aided General William Nott in evacuating the British forces from Qandahār in July 1842. The Āghā Khān himself soon headed southwards to Sind. He left his brother Sardār Abu'l-Ḥasan Khān behind in Qandahār, where the imām had been visited during his stay by Nizārī deputations from Kābul, Badakhshān, Bukhārā, and Sind.

Āghā Khān I rendered further services to the British in Sind.[161] In particular, he placed his cavalry at their disposal and endeavoured to convince Nāṣir Khān, the Tālpur *amīr* of Kalāt, to cede Karachi to the British. As Nāṣir Khān refused to co-operate, the Āghā Khān disclosed his battle plans to Major James Outram, the British political agent in Sind. As a result, the British camp was saved from a night attack, and, following the battle of Miyānī in February 1843, Ḥaydarābād and then all of Sind became annexed to British India. For his services in Sind, the Āghā Khān received an annual pension of £2,000 from General Charles Napier, the British conqueror of Sind who maintained a friendly relationship with the Nizārī Imām from the time of the latter's arrival in Sind in the autumn of 1842.

After the conquest of Sind in 1259/1843, the British attempted to subjugate neighbouring Balūchistān; the Āghā Khān again helped them militarily and diplomatically. From Jerruck, where he was staying after February 1843, the Āghā Khān contacted the various Balūchī chieftains and advised them to submit to British rule. He also despatched his brother Muḥammad Bāqir Khān together with a number of his horsemen in order to help the British defeat Mīr Shīr Khān, one of the important Balūchī *amīrs*. Meanwhile, the Āghā Khān himself became the target of a Balūchī raid, perhaps in reprisal for his assistance to the British, and his possessions were plundered. However, he continued to help the British, always hoping that they would arrange for his safe return to Persia. It was with the approval of the British, and perhaps on their behalf, that in Rabīʿ I 1260/ April 1844 the Āghā Khān sent Muḥammad Bāqir Khān to capture the fortress of Bampūr (Banfahl), in Persian Balūchistān. Later, he despatched his other brother, Sardār Abu'l-Ḥasan Khān, who finally occupied Bampūr and won other military successes in Balūchistān while Muḥammad Bāqir Khān was relieved to join the Āghā Khān in India.[162]

After controlling certain parts of Balūchistān for about two years, Sardār Abu'l-Ḥasan Khān was defeated in battle in 1262/1846 by a Qājār army sent against him from Kirmān. The Āghā Khān's brother was taken as a prisoner to Tehran, where he arrived in Rajab 1262 A.H. After spending some time in detention, Sardār Abu'l-Ḥasan Khān was pardoned by Nāṣir al-Dīn Shāh Qājār (1264–1313/1848–1896), Muḥammad Shāh's son and successor. Impressed by the Sardār's military and hunting expertise, the Qājār monarch subsequently received him amongst his entourage and gave him a Qājār princess, Mihr-i Jahān Khānum, in marriage. Sardār Abu'l-Ḥasan Khān spent the remainder of his life in Persia, managing the family lands in Maḥallāt and occasionally performing services for the Āghā Khān. He died in 1297/1880 and was buried in the mausoleum of his father, Imām Shāh Khalīl Allāh III, at Najaf. Sardār Abu'l-Ḥasan Khān's son, Mīrzā Ismāʿīl Khān Iʿtibār al-Salṭana (d. 1346/ 1928), the author's maternal great-grandfather, also received the favour of Nāṣir al-Dīn Shāh and handled the affairs of the Āghā Khān's properties in Maḥallāt and Kirmān. A number of the descendants of Sardār Abu'l-

Ḥasan Khān, through Iʿtibār al-Salṭana and other sons and daughters, are still living in Tehran and Maḥallāt.

In the meantime, in Ramaḍān 1260/October 1844, Āghā Khān I had left Sind via the port of Karachi for Bombay.[163] He passed through Cutch and Kathiawar, where he arrived in Muḥarram 1261/January 1845. He spent a year at Kathiawar and visited the Nizārī communities of the area, as he had done all along his route. He then travelled through Sūrat and Daman, and arrived in Bombay in Ṣafar 1262/February 1846. Soon after his arrival in Bombay, the Persian government, then still controlled by the chief minister Ḥājjī Mīrzā Āqāsī, demanded the Āghā Khān's extradition from India, citing the Anglo-Persian Treaty of 1229/1814.[164] The British, however, refused to comply and only promised to transfer the Āghā Khān's residence to Calcutta, farther removed from Persia where it would be more difficult for him to launch new activities against the Persian government. Meanwhile, the British entered into a series of negotiations with the Persian government for the safe return of the Āghā Khān to Persia, which was the imām's own wish. In Ṣafar 1263/February 1847, Justin Sheil, the British minister in Tehran, forwarded yet another unsuccessful appeal to this effect on behalf of the Governor-General of India. Ḥājjī Mīrzā Āqāsī now consented to the Āghā Khān's return to Persia, on the condition that he would avoid passing through Balūchistān and Kirmān, where he could start new anti-government activities. Furthermore, the Āghā Khān was to settle down peacefully in Maḥallāt.

Āghā Khān Maḥallātī was eventually obliged, in Jumādā I 1263/April 1847, to leave for Calcutta, where he remained until receiving the news of the death of Muḥammad Shāh Qājār in Dhu'l-Ḥijja 1264/November 1848, which had actually occurred two months earlier. Hoping that Muḥammad Shāh's successor Nāṣir al-Dīn Shāh would be more lenient towards him, the Āghā Khān left Calcutta for Bombay in Muḥarram 1265/December 1848. On arriving in Bombay a few weeks later, the British made new efforts to win permission for his return to Persia, while the Āghā Khān himself wrote a letter on the subject to Nāṣir al-Dīn Shāh's first chief minister, Amīr Kabīr. Amīr Kabīr proved even less responsive than his predecessor, insisting that the Āghā Khān would be arrested at the borders as a fugitive.[165] After the downfall and execution of Amīr Kabīr in 1268/1852, the Āghā Khān made a final plea from Bombay to return to his ancestral homeland, and sent Nāṣir al-Dīn Shāh an elephant and a giraffe as gifts.[166] He also sent presents to Amīr Kabīr's successor Mīrzā Āqā Khān Nūrī, who was a personal friend of the Āghā Khān. Some of the imām's family lands in Persia were now restored to the control of his relatives, but the new chief minister was unable to arrange for his return. By then, the Nizārī Imām had resigned himself to permanent residence in India, though he maintained his contacts with the Qājār court and sent Nāṣir al-Dīn Shāh another gift of three elephants and a rhinoceros in 1284/1867–1868.[167] Still later in 1287/1870, when Nāṣir al-Dīn Shāh was on pilgrimage to the Shīʿī shrines in ʿIrāq, Āghā Khān I sent one of his sons, Jalāl Shāh, with a number of presents including a hunting rifle, to the Qājār monarch in Baghdād.[168] As an indication of royal favour towards the Āghā Khān, Nāṣir al-Dīn Shāh had now consented to give one of his daughters in marriage to Jalāl Shāh who accompanied the monarch to Tehran. However, the youthful Jalāl Shāh was taken ill and died in Tehran the following year.

Āghā Khān Maḥallātī's settlement in Bombay in effect initiated the modern period in the history of Nizārī Ismāʿīlism. The Nizārī Imāmate was now transferred, after almost seven centuries, from Persia to India, and henceforth Bombay became the seat of the Qāsim-Shāhī Nizārī Imāms. Āghā Khān I was the first imām of his line to set foot in India and his presence there was greatly rejoiced by the Nizārī Khojas who gathered enthusiastically to his side to pay their homage and receive his blessings. The Nizārīs of many regions had regularly visited the Āghā Khān and given him their tributes when he was in Persia or wandering in Afghanistan and Sind. However, the Khojas had for several centuries comprised the most important section of the Nizārī community, and they often found it difficult to make the hazardous journey to Anjudān, Kahak, Shahr-i Bābak, Kirmān, or Maḥallāt, to see the imām. When the Nizārī Khojas found direct access to the imām for the first time, they more readily began to send their religious dues to his *durkhana* (Persian, *darb-i khāna*), or chief place of residence, in Bombay. As a result, the Āghā Khān was enabled to establish elaborate headquarters and residences in Bombay, Poona and Bangalore. He also supported numerous relatives, who gradually joined him in Bombay, and a large retinue of attendants and servants who were lodged in suitable living quarters. Āghā Khān I attended the *jamāʿat-khāna* in Bombay on special religious occasions, and led the public prayers of the Khojas there. Every Saturday when in Bombay, he held *durbar* (Persian, *darbār*), giving audience to his followers who received his blessings. In India, the Āghā Khān retained his close association with the British, and on a rare occasion he was visited in his Bombay home, the Aga Hall, by the Prince of Wales when the future King Edward VII (1901–

1910) was on a state visit to India. Āghā Khān I also came to be addressed as His Highness by the British.

Āghā Khān I received government protection in British India as the spiritual head of a Muslim sect, which strengthened his position and helped him in the exercise of his authority. During three decades of residency in Bombay, he succeeded in exerting a great degree of direct control over the Indian Nizārīs, who had remained without any *pīr* or chief representative of the imām for quite some time. He also organized the Nizārī Khojas more tightly through the network of officers called *mukhi*, treasurer, and *kamdia* or *kamadia* (pronounced *kāmriyā* or *kāmariyā*), accountant, who were often appointed by the Āghā Khān himself, especially in the case of Bombay and other major Khoja centres. The *mukhi* normally acted as the social and religious head of any local Khoja congregation or *jamāʿat*, and he was assisted by a *kamadia*. These functionaries were found in every Khoja *jamāʿat*, who also possessed a *jamāʿat-khāna* or assembly hall. The *mukhi*s and *kamadia*s also collected the religious dues, notably the *dassondh* or tithe, and forwarded the funds to the imām, who was addressed as Sarkār Ṣāḥib and Pīr Salāmat by his Indian followers.

The first Āghā Khān established his religious authority in India after some difficulties. He did, in fact, face periodical troubles from certain dissident members of the Khoja community.[169] In 1829, while the Āghā Khān was still in Persia, some Nizārī Khojas of Bombay had refused to pay the customary *dassondh* to him. As a result, the Āghā Khān sent to Bombay a special representative, accompanied by his maternal grandmother, who filed a suit against the dissidents in the Bombay High Court. The suit was withdrawn in 1830. But the recusants were summoned before the *jamāʿat-khāna* in Bombay and, since they persisted in their refusal to pay the dues, they were outcast by the whole Khoja *jamāʿat* assembled there for the occasion. The dissidents, headed by a certain Ḥabīb Ibrāhīm, became known as the Barbhai, or the twelve brethren, because they were originally twelve in number. They were readmitted in 1835 to the Khoja *jamāʿat* of Bombay on the payment of their arrears. The Barbhai had, however, laid the foundation of a dissident party which subsequently posed doctrinal and financial objections to the position of the Āghā Khāns. In 1847, when the imām was in Calcutta, another conflict broke out in the Khoja community of Bombay. A legal case was initiated by two Khoja sisters for a share in their deceased father's estate against the will of the deceased. In this litigation, the Āghā Khān, then represented in court by his brother Muḥammad Bāqir Khān (d. 1296/1879), upheld the rules of female inheritance as laid down in Islamic law, while his Barbhai opponents supported the Khoja custom that essentially deprived the females from such inheritance. In the resulting judgement, Sir Erskine Perry, the presiding judge, ruled that the custom of the Khojas should prevail even though it might be in conflict with the provisions of Islamic law. This judgement in effect recognized the Khojas as a distinct community. In view of their unwillingness to acknowledge the imām's leadership, Ḥabīb Ibrāhīm and his supporters were again excommunicated in 1848. The Barbhai dissidents, with their tacit Sunnī leanings, now seceded from the Khoja community and established themselves in a separate *jamāʿat-khāna* in Bombay, but in Mahim they used the upper floor of the existing *jamāʿat-khāna* while the Khoja followers of the Āghā Khān held the lower floor. It was at the *jamāʿat-khāna* of Mahim that, in 1267/1850, four members of the Barbhai party were murdered by the Khojas loyal to the Āghā Khān. Nineteen Khojas were brought to trial for this murder, and four of them were sentenced to death. Later, the Barbhai dissidents were once again admitted into the Nizārī Khoja *jamāʿat* of Bombay.

It was under such circumstances that the Āghā Khān decided in 1861 to secure what amounted to a pledge of loyalty to himself and to the Nizārī religion, from the members of the Khoja community. He circulated a document in the Bombay *jamāʿat* summarizing the practices of the Nizārī Shīʿīs, especially regarding marriage, ablution and funeral rites, and requiring all those in agreement to sign it. The document, copies of which were sent to the Nizārīs of other places in India and elsewhere, was issued because there had appeared in print statements representing the Khojas as Sunnīs, alleging that the Āghā Khān had been attempting by coercion to make them Shīʿīs. In opposition to this document, the dissenting Khojas of the Barbhai party held that the Khojas had always been Sunnīs and that no Shīʿī, including the Nizārī Imām, could be entitled to any share or voice in the management of the public property belonging to the Khoja community. As a result, the Barbhai party was again outcast in 1862 by the unanimous vote of all the Khojas assembled in the *jamāʿat-khāna* of Bombay. Matters came to a head in 1866 when the dissenting Khojas filed a suit in the Bombay High Court against the Āghā Khān, emphasizing that the Khojas had been Sunnīs from the beginning, since their conversion from Hinduism to Islam by Pīr Ṣadr al-Dīn. More specifically, the Barbhai plaintiffs, led by Ḥabīb Ibrāhīm's son Ahmed Habibbhai, demanded that an account be made of all the communal property and dues collected from the Khojas; that the property of the community be held in trust for charitable, religious and public uses for the sole benefit of the Khojas and that no Shīʿī person be entitled to any share or interest in them; that the *mukhi*s and *kamadia*s be elected periodically; and that the Āghā Khān refrain from interfering in the management of communal property, appointing the functionaries of the Khoja *jamāʿat*s, excommunicating any Khojas from the community, and charging fees for the discharge of his functions as spiritual leader. This case, generally known as the Aga Khan Case, was heard by Sir Joseph Arnould. After a hearing of several weeks, in the course of which the Āghā Khān himself testified and the history of the Khoja community was fully reviewed, in November 1866 Justice Arnould rendered a detailed judgement against the plaintiffs and in favour of the Āghā Khān and other defendants on all points.[170] This judgement legally established the status of the Khojas as a community of Nizārīs, referred to as 'Shia Imami Ismailis', and of the Āghā Khān as the *murshid* or spiritual head of that community and heir in lineal descent to the imāms of Alamūt. It also established, for the first time in a British court, the rights of the Āghā Khān to all the customary dues collected from the Khojas, and placed all the community property of the Nizārī Ismāʿīlīs in his name and under his absolute control. The first Āghā Khān's authority was never seriously challenged again.

Āghā Khān Maḥallātī spent his final years peacefully in Bombay, with seasonal stays in Poona. He had maintained excellent stables and became a familiar figure in the Bombay racecourse. Āghā Khān I's interest in horse racing and horse breeding was retained and further developed in Europe by his successors. Muḥammad Ḥasan al-Ḥusaynī (Ḥasan ʿAlī Shāh), Āghā Khān I, the forty-sixth Qāsim-Shāhī Nizārī Imām, died after an eventful imāmate of sixty-four years in Jumādā I 1298/April 1881. He was buried in a specially erected shrine at Ḥasanābād in the Mazagon area of Bombay. Āghā Khān I married seven times and was survived by three sons, Āqā ʿAlī Shāh, Āqā Jangī Shāh, and Āqā Akbar Shāh, and five daughters.

Āghā Khān I was succeeded as imām by his eldest son Āqā ʿAlī Shāh, his only son by Sarv-i Jahān Khānum.[171] Āqā ʿAlī Shāh, who became known as Āghā Khān II, was born in 1246/1830 at Maḥallāt, where he spent his early years. At the beginning of Āghā Khān I's rebellion in 1256/1840, ʿAlī Shāh was taken to ʿIrāq where he stayed for a few years with his mother and studied Arabic, Persian and the doctrines of the Nizārīs. During the late 1840s, Āqā ʿAlī Shāh was apparently permitted by the Qājār regime to take up temporary residence in Persia and assume certain responsibilities on behalf of his father. Sarv-i Jahān Khānum (d. 1299/1882) and ʿAlī Shāh eventually joined Āghā Khān I in Bombay in 1269/1853. Henceforth, ʿAlī Shāh, as the imām's heir apparent, regularly visited different Nizārī Khoja communities, especially in Sind and Kathiawar, and organized their *jamāʿat-khānas*. Āqā ʿAlī Shāh in fact lived for some time in Karachi, where his third son and future successor was born in 1294/1877.

On succeeding to the imāmate in 1298/1881, Āghā Khān II maintained the friendly relations that his father had cultivated with the British. He was appointed to the Bombay Legislative Council when Sir James Fergusson was the governor of Bombay. Āghā Khān II was distinctly concerned about the welfare of the Nizārī Khojas and opened a number of schools for the Khoja children in Bombay and elsewhere, also assisting needy Khoja families. During his brief imāmate, ʿAlī Shāh increased his contacts with the Nizārī communities outside of the Indian subcontinent, showing particular interest in his followers in the upper Oxus districts, Burma and East Africa. The growing prosperity of the Nizārī Khoja community and his own policies earned Āghā Khān II prestige among the Muslim population of India. He was elected president of a body called the Muhammadan National Association. In that position, which he held until his death, Āghā Khān II promoted educational and philanthropic institutions for the benefit of the Indian Muslims.

Āqā ʿAlī Shāh, like his father, was closely associated with the Niʿmat Allāhī order.[172] Before going to India, he had developed close ties with Raḥmat ʿAlī Shāh, the *quṭb* of one of the branches of this Ṣūfī *ṭarīqa* who had been Āghā Khān I's guest in Maḥallāt in 1249/1833. Subsequently, Āqā ʿAlī Shāh maintained his friendship with Raḥmat ʿAlī, and after Raḥmat's death in 1278/1861, he regularly sent money from India for the recitation of the Qur'ān at the Ṣūfī master's grave in Shīrāz. ʿAlī Shāh maintained close relations also with Raḥmat ʿAlī's uncle and one of his successors as *quṭb*, Munawwar ʿAlī Shāh (d. 1301/1884). He entertained several notable Persian Niʿmat Allāhīs in Bombay, including Raḥmat ʿAlī's son Muḥammad Maʿṣūm Shīrāzī, Nā'ib al-Ṣadr (d. 1344/1926), the author of the *Ṭarā'iq al-ḥaqā'iq*. This Ṣūfī, carrying the *ṭarīqa* name of Maʿṣūm ʿAlī Shāh, visited India in 1298/1881 and stayed with Āqā ʿAlī Shāh for an entire year. Ṣafī ʿAlī Shāh (d. 1316/1898), the eponymous founder of one of the most important branches of the order, was another outstanding Niʿmat Allāhī to enjoy ʿAlī Shāh's hospitality in Bombay. In 1280/1863 he went to India, for the first time, at the invitation of ʿAlī Shāh.

On his second visit a few years later, Ṣafī ʿAlī Shāh spent four years in India, during which time he completed and lithographed his well-known versified Ṣūfī work, the *Zubdat al-asrār*, at Āghā Khān II's request. On his return to Persia, Ṣafī ʿAlī spent some time in ʿIrāq, staying at the Aghā Khān's houses in Najaf and Karbalāʾ and winning the approval of certain local Ithnāʿasharī *ʿulamāʾ* for ʿAlī Shāh's marriage to a Qājār princess, Shams al-Mulūk. The *ʿulamāʾ* had previously raised objections to this marriage on account of ʿAlī Shāh's Ismāʿīlī faith.

Shams al-Mulūk, the daughter of Mīrzā ʿAlī Muḥammad Niẓām al-Dawla by one of Fatḥ ʿAlī Shāh's daughters, became ʿAlī Shāh's third wife and bore him his sole surviving son and successor, Sulṭān Muḥammad Shāh. Both of ʿAlī Shāh's sons by a previous marriage predeceased him. His eldest son, Shihāb al-Dīn Shāh, also known as Khalīl Allāh, who was expected to succeed to the imāmate, was born around 1268/1851–1852. He acquired some learning and composed a few treatises in Persian dealing with the doctrines of the Nizārī Ismāʿīlīs.[173] Shihāb al-Dīn Shāh died in Ṣafar 1302/December 1884, and was taken for burial to Najaf. Shihāb al-Dīn's only son, Abu'l-Ḥasan, too, died shortly afterwards; he was buried at the mausoleum in Ḥasanābād next to Āghā Khān I. Shihāb al-Dīn Shāh's full-brother, Nūr al-Dīn Shāh, was killed in his youth early in 1302 A.H. in a riding accident at Poona. Āqā ʿAlī Shāh, Āghā Khān II, the forty-seventh imām of the Qāsim-Shāhī Nizārīs, was also a sportsman and a hunter, with particular renown for his tiger hunting in India. After an imāmate of four years, he died in Dhu'l-Qaʿda 1302/August 1885 of pneumonia contracted in a day's hunting near Poona. Āghā Khān II's body was later buried in the family mausoleum in Najaf.

Āghā Khān II was succeeded by his sole surviving son Sulṭān Muḥammad Shāh al-Ḥusaynī, Āghā Khān III, whose life is well documented.[174] Born in Karachi in Shawwāl 1294/November 1877, he was eight years-old when installed in 1302/1885 at Bombay as the forty-eighth Qāsim-Shāhī Nizārī Imām. His nominal guardian was his uncle Āqā Jangī Shāh, but the Āghā Khān grew up under the close supervision of his capable mother, Shams al-Mulūk, known as Lady ʿAlī Shāh in the social circles of British India. Until the age of eighteen, Āghā Khān III received a rigorous education in Bombay and Poona under the guidance of his mother, taking lessons in Arabic, Persian literature, Ismāʿīlī doctrine, and calligraphy. During the imām's youth, Lady ʿAlī Shāh played an active part in the administration of the affairs of the Nizārī community through a council, also investing the family wealth shrewdly. Lady ʿAlī Shāh, who had a lasting influence on her son, died in 1356/1938 and was buried next to the tomb of her husband in Najaf. Āghā Khān III's closest childhood companions were his cousins Āqā Shams al-Dīn and ʿAbbās, sons of Āqā Jangī Shāh; he was greatly disturbed when Jangī Shāh and ʿAbbās were murdered in 1314/1896, under obscure circumstances, at Jidda. Jangī Shāh and his family had gone for pilgrimage to Mecca, and the murderers, who were apparently religious fanatics, did not live long enough to divulge the names of the instigators of their crime.[175] The young Āghā Khān was shocked again when his nephew Hāshim Shāh, son of his half-brother Nūr al-Dīn Shāh, was assassinated in 1316/1898 at Poona by a family steward.[176] In 1315/1897, Āghā Khān III married his cousin Shahzāda Begum, one of Jangī Shāh's daughters who had witnessed the murders at Jidda. This marriage, which lasted briefly, was the first of his four marriages.

In 1898, Āghā Khān III set out from Bombay on his first journey to Europe, which later became his chief place of residence. He visited France and Britain, where he dined with Queen Victoria at Windsor Castle, and met the future King Edward VII, who was to become his friend. On his return journey to India, he paid the first of several visits to the Nizārī Khojas of East Africa. Soon after, the Āghā Khān travelled to Burma and met his followers there. On his second European journey in 1900, the Āghā Khān made the acquaintance of Nāṣir al-Dīn Shāh's son and successor Muẓaffar al-Dīn Shāh Qājār (1313–1324/1896–1907), who was in Paris at the time. By then, the old animosities between the Nizārī Imāms and the Qājār dynasty of Persia had been forgotten, and the Persian monarch gave valuable gifts and one of his highest decorations to the Āghā Khān. However, the Āghā Khān, who remained aware of his Persian and Qājār ancestry, was disturbed by Muẓaffar al-Dīn Shāh's childish disposition and political incompetence.[177] On that journey, he also met Kaiser William II in Potsdam and Sultan ʿAbd al-Ḥamīd II in Istanbul, which was a historic meeting between an Ismāʿīlī Imām and a Sunnī ruler claiming the heritage of the ʿAbbāsid caliphs.

Āghā Khān III returned once again to Europe in 1902 as the personal guest of Edward VII at his coronation, and the new Emperor King advanced the Nizārī Imām from the rank of Knight (K.C.I.E.) to that of Grand Knight Commander of the Indian Empire (G.C.I.E.) in his coronation honours.[178] The Āghā Khān returned to India in November 1902, and, as a further sign of esteem in which he was now held by the British, he was appointed by Lord Curzon, the Viceroy of India, to a seat on his Legislative Council. He served two years on that council in Calcutta, then the seat of British power in India. The Āghā Khān paid another visit to Europe in 1904, and in 1905 he saw his followers in East Africa for the second time. While the Āghā Khān was in East Africa, a suit was filed against him in the Bombay High Court by certain discontented members of his family led by Ḥājjī Bībī, a daughter of Jangī Shāh, and her son Ṣamad Shāh. The litigants had certain financial grievances regarding their shares in the estate of Āghā Khān I, and they also raised claims to the current Āghā Khān's income and status. After lengthy hearings, Justice Russell, the presiding judge, ruled against the plaintiffs, confirming the Āghā Khān's rights to the estate of his grandfather and to the offerings made to him by the Nizārīs. This ruling also established that the Nizārī Khojas were distinct from the Shīʿīs of the Ithnāʿasharī school.[179] From 1907 onwards, the Āghā Khān visited Europe every year, and eventually established his chief places of residence there. Gradually, he came to know most of the royal families of Europe and that continent's foremost political figures and artists. In 1908, he married Mlle Theresa Magliano (d. 1926) in Cairo. She bore Aly Khan, the first of Āghā Khān III's two surviving sons, in 1911 in Turin, her native city.

Meanwhile, the Āghā Khān had increasingly concerned himself with the affairs of the Muslim community of India, beyond the immediate interests of his own followers. As a result, he gained much popularity amongst the Indian Muslims and their spokesmen. He participated actively in the first All-India Muslim Educational Conference, held at Bombay in 1903, and became the president of the second one, held at Delhi the following year. In 1906, he headed the Muslim delegation that met with Lord Minto at Simla, asking the Viceroy to regard the Indian Muslims not as a minority but as a nation within a nation whose members deserved adequate representation on both local and legislative councils of the land. In 1907, he joined in the founding of the All-India Muslim League, and served as the permanent president of that body until he resigned from the position in 1912. The Āghā Khān campaigned most energetically for various educational projects, for Khojas and other Indian Muslims. He played a leading part in the elevation of the Muhammadan Anglo-Oriental College at Aligarh to university status, a measure that came about in 1912.[180] In the same year, King George V, who had gone to India for his coronation *durbar*, bestowed upon the Āghā Khān the highest decoration that could be given to any Indian subject of the British Empire, making him a Knight Grand Commander of the Star of India (G.C.S.I.).

In 1914, Āghā Khān III paid his second visit to Burma and advised his followers there to adopt measures, such as giving up their Indo-Muslim names and habits, that would facilitate their socio-cultural assimilation in Burma.[181] In later years, the Āghā Khān recommended similar assimilatory measures to his followers in other parts of the world; a policy designed to reduce the local difficulties of the Nizārīs who lived as minorities in many countries.

On the outbreak of World War I, the Āghā Khān went to Europe and offered his services to the British government, also urging his followers to aid the British authorities in their territories. For his valuable services, the Āghā Khān was accorded in 1916 the status of a first-class ruling prince of the Bombay Presidency, although unlike other native rulers of India he did not possess a territorial principality. In the same year, the Āghā Khān lost a cousin in the pursuit of his pro-British policies during the war. He had despatched Āqā Farrukh Shāh, the son of Āqā Akbar Shāh (d. 1322/1904), on a pro-Allies political mission to the tribesmen and the Nizārīs of Kirmān, where he was assassinated at the instigation of German agents.[182] In 1917, the German agents evidently made an unsuccessful attempt on the life of the Āghā Khān himself in Switzerland. Suffering from an illness that prevented him from undertaking any political activity, the Āghā Khān rested in Switzerland for three years until 1919, during which time he wrote a book setting forth his views on the future of India.[183]

For a decade after World War I, the Aghā Khān stayed away from the international and Indian political scenes, devoting his time mainly to the affairs of his Nizārī followers. Having established permanent homes in Switzerland and the French Riviera, he now visited India every year. Soon, he also acquired an international fame for owning, breeding and racing horses. In 1928, the Āghā Khān presided over the All-India Muslim Conference held at Delhi, which was to formulate Muslim views on how independence should evolve for India. Under the guidance of the Āghā Khān, the assembly demanded guaranteed rights for Indian Muslims in the framework of a federal and self-governing India.[184] In 1930, he led the Muslim delegation to the first Round Table Conference that was convened in London to consider the future of India. Muhammad Ali Jinnah, who came from a Khoja family and later became the founder of the state of Pakistan, was amongst the other members of this Muslim delegation. In the course of the second Round Table Conference, held in London in 1931, Āghā Khān III had lengthy discussion sessions with Mahatma Gandhi who was then the sole representative of the Congress Party. These conferences, lasting until 1934, marked the climax of the Āghā Khān's involvement in Indian politics. Soon afterwards, at the insistence of his Indian followers, the Āghā Khān approached the government of India and asked to be given a territorial state, like other ruling princes of the land. This petition was, however, rejected.[185] Meanwhile, the Āghā Khān had served, since 1932, as India's delegate at the Disarmament Conference and at successive sessions of the Assembly of the League of Nations in Geneva. The Āghā Khān's involvement in international affairs at Geneva culminated in his election in 1937 as president of the League of Nations for a session.

In 1929, the Āghā Khān had married his third wife, Mlle Andrée Carron, who bore his second son Ṣadr al-Dīn in 1933. In 1935, he celebrated the golden jubilee of his imāmate in Bombay and Nairobi. By then, Āghā Khān III had been the imām of the Nizārīs for half a century and the celebrations culminated in the weighing of the imām against gold. In 1936, Aly Khan married Mrs Loel Guiness, formerly the Hon. Joan Yarde-Buller, a daughter of Lord Churston. On 13 December 1936, she bore Aly Khan's first of two sons, Karīm, who was to succeed his grandfather in the imāmate.

The outbreak of World War II found the Āghā Khān in Switzerland, where he once again urged his followers everywhere to support the British cause in the war. The Āghā Khān spent the war years in Geneva, where he divorced his third wife in 1943. In the following year, he married his fourth and last wife, Mlle Yvette Labrousse, who became known as the Begum Aga Khan. The sixtieth anniversary of the Āghā Khān's imāmate was celebrated, with a year's delay, in Bombay in 1946, when he was weighed against diamonds rented by the community for the occasion. A few months later, the diamond jubilee celebrations were repeated in Dar-es-Salaam. The platinum jubilee celebrations, marking the seventieth anniversary of Āghā Khān III's imāmate, were held during 1954–1955 in Karachi and elsewhere. These jubilee celebrations reflected the deep devotion of the Nizārīs to their present (*ḥāḍir*) imām, to whom they refer as Mawlānā Ḥāḍir Imām (Mawlana Hazar Imam). A few years earlier in 1951, Āghā Khān III had paid his first and only visit to Persia, his ancestral land, and was warmly received at Maḥallāt by thousands of his Persian followers, known generally as the Murīdān-i Āqā Khān.

During his long imāmate, Āghā Khān III devoted much of his time and financial resources to consolidating and organizing the Nizārī community, especially in India and East Africa. He was particularly concerned with introducing socio-economic reforms that would transform his Shīʿī

Muslim followers into a modern, self-sufficient community with high standards of education and welfare. The successful attainment of these objectives, however, required an appropriate administrative organization, over and beyond the existing *jamāʿat* structure of the Nizārī community; an organization through which the imām could implement his reform policies and modernize the Nizārī community without destroying the traditions and the identity of that community. The development of a new communal organization, thus, became one of Āghā Khān III's major tasks. The court decisions in Bombay had already laid the foundations in British India for the Āghā Khān's institutional and administrative reforms. They had delineated the Nizārī Khojas from those Khojas who preferred to be Sunnīs or Ithnāʿasharīs, while clarifying the status of the Āghā Khān with respect to his followers and to all the communal property. At the same time, the deep devotion of the Nizārī Khojas to their imām permitted the sectarians to readily accept the Āghā Khān's reform policies. On the basis of such assets and the existing *jamāʿat* structure of the community, and enjoying the support of the British government of India, Āghā Khān III developed an elaborate administrative system of councils for the Nizārīs of the Indian subcontinent and East Africa. The powers, functions and compositions of different categories of councils were in due course specified in written constitutions for the Āghā Khān's Nizārī followers in those regions, designated officially as the Shia Imami Ismailis. Similar constitutions were promulgated for the councils and *jamāʿat*s of India and East Africa, and when India was partitioned in 1947, a separate but still similar constitution and council system was developed for Pakistan. The workings of the Ismāʿīlī administrative system of councils can perhaps be best shown in the case of the community in East Africa, where the Nizārī Khojas have been scattered through the independent states of Kenya, Uganda and Tanzania, formerly representing three colonial territories.[186] Furthermore, East Africa provides a suitable case study for evaluating the achievements of the Nizārīs against the conditions of other Asian communities settled in the region, including the Bohras and non-Nizārī Khojas.

The Nizārī Khojas had been active as traders between western India and East Africa at least since the seventeenth century; and they began to settle permanently in the region during the earliest decades of the nineteenth century. The early Indian Nizārī immigrants came mainly from Cutch, Kathiawar, Sūrat and Bombay, located in western India, and they originally settled on the island of Zanzibar. By 1820, a small community of

Nizārī Khojas had settled in Zanzibar. They had built a *jamāʿat-khāna* on the island and the *jamāʿat*'s affairs were administered by two local functionaries, a *mukhi* and his assistant, a *kamadia*. This traditional pattern of local organization and administration, brought over from India, was in due course adopted by other Nizārī settlements in East Africa. As in the case of the Ismāʿīlī Bohras and other Asian immigrants, the Nizārī Khojas went to East Africa in large numbers after 1840, when the ʿUmānī sultan Sayyid Saʿīd transferred his capital from Muscat to Zanzibar. Sultan Saʿīd, who was interested in the development of foreign trade in his dominions, encouraged the immigration of Asian traders to Zanzibar. The settlement of Nizārī Khojas and other Indian sectarians in Zanzibar increased significantly between 1840 and the 1870s. This period of economic prosperity and trading opportunities in Zanzibar coincided with the period of improved travelling facilities between India and East Africa. At the same time, severe droughts and famines in Gujarāt induced many Khoja farmers there to join the caravans of the Khoja traders immigrating to East Africa. By the end of the nineteenth century, when the interior of East Africa was becoming more accessible through the construction of roads and railways, an increasing number of Nizārī trading establishments moved from Zanzibar to the mainland. Later, the Nizārī Khoja immigrants came to be found even in more remote rural areas of the East African mainland. By World War I, Nizārī *jamāʿats* of Indian origins existed in many parts of East Africa, while the bulk of the Nizārī settlers were concentrated in the region's growing urban areas, including Zanzibar, Mombasa, Dar-es-Salaam, Nairobi, Kampala and Tanga.

Āghā Khān III, as noted, first visited his East African followers in 1899. By that time, the Nizārīs of Zanzibar had come to experience their own internal conflicts, like the Khojas of Bombay a few decades earlier. The conflict centred around the same issues that had brought about the Arnould judgement of 1866. Some of the dissident East African Nizārīs, who raised questions regarding the Āghā Khān's claims and privileges, seceded from the community during the last quarter of the nineteenth century. The seceders mainly joined the Ithnāʿasharī Khojas of Zanzibar, who were the least organized group amongst the Asian immigrants to East Africa.[187] The imām's visit did not end the rift in the community and defections continued for a while longer. It was under such circumstances that on the occasion of his second visit to the region in 1905, the Āghā Khān issued a set of written rules and regulations that in effect comprised the first constitution of the East African Nizārī community.[188] This constitution foresaw a new administrative organization in the form of a hierarchy of councils; it also established rules for governing the personal relations in the community, especially with respect to marriage, divorce and inheritance. Around the same time, the first Ismāʿīlī council was established in Zanzibar, then the seat of the East African Nizārī community, with the local *mukhi* acting as its president. This council not only took over the administration of the local *jamāʿat-khāna* and defended its interests against the dissenters, but also supervised the affairs of the congregations on the mainland. These steps initiated the Āghā Khān's continuing programme of reorganizing and modernizing the Nizārī community of East Africa.

By the early 1920s, new centres of economic activity had appeared on mainland East Africa, where the Nizārī Khojas had gradually moved with the Āghā Khān's encouragement. Having lost its importance as the main commercial centre of the region, Zanzibar had now also ceased to be the seat of the East African Nizārī community. Accordingly, the widely scattered Nizārī congregations of the mainland had to be provided with appropriate administrative organizations of their own. It was in recognition of these changed realities that Āghā Khān III revised the first constitution in 1926, instituting separate central councils in the three territories of Tanganyika, Kenya and Uganda. The members of these councils were carefully selected by the Āghā Khān, who personally supervised much of their operations. The original council in Zanzibar continued for some time to co-ordinate the activities of the Territorial Councils in matters of common interest. These central functions were later delegated to a Supreme Council, separate from the council in Zanzibar; and subordinate committees with responsibilities in particular fields such as education, welfare and health, came to be attached to each Territorial Council. During the final three decades of Āghā Khān III's imāmate, the hierarchical system of councils, with its subsidiary bodies, was further developed on the basis of periodical revisions of the constitution for the East African Nizārī councils and *jamāʿats*; the revisions occurring in 1937, 1946, and 1954. The Constitution of 1954 was promulgated after the Āghā Khān had called a special conference of the East African councillors at Evian in 1952 to discuss the existing problems and the future prospects of the community. By that time, the East African followers of the Āghā Khān numbered to around 50,000, with almost one half of the total residing in Tanganyika.[189]

All of the Ismāʿīlī constitutions, including those pertaining to the Indian subcontinent, revolved around the person of the Āghā Khān, who acted as the religious and administrative head of the community. He was the sole person who could change or revise the constitutions. After the earliest challenges to his status, Āghā Khān III's leadership was accepted unquestionably by his followers. He remained in direct contact with many Nizārīs in different lands and guided the community frequently in the form of *firmans* (*farmāns*), or written directives read in the local *jamāʿat-khānas*. The *firmans* of the Āghā Khān guided the Nizārīs in specific directions, especially in the areas of education, social welfare, co-operative economic enterprises and female emancipation, also guiding the community in terms of religious practices, social relations, and personal conduct.[190] Numerous *firmans* dealt with the abolition of the veil (*pardah* or *chādur*), worn until recent times by Nizārī women, like other women in many parts of the Muslim world, and the participation of the Nizārī women in communal affairs.

Āghā Khān III increasingly utilized the offerings submitted to him, including the tithes and the funds collected at the jubilee celebrations, for the implementation of socio-economic policies and projects that would benefit his followers. At the same time, he created a number of financial institutions which acted as vehicles for the realization of his multi-purpose programmes. In East Africa, the Āghā Khān founded an insurance company in 1935, and an investment trust company in 1946. The latter body and its subsidiaries provided loans, at low rates of interest, to Nizārī traders and co-operative organizations and to those needing financial assistance for building their own houses. Around the same time, the Āghā Khān became one of the founding members of the East African Muslim Welfare Society, devoted to building schools and mosques for the indigenous Muslim communities of East Africa. The Āghā Khān was deeply concerned with the housing problems of his followers and aimed to provide an adequate number of dwellings for the Nizārī Khojas. For this purpose, he established a number of housing societies in the major Nizārī centres of East Africa. He also paid special attention to the health and education standards of the community. Thus, the Āghā Khān created and maintained a network of schools, vocational institutions, libraries, sports and recreational clubs, hospitals and dispensaries for the benefit of his followers in East Africa, India and Pakistan. Appropriate bodies were created within the system of councils to supervise the operations of these institutions, whose services were often made available also to non-Ismāʿīlīs.

Resuming our discussion of the administrative system of councils in East Africa, it may be noted that the Constitution of 1954 was again revised in 1962, in the imāmate of Āghā Khān III's successor Karīm Āghā Khān IV. The 1962 Constitution of the East African Nizārīs was issued after considerable consultation with many councillors and knowledgeable members of the community, supplemented by the studies of specially appointed constitutional committees in Tanganyika, Kenya and Uganda. According to the Constitution of 1962,[191] which remained operative for twenty-five years, the administrative hierarchy was headed, after the imām, by a Supreme Council for Africa, an interterritorial body that directed, supervised and co-ordinated the activities of the three Territorial Councils. The Supreme Council, with its changing headquarters in Nairobi and other major cities of East Africa, was also empowered to act as a judicial tribunal of the second degree, the highest judicial authority being the imām himself. Members of the Supreme Council were appointed by the imām, who accorded some representation to each of the three East African territories. Below the Supreme Council, there were the Territorial Councils in the states of Tanzania, Kenya and Uganda, each enjoying a great degree of local autonomy; the headquarters of these councils were located in Dar-es-Salaam, Nairobi and Kampala, respectively. Before the formation of Tanzania in 1964, Zanzibar had its own Territorial Council, but subsequently the island was placed under the jurisdiction of the Territorial Council for Tanzania. In each of the three states, there were a number of Provincial Councils charged with directing the affairs of the various districts and local *jamāʿat*s under their jurisdiction. The members of the Provincial Councils were appointed by the imām from amongst the Nizārīs of each particular province. A number of auxiliary bodies, such as economic committees, welfare societies and women's associations, operated under the supervision of the Provincial Councils.

The Constitution of 1962 was concerned, much more than its predecessors, with matters related to marriage, betrothal, dower and compensation, divorce, restitution of conjugal rights, maintenance, guardianship, apostasy and marriage with non-Nizārīs. These matters were covered in numerous articles which in effect represented the personal law of the community. The Ismāʿīlī councils and their affiliated tribunals have frequently passed out decisions on such personal matters and the related disputes brought before them. The 1962 Constitution also established an Executive Council for Africa with the main function of allocating funds to various organizations, including those operating in the fields of education, health and religious instruction. At the same time, in each of the three states, Education and Health Administrations were established. These bodies, entrusted to ministers and charged with providing services in their fields and supervising the relevant institutions in each state, were ultimately under the direction of the imām himself. All councillors and other important officeholders have been appointed by the imām for an initial period of two years, renewable at his discretion. The officeholders in the council system, comprised mainly of lawyers and other professional men, do not receive any salaries but are rewarded by receiving special blessings, titles, etc., from the imām. Āghā Khān III instituted an elaborate system of titles, maintained by his successor, which now includes designations such as *diwan*, *vazir*, *rai*, and *alijah*, for the eligible members of the community.

The Nizārī community in East Africa had, meanwhile, retained its traditional pattern of organization in terms of local *jamāʿat*s, each having a *jamāʿat-khāna* where religious and social ceremonies continue to be performed. At the *jamāʿat* level, the communal affairs are under the jurisdiction of a *mukhi* and a *kamadia*, who until 1987 were selected for each *jamāʿat-khāna* by the relevant Provincial Councils. These functionaries officiate on various occasions, such as marriage ceremonies, funeral rites, and communal prayers on special occasions. They also collect the religious dues, including the *dassondh* and the *memani*, a voluntary offering to the imām. Religious matters of general interest to the community, including especially the religious education of the Nizārīs themselves, have been the responsibility of an Ismailia Association, now called the Tariqah and Religious Education Board, in each of the three East African states, which operate independently of the secular councils and are accountable directly to the Āghā Khān. These bodies have also been responsible for the publication and distribution of the religious literature of the Nizārīs, notably the imāms' *firman*s and speeches. The Ismailia Associations (Tariqah Boards), as well as *mukhi*s and *kamadia*s, have not conducted any proselytizing activities, though on rare occasions some native Africans and European residents of East Africa have embraced Nizārī Ismāʿīlism. There are, however, religious functionaries, comparable to the *dāʿī*s of the earlier times, active in most Nizārī communities of today. The modern-day missionaries, usually called religious teachers (*muʿallim*s) and preachers (*waezeen*), perform the vital function of instructing the members of the community in their own religion. In East Africa, they work mainly in the Ismāʿīlī schools or amongst the local groups. They do not attempt to spread the Nizārī doctrines and practices among the adherents of other religions. Formerly, many Nizārī teachers of East Africa received their education in India and Pakistan, but since 1964 a missionary centre in Dar-es-Salaam has provided the required training for them. The elaborate administrative organization of the Nizārī community in East Africa has represented essentially a carefully developed system of checks and balances. This system, together with its governing constitution, has safeguarded the absolute authority of the imām and the traditional *jamāʿat* fabric of the community, while at the same time it has served to modernize the community and produce substantial socio-economic gains for the Āghā Khān's followers. The Nizārī Khojas have, indeed, emerged as the best organized and the most progressive of the Muslim communities of East Africa.

Council systems with affiliated central and subordinate bodies, similar to those existing in East Africa, were also developed for the Nizārī communities of Pakistan and India.[192] Allowing for special local conditions, the organizations of the councils and *jamāʿat*s of Pakistan and India were specified in written constitutions, which were revised several times until the most recent constitution issued in 1986 for all the Nizārī *jamāʿat*s of the world. According to these earlier constitutions, the Shia Imami Ismailis of Pakistan and India were organized hierarchically in a series of councils under the overall administrative and religious leadership of the present imām of the Nizārī Ismāʿīlīs, the Mawlana Hazar Imam. In Pakistan, the communal administration was headed by a Federal Council located at Karachi. The Federal Council co-ordinated the activities of five Supreme Councils for the different regions of the country, including one that was charged with the affairs of East Pakistan until that region gained independence as the state of Bangladesh in 1972. On the basis of the Constitution of 1962 for Pakistan, each Supreme Council was responsible for supervising the activities of some of the twenty-three Divisional, District and Local Councils throughout the country. The Supreme Councils were also empowered to hear the appeals of the lower councils and to communicate instructions to *mukhi*s and *kamadia*s of the *jamāʿat*s in their regions. The *jamāʿat*s were represented on the Local Councils, and the latter selected the *mukhi*s and *kamadia*s of the districts under their jurisdiction. In India, the Federal Council, located at Bombay, directed the affairs of four Regional Councils for Maharashtra, Gujarāt, southern India and eastern India. At the bottom of the hierarchy, there were twenty-eight

Local Councils in India, for south Bombay, north Bombay, Jamnagar, Cutch, Sūrat, Hyderabad, and so forth. Every council had its own president and members, appointed by the imām or selected with his approval. All the councils also acted as judiciary tribunals for settling the various communal disputes.

As in the East African states, the general religious policies, the publication and distribution of religious literatures, and the supervision of the activities of the religious teachers in Pakistan and India have been entrusted to Ismailia Associations, renamed Ismaili Tariqah and Religious Education Boards in 1987, with headquarters in Karachi and Bombay. Until the late 1970s, these Ismailia Associations, like those in East Africa, operated rather autonomously, especially in their publishing activities. Furthermore, in each country there developed a number of central boards in charge of communal activities in the fields of education, health, social welfare, housing and economic planning. These boards, acting under the general supervision of the Federal Council in each country, have been responsible for the provision of the services in their respective fields of operation. In the Indo-Pakistan subcontinent too, the followers of the Āghā Khāns have received substantial socio-economic benefits from various communal programmes. Nonetheless, sporadic dissension occurred in the Khoja community of the subcontinent after 1901. Some of the dissenters, raising particular doctrinal and financial objections, periodically seceded from the Nizārī community. They mainly embraced Twelver Shīʿism. Other dissidents, a small minority, stayed within the community, forming the Khojah Reformers' Society, with headquarters in Karachi.[193]

Most recently in Rabīʿ II 1407/December 1986, Āghā Khān IV issued a universal constitution entitled 'The Constitution of the Shia Imami Ismaili Muslims' for all his Nizārī followers throughout the world. The new Constitution was to be enforced by December 1987, while the new rules and regulations applicable to different Nizārī territories were to be formulated in due time. The preamble of the new Constitution affirms all the fundamental Islamic beliefs and then clearly focuses on the doctrine of the imāmate upheld by the Nizārī Ismāʿīlīs, like other Shīʿī Muslims; it also emphasizes the imām's *taʿlīm* or teaching which guides his followers along the path of spiritual enlightenment and improved temporal life. The new Constitution, indeed, stresses the all-important teaching and guiding role of the present imām of the Nizārīs by affirming that by the virtue of his office and in accordance with the belief of his followers, the imām enjoys full authority of governance in respect to all the religious and communal matters of the Nizārīs.

The hierarchical administrative system of councils is somewhat simplified in the Constitution of 1986, which envisages a uniform system of councils for a selection of the Nizārī territories in the Eastern and Western hemispheres of the world. Taking account of the fact that large numbers of Nizārīs have immigrated during the last two decades to Europe and America as well as to the Persian Gulf region, the new Constitution has established the council system for a number of these newly-founded Nizārī communities in addition to modifying the system for several communities in the traditional abodes of the Nizārīs in Asia and Africa. The particular Nizārī communities having the council system under the new Constitution are located in fourteen territories, including India, Pakistan, Bangladesh, Malaysia and Singapore, the Gulf Co-operation Council Countries (namely, Bahrain, Kuwait, Oman, Qatar, Saudi Arabia, and the United Arab Emirates), Syria, the Malagasy Republic, Kenya, Tanzania, France, Portugal, the United Kingdom, Canada and the United States. In each of these fourteen Nizārī territories a National Council will direct and supervise the affairs of a network of Regional and Local Councils. At the discretion of the Āghā Khān, the jurisdiction of each National Council may be extended to geographical areas where the Nizārī *jamāʿat*s do not have their own council system.

The Constitution of 1986 envisages a number of additional organizations for the Nizārī territories having National Councils. Each of these territories will also come to possess a Tariqah and Religious Education Board (formerly called Ismailia Association), for the provision of religious education at all levels of the *jamāʿat*, for the training of religious teachers, and for research and publication of materials on different aspects of Islam and Ismāʿīlism. It is interesting to note that the new Constitution officially refers to Nizārī Ismāʿīlism as 'the Ismaili Tariqah,' defining *tariqah* as persuasion, path or way in faith analogous to the designation of a Ṣūfī *ṭarīqa*. The Tariqah Boards will also be responsible for guiding the *mukhi*s and *kamadia*s in matters of religious rites and practices of Nizārī Ismāʿīlism. Furthermore, the new Constitution has established Grants and Review Boards in eleven of the Nizārī territories to ensure the observance of proper standards of financial discipline by those institutions, such as the Councils, the Tariqah Boards and other central bodies, which receive financial support from the imām or the Nizārī community. Finally, the new Constitution has set up National Conciliation and Arbitration Boards in eleven of the fourteen territories with National Councils. These Boards will act as judicial tribunals to arbitrate between parties or on disputes arising from commercial and other civil liability matters as well as domestic and family matters; they are also empowered to take disciplinary action against the Nizārīs. An International Conciliation and Arbitration Board will act as a judicial tribunal of the first degree, after the present imām, for hearing appeals from decisions of the National Conciliation Boards. In all matters related to the governance of the Nizārī *jamāʿat*s, however, the ultimate authority is vested in the imām. The appointment of *mukhi*s and *kamadia*s and their functions and terms of office, too, are now placed strictly at the discretion of the imām. The new Constitution lists a number of grounds on the basis of which disciplinary action, including expulsion from the community, may be taken against Nizārīs. These grounds include the ridiculing of the Qur'ān, the Prophet, the Ahl al-Bayt, the person of the Hazar Imam, the new Constitution, and any Ismāʿīlī religious literature or practice, amongst other unacceptable behaviour and activities.

The administrative system of Ismāʿīlī councils has not been extended to several countries and regions of the Near East and Asia, such as Persia, Afghanistan, and the upper Oxus region, where scattered Nizārī communities exist; while the Syrian Nizārīs following the Āghā Khānī line of imāms acquired the council system only under the terms of the 1986 Constitution. These Nizārī communities, engaged mainly in agricultural activities, have been led by their hereditary dynasties of *pīr*s, *amīr*s or *mīr*s. In some cases, the Āghā Khāns have appointed their own special representatives, who sometimes have been the same hereditary local leaders. In Syria, as noted, the community had mainly acknowledged the Muḥammad-Shāhī (Mu'minī) line of imāms until the latter part of the nineteenth century.[194] The Syrian Nizārīs remained loyal subjects of the Mamlūks and their Ottoman successors, to whom they paid a special tax. The Nizārīs had recurrent military entanglements with their neighbours in Syria, especially with the numerically stronger Nuṣayrīs who repeatedly occupied their fortresses and destroyed their religious literature. A number of such clashes took place between the latter part of the eighteenth century and the opening decades of the nineteenth century. Intense rivalries between the two ruling Nizārī families centred at Maṣyāf and Qadmūs further weakened the Nizārī community of Syria. In 1808, the Nuṣayrīs succeeded by trickery in murdering Muṣṭafā Mulḥim, the Nizārī *amīr* of Maṣyāf, also seizing his fortress. Thereupon, Shaykh Sulaymān b.

Ḥaydar, the senior *dāʿī* at Maṣyāf, left the locality with many Nizārīs to settle in Ḥimṣ, Ḥamāt and elsewhere. As in other instances, the Nizārīs later regained possession of Maṣyāf on the intercession of the Ottoman authorities. However, the Syrian Nizārīs continued to be divided by rivalries between the *amīr*s of Maṣyāf and Qadmūs, and the whole community received a devastating blow in the 1830s from an Ottoman expedition led by Ibrāhīm Pasha, who caused much damage to Nizārī castles and villages.

By the 1840s, Amīr Ismāʿīl b. Amīr Muḥammad, the Nizārī *amīr* of Qadmūs, succeeded in establishing his authority over the greater section of the Syrian community. He also managed to win the friendship of the Ottoman authorities in the time of Sultan ʿAbd al-Majīd I (1255–1277/1839–1861). Amīr Ismāʿīl had decided to gather his Nizārī co-religionists in Salamiyya, the town that had served as the central headquarters of the early Ismāʿīlī movement. In 1843, he petitioned the Ottoman authorities to permit the Syrian Nizārīs to restore Salamiyya, then in ruins, for their permanent settlement. The Ottomans later granted the request, allowing Amīr Ismāʿīl to gather the Syrian Nizārīs from different localities and settle them in Salamiyya and in the nearby villages east of Ḥamāt. This initiated a new era in the history of the Syrian Nizārī community. In 1850, the Ottomans granted a further favour to the Nizārīs of Salamiyya by exempting them from military service. Meanwhile, the Syrian Muḥammad-Shāhīs had lost contact with their fortieth imām, Amīr Muḥammad al-Bāqir. Since 1210/1796, as noted, they had not heard from this imām, who, like his predecessors, had been living in India. In 1304/1887, the Syrian Muḥammad-Shāhī Nizārīs sent a delegation to India to locate the descendants of Amīr Muḥammad al-Bāqir, who was thought to have gone into concealment. The delegation failed in its search, and soon afterwards the majority of the Syrian Muḥammad-Shāhī Nizārīs transferred their allegiance to the Qāsim-Shāhī line, then represented by Āghā Khān III who had shortly earlier assumed the imāmate in Bombay. A minority remained loyal to the Muḥammad-Shāhī (Mu'minī) line of imāms, even though that line had apparently become discontinued.

The Syrian Muḥammad-Shāhīs, who like the bulk of that country's Qāsim-Shāhīs are mainly engaged in agriculture, have not prospered in their difficult mountainous terrain west of Ḥamāt. Lacking proper leadership and organization, they also suffered from further clashes with the Nuṣayrīs. The last Nuṣayrī attacks on the Syrian Muḥammad-Shāhīs occurred during 1919–1920, when Qadmūs was taken and much damage was caused to the sectarian houses, possessions and manuscripts. At present some 15,000 Muḥammad-Shāhīs, locally known as the Jaʿfariyya, live in Maṣyāf, Qadmūs and a few surrounding villages. They are evidently the sole surviving members of the Muḥammad-Shāhī Nizārī sub-sect. By contrast to the Muḥammad-Shāhīs, the Syrian Qāsim-Shāhīs have enjoyed a rising standard of living. Their agricultural activities have yielded better results in the plains around Salamiyya; they have also benefited from better leadership and greater access to educational services. Āghā Khān III built several schools in Salamiyya and elsewhere, including an agricultural institution, for his Syrian followers, whom he visited in 1951. He also despatched religious instructors there from Africa. The Syrian Qāsim-Shāhī Nizārīs were in the past particularly attached to Āghā Khān III's son Aly Khan, then the heir apparent to the imāmate, who visited the Syrian community several times. Today, the Nizārī adherents of the Āghā Khānī line in Syria, numbering to around 60,000, live in Salamiyya and its surrounding villages. Most are the descendants of those Nizārīs who restored the town in the middle of the last century. They carry family names, such as ʿAkkārī and Jandalī, indicative of the districts from which their ancestors moved to Salamiyya. Until recently, the leadership of the Qāsim-Shāhī community in Syria had remained hereditary in the family of Amīr Ismāʿīl; a recent leader, Amīr Sulaymān, was Ismāʿīl's grandson and an uncle of the late Syrian Ismāʿīlī scholar Muṣṭafā Ghālib. These hereditary *amīr*s loyally represented the last two Āghā Khāns in the Syrian community. In the administration of the communal affairs, the *amīr*s were assisted by a number of functionaries, including *mukhi*s (*mukī*s) and *kamadia*s (*kāmariyā*s); designations originally adopted by the Nizārī Khojas and later used also by the non-Khoja Nizārī communities outside of India, Pakistan and East Africa. As noted, the Syrian Nizārīs following the Āghā Khān now have their own council system of administration under the terms of the 1986 Constitution of the Nizārī Ismāʿīlīs.

When Āghā Khān I left Persia permanently in 1257/1841, the Persian Nizārīs were left without effective leadership, as the bulk of the senior leaders of the community had also migrated with their imām. More significantly, the Persian Nizārīs were now deprived, for the first time in almost seven centuries, of direct access to the imām and the headquarters of the *daʿwa*. Under these circumstances, the different Nizārī communities of Khurāsān, Kirmān and elsewhere in the country, separated from one another by relatively long distances, became highly disorganized, each community developing autonomously on the basis of its own resources and local initiative. Deprived of the guidance and protection of the Nizārī Imām, who had clashed with the Qājār regime prior to establishing his permanent seat in Bombay, the scattered Nizārī communities of Persia were now also subjected to periodical persecutions at the hands of their hostile neighbours, who were often manipulated by the local officials and the powerful Twelver *ʿulamāʾ*. It was only during the first quarter of the present century that the Nizārīs of Persia began to experience stability and improvements in their overall situation.[195]

According to the oral traditions of the Persian Nizārīs, Āghā Khān I made certain provisional arrangements for the administration of the affairs of his Persian followers a few years after his migration to India. A certain Mīrzā Ḥasan, whose family had served the imāms, was apparently made responsible for collecting the religious dues and managing the community in Persia for a period of forty years. The seat of Mīrzā Ḥasan's family was in Sidih, a village located between Qā'in and Bīrjand in southern Khurāsān, the region formerly known as Quhistān. Mīrzā Ḥasan's father, Mīrzā Ḥusayn b. Yaʿqūb Shāh Qā'inī, who is named in the sectarian traditions as the *dāʿī* of Quhistān, composed numerous religious poems.[196] Mīrzā Ḥasan died around 1305/1887–1888, and his privileged position in the community was inherited by his son Murād Mīrzā, who had his own rebellious ideas regarding the affairs of the Persian Nizārīs.

From early on, Murād Mīrzā seems to have aimed at completely severing the ties between the Persian Nizārīs and their new imām, Āghā Khān III. He was particularly encouraged in his designs by the fact that the bulk of the Nizārīs of Persia had lost direct contact with their imām, whose place of residence was then unknown to most of them. Murād Mīrzā soon began to lead the community, especially in Khurāsān where the majority of the Qāsim-Shāhī Nizārīs were concentrated, in an autonomous fashion, also refusing to remit the tithes to the imām in Bombay. He evidently claimed the rank of *ḥujja* for himself, and accorded a greater significance to this position than had been expressed on the subject by Khayrkhwāh. Murād Mīrzā asserted that now only the *ḥujja* was capable of having access to the imām, and that it was beyond the station of the ordinary Nizārīs to know the imām or even his place of residence. The *ḥujja* was, therefore, to be obeyed, without hesitation, by the ordinary members of the sect. Murād Mīrzā, who prevented the Nizārīs of Khurāsān from visiting the imām in India, became duly informed of the conflicts within Āghā Khān III's family; conflicts that led to the Hajji Bibi Case brought before the

Bombay High Court in 1908. Murād Mīrzā sided with Ḥājjī Bībī, Āghā Khān III's cousin. Soon, he went further and claimed that the rightful imām of the time was Ḥājjī Bībī's son Ṣamad Shāh, whose father Mūchūl Shāh (d. 1321/1903) was a grandson of Āghā Khān I. A faction of the Persian Nizārī community, especially in southern Khurāsān, accepted Murād Mīrzā's claims and acknowledged Ṣamad Shāh as their imām. They split off from the Qāsim-Shāhī Nizārīs and later became generally known as Murād Mīrzā'īs. Ṣamad Shāh spent twenty years in the armed forces of British India, also serving with the British army in ʿIrāq during World War I. It was around that time that he visited the Murād Mīrzā'īs of Sidih, and on leaving Persia he promised to return. Murād Mīrzā died after 1925, and his descendants have continued to lead the surviving Murād Mīrzā'īs of Sidih and a few other villages in southern Khurāsān. It is not clear whether Ṣamad Shāh himself ever claimed the imāmate. At any rate, he seems to have eventually reconciled his differences with Āghā Khān III, as the latter sent Ṣamad Shāh on at least one mission to Hunza in the 1930s. When Ṣamad Shāh died without a son around World War II, most of the Murād Mīrzā'īs embraced Twelver Shīʿism, while a small number around Sidih refused to accept his death and began to await his reappearance.

In the meantime, Āghā Khān III had endeavoured to establish direct contacts with his followers in Persia to undermine the rebellious activities of Murād Mīrzā. He eventually succeeded in asserting his authority over the Persian Nizārī community through the efforts of Muḥammad b. Zayn al-ʿĀbidīn b. Karbalā'ī Dā'ūd Khurāsānī, better known as Fidā'ī Khurāsānī, who was the most learned Persian Nizārī of the time. Born around 1266/1850 in the Ismāʿīlī village of Dizbād, between Mashhad and Nīshāpūr, Fidā'ī, a descendant of Khākī Khurāsānī, studied the religious sciences at the Bāqiriyya Madrasa in Mashhad.[197] Fidā'ī set off on his first journey to India for the *dīdār* of the imām in 1313/1896. Accompanied by two other Nizārīs from Dizbād, he stayed in Bombay for two years before returning to Persia. In 1317/1900, Fidā'ī paid his second visit to Bombay, where he remained a few years to see the imām who was then in Europe. Whilst waiting to see the imām, Fidā'ī found access to the Āghā Khān's library and read many Ismāʿīlī books. He finally saw the imām, who, in 1321/1903, gave Fidā'ī a *firman*, appointing him as the *muʿallim* in charge of the religious affairs of the Persian Nizārī community. At the same time, Āghā Khān III made a certain Muḥammad Ḥusayn Maḥmūdī responsible for the community's dealings with the Persian government, and instructed his Persian followers to stop paying their tithes to Murād Mīrzā. These measures posed a direct challenge to Murād Mīrzā, who was now officially deprived of any authority. On returning to Persia, Fidā'ī passed through Arabia and made the *ḥajj* pilgrimage, which later won him the popular designation of Ḥājjī Ākhūnd in Khurāsān. Henceforth, Fidā'ī frequently visited the various Nizārī communities in Persia, guiding them in religious matters and winning their renewed allegiance to Āghā Khān III. It was also at the Āghā Khān's suggestion that Fidā'ī composed his history of Ismāʿīlism, the *Hidāyat al-mu'minīn* (*Guiding the Faithful*). In 1324/1906, Fidā'ī, accompanied by twelve Nizārīs from Dizbād, paid his third and last visit to Bombay, where he found the occasion to testify in favour of Āghā Khān III during the hearings of the Hajji Bibi Case. On returning to Khurāsān in 1326/1908, Fidā'ī continued to campaign on behalf of Āghā Khān III, whose authority was being increasingly extended throughout the Persian community. For instance, the Persian Nizārīs of different *jamāʿat*s, who hitherto possessed hereditary local leaders, were now instructed by the imām to choose their *mukhi*s from amongst the trusted elders of their communities for terms of tenure not exceeding five years. The new local leaders were to make special efforts to collect the tithes and remit them regularly to the imām in Bombay.

Around 1910, in line with the directives issued to the Qāsim-Shāhī Nizārīs of other countries, Āghā Khān III began to introduce certain changes in the religious practices and rituals of his Persian followers. In particular, he changed or simplified some of those religious rituals that the Persian Shīʿīs, like other Muslims, had categorized as the *furūʿ-i dīn*, comprising the positive rules of the Islamic law, such as the rituals of praying, ablution, fasting, the *ḥajj* pilgrimage, and so forth.[198] The Persian Nizārīs had hitherto observed these rituals mainly in the fashion of the Twelver Shīʿīs, perhaps for the sake of *taqiyya*. But now they were required to set themselves drastically apart from the Twelvers, asserting their own identity as a religious community. For instance, they now recited the entire list of the Nizārī Imāms recognized by the Qāsim-Shāhīs at the end of their daily prayers. They were also discouraged from joining the Twelvers at their mosques on special occasions, and from participating in the Shīʿī mourning rituals of Muḥarram, because the Nizārīs had a living and present (*mawjūd wa ḥāḍir*) imām and did not need to commemorate any of their dead imāms. Indeed, they were now required to observe only those religious prescriptions that were directly endorsed or issued by their living imām. The Āghā Khān, however, asked his followers to be aware of the true, *bāṭinī* significance of the rituals, also emphasizing that all Muslims essentially shared the same basic pillars of Islam irrespective of their sectarian persuasions.[199]

In the meantime, Murād Mīrzā had not remained idle. Taking advantage of the breakdown of the Persian government's central authority during the years of the Constitutional Revolution, lasting throughout the first decade of the twentieth century, and capitalizing on the enmity of the Twelver *ʿulamāʾ* towards the Ismāʿīlīs, Murād Mīrzā incessantly intrigued against the followers of the Āghā Khān. Fidāʾī's house in Dizbād was pillaged when he was on missionary work in Qāʾin and elsewhere. Later, a Twelver *ʿālim*, Mullā Muḥammad Bāqir, collected a mob and attacked Dizbād to capture the Khurāsānī Nizārī leaders who were supporting the Āghā Khān. Fidāʾī himself was in southern Khurāsān at the time but his brother, Mullā Ḥasan, and a few others were seized and taken to Darrūd, a village near Nīshāpūr. Subsequently, the captured Nizārīs, refusing to curse the Āghā Khān publicly, were sentenced to death by a group of local Twelver *mullās*. In 1327/1909, two of the Nizārī prisoners were actually executed in Darrūd. The Āghā Khān prevented further persecution of his Khurāsānī followers through the intervention of the British Consul at Mashhad. Fidāʾī died in 1342/1923, and was succeeded as the *muʿallim* of the Nizārīs by Sayyid Sulaymān Badakhshānī, another senior sectarian leader from Dizbād. By that time, Āghā Khān III had established his authority over the Persian Nizārīs, who had clearly set themselves apart from the country's Twelver Shīʿīs as well as the Murād Mīrzāʾīs, who observed all their religious rituals in the manner of the Ithnāʿasharīs. By the 1930s, Āghā Khān III began to concern himself with the socio-economic conditions of his followers in Persia, especially with the Khurāsānī Nizārīs, who comprised the bulk of the community and possessed adequate local initiative for implementing the imām's modernization policies. As instructed by the Āghā Khān, the sectarians launched a programme of building a school in every Ismāʿīlī village in Khurāsān. The first school, constructed in 1932 in Dizbād, was named after Nāṣir-i Khusraw, who is particularly revered by the Nizārīs of Khurāsān. Later, Dizbād became the first village in Khurāsān to have a secondary school. The schools were built with local funds under the supervision of the trusted members of each village. Āghā Khān III had permitted the sectarians to set aside 80 per cent of their tithes for this purpose; only the remaining 20 per cent was to be sent to the imām. The sectarians were also encouraged to form special groups for undertaking communal ventures, including agricultural extension projects. Soon, the

Ismāʿīlī villages of Khurāsān attained high rates of literacy, with a growing number of the province's Ismāʿīlī students attending the institutions of higher learning in Mashhad and Tehran. Many educated Khurāsānī Nizārīs gradually settled down in those cities mainly as teachers and civil servants, thus changing the traditionally rural structure of the Persian Nizārī community. Northern Khurāsān took the lead in supplying the bulk of the educated urban elite of the Persian Nizārī community.

Āghā Khān III was pleased by the progress made by his Persian followers when he visited them in 1951. He was particularly glad to see that the Ismāʿīlī women had abandoned the *chādur*, the traditional Muslim veil worn in Persia.[200] It was in 1372/1953 that the Āghā Khān chose a distant cousin, Amīr Asʿad Shāh Khalīlī, to be his chief representative (*wazīr*) in Iran. Shāh Khalīlī, who had replaced another relative, managed the affairs of the community in an obedient manner whilst Āghā Khān III was alive. But soon after the accession of Āghā Khān IV, he began to act rather autonomously, issuing religious orders that were contradictory to the *firmans* of the Āghā Khāns. In particular, he instructed the community to revert back to the ritual practices of the Twelver Shīʿīs. During the 1960s, several clashes occurred between Āghā Khān IV and Shāh Khalīlī.

Āghā Khān IV finally decided to remove Shāh Khalīlī and to reorganize the local leadership of the Persian Nizārī community. He sent two trusted Khoja Nizārīs to Persia with a *firman* dismissing Shāh Khalīlī and ordering his followers to stop paying their tithes until further notice. Later, Āghā Khān IV despatched another *firman*, entrusting the affairs of the Persian Nizārīs to two committees to be located in Mashhad and Tehran. The committees were actually set up in 1973. The twelve members of each committee, designated as the Kumita-yi Ḥaḍrat-i Vālā Āqā Khān, were chosen by the imām himself from amongst the candidates proposed by the community. The control of the committees has remained chiefly in the hands of the educated members of the community, appointed periodically by the Āghā Khān, who supervises their operations. The Mashhad Committee, responsible for the country's largest and best educated Nizārī community in Khurāsān, has been rather successful in implementing different socio-economic projects while continuing to emphasize the community's educational progress. The Mashhad Committee, whose headquarters are located at the newly constructed *jamāʿat-khāna* in Mashhad, also supervises the operations of the Ikhwān al-Ṣafāʾ Co-operative Society, founded in 1965 at Mashhad. This body extends loans, at low

17 Sulṭān Muḥammad Shāh, Āghā Khān III

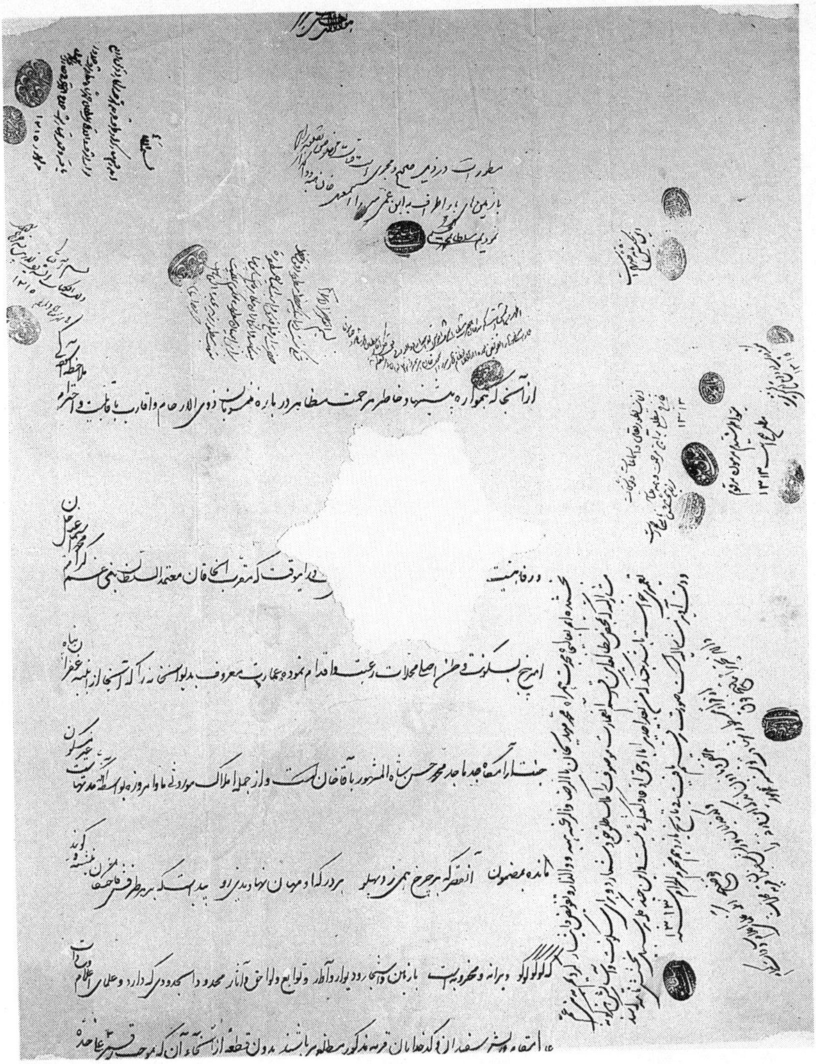

18 A document, dated 1313/1895, issued by Āghā Khān III, granting some ancestral properties in Maḥallāt to his cousin Mīrzā Ismāʿīl Khān Iʿtibār al-Salṭana, the author's maternal great-grandfather

19 His Highness Shāh Karīm al-Ḥusaynī, Āghā Khān IV

rates of interest, to the Nizārīs of Khurāsān. The Tehran Committee, responsible for the affairs of a number of scattered Nizārī groups in Tehran, Maḥallāt, Yazd and Kirmān, has been less successful in the discharge of its duties. The leaders of both committees have access to the Āghā Khān and periodically see him in Europe or Pakistan. Āghā Khān IV also guides his Persian followers directly through his *firmans*. The Nizārīs of Persia, as elsewhere, have been traditionally organized in terms of *jamāʿats*, often representing the Nizārī inhabitants of single villages. Each *jamāʿat* has its own *mukhi*, acting usually as the chief religious headman of the village, and *kamadia*, the treasurer responsible for keeping record of the tithes. These functionaries are normally elected by the members of the local *jamāʿat*, but the Āghā Khān's endorsement is sometimes required.

There are no reliable figures on the size of the Nizārī population of Iran, with different available estimates ranging from 10,000 to 100,000 persons. At present, there are probably about 20,000–30,000 Nizārīs living in various towns and rural areas of Iran, with nearly half of the total concentrated in the province of Khurāsān. The Khurāsānī Nizārīs are located mainly in the southern part of the province, in the towns of Qā'in, Bīrjand and a few surrounding villages like Khushk, where the Mashhad Committee has established a branch, Mu'minābād, Naṣrābād and Mazdāb. In northern Khurāsān, aside from some 1,500 Nizārīs engaged in urban jobs in Mashhad, the sectarians are to be found in Nīshāpūr, Turbat-i Ḥaydariya and a few smaller towns as well as in Dizbād (Dīzbād), Qāsimābād, Shāh Taqī and other villages. Most of the Nizārīs of northern Khurāsān have maintained houses in Dizbād, their ancestral home, where the remainders of some old Ismāʿīlī fortresses are still preserved. The Khurāsānī Nizārīs, joined by their co-religionists from other parts of the country, participate in the pilgrimage ceremonies of *Naw-ḥiṣār*, held annually at the end of summer in Dizbād. In 1985, when the author visited Dizbād on the occasion of the *Naw-ḥiṣār* ceremonies, some 3,000 Nizārīs had gathered there. The ceremonies included Ṣūfī-like *dhikr*s or incantations, which are recited by the Persian Nizārīs on other occasions as well. After Khurāsān, the largest number of Persian Nizārīs are to be found in the country's central province, especially in Tehran where a *jamāʿat-khāna* has been established, and in some nine villages around Maḥallāt. Smaller numbers reside in the province of Kirmān, mainly in the towns of Kirmān, Sīrjān and Shahr-i Bābak and their surrounding villages, as well as in Yazd. In the largest Ismāʿīlī villages of Iran, like Khushk and Dizbād, the sectarians now have friendly relations with the numerically fewer Twelver Shīʿīs who live amongst them and are often related to them.

Nizārī communities following the Āghā Khānī line have survived in Kābul and other parts of Afghanistan as well as in Badakhshān and the adjacent districts in the upper Oxus region, notably in the Shughnān and Rushān districts of western Pāmīr. Small Nizārī communities are also located in Yarkand and Kāshghar, a town in Chinese Turkistān. Most of these remote Nizārī communities have been led by their hereditary *amīrs* and *pīrs*. During the twentieth century, the Āghā Khāns have not had any contacts with their followers in Central Asia and Chinese Turkistān, following the establishment of Communist regimes in those regions.[201] On the other hand, the Nizārī communities in Chitral, Gilgit and Hunza, in northern Pakistan where the sectarians are known as Mawlā'īs, have maintained close relations with the Āghā Khāns. They often send deputations to their imām. The Mawlā'īs of Hunza have been ruled for several generations by an Ismāʿīlī dynasty of *mīrs*, centred at Bāltīt.

Sir Sulṭān Muḥammad Shāh, Āghā Khān III, died at his villa in Versoix, near Geneva, in Dhu'l-Ḥijja 1376/July 1957. He had led the Nizārī Ismāʿīlī community for seventy-two years, perhaps longer than any of his predecessors. He was subsequently buried in a permanent mausoleum at Aswan, overlooking the Nile in Egypt, the seat of the Fāṭimid caliph-imāms. In accordance with Āghā Khān III's last will and testament, made in 1955, his grandson Karīm succeeded to the imāmate as the forty-ninth Mawlana Hazar Imām of the Nizārī Ismāʿīlīs.[202] Āghā Khān III had explained in his last will that due to the changed conditions of the world, it would be in the best interest of the Nizārī community that their next imām be a young man brought up and educated during recent years. Consequently, he designated his grandson Karīm as his successor, in preference to both his own sons. It may be added that Aly Khan, the elder of Āghā Khān III's two sons and Karīm's father, who led a controversial private life (and who later represented Pakistan at the United Nations) had been expected by many to succeed to the imāmate. Shāh Karīm al-Ḥusaynī, Āghā Khān IV, generally designated in the western world as His Highness Prince Karim Aga Khan IV, was immediately acclaimed as the new imām in Switzerland in the presence of the representatives of the Nizārīs of Asia and Africa. In due course, all the Nizārī communities offered their *bayʿa* to Āghā Khān IV. Aly Khan, who personally did not question his father's designation, lost his life in a car accident in 1960; he was buried in a permanent mausoleum at Salamiyya in 1972. Born in 1936 in Geneva, Āghā Khān IV had attended Le Rosey, the famous boarding school in Switzerland, for nine years before entering Harvard University. Upon his accession to the imāmate at the age of twenty, Āghā Khān IV interrupted his undergraduate studies at Harvard for a one-year visit to the various Nizārī communities, during which time he was officially installed to the imāmate in a number of enthronement (*takht-nishīnī*) ceremonies held in Dar-es-Salaam, Nairobi, Kampala, Karachi and Bombay. He completed his final year of studies at Harvard during 1958–1959, receiving a B.A. in Islamic history, and thereafter concerned himself with his duties as the imām of the Nizārīs of many lands.

Āghā Khān IV has continued and extended the modernization policies of his grandfather. He has closely supervised the religious and temporal affairs of his followers, especially in India, Pakistan and Africa, mainly through their council systems and by paying regular visits to them. Āghā Khān IV has shown a particular interest in improving the socio-economic and educational conditions of his followers. In the field of education, he has encouraged the Nizārīs to acquire specialized and technical skills, also providing numerous scholarships in Western institutions for eligible students. Āghā Khān IV currently supports a network of some 300 educational institutions and programmes in India, Pakistan, Kenya, Tanzania and elsewhere, ranging from day-care centres and elementary schools to specialized projects such as the Aga Khan School of Commerce in Dar-es-Salaam. In 1983, the Aga Khan University, with a medical college and a nursing school, was founded in Pakistan. Similarly, the Aga Khan Health Services consist of an elaborate network of approximately 200 health programmes and institutions, including six general hospitals, in different Asian and African countries as well as in the West. The Āghā Khān's health and education services are available to all people regardless of their race or religion. Many new projects in these fields were launched during 1982–1983, when the twenty-fifth anniversary of Āghā Khān IV's imāmate was celebrated. On the occasion of his silver jubilee, however, the present imām of the Nizārīs was not weighed against silver. Being keenly concerned with the administrative and economic efficiency of his programmes, the Āghā Khān promotes and finances many of his different projects in the areas of health, education, rural development and social welfare through the Aga Khan Foundation, established in 1967. With headquarters in Geneva and branches in several countries, the Aga Khan

20 A group of Persian Nizārī Ismāʿīlīs, with the author (bespectacled) standing in the middle, Dizbād, Khurāsān

Foundation now collaborates with more than thirty national and international organizations for the implementation of numerous programmes in the Third World.

Āghā Khān IV has also formulated and implemented many economic projects and services for the benefit of his followers, who have been increasingly encouraged to participate in industrial ventures in addition to their traditional activities in commerce and agriculture. For the realization of his economic programmes, in 1963 the Āghā Khān set up the Industrial Promotion Services. This development corporation now operates in several Asian and African countries as well as in Canada. With the participation of various private and public organizations, this corporation has launched more than one hundred projects in areas ranging from textiles to modern enterprises in tourism, providing direct employment for some 10,000 persons. All of the Āghā Khān's existing projects and institutions related to economic activities, including the Industrial Promotion Services, are now absorbed into the Aga Khan Fund for Economic Development. The Fund, established in 1984, particularly seeks to promote economic projects in the Third World.

As a modern Muslim leader with an international outlook, Āghā Khān IV has shown a profound interest in promoting a better understanding of Islam and its cultural heritage. In pursuit of these aims, he has established a number of specific institutions and programmes. In 1977, the Institute of Ismaili Studies, London, was founded to promote Islamic studies. There is also the Aga Khan Trust for Culture, based in Geneva, which encourages projects and scholarship for a better understanding of Islamic civilization. The Aga Khan Award for Architecture, established in 1976, seeks to encourage architectural excellence for the Islamic world. Furthermore, students from different Islamic countries continue to benefit from the Aga Khan Program for Islamic Architecture, established in 1979 at Harvard University and the Massachusetts Institute of Technology. Thus, Āghā Khān IV has been responsible not only for guiding a progressive community of Shīʿī Muslims scattered in more than twenty countries of Asia, Africa, Europe and America, but he has also managed a vast complex of administrative, social, economic and cultural enterprises while concerning himself with a better understanding of the Islamic culture in the world today. In 1976, he moved his headquarters, the Secrétariat de Son Altesse l'Aga Khan, from Switzerland to Aiglemont, Gouvieux, near Paris. In 1969, Āghā Khān IV married Lady James Crichton-Stuart, née Sarah

Crocker-Poole; they have two sons, Raḥīm and Ḥusayn, and a daughter, Zahrā.

Since the 1970s, thousands of Nizārīs have immigrated to the West. Many of these immigrants, belonging mainly to the Khoja families of East Africa, have been forced to leave their native countries due to the unfavourable policies of certain African governments towards the Asian minorities. The Nizārīs who have established new homes in Europe and North America, especially in Britain, Canada and the United States, have been able to find employment in various professional occupations.[203] The largest single community of such Nizārī expatriates, numbering to around 10,000 persons, has come to be concentrated in London, where the Āghā Khān recently built a religious and socio-cultural centre for them. Different Asian groups of Nizārī immigrants, too, have found employment in the Arab countries of the Persian Gulf region and in the Far East. At the same time, in every country of Asia and Africa where the Nizārīs live as indigenous religious minorities and loyal citizens, the sectarians enjoy exemplary standards of living. These realities attest to the Nizārī successes achieved in modern times under the leadership of the last two Āghā Khāns. The Nizārīs have successfully entered the modern world while cherishing their heritage and retaining their doctrines and identity as a religious sect.

Having withstood the Mongol massacres and many later persecutions, the Nizārīs have, indeed, passed the test of time, and they have emerged in the twentieth century as a prosperous and progressive community. The experience of the modern Nizārī Ismāʿīlī community, which numbers several million, represents an exceptional record of achievement in the Muslim world, which is still deeply plagued by poverty, illiteracy and religious fanaticism.

GENEALOGICAL TABLES AND LISTS

The Hāshimids and the early Shīʿī imāms

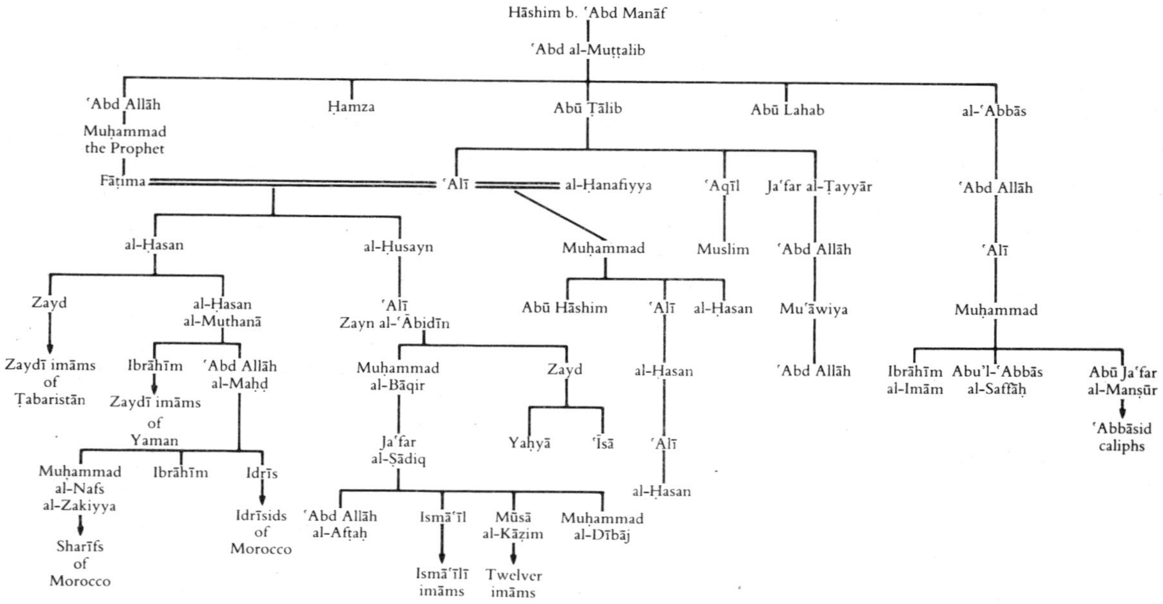

The early Ismāʿīlī imāms

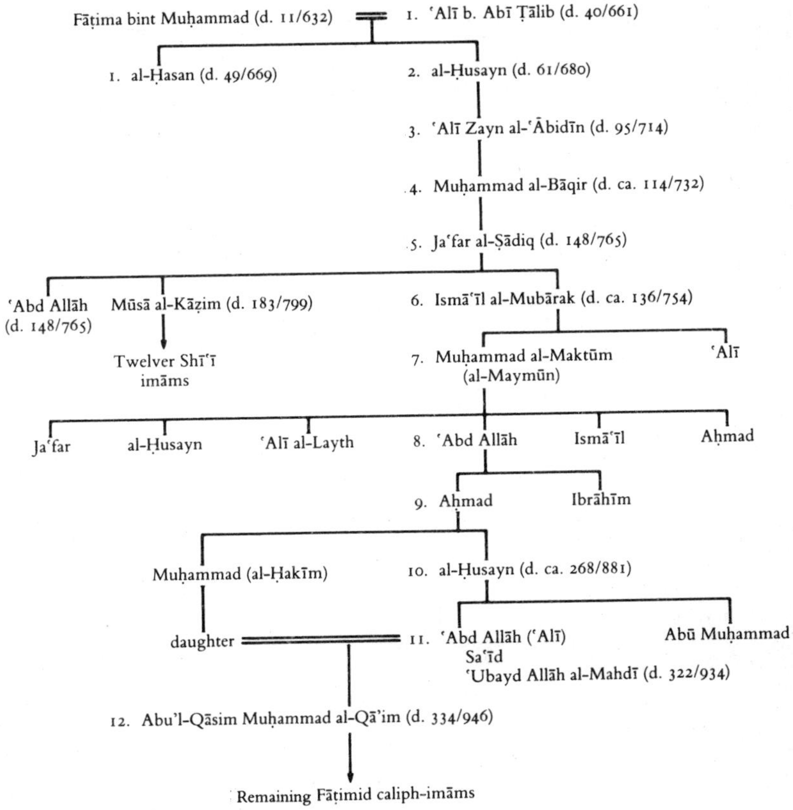

Originally ʿAlī was counted as the first imām. Later, ʿAlī acquired the higher rank of *asās* and al-Ḥasan was counted as the first imām. Still later, the Nizārīs omitted al-Ḥasan and started the list with ʿAlī, counting al-Ḥusayn as their second imām.

The Fāṭimid Ismāʿīlī caliph-imāms

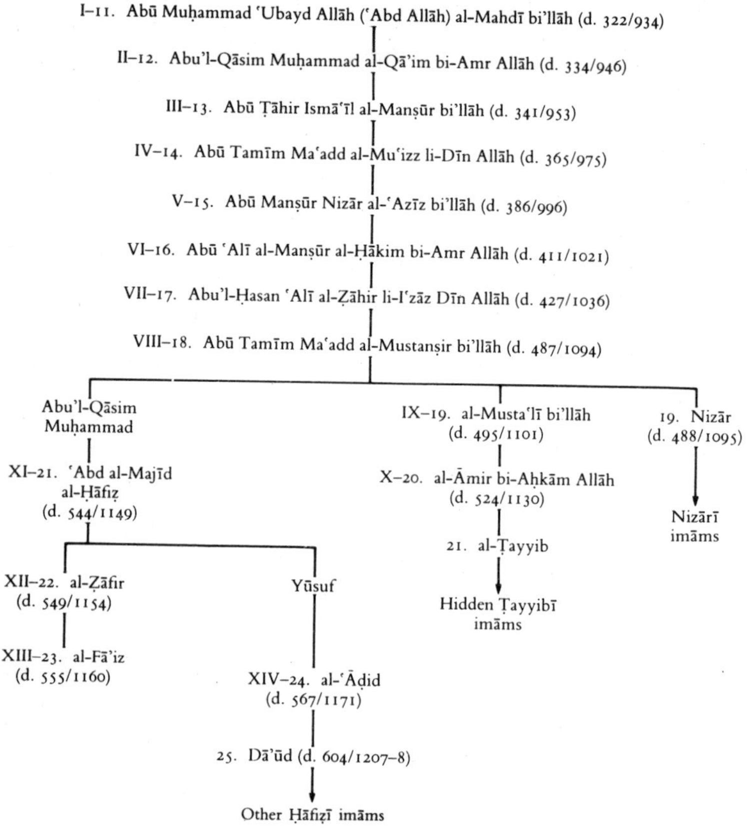

Roman numbers designate the succession order of the Fāṭimid caliphs. Arabic numbers designate the order of the Ismāʿīlī Imāms. After al-Mustanṣir, the Nizārīs and Mustaʿlians followed different lines of imāms. After al-Āmir, the Mustaʿlians themselves split into the Ṭayyibī and Ḥāfiẓī factions, recognizing different imāms.

NIZĀRĪ IMĀMS

Qāsim-Shāhī Nizārī Imāms

19. Nizār b. al-Mustanṣir bi'llāh (d. 488/1095)
20. al-Hādī
21. al-Muhtadī
22. al-Qāhir
23. Ḥasan II *ʿalā dhikrihi'l-salām* (d. 561/1166)
24. Nūr al-Dīn Muḥammad II (d. 607/1210)
25. Jalāl al-Dīn Ḥasan III (d. 618/1221)
26. ʿAlā' al-Dīn Muḥammad III (d. 653/1255)
27. Rukn al-Dīn Khurshāh (d. 655/1257)
28. Shams al-Dīn Muḥammad (d. ca. 710/1310)
29. Qāsim Shāh
30. Islām Shāh
31. Muḥammad b. Islām Shāh
32. Mustanṣir bi'llāh II (d. 885/1480)
33. ʿAbd al-Salām Shāh
34. Gharīb Mīrzā (Mustanṣir bi'llāh III) (d. 904/1498)
35. Abū Dharr ʿAlī (Nūr al-Dīn)
36. Murād Mīrzā (d. 981/1574)
37. Dhu'l-Faqār ʿAlī (Khalīl Allāh I) (d. 1043/1634)
38. Nūr al-Dahr (Nūr al-Dīn) ʿAlī (d. 1082/1671)
39. Khalīl Allāh II ʿAlī (d. 1090/1680)
40. Shāh Nizār II (d. 1134/1722)
41. Sayyid ʿAlī
42. Ḥasan ʿAlī
43. Qāsim ʿAlī (Sayyid Jaʿfar)
44. Abu'l-Ḥasan ʿAlī (Bāqir Shāh) (d. 1206/1792)
45. Shāh Khalīl Allāh III (d. 1232/1817)
46. Ḥasan ʿAlī Shāh, Āghā Khān I (d. 1298/1881)
47. Āqā ʿAlī Shāh, Āghā Khān II (d. 1302/1885)
48. Sulṭān Muḥammad Shāh, Āghā Khān III (d. 1376/1957)
49. H.H. Shāh Karīm al-Ḥusaynī, Āghā Khān IV, the present *ḥāḍir* imām

Muḥammad-Shāhī (Mu'minī) Nizārī Imāms

19. Nizār b. al-Mustanṣir bi'llāh (d. 488/1095)
20. Ḥasan b. Nizār (d. 534/1139)
21. Muḥammad b. Ḥasan (d. 590/1194)
22. Jalāl al-Dīn Ḥasan b. Muḥammad (d. 618/1221)
23. ʿAlā' al-Dīn Muḥammad b. Ḥasan (d. 653/1255)
24. Rukn al-Dīn Maḥmūd b. Muḥammad (d. 655/1257)

*25. Shams al-Dīn Muḥammad b. Maḥmūd (d. ca. 710/1310)

* Some Muḥammad-Shāhī sources add the name of Aḥmad al-Qā'im between the 24th and the 25th imāms.

26. ʿAlāʾ al-Dīn Muʾmin Shāh b. Muḥammad
27. Muḥammad Shāh b. Muʾmin Shāh
28. Raḍī al-Dīn b. Muḥammad Shāh
29. Ṭāhir b. Raḍī al-Dīn
30. Raḍī al-Dīn II b. Ṭāhir (d. 915/1509)
31. Shāh Ṭāhir b. Raḍī al-Dīn II al-Ḥusaynī al-Dakkanī (d. ca. 956/1549)
32. Ḥaydar b. Shāh Ṭāhir (d. 994/1586)
33. Ṣadr al-Dīn Muḥammad b. Ḥaydar (d. 1032/1622)
34. Muʿīn al-Dīn b. Ṣadr al-Dīn (d. 1054/1644)
35. ʿAṭiyyat Allāh b. Muʿīn al-Dīn (Khudāybakhsh) (d. 1074/1663)
36. ʿAzīz Shāh b. ʿAṭiyyat Allāh (d. 1103/1691)
37. Muʿīn al-Dīn II b. ʿAzīz Shāh (d. 1127/1715)
38. Amīr Muḥammad b. Muʿīn al-Dīn II al-Musharraf (d. 1178/1764)
39. Ḥaydar b. Muḥammad al-Muṭahhar (d. 1201/1786)
40. Amīr Muḥammad b. Ḥaydar al-Bāqir, the final imām of this line

MUSTAʿLĪ-ṬAYYIBĪ *DĀʿĪS*

In Yaman

1. al-Dhu'ayb b. Mūsā al-Wādiʿī (d. 546/1151)
2. Ibrāhīm b. al-Ḥusayn al-Ḥāmidī (d. 557/1162)
3. Ḥātim b. Ibrāhīm al-Ḥāmidī (d. 596/1199)
4. ʿAlī b. Ḥātim al-Ḥāmidī (d. 605/1209)
5. ʿAlī b. Muḥammad b. al-Walīd (d. 612/1215)
6. ʿAlī b. Ḥanẓala al-Wādiʿī (d. 626/1229)
7. Aḥmad b. al-Mubārak b. Muḥammad b. al-Walīd (d. 627/1230)
8. al-Ḥusayn b. ʿAlī b. Muḥammad b. al-Walīd (d. 667/1268)
9. ʿAlī b. al-Ḥusayn b. ʿAlī b. al-Walīd (d. 682/1284)
10. ʿAlī b. al-Ḥusayn b. ʿAlī b. Ḥanẓala (d. 686/1287)
11. Ibrāhīm b. al-Ḥusayn b. ʿAlī b. al-Walīd (d. 728/1328)
12. Muḥammad b. Ḥātim b. al-Ḥusayn b. al-Walīd (d. 729/1329)
13. ʿAlī b. Ibrāhīm b. al-Ḥusayn b. al-Walīd (d. 746/1345)
14. ʿAbd al-Muṭṭalib b. Muḥammad b. Ḥātim b. al-Walīd (d. 755/1354)
15. ʿAbbās b. Muḥammad b. Ḥātim b. al-Walīd (d. 779/1378)
16. ʿAbd Allāh b. ʿAlī b. Muḥammad b. al-Walīd (d. 809/1407)
17. al-Ḥasan b. ʿAbd Allāh b. ʿAlī b. al-Walīd (d. 821/1418)
18. ʿAlī b. ʿAbd Allāh b. ʿAlī b. al-Walīd (d. 832/1428)
19. Idrīs b. al-Ḥasan b. ʿAbd Allāh b. al-Walīd (d. 872/1468)
20. al-Ḥasan b. Idrīs b. al-Ḥasan b. al-Walīd (d. 918/1512)
21. al-Ḥusayn b. Idrīs b. al-Ḥasan b. al-Walīd (d. 933/1527)
22. ʿAlī b. al-Ḥusayn b. Idrīs b. al-Walīd (d. 933/1527)
23. Muḥammad b. al-Ḥasan (al-Ḥusayn) b. Idrīs b. al-Walīd (d. 946/1539)

In India

24. Yūsuf b. Sulaymān (d. 974/1567)
25. Jalāl b. Ḥasan (d. 975/1567)
26. Dā'ūd b. ʿAjabshāh (d. 999/1591)

Dā'ūdī *Dāʿīs*

27. Dā'ūd Burhān al-Dīn b. Quṭbshāh (d. 1021/1612)
28. Shaykh Ādam Ṣafī al-Dīn b. Ṭayyibshāh (d. 1030/1621)
29. ʿAbd al-Ṭayyib Zakī al-Dīn b. Dā'ūd b. Quṭbshāh (d. 1041/1631)
30. ʿAlī Shams al-Dīn b. al-Ḥasan b. Idrīs b. al-Walīd (d. 1042/1632)

31. Qāsim Zayn al-Dīn b. Pīrkhān (d. 1054/1644)
32. Quṭbkhān Quṭb al-Dīn b. Dā'ūd (d. 1056/1646)
33. Pīrkhān Shujā' al-Dīn b. Aḥmadjī (d. 1065/1655)
34. Ismā'īl Badr al-Dīn b. Mullā Rāj b. Ādam (d. 1085/1674)
35. 'Abd al-Ṭayyib Zakī al-Dīn b. Ismā'īl Badr al-Dīn (d. 1110/1699)
36. Mūsā Kalīm al-Dīn b. 'Abd al-Ṭayyib Zakī al-Dīn (d. 1122/1710)
37. Nūr Muḥammad Nūr al-Dīn b. Mūsā Kalīm al-Dīn (d. 1130/1718)
38. Ismā'īl Badr al-Dīn b. Shaykh Ādam Ṣafī al-Dīn (d. 1150/1737)
39. Ibrāhīm Wajīh al-Dīn b. 'Abd al-Qādir Ḥakīm al-Dīn (d. 1168/1754)
40. Hibat Allāh al-Mu'ayyad fi'l-Dīn b. Ibrāhīm Wajīh al-Dīn (d. 1193/1779)
41. 'Abd al-Ṭayyib Zakī al-Dīn b. Ismā'īl Badr al-Dīn (d. 1200/1785)
42. Yūsuf Najm al-Dīn b. 'Abd al-Ṭayyib Zakī al-Dīn (d. 1213/1798)
43. 'Abd 'Alī Sayf al-Dīn b. 'Abd al-Ṭayyib Zakī al-Dīn (d. 1232/1817)
44. Muḥammad 'Izz al-Dīn b. Shaykh Jīwanjī Awrangābādī (d. 1236/1821)
45. Ṭayyib Zayn al-Dīn b. Shaykh Jīwanjī Awrangābādī (d. 1252/1837)
46. Muḥammad Badr al-Dīn b. 'Abd 'Alī Sayf al-Dīn (d. 1256/1840)
47. 'Abd al-Qādir Najm al-Dīn b. Ṭayyib Zayn al-Dīn (d. 1302/1885)
48. 'Abd al-Ḥusayn Ḥusām al-Dīn b. Ṭayyib Zayn al-Dīn (d. 1308/1891)
49. Muḥammad Burhān al-Dīn b. 'Abd al-Qādir Najm al-Dīn (d. 1323/1906)
50. 'Abd Allāh Badr al-Dīn b. 'Abd al-Ḥusayn Ḥusām al-Dīn (d. 1333/1915)
51. Ṭāhir Sayf al-Dīn b. Muḥammad Burhān al-Dīn (d. 1385/1965)
52. Muḥammad Burhān al-Dīn b. Ṭāhir Sayf al-Dīn, the present *dā'ī*

Sulaymānī *Dā'īs*

27. Sulaymān b. Ḥasan (d. 1005/1597)
28. Ja'far b. Sulaymān (d. 1050/1640)
29. 'Alī b. Sulaymān (d. 1088/1677)
30. Ibrāhīm b. Muḥammad b. al-Fahd al-Makramī (d. 1094/1683)
31. Muḥammad b. Ismā'īl (d. 1109/1697)
32. Hibat Allāh b. Ibrāhīm (d. 1160/1747)
33. Ismā'īl b. Hibat Allāh (d. 1184/1770)
34. al-Ḥasan b. Hibat Allāh (d. 1189/1775)
35. 'Abd al-'Alī b. al-Ḥasan (d. 1195/1781)
36. 'Abd Allāh b. 'Alī (d. 1225/1810)
37. Yūsuf b. 'Alī (d. 1234/1819)
38. al-Ḥusayn b. al-Ḥasan (d. 1241/1826)
39. Ismā'īl b. Muḥammad (d. 1256/1840)
40. al-Ḥasan b. Muḥammad (d. 1262/1846)
41. al-Ḥasan b. Ismā'īl (d. 1289/1872)
42. Aḥmad b. Ismā'īl (d. 1306/1889)
43. 'Abd Allāh b. 'Alī (d. 1323/1905)
44. 'Alī b. Hibat Allāh (d. 1331/1913)
45. 'Alī b. Muḥsin (d. 1355/1936)

46. Ḥusām al-Dīn al-Ḥājj Ghulām Ḥusayn (d. 1357/1938)
47. Sharaf al-Dīn al-Ḥusayn b. Aḥmad al-Makramī (d. 1358/1939)
48. Jamāl al-Dīn ʿAlī b. Sharaf al-Dīn al-Ḥusayn al-Makramī (d. 1396/1976)
49. al-Sharafī al-Ḥusayn b. al-Ḥasan al-Makramī, the present *dāʿī*

GLOSSARY

Listings in the glossary are selected terms and names, chiefly of Arabic and Persian origins, frequently appearing in the text. The meanings given often refer to the technical and religious senses of the words, reflecting their main applications in the text, especially as adopted by the Ismāʿīlīs. More detailed definitions and explanations of the Ismāʿīlī terms and doctrines, which appear in different chapters, may be located by consulting the Index. In this glossary, pl. and lit. are the abbreviated forms for the words 'plural' and 'literally'; and q.v. (*quod vide*) is used for cross-reference in the glossary.

ʿAbbāsids: descendants of the Prophet's uncle al-ʿAbbās b. ʿAbd al-Muṭṭalib; also the name of the dynasty of caliphs from 132/749 to 656/1258.

adhān: Muslim call to prayer. The *adhān* of the Shīʿīs differs slightly from that of the Sunnīs.

Ahl al-Bayt: lit., the people of the house; members of the household of the Prophet, including especially, besides Muḥammad, ʿAlī, Fāṭima, al-Ḥasan, al-Ḥusayn, and their progeny. The Prophet's family is also designated as āl Muḥammad.

ʿAlids: descendants of ʿAlī b. Abī Ṭālib, cousin and son-in-law of the Prophet, and also the fourth caliph and the first Shīʿī Imām (q.v.). The Shīʿīs believed certain ʿAlids should be imāms, and they acknowledged ʿAlī as the first amongst their imāms. ʿAlī's first spouse was Fāṭima, the Prophet's daughter, and ʿAlī's descendants by Fāṭima (the only descendants of the Prophet) are in particular called Fāṭimids (q.v.). Descendants of ʿAlī and Fāṭima through their sons al-Ḥasan and al-Ḥusayn are also called Ḥasanids and Ḥusaynids. Descendants of al-Ḥasan and al-Ḥusayn are often also designated, respectively, as *sharīfs* and *sayyids*.

ʿālim (pl., *ʿulamāʾ*): a learned man; specifically a scholar in Islamic religious sciences.

amīr (pl., *umarāʾ*): military commander, prince; many independent rulers also held this title in the Islamic world.

amr: command; specifically the divine command or volition.

Anṣār: lit., helpers; name given collectively to those Medinese who supported the

Prophet after his emigration (*hijra*) from Mecca to Medina, in distinction from the Muhājirūn (q.v.).

ʿaql: intellect, intelligence.

asās: lit., foundation; successor to a speaking prophet, *nāṭiq* (q.v.).

atabeg (or *atābak*): lit., 'father-lord'; a Turkish title given to tutors or guardians of Saljūq and other Turkish rulers. The *atabeg*s became powerful officers of state and some of them founded independent dynasties in Islamic lands.

ʿawāmm (or *ʿāmm*): the common people, the masses, in distinction from the *khawāṣṣ* (q.v.).

bāb: lit., gate; the Ismāʿīlī religious term for the administrative head of the *daʿwa* (q.v.) under the Fāṭimids, sometimes also called *bāb al-abwāb*; the highest rank, after the imām, in the *daʿwa* hierarchy of the Fāṭimid Ismāʿīlīs; the equivalent of the official term *dāʿī al-duʿāt* (q.v.), mentioned especially in non-Ismāʿīlī sources; also a chapter or short treatise.

bāṭin: the inward, hidden or esoteric meaning behind the literal wording of sacred texts and religious prescriptions, notably the Qur'ān and the Sharīʿa (q.v.), in distinction from the *ẓāhir* (q.v.); hence, Bāṭinīs, Bāṭiniyya, the groups associated with such ideas. Most of these groups were Shīʿīs, particularly Ismāʿīlīs.

bayʿa: recognition of authority, especially the act of swearing allegiance to a new sovereign or leader.

bayt al-māl: lit., the house of wealth; treasury of the Muslim state.

dāʿī (pl., *duʿāt*): lit., he who summons; a religious propagandist or missionary of various Muslim groups, especially amongst the Ismāʿīlīs and other Shīʿī groups; a high rank in the *daʿwa* (q.v.) hierarchy of the Ismāʿīlīs. The term *dāʿī* came to be used generically from early on by the Ismāʿīlīs in reference to any authorized representative of their *daʿwa*; a propagandist responsible for spreading the Ismāʿīlī religion and for winning suitable converts.

dāʿī al-duʿāt: chief *dāʿī*; a non-technical term used mainly in non-Ismāʿīlī sources; see *bāb*.

dāʿī muṭlaq: a rank in the *daʿwa* (q.v.) hierarchy of the Fāṭimid Ismāʿīlīs; it later became the highest rank in the Mustaʿlī-Ṭayyibī *daʿwa* organization; the administrative head of the Ṭayyibī *daʿwa* during its Yamanī phase, enjoying absolute authority in the community. It was also adopted by the administrative heads of the Dā'ūdī and Sulaymānī branches of the Ṭayyibī *daʿwa*.

darwīsh (Anglicized dervish): a term meaning 'poor' applied to a practising Ṣūfī (q.v.), with special reference to his poor or wandering life.

dassondh: lit;, tithe, a tenth; equivalent of the Arabic word *ʿushr*; the religious tithe paid annually by the Nizārī Khojas to their imām. Amongst the Persian Nizārīs it is called *dah-yik*, sometimes more generally referred to as *ḥaqq-i imām*.

daʿwa: mission or propaganda; in the religio-political sense, *daʿwa* is the invitation or call to adopt the cause of an individual or family claiming the right to the imāmate; it also refers to the entire hierarchy of ranks, sometimes called *ḥudūd* (q.v.), within the particular religious organization developed for this purpose, especially amongst the Ismāʿīlīs. The Ismāʿīlīs often referred to their movement simply as *al-daʿwa*, or more formally as *al-daʿwa al-hādiya*, 'the rightly-guiding mission'.

dawr (pl., *adwār*): period, era, cycle of history; the Ismāʿīlīs held that the hiero-history of mankind consisted of seven *adwār*, each inaugurated by a speaking prophet or *nāṭiq* (q.v.) who brought a revealed message in the form of a religious law.

dīwān: a public financial register; or a government department; also the collected works of a poet.

faqīh (pl., *fuqahā'*): in its technical meaning it denotes an exponent of *fiqh* (q.v.); a specialist in Islamic jurisprudence; a Muslim jurist in general.

farmān: royal decree; written edict; also called *firman* by the Nizārī Khojas. For the Nizārī Ismāʿīlīs, it refers to any pronouncement, order or ruling made by their imām.

Fāṭimids: descendants of ʿAlī b. Abī Ṭālib and Fāṭima, the Prophet's daughter, corresponding to Fāṭimid ʿAlids (q.v.); also the name of the Ismāʿīlī dynasty of caliph-imāms, claiming Fāṭimid descent, from 297/909 to 567/1171.

fidā'ī (or *fidāwī*): one who offers his life for a cause; a term used for special devotees in several religio-political Muslim groups; particularly those Nizārī Ismāʿīlīs of Persia and Syria who, during the Alamūt period, risked their lives to assassinate the enemies of their sect.

fiqh: the technical term for Islamic jurisprudence; the science of law in Islam; the discipline of elucidating the Sharīʿa (q.v.).

ghayba: lit., absence; the word has been used in a technical sense for the condition of anyone who has been withdrawn by God from the eyes of men and whose life during that period of occultation (called his *ghayba*) may be miraculously prolonged. In this sense, a number of Shīʿī groups have recognized the *ghayba* of one or another imām (q.v.), with the implication that no further imām was to succeed him and he was to return at a foreordained time before the Day of Resurrection, *qiyāma* (q.v.), as Mahdī (q.v.).

Ghulāt (pl. of *ghālī*): exaggerator, extremist; a term of disapproval for individuals accused of exaggeration (*ghuluww*) in religion and in respect to the imāms (q.v.); it was particularly applied to those Shīʿī personalities and groups whose doctrines were offensive to the Twelver Imāmī Shīʿīs.

ginān (*gnān*): derived from a Sanskrit word meaning meditative or contemplative knowledge; a general term used for the corpus of the poetical, religious compositions of the Nizārī Khojas and some related groups. The *ginān* literature exists in a number of Indian languages.

ḥadīth: a report, sometimes translated as tradition, relating an action or saying of the Prophet, or the corpus of such reports collectively, constituting one of the major sources of Islamic law. For the Shīʿīs, it generally also refers to the actions and sayings of their imāms (q.v.). The Shīʿīs accepted those *ḥadīth*s related from the Prophet which had been handed down or sanctioned by their imāms in conjunction with those *ḥadīth*s related from the imāms recognized by them. The Shīʿīs also use the terms *riwāyāt* and *akhbār* as synonyms of *ḥadīth*.

ḥajj: the annual pilgrimage to Mecca and some other sacred localities in the Ḥijāz in the month of Dhu'l-Ḥijja, the last month of the Muslim calendar; required of every Muslim at least once in his lifetime if possible. One who has performed the *ḥajj* is called Ḥājj in Arabic and Ḥājjī in Persian and Turkish.

Ḥanafids: descendants of Muḥammad b. al-Ḥanafiyya, a non-Fāṭimid (q.v.) son of ʿAlī b. Abī Ṭālib.

ḥaqāʾiq (pl. of *ḥaqīqa*): truths; as a technical term it denotes the gnostic system of the Ismāʿīlīs. In this sense, the *ḥaqāʾiq* are the unchangeable truths contained in the *bāṭin* (q.v.); while the law changes with every law-announcing prophet or *nāṭiq* (q.v.), the *ḥaqāʾiq* remain eternal.

Ḥasanids: see ʿAlids.

Hāshimids: descendants of Hāshim b. ʿAbd Manāf, the common ancestor of the Prophet, ʿAlī and al-ʿAbbās. The chief Hāshimid branches were the ʿAlids (q.v.) and the ʿAbbāsids (q.v.). Hāshimid also refers to those Shīʿīs who acknowledged the imāmate of Abū Hāshim, the son of Muḥammad b. al-Ḥanafiyya, and other Ḥanafids (q.v.).

ḥudūd (pl. of *ḥadd*): ranks; a technical term denoting the various ranks in the *daʿwa* (q.v.) hierarchy of the Ismāʿīlīs, also called *ḥudūd al-dīn*.

ḥujja: proof or the presentation of proof. Amongst the Shīʿīs, the term has been used in different senses. Initially, it meant the proof of God's presence or will and as such, it referred to that person who at any given time served as evidence among mankind of God's will. In this sense, the application of the term was systematized by the Imāmī Shīʿīs to designate the category of prophets and imāms (q.v.) and, after the Prophet Muḥammad, more particularly of the imāms. The original Shīʿī application of the term *ḥujja* was retained by the pre-Fāṭimid Ismāʿīlīs who also used *ḥujja* in reference to a dignitary in their religious hierarchy, notably one through whom the inaccessible Mahdī (q.v.) could become accessible to his adherents. The *ḥujja* was also a high rank in the *daʿwa* (q.v.) hierarchy of the Fāṭimid Ismāʿīlīs; there were twelve such *ḥujja*s, each one in charge of a separate *daʿwa* region called *jazīra* (q.v.). In Nizārī Ismāʿīlī *daʿwa*, the term generally denoted the chief representative of the imām, sometimes also called *pīr* (q.v.)

ḥulūl: infusion or incarnation of the divine essence in the human body; amongst some Shīʿī groups, notably the Ghulāt (q.v.), it particularly referred to the incarnation of the divine essence in one or another imām (q.v.).

Ḥusaynids: see ʿAlids.

ilḥād: heresy in religion. The Ismāʿīlīs and related groups were often accused of *ilḥād* by the Twelver Shīʿīs and other Muslim groups amongst their enemies. A person accused of *ilḥād* is called *mulḥid* (pl., *malāḥida*).

ʿilm: knowledge, more specifically religious knowledge. Amongst the Shīʿīs, it was held that every imām (q.v.) possessed a special secret knowledge, *ʿilm*, which was divinely inspired and transmitted through the *naṣṣ* (q.v.) of the preceding imām.

imām (pl., *a'imma*): leader of a group of Muslims in prayer, *ṣalāt*; or the supreme leader of the Muslim community. The title was particularly used by the Shīʿīs in reference to the persons recognized by them as the heads of the Muslim community after the Prophet. The Shīʿīs regard ʿAlī b. Abī Ṭālib and certain of his descendants as such leaders, imāms, the legitimate successors to the Prophet. The imāms are held to be *maʿṣūm*, fully immune from sin and error; they are generally held to be also divinely appointed, and divinely guided in the discharge of their special spiritual functions. Amongst the Sunnīs, the term is used in reference to any great *ʿālim* (q.v.), especially the founder of a legal *madhhab* (q.v.). The office of imām is called imāmate (Arabic, *imāma*).

iqṭāʿ: an administrative grant of land or of its revenues by a Muslim ruler to an individual, usually in recompense for service.

jamāʿa: assembly, religious congregation; also pronounced *jamāʿat* and used by the Nizārī Ismāʿīlīs of the post-Alamūt period in reference to their individual communities.

jamāʿat-khāna: assembly house; congregation place used by the Nizārī Ismāʿīlīs for their religious and communal activities.

jazīra (pl., *jazāʾir*): lit., island; a term denoting a particular *daʿwa* (q.v.) region. The Ismāʿīlīs, specifically the Fāṭimid Ismāʿīlīs, in theory divided the world into twelve regions, sometimes called *jazāʾir al-arḍ*, each *jazīra* representing a separate region for the penetration of their *daʿwa*, and placed under the charge of a *ḥujja* (q.v.).

kalima: word; specifically the divine word, logos; a synonym of *kalimat Allāh*.

kamadia: see *mukhi*.

kashf: manifestation, unveiling; in Ismāʿīlī doctrine, it is used specifically in reference to a period, called *dawr al-kashf*, when the imāms (q.v.) were manifest, or when the *ḥaqāʾiq* (q.v.) would be no longer concealed in the *bāṭin* (q.v.), in distinction from *satr* (q.v.).

khān: Turkish title originally a contraction of *khāqān*, which as a title of sovereignty denoted supremacy over a group of tribes or territories. The title *khān* was used by Turkish Muslim rulers in Central Asia from the 4th/10th century onwards; in time it came to be applied to subordinate rulers and important local officials; also an honorific appellation.

khawāss (or *khāṣṣ*): the elite, the privileged people, in distinction from the *ʿawāmm* (q.v.).

Khoja: see *khwāja*.

khudāwand: lord, master; it was used as a term in reference to the rulers of the Nizārī state in Persia.

khuṭba: an address or sermon delivered (by a *khāṭib*) at the Friday midday public prayers in the mosque; since it includes a prayer for the ruler, mention in the *khuṭba* is a mark of sovereignty in Islam.

khwāja: master; a title used in different senses in Islamic lands; it was frequently accorded to scholars, teachers, merchants, and *wazīrs* (q.v.); in India, it was transformed to Khoja (Khōja), denoting an Indian caste consisting mostly of

Nizārī Ismāʿīlīs. In a looser sense, Khoja is used in reference to an Indian Nizārī, or a Nizārī of Indian origins, in general.

laqab (pl., *alqāb*): nickname, sobriquet, honorific title.

madhhab (pl., *madhāhib*): a system or school of religious law in Islam; in particular it is applied to the four main systems of *fiqh* (q.v.) that arose among the Sunnī Muslims, namely, Ḥanafī, Mālikī, Shāfiʿī and Ḥanbalī, named after the jurists who founded them. Different Shīʿī sects have had their own *madhāhib*. In Persian, the word *madhhab* is also used to mean religion, a synonym of *dīn*.

ma'dhūn: lit., licentiate; a rank in the *daʿwa* (q.v.) hierarchy of the Ismāʿīlīs following that of the *dāʿī*. In post-Fāṭimid period in particular, *ma'dhūn* came to be used generically by the Ismāʿīlīs in reference to the assistant of the *dāʿī*.

madrasa: a college or seminary of higher Muslim learning, frequently attached to a mosque.

Mahdī: the rightly guided one; a name applied to the restorer of religion and justice who, according to a widely held Muslim belief, will appear and rule before the end of the world. This name with its various messianic connotations has been applied to different individuals by Shīʿīs and Sunnīs in the course of the centuries. Belief in the coming of the Mahdī of the family of the Prophet, Ahl al-Bayt (q.v.), became a central aspect of the faith in radical Shīʿism in contrast to Sunnism. Distinctively Shīʿī was also the common belief in a temporary absence or occultation, *ghayba* (q.v.), of the Mahdī and his eventual return, *rajʿa* (q.v.), in glory. In Shīʿī terminology, at least from the 2nd/8th century, the Mahdī was commonly given the epithet al-Qā'im (q.v.), 'riser', also called Qā'im āl Muḥammad, denoting a member of the Prophet's family who would rise and restore justice on earth. Various early Shīʿī groups expected the return of the last imām (q.v.) recognized by them in the role of the Qā'im. In Imāmī and Ismāʿīlī usage, the term Qā'im widely replaced that of Mahdī.

malāḥida (pl. of *mulḥid*): see *ilḥād*.

mawlā (pl., *mawālī*): master, freed slave, or client of an Arab tribe; more specifically a non-Arab convert to Islam who acquired status by attachment to an Arab tribal group. In the early Islamic centuries, the term *mawālī* was applied generally to the non-Arab converts to Islam.

minbar: the pulpit in a mosque, from which the *khuṭba* (q.v.) is delivered.

muʿallim: teacher, specifically religious teacher; also a rank in the *daʿwa* (q.v.) hierarchy of the post-Alamūt Nizārī Ismāʿīlīs.

Muhājirūn: lit., emigrants; name given collectively to those Meccan followers of the Prophet who accompanied him in his emigration (*hijra*) from Mecca to Medina, in distinction from the Anṣār (q.v.).

muḥtashim: a title used commonly in reference to the leader of the Nizārī Ismāʿīlīs of Quhistān in Persia during the Alamūt period.

mukhi: a name originally used by the Indian Nizārīs in reference to the head of a local Nizārī community, *jamāʿa* (q.v.), who acted as treasurer and also officiated on various occasions in the local *jamāʿat-khāna* (q.v.). The *mukhi*'s assistant was called *kamadia* (pronounced *kāmariyā*). The terms *mukhi* and *kamadia*, with various pronunciations, were in time adopted by the Nizārī Ismāʿīlī communities outside of the Indian subcontinent.

mulḥid: see *ilḥād*.

murīd: disciple; specifically, disciple of a Ṣūfī (q.v.) master; member of a Ṣūfī order in general; also frequently used in reference to an ordinary Nizārī Ismāʿīlī in Persia and elsewhere during the post-Alamūt period.

murshid: guide, Ṣūfī master; also used in reference to the imāms of the Nizārī Ismāʿīlīs during the post-Alamūt period.

mustajīb: lit., respondent; a term denoting an ordinary Ismāʿīlī initiate or neophyte.

nabī (pl., *anbiyāʾ*): prophet. The office of *nabī* is called *nubuwwa*.

nafs: soul, often used as a synonym of *rūḥ*.

naṣṣ: explicit designation of a successor by his predecessor, particularly relating to the Shīʿī view of succession to the imāmate, whereby each imām (q.v.), under divine guidance, designates his successor. The Mustaʿlī-Ṭayyibī *dāʿīs* are also designated by the rule of the *naṣṣ*. One who has received the *naṣṣ* is called *manṣūṣ*.

nāṭiq (pl., *nuṭaqāʾ*): lit., speaker, one gifted with speech; in Ismāʿīlī thought, a speaking or law-announcing prophet who brings a new religious law (*sharīʿa*), abrogating the previous law and, hence, initiating a new *dawr* (q.v.) in the hierohistory of mankind. According to the early Ismāʿīlīs, the hierohistory of mankind was comprised of seven eras of various durations, each one inaugurated by a speaker-prophet or enunciator, *nāṭiq*. The early Ismāʿīlīs further maintained that each of the first six *nāṭiqs* was succeeded by a spiritual legatee or executor (*waṣī*), also called foundation (*asās*) or silent one (*ṣāmit*), who interpreted the inner, esoteric, *bāṭin* (q.v.), meaning of the revealed message of that era to the elite. This cyclical prophetic view of religious history was essentially maintained, with various modifications, by the later Ismāʿīlīs.

Nizārids: descendants of Nizār b. al-Mustanṣir, the nineteenth imām of the Nizārī Ismāʿīlīs, to whom the subsequent Nizārī Imāms traced their descent. The followers of the *daʿwa* (q.v.) of the Nizārī Imāms were designated as Nizārīs (Nizāriyya), in distinction from Mustaʿlians (Mustaʿlawiyya or Mustaʿliyya) who recognized Nizār's younger brother al-Mustaʿlī and the latter's descendants as their imāms. In 487/1094, the Fāṭimid Ismāʿīlīs split into Nizārī and Mustaʿlian branches, following different lines of imāms.

pīr: the Persian equivalent of the Arabic word *shaykh* in the sense of a spiritual guide, Ṣūfī (q.v.) master or *murshid* (q.v.), qualified to lead disciples, *murīds* (q.v.), on the mystical path, *ṭarīqa* (q.v.), to truth (*ḥaqīqa*); also used loosely in reference to the imām and the holders of the highest ranks in the *daʿwa* (q.v.) hierarchy of the post-Alamūt Nizārī Ismāʿīlīs; also a chief Nizārī *dāʿī* in a certain territory, in this sense it was particularly used by the Indian Nizārīs in reference to the administrative heads of the *daʿwa* in India.

qāḍī (pl., *quḍāt*): a religious judge administering the sacred law of Islam, the Sharīʿa (q.v.).

qāḍī al-quḍāt: chief *qāḍī*; the highest judiciary officer of the Fāṭimid state.

Qā'im: 'riser'; the eschatological Mahdī (q.v.). In pre-Fāṭimid Ismāʿīlism, the terms Mahdī and Qā'im were both used, as in Imāmī Shīʿism, for the expected messianic imām. After the rise of the Fāṭimids, the name al-Mahdī was reserved for the first Fāṭimid caliph-imām, while the eschatological imām and seventh *nāṭiq* (q.v.) still expected for the future was called the Qā'im by the Ismāʿīlīs.

qaṣīda: a poetic genre of a certain length, normally concerned with the eulogy of a personality; in Persian, it is a lyric poem, most frequently panegyric.

qiyāma: Resurrection and the Last Day, when mankind would be judged and committed forever to either Paradise or Hell; in Ismāʿīlī doctrine, it also came to be used in reference to the end of any partial cycle in the history of mankind, with the implication that the entire hierohistory of mankind consisted of many such partial cycles and partial *qiyāma*s, leading to the final *qiyāma*, sometimes called *qiyāmat al-qiyāmāt*. The Nizārīs of the Alamūt period interpreted the *qiyāma* spiritually as the manifestation of the unveiled truth in the spiritual reality of the current imām (q.v.), who was also called the *Qā'im al-qiyāma*. Thus, the recognition of the true essence of the imām actualized Paradise for the faithful while the imām's opponents were condemned to the Hell of spiritual non-existence.

quṭb (pl., *aqṭāb*): lit., pole; in Islamic mysticism, it denotes the most perfect human being, or *al-insān al-kāmil*; also the head of a Ṣūfī order, *ṭarīqa* (q.v.).

rafīq (pl., *rafīqān*): comrade, friend; the Nizārī Ismāʿīlīs of Persia commonly addressed one another by this term during the Alamūt period.

rajʿa: lit., return; the word has been used in a technical sense to denote the return or reappearance of a messianic personality, specifically one considered as the Mahdī (q.v.). A number of early Shīʿī groups awaited the return of one or another imām as the Mahdī, often together with many of his supporters, from the dead or from occultation, *ghayba* (q.v.), before the Day of Resurrection, *qiyāma* (q.v.).

risāla (pl., *rasā'il*): treatise, letter, epistle.

Ṣaḥāba: companions; as a technical term it denotes the Companions of the Prophet, including the Muhājirūn (q.v.) and the Anṣār (q.v.), amongst other categories.

ṣāmit: lit., silent one; successor to a speaking prophet, *nāṭiq* (q.v.).

satr: concealment, veiling; in Ismāʿīlī doctrine, it is used specifically in reference to a period, called *dawr al-satr*, when the imāms (q.v.) were hidden from the eyes of their followers, or when the *ḥaqā'iq* (q.v.) were concealed in the *bāṭin* (q.v.), in distinction from *kashf* (q.v.).

sayyid (pl., *sādāt*): lord, master; an honorific appellation for men of authority; the term has been used extensively, but not exclusively, for the descendants of the Prophet, particularly in the Ḥusaynid line; see ʿAlids.

Shāh: an Iranian royal title denoting a king; it is often also added to the names of Ṣūfī (q.v.) saints and Nizārī Imāms of the post-Alamūt period.

Sharīʿa (or Sharʿ): the divinely revealed sacred law of Islam; the whole body of rules guiding the life of a Muslim. The provisions of the Sharīʿa are worked out through the discipline of *fiqh* (q.v.).

sharīf (pl., *ashrāf*): noble; at first used generally of the leading Arab families, then more particularly of the descendants of the Prophet, particularly in the Ḥasanid line; see ʿAlids.

shaykh: old man, elder; the chief of a tribe, any religious dignitary; in particular, an independent Ṣūfī (q.v.) master or spiritual guide, qualified to lead aspirants on the Ṣūfī path, *ṭarīqa* (q.v.); in this sense called *pīr* in Persian; *shaykh* (pl., *mashāyikh*) is also a high rank in the *daʿwa* organization of the Dāʾūdī Ṭayyibīs.

Ṣūfī: an exponent of Ṣūfism (*taṣawwuf*), the commonest term for that aspect of Islam which is based on the mystical life; hence, it denotes a Muslim mystic; more specifically, a member of an organized Ṣūfī order, *ṭarīqa* (q.v.).

sulṭān (Anglicized, sultan): a Muslim term for sovereign; the supreme political and military authority in a Muslim state.

sunna: custom, practice; particularly that associated with the exemplary life of the Prophet, comprising his deeds, utterances and his unspoken approval; it is embodied in *ḥadīth* (q.v.).

tafsīr: lit., explanation, commentary; particularly the commentaries on the Qurʾān; the external, philological exegesis of the Qurʾān, in distinction from *taʾwīl* (q.v.).

Ṭālibids: descendants of Abū Ṭālib b. ʿAbd al-Muṭṭalib, the father of ʿAlī and full-brother of the Prophet's father ʿAbd Allāh; including particularly the ʿAlids (q.v.) and the descendants of ʿAlī's brother Jaʿfar al-Ṭayyār.

taʿlīm: teaching, instruction; in Shīʿism, authoritative teaching in religion which could be carried out only by an imām (q.v.) in every age after the Prophet.

tanāsukh: metempsychosis, transmigration of souls; passing of the soul (*nafs* or *rūḥ*) from one body to another; reincarnation of the soul of an individual in a different human body or in a different creature.

taqiyya: precautionary dissimulation of one's true religious beliefs, especially in time of danger; used especially by the Shīʿīs.

ṭarīqa: way, path; the mystical path followed by Ṣūfīs (q.v.); also any one of the organized Ṣūfī orders.

taʾwīl: the educing of the inner meaning from the literal wording or apparent meaning of a text or a ritual, religious prescription; as a technical term among the Shīʿīs, particularly the Ismāʿīlīs, it denotes the method of educing the *bāṭin* (q.v.) from the *ẓāhir* (q.v.); as such it was extensively used by the Ismāʿīlīs for the allegorical, symbolic or esoteric interpretation of the Qurʾān, the Sharīʿa, historical events and the world of nature. Translated also as spiritual or hermeneutic exegesis, *taʾwīl* may be distinguished from *tafsīr* (q.v.).

ʿulamāʾ: see *ʿālim*.

umma: community, any people as followers of a particular religion or prophet; in particular, the Muslims as forming a religious community.

walī al-ʿahd: heir designate, designated successor to a sovereign.

waṣī (pl., *awṣiyā'*): legatee, executor of a will; also the immediate successor to a prophet; in this sense, it was the function of *awṣiyā'* to interpret and explain the messages brought by prophets, *anbiyā'*; see *nāṭiq*.

wazīr (Anglicized vizier): a high officer of state, the equivalent of a chief minister. The power and status of the office of *wazīr*, called *wizāra* (Anglicized vizierate), varied greatly.

ẓāhir: the outward, apparent, or literal meaning of sacred texts and religious prescriptions, notably the Qur'ān and the Sharī'a (q.v.), in distinction from the *bāṭin* (q.v.).

NOTES

The following abbreviations are used in the notes and bibliography.

AIEO	*Annales de l'Institut d'Études Orientales*
AI(U)ON	*Annali dell' Istituto (Universitario) Orientale di Napoli*
BIFAO	*Bulletin de l'Institut Français d'Archéologie Orientale*
BSO(A)S	*Bulletin of the School of Oriental (and African) Studies*
EI	*Encyclopaedia of Islam*, 1st edition
EI2	*Encyclopaedia of Islam*, New edition
EII	*Encyclopaedia of Iran and Islam*
EIR	*Encyclopaedia Iranica*
EJ	*Eranos Jahrbuch*
ERE	*Encyclopaedia of Religion and Ethics*
GJ	*Geographical Journal*
IC	*Islamic Culture*
IJMES	*International Journal of Middle East Studies*
JA	*Journal Asiatique*
JAOS	*Journal of the American Oriental Society*
JASB	*Journal and Proceedings of the Asiatic Society of Bengal*
JBBRAS	*Journal of the Bombay Branch of the Royal Asiatic Society*
JESHO	*Journal of the Economic and Social History of the Orient*
JRAS	*Journal of the Royal Asiatic Society of Great Britain and Ireland*
MW	*Muslim World*
NS	*New Series, Nuova Serie*
REI	*Revue des Études Islamiques*
RHC	*Recueil des Historiens des Croisades*
RHCHO	*Recueil des Historiens des Croisades: Historiens Orientaux*
RSO	*Rivista degli Studi Orientali*
SEI	*Shorter Encyclopaedia of Islam*
SI	*Studia Islamica*
ZDMG	*Zeitschrift der Deutschen Morgenländischen Gesellschaft*

1. *Introduction: Western progress in Ismāʿīlī studies*

1. For the treatment of the Ismāʿīlīs, and especially the Nizārīs, in mediaeval European writings, see Camille Falconet, 'Dissertation sur les Assassins, peuple d'Asie', *Mémoires de Littérature, tirés des Registres de l'Académie Royale des Inscriptions et Belles Lettres*, 17 (1751), pp. 127–170; translated into English as an appendix in Jean de Joinville, *Memoirs of John Lord de Joinville*, tr. T. Johnes (Hafod, 1807), vol. 2, pp. 287–328; Charles E. Nowell, 'The Old Man of the Mountain', *Speculum*, 22 (1947), pp. 497–519; B. Lewis, *The Assassins: A Radical Sect in Islam* (London, 1967), pp. 1–9; J. Hauziński, *Muzulmánska sekta asasynów w europejskim piśmiennictwie wieków średnich* (Poznan, 1978), and Leopold Hellmuth, *Die Assassinenlegende in der österreichischen Geschichtsdichtung des Mittelalters* (Vienna, 1988), the most comprehensive modern survey of the subject.
2. Benjamin of Tudela, *The Itinerary*, ed. and tr. Marcus N. Adler (London, 1907), translation pp. 16–17.
3. Ibid., translation pp. 53–54.
4. The Latin text of this report is incorporated in Arnold of Lübeck's *Chronica Slavorum*, book 7, chap. 8, in *Monumenta Germaniae Historica: Scriptores*, ed. Georg H. Pertz et al. (Hanover, 1869), vol. 21, p. 240.
5. William of Tyre, *Historia rerum in patribus transmarinis gestarum*, book 20, chap. 29, in *RHC: Historiens Occidentaux* (Paris, 1844–1895), vol. 1, pp. 995–996; English translation, *A History of Deeds Done Beyond the Sea*, tr. E. A. Babcock and A. C. Krey (New York, 1943), vol. 2, pp. 390–392.
6. See, for example, Ambroise, *L'Estoire de la guerre Sainte*, ed. G. Paris (Paris, 1897), cols. 233–239, and the old French continuations of William of Tyre (Guillaume de Tyr), namely *L'Estoire de Eracles empereur et la conqueste de la Terre d'Outremer*, book 24, chap. 15, in *RHC: Historiens Occidentaux*, vol. 2, pp. 192–194, and *La Chronique d'Ernoul et de Bernard le Trésorier*, ed. L. de Mas Latrie (Paris, 1871), pp. 288–289. For further accounts, by Anglo-Norman chroniclers, see William of Newburgh, *Historia rerum Anglicarum*, ed. Hans C. Hamilton (London, 1856), pp. 165–166; Roger of Hoveden, *Chronica*, ed. W. Stubbs (London, 1870), vol. 3, p. 181, published as volume 51 in the monumental collection of British mediaeval chronicles officially entitled Rerum Britannicarum medii aevi scriptores, and popularly known as the Rolls Series; the chronicle (possibly written by a certain Londoner, Richard of Holy Trinity) *Itinerarium peregrinorum et gesta regis Ricardi*, ed. W. Stubbs, in *Chronicles and Memorials of the Reign of Richard I*, Rolls Series 38 (London, 1864), pp. 337–342 and 444–445, and the work attributed to Geoffrey Vinsauf, *Itinerary of Richard I and Others to the Holy Land*, in *Chronicles of the Crusades; being Contemporary Narratives of the Crusade of Richard Cœur de Lion and of the Crusade of Saint Louis* (London, 1848), pp. 276–277.
7. Arnold of Lübeck, *Chronica*, book 4, chap. 16, in *Monumenta Germaniae*, vol. 21, p. 179.
8. *L'Estoire de Eracles*, pp. 216 and 230–231; *Chronique d'Ernoul*, pp. 323–324; Marino Sanudo Torsello, *Liber secretorum fidelium Crucis*, in *Gesta Dei per*

Francos, ed. J. Bongars (Hanover, 1611), vol. 2, p. 207; Sanudo completed and presented this work in 1321 to Pope John XXII; friar Pipino, who also wrote in the early decades of the fourteenth century, is the author of a lengthy *Chronica* down to 1314 in which (chaps. 38–41) he repeats what his predecessors had said about the Ismāʿīlīs. Extracts of this chronicle are to be found in *Rerum Italicarum scriptores*, ed. Ludovico A. Muratori (Milan, 1723–1751), vol. 9, where the leap story is mentioned on p. 705. The same story appears as an incident in the poetical French romance of Bauduin de Sebourc, a work ascribed to the early fourteenth century, namely *Li romans de Bauduin de Sebourc IIIe, Roy de Jherusalem* (Valenciennes, 1841), vol. 1, p. 359, where the sectarians are called the *Hauts-Assis*, and also at the end of an Italian collection of old stories, *Cento novelle antiche* (Florence, 1572), p. 92, where the German emperor Frederick wrongly replaces Henry of Champagne as the dignitary who visited the Old Man (*Veglio*).

9. James of Vitry (Jacques de Vitri), *Historia Orientalis seu Hierosolymitana*, in *Gesta Dei per Francos*, vol. 1, pp. 1062 and 1095.
10. He insisted, however, that these sectarians, despite their Jewish descent, did not adhere to Jewish law; see *Magistri Thietmari Peregrinatio*, ed. J. C. M. Laurent (Hamburg, 1857), p. 52.
11. Matthew Paris, *Chronica majora*, ed. Henry R. Luard, Rolls Series 57 (London, 1876), vol. 3, pp. 487–489; English translation, *Matthew Paris's English History*, tr. John A. Giles (London, 1852), vol. 1, pp. 131–132; where it is also related that whilst the Ismāʿīlī envoy was presenting his case before the king of England, the bishop of Winchester who was at the audience interrupted the proceedings and remarked: 'Let us leave these dogs to devour one another, that they may all be consumed, and perish; and we, when we proceed against the enemies of Christ who remain, will slay them, and cleanse the face of the earth, so that all the world will be subject to the one Catholic Church.'
12. Jean de Joinville, *Histoire de Saint Louis*, ed. Natalis de Wailly (Paris, 1874), pp. 88, 160ff. and 246ff. In English translation, the main section on the exchange of the embassies is to be found in Joinville, *Memoirs*, vol. 1, pp. 194–197, which is based on the 1668 edition of the old French text prepared by Charles du Fresne du Cange, also reprinted in *Chronicles of the Crusades*, pp. 470–474.
13. Falconet notes, however, that the word Bedouin, occurring in du Cange's and in later editions, may only represent a scribal misreading since it does not occur in Joinville's original manuscript, which had found its way to the Bibliothèque du Roi; see Falconet, 'Dissertation', p. 165. Du Cange himself seems to have been aware of the issue when he accused Joinville of confounding the Bedouins with the Assassins; see his note in Joinville, *Memoirs*, vol. 1, pp. 331–332.
14. Joinville, *Memoirs*, vol. 1, pp. 148–149, reprinted in *Chronicles of the Crusades*, pp. 420–421.
15. William of Rubruck (Willem van Ruysbroeck), *The Journey of William of*

Rubruck to the Eastern Parts of the World, 1253–55, ed. and tr. William W. Rockhill (London, 1900), pp. 118 and 221–222.

16. Marco Polo, *The Book of Ser Marco Polo*, ed. and tr. Henry Yule, third revised edition by Henri Cordier (London, 1903), vol. 1, pp. 139–146, utilized as our main source of reference. See also the English edition of A. C. Moule and P. Pelliot, entitled *Marco Polo, the Description of the World* (London, 1938), vol. 1, pp. 128–133, based on a Latin version discovered in 1932 at the Cathedral Library in Toledo, but also containing collated passages drawn from other important manuscripts of this work.
17. For various corruptions of *mulḥid* in different texts of Marco Polo, see Paul Pelliot, *Notes on Marco Polo* (Paris, 1959–1973), vol. 2, pp. 785–787.
18. See Yule's comments in his valuable introduction to the *Book of Ser Marco Polo*, vol. 1, p. 142, and Pelliot, *Notes*, vol. 1, pp. 52–55, where other forms of this name, appearing in different manuscript copies of Marco Polo, are cited.
19. On this point, see Freya Stark, 'The Assassins' Valley and the Salambar Pass', *GJ*, 77 (1931), especially pp. 53–54.
20. *Book of Ser Marco Polo*, vol. 1, p. 148. See also Norman M. Penzer's introductory remarks in his edition of Marco Polo, based on the first English translation of this work undertaken in the sixteenth century by John Frampton, entitled *The Most Noble and Famous Travels of Marco Polo* (London, 1929), pp. xxxviii–xxxix.
21. See *Book of Ser Marco Polo*, vol. 1, p. 149, where this castle is alluded to.
22. For the reconstruction of Marco Polo's disputable itinerary in eastern Persia, see Percy M. Sykes, *Ten Thousand Miles in Persia* (New York, 1902), pp. 260–273; also his *History of Afghanistan* (London, 1940), vol. 1, pp. 245–246, where Tūn is suggested as the locality of the Nizārī castle; Sven A. Hedin, *Overland to India* (London, 1910), vol. 2, pp. 67–77; H. Cordier, 'L'Itinéraire de Marco Polo en Perse', in his *Mélanges d'histoire et de géographie Orientales* (Paris, 1920), vol. 2, pp. 40–52, and his *Ser Marco Polo, Notes and Addenda to Sir Henry Yule's Edition* (London, 1920), pp. 32–34.
23. In some versions of Marco Polo the term *Assassin* does not appear at all; see, for example, *The Travels of Marco Polo*, ed. Thomas Wright (London, 1854), pp. 73–77, which is a revised edition of William Marsden's well-known English edition published in 1818 and itself translated from the Italian version prepared by Giovanni B. Ramusio and published in Venice in 1559.
24. For more details, see B. Lewis, 'Assassins of Syria and Ismāʿīlīs of Persia', in Accademia Nazionale dei Lincei, *Atti del convegno internazionale sul tema: La Persia nel medioevo* (Rome, 1971), especially pp. 573–576, reprinted in his *Studies in Classical and Ottoman Islam (7th–16th Centuries)* (London, 1976).
25. F. M. Chambers, 'The Troubadours and the Assassins', *Modern Language Notes*, 64 (1949), pp. 245–251.
26. Cited in Nowell, 'Old Man of the Mountain', p. 515, and Lewis, *Assassins*, pp. 2 and 142.
27. Lewis, *Assassins*, p. 8.

28. Lewis, 'Assassins of Syria', p. 575.
29. Bauduin de Sebourc, *Li romans*, vol. 1, pp. 319–364.
30. Jacopo d'Acqui, *Imago mundi*, in *Monumenta Historia Patriae* (Turin, 1848), vol. 3, pp. 1557ff.
31. Pelliot, *Notes*, vol. 2, p. 785.
32. Odoric of Pordenone (Odorico da Pordenone), *The Journal of Friar Odoric*, in *The Travels of Sir John Mandeville . . . With Three Narratives*, ed. A. W. Pollard (London, 1900), pp. 356–357; Odoric's narrative here is reprinted from the English translation first published in the second volume of Richard Hakluyt's *Principal Navigations* (London, 1599).
33. *Directorium ad passagium faciendum*, in *RHC*: *Documents Arméniens* (Paris, 1869–1906), vol. 2, pp. 496–497.
34. F. Fabri, *Evagatorium in Terrae Sanctae, Arabiae et Egypti peregrinationem*, ed. C. D. Hassler (Stuttgart, 1843–1849), vol. 2, pp. 323–328.
35. *The Book of Wanderings of Brother Felix Fabri*, tr. A. Stewart (London, 1893), p. 390.
36. Denis Lebey de Batilly, *Traicté de l'origine des anciens Assasins porte-couteaux; avec quelques exemples de leurs attentats et homicides és personnes d'aucuns Roys, Princes, et Seigneurs de la Chrestienté* (Lyon, 1603); apparently published separately also in Paris in the same year; reprinted in *Collection des Meilleurs Dissertations, Notices et traités particuliers relatifs à l'Histoire de France*, ed. C. Leber (Paris, 1838), vol. 20, pp. 453–501.
37. Arnold of Lübeck, *Chronica Slavorum*, ed. H. Bengertus (Lübeck, 1659), pp. 379–382 and 550–551.
38. See *Voyage de Rabbi Benjamin*, tr. J. P. Baratier (Amsterdam, 1733), notes to chaps. 7 and 15.
39. Du Cange, *Glossarium ad scriptores mediae et infimae Latinitatis, cum supplementis integris D. P. Carpenterii*, ed. L. Favre (Niort, 1883), vol. 1, p. 428. Du Cange had previously taken up the matter in one of his notes to his edition of Joinville's work; see Joinville, *Memoirs*, vol. 1, pp. 357–358.
40. Barthélemy d'Herbelot de Molainville, *Bibliothèque orientale, ou dictionnaire universel, contenant généralement tout ce qui regarde la connoissance des peuples de l'Orient* (Paris, 1697).
41. T. Hyde, *Historia religionis veterum Persarum* (Oxford, 1700), pp. 36 and 493.
42. J. S. Assemani, *Bibliotheca Orientalis Clementino-Vaticana* (Rome, 1719–1728), vol. 2, pp. 214–215 and 318–320.
43. See, for example, *Mémoires des missions dans le Levant* (Paris, 1727), vol. 6, pp. 208–209; Joseph de Guignes, *Histoire générale de Huns* (Paris, 1757), vol. 3, pp. 128–129; Carsten Niebuhr, *Reisebeschreibung nach Arabien und andern umliegenden landern* (Copenhagen, 1778), vol. 2, pp. 444–445, which contains this famous traveller's notes on the Syrian Ismāʿīlīs, and G. F. Mariti, *Voyage dans l'isle de Chypre, la Syrie, et la Paléstine avec l'histoire générale du Levant* (Paris, 1791), vol. 2, pp. 22, 24 and 52, originally published in Italian in 1769.
44. Lévesque de la Ravalière, 'Éclaircissemens sur quelques circonstances de l'histoire du Vieux de la Montagne, Prince des Assassins', *Histoire de l'Académie Royale des Inscriptions et Belles Lettres*, 16 (1751), pp. 155–164;

translated into English as an appendix in Joinville, *Memoirs*, vol. 2, pp. 275–285.

45. See, for example, Puget de Saint Pierre, *Histoire des Druses* (Paris, 1763); Johann G. Eichhorn, 'Von der religion der Drusen', *Repertorium für Biblische und Morgenländishe Litteratur*, 12 (1783), pp, 108ff., and J. G. Worbs, *Geschichte und beschreibung des landes der Drusen in Syrien* (Görlitz, 1799).
46. S. Assemani, 'Ragguaglio storico-critico sopra la setta Assissana, detta volgarmente degli Assassini', *Giornale dell' Italiana Letteratura*, 13 (1806), pp. 241–262, also published separately in Padua in 1806.
47. Giovanni F. Mariti, *Memorie istoriche del popolo degli Assassini e del Vecchio della Montagna, loro capo-signore* (Leghorn, 1807). According to this Italian abbot's work, which may have been a reprint of an earlier 1787 edition, the name *Assassins* derived from *Arsasids*; the latter being the designation for the inhabitants of the Kurdish town of Arsacia from where the first Ismāʿīlīs had allegedly migrated to Syria.
48. G. Bokti, 'Notizie sull' origine della religione dei Drusi raccolte da vari istorici arabi', *Fundgruben des Orients*, 1 (1809), p. 31.
49. For further details on the life and academic accomplishments of de Sacy, see J. Reinaud, 'Notice historique et littéraire sur M. le baron Silvestre de Sacy', *JA*, 3 série, 6 (1838), pp. 113–195; H. Derenbourg, *Silvestre de Sacy* (Paris, 1895), and H. Dehérain, *Silvestre de Sacy, 1758–1838, ses contemporains et ses disciples* (Paris, 1938).
50. De Sacy's works on the Druzes include editions of a number of extracts with French translations from Druze manuscripts, published in his *Chrestomathie Arabe* (Paris, 1806), vol. 1, pp. 260–309, and vol. 2, pp. 334–403; 'Mémoire sur l'origine du culte que les Druzes rendent à la figure d'un veau', *Mémoires de l'Institut Royal de France*, 3 (1818), pp. 74–128, where the earlier European literature on the Druzes is also reviewed; and most importantly *Exposé de la religion des Druzes* (Paris, 1838), 2 vols., partial German translation, *Die Drusen und ihre Vorläufer*, tr. Philipp Wolff (Leipzig, 1845).
51. Silvestre de Sacy, 'Mémoire sur la dynastie des Assassins, et sur l'étymologie de leur nom', *Mémoires de l'Institut Royal de France*, 4 (1818), pp. 1–84; shorter versions of this memoir were published earlier in the *Moniteur*, 210 (1809), pp. 828–830, and in *Annales des Voyages*, 8 (1809), pp. 325–343.
52. Lewis, *Assassins*, p. 11, and also his 'Assassins of Syria', pp. 573–574.
53. An elaborate version of this story on the use of *ḥashīsh* to stimulate ecstatic visions of paradise is contained in an Arabic novel about the Syrian Ismāʿīlīs. This novel was discovered by von Hammer, who took it seriously and later cited it to reject de Sacy's doubts regarding the existence of an actual Nizārī garden of paradise; see J. von Hammer-Purgstall, 'Sur le paradis du Vieux de la Montagne', *Fundgruben des Orients*, 3 (1813), pp. 201–206.
54. Marshall G. S. Hodgson, *The Order of Assassins; the Struggle of the Early Nizārī Ismāʿīlīs against the Islamic World* (The Hague, 1955), pp. 133–137; B. Lewis, 'Ḥashīshiyya', *EI2*, vol. 3, pp. 267–268, and also his *Assassins*, pp. 11–12.
55. For the application of the term to the Syrian Nizārīs, see al-Bundārī, *Zubdat al-nuṣra*, ed. M. Th. Houtsma, in his Recueil de textes relatifs à l'histoire des

Seldjoucides II (Leiden, 1889), pp. 169 and 195; Ibn Muyassar, *Akhbār Miṣr*, ed. H. Massé (Cairo, 1919), p. 68; ed. A. Fu'ād Sayyid (Cairo, 1981), p. 102; M. T. Dānishpazhūh, 'Dhaylī bar ta'rīkh-i Ismā'īliyya', *Revue de la Faculté des Lettres, Université de Tabriz*, 17 (1344/1965), p. 312, and Rashīd al-Dīn, *Histoire des Mongols de la Perse*, ed. and tr. É. Quatremère (Paris, 1836), notes on pp. 122–128. Professor Madelung has informed the author that the Persian Nizārīs, too, are called *ḥashīshīs* in some Caspian Zaydī sources of the early seventh/thirteenth century; these sources include the letter of Yūsuf al-Jīlānī to the Yamanī Zaydī scholar ʿImrān b. al-Ḥasan al-Hamdānī, and Ḥumayd al-Muḥallī's *Kitāb al-ḥadā'iq al-wardiyya*, which are now contained in W. Madelung, ed., *Arabic Texts Concerning the History of the Zaydī Imāms of Ṭabaristān, Daylamān and Gīlān* (Beirut, 1987), pp. 146 and 329. Thus, B. Lewis has not been accurate in arguing that the Muslims have used the term *ḥashīshiyya* exclusively in reference to the Nizārīs of Syria.

56. *Al-Hidāyatu'l-Āmirīya*, ed. Asaf A. A. Fyzee (London, etc., 1938), text pp. 27 and 32, reprinted in Jamāl al-Dīn al-Shayyāl, ed., *Majmūʿat al-wathā'iq al-Fāṭimiyya* (Cairo, 1958), pp. 233 and 239.
57. See the following works by É. Quatremère: 'Notice historique sur les Ismaëliens', *Fundgruben des Orients*, 4 (1814), pp. 339–376; 'Mémoires historiques sur la dynastie des Khalifes Fatimites', *JA*, 3 série, 2 (1836), pp. 97–142, and 'Vie du khalife Fatimite Möezz-li-din-Allah', *JA*, 3 série, 2 (1836), pp. 401–439, and 3 (1837), pp. 44–93 and 165–208.
58. Am. Jourdain, 'Histoire de la dynastie des Ismaéliens de Perse', *Notices et Extraits des Manuscrits*, 9 (1813), translation pp. 143–182, text pp. 192–248, and also his 'Sur les Assassins', in Joseph F. Michaud, *Histoire des Croisades* (Paris, 1825), vol. 2, pp. 449–477, reprinted in the enlarged edition of this work prepared by M. Huillard Bréholles (Paris, 1849), vol. 1, pp. 472–488; English translation, *Michaud's History of the Crusades*, tr. W. Robson (London, 1852), vol. 3, pp. 413–431.
59. Silvestre de Sacy, *Exposé*, vol. 1, introduction pp. 20–246; see also his 'Recherches sur l'initiation à la secte des Ismaéliens', *JA*, 1 série, 4 (1824), pp. 298–311 and 321–331.
60. See Hodgson, *Order of Assassins*, pp. 22ff.
61. Joseph von Hammer, *Die Geschichte der Assassinen aus Morgenländischen Quellen* (Stuttgart–Tübingen, 1818).
62. French translation, *Histoire de l'ordre des Assassins*, tr. J. Hellert and P. A. de la Nourais (Paris, 1833), reprinted (Paris, 1961); English translation, *The History of the Assassins*, tr. Oswald C. Wood (London, 1835), reprinted with an introduction by S. Shraddhananda Sanyasi (Benares, 1926) and more recently (New York, 1968). It should also be mentioned that only the English edition contains, at its end as Note D, the translation of de Sacy's famous memoir on the Assassins, as it had appeared in the *Moniteur*.
63. For example, von Hammer is cited as a main authority by Freya Stark, the noted traveller to the Alamūt valley, in her *The Valleys of the Assassins* (London, 1934), p. 228, and in Betty Bouthoul's celebrated historical

romance entitled *Le Grand Maître des Assassins* (Paris, 1936), reproduced as *Le Vieux de la Montagne* (Paris, 1958). Some authors of popular works on the subject still continue to take von Hammer seriously; see Jean-Claude Frère, *L'Ordre des Assassins* (Paris, 1973).

64. See von Hammer, *History of the Assassins* (London, 1835), pp. 136–138.
65. Ibid., pp. 1–2.
66. Ibid., p. 218.
67. Ibid., pp. 216–217.
68. C. Defrémery, 'Histoire des Seldjoukides, extraite du Tarikh-i guzideh, ou Histoire choisie, d'Hamd Allah Mustaufi', *JA*, 4 série, 13 (1849), pp. 26–49.
69. C. Defrémery, 'Nouvelles recherches sur les Ismaéliens ou Bathiniens de Syrie, plus connus sous le nom d'Assassins', *JA*, 5 série, 3 (1854), pp. 373–421, and 5 (1855), pp. 5–76, and also his 'Essai sur l'histoire des Ismaéliens ou Batiniens de la Perse, plus connus sous le nom d'Assassins', *JA*, 5 série, 8 (1856), pp. 353–387, and 15 (1860), pp. 130–210.
70. R. Dozy, *Histoire des Musulmans d'Espagne* (Leiden, 1861), vol. 3, pp. 7ff., and his *Essai sur l'histoire de l'Islamisme*, tr. V. Chauvin (Leiden–Paris, 1879), pp. 257–313.
71. See the following works by M. J. de Goeje: *Mémoire sur les Carmathes du Bahraïn et les Fatimides* (Leiden, 1862; 2nd ed., Leiden, 1886); 'La Fin de l'empire des Carmathes du Bahraïn', *JA*, 9 série, 5 (1895), pp. 5–30, and 'Carmaṭians', *ERE*, vol. 3, pp. 222–225.
72. F. Wüstenfeld, 'Geschichte der Faṭimiden chalifen nach den Arabischen Quellen', *Abhandlungen der Königlichen Gesellschaft der Wissenschaften zu Göttingen, Historich-philologische Classe*, 26 (1880), pp. 1–97, and 27 (1881), pp. 1–130 and 1–126, reprinted (Hildesheim–New York, 1976).
73. H. Guys, *La nation Druse* (Paris, 1863); also by Guys, *Théogonie des Druses* (Paris, 1863); F. Wüstenfeld, *Fachr ed-dīn der Drusenfürst und seine Zeitgenossen* (Göttingen, 1886); and also some travel accounts such as Henry H. M. Carnarvon, *Recollections of the Druses of Lebanon* (2nd ed., London, 1860); and Charles H. Churchill, *The Druzes and the Maronites under the Turkish Rule* (London, 1862).
74. E. G. Browne, *A Literary History of Persia, from the Earliest Times until Firdawsi* (London, 1902), pp. 391–415; and also his *A Literary History of Persia, from Firdawsi to Saʿdi* (London, 1906), pp. 190–211 and 453–460. See also the anonymous article 'Assassins', *EI*, vol. 1, pp. 491–492, and David S. Margoliouth, 'Assassins', *ERE*, vol. 2, pp. 138–141, where a more balanced view is presented.
75. See the following works by Silvestre de Sacy: 'Notice des manuscrits des livres sacrés des Druzes, qui se trouvent dans diverses bibliothèques de l'Europe', *JA*, 1 série, 5 (1824), pp. 3–18, and *Exposé*, vol. 1, introduction pp. 454–465.
76. J. B. L. J. Rousseau, 'Mémoire sur l'Ismaélis et les Nosaïris de Syrie, adressé à M. Silvestre de Sacy', *Annales des Voyages*, 14 (1811), pp. 271–303, which contains some explanatory notes by de Sacy himself. This memoir was later

incorporated into Rousseau's expanded work entitled *Mémoire sur les trois plus fameuses sectes du Musulmanisme; les Wahabis, les Nosaïris et les Ismaélis* (Paris, 1818), pp. 51ff.

77. Rousseau, 'Mémoire', pp. 279–280. Rousseau had already communicated, in 1808, some of this information to de Sacy who added it to the end of his own 'Mémoire sur la dynastie des Assassins', p. 84, published after a delay of some ten years; the same details were subsequently cited repeatedly by von Hammer, Defrémery, Guyard and others.
78. J. B. Fraser, *Narrative of a Journey into Khorasān, in the years 1821 and 1822* (London, 1825), pp. 376–377.
79. For a brief account of these events from the pen of an Englishman attached to the British legation in Tehran, see Robert G. Watson, *A History of Persia* (London, 1866), pp. 191–192 and 331–334.
80. J. L. Burckhardt, *Travels in Syria and the Holy Land* (London, 1822), pp. 150–156.
81. J. B. L. J. Rousseau, 'Extraits d'un livre qui contient la doctrine des Ismaélis', *Annales des Voyages*, 18 (1812), pp. 222–249.
82. S. Guyard, 'Fragments relatifs à la doctrine des Ismaélîs', *Notices et Extraits des Manuscrits*, 22 (1874), pp. 177–428, published also separately (Paris, 1874).
83. S. Guyard, 'Un Grand Maître des Assassins au temps de Saladin', *JA*, 7 série, 9 (1877), pp. 324–489.
84. A preliminary note on the contents of this manuscript had been published earlier by its original discoverer, J. Catafago, a dragoman at the Prussian consulate in Syria; see 'Lettre de M. Catafago à M. Mohl', *JA*, 4 série, 12 (1848), pp. 485–493.
85. Edward E. Salisbury, 'Translation of Two Unpublished Arabic Documents Relating to the Doctrines of the Ismāʿilis and other Bāṭinian Sects', *JAOS*, 2 (1851), pp. 257–324, and also his 'Translation of an Unpublished Arabic Risāleh by Khālid Ibn Zeid el-Juʿfy', *JAOS*, 3 (1852), pp. 165–193.
86. *Sefer nameh; relation du voyage de Nassiri Khosrau en Syrie, en Palestine, en Égypte, en Arabie et en Perse*, ed. and tr. Charles Schefer (Paris, 1881); English translation, *Nāṣer-e Khosraw's Book of Travels (Safarnāma)*, tr. W. M. Thackston, Jr. (Albany, N.Y., 1986); Hermann Ethé, 'Nāsir Chusrau's Rūšanāināma oder Buch der Erleuchtung, in Text und Uebersetzung', *ZDMG*, 33 (1879), pp. 645–665, and 34 (1880), pp. 428–464 and 617–642, and Edmond Fagnan, 'Le Livre de la félicité, par Nāçir ed-Dīn ben Khosroū', *ZDMG*, 34 (1880), pp. 643–674, containing the text and French translation of a work, the *Saʿādat-nāma*, wrongly attributed until recently to Nāṣir-i Khusraw.
87. P. Casanova, 'Notice sur un manuscrit de la secte des Assassins', *JA*, 9 série, 11 (1898), pp. 151–159; see also his 'Une date astronomique dans les Épîtres des Ikhwān aṣ-Ṣafā', *JA*, 11 série, 5 (1915), pp. 5–17.
88. P. Casanova, 'Monnaie des Assassins de Perse', *Revue Numismatique*, 3 série, 11 (1893), pp. 343–352.
89. Fr. Dieterici, *Die Abhandlungen der Ichwān es-Safā in Auswahl; zum ersten Mal aus arabischen Handschriften* (Leipzig, 1883–1886), 2 vols.; also published as

vols. 13 and 14 of his *Die Philosophie der Araber* (Leipzig–Berlin, 1858–1891), containing an almost complete German translation of the *Epistles*.

90. W. Monteith, 'Journal of a Tour through Azerdbijan and the Shores of the Caspian', *Journal of the Royal Geographical Society*, 3 (1833), especially pp. 15–16; J. Shiel, 'Itinerary from Tehrān to Alamūt and Khurrem-ābād in May 1837', *Journal of the Royal Geographical Society*, 8 (1838), pp. 430–434, which contains the account of the first Westerner in modern times who correctly identified the site of the fortress itself; and A. Eloy, *Relations de voyage en Orient* (Paris, 1843), p. 774.
91. M. van Berchem, 'Épigraphie des Assassins de Syrie', *JA*, 9 série, 9 (1897), pp. 453–501, reprinted in his *Opera Minora* (Geneva, 1978), vol. 1, pp. 453–501.
92. M. van Berchem, 'Notes d'archéologie Arabe: Monuments et inscriptions Fatimites', *JA*, 8 série, 17 (1891), pp. 411–495, and 18 (1891), pp. 46–86, and also his 'Notes d'archéologie Arabe, deuxième article: Toulounides et Fatimites', *JA*, 8 série, 19 (1892), especially pp. 392–407; both articles reprinted in his *Opera Minora*, vol. 1, pp. 77–233.
93. 'Judgment of the Honourable Sir Joseph Arnould in the Khodjah Case, otherwise known as the Aga Khan Case, heard in the High Court of Bombay, during April and June 1866; Judgment delivered 12th November, 1866' (Bombay, 1867); see also *Bombay High Court Reports*, 12 (1866), pp. 323–363. This case has been summarized in H. B. E. Frere, 'The Khodjas, the Disciples of the Old Man of the Mountain', *Macmillan Magazine*, 34 (1876), pp. 342ff.; and more fully in Abdus Salam Picklay, *History of the Ismailis* (Bombay, 1940), pp. 113–170, and also in Asaf A. A. Fyzee, *Cases in the Muhammadan Law of India and Pakistan* (Oxford, 1965), pp. 504–549.
94. E. Griffini, 'Die jüngste ambrosianische Sammlung arabischer Handschriften', *ZDMG*, 69 (1915), especially pp. 80–88. For the description of another early manuscript of lesser Ismāʿīlī items coming from Yaman, see R. Strothmann, 'Kleinere ismailitische Schriften', in Islamic Research Association, *Miscellany* (Bombay, 1949), vol. 1, pp. 121–163.
95. A. A. Bobrinskoy, 'Sekta Ismailiya v Russkikh i Bukharskikh predelakh Srednej Azii', *Etnograficheskoye Obozrenie*, 2 (1902), pp. 1–20, published also separately (Moscow, 1902), and his *Gortsy verkhovjev Pyandzha* (Moscow, 1908).
96. *Ummu'l-kitāb*, ed. W. Ivanow, in *Der Islam*, 23 (1936), pp. 1–132; translated into Italian, with a valuable introduction, by Pio Filippani-Ronconi (Naples, 1966).
97. See A. A. Semenov, 'Iz oblasti religioznuikh verovany Shughnanskikh Ismailitov', *Mir Islama*, 1 (1912), pp. 523–561, and his two articles, 'Sheikh Dzhelāl-ud-Dīn-Rūmī po predstavleniyam Shughnanskikh Ismailitov', and 'Razskaz Shughnanskikh Ismailitov o Bukharskom Sheikh Bekhā-ud-Dīne', appearing in *Zapiski Vostochnago Otdyeleniya Imperatorskago Russkago Arkheologicheskago Obshchestva*, 22 (1913–1914), pp. 247–256 and 321–326, respectively.
98. For descriptions of these two collections, see V. A. Ivanov, 'Ismailitskiya

rukopisi Aziatskago Muzeya. Sobranie I. Zarubina, 1916 g.', *Bulletin de l'Académie des Sciences de Russie*, 6 série, 11 (1917), pp. 359–386, summarized in E. Denison Ross, 'W. Ivanow, Ismaili MSS in the Asiatic Museum, Petrograd, 1917', *JRAS* (1919), pp. 429–435, and A. A. Semenov, 'Opisanie Ismailitskikh rukopisei, sobrannuikh A. A. Semenovuim', *Bulletin de l'Académie des Sciences de Russie*, 6 série, 12 (1918), pp. 2171–2202. These Ismāʿīlī manuscripts are currently kept at the Leningrad branch of the Institute of Oriental Studies, formerly the Institute of the Peoples of Asia, which has absorbed the Asiatic Museum and other oriental institutions of the Academy of Sciences of the USSR (Akaedmiia Nauk SSSR); see O. F. Akimushkin et al., *Persidskie i Tadzhiskie rukopisi, Instituta Narodov Azii an SSSR*, ed. N. D. Muklukho-Maklai (Moscow, 1964), vol. 1, pp. 54–55, 208, 259, 313, 356, 530, 541, 600 and 608.

99. L. Massignon, 'Esquisse d'une bibliographie Qarmaṭe', in *A Volume of Oriental Studies Presented to Edward G. Browne*, ed. T. W. Arnold and R. A. Nicholson (Cambridge, 1922), pp. 329–338, which does not include the Asiatic Museum's then newly acquired Ismāʿīlī items.

100. See Asaf A. A. Fyzee, 'Materials for an Ismaili Bibliography: 1920–1934', *JBBRAS*, NS, 11 (1935), pp. 60–62.

101. This commencement is clearly marked by the appearance of an unprecedented number of publications on Ismāʿīlī subjects during the 1930s; see Asaf A. A. Fyzee's works, 'Materials for an Ismaili Bibliography: 1920–1934', pp. 59–65; 'Additional Notes for an Ismaili Bibliography', *JBBRAS*, NS, 12 (1936), pp. 107–109 and 'Materials for an Ismaili Bibliography: 1936–1938', *JBBRAS*, NS, 16 (1940), pp. 99–101. For further bibliographies of Ismāʿīlī works, published earlier and subsequently, see Jean Sauvaget, *Introduction à l'histoire de l'Orient Musulman* (Paris, 1943), pp. 136–139; also his *Introduction to the History of the Muslim East*, based on the second edition as recast by Claude Cahen (Berkeley, 1965), pp. 146–150; Cl. Cahen, *Introduction à l'histoire du monde Musulman médiéval: VIIe–XVe siècle* (Paris, 1982), pp. 136, 139–142, 149 and 186; Hasan I. Hasan, 'Contributions to the Study of Fāṭimid History in Egypt during the last 12 Years', *Bulletin of the Faculty of Arts, Fouad I University*, 13 (1951), pp. 129–140; B. Lewis, 'The Sources for the History of the Syrian Assassins', *Speculum*, 27 (1952), pp. 475–489, reprinted in his *Studies in Classical and Ottoman Islam*, where both Muslim and non-Muslim sources on the Nizārīs are reviewed; James D. Pearson's most valuable *Index Islamicus*, 1906–1955 (Cambridge, 1958), pp. 89–90, 108, 425 and 479–480, and the relevant sections in its *Supplements* for 1956–1960, 1961–1965, 1966–1970, 1971–1975, 1976–1980, and in the issues of the *Quarterly Index Islamicus* published since 1981.

102. Arthur S. Tritton, 'Notes on Some Ismaïli Manuscripts, from information supplied by Dr. Paul Kraus', *BSOS*, 7 (1933), pp. 33–39; and A. Gacek, *Catalogue of the Arabic Manuscripts in the Library of the School of Oriental and African Studies* (London, 1981), pp. 16–17, 30, 39, 86, 94–95, 115, 118–121, 172, 181, 188, 218 and 239–240.

103. A. Berthels and M. Baqoev, *Alphabetic Catalogue of Manuscripts found by*

1959–1963 Expedition in Gorno–Badakhshan Autonomous Region, ed. B. G. Gafurov and A. M. Mirzoev (in Russian, Moscow, 1967).

104. The first such account of Ismāʿīlī literature by an Ismāʿīlī, belonging to a distinguished Dāʾūdī Bohra family with an important collection of manuscripts preserved originally at Sūrat, Gujarāt, was provided by Ḥ. F. al-Hamdānī in his 'Some Unknown Ismāʿīlī Authors and their Works', *JRAS* (1933), pp. 359–378. For a similar later instance, see Asaf A. A. Fyzee, 'The Study of the Literature of Fatimid Daʿwa', in *Arabic and Islamic Studies in Honor of Hamilton A. R. Gibb*, ed. G. Makdisi (Leiden, 1965), pp. 232–249.

105. M. Goriawala, *A Descriptive Catalogue of the Fyzee Collection of Ismaili Manuscripts* (Bombay, 1965); see also Asaf A. A. Fyzee, 'A Collection of Fatimid Manuscripts', in *Comparative Librarianship: Essays in Honour of Professor D. N. Marshall*, ed. N. N. Gidwani (Delhi, 1973), pp. 209–220, which describes the residue of Fyzee's private collection.

106. W. Ivanow, *Ismaili Literature: A Bibliographical Survey* (Tehran, 1963), covering 929 titles.

107. W. Ivanow, *A Guide to Ismaili Literature* (London, 1933), covering 691 titles by some 150 authors and based partly on the *Fahrasat al-kutub wa'l-rasāʾil* of Ismāʿīl b. ʿAbd al-Rasūl al-Majdūʿ, a learned Indian Dāʾūdī Ismāʿīlī who died in 1183 or 1184/1769–1770. The Arabic text of the latter work, commonly known as the *Fihrist al-Majdūʿ*, has now been edited by ʿAlī Naqī Munzavī (Tehran, 1966). See also P. Kraus, 'La Bibliographie Ismaëlienne de W. Ivanow', *REI*, 6 (1932), pp. 483–490, which contains some useful additions and corrections in respect to Ivanow's *Guide*.

108. Ismail K. Poonawala, *Biobibliography of Ismāʿīlī Literature* (Malibu, California, 1977). This excellent compendium provides detailed information on more than 200 authors and 1,300 titles; it also supplies all the particulars regarding the Ismāʿīlī texts edited and published until the 1970s, in addition to indicating the locations of a large number of Ismāʿīlī manuscripts and including, pp. 383–463, a select bibliography of published works on Ismāʿīlī subjects; hereafter cited as *Bio*.

109. Asaf A. A. Fyzee, 'W. Ivanow (1886–1970)', *Indo-Iranica*, 23 (1970), p. 23, also in *Journal of the Asiatic Society of Bombay*, 45–46 (1970–1971), p. 93.

110. W. Ivanow, 'Ismailitica', *Memoirs of the Asiatic Society of Bengal*, 8 (1922), pp. 1–76.

111. Hodgson, *Order of Assassins*, pp. 30–32. For more details on the life and works of Ivanow, see F. Daftary, 'W. Ivanow: A Biographical Notice', *Middle Eastern Studies*, 8 (1972), pp. 241–244; also his 'Bibliography of the Publications of the late W. Ivanow', *IC*, 45 (1971), pp. 56–67, and 56 (1982), pp. 239–240, summarized in *Ayandeh*, 9 (1983), pp. 665–674, and Daftary's 'Anǰoman-e Esmāʿīlī', *EIR*, vol. 2, p. 84.

112. W. Ivanow, *Brief Survey of the Evolution of Ismailism* (Leiden, 1952), p. 29.

2. Origins and early development of Shīʿism

1. I. Friedlaender, 'The Heterodoxies of the Shiites in the Presentation of Ibn Ḥazm', *JAOS*, 28 (1907), p. 3.
2. E. G. Browne, *A History of Persian Literature in Modern Times* (Cambridge, 1924), p. 418.
3. R. Strothmann, 'Shīʿa', *EI*, vol. 4, p. 357.
4. B. Lewis, *The Origins of Ismāʿīlism: A Study of the Historical Background of the Fāṭimid Caliphate* (Cambridge, 1940), p. 23; W. Ivanow, 'Early Shiʿite Movements', *JBBRAS*, NS, 17 (1941), p. 1; Asaf A. A. Fyzee, *Conférences sur l'Islam*, tr. E. Meyerovitch (Paris, 1956), p. 45; H. Corbin, *Spiritual Body and Celestial Earth*, tr. N. Pearson (Princeton, N.J., 1977), p. 57, and Poonawala, *Bio*, p. 4.
5. See S. Hossein Nasr, 'Henry Corbin, the Life and Works of the Occidental Exile in Quest of the Orient of Light', *Sophia Perennis*, 3 (1977), pp. 88–127, reproduced, with the biographical section in French, in *Mélanges offerts à Henry Corbin*, ed. S. H. Nasr (Tehran, 1977), pp. iii–xxxii and 3–27.
6. Sayyid Muḥammad Ḥusayn Ṭabāṭabāʾī was one of the most respected Twelver Shīʿī scholars of Persia and also the country's foremost Islamic theosopher. In his *Shīʿa dar Islām* (Tehran, 1348/1969), he produced the first authoritative introduction to Shīʿism written in modern times; now also available in English as *Shiʿite Islam*, ed. and tr. S. H. Nasr (London, 1975). It may be noted that until the translation of Ṭabāṭabāʾī's work, Dwight M. Donaldson's *The Shiʿite Religion* (London, 1933), written by a Christian missionary in Persia, was considered as the standard work on the subject in the English language. See also M. Momen, *An Introduction to Shiʿi Islam* (New Haven, 1985), and *Shiʿism: Doctrines, Thought and Spirituality*, ed. S. H. Nasr et al. (Albany, N.Y., 1988).
7. See P. Crone and M. Hinds, *God's Caliph: Religious Authority in the First Centuries of Islam* (Cambridge, 1986).
8. Henri Lammens (1862–1937), the Belgian Islamist and Jesuit missionary in Lebanon, in line with his generally unsympathetic attitude towards Shīʿism and his high regard for the Umayyads, produced an unfavourable account of Fāṭima in his *Fāṭima et les filles de Mahomet* (Rome, 1912), especially pp. 109–140; and 'Fāṭima', EI, vol. 2, pp. 85–88. An objective and thorough study is now to be found in L. Veccia Vaglieri, 'Fāṭima', *EI2*, vol. 2, pp. 841–850. The particular importance and reverence accorded to Fāṭima in Shīʿī thought has been studied in a number of works by L. Massignon, especially in his 'Der Gnostische Kult der Fatima im Schiitischen Islam', *EJ*, 6 (1938), pp. 161–173, reprinted in his *Opera Minora*, ed. Y. Moubarac (Paris, 1969), vol. 1, pp, 514–522, which contains most of Massignon's scattered writings on Shīʿism. H. Corbin has also treated this subject in his *Spiritual Body*, pp. 51–73, and elsewhere.
9. S. H. Nasr, *Ideals and Realities of Islam* (New York, 1967), pp. 147 ff.
10. See, for example, W. M. Watt, *The Majesty that was Islam* (London, 1974), pp. 65–66.

11. The best exposition of this view in the English language is to be found in Ṭabāṭabā'ī's *Shiʿite Islam*, especially pp. 39–50 and 173ff., and in S. H. Nasr's introductory comments therein. Many of H. Corbin's works are also relevant here; see especially his 'Le combat spirituel du Shīʿisme', *EJ*, 30 (1961), pp. 69–125; *Histoire de la philosophie Islamique* I: *Des origines jusqu'à la mort d'Averroës (1198)* (Paris, 1964), pp. 62–79, hereafter cited as *Histoire*, and *En Islam Iranien: Aspects spirituels et philosophiques* (Paris, 1971–1972), vol. 1, pp. 39–53 and 219–235.
12. See L. Veccia Vaglieri, 'Ghadīr Khumm', *EI2*, vol. 2, pp. 993–994, where additional references are given.
13. For more details on ʿAlī's activities during this period, see Abū ʿAbd Allāh Muḥammad al-Mufīd, *Kitāb al-Irshād*, tr. I. K. A. Howard (London, 1981), pp. 143ff., and S. Husain M. Jafri, *Origins and Early Development of Shīʿa Islam* (London, 1979), pp. 58–79; this work, hereafter cited as *Origins*, is a major contribution to the study of the early history of Shīʿism.
14. Some of the best results of modern research on the roots of discontent with ʿUthmān's caliphate are to be found in Hamilton A. R. Gibb, 'An Interpretation of Islamic History', *Journal of World History*, 1 (1953), pp. 39ff.; M. A. Shaban, *Islamic History: A New Interpretation* (Cambridge, 1971–1976), vol. 1, pp. 60–70, and M. Hinds, 'The Murder of the Caliph ʿUthmān', *IJMES*, 3 (1972), pp. 450–469.
15. For many interesting details of the garrison towns in the broader context of early Islamic history and society, see Marshall G. S. Hodgson, *The Venture of Islam* (Chicago, 1974), vol. 1, pp. 206–217.
16. Jafri, *Origins*, pp. 117–123; M. Hinds, 'Kūfan Political Alignments and their Background in the Mid-Seventh Century A.D.', *IJMES*, 2 (1971), pp. 358–365, and H. Djait, 'Les Yamanites à Kūfa au Ier siècle de l'Hégire', *JESHO*, 19 (1976), especially pp. 148–174. See also Shaban, *Islamic History*, vol. 1, pp. 50–51; G. H. A. Juynboll, 'The Qurrā' in Early Islamic History', *JESHO*, 16 (1973), pp. 113–129, and T. Nagel, 'Ḳurrā'', *EI2*, vol. 5, pp. 499–500.
17. The classical treatment of the first civil war, and the events of the subsequent Umayyad period, is still to be found in J. Wellhausen, *The Arab Kingdom and its Fall*, tr. M. G. Weir (Calcutta, 1927), pp. 75–112, originally published in German, *Das arabische Reich und sein Sturz* (Berlin, 1902). The ʿAlī-Muʿāwiya conflict has been studied more recently by Erling L. Petersen; see especially his *ʿAlī and Muʿāwiya in Early Arabic Tradition* (Copenhagen, 1964), where a full bibliography is given on pp. 188–192. The same events have been examined on the basis of some Khārijī sources discovered in the present century, by a number of Italian Islamists, notably L. Veccia Vaglieri, who is also the foremost Western authority on the Khawārij; see her 'Il conflitto ʿAlī-Muʿāwiya e la secessione khārigita riesaminati alla luce di fonti ibāḍite', *AIUON*, NS, 4 (1952), pp. 1–95, and 5 (1953), pp. 1–98; 'ʿAlī b. Abī Ṭālib', *EI2*, vol. 1, pp. 381–386; G. Levi Della Vida 'Khāridjites', *EI2*, vol. 4, pp. 1074–1077, and I. K. Poonawla and E. Kohlberg, ''Alī b. Abī Ṭāleb'', *EIR*, vol. 1, pp. 838–848.
18. See M. Guidi, 'Sui Ḫarigiti', *RSO*, 21 (1944), pp. 1–14; L. Veccia Vaglieri,

'Sulla denominazione Ḫawārig', *RSO*, 26 (1951), pp. 41–46; W. M. Watt, 'Khārijite Thought in the Umayyad Period', *Der Islam*, 36 (1961), pp. 215–231, and also his *The Formative Period of Islamic Thought* (Edinburgh, 1973), pp. 9–37. On the Ibāḍīs, one of the main branches and today the only survivors of the Khawārij, see T. Lewicki, 'al-Ibāḍiyya', *EI2*, vol. 3, pp. 648–660.

19. Abū Jaʿfar Muḥammad b. Jarīr al-Ṭabarī, *Ta'rīkh al-rusul wa'l-mulūk*, ed. M. J. de Goeje et al. (Leiden, 1879–1901), I, pp. 3350ff.
20. W. M. Watt, *Islamic Philosophy and Theology* (Edinburgh, 1962), pp. 2–9, which reflects the author's emphasis on social factors in the genesis of Shīʿism. For Watt's different hypothesis contending how for the Khawārij, the community rather than any individual came to acquire the charisma of leadership, see his 'The Conception of the Charismatic Community', *Numen*, 7 (1960), pp. 77–90; arguments relevant to both types of charismata are to be found also in his *Formative Period*, pp. 36–37 and 42–44; 'Shīʿism under the Umayyads', *JRAS* (1960), pp. 158–172, and his *Islam and the Integration of Society* (Evanston, 1961), pp. 103–106 and 110–114.
21. For some details, see Wellhausen, *Arab Kingdom*, pp. 104–112; Jafri, *Origins*, pp. 130–154, and L. Veccia Vaglieri, 'al-Ḥasan b. ʿAlī b. Abī Ṭālib', *EI2*, vol. 3, pp. 241–242.
22. L. Veccia Vaglieri, 'Sulla origine della denominazione Sunniti', in *Studi Orientalistici in onore di Giorgio Levi Della Vida* (Rome, 1956), vol. 2, pp. 573–585, and L. Gardet, 'Djamāʿa', *EI2*, vol. 2, pp. 411–412.
23. J. Wellhausen, *The Religio-Political Factions in Early Islam*, tr. R. C. Ostle and S. M. Walzer (Amsterdam, 1975), pp. 96–101; this is a long overdue translation of *Die religiös-politischen Oppositionspartheien im alten Islam* (Berlin, 1901), an important study of the major events in the early history of the Khārijī and Shīʿī movements.
24. Abū Mikhnaf (d. 157/774) is the earliest Muslim historian who recorded the Shīʿī risings of the Umayyad period. But his detailed narratives have been preserved mainly in the famous chronicles of the Sunnī authors al-Balādhurī (d. 279/892) and al-Ṭabarī (d. 310/923). These historians have provided the chief sources for the thorough accounts of al-Ḥusayn's martyrdom given in Wellhausen, *Religio-Political Factions*, pp. 105–120; Jafri, *Origins*, pp. 174–221, and L. Veccia Vaglieri, 'al-Ḥusayn b. ʿAlī b. Abī Ṭālib', *EI2*, vol. 3, pp. 607–615. See also the accounts of Abu'l-Ḥasan ʿAlī b. al-Ḥusayn al-Masʿūdī (d. 345/956), another noteworthy early Muslim historian, in his *Murūj al-dhahab* (*Les Prairies d'or*), ed. and tr. C. Barbier de Meynard and A. Pavet de Courteille (Paris, 1861–1876), vol. 5, pp. 127–147; Abu'l-Faraj ʿAlī b. al-Ḥusayn al-Iṣfahānī, *Maqātil al-Ṭālibiyyīn*, ed. A. Ṣaqr (Cairo, 1368/1949), pp. 78–122, which is an important work containing the biographies of many Ṭālibid martyrs, written by a Shīʿī author who died in 356/967, and al-Mufīd, *al-Irshād*, pp. 299–374.
25. See, however, Jafri, *Origins*, pp. 229–230 and 244–245, where it is argued that the Tawwābūn did probably consider al-Ḥusayn's son Zayn al-ʿĀbidīn as their imām; but, as he refused to make any public claims, or to allow any

claims to be made on his behalf, they were obliged to refrain from mentioning his name.

26. The most detailed account of al-Mukhtār's revolt is related in al-Ṭabarī, *Ta'rīkh*, II, pp. 520–752; see also Wellhausen, *Religio-Political Factions*, pp. 125–145, based mainly on al-Ṭabarī, and G. Levi Della Vida, 'al-Mukhtār', *EI*, vol. 3, pp. 715–717. No serious study has so far been made of al-Mukhtār and his enigmatic background, aside from H. D. van Gelder's *Muḫtār de valsche Profeet* (Leiden, 1888), still available only in Dutch, and K. A. Fariq's more recent and sketchy account, 'The Story of an Arab Diplomat', *Studies in Islam*, 3 (1966), pp. 53–80, 119–142 and 227–241, and 4 (1967), pp. 50–59, published also separately (New Delhi, 1967).

27. The classical study of the *mawālī* and their problems was undertaken by the Austrian orientalist Alfred von Kremer (1828–1889), notably in his *Culturgeschichtliche Streifzüge auf dem gebiete des Islam* (Leipzig, 1873), and *Culturgeschichte des Orients unter den Chalifen* (Vienna, 1875–1877), vol. 2., pp. 154ff.; English translations of the relevant sections are to be found, respectively, in S. Khuda Bukhsh, *Contributions to the History of Islamic Civilization* (3rd ed., Calcutta, 1959), vol. 1, pp. 68–86; and in A. von Kremer, *The Orient under the Caliphs*, tr. S. Khuda Bukhsh (Calcutta, 1920), vol. 2, pp. 107ff. The subject has been treated also by I. Goldziher in his *Muhammedanische Studien* (Halle, 1889–1890), vol. 1, pp. 104–146; English translation, *Muslim Studies*, tr. C. R. Barber and S. M. Stern (London, 1967–1971), vol. 1, pp. 101–136; see also B. Lewis, *The Arabs in History* (Rev. ed., New York, 1960), pp. 70ff.; E. Ashtor, *A Social and Economic History of the Near East in the Middle Ages* (London, 1976), pp. 22–29, and A. J. Wensinck, 'Mawlā', *EI*, vol. 3, pp. 417–418, where different meanings of the term are considered.

28. See Jafri, *Origins*, pp. 113–116, and W. Ivanow, *Studies in Early Persian Ismailism* (Leiden, 1948), pp. 12–20. The situation of the Persian *mawālī* has been investigated extensively by ʿAbd al-Ḥusayn Zarrīnkūb, the noted contemporary authority on the history of Arab rule over Persia; see especially his *Ta'rīkh-i Īrān baʿd az Islām* (2nd ed., Tehran, 1355/1976), vol. 1, pp. 283–384, and 'The Arab Conquest of Iran and its Aftermath', in *The Cambridge History of Iran*: Volume 4, *The Period from the Arab Invasion to the Saljuqs*, ed. Richard N. Frye (Cambridge, 1975), pp. 1–38. See also M. Azizi, *La domination Arabe et l'épanouissement du sentiment national en Iran* (Paris, 1938), pp. 28–72.

29. Most contemporary Western Islamists, such as B. Lewis, 'Some Observations on the Significance of Heresy in the History of Islam', *SI*, 1 (1953), pp. 44ff., by drawing on the findings of modern scholarship, have argued that although racial elements did play a part in the development of the Shīʿī movement, Shīʿism was nevertheless of Arab origin and it was in fact introduced into Persia (e.g., to the garrison town of Qumm) by the Arabs. As a corollary, they have concluded that Shīʿism should not be regarded as having been the expression of Persian national aspirations. The latter view was held by a number of the nineteenth-century orientalists who were

influenced by the then current racial theories of Joseph A. Gobineau (1816–1882) and others; see, for instance, Dozy, *Essai sur l'histoire de l'Islamisme*, pp. 189–221.

30. See Aḥmad b. ʿAlī b. ʿInaba, *ʿUmdat al-ṭālib fī ansāb āl Abī Ṭālib*, ed. M. Ḥ. Āl al-Ṭāliqānī (Najaf, 1961), written by an important Imāmī genealogist who died in 828/1424, and B. Lewis, ''ʿAlids', *EI2*, vol. 1, pp. 400–403.
31. Jafri, *Origins*, pp. 269–270; Hodgson, *Venture of Islam*, vol. 1, pp. 259–260; W. M. Watt, *Islamic Political Thought* (Edinburgh, 1968), p. 45; I. Goldziher, C. van Arendonk and A. S. Tritton, 'Ahl al-Bayt', *EI2*, vol. 1, pp. 257–258, and I. K. A. Howard, 'Ahl-e Bayt', *EIR*, vol. 1, p. 635.
32. Lewis, *Origins*, p. 24.
33. See especially Claude Cahen, 'Points de vue sur la "Révolution ʿAbbāside"', in his *Les peuples Musulmans dans l'histoire médiévale* (Damascus, 1977), pp. 120 and 128; an important study on early Shīʿism originally published in *Revue Historique*, 230 (1960), pp. 295–338, hereafter references are to the paginations of the reprinted text. In line with the opinion of many Western Islamists, Cahen has further argued that during the Umayyad period ʿAlid claims to the imāmate were based on descent from ʿAlī, rather than from Fāṭima and ʿAlī; since direct descent from the Prophet in the female (Fāṭimid) line had still not acquired its later Shīʿī significance. See also W. Madelung, ''ʿAlī b. al-Ḥosayn', *EIR*, vol. 1, pp. 849–850.
34. The most detailed and accurate accounts of the Kaysāniyya, often used by the heresiographers as a collective name for all the Shīʿī groups evolving out of al-Mukhtār's movement, are contained in al-Ḥasan b. Mūsā al-Nawbakhtī, *Firaq al-Shīʿa*, ed. H. Ritter (Istanbul, 1931), pp. 20–37 and 41–47; French translation, *Les Sectes Shiites*, tr. M. J. Mashkūr (2nd ed., Tehran, 1980), pp. 37–58 and 63–69, and in Saʿd b. ʿAbd Allāh al-Qummī, *al-Maqālāt wa'l-firaq*, ed. M. J. Mashkūr (Tehran, 1963), pp. 21–23, 25–44, 55–56 and 64–70; see also W. Madelung, 'Kaysāniyya', *EI2*, vol. 4, pp. 836–838, which presents an excellent survey of the main Kaysānī groups. It may be pointed out here that after the arguments of the late ʿAbbās Iqbāl, in his *Khānidān-i Nawbakhtī* (Tehran, 1311/1932), pp. 143–161, many scholars had come to consider al-Qummī as the real author of al-Nawbakhtī's *Firaq*; but, with the recent discovery of al-Qummī's own partial heresiography on the Shīʿī sects, the genuineness of al-Nawbakhtī's authorship of the *Firaq* should no longer be doubted; for further comments on the two sources in question, see W. Madelung, 'Bemerkungen zur imamitischen Firaq-Literatur', *Der Islam*, 43 (1967), pp. 37ff., reprinted in his *Religious Schools and Sects in Medieval Islam* (London, 1985).
35. See al-Nawbakhtī, *Firaq*, pp. 20–21; al-Qummī, *al-Maqālāt*, pp. 21–22; I. Friedlaender, 'The Heterodoxies of the Shiites in the Presentation of Ibn Ḥazm: Commentary', *JAOS*, 29 (1908), pp. 33–34 and 93–95; H. Halm, *Die islamische Gnosis* (Zürich, 1982), pp. 43ff., and A. A. Dixon, 'Kaysān', *EI2*, vol. 4, p. 836. The Kaysāniyya were sometimes also called the Khashabiyya, originally an abusive name for al-Mukhtār's *mawālī* followers who were mainly armed with wooden clubs (singular, *khashaba*); see C. van Arendonk, 'Khashabiyya', *EI2*, vol. 4, p. 1086.

36. For the situation of the Kaysānīs between the deaths of al-Mukhtār and Ibn al-Ḥanafiyya, see W. al-Qāḍī, *al-Kaysāniyya fi'l-ta'rīkh wa'l-adab* (Beirut, 1974), pp. 139–201. See also J. van Ess, 'al-Ḥasan b. Muḥammad b. al-Ḥanafiyya', *EI2*, Supplement, pp. 357–358.
37. As noted, the most reliable sources on the Kaysāniyya and other early Shīʿī groups are al-Nawbakhtī and al-Qummī, who are well-informed and free from the unfavourable biases of the Sunnī heresiographers. The earliest works in the latter category with the relevant sections on the Kaysāniyya and its sub-divisions, are: Abu'l-Ḥasan ʿAlī b. Ismāʿīl al-Ashʿarī, *Maqālāt al-Islāmiyyīn*, ed. H. Ritter (Istanbul, 1929–1930), pp. 18–23; Muḥammad b. Aḥmad al-Malaṭī, *Kitāb al-tanbīh wa'l-radd*, ed. S. Dedering (Istanbul, 1936), which is an unreliable work concerned mainly with refuting rather than explaining; ʿAbd al-Qāhir b. Ṭāhir al-Baghdādī has a detailed, though extremely hostile treatment of the Kaysānī-related groups in his *al-Farq bayn al-firaq*, ed. M. Badr (Cairo, 1328/1910), pp. 27–38, 227–228, 234–236 and 253ff.; English translation, *Moslem Schisms and Sects*, part I, tr. K. C. Seelye (New York, 1919), pp. 47–60, containing numerous errors, and part II, tr. A. S. Halkin (Tel Aviv, 1935), pp. 46–48, 56–61 and 91ff.; Abū Muḥammad ʿAlī b. Aḥmad b. Ḥazm, *al-Fiṣal fi'l-milal* (Cairo, 1317–1321/1899–1903), vol. 4, pp. 179ff.; Friedlaender has provided useful notes to Ibn Ḥazm in his already-cited English translation of the latter's sections on the Shīʿīs, in *JAOS*, 28 (1907), pp. 44ff. and 77–78, and in his commentary thereto, *JAOS*, 29 (1908), pp. 33–39; and finally, Muḥammad b. ʿAbd al-Karīm al-Shahrastānī, who is of a late date but rather well-balanced, supplies a few doctrinal details in his *Kitāb al-milal wa'l-niḥal*, ed. ʿA. M. al-Wakīl (Cairo, 1968), vol. 1, pp. 147–154; German translation, *Religionspartheien und Philosophen-Schulen*, tr. T. Haarbrücker (Halle, 1850–1851), vol. 1, pp. 165–174; partial French translations, *Kitāb al-milal, Les dissidences de l'Islam*, tr. Jean Claude Vadet (Paris, 1984), pp. 262–269; *Livre des religions et des sectes*, tr. D. Gimaret and G. Monnot (Paris, 1986), pp. 437–456; partial English translation, *Muslim Sects and Divisions*, tr. A. K. Kazi and J. G. Flynn (London, 1984), pp. 126–132.
38. For brief surveys of the concept of the Mahdī, see D. S. Margoliouth, 'On Mahdis and Mahdism', *Proceedings of the British Academy*, 7 (1915–1916), pp. 213–233; also his 'Mahdī', *ERE*, vol. 8, pp. 336–340; D. B. Macdonald, 'al-Mahdī', *EI*, vol. 3, pp. 111–115, and W. Madelung, 'al-Mahdī', *EI2*, vol. 5, pp. 1230–1238. More detailed studies of messianism in Islam are to be found in I. Friedlaender, 'Die Messiasidee im Islam', in *Festschrift zum siebzigsten Geburtstage A. Berliner's*, ed. A. Freimann and M. Hildesheimer (Frankfurt-am-Main, 1903), pp. 116–130; Edgar Blochet, *Le Messianisme dans l'hétérodoxie Musulmane* (Paris, 1903), and more recently, A. A. Sachedina, *Islamic Messianism* (Albany, N.Y., 1981); J. M. Hussain, *The Occultation of the Twelfth Imam* (London, 1982), and Jan-Olaf Blichfeldt, *Early Mahdism* (Leiden, 1985).
39. James Darmesteter, *Le Mahdi* (Paris, 1885), especially pp. 26–32; B. Carra de Vaux, *Les Penseurs de l'Islam* (Paris, 1921–1926), vol. 5, pp. 12ff.; Corbin, *Spiritual Body*, pp. 13–16, 36–50 and 68–73; and also his 'L'idée du Paraclet en

philosophie Iranienne', in Accademia Nazionale dei Lincei, *La Persia nel medioevo*, pp. 37–68. H. Corbin has devoted numerous studies to the role of the Mahdī in Twelver Shīʿism; see especially his 'Sur le Douzième Imām', *La Table Ronde*, 110 (1957), pp. 7–20; 'L'Imām caché et la rénovation de l'homme en théologie Shīʿite', *EJ*, 28 (1959), pp. 47–87; 'Au pays de l'Imām caché', *EJ*, 32 (1963), pp. 31–87; *Histoire*, pp. 101–109, and *En Islam*, vol. 4, pp. 303–460.

40. C. Snouck Hurgronje, 'Der Mahdi', *Revue Coloniale Internationale*, 1 (1886), pp. 25–59, reprinted in his *Verspreide Geschriften*, ed. J. W. Wensinck (Bonn–Leipzig, 1923), vol. 1, pp. 147–181; I. Goldziher, *Introduction to Islamic Theology and Law*, tr. A. and R. Hamori (Princeton, N.J., 1981), pp. 192–202 and 211–212; this is a most valuable translation of Goldziher's important lectures first published in German as *Vorlesungen über den Islam* (Heidelberg, 1910); see also Friedlaender, 'Heterodoxies: Commentary', pp. 23–30, and Ivanow, *Studies*, pp. 10–11.
41. S. Moscati, 'Abū Hāshim', *EI2*, vol. 1, pp. 124–125, and T. Nagel, 'Abū Hāšem ʿAbdallāh', *EIR*, vol. 1, pp. 314–315.
42. Al-Nawbakhtī, *Firaq*, pp. 30–31; al-Qummī, *al-Maqālāt*, pp. 37–38; al-Ashʿarī, *Maqālāt*, pp. 5–6 and 23, and al-Baghdādī, *al-Farq*, pp. 227–228; tr. Halkin, pp. 46–48. See also William F. Tucker, 'Bayān b. Samʿān and the Bayāniyya', *MW*, 65 (1975), pp. 241–253; Halm, *Islamische Gnosis*, pp. 55–64, and M. G. S. Hodgson, 'Bayān b. Samʿān al-Tamīmī', *EI2*, vol. 1, pp. 1116–1117.
43. Al-Nawbakhtī, *Firaq*, p. 28, where they are also referred to as al-Mukhtāriyya. See also al-Qāḍī, *al-Kaysāniyya*, pp. 212–237.
44. Al-Nawbakhtī, *Firaq*, pp. 29–30 and 46–47, and al-Qummī, *al-Maqālāt*, pp. 39–40 and 69.
45. The relevant issues and sources have been particularly investigated by Sabatino Moscati in his 'Il testamento di Abū Hāšim', *RSO*, 27 (1952), pp. 28–46, and 'Per una storia dell' antica Šīʿa', *RSO*, 30 (1955), pp. 258ff.
46. See especially Wellhausen, *Arab Kingdom*, pp. 503ff.
47. Cahen, 'Points', pp. 125–127, and B. Lewis, 'Hāshimiyya', *EI2*, vol. 3, p. 265.
48. Al-Nawbakhtī, *Firaq*, pp. 29–32 and 35; al-Qummī, *al-Maqālāt*, pp. 26–27, 39–40 and 56; al-Baghdādī, *al-Farq*, p. 234; tr. Halkin, p. 56; Friedlaender, 'Heterodoxies: Commentary', pp. 44–45 and 124–126; al-Qāḍī, *al-Kaysāniyya*, pp. 208ff., and Halm, *Islamische Gnosis*, pp. 64ff. and 69ff.
49. On the death of Ibn Muʿāwiya, shortly before the accession of the ʿAbbāsids, the Janāḥiyya split into several groups. Aside from the sources cited above, see al-Ashʿarī, *Maqālāt*, pp. 6 and 22; al-Baghdādī, *al-Farq*, pp. 235–236; tr. Halkin, pp. 59–61; al-Shahrastānī, *al-Milal*, vol. 1, pp. 151–152; tr. Kazi, pp. 129–130; Moscati, 'Il testamento', pp. 32–33 and 46; William F. Tucker, ''Abd Allāh ibn Muʿāwiya and the Janāḥiyya: Rebels and Ideologies of the late Umayyad Period', *SI*, 51 (1980), especially pp. 49–55, and Marshall G. S. Hodgson and M. Canard, 'al-Djanāḥiyya', *EI2*, vol. 2, p. 441.
50. Al-Nawbakhtī, *Firaq*, pp. 32 and 41ff.; al-Qummī, *al-Maqālāt*, p. 44; al-

Baghdādī, *al-Farq*, pp. 251–252; tr. Halkin, pp. 87–90; Azizi, *La domination*, pp. 136ff.; G. H. Sadighi, *Les Mouvements religieux Iraniens au IIe et au IIIe siècle de l'hégire* (Paris, 1938), especially pp. 163–280; B. S. Amoretti, 'Sects and Heresies', in *Cambridge History of Iran*, vol. 4, pp. 494–519; Richard N. Frye, *The Golden Age of Persia* (London, 1975), pp. 126–137, and W. Madelung, 'Khurramiyya', *EI2*, vol. 5, pp. 63–65.

51. Our discussion of the Ghulāt owes much to the views of Marshall G. S. Hodgson, as expounded especially in his *Venture of Islam*, vol. 1, pp. 258–267, also his 'How did the Early Shīʿa become Sectarian?', *JAOS*, 75 (1955), pp. 4–8, and 'Ghulāt', *EI2*, vol. 2, pp. 1093–1095.
52. I. Friedlaender, ''ʿAbdallāh b. Saba', der Begründer der Šīʿa, und sein jüdischer Ursprung', *Zeitschrift für Assyrologie*, 23 (1909), pp. 296–327, and 24 (1910), pp. 1–46; Halm, *Islamische Gnosis*, pp. 32–42, and Marshall G. S. Hodgson, ''ʿAbd Allāh b. Saba'', *EI2*, vol. 1, p. 51.
53. Al-Nawbakhtī, *Firaq*, pp. 19–20; al-Qummī, *al-Maqālāt*, pp. 19–21 and 44–45; al-Ashʿarī, *Maqālāt*, p. 15; al-Malaṭī, *Kitāb al-tanbīh*, pp. 14 and 18–19; al-Baghdādī, *al-Farq*, pp. 223–226, 241 and 254; tr. Halkin, pp. 41–45, 73–74 and 92–93; Ibn Ḥazm, *al-Fiṣal*, vol. 4, p. 180; Friedlaender, 'Heterodoxies', pp. 45–46, and al-Shahrastānī, *al-Milal*, vol. 1, p. 174; tr. Kazi, pp. 150–151.
54. See J. Wellhausen, *Skizzen und Vorarbeiten* (Berlin, 1889), vol. 6, pp. 124–125 and 133; Friedlaender, ''ʿAbdallāh b. Saba'' (1910), pp. 7–8, and Lewis, *Origins*, p. 25.
55. For an excellent survey of the changing criteria of *ghuluww* during the first three Islamic centuries, see W. al-Qāḍī, 'The Development of the Term Ghulāt in Muslim Literature with Special Reference to the Kaysāniyya', in *Akten des VII. Kongresses für Arabistik und Islamwissenschaft*, ed. A. Dietrich (Göttingen, 1976), pp. 295–319; also his *al-Kaysāniyya*, pp. 238–267.
56. Our discussion is mainly based on al-Nawbakhtī, *Firaq*, pp. 32–34 and 35–37, and al-Qummī, *al-Maqālāt*, pp. 44–46 and 48–50. Useful details are to be found also in al-Baghdādī, *al-Farq*, pp. 214–217, and 253ff.; tr. Halkin, pp. 31–35 and pp. 91ff.
57. For the central Manichaean doctrine of redemption, whereby the transmigrating soul is the focus of the all-important salvational process, see Henri C. Puech, 'Der Begriff der Erlösung im Manichäismus', *EJ*, 4 (1936), pp. 183–286; G. Widengren, *Mani and Manichaeism*, tr. C. Kessler (New York, 1965), especially pp. 59–69, and Jes P. Asmussen, *Manichaean Literature* (Delmar, N.Y., 1975), pp. 6–8, 47–53 and 78–97.
58. See Jafri, *Origins*, pp. 246–247; Hodgson, 'How', p. 10, and Corbin, *En Islam*, vol. 1, pp. 53ff.
59. Al-Nawbakhtī, *Firaq*, pp. 52–53, and al-Qummī, *al-Maqālāt*, pp. 74–76.
60. The influence of the Muʿtazilīs on the Zaydī Shīʿīs is investigated in W. Madelung, *Der Imam al-Qāsim ibn Ibrāhīm und die Glaubenslehre der Zaiditen* (Berlin, 1965), pp. 7–43; while a discussion of the connection between Muʿtazilism and Imāmī Shīʿism is to be found in Madelung, 'Imamism and Muʿtazilite Theology', in *Le Shīʿisme Imāmite*, Colloque de Strasbourg, ed. T. Fahd (Paris, 1970), pp. 13–29, reprinted in his *Religious Schools and Sects*.

61. The Zaydīs managed, by the second half of the third/ninth century, to establish two states, one in the southern coastal regions of the Caspian Sea and another in Yaman. Only the latter has survived to the present, under the Zaydī Imāms of Ṣanʿāʾ. For further details on the history and doctrines of the Zaydiyya, see R. Strothmann, *Das Staatsrecht der Zaiditen* (Strassburg, 1912); also his 'al-Zaidīya', *EI*, vol. 4, pp. 1196–1198; C. van Arendonk, *Les débuts de l'Imāmat Zaidite au Yémen*, tr. J. Ryckmans (Leiden, 1960), originally published in Dutch (Leiden, 1919); Madelung, *Der Imam al-Qāsim*, pp. 44–152; and his 'The Alid rulers of Ṭabaristān, Daylamān and Gīlān', in *Atti del Terzo Congresso di Studi Arabi e Islamici* (Naples, 1967), pp. 483–492; M. S. Khan, 'The Early History of Zaydī Shīʿism in Daylamān and Gīlān', in *Mélanges H. Corbin*, pp. 257–277, and R. B. Serjeant, 'The Zaydīs', in *Religion in the Middle East*, ed. A. J. Arberry (Cambridge, 1969), vol. 2, pp. 285–301, where more recent developments are also covered.
62. Abū ʿAmr Muḥammad b. ʿUmar al-Kashshī, *Ikhtiyār maʿrifat al-rijāl*, abridged by Muḥammad b. al-Ḥasan al-Ṭūsī, ed., Ḥasan al-Muṣṭafawī (Mashhad, 1348/1969); hereafter cited as *al-Rijāl*.
63. Aḥmad b. ʿAlī al-Najāshī, *Kitāb al-rijāl* (Bombay, 1317/1899); the Shaykh al-Ṭāʾifa Abū Jaʿfar Muḥammad b. al-Ḥasan al-Ṭūsī, *Fihrist kutub al-Shīʿa*, ed. A. Sprenger et al. (Calcutta, 1853–1855); also his *Rijāl al-Ṭūsī*, ed. M. Ṣ. *Āl* Baḥr al-ʿUlūm (Najaf, 1381/1961), and Muḥammad b. ʿAlī b. Shahrāshūb, *Maʿālim al-ʿulamāʾ*, ed. ʿA. Iqbāl (Tehran, 1353/1934); more recently some of these works have been reprinted in Najaf, Qumm, Mashhad and Tehran.
64. For further details and references, see Goldziher, *Muslim Studies*, vol. 2, pp. 17–43 and 77–85; also his *Introduction*, pp. 30–66, and J. Robson, 'Ḥadīth', *EI2*, vol. 3, pp. 23–28. The early period of Islamic jurisprudence has been traced in numerous works by Joseph Schacht (1902–1969), the foremost Western authority on the subject; see especially his *Esquisse d'une histoire du droit Musulman* (Paris, 1953), pp. 9–50; *An Introduction to Islamic Law* (Oxford, 1964), pp. 10–56, and 'Fiḳh', *EI2*, vol. 2, pp. 887–891.
65. Al-Nawbakhtī, *Firaq*, pp. 37, 52 and 54–55; al-Qummī, *al-Maqālāt*, pp. 43–44, 55, 74 and 76–77; al-Ashʿarī, *Maqālāt*, pp. 6–9 and 23–24; al-Malaṭī, *Kitāb al-tanbīh*, pp. 123ff.; al-Baghdādī, *al-Farq*, pp. 229–233; tr. Halkin, pp. 49–55; Ibn Ḥazm, *al-Fiṣal*, vol. 4, pp. 184–185; Friedlaender, 'Heterodoxies', pp. 59–60, and al-Shahrastānī, *al-Milal*, vol. 1, pp. 176–178; tr. Kazi, pp. 152–153. See also al-Kashshī, *al-Rijāl*, pp. 191–192, 223–228, 290–291, 302, 305 and 483.
66. On the sources of al-Mughīra's ideas, see Friedlaender, 'Heterodoxies: Commentary', pp. 79–85 and 91; William F. Tucker, 'Rebels and Gnostics: Al-Muġīra Ibn Saʿīd and the Muġīriyya', *Arabica*, 22 (1975), especially pp. 39–44, and Halm, *Islamische Gnosis*, pp. 89–96.
67. Corbin, *Histoire*, p. 112.
68. The Mandaeans, who appear in Arabic literature as the Ṣābiʾa, were numerous in southern ʿIrāq in al-Mughīra's time; and their few survivors are still to be found there as well as in southwestern Persia. For more details on this peculiar gnostic sect, also identified with the Sabaeans, and their obscure Iranian and Judaeo-Christian religious origins, see W. Brandt, *Die mandäische*

Religion (Leipzig, 1889); B. Carra de Vaux, 'al-Ṣābi'a', *EI*, vol. 4, pp. 21–22, and K. Rudolph's more recent studies, especially his *Die Mandäer* (Göttingen, 1960–1961), 2 vols.

69. Corbin, *Histoire*, pp. 111–112. On the Valentinian school of Gnosticism, founded in the second century A.D. by Valentinus and later developed, in different trends, by Marcus and other disciples, see E. F. Scott, 'Valentinianism', *ERE*, vol. 12, pp. 572–576; H. Jonas, *The Gnostic Religion* (2nd ed., Boston, 1963), pp. 174–197, and *The Rediscovery of Gnosticism*: Volume One, *The School of Valentinus*, ed. B. Layton (Leiden, 1980).
70. On the Shīʿī Jafr or the mystical science of letters, see Corbin, *Histoire*, pp. 187 and 204–207, and T. Fahd, 'Djafr', *EI2*, vol. 2, pp. 375–377. See also L. Massignon, 'La Philosophie orientale d'Ibn Sīna et son alphabet philosophique', in his *Opera Minora*, vol. 2, pp. 591, 594 and 603–604, where it is argued, after the earlier ideas of Paul Kraus, that it is in the Greek Gnosis of Asia (reflecting Aramaean influence) that we see the first systematic efforts to investigate the symbolic meaning of the letters of the alphabet. This is contrary to the commonly accepted view that ascribes the origins of such efforts to the Jewish cabala.
71. Tucker, 'Rebels and Gnostics', pp. 36 and 45–46.
72. Al-Nawbakhtī, *Firaq*, pp. 34–35; al-Qummī, *al-Maqālāt*, pp. 46–47; al-Ashʿarī, *Maqālāt*, pp. 9–10 and 24–25; al-Malaṭī, *Kitāb al-tanbīh*, p. 120; al-Baghdādī, *al-Farq*, pp. 234–235; tr. Halkin, pp. 57–58; Ibn Ḥazm, *al-Fiṣal*, vol. 4, pp. 185–186; Friedlaender, 'Heterodoxies', pp. 62–65; also his 'Heterodoxies: Commentary', pp. 89ff. and 96; al-Shahrastānī, *al-Milal*, vol. 1, pp. 178–179; tr. Kazi, pp. 153–154; Halm, *Islamische Gnosis*, pp. 86–89, and W. Madelung, 'Manṣūriyya', *EI2*, vol. 6, pp. 441–442.
73. See William F. Tucker, 'Abū Manṣūr al-ʿIjlī and the Manṣūriyya: A Study in Medieval Terrorism', *Der Islam*, 54 (1977), pp. 66–76.
74. It is interesting to note that whereas in al-Mughīra's cosmogony, Muḥammad and ʿAlī were the first persons created by God, Jesus and ʿAlī were the primordial men for Abū Manṣūr, reflecting Christian influences; see Friedlaender, 'Heterodoxies: Commentary', pp. 89–92.
75. This is the most frequently cited year; for other dates and their sources, see Jafri, *Origins*, pp. 255 and 258, and W. Madelung, 'al-Bāqer, Abū Jaʿfar Moḥammad', *EIR*, vol. 3, pp. 725–726.
76. Al-Nawbakhtī, *Firaq*, pp. 34 and 53–55, and al-Qummī, *al-Maqālāt*, pp. 76–78.
77. Al-Ṭabarī, *Ta'rīkh*, II, p. 1700. For the meaning and different applications of this term, see Friedlaender, 'Heterodoxies: Commentary', pp. 137–159; J. H. Kramers, 'Rāfiḍites', *SEI*, p. 466; W. M. Watt, 'The Rāfiḍites: A Preliminary Study', *Oriens*, 16 (1963), pp. 110–121; and also his *Formative Period*, pp. 157ff.
78. See al-Iṣfahānī, *Maqātil*, pp. 178–184, and K. V. Zetterstéen, 'ʿAbd Allāh b. al-Ḥasan', *EI2*, vol. 1, p. 45.
79. For a brief survey of these risings, see Ivanow, 'Early Shiʿite Movements', pp. 5ff., and H. Laoust, *Les Schismes dans l'Islam* (Paris, 1965), pp. 33ff.
80. On Zayd's revolt, see al-Ṭabarī, *Ta'rīkh*, II, pp. 1667–1688 and 1698–1716;

al-Masʿūdī, *Murūj*, vol. 5, pp. 467ff., al-Iṣfahānī, *Maqātil*, pp. 133–151; Wellhausen, *Arab Kingdom*, pp. 337–338; also his *Religio-Political Factions*, pp. 162–163; Arendonk, *Les débuts*, pp. 28–33, and R. Strothmann, 'Zaid b. ʿAlī', *EI*, vol. 4, pp. 1193–1194.

81. Al-Ṭabarī, *Ta'rīkh*, II, pp. 1710 and 1770–1774; al-Masʿūdī, *Murūj*, vol. 6, pp. 2–4; al-Iṣfahānī, *Maqātil*, pp. 152–158; Wellhausen: *Arab Kingdom*, pp. 338–339, 359 and 499–500; also his *Religio-Political Factions*, pp. 163–164; Arendonk, *Les débuts*, pp. 33–34; and his 'Yaḥyā b. Zaid al-Ḥusainī', *EI*, vol. 4, pp. 1151–1152.
82. Al-Ṭabarī, *Ta'rīkh*, III, pp. 143ff., and al-Iṣfahānī, *Maqātil*, pp. 206–209, 253 and 256.
83. The most detailed account of this Ḥasanid movement is contained in al-Iṣfahānī, *Maqātil*, pp. 205–229, 232–309 and 315–389; see also al-Ṭabarī, *Ta'rīkh*, III, pp. 66, 143–265, 282–318 and 359ff.; al-Masʿūdī, *Murūj*, vol. 6, pp. 189–197; Theodor Nöldeke, *Sketches from Eastern History*, tr. J. S. Black (London, 1892), pp. 120–128; Arendonk, *Les débuts*, pp. 45–48; R. Traini, 'La corrispondenza tra al-Manṣūr e Muḥammad an-Nafs az-Zakiyyah', *AIUON*, NS, 14 (1964), pp. 773–798; L. Veccia Vaglieri, 'Divagazioni su due rivolti Alidi', in *A Francesco Gabrieli, Studi Orientalistici* (Rome, 1964), pp. 315–324, 328–332 and 337–347; also see her 'Ibrāhīm b. ʿAbd Allāh', *EI2*, vol. 3, pp. 983–985, and F. Buhl, 'Muḥammad b. ʿAbd Allāh', *EI*, vol. 3, pp. 665–666.
84. On Ibn Muʿāwiya's movement, see al-Ṭabarī, *Ta'rīkh*, II, pp. 1879–1887, 1947–1948 and 1976–1981; al-Iṣfahānī, *Maqātil*, pp. 161–169; Wellhausen, *Arab Kingdom*, pp. 383–386 and 393–395; also see his *Religio-Political Factions*, pp. 164–165; Shaban, *Islamic History*, vol. 1, pp. 161–163; Tucker, 'ʿAbd Allāh ibn Muʿāwiya', pp. 39–49 and 55–56; Clifford E. Bosworth, *Sīstān under the Arabs* (Rome, 1968), pp. 76–77; K. V. Zetterstéen, 'ʿAbd Allāh b. Muʿāwiya', *EI2*, vol. 1, pp. 48–49, and D. M. Dunlop, 'ʿAbdallāh b. Moʿāvīa', *EIR*, vol. 1, pp. 183–184.
85. New details of the ʿAbbāsid movement came to light with the discovery and publication of the anonymous *Akhbār al-dawla al-ʿAbbāsiyya*, ed. ʿA. ʿA. Dūrī and A. J. Muṭṭalibī (Beirut, 1971). Much useful information on the ʿAbbāsid revolution can still be derived from Gerlof van Vloten's classic studies, *De Opkomst der Abbasiden in Chorasan* (Leiden, 1890), and *Recherches sur la domination Arabe, le Chiitisme et les croyances messianiques sous le khalifat des Omayades* (Amsterdam, 1894), and from Wellhausen's *Arab Kingdom*, pp. 492–566. More recently, the subject has been treated in a number of monographs, notably F. Omar, *The ʿAbbāsid Caliphate, 132/750–170/786* (Baghdad, 1969); M. A. Shaban, *The ʿAbbāsid Revolution* (Cambridge, 1970), especially pp. 149–168; Elton L. Daniel, *The Political and Social History of Khurasan under Abbasid Rule, 747–820* (Minneapolis, 1979), pp. 25–99; H. Kennedy, *The Early Abbasid Caliphate* (London, 1981), pp. 18–56, and J. Lassner, *The Shaping of ʿAbbāsid Rule* (Princeton, N.J., 1980), which contains a variety of interesting details. Briefer but important surveys are to be found in Cahen, 'Points', pp. 136–160; B. Lewis, 'ʿAbbāsids', *EI2*, vol. 1,

pp. 15ff., and C. E. Bosworth, ''Abbāsid Caliphate', *EIR*, vol. 1, pp. 89ff.

86. For a somewhat different view on the origins of the ʿAbbāsid movement, challenging the traditional account, see T. Nagel, *Untersuchungen zur Entstehung des abbasidischen Kalifates* (Bonn, 1972), and M. Sharon, *Black Banners from the East: The Establishment of the ʿAbbāsid State – Incubation of a Revolt* (Jerusalem–Leiden, 1983).
87. Zarrīnkūb, *Ta'rīkh-i Īrān*, vol. 1, pp. 390–404; Richard N. Frye, 'The Role of Abū Muslim in the ʿAbbāsid Revolt', *MW*, 37 (1947), pp. 28–38; S. Moscati, 'Studi su Abū Muslim', *Rendiconti della Reale Accademia dei Lincei, Classe di Scienze Morali, Storiche e Filologiche*, serie 8, 4 (1949–1950), pp. 323–335 and 474–495, and 5 (1950–1951), pp. 89–105; also his 'Abū Muslim', *EI2*, vol. 1, p. 141; Sharon, *Black Banners*, pp. 201–226, and Ḡ. Ḥ. Yūsofī, 'Abū Moslem Ḵorāsānī', *EIR*, vol. 1, pp. 340–344.
88. See M. Sharon, 'Ḳaḥṭaba', *EI2*, vol. 4, pp. 445–447.
89. Al-Ṭabarī, *Ta'rīkh*, III, pp. 27ff.; al-Masʿūdī, *Murūj*, vol. 6, pp. 93–96 and 133ff.; Arendonk, *Les débuts*, p. 43; Laoust, *Schismes*, pp. 56–58 and 61; Shaban, *Islamic History*, vol. 1, pp. 185–187; Jafri, *Origins*, pp. 273–274; Hodgson, *Venture of Islam*, vol. 1, pp. 275–276; Lassner, *Shaping*, pp. 59–60, 84, 145–147 and 151–152; F. Omar, *ʿAbbāsid Caliphate*, pp. 139ff.; also his 'Some Aspects of the ʿAbbāsid–Ḥusaynid Relations during the Early ʿAbbāsid Period, 132–193 A.H./750–809 A.D.', *Arabica*, 22 (1975), pp. 172–173; S. Moscati, 'Abū Salama', *EI2*, vol. 1, p. 149, and R. W. Bulliet, 'Abū Salama Ḵallāl', *EIR*, vol. 1, pp. 382–383.
90. Al-Ṭabarī, *Ta'rīkh*, III, p. 74, and Muḥammad b. Jaʿfar al-Narshakhī, *Ta'rīkh-i Bukhārā*, ed. M. T. Mudarris Raḍavī (2nd ed., Tehran, 1363/1984), pp. 86–89, and its English translation, *The History of Bukhara*, tr. Richard N. Frye (Cambridge, Mass., 1954), pp. 62–65.
91. Al-Ṭabarī, *Ta'rīkh*, III, pp. 129–133 and 418–419; Friedlaender, 'Heterodoxies: Commentary', pp. 100–101 and 121–124, and Lassner, *Shaping*, pp. 109–111 and 159–160.
92. Marshall G. S. Hodgson, 'Djaʿfar al-Ṣādiḳ', *EI2*, vol. 2, pp. 374–375.
93. See J. Schacht, *The Origins of Muhammadan Jurisprudence* (Oxford, 1950), pp. 262–268; Asaf A. A. Fyzee, 'Shīʿī Legal Theories', in *Law in the Middle East*, ed. M. Khaduri and H. J. Liebesny (Washington, D.C., 1955), vol. 1, pp. 113–131, and Fyzee, *Outlines of Muhammadan Law* (4th ed., Delhi, 1974), pp. 43–48 and 80–87.
94. Hodgson, 'How', pp. 10–13; also see Hodgson's *Venture of Islam*, vol. 1, pp. 259–260 and 374–376; and Jafri, *Origins*, pp. 289–300. Summary English expositions of the Imāmī Shīʿī doctrine of the imāmate are to be found in Ṭabāṭabā'ī, *Shiʿite Islam*, pp. 173–190; Momen, *Introduction to Shiʿi Islam*, pp. 147–160, and W. Madelung, 'Imāma', *EI2*, vol. 3, pp. 1166–1167.
95. See al-Ṭabarī, *Ta'rīkh*, III, pp. 169–189 and 445–446; al-Masʿūdī, *Murūj*, vol. 6, pp. 198–203; al-Iṣfahānī, *Maqātil*, pp. 178ff.; Cahen, 'Points', pp. 155–156, and Omar, 'Some Aspects', pp. 173–175.
96. Hodgson, *Venture of Islam*, vol. 1, p. 260.

97. Hodgson, 'How', p. 11.
98. Al-Nawbakhtī, *Firaq*, pp. 56–57; al-Qummī, *al-Maqālāt*, pp. 78–79; Muḥammad b. Yaʿqūb al-Kulaynī (or al-Kulīnī), *al-Uṣūl min al-Kāfī*, ed. ʿAlī Akbar al-Ghaffārī (Tehran, 1388/1968), vol. 2, pp. 217–226. See also I. Goldziher, 'Das Prinzip der Taḳijja im Islam', *ZDMG*, 60 (1906), pp. 213–226; R. Strothmann, 'Taḳīya', *EI*, vol. 4, pp. 628–629; Corbin, *En Islam*, vol. 1, pp. 6, 87 and 117; Ṭabāṭabāʾī, *Shīʿite Islam*, pp. 223–225; and E. Kohlberg, 'Some Imāmī-Shīʿī Views on Taqiyya', *JAOS*, 95 (1975), pp. 395–402.
99. These *ḥadīths* are to be found in the *Kitāb al-ḥujja*, the opening book in al-Kulaynī's *al-Uṣūl min al-Kāfī*, vol. 1, pp. 168–548, of which a list of contents in English is given in Sachedina, *Islamic Messianism*, pp. 184–193.
100. See, for example, Abū Ḥanīfa al-Nuʿmān b. Muḥammad, *Daʿāʾim al-Islām*, ed. Asaf A. A. Fyzee (Cairo, 1951–1961), vol. 1, pp. 1–98; this is the important opening chapter, the *Kitāb al-walāya*, based mainly on *ḥadīths* reported from the Imām al-Ṣādiq, now available separately also in English translation under the title of *The Book of Faith*, tr. Asaf A. A. Fyzee (Bombay, 1974). The *Daʿāʾim* is one of the principal works of al-Qāḍī al-Nuʿmān (d. 363/974), the foremost Ismāʿīlī jurist of the Fāṭimid period. See also A. Nanji, 'An Ismāʿīlī Theory of Walāyah in the Daʿāʾim al-Islām of Qāḍī al-Nuʿmān', in *Essays on Islamic Civilization Presented to Niyazi Berkes*, ed. D. P. Little (Leiden, 1976), pp. 260–273.
101. Al-Kulaynī, *al-Uṣūl*, vol. 1, pp. 376–377.
102. H. Corbin has investigated the various aspects of the subject of *walāya*, to be distinguished from *wilāya* meaning sanctity and guardianship, more than any other Western scholar; see especially his 'L'Imām caché', pp. 87ff.; *Histoire*, pp. 45ff., 59–62, 66–70 and 78–92; 'De la philosophie prophétique en Islam Shīʿite', *EJ*, 31 (1962), pp. 67ff. and 78–91; 'Sur la notion de "walāyat" en Islam Shīʿite', in *Normes et valeurs dans l'Islam contemporain*, ed. J. P. Charnay (Paris, 1966), pp. 38–47; 'Imamologie et philosophie', in *Le Shīʿisme Imāmite*, pp. 161–172, and *En Islam*, vol. 1, pp. 39ff., 51 and 235–284. See also Ṭabāṭabāʾī, *Shīʿite Islam*, pp. 10 and 78–79; and Nasr, *Ideals*, pp. 86–88 and 160–162.
103. For the different meanings and applications of the term *awliyāʾ* (singular, *walī*), see Goldziher, *Muslim Studies*, vol. 2, pp. 255ff.; W. M. Patton, 'Saints and Martyrs (Muhammadan)', *ERE*, vol. 11, pp. 63–68; and B. Carra de Vaux, 'Walī', *EI*, vol. 4, pp. 1109–1111.
104. See al-Kashshī, *al-Rijāl*, pp. 167, 251–252, 316–317, 345, 352, 375 and 382–383; al-Najāshī, *al-Rijāl*, pp. 10, 92, 103–104, 148–149 and 154; al-Ṭūsī, *Rijāl*, pp. 142–341; Ibn Shahrāshūb, *Manāqib āl Abī Ṭālib* (Bombay, 1313/1896), vol. 5, p. 55, and Jafri, *Origins*, pp. 309–310.
105. Al-Kashshī, *al-Rijāl*, pp. 133–161, 185–191, 213, 255–280 and 281–285; al-Najāshī, *al-Rijāl*, pp. 176, 228 and 304–305; al-Ṭūsī, *Fihrist*, pp. 141–143, 212, 323 and 355–356, and Ibn Shahrāshūb, *Maʿālim*, p. 115. See also Jafri, *Origins*, pp. 305–308; T. Fahd, 'Ǧaʿfar aṣ-Ṣādiq et la tradition scientifique Arabe', in *Le Shīʿisme Imāmite*, pp. 131–141; W. Madelung, 'The Shiite and Khārijite Contribution to Pre-Ashʿarite Kalām', in *Islamic Philosophical*

Theology, ed. P. Morewedge (Albany, N.Y., 1979), pp. 120–139, and Madelung, 'Hishām b. al-Ḥakam', *EI2*, vol. 3, pp. 496–498.

106. J. Ruska, 'Ǧābir ibn Ḥajjān und seine Beziehungen zum Imām Ǧaʿfar aṣ-Ṣādiq', *Der Islam*, 16 (1927), pp. 264–266; also his 'The History of the Jābir Problem', *IC*, 11 (1937), pp. 303–312; P. Kraus, 'Dschābir ibn Ḥajjān und die Ismaʿīlijja', in *Der Zusammenbruch der Dschābir-legende, Dritter Jahresbericht des Forschungs-Institut für Geschichte der Naturwissenschaften* (Berlin, 1930), pp. 23–42; H. Corbin, 'Le Livre du Glorieux de Jābir ibn Ḥayyān', *EJ*, 18 (1950), especially pp. 47–86; reprinted in Corbin, *L'Alchimie comme art hiératique* (Paris, 1986), pp. 145–182; also his *Histoire*, pp. 184–190; F. Sezgin, 'Das Problem des Ǧābir ibn Ḥayyān im Lichte neu gefundener Handschriften', *ZDMG*, 114 (1964), pp. 255–268; also his *Geschichte des arabischen Schrifttums* (Leiden, 1967–), vol. 4, pp. 132–269, and P. Kraus and M. Plessner, 'Djābir b. Ḥayyān', *EI2*, vol. 2, pp. 357–359.

107. Al-Kashshī, *al-Rijāl*, pp. 191–198, 373 and 485; al-Najāshī, *al-Rijāl*, pp. 93–94; Halm, *Islamische Gnosis*, pp. 96ff., and W. Madelung, 'Djābir al-Djuʿfī', *EI2*, Supplement, pp. 232–233.

108. Jafri, *Origins*, pp. 301–303.

109. The most detailed and accurate accounts of Abu'l-Khaṭṭāb and his ideas, as well as the various Khaṭṭābī sub-groups, are to be found in al-Nawbakhtī, *Firaq*, pp. 37–41 and 58–60; al-Qummī, *al-Maqālāt*, pp. 50–55, 63–64 and 81–82, and al-Kashshī, *al-Rijāl*, pp. 224–226, 228, 290–308, 324, 344, 352–353, 365–366, 370, 482–483, 528–529 and 571. See also Muḥammad b. Yaʿqūb al-Kulaynī, *al-Rawḍa min al-Kāfī*, ed. M. B. al-Bihbūdī and ʿA. A. al-Ghaffārī (Tehran, 1397/1977), vol. 2, pp. 42–43; al-Ashʿarī, *Maqālāt*, pp. 10–13; al-Baghdādī, *al-Farq*, pp. 236–237; tr. Halkin, pp. 62–66; Ibn Ḥazm, *al-Fiṣal*, vol. 4, p. 187; Friedlaender, 'Heterodoxies', pp. 68–69; also his 'Heterodoxies: Commentary', pp. 95–96 and 111–113; al-Shahrastānī, *al-Milal*, vol. 1, pp. 179–181; tr. Kazi, pp. 154–155; Lewis, *Origins*, pp. 32ff.; also his 'Abu'l-Khaṭṭāb', *EI2*, vol. 1, p. 134. W. Ivanow, *The Alleged Founder of Ismailism* (Bombay, 1946), pp. 113–137; H. Corbin, *Étude préliminaire pour le 'Livre réunissant les deux sagesses' de Nasir-e Khosraw* (Tehran-Paris, 1953) pp. 14ff., hereafter cited as *Étude*; Corbin, 'Une liturgie Shīʿite du Graal', in *Mélanges d'histoire des religions offerts à Henri Charles Puech* (Paris, 1974), especially pp. 83–93; Halm, *Islamische Gnosis*, pp. 199–217; D. S. Margoliouth, 'Khaṭṭābīya', *EI*, vol. 2, pp. 931–932; A. A. Sachedina, 'Abu'l-Khaṭṭāb', *EII*, vol. 1, pp. 951–952; also his 'Abu'l-Ḵaṭṭāb', *EIR*, vol. 1, pp. 329–330, and W. Madelung, 'Khaṭṭābiyya', *EI2*, vol. 4, pp. 1132–1133.

110. Hodgson, 'How', p. 8.

3. Early Ismāʿīlism

1. Corbin, *Étude*, p. 7.
2. Asaf A. A. Fyzee, 'The Ismāʿīlīs', in *Religion in the Middle East*, vol. 2, p. 328.
3. *Kitāb al-rushd wa'l-hidāya*, ed. M. Kāmil Ḥusayn, in *Collectanea*: Vol. 1, ed. W. Ivanow (Leiden, 1948), pp. 185–213, and its English translation, 'The

Book of Righteousness and True Guidance', in W. Ivanow, *Studies in Early Persian Ismailism* (2nd ed., Bombay, 1955), pp. 29–59, hereafter cited as *Studies* 2.

4. The Arabic text of this work has appeared in *Arbaʿ kutub ḥaqqāniyya*, ed. M. Ghālib (Beirut, 1983), pp. 13–75, and its abridged English translation entitled 'The Book of the Teacher and the Pupil' is to be found in Ivanow, *Studies* 2, pp. 61–86; it is studied extensively in H. Corbin, 'Un roman initiatique Ismaélien', *Cahiers de Civilisation Médiévale*, 15 (1972), pp. 1–25 and 121–142, and in his 'L'Initiation Ismaélienne ou l'ésotérisme et le Verbe', *EJ*, 39 (1970), pp. 41–142, reprinted in his *L'Homme et son age* (Paris, 1983), pp. 81–205. See also Kraus, 'Bibliographie Ismaëlienne', p. 486; Ivanow, *Ismaili Literature*, p. 18, and Poonawala, *Bio*, p. 74.
5. Al-Nuʿmān b. Muḥammad, *Iftitāḥ al-daʿwa*, ed. W. al-Qāḍī (Beirut, 1970), also edited by F. Dachraoui (Tunis, 1975); hereafter references are to Wadād al-Qāḍī's edition. This work has been utilized thoroughly in T. Nagel, *Frühe Ismailiya und Fatimiden im lichte der Risālat Iftitāḥ ad-Daʿwa* (Bonn, 1972).
6. Idrīs ʿImād al-Dīn, *ʿUyūn al-akhbār wa funūn al-āthār*, ed. M. Ghālib (Beirut, 1973–1978), vols. 4–6; these are the only volumes published so far, carrying the narrative from the biography of the Imām al-Ḥasan b. ʿAlī, and the subsequent imāms recognized by the Ismāʿīlīs, to the rule of the Fāṭimid caliph-imām al-Mustanṣir; see Ivanow, *Ismaili Literature*, pp. 77–79, and Poonawala, *Bio*, pp. 169–172.
7. Samuel M. Stern had a special interest in early Ismāʿīlism, which he pursued over a twenty-year period at Oxford until his untimely death in 1969. His views on the subject can be found in several major articles, notably in 'Heterodox Ismāʿīlism at the time of al-Muʿizz', *BSOAS*, 17 (1955), pp. 10–33, 'The Early Ismāʿīlī Missionaries in North-West Persia and in Khurāsān and Transoxania', *BSOAS*, 23 (1960), pp. 56–90, and 'Ismāʿīlīs and Qarmaṭians', in *L'Élaboration de l'Islam*, Colloque de Strasbourg (Paris, 1961), pp. 99–108. These articles, and some others, have been reprinted in Stern's recently published collection of works entitled *Studies in Early Ismāʿīlism* (Jerusalem–Leiden, 1983), in which several essays on the various aspects of early Ismāʿīlī thought are also published for the first time. Unfortunately, Stern's promised book on early Ismāʿīlism was found to be in an unfinished form, aside from having been largely superseded by the subsequent studies of other scholars, notably W. Madelung. For Stern's contributions to Ismāʿīlī studies, and his life and varied works, see J. D. Latham and H. W. Mitchell, 'The Bibliography of S. M. Stern', *Journal of Semitic Studies*, 15 (1970), pp. 226–238; R. Walzer, 'Samuel M. Stern', *Israel Oriental Studies*, 2 (1972), pp. 1–14, and David R. W. Bryer, 'An Analysis of Samuel M. Stern's Writings on Ismāʿīlism', in Stern, *Studies*, pp. ix–xii.
8. The contributions of W. Madelung to early Ismāʿīlism are contained in two long articles written in German, 'Fatimiden und Baḥrainqarmaṭen', *Der Islam*, 34 (1959), pp. 34–88, and 'Das Imamat in der frühen ismailitischen Lehre', *Der Islam*, 37 (1961), pp. 43–135, hereafter cited as 'Imamat'.

Madelung has also contributed the major Ismāʿīlī entries, 'Ismāʿīliyya', and 'Ḳarmaṭī', to *EI2*, vol. 4, pp. 198–206 and 660–665, amongst many other articles on different aspects of Imāmī, Ismāʿīlī and Zaydī Shīʿism. Recently, W. Madelung has summarized his views on these sects and some other movements in his *Religious Trends in Early Islamic Iran* (Albany, N.Y., 1988).

9. *Kitāb al-rushd*, p. 212; tr. Ivanow in *Studies* 2, p. 58, and Stern, 'Ismāʿīlīs', p. 100.
10. Abū Tamīm Maʿadd al-Mustanṣir bi'llāh, *al-Sijillāt al-Mustanṣiriyya*, ed. ʿA. M. Mājid (Cairo, 1954), pp. 157, 168, 176, 178 and 179; see also Ḥ. F. al-Hamdānī, 'The Letters of al-Mustanṣir bi'llāh', *BSOS*, 7 (1934), pp. 307ff. and 320–322.
11. *Al-Hidāyatu'l-Āmirya*, text p. 7.
12. See al-Majdūʿ, *Fihrist*, p. 3, and Aḥmad b. ʿAlī al-Qalqashandī, *Ṣubḥ al-aʿshā fī ṣināʿat al-inshā'*, ed. M. ʿA. Ibrāhīm (Cairo, 1331–1338/1913–1920), vol. 9, pp. 18–20, vol. 10, pp. 434–435, and vol. 13, pp. 238 and 246, containing references to the designation *al-daʿwa al-hādiya* used in certain Ismāʿīlī oaths and investiture diplomas which are quoted in this secretarial encyclopaedia completed in 814/1412 by the celebrated secretary in the chancery of the Mamlūks in Cairo. See also Ivanow, *Guide*, pp. 5–8; also his *Studies* 2, pp. 108–109; Fyzee, 'Study', p. 233; M. Kāmil Ḥusayn's introductory remarks in his edition of *al-Majālis al-Mustanṣiriyya* (Cairo, 1947), which are the lectures of the Fāṭimid chief *qāḍī* Abu'l-Qāsim al-Mālījī, and B. Lewis, 'Ismāʿīlī Notes', *BSOAS*, 12 (1948), pp. 597–598.
13. Al-Nawbakhtī, *Firaq*, p. 55; al-Qummī, *al-Maqālāt*, p. 78, and Sachedina, *Islamic Messianism*, pp. 153–154.
14. Lewis, *Origins*, pp. 38–39; Ivanow, *Alleged*, p. 159, and Madelung, 'Imamat', p. 44.
15. See al-Kulaynī, *al-Uṣūl*, vol. 1, pp. 307–311; al-Kashshī, *al-Rijāl*, pp. 451 and 462; al-Mufīd, *al-Irshād*, pp. 436–440 and 510, and Ṭabāṭabā'ī, *Shiʿite Islam*, pp. 75, 190, 205 and 221, where additional Twelver sources are cited.
16. These groups are covered in the earliest extant Imāmī works on the Shīʿī sects; the relevant passages (excluding those on the two earliest Ismāʿīlī groups that will be discussed later) are to be found in al-Nawbakhtī, *Firaq*, pp. 57, 64–67 and 71–72, and al-Qummī, *al-Maqālāt*, pp. 79–80 and 86–89, both drawing on an earlier account by Hishām b. al-Ḥakam. See also al-Ashʿarī, *Maqālāt*, pp. 25 and 27–29; Ibn Ḥazm, *al-Fiṣal*, vol. 4, pp. 93 and 180; Friedlaender, 'Heterodoxies', pp. 44 and 76; also his 'Heterodoxies: Commentary', pp. 39–40, 41, 50ff. and 114; al-Shahrastānī, *al-Milal*, vol. 1, pp. 165–169; tr. Kazi, pp. 142–145; Omar, 'Some Aspects', pp. 178–179; W. M. Watt, 'The Reappraisal of Abbasid Shiʿism', in *Arabic and Islamic Studies in Honor of H. A. R. Gibb*, pp. 638–639 and 645ff.; also his 'Sidelights on Early Imāmite Doctrine', *SI*, 31 (1970), pp. 293–298, and R. Strothmann, 'Mūsā al-Kāẓim', *EI*, vol. 3, p. 741.
17. On this revolt, see al-Ṭabarī, *Ta'rīkh*, III, pp. 551–568; al-Masʿūdī, *Murūj*, vol. 6, pp. 266–268; al-Iṣfahānī, *Maqātil*, pp. 431ff. and 442–460; Arendonk,

Les débuts, pp. 62–65; Veccia Vaglieri, 'Divagazioni su due rivolti Alidi', pp. 315–316, 320–322, 335–339 and 341–350, and her 'al-Ḥusayn b. ʿAlī, Ṣāḥib Fakhkh', *EI2*, vol. 3, pp. 615–617.

18. Al-Nawbakhtī, *Firaq*, pp. 67 and 72ff.; al-Qummī, *al-Maqālāt*, pp. 89 and 93ff.; al-Kulaynī, *al-Uṣūl*, vol. 1, pp. 311–319; al-Iṣfahānī, *Maqātil*, pp. 561–562; Ṭabāṭabāʾī, *Shiʿite Islam*, pp. 63–64 and 205–207; Laoust, *Schismes*, pp. 98–100; F. Gabrieli, *al-Maʾmūn e gli ʿAlidi* (Leipzig, 1929), pp. 35ff.; B. Lewis, 'ʿAlī al-Riḍā', *EI2*, vol. 1, pp. 399–400, and W. Madelung, 'ʿAlī al-Reżā', *EIR*, vol. 1, pp. 877–880. The tomb of the Imām al-Riḍā, situated at Mashhad, the capital of the modern-day province of Khurāsān, is the most sacred Shīʿī shrine in Persia.

19. With the formulation in the first half of the fourth/tenth century of the doctrine of the twelve imāms, the Imāmī Shīʿī doctrine of the imāmate acquired its final important characteristic. It is this belief in a line of twelve imāms, already reflected in al-Nawbakhtī, *Firaq*, pp. 90–93, al-Qummī, *al-Maqālāt*, pp. 102–106, al-Kulaynī, *al-Uṣūl*, vol. 1, pp. 328ff., and later refined by Ibn Bābawayh (d. 381/991), al-Mufīd (d. 413/1022), and others, which distinguishes Twelver Shīʿism from the earlier Imāmiyya. With the rising predominance of the Twelvers, the terms Imāmiyya and Ithnāʿashariyya gradually became synonymous, though the Ismāʿīlīs also referred to themselves as Imāmī Shīʿīs. See Laoust, *Schismes*, pp. 146ff. and 181–184; Watt, *Formative Period*, pp. 274–278; Nasr, *Ideals*, pp. 155–157 and 164ff.; also his 'Ithnāʿashariyya', *EI2*, vol. 4, pp. 277–279; E. Kohlberg, 'From Imāmiyya to Ithnā-ʿashariyya', *BSOAS*, 39 (1976), pp. 521–534, and Sachedina, *Islamic Messianism*, pp. 39–179. For brief biographical notices on these twelve imāms, see al-Kulaynī, *al-Uṣūl*, vol. 1, pp. 452–458 and 461–525; al-Mufīd, *al-Irshād*, pp. 279–568; Ṭabāṭabāʾī, *Shiʿite Islam*, pp. 190–211 and 220–222, where additional Shīʿī sources are cited; J. Eliash, 'Ḥasan al-ʿAskarī', *EI2*, vol. 3, pp. 246–247, and W. Madelung, 'ʿAlī al-Hādī', *EIR*, vol. 1, pp. 861–862. Many of Corbin's works are highly valuable for the study of Twelver Shīʿism.

20. W. Ivanow, 'Ismāʿīlīya', *SEI*, p. 179, and Corbin, *Étude*, p. 6.

21. Al-Nawbakhtī, *Firaq*, pp. 57–58, and al-Qummī, *al-Maqālāt*, p. 80.

22. Al-Shahrastānī, *al-Milal*, vol. 1, pp. 27 and 167–168; tr. Kazi, pp. 23 and 144; tr. Vadet, p. 284; tr. Gimaret and Monnot, pp. 491–492. See also Friedlaender, 'Heterodoxies: Commentary', pp. 26, 40 and 51.

23. Al-Nawbakhtī, *Firaq*, p. 58, and al-Qummī, *al-Maqālāt*, pp. 80–81. See also al-Ashʿarī, *Maqālāt*, pp. 26–27; al-Baghdādī, *al-Farq*, pp. 46–47; tr. Seelye, pp. 65–66; al-Shahrastānī, *al-Milal*, vol. 1, pp. 27–28, 168 and 191ff.; tr. Kazi, pp. 23, 144 and 163ff.; al-Mufīd, *al-Irshād*, p. 431, and al-Ṭūsī, *Rijāl*, p. 310.

24. Ivanow, *Alleged*, pp. 108–112.

25. See Abū Yaʿqūb al-Sijistānī, *Ithbāt al-nubūʾāt [al-nubūwāt]*, ed. ʿĀ. Tāmir (Beirut, 1966), p. 190. Mubārak is also mentioned as a pseudonym of Ismāʿīl in a letter sent by the first Fāṭimid caliph to the Ismāʿīlīs in Yaman. This letter, as reported in the book *al-Farāʾiḍ wa ḥudūd al-dīn* by Jaʿfar b. Manṣūr al-Yaman, has been published and translated in Ḥusayn F. al-Hamdānī, *On the Genealogy of Fatimid Caliphs* (Cairo, 1958), hereafter cited as *Genealogy*; the

relevant passage on Mubārak is found in text p. 10, translation p. 12. For a detailed analysis of this letter and its more precise translation, and an interesting hypothesis regarding the descent of the early Ismāʿīlī Imāms, see A. Hamdani and F. de Blois, 'A Re-Examination of al-Mahdī's Letter to the Yemenites on the Genealogy of the Fatimid Caliphs', *JRAS* (1983), pp. 173–207.

26. See al-Nawbakhtī, *Firaq*, p. 62, and al-Qummī, *al-Maqālāt*, p. 84; this can be gathered also from the earliest extant Zaydī reference to the nascent Ismāʿīliyya by the Zaydī Imām al-Qāsim b. Ibrāhīm (d. 246/860), in a treatise entitled *al-Radd ʿalā'l-Rawāfiḍ*, cited in Madelung, 'Imamat', p. 46.
27. Al-Qummī, *al-Maqālāt*, p. 81, and al-Nawbakhtī, *Firaq*, pp. 58–59, where the group al-Ismāʿīliyya is identified with al-Khaṭṭābiyya. However, since al-Nawbakhtī does not discuss a group called *al-Ismāʿīliyya*, it seems that by the latter designation, similarly to al-Qummī, he is referring to *al-Ismāʿīliyya al-khāliṣa*, one of the two proto-Ismāʿīlī groups covered in his work.
28. Al-Nawbakhtī, *Firaq*, pp. 60–61, and al-Qummī, *al-Maqālāt*, p. 83.
29. See Lewis, *Origins*, pp. 33–35.
30. See al-Nawbakhtī, *Firaq*, p. 90, and al-Qummī, *al-Maqālāt*, p. 103, where the claims of Ismāʿīl and Muḥammad b. Ismāʿīl are rejected; see also al-Kashshī, *al-Rijāl*, pp. 473–474, where Ismāʿīl is accused of being inclined to drink.
31. See Jaʿfar b. Manṣūr al-Yaman, *Asrār al-nuṭaqā'*, in W. Ivanow, *Ismaili Tradition Concerning the Rise of the Fatimids* (London, etc., 1942), text p. 98, translation p. 295, hereafter cited as *Rise*; Jaʿfar b. Manṣūr al-Yaman, *Sarā'ir wa asrār al-nuṭaqā'*, ed. M. Ghālib (Beirut, 1984), p. 258, and Ivanow, *Alleged*, pp. 155–156. ʿĀrif Tāmir places Ismāʿīl's birth in 101/719–720, in his *al-Imāma fi'l-Islām* (Beirut, 1964?), p. 180; the same date is repeated in some Ismāʿīlī sources cited in M. T. Dānishpazhūh, 'Dhaylī bar ta'rīkh-i Ismāʿīliyya', *Revue de la Faculté des Lettres, Université de Tabriz*, 18 (1345/1966), p. 21. But M. Ghālib mentioned the year 110/728–729 in his biographical work *Aʿlām al-Ismāʿīliyya* (Beirut, 1964), p. 161.
32. Cited in Ivanow, *Rise*, p. 30. According to Muḥammad Ḥusayn Farāhānī, *Safar-nāma*, ed. Ḥ. Farmān-Farmā'īyān (Tehran, 1342/1963), p. 288, Ismāʿīl's mausoleum still existed in 1302/1885.
33. Jaʿfar b. Manṣūr al-Yaman, *Asrār al-nuṭaqā'*, in Ivanow, *Rise*, text pp. 103–104, translation pp. 301–302; ed. Ghālib, p. 262; Idrīs, *ʿUyūn*, vol. 4, p. 334; also his *Zahr al-maʿānī*, in Ivanow, *Rise*, text pp. 47ff., translation pp. 232ff., and al-Mufīd, *al-Irshād*, p. 431; this story is also related by the celebrated Persian historian Rashīd al-Dīn in his *Jāmiʿ al-tawārīkh*; *qismat-i Ismāʿīliyān*, ed. M. T. Dānishpazhūh and M. Mudarrisī Zanjānī (Tehran, 1338/1959), p. 10, hereafter cited as *Ismāʿīliyān*; see also R. Levy, 'The Account of the Ismaʿili Doctrines in the Jamiʿ al-Tawarikh of Rashid al-Din Fadlallah', *JRAS* (1930), pp. 514–515 and 521.
34. Al-Kashshī, *al-Rijāl*, pp. 376–382; see also Idrīs, *ʿUyūn*, vol. 4, pp. 326–327; al-Najāshī, *al-Rijāl*, p. 296; al-Ṭūsī, *Fihrist*, pp. 334–335; also his *Rijāl*, p. 310, and Ibn Shahrāshūb, *Manāqib*, vol. 5, p. 29.
35. Ibn ʿInaba, *ʿUmdat al-ṭālib*, p. 233. The late Zāhid ʿAlī, a learned Dā'ūdī Bohra

from Hyderabad, also mentions the same year in his *Ta'rīkh-i Fāṭimiyyīn-i Miṣr* (2nd ed., Karachi, 1963), vol. 1, pp. 41, 43 and 63.

36. The year 138/755–756 is mentioned in Aḥmad b. ʿAlī al-Maqrīzī, *Ittiʿāẓ al-ḥunafā'*, ed. H. Bunz (Leipzig, 1909), p. 6, ed. Jamāl al-Dīn al-Shayyāl (Cairo, 1967), vol. 1, p. 15. Other sources place Ismāʿīlī's death in 145/762–763; see ʿAlā' al-Dīn ʿAṭā-Malik Juwaynī, *Ta'rīkh-i jahān-gushāy*, ed. Muḥammad Qazvīnī (London, 1912–1937), vol. 3, p. 146, and Qazvīnī's commentary therein on p. 309; English translation, *The History of the World-Conqueror*, tr. John A. Boyle (Cambridge, Mass., 1958), vol. 2, p. 643; Rashīd al-Dīn, *Ismāʿīliyān*, p. 10, and Dānishpazhūh, 'Dhaylī' (1345/1966), p. 21. An anonymous Ismāʿīlī treatise, *Dastūr al-munajjimīn*, quoted in de Goeje, *Mémoire sur les Carmathes du Bahraïn* (2nd ed., Leiden, 1886), p. 203, hereafter cited as *Mémoire*, mentions 145 A.H. as the year of Ismāʿīl's disappearance; on this work, perhaps written by a Nizārī Ismāʿīlī towards the end of the fifth/eleventh century, see P. Casanova, 'Un nouveau manuscrit de la secte des Assassins', *JA*, 11 série, 19 (1922), pp. 126–135, and M. Qazvīnī, *Yāddāshthā-yi Qazvīnī*, ed. I. Afshār (Tehran, 1332–1354/1953–1975), vol. 8, pp. 110–143, both Casanova and Qazvīnī were of the opinion that the unique manuscript copy of the *Dastūr* now preserved at the Bibliothèque Nationale, Paris, probably once belonged to the famous Ismāʿīlī library at Alamūt.

37. Al-Kashshī, *al-Rijāl*, pp. 217–218, 321, 325–326, 354–356 and 390; some of these traditions are examined in W. Ivanow, 'Imam Ismail', *JASB*, NS, 19 (1923), pp. 305–310.

38. The most famous one amongst such works attributed to al-Mufaḍḍal b. ʿUmar al-Juʿfī is the *Kitāb al-haft wa'l-aẓilla*, ed. ʿĀ. Tāmir and Ign. A. Khalifé (2nd ed., Beirut, 1970), also edited by M. Ghālib (4th ed., Beirut, 1983), reporting the views of the Imām al-Ṣādiq; see Ivanow, *Guide*, p. 30, where it is wrongly stated that al-Mufaḍḍal was executed in 145/762; also by Ivanow, *Ismaili Literature*, pp. 59, 64 and 101, and L. Massignon, 'Esquisse d'une bibliographie Nusayrie', in *Mélanges Syriens offerts à M. René Dussaud* (Paris, 1939), vol. 2, pp. 914–915.

39. On al-Mufaḍḍal and his group, see al-Kashshī, *al-Rijāl*, pp. 321–329, 509 and 530–531; al-Najāshī, *al-Rijāl*, pp. 295–296; al-Ṭūsī, *Fihrist*, p. 337; also by al-Ṭūsī, *Rijāl*, pp. 314 and 360; al-Ashʿarī, *Maqālāt*, pp. 13 and 29; al-Baghdādī, *al-Farq*, p. 236; tr. Halkin, p. 65, and al-Shahrastānī, *al-Milal*, vol. 1, p. 168; tr. Kazi, p. 144; see also H. Halm, 'Das Buch der Schatten. Die Mufaḍḍal-Tradition der Gulāt und die Ursprünge des Noṣairiertums', *Der Islam*, 55 (1978), pp. 219–267, and 58 (1981), pp. 15–86, and also by Halm, *Islamische Gnosis*, pp. 240–274.

40. Al-Kashshī, *al-Rijāl*, pp. 244–245; see also al-Najāshī, *al-Rijāl*, pp. 81–82; Lewis, *Origins*, p. 39, and Omar, 'Some Aspects', p. 177.

41. L. Massignon, 'Explication du plan de Kūfa', in his *Opera Minora*, vol. 3, p. 50. Al-Saffāḥ had established his capital at al-Anbār in 134/752; he died and was buried in his palace there in 136/754. Al-Manṣūr moved his capital from al-Anbār to al-Ḥīra shortly after taking power, which lends further support

to the reports contending that Ismāʿīl's death occurred after 136/754; see Lassner, *Shaping*, pp. 155 and 158–159.

42. See the following works by L. Massignon: 'Bibliographie Qarmaṭe', pp. 329–330; 'Les Origines Shīʿites de la famille vizirale des Banū'l Furāt', in *Mélanges Gaudefroy-Demombynes* (Cairo, 1935–1945), p. 26; and 'Ḳarmaṭians', *EI*, vol. 2, p. 770, where Abu'l-Khaṭṭāb's death is wrongly placed in 167/783, later changed to 145–147/762–764 in *SEI*, p. 221; Corbin, *Étude*, pp. 15–16, and also his 'Une liturgie Shīʿite', pp. 83 and 85.
43. L. Massignon, *Salmān Pāk et les prémices spirituelles de l'Islam Iranien* (Tours, 1934), pp. 16–19; English translation, *Salmān Pāk and the Spiritual Beginnings of Iranian Islam*, tr. J. M. Unvala (Bombay, 1955), pp. 10–12.
44. Lewis, *Origins*, pp. 42ff. The *Asrār al-nuṭaqā'* of Jaʿfar b. Manṣūr al-Yaman, cited in Ivanow, *Rise*, text pp. 95–96, translation pp. 292–293, ed. Ghālib, pp. 256–257, reports that Ismāʿīl at one time, before Abu'l-Khaṭṭāb's denouncement by the Imām al-Ṣādiq, had attended a school directed by Abu'l-Khaṭṭāb. For a criticism of Massignon's hypothesis, see Ivanow, *Alleged*, pp. 165–169.
45. Ivanow, *Alleged*, pp. 138ff. See also al-Qāḍī, *al-Kaysāniyya*, pp. 289ff.
46. See several works by al-Nuʿmān: *Daʿā'im*, vol. 1, pp. 49–50; *Book of Faith*, pp. 58–59, and *Kitāb al-majālis wa'l-musāyarāt*, ed. al-Ḥabīb al-Faqī et al. (Tunis, 1978), pp. 84–85.
47. See W. Ivanow, 'Notes sur l'Ummu'l-Kitab des Ismaëliens de l'Asie Centrale', *REI*, 6 (1932), pp. 419–481; also his *Ismaili Literature*, pp. 193–195, and L. Massignon, 'Die Ursprünge und die Bedeutung des Gnostizismus im Islam', *EJ*, 5 (1937), pp. 55ff.
48. *Ummu'l-kitāb*, text p. 11; Italian translation, *Ummu'l-Kitāb, introduzione, traduzione e note*, tr. Pio Filippani-Ronconi (Naples, 1966), p. 23.
49. Ivanow, *Alleged*, pp. 99–100, and Corbin, *Étude*, p. 16.
50. Ivanow, 'Notes sur l'Ummu'l-Kitab', pp. 422–425; also by Ivanow, *Studies* 2, pp. 8 and 82, where it is stated that the original Arabic text of the treatise was probably composed in the second/eighth century; Corbin, *Étude*, pp. 12 and 14; also his *Histoire*, pp. 111–112, and Madelung's review of Filippani-Ronconi's translation in *Oriens*, 25–26 (1976), pp. 352–358.
51. H. Halm, *Kosmologie und Heilslehre der frühen Ismāʿīlīya* (Wiesbaden, 1978), pp. 142–168, an excellent study of early Ismāʿīlī thought, and also his *Islamische Gnosis*, pp. 113–198; see also E. F. Tijdens, 'Der mythologisch-gnostische Hintergrund des Umm al-Kitāb', *Acta Iranica*, 16 (1977), pp. 241–526, which was left unfinished by the death of its author.
52. Al-Qummī, *al-Maqālāt*, pp. 56–59; see also L. Massignon, 'Recherches sur les Shiʿite extrémistes à Bagdad', *ZDMG*, 92 (1938), pp. 378–382; Halm, *Kosmologie*, pp. 157ff., and also his *Islamische Gnosis*, pp. 218ff.
53. Al-Qummī, *al-Maqālāt*, pp. 59–60 and 63. See also al-Kashshī, *al-Rijāl*, pp. 305 and 398–401; Ibn Ḥazm, *al-Fiṣal*, vol. 4, p. 186; Friedlaender, 'Heterodoxies', pp. 65–66; also his 'Heterodoxies: Commentary', pp. 101–103; al-Shahrastānī, *al-Milal*, vol. 1, pp. 175–176; tr. Kazi, pp. 151–152; Massignon, *Salmān Pāk*, pp. 44–45; tr. Unvala, p. 32; R. Strothmann,

'Morgenländische Geheimsekten in abendländischer Forschung und die Handschrift Kiel arab. 19', *Abhandlungen der Deutschen Akademie der Wissenschaften zu Berlin, Klasse für Sprachen, Literatur und Kunst*, 5 (1952), pp. 41–42, text pp. 25–27; Halm, *Islamische Gnosis*, pp. 225ff., and B. Lewis, 'Bashshār al-Shaʿīrī', *EI2*, vol. 1, p. 1082.

54. On the Nuṣayrīs, also known as the ʿAlawīs, see al-Nawbakhtī, *Firaq*, p. 78; al-Qummī, *al-Maqālāt*, pp. 100–101; al-Ashʿarī, *Maqālāt*, p. 15; al-Baghdādī, *al-Farq*, pp. 239–242; tr. Halkin, pp. 70–74; Ibn Ḥazm, *al-Fiṣal*, vol. 4, p. 188; Friedlaender, 'Heterodoxies', pp. 71–72; also his 'Heterodoxies: Commentary', pp. 126–128, and al-Shahrastānī, *al-Milal*, vol. 1, pp. 188–189; tr. Kazi, pp. 161–162. Amongst the modern authorities, aside from the standard studies of R. Dussaud, *Histoire et religion des Noṣairīs* (Paris, 1900), with a full bibliography, and R. Basset, 'Nusairis', *ERE*, vol. 3, pp. 417–419, reference may be made to R. Strothmann, 'Seelenwanderung bei den Nuṣairī', *Oriens*, 12 (1959), pp. 89–114, and other relevant articles of this scholar listed in Halm, *Kosmologie*, p. 203. L. Massignon, who regarded both the Nuṣayrīs and the Ismāʿīlīs as the heirs of the Khaṭṭābīs, has also produced valuable work here; see especially his 'Bibliographie Nuṣayrie', pp. 913–922; 'Nuṣairī', *EI*, vol. 3, pp. 963–967, and 'Les Nusayrīs', in *L'Élaboration de l'Islam*, pp. 109–114. See also Halm, *Islamische Gnosis*, pp. 284–355, and W. Kadi, 'ʿAlawī', *EIR*, vol. 1, pp. 804–806.

55. See L. Massignon, *La Mubāhala de Médine et l'hyperdulie de Fatima* (Paris, 1955), pp. 19–26; also his *Salmān Pāk*, pp. 30–39; tr. Unvala, pp. 20–28; J. Horvitz, 'Salmān al-Fārisī', *Der Islam*, 12 (1922), pp. 178–183, and G. Levi Della Vida, 'Salmān al-Fārisī', EI, vol. 4, pp. 116–117.

56. According to P. Filippani-Ronconi the *Umm al-kitāb* was originally produced by a Gnostic-Manichaean sect with cabalistic and Mazdaean strains in some Aramaic-Mesopotamian milieu. Later in the second/eighth century, the members of this sect became subjected to Muslim persecutions and fled to Khurāsān and Central Asia where the treatise was now influenced by Buddhist ideas. Still later, the sectarians in question became Muslims, and more specifically extremist Shīʿīs of the Mughīrī-Khaṭṭābī tradition. Eventually, during the fifth–sixth/tenth–eleventh centuries, these Central Asian Shīʿīs were converted to Ismāʿīlism, without incorporating any Ismāʿīlī doctrines into the *Umm al-kitāb* which they continued to preserve; see Filippani-Ronconi's introductory section in his Italian translation of *Ummu'l-kitāb*, pp. xvii–lv, and his 'Note sulla soteriologica e sul simbolismo cosmico dell'Ummu'l-Kitāb', *AIUON*, NS, 14 (1964), pp. 111–134, and 'The Soteriological Cosmology of Central-Asiatic Ismāʿīlism', in *Ismāʿīlī Contributions to Islamic Culture*, ed. S. H. Nasr (Tehran, 1977), pp. 101–120.

57. Idrīs, *ʿUyūn*, vol. 4, pp. 351–356; also by Idrīs, *Zahr al-maʿānī*, in Ivanow, *Rise*, text pp. 53–58, translation pp. 240–248; English summary, based mainly on the *ʿUyūn*, in W. Ivanow, 'Ismailis and Qarmatians', *JBBRAS*, NS, 16 (1940), pp. 60–63.

58. In the *Asrār al-nuṭaqāʾ*, cited in Ivanow, *Rise*, text p. 99, translation p. 296, ed.

Ghālib, p. 259, it is furthermore mentioned that Muḥammad was fourteen years old when his father died. On this basis, it can be inferred, therefore, that Ismāʿīl b. Jaʿfar had predeceased his father by some twelve years, or around 136 A.H.

59. Cited in Qazvīnī's notes in Juwaynī, *Ta'rīkh*, vol. 3, pp. 148 and 310–312, and in Dānishpazhūh, 'Dhaylī' (1345/1966), p. 22.
60. Ivanow, 'Early Shiʿite Movements', p. 17; Ivanow, *Brief*, p. 9, and M. Kāmil Ḥusayn, *Ṭā'ifat al-Ismāʿīliyya* (Cairo, 1959), p. 12.
61. The *Dastūr al-munajjimīn*, cited in de Goeje, *Mémoire*, p. 203, mentions India as the farthest region reached by Muḥammad; but according to Ibn ʿInaba, *ʿUmdat al-ṭālib*, p. 233, he left Medina much later, in the company of the caliph Hārūn al-Rashīd, for Baghdād, where he eventually died. On the other hand, Idrīs, in his *ʿUyūn*, vol. 4, pp. 353–354, and his *Zahr al-maʿānī*, cited in Ivanow, *Rise*, text p. 54, translation p. 241, names several towns in Persia ultimately reached by Muḥammad; he also reports that the remains of Muḥammad were transferred from Persia to Cairo during the rule of the Fāṭimid caliph al-Muʿizz. See also Juwaynī, *Ta'rīkh*, vol. 3, p. 148; tr. Boyle, vol. 2, p. 645; Rashīd al-Dīn, *Ismāʿīliyān*, p. 11, and P. H. Mamour, *Polemics on the Origin of the Fatimi Caliphs* (London, 1934), pp. 66–68.
62. See Qazvīnī's comments in Juwaynī, *Ta'rīkh*, vol. 3, p. 311, and Ivanow, *Rise*, p. 67. Zāhid ʿAlī in his *Ta'rīkh*, vol. 1, pp. 43 and 65, places Muḥammad's death in 183/799, while both Tāmir, *al-Imāma*, p. 181, and M. Ghālib, *Ta'rīkh al-daʿwa al-Ismāʿīliyya* (2nd ed., Beirut, 1965), p. 46, mention the year 193/808–809.
63. Al-Kulaynī, *al-Uṣūl*, vol. 1, pp. 485–486; al-Kashshī, *al-Rijāl*, pp. 263–265, and Ibn Shahrāshūb, *Manāqib*, vol. 5, p. 77.
64. Ibn ʿInaba, *ʿUmdat al-ṭālib*, pp. 234ff.; Idrīs, *ʿUyūn*, vol. 4, p. 356; *Dastūr al-munajjimīn*, quoted in de Goeje, *Mémoire*, pp. 8–9 and 203, and Ivanow, *Rise*, pp. 38–39. Ismāʿīlī sources avoid mentioning Muḥammad's first two sons, with the main exception of Idrīs, *Zahr al-maʿānī*, cited in Ivanow, *Rise*, text pp. 53–54, translation p. 241.
65. Al-Nawbakhtī, *Firaq*, p. 61, and al-Qummī, *al-Maqālāt*, p. 83. Just prior to their discussion of the Qarāmiṭa, these authors also refer to a Khaṭṭābī subgroup recognizing a line of imāms descended from Muḥammad b. Ismāʿīl. See also Lewis, *Origins*, pp. 40–41 and 78, and Ivanow, 'Ismailis and Qarmatians', pp. 79ff.
66. See Ivanow, *Studies* 2, p. 24, and W. Madelung, 'Ḳā'im Āl Muḥammad', *EI2*, vol. 4, pp. 456–457.
67. Al-Nawbakhtī, *Firaq*, pp. 61–64; al-Qummī, *al-Maqālāt*, pp. 83–86; English translation in Stern, *Studies*, pp. 47–53, with a note therein by W. Madelung. See also Stern, 'Ismāʿīlīs', pp. 102–103 and 108, and Madelung, 'Imamat', pp. 48ff.
68. R. Strothmann, 'Sabʿīya', *EI*, vol. 4, pp. 23–25.
69. Al-Hamdānī, *Genealogy*, text pp. 10–11, translation p. 13.
70. *Kitāb al-rushd*, pp. 198ff.; tr. Ivanow in *Studies* 2, pp. 43ff.
71. Jaʿfar b. Manṣūr al-Yaman, *Kitāb al-kashf*, ed. R. Strothmann (London, etc.,

1952), pp. 62, 77, 103–104, 109–110, 135, 160, 170 and elsewhere. This important early Ismāʿīlī text, compiled probably during the reign of the second Fāṭimid caliph-imām, al-Qā'im, has been edited also by M. Ghālib (Beirut, 1984), but our references are to Strothmann's edition. See also Jaʿfar b. Manṣūr al-Yaman, *Asrār al-nuṭaqā'*, ed. Ghālib, pp. 21, 39, 109 and 112.

72. *Ummu'l-kitāb*, text pp. 91–92; tr. Filippani-Ronconi, pp. 229–230; this is the only clear Ismāʿīlī idea found in the treatise. For similar ideas held by the Mukhammisa, see al-Qummī, *al-Maqālāt*, pp. 56 and 59.
73. Stern, 'Ismāʿīlīs', p. 101; see also Madelung, *Religious Trends*, p. 93.
74. Al-Nawbakhtī, *Firaq*, p. 64, and al-Qummī, *al-Maqālāt*, p. 86.
75. See Massignon, 'Bibliographie Qarmaṭe', p. 334, and Qazvīnī's comments in Juwaynī, *Ta'rīkh*, vol. 3, p. 327. According to al-Muṭahhar b. Ṭāhir al-Muqaddasī (al-Maqdisī), *al-Bad' wa'l-ta'rīkh*, ed. Cl. Huart (Paris, 1899–1919), vol. 1, p. 137, the title of Ibn Rizām's book was *al-Naqḍ ʿalā'l-Bāṭiniyya*; but in al-Maqrīzī, *Ittiʿāẓ*, ed. Bunz, p. 12, ed. al-Shayyāl, vol. 1, p. 23, the book is mentioned as the *Kitāb radd ʿalā'l-Ismāʿīliyya*. See also C. H. Becker, *Beiträge zur Geschichte Ägyptens unter dem Islam* (Strassburg, 1902–1903), vol. 1, p. 6; I. Goldziher, *Streitschrift des Ġazālī gegen die Bāṭinijja-Sekte* (Leiden, 1916), p. 15; Ivanow, *Alleged*, p. 2, and Ṭāhā al-Walī, *al-Qarāmiṭa* (Beirut, 1981), pp. 235–239.
76. Al-Ṭabarī, *Ta'rīkh*, III, pp. 2124ff.; English translation, *The History of al-Ṭabarī*: Volume 37, *The ʿAbbāsid Recovery*, tr. Philip M. Fields (Albany, N.Y., 1987), pp. 169ff.
77. Idrīs, *ʿUyūn*, vol. 4, pp. 357–367 and 390–404; English summary in Ivanow, 'Ismailis and Qarmatians', pp. 63ff., and in Ivanow, *Rise*, pp. 33ff. Another succinct Ismāʿīlī account of the ancestors of ʿUbayd Allāh is found in the first volume of the *Kitāb al-azhār* of Ḥasan b. Nūḥ al-Bharūchī, in *Muntakhabāt Ismāʿīliyya*, ed. ʿĀ. al-ʿAwwā (Damascus, 1958), pp. 232–236, English summary in Ivanow, *Rise*, pp. 29ff.
78. The earliest Ismāʿīlī source relating these details is apparently the *Istitār al-imām* written by Aḥmad b. Ibrāhīm (or Muḥammad) al-Nīsābūrī, who flourished towards the end of the fourth/tenth century; this work has been edited, together with another Ismāʿīlī text, by Ivanow in *Bulletin of the Faculty of Arts, University of Egypt*, 4 (1936), pp. 93–107; English translation in Ivanow, *Rise*, translation pp. 157–183. The Arabic text of the *Istitār* is reproduced in *Akhbār al-Qarāmiṭa*, ed. S. Zakkār (2nd ed., Damascus, 1982), pp. 111–132, not referred to hereafter.
79. Zāhid ʿAlī, *Ta'rīkh*, vol. 1, p. 43; Ḥusayn, *Ṭā'ifat*, p. 17; Tāmir, *al-Imāma*, p. 182, and Ghālib, *Aʿlām*, pp. 342–344.
80. Ivanow, *Rise*, pp. 41 and 57; Zāhid ʿAlī, *Ta'rīkh*, vol. 1, p. 43; Ḥusayn, *Ṭā'ifat*, p. 18; Tāmir, *al-Imāma*, p. 183. On ʿUbayd Allāh, see Ibn Khallikān, *Biographical Dictionary*, tr. William MacGuckin de Slane (Paris, 1842–1871), vol. 2, pp. 77–79; Ḥ. I. Ḥasan and Ṭ. A. Sharaf, *ʿUbayd Allāh al-Mahdī* (Cairo, 1947); Ghālib, *Aʿlām*, pp. 348–358; J. Walker, 'al-Mahdī ʿUbaid Allāh', *EI*, vol. 3, pp. 119–121, and F. Dachraoui, 'al-Mahdī ʿUbayd Allāh', *EI2*, vol. 5, pp. 1242–1244.

81. In ʿUbayd Allāh's letter cited in al-Hamdānī, *Genealogy*, text pp. 10–11, translation p. 13, he is named as an imām, while ʿUbayd Allāh's father al-Ḥusayn b. Aḥmad is not included among the 'hidden imāms'; his imāmate is also implied in Jaʿfar b. Manṣūr al-Yaman, *Kitāb al-kashf*, pp. 98–99. See Ivanow, *Rise*, pp. 42–43 and 59; and Madelung, 'Imamat', pp. 55 and 71ff., where it is suggested that ʿUbayd Allāh's father may have been elevated to the imāmate retrospectively, and H. Halm, 'Aḥmad b. ʿAbdallāh', *EIR*, vol. 1, pp. 638–639.
82. Al-Nīsābūrī, *Istitār*, pp. 95–96; tr. Ivanow in *Rise*, translation pp. 37 and 162–163, and al-Mālījī, *al-Majālis al-Mustanṣiriyya*, p. 143.
83. Ivanow, *Rise*, p. 28.
84. See Mamour, *Polemics*, especially pp. 60–64, 124–155 and 189–219; Zāhid ʿAlī, *Taʾrīkh*, vol. 1, pp. 74–75; Sami N. Makarem, 'The Hidden Imāms of the Ismāʿīlīs', *al-Abhath*, 22 (1969), pp. 23–37, and Nagel, *Frühe Ismailiya*, pp. 56–72, examining also the main recent contributions.
85. Al-Hamdānī, *Genealogy*, text pp. 11–12, translation p. 14. See also al-Qummī, *al-Maqālāt*, p. 88, which somehow seems to support this claim; Madelung, 'Imamat', pp. 69–70; Madelung, 'Bemerkungen', pp. 38–39, and Hamdani and de Blois, 'A Re-Examination', pp. 179–183 and 200–201, arguing that the imāms listed by ʿUbayd Allāh al-Mahdī in fact belong to two parallel lines of descendants of Jaʿfar al-Ṣādiq, representing the progenies of ʿAbd Allāh and his brother Ismāʿīl b. Jaʿfar. The authors of this interesting article further argue that the official Fāṭimid genealogy was later derived by combining the two lines and rearranging the genealogy claimed by al-Mahdī.
86. Ibn al-Nadīm, *Kitāb al-Fihrist*, ed. G. Flügel (Leipzig, 1871–1872), vol. 1, pp. 186–187; English translation, *The Fihrist of al-Nadīm*, ed. and tr. B. Dodge (New York, 1970), vol. 1, pp. 462–467; Persian translation, based on additional manuscripts, *Kitāb al-Fihrist*, M. R. Tajaddud (2nd ed., Tehran, 1346/1967), pp. 348–351. The late M. R. Tajaddud also prepared an Arabic edition of *al-Fihrist* (Tehran, 1971) which will not be referred to.
87. See al-Maqrīzī, *Ittiʿāẓ*, ed. Bunz, pp. 11–12, ed. al-Shayyāl, vol. 1, p. 22; Becker, *Beiträge*, vol. 1, pp. 4ff.; Massignon, 'Bibliographie Qarmaṭe', p. 334; Mamour, *Polemics*, pp. 35–36 and 159ff.; Qazvīnī's notes in Juwaynī, *Taʾrīkh*, vol. 3, pp. 328–329; Lewis, *Origins*, pp. 6–8; Madelung, 'Fatimiden', pp. 68ff.; Madelung, 'Imamat', pp. 58–59, and Stern, *Studies*, pp. 61–62.
88. Aḥmad b. ʿAbd al-Wahhāb al-Nuwayrī, *Nihāyat al-arab*, ed. M. Jābir ʿAbd al-ʿĀl al-Ḥīnī et al. (Cairo, 1984), vol. 25, pp. 187–317; partially translated into French in de Sacy, *Exposé*, vol. 1, introduction pp. 74–171, 184–238 and 438ff.
89. Ibn al-Dawādārī, *Kanz al-durar*, ed. Ṣ. al-Munajjid (Cairo, 1961), vol. 6, pp. 6ff., 17–21 and 44–156.
90. Al-Maqrīzī utilized the historical part of Akhū Muḥsin's work in his history of the Fāṭimids, *Ittiʿāẓ al-ḥunafāʾ*, ed. Bunz, pp. 11–14 and 101–143, ed. al-Shayyāl, vol. 1, pp. 22–29 and 151–201 (reproduced in *Akhbār al-Qarāmiṭa*,

pp. 325–383), and in his unfinished history of Egypt, *al-Muqaffā*, partially reproduced in *Akhbār al-Qarāmiṭa*, pp. 391ff.; French translation of a relevant section from *al-Muqaffā* is contained in É. Quatremère, 'Mémoires historiques sur la dynastie des khalifes Fatimites', pp. 117–123, and in E. Fagnan, 'Nouveaux textes historiques relatifs à l'Afrique du Nord et à la Sicile: I, Traduction de la biographie d'Obeyd Allāh', in *Centenario della nascita di Michele Amari* (Palermo, 1910), vol. 2, pp. 35–86. The doctrinal part of Akhū Muḥsin's book is given in al-Maqrīzī's *Kitāb al-mawāʿiẓ wa'l-iʿtibār bi-dhikr al-khiṭaṭ wa'l-āthār* (Būlāq, 1270/1853), vol. 1, pp. 391–397; French translation, *Description historique et topographique de l'Égypte*, tr. U. Bouriant and P. Casanova, in Mémoires publiés par les membres de l'Institut Français d'Archéologie Orientale du Caire (Cairo, 1895–1920), vol. 4, pp. 122–144, reproduced in P. Casanova, 'La Doctrine secrète des Fatimides d'Égypte', *BIFAO*, 18 (1921), pp. 130–165.

91. Al-Masʿūdī, *Kitāb al-tanbīh wa'l-ishrāf*, ed. M. J. de Goeje (Leiden, 1894), p. 396; French translation, *Le Livre de l'avertissement et de la revision*, tr. B. Carra de Vaux (Paris, 1896), p. 502; this work was completed in 345/956.
92. It is used in the chapter on the Bāṭiniyya in al-Baghdādī, *al-Farq*, pp. 266ff.; tr. Halkin, pp. 108ff.; it also provided one of the sources of Ismāʿīl b. Aḥmad al-Bustī, a Muʿtazilī author who around 400/1009 produced an anti-Ismāʿīlī book entitled *Min kashf asrār al-Bāṭiniyya*, see S. M. Stern, 'Abu'l-Qasim al-Bustī and his Refutation of Ismāʿīlism', *JRAS* (1961), pp. 14–35. Ibn al-Jawzī (d. 597/1200), a historian and one of the most famous Ḥanbalī jurists of Baghdād, utilized the Ibn Rizām-Akhū Muḥsin account in his treatise on the Qarmaṭīs, included in his major historical work *al-Muntaẓam*. This small treatise, *al-Qarāmiṭa* included in *Akhbār al-Qarāmiṭa*, pp. 253–268, is also edited and translated in J. de Somogyi, 'A Treatise on the Qarmaṭians', *RSO*, 13 (1932), pp. 248–265. Many important later sources, such as Juwaynī, *Ta'rīkh*, vol. 3, pp. 152ff.; tr. Boyle, vol. 2, pp. 647ff., and Rashīd al-Dīn, *Ismāʿīliyān*, pp. 11ff., have drawn on the same account; for more references, see Lewis, *Origins*, pp. 58–60.
93. The text, and the list of the signatories of the manifesto with slight variations, may be found in Ibn al-Jawzī, *al-Muntaẓam*, ed. F. Krenkow (Hyderabad, 1357–1362/1938–1943), vol. 7, p. 255; Juwaynī, *Ta'rīkh*, vol. 3, pp. 174–177; tr. Boyle, vol. 2, pp. 658–660; Ibn Khaldūn, *The Muqaddimah*, tr. F. Rosenthal (2nd ed., Princeton, 1967), vol. 1, pp. 45–46; al-Maqrīzī, *Ittiʿāẓ*, ed. Bunz, pp. 22–23, ed. al-Shayyāl, vol. 1, pp. 43–44, and Ibn Taghrībirdī, *al-Nujūm al-zāhira fī mulūk Miṣr wa'l-Qāhira* (Cairo, 1348–1391/1929–1972), vol. 4, pp. 229–231; see also Mamour, *Polemics*, pp. 16–29; Lewis, *Origins*, pp. 8 and 60–61, and al-Walī, *al-Qarāmiṭa*, pp. 361ff.
94. See Mamour, *Polemics*, pp. 30–42; Ivanow, *Alleged*, pp. 83–103, and A. Abel, 'Dayṣāniyya', *EI2*, vol. 2, p. 199.
95. This was a flourishing mediaeval town in Khūzistān founded at the beginning of the second/eighth century, and today its ruins to the south of Shūshtar are known as Band-i Qīr; see the anonymous *Ḥudūd al-ʿālam, the Regions of the World*, tr. V. Minorsky (2nd ed., London, 1970), pp. 75 and 130, an important geographical work of the second half of the fourth/tenth

century; Yāqūt al-Ḥamawī, *Muʿjam al-buldān*, ed. F. Wüstenfeld (Leipzig, 1866–1973), vol. 3, p. 676; partial French translation, *Dictionnaire géographique, historique et littéraire de la Perse*, tr. C. Barbier de Meynard (Paris, 1861), pp. 402–403; G. Le Strange, *The Lands of the Eastern Caliphate* (2nd ed., Cambridge, 1930), pp. 233, 236–237, 242 and 246–247, and M. Streck and L. Lockhart, 'ʿAskar Mukram', *EI2*, vol. 1, p. 711.

96. This is the title reported by al-Nuwayrī, *Nihāyat al-arab*, vol. 25, p. 220; tr. de Sacy, *Exposé*, vol. 1, introduction p. 148. The same book has been referred to under other titles, such as *Kitāb al-balāgh al-akbar*, mentioned by the Zaydī author Muḥammad b. al-Ḥasan al-Daylamī in his *Bayān madhhab al-Bāṭiniyya*, ed. R. Strothmann (Istanbul, 1939), pp. 15, 30, 42, 59, 72–73, 75–76, 78–81, 84, 86 and 91–94, an anti-Ismāʿīlī treatise forming part of a larger work completed in 707/1308, while al-Baghdādī, *al-Farq*, p. 278, knows the book as the *Kitāb al-siyāsa wa'l-balāgh*. S. M. Stern in a chapter entitled 'The Book of the Highest Initiation and other anti-Ismāʿīlī Travesties' included in his *Studies*, pp. 56–83, has partially reconstructed the Arabic text of the treatise in question with an English translation, from quotations preserved by different authors including al-Nuwayrī, al-Baghdādī and al-Daylamī.

97. Ibn al-Nadīm, *al-Fihrist*, vol. 1, p. 189; tr. Dodge, vol. 1, p. 471; tr. Tajaddud, p. 353.

98. See Ivanow, *Guide*, pp. 41 and 78; also his *Ismaili Literature*, pp. 38, 44 and 97, and Poonawala, *Bio*, pp. 44 and 56.

99. Becker, *Beiträge*, vol. 1, p. 7; Massignon, 'Bibliographie Qarmaṭe', pp. 332 and 336; Ivanow, *Studies* 2, p. 125; Madelung, 'Fatimiden', pp. 69–73; also his 'Imamat', 112–114, and Stern, *Studies*, pp. 61 and 64.

100. As preserved, for example, by al-Nuwayrī, *Nihāyat al-arab*, vol. 25, p. 216; tr. de Sacy, *Exposé*, vol. 1, introduction pp. 137–138.

101. Massignon, 'Bibliographie Qarmaṭe', pp. 330–331; also his 'Ḳarmaṭians', p. 768; Qazvīnī's notes in Juwaynī, *Ta'rīkh*, vol. 3, pp. 312–343, and Lewis, *Origins*, pp. 62–65.

102. Ivanow, *Rise*, pp. 127ff. and 140–156, and also, *Alleged*, especially pp. 28–82.

103. Ivanow, 'Ismailis and Qarmatians', p. 70, and also, *Alleged*, p. 2.

104. Al-Kashshī, *al-Rijāl*, pp. 245–246 and 389; al-Najāshī, *al-Rijāl*, p. 148; al-Ṭūsī, *Fihrist*, pp. 197–198; al-Ṭūsī, *Rijāl*, pp. 135 and 225; Ibn Shahrāshūb, *Maʿālim*, p. 65, and his *Manāqib*, vol. 5, p. 19. See also S. M. Stern, 'ʿAbd Allāh b. Maymūn', *EI2*, vol. 1, p. 48; H. Halm, 'ʿAbdallāh b. Maymūn al-Qaddāḥ', *EIR*, vol. 1, pp. 182–183, and B. Lewis, 'Dindān', *EI2*, vol. 2, p. 301.

105. Al-Hamdānī, *Genealogy*, text pp. 9–10, translation p. 12.

106. Ivanow had already made this inference in his *Alleged*, pp. 110–112, before this letter had come to light; see also Mamour, *Polemics*, pp. 68ff.

107. Cited in Ibn ʿInaba, *ʿUmdat al-ṭālib*, p. 233; see also Ivanow, *Alleged*, p. 106.

108. This epistle has been preserved in Idrīs, *ʿUyūn*, vol. 5, pp. 160–162; it is published and translated in Ivanow, 'Ismailis and Qarmatians', pp. 74–76, and also in Stern, 'Heterodox Ismāʿīlism at the Time of al-Muʿizz', pp. 11–13 and 26–27, hereafter cited as 'Heterodox'.

109. Al-Nuʿmān, *al-Majālis*, pp. 405–411 and 523–525. The text and English

translation of the relevant passages are also to be found in Stern, 'Heterodox', pp. 14–17 and 28–33.

110. See Lewis, *Origins*, pp. 47–50, 53–54 and 65–67; W. Ivanow, *Ibn al-Qaddah* (2nd ed., Bombay, 1957), pp. 135–141; Madelung, 'Imamat', pp. 73ff., and Ghālib, *Aʿlām*, pp. 345–347 and 559–561.
111. See Stern, 'Heterodox', pp. 18–22.
112. For more details on the work of this Zaydī author and its refutation by al-Kirmānī, entitled *al-Kāfiya fi'l-radd ʿalā'l-Hārūnī al-Ḥasanī*, included in al-Kirmānī, *Majmūʿat rasā'il*, ed. M. Ghālib (Beirut, 1983), pp. 148–182, see Ivanow, *Rise*, pp. 142–143, and also by Ivanow, *Ismaili Literature*, p. 44.
113. See, for example, de Sacy, *Exposé*, vol. 1, pp. 83ff.
114. Quoted in Ibn al-Nadīm, *al-Fihrist*, vol. 1, p. 187; tr. Dodge, vol. 1, p. 465; tr. Tajaddud, p. 350.
115. The relevant passage, quoted from a faulty manuscript, appears in Lewis, *Origins*, pp. 51–52 and (Arabic text) p. 109; a more complete excerpt of the same passage may be found in Ivanow, *Rise*, text pp. 35–39.
116. Ibrāhīm b. al-Ḥusayn al-Ḥāmidī, *Kitāb kanz al-walad*, ed. M. Ghālib (Wiesbaden, 1971), pp. 208 and 211.
117. Idrīs, *ʿUyūn*, vol. 4, p. 335, and also by Idrīs, *Zahr al-maʿānī*, in Ivanow, *Rise*, text pp. 47, 49, 59–60 and 64, translation pp. 233, 236, 248, 250 and 256.
118. Idrīs, *Zahr al-maʿānī*, in Ivanow, *Rise*, text pp. 66ff., translation pp. 258ff., and Madelung, 'Imamat', pp. 77–78; however, see also Idrīs, *ʿUyūn*, vol. 5, p. 89, and Hamdani and de Blois, 'A Re-Examination', p. 190.
119. Qazvīnī's notes in Juwaynī, *Ta'rīkh*, vol. 3, pp. 335ff.; Stern, 'Heterodox', pp. 20–21, and also his 'ʿAbd Allāh b. Maymūn', p. 48.
120. Lewis, *Origins*, pp. 44ff. and 71–73.
121. Ḥasan and Sharaf, *ʿUbayd Allāh al-Mahdī*, pp. 25ff., 37ff., 47–92 and 143–169, and Zāhid ʿAlī, *Ta'rīkh*, vol. 1, pp. 73–88. See also Fyzee, 'Ismāʿīlīs', in *Religion in the Middle East*, vol. 2, pp. 319 and 329.
122. See Ivanow, *Rise*, pp. 54ff., 129 and 151–152, and also his *Alleged*, pp. 169–174.
123. As preserved by al-Nuwayrī, *Nihāyat al-arab*, vol. 25, p. 191; tr. de Sacy, *Exposé*, vol. 1, introduction p. 171; Ibn al-Dawādārī, *Kanz*, vol. 6, p. 46, and al-Maqrīzī, *Ittiʿāẓ*, ed. Bunz, p. 102, ed. al-Shayyāl, vol. 1, p. 153. It may be added that al-Masʿūdī mentions the year 260/873–874 in his *Kitāb al-tanbīh*, p. 395, tr. Carra de Vaux, p. 501.
124. The Ibn Rizām-Akhū Muḥsin account of the *daʿwa* in southern ʿIrāq, aside from the already-noted direct quotation in Ibn al-Nadīm, may be found in al-Nuwayrī, *Nihāyat al-arab*, vol. 25, pp. 189ff.; tr. de Sacy, *Exposé*, vol. 1, introduction pp. 166ff.; and in Ibn al-Dawādārī, *Kanz*, vol. 6, pp. 44ff., and al-Maqrīzī, *Ittiʿāẓ*, ed. Bunz, pp. 101ff., ed. al-Shayyāl, vol. 1, pp. 151ff. Al-Ṭabarī's account is to be found in his *Ta'rīkh*, III, pp. 2124ff.; tr. Fields, pp. 169ff. Relevant extracts from Thābit b. Sinān's history and Ibn al-ʿAdīm's *Bughyat al-ṭalab* are contained in *Akhbār al-Qarāmiṭa*, pp. 3ff. and 273ff. See also de Goeje, *Mémoire*, pp. 16ff. and 199–203; Madelung, 'Fatimiden', pp. 37ff., and also his 'Ḥamdān Ḳarmaṭ', *EI2*, vol. 3, pp. 123–124; a general

treatment of the Qarmaṭī movement in ʿIrāq is contained in M. ʿA. ʿAlyān, *Qarāmiṭat al-ʿIrāq* (Cairo, 1970).

125. Al-Ṭabarī, *Ta'rīkh*, III, pp. 2129–2130; tr. Fields, p. 175; de Goeje, *Mémoire*, p. 26, and A. Popovic, *La révolte des esclaves en Iraq au IIIᵉ/IXᵉ siècle* (Paris, 1976), pp. 122, 167 and 179–180.

126. See al-Kashshī, *al-Rijāl*, pp. 537–544; al-Najāshī, *al-Rijāl*, pp. 216–217; al-Ṭūsī, *Fihrist*, pp. 254–255, and Ibn Shahrāshūb, *Maʿālim*, pp. 80–81.

127. Ibn al-Nadīm, *al-Fihrist*, vol. 1, pp. 187, 188 and 189; tr. Dodge, vol. 1, pp. 464, 468, 470 and 472; tr. Tajaddud, pp. 349, 352, 353 and 354; al-Nuwayrī, *Nihāyat al-arab*, vol. 25, pp. 191ff; tr. de Sacy, *Exposé*, vol. 1, introduction pp. 184ff.; Ibn al-Dawādārī, *Kanz*, vol. 6, pp. 46–47 and 79; al-Maqrīzī, *Ittiʿāẓ*, ed. Bunz, pp. 103–104 and 130, ed. al-Shayyāl, vol. 1, pp. 155 and 185, and al-Maqrīzī, *al-Muqaffā*, cited in *Akhbār al-Qarāmiṭa*, pp. 395 and 398. See also Ivanow, *Ismaili Literature*, p. 17; Poonawala, *Bio*, pp. 31–33; S. M. Stern, ''ʿAbdān', *EI2*, vol. 1, pp. 95–96, and W. Madelung, ''ʿAbdān b. al-Rabīṭ', *EIR*, vol. 1, pp. 207–208.

128. Al-Ṭabarī, *Ta'rīkh*, III, pp. 2126–2127; tr. Fields, pp. 171–173.

129. See de Goeje, *Mémoire*, pp. 33–34; B. Carra de Vaux and M. G. S. Hodgson, 'al-Djannābī, Abū Saʿīd', *EI2*, vol. 2, p. 452, and W. Madelung, 'Abū Saʿīd Jannābī', *EIR*, vol. 1, pp. 380–381.

130. Al-Daylamī, *Bayān*, p. 21.

131. Al-Nuʿmān, *Iftitāḥ*, pp. 32–47; partial French translation, Quatremère, 'Mémoires historiques sur la dynastie des khalifes Fatimites', pp. 123–131; see also Idrīs, *ʿUyūn*, vol. 4, pp. 396ff.; Zāhid ʿAlī, *Ta'rīkh*, vol. 1, pp. 68–71; Ḥ. F. al-Hamdānī, *al-Ṣulayḥiyyūn wa'l-ḥaraka al-Fāṭimiyya fi'l-Yaman* (Cairo, 1955), pp. 27ff.; Friedlaender, 'Heterodoxies: Commentary', pp. 109–110; Arendonk, *Les débuts*, pp. 119–126 and 237–249; Ghālib, *Aʿlām*, pp. 233–241 and 386–391; H. Halm, 'Die Sīrat Ibn Ḥaušab: Die ismailitische daʿwa im Jemen und die Fatimiden', *Die Welt des Orients*, 12 (1981), pp. 107–135, and W. Madelung, 'Manṣūr al-Yaman', *EI2*, vol. 6, pp. 438–439. The establishment of the *daʿwa* in Yaman is also discussed in some detail by the Shāfiʿī jurist Bahā' al-Dīn al-Janadī (d. 732/1332) in his *Kitāb al-sulūk*; its relevant section on the Qarāmiṭa of Yaman, *Akhbār al-Qarāmiṭa bi'l-Yaman*, is to be found in Henry C. Kay, ed., *Yaman, its Early Mediaeval History* (London, 1892), text pp. 139–152, translation pp. 191–212. Al-Janadī quotes solely from Muḥammad b. Mālik al-Yamānī, a Yamanī Sunnī jurist who became an Ismāʿīlī in the latter part of the fifth/eleventh century, but who later abjured and wrote an anti-Ismāʿīlī treatise, *Kashf asrār al-Bāṭiniyya wa akhbār al-Qarāmiṭa*, ed. M. Z. al-Kawtharī (Cairo, 1939), reproduced in *Akhbār al-Qarāmiṭa*, pp. 201–251; this work apparently served as the primary source on early Ismāʿīlism in Yaman for all subsequent Sunnī historians of Yaman. See also al-Walī, *al-Qarāmiṭa*, pp. 250–257.

132. Al-Nuʿmān, *Iftitāḥ*, pp. 45 and 47; Lewis, 'Ismāʿīlī Notes', pp. 599–600; S. M. Stern, 'Ismāʿīlī Propaganda and Fatimid Rule in Sind', *IC*, 23 (1949), pp. 298ff.; A. Hamdani, *The Beginnings of the Ismāʿīlī Daʿwa in Northern India* (Cairo, 1956), and also his 'The Daʿi Jalam b. Shayban and the Ismaili State of

Multan', in *The Great Ismaili Heroes*, ed. A. R. Kanji (Karachi, 1973), pp. 14–15.

133. The standard work on the Qarmaṭīs of Baḥrayn remains de Goeje's *Mémoire*, especially pp. 33–47 and 69ff., covering the earliest phase of the *daʿwa* there; de Sacy also has a valuable discussion, based on various sources including Akhū Muḥsin, in his *Exposé*, vol. 1, introduction pp. 211ff.; the relevant portion of the Ibn Rizām-Akhū Muḥsin account may be found in Ibn al-Dawādārī, *Kanz*, vol. 6, pp. 55–62 and 91ff.; al-Nuwayrī, *Nihāyat al-arab*, vol. 25, pp. 233ff., and al-Maqrīzī, *Ittiʿāẓ*, ed. Bunz, pp. 107ff., ed. al-Shayyāl, vol. 1, pp. 159ff. Relevant extracts from Thābit b. Sinān's *Ta'rīkh* and al-Maqrīzī's *al-Muqaffā* are included in *Akhbār al-Qarāmiṭa*, pp. 12–16, 35ff. and 400ff. See also Lewis, *Origins*, pp. 76ff., and Madelung, 'Fatimiden', pp. 34ff., which is the best modern survey of the sources and of the later history of the Qarmaṭīs of Baḥrayn.

134. Al-Ṭabarī, *Ta'rīkh*, III, pp. 2188ff., 2196–2197, 2205, 2232 and 2291; English translation, *The History of al-Ṭabarī*: Volume 38, *The Return of the Caliphate to Baghdad*, tr. F. Rosenthal (Albany, N.Y., 1985), pp. 77ff., 86–89, 98, 128–129 and 202, and al-Masʿūdī, *Murūj*, vol. 8, pp. 191ff.

135. Ibn Ḥawqal, *Kitāb ṣūrat al-arḍ*, ed. J. H. Kramers (2nd ed., Leiden, 1938–1939), pp. 25–27; Nāṣir-i Khusraw, *Safar-nāma*, ed. and tr. Schefer, text pp. 81–84, translation pp. 225–230, ed. M. Dabīr Siyāqī (5th ed., Tehran, 1356/1977), pp. 147–151. See also de Goeje, *Mémoire*, pp. 150ff., and Lewis, *Origins*, pp. 98–99.

136. Niẓām al-Mulk, *Siyar al-mulūk (Siyāsat-nāma)*, ed. H. Darke (2nd ed., Tehran, 1347/1968), pp. 282–295 and 297–305; English translation, *The Book of Government or Rules for Kings*, tr. H. Darke (2nd ed., London, 1978), pp. 208–218 and 220–226. Darke's edition supersedes Schefer's pioneering edition and French translation of this work, *Siasset Namèh, traité de gouvernement* (Paris, 1891–1893), vol. 1, pp. 183–193 and 194–195, and vol. 2, pp. 268–281 and 283–284, and also the later Persian editions by ʿA. R. Khalkhālī (Tehran, 1310/1931), pp. 157ff., ʿA. Iqbāl (Tehran, 1320/1941), pp. 260ff., and by M. Mudarrisī Chahārdihī (Tehran, 1334/1955), pp. 215ff. It may be noted that Darke's second edition, adopted as our reference, is based on the oldest known, and hitherto most complete, manuscript of the text dated 673/1274 and preserved at the National Library of Tabrīz; this manuscript has been utilized also in the edition of J. Shuʿār (Tehran, 1348/1969), pp. 322–338 and 340–351. Besides a Russian translation by B. N. Zakhoder (Moscow, 1949), there is also a German translation of this work, *Siyāsatnāma: Gedanken und Geschichten*, tr. K. E. Schabinger (Munich, 1960), pp. 306–316 and 317–319, based on Schefer's incomplete text. Niẓām al-Mulk is used as the main authority in Stern's articles on the subject, 'The Early Ismāʿīlī Missionaries in North-West Persia and in Khurāsān and Transoxania', hereafter cited as 'Early', and 'The First appearance of Ismāʿīlism in Iran', text of a lecture delivered at Tehran University, translated into Persian by S. H. Nasr and published in *Revue de la Faculté des Lettres, Université de Téhran*, 9 (1340/1961), pp. 1–13; published also separately, with the English text (Tehran, 1961).

137. Ibn al-Nadīm, *al-Fihrist*, vol. 1, p. 188; tr. Dodge, vol. 1, pp. 467–468; tr. Tajaddud, pp. 351–352; al-Baghdādī, *al-Farq*, p. 267; tr. Halkin, pp. 112–113; al-Daylamī, *Bayān*, pp. 20–21; Ibn al-Dawādārī, *Kanz*, vol. 6, pp. 95–96; al-Maqrīzī, *Itti'āẓ*, ed. Bunz, pp. 130–131, ed. al-Shayyāl, vol. 1, p. 186. Excerpts from some of these sources are to be found in Stern, 'Early', pp. 82–90.
138. Poonawala, *Bio*, p. 33, and L. Massignon, *La Passion d'al-Hosayn Ibn Mansour al-Hallaj, martyr mystique de l'Islam* (Paris, 1922), vol. 1, pp. 77–80, where some parallels are drawn between Ghiyāth and Manṣūr al-Ḥallāj, the famous mystic who was suspected of Ismā'īlī affiliations and was executed in 309/922; this discussion does not appear in the second revised edition of this important work by Massignon, published posthumously in 1975, and subsequently translated into English (Princeton, 1982).
139. On Abū Ḥātim and his works, see al-Hamdānī, 'Some Unknown Ismā'īlī Authors', pp. 365–369; al-Hamdānī's introductory comments in his incomplete edition of Abū Ḥātim's *Kitāb al-zīna* (Cairo, 1957–1958), vol. 1, pp. 14ff.; Ivanow, *Ismaili Literature*, pp. 24–26; Sezgin, *Geschichte*, vol. 1, p. 573; Poonawala, *Bio*, pp. 36–39; Ghālib, *A'lām*, pp. 97–98; S. M. Stern, 'Abū Ḥātim al-Rāzī', *EI2*, vol. 1, p. 125, and H. Halm, 'Abū Ḥātem Rāzī', *EIR*, vol. 1, p. 315.
140. See al-Mas'ūdī, *Murūj*, vol. 9, pp. 6–19; Ḥamza al-Iṣfahānī, *Ta'rīkh sinī mulūk al-arḍ*, ed. J. Īrānī Tabrīzī (Berlin, 1340/1921), pp. 152–153; al-Baghdādī, *al-Farq*, p. 267; tr. Halkin, pp. 112–113; Ibn Isfandiyār, *Ta'rīkh-i Ṭabaristān*, ed. 'A. Iqbāl (Tehran, 1320/1941), vol. 1, pp. 285–295; abridged English translation, *History of Ṭabaristān*, tr. E. G. Browne (Leiden–London, 1905), pp. 209–217; Ẓahīr al-Dīn Mar'ashī, *Ta'rīkh-i Ṭabaristān va Rūyān va Māzandarān*, ed. M. Ḥ. Tasbīḥī (Tehran, 1345/1966), pp. 68–72; H. L. Rabino, 'Les Dynasties Alaouides du Mazandéran', *JA*, 210 (1927), pp. 256–258; George C. Miles, *The Numismatic History of Rayy* (New York, 1938), pp. 143ff., and W. Madelung, 'The Minor Dynasties of Northern Iran', in *Cambridge History of Iran*, vol. 4, pp. 206–212.
141. Ḥamīd al-Dīn al-Kirmānī, *al-Aqwāl al-dhahabiyya*, ed. Ṣ. al-Ṣāwī (Tehran, 1977), pp. 2–3. See also P. Kraus, ed., *Rasā'il falsafiyya li-Abī Bakr Muḥammad ibn Zakariyyā' al-Rāzī* (Cairo, 1939), pp. 291ff.; Corbin, *Étude*, pp. 128ff.; also by Corbin, *Histoire*, pp. 194ff., and M. Muḥaqqiq, *Fīlsūf-i Rayy* (2nd ed., Tehran, 1352/1973), pp. 3–8, 155ff., 166–167 and 276.
142. During the caliphate of al-Rāḍī (322–329/934–940), when contemplating a march on Baghdād, Mardāwīj was accused of collaboration with Abū Ṭāhir, the leader of the Qarmaṭīs of Baḥrayn; see Muḥammad b. Yaḥyā al-Ṣūlī, *Akhbār ar-Rāḍī billāh wa'l-Muttaqī billāh*, tr. M. Canard (Algiers, 1946–1950), vol. 1, pp. 71–73.
143. Abu'l-Ma'ālī Muḥammad b. 'Ubayd Allāh, *Bayān al-adyān*, ed. H. Raḍī (Tehran, 1342/1963), pp. 67–69; al-Shahrastānī, *al-Milal*, vol. 1, pp. 181–184; tr. Kazi, pp. 156–158; Abu'l-Ḥasan 'Alī b. Zayd al-Bayhaqī, *Ta'rīkh-i Bayhaq*, ed. A. Bahmanyār (Tehran, 1317/1938), p. 253, ed. Q. S. K. Husaini (Hyderabad, 1968), p. 438; Muḥaqqiq, *Fīlsūf-i Rayy*, pp. 48–49; Madelung, 'Fatimiden', pp. 44–45, and his 'al-Kayyāl', *EI2*, vol. 4, p. 847. See also Idrīs,

ʿUyūn, vol. 4, pp. 357–358, and Ivanow, 'Ismailis and Qarmatians', pp. 64–65, which adopts the account of Idrīs and wrongly presents Ibn al-Kayyāl as a dissenting *dāʿī* of the Imām ʿAbd Allāh b. Muḥammad b. Ismāʿīl.

144. See ʿAbd al-Ḥayy b. al-Ḍaḥḥāk Gardīzī, *Zayn al-akhbār*, ed. ʿA. Ḥabībī (Tehran, 1347/1968), pp. 148–149; *Ta'rīkh-i Sīstān*, ed. M. T. Bahār (Tehran, 1314/1935), pp. 290–294 and 300–302; English translation, *The Tārikh-e Sistān*, tr. M. Gold (Rome, 1976), pp. 233–237 and 243–244; Mīrkhwānd, *Rawḍat al-ṣafā'* (Tehran, 1338–1339/1960), vol. 4, pp. 40–42; also by Mīrkhwānd, *Historie des Samanides*, ed. and tr. Ch. Defrémery (Paris, 1845), text pp. 21–24, translation pp. 133–136, and V. V. Barthold, *Turkestan down to the Mongol Invasion*, ed. C. E. Bosworth (3rd ed., London, 1968), p. 241.

145. On al-Nasafī and his works, see Barthold, *Turkestan*, pp. 242–245; Ivanow, *Studies* 2, pp. 87ff.; also his *Ismaili Literature*, pp. 23–24; Sezgin, *Geschichte*, vol. 1, pp. 573–574; Poonawala, *Bio*, pp. 40–43, and Ghālib, *Aʿlām*, pp. 336–338.

146. See Nāṣir-i Khusraw, *Khwān al-ikhwān*, ed. Y. al-Khashshāb (Cairo, 1940), pp. 112 and 115, ed. ʿA. Qavīm (Tehran, 1338/1959), pp. 131 and 135, where al-Nasafī is referred to as the martyred *shaykh* and *khwāja*; Stern, 'Early', pp. 80–81, and also his 'Abu'l-Qasim al-Bustī', p. 23.

147. See Goldziher, *Streitschrift*, pp. 14–16 and 23–24; Lewis, *Origins*, pp. 92–93, and also by Lewis, *Arabs in History*, pp. 108ff.

148. Cl. Cahen, 'La Changeante portée sociale de quelques doctrines religieuses', in *L'Élaboration de l'Islam*, pp. 12–15 and 20–21, and Ashtor, *A Social and Economic History*, pp. 160ff.; see also I. P. Petrushevsky, *Islām dar Īrān*, tr. K. Kishāvarz (Tehran, 1351/1972), pp. 293ff.; English translation, *Islam in Iran*, tr. H. Evans (London, 1985), pp. 234ff., which reflects a characteristically Marxist approach emphasizing class conflicts.

149. Massignon repeated this hypothesis in various writings which have been reprinted in his *Opera Minora*, vol. 1, pp. 369–422; see also his 'Ṣinf', *EI*, vol. 4, pp. 436–437. Massignon's ideas on the subject were pursued by B. Lewis, especially in his 'The Islamic Guilds', *Economic History Review*, 8 (1937), pp. 20–37; but Lewis advocated the milder opinion that if not actually created by the Ismāʿīlīs, the guilds were certainly used by them as instruments in their organization.

150. S. M. Stern, 'The Constitution of the Islamic City', and Cl. Cahen, 'Y a-t-il eu des corporations professionnelles dans le monde Musulman classique?', both in *The Islamic City*, ed. A. H. Hourani and S. M. Stern (Oxford, 1970), pp. 36–50 and 51–63, and G. Baer, 'Guilds in Middle Eastern History', in *Studies in the Economic History of the Middle East*, ed. M. A. Cook (London, 1970), especially pp. 11–17 and 27–30.

151. See *Ḥudūd al-ʿālam*, p. 89; Gardīzī, *Zayn al-akhbār*, pp. 178–180; Muḥammad b. Aḥmad al-Muqaddasī (al-Maqdisī), *Aḥsan al-taqāsīm*, ed. M. J. de Goeje (2nd ed., Leiden, 1906), pp. 481–482 and 485, in which this famous geographer-traveller relates the account of a visit he made in 375/985 to Multān, then under Ismāʿīlī rule; Nāṣiḥ b. Ẓafar al-Jurbādhaqānī, *Tarjuma-yi*

ta'rīkh-i Yamīnī, ed. J. Shuʿār (Tehran, 1345/1966), pp. 278–280; Mīrkhwānd, *Raḍwat al-ṣafā'*, vol. 4, pp. 96–97; Hamdani, *Ismāʿīlī Daʿwa*, pp. 3–6, and A. Z. Khan, 'Ismaʿilism in Multan and Sind', *Journal of the Pakistan Historical Society*, 23 (1975), pp. 36–57.

152. As preserved by al-Nuwayrī, *Nihāyat al-arab*, vol. 25, pp. 229–232; tr. in de Sacy, *Exposé*, vol. 1, introduction pp. 193–200; Ibn al-Dawādārī, *Kanz*, vol. 6, pp. 65–68, and al-Maqrīzī, *Ittiʿāẓ*, ed. Bunz, pp. 114–115, ed. al-Shayyāl, vol. 1, pp. 167–168. See also de Goeje, *Mémoire*, pp. 58–59; Ivanow, *Rise*, pp. 48ff.; Stern, 'Ismāʿīlīs', pp. 104–106, and Madelung, 'Imamat', pp. 59–60.

153. Ibn Ḥawqal, *Ṣūrat al-arḍ*, p. 295.

154. According to Ibn Mālik al-Yamānī, *Kashf asrār al-Bāṭiniyya*, ed. al-Kawtharī, p. 18, also in *Akhbār al-Qarāmiṭa*, p. 213, Ḥamdān was killed in Baghdād.

155. Jaʿfar b. Manṣūr al-Yaman, *Kitāb al-kashf*, pp. 97ff. and 102ff. See also Madelung, 'Imamat', pp. 54–58.

156. Jaʿfar b. Manṣūr al-Yaman, *Kitāb al-kashf*, pp. 12 and 60.

157. Ivanow, *Studies* 2, pp. 15–19; Corbin, *Histoire*, pp. 64ff. and 146ff.; Madelung, 'Imamat', pp. 61ff., and M. G. S. Hodgson, 'Ḥudjdja: In Shīʿī Terminology', *EI2*, vol. 3, pp. 544–545.

158. Al-Shahrastānī, *al-Milal*, vol. 1, p. 192; tr. Kazi, p. 164.

159. Ibn Ḥawshab, *Kitāb al-rushd*, p. 209; tr. Ivanow in *Studies* 2, p. 54, and Jaʿfar b. Manṣūr al-Yaman, *Kitāb al-kashf*, pp. 55, 60 and 125.

160. *Kitāb al-rushd*, p. 201, tr. Ivanow in *Studies* 2, p. 46.

161. Jaʿfar b. Manṣūr al-Yaman, *Kitāb al-kashf*, p. 119.

162. Al-Nawbakhtī, *Firaq*, p. 63, and al-Qummī, *al-Maqālāt*, pp. 84–85.

163. Al-Hamdānī, *Genealogy*, text p. 10, translation p. 13.

164. Ibid., text pp. 12–13.

165. See Madelung, 'Imamat', pp. 80–86.

166. Some of these traditions are cited in Ivanow, *Rise*, pp. 61–65, 95–122, and text pp. 1–31.

167. See Madelung, 'Imamat', pp. 65ff. and 71–73.

168. Al-Nuʿmān, *al-Urjūza al-mukhtāra*, ed. I. K. Poonawala (Montreal, 1970), pp. 194–203; see also T. Nagel, 'Die Urǧūza al-Muḫtāra des Qāḍī an-Nuʿmān', *Die Welt des Islam*, 15 (1974), pp. 96–128.

169. Al-Masʿūdī, *al-Tanbīh*, p. 391; tr. Carra de Vaux, p. 496; ʿArīb b. Saʿd al-Qurṭubī, *Ṣilat ta'rīkh al-Ṭabarī*, ed. M. J. de Goeje (Leiden, 1897), p. 137; Ibn al-Jawzī, *al-Muntaẓam*, vol. 6, p. 195; al-Daylamī, *Bayān*, p. 20; al-Maqrīzī, *Ittiʿāẓ*, ed. Bunz, p. 130, ed. al-Shayyāl, vol. 1, p. 185, and Madelung, 'Fatimiden', pp. 84–85.

170. Al-Nuʿmān, *al-Risāla al-mudhhiba*, in *Khams rasā'il Ismāʿīliyya*, ed. ʿĀ. Tāmir (Salamiyya, 1956), p. 41. For one such work attributed wrongly to ʿAbdān, see *Kitāb shajarat al-yaqīn*, ed. ʿĀ. Tāmir (Beirut, 1982).

171. Ibn Ḥawqal, *Ṣūrat al-arḍ*, p. 295; see also Madelung, 'Fatimiden', pp. 39–40 and 45–46.

172. On the Musāfirids, also called Sallārids and Langarids, who held the key fortress of Shamīrān, in Ṭārum, and who were eventually uprooted by the Nizārīs, see A. Kasravī, *Shahriyārān-i gum-nām* (2nd ed., Tehran, 1335/1956),

pp. 36–120; Cl. Huart, 'Les Mosāfirides de l'Adherbaïdjān', in *Oriental Studies Presented to Edward G. Browne*, pp. 228–256; V. Minorsky, *Studies in Caucasian History* (London, 1953), pp. 159–166, and also his 'Musāfirids', *EI*, vol. 3, pp. 743–745.

173. See Stern, 'Early', pp. 70–74.

174. Al-Nīsābūrī, *Istitār*, pp. 96ff.; tr. Ivanow in *Rise*, pp. 163ff.; al-Ṭabarī, *Ta'rīkh*, III, pp. 2218–2226, 2230–2232, 2237–2246, 2255–2266 and 2269–2275; tr. Rosenthal, pp. 113–123, 126–129, 134–144, 157–168 and 172–179; ʿArīb, *Ṣilat*, pp. 4–6 and 9–18; al-Masʿūdī, *al-Tanbīh*, pp. 370–376; tr. Carra de Vaux, pp. 475–480; excerpts from Thābit b. Sinān's *Ta'rīkh* and Ibn al-ʿAdīm's *Bughyat* in *Akhbār al-Qarāmiṭa*, pp. 16–35, 275ff. and 287ff.; al-Nuwayrī, *Nihāyat al-arab*, vol. 25, pp. 246–275; tr. de Sacy, *Exposé*, vol. 1, introduction pp. 200–209; Ibn al-Dawādārī, *Kanz*, vol. 6, pp. 69–89, and al-Maqrīzī, *Ittiʿāẓ*, ed. Bunz, pp. 115ff., ed. al-Shayyāl, vol. 1, pp. 168ff. Of the secondary sources on Zikrawayh and his activities, see de Goeje, *Mémoire*, pp. 47–58; Lewis, *Origins*, pp. 73–74; Ivanow, *Rise*, pp. 76–94; Hodgson, *Venture of Islam*, vol. 1, pp. 488–492; H. Halm, 'Die Söhne Zikrawaihs und das erste fatimidische Kalifat (290/903)', *Die Welt des Orients*, 10 (1979), pp. 30–53; I. A. Bello, 'The Qarmaṭians', *IC*, 54 (1980), especially pp. 233–236; K. V. Zetterstéen, 'Zikrawaih b. Mihrawaih', *EI*, vol. 4, pp. 1226–1227, and Madelung, 'Ḳarmaṭī', pp. 660–661.

175. Al-Masʿūdī, *al-Tanbīh*, p. 391; tr. Carra de Vaux, p. 496; ʿArīb, *Ṣilat*, p. 137; al-Nuwayrī, *Nihāyat al-arab*, vol. 25, pp. 275–276; tr. de Sacy, *Exposé*, vol. 1, introduction p. 210; Ibn al-Dawādārī, *Kanz*, vol. 6, p. 90; al-Maqrīzī, *Ittiʿāẓ*, ed. Bunz, p. 124, ed. al-Shayyāl, vol. 1, pp. 179–180; de Goeje, *Mémoire*, pp. 99–100; Friedlaender, 'Heterodoxies: Commentary', pp. 110–111; Madelung, 'Fatimiden', pp. 82–84; and M. G. S. Hodgson, 'Baḳliyya', *EI2*, vol. 1, p. 962.

176. The most detailed account of ʿUbayd Allāh's flight from Salamiyya to the Maghrib, and the establishment of the Ismāʿīlī mission in North Africa, used as the main source by later historians, is contained in al-Nuʿmān, *Iftitāḥ*, pp. 54–258; excerpts in Ivanow, *Rise*, text pp. 40–46, translation pp. 224–231. Other early Ismāʿīlī accounts, written shortly after 346 A.H. (the date of the composition of the *Iftitāḥ*), may be found in al-Nīsābūrī, *Istitār*, pp. 96ff.; English translation, Ivanow, *Rise*, pp. 164ff., and in the *Sīrat al-Ḥājib Jaʿfar b. ʿAlī*, the autobiography of ʿUbayd Allāh's chamberlain, as compiled by a certain Muḥammad b. Muḥammad al-Yamānī, edited and published by Ivanow in *Bulletin of the Faculty of Arts, University of Egypt*, 4 (1936), pp. 107–133; English translation, Ivanow, *Rise*, pp. 184–223; French translation, M. Canard, 'L'autobiographie d'un chambellan du Mahdī ʿObeidallāh le Fāṭimide', *Hespéris*, 39 (1952), pp. 279–324. Canard has added to the end of this article (pp. 324–328) a French translation of the above-mentioned excerpts from the *Iftitāḥ*, published by Ivanow. These Ismāʿīlī sources were later used extensively in Idrīs, *ʿUyūn*, vol. 5, pp. 44–112. There are numerous non-Ismāʿīlī sources on the subject; see ʿArīb, *Ṣilat*, pp. 51–52; Ibn Ḥammād, *Histoire des rois ʿObaidides*, ed. and tr. M. Vonderheyden (Algiers–Paris,

1927), text pp. 7ff., translation pp. 18ff.; excerpts in A. Cherbonneau, 'Documents inédits sur Obeïd Allah', *JA*, 5 série, 5 (1855), pp. 529–547; Ibn Khallikān, *Biographical Dictionary*, vol. 1, pp. 465–466; Ibn ʿIdhārī, *al-Bayān al-mughrib*, ed. G. S. Colin and É. Lévi-Provençal (New ed., Leiden, 1948–1951), vol. 1, pp. 124ff.; Ibn Khaldūn, *Histoire des Berbères*, tr. W. MacGuckin de Slane, new edition by P. Casanova (Paris, 1968–1969), vol. 1, pp. 262ff., 291ff., 441ff., and vol. 2, pp. 506–521; al-Maqrīzī, *Ittiʿāẓ*, ed. Bunz, pp. 31–39, ed. al-Shayyāl, vol. 1, pp. 55–66, and al-Maqrīzī, *al-Muqaffā*, in Fagnan, 'Nouveaux textes', pp. 35ff. Of the secondary sources, mention may be made of de Goeje, *Mémoire*, pp. 49 and 64ff.; Qazvīnī's notes in Juwaynī, *Ta'rīkh*, vol. 3, pp. 349–355; Ḥasan and Sharaf, *ʿUbayd Allāh al-Mahdī*, pp. 124–143; A. Gateau, 'La Sīrat Jaʿfar al-Ḥājib', *Hespéris*, 34 (1947), pp. 375–396; F. Dachraoui, 'Contribution à l'histoire des Fāṭimides en Ifrīqiya', *Arabica*, 8 (1961), pp. 189–203; also by Dachraoui, 'Les Commencements de la prédication Ismāʿīlienne en Ifrīqiya', *SI*, 20 (1964), pp. 89–102; Nagel, *Frühe Ismailiya*, pp. 11–55; W. Madelung, 'Some Notes on Non-Ismāʿīlī Shiism in the Maghrib', *SI*, 44 (1976), pp. 87–97, reprinted in his *Religious Schools and Sects*; Ghālib, *Aʿlām*, pp. 246–253, and S. M. Stern, 'Abū ʿAbd Allāh al-Shīʿī', *EI2*, vol. 1, pp. 103–104.

177. On the *bāṭinī ta'wīl*, and the Ismāʿīlī distinction between the exoteric and the esoteric dimensions of religion, see Goldziher, *Introduction*, pp. 221–224; Ivanow, *Brief*, pp. 23–25 and 33–36. Many studies by H. Corbin are also relevant here, including his 'Rituel Sabéen et exégèse Ismaélienne du rituel', *EJ*, 19 (1950), especially pp. 181–188 and 229–246, reprinted in his *Temple et contemplation* (Paris, 1980), pp. 143–149 and 183–196; English translation, 'Sabian Temple and Ismailism', in H. Corbin, *Temple and Contemplation*, tr. Philip Sherrard (London, 1986), pp. 132–138 and 170–182; 'Herméneutique spirituelle comparée: I. Swedenborg – II. Gnose Ismaélienne', *EJ*, 33 (1964), pp. 122–153, reprinted in his *Face de Dieu, Face de l'homme* (Paris, 1983), pp. 108–151; *Étude*, pp. 65–73; *Histoire*, pp. 27ff.; 'L'Initiation Ismaélienne', pp. 63–84; and *En Islam*, vol. 1, pp. 212–218, and vol. 3, pp. 214ff. Also see Naṣr, *Ideals*, pp. 58ff., 160ff. and 168ff.; R. Paret, 'Ta'wīl', *EI*, vol. 4, pp. 704–705; M. G. S. Hodgson, 'Bāṭiniyya', *EI2*, vol. 1, pp. 1098–1100, and F. Daftary, 'Bāṭiniyya', *Encyclopaedia Islamica* (Tehran, forthcoming).

178. For a general discussion of time and cyclicism in Ismāʿīlī thought, see H. Corbin, 'Le Temps cyclique dans le Mazdéisme et dans l'Ismaélisme', *EJ*, 20 (1951), especially pp. 183–217, reprinted in his *Temps cyclique et gnose Ismaélienne* (Paris, 1982), pp. 39–69; English translation, 'Cyclical Time in Mazdaism and Ismailism', in *Papers from the Eranos Yearbooks*: Vol. 3, *Man and Time* (Princeton, 1957), pp. 144–172, reprinted in H. Corbin, *Cyclical Time and Ismaili Gnosis* (London, 1983), pp. 30–58, and Paul E. Walker, 'Eternal Cosmos and the Womb of History: Time in Early Ismaili Thought', *IJMES*, 9 (1978), pp. 355–366.

179. The cyclical division of history into eras, and other related details, are clearly outlined in the *Kitāb al-rushd*, pp. 189 and 197ff., tr. Ivanow in *Studies* 2, pp. 33 and 41ff., in Jaʿfar b. Manṣūr al-Yaman, *Kitāb al-kashf*, pp. 14ff., 104, 113–

114, 132–133, 138, 143, 150 and 169–170, as well as in many Fāṭimid Ismāʿīlī works, such as al-Nuʿmān, *Asās al-taʾwīl*, ed. ʿĀ. Tāmir (Beirut, 1960), with an unpublished Persian version entitled *Bunyād-i taʾwīl*, prepared by the *dāʿī* al-Muʾayyad fi'l-Dīn al-Shīrāzī; and al-Sijistānī, *Ithbāt*, especially pp. 181–193. The Ibn Rizām-Akhū Muḥsin description of the subject may be found, for example, in al-Nuwayrī, *Nihāyat al-arab*, vol. 25, pp. 205–207; tr. de Sacy, *Exposé*, vol. 1, introduction pp. 103–110. See also Zāhid ʿAlī, *Hamārē Ismāʿīlī madhhab kī ḥaqīqat aur us kā niẓām* (Hyderabad, 1373/1954), pp. 576ff.; Ivanow, *Studies* 2, pp. 3ff.; Madelung, 'Imamat', pp. 51ff.; Paul E. Walker, 'An Early Ismaili Interpretation of Man, History and Salvation', *Ohio Journal of Religious Studies*, 3 (1975), pp. 29–35; Hodgson, *Venture of Islam*, vol. 1, pp. 378–384; Corbin, *Histoire*, pp. 92ff., 127 and 132; also his 'La Prophétologie Ismaélienne', in *Les Cahiers de l'Herne: Henry Corbin*, ed. Ch. Jambet (Paris, 1981), pp. 138–149; Stern, *Studies*, pp. 30ff. and 53–55; Halm, *Kosmologie*, pp. 18–37, and also his 'Dawr', *EI2*, Supplement, pp. 206–207.

180. For these and other terms used by the early Ismāʿīlīs, see Ivanow, *Studies* 2, pp. 9–27.

181. See Madelung, 'Imamat', pp. 82–90, and Y. Marquet, 'Le Qāḍī Nuʿmān à propos des heptades d'imāms', *Arabica*, 25 (1978), pp. 225–232.

182. Extracts from Abū Ḥātim's *Kitāb al-iṣlāḥ* and from other Ismāʿīlī works on the subject are to be found in Halm, *Kosmologie*, pp. 206–227. See also al-Sijistānī, *Kitāb al-iftikhār*, ed. M. Ghālib (Beirut, 1980), pp. 43–56.

183. The full Arabic text of this small treatise, discovered by S. M. Stern at the end of a manuscript belonging to Asaf A. A. Fyzee, is printed in Stern, *Studies*, pp. 6–16; see also Goriawala, *Catalogue*, p. 69.

184. For the Zaydī references, notably those contained in the biography of the Zaydī Imām al-Nāṣir Aḥmad b. Yaḥyā (d. 322/934) produced by ʿAbd Allāh b. ʿUmar al-Hamdānī and preserved by the later historian al-Laḥjī, see Arendonk, *Les débuts*, pp. 330–334; Stern, *Studies*, pp. 3–5, and Halm, *Kosmologie*, pp. 58–60.

185. Stern, *Studies*, pp. 17–29, based chiefly on al-Murshid's treatise, and Halm, *Kosmologie*, pp. 38–127; see also Y. Marquet, 'Quelques remarques à propos de Kosmologie und Heilslehre der frühen Ismāʿīliyya de Heinz Halm', *SI*, 55 (1982), pp. 115–135.

186. For the treatment of this triad by different Ismāʿīlī authors, see al-Sijistānī, *al-Iftikhār*, pp. 43–46; Jaʿfar b. Manṣūr al-Yaman, *Asrār al-nuṭaqāʾ*, ed. Ghālib, pp. 24–26 and 81–82, both quoted in Halm, *Kosmologie*, pp. 206–209 and 220–222; al-Ḥāmidī, *Kanz*, p. 165; Nāṣir-i Khusraw, *Khwān al-ikhwān*, ed. al-Khashshāb, pp. 170ff., ed. Qavīm, pp. 199ff., and Corbin, *Étude*, pp. 91–112.

187. Halm, *Kosmologie*, pp. 120–127. See also G. Vajda, 'Melchisédec dans la mythologie Ismaélienne', *JA*, 234 (1943–1945), pp. 173–183, and W. Ivanow, 'Noms Bibliques dans la mythologie Ismaélienne', *JA*, 237 (1949), pp. 249–255.

188. Rudolph, *Die Mandäer*, vol. 1, pp. 145 and 248ff.

4. Fāṭimid Ismāʿīlism

1. L. Massignon, 'Mutanabbi, devant le siècle Ismaélien de l'Islam', in *Al Mutanabbi: Recueil publié à l'occasion de son millénaire* (Beirut, 1936), p. 1.
2. See Richard J. H. Gottheil, 'Al-Ḥasan ibn Ibrāhīm ibn Zūlāḳ', *JAOS*, 28 (1907), pp. 254–270; Becker, *Beiträge*, vol. 1, pp. 13–15; Ivanow, *Guide*, p. 42; also by Ivanow, *Ismaili Literature*, p. 39, and Ghālib, *Aʿlām*, pp. 205–206.
3. The extant volume forty of Muḥammad b. ʿUbayd Allāh al-Musabbiḥī's *Akhbār Miṣr* consists of historical and literary parts. The historical part has been edited by A. Fu'ād Sayyid and Th. Bianquis (Cairo, 1978), and the literary part has been edited by Ḥusayn Naṣṣār (Cairo, 1984); both parts are also contained in a separate edition prepared by W. G. Millward (Cairo, 1980). A small extract of al-Musabbiḥī's extant fragment, covering the last two months of the year 415 A.H., was first published in Becker, *Beiträge*, vol. 1, pp. 59–80.
4. Yaḥyā b. Saʿīd al-Anṭākī, *Ta'rīkh*, ed. L. Cheikho, B. Carra de Vaux and H. Zayyat (Paris–Beirut, 1909); a later partial edition with French translation by I. Kratchkovsky and A. A. Vasiliev entitled *Histoire de Yahya Ibn Saʿïd d'Antioche*, appeared in *Patrologia Orientalis*, 18 (1924), pp. 699–833, and 23 (1932), pp. 347–520.
5. These include his *al-Ishāra ilā man nāl al-wizāra*, ed. ʿAbd Allāh Mukhliṣ, in *BIFAO*, 25 (1925), pp. 49–112, and 26 (1926), pp. 49–70, a history of Fāṭimid viziers from Ibn Killis to al-Baṭā'iḥī; see G. el-Din el-Shayyal, 'Ibn al-Ṣayrafī', *EI2*, vol. 3, p. 932.
6. Jamāl al-Dīn ʿAlī b. Ẓāfir al-Azdī, *Akhbār al-duwal al-munqaṭiʿa, La section consacrée aux Fatimides*, ed. A. Ferré (Cairo, 1972).
7. Ibn Muyassar's *Akhbār Miṣr*, as noted, was first edited by H. Massé in 1919; more recently, a better edition from the same incomplete manuscript was prepared by A. Fu'ād Sayyid (Cairo, 1981). The latter edition, along with the above-mentioned histories of al-Musabbiḥī and Ibn Ẓāfir, have appeared in the valuable series, entitled Textes Arabes et Études Islamiques, published by the Institut Français d'Archéologie Orientale du Caire.
8. Ibn Taghrībirdī, *al-Nujūm al-zāhira*, ed. W. Popper (Berkeley, 1909–1913), vol. 2, part 2, and vol. 3, part 1; Cairo ed., vols. 4 and 5; hereafter our references are to the Cairo edition.
9. See A. R. Guest, 'A List of Writers, Books and other Authorities Mentioned by El Maqrizi in his Khitat', *JRAS* (1902), pp. 103–125; Muḥammad ʿAbd Allāh ʿInān, *Miṣr al-Islāmiyya* (2nd ed., Cairo, 1969), pp. 49–63, and Cl. Cahen, 'Les Éditions de l'Ittiʿāẓ al-Ḥunafā' (Histoire Fatimide) de Maqrīzī', *Arabica*, 22 (1975), pp. 302–320.
10. Jalāl al-Dīn al-Suyūṭī, *Ḥusn al-muḥāḍara fī akhbār Miṣr wa'l-Qāhira* (Cairo, 1327/1909), and other editions; Ibn Iyās (Ayās), *Badā'iʿ al-zuhūr fī waqā'iʿ al-duhūr* (Cairo, 1301–1306/1884–1888; reprinted, Būlāq, 1311–1312/1893–1894), of which the first volume covers the history of Egypt from the beginning to the year 815/1412.

11. Parts of Miskawayh's *Tajārib al-umam*, covering the period 295–369 A.H., together with al-Rūdhrāwarī's continuation (*Dahyl*) down to 389 A.H. and the extant fragment of Hilāl's *Ta'rīkh*, have been edited by H. F. Amedroz and translated into English by D. S. Margoliouth, under the title of *The Eclipse of the 'Abbasid Caliphate* (Oxford–London, 1920–1921), 7 vols. Earlier, L. Caetani had published, in the E. J. W. Gibb Memorial Series, a facsimile edition of the first, fifth and sixth volumes of the Istanbul manuscript of the *Tajārib* (Leiden–London, 1909–1917), the last two volumes covering the period 284–369/897–979; our references are to the Arabic text of the edition in three volumes prepared by Amedroz.
12. Ibn al-Athīr, *Kitāb al-kāmil fi'l-ta'rīkh*, ed. Carl J. Tornberg (Leiden, 1851–1876), 12 vols., and indices, reprinted (Beirut, 1982); the Fāṭimids are covered in volume eight and the subsequent volumes. At least three other editions of this work were published in Cairo, in 1290/1873, 1301/1883, and 1303/1885; hereafter our references are to the Cairo edition, entitled *Ta'rīkh al-kāmil*, published in 1303 A.H.
13. For further details on Fāṭimid historiography, see Becker, *Beiträge*, vol. 1, pp. 1–31; Cl. Cahen, 'Quelques chroniques anciennes relatives aux derniers Fatimides', *BIFAO*, 37 (1937–1938), pp. 1–27; also by Cahen, 'Les chroniques Arabes concernant la Syrie, l'Égypte et la Mésopotamie', *REI*, 10 (1936), pp. 333–358; M. Kāmil Ḥusayn, *Fī adab Miṣr al-Fāṭimiyya* (Cairo, 1950), pp. 108ff.; A. Hamdani, 'The Discovery of a Lost literature (Fāṭimid)', *Proceedings of the Pakistan History Conference*, 8 (1958), pp. 61–73; Sauvaget, *Introduction to the History of the Muslim East*, pp. 146ff.; 'Inān, *Miṣr al-Islāmiyya*, pp. 37–49 and 63–76, and A. Fu'ād Sayyid, 'Lumières nouvelles sur quelques sources de l'histoire Fatimide en Égypte', *Annales Islamologiques*, 13 (1977), pp. 1–41. Much information may also be found in the relevant sections of Carl Brockelmann, *Geschichte der arabischen Litteratur* (Weimar, 1898–1902), 2 vols., (2nd ed., Leiden, 1943–1949), 2 vols., with three supplementary volumes (Leiden, 1937–1942), and in Sezgin, *Geschichte*, vol. 1, pp. 323ff. and 354ff.
14. See G. el-Din el-Shayyal, 'The Faṭimid Documents as a Source for the History of the Faṭimids and their Institutions', *Bulletin of the Faculty of Arts, Alexandria University*, 8 (1954), pp. 3–12, and Sauvaget, *Introduction to the History of the Muslim East*, pp. 16ff.
15. The late Professor Jamāl al-Dīn al-Shayyāl published some twenty-three such Fāṭimid documents in his already-cited *Majmū'at al-wathā'iq al-Fāṭimiyya*, the majority having been preserved by al-Qalqashandī. Another collection comprised of sixty-six letters and epistles issued on the orders of the Fāṭimid caliph al-Mustanṣir, was edited by 'Abd al-Mun'im Mājid and published under the title of *al-Sijillāt al-Mustanṣiriyya* (Cairo, 1954).
16. More than any other scholar, Solomon D. Goitein (1900–1985) has written on the Cairo Geniza and its importance, see especially his 'The Cairo Geniza as a Source for the History of Muslim Civilization', *SI*, 3 (1955), pp. 75–91; 'The Documents of the Cairo Geniza as a Source for Mediterranean Social Studies', *JAOS*, 80 (1960), pp. 91–100; *Studies in Islamic History and Institu-*

tions (Leiden, 1966), pp. 279–295, and 'Geniza', *EI2*, vol. 2, pp. 987–989. Professor Goitein also undertook a monumental socio-economic study, based on the Geniza records, in his *A Mediterranean Society* (Berkeley, 1967–1988), 5 vols. See also Paul E. Kahle, *The Cairo Geniza* (London, 1947), pp. 1–20, and S. Shaked, *A Tentative Bibliography of Geniza Documents* (The Hague–Paris, 1964).

17. For details on some of these documents, see S. M. Stern, 'An Original Document from the Fāṭimid Chancery concerning Italian Merchants', in *Studi Orientalistici in onore di Giorgio Levi Della Vida*, vol. 2, pp. 529–538; also by Stern, 'Three Petitions of the Fāṭimid Period', *Oriens*, 15 (1962), pp. 172–209, and also Stern's 'A Petition to the Fāṭimid Caliph al-Mustanṣir concerning a Conflict within the Jewish Community', *Revue des Études Juives*, 128 (1969), pp. 203–222; all three articles are reprinted in S. M. Stern, *Coins and Documents from the Medieval Middle East* (London, 1986). See also S. D. Goitein, 'Petitions to Fatimid Caliphs from the Cairo Geniza', *Jewish Quarterly Review*, NS, 45 (1954–1955), pp. 30–38, and J. Mann, *The Jews in Egypt and in Palestine under the Fāṭimid Caliphs* (Oxford, 1920–1922), 2 vols., a classic study (reprinted, New York, 1970) utilizing a large number of the Hebrew records of the Cairo Geniza.

18. The Arabic texts and English translations of these ten documents, together with a full commentary, may be found in S. M. Stern, *Fāṭimid Decrees: Original Documents from the Fāṭimid Chancery* (London, 1964). Some of the documents in question had been published earlier in Richard J. H. Gottheil, 'A Decree in Favour of the Karaites of Cairo dated 1024', in *Festschrift zu Ehren des Dr. A. Harkavy*, ed. D. von Günzburg and I. Markon (St Petersburg, 1908), pp. 115–125; N. Shuqayr, *Ta'rīkh Sīnā* (Cairo, 1916), pp. 503–504; A. Grohmann and P. Labib, 'Ein Fāṭimidenerlass vom Jahre 415 A.H. (1024 A.D.) im Koptischen Museum in Alt-Kairo', *RSO*, 32 (1957), pp. 641–654, and S. M. Stern, 'A Fāṭimid Decree of the Year 524/1130', *BSOAS*, 23 (1960), pp. 439–455. See also Joseph N. Youssef, 'A Study of the Fāṭimid and Ayyūbid Documents in the Monastery of Mt. Sinai', *Bulletin of the Faculty of Arts, Alexandria University*, 18 (1964), pp. 179ff., and Donald S. Richards, 'A Fāṭimid Petition and Small Decree from Sinai', *Israel Oriental Studies*, 3 (1973), pp. 140–158.

19. De Lacy O'Leary, *A Short History of the Fatimid Khalifate* (London, 1923). The Fāṭimids were treated briefly also in Stanley Lane-Poole, *A History of Egypt in the Middle Ages* (London, 1901), with later revised editions, and in Gaston Wiet, *Histoire de la nation Égyptienne*: IV, *L'Égypte Arabe* (Paris, 1937). These works, as well as E. Graefe's 'Fāṭimids', *EI*, vol. 2, pp. 88–92, were produced before the modern progress in Ismāʿīlī studies.

20. A. Hamdani, *The Fatimids* (Karachi, 1962). Earlier, Abdus Salam Picklay, an Ismāʿīlī author, had presented a brief popular account in his *Rise and Fall of the Fatimid Empire* (Bombay, 1944), and subsequently, there appeared two detailed studies in Urdu: Qudrat Allāh Khān, *Fāṭimī khilāfat-i Miṣr* (Karachi, 1962), and S. R. Aḥmad Jaʿfarī, *Ta'rīkh-i dawlat-i Fāṭimiyya* (Lahore, 1965).

21. Amongst such works, Ḥasan Ibrāhīm Ḥasan's *Ta'rīkh al-dawla al-Fāṭimiyya*

(3rd ed., Cairo, 1964), which was originally written in English and submitted in 1928 as a doctoral thesis to the University of London, is the most comprehensive study of Fāṭimid history and institutions; see also Muḥammad J. Surūr, *Miṣr fī ʿaṣr al-dawla al-Fāṭimiyya* (Cairo, 1960), and ʿAbd al-Munʿim Mājid (Magued), *Ẓuhūr khilāfat al-Fāṭimiyyīn wa suqūṭuhā fī Miṣr* (Alexandria, 1968). See also Hasan, 'Contributions to the Study of Fāṭimid History in Egypt during the Last 12 Years', pp. 129ff.

22. See, for example, Panayiotis J. Vatikiotis, *The Fatimid Theory of State* (Lahore, 1957), originally submitted in 1954 as a doctoral thesis to the Johns Hopkins University; B. I. Beshir, 'The Fatimid Caliphate: 386–487 A.H./ 996–1094 A.D.' (Ph.D. thesis, University of London, 1970); Hussain A. Ladak, 'The Fāṭimid Caliphate and the Ismāʿīlī Daʿwa from the Appointment of Mustaʿlī to the Suppression of the Dynasty' (Ph.D. thesis, University of London, 1971), and Sadik A. Assaad, *The Reign of al-Hakim bi Amr Allah, 386/996–411/1021* (Beirut, 1974), initially submitted in 1971 to the University of London. More recently, there has appeared, after a long delay, Farhat Dachraoui's *Le Califat Fatimide au Maghreb, 296–365 H./909–975 Jc.* (Tunis, 1981), a comprehensive study of the history and institutions of the Fāṭimid Caliphate during its North African phase, originally completed in 1970 as a doctoral thesis at the Sorbonne, Paris.

23. M. Canard, 'Fāṭimids', *EI2*, vol. 2, pp. 850–862; several of Canard's articles on the Fāṭimids have been reprinted in his *Miscellanea Orientalia* (London, 1973). For further details, see F. Daftary, 'Marius Canard (1888–1982): A Bio-bibliographical Notice', *Arabica*, 33 (1986), pp. 251–262.

24. *Colloque international sur l'histoire du Caire*, sponsored by the Ministry of Culture of the Arab Republic of Egypt (Cairo, 1972); hereafter cited as *Colloque du Caire*.

25. Valuable details on the reigns of the first three Fāṭimids are contained in al-Nuʿmān, *Iftitāḥ*, pp. 249–282, and also his *al-Majālis*, which is a rich source of information. The fullest Ismāʿīlī account of this period, however, is contained in Idrīs, *ʿUyūn*, vol. 5, pp. 112–350, based on al-Nuʿmān and a number of Fāṭimid chronicles which have not survived. The section from the *ʿUyūn* on the North African phase of the Fāṭimid Caliphate has been edited separately, *al-Khulafāʾ al-Fāṭimiyyīn biʾl-Maghrib*, ed. M. al-Yaʿlāwī (Tunis, 1985); extracts from the *ʿUyūn*, on al-Mahdī's reign, are included in Stern, *Studies*, pp. 96–145. Numerous Fāṭimid documents from this period are contained in Abū ʿAlī Manṣūr al-ʿAzīzī al-Jawdharī, *Sīrat al-ustādh Jawdhar*, ed. M. Kāmil Ḥusayn and M. ʿAbd al-Hādī Shaʿīra (Cairo, 1954), pp. 33–86; French translation, *Vie de l'ustadh Jaudhar (Contenant sermons, lettres et rescrits des premiers califes Fātimides)*, tr. M. Canard (Algiers, 1958), pp. 41–126. On this important Ismāʿīlī work compiled by al-Jawdharī, the private secretary to Jawdhar (d. 363/973) who held various posts under the first four Fāṭimids, see Idrīs, *Zahr al-maʿānī*, in Ivanow, *Rise*, text pp. 70–72 and 79, translation pp. 263–266 and 279; see also Canard's introduction to his translation of Jawdhar's *Sīrat*, pp. 8–24; Ḥusayn, *Fī adab*, pp. 114–116; Ghālib, *Aʿlām*, pp. 546–547; Poonawala, *Bio*, pp. 90–91, and M. Canard, 'Djawdhar', *EI2*, vol.

2, p. 491. The North African phase of the Fāṭimid Caliphate is covered in varying details in the already-cited Sunnī historical sources, which will be referred to in connection with specific events. Aside from Ibn ʿIdhārī's *al-Bayān*, an important place is occupied by al-Maqrīzī's *Ittiʿāẓ*, ed. Bunz, pp. 38–58, ed. al-Shayyāl, vol. 1, pp. 65–92, for the period in question; see also Ibn Ẓāfir, *Akhbār*, pp. 6–20; Ibn Ḥammād, *Histoire*, text pp. 6–39, translation pp. 17–61, and Ibn Khallikān, *Biographical Dictionary*, vol. 1, pp. 218–221, and vol. 3, pp. 181–182. Of the secondary sources, mention may be made of Ḥasan, *Ta'rīkh*, pp. 80–92; Zāhid ʿAlī, *Ta'rīkh*, vol. 1, pp. 123–147; O'Leary, *Fatimid Khalifate*, pp. 74–92; Shaban, *Islamic History*, vol. 2, pp. 188–195; ʿĀdala ʿA. al-Ḥammad, *Qiyām al-dawla al-Fāṭimiyya bi-bilād al-Maghrib* (Cairo, 1980), pp. 125–225; Dachraoui, *Califat Fatimide*, pp. 57–218, covering also the background to the establishment of the dynasty; also by Dachraoui, 'al-Ḳā'im', *EI2*, vol. 4, pp. 458–460, and 'al-Manṣūr Bi'llāh', *EI2*, vol. 6, pp. 434–435, and Ghālib, *Aʿlām*, pp. 166–170 and 495–498.

26. Al-Hamdānī, 'Some Unknown Ismāʿīlī Authors', p. 366.
27. Al-Nuʿmān, *Iftitāḥ*, pp. 259ff.; al-Nuʿmān, *al-Majālis*, pp. 183–184; Idrīs, *ʿUyūn*, vol. 5, pp. 116–123; Ibn ʿIdhārī, *al-Bayān*, vol. 1, pp. 150–151, 161 and 163–165; Ibn Khaldūn, *Histoire*, vol. 2, pp. 521–523; al-Maqrīzī, *al-Khiṭaṭ*, vol. 1, pp. 350–351, and vol. 2, pp. 10–11; French tr., vol. 4, pp. 11–12; al-Maqrīzī, *Ittiʿāẓ*, ed. Bunz, pp. 40–41, ed. al-Shayyāl, vol. 1, pp. 67–68; Ibn Taghrībirdī, *al-Nujūm*, vol. 3, p. 174; Ḥasan and Sharaf, *ʿUbayd Allāh*, pp. 263–269; Zāhid ʿAlī, *Ta'rīkh*, vol. 1, pp. 115–122; Madelung, 'Imamat', pp. 66 and 80; al-Ḥammad, *Qiyām*, pp. 229–248, and Dachraoui, *Califat Fatimide*, pp. 127–132.
28. For more details, see Ibn Ḥawqal, *Ṣūrat al-arḍ*, pp. 60ff., 83ff., 93ff. and 100–107; al-Idrīsī, *Description de l'Afrique et de l'Espagne*, ed. and tr. R. Dozy and M. J. de Goeje (Leiden, 1866), text pp. 56ff., 70, 75–76, 85, 87–88 and 98–99, translation pp. 65ff., 80–81, 86–87, 98, 100–102 and 115–116; Ibn Faḍl Allāh al-ʿUmarī, *Masālik el abṣār fī mamālik el amṣār*: I, *L'Afrique, moins l'Égypte*, tr. M. Gaudefroy-Demombynes (Paris, 1927), pp. 96ff. and 137ff.; Ibn Khaldūn, *Histoire*, vol. 1, pp. 37, 45, 169–170, 178, 182, 186ff., 194–197, 291–299, vol. 2, pp. 1ff., and vol. 3, pp. 179ff., 188ff., 196–197 and 300ff.; E. Fagnan, *Extraits inédits relatifs au Maghreb* (Algiers, 1924), pp. 17–18, 41ff. and 153–154; G. Marçais, *La Berbérie Musulmane et l'Orient au moyen-âge* (Paris, 1946), the fullest modern treatment of the subject; Émile F. Gautier, *Le passé de l'Afrique du Nord* (Paris, 1952), pp. 201ff., 322ff. and 337–345; T. Lewicki, 'Le Répartition géographique des groupements ibāḍites dans l'Afrique du Nord au moyen-âge', *Rocznik Orientalistyczny*, 21 (1957), pp. 301–343, and Dachraoui, *Califat Fatimide*, pp. 31ff. and 364ff.
29. See al-Nuʿmān, *al-Majālis*, pp. 115–116, 164ff., 173ff. and 189ff.; Ibn ʿIdhārī, *al-Bayān*, vol. 1, pp. 175, 178ff., 185, 197–200 and 209–216; Ibn Khaldūn, *Histoire*, vol. 1, pp. 258–260, 265ff., and vol. 2, pp. 145ff., 526–527 and 567–571; Dozy, *Histoire des Musulmans d'Espagne*, vol. 3, pp. 13–21, 29–30, 33–49, 66–71 and 76–79; H. I. Hasan, 'Relations between the Fāṭimids in North Africa and Egypt and the Umayyads in Spain during the 4th Century A.H.

(10th Century A.D.)', *Bulletin of the Faculty of Arts, Fouad I University*, 10 (1948), pp. 39–83; M. Canard, 'L'impérialisme des Fatimides et leur propagande', *AIEO*, 6 (1942–1947), pp. 156ff.; Muḥammad J. Surūr, *Siyāsat al-Fāṭimiyyīn al-khārijiyya* (Cairo, 1967), pp. 221–224; M. Yalaoui, 'Les Relations entre Fāṭimides d'Ifriqiya et Omeyyades d'Espagne', *Actas del II Coloquio Hispano-Tunecino de Estudios Históricos* (Madrid, 1973), pp. 13–30; also his 'Controverse entre le Fatimide al-Muʿizz et l'Omeyyade al-Nasir', *Cahiers de Tunisie*, 26 (1978), pp. 7–33, and Dachraoui, *Califat Fatimide*, pp. 138ff., 150ff. and 163.

30. See Idrīs, *ʿUyūn*, vol. 5, pp. 125–136; Muḥammad b. Yūsuf al-Kindī, *The Governors and Judges of Egypt; or, Kitāb el Umarā' (el wulāh) wa Kitāb el quḍāh*, together with an appendix derived mostly from *Rafʿ el iṣr* by Ibn Ḥajar, ed. R. Guest (Leiden–London, 1912), pp. 268ff.; ʿArīb, *Ṣilat*, pp. 51ff., 79 and 80–86; Ibn ʿIdhārī, *al-Bayān*, vol. 1, pp. 170–173, 181–182 and 209; al-Maqrīzī, *al-Khiṭaṭ*, vol. 1, pp. 327–329; French tr., vol. 3, pp. 251–253 and 255; al-Maqrīzī, *Ittiʿāẓ*, ed. Bunz, pp. 41–43 and 45, ed. al-Shayyāl, vol. 1, pp. 68–69, 71–72 and 74; Ibn Taghrībirdī, *al-Nujūm*, vol. 3, pp. 172–173, 184, 187, 196 and 252; Ḥasan and Sharaf, *ʿUbayd Allāh*, pp. 172–186; Ḥasan, *Ta'rīkh*, pp. 112ff.; Surūr, *Miṣr*, pp. 27ff., and Canard, 'L'impérialisme', pp. 169ff.

31. On Fāṭimid Sicily, see Ibn Ḥawqal, *Ṣūrat al-arḍ*, pp. 118–131, relating the account of his visit to the island in 362/973; al-Jawdharī, *Sīrat*, pp. 70–72, 87–89, 103–104, 114–117, 121, 125, 128–129 and 135–137; tr. Canard, pp. 102–105, 127–130, 156–157, 172–177, 183, 189–190, 195–197 and 207–209; these documents, preserved by Jawdhar who himself had close relations with the Kalbids, are also discussed and analyzed in M. Canard, 'Quelques notes relatives à la Sicile sous les premiers califes Fatimites', in *Studi Medievali in onore di Antonino de Stefano* (Palermo, 1956), pp. 569–576. The classical work here was produced by the great Italian orientalist Michele Amari (1806–1889), under the title of *Storia dei Musulmani di Sicilia*, second ed. by Carlo A. Nallino (Catania, 1933–1939), especially vol. 2, pp. 165–436; this study, first published in 1854–1872, has now been supplemented by Nallino's notes to his revised edition and by several articles in *Centenario della nascita di Michele Amari*. See also Fagnan, *Extraits*, pp. 110–115 and 285–288; Ḥasan and Sharaf, *ʿUbayd Allāh*, pp. 199–204; Ḥasan, *Ta'rīkh*, pp. 97–109 and 250–257; Surūr, *Siyāsat*, pp. 231–236; Aziz Ahmad, *A History of Islamic Sicily* (Edinburgh, 1975), pp. 25–47, and several studies by Professor U. Rizzitano of the University of Palermo, especially his 'Nuove fonti Arabe per la storia dei Musulmani di Sicilia', *RSO*, 32 (1957), pp. 531–555; 'Gli Arabi in Italia', in *L'Occidente e l'Islam nell' alto medio evo* (Spoleto, 1965), vol. 1, pp. 93–114, and 'Kalbids', *EI2*, vol. 4, pp. 496–497.

32. On Fāṭimid–Byzantine relations, especially in the western Mediterranean and during the North African phase of the Fāṭimid Caliphate, see al-Nuʿmān, *Iftitāḥ*, p. 281; also by al-Nuʿmān, *al-Majālis*, pp. 167, 179, 366ff. and 442–444; al-Jawdharī, *Sīrat*, pp. 60–61 and 125; tr. Canard, pp. 88–89 and 189–190; Idrīs, *ʿUyūn*, vol. 5, pp. 139, 151, 170–171, 328 and 337–338, and

Ibn Ḥawqal, *Ṣūrat al-arḍ*, pp. 200–201. See also Amari, *Storia*, vol. 2, pp. 279ff., 288ff., 296–311 and 318–322; M. Canard, 'Arabes et Bulgares au début du Xe siècle', *Byzantion*, 11 (1938), pp. 213–223; and other works by M. Canard, 'L'impérialisme', pp. 185–193; and 'Les Sources Arabes de l'histoire Byzantine aux confins des Xe et XIe siècles', *Revue des Études Byzantines*, 19 (1961), especially pp. 284–292; S. M. Stern, 'An Embassy of the Byzantine Emperor to the Fatimid Caliph al-Muʿizz', *Byzantion*, 20 (1950), pp. 239–258; F. Dachraoui, 'La Crète dans le conflit entre Byzance et al-Muʿizz', *Cahiers de Tunisie*, 7 (1959), pp. 307–318; also his *Califat Fatimide*, pp. 155–157; A. Hamdani, 'Some Considerations on the Fāṭimid Caliphate as a Mediterranean Power', in *Atti del Terzo Congresso di Studi Arabi*, pp. 385–396, and also by Hamdani, 'Byzantine–Fāṭimid Relations before the Battle of Manzikert', *Byzantine Studies*, 1 (1974), pp. 169–179.

33. On anti-Fāṭimid grievances of the North African Mālikī Sunnīs, the most important sources, produced by contemporary Mālikī *faqīhs*, are Abu'l-ʿArab's *Ṭabaqāt ʿulamāʾ Ifrīqiya*, and its continuation under the same title by al-Khushanī, both of which are contained in *Classes des savants de l'Ifrīqīya*, ed. and tr. M. Ben Cheneb (Algiers, 1915–1920). See also al-Muqaddasī, *Aḥsan al-taqāsīm*, pp. 236–238; Abū Bakr al-Mālikī, *Riyāḍ al-nufūs*, ed. Ḥ. Mu'nis (Cairo, 1951–1960), vol. 2, pp. 43–83, also citing the accounts of the disputations between the first Fāṭimid caliph and some of the Mālikī jurists of Qayrawān, as preserved by this distinguished Mālikī jurist-historian of the second half of the fifth/eleventh century; Hady R. Idris, 'Contribution à l'histoire de l'Ifrikiya: Tableau de la vie intellectuelle et administrative à Kairouan sous les Aġlabites et Fatimites', *REI*, 9 (1935), especially pp. 122–129, 144–152, and 10 (1936), pp. 72–88, based on al-Mālikī's *Riyāḍ*; Marçais, *Berbérie Musulmane*, pp. 131–156; H. Monès, 'Le Malékisme et l'échec des Fatimides en Ifrikiya', in *Études d'Orientalisme dédiées à la mémoire de Lévi-Provençal* (Paris, 1962), vol. 1, pp. 197–220, and Dachraoui, *Califat Fatimide*, pp. 397ff.

34. On Abū Yazīd and his revolt, see al-Nuʿmān, *al-Majālis*, pp. 72ff., 113–114, 214, 245, 323ff., 336–337, 429, 447, 492, 542 and 555; al-Jawdharī, *Sīrat*, pp. 44–58 and 69; tr. Canard, pp. 62–66, 68–74, 76–80, 82–84 and 100; Idrīs, *ʿUyūn*, vol. 5, pp. 172–318, based mainly on a contemporary Fāṭimid chronicle that has not survived; Idrīs, *Zahr al-maʿānī*, in Ivanow, *Rise*, text pp. 78–80, translation pp. 272–274; Abū Zakariyyā' al-Warjalānī, *Chronique d'Abou Zakaria*, tr. Émile Masqueray (Algiers–Paris, 1878), especially pp. 226–248, a partial translation of the oldest extant history of the Ibāḍīs of the Maghrib written in the second half of the fifth/eleventh century by a member of the sect; a better French translation of this work may be found in R. Le Tourneau, 'La Chronique d'Abū Zakariyyā' al-Wargalānī (m. 471 H = 1078 J.C.): Traduction annotée', *Revue Africaine*, 104 (1960), pp. 99–176, 322–390, and 105 (1961), pp. 117–176 and 323–374; Ibn al-Athīr, *al-Kāmil*, vol. 8, pp. 62 and 138–145, apparently drawing on the same Fāṭimid chronicle used by Idrīs; Ibn ʿIdhārī, *al-Bayān*, vol. 1, pp. 216–220, and vol. 2, pp. 212–214 and 216; Ibn Khaldūn, *Histoire*, vol. 1, pp. 203–204, vol. 2, pp. 5–6, 530–540,

553ff., and vol. 3, pp. 201–212; al-Maqrīzī, *al-Khiṭaṭ*, vol. 1, p. 35; French tr., vol. 4, p. 14; al-Maqrīzī, *Ittiʿāẓ*, ed. Bunz, pp. 45–54 and 56–57, ed. al-Shayyāl, vol. 1, pp. 75–85 and 88–89. See also H. Fournel, *Les Berbères* (Paris, 1875–1881), vol. 2, pp. 223–276; Marçais, *Berbérie Musulmane*, pp. 147ff.; Gautier, *Le passé*, pp. 363ff.; Zāhid ʿAlī, *Ta'rīkh*, vol. 1, pp. 138–145; R. Le Tourneau, 'La Révolte d'Abū-Yazīd au Xme siècle', *Cahiers de Tunisie*, 1 (1953), pp. 103–125; Dachraoui, *Califat Fatimide*, pp. 165–183 and 188–206; H. Halm, 'Der Mann auf dem Esel: Der Aufstand des Abū Yazīd gegen die Fatimiden nach einem Augenzeugenbericht', *Die Welt des Orients*, 15 (1984), pp. 144–204, and S. M. Stern, 'Abū Yazīd al-Nukkārī', *EI2*, vol. 1, pp. 163–164.

35. According to al-Masʿūdī, *al-Tanbīh*, pp. 391 and 394–395, tr. Carra de Vaux, pp. 496 and 500–501, Abū Saʿīd was killed in Dhu'l-Qaʿda 300/June–July 913. If this date is correct, then his death must have been kept secret for some time, since it was officially reported in Baghdād only towards the end of 301 A.H. Abū Saʿīd's death is placed in 300 A.H. also by ʿAbd al-Raḥīm al-Jawbarī, cited in de Goeje, *Mémoire*, p. 208, a writer and traveller who flourished in the first half of the seventh/thirteenth century. ʿAbd al-Jabbār al-Hamadhānī, *Tathbīt dalā'il al-nubuwwa*, in *Akhbār al-Qarāmiṭa*, p. 151, also mentions the year 300 A.H.

36. Louis Massignon, more than any other modern scholar produced detailed studies on al-Ḥallāj and his thought; see especially his *La Passion d'al-Hosayn Ibn Mansour al-Hallaj*, vol. 1, pp. 71–80, 138–146, 151–159, 252–257, 264, 275–279, 349–352, and vol. 2, pp. 586 and 730–736, where the alleged relations and ideological affinities between al-Ḥallāj and the Qarmaṭīs are discussed in the wider perspective of Shīʿī-gnostic thought; the relevant arguments are not entirely reproduced in the revised edition of this classic work (Paris, 1975), vol. 1, pp. 213ff., 245–249, 342–350, 369–374, 559–560, vol. 3, pp. 205–209, and vol. 4, pp. 8–133, containing a comprehensive bibliography; see also L. Massignon and L. Gardet, 'al-Ḥallādj', *EI2*, vol. 3, pp. 99–104. Most of Massignon's scattered writings on al-Ḥallāj are collected in his *Opera Minora*, vol. 2, pp. 9–342.

37. On the Qarmaṭīs of Baḥrayn, and their relations with the early Fāṭimids, see al-Masʿūdī, *Murūj*, vol. 8, pp. 285–286, 346, 374, and vol. 9, pp. 32 and 76–77; al-Masʿūdī, *al-Tanbīh*, pp. 104–105, 378–387 and 389–396; tr. Carra de Vaux, pp. 149, 483–492 and 494–502; al-Ṣūlī, *Akhbār*, vol. 1, pp. 77, 122–124, 148–149, 152, 163, 184, 187, 195–196, 207, 217–218, 221, 223, 231–232, and vol. 2, pp. 27, 50, 66, 78, 88, 90, 92–93, 99, 103, 108, 110 and 129; ʿArīb, *Ṣilat*, pp. 38, 59, 101, 110–111, 113, 118–120, 123–124, 127, 128, 130, 132–133, 134, 136–137, 139, 159, 162–163, 168 and 184; Ibn Ḥawqal, *Ṣūrat al-arḍ*, pp. 295–296; ʿAbd al-Jabbār al-Hamadhānī, *Tathbīt dalā'il al-nubuwwa*, ed. ʿAbd al-Karīm Uthmān (Beirut, 1966), pp. 129–130, 342, 378–381, 386–399 and 594ff.; al-Baghdādī, *al-Farq*, pp. 270–275, 278–282, 288; tr. Halkin, pp. 118–127, 131–138 and 145–146; al-Daylamī, *Bayān*, pp. 71–96; Miskawayh, *Tajārib*, vol. 1, pp. 33–35, 104–105, 109, 119, 120–122, 139–140, 145–146, 147–148, 165, 167–168, 172–183, 184–186, 201, 263, 284, 330, 367–370, 405,

408, and vol. 2, pp. 24, 55–57, 60–61, 126–127 and 129; Ibn al-Athīr, *al-Kāmil*, vol. 8, pp. 27, 45–47, 49–50, 53–58, 65, 67, 79, 93–94, 99, 107, 113–114, 123, 135 and 161; Ibn Khallikān, *Biographical Dictionary*, vol. 1, pp. 426–430; al-Nuwayrī, *Nihāyat al-arab*, vol. 25, pp. 243–244 and 276ff.; tr. de Sacy, *Exposé*, vol. 1, introduction pp. 216ff.; Ibn al-Dawādārī, *Kanz*, vol. 6, pp. 61–62 and 91–94; al-Maqrīzī, *Ittiʿāẓ*, ed. Bunz, pp. 112–113, 124–130, ed. al-Shayyāl, vol. 1, pp. 164–165 and 180–185; Ibn Khaldūn's account in his *Kitāb al-ʿibar* (Beirut, 1958), vol. 4, pp. 181–195, which differs from other sources in some important respects, does not seem to be reliable; and Ibn Taghrībirdī, *al-Nujūm*, vol. 3, pp. 182, 197, 207–208, 211–213, 215, 217, 220, 224–226, 228, 232, 245, 260, 264, 278–279, 281, 287, 295, 301–302 and 304–305. Of the secondary sources, aside from the pioneering study of de Goeje, *Mémoire*, pp. 69–115 and 129–150, and Madelung's 'Fatimiden und Baḥrainqarmaṭen', pp. 34–54, 59–63, 66–67, 74–85 and 88, which is a thorough survey of the various arguments regarding the Fāṭimid–Qarmaṭī relations and the relevant sources, see H. Bowen, *The Life and Times of ʿAlī Ibn ʿĪsā* (Cambridge, 1928), pp. 50–56, 136–141, 191–195, 205–206, 210–211, 237, 249, 261–263, 266–275, 279–280, 302, 350 and 357–358; Lewis, *Origins*, pp. 80–89; Ivanow, 'Ismailis and Qarmatians', pp. 77–85; Ḥasan and Sharaf, *ʿUbayd Allāh*, pp. 94, 176, 180, 211–232, 277–279 and 295ff.; Ḥasan, *Ta'rīkh*, pp. 385–394; Stern, 'Ismāʿīlīs', pp. 105–107; Stern, 'Early', pp. 75–76; G. T. Scanlon, 'Leadership in the Qarmaṭian Sect', *BIFAO*, 59 (1960), pp. 29–48; M. Canard, *Histoire de la dynastie des H'amdanides de Jazīra et de Syrie* (Paris, 1953), pp. 352–357, and Canard, 'al-Djannābī, Abū Ṭāhir', *EI2*, vol. 2, pp. 452–454.

38. On the Justānids, about whom only fragmentary information is available in the general chronicles and in some of the mediaeval local histories of the Caspian provinces, see Ibn Isfandiyār, *Ta'rīkh*, vol. 1, pp. 235, 243–244, 253–254, 256, 262, 274 and 281; tr. Browne, pp. 169, 178–179, 190–191, 193, 196, 202–203 and 206; Awliyā' Allāh Āmulī, *Ta'rīkh-i Rūyān*, ed. M. Sutūda (Tehran, 1348/1969), pp. 92, 96, 99, 104, 106 and 109; Marʿashī, *Ta'rīkh-i Ṭabaristān*, pp. 133, 136, 139, 141, 145–146 and 150; B. Dorn, ed., *Auszüge aus Muhammedanischen schriftstellern* (St Petersburg, 1858), pp. 26, 52, 450, 474–475 and 498, containing a number of extracts from Arabic and Persian sources. See also R. Vasmer, 'Zur chronologie der Ǧastāniden und Sallāriden', *Islamica*, 3 (1927), pp. 165–186 and 482–485; H. L. Rabino, 'Les Provinces Caspiennes de la Perse, le Guīlān', *Revue du Monde Musulman*, 32 (1915–1916), pp. 387–392; also by Rabino, 'Rulers of Gilan', *JRAS* (1920), pp. 291–293; and his 'Les Dynasties locales du Gīlān et du Daylam', *JA*, 237 (1949), pp. 308–309; Qazvīnī's notes in Juwaynī, *Ta'rīkh*, vol. 3, pp. 432–435; Kasravī, *Shahriyārān*, pp. 21–34 and 111; V. Minorsky, *La domination des Dailamites* (Paris, 1932), pp. 6ff.; Minorsky, 'Daylam', *EI2*, vol. 2, especially pp. 191–192, and W. Madelung, 'Abū Isḥāq al-Ṣābī on the Alids of Ṭabaristān and Gīlān', *Journal of Near Eastern Studies*, 26 (1967), especially pp. 52–57.

39. Ibn Ḥawqal, *Ṣūrat al-arḍ*, pp. 348–349 and 354. See also Kasravī, *Shahriyārān*,

pp. 88–94 and 118–119, and V. Minorsky, 'Caucasica IV', *BSOAS*, 14 (1952), pp. 514–529, containing commentaries on Ibn Ḥawqal's passages regarding the tributaries of Marzubān b. Muḥammad.

40. On the history of the Musāfirids under Marzubān and Wahsūdān, aside from the sources cited previously, see Ibn Ḥawqal, *Ṣūrat al-arḍ*, pp. 331ff.; Miskawayh, *Tajārib*, vol. 2, pp. 31–37, 62–67, 115, 135–136, 148–154, 166–167, 177–180 and 219–220; Ibn al-Athīr, *al-Kāmil*, vol. 8, pp. 125–126, 158–159, 165–167, 172 and 175, based on Miskawayh; Rabino, 'Dynasties locales', pp. 310–313; Kasravī, *Shahriyārān*, pp. 59–63; V. Minorsky, *A History of Sharvān and Darband* (Cambridge, 1958), pp. 27, 60–62, 71, 76, 85 and 112; Stern, 'Early', pp. 70ff.; Madelung, 'Minor Dynasties', pp. 224–225 and 231ff.; G. C. Miles, 'Numismatics', in *Cambridge History of Iran*, vol. 4, p. 373, where the author mentions the existence of more specimens of Wahsūdān's coin dating from 343 A.H., bearing the names of the early Ismāʿīlī Imāms up to Muḥammad b. Ismāʿīl. See also Nāṣir-i Khusraw, *Safar-nāma*, ed. and tr. Schefer, text pp. 4–5, translation pp. 12–16, ed. Dabīr Siyāqī, pp. 6–8, where Nāṣir relates his visit to Shamīrān in 438/1046; Yāqūt, *Muʿjam*, vol. 1, p. 239, and vol. 3, pp. 148–150; tr. Barbier de Meynard, pp. 318–321; M. Sutūda, 'Shamīrān', in *Yād-nāma-yi Nāṣir-i Khusraw* (Mashhad, 1976), pp. 253–262, and M. Kervran, 'Une fortresse d'Azerbaidjan: Samīrān', *REI*, 41 (1973), pp. 71ff.

41. Madelung, 'Ḳarmaṭī', p. 622.

42. On al-Sijistānī and his contributions to Ismāʿīl thought, see al-Hamdānī, 'Some Unknown Ismāʿīlī Authors', pp. 367–368; H. Corbin's introduction to his edition of al-Sijistānī's *Kashf al-maḥjūb* (Tehran–Paris, 1949), pp. 5–25, the *dāʿī*'s only extant work in Persian; Ivanow, *Studies* 2, pp. 87ff.; also his *Ismaili Literature*, pp. 27–30; Sezgin, *Geschichte*, vol. 1, pp. 574–575; Poonawala, *Bio*, pp. 82–89; and his 'Al-Sijistānī and his Kitāb al-Maqālīd', in *Essays on Islamic Civilization*, pp. 274–283; Ghālib, *Aʿlām*, pp. 154–156; several works by Stern, including 'Early', pp. 67–70 and 80–81; 'Arabico–Persica', in *W. B. Henning Memorial Volume* (London, 1970), pp. 415–416; 'Abū Yaʿḳūb al-Sidjzī', *EI2*, vol. 1, p. 160, and see Paul E. Walker, 'Abū Yaʿqūb Sejestānī', *EIR*, vol. 1, pp. 396–398. Professor Walker has undertaken a detailed study of al-Sijistānī in his 'Abū Yaʿqūb al-Sijistānī and the Development of Ismaili Neoplatonism' (Ph.D. thesis, University of Chicago, 1974), and in a number of articles; see also H. Corbin, 'L'Ismaélisme et le symbole de la Croix', *La Table Ronde*, 120 (December, 1957), pp. 122–134, and Y. Marquet, 'La Pensée d'Abū Yaʿqūb as-Sijistānī à travers l'Iṯbāt an-Nubuwwāt et la Tuḥfat al-Mustajībīn', *SI*, 54 (1981), pp. 95–128.

43. See Muḥammad b. Surkh al-Nīshāpūrī, *Commentaire de la qasida Ismaélienne d'Abu'l-Haitham Jorjani*, ed. H. Corbin and M. Muʿīn (Tehran–Paris, 1955), and Corbin's French introduction thereto. Abu'l-Haytham's original *qaṣīda* may also be found in Nāṣir-i Khusraw, *Kitāb-i jāmiʿ al-ḥikmatayn*, ed. H. Corbin and M. Muʿīn (Tehran–Paris, 1953), pp. 19–31, which is another commentary on the *qaṣīda* in question. See also G. Lazard, *Les premiers poètes Persans* (Tehran–Paris, 1964), vol. 1, pp. 24–25, 78–84, and vol. 2, pp. 52–63;

Corbin, *Étude*, pp. 46–52, and also his 'Abu'l-Haytam Gorgānī', *EIR*, vol. 1, pp. 316–317.

44. This mistake probably resulted from misreading a statement in al-Baghdādī, *al-Farq*, p. 267, tr. Halkin, p. 113; see Massignon, 'Bibliographie Qarmaṭe', p. 332; al-Hamdānī, 'Some Unknown Ismāʿīlī Authors', p. 368, and Ivanow, *Guide*, p. 33.

45. Ibn al-Nadīm, *al-Fihrist*, vol. 1, pp. 139 and 189–190; tr. Dodge, vol. 1, pp. 306 and 472–473; tr. Tajaddud, pp. 230 and 354–355. See also Niẓām al-Mulk, *Siyar*, p. 287; tr. Darke, p. 212; Yāqūt al-Ḥamawī, *Irshād al-arīb ilā maʿrifat al-adīb*, ed. D. S. Margoliouth (Leiden–London, 1907–1927), vol. 5, p. 435, and Ghālib, *Aʿlām*, pp. 377–378.

46. Rashīd al-Dīn, *Ismāʿīliyān*, p. 12. This point is also mentioned by Rashīd al-Dīn's contemporary Abu'l-Qāsim ʿAbd Allāh b. ʿAlī Kāshānī (al-Qāshānī), *Zubdat al-tawārīkh; ta'rīkh-i Ismāʿīliyya va Nizāriyya*, ed. M. T. Dānish-pazhūh, in *Revue de la Faculté des Lettres, Université de Tabriz*, Supplément no. 9 (1343/1964), p. 21. It may also be noted that Kāshānī, p. 24, like al-Maqrīzī, places the Imām Ismāʿīl b. Jaʿfar's death in the year 138 A.H.

47. Al-Sijistānī, *al-Iftikhār*, p. 82.

48. On al-Muʿizz and his reign, see al-Nuʿmān, *al-Majālis*, containing many valuable details; al-Jawdharī, *Sīrat*, pp. 87–148; tr. Canard, pp. 127–255; Idrīs, *ʿUyūn*, vol. 6, pp. 9–204; Ibn Ẓāfir, *Akhbār*, pp. 21–30; Ibn Ḥammād, *Histoire*, text pp. 40–48, translation pp. 62–72; Ibn Muyassar, *Akhbār*, ed. Massé, pp. 43–47, ed. Sayyid, pp. 159–168, covering only the years 363–365 A.H.; Ibn al-Athīr, *al-Kāmil*, vol. 8, pp. 164–165, 173–174, 194–195, 204, 211–212, 214 and 217–219; Ibn Khallikān, *Biographical Dictionary*, vol. 2, pp. 47–49, and vol. 3, pp. 377–381; Ibn ʿIdhārī, *al-Bayān*, vol. 1, pp. 221–223; Ibn al-Dawādārī, *Kanz*, vol. 6, pp. 119–173; Ibn Khaldūn, *Histoire*, vol. 2, pp. 541–551; al-Maqrīzī, *al-Khiṭaṭ*, vol. 1, pp. 351–354, 361ff. and 407–408; French tr., vol. 4, pp. 15–21 and 42ff.; al-Maqrīzī, *Ittiʿāẓ*, ed. Bunz, pp. 59–101, 131–143, ed. al-Shayyāl, vol. 1, pp. 93–150 and 186–235, and Ibn Taghrībirdī, *al-Nujūm*, vol. 4, pp. 21ff., 28–42, 54ff., 58–59, 62, 69–79, 102–112 and 128. Of the secondary sources, mention may be made of Ḥasan, *Ta'rīkh*, pp. 93–97 and 122–151; Zāhid ʿAlī, *Ta'rīkh*, vol. 1, pp. 148–188; Surūr, *Miṣr*, pp. 22–24, 34–44 and 47ff.; Mājid, *Ẓuhūr*, pp. 103–117 and 124ff.; Ḥasan I. Ḥasan and Ṭāhā A. Sharaf, *al-Muʿizz li-Dīn Allāh* (2nd ed., Cairo, 1963); Ghālib, *Aʿlām*, pp. 526–541; ʿĀ. Tāmir, *al-Muʿizz li-Dīn Allāh al-Fāṭimī* (Beirut, 1982); Quatremère, 'Vie du khalife Fatimite Möezz-li-din Allah'; O'Leary, *Fatimid Khalifate*, pp. 93–114; Shaban, *Islamic History*, vol. 2, pp. 194ff.; Th. Bianquis, 'La prise du pouvoir par les Fatimides en Égypte (357–363/968–974)', *Annales Islamologiques*, 11 (1972), pp. 49–108; Dachraoui, *Califat Fatimide*, pp. 219–275, and H. A. R. Gibb, 'al-Muʿizz li-Dīn Allāh', *EI*, vol. 3, pp. 706–707.

49. On Jawhar, see al-Nuʿmān, *al-Majālis*, pp. 217, 256 and 546; al-Jawdharī, *Sīrat*, pp. 40, 51, 95, 99, 119, 122 and 135; tr. Canard, pp. 55–56, 74, 142, 148, 179, 184–185 and 206; Idrīs, *ʿUyūn*, vol. 6, pp. 80ff. and 135–170; Ibn Khallikān, *Biographical Dictionary*, vol. 1, pp. 340–347; al-Maqrīzī, *al-Khiṭaṭ*,

vol. 1, pp. 377–379; French tr., vol. 4, pp. 83–87; ʿAlī I. Ḥasan, *Ta'rīkh Jawhar al-Ṣiqillī* (Cairo, 1933); I. Hrbek, 'Die Slawen im Dienste der Fāṭimiden', *Archiv Orientální*, 21 (1953), pp. 543–581; Ghālib, *Aʿlām*, pp. 194–196; Zawahir Noorally, 'Jawhar as-Siqilli', in *Great Ismaili Heroes*, pp. 23–30, and H. Monés, 'Djawhar al-Ṣiḳillī', *EI2*, vol. 2, pp. 494–495.

50. On Zīrī b. Manād, his son Buluggīn, and the Zīrids, see Ibn al-Athīr, *al-Kāmil*, vol. 8, pp. 140, 197–198, 203, 205–206, 220–221, and vol. 9, p. 12; Ibn Khallikān, *Biographical Dictionary*, vol. 1, pp. 267–268 and 550; Ibn ʿIdhārī, *al-Bayān*, vol. 1, pp. 228ff., 239ff., and vol. 2, pp. 242–243 and 293–294; Ibn Khaldūn, *Histoire*, vol. 2, pp. 4ff., 9ff., 43ff., 131, 149, 483–493 (quoting al-Nuwayrī), 532–533, 540, 542, 544, 548, 550, and vol. 3, pp. 211, 218, 233–234, 236, 256ff., 262 and 294; Fournel, *Berbères*, vol. 2, pp. 205–206, 349ff. and 355–363; L. Golvin, *Le Magrib central à l'époque des Zirides* (Paris, 1957); M. Yalaoui, 'Sur une possible régence du prince Fatimide ʿAbdallāh b. Muʿizz en Ifriqiya au IVe/Xe siècle', *Cahiers de Tunisie*, 22 (1974), pp. 7–22; Dachraoui, *Califat Fatimide*, pp. 269ff.; H. R. Idris, *La Berbérie orientale sous les Zīrīdes*, Xe–XIIe siècles (Paris, 1962), 2 vols., the most comprehensive study of the subject; H. R. Idris, 'Buluggīn b. Zīrī', *EI2*, vol. 1, p. 1309, and G. Marçais, 'Zīrids', *EI*, vol. 4, pp. 1229–1230.

51. On ʿAlī b. Ḥamdūn and his sons, see al-Jawdharī, *Sīrat*, pp. 75, 100–102, 123–124, 129–131 and 140–141; tr. Canard, pp. 109–110, 152–154, 187–188, 197–199 and 216–217; Ibn al-Athīr, *al-Kāmil*, vol. 8, pp. 142 and 206; Ibn Khallikān, *Biographical Dictionary*, vol. 1, p. 326; Ibn ʿIdhārī, *al-Bayān*, vol. 2, pp. 242–244, 249, 278 and 280; Ibn Khaldūn, *Histoire*, vol. 2, pp. 8, 11, 130, 151–152, 534, 542, 553–557, and vol. 3, pp. 234–235 and 291; M. Canard, 'Une famille de partisans, puis d'adversaires, des Fatimides en Afrique du Nord', in *Mélanges d'histoire et d'archéologie de l'Occident Musulman*: II, *Hommage à Georges Marçais* (Algiers, 1957), pp. 33–49, where further sources are mentioned, and Dachraoui, *Califat Fatimide*, pp. 238ff.

52. Al-Maqrīzī, *al-Khiṭaṭ*, vol. 2, p. 27; also his *Ittiʿāẓ*, ed. Bunz, pp. 66–67, ed. al-Shayyāl, vol. 1, pp. 102–103, and Ibn Taghrībirdī, *al-Nujūm*, vol. 4, pp. 24, 30 and 72–73.

53. On Shīʿism in pre-Fāṭimid Egypt, see al-Maqrīzī, *al-Khiṭaṭ*, vol. 2, pp. 331ff.; Ḥasan, *Ta'rīkh*, pp. 117–122 and 138ff.; Ḥasan and Sharaf, *al-Muʿizz*, pp. 69–76, and M. Kamil Hussein, 'Shiism in Egypt before the Fatimids', in Islamic Research Association, *Miscellany*, pp. 73–85.

54. Al-Maqrīzī is the foremost authority on the antiquities of Cairo. See his *al-Khiṭaṭ*, vol. 1, pp. 361–364, 377ff., and vol. 2, pp. 273–277; French tr., vol. 4, pp. 42–49 and 81ff.; see also P. Ravaisse, 'Essai sur l'histoire et la topographie du Caire d'après Maqrizi', *Mémoires de la Mission Archéologique Française du Caire*, 1 (1886), pp. 409–480, and 3 (1889), pp. 33–114; P. Casanova, 'Histoire et description de la Citadelle du Caire', *Mémoires de la Mission Archéologique Française du Caire*, 6 (1897), pp. 509–781; K. A. C. Creswell, 'The Foundation of Cairo', *Bulletin of the Faculty of Arts, Fouad I University*, 1 (1933), pp. 258–281, and also Creswell's 'The Founding of Cairo', in *Colloque du Caire*, pp. 125–130.

55. On Ibn Hānī', see Ibn Khallikān, *Biographical Dictionary*, vol. 3, pp. 123–127; A. von Kremer, 'Über den shi'itischen Dichter Abū'l-Ḳāsim Muḥammad ibn Hāni'', *ZDMG*, 24 (1870), pp. 481–494; Canard, 'L'impérialisme', pp. 176–185; Ḥasan, *Ta'rīkh*, pp. 439–443; Ḥasan and Sharaf, *al-Mu'izz*, pp. 225–230; 'Ā. Tāmir, *Ibn Hāni' al-Andalusī Mutanabbī al-Maghrib* (Beirut, 1961); M. Nājī, *Ibn Hāni' al-Andalusī* (Beirut, 1962); Ghālib, *A'lām*, pp. 499–504; M. Yalaoui, *Un poète chiite d'Occident au IVème/Xème siècle: Ibn Hāni' al-Andalusī* (Tunis, 1976); Ivanow, *Ismaili Literature*, p. 37; Poonawala, *Bio*, pp. 47–48, and F. Dachraoui, 'Ibn Hāni' al-Andalusī', *EI2*, vol. 3, pp. 785–786. Ibn Hāni''s *Dīwān*, first lithographed at Būlāq in 1274/1858, has been published several times in Beirut, the latest edition appearing in 1964; its critical edition, however, remains the one prepared by Zāhid 'Alī under the title of *Tabyīn al-ma'ānī fī sharḥ dīwān Ibn Hāni' al-Andalusī al-Maghribī* (Cairo, 1352/1933), originally submitted to the University of Oxford as a doctoral thesis. Several of Ibn Hāni''s poems are translated in R. P. Dewhurst, 'Abu Tammam and Ibn Hani', *JRAS* (1926), pp. 629 and 639–642, and in H. Massé, 'Le Poème d'Ibn Hāni al-Andalusi sur la conquête de l'Égypte (969)', in *Mélanges d'histoire et d'archéologie*, pp. 121–127, and a more complete English translation of his poems appears in *The Diwan of Abu Qasim Muhammad ibn Hani al-Azdi al-Andalusi*, tr. A. Wormhoudt (Oskaloosa, Iowa, 1985).
56. Ibn Hānī', *Dīwān*, ed. Zāhid 'Alī, the *qaṣīdas* starting on pages 42, 143, 183, 205, 335, 352, 365, 390, 429, 503, 540, 560, 593, 612, 649, 657, 728 and 773.
57. Ḥasan, *Ta'rīkh*, pp. 151–156; Muḥammad J. Surūr, *al-Nufūdh al-Fāṭimī fī Jazīrat al-'Arab* (4th ed., Cairo, 1964), pp. 9–30, and also his *Siyāsat*, pp. 19–37.
58. See Ibn al-Athīr, *al-Kāmil*, vol. 8, p. 228.
59. The most complete text of this letter may be found in al-Maqrīzī, *Itti'āẓ*, ed. Bunz, pp. 133–143, omitting the end of the letter; ed. al-Shayyāl, vol. 1, pp. 189–202, reproduced in Ḥasan and Sharaf, *al-Mu'izz*, pp. 301–307; *Akhbār al-Qarāmiṭa*, pp. 367–383, and also in al-Walī, *al-Qarāmiṭa*, pp. 289–300; briefer versions are preserved in Ibn al-Dawādārī, *Kanz*, vol. 6, pp. 149–156, and in al-Nuwayrī, *Nihāyat al-arab*, vol. 25, pp. 307–311; tr. de Sacy, *Exposé*, vol. 1, introduction pp. 227–238. The contemporary Thābit b. Sinān also mentions this letter under the events of the year 363 A.H., see Lewis, *Origins*, pp. 81–82.
60. Madelung, 'Fatimiden', pp. 68–69 and 85–88, and also his 'Imamat', p. 101.
61. On al-A'ṣam and the hostilities between the Qarmaṭīs and the Fāṭimids in the time of al-Mu'izz, in addition to the references cited in connection with the latter's caliphate, see Ibn al-Qalānisī, *Dhayl ta'rīkh Dimashq*, ed. Henry F. Amedroz (Leiden, 1908), pp. 1–11; relevant extracts from Thābit b. Sinān, al-Nuwayrī, and al-Maqrīzī's *al-Muqaffā*, in *Akhbār al-Qaramiṭā*, pp. 57ff., 68, 73–74, 315–321, 393 and 402ff.; al-Nuwayrī, *Nihāyat al-arab*, vol. 25, pp. 304ff.; tr. de Sacy, *Exposé*, vol. 1, introduction pp. 219ff.; Quatremère, 'Vie du khalife Fatimite Möezz' (1837), pp. 76ff. and 175ff.; Defrémery, 'Ismaéliens de la Perse' (1856), pp. 376–380; de Goeje, *Mémoire*, pp. 180–192;

Madelung, 'Fatimiden', pp. 54–58, 63–65 and 73–74; Ḥasan, *Taʾrīkh*, pp. 394ff.; Ḥasan and Sharaf, *al-Muʿizz*, pp. 106–127; M. J. Surūr, *al-Nufūdh al-Fāṭimī fī bilād al-Shām wa'l-ʿIrāq* (3rd ed., Cairo, 1964), pp. 10–38; also his *Siyāsat*, pp. 111–134; Canard, *Histoire*, pp. 632ff. and 677ff., and also by Canard, 'al-Ḥasan al-Aʿṣam', *EI2*, vol. 3, p. 246.

62. For a review of the doctrinal reform of al-Muʿizz, see Madelung, 'Imamat', pp. 86–101.
63. See, for example, al-Nuʿmān's *Asās*, pp. 316–317, 333, 337–338 and 351, and his *Taʾwīl al-daʿāʾim*, ed. Muḥammad Ḥasan al-Aʿẓamī (Cairo, 1967–1972), vol. 1, pp. 235, 269, and vol. 3, pp. 109, 130 and 222–223. See also Madelung, 'Imamat', pp. 84–85.
64. Al-Nuʿmān, *al-Risāla al-mudhhiba*, in *Khams rasāʾil Ismāʿīliyya*, pp. 45ff.
65. Ibid., pp. 70–71.
66. Ibid., pp. 66, 74ff. and 79.
67. Some excerpts of *al-Munājāt* are contained in Guyard, 'Fragments', *Notices et Extraits*, text pp. 224–229, translation pp. 344–358; see also L. Massignon, *Recueil de textes inédits concernant l'histoire de la mystique en pays d'Islam* (Paris, 1929), pp. 215–217.
68. Excerpts from the *Adʿiyat al-ayyām al-ṣabʿa* of al-Muʿizz may be found in Zāhid ʿAlī, *Hamārē*, pp. 90ff., and in Zāhid ʿAlī's *Taʾrīkh*, vol. 2, pp. 254ff.
69. See al-Muʿizz (supposed author), *Taʾwīl al-sharīʿa*, quoted in Zāhid ʿAlī, *Hamārē*, pp. 134ff., and in al-Daylamī, *Bayān*, pp. 43 and 46; see also Idrīs, *Zahr al-maʿānī*, in Ivanow, *Rise*, text pp. 56–69, translation pp. 244–248, and G. Troupeau, 'Un traité christologique attribué au calife Fatimide al-Muʿizz', *Annales Islamologiquès*, 15 (1979), pp. 11–24. On the writings of al-Muʿizz, see Ivanow, *Ismaili Literature*, p. 31; Sezgin, *Geschichte*, vol. 1, p. 574, and Poonawala, *Bio*, pp. 68–70.
70. *Taʾwīl al-sharīʿa*, in Zāhid ʿAlī, *Hamārē*, p. 135.
71. Quotations from these works may be found in Zāhid ʿAlī, *Taʾrīkh*, vol. 2, pp. 257ff., Madelung, 'Imamat', pp. 95ff., and H. Corbin, 'Épiphanie divine et naissance spirituelle dans la gnose Ismaélienne', *EJ*, 23 (1954), pp. 193ff., reprinted in his *Temps cyclique*, pp. 116ff.; English translation, 'Divine Epiphany and Spiritual Birth in Ismailian Gnosis', in *Papers from the Eranos Yearbooks*: Vol. 5, *Man and Transformation* (Princeton, 1964), pp. 113ff., reprinted in Corbin, *Cyclical Time*, pp. 103ff.
72. Quoted in Idrīs, *ʿUyūn*, vol. 5, pp. 206, 274–276, 319–320 and 329–330, reproduced in Stern, *Studies*, pp. 148–152.
73. Al-Jawdharī, *Sīrat*, pp. 126–127; tr. Canard, pp. 193–194.
74. For further details on the life and works of Jaʿfar b. Manṣūr al-Yaman, see Idrīs, *ʿUyūn*, vol. 6, pp. 49ff.; Ibn Mālik al-Yamānī, *Kashf asrār al-Bāṭiniyya*, p. 40; al-Hamdānī, 'Some Unknown Ismāʿīlī Authors', pp. 370–371; Ḥasan, *Taʾrīkh*, pp. 483–488; Ḥasan and Sharaf, *al-Muʿizz*, pp. 268–272; Ghālib, *Aʿlām*, pp. 185–186; Madelung, 'Imamat', pp. 94–95; Stern, *Studies*, pp. 146–147; Ivanow, *Ismaili Literature*, pp. 21–22; Sezgin, *Geschichte*, vol. 1, pp. 578–579; Poonawala, *Bio*, pp. 70–75; H. Halm, 'Zur Datierung des ismāʿīlitischen Buches der Zwischenzeiten und der zehn Konjunktionen (*Kitāb al-fatarāt wal-*

qirānāt al-ʿašra)', *Die Welt des Orients*, 8 (1975), pp. 91–107, and also his 'Djaʿfar b. Manṣūr al-Yaman', *EI2*, Supplement, pp. 236–237.

75. On the Fāṭimid vassal state of Multān, in addition to the sources cited previously, see Ibn Ḥawqal, *Ṣurāt al-arḍ*, pp. 321ff.; al-Baghdādī, *al-Farq*, p. 277; tr. Halkin, p. 130; Ibn al-Athīr, *al-Kāmil*, vol. 9, p. 64; Rashīd al-Dīn, *Jāmiʿ al-tawārīkh, tawārīkh-i Diyālama va āl Būya va āl Sāmān*, ed. Ahmed Ateş (Ankara, 1957), pp. 146–148; M. Nāẓim, *The Life and Times of Sulṭān Maḥmūd of Ghazna* (Cambridge, 1931), pp. 96–99; Andrei E. Bertel's, *Nasir-i Khosrov i ismailizm* (Moscow, 1959), pp. 85ff.; Persian translation, *Nāṣir-i Khusraw va Ismāʿīliyān*, tr. Yaḥyā Āriyanpūr (Tehran, 1346/1967), pp. 91ff.; C. E. Bosworth, *The Ghaznavids* (Edinburgh, 1963), pp. 52–53, 76, 199–200 and 235; M. Habib, *Sultan Mahmud of Ghaznin* (2nd ed., Delhi, 1967), pp. 6–8, 25ff., 34, 71 and 90–91, and A. Hamdani, 'The Fāṭimid-ʿAbbāsid Conflict in India', *IC*, 41 (1967), pp. 185ff.

76. Ibn al-Athīr, *al-Kāmil*, vol. 9, p. 119; Nāẓim, *Maḥmūd of Ghazna*, p. 120, and Hamdani, *Ismāʿīlī Daʿwa*, pp. 6–8.

77. See Mīr Muḥammad Maʿṣūm Nāmī, *Taʾrīkh-i Sind*, ed. U. M. Daudpota (Poona, 1938), pp. 60, 148 and 270–271, and Hamdani, *Ismāʿīlī Daʿwa*, pp. 8ff.

78. On the caliphate of al-ʿAzīz, see Idrīs, *ʿUyūn*, vol. 6, pp. 205–248; al-Anṭākī, *Taʾrīkh*, ed. Cheikho et al., pp. 146–180, ed. Kratchkovsky and Vasiliev, in *Patrologia Orientalis* (1932), pp. 371–450; Miskawayh, *Tajārib*, vol. 2, pp. 401–404; al-Rūdhrāwarī, *Dhayl kitāb tajārib al-umam*, as vol. 3 of *The Eclipse of the ʿAbbasid Caliphate*, pp. 208ff.; Ibn al-Qalānisī, *Dhayl*, pp. 14–44; Ibn Ẓāfir, *Akhbār*, pp. 31–42; Ibn Ḥammād, *Histoire*, text pp. 48–49, translation pp. 73–75; Ibn Muyassar, *Akhbār*, ed. Massé, pp. 47–52, ed. Sayyid, pp. 168–176, covering the years 381–382 and 385–386 A.H.; Ibn al-Athīr, *al-Kāmil*, vol. 8, pp. 230, 231–232, 236, and vol. 9, pp. 2–3, 6, 13, 14–15, 18, 19–20, 23–24, 27, 29, 31 and 40; Ibn Khallikān, *Biographical Dictionary*, vol. 3, pp. 525–530; Ibn ʿIdhārī, *al-Bayān*, vol. 1, pp. 229–232, 238 and 247; Ibn al-Dawādārī, *Kanz*, vol. 6, pp. 174–180 and 186–239; al-Maqrīzī, *al-Khiṭaṭ*, vol. 1, pp. 378–379, 408, and vol. 2, pp. 284–285 and 341; French tr., vol. 4, pp. 85–87; al-Maqrīzī, *Ittiʿāẓ*, ed. al-Shayyāl, vol. 1, pp. 236–299; Ibn Taghrībirdī, *al-Nujūm*, vol. 4, pp. 112–176. See also Ḥasan, *Taʾrīkh*, pp. 156–163; Zāhid ʿAlī, *Taʾrīkh*, vol. 1, pp. 189–205; Ghālib, *Aʿlām*, pp. 577–582; Surūr, *Bilād al-Shām*, pp. 38ff.; also by Surūr, *Siyāsat*, pp. 134ff., 142ff. and 240–241; Mājid, *Ẓuhūr*, pp. 134ff.; ʿAlī Ḥusnī al-Kharbūṭlī, *al-ʿAzīz bi'llāh al-Fāṭimī* (Cairo, 1968); ʿĀrif Tāmir, *al-Khalīfa al-Fāṭimī al-khāmis, al-ʿAzīz bi'llāh* (Beirut, 1982); O'Leary, *Fatimid Khalifate*, pp. 115–122; Poonawala, *Bio*, p. 82; Canard, *Histoire*, pp. 677–690, 696–705 and 853–858, and also his 'al-ʿAzīz bi'llāh', *EI2*, vol. 1, pp. 823–825. A full account of the Fāṭimid conquest and domination of Syria is contained in Thierry Bianquis, *Damas et la Syrie sous la domination Fatimide, 359–468/969–1076* (Damascus, 1986), vol. 1.

79. Al-Jawdharī, *Sīrat*, pp. 62ff., 69, 74, 98, 105–106 and 115; tr. Canard, pp. 91ff., 99–100, 107, 147, 159–160 and 174.

80. See al-Jawdharī, *Sīrat*, pp. 99–100 and 120; tr. Canard, pp. 149–150 and 181–

182. On the other hand, according to Ibn Ḥammād, *Histoire*, text p. 47, al-Muʿizz had at one time designated Tamīm as his heir apparent, but had later revoked this nomination. Ibn Ḥammād is apparently the only source relating this nomination.

81. Al-Jawdharī, *Sīrat*, pp. 139–140; tr. Canard, pp. 213–216.
82. On Tamīm, see Ibn Khallikān, *Biographical Dictionary*, vol. 1, pp. 279–281; Ḥasan and Sharaf, *al-Muʿizz*, pp. 230–232; Ḥusayn, *Fī adab*, pp. 170–173 and 247–252; Ghālib, *Aʿlām*, pp. 173–179; Muḥammad Ḥasan al-Aʿẓamī, *ʿAbqariyyat al-Fāṭimiyyīn* (Beirut, 1960), pp. 133–209 and 235–240, containing also some of his poems; Ḥ. Sharaf, *Tamīm ibn al-Muʿizz* (Cairo, 1967); ʿĀrif Tāmir, *Tamīm al-Fāṭimī* (Beirut, 1982); Ivanow, *Ismaili Literature*, p. 38; Poonawala, *Bio*, pp. 76–78, and J. Walker, 'Tamīm b. al-Muʿizz', *EI*, vol. 4, p. 646. Tamīm's *Dīwān*, which is devoted mainly to the praise of al-Muʿizz and al-ʿAzīz, was first edited by M. Ḥ. al-Aʿẓamī et al. (Cairo, 1957); it was reprinted, with some additional introductory materials, by Muḥammad Ḥasan al-Aʿẓamī (Beirut, 1970).
83. See Canard, *Histoire*, pp. 541–572, and also his 'Abū Taghlib', *EI2*, Supplement, pp. 36–37.
84. On Abu'l-Fawāris al-Ḥasan b. Muḥammad al-Mīhadhī, one of the Fāṭimid *dāʿīs* sent to Rayy in the time of al-ʿAzīz, and the ideas preached by him, see Ivanow, *Studies* 2, pp. 123–140; and also Ivanow's *Ismaili Literature*, pp. 38–39; Sezgin, *Geschichte*, vol. 1, p. 578, and Poonawala, *Bio*, pp. 80–81.
85. On Ibn Killis, see Ibn al-Ṣayrafī, *al-Ishāra*, in *BIFAO* (1925), pp. 90–94 (19–23); Ibn Khallikān, *Biographical Dictionary*, vol. 4, pp. 359–368; al-Maqrīzī, *al-Khiṭaṭ*, vol. 2, pp. 5–8 and 341; Ḥasan, *Taʾrīkh*, pp. 270–272, 298–300 and 426–427; Zāhid ʿAlī, *Taʾrīkh*, vol. 1, pp. 197–198, and vol. 2, pp. 111–112 and 130–131; Ḥusayn, *Fī adab*, pp. 54–59 and 174–176; Ghālib, *Aʿlām*, pp. 607–610; Muḥammad Ḥ. al-Manāwī, *al-Wizāra wa'l-wuzarāʾ fi'l-ʿaṣr al-Fāṭimī* (Cairo, 1970), pp. 35ff., 52, 74, 85–86, 94–96, 103–104, 126, 133–134, 143–144, 172–173, 193–195 and 241; Walter J. Fischel, *Jews in the Economic and Political Life of Mediaeval Islam* (London, 1937), pp. 45–68; B. Lewis, 'Palṭiel: A Note', *BSOAS*, 30 (1967), pp. 179–181; Ivanow, *Ismaili Literature*, p. 38; Sezgin, *Geschichte*, vol. 1, p. 579; Poonawala, *Bio*, pp. 78–79, and M. Canard, 'Ibn Killis', *EI2*, vol. 3, pp. 840–841.
86. Ibn al-Ṣayrafī, *al-Ishāra*, in *BIFAO* (1925), pp. 87–90 (23–26), and al-Manāwī, *al-Wizāra*, pp. 241–244.
87. Al-Maqrīzī, *al-Khiṭaṭ*, vol. 1, pp. 388–389 and 430–431; French tr., vol. 4, pp. 111ff.
88. On al-Ḥākim's reign, see Idrīs, *ʿUyūn*, vol. 6, pp. 248–304; al-Anṭākī, *Taʾrīkh*, ed. Cheikho et al., pp. 180–234, ed. Kratchkovsky and Vasiliev, in *Patrologia Orientalis* (1932), pp. 450–520, the latter edition ends with the events of the year 404 A.H.; al-Rūdhrāwarī, *Dhayl*, pp. 221–239; Ibn al-Ṣayrafī, *al-Ishāra*, in *BIFAO* (1925), pp. 80–87 (26–33); Ibn al-Qalānisī, *Dhayl*, pp. 44–71 and 79; Ibn Ẓāfir, *Akhbār*, pp. 43–62; Ibn Ḥammād, *Histoire*, text pp. 49–58, translation pp. 76–86; Ibn Muyassar, *Akhbār*, ed. Massé, pp. 52–56, ed. Sayyid, pp. 176–183, covering the years 386–387

A.H.; Ibn al-Athīr, *al-Kāmil*, vol. 9, pp. 40–42, 44, 52–54, 68–70, 72–73, 75, 76–77, 79, 81, 86–89, 102 and 108–109; Ibn Khallikān, *Biographical Dictionary*, vol. 3, pp. 449–454; Ibn ʿIdhārī, *al-Bayān*, vol. 1, pp. 247ff., 257ff. and 267–270; al-Nuwayrī, in de Sacy, *Exposé*, vol. 1, introduction pp. 430–437; Ibn al-Dawādārī, *Kanz*, vol. 6, pp. 256–312; al-Maqrīzī, *al-Khiṭaṭ*, vol. 2, pp. 14–15, 31, 36–37, 277ff., 282–283 and 285–289, the last section also in de Sacy, *Chrestomathie*, vol. 1, pp. 74–104, French translation and notes in vol. 2, pp. 67–114 and 410–462; al-Maqrīzī, *Ittiʿāẓ*, ed. Aḥmad, vol. 2, pp. 3–123, and Ibn Taghrībirdī, *al-Nujūm*, vol. 4, pp. 176–247. Besides the detailed biography of al-Ḥākim contained in de Sacy, *Exposé*, vol. 1, introduction pp. 278–429, which is still valuable, mention may be made of the following more recent monographs on this Fāṭimid caliph-imām: Muḥammad ʿAbd Allāh ʿInān, *al-Ḥākim bi-Amr Allāh wa asrār al-daʿwa al-Fāṭimiyya* (2nd ed., Cairo, 1959); ʿAbd al-Munʿim Mājid, *al-Ḥākim bi-Amr Allāh* (Cairo, 1959); ʿĀrif Tāmir, *al-Ḥākim bi-Amr Allāh* (Beirut, 1982); Sadik A. Assaad, *Reign of al-Hakim bi Amr Allah*, and Josef van Ess, *Chiliastische Erwartungen und die Versuchung der Göttlichkeit: Der Kalif al-Ḥākim (386–411H.)* (Heidelberg, 1977). See also Ḥasan, *Taʾrīkh*, pp. 164–168, 205–209, 219–225, 228ff., 234ff., 272ff., 310ff., 378–379, 428, 443–445 and 538–539; Zāhid ʿAlī, *Taʾrīkh*, vol. 1, pp. 206–261; Surūr, *Miṣr*, pp. 59–71, 122ff. and 164ff.; Surūr, *Bilād al-Shām*, pp. 44ff. and 84–85; and also his *Siyāsat*, pp. 139ff., 147–148 and 242–243; Mājid, *Ẓuhūr*, pp. 162ff., 244ff. and 339ff.; al-Manāwī, *al-Wizāra*, pp. 245–251; Ghālib, *Aʿlām*, pp. 548–554; O'Leary, *Fatimid Khalifate*, pp. 123–188; P. J. Vatikiotis, 'Al-Hakim bi-Amrillah: The God-King Idea Realised', *IC*, 29 (1955), pp. 1–8, revised in Vatikiotis, *Fatimid Theory of State*, pp. 149–159; Shaban, *Islamic History*, vol. 2, pp. 206–210; Y. Rāġib, 'Un épisode obscur d'histoire Fatimide', *SI*, 48 (1978), pp. 125–132; Th. Bianquis, 'al-H'ākim bi Amr Allāh', in *Les Africains*, sous les direction de Ch. A. Julien et al. (Paris, 1978), vol. 11, pp. 103–133; Canard, *Histoire*, pp. 706–713, and also his 'al-Ḥākim bi-Amr Allāh', *EI2*, vol. 3, pp. 76–82.

89. On Barjawān, see Ibn al-Ṣayrafī, *al-Ishāra*, in *BIFAO* (1925), pp. 85–86 (27–28); Ibn Khallikān, *Biographical Dictionary*, vol. 1, p. 253; al-Maqrīzī, *al-Khiṭaṭ*, vol. 2, pp. 3–4; de Sacy, *Exposé*, vol. 1, introduction pp. 284ff.; al-Manāwī, *al-Wizāra*, p. 245, and B. Lewis, 'Bardjawān', *EI2*, vol. 1, pp. 1041–1042.
90. See H. R. Idris, 'Ḥammādids', *EI2*, vol. 3, pp. 137–139.
91. See M. Canard, 'La destruction de l'Église de la Résurrection par le calife Ḥākim et l'histoire de la descente du feu sacré', *Byzantion*, 35 (1965), pp. 16–43.
92. Al-Maqrīzī, *al-Khiṭaṭ*, vol. 1, pp. 391, 458–460, and vol. 2, pp. 342 and 363; French tr., vol. 4, pp. 118–121; É. Quatremère, *Mémoires géographiques et historiques sur l'Égypte* (Paris, 1811), vol. 1, pp. 474–484, and D. Sourdel, 'Dār al-Ḥikma', *EI2*, vol. 2, pp. 126–127.
93. Ibn Taghrībirdī, *al-Nujūm*, vol. 4, pp. 222–223.
94. Muḥammad b. Aḥmad al-Fāsī, *al-ʿIqd al-thāmin fī taʾrīkh al-balad al-amīn*, ed. A. Fuʾād Sayyid (Cairo, 1384/1965), vol. 4, pp. 69–79.

95. See M. Canard, 'Djarrāḥids', *EI2*, vol. 2, pp. 482–485.
96. See Idris, *Berbérie orientale*, vol. 1, pp. 143–149.
97. Abu'l-Fawāris Aḥmad b. Yaʿqūb, *al-Risāla fi'l-imāma*, ed. and tr. Sami N. Makarem (New York, 1977); see also Ghālib, *Aʿlām*, pp. 126–127; Ivanow, *Ismaili Literature*, p. 39; Sezgin, *Geschichte*, vol. 1, p. 579, and Poonawala, *Bio*, p. 94.
98. On al-Kirmānī's life and works, see Idrīs, *ʿUyūn*, vol. 6, pp. 283–288 and 306; al-Hamdānī, 'Some Unknown Ismāʿīlī Authors', pp. 372–375; also his *al-Ṣulayḥiyyūn*, pp. 258–261; the introductory comments of M. Kāmil Ḥusayn and M. Muṣṭafā Ḥilmī in their edition of al-Kirmānī's *Rāḥat al-ʿaql* (Cairo, 1953); M. Ghālib's introduction to his edition of *Rāḥat al-ʿaql* (Beirut, 1967), but hereafter our references are to the Cairo edition of this work; Ḥasan, *Ta'rīkh*, pp. 488–492; Zāhid ʿAlī, *Ta'rīkh*, vol. 2, pp. 114–115; Ghālib, *Aʿlām*, pp. 99–102; S. I. Assaad, 'Sayyidna Hamid ad-Din al-Kirmani', in *Great Ismaili Heroes*, pp. 39–40; Ivanow, *Guide*, pp. 43–46; Ivanow, *Ismaili Literature*, pp. 44–45; Sezgin, *Geschichte*, vol. 1, pp. 580–582; Poonawala, *Bio*, pp. 94–102, and J. T. P. de Bruijn, 'al-Kirmānī', *EI2*, vol. 5, pp. 166–167.
99. See P. Kraus, 'Hebräische und syrische Zitate in ismāʿīlitischen Schriften', *Der Islam*, 19 (1931), pp. 243–263, explaining that al-Kirmānī was familiar with the Hebrew text of the Old Testament, the Syriac version of the New Testament, and the post-Biblical Jewish writings; see also A. Baumstark, 'Zu den Schriftzitaten al-Kirmānīs', *Der Islam*, 20 (1932), pp. 308–313, which is a note on the previous article, and Stern, *Studies*, pp. 84–95.
100. Gardīzī, *Zayn al-akhbār*, p. 181; al-Jurbādhaqānī, *Ta'rīkh-i Yamīnī*, pp. 369–373, containing the fullest details of a Fāṭimid embassy sent to Sultan Maḥmūd; Ibn Taghrībirdī, *al-Nujūm*, vol. 4, p. 232, and Bertel's *Nasir-i Khosrov*, pp. 94–104; tr. Āriyanpūr, pp. 98–108.
101. See Sami N. Makarem, 'Al-Ḥākim bi-Amrillāh's Appointment of his Successors', *al-Abhath*, 23 (1970), pp. 319–325.
102. The classical treatment of the early history and doctrines of the Druzes is found in Silvestre de Sacy's *Exposé de la religion des Druzes*, which also describes the Druze literature then available in European libraries; a number of excerpts from the sacred scriptures of the Druzes are published and translated into French in de Sacy's *Chrestomathie Arabe*, vol. 1, pp. 260–309, and vol. 2, pp. 334–403. Further Druze writings are to be found in Guys, *Théogonie des Druses*, and in other early European studies. A list of the Druze epistles, which are usually copied in the same traditional sequence and collected in the same number of volumes, may be found in Ivanow, *Ismaili Literature*, pp. 112–125. Amongst the more recent studies, mention may be made of Philip K. Hitti, *The Origins of the Druze People and Religion* (New York, 1928), containing numerous inaccuracies; N. Bourn, *Les Druzes* (Paris, 1930); M. Kāmil Ḥusayn, *Ṭā'ifat al-Durūz* (Cairo, 1962); A. A. Najjār, *Madhhab al-Durūz wa'l-tawḥīd* (Cairo, 1965); Sami N. Makarem, *The Druze Faith* (New York, 1974), and Nejla M. Abu-Izzeddin, *The Druzes: A New Study of their History, Faith and Society* (Leiden, 1984), the best modern

survey written by a Druze scholar. See also H. Z. Hirschberg, 'The Druzes', in *Religion in the Middle East*, vol. 2, pp. 330–348 and 685; D. R. W. Bryer, 'The Origins of the Druze Religion', *Der Islam*, 52 (1975), pp. 47–84, 239–262, and 53 (1976), pp. 5–27; P. Filippani-Ronconi, *Ismaeliti ed 'Assassini'* (Milan, 1973), pp. 91–105; Madelung, 'Imamat', pp. 114–127; also his 'Ḥamza b. ʿAlī', *EI2*, vol. 3, p. 154; M. G. S. Hodgson, 'Al-Darazī and Ḥamza in the Origin of the Druze Religion', *JAOS*, 82 (1962), pp. 5–20; Hodgson, 'al-Darazī', *EI2*, vol. 2, pp. 136–137; and also his 'Durūz', *EI2*, vol. 2, pp. 631–634; Ign. Kratschkowsky, 'al-Muḳtanā', *EI*, vol. 3, pp. 720–721, and H. Halm, 'Der Treuhänder Gottes', *Der Islam*, 63 (1986), pp. 11–72.

103. Ḥamīd al-Dīn al-Kirmānī, *al-Maṣābīḥ fī ithbāt al-imāma*, ed. M. Ghālib (Beirut, 1969), some excerpts in Kraus, 'Hebräische', pp. 245–247.

104. Al-Kirmānī, *Mabāsim al-bishārāt bi'l-Imām al-Ḥākim bi-Amr Allāh*, ed. M. Kāmil Ḥusayn in his *Ṭā'ifat al-Durūz*, pp. 55–74, also in al-Kirmānī, *Majmūʿat rasā'il*, pp. 113–133, excerpts in Kraus, 'Hebräische', pp. 253–254.

105. Al-Kirmānī, *al-Risāla al-wāʿiẓa*, ed. M. Kāmil Ḥusayn, in *Bulletin of the Faculty of Arts, Fouad I University*, 14, part 1 (1952), pp. 1–29, also in al-Kirmānī, *Majmūʿat rasā'il*, pp. 134–147.

106. Al-Kirmānī, *al-Risāla al-durriyya*, ed. M. Kāmil Ḥusayn (Cairo, 1952), edited together with his *al-Risāla al-naẓm*, containing further discussions of the issues raised in *al-Durriyya*; both of these short works are included in al-Kirmānī, *Majmūʿat rasā'il*, pp. 19–34.

107. See de Sacy, *Exposé*, vol. 2, pp. 335–348, and Abu-Izzeddin, *Druzes*, pp. 73, 108 and 236.

108. See, for instance, the epistle called *Maʿrifat al-imām*, in the second volume of the Druze canon. In the personal manuscript copy of the author, this epistle is only three pages long.

109. On al-Ẓāhir's caliphate, see Idrīs, *ʿUyūn*, vol. 6, pp. 304–322; al-Musabbiḥī, *Akhbār*, ed. Sayyid and Bianquis, vol. 1, pp. 3–112, ed. Millward, pp. 21–62 and 171–248, covering parts of the years 414–415 A.H., and in both editions, some gaps are filled by relevant extracts from al-Maqrīzī's *Ittiʿāẓ*; al-Anṭākī, ed. Cheikho et al., pp. 234ff.; Ibn al-Ṣayrafī, *al-Ishāra*, in *BIFAO* (1925), pp. 77–80 (33–36); Ibn al-Qalānisī, *Dhayl*, pp. 71–83; Ibn Ẓāfir, *Akhbār*, pp. 63–66; Ibn Ḥammād, *Histoire*, text p. 58, translation pp. 87–88; Ibn al-Athīr, *al-Kāmil*, vol. 9, pp. 110, 111, 113, 114–115, 117, 121, 123, 128, 136 and 154; Ibn Khallikān, *Biographical Dictionary*, vol. 2, pp. 340–341; Ibn ʿIdhārī, *al-Bayān*, vol. 1, pp. 270ff.; Ibn al-Dawādārī, *Kanz*, vol. 6, pp. 313–341; al-Maqrīzī, *al-Khiṭaṭ*, vol. 1, pp. 354–355; French tr., vol. 4, pp. 22–26; al-Maqrīzī, *Ittiʿāẓ*, ed. Aḥmad, vol. 2, pp. 124–183, and Ibn Taghrībirdī, *al-Nujūm*, vol. 4, pp. 247–283. Of the secondary sources, see Ḥasan, *Ta'rīkh*, pp. 168–169, 225, 237 and 445–448; Zāhid ʿAlī, *Ta'rīkh*, vol. 1, pp. 262–272; Surūr, *Bilād al-Shām*, pp. 47ff., 55 and 89; also his *Siyāsat*, pp. 141–142, 148–149, 177 and 243ff.; Mājid, *Ẓuhūr*, pp. 145ff., 209, 220, 257–258 and 282–283; al-Manāwī, *al-Wizāra*, pp. 251–253; Ghālib, *Aʿlām*, pp. 414–416; O'Leary, *Fatimid Khalifate*, pp. 189–192, and J. Walker, 'Sitt al-Mulk', *EI*, vol. 4, pp. 461–462.

110. On the reign of al-Mustanṣir, see Idrīs, *ʿUyūn*, vol. 6, pp. 322–359 and the beginning of vol. 7, still in manuscript form; Ibn al-Ṣayrafī, *al-Ishāra*, in *BIFAO* (1925), pp. 59–77 (36–54) and (1926), pp. 66–67 (68–69); Ibn al-Qalānisī, *Dhayl*, pp. 83–128; Ibn Ẓāfir, *Akhbār*, pp. 67–81; Ibn Muyassar, *Akhbār*, ed. Massé, pp. 1–34, ed. Sayyid, pp. 3–59; Ibn Ḥammād, *Histoire*, text p. 59, translation pp. 89–90; Ibn al-Athīr, *al-Kāmil*, vol. 9, pp. 154–155, 158–159, 160, 170, 173, 177, 186–187, 189–190, 193, 200, 221–222, and vol. 10, pp. 4, 28–30, 35–36, 38, 43, 49, 60, 70 and 77; Ibn Khallikān, *Biographical Dictionary*, vol. 3, pp. 381–384; Ibn ʿIdhārī, *al-Bayān*, vol. 1, pp. 275–301; Ibn al-Dawādārī, *Kanz*, vol. 6, pp. 342–442; al-Maqrīzī, *al-Khiṭaṭ*, vol. 1, pp. 355–356; French tr., vol. 4, pp. 26–29; al-Maqrīzī, *Ittiʿāẓ*, ed. Aḥmad, vol. 2, pp. 184–334, and Ibn Taghrībirdī, *al-Nujūm*, vol. 5, pp. 1–141. Amongst the modern sources, see Ḥasan, *Ta'rīkh*, pp. 169–171, 210–211, 239ff., 252ff. and 259–261; Zāhid ʿAlī, *Ta'rīkh*, vol. 1, pp. 273–323; Surūr, *Miṣr*, pp. 72ff., 87ff., 125ff., 133–139, 144–151 and 169ff.; Surūr, *Bilād al-Shām*, pp. 56ff. and 124ff.; Surūr, *Jazīrat al-ʿArab*, pp. 19ff., 54ff. and 75ff.; and also his *Siyāsat*, pp. 79ff., 149ff., 207ff., 228–230 and 245–246; ʿAbd al-Munʿim Mājid, *al-Imām al-Mustanṣir bi'llāh al-Fāṭimī* (Cairo, 1961), also his *Ẓuhūr*, pp. 147–154, 162ff., 176–192, 196–205, 212ff., 220–229, 258–273, 283ff. and 365ff.; al-Manāwī, *al-Wizāra*, pp. 253–271; Ghālib, *Aʿlām*, pp. 520–525; O'Leary, *Fatimid Khalifate*, pp. 193–210; Fischel, *Jews*, pp. 68–89; G. Wiet, 'Yāzūrī', *EI*, vol. 4, pp. 1172–1173, and H. A. R. Gibb and P. Kraus, 'al-Mustanṣir Bi'llāh', *EI*, vol. 3, pp. 768–771.

111. See the detailed account of al-Maqrīzī in his *al-Khiṭaṭ*, vol. 1, pp. 335–337; French tr., vol. 3, pp. 275–283, and in his *Ighāthat al-umma bi-kashf al-ghumma*, ed. Muḥammad M. Ziyāda and Jamāl al-Dīn al-Shayyāl (Cairo, 1940), pp. 18–26; French translation, *Le Traité des famines de Maqrīzī*, tr. G. Wiet (Leiden, 1962), pp. 18–27.

112. Al-Maqrīzī, *al-Khiṭaṭ*, vol. 1, pp. 408–409, and also his *Ittiʿāẓ*, ed. Aḥmad, vol. 2, pp. 294–295.

113. On Badr al-Jamālī, see Ibn al-Ṣayrafī, *al-Ishāra*, in *BIFAO* (1925), pp. 57–58 (55–56); Ibn al-Qalānisī, *Dhayl*, pp. 84 and 91ff.; Ibn al-Athīr, *al-Kāmil*, vol. 10, pp. 81–82; al-Maqrīzī, *al-Khiṭaṭ*, vol. 1, pp. 381–382; French tr., vol. 4, pp. 92–95; al-Maqrīzī, *Ittiʿāẓ*, ed. Aḥmad, vol. 2, pp. 268, 272 and 311ff.; Mājid, *al-Mustanṣir*, pp. 179ff.; also his *Ẓuhūr*, pp. 392ff., and C. H. Becker, 'Badr al-Djamālī', *EI2*, vol. 1, pp. 869–870.

114. On al-Basāsīrī and his pro-Fāṭimid activities, see al-Mu'ayyad fi'l-Dīn al-Shīrāzī, *Sīrat al-Mu'ayyad fi'l-Dīn dāʿī al-duʿāt*, ed. M. Kāmil Ḥusayn (Cairo, 1949), especially pp. 94–184; partial English translation in Abbas H. al-Hamdani, 'The Sīra of al-Mu'ayyad fi'd-Dīn ash-Shīrāzī' (Ph.D. thesis, University of London, 1950), pp. 58–105; Ẓahīr al-Dīn Nīshāpūrī, *Saljūq-nāma* (Tehran, 1332/1953), pp. 19–20; Muḥammad b. ʿAlī al-Rāwandī, *Rāḥat al-ṣudūr*, ed. M. Iqbāl (London, 1921), pp. 107–110; al-Fatḥ b. ʿAlī al-Bundārī, *Zubdat al-nuṣra*, ed. M. Th. Houtsma, pp. 12–18; Ibn al-Athīr, *al-Kāmil*, vol. 9, pp. 208, 211ff., 217ff. and 222–229; Yāqūt, *Muʿjam*, vol. 1, pp.

608–609, and vol. 3, p. 595; Ibn Khallikān, *Biographical Dictionary*, vol. 1, pp. 172–174; Rashīd al-Dīn, *Jāmiʿ al-tawārīk; āl Saljūq*, ed. A. Ateş (Ankara, 1960), pp. 22–24 and 180; al-Maqrīzī, *Ittiʿāẓ*, ed. Aḥmad, vol. 2, pp. 232–234 and 252–258, and Ibn Taghrībirdī, *al-Nujūm*, vol. 5, pp. 5–12. See also Ḥasan, *Taʾrīkh*, pp. 232–234; Surūr, *Bilād al-Shām*, pp. 91–123; also his *Siyāsat*, pp. 179–206; Ghālib, *Aʿlām*, pp. 140–142; Mājid, *Ẓuhūr*, pp. 169ff., and M. Canard, 'al-Basāsīrī', *EI2*, vol. 1, pp. 1073–1075.

115. The *dāʿī* Idrīs has detailed accounts of the Ṣulayḥids, and the revitalization of the Ismāʿīlī *daʿwa* in Yaman in al-Mustanṣir's time, in his *ʿUyūn al-akhbār*, vol. 7, and *Nuzhat al-afkār*, vol. 1, which still remain unpublished. The works of Idrīs have been utilized extensively by Ḥusayn F. al-Hamdānī in his 'The Doctrines and History of the Ismāʿīlī Daʿwat in Yemen' (Ph.D. thesis, University of London, 1931), especially chapter 2, and in *al-Ṣulayḥiyyūn*, chapters 4 and 5, which is still the best modern study on the subject. However, the earliest and most detailed account has been produced by ʿUmāra b. ʿAlī al-Ḥakamī (d. 569/1174), the famous Yamanī historian and poet, in his *Taʾrīkh al-Yaman*, published in Kay, *Yaman*, text pp. 14–48, translation pp. 19–64; more recently, this work has been edited by Ḥasan Sulaymān Maḥmūd (Cairo, 1957) and also by Muḥammad b. ʿAlī al-Akwaʿ (Cairo, 1967), but our references are to Kay's edition. Information on the early Ṣulayḥids is to be found also in Ibn Khallikān, *Biographical Dictionary*, vol. 2, pp. 344–349, and in Ibn Khaldūn, *Taʾrīkh al-Yaman*, an extract from the *ʿIbar*, in Kay, *Yaman*, text pp. 107–111, translation pp. 145–151, amongst other sources. See also Ḥ. F. al-Hamdānī, 'The Life and Times of Queen Saiyidah Arwā the Ṣulaiḥid of the Yemen', *Journal of the Royal Central Asian Society*, 18 (1931), pp. 505–517; A. al-Hamdani, 'Sīra', pp. 137–164; Ḥasan, *Taʾrīkh*, pp. 239–248; Surūr, *Jazīrat al-ʿArab*, pp. 75–106; also his *Siyāsat*, pp. 82–107; Mājid, *Ẓuhūr*, pp. 196ff.; Ghālib, *Aʿlām*, pp. 118–125, 143–154, 402–407 and 439–441; Poonawala, *Bio*, pp. 103 and 110–111, and F. Krenkow, 'Ṣulaiḥī', *EI*, vol. 4, pp. 515–517.

116. For these names, derived from Idrīs, see H. al-Hamdānī, 'Doctrines', pp. 30ff. For other lists, see Ibn Mālik al-Yamānī, *Kashf asrār al-Bāṭiniyya*, pp. 39–42, written by a Yamanī contemporary of the founder of the Ṣulayḥid dynasty, and al-Janadī's later work *Akhbār al-Qarāmiṭa*, in Kay, *Yaman*, text p. 152, translation pp. 211–212.

117. The date 429 A.H. is mentioned by Idrīs, ʿUmāra and Ibn Khallikān; but Ibn Mālik, *Kashf*, p. 43, and some other sources, give the later date 439 A.H. for the accession of the Ṣulayḥids.

118. On Lamak's Egyptian embassy, and its purposes, see A. al-Hamdani, 'Sīra', pp. 155–160, and also his 'The Dāʿī Ḥātim Ibn Ibrāhīm al-Ḥāmidī (d. 596 H./1199 A.D.) and his Book Tuḥfat al-Qulūb', *Oriens*, 23–24 (1970–1971), pp. 260–263.

119. See the already-cited *al-Sijillāt al-Mustanṣiriyya*, ed. Mājid, and al-Hamdānī, 'Letters of al-Mustanṣir', pp. 307ff., describing the contents of his letters. Some additional letters of al-Mustanṣir, not included in Mājid's collection,

are preserved in Idrīs, *ʿUyūn*, vol. 7, of which five have been reproduced in al-Hamdānī, *al-Ṣulayḥiyyūn*, pp. 302–307 and 319–320. See also Ivanow, *Ismaili Literature*, p. 49, and Poonawala, *Bio*, pp. 126–127.

120. Until recently, there was controversy on the date of this event. According to Idrīs, *ʿUyūn*, vol. 7, and Ibn al-Athīr, *al-Kāmil*, vol. 10, p. 19, it occurred in 459 A.H., a date endorsed also by ʿUmāra. On the other hand, Ibn Khallikān placed the event in 473 A.H. In the light of al-Mustanṣir's *Sijillāt*, pp. 137–140 and 196–200, issued in 460–461 A.H. and in which the Fāṭimid caliph expresses his sorrow about ʿAlī's assassination, now there remains no doubt that the correct year was 459 A.H.; see also al-Hamdānī, 'Letters of al-Mustanṣir', pp. 307, 319 and 323.

121. Abu'l-Faḍl Muḥammad b. Ḥusayn Bayhaqī, *Ta'rīkh-i Bayhaqī*, ed. ʿAlī Akbar Fayyāḍ (2nd ed., Mashhad, 1356/1977), pp. 71–72 and 220–236; English translation in H. M. Elliot and J. Dowson, *The History of India as told by its own Historians* (London, 1867–1877), vol. 2, pp. 88–100; Gardīzī, *Zayn al-akhbār*, pp. 196–197; Bosworth, *Ghaznavids*, pp. 182–184, and B. Spuler, 'Ḥasanak', *EI2*, vol. 3, pp. 255–256.

122. See the anonymous Arabic treatise entitled *al-Tarjama al-ẓāhira li-firqat Bohrat al-bāhira*, ed. H. M. Fakhr, in *JBBRAS*, NS, 16 (1940), pp. 87–98; English translation and additional materials in K. M. Jhaveri, 'A Legendary History of the Bohoras', *JBBRAS*, NS, 9 (1933), pp. 37–52; ʿAlī Muḥammad Khān, *Mirat-i Ahmadi*, ed. and tr. Syed Nawab Ali et al. (Baroda, 1928–1965), Supplement, English translation, pp. 107–110. See also R. E. Enthoven, *The Tribes and Castes of Bombay* (Bombay, 1920–1922), vol. 1, pp. 197–200; A. al-Hamdani, 'Sīra', pp. 166–177, and Satish C. Misra, *Muslim Communities in Gujarat* (Bombay, 1964), pp. 9ff.

123. Al-Mustanṣir, *al-Sijillāt*, pp. 167–169 and 203–206, and al-Hamdani, 'Letters of al-Mustanṣir', pp. 321 and 324.

124. See Ḥasan, *Ta'rīkh*, pp. 608ff.; Rāshid al-Barrāwī, *Ḥālat Miṣr al-iqtiṣādiyya fī ʿahd al-Fāṭimiyyīn* (Cairo, 1948); B. Lewis, 'The Fatimids and the Route to India', *Revue de la Faculté des Sciences Économiques de l'Université d'Istanbul*, 11 (1949–1950), pp. 50–54; S. D. Goitein, 'From the Mediterranean to India: Documents on the Trade to India, South Arabia and East Africa from the Eleventh and Twelfth Centuries', *Speculum*, 29 (1954), pp. 181–197; also see his *Studies in Islamic History and Institutions*, pp. 329–350, and G. T. Scanlon, 'A Note on Fāṭimid–Saljūq Trade', in *Islamic Civilisation, 950–1150*, ed. D. S. Richards (Oxford, 1973), pp. 265–274.

125. On these events, see Ibn al-Athīr, *al-Kāmil*, vol. 9, pp. 180 and 195–197; Ibn Khallikān, *Biographical Dictionary*, vol. 3, pp. 386–388; Ibn ʿIdhārī, *al-Bayān*, vol. 1, pp. 277–279 and 288ff.; Ibn Khaldūn, *Histoire*, vol. 1, pp. 29–46, and vol. 2, pp. 29ff.; al-Maqrīzī, *Ittiʿāẓ*, ed. Aḥmad, vol. 2, pp. 214ff., and Ibn Taghrībirdī, *al-Nujūm*, vol. 5, pp. 50–51. See also R. Le Tourneau, 'Nouvelles orientations des Berbères d'Afrique du Nord (950–1150)', in *Islamic Civilisation*, pp. 135ff., H. R. Idris, 'Sur le retour des Zīrīdes à l'obédience Fāṭimide', *AIEO*, 11 (1953), pp. 25–39; also his *Berbérie orientale*, pp. 172–203, where the various dates mentioned by the chroniclers for the

Zīrid renouncement of their Fāṭimid allegiance are also considered, and his 'Hilāl', *EI2*, vol. 3, pp. 385–387.

126. See Amari, *Storia*, vol. 3, pp. 52–133 and 372ff., M. Canard, 'Une lettre du calife Fāṭimite al-Ḥāfiẓ (524–544/1130–1149) à Roger II', in *Atti del convegno internazionale di studi Ruggeriani* (Palermo, 1955), vol. 1, pp. 125–146, and Aziz Ahmad, *History of Islamic Sicily*, pp. 48–62.

127. These points can be gathered from Ibn Sīnā's autobiography, called *Sīrat al-Shaykh al-Ra'īs*, which was completed by one of his disciples Abū ʿUbayd al-Juzjānī; see the Arabic text and English translation of this work entitled *The Life of Ibn Sina*, ed. and tr. William E. Gohlman (Albany, N.Y., 1974), pp. 17–20. Professor Saʿīd Nafīsī (1897–1966) also prepared an edition together with a Persian translation of this biography, *Sargudhasht-i Ibn Sīnā* (Tehran, 1331/1952); while an earlier English translation may be found in A. J. Arberry, *Avicenna on Theology* (London, 1951), pp. 4–5 and 9. See also S. Nafīsī, *Pūr Sīnā* (Tehran, 1333/1954), pp. 2ff., 63, 101, 107–108, 152, 205–214 and 218; W. Ivanow, 'Abū ʿAlī Sīnā va Ismāʿīliyān-i makhfī', in *Jashn-nāma-yi Ibn Sīnā* (Tehran, 1334/1955), vol. 2, pp. 450–454; H. Corbin, *Avicenna and the Visionary Recital*, tr. W. R. Trask (New York, 1960), pp. 243–257 and 314–318, and also his *Histoire*, pp. 238ff.

128. Ibn al-Athīr, *al-Kāmil*, vol. 9. pp. 180–181, and vol. 10, pp. 58–59 and 84; al-Maqrīzī, *Ittiʿāẓ*, ed. Aḥmad, vol. 2, pp. 191–192, and Barthold, *Turkestan*, pp. 251, 304–305 and 316–318.

129. The principal sources on the life and activities of al-Mu'ayyad are his already-cited autobiography, *Sīrat al-Mu'ayyad*, and his *Dīwān*, ed. M. Kāmil Ḥusayn (Cairo, 1949); with much information in Ḥusayn's introductions to both works. ʿĀrif Tāmir has more recently prepared another edition of al-Mu'ayyad's autobiography under the title of *Mudhakkirāt dāʿī duʿāt al-dawla al-Fāṭimiyya al-Mu'ayyad fi'l-Dīn* (Beirut, 1983). The *dāʿī* Idrīs devotes large sections to al-Mu'ayyad in his *ʿUyūn*, vol. 6, pp. 329–359, and at the beginning of vol. 7. Briefer though valuable references may also be found in Ibn al-Balkhī, *The Fārs-nāma*, ed. G. Le Strange and R. A. Nicholson (London, 1921), p. 119, a local history of Fārs written around 498/1105, and in Ibn al-Ṣayrafī, *al-Ishāra*, in *BIFAO* (1925), pp. 61, 65 and 69 (44, 48 and 52). In modern times, Ḥusayn al-Hamdānī was the first person to call the attention of researchers to the important role of this *dāʿī* in the events of the Fāṭimid state; see especially his 'Doctrines and History', pp. 97ff.; 'Some Unknown Ismāʿīlī Authors', pp. 375–377; 'The History of the Ismāʿīlī Daʿwat and its Literature during the last phase of the Fāṭimid Empire', *JRAS* (1932), pp. 129–135; *al-Ṣulayḥiyyūn*, pp. 175–179 and 261–265, and 'al-Mu'aiyad fi'l-Dīn', *EI*, vol. 3, p. 615. See also Ḥasan, *Ta'rīkh*, pp. 492–500; Zāhid ʿAlī, *Ta'rīkh*, vol. 1, pp. 116–118; Ḥusayn, *Fī adab*, pp. 59–65; Ḥusayn V. Ḥakīm Ilāhī, 'Hibat Allāh Shīrāzī', *Dānish*, 1 (1949–1950), pp. 501–508, 594–595, 635–641, and 2 (1950), pp. 22–23; Ghālib, *Aʿlām*, pp. 596–604; J. Muscati and A. M. Moulvi, *Life and Lectures of the Grand Missionary al-Muayyad fid-Din al-Shirazi* (Karachi, 1950), pp. 3–77, a somewhat popular account; A. al-Hamdani draws extensively on al-Mu'ayyad's autobiography

in his dissertation, 'Sīra', especially pp. 19–135, and he has now provided a good summary exposition in his 'The Fatimid Daʿi al-Mu'ayyad: His Life and Work', in *Great Ismaili Heroes*, pp. 41–47. Al-Mu'ayyad's writings are listed in Ivanow, *Ismaili Literature*, pp. 45–47, and Poonawala, *Bio*, pp. 103–109.

130. Al-Mu'ayyad, *Dīwān*, pp. 256–258, and Ibn al-Athīr, *al-Kāmil*, vol. 9, p. 199.

131. This victory is commemorated in a *qaṣīda* by al-Mu'ayyad; see his *Dīwān*, p. 281.

132. Muṣṭafā Ghālib had started to prepare a complete edition of *al-Majālis al-Mu'ayyadiyya* (Beirut, 1974–), of which only the first and third volumes had appeared by 1984 when this Ismāʿīlī scholar had passed away. A separate edition of the first volume was undertaken by Ḥātim Ḥamīd al-Dīn (Bombay, 1395/1975); but hereafter our references are to Ghālib's edition. The first volume of these *Majālis*, as abridged in two volumes by Ḥātim b. Ibrāhīm al-Ḥāmidī, has been edited by Muḥammad ʿAbd al-Qādir ʿAbd al-Nāṣir (Cairo, 1975). An English summary of some of al-Mu'ayyad's lectures may be found in Muscati and Moulvi, *Life and Lectures*, pp. 78–183.

133. This correspondence, included in the 13th *Majlis* of the 6th volume, is reproduced in Yāqūt, *Muʿjam al-udabā'* (Cairo, 1936–1938), vol. 3, pp. 176–213, and also in his *Irshād*, vol. 1, pp. 194–214; it is edited, translated and analyzed in D. S. Margoliouth, 'Abu'l-ʿAlā al-Maʿarrī's Correspondence on Vegetarianism', *JRAS* (1902), pp. 289–332. See also R. A. Nicholson, *Studies in Islamic Poetry* (Cambridge, 1921), pp. 134–136 and 141–142.

134. See P. Kraus, 'Beiträge zur islamischen Ketzergeschichte: Das Kitāb az-Zumurrud des Ibn ar-Rāwandī', *RSO*, 14 (1933–1934), pp. 93–129 and 335–379, where the relevant lectures, 17th through 22nd of the 5th volume, are reproduced on pp. 96–109.

135. This spurious autobiography was used by Luṭf ʿAlī Beg Ādhar (d. 1195/1781) in his *Ātashkada* (Bombay, 1299/1881–1882), pp. 202–208; in more recent times, only one reprint edition of this work, based on the one lithographed in Calcutta in 1277/1860, has appeared (Tehran, 1337/1958), pp. 202–208. An abridgement of this autobiography was included in the introduction to the first lithographic edition of Nāṣir's *Dīwān* (Tabrīz, 1280/1863); it also appeared in a subsequent undated edition of his *Dīwān* lithographed in Bombay, pp. 2–14. Copies of this work, entitled *Sargud-hasht-i Nāṣir-i Khusraw*, are still preserved by the Central Asian Ismāʿīlīs; see Berthels and Baqoev, *Alphabetic Catalogue*, pp. 64–65.

136. After several lithographic editions, the first critical edition of Nāṣir-i Khusraw's *Dīwān* was prepared by the late Persian judge and scholar Sayyid Naṣr Allāh Taqavī, assisted by ʿAlī Akbar Dihkhudā and Mujtabā Mīnuvī (Tehran, 1304–1307/1925–1928), containing a valuable biographical introduction by the Persian scholar-politician Sayyid Ḥasan Taqizadeh (1878–1970). More recently, an improved edition of the *Dīwān*, based on the oldest known manuscript copy dated 736/1335, was prepared by M. Mīnuvī and M. Muḥaqqiq (Tehran, 1353/1974); but the death of Professor Mīnuvī

(1903–1977) prevented the publication of a second volume which was planned to be devoted to Nāṣir's life and work. Some of Nāṣir's odes have been translated into English in a volume entitled *Forty Poems from the Divan*, tr. Peter L. Wilson and G. R. Aavani (Tehran, 1977). In the case of Nāṣir's *Safar-nāma*, besides the edition prepared by Schefer which provided the basis for several later editions produced in India and Persia, and that of Dabīr Siyāqī, mention may also be made of M. Ghanīzāda's edition (Berlin, 1341/1922). Aside from Schefer's French translation and Thackston's English translation, the *Safar-nāma* has been translated into Russian, tr. A. E. Bertel's (Leningrad, 1933); Urdu, tr. M. Tharvat Allāh (Lucknow, 1937); Arabic, tr. Y. al-Khashshāb (Cairo, 1945; 2nd ed., Beirut, 1970), and Turkish, tr. A. Tarzi (Istanbul, 1950). In order to understand Nāṣir-i Khusraw's ideas, it is also essential to study his prose writings. These include the small corpus preserved by the Ismāʿīlīs of Central Asia, notably his *Wajh-i dīn*, ed. M. Ghanīzāda and M. Qazvīnī (Berlin, 1343/1924), with a better edition by Gholam Reza Aavani (Tehran, 1977), and his *Six Chapters, or Shish faṣl*, also called *Rawshanāʾī-nāma*, ed. and tr. W. Ivanow (Leiden, 1949); as well as other works, found in Istanbul libraries and elsewhere, such as his *Khwān al-ikhwān*, *Jāmiʿ al-ḥikmatayn*, and *Zād al-musāfirīn*, ed. M. Badhl al-Raḥmān (Berlin, 1341/1923).

137. See, for instance, Nāṣir-i Khusraw's *Gushāʾish va rahāʾish*, ed. S. Nafīsī (Leiden, 1950), pp. 82, 121 and 123; Italian translation, *Il libro dello scioglimento e della liberazione*, tr. P. Filippani-Ronconi (Naples, 1959), pp. 68, 99 and 100, where the scribe clearly admits his censorship of certain passages in the original text. On the other hand, those works preserved by the Ismāʿīlīs seem to have escaped such interferences.

138. On Nāṣir-i Khusraw's life, thought and works, aside from his own writings, see Dawlatshāh b. ʿAlāʾ al-Dawla, *Tadhkirat al-shuʿarāʾ*, ed. E. G. Browne (London–Leiden, 1901), pp. 61–64; partial English translation, *Memoirs of the Poets*, tr. P. B. Vachha (Bombay, 1909), pp. 29–33, amongst other mediaeval biographical works on Persian poets; H. Ethé, 'Neupersische Litteratur', in *Grundriss der iranischen philologie*, ed. W. Geiger and E. Kuhn (Strassburg, 1895–1904), vol. 2, pp. 278–282; Edward G. Browne, 'Nasir-i-Khusraw, Poet, Traveller, and Propagandist', *JRAS* (1905), especially pp. 313–352; Browne, *A Literary History of Persia, from Firdawsi to Saʿdi*, pp. 218–246; J. Rypka, *History of Iranian Literature*, ed. K. Jahn (Dordrecht, 1968), pp. 185–189; Z. Ṣafā, *Ta'rīkh-i adabiyyāt dar Īrān* (4th ed., Tehran, 1342– /1963–), vol. 2, pp. 165–166, 443–456 and 893–898; and a number of studies by Mahdī Muḥaqqiq, including his *Taḥlīl-i ashʿār-i Nāṣir-i Khusraw* (3rd ed., Tehran, 1359/1980), and articles reprinted in his *Bīst guftār* (Tehran, 1976), pp. 279–300 and 359–364. After the initial efforts of Éthe, Browne, and Taqizadeh, a number of modern scholars have attempted to shed light on aspects of Nāṣir's life and role in the Ismāʿīlī movement; see especially Y. el-Khachab, *Nāṣir-é Khosraw, son voyage, sa pensée religieuse, sa philosophie et sa poésie* (Cairo, 1940); W. Ivanow, *Nasir-i Khusraw and Ismailism* (Bombay, 1948); also, Ivanow, *Problems in Nasir-i Khusraw's Biography* (Bombay, 1956);

Corbin, *Étude*, pp. 25–39, 46–48 and 128–144; Corbin, 'Nāṣir-i Khusrau and Iranian Ismā'īlism', in *Cambridge History of Iran*, vol. 4, pp. 520–542; Bertel's *Nasir-i Khosrov*, especially pp. 148–264; tr. Āriyanpūr, pp. 149–256; Filippani-Ronconi, *Ismaeliti*, pp. 121–127; and a number of shorter studies by Bertel's, Dabīr Siyāqī, and others, in *Yād-nāma-yi Nāṣir-i Khusraw*, produced on the occasion of Nāṣir's millenary. See also Charles A. Storey, *Persian Literature: A Bio-bibliographical Survey* (London, 1927–), vol. 1, part 2, pp. 1138–1141; Ghālib, *Aʿlām*, pp. 562–572; Ivanow, *Guide*, pp. 89–96; Ivanow, *Ismaili Literature*, pp. 159–163; Poonawala, *Bio*, pp. 111–125 and 430–436, and E. Berthels, 'Nāṣir-i Khusraw', *EI*, vol. 3, pp. 869–870.

139. *Dīwān*, ed. Taqavī, p. 173; ed. Mīnuvī, p. 507.
140. *Safar-nāma*, ed. Schefer, text pp. 1–2, translation pp. 3–4; ed. Ghanīzāda, p. 3; ed. Dabīr Siyāqī, p. 2.
141. *Dīwān*, ed. Taqavī, pp. 172–177; ed. Mīnuvī, pp. 505–515; translated and analyzed in Ivanow, *Nasir-i Khusraw*, pp. 17–35, and also his *Problems*, pp. 21–40.
142. *Safar-nāma*, ed. Schefer, text pp. 42–56, translation pp. 124–160; ed. Ghanīzāda, pp. 59–81; ed. Dabīr Siyāqī, pp. 74–100.
143. See three works by Nāṣir-i Khusraw: *Zād al-musāfirīn*, p. 397; *Jāmiʿ al-ḥikmatayn*, pp. 15 and 16–17, and *Dīwān*, ed. Taqavī, pp. 309, 313, 321, 402, 404, 413, 420, 439, 451, 472 and 478; ed. Mīnuvī, pp. 8, 10, 17, 51, 56, 86, 92, 366, 416, 459, 490 and elsewhere. See, however, Ivanow, *Nasir-i Khusraw*, pp. 43–45, and also his *Problems*, pp. 48–49, where it is argued that Nāṣir may only have aspired to that position in the *daʿwa* organization.
144. Abu'l-Maʿālī, *Bayān al-adyān*, pp. 39–40. The passages in question are also contained in the partial edition of this work in Charles Schefer, *Chrestomathie Persane* (Paris, 1883–1885), vol. 1, p. 161. For Nāṣir's own references to his visit to Māzandarān, see his *Dīwān*, ed. Taqavī, pp. 413 and 506; ed. Mīnuvī, pp. 56 and 516.
145. Nāṣir-i Khusraw, *Zād al-musāfirīn*, pp. 3 and 402, and also his *Dīwān*, ed. Taqavī, pp. 110, 217, 430 and 448; ed. Mīnuvī, pp. 162, 234, 287 and 436; tr. Wilson and Aavani, pp. 73 and 113.
146. Nāṣir refers to these unhappy events in many of his odes; see his *Dīwān*, ed. Taqavī, especially pp. 5, 190–191, 205, 272–273, 287, 289, 294, 331, 387, 429, 465, 467, 469 and 489; ed. Mīnuvī, pp. 11, 138–139, 153, 156–157, 209, 303, 310, 343, 351, 400–401, 419, 435, 446 and 539; tr. Wilson and Aavani, pp. 62, 97 and 113.
147. See *Zād al-musāfirīn*, p. 280.
148. *Dīwān*, ed. Taqavī, p. 281; ed. Mīnuvī, p. 195; tr. Wilson and Aavani, p. 115, where *pānzdah*, or fifteen, is erroneously translated as fifty.
149. See *Jāmiʿ al-ḥikmatayn*, pp. 15, 17, 314 and 316, and ʿA. Ḥabībī, 'ʿAlī b. Asad', *EIR*, vol. 1, p. 848.
150. *Dīwān*, ed. Taqavī, pp. 8, 36, 106, 144, 203, 253–254, 271, 275–276, 281–282, 285–286, 290, 305, 326, 329–330, 354, 392, 416, 429, 441, 492 and 497; ed. Mīnuvī, pp. 17, 60, 96, 108, 113, 116, 135, 144–145, 151, 170–171, 195–196, 228, 326, 348, 368, 372, 417–418, 433, 435, 469–470 and 487; tr. Wilson and

Aavani, pp. 97, 100–101, 106, 113 and 115. See also Nāṣir-i Khusraw, *Wajh-i dīn*, ed. Ghanīzāda, p. 210; ed. Aavani, pp. 242–243.

151. *Dīwān*, ed. Taqavī, p. 98; ed. Mīnuvī, p. 61.

152. In some Nizārī works, seen by Ivanow, the date of Nāṣir's death is put as late as 498/1104; see Ivanow, *Problems*, pp. 15–16, and also his *Ismaili Literature*, p. 159.

153. See Ivanow, *Problems*, p. 43; Bertel's, *Nasir-i Khosrov*, p. 190; tr. Āriyanpūr, p. 187, and Khalīl Allāh Khalīlī, 'Mazār-i Nāṣir-i Khusraw', *Yaghmā*, 20, no. 9 (1346/1967), pp. 472–476, a detailed description of the site by the late Afghan diplomat-poet.

154. See Madelung, 'Imamat', pp. 127–132, where the different variants of this doctrine are also discussed. See also Aḥmad b. Ibrāhīm al-Nīsābūrī, *Ithbāt al-imāma*, ed. M. Ghālib (Beirut, 1984), written by a renowned Fāṭimid *dāʿī* who flourished during the reigns of al-ʿAzīz and al-Ḥākim.

155. Al-Kirmānī develops his interpretation of the doctrine of the imāmate in his *Mabāsim*, ed. Ḥusayn, pp. 56–59, 61, 63–64 and 66, and in his *al-Risāla al-wāʿiẓa*, ed. Ḥusayn, pp. 11–14 and 21ff.; both appearing also in al-Kirmānī, *Majmūʿat rasāʾil*, pp. 114–117, 119, 121–123, 124, 134–136 and 142ff., and in a major portion of the second *maqāla* in his *al-Maṣābīḥ fī ithbāt al-imāma*; see also al-Kirmānī's *Rāḥat al-ʿaql*, pp. 127, 145, 159–160, 167–168, 261, 379ff., 390ff. and 424–430.

156. Al-Mu'ayyad, *al-Majālis*, vol. 1, p. 363.

157. Al-Ṣūrī, *al-Qaṣīda al-Ṣūriyya*, ed. ʿĀrif Tāmir (Damascus, 1955), especially pp. 41–71. On this *dāʿī*, see Ghālib, *Aʿlām*, pp. 282–283; Ivanow, *Ismaili Literature*, p. 171, and Poonawala, *Bio*, p. 110.

158. Al-Ṣūrī, *al-Qaṣīda*, p. 68.

159. Ibid., pp. 67ff.

160. Ismāʿīlī tradition ascribes this already-cited work to Badr al-Jamālī, though in some copies of the *Fihrist* of al-Majdūʿ, such as the one underlying Munzavī's edition, pp. 136–137, it is instead attributed to al-Mu'ayyad al-Shīrāzī. M. Kāmil Ḥusayn, the learned editor of the published text of *al-Majālis al-Mustanṣiriyya*, has, in his introductory comments, ascribed it to an anonymous *dāʿī*. However, it has now been demonstrated by S. M. Stern in his 'Cairo as the Centre of the Ismāʿīlī Movement', in *Colloque du Caire*, pp. 439–440, that the author of these lectures was Abu'l-Qāsim ʿAbd al-Ḥākim b. Wahb al-Mālījī, chief *qāḍī* in Cairo during 450–452 A.H., in al-Mustanṣir's caliphate. See also Vatikiotis, *Fatimid Theory of State*, pp. 201–203; Ivanow, *Ismaili Literature*, pp. 46–47 and 49, and Poonawala, *Bio*, pp. 319–320.

161. Al-Mālījī, *al-Majālis al-Mustanṣiriyya*, p. 30.

162. Ibid., pp. 30–31, 32, 36–37, 64 and 117. The author is aware of the fact that al-Mustanṣir was, in his own words, the nineteenth imām after the Prophet. Nevertheless, he also seems to have started a different enumeration of the imāms, starting with the establishment of the Fāṭimid Caliphate and, consequently, ranking al-Mustanṣir as the eighth imām and the eighth amongst the *khulafāʾ*, which in his terminology apparently referred to the Fāṭimid caliph-imāms.

163. *Al-Majālis al-Mustanṣiriyya*, especially pp. 43–47.
164. Nāṣir-i Khusraw, *Wajh-i dīn*, ed. Ghanīzāda, pp. 9, 12, 33, 42, 110–112, 127, 128, 146, 151, 182, 203 and 245; ed. Aavani, 13, 16, 43, 54, 127–129, 148, 150, 169, 175, 212 and 335.
165. *Wajh-i dīn*, ed. Ghanīzāda, pp. 76, 80, 94, 109, 122, 130, 132, 138, 154, 161–163, 164, 173, 194, 196–198 and 231; ed. Aavani, pp. 94, 98, 111, 126–127, 141, 152, 154, 160, 177, 186–188, 189, 202, 225, 227–228 and 265.
166. *Wajh-i dīn*, ed. Ghanīzāda, p. 212; ed. Aavani, pp. 244–245.
167. *Wajh-i dīn*, ed. Ghanīzāda, pp. 86–88, 136, 138, 163, 212 and 223; ed. Aavani, pp. 104–105, 158, 161, 187–188, 244–245 and 256–257.
168. *Wajh-i dīn*, ed. Ghanīzāda, pp. 46–51 and 147; ed. Aavani, pp. 60–65 and 169–170; see also Nāṣir's *Jāmiʿ al-ḥikmatayn*, pp. 111–112.
169. *Wajh-i dīn*, ed. Ghanīzāda, pp. 109, 135 and 293; ed. Aavani, pp. 126–127, 157 and 331, and *Jāmiʿ al-ḥikmatayn*, p. 163.
170. *Wajh-i dīn*, ed. Ghanīzāda, p. 215; ed. Aavani, p. 248.
171. *Khalqān* is, however, taken by Madelung, 'Imamat', p. 131, to be a corruption of *khulafāʾ* or vicegerents of the Qā'im. But elsewhere, *Wajh-i dīn*, ed. Ghanīzāda, pp. 131 and 154, ed. Aavani, pp. 153 and 177, Nāṣir himself explicitly speaks of the Qā'im's *khalīfa*.
172. See *Wajh-i dīn*, ed. Ghanīzāda, pp. 51, 152–154, 166, 171, 209, 212 and 241; ed. Aavani, pp. 65, 176–177, 192, 200, 242, 245 and 276. See also the following works of Nāṣir-i Khusraw: *Six Chapters*, text pp. 29, 38 and 39–44, translation pp. 66, 79 and 80–87; *Gushāʾish*, p. 92; tr. Filippani-Ronconi, p. 74; *Khwān al-ikhwān*, ed. al-Khashshāb, pp. 245ff.; ed. Qavīm, pp. 281ff.; *Zād al-musāfirīn*, pp. 476–484, and *Jāmiʿ al-ḥikmatayn*, pp. 121–122 and 163–165.
173. Madelung, 'Imamat', p. 132.
174. Ibn al-Athīr, *al-Kāmil*, vol. 9, p. 205; Ibn Muyassar, *Akhbār*, ed. Massé, p. 6, ed. Sayyid, p. 13; al-Maqrīzī, *Ittiʿāẓ*, ed. Aḥmad, vol. 2, p. 223; Ibn Taghrībirdī, *al-Nujūm*, vol. 5, p. 53. See also H. Laoust, 'Les Agitations religieuses à Baghdād aux IVe et Ve siècles de l'hégire', in *Islamic Civilisation*, pp. 175ff.
175. Selections from al-Ghazālī's *al-Mustaẓhirī*, together with an analysis of the cited passages, were first published by I. Goldziher in his *Streitschrift des Ġazālī gegen die Bāṭinijja-Sekte*, text pp. 1–81, analysis pp. 36–112; but the complete edition of this text, in ten chapters, entitled *Faḍāʾiḥ al-Bāṭiniyya*, has been prepared by ʿAbd al-Raḥmān Badawī (Cairo, 1964). See also al-Ghazālī, *al-Munqidh min al-ḍalāl*, ed. J. Ṣalībā and K. ʿAyād (11th ed., Beirut, 1983), pp. 89, 117–129 and 154ff.; ed. and tr. F. Jabre (Beirut, 1959), text pp. 15, 28–34 and 46ff., French translation pp. 67, 85–94 and 108ff., and W. Montgomery Watt, *The Faith and Practice of al-Ghazālī* (London, 1953), pp. 26, 43–54 and 71ff., containing the translation of al-Ghazālī's spiritual autobiography, *al-Munqidh min al-ḍalāl*, under the title of *Deliverance from Error*; F. Jabre, *La notion de certitude selon Ghazali* (Paris, 1958), pp. 294–326, 335ff. and 348–368, and M. Bouyges, *Essai de chronologie des œuvres de al-Ghazali*, ed. M. Allard (Beirut, 1959), pp. 30–32; W. M. Watt, *Muslim Intellectual: A Study of al-Ghazali* (Edinburgh, 1963), pp. 73–86 and 174–175;

Corbin, *Histoire*, pp. 251–261; Hodgson, *Venture of Islam*, vol. 2, pp. 183–188; ʿAbd al-Ḥusayn Zarrīnkūb, *Farār az madrasa: Dar bāra-yi Abū Ḥāmid Ghazālī* (2nd ed., Tehran, 1356/1977), pp. 44–45, 53–54, 65–66, 72–73, 76–80 and 150–152; G. Makdisi, 'The Sunnī Revival', in *Islamic Civilisation*, pp. 155–168, and F. Daftary, 'Ghazālī va Ismāʿīliyya', *Maʿārif*, 1 (March, 1985), pp. 179–198.

176. See Bouyges, *Oeuvres de al-Ghazali*, pp. 32–33, 45–46, 56–57, 85–86, 88 and 113. Al-Ghazālī's short anti-Ismāʿīlī tract *Qawāṣim al-Bāṭiniyya* was edited and translated into Turkish by Ahmed Ateş in *Ilāhiyāt Fakültesi Dergisi, Ankara University*, 1–2 (1954), pp. 23–54.

177. ʿAlī b. Muḥammad b. al-Walīd, *Dāmigh al-bāṭil*, ed. M. Ghālib (Beirut, 1982), 2 vols.; see also H. Corbin, 'The Ismāʿīlī Response to the Polemic of Ghazālī, tr. J. Morris', in *Ismāʿīlī Contributions*, pp. 69–98; Ivanow, *Ismaili Literature*, pp. 69–70, and Poonawala, *Bio*, p. 159.

178. Nāṣir-i Khusraw, *Safar-nāma*, ed. Schefer, text pp. 81ff., translation pp. 225ff.; ed. Ghanīzāda, pp. 122ff.; ed. Dabīr Siyāqī, pp. 147ff. See also de Goeje, *Mémoire*, pp. 155ff., and Lewis, *Origins*, pp. 99–100.

179. See M. J. de Goeje, 'La Fin de l'empire des Carmathes du Bahraïn', pp. 5–30, and Madelung, 'Ḳarmaṭī', p. 664.

180. Al-Mustanṣir, *al-Sijillāt*, p. 179, and al-Hamdānī, 'Letters of al-Mustanṣir', p. 332.

181. Aside from Ibn al-Ṣayrafī's *al-Ishāra*, which is the chief primary source on the subject, see al-Qalqashandī, *Ṣubḥ*, vol. 3, pp. 485–486, and vol. 7, pp. 78–81 and 107ff., and al-Maqrīzī, *al-Khiṭaṭ*, vol. 1, pp. 438ff. See also ʿAbd al-Munʿim Mājid, *Nuẓum al-Fāṭimiyyīn wa rusūmuhum fī Miṣr* (Cairo, 1953–1955), vol. 1, pp. 78–93; Ḥasan, *Taʾrīkh*, pp. 268–279; al-Manāwī, *al-Wizāra*, especially pp. 33–99, and Dachraoui, *Califat Fatimide*, pp. 303–309.

182. For the distinction between these two categories of viziers, see Abu'l-Ḥasan ʿAlī al-Māwardī, *al-Aḥkām al-sulṭāniyya* (Beirut, 1978), pp. 22–29. See also Vatikiotis, *Fatimid Theory of State*, pp. 95–98.

183. See M. Canard, 'Notes sur les Arméniens en Égypte à l'époque Fāṭimite', *AIEO*, 13 (1955), pp. 143–157. Canard also explains how the policies of the Armenian viziers Badr al-Jamālī and Bahrām encouraged the immigration of large numbers of Armenians to Fāṭimid Egypt, where many of them secured important posts.

184. For the most detailed discussion of the organization of the Fāṭimid state in North Africa, and the relevant sources, see Dachraoui, *Califat Fatimide*, pp. 279–395 and 473–491.

185. For the organization of the state and its different institutions in Fāṭimid Egypt, see Ibn al-Ṣayrafī, *Qānūn dīwān al-rasāʾil*, ed. ʿAlī Bahjat (Cairo, 1905), which is the main source on chancery practices; French translation, H. Massé, 'Ibn El-Çaïrafī, Code de la Chancellerie d'État (période Fāṭimide)', *BIFAO*, 11 (1914), pp. 65–120; al-Qalqashandī, *Ṣubḥ*, vol. 1, pp. 89ff., 101ff., 130–139, and vol. 3, pp. 467–528, the latter section is reproduced in M. Canard, *Les institutions des Fāṭimides en Égypte* (Algiers, 1957), pp. 3–60, and al-Maqrīzī, *al-Khiṭaṭ*, vol. 1, pp. 397–403, 408ff., 490ff., and vol. 2, pp.

225ff., 280ff. and 295ff. Of the secondary sources, mention may be made of Mājid, *Nuẓum*, vol. 1, pp. 94–134, 191ff., and vol. 2, pp. 9–136, containing a detailed discussion of Fāṭimid ceremonial; Mājid, *Ẓuhūr*, pp. 289ff.; and also his 'L'organisation financière en Égypte sous les Fatimides', *L'Égypte Contemporaine*, 53, no. 308 (1962), pp. 47–57; ʿA. Muṣṭafā Musharrafa, *Nuẓum al-ḥukm bi-Miṣr fī ʿaṣr al-Fāṭimiyyīn* (2nd ed., Cairo, n.d.); Ḥasan, *Ta'rīkh*, pp. 264ff., 279–305 and 628–673; Zāhid ʿAlī, *Ta'rīkh*, vol. 2, pp. 87ff., 99–103 and 126ff.; Ḥusayn, *Fī adab*, pp. 311–323; Surūr, *Miṣr*, pp. 179–195 and 205–217, and S. M. Imamuddin, 'Administration under the Fatimids', *Journal of the Asiatic Society of Pakistan*, 14 (1969), pp. 253–269. Elaborate studies of Fāṭimid ceremonial may also be found in K. Inostrantsev, 'Torzhestvennuy vuiezd fatuimidskikh khalifov', *Zapiski Vostochnago Otdyeleniya Imperatorskago Russkago Arkheologicheskago Obshchestva*, 17 (1906), pp. 1–113; P. Kahle, 'Die Schätze der Fatimiden', *ZDMG*, 14 (1935), pp. 329–362; M. Canard, 'Le cérémonial Fatimite et le cérémonial Byzantin: Essai de comparison', *Byzantion*, 21 (1951), pp. 355–420, and also his 'La procession du Nouvel An chez les Fatimides', *AIEO*, 10 (1952), pp. 364–395. See also B. J. Beshir, 'Fatimid Military Organization', *Der Islam*, 55 (1978), pp. 37–56, and Y. Lev, 'Army, Regime, and Society in Fatimid Egypt, 358–487/968–1094', *IJMES*, 19 (1987), pp. 337–365.

186. See W. Ivanow, 'The Organization of the Fatimid Propaganda', *JBBRAS*, NS, 15 (1939), pp. 1–35; and his *Brief*, pp. 64ff.; Ḥusayn, *Fī adab*, pp. 19ff. and 33ff.; Ḥasan, *Ta'rīkh*, pp. 326–354, 371–384; Zāhid ʿAlī, *Ta'rīkh*, vol. 2, pp. 211–225; Mājid, *Nuẓum*, vol. 1, pp. 177–190; also his *Ẓuhūr*, pp. 319–339; S. M. Stern, 'Cairo as the Centre of the Ismāʿīlī Movement', in *Colloque du Caire*, pp. 437–450, reprinted in his *Studies*, pp. 234–253; A. Hamdani, 'Evolution of the Organisational Structure of the Fāṭimī Daʿwah', *Arabian Studies*, 3 (1976), pp. 85–114; B. Lewis, 'Bāb', *EI2*, vol. 1, p. 832; M. G. S. Hodgson, 'Dāʿī', *EI2*, vol. 2, pp. 97–98, and M. Canard, 'Daʿwa', *EI2*, vol. 2, pp. 168–170.

187. Al-Maqrīzī, *al-Khiṭaṭ*, vol. 1, pp. 390–391, and vol. 2, pp. 341–342; French tr., vol. 4, pp. 118–121. See also al-Qalqashandī, *Ṣubḥ*, vol. 10, pp. 434–439; Ḥusayn, *Fī adab*, pp. 23ff. and 33–41, and W. Madelung, 'Madjlis: In Ismāʿīlī Usage', *EI2*, vol. 5, p. 1033.

188. The treatise in question is al-Nuʿmān's *Kitāb al-iqtiṣār*, ed. M. Wahid Mirza (Damascus, 1957).

189. A polemical work on the principles of Islamic law according to different schools of jurisprudence, this book is al-Nuʿmān's *Ikhtilāf uṣūl al-madhāhib*, ed. S. T. Lokhandwalla (Simla, 1972), also edited by M. Ghālib (Beirut, 1973).

190. See al-Qalqashandī, *Ṣubḥ*, vol. 8, pp. 239–241 (reprinted in al-Shayyāl, *Majmūʿat al-wathā'iq*, pp. 199–202), and vol. 11, pp. 61–66, citing letters of appointment for Fāṭimid governors of Faramā, ʿAsqalān and elsewhere, and in which the governors are also instructed to assist the local resident *dāʿī*s, designated as the representatives of *al-daʿwa al-hādiya* (the rightly-guiding mission).

191. Al-Qalqashandī, *Ṣubḥ*, vol. 3, p. 483, and al-Maqrīzī, *al-Khiṭaṭ*, vol. 1, pp. 391 and 403.
192. See Ḥusayn's introduction to al-Mu'ayyad's *Dīwān*, pp. 48–57, and A. al-Hamdani, 'Sīra', pp. 107ff. But it may be noted that the term *dāʿī al-duʿāt* is also applied to al-Mu'ayyad, as an official title, in two of al-Mustanṣir's letters, dated 461/1069, issued to the Ṣulayḥids; see al-Hamdānī, 'Letters of al-Mustanṣir', pp. 322 and 324, and also al-Majdūʿ, *Fihrist*, p. 40.
193. See, for example, Ibn Muyassar, *Akhbār*, ed. Massé, p. 10; ed. Sayyid, p. 18, and al-Maqrīzī, *Ittiʿāẓ*, ed. Aḥmad, vol. 2, p. 251.
194. Al-Kirmānī, *Rāḥat al-ʿaql*, pp. 135, 138, 143, 152, 205–208, 212–214, 224, 260–262 and 349; English summary in Ivanow, *Studies* 2, pp. 19–23. See also al-Mu'ayyad, *al-Majālis*, vol. 3, pp. 220, 256–257 and 263–264. The *bāb*'s status is also described in various post-Fāṭimid Ismāʿīlī sources produced in Yaman; see, for instance, the references in *Gnosis-Texte der Ismailiten*, ed. R. Strothmann (Göttingen, 1943), pp. 8, 82, 102, 154 and 175.
195. Al-Nuʿmān, *Ta'wīl al-daʿā'im*, vol. 2, p. 74, and vol. 3, pp. 48–49. See also al-Sijistānī, *Ithbāt*, p. 172, where seven of these *jazā'ir* are named, together with al-Turk, as some of the main regions of the world.
196. The reference in question, the only one of its kind known to Ivanow, is cited in the latter's *Rise*, pp. 20–21; see also Ivanow, *Studies* 2, pp. 15ff. On this Ismāʿīlī author and his *Risālat al-basmala*, see Ivanow, *Ismaili Literature*, pp. 54 and 56, and Poonawala, *Bio*, pp. 130–140 and 146.
197. Ibn Ḥawqal, *Ṣūrat al-arḍ*, p. 310.
198. Al-Nuʿmān, *Ta'wīl al-daʿā'im*, vol. 1, pp. 114–116, 147, 297, vol. 2, pp. 116–117, and vol. 3, pp. 86–88, and also his *Asās*, pp. 79–80, 127, 190 and 224. Some sources mention twelve *ḥujja*s of the day and twelve *ḥujja*s of the night; see Jaʿfar b. Manṣūr al-Yaman, *Asrār al-nuṭaqā'*, ed. Ghālib, pp. 42 and 216–217. See also the remarks of al-Ḥusayn b. ʿAlī b. al-Walīd (d. 667/1268) in his *Risālat al-mabda' wa'l-maʿād*, in *Trilogie Ismaélienne*, ed. and tr. H. Corbin (Tehran–Paris, 1961), text pp. 114–115, translation pp. 167–168, and other post-Fāṭimid Yamanī texts in *Gnosis-Texte*, pp. 102–175.
199. There may have been as many as thirty *dāʿī*s in every *jazīra*, see Nāṣir-i Khusraw, *Wajh-i dīn*, ed. Ghanīzāda, p. 154. ed. Aavani, p. 178.
200. Al-Kirmānī, *Rāḥat al-ʿaql*, pp. 134–139 and 224–225, quoted with commentary in Corbin, 'Épiphanie divine', pp. 178–184, reprinted in his *Temps cyclique*, pp. 103–108; English translation, 'Divine Epiphany', in *Papers from the Eranos Yearbooks*, vol. 5, pp. 100–105, reprinted in Corbin, *Cyclical Time*, pp. 90–95.
201. See Nāṣir-i Khusraw, *Six Chapters*, text pp. 34–36, translation pp. 74–77, and also his *Wajh-i dīn*, ed. Ghanīzāda, p. 221; ed. Aavani, p. 255; see also the hierarchy enumerated by Strothmann in his *Gnosis-Texte*, p. 57, derived from various Yamanī Ismāʿīlī works, including some in the same collection, pp. 82 and 174ff.
202. See Abū Ḥātim al-Rāzī, *Kitāb al-iṣlāḥ*, excerpt in Hamdani, 'Evolution', p. 109; al-Sijistānī, *Ithbāt*, pp. 91, 100 and 128, and also his *Kitāb al-yanābīʿ*, in *Trilogie Ismaélienne*, text p. 8, translation p. 21. Al-Sijistānī's *al-Yanābīʿ* has

also been edited by M. Ghālib (Beirut, 1965); but our references are to Corbin's edition. See also Jaʿfar b. Manṣūr al-Yaman, *Asrār al-nuṭaqā'*, ed. Ghālib, pp. 159, 160 and 220.

203. Al-Nuʿmān, *Kitāb al-himma fī ādāb atbāʿ al-a'imma*, ed. M. Kāmil Ḥusayn (Cairo, 1948), pp. 136–140; abridged English translation, *Selections from Qazi Noaman's Kitab-ul-Himma; or, Code of Conduct for the Followers of Imam*, tr. J. Muscati and A. M. Moulvi (Karachi, 1950), pp. 134–135.

204. Al-Nīsābūrī's lost *al-Risāla al-mūjaza al-kāfiya fī ādāb al-duʿāt* is reproduced in full, except for a short introduction, by Ḥātim b. Ibrāhīm al-Ḥāmidī (d. 596/1199) at the end of his *Tuḥfat al-qulūb*, a treatise on Ismāʿīlī doctrine which has not been published; it is also quoted in Ḥasan b. Nūḥ al-Bharūchī's Ismāʿīlī chrestomathy *Kitāb al-azhār*, vol. 2, still in manuscript form. The main points of this treatise may be found in Ivanow, 'Organization of the Fatimid Propaganda', pp. 18–35.

205. See al-Nuwayrī, *Nihāyat al-arab*, vol. 25, pp. 195ff.; translated in de Sacy, *Exposé*, vol. 1, introduction pp. 74ff.; Ibn al-Dawādārī, *Kanz*, vol. 6, pp. 97ff., and al-Maqrīzī, *al-Khiṭaṭ*, vol. 1, pp. 391ff. See also O'Leary, *Fatimid Khalifate*, pp. 21–29.

206. Al-Baghdādī, *al-Farq*, pp. 282ff.; tr. Halkin, pp. 138ff., and al-Ghazālī, *Faḍā'iḥ al-Bāṭiniyya*, pp. 21–32; also in Goldziher, *Streitschrift*, text pp. 4ff., analysis pp. 40ff.

207. This official Fāṭimid viewpoint is well reflected in the works of al-Kirmānī, notably in his *al-Wāʿiẓa*, written in refutation of the Druze ideas. It is also reiterated in the writings of other major authors who represented the views of the Fāṭimid headquarters; see, for instance, al-Nuʿmān, *Daʿā'im*, vol. 1, p. 53; also his *Asās*, pp. 33ff., 347ff. and 364ff.; and his *Ta'wīl al-daʿā'im*, vol. 1, pp. 69–71; al-Mu'ayyad, *al-Majālis*, vol. 1, pp. 114, 124, 162, 189, 192, 260, 332 and 351, and Nāṣir-i Khusraw, *Wajh-i dīn*, ed. Ghanīzāda, pp. 61–67 and 280–281; ed. Aavani, pp. 77–83 and 318–319, where antinomianism is severely condemned. See also Ivanow, *Brief*, pp. 23ff., 31ff. and 36ff., and Ḥusayn, *Ṭā'ifat al-Ismāʿīliyya*, pp. 147ff.

208. According to Ibn al-Nadīm, *al-Fihrist*, vol. 1, p. 189; tr. Dodge, vol. 1, pp. 471–472, Ismāʿīlī works were scarce even during the second half of the fourth/tenth century. The works of some of the most eminent Ismāʿīlī authors of the Fāṭimid period are listed in al-Kirmānī, *Rāḥat al-ʿaql*, pp. 21–23, but the fullest Ismāʿīlī bibliography of the literature of the Fāṭimid *daʿwa*, arranged in terms of some eleven categories in ascending order of secrecy from works on *fiqh* to the most secret writings on the *ḥaqā'iq*, may be found in the *Fihrist* of al-Majdūʿ, which provided the basis of Ivanow's *Guide*. See also Zāhid ʿAlī, *Ta'rīkh*, vol. 2, pp. 181ff.; Ivanow, *Guide*, pp. 19–24; also his *Ismaili Literature*, pp. 1ff. and 13–16, and Fyzee, 'Study', especially pp. 235ff.

209. Al-Nuʿmān, *Daʿā'im*, vol. 1, pp. 25–27 and 31ff.; tr. Fyzee, *Book of Faith*, pp. 29–32 and 36ff.; al-Mu'ayyad, *al-Majālis*, vol. 1, pp. 410–411, and al-Mālījī, *al-Majālis al-Mustanṣiriyya*, pp. 29–30.

210. Summarized in Ivanow, *Studies* 2, pp. 87–122, which unfortunately contains erroneous translations of the original texts.

211. Al-Kirmānī, *Kitāb al-riyāḍ*, ed. ʿĀrif Tāmir (Beirut, 1960).
212. The author has had access to an unnumbered copy of Abū Ḥātim's *al-Iṣlāḥ* transcribed in India during the nineteenth century, and to the photocopy of the manuscript in the Fyzee collection of the University of Bombay presented, along with the photocopies of other items in this collection, to the Institute of Ismaili Studies, London; see Goriawala, *Catalogue of the Fyzee Collection*, p. 8.
213. See, for instance, Idrīs, *ʿUyūn*, vol. 5, pp. 168–169, where the author cites the praise of al-Muʿizz for Abū Ḥātim's *Kitāb al-zīna*.
214. Nāṣir-i Khusraw, *Khwān al-ikhwān*, ed. al-Khashshāb, pp. 112ff.; ed. Qavīm, pp. 131ff., and also his *Zād al-musāfirīn*, pp. 421–422. See also Corbin's remarks in his edition of al-Sijistānī's *Kashf al-maḥjūb*, pp. 15–18.
215. See al-Kirmānī, *al-Riyāḍ*, pp. 176–212; see also Madelung, 'Imamat', pp. 101–106.
216. Al-Sijistānī, *Ithbāt*, pp. 82–83.
217. Many of Abū Ḥātim's ideas on prophecy and on different religions, elaborated in the *Iṣlāḥ*, find their first expressions in his *Aʿlām al-nubuwwa*, ed. Ṣ. al-Ṣāwī and G. R. Aʿvānī (Tehran, 1977), especially pp. 52ff., 59, 69ff., 160ff., 171–177 and 267; sections of this important work are reproduced in P. Kraus, 'Raziana II', *Orientalia*, NS, 5 (1936), pp. 35–56 and 358–378, with briefer extracts in Kraus, ed., *Rasāʾil falsafiyya li-Abī Bakr Muḥammad ibn Zakariyyāʾ al-Rāzī*, pp. 219–313. Al-Kirmānī also quotes with approval passages on prophecy from Abū Ḥātim's *Aʿlām* in his *al-Aqwāl al-dhahabiyya*, pp. 9–19, extracts in Kraus, *Rasāʾil falsafiyya*, pp. 295–299 and 313–316. See also Ivanow, *Alleged*, pp. 87–89; also his *Studies* 2, pp. 116ff., representing some misinterpretations of Abū Ḥātim's views; H. Corbin, 'De la gnose antique à la gnose Ismaélienne', in *Oriente ed Occidente nel medio evo: Atti del XII convegno Volta* (Rome, 1957), pp. 138–143, reprinted in his *Temps cyclique*, pp. 203–208; English translation, 'From the Gnosis of Antiquity to Ismaili Gnosis, tr. James W. Morris', in Corbin, *Cyclical Time and Ismaili Gnosis*, pp. 187–193, and Stern, *Studies*, pp. 30–46.
218. *Al-Nuṣra* quoted in *al-Riyāḍ*, pp. 176ff.; al-Sijistānī, *Ithbāt*, pp. 166 and 181ff.; al-Sijistānī, *al-Iftikhār*, p. 59, and also his *Kashf al-maḥjūb*, pp. 69ff. and 81–83. See also Madelung, 'Imamat', pp. 106–109.
219. *Al-Nuṣra* quoted in *al-Riyāḍ*, p. 204.
220. See al-Sijistānī, *Kashf al-maḥjūb*, pp. 53 and 79, where the author conveys a modified position by referring to Muḥammad as the master of his era.
221. Al-Sijistānī, *Ithbāt*, pp. 51–53.
222. Ibid., pp. 177ff. As Professor Madelung has mentioned to the author, in this context the correct reading of *waṣfī* should probably be *waḍʿī*.
223. Ibid., p. 180.
224. Ibid., pp. 178 and 186–187. Compare these ideas with those expressed in his *al-Iftikhār*, pp. 72–73.
225. See Madelung, 'Imamat', pp. 112–114.
226. See P. Kraus, 'Plotin chez les Arabes', *Bulletin de l'Institut d'Égypte*, 23 (1941), pp. 263–295; S. Pines, 'La longue récension de la Théologie d'Aristote dans

ses rapports avec la doctrine Ismaélienne', *REI*, 22 (1954), pp. 7–20, and S. M. Stern, 'Ibn Ḥasdāy's Neoplatonist', *Oriens*, 13–14 (1960–1961), especially pp. 58–98, reprinted in Stern, *Medieval Arabic and Hebrew Thought* (London, 1983).

227. *Al-Nuṣra* cited in *al-Riyāḍ*, pp. 99–100 and 147.

228. Stern, 'Early', p. 79, and also his 'Ismāʿīlīs', p. 107. See also A. Altmann and S. M. Stern, *Isaac Israeli: A Neoplatonic Philosopher of the Early Tenth Century* (Oxford, 1958), which discusses a parallel Neoplatonic system expounded by al-Nasafī's contemporary Isḥāq b. Sulaymān al-Isrā'īlī, the earliest Jewish Neoplatonist who also served as a physician to the first Fāṭimid caliph in Ifrīqiya.

229. *Al-Maḥṣūl* quoted in *al-Riyāḍ*, especially pp. 213–229.

230. See Stern, 'Abu'l-Qasim al-Bustī and his Refutation of Ismāʿīlism', pp. 14ff., 20ff. and 29–35, reprinted in his *Studies*, pp. 299ff., 307ff., 307ff. and 315–320, and also his 'The First in Thought is the Last in Action: The History of a Saying Attributed to Aristotle', *Journal of Semitic Studies*, 7 (1962), pp. 243ff., reprinted in Stern, *Medieval Arabic*. A relevant excerpt from al-Bustī's treatise may be found in Halm, *Kosmologie*, pp. 222–224.

231. Al-Sijistānī's cosmological doctrine may be reconstructed on the basis of the fragments of his *al-Nuṣra* preserved in al-Kirmānī's *al-Riyāḍ*, and a number of his published works, including the *Kashf al-maḥjūb*; *Ithbāt al-nubūwāt*; *al-Iftikhār*; and *Tuḥfat al-mustajībīn*, in *Khams rasā'il Ismāʿīliyya*, pp. 145–156, reprinted with some changes in *al-Mashriq* (March–April, 1967), pp. 136–146, also in *Thalāth rasā'il Ismāʿīliyya*, ed. ʿĀ. Tāmir (Beirut, 1983), pp. 10–20, and above all his *Kitāb al-yanābīʿ*, in *Trilogie Ismaélienne*, text pp. 2–97, partial French translation and commentary pp. 5–127. The *Yanābīʿ* has been edited also by M. Ghālib (Beirut, 1965); but our references are to Corbin's edition. A number of al-Sijistānī's unpublished works, notably his *Sullam al-najāt* and *al-Maqālīd* are also important here. Paul E. Walker has produced a number of studies on al-Sijistānī's cosmological doctrine; aside from his already-cited doctoral dissertation, see his 'The Ismaili Vocabulary of Creation', *SI*, 40 (1974), pp. 75–85; 'An Ismāʿīlī Answer to the Problem of Worshiping the Unknowable, Neoplatonic God', *American Journal of Arabic Studies*, 2 (1974), pp. 7–21; 'Cosmic Hierarchies in Early Ismāʿīlī Thought: The View of Abū Yaʿqūb al-Sijistānī', *MW*, 66 (1976), pp. 14–28, and 'Eternal Cosmos and the Womb of History', pp. 360ff. See also Mohamed Abualy Alibhai, 'Abū Yaʿqūb al-Sijistānī and Kitāb Sullam al-Najāt: A Study in Islamic Neoplatonism' (Ph.D. thesis, Harvard University, 1983).

232. Various aspects of this Ismāʿīlī Neoplatonic cosmology have been studied by H. Corbin in his *Étude*, pp. 112–128; 'Épiphanie divine', pp. 162ff. and 193ff., reprinted in his *Temps cyclique*, pp. 88ff. and 116ff.; English translation, 'Divine Epiphany', in *Papers from the Eranos Yearbooks*, vol. 5, pp. 86ff. and 113ff., reprinted in Corbin, *Cyclical Time*, pp. 76ff. and 103ff.; 'De la gnose antique', pp. 105ff., 110ff., 114–120 and 126–138, reprinted in his *Temps cyclique*, pp. 167ff., 172ff., 176–183 and 189–203; English translation, 'From the Gnosis of Antiquity', in Corbin's *Cyclical Time*, pp. 151ff., 156ff.,

161–167 and 173–187, and *Histoire*, pp. 118–124. See also Ivanow, *Brief*, pp. 39–54 and 58ff.; A. S. Tritton, 'Theology and Philosophy of the Isma'ilis', *JRAS* (1958), pp. 178–188; B. Dodge, 'Aspects of the Fāṭimid Philosophy', *MW*, 50 (1960), pp. 182–192; S. N. Makarem, 'The Philosophical Significance of the Imām in Ismāʿīlism', *SI*, 27 (1967), pp. 41ff.; Filippani-Ronconi, *Ismaeliti*, pp. 75ff.; W. Madelung, 'Aspects of Ismāʿīlī Theology: The Prophetic Chain and the God Beyond Being', in *Ismāʿīlī Contributions*, pp. 53–65, reprinted in Madelung, *Religious Schools and Sects*, and Halm, *Kosmologie*, pp. 53–62, 67ff. and 128–138.

233. Al-Sijistānī, *Kashf al-maḥjūb*, pp. 4–15.
234. On this term, see Nāṣir-i Khusraw, *Jāmiʿ al-ḥikmatayn*, pp. 210–232; Altmann and Stern, *Isaac Israeli*, pp. 66–74; L. Gardet, 'Ibdāʿ', *EI2*, vol. 3, pp. 663–665, and R. Arnaldez, 'Khalḳ', *EI2*, vol. 4, pp. 980–988.
235. Al-Sijistānī, *al-Yanābīʿ*, text pp. 22–29 and 61ff., translation pp. 42–48 and 84ff., and also his *Ithbāt*, p. 145.
236. Al-Sijistānī, *Ithbāt*, p. 3.
237. Al-Sijistānī's *al-Yanābīʿ*, text pp. 32ff., translation pp. 49ff.; and his *Ithbāt*, pp. 18 and 145, and *al-Nuṣra* quoted in *al-Riyāḍ*, pp. 59–65 and 68–69.
238. *Al-Maḥṣūl* cited in *al-Riyāḍ*, p. 220; *al-Yanābīʿ*, text p. 56, translation p. 74, and *Ithbāt*, pp. 2–3 and 28.
239. *Kashf al-maḥjūb*, pp. 29–31, and *al-Nuṣra* in *al-Riyāḍ*, pp. 102ff.
240. *Ithbāt*, p. 44.
241. Ibid., pp. 127–128.
242. See al-Sijistānī, *Tuḥfat al-mustajībīn*, in *Khams rasāʾil*, pp. 148ff., in *Thalāth rasāʾil*, pp. 13ff., and also his *al-Iftikhār*, pp. 38–42.
243. *Al-Yanābīʿ*, text pp. 17–19, translation pp. 37–39, and *al-Iftikhār*, pp. 47–56.
244. The original Arabic passage is quoted in Arendonk, *Les débuts*, p. 333. See also al-Baghdādī, *al-Farq*, pp. 269–270 and 277–278; tr. Halkin, pp. 115–117 and 131, and al-Daylamī, *Bayān*, pp. 5–6 and 72–73.
245. Al-Sijistānī, *al-Iftikhār*, pp. 43ff., and also his *Ithbāt*, p. 128. See also Jaʿfar b. Manṣūr al-Yaman, *Asrār al-nuṭaqāʾ*, ed. Ghālib, pp. 24ff. and 81.
246. Walker, 'Cosmic Hierarchies', pp. 14ff.
247. Al-Sijistānī, *al-Yanābīʿ*, text pp. 44–47, translation pp. 65–68.
248. Ibid., text pp. 83–85 and 87–90, translation pp. 107–118.
249. Al-Nuʿmān, *al-Mudhhiba*, in *Khams rasāʾil*, pp. 60ff. and 81. See also Halm, *Kosmologie*, pp. 135ff.
250. Nāṣir-i Khusraw's metaphysical system may be traced through his *Six Chapters*, *Gushāʾish va rahāʾish*, *Khwān al-ikhwān*, *Zād al-musāfirīn* and, above all, his *Jāmiʿ al-ḥikmatayn*, which analyzes agreements and disagreements between the views of Muslim philosophers and the wisdom of the Ismāʿīlī gnosis.
251. See al-Kirmānī, *Rāḥat al-ʿaql*, p. 20.
252. Ibid., pp. 134ff. See also Corbin, *Avicenna and the Visionary Recital*, pp. 25, 46ff., 56ff., 68ff., 120, 254ff., 262 and 314ff.
253. See L. Gardet, 'Hayūlā', *EI2*, vol. 3, pp. 328–330.
254. *Rāḥat al-ʿaql*, pp. 121–131.

255. *Al-Riyāḍ*, p. 157.
256. Three complete editions of the *Epistles* have appeared so far. These are *Kitāb Ikhwān al-Ṣafā'* (Bombay, 1305–1306/1887–1889), 4 vols.; *Rasā'il Ikhwān al-Ṣafā'*, ed. Khayr al-Dīn al-Ziriklī (Cairo, 1347/1928), 4 vols., and *Rasā'il Ikhwān al-Ṣafā'* (Beirut, 1957), 4 vols. See also David R. Blumenthal, 'A Comparative Table of the Bombay, Cairo, and Beirut Editions of the Rasā'il Ihwān al-Ṣafā'', *Arabica*, 21 (1974), pp. 186–203. A partial French translation, with extensive analysis, of the *Epistles* may be found in Y. Marquet, *La Philosophie des Ihwān al-Ṣafā'* (Algiers, 1975), and a partial Italian translation is contained in A. Bausani, *L'Enciclopedia dei Fratelli della Purità* (Naples, 1978). Susanne Diwald is preparing a comprehensive German translation, with commentary, of the *Rasā'il*, of which one volume (dealing with the third book of the *Epistles*) has now appeared under the title of *Arabische Philosophie und Wissenschaft in der Enzyklopädie Kitāb Ihwān aṣ-ṣafā' (III): Die Lehre von Seele und Intellekt* (Wiesbaden, 1975), containing an extensive bibliography, pp. 557–592.
257. Idrīs, *'Uyūn*, vol. 4, pp. 367–393, with a detailed description of the *Epistles*; see also al-Majdū', *Fihrist*, pp. 154–158; Ḥ. F. al-Hamdānī, 'Rasā'il Ikhwān aṣ-Ṣafā' in the Literature of the Ismā'īlī Ṭaiyibī Da'wat', *Der Islam*, 20 (1932), pp. 281–300; also his *Baḥth ta'rīkhī fī Rasā'il Ikhwān al-Ṣafā'* (Bombay, 1354/1935), and Abbas Hamdani, 'An Early Fāṭimid Source on the Time and Authorship of the Rasā'il Ihwān al-Ṣafā'', *Arabica*, 26 (1979), pp. 62–75.
258. See Abū Ḥayyān al-Tawḥīdī, *al-Imtā' wa'l-mu'ānasa*, ed. A. Amīn and A. al-Zayn (Cairo, 1939–1944), vol. 2, pp. 4ff. and 157–160, reproduced in Ibn al-Qifṭī, *Ta'rīkh al-ḥukamā'*, ed. J. Lippert (Leipzig, 1903), pp. 82–88, and 'Abd al-Jabbār al-Hamadhānī, *Tathbīt dalā'il al-nubuwwa*, ed. 'Uthmān, pp. 610ff. See also several works by S. M. Stern: 'The Authorship of the Epistles of the Ikhwān-aṣ-Ṣafā', *IC*, 20 (1946), pp. 367–372; 'Additional Notes to the Article: The Authorship of the Epistles of the Ikhwan aṣ-Ṣafā', *IC*, 21 (1947), pp. 403–404; 'New Information about the Authors of the Epistles of the Sincere Brethren', *Islamic Studies*, 3 (1964), pp. 405–428; *Studies*, pp. 85–87 and 155–176. Martin M. Plessner, 'Beiträge zur islamischen Literaturgeschichte IV: Samuel Miklos Stern, die Ikhwān aṣ-Ṣafā' und die Encyclopaedia of Islam', *Israel Oriental Studies*, 2 (1972), pp. 353–361; Abbas Hamdani, 'Abū Ḥayyān al-Tawḥīdī and the Brethren of Purity', *IJMES*, 9 (1978), pp. 345–353, also his 'The Arrangement of the Rasā'il Ikhwān al-Ṣafā' and the Problem of Interpolations', *Journal of Semitic Studies*, 29 (1984), pp. 97–110. For a general discussion of the various opinions on the authorship of the *Epistles*, see A. L. Tibawi, 'Ikhwān aṣ-Ṣafā and their Rasā'il', *Islamic Quarterly*, 2 (1955), pp. 28–46, and also his 'Further Studies on Ikhwān aṣ-Ṣafā', *Islamic Quarterly*, 22 (1978), pp. 57–67.
259. This approximate date was first suggested by Fr. Dieterici, the German orientalist who pioneered the Ikhwān studies in modern times, see his *Die Philosophie der Araber*, vol. 1, pp. 142ff.
260. *Rasā'il*, Bombay ed., vol. 3, pp. 2–24; Cairo ed., vol. 3, pp. 182–210; Beirut ed., vol. 3, pp. 178–211. See also Seyyed H. Nasr, *An Introduction to Islamic*

Cosmological Doctrines (Cambridge, Mass., 1964), pp. 44–74; Marquet, *Philosophie*, pp. 41–226; Diwald, *Arabische Philosophie*, pp. 31–128, and Bausani, *L'Enciclopedia*, pp. 211–215.

261. *Rasā'il*, Bombay ed., vol. 1, p. 15, vol. 2, p. 189, and vol. 4, pp. 181–182; Cairo ed., vol. 1, p. 16, vol. 2, p. 244, and vol. 4, p. 179; Beirut ed., vol. 1, p. 40, vol. 2, p. 290, and vol. 4, p. 125.

262. See al-Ḥāmidī, *Kanz al-walad*, pp. 111ff.

263. See Ikhwān al-Ṣafā', *al-Risāla al-jāmiʿa*, ed. Jamīl Ṣalībā (Damascus, 1949), 2 vols., also edited by M. Ghālib (Beirut, 1974). Of the more scarce *Jāmiʿat al-jāmiʿa*, there has appeared an edition prepared by ʿĀrif Tāmir (Beirut, 1959; 2nd ed., Beirut, 1970).

264. The *Epistles*, for instance, refer (Beirut, ed., vol. 2, p. 282, and vol. 4, pp. 58, 148ff., 152ff., 162ff. and 175) to the ancient Indian legend of Bilawhar and Yūdāsaf (Būdhāsf), known in mediaeval Europe as Barlaam and Joasaph. The full Arabic version of the *Kitāb Bilawhar wa Būdhāsf*, preserved in the Ismāʿīlī libraries of India, was first lithographed in Bombay in 1306/1889, and more recently, it was edited by Daniel Gimaret (Beirut, 1972). Gimaret has also prepared a French translation of this work entitled *Le Livre de Bilawhar et Būḏāsf, selon la version Arabe Ismaélienne* (Geneva, 1971). See also S. M. Stern and S. Walzer, *Three Unknown Buddhist Stories in an Arabic Version* (Oxford, 1971); al-Majdūʿ, *Fihrist*, pp. 11–15; Ivanow, *Ismaili Literature*, p. 91; Poonawala, *Bio*, p. 360, and D. M. Lang, 'Bilawhar wa-Yūdāsaf', *EI2*, vol. 1, pp. 1215–1217.

265. Various aspects of the Ikhwān al-Ṣafā' and their *Rasā'il* are treated in Zāhid ʿAlī, *Ta'rīkh*, vol. 2, pp. 226–249; A. Awa, *L'Esprit critique des Frères de la Pureté* (Beirut, 1948); ʿUmar Farrūkh, *Ikhwān al-Ṣafā'* (2nd ed., Beirut, 1953); also his 'Ikhwān al-Ṣafā', in *A History of Muslim Philosophy*, ed. M. M. Sharif (Wiesbaden, 1963–1966), vol. 1, pp. 289–310; Corbin, 'Rituel Sabéen', pp. 181ff. and 214–229; Corbin, *Histoire*, pp. 190–194; Nasr, *Islamic Cosmological Doctrines*, pp. 25–104; M. Fakhry, *A History of Islamic Philosophy* (New York, 1970), pp. 185–204; A. Bausani, 'Scientific Elements in Ismāʿīlī Thought: The Epistles of the Brethren of Purity', in *Ismāʿīlī Contributions*, pp. 123–140; G. Widengren, 'The Pure Brethren and the Philosophical Structure of their System', in *Islam: Past Influence and Present Challenge*, ed. A. T. Welch and P. Cachia (Edinburgh, 1979), pp. 57–69, and Ian R. Netton, *Muslim Neoplatonists: An Introduction to the Thought of the Brethren of Purity* (London, 1982). Besides his already-cited monograph, Yves Marquet has produced a number of shorter studies on the subject, including his 'Imamat, résurrection et hiérarchie selon les Ikhwan as-Safa', *REI*, 30 (1962), pp. 49–142; 'Les Cycles de la souveraineté selon les épîtres des Iḫwān al-Ṣafā', *SI*, 36 (1972), pp. 47–69; 'Iḫwān al-Ṣafā', Ismaïliens et Qarmaṭes', *Arabica*, 24 (1977), pp. 233–257; 'Les ĕpîtres des Ikhwān al-Safā'', *SI*, 61 (1985), pp. 57–79, and his 'Ikhwān al-Ṣafā'', *EI2*, vol. 3, pp. 1071–1076, which does not accept Stern's views on the subject. See also Brockelmann, *Geschichte*, 1st ed., vol. 1, pp. 213–214; 2nd ed., vol. 1, pp. 236–238, and Ivanow, *Ismaili Literature*, pp. 18–20.

266. On al-Qāḍī al-Nuʿmān's life, works and family, see Idrīs, *ʿUyūn*, vol. 5, pp.

331ff., 346–347, and vol. 6, pp. 38–50, 185, 192, 195, 200, 215–216, 232, 276, 280, 311, 315 and 322; al-Majdūʿ, *Fihrist*, pp. 18–37, 50–53, 65–72, 82, 96–97, 111–112, 134, 135–136 and 187; Ibn Khallikān, *Biographical Dictionary*, vol. 3, pp. 565–574; Aḥmad b. ʿAbd al-Raḥmān b. Burd's *Dhayl* to al-Kindī's *Governors*, pp. 494ff.; Ibn Ḥajar al-ʿAsqalānī, *Rafʿ al-iṣr*, in al-Kindī, *Governors*, pp. 586–587, 589–603 and 613, reproduced with English translation in Richard Gottheil, 'A Distinguished Family of Fatimide Cadis (al-Nuʿmān) in the Tenth Century', *JAOS*, 27 (1906), pp. 217–296; al-Hamdānī, 'Some Unknown Ismāʿīlī Authors', pp. 368–370; also his *al-Ṣulayḥiyyūn*, pp. 253–256; Ḥasan, *Ta'rīkh*, pp. 474–483; Ḥasan and Sharaf, *al-Muʿizz*, pp. 258–268; Zāhid ʿAlī, *Ta'rīkh*, vol. 2, pp. 109–111; Ḥusayn, *Fī adab*, pp. 42–54; Ḥusayn's introduction to his edition of al-Nuʿmān's *Kitāb al-himma*; Ghālib, *Aʿlām*, pp. 589–595; Brockelmann, *Geschichte*, 1st ed., vol. 1, pp. 187–188; 2nd ed., vol. 1, p. 201, and Supplement, vol. 1, pp. 324–325; Ivanow, *Guide*, pp. 37–40; Ivanow, *Ismaili Literature*, pp. 32–37, and Sezgin, *Geschichte*, vol. 1, pp. 575–578. Asaf Fyzee was the modern Ismāʿīlī scholar who initiated the study of al-Nuʿmān's life, see especially his 'Qadi an-Nuʿman, the Fatimid Jurist and Author', *JRAS* (1934), pp. 1–32; 'Ismaʿili Law and its Founder', *IC*, 9 (1935), pp. 107–112; 'Qadi an-Nuʿman', in *Great Ismaili Heroes*, pp. 18–20, and 'al-Nuʿmān', *EI*, vol. 3, pp. 953–954. More recently, Ismail K. Poonawala has produced some valuable results in his 'Al-Qāḍī al-Nuʿmān's Works and the Sources', *BSOAS*, 36 (1973), pp. 109–115; 'A Reconsideration of al-Qāḍī al-Nuʿmān's Madhhab', *BSOAS*, 37 (1974), pp. 572–579, and *Bio*, pp. 48–68, containing a full description of al-Nuʿmān's published and unpublished works.

267. Ibn Shahrāshūb, *Maʿālim*, p. 113.
268. Nūr Allāh al-Shūshtarī, *Majālis al-mu'minīn* (Tehran, 1375–1376/1955–1956), vol. 1, pp. 538–539.
269. Muḥammad b. al-Ḥasan al-Ḥurr al-ʿĀmilī, *Amal al-āmil*, ed. A. al-Ḥusaynī (Baghdād, 1385/1965), vol. 2, p. 335; Muḥammad Bāqir al-Majlisī, *Biḥār al-anwār* (2nd ed., Beirut, 1983), vol. 1, pp. 20 and 38–39; Muḥammad al-Mahdī Baḥr al-ʿUlūm al-Ṭabāṭabā'ī, *Rijāl*, ed. Muḥammad Ṣādiq and Ḥusayn Baḥr al-ʿUlūm (Najaf, 1385–1386/1965–1966), vol. 4, pp. 5–14, and Ḥusayn b. Muḥammad Taqī al-Nūrī, *Mustadrak al-wasā'il* (Tehran, 1318–1321/1900–1903), vol. 3, pp. 291 and 313–322.
270. Muḥammad Muḥsin Āghā Buzurg al-Ṭihrānī, *al-Dharīʿa ilā taṣānīf al-Shīʿa* (Tehran–Najaf, 1353–1398/1934–1978), vol. 1, p. 60.
271. Muḥammad Bāqir al-Khwānsārī, *Kitāb rawḍāt al-jannāt* (Tehran, 1367/1948), pp. 727–728.
272. See F. Daftary, 'Professor Asaf A. A. Fyzee (1899–1981)', *Arabica*, 31 (1984), pp. 327–330, and also his 'The Bibliography of Asaf A. A. Fyzee', *Indo-Iranica*, 37 (1984), pp. 49–63.
273. For summary discussions of the Imāmī sources of law, see R. Brunschvig, 'Les uṣūl al-fiqh imāmites à leur stade ancien (Xe et XIe siècles)', in *Le Shīʿisme Imāmite*, pp. 201–213; Fyzee, *Outlines of Muhammadan Law*, pp. 43–48; W. Madelung, 'Authority in Twelver Shiism in the Absence of the

Imam', in *La Notion d'autorité au Moyen Age: Islam, Byzance, Occident*, Colloques internationaux de la Napoule, 1978 (Paris, 1982), pp. 163–173, reprinted in his *Religious Schools and Sects*, and H. Modarressi Tabāṭabā'i, *An Introduction to Shī'ī Law: A Bibliographical Study* (London, 1984), especially pp. 2–6, 9–10 and 29–43, containing also an extensive survey of the relevant sources.

274. Al-Nu'mān, *Ikhtilāf uṣūl al-madhāhib*, ed. Lokhandwalla, pp. 25 and 230; ed. Ghālib, pp. 51 and 226.

275. The chief legal compendium of the Fāṭimid Ismā'īlīs, the *Da'ā'im al-Islām*, has been edited by Asaf A. A. Fyzee (Cairo, 1951–1961), 2 vols., reprinted several times; partial English translations of the *Da'ā'im* have been produced by Fyzee under the titles of *The Ismaili Law of Wills* (London, etc., 1933), and *The Book of Faith*. Asaf Fyzee produced a number of valuable studies, based on al-Nu'mān's writings, on Fāṭimid Ismā'īlī law, still observed by the Ṭayyibī Ismā'īlīs; see especially his 'Studies in Ismā'īlī Law', *Bombay Law Reporter, Journal*, 31 (1929), pp. 84–87, 33 (1931), pp. 30–32, 34 (1932), pp. 89–92 and 38 (1936), pp. 41–43; *Conférences sur l'Islam*, pp. 45–67; 'The Fatimid Law of Inheritance', *SI*, 9 (1958), pp. 61–69; 'Aspects of Fāṭimid Law', *SI*, 31 (1970), pp. 81–91; 'The Religion of the Ismailis', in *India and Contemporary Islam*, ed. S. T. Lokhandwalla (Simla, 1971), pp. 70–87, and his *Compendium of Fatimid Law* (Simla, 1969). See also S. T. Lokhandwalla, 'The Origins of Ismā'īlī Law' (D.Phil. thesis, Oxford University, 1951); Lokhandwalla's introduction to his edition of al-Nu'mān's *Ikhtilāf uṣūl al-madhāhib*; R. Strothmann, 'Recht der Ismailiten', *Der Islam*, 31 (1954), pp. 131–146; R. Brunschvig, 'Fiqh Fatimide et histoire de l'Ifriqiya', in *Mélanges d'histoire et d'archéologie*, pp. 13–20; Vatikiotis, *Fatimid Theory of State*, pp. 69–85; F. Castro, 'Su Ġasb e Ta'addī nel Fiqh Fatimida', *Annali di Ca' Foscari*, serie orientale, 6 (1975), pp. 95–100, and W. Madelung, 'The Sources of Ismā'īlī Law', *Journal of Near Eastern Studies*, 35 (1976), pp. 29–40, reprinted in his *Religious Schools and Sects*. The judiciary organization of the Fāṭimid state is discussed in Ḥasan, *Ta'rīkh*, pp. 306–325; Dachraoui, *Califat Fatimide*, pp. 397–422, and Amin Haji, 'Institutions of Justice in Fatimid Egypt (358–567/969–1171)', in *Islamic Law*, ed. A. al-Azmeh (London, 1988), pp. 198–214.

276. For different interpretations and evaluations of Fāṭimid achievements, see Hodgson, *Venture of Islam*, vol. 2, pp. 21–28; and the articles, B. Lewis, 'An Interpretation of Fāṭimid History', Gustav E. von Grunebaum, 'The Nature of the Fāṭimid Achievement', and Oleg Grabar, 'Imperial and Urban Art in Islam: The Subject Matter of Fāṭimid Art', all in *Colloque du Caire*, pp. 173–189, 199–215 and 287–295.

277. See especially K. A. C. Creswell, *The Muslim Architecture of Egypt*: I, *Ikhshīds and Fāṭimids, A.D. 939–1171* (Oxford, 1952).

278. See Zakī Muḥammad Ḥasan, *al-Fann al-Islāmī fī Miṣr* (Cairo, 1935); also his *Kunūz al-Fāṭimiyyīn* (Cairo, 1937); C. J. Lamm, 'Fāṭimid Woodwork, its Style and Chronology', *Bulletin de l'Institut d'Égypte*, 18 (1936), pp. 59–91; F. Massoul, *Le Céramique Musulmane d'Égypte* (Cairo, 1930); R. Ettinghausen,

'Painting in the Fāṭimid Period: A Reconstruction', *Ars Islamica*, 9 (1942), pp. 112–124; O. Grabar, 'Fāṭimid Art, Precursor or Culmination', in *Ismāʿīlī Contributions*, pp. 209–224; Aḥmad Fikrī, *Masājid al-Qāhira wa madārisuhā*: I, *al-ʿaṣr al-Fāṭimī* (Cairo, 1965), and G. Marçais, 'Fāṭimid Art', *EI2*, vol. 2, pp. 862–864.

5. *Mustaʿlian Ismāʿīlism*

1. Ayman Fu'ād Sayyid, *Maṣādir ta'rīkh al-Yaman fi'l-ʿaṣr al-Islāmī* (Cairo, 1974), especially pp. 99–219.
2. See Ibn Khallikān, *Biographical Dictionary*, vol. 2, pp. 367–372; Ḥusayn, *Fī adab*, pp. 348–354; Ghālib, *Aʿlām*, pp. 420–422, and Sayyid, *Maṣādir*, pp. 108–110, where additional sources are cited. The most detailed study of ʿUmāra's life and works may be found in Hartwig Derenbourg, *ʿOumāra du Yémen, sa vie et son œuvre* (Paris, 1897–1904), 3 vols., also containing editions of his *Dīwān* of poetry and his book entitled *al-Nukat al-ʿaṣriyya fī akhbār al-wuzarā' al-Miṣriyya*, especially valuable on the Fāṭimid viziers of ʿUmāra's time.
3. The works of Idrīs are fully described in Ivanow, *Ismaili Literature*, pp. 77–82, and Poonawala, *Bio*, pp. 169–175. The unpublished *Tuḥfat al-qulūb* of Ḥātim b. Ibrāhīm al-Ḥāmidī (d. 596/1199) is also an important source for the history of the early Ṭayyibī and pre-Ṭayyibī *dāʿīs* in Yaman.
4. Muḥammad ʿAlī b. Mullā Jīwābhā'ī, *Mawsim-i bahār fī akhbār al-ṭāhirīn al-akhyār* (Bombay, 1301–1311/1884–1893), 3 vols. The first two volumes were reprinted in Bombay in 1335/1916–1917 and subsequently, while the long-prohibited and scarce third volume was reprinted only recently in Bombay; our references are to the original edition. On this important work, considered by the Dā'ūdī Bohras to represent their authentic history, see Ivanow, *Guide*, p. 76; also his *Ismaili Literature*, p. 96, and Poonawala, *Bio*, p. 229.
5. Mian Bhai Mulla Abdul Husain, *Gulzare Daudi, for the Bohras of India* (Ahmedabad, 1920).
6. On al-Mustanṣir's succession dispute and Nizār's brief revolt, see al-Mustanṣir, *al-Sijillāt*, pp. 109–118, containing letters of al-Mustaʿlī and his mother, written in 489/1096 to the Ṣulayḥid al-Malika al-Sayyida, describing Nizār's revolt; Ibn al-Qalānisī, *Dhayl*, p. 128; Ibn Muyassar, *Akhbār*, ed. Massé, pp. 34ff., ed. Sayyid, pp. 59ff.; Ibn al-Athīr, *al-Kāmil*, vol. 10, p. 82; Ibn al-Dawādārī, *Kanz*, vol. 6, pp. 443ff.; al-Maqrīzī, *al-Khiṭaṭ*, vol. 1, pp. 422–423; al-Maqrīzī, *Ittiʿāẓ*, ed. Aḥmad, vol. 3, pp. 11ff., and Ibn Taghrībirdī, *al-Nujūm*, vol. 5, pp. 142–145; see also Zāhid ʿAlī, *Ta'rīkh*, vol. 1, pp. 324ff.; Mājid, *Ẓuhūr*, pp. 409ff.; Ghālib, *Ta'rīkh*, pp. 253–255; also his *Aʿlām*, pp. 583–586; Hodgson, *Order of Assassins*, pp. 62ff.; Ladak, 'Fāṭimid Caliphate', pp. 1–138, and H. A. R. Gibb, 'Nizār b. al-Mustanṣir', *EI*, vol. 3, p. 941.
7. See, for instance, al-Shahrastānī, *al-Milal*, vol. 1, pp. 192 and 195; tr. Kazi, pp. 165 and 167, and Juwaynī, *Ta'rīkh*, vol. 3, p. 195; tr. Boyle, vol. 2, p. 671.

8. Ivanow, *Guide*, p. 6, and Ḥusayn, *Ṭā'ifat al-Ismā'īliyya*, pp. 46 and 62.
9. On al-Musta'lī's caliphate, see Ibn al-Qalānisī, *Dhayl*, pp. 128–141, containing the fullest details on the events of this period in Fāṭimid Syria and on the confrontations between the Fāṭimids and the earliest Crusaders; partial English translation, *The Damascus Chronicle of the Crusades*, tr. H. A. R. Gibb (London, 1932), pp. 41–56; partial French translation, without the omissions of the Gibb's translation for the overlapping years, entitled *Damas de 1075 à 1154*, tr. Roger Le Tourneau (Damascus, 1952), pp. 30–49; see also Ibn Ẓāfir, *Akhbār*, pp. 82–86; Ibn Muyassar, *Akhbār*, ed. Massé, pp. 34–40, ed. Sayyid, pp. 59–70; Ibn al-Athīr, *al-Kāmil*, vol. 10, pp. 82, 83, 91, 93, 99 and 114; Ibn Khallikān, *Biographical Dictionary*, vol. 1, pp. 159–162; Ibn al-Dawādārī, *Kanz*, vol. 6, pp. 443–460; al-Maqrīzī, *al-Khiṭaṭ*, vol. 1, pp. 356–357; French tr., vol. 4, pp. 29–30; also his *Itti'āẓ*, vol. 3, pp. 11–28, and Ibn Taghrībirdī, *al-Nujūm*, vol. 5, pp. 142–169. Of the secondary sources, see Ḥasan, *Ta'rīkh*, pp. 171–173; Zāhid 'Alī, *Ta'rīkh*, vol. 1, pp. 324–332; Surūr, *Miṣr*, pp. 87ff., 128–130 and 139ff.; also his *Bilād al-Shām*, pp. 64ff., and *Siyāsat*, pp. 155ff.; Mājid, *Ẓuhūr*, pp. 409–415; O'Leary, *Fatimid Khalifate*, pp. 211–217; Ladak, 'Fāṭimid Caliphate', pp. 87ff., and H. A. R. Gibb, 'al-Musta'lī Bi'llāh', *EI*, vol. 3, p. 767.
10. See 'Umāra, *Ta'rīkh al-Yaman*, in Kay, *Yaman*, text pp. 28ff., translation pp. 38ff.; al-Hamdānī, *al-Ṣulayḥiyyūn*, pp. 142ff., 181 and 268–269; Surūr, *Jazīrat al-'Arab*, pp. 88ff., and Surūr, *Siyāsat*, pp. 92ff.
11. On al-Āmir's reign, see al-Shayyāl, *Majmū'at al-wathā'iq*, text pp. 181–202 and 323–325, commentaries pp. 37–46 and 140–143, containing some of al-Āmir's epistles, two of which have been preserved in al-Qalqashandī, *Ṣubḥ*, vol. 8, pp. 237–241; Ibn al-Ṣayrafī, *al-Ishāra*, in *BIFAO* (1925), pp. 98–100 (13–15); Ibn al-Ma'mūn al-Baṭā'iḥī, *Nuṣūṣ min akhbār Miṣr*, ed. A. F. Sayyid (Cairo, 1983), pp. 3–105; Ibn-al-Qalānisī, *Dhayl*, pp. 141ff. and 228–229; tr. Gibb, pp. 56ff.; tr. Le Tourneau, pp. 49ff. and 190–191; Ibn Ẓāfir, *Akhbār*, pp. 87–93; Ibn Muyassar, *Akhbār*, ed. Massé, pp. 40–43 and 56–74, ed. Sayyid, pp. 70–112; Ibn al-Athīr, *al-Kāmil*, vol. 10, pp. 114, 127, 137–138, 142, 145, 167–168, 169–170, 191, 219–221 and 237; Ibn Khallikān, *Biographical Dictionary*, vol. 3, pp. 455–457; Ibn al-Dawādārī, *Kanz*, vol. 6, pp. 461–505; al-Maqrīzī, *al-Khiṭaṭ*, vol. 1, pp. 357, 466, 468ff., 483ff., and vol. 2, pp. 181 and 290; also his *Itti'āẓ*, vol. 3, pp. 29–133, and Ibn Taghrībirdī, *al-Nujūm*, vol. 5, pp. 170–236; see also Ḥasan, *Ta'rīkh*, pp. 173–176; Zāhid 'Alī, *Ta'rīkh*, vol. 2, pp. 13–22; Surūr, *Miṣr*, pp. 93ff.; Surūr, *Jazīrat al-'Arab*, pp. 94–100; Mājid, *Ẓuhūr*, pp. 415 and 422ff.; O'Leary, *Fatimid Khalifate*, pp. 218–221, and S. M. Stern, 'al-Āmir bi-Aḥkām Allāh', *EI2*, vol. 1, p. 440.
12. On al-Afḍal, aside from the sources cited in connection with al-Musta'lī and al-Āmir, see Ibn al-Ṣayrafī, *al-Ishāra*, in *BIFAO* (1925), pp. 52–56 (57–61); Ibn al-Qalānisī, *Dhayl*, pp. 160–161, 172–173, 178, 182, 188–189 and 203–204; tr. Gibb, pp. 84, 86, 109–110, 120, 129–130, 142, 144 and 163–164; tr. Le Tourneau, pp. 81–82, 102–103, 110, 118, 128–129 and 153–155; Ibn al-Athīr, *al-Kāmil*, vol. 10, pp. 209–210; Ibn Khallikān, *Biographical Dictionary*, vol. 1, pp. 612–615; Ḥusayn, *Fī adab*, pp. 179ff.; al-Manāwī, *al-Wizāra*, pp. 56ff.,

68, 75, 79, 81, 89–92, 106, 117–119, 137, 148–149, 159, 178, 203–204, 225ff. and 271–272; Mājid, *Ẓuhūr*, pp. 408ff., and G. Wiet, 'al-Afḍal b. Badr al-Djamālī', *EI2*, vol. 1, pp. 215–216. According to the Nizārī chronicles used by Rashīd al-Dīn, *Ismāʿīliyān*, pp. 133 and 137, and other Persian historians, al-Afḍal was murdered by three Syrian Nizārīs.

13. See Ibn al-Ṣayrafī, *al-Ishāra*, in *BIFAO* (1925), pp. 49–52 (61–64); Ibn al-Athīr, *al-Kāmil*, vol. 10, p. 224; al-Maqrīzī, *al-Khiṭaṭ*, vol. 1, pp. 125–128 and 462–463; al-Manāwī, *al-Wizāra*, pp. 272–275, and D. M. Dunlop, 'al-Baṭā'iḥī', *EI2*, vol. 1, pp. 1091–1092.
14. Ibn Muyassar, *Akhbār*, ed. Massé, pp. 65 and 68–69, ed. Sayyid, pp. 97 and 103, and Hodgson, *Order of Assassins*, pp. 69–72.
15. Ibn Muyassar, *Akhbār*, ed. Massé, pp. 66–67, ed. Sayyid, pp. 99–101; see also al-Maqrīzī, *Ittiʿāẓ*, vol. 3, pp. 84–87.
16. *Al-Hidāyatu'l-Āmirīya*, ed. Fyzee, text pp. 3–26, reprinted in al-Shayyāl, *Majmūʿat al-wathāʾiq*, text pp. 203–230, commentaries pp. 47–67. This epistle is fully analyzed in S. M. Stern, 'The Epistle of the Fatimid Caliph al-Āmir (al-Hidāya al-Āmiriyya) – its Date and its Purpose', *JRAS* (1950), pp. 20–31, reprinted in his *History and Culture in the Medieval Muslim World* (London, 1984). Stern was the first modern scholar who, on the basis of Ibn Muyassar's account, identified Ibn al-Ṣayrafī as the scribe of the *Hidāya*. See also al-Majdūʿ, *Fihrist*, pp. 116 and 260; Fyzee's introductory remarks in his edition of *al-Hidāya*, pp. 1–16; Ivanow, *Guide*, p. 50; Ivanow, *Ismaili Literature*, p. 49, and Poonawala, *Bio*, pp. 130–131.
17. *Al-Hidāyatu'l-Āmirīya*, text p. 21.
18. Ibid., text pp. 10, 13, 14, 16, 18, 22, 23 and 24.
19. This additional epistle, the *Īqāʿ ṣawāʿiq al-irghām*, appears as an appendix to *al-Hidāyatu'l-Āmirīya*, text pp. 27–39, reprinted in al-Shayyāl, *Majmūʿat al-wathāʾiq*, text pp. 231–247, commentaries pp. 68–70. See also al-Majdūʿ, *Fihrist*, pp. 280 and 284; Stern, 'Epistle of the Fatimid Caliph al-Āmir', pp. 30–31, and Poonawala, *Bio*, p. 131.
20. This *sijill* is preserved in the first volume of the *Majmūʿ al-tarbiya*, a chrestomathy of Ismāʿīlī literature compiled by Muḥammad b. Ṭāhir al-Ḥārithī (d. 584/1188), and in the seventh volume of the *ʿUyūn al-akhbār* of Idrīs; it is also quoted in ʿUmāra, *Ta'rīkh*, text pp. 100–102, translation pp. 135–136.
21. Ibn Muyassar, *Akhbār*, ed. Massé, p. 72, ed. Sayyid, pp. 109–110.
22. See S. M. Stern, 'The Succession to the Fatimid Imam al-Āmir, the Claims of the Later Fatimids to the Imamate, and the Rise of Ṭayyibī Ismailism', *Oriens*, 4 (1951), pp. 193ff., reprinted in his *History and Culture in the Medieval Muslim World*, and hereafter cited as 'Succession'; this is the most detailed modern investigation of the events following al-Āmir's assassination and of the origins of the Ṭayyibī–Ḥāfiẓī schism. See also G. Wiet, *Matériaux pour un corpus Inscriptionum Arabicarum*: vol. 2, in *Mémoires de l'Institut Français d'Archéologie Orientale*, 52 (1930), pp. 83ff.
23. Ibn Taghrībirdī, *al-Nujūm*, vol. 5, pp. 240–241, quoting a report by Ibn al-

Ṭuwayr according to which al-Āmir, shortly before his death, had prophesied his assassination and had in effect revoked his *naṣṣ* for al-Ṭayyib in favour of the expected posthumous child.

24. Ibn Muyassar, *Akhbār*, ed. Massé, p. 74, ed. Sayyid, p. 113, merely stating that the matter of al-Āmir's child, born in 524 A.H., was concealed by 'Abd al-Majīd.
25. See Stern, 'A Fāṭimid Decree of the Year 524/1130', pp. 446–455, and also his *Fāṭimid Decrees*, pp. 35ff.
26. See H. Sauvaire and S. Lane-Poole, 'The Name of the Twelfth Imam on the Coinage of Egypt', *JRAS*, NS, 7 (1875), pp. 140–151; P. Balog, 'Quatre dinars du Khalife Fatimide al-Mountazar li-amr-illah', *Bulletin de l'Institut d'Égypte*, 33 (1950–1951), pp. 375–378, and George C. Miles, *Fāṭimid Coins in the Collections of the University Museum, Philadelphia, and the American Numismatic Society* (New York, 1951), pp. 44–45. See also M. Jungfleisch, 'Jetons (ou poids?) en verre de l'Imam El Montazer', *Bulletin de l'Institut d'Égypte*, 33 (1950–1951), pp. 359–374, describing Fāṭimid glass weights bearing inscriptions in the name of the expected imām.
27. Al-Maqrīzī, *al-Khiṭaṭ*, vol. 1, pp. 357 and 490.
28. On al-Ḥāfiẓ and his turbulent times, see Ibn al-Qalānisī, *Dhayl*, pp. 203, 229, 242ff., 262, 270, 272–273, 282, 295–296, 302 and 308; tr. Le Tourneau, pp. 154, 191, 213ff., 241, 253–254, 258, 271, 291–292, 301 and 311; Ibn Ẓāfir, *Akhbār*, pp. 94–101; Ibn Muyassar, *Akhbār*, ed. Massé, pp. 74–89, ed. Sayyid, pp. 113–141; Ibn al-Athīr, *al-Kāmil*, vol. 10, pp. 237, 240, and vol. 11, pp. 8–9, 18–19, 34 and 53; Ibn Khallikān, *Biographical Dictionary*, vol. 2, pp. 179–181; Ibn al-Dawādārī, *Kanz*, vol. 6, pp. 506–556; al-Maqrīzī, *al-Khiṭaṭ*, vol. 1, pp. 357, 490–491, and vol. 2, pp. 17–18; French tr., vol. 4, pp. 30–32; also his *Ittiʿāẓ*, vol. 3, pp. 135–192, and Ibn Taghrībirdī, *al-Nujūm*, vol. 5, pp. 237–287; see also Ḥasan, *Ta'rīkh*, pp. 176–181, 213–215 and 247–248; Zāhid ʿAlī, *Ta'rīkh*, vol. 2, pp. 23–35; Surūr, *Miṣr*, pp. 95–101; Mājid, *Ẓuhūr*, pp. 425–434; al-Manāwī, *al-Wizāra*, pp. 276–281; O'Leary, *Fatimid Khalifate*, pp. 222–226; M. Canard, 'Fāṭimides et Būrides à l'époque du calife al-Ḥāfiẓ li-Dīn-Illāh', *REI*, 35 (1967), pp. 103–117; S. M. Stern, 'al-Afḍal Kutayfāt', *EI2*, vol. 1, p. 216, and A. M. Magued, 'al-Ḥāfiẓ', *EI2*, vol. 3, pp. 54–55.
29. Al-Qalqashandī, *Ṣubḥ*, vol. 9, pp. 291–297, reproduced in al-Shayyāl, *Majmūʿat al-wathā'iq*, text pp. 249–260, commentaries pp. 71–102; see also Stern, 'Succession', pp. 207ff.
30. See al-Qalqashandī, *Ṣubḥ*, vol. 6, p. 450, vol. 7, p. 108, and vol. 8, p. 344, and a decree of al-Ḥāfiẓ cited in Stern, *Fāṭimid Decrees*, p. 59.
31. Al-Qalqashandī, *Ṣubḥ*, vol. 9, pp. 377–379, reproduced in al-Shayyāl, *Majmūʿat al-wathā'iq*, text pp. 261–265, commentaries pp. 103–107.
32. On Bahrām and his career, see al-Qalqashandī, *Ṣubḥ*, vol. 6, pp. 458–463, vol. 8, pp. 260–262, and vol. 13, pp. 325–326, and the studies of M. Canard, including his 'Un vizir chrétien à l'époque Fāṭimite: l'Arménien Bahrām', *AIEO*, 12 (1954), pp. 84–113; 'Une lettre du calife Fāṭimite al-Ḥāfiẓ',

especially pp. 136ff.; 'Notes sur les Arméniens en Égypte', pp. 151ff., all three articles reprinted in his *Miscellanea Orientalia*, and 'Bahrām', *EI2*, vol. 1, pp. 939–940.

33. See M. Canard, 'Ibn Maṣāl', *EI2*, vol. 3, p. 868.

34. On the last three Fāṭimids and the downfall of their dynasty, see Ibn al-Qalānisī, *Dhayl*, pp. 308, 311, 312, 316, 319–320, 321, 329–330, 331, 351, 353 and 360–361; tr. Le Tourneau, pp. 311, 316, 318, 325, 330 and 332; Ibn Ẓāfir, *Akhbār*, pp. 102–117; Ibn Muyassar, ed. Massé, pp. 89–98, ed. Sayyid, pp. 141–157, covering the events until 553/1158; Ibn al-Athīr, *al-Kāmil*, vol. 11, pp. 53–54, 70, 72–73, 96, 99, 103, 108–109, 111–112, 121–122, 125–129, 131–132 and 137–139; Ibn Khallikān, *Biographical Dictionary*, vol. 1, pp. 222–223, and vol. 2, pp. 72–74 and 425–427; Ibn al-Dawādārī, *Kanz*, vol. 6, pp. 557–572, ending his narrative with the year 554/1159; al-Maqrīzī, *al-Khiṭaṭ*, vol. 1, pp. 338–339, 357–359, 496–498, and vol. 2, pp. 2–3, 12–13, 30 and 233; French tr., vol. 3, pp. 283–288, and vol. 4, pp. 32–36; al-Maqrīzī, *Ittiʿāẓ*, vol. 3, pp. 193–334; Ibn Taghrībirdī, *al-Nujūm*, vol. 5, pp. 288–389, and vol. 6, pp. 3ff. The famous memoirs of Usāma b. Munqidh (d. 584/1188), a Syrian author and warrior who was in Egypt during 539–549/1144–1154 and personally knew al-Ḥāfiẓ and the viziers Ibn al-Salār and ʿAbbās, also contain important details on the closing period of the Fāṭimid dynasty; see the English translation of this work entitled *Memoirs of an Arab–Syrian Gentleman*, tr. Philip K. Hitti (Beirut, 1964), especially pp. 30–59, originally published in 1927 with a different title; Professor Hitti (1886–1978) also prepared an edition of the Arabic text of Usāma's memoirs, *Kitāb al-iʿtibār* (Princeton, 1930), pp. 6–42. More recently, A. Miquel has prepared an edition and French translation of this work under the title of *Kitāb al-Iʿtibār: Des enseignements de la vie; Souvenirs d'un gentilhomme Syrien du temps des Croisades* (Paris, 1983). See also Ḥasan, *Ta'rīkh*, pp. 179–201; Zāhid ʿAlī, *Ta'rīkh*, vol. 2, pp. 36–66; Surūr, *Miṣr*, pp. 101–116; Mājid, *Ẓuhūr*, pp. 434–496; al-Manāwī, *al-Wizāra*, pp. 56ff., 70, 108ff., 140–141, 164ff., 181–182, 225–234 and 282–291; O'Leary, *Fatimid Khalifate*, pp. 227–245, and G. Wiet, 'al-ʿĀḍid li-Dīn Allāh', *EI2*, vol. 1, pp. 196–197.

35. Ibn Khallikān, *Biographical Dictionary*, vol. 2, pp. 350–353; Nikita Elisséeff, *Nūr ad-Dīn, un grand prince Musulman de Syrie au temps des Croisades* (Damascus, 1967), vol. 2, pp. 474ff., and G. Wiet, 'al-ʿĀdil b. al-Salār', *EI2*, vol. 1, p. 198.

36. See C. H. Becker and S. M. Stern, 'ʿAbbās b. Abi'l-Futūḥ', *EI2*, vol. 1, p. 9.

37. On Ṭalā'iʿ and his son and successor Ruzzīk, see al-Shayyāl, *Majmūʿat al-wathā'iq*, text pp. 335–353, commentaries pp. 151–154; Stern, *Fāṭimid Decrees*, pp. 70–79; Derenbourg, *ʿOumāra*, vol. 1, pp. 32–37, 40–60, 62–64, 174–176, 229–235, 243–248, 294–298, 312–315, 388–391, and vol. 2 (partie française), pp. 119–253; Ibn Khallikān, *Biographical Dictionary*, vol. 1, pp. 657–661; Ibn al-Dawādārī, *Kanz al-durar*, ed. Saʿīd ʿAbd al-Fattāḥ ʿĀshūr (Cairo, 1972), vol. 7, pp. 16–18; Ḥusayn, *Fī adab*, pp. 193ff.; J. Walker, 'Ṭalā'iʿ b. Ruzzīk', *EI*, vol. 4, pp. 635–636, and H. A. R. Gibb, 'Ruzzīk b. Ṭalā'iʿ', *EI*, vol. 3, p. 1190.

38. On Shāwar and Ḍirghām, see al-Qalqashandī, *Ṣubḥ*, vol. 10, pp. 310–325,

reproduced in al-Shayyāl, *Majmūʿat al-wathāʾiq*, text pp. 355–379, commentaries pp. 155–170; Derenbourg, *ʿOumāra*, vol. 1, pp. 66–92, 146–148, 167–169, 274–278, 367–369, and vol. 2, pp. 255–347; Ibn Khallikān, *Biographical Dictionary*, vol. 1, pp. 608–612; Ibn al-Dawādārī, *Kanz*, vol. 7, pp. 18–19 and 25–39; M. Canard, 'Ḍirghām', *EI2*, vol. 2, pp. 317–319, and G. Wiet, 'Shāwar', *EI*, vol. 4, pp. 339–340.

39. For Amalric's Egyptian expeditions and his relations with the Fāṭimids and Zangids, see G. Schlumberger, *Campagnes du roi Amaury Ier en Égypte* (Paris, 1906); René Grousset, *Histoire des Croisades* (Paris, 1934–1936), vol. 2, pp. 436–458 and 478–551, and Marshall W. Baldwin, 'The Latin States under Baldwin III and Amalric I, 1143–1174', in *A History of the Crusades*, ed. Kenneth M. Setton: Volume 1, *The First Hundred Years*, ed. M. W. Baldwin (2nd ed., Madison, Wisconsin, 1969), pp. 548–561. For the relationships between the Crusaders and Fāṭimid Egypt, and the relevant occidental sources on the subject, see Steven Runciman, *A History of the Crusades* (Cambridge, 1951–1954), vol. 2, pp. 362–400; see also E. Sivan, *L'Islam et la Croisade* (Paris, 1968), pp. 59–91 and 93ff.

40. The account of this embassy, not recorded by Muslim chroniclers, is related in William of Tyre, *Historia rerum in patribus transmarinis gestarum*, book 19, chaps. 19–20.

41. On Shīrkūh and Saladin, see al-Qalqashandī, *Ṣubḥ*, vol. 9, pp. 406–407, and vol. 10, pp. 80–98, reproduced in al-Shayyāl, *Majmūʿat al-wathāʾiq*, text pp. 381–419, commentaries pp. 171–178; Stern, *Fāṭimid Decrees*, pp. 80–84; Derenbourg, *ʿOumāra*, vol. 1, pp. 78–80, 260–262, and vol. 2, pp. 349–388; Ibn Khallikān, *Biographical Dictionary*, vol. 1, pp. 626–629, and vol. 4, pp. 479–563, and Ibn al-Dawādārī, *Kanz*, vol. 7, pp. 39ff. and 47ff. Hamilton A. R. Gibb has produced a number of studies on Saladin, with analysis of the relevant sources, in his 'The Rise of Saladin, 1169–1189', in *A History of the Crusades*: Volume 1, pp. 563–589; 'The Arabic Sources for the Life of Saladin', *Speculum*, 25 (1950), pp. 58–72, and *The Life of Saladin, from the works of ʿImād ad-Dīn and Bahāʾ ad-Dīn* (Oxford, 1973). From amongst other modern works on Saladin, mention may be made of Stanley Lane-Poole, *Saladin and the Fall of the Kingdom of Jerusalem* (London, 1898); Andrew S. Ehrenkreutz, *Saladin* (Albany, N.Y., 1972), and his 'Saladin's Coup d'État in Egypt', in *Medieval and Middle Eastern Studies in Honor of Aziz Suryal Atiya*, ed. Sami A. Hanna (Leiden, 1972), pp. 144–157. Much relevant information on these two personalities and the final years of the Fāṭimid dynasty is also contained in Elisséeff, *Nūr ad-Dīn*, vol. 2, pp. 563–674. See also G. Wiet, 'Shīrkūh', *EI*, vol. 4, pp. 381–382, and M. Sobernheim, 'Saladin', *EI*, vol. 4, pp. 84–89.

42. See Ibn Muyassar, *Akhbār*, ed. Massé, pp. 76, 84, 88 and 93, ed. Sayyid, pp. 118, 120, 132, 139 and 148, and al-Maqrīzī, *al-Khiṭaṭ*, vol. 1, p. 391.

43. The extant anonymous *al-Qaṣīda al-Shāfiya*, ed. and tr. S. N. Makarem (Beirut, 1966), also edited by ʿĀ. Tāmir (Beirut, 1967), was, however, originally composed by a Ḥāfiẓī poet and then revised by a Nizārī author. See W. Madelung's review of these editions in *ZDMG*, 118 (1968), pp. 423–424, and *Oriens*, 23–24 (1970–1971), pp. 517–518.

44. For the fullest account of these pro-Fāṭimid revolts, and the situation of the Fāṭimids after the fall of their dynasty, see P. Casanova, 'Les Derniers Fāṭimides', *Mémoires de la Mission Archéologique Française du Caire*, 6 (1897), pp. 415–445.
45. Ibn al-Athīr, *al-Kāmil*, vol. 11, pp. 149–150; Ibn Wāṣil, *Mufarrij al-kurūb*, ed. J. al-Shayyāl (Cairo, 1953–1960), vol. 1, pp. 236, 244 and 246–247; Ibn al-Dawādārī, *Kanz*, vol. 7, p. 55; al-Maqrīzī, *Histoire d'Égypte*, tr. E. Blochet, in *Revue de l'Orient Latin*, 6–11 (1898–1908), pp. 58–60 (continuous pagination), also printed separately (Paris, 1908), being the French translation of the part dealing with the Ayyūbids in al-Maqrīzī's history entitled *al-Sulūk*; English translation, *A History of the Ayyūbid Sultans of Egypt*, tr. Ronald J. C. Broadhurst (Boston, 1980), pp. 46–47; Ibn Taghrībirdī, *al-Nujūm*, vol. 6, pp. 70–71 and 73, and Elisséeff, *Nūr ad-Dīn*, vol. 2, pp. 688–691.
46. Ibn al-Athīr, *al-Kāmil*, vol. 11, p. 156; Ibn al-Dawādārī, *Kanz*, vol. 7, p. 58; al-Maqrīzī, *Histoire d'Égypte*, pp. 55–56 and 63–64, and al-Maqrīzī, *Ayyūbid Sultans of Egypt*, pp. 44 and 50–51.
47. Al-Maqrīzī, *al-Khiṭaṭ*, vol. 1, p. 233, and Ibn Taghrībirdī, *al-Nujūm*, vol. 6, p. 78.
48. See Ibn al-Athīr, *al-Kāmil*, vol. 12, pp. 9–10; al-Maqrīzī, *Histoire d'Égypte*, pp. 136 and 158–159, and also his *Ayyūbid Sultans of Egypt*, pp. 89 and 97–98.
49. Al-Maqrīzī, *Ittiʿāẓ*, vol. 3, pp. 347–348, and also his *Ayyūbid Sultans of Egypt*, p. 151.
50. Ibn al-Dawādārī, *Kanz*, vol. 7, p. 363.
51. Al-Maqrīzī, *Histoire d'Égypte*, p. 237, and also his *Ayyūbid Sultans of Egypt*, p. 151.
52. Stern, 'Succession', pp. 211–212.
53. ʿUmāra, *Ta'rīkh*, text pp. 48–59, translation pp. 64–80, based on the only known extant manuscript copy of this work, which is very faulty. ʿUmāra's chapter on the Zurayʿids is cited in more correct form by Ibn al-Mujāwir (d. 690/1291) in his *Ta'rīkh al-Mustabṣir*; the relevant extract is contained in *Arabische Texte zur Kenntnis der Stadt Aden im Mittelalter*, ed. O. Löfgren (Uppsala, 1936–1950), vol. 1, pp. 24–70. The complete text of Ibn al-Mujāwir's *al-Mustabṣir* has been edited by O. Löfgren (Leiden, 1951–1954), 2 vols.
54. For some relevant extracts on the Zurayʿids from Abu'l-Ḥasan ʿAlī b. al-Ḥasan al-Khazrajī's still unpublished dynastic history of Yaman, entitled *al-Kifāya wa'l-iʿlām fī man waliya al-Yaman*, together with valuable notes, see Kay, *Yaman*, pp. 266–278. See also Redhouse's introduction to his translation of al-Khazrajī's *al-ʿUqūd al-lu'lu'iyya*, the history of the Rasūlids from *al-Kifāya*, under the title of *The Pearl-Strings; a History of the Resūliyy Dynasty of Yemen*, tr. J. W. Redhouse, ed. E. G. Browne et al. (Leiden–London, 1906–1908), vol. 1, pp. 18–19, 21 and 23, and G. R. Smith, *The Ayyūbids and Early Rasūlids in the Yemen (567–694/1173–1295)* (London, 1974–1978), vol. 2, pp. 63–67.
55. See C. L. Geddes, 'Bilāl b. Djarīr al-Muḥammadī', *EI2*, vol. 1, pp. 1214–1215.

56. On this investiture and the dāʿīship of the Zurayʿids, see ʿUmāra, *Ta'rīkh*, text pp. 50 and 55, translation pp. 67 and 74; Abū Makhrama ʿAbd Allāh al-Ṭayyib b. ʿAbd Allāh, *Ta'rīkh thaghr ʿAdan*, in *Arabische Texte*, vol. 2, pp. 32 and 216ff., and Yaḥyā b. al-Ḥusayn b. al-Qāsim, *Ghāyat al-amānī fī akhbār al-quṭr al-Yamānī*, ed. Saʿīd ʿA. ʿĀshūr (Cairo, 1968), pp. 297–298, written by a Zaydī author who died around 1100/1688. See also Ibn al-Mujāwir, *Ta'rīkh al-Mustabṣir*, ed. Löfgren, vol. 1, pp. 126–127; Stern, 'Succession', pp. 214ff., 226–227 and 229–230, and Hamdani, 'Dāʿī Ḥātim', pp. 270 and 273–274.
57. See ʿUmāra, *Ta'rīkh*, text p. 27, translation p. 37, the author having been on friendly terms with ʿImrān and his father; S. Lane-Poole, *Catalogue of the Oriental Coins in the British Museum* (London, 1875-1890), vol. 5, p. 121; N. M. Lowick, 'Some Unpublished Dinars of the Ṣulayḥids and Zurayʿids', *Numismatic Chronicle*, 7th series, 4 (1964), pp. 261ff., suggesting a different view, and M. L. Bates, 'Notes on some Ismāʿīlī Coins from Yemen', *American Numismatic Society Notes*, 18 (1972), pp. 149ff.
58. See Kay's notes in his *Yaman*, pp. 274ff., and Abū Makhrama, *Ta'rīkh*, in *Arabische Texte*, vol. 2, pp. 41–43.
59. On the Hamdānids of Ṣanʿā', see Kay's notes, based on al-Khazrajī, in his *Yaman*, pp. 230, 294–297 and 299; Redhouse's introduction to al-Khazrajī, *Pearl-Strings*, vol. 1, pp. 13–18, 20 and 22ff.; Stern, 'Succession', pp. 231–232 and 249–253, also containing relevant extracts from the *ʿUyūn al-akhbār* of Idrīs; Hamdani, 'Dāʿī Ḥātim', pp. 259, 263–265, 266, 268–270 and 280, utilizing extensively the *ʿUyūn al-akhbār* and the *Nuzhat al-afkār* of Idrīs; Smith, *Ayyūbids*, vol. 2, pp. 68–75, and C. L. Geddes, 'Hamdānids', *EI2*, vol. 3, pp. 125–126.
60. Yaḥyā b. al-Ḥusayn, *Ghāyat al-amānī*, pp. 279, 280, 282 and 285.
61. Ibid., pp. 301–303.
62. This episode is related by Idrīs in the seventh volume of his *ʿUyūn al-akhbār*; the relevant passage is quoted in Stern, 'Succession', pp. 252–253.
63. The hostilities between the *dāʿī* Ḥātim and the Hamdānid ruler are described in Idrīs, *Nuzhat al-afkār*, vol. 1, extract in Hamdani, 'Dāʿī Ḥātim', pp. 288–289; in a passage in al-Khazrajī's *al-Kifāya*, cited in Stern, 'Succession', p. 253, and in Yaḥyā b. al-Ḥusayn, *Ghāyat al-amānī*, p. 317.
64. The Zurayʿid Muḥammad b. Saba' had refused, in 549/1154, to help ʿAlī b. Mahdī in his conquest of Zabīd; see ʿUmāra, *Ta'rīkh*, text p. 95, translation pp. 127–128. ʿUmāra was present at the Zurayʿid court in Dhū Jibla when the Mahdid arrived seeking assistance.
65. ʿUmāra, *Ta'rīkh*, text pp. 96ff., translation pp. 129ff., and Kay's notes therein pp. 294–295; Yaḥyā b. al-Ḥusayn, *Ghāyat al-amānī*, pp. 319–320, and Smith, *Ayyūbids*, vol. 2, pp. 60–62.
66. Badr al-Dīn Muḥammad b. Ḥātim al-Yāmī, *Kitāb al-simṭ al-ghālī al-thaman*, ed. Smith, in his *Ayyūbids*, vol. 1, especially pp. 15–42, 48, 64–65, 69–70, 91, 100, 119, 139, 203, 449–450 and 460; see also Redhouse's introduction to al-Khazrajī, *Pearl-Strings*, vol. 1, pp. 20 and 22–25.
67. This treatise, the *Tuḥfat al-murtād*, may be found in *Gnosis-Texte der Ismailiten*, ed. Strothmann, pp. 159–170.

68. For a vague reference to the existence of an isolated Ṭayyibī community in Egypt mentioned in an anonymous Syrian chronicle written towards the end of the sixth/twelfth century, see Cl. Cahen, 'Une chronique Syrienne du VIe–XIIe siècle: *Le Bustān al-Jāmiʿ*', *Bulletin d'Études Orientales*, 7–8 (1937–1938), pp. 121–122, hereafter cited as *Bustān*, and Stern, 'Succession', p. 198.
69. Cited in Stern, 'Succession', p. 198.
70. For the most detailed modern account of the establishment of the Ṭayyibī *daʿwa* in Yaman, see al-Hamdānī, 'Doctrines and History of the Ismāʿīlī Daʿwat in Yemen', and also his *al-Ṣulayḥiyyūn*. The late Ḥusayn al-Hamdānī, who had access to a family collection of Ismāʿīlī manuscripts, was the first modern Ismāʿīlī scholar to base his pioneering studies of Yamanī Ismāʿīlism on genuine sectarian sources.
71. *Bustān*, pp. 121–122.
72. The relevant extract from Idrīs, quoting Ibrāhīm al-Ḥāmidī, is reproduced in Stern, 'Succession', pp. 232–233; see also al-Hamdānī, 'Doctrines and History', pp. 41ff.; Zāhid ʿAlī, *Ta'rīkh*, vol. 2, pp. 25–28, and Stern, 'Succession', pp. 199–201.
73. According to a legend, known to the Ṭayyibīs, al-Ṭayyib lived in a remote district of the Maghrib; see Stern, 'Succession', pp. 201–202.
74. The relevant passage from al-Khaṭṭāb's *Ghāyat al-mawālīd* is contained in Ivanow, *Rise*, text pp. 37–38; English translation in Stern, 'Succession', pp. 223–224.
75. The passages regarding these sermons, as preserved in the *ʿUyūn al-akhbār* of Idrīs, are translated in Stern, 'Succession', pp. 224–225.
76. Cited in Stern, 'Succession', p. 226.
77. ʿUmāra, *Ta'rīkh*, text p. 100, translation p. 134.
78. See Hamdani, 'Dāʿī Ḥātim', pp. 262–263.
79. The testimonies of al-Khaṭṭāb and Idrīs for this designation are cited in Stern, 'Succession', pp. 221 and 227–228, and Hamdānī, 'Dāʿī Ḥātim', p. 271.
80. See ʿUmāra, *Ta'rīkh*, text pp. 42–48 and 99, translation pp. 57–64 and 134, and Kay's notes therein pp. 297–299. Stern, utilizing ʿUmāra and al-Janadī, made the same error in his 'Succession', pp. 214–223. On ʿAlī b. Ibrāhīm b. Najīb al-Dawla, see al-Hamdānī, *al-Ṣulayḥiyyūn*, pp. 168–174.
81. Some relevant extracts from the *Tuḥfat al-qulūb* of Ḥātim b. Ibrāhīm and the *Nuzhat al-afkār* of Idrīs are contained in Stern, 'Succession', pp. 233–243, and in Hamdani, 'Dāʿī Ḥātim', pp. 286–298.
82. This testament, also containing a detailed description of her jewellery, has been preserved in the *ʿUyūn al-akhbār*, vol. 7, quoted in al-Hamdānī, *al-Ṣulayḥiyyūn*, pp. 323–330. The mausoleum of this celebrated queen, who ruled for more than sixty years, still exists in Dhū Jibla and is visited by members of different Muslim sects, see al-Hamdānī, 'Doctrines and History', pp. 45–46, and also his 'Life and Times of Queen Saiyidah', p. 515.
83. The earliest history of the Ṭayyibī *daʿwa* in Yaman is related by Ḥātim b. Ibrāhīm in his unpublished *Tuḥfat al-qulūb*. Idrīs, too, has biographical details on al-Dhu'ayb and his successors in his *ʿUyūn al-akhbār*, vol. 7, and *Nuzhat al-afkār*, both still in manuscript form. On al-Dhu'ayb's life and

works, see also al-Majdūʿ, *Fihrist*, pp. 130 and 201; Muḥammad ʿAlī, *Mawsim-i bahār*, vol. 3, pp. 46–50; Zāhid ʿAlī, *Ta'rīkh*, vol. 2, pp. 74–77; al-Hamdānī, *al-Ṣulayḥiyyūn*, pp. 181ff., 193 and 268–269; Ghālib, *Aʿlām*, pp. 293–294; Hamdani, 'Dāʿī Ḥātim', pp. 259 and 271–272; Ivanow, *Ismaili Literature*, p. 52, and Poonawala, *Bio*, pp. 137–139.

84. On al-Khaṭṭāb, see Ibrāhīm al-Ḥāmidī, *Kanz al-walad*, pp. 100–101 and 106–108; Stern, 'Succession', pp. 244–249, containing extracts from the *ʿUyūn al-akhbār*; Yaḥyā b. al-Ḥusayn, *Ghāyat al-amānī*, p. 281; al-Majdūʿ, *Fihrist*, pp. 41, 132, 198–199, 204 and 240; Muḥammad ʿAlī, *Mawsim-i bahār*, vol. 3, pp. 48–49; al-Hamdānī, 'Doctrines and History', pp. 46–47; also his *al-Ṣulayḥiyyūn*, pp. 193–204 and 269–270; Strothmann, 'Kleinere ismailitische Schriften', pp. 136–139 and 152–153; Ghālib, *Aʿlām*, pp. 280–282; Ivanow, *Ismaili Literature*, pp. 51–52; Poonawala, *Bio*, pp. 133–137, and also his *al-Sulṭān al-Khaṭṭāb* (Cairo, 1967), containing an edition of al-Khaṭṭāb's *Dīwān* of poetry, pp. 97–241, and a detailed study of his life, pp. 29–95.

85. See Ivanow, *Rise*, pp. 20–23, questioning al-Khaṭṭāb's authorship of the *Ghāyat*; Stern, 'Succession', pp. 227–228, and Poonawala, *al-Sulṭān al-Khaṭṭāb*, pp. 73–75 and 78–80.

86. See ʿUmāra, *Ta'rīkh*, text p. 102, translation p. 137, where it is stated that al-Sayyida in 526 A.H. nominated Ibrāhīm as the chief *dāʿī* before transferring the headship of the *daʿwa* on behalf of al-Ḥāfiẓ to the Zurayʿids. These statements are not corroborated by the Ṭayyibī tradition and this confused passage of ʿUmāra seems to have been subjected to later interpolations; see also Stern, 'Succession', pp. 215ff. and 228, and Hamdani, 'Dāʿī Ḥātim', pp. 273–274.

87. On Ibrāhīm al-Ḥāmidī, see al-Majdūʿ, *Fihrist*, pp. 237–239, 269, 270 and 279; Muḥammad ʿAlī, *Mawsim-i bahār*, vol. 3, pp. 50–51; al-Hamdānī, 'Doctrines and History', p. 48; and his *al-Ṣulayḥiyyūn*, pp. 270–273; Ghālib, *Aʿlām*, pp. 87–88; H. Feki, 'Trois traités Ismaéliens Yéménites' (Thèse de doctorat de 3e cycle, Sorbonne, Paris IV, 1970), pp. 22–28; Ivanow, *Ismaili Literature*, pp. 52–54; Poonawala, *Bio*, pp. 141–143, and W. Madelung, 'al-Ḥāmidī', *EI2*, vol. 3, p. 134, also containing notices on Ḥātim b. Ibrāhīm and ʿAlī b. Ḥātim al-Ḥāmidī.

88. On Ḥātim b. Ibrāhīm, see a section of his own *Tuḥfat al-qulūb*, cited in Stern, 'Succession', pp. 236ff., while the most detailed account is contained in Idrīs, *Nuzhat al-afkār*, quoted in Hamdani, 'Dāʿī Ḥātim', pp. 287–298; see also ʿUmāra, *Ta'rīkh*, text p. 102, translation p. 137; Yaḥyā b. al-Ḥusayn, *Ghāyat al-amānī*, p. 320, al-Bharūchī, *Kitāb al-azhār*, vol. 1, in *Muntakhabāt Ismāʿīliyya*, ed. al-ʿAwwā, pp. 184, 193ff. and 247; al-Majdūʿ, *Fihrist*, pp. 47–48, 53–54, 68–69, 84, 173–175, 180, 191–193, 199–200, 253–254, 261–263, 271–273 and 279; Muḥammad ʿAlī, *Mawsim-i bahār*, vol. 3, pp. 52–56; al-Hamdānī, 'Doctrines and History', pp. 48–52 and 104–105; also his *al-Ṣulayḥiyyūn*, pp. 273–280; Stern, 'Succession', pp. 215, 218, 220 and 228; Ghālib, *Aʿlām*, pp. 197–200; Hamdani, 'Dāʿī Ḥātim', pp. 279–286; also his 'The Ṭayyibī–Fāṭimid Community of the Yaman at the Time of the Ayyūbid Conquest of Southern Arabia', *Arabian Studies*, 7 (1985), pp. 151–

160; Ivanow, *Ismaili Literature*, pp. 61–68; Poonawala, *Bio*, pp. 151–155, and Madelung, 'al-Ḥāmidī', *EI2*, vol. 3, p. 134.

89. Idrīs, *Nuzhat al-afkār*, cited in Hamdani, 'Dāʿī Ḥātim', p. 290. On this region, see A. K. Irvine, 'Ḥarāz', *EI2*, vol. 3, pp. 178–179.

90. Some of these poems are cited in Stern, 'Succession', pp. 231–232 and 254. On Muḥammad b. Ṭāhir, see al-Majdūʿ, *Fihrist*, pp. 41–42, 129–134, 204, 246–253, 270 and 278; Muḥammad ʿAlī, *Mawsim-i bahār*, vol. 3, pp. 54–55; Ivanow, *Ismaili Literature*, pp. 54–61, and Poonawala, *Bio*, pp. 143–150.

91. On ʿAlī b. Muḥammad b. al-Walīd, see al-Bharūchī, *Kitāb al-azhār*, vol. 1, pp. 191, 193–194, 198 and 247; al-Majdūʿ, *Fihrist*, pp. 41–42, 80, 93–95, 123–127, 131, 140, 153, 200–201, 229–237, 244–246, 257 and 278; Muḥammad ʿAlī, *Mawsim-i bahār*, vol. 3, pp. 55 and 57–63; al-Hamdānī, 'Doctrines and History', pp. 53–55 and 105–106; also his *al-Ṣulayḥiyyūn*, pp. 284–291; Strothmann, 'Kleinere ismailitische Schriften', pp. 139–146; Feki, 'Trois traités', pp. 38–52; Ghālib, *Aʿlām*, pp. 408–411; Ivanow, *Ismaili Literature*, pp. 69–74; Poonawala, *Bio*, pp. 156–161, and also his 'ʿAlī b. Muḥammad b. Djaʿfar', *EI2*, Supplement, p. 62.

92. See especially ʿAlī b. Muḥammad's *Tāj al-ʿaqāʾid*, ed. ʿĀrif Tāmir (Beirut, 1967); summary English translation, W. Ivanow, *A Creed of the Fatimids* (Bombay, 1936); *Lubb al-maʿārif*, and *Mulḥiqāt al-adhhān*, in Feki, 'Trois traités', text pp. 1–45, French translation pp. 151–259; *Kitāb al-dhakhīra*, ed. Muḥammad Ḥasan al-Aʿẓamī (Beirut, 1971); *Jalāʾ al-ʿuqūl*, in *Muntakhabāt Ismāʿīliyya*, pp. 89–153, and *al-Īḍāḥ wa'l-tabyīn*, in *Gnosis-Texte*, pp. 137–158. As noted, he also produced a detailed refutation of al-Ghazālī's *al-Mustaẓhirī* in his *Dāmigh al-bāṭil*. ʿAlī b. Muḥammad was also a poet and excerpts of his poetry are cited in Strothmann, 'Kleinere ismailitische Schriften', pp. 153–163.

93. On ʿAlī b. Ḥanẓala, see al-Bharūchī, *Kitāb al-azhār*, vol. 1, pp. 195 and 247; al-Majdūʿ, *Fihrist*, pp. 196–197 and 269–270; Muḥammad ʿAlī, *Mawsim-i bahār*, vol. 3, pp. 61–65; al-Hamdānī, 'Doctrines and History', pp. 55–56; also his *al-Ṣulayḥiyyūn*, pp. 291–297; Ghālib, *Aʿlām*, pp. 379–380; Ivanow, *Ismaili Literature*, pp. 74–75; Poonawala, *Bio*, pp. 162–163, also his 'ʿAlī b. Ḥanẓala b. Abī Sālim', *EI2*, Supplement, p. 61. ʿAlī b. Ḥanẓala's important work in verse, on the *ḥaqāʾiq*, the *Simṭ al-ḥaqāʾiq* has been edited by ʿAbbās al-ʿAzzāwī (Damascus, 1953).

94. This treatise is contained in *Trilogie Ismaélienne*, ed. and tr. H. Corbin, text pp. 99–130, French translation pp. 148–200; see also Corbin's introductory remarks therein pp. 131–147. On al-Ḥusayn b. ʿAlī b. al-Walīd, see al-Bharūchī, *Kitāb al-azhār*, vol. 1, pp. 195 and 248; al-Majdūʿ, *Fihrist*, pp. 98, 149–150, 152–153, 207–223 and 279; Muḥammad ʿAlī, *Mawsim-i bahār*, vol. 3, pp. 66–74; al-Hamdānī, 'Doctrines and History', pp. 57–61; Ivanow, *Ismaili Literature*, pp. 75–76, and Poonawala, *Bio*, pp. 163–165.

95. On Idrīs and his works, see al-Bharūchī, *Kitāb al-azhār*, vol. 1, pp. 188, 196, 202 and 250; al-Majdūʿ, *Fihrist*, pp. 34, 44, 73–77, 85, 97, 103–104, 150–151, 239–242, 270 and 275–277; Muḥammad ʿAlī, *Mawsim-i bahār*, vol. 3, pp. 107–108 and 138–146; al-Hamdānī, 'Doctrines and History', pp. 1–26, 127ff. and 137–253, drawing extensively on the writings of Idrīs; Zāhid ʿAlī,

Ta'rīkh, vol. 2, pp. 77–78; Ghālib, *Aʿlām*, pp. 137–139; Sayyid, *Maṣādir*, pp. 180–183; Ivanow, *Guide*, pp. 62–65; also his *Ismaili Literature*, pp. 77–82; Poonawala, *Bio*, pp. 169–175, and also his 'Idrīs b. al-Ḥasan', *EI2*, Supplement, p. 407.

96. For elaborations of the Ṭayyibī *ḥaqā'iq* system, with its cosmological doctrine, eschatology, anthropology, as well as its conceptions of mythohistory, prophetology and imamology, see Ibrāhīm b. al-Ḥusayn al-Ḥāmidī, *Kanz al-walad*; also his *al-Ibtidā' wa'l-intihā'*, in Feki, 'Trois traités', text pp. 46ff., French translation pp. 260ff.; ʿAlī b. Muḥammad b. al-Walīd, *Lubb al-maʿārif*, in Feki, 'Trois traités', text pp. 1ff., translation pp. 151ff.; also his *al-Īḍāḥ*, in *Gnosis-Texte*, pp. 137ff., and his *Kitāb al-dhakhīra*; al-Ḥusayn b. ʿAlī b. al-Walīd, *al-Mabda' wa'l-maʿād*, in *Trilogie Ismaélienne*, text pp. 99–130, translation pp. 148–200, containing an excellent summary of the subject by the eighth *dāʿī muṭlaq*; excerpts from this *dāʿī*'s *Kitāb al-īḍāḥ wa'l-bayān* are contained in B. Lewis, 'An Ismaili Interpretation of the Fall of Adam', *BSOS*, 9 (1938), pp. 691–704; see also al-Khaṭṭāb b. al-Ḥasan, *Dīwān*, in Poonawala, *al-Sulṭān al-Khaṭṭāb*, pp. 69ff. and 319–326, and the anonymous work entitled *Masā'il majmūʿa min al-ḥaqā'iq*, a collection of several small treatises, in *Gnosis-Texte*, pp. 4–136. The works of Ibrāhīm al-Ḥāmidī and his successors are synthesized and reproduced in Idrīs ʿImād al-Dīn's still unpublished *Zahr al-maʿānī* (personal copy), especially chapters 4–11 which deal with cosmogony. A summarized English description of the contents of the *Zahr al-maʿānī* may be found in al-Hamdānī, 'Doctrines and History', pp. 137–253; see also al-Hamdānī, 'A Compendium of Ismāʿīlī Esoterics', *IC*, 11 (1937), pp. 210–220. More than any other modern scholar, Henry Corbin has studied the various aspects of Ṭayyibī thought, especially the Ṭayyibī cosmology with its so-called *le drame dans le ciel*, and eschatology, also discussing the parallels between the Ṭayyibī doctrines and those found in Manichaeism and other pre-Islamic Iranian religions; see especially his introductory remarks in his *Trilogie Ismaélienne*, pp. 131–147; *Histoire*, pp. 124–136; 'Le temps cyclique', pp. 192–217; 'Épiphanie divine', pp. 148ff., 162ff., 171ff. and 193ff., and 'De la gnose antique', pp. 114ff. and 126–133, all three articles are reprinted in his *Temps cyclique et gnose Ismaélienne*, pp. 47–69, 76ff., 88ff., 97ff., 116ff., 176ff. and 189–197, and translated into English in his *Cyclical Time and Ismaili Gnosis*, pp. 37–58, 65ff., 76ff., 84ff., 103ff., 161ff. and 173–181. See also Zāhid ʿAlī, *Hamārē*, pp. 576ff.; also his *Ta'rīkh*, vol. 2, pp. 195–210; Madelung, 'Imamat', pp. 132–135; David R. Blumenthal, 'An Example of Ismaili Influence in Post-Maimonidean Yemen', in *Studies in Judaism and Islam presented to S. D. Goitein*, ed. Shelomo Morag et al. (Jerusalem, 1981), pp. 155–174, and H. Feki, *Les idées religieuses et philosophiques de l'Ismaélisme Fatimide* (Tunis, 1978), especially pp. 109–138.

97. Al-Ḥāmidī, *Kanz al-walad*, pp. 66, 68, 78ff. and 132.

98. Corbin, 'Cyclical Time in Mazdaism and Ismailism', in *Papers from the Eranos Yearbooks*, vol. 3, pp. 134ff., 143, 149 and 153ff., reprinted in his *Cyclical Time*, pp. 20ff., 29, 35 and 39ff. See also al-Shahrastānī, *al-Milal*, vol. 2, pp.

39–41; tr. Haarbrücker, vol. 1, pp. 277–280; tr. Gimaret and Monnot, pp. 638–641; English translation in R. C. Zaehner, *Zurvan: A Zoroastrian Dilemma* (New York, 1972), pp. 433–434.

99. Corbin, 'Cyclical Time in Mazdaism and Ismailism', pp. 161–162, reprinted in his *Cyclical Time*, pp. 47–48.

100. Al-Kirmānī, *Rāḥat al-ʿaql*, pp. 224–225.

101. Al-Hamdānī, 'Doctrines and History', pp. 236–243; A. Hamdani, 'Dāʿī Ḥātim', pp. 275ff., also his 'Evolution of the Organisational Structure of the Fāṭimī Daʿwah', pp. 94–95, 102–103 and 111, citing excerpts from the *Tuḥfat al-qulūb*. See also R. Strothmann's introductory remarks in his partial edition of Ismāʿīl b. Hibat Allāh's *Mizāj al-tasnīm* (Göttingen, 1944–1955), pp. 16ff., a commentary of the Qur'ān by the thirty-third Sulaymānī *dāʿī*, who was a learned religious scholar and made some original contributions to Ṭayyibī Ismāʿīlī thought.

102. For these traditional accounts of the opening phase of Ismāʿīlism in Gujarāt, mixing reality with legend, see Muḥammad ʿAlī, *Mawsim-i bahār*, vol. 3, pp. 328–345; Ḥasan ʿAlī Badripresswala Ismāʿīljī, *Akhbār al-duʿāt al-akramīn* (Rajkot, 1937), pp. 53–60, a work in Gujarātī drawing on earlier *daʿwa* works as well as on the *Mawsim-i bahār*; Jhaveri, 'Legendary History of the Bohoras', pp. 39ff.; Abdul Husain, *Gulzare Daudi*, pp. 30ff., and Najm al-Ghanī Khān, *Madhāhib al-Islām* (Lucknow, 1924), pp. 270ff. Amongst more recent works, mention may be made of Zāhid ʿAlī, *Ta'rīkh*, vol. 2, pp. 80ff.; John N. Hollister, *The Shīʿa of India* (London, 1953), pp. 267ff.; Misra, *Muslim Communities*, pp. 8ff. and 19ff., and Asghar Ali Engineer, *The Bohras* (New Delhi, 1980), pp. 100ff.

103. Abdul Husain, *Gulzare Daudi*, p. 113.

104. For the succession of the Indian *wālīs*, see Muḥammad ʿAlī, *Mawsim-i bahār*, vol. 3, p. 327; Ismāʿīljī, *Akhbār*, p. 221, Najm al-Ghanī Khān, *Madhāhib*, p. 277, and Hollister, *Shīʿa*, p. 270.

105. On this schism in the Bohra community, see Muḥammad ʿAlī, *Mawsim-i bahār*, vol. 3, pp. 117–127; Ismāʿīljī, *Akhbār*, pp. 61–66; Najm al-Ghanī Khān, *Madhāhib*, pp. 316–317; Abdul Husain, *Gulzare Daudi*, p. 45; Zāhid ʿAlī, *Hamārē*, pp. 292–293; Misra, *Muslim Communities*, pp. 22–23, and Engineer, *Bohras*, pp. 108ff.

106. ʿAlī Muḥammad Khān, *Mirat-i Ahmadi*, Supplement, Persian text, pp. 130–131, English translation, p. 109.

107. Ismāʿīljī, *Akhbār*, pp. 67–69.

108. On al-Bharūchī, see his own *Kitāb al-azhār*, vol. 1, pp. 186ff.; al-Majdūʿ, *Fihrist*, pp. 77–88; Muḥammad ʿAlī, *Mawsim-i bahār*, vol. 3, pp. 155–156; Fyzee, 'Study of the Literature of the Fatimid Daʿwa', pp. 238–242; Ivanow, *Ismaili Literature*, pp. 83–88; Poonawala, *Bio*, pp. 178–183, and also his 'Ḥasan b. Nūḥ', *EI2*, Supplement, p. 358.

109. Muḥammad ʿAlī, *Mawsim-i bahār*, vol. 3, pp. 153–161; Ismāʿīljī, *Akhbār*, pp. 85–86; Misra, *Muslim Communities*, pp. 25–26; Ivanow, *Ismaili Literature*, p. 88, and Poonawala, *Bio*, p. 184.

110. See al-Majdūʿ, *Fihrist*, pp. 37–38; Muḥammad ʿAlī, *Mawsim-i bahār*, vol. 3,

pp. 206, 237–238, 252 and 257; Ivanow, *Ismaili Literature*, pp. 88–89; Poonawala, *Bio*, pp. 185–186; also his 'Amīndjī b. Djalāl b. Ḥasan', *EI2*, Supplement, p. 70, and his 'Amīnjī b. Jalāl', *EIR*, vol. 1, p. 956.

111. On the Dā'ūdī–Sulaymānī schism, see Muḥammad ʿAlī, *Mawsim-i bahār*, vol. 3, pp. 169–259; Ismāʿīljī, *Akhbār*, pp. 110–112 and 144–168; Najm al-Ghanī Khān, *Madhāhib*, pp. 312–314; Misra, *Muslim Communities*, pp. 27–31, and Engineer, *Bohras*, pp. 117–122.

112. Biographical details on the Dā'ūdī *dāʿīs* are contained in Quṭb al-Dīn Burhānpūrī's *Muntazaʿ al-akhbār*, vol. 2, and in Muḥammad ʿAlī, *Mawsim-i bahār*, vol. 3. The Sulaymānīs have produced very few works, and information on their *dāʿīs* is rather scarce. Lists of the Mustaʿlī–Ṭayyibī *dāʿīs* and the separate *dāʿīs* of the Dā'ūdīs and Sulaymānīs may be found in the prayer books, the *Ṣaḥīfat al-ṣalāt*, of the Dā'ūdīs (Bombay, 1344/1925), pp. 277–342 and the Sulaymānīs (Bombay, 1340/1921), pp. 547–552, with more recent editions available of both documents; in Abdul Husain, *Gulzare Daudi*, pp. 39–43, and in A. A. A. Fyzee, 'A Chronological List of the Imams and Daʿis of the Mustaʿlian Ismailis', *JBBRAS*, NS, 10 (1934), pp. 8–16; also his 'Three Sulaymani Daʿīs: 1936–1939', *JBBRAS*, NS, 16 (1940), pp. 101–104; Hollister, *Shiʿa*, pp. 266–267 and 274–275; Ghālib, *Aʿlām*, table no. 3 in appendix, and Poonawala, *Bio*, pp. 364–369.

113. Najm al-Ghanī Khān, *Madhāhib*, p. 314, and Zāhid ʿAlī, *Hamārē*, pp. 293–294. For the ʿAliyya and some of the other minor schisms in the Dā'ūdī Bohra community, see Abdul Husain, *Gulzare Daudi*, pp. 46–47; Enthoven, *Tribes and Castes of Bombay*, vol. 1, pp. 200ff., and Ivanow, *Ismaili Literature*, pp. 109–111.

114. For the complete list, supplied by the present *dāʿī* of the ʿAliyya, see Poonawala, *Bio*, pp. 369–370.

115. Quṭbkhān is highly revered by the Dā'ūdīs as a *shahīd* or martyr, and his tomb is a well-known Bohra shrine at Aḥmadābād; see Muḥammad ʿAlī, *Mawsim-i bahār*, vol. 3, pp. 280–296, and Misra, *Muslim Communities*, pp. 32–34.

116. Muḥammad ʿAlī, *Mawsim-i bahār*, vol. 3, pp. 316–317; Ismāʿīljī, *Akhbār*, pp. 230ff., and Misra, *Muslim Communities*, pp. 35–36.

117. ʿAlī Muḥammad Khān, *Mirat-i Ahmadi*, Persian text, vol. 1, pp. 356 and 358–359, English translation, tr. Lokhandwala, pp. 315 and 317.

118. On the Hiptias and their leaders, see al-Majdūʿ, *Fihrist*, pp. 108–109 and 119; Muḥammad ʿAlī, *Mawsim-i bahār*, vol. 3, pp. 440–526; Zāhid ʿAlī, *Hamārē*, pp. 294–295; Misra, *Muslim Communities*, pp. 41–42; Ivanow, *Ismaili Literature*, pp. 93–94; Poonawala, *Bio*, pp. 13 and 204–206, and also his 'Luḳmāndjī', *EI2*, vol. 5, pp. 814–815.

119. For the controversy surrounding the succession to the forty-sixth Dā'ūdī *dāʿī*, and the ensuing events, see Muḥammad ʿAlī, *Mawsim-i bahār*, vol. 3, pp. 693–767; Ismāʿīljī, *Akhbār*, pp. 362ff.; Zāhid ʿAlī, *Hamārē*, pp. 295ff.; Misra, *Muslim Communities*, pp. 47–49; Engineer, *Bohras*, pp. 135ff., and Poonawala, *Bio*, pp. 14, 219–221 and 224–228.

120. On this document known as the *ʿAhd-nāma*, which was subsequently

destroyed, see Fayḍ Allāh b. Muḥammad ʿAlī al-Hamdānī, *ʿAqīda-yi Burhāniyya* (Sūrat, 1966), containing the Gujarātī translation and analysis of the document in question; see also Poonawala, *Bio*, pp. 230 and 238–239.

121. Abdul Husain, *Gulzare Daudi*, pp. 49–53; Ismāʿīljī, *Akhbār*, p. 378; Zāhid ʿAlī, *Hamārē*, p. 295; Hollister, *Shiʿa*, pp. 295–296; Misra, *Muslim Communities*, pp. 51–52, and Engineer, *Bohras*, pp. 138–139.
122. For a reference to one of these treatises, written by Muḥammad ʿAlī al-Hamdānī, see Poonawala, *Bio*, p. 228.
123. For a detailed account of the history of the reformist movement in the Dā'ūdī Bohra community, written by an active reformer, see Engineer, *Bohras*, pp. 165–281 and 303–323.
124. Engineer, *Bohras*, pp. 142ff., and S. K. Rayaq, *Gulshan-i maʿlūmāt* (Ujjain, 1975), p. 350.
125. On the settlement of the Bohras in East Africa, and their religious organization, see Chanan Singh, 'The Historical Background', in *Portrait of a Minority: Asians in East Africa*, ed. Dharam P. Ghai (Nairobi, 1965), pp. 1–12; and the late Professor Hatim M. Amiji's valuable studies, 'The Asian Communities', in *Islam in Africa*, ed. J. Kritzeck and William H. Lewis (New York, 1969), pp. 141–144, 155–164 and 168ff., and 'The Bohras of East Africa', *Journal of Religion in Africa*, 7 (1975), pp. 27–61. More general investigations of the Ismāʿīlīs and other Muslims in East Africa may be found in L. W. Hollingsworth, *Asians of East Africa* (London, 1960); G. Delf, *Asians in East Africa* (New York, 1963), and J. Mangat, *A History of the Asians of East Africa* (Oxford, 1969); see also J. Schacht, 'Notes on Islam in East Africa', *SI*, 23 (1965), pp. 91–136; J. Spencer Trimingham, *Islam in East Africa* (Oxford, 1964), especially pp. 1–111, and J. N. D. Anderson, *Islamic Law in Africa* (London, 1970), especially pp. 58–161 and 322–331.
126. For the *daʿwa* organization of the Dā'ūdīs, see Najm al-Ghanī Khān, *Madhāhib*, pp. 309ff.; Abdul Husain, *Gulzare Daudi*, pp. 63ff.; S. V. Molvi, *An Authentic Account of the Pontifical Office of Daʿi Mutlaq* (Bombay, 1914); Hollister, *Shiʿa*, pp. 279ff.; The Dawoodi Bohra Friendship Guild, *The History and Faith of the Dawoodi Bohras* (Bombay, 1964), and Amiji, 'Bohras of East Africa', pp. 41ff.
127. Hollister, *Shiʿa*, pp. 282–284, and 'Why Misaq, for Whom and to Whom', *Dawoodi Bohra Bulletin* (18 March 1961), p. 261.
128. See Abdul Husain, *Gulzare Daudi*, pp. 92–100; Hollister, *Shiʿa*, pp. 287–289, and Amiji, 'Bohras of East Africa', pp. 45–46.
129. On religious beliefs and customs of the Dā'ūdīs and their conditions in more recent times, aside from details found in Abdul Husain, *Gulzare Daudi*, and in Zāhid ʿAlī, *Hamārē*, see D. Menant, 'Les Bohoras du Guzarate', *Revue du Monde Musulman*, 10 (1910), pp. 465–493; Enthoven, *Tribes and Castes of Bombay*, vol. 1, pp. 200ff.; Murray T. Titus, *Indian Islam* (London, etc., 1930), pp. 97ff.; Hollister, *Shiʿa*, pp. 285ff. and 293–305; S. T. Lokhandwalla, 'The Bohras, a Muslim Community of Gujarat', *SI*, 3 (1955), pp. 117–135; also his 'Islamic Law and Ismāʿīlī Communities (Khojas and Bohras)', in *India and Contemporary Islam*, especially pp. 379–380 and 388–396; Engineer,

Bohras, pp. 145–164; Ivanow, *Guide*, pp. 10ff. and 24–25; Ivanow, 'Bohoras', *SEI*, pp. 64–65, and the studies of Asaf Fyzee, especially his *Outlines of Muhammadan Law*, pp. 73–75; *Compendium of Fatimid Law*, introduction pp. 35–50 and the chapters dealing with marriage, divorce, gifts, wills, inheritance, food, and dress, and his 'Bohorās', *EI2*, vol. 1, pp. 1254–1255.

130. See al-Majdūʿ, *Fihrist*, p. 98; Ivanow, *Guide*, pp. 86–87; Ivanow, *Ismaili Literature*, pp. 106–107; Goriawala, *Catalogue of the Fyzee Collection*, p. 127; Poonawala, *Bio*, pp. 244–246; also his 'al-Makramī', *EI2*, vol. 6, pp. 190–191, and W. Madelung, 'Makramids', *EI2*, vol. 6, pp. 191–192.

131. Fyzee, tr., *Ismaili Law of Wills*, p. 6; also his 'Three Sulaymani Daʿīs', pp. 102–103; Hollister, *Shiʿa*, p. 302, and Poonawala, *Bio*, p. 250.

132. This estimate is based on the adjustment of some older figures, allowing for natural population increases at an average annual rate of 3 per cent during the intervening years; see Fyzee, 'A Chronological List', p. 16; also his *Outlines of Muhammadan Law*, p. 73, and William H. Ingrams, 'Yemen', *Encyclopaedia Britannica* (1968 edition), vol. 23, p. 887. On the present situation of the Ṭayyibīs of Yaman, see T. Gerholm, *Market, Mosque and Mafrag* (Stockholm, 1977).

133. Ivanow, *Guide*, p. 10, and Hollister, *Shiʿa*, p. 300.

134. See P. J. E. Damishky, 'Moslem Population of India', *MW*, 1 (1911), p. 123; Menant, 'Bohoras du Guzarate', pp. 482–483; Enthoven, *Tribes and Castes of Bombay*, vol. 1, pp. 204–205; F. B. Tyabji, 'Social Life in 1804 and 1929 amongst Muslims in Bombay', *JBBRAS*, NS, 6 (1930), especially pp. 288ff.; Hollister, *Shiʿa*, p. 300; Lokhandwalla, 'Islamic Law and Ismāʿīlī Communities', pp. 391–392; Ivanow, *Ismaili Literature*, p. 102, and Fyzee, 'Study of the Literature of the Fatimid Daʿwa', pp. 236ff.

6. *Nizārī Ismāʿīlism of the Alamūt period*

1. See Ivanow, *Ismaili Literature*, pp. 127–136, and Poonawala, *Bio*, pp. 251–263.
2. For modern descriptions of the mediaeval Nizārī strongholds in Persia, see L. Lockhart, 'Hasan-i-Sabbah and the Assassins', *BSOS*, 5 (1928–1930), pp. 689–696; also his 'Some Notes on Alamut', *GJ*, 77 (1931), pp. 46–48; F. Stark, *Valleys of the Assassins*, pp. 197–251; French translation, *La Vallée des Assassins*, tr. M. Metzger (Paris, 1946), pp. 196–240; Persian translation, *Safarī bi diyār-i Alamūt*, tr. ʿAlī M. Sākī (Tehran, 1364/1985), pp. 223–286; W. Ivanow, 'Alamut', *GJ*, 77 (1931), pp. 38–45; also his 'Some Ismaili Strongholds in Persia', *IC*, 12 (1938), pp. 383–396; and his *Alamut and Lamasar* (Tehran, 1960); Peter Willey, *The Castles of the Assassins* (London, 1963); also his 'Further Expeditions to the Valleys of the Assassins', *Royal Central Asian Journal*, 54 (1967), pp. 156–162; and his 'The Assassins in Quhistan', *Royal Central Asian Journal*, 55 (1968), pp. 180–183; M. Sutūda, 'Qalʿa-yi Girdkūh', *Mihr*, 8 (1331/1952), pp. 339–343 and 484–490; also his 'Qalʿa-yi Alamūt', *Farhang-i Īrān Zamīn*, 3 (1334/1955), pp. 5–21; and his *Qilāʿ-i Ismāʿīliyya* (Tehran, 1345/1967); S. M. Stern, E. Beazley and A.

Dobson, 'The Fortress of Khān Lanjān', *Iran, Journal of the British Institute of Persian Studies*, 9 (1971), pp. 45–57; Caro O. Minasian, *Shah Diz of Isma'ili Fame, its Siege and Destruction* (London, 1971), W. Kleiss, 'Bericht über Erkundungsfahrten in Iran im Jahre 1970', in *Archäologische Mitteilungen aus Iran*, 4 (1971), pp. 88–96, and M. Kervran, 'Une fortresse d'Azerbaidjan: Samīrān', pp. 71–93. Between 1983 and 1986, the author visited several of these fortresses, including Alamūt, Lamasar, Shamīrān (Samīrān) and Girdkūh. The Mongol debacle, the passage of time, and the continuous damage inflicted by fortune hunters have taken their toll on these historic Nizārī sites, which are now rapidly disappearing.

3. Juwayni, *Ta'rīkh-i jahān-gushāy*, ed. M. Qazvīnī (Leiden–London, 1912–1937), 3 vols., reprinted several times in Tehran, during 1311–1314/1932–1935 and in 1337/1958. A facsimile edition of the third volume, containing the history of the Ismā'īlīs, was first prepared for publication by E. Denison Ross (London, 1931), and recently a new text of the entire work, based on Qazvīnī's edition and cast in simplified, modern Persian has been produced by Manṣūr Tharvat under the title of *Taḥrīr-i nuvīn-i ta'rīkh-i jahān-gushāy* (Tehran, 1362/1983). Boyle's English translation, as noted, appeared in 1958 under the title of *The History of the World-Conqueror*, 2 vols., the sections on the Ismā'īlīs appearing at the end of the second volume. Boyle's version has been translated into Italian, *Gengiskhan, il conquistatore del mondo*, tr. G. Scarcia (Milan, 1962), while parts of Juwaynī's sections on the Ismā'īlīs have been translated into Arabic in Muḥammad al-Sa'īd Jamāl al-Dīn, *Dawlat al-Ismā'īliyya fī Īrān* (Cairo, 1975), pp. 150–255. Our references to Juwaynī are to Qazvīnī's edition and to Boyle's English translation of *Ta'rīkh-i jahān-gushāy*.

4. Rashīd al-Dīn's entire section on the Ismā'īlīs, covering the earlier history of the sect, the Fāṭimid caliphs and the Nizārī state in Persia, entitled *Jāmi' al-tawārīkh; qismat-i Ismā'īliyān va Fāṭimiyān va Nizāriyān va dā'īyān va rafīqān*, has been edited, as noted, by Dānishpazhūh and Mudarrisī Zanjānī (Tehran, 1338/1959). Earlier, a partial edition of this section, covering only the history of the Persian Nizārī state, based on a text prepared by W. Ivanow, was produced by M. Dabīr Siyāqī under the title of *Faṣlī az jāmi' al-tawārīkh; ta'rīkh-i firqa-yi rafīqān va Ismā'īliyān-i Alamūt* (Tehran, 1337/1958). Excerpts from Rashīd al-Dīn's history of the Ismā'īlīs, with English translations, first appeared in Levy's already-cited article 'Account of the Isma'ili doctrines in the Jami' al-Tawarikh of Rashid al-Din Fadlallah', pp. 509–536. Unless otherwise specified, our references to Rashīd al-Dīn are to the edition prepared by Dānishpazhūh and Mudarrisī. See also L. V. Stroeva, 'Rashid-ad-din kak istochnik po istorii Ismailitov Alamuta (izdani neopublikovannoy chasti Dzami at-tavarikh)', in *Vopruosui istorii stran Azii* (Leningrad, 1965), pp. 123–142.

5. Abu'l-Qāsim Kāshānī (al-Qāshānī), *Ta'rīkh-i Uljāytū*, ed. M. Hambly (Tehran, 1348/1969), pp. 4–5, 54–55 and 240–241, and also his *Ta'rīkh-i Ismā'īliyya*, pp. 3–4; see also M. Murtaḍavī, 'Jāmi' al-tawārīkh va mu'allif-i vaqi'ī-yi ān', *Revue de la Faculté des Lettres, Université de Tabriz*, 13 (1340/1961), pp. 31ff., 323ff. and 517ff.

6. As noted, M. T. Dānishpazhūh prepared an edition of Abu'l-Qāsim Kāshānī's history of the Ismā'īlīs, on the basis of a single manuscript copy, under the title of *Zubdat al-tawārīkh; ta'rīkh-i Ismā'īliyya va Nizāriyya va Malāḥida*, which appeared in *Revue de la Faculté des Lettres, Université de Tabriz*, Supplément no. 9 (1343/1964), pp. 1–215. More recently, Dānishpazhūh has produced a better edition of this history, based on the same manuscript copy dated 989/1581; see Kāshānī, *Zubdat al-tawārīkh; bakhsh-i Fāṭimiyān va Nizāriyān*, ed. M. T. Dānishpazhūh (2nd ed., Tehran, 1366/1987). Our references in this book are to the first edition of Kāshānī's history. Juwaynī's *Ta'rīkh* was introduced to the orientalists of the nineteenth century by Constantin M. d'Ohsson (1779–1851), who made extensive use of it in his *Histoire des Mongols* (1st ed., Paris, 1824; 2nd ed., The Hague–Amsterdam, 1834–1835), while Rashīd al-Dīn's section on the Ismā'īlīs was known in manuscript form long before it was published. But Kāshānī's version does not seem to have been utilized by scholars until its publication in 1964.
7. Ḥamd Allāh Mustawfī's section on the Persian Nizārīs first appeared in French translation in Defrémery, 'Histoire des Seldjoukides', pp. 26–49. A partial edition with French translation of the *Ta'rīkh-i guzīda*, including the sections on the Fāṭimid caliphs and the lords of Alamūt, was published by Jules Gantin (Paris, 1903), but it was E. G. Browne who provided a complete facsimile edition of this history for the E. J. W. Gibb Memorial Series, *The Ta'rīkh-i Guzīda; or, 'Select History'* (Leiden–London, 1910), and he later produced an abridged English translation of the work in the same series (Leiden–London, 1913). More recently, 'Abd al-Ḥusayn Navā'ī has prepared a complete edition of the *Ta'rīkh-i guzīda* (Tehran, 1339/1960).
8. Muḥammad b. 'Alī al-Shabānkāra'ī, *Majma' al-ansāb*, ed. Mīr Hāshim Muḥaddith (Tehran, 1363/1984), pp. 125–133.
9. Ḥāfiẓ Abrū, *Majma' al-tawārīkh al-sulṭāniyya; qismat-i khulafā'-i 'Alawiyya-yi Maghrib va Miṣr va Nizāriyān va rafīqān*, ed. Muḥammad Mudarrisī Zanjānī (Tehran, 1364/1985), hereafter cited as Ḥāfiẓ Abrū; see F. Daftary's review of this work in *Nashr-i Dānish*, 6 (June–July, 1986), pp. 34–37.
10. Mīrkhwānd, *Rawḍat al-ṣafā'* (Tehran, 1338–1339/1960), vol. 4, pp. 181–235. Am. Jourdain, as noted, had earlier published the Persian text with French translation of Mīrkhwānd's history of the Persian Nizārīs in *Notices et Extraits des Manuscrits de la Bibliothèque Impériale*, 9 (1813), text pp. 192–248, translation pp. 143–182.
11. Khwānd Amīr, *Ḥabīb al-siyar* (Tehran, 1333/1954), vol. 2, pp. 450–479.
12. See, for instance, Yaḥyā b. 'Abd al-Laṭīf Qazwīnī, *Lubb al-tawārīkh*, ed. S. Jalāl al-Dīn Ṭihrānī (1314/1936), pp. 125–133, and the more recent edition of the same history (Tehran, 1363/1984), pp. 206–219, a work written in 948/1541; Qāḍī Aḥmad b. Muḥammad al-Ghaffārī, *Ta'rīkh-i nigāristān* (Bombay, 1275/1859), pp. 233–234; ed. M. Mudarris Gīlānī (Tehran, 1340/1961), pp. 199–200, and also his *Jahān-ārā* (Tehran, 1343/1964), pp. 66–69 and 70–71, containing brief chronological listings by this famous historian who died in 975/1567–1568.
13. Ṣadr al-Dīn Abu'l-Ḥasan 'Alī b. Nāṣir al-Ḥusaynī, *Akhbār al-dawla al-Saljūqiyya*, ed. M. Iqbāl (Lahore, 1933). For more details on this work and

other early Saljūq chronicles, see Cl. Cahen, 'The Historiography of the Seljuqid Period', in *Historians of the Middle East*, ed. B. Lewis and P. M. Holt (London, 1964), especially pp. 68–76.

14. Lewis, 'Sources for the History of the Syrian Assassins', pp. 475–489, reprinted in his *Studies in Classical and Ottoman Islam.*
15. See Ivanow, *Ismaili Literature*, pp. 168–173, and Poonawala, *Bio*, pp. 287–297 and 348–350.
16. Most of these inscriptions were studied by Max van Berchem who presented the results in his 'Épigraphie des Assassins de Syrie', pp. 453–501, reprinted in his *Opera Minora*, vol. 1, pp. 453–501.
17. Claude Cahen has listed and analyzed most of these Arabic sources in his *La Syrie du Nord à l'époque des Croisades* (Paris, 1940), pp. 33–93. See also Sauvaget, *Introduction to the History of the Muslim East*, pp. 162ff.; F. Gabrieli, 'The Arabic Historiography of the Crusades', in *Historians of the Middle East*, pp. 98–107, and Elisséeff, *Nūr ad-Dīn*, vol. 1, pp. 9–81.
18. Ibn al-ʿAdīm's history of Aleppo from early times to 641/1243 entitled the *Zubdat al-ḥalab min ta'rīkh Ḥalab* has been critically edited by Sāmī Dahān (Damascus, 1951–1968), 3 vols.; extracts of this history with French translation appeared earlier in *RHC: Historiens Orientaux* (Paris, 1872–1906), vol. 3, pp. 571–690, hereafter cited as *RHCHO*. Other passages of this work were translated into French by E. Blochet under the title of *L'Histoire d'Alep de Kamal-ad-Dīn*, in *Revue de l'Orient Latin*, 3 (1895), pp. 509–565, 4 (1896), pp. 145–225, 5 (1897), pp. 37–107, and 6 (1898), pp. 1–49.
19. Sibṭ Ibn al-Jawzī, *Mir'āt al-zamān*, ed. J. R. Jewett (Chicago, 1907), a partial facsimile edition covering the period 495–658/1101–1260, also published at Hyderabad, 1370–1371/1951–1952, 2 vols.; extracts of the *Mir'āt* with French translation are contained in *RHCHO*, vol. 3, pp. 511–570; hereafter cited as Sibṭ.
20. An extract of al-ʿAẓīmī's history, dealing mainly with Syrian events during 455–538/1063–1143, was published by Claude Cahen under the title of 'La Chronique abrégée d'al-ʿAẓīmī', *JA*, 230 (1938), pp. 353–448, hereafter cited as al-ʿAẓīmī.
21. Passages from this chronicle, as noted, appeared in Cl. Cahen's 'Une chronique Syrienne du VIe/XIIe siècle: Le *Bustān al-Jāmiʿ*', pp. 113–158, hereafter referred to as *Bustān*.
22. Extracts of Ibn al-ʿAdīm's *Bughyat al-ṭalab fī ta'rīkh Ḥalab*, a biographical dictionary of personalities connected with Aleppo, are included in *RHCHO*, vol. 3, pp. 691–732. Passages on Rāshid al-Dīn Sinān, and two of the Syrian rulers killed by Nizārīs, are contained in B. Lewis, 'Three Biographies from Kamāl ad-Dīn', in *Fuad Köprülü Armağani* (Istanbul, 1953), pp. 330–344, and in his 'Kamāl al-Dīn's Biography of Rāšid al-Dīn Sinān', *Arabica*, 13 (1966), pp. 260–267.
23. As noted, the title of this book, published in 1955 and reprinted with the same pagination (New York, 1980), is *The Order of Assassins; the Struggle of the Early Nizārī Ismāʿīlīs against the Islamic World*, hereafter cited as *Order*; Persian translation, *Firqa-yi Ismāʿīliyya*, tr. F. Badra'ī (Tabrīz, 1343/1964; 2nd ed.,

Tabrīz, 1346/1967). Hodgson summarized the contents of this book, with many revisions and improved interpretations, in his 'The Ismāʿīlī State', in *The Cambridge History of Iran*: Volume 5, *The Saljuq and Mongol Periods*, ed. J. A. Boyle (Cambridge, 1968), pp. 422–482, hereafter cited as 'State'; Persian translation of this article is included in B. Lewis et al., *Ismāʿīliyān dar ta'rīkh*, tr. Y. Āzhand (Tehran, 1363/1984), pp. 255–340.

24. Lewis's *The Assassins: A Radical Sect in Islam* has also been translated into Persian by F. Badra'ī, *Fidā'īyān-i Ismāʿīlī* (Tehran, 1348/1969), reproduced with some revisions, under the title of *Ismāʿīliyān-i Nizārī*, in B. Lewis, *Ta'rīkh-i Ismāʿīliyān*, tr. F. Badra'ī (Tehran, 1362/1984), pp. 135–319, also containing the Persian translation of Lewis's *The Origins of Ismāʿīlism*, pp. 1–133; French translation, *Les Assassins: Terrorisme et politique dans l'Islam médiéval*, tr. A. Pélissier (Paris, 1982), also (Brussels, 1984). P. Filippani-Ronconi devoted the greater part of his book, *Ismaeliti ed 'Assassini'*, pp. 107–265, to the history of the Nizārī state. For the sake of completeness, mention may also be made of A. S. Picklay, *History of the Ismailis* (Bombay, 1940), a popular account written by an Indian Ismāʿīlī; the already-cited Jean-Claude Frère's *L'Ordre des Assassins*, another popular account, and E. Franzius, *History of the Order of Assassins* (New York, 1969), a brief but scholarly treatment of the Nizārīs of the Alamūt and post-Alamūt periods. It may also be noted here that I. P. Petrushevsky (1898–1977) in the chapter dealing with the Ismāʿīlīs, the Qarmaṭīs and the Shīʿī Ghulāt in his *Islam in Iran* adopted a Marxist approach and viewed the struggles of the Nizārīs in terms of class conflicts. According to him, the Nizārīs represented the rural and the lower social classes in the urban areas who fought against the Saljūqs and other feudal rulers; see Petrushevsky, *Islām dar Īrān*, pp. 309–320; tr. Evans, *Islam in Iran*, pp. 248–258; for similar views see L. V. Stroeva's chapter on the Persian Ismāʿīlīs in N. V. Pigulevskaya et al., *Istoriya Irana* (Leningrad, 1958); Persian translation, *Ta'rīkh-i Īrān*, tr. Karīm Kishāvarz (Tehran, 1354/1975), pp. 276ff.

25. See Corbin, *Histoire*, pp. 137ff.; Hodgson, *Order*, pp. 41–42; also his 'State', pp. 422 and 428–429; and his 'Alamūt: The Dynasty', *EI2*, vol. 1, pp. 353–354, and B. Hourcade, 'Alamūt', *EIR*, vol. 1, pp. 799–801.

26. For the meagre biographical information available on this *dāʿī*, see Nasseh Ahmad Mirza, 'The Syrian Ismāʿīlīs at the Time of the Crusades' (Ph.D. thesis, University of Durham, 1963), pp. 186–187; Shaykh M. Iqbal, 'Abdul Malik bin Attash', in *Great Ismaili Heroes*, pp. 56–57, and B. Lewis, 'Ibn ʿAṭṭāsh', *EI2*, vol. 3, p. 725.

27. Juwaynī, vol. 3, pp. 187ff.; tr. Boyle, vol. 2, pp. 666ff.; Rashīd al-Dīn, pp. 97ff.; Kāshānī, pp. 120ff., and Ḥāfiẓ Abrū, pp. 191ff. Rashīd al-Dīn and Kāshānī have fuller quotations from this biography than Juwaynī. See also Ḥamd Allāh, *Ta'rīkh*, ed. and tr. Gantin, pp. 486ff.; ed. and tr. Browne, vol. 1, pp. 517ff., and vol. 2, pp. 127–128; ed. Navā'ī, pp. 518ff.; Mīrkhwānd, *Rawḍat al-ṣafā'*, ed. and tr. Jourdain, translation pp. 151ff., text pp. 202ff.; Tehran ed., vol. 4, pp. 205ff., and Khwānd Amīr, *Ḥabīb al-siyar*, vol. 2, pp. 464ff. Briefer details, from a different source, on Ḥasan's biography are

related in Ibn al-Athīr, *al-Kāmil*, vol. 9, pp. 154–155, and vol. 10, pp. 82 and 109–110. In modern times, no scholarly work has been written on Ḥasan-i Ṣabbāḥ and his career; for some popular accounts, see Jawad al-Muscati, *Hasan bin Sabbah*, translated into English by A. H. Hamdani (Karachi, 1953); ʿĀrif Tāmir, *ʿAlā abwāb Alamūt* (Ḥarīṣa, 1959); Muṣṭafā Ghālib, *al-Thāʾir al-Ḥimyarī al-Ḥasan b. al-Ṣabbāḥ* (Beirut, 1966); ʿAbd al-Ḥalīm Sharar, *Ḥasan ibn Ṣabbāḥ* (Lucknow, n.d.), in Urdu, and Karīm Kishāvarz, *Ḥasan-i Ṣabbāḥ* (Tehran, 1344/1965), a semi-popular but documented biography. A briefer account, with some relevant documents, is contained in Naṣr Allāh Falsafī, *Hasht maqāla* (Tehran, 1330/1951), pp. 197–223, reproduced in his *Chand maqāla-yi taʾrīkhī va adabī* (Tehran, 1342/1963), pp. 403–434; see also M. Mīnuvī, *Taʾrīkh va farhang* (Tehran, 1352/1973), pp. 170–225. The best succinct modern accounts of Ḥasan-i Ṣabbāḥ may be found in three works by Hodgson, *Order*, pp. 43ff., 'State', pp. 429ff., and 'Ḥasan-i Ṣabbāḥ', *EI2*, vol. 3, pp. 253–254. See also Zāhid ʿAlī, *Taʾrīkh*, vol. 2, pp. 167ff.; Lockhart, 'Hasan-i-Sabbah and the Assassins', pp. 675ff.; Anonymous, 'al-Ḥasan b. al-Ṣabbāḥ', *SEI*, pp. 136–137; Lewis, *Assassins*, pp. 38ff.; Filippani-Ronconi, *Ismaeliti*, pp. 131ff.; Ghālib, *Taʾrīkh*, pp. 262–265; Ghālib, *Aʿlām*, pp. 222–228, and Poonawala, *Bio*, pp. 251–254.

28. Rashīd al-Dīn, pp. 110–112, and Kāshānī, pp. 132–134, quote the tale from the *Sargudhasht-i Sayyidnā*, while Juwaynī omits it. See also Dozy, *Essai sur l'histoire de l'Islamisme*, pp. 296ff.; E. G. Browne, 'Yet More Light on ʿUmar-i-Khayyām', *JRAS* (1899), pp. 409–420; also his *A Literary History of Persia from Firdawsi to Saʿdi*, pp. 190–193; H. Bowen, 'The *sar-gudhasht-i sayyidnā*, the Tale of Three Schoolfellows and the *wasaya* of the Niẓām al-Mulk', *JRAS* (1931), pp. 771–782; Hodgson, *Order*, pp. 137–138; Kishāvarz, *Ḥasan-i Ṣabbāḥ*, pp. 54–57; Lewis, *Assassins*, pp. 39–40, and Filippani-Ronconi, *Ismaeliti*, pp. 133–134. Falsafī was one of the few scholars defending the authenticity of this tale, see his *Hasht maqāla*, pp. 200–203, and *Chand maqāla*, pp. 406–410. This tale is reproduced in von Hammer-Purgstall, *History of the Assassins*, pp. 42ff.; Bouthoul, *Le Grand Maître des Assassins*, pp. 14ff.; also her *Le Vieux de la Montagne*, pp. 15ff., and Frère, *L'Ordre des Assassins*, pp. 79ff.; it also finds expression in a number of popular works, written in the Persian language, on Ḥasan-i Ṣabbāḥ and the Nizārī movement.
29. See, for instance, *Rubāiyāt of Omar Khayyām*, rendered into English verse by Edward FitzGerald (5th ed., London, 1898), pp. 1–6.
30. Mīrkhwānd, *Rawḍat al-ṣafāʾ*, ed. and tr. Jourdain, translation pp. 143–150, text pp. 192–201; Tehran ed., vol. 4, pp. 199–204. Mīrkhwānd's recension of the tale, based on the Niẓām al-Mulk's *Waṣāyā*, is reproduced in Khwānd Amīr, *Ḥabīb al-siyar*, vol. 2, pp. 460–464, and also his *Dastūr al-wuzarāʾ*, ed. S. Nafīsī (Tehran, 1317/1938), pp. 168–178, amongst other later Persian sources. See also Charles Schefer, *Siasset Namèh*, Supplément (Paris, 1897), pp. 48–56, and *Dabistān-i madhāhib*, attributed to Kaykhusraw Isfandiyār, ed. R. Riḍāzāda Malik (Tehran, 1362/1983), vol. 1, pp. 258–260.
31. Ibn al-Athīr, *al-Kāmil*, vol. 10, p. 82; see also Rashīd al-Dīn, p. 77; Kāshānī, p. 103; Ḥāfiẓ Abrū, p. 162, and al-Maqrīzī, *Ittiʿāẓ*, vol. 2, p. 323, and vol. 3, p. 15.

32. Juwaynī, vol. 3, pp. 189–191; tr. Boyle, vol. 2, pp. 668–669; Rashīd al-Dīn, pp. 99–103; Kāshānī, pp. 122–124, and Ḥāfiẓ Abrū, pp. 192–193.
33. Juwaynī, vol. 3, pp. 191–193; tr. Boyle, vol. 2, p. 669; Rashīd al-Dīn, p. 103; Kāshānī, p. 125, and Ḥāfiẓ Abrū, pp. 193–194.
34. Rabino, 'Les Dynasties Alaouides du Mazandéran', p. 261; also his *Māzandarān and Astarābād* (London, 1928), pp. 139 and 166, and Abu'l-Fatḥ Ḥakīmiyān, *ʿAlawiyān-i Ṭabaristān* (Tehran, 1348/1969), p. 116. On ʿAlid rule in Ṭabaristān and the history of the Caspian Zaydī community, which came under increasing pressure with the rise of Nizārī Ismāʿīlism in northern Persia, see several works by Madelung, *Der Imam al-Qāsim*, pp. 153–220; 'The Alid Rulers of Ṭabaristān, Daylamān and Gīlān', pp, 483–492; 'Abū Isḥāq al-Ṣābī on the Alids of Ṭabaristān and Gīlān', pp. 17–57; 'Minor Dynasties', pp. 206–212 and 219–222, and 'ʿAlids of Ṭabarestān, Daylamān, and Gīlān', *EIR*, vol. 1, pp. 881–886.
35. Juwaynī, vol. 3, pp. 193–195; tr. Boyle, vol. 2, pp. 669–671; Rashīd al-Dīn, pp. 104–105; Kāshānī, pp. 125–128, and Ḥāfiẓ Abrū, p. 194.
36. Ibn al-Athīr, *al-Kāmil*, vol. 10, p. 110.
37. Juwaynī, vol. 3, pp. 269–273; tr. Boyle, vol. 2, pp. 719–721; Rashīd al-Dīn, p. 105; Kāshānī, p. 128; Ḥāfiẓ Abrū, p. 195, and Ḥamd Allāh Mustawfī Qazwīnī, *The Geographical Part of the Nuzhat al-Qulūb*, ed. and tr. G. Le Strange (Leiden–London, 1915–1919), vol. 1, pp. 60–61, and vol. 2, p. 66. See also G. Le Strange, *Lands of the Eastern Caliphate*, pp. 220–221; Qazvīnī, *Yāddāshthā*, vol. 1, pp. 102–107; Ivanow, *Alamut and Lamasar*, pp. 1ff. and 35–59; Willey, *Castles of the Assassins*, pp. 204–226; Sutūda, *Qilāʿ*, pp. 72–108; P. Varjāvand, *Sarzamīn-i Qazvīn* (Tehran, 1349/1970), pp. 173ff. and 181–205, and Hourcade, 'Alamūt', pp. 797–799.
38. For the activities of Ḥasan-i Ṣabbāḥ during the years immediately following the seizure of Alamūt, the Nizārī sources are quoted in Juwaynī, vol. 3, pp. 195 and 199–207; tr. Boyle, vol. 2, pp. 671 and 673–678; Rashīd al-Dīn, pp. 105 and 107–110; Kāshānī, pp. 128 and 130–132, and Ḥāfiẓ Abrū, pp. 200–202.
39. *Ta'rīkh-i Sīstān*, p. 386; tr. Gold, p. 315, and Ḥamd Allāh, *Nuzhat al-qulūb*, vol. 1, p. 146, and vol. 2, p. 144.
40. On this assassination, reported by Ibn al-Athīr to have been an act of revenge for Ṭāhir al-Najjār, an Ismāʿīlī from Sāwa near Qumm, executed earlier on Niẓām al-Mulk's orders, see Juwaynī, vol. 3, pp. 203–204; tr. Boyle, vol. 2, pp. 676–677; Rashīd al-Dīn, pp. 109–110; Kāshānī, p. 132; Ḥāfiẓ Abrū, p. 202, and Ibn al-Athīr, *al-Kāmil*, vol. 10, pp. 70–71 and 108–109. See also M. Th. Houtsma, 'The Death of Nizam al-Mulk and its Consequences', *Journal of Indian History*, 3 (1924), pp. 147–160, and Hodgson, *Order*, pp. 47–48 and 75.
41. On these castles, see Yāqūt, *Muʿjam*, vol. 1, p. 244; tr. Barbier de Meynard, p. 33; Ibn al-Athīr, *al-Kāmil*, vol. 10, p. 110; Ibn Isfandiyār, *Ta'rīkh*, vol. 1, p. 111, and vol. 2 (continuation), pp. 11, 27–29 and 35; tr. Browne, pp. 4, 231, 240 and 243; Ẓahīr al-Dīn Marʿashī, *Ta'rīkh-i Ṭabaristān va Rūyān va Māzandarān*, ed. B. Dorn, in his Muhammedanische Quellen zur Geschichte der Südlichen Küstenländer des Kaspischen Meeres 1 (St Petersburg, 1850),

pp. 61–62, 196, 242, 261 and 263; ed. Tasbīḥī, pp. 19, 86 and 116, and Sutūda, *Qilā'*, pp. 138–142 and 160–162.

42. On the seizure of Girdkūh, earlier evidently also called Diz-i Gunbadān, see Juwaynī, vol. 3, pp. 207–208; tr. Boyle, vol. 2, pp. 678–679; Rashīd al-Dīn, pp. 116–120; Kāshānī, pp. 137–141, Ḥāfiẓ Abrū, pp. 208–210; Ḥamd Allāh, *Nuzhat al-qulūb*, vol. 1, p. 161, and vol. 2, p. 158; *Mujmal al-tawārīkh wa'l-qiṣaṣ*, ed. Muḥammad Taqī Bahār (Tehran, 1318/1939), p. 52; al-Ḥusaynī, *Akhbār*, p. 87, and Hodgson, *Order*, pp. 86–87.

43. Ibn al-Balkhī, *Fārs-nāma*, pp. 84, 121, 148 and 162; Ḥamd Allāh, *Nuzhat al-qulūb*, vol. 1, pp. 129–130, and vol. 2, p. 129; Ibn al-Athīr, *al-Kāmil*, vol. 10, p. 111; Hodgson, *Order*, p. 76, and H. Gaube, 'Arrajān', *EIR*, vol. 2, pp. 519–520.

44. Muḥammad b. Ibrāhīm, *Ta'rīkh-i Saljūqiyān-i Kirmān*, ed. M. Th. Houtsma, in his Recueil de textes relatifs à l'histoire des Seldjoucides I (Leiden, 1886), pp. 21–25; the same work has been edited by M. I. Bāstānī Pārīzī under the title of *Saljūqiyān va Ghuzz dar Kirmān* (Tehran, 1343/1964), pp. 29–32; Nāṣir al-Dīn Munshī Kirmānī, *Simṭ al-'ulā*, ed. 'Abbās Iqbāl (Tehran, 1328/1949), p. 17; Ibn al-Athīr, *al-Kāmil*, vol. 10, p. 111; al-Ghaffārī, *Jahān-ārā*, p. 117, and Hodgson, *Order*, p. 87.

45. Ibn al-Athīr, *al-Kāmil*, vol. 10, pp. 97, 100–101 and 146–147.

46. Rashīd al-Dīn, pp. 114–115; Kāshānī, pp. 135–136; Ḥāfiẓ Abrū, p. 203, and 'Abd al-Jalīl al-Qazwīnī al-Rāzī, *Kitāb al-naqḍ*, ed. Mīr Jalāl al-Dīn Muḥaddith (2nd ed., Tehran, 1358/1980), pp. 313–314 and 478–479, a polemical work written around 565/1170 by an Imāmī scholar from Rayy.

47. Juwaynī, vol. 3, pp. 208–209; tr. Boyle, vol. 2, p. 679; Rashīd al-Dīn, pp. 115–116; Kāshānī, pp. 136–137; Ḥāfiẓ Abrū, p. 206; Ivanow, *Alamut and Lamasar*, pp. 60–74; Willey, *Castles of the Assassins*, pp. 269–279; Sutūda, *Qilā'*, pp. 54–71; Varjāvand, *Sarzamīn-i Qazvīn*, pp. 212ff. and 216–233, and C. E. Bosworth, 'Lanbasar', *EI2*, vol. 5, p. 656.

48. See Amin Haji, 'The succession to the Fatimid Imam al-Mustansir Bi-llah (427–487/1036–1094) and the Rise of Nizari Ismailism', in *Proceedings of the Symposium on Fāṭimid History and Art*, ed. M. Brett and G. Fehérvári (forthcoming), where it is also argued that a group of the Nizārīs refused to accept Nizār's death and awaited his return as the Mahdī until shortly after the declaration of the *qiyāma* at Alamūt.

49. Various non-Ismā'īlī sources allude, in different forms, to the existence of an unnamed imām at that time in Alamūt; see, for instance, Juwaynī, vol. 3, p. 231; tr. Boyle, vol. 2, pp. 691–692; Rashīd al-Dīn, p. 166; Kāshānī, p. 186; Ibn al-Qalānisī, *Dhayl*, pp. 127–129, with a quotation on the subject from al-Fāriqī, a historian writing shortly after the capture of Alamūt, and Ibn Muyassar, *Akhbār*, ed. Massé, p. 68; ed. Sayyid, p. 102. Al-Ghazālī in his *al-Munqidh*, ed. and tr. Jabre, text p. 33, translation pp. 93–94; ed. Ṣalībā, p. 127; tr. Watt, pp. 52–53, also speaks of the imām as being hidden and yet accessible to his followers. See also *al-Hidāyatu'l-Āmirīya*, p. 23.

50. Casanova, 'Monnaie des Assassins de Perse', p. 345. See also G. C. Miles,

'Coins of the Assassins of Alamut', *Orientalia Lovaniensia Periodica*, 3 (1972), pp. 155–162.

51. *Haft bāb-i Bābā Sayyidnā*, in *Two Early Ismaili Treatises*, ed. W. Ivanow (Bombay, 1933), p. 21; English translation in Hodgson, *Order*, p. 301. In later Nizārī sources, too, Ḥasan-i Ṣabbāḥ is given the title of *ḥujja* or chief *ḥujja*; see Naṣīr al-Dīn Abū Jaʿfar Muḥammad b. Muḥammad al-Ṭūsī, *Rawḍat al-taslīm, yā taṣawwurāt*, ed. and tr. W. Ivanow (Leiden, 1950), text p. 148, translation p. 173; Sayyid Suhrāb Valī Badakhshānī, *Sī va shish ṣaḥīfa*, ed. H. Ujāqī (Tehran, 1961), p. 55; Abū Isḥāq Quhistānī, *Haft bāb; or, Seven Chapters*, ed. and tr. W. Ivanow (Bombay, 1959), text pp. 23 and 43, translation pp. 23 and 43; Muḥammad Riḍā b. Sulṭān Ḥusayn Harātī, better known as Khayrkhwāh-i Harātī, *Kalām-i pīr: A Treatise on Ismaili Doctrine*, ed. and tr. W. Ivanow (Bombay, 1935), text pp. 51 and 68, translation pp. 44 and 63, and also his *Taṣnīfāt-i Khayrkhwāh-i Harātī*, ed. W. Ivanow (Tehran, 1961), pp. 52 and 102. As Ivanow has shown, the *Kalām-i pīr* is a plagiarized version of Abū Isḥāq Quhistānī's *Haft bāb* produced by Khayrkhwāh-i Harātī, a Nizārī *dāʿī* and author who flourished in the first half of the tenth/sixteenth century. Khayrkhwāh attributed the authorship of his *Kalām-i pīr*, written a few decades after the original *Haft bāb*, to Nāṣir-i Khusraw; see Ivanow's introductory remarks in the *Kalām-i pīr*, introduction pp. 11–26 and 59–68; Ivanow, *Guide*, pp. 93–94; also his *Ismaili Literature*, pp. 141, 142–143 and 162–163, and Poonawala, *Bio*, pp. 270 and 276.
52. Hodgson, *Order*, pp. 66–69.
53. Our discussion here draws on the exposition of Hodgson, *Order*, pp. 77–84, 87–89 and 110–115, and his 'State', pp. 439–443. See also Lewis, *Assassins*, pp. 125–140 and 158–160, where the social bases of the movement are also discussed.
54. See W. Ivanow, 'An Ismaili Poem in Praise of Fidawis', *JBBRAS*, NS, 14 (1938), pp. 63–72, containing excerpts of poems composed by the *raʾīs* Ḥasan b. Ṣalāḥ Bīrjandī, a secretary (*munshī*) to Shihāb al-Dīn, the Nizārī chief of Quhistān during the first half of the seventh/thirteenth century. This Nizārī author-poet had evidently also written a history of the Nizārī state in Persia, which has not survived but was used by Rashīd al-Dīn, as stated in his history of Ismāʿīlism, pp. 153 and 161. See Ivanow, *Ismaili Literature*, p. 134, and Poonawala, *Bio*, pp. 259–260.
55. Rashīd al-Dīn, pp. 134–137, 144–145 and 160–161; Kāshānī, pp. 154–157, 167–168, 182 and 216–218, and Ḥāfiẓ Abrū, pp. 223–225, 230–231 and 243–244.
56. Juwaynī, vol. 3, pp. 129 and 135; tr. Boyle, vol. 2, pp. 631 and 635, where the term *fidāʾī* is seemingly used to designate a special group. See also M. G. S. Hodgson, 'Fidāʾī', *EI2*, vol. 2, p. 882.
57. See, for instance, Ẓahīr al-Dīn Nīshāpūrī, *Saljūq-nāma*, pp. 40–41; al-Rāwandī, *Rāḥat al-ṣudūr*, pp. 157–158, and Ḥamd Allāh, *Taʾrīkh*, ed. and tr. Gantin, pp. 250–252; ed. and tr. Browne, vol. 1, pp. 454–456, and vol. 2, p. 100; ed. Navāʾī, pp. 445–446.

58. Ibn al-Athīr, *al-Kāmil*, vol. 10, pp. 109, 112–113 and 132.
59. Ibid., vol. 10, p. 137.
60. The renewed Nizārī activities in the Iṣfahān region, and the capture of Shāhdiz, received very limited treatment by our chief Persian historians. Juwaynī has nothing on the subject, while Rashīd al-Dīn, p. 120, and Kāshānī, p. 142, have brief references. Rashīd al-Dīn has more details in his *Jāmiʿ al-tawārīkh; taʾrīkh-i āl Saljūq*, pp. 69–74. There are also summary accounts in Ibn al-Athīr, *al-Kāmil*, vol. 10, pp. 109–110 and other general chronicles; but fuller details are contained in Ẓahīr al-Dīn Nāshāpūrī, *Saljūq-nāma*, pp. 40–41; al-Rāwandī, *Rāḥat al-ṣudūr*, pp. 155ff.; Mīrkhwānd, *Rawḍat al-ṣafāʾ*, Tehran ed., vol. 4, pp. 306ff.; also his *Mirchondi Historia Seldschukidarum Persice*, ed. Johann A. Vullers (Giessen, 1838), pp. 163ff., and Khwānd Amīr, *Ḥabīb al-siyar*, vol. 2, pp. 504ff. See also Yāqūt, *Muʿjam*, vol. 3, p. 246; tr. Barbier de Meynard, p. 344; Ghālib, *Taʾrīkh*, pp. 256–258, also his *Aʿlām*, pp. 114–115. In modern times, the sites of the castles of Shāhdiz and Khānlanjān were first identified by Dr. Caro O. Minasian (1897–1972), a resident of Iṣfahān who had a thorough knowledge of that city and its surroundings; see his *Shah Diz*; and Muḥammad Mihryār, 'Shāhdiz kujāst?', *Revue de la Faculté des Lettres d'Isfahan*, 1 (1343/1964–1965), pp. 87–157, and Stern et al., 'Fortress of Khān Lanjān', pp. 45–57.
61. Ibn al-Athīr, *al-Kāmil*, vol. 10, p. 112.
62. Bernard Lewis is the foremost modern authority on the history of the Syrian Nizārīs; on the opening phase of the Nizārī *daʿwa* in Syria, see his 'The Ismāʿīlites and the Assassins', in *A History of the Crusades*, ed. Setton, vol. 1, pp. 99–114; Persian translation in Lewis et al., *Ismāʿīliyān dar taʾrīkh*, pp. 341–388, and Lewis, *Assassins*, pp. 97–104. Defrémery's 'Nouvelles recherches sur les Ismaéliens ou Bathiniens de Syrie', *JA* (1854), pp. 373–397, is still valuable; see also Hodgson, *Order*, pp. 89–95; Mirza, 'Syrian Ismāʿīlīs', pp. 12–20, and Usāma Zakī Zaydī *al-Ṣalībiyyūn wa Ismāʿīliyya al-Shām fī ʿaṣr al-ḥurūb al-Ṣalībiyya* (Alexandria, 1980), containing a general discussion on the relations between the Syrian Nizārīs and the Crusaders.
63. Ibn al-Qalānisī, *Dhayl*, p. 133; tr. Le Tourneau, p. 37; al-ʿAẓīmī, p. 372; Ibn al-ʿAdīm, *Zubdat al-ḥalab*, ed. Dahān, vol. 2, p. 128; Ibn Muyassar, *Akhbār*, ed. Massé, pp. 37–38; ed. Sayyid, p. 64, extract with French translation in *RHCHO*, vol. 3, pp. 461–462; Ibn al-Athīr, *al-Kāmil*, vol. 10, p. 93, and Ibn Taghrībirdī, *al-Nujūm*, vol. 5, p. 158, extract in *RHCHO*, vol. 3, p. 486, placing the event in the year 489 A.H.
64. Sibṭ, *Mirʾāt*, in *RHCHO*, vol. 3, pp. 548–549, and Ibn Taghrībirdī, *al-Nujūm*, vol. 5, p. 205, in *RHCHO*, vol. 3, p. 497.
65. Ibn al-Qalānisī, *Dhayl*, p. 142, tr. Gibb, pp. 57–58; tr. Le Tourneau, pp. 51–52; al-ʿAẓīmī, p. 375, simply mentions the event without naming the Nizārīs; *Bustān*, p. 115; Ibn al-ʿAdīm, *Zubdat al-ḥalab*, in *RHCHO*, vol. 3, pp. 589–591; also his *Bughyat* in Lewis, 'Three Biographies', pp. 330–332; Ibn al-Athīr, *al-Kāmil*, vol. 10, p. 120, in *RHCHO*, vol. 1, p. 213, placing the murder in 495 A.H.; Sibṭ, *Mirʾāt*, ed. Jewett, pp. 3–4, in *RHCHO*, vol. 3, pp. 525–526, and Ibn Taghrībirdī, *al-Nujūm*, vol. 5, pp. 168–169, also recording

the event a year earlier. See also Lewis, 'Sources', pp. 485–486, relating the accounts of different authorities; Grousset, *Croisades*, vol. 1, pp. 338–340 and 387, and Runciman, *A History of the Crusades*, vol. 2, pp. 119–120.

66. Ibn al-Qalānisī, *Dhayl*, pp. 149–150; tr. Gibb, pp. 72–73; tr. Le Tourneau, pp. 63–64; al-ʿAẓīmī, p. 378; Ibn al-ʿAdīm, *Zubdat al-ḥalab*, ed. Dahān, vol. 2, pp. 151–152, in *RHCHO*, vol. 3, pp. 594–595; also his *Bughyat* in Lewis, 'Three Biographies', pp. 333–336; Ibn Muyassar, *Akhbār*, ed. Massé, pp. 37 and 41; ed. Sayyid, pp. 63 and 76, in *RHCHO*, vol. 3, pp. 461 and 466; Ibn al-Athīr, *al-Kāmil*, vol. 10, pp. 142–143, in *RHCHO*, vol. 1, pp. 232–235; Sibṭ, *Mirʾāt*, in *RHCHO*, vol. 3, p. 530; Ibn Taghrībirdī, *al-Nujūm*, vol. 5, p. 192; William B. Stevenson, *The Crusaders in the East* (Cambridge, 1907), p. 82; Grousset, *Croisades*, vol. 1, pp. 423–426, and Runciman, *Crusades*, vol. 2, pp. 52–53.

67. Ibn al-Qalānisī, *Dhayl*, pp. 174–175; tr. Gibb, pp. 114–115; tr. Le Tourneau, pp. 106–107, and Ibn al-ʿAdīm, *Zubdat al-ḥalab*, in *RHCHO*, vol. 3, pp. 599–600.

68. Ibn al-Qalānisī, *Dhayl*, pp. 187–188; tr. Gibb, pp. 139–141; tr. Le Tourneau, pp. 126–127; al-ʿAẓīmī, p. 382; *Bustān*, p. 117; Ibn al-Athīr, *al-Kāmil*, vol. 10, p. 174, in *RHCHO*, vol. 1, pp. 289–290; Ibn al-Athīr, *Taʾrīkh al-dawla al-Atābakiyya mulūk al-Mawṣil*, in *RHCHO*, vol. 2, part 2, pp. 35–36; Sibṭ, *Mirʾāt*, ed. Jewett, p. 31, in *RHCHO*, vol. 3, p. 550, and Ibn Khallikān, *Biographical Dictionary*, vol. 1, p. 227. See also Grousset, *Croisades*, vol. 1, pp. 483ff., and Runciman, *Crusades*, vol. 2, pp. 126–127.

69. On the persecution of the Nizārīs of Aleppo in the year 507 A.H., see Ibn al-Qalānisī, *Dhayl*, pp. 189–190; tr. Gibb, pp. 145–146; tr. Le Tourneau, pp. 130–131; al-ʿAẓīmī, p. 382; Ibn al-ʿAdīm, *Zubdat al-ḥalab*, ed. Dahān, vol. 2, pp. 532–533, in *RHCHO*, vol. 3, pp. 603–604; Ibn al-Athīr, *al-Kāmil*, vol. 10, p. 175, in *RHCHO*, vol. 1, p. 291; Sibṭ, *Mirʾāt*, in *RHCHO*, vol. 3, pp. 549–550, and Grousset, *Croisades*, vol. 1, pp. 478ff.

70. Ibn al-Qalānisī, *Dhayl*, pp. 190–191; tr. Gibb, pp. 147–148; tr. Le Tourneau, pp. 132–133; al-ʿAẓīmī, p. 382; Ibn al-Athīr, *al-Kāmil*, vol. 10, p. 166, in *RHCHO*, vol. 1, p. 272; Abu'l-Fidā, *al-Mukhtaṣar taʾrīkh al-bashar*, in *RHCHO*, vol. 1, p. 10, who like his source Ibn al-Athīr places this event in the year 502/1108–1109; Sibṭ, *Mirʾāt*, in *RHCHO*, vol. 3, p. 548, and Usāma, *Memoirs*, pp. 107, 146 and 153–154.

71. Ibn al-Athīr, *al-Kāmil*, vol. 10, pp. 146–147.

72. Our Persian historians have only brief accounts of the fall of Shāhdiz; see Rashīd al-Dīn, pp. 121–122; Kāshānī, pp. 142–143, and Ḥāfiẓ Abrū, p. 211. Ibn al-Athīr, *al-Kāmil*, vol. 10, pp. 151–152, has the fullest details. See also Ibn al-Qalānisī, *Dhayl*, pp. 151–156, containing also the text of the victory statement issued on the occasion; tr. Le Tourneau, pp. 66–73; Ẓahīr al-Dīn Nīshāpūrī, *Saljūq-nāma*, pp. 41–42; al-Rāwandī, *Rāḥat al-ṣudūr*, pp. 158--161; al-Bundārī, *Zubdat al-nuṣra*, pp. 90–91; Hodgson, *Order*, pp. 95–96, and Lewis, *Assassins*, pp. 53–55. See also J. van Ess, 'ʿAṭṭāš', *EIR*, vol. 3, p. 26.

73. Ibn al-Balkhī, *Fārs-nāma*, pp. 148 and 158.

74. On Muḥammad Tapar's campaigns against the Nizārīs of Rūdbār, see

Juwaynī, vol. 3, pp. 211–212; tr. Boyle, vol. 2, pp. 680–681; Rashīd al-Dīn, pp. 124–132; Kāshānī, pp. 145–152; Ḥāfiẓ Abrū, pp. 213–217; Ibn al-Qalānisī, *Dhayl*, p. 162; tr. Le Tourneau, pp. 83–84; al-Bundārī, *Zubdat al-nuṣra*, p. 117; al-Ḥusaynī, *Akhbār*, pp. 81–82; Ibn al-Athīr, *al-Kāmil*, vol. 10, pp. 168 and 185–186; Hodgson, *Order*, pp. 97–98, and Lewis, *Assassins*, pp. 55–57.

75. Ibn Isfandiyār, *Ta'rīkh*, vol. 2, p. 33; tr. Browne, p. 241; Marʿashī, *Ta'rīkh-i Ṭabaristān*, ed. Dorn, pp. 210–211; ed. Tasbīḥī, p. 96, and H. L. Rabino, 'Les Dynasties du Māzandarān', *JA*, 228 (1936), p. 422.
76. Al-Bundārī, *Zubdat al-nuṣra*, pp. 123 and 144–147.
77. Hodgson, *Order*, pp. 99ff. and 145, and his 'State', pp. 428 and 447ff.
78. Juwaynī, vol. 3, pp. 214–215; tr. Boyle, vol. 2, p. 682.
79. Juwaynī, vol. 3, pp. 213–214; tr. Boyle, vol. 2, pp. 681–682; Rashīd al-Dīn, p. 123; Kāshānī, p. 144, and Ḥāfiẓ Abrū, p. 212.
80. Rashīd al-Dīn, pp. 133 and 137; Kāshānī, pp. 153 and 156, and Ḥāfiẓ Abrū, pp. 217 and 225.
81. Ibn Muyassar, *Akhbār*, ed. Massé, pp. 65–69; ed. Sayyid, pp. 97–103. See also Ibn al-Ṣayrafī, *al-Ishāra*, p. 49 (64); Stern, 'Epistle of the Fatimid Caliph al-Āmir', pp. 20ff.; Hodgson, *Order*, pp. 107–109, and Lewis, *Assassins*, pp. 59–61.
82. Juwaynī, vol. 3, p. 215; tr. Boyle, vol. 2, p. 682; Rashīd al-Dīn, p. 133; Kāshānī, p. 153, and Ḥāfiẓ Abrū, pp. 217–218.
83. See W. Madelung, 'Amr Be Maʿrūf', *EIR*, vol. 1, pp. 992–995.
84. Juwaynī, vol. 3, pp. 209–211; tr. Boyle, vol. 2, pp. 679–680; Rashīd al-Dīn, pp. 123–124; Kāshānī, p. 145, and Ḥāfiẓ Abrū, p. 212.
85. See Juwaynī, vol. 3, pp. 195–199; tr. Boyle, vol. 2, pp. 671–673; Rashīd al-Dīn, pp. 105–107, reproduced with English translation in Levy, 'Account of the Ismaʿili doctrines', pp. 532–536, and Kāshānī, pp. 128–129. Ḥāfiẓ Abrū, p. 200, as in many other instances, summarizes Rashīd al-Dīn's account.
86. Al-Shahrastānī, *Kitāb al-milal wa'l-niḥal*, ed. W. Cureton (London, 1842), pp. 150–152; ed. Cairo, 1317–1321/1899–1903 (on the margin of Ibn Ḥazm's *al-Fiṣal*), vol. 2, pp. 32–36; ed. A. Fahmī Muḥammad (Cairo, 1948), vol. 1, pp. 339ff.; ed. Muḥammad b. Fatḥ Allāh Badrān (2nd ed., Cairo, 1375/1955), vol. 1, pp. 176–178; ed. al-Wakīl, vol. 1, pp. 195–198. The Arabic text of al-Shahrastānī's *al-Milal* was translated into Persian in 843/1439 by Afḍal al-Dīn Ṣadr Turka-yi Iṣfahānī (d. 850/1446), who probably produced a version of the *Four Chapters* closer to the original text of Ḥasan-i Ṣabbāḥ; this translation has been edited by Sayyid Muḥammad Riḍā Jalālī Nā'īnī (3rd ed., Tehran, 1350/1972), pp. 155–157. Afḍal al-Dīn's Persian version of the work was revised in 1021/1612 in India, for the Mughal emperor Jahāngīr, by Muṣṭafā b. Khāliqdād al-Hāshimī; this revised Persian translation has also been edited by M. R. Jalālī Nā'īnī (2nd ed., Tehran, 1358/1979), vol. 1, pp. 264–269. Amongst other translations of this work, mention may be made of the German translation, *Religionspartheien*, tr. Haarbrücker, vol. 1, pp. 225–230; English translation, *Muslim Sects*, tr. Kazi and Flynn, pp. 167–170; the relevant section on Ḥasan-i Ṣabbāḥ's doctrine was earlier translated into

English in Salisbury, 'Translation of Two Unpublished Arabic Documents', pp. 267–272, and in Hodgson, *Order*, pp. 325–328; French translations, *Les dissidences de l'Islam*, tr. Vadet, pp. 315–319; *Livre des religions et des sectes*, tr. Gimaret and Monnot, pp. 560–565. For a summary exposition of the doctrine of *taʿlīm*, see Hodgson, *Order*, pp. 51–61, and his 'State', pp. 433–437. See also P. Kraus, 'The Controversies of Fakhr al-Dīn Rāzī', *IC*, 12 (1938), pp. 146–153.

87. See M. R. Jalālī Nā'īnī, *Sharḥ-i ḥāl va āthār-i ḥujjat al-ḥaqq Abu'l-Fatḥ Muḥammad b. ʿAbd al-Karīm b. Aḥmad Shahrastānī* (Tehran, 1343/1964), pp. 9–10, 33, 45, 47, 51 and 75, and M. T. Dānishpazhūh, 'Dāʿī al-duʿāt Tāj al-Dīn Shahrastāna', *Nāma-yi Āstān-i Quds*, 7 (1346/1967), pp. 71–80, and 8 (1347/1968), pp. 61–71, where the author examines the available evidence and concludes that al-Shahrastānī adhered to Ismāʿīlism.

88. Naṣīr al-Dīn al-Ṭūsī, *Sayr va sulūk*, in his *Majmūʿa-yi rasā'il*, ed. M. T. Mudarris Raḍavī (Tehran, 1335/1956), pp. 38 and 120–121.

89. Jalālī Nā'īnī, *Sharḥ-i ḥāl*, pp. 47–52 and 75–76, and Poonawala, *Bio*, pp. 254–257.

90. See two articles by W. Madelung, 'Aš-Šahrastānīs Streitschrift gegen Avicenna und ihre Widerlegung durch Naṣīr ad-Dīn aṭ-Ṭūsī', in *Akten des VII: Kongresses für Arabistik und Islamwissenschaft*, pp. 250–259, and 'Aspects of Ismāʿīlī Theology', pp. 59ff., both articles reprinted in his *Religious Schools and Sects*; see also al-Shahrastānī, *Muṣāraʿat al-falāsifa*, ed. S. M. Mukhtār (Cairo, 1976).

91. On Buzurg-Ummīd's reign, see Juwaynī, vol. 3, pp. 216ff.; tr. Boyle, vol. 2, pp. 683ff.; Rashīd al-Dīn, pp. 137ff.; Kāshānī, pp. 157ff., the latter two sources drawing primarily on an anonymous Nizārī chronicle; Ḥāfiẓ Abrū, pp. 227ff.; Mīrkhwānd, *Rawḍat al-ṣafā'*, ed. and tr. Jourdain, translation pp. 161–163, text pp. 218–221; Tehran ed., vol. 4, pp. 215–217, and Khwānd Amīr, *Ḥabīb al-siyar*, vol. 2, pp. 469–470. See also three works by Hodgson, *Order*, pp. 99–104 and 117–119; 'State', pp. 449–450; 'Buzurg-Ummīd', *EI2*, vol. 1, p. 1359; Lewis, *Assassins*, pp. 64–67; Filippani-Ronconi, *Ismaeliti*, pp. 167–174; Ghālib, *Aʿlām*, pp. 437–438, and A. M. Rajput, 'Kiya Buzurg Ummid', in *Great Ismaili Heroes*, pp. 67–69.

92. On relations between these rulers and the Nizārīs, see Ibn Isfandiyār, *Ta'rīkh*, vol. 1, p. 111, and vol. 2, pp. 68 and 85–87; tr. Browne, p. 64; Āmulī, *Ta'rīkh*, pp. 127–129 and 131; Marʿashī, *Ta'rīkh-i Ṭabaristān*, ed. Dorn, pp. 57–58, 61–62 and 74–77; ed. Tasbīḥī, pp. 17, 19 and 27–28; Ferdinand Justi, *Iranisches Namenbuch* (Marburg, 1895), pp. 433 and 457; Rabino, 'Dynasties du Māzandarān', pp. 427–428 and 450–452, and W. Madelung, 'Baduspanids', *EIR*, vol. 3, p. 386.

93. Ibn al-Athīr, *al-Kāmil*, vol. 10, p. 222, and Sibṭ, *Mir'āt*, ed. Jewett, p. 69.

94. Al-Bayhaqī, *Ta'rīkh-i Bayhaq*, ed. Bahmanyār, pp. 271 and 276; ed. Husaini, pp. 472 and 480, and Ibn al-Athīr, *al-Kāmil*, vol. 10, pp. 224–225.

95. Rashīd al-Dīn, p. 138, and Kāshānī, p. 158; while Ḥāfiẓ Abrū does not mention this detail. Both Rashīd al-Dīn, p. 122, and Kāshānī, p. 144, also give earlier dates, 490 and 497 A.H., respectively, for the construction of

Maymūndiz. According to Juwaynī, vol. 3, pp. 122–123, tr. Boyle, vol. 2, p. 627, Maymūndiz was built sometime during the reign of ʿAlāʾ al-Dīn Muḥammad III (618–653/1221–1255), the penultimate lord of Alamūt. The site of Maymūndiz, located to the north of the present-day village of Shams Kilāya and westward from Alamūt, was identified in 1960 by an expeditionary group organized at Oxford University for exploring the Nizārī castles of northern Persia; see Willey, *Castles of the Assassins*, pp. 158–192. For other views on the site of Maymūndiz, see Ivanow, *Alamut and Lamasar*, pp. 75–81; Varjāvand, *Sarzamīn-i Qazvīn*, pp. 207 and 234–240, and Sutūda, *Qilāʿ*, pp. 108–122. Dr Sutūda, who is well acquainted with the area, rejects the validity of the identification made by Willey's expedition.

96. Ibn al-Athīr, *al-Kāmil*, vol. 10, p. 231, Khwānd Amīr, *Dastūr al-wuzarāʾ*, pp. 194–198, and ʿAbbās Iqbāl, *Vizārat dar ʿahd-i salāṭīn-i buzurg-i Saljūqī* (Tehran, 1338/1959), pp. 254–260.
97. *Taʾrīkh-i Sīstān*, p. 391; tr. Gold, p. 319.
98. Rashīd al-Dīn, p. 140; Kāshānī, p. 159; Ḥāfiẓ Abrū, p. 228, and Ibn al-Athīr, *al-Kāmil*, vol. 10, p. 238.
99. Kāshānī, pp. 160–164, containing the fullest account; see also Rashīd al-Dīn, p. 141, and Ḥāfiẓ Abrū, p. 229.
100. See Rashīd al-Dīn, pp. 144–145; Kāshānī, pp. 167–168, and Ḥāfiẓ Abrū, pp. 230–231.
101. Juwaynī, vol. 3, pp. 217–221; Boyle, vol. 2, pp. 683–685; Rashīd al-Dīn, pp. 141–142; also his *Āl Saljūq*, pp. 114–115; Kāshānī, pp. 164–165; Ḥamd Allāh, *Taʾrīkh*, ed. and tr. Gantin, pp. 280–281; ed. and tr. Browne, vol. 1, pp. 361–362 and 465, and vol. 2, pp. 69–70 and 103; ed. Navāʾī, pp. 358–360 and 455; Ḥāfiẓ Abrū, p. 229; Ẓahīr al-Dīn Nīshāpūrī, *Saljūq-nāma*, p. 56; al-Bundārī, *Zubdat al-nuṣra*, pp. 176–178, accusing Sanjar himself of this murder; al-Rāwandī, *Rāḥat al-ṣudūr*, pp. 227–228; al-Ḥusaynī, *Akhbār*, p. 107; Ibn al-Athīr, *al-Kāmil*, vol. 11, pp. 9–11, in *RHCHO*, vol. 1, pp. 408–409; Ibn al-Athīr, *al-Atābakiyya*, in *RHCHO*, vol. 2, part 2, pp. 87–91; Ibn Khallikān, *Biographical Dictionary*, vol. 1, p. 506, and vol. 3, pp. 355–356, and Hindūshāh b. Sanjar Nakhjavānī, *Tajārib al-salaf*, ed. ʿAbbās Iqbāl (2nd ed., Tehran, 1344/1965), pp. 294–296.
102. See Defrémery, 'Ismaéliens de Syrie' (1854), pp. 397–416; Lewis, 'Ismāʿīlites and the Assassins', pp. 114–119; also his *Assassins*, pp. 104–108; Hodgson, *Order*, pp. 104ff., and Mirza, 'Syrian Ismāʿīlīs', pp. 20–27.
103. Al-ʿAẓīmī, p. 386, and Ibn al-ʿAdīm, *Zubdat al-ḥalab*, in *RHCHO*, vol. 3, p. 616.
104. Ibn al-ʿAdīm, *Zubdat al-ḥalab*, in *RHCHO*, vol. 3, p. 640.
105. Ibn al-Qalānisī, *Dhayl*, p. 215; tr. Gibb, p. 179; tr. Le Tourneau, p. 169.
106. Ibn al-Qalānisī, *Dhayl*, p. 214; tr. Gibb, p. 177; tr. Le Tourneau, p. 167; al-ʿAẓīmī, p. 397; *Bustān*, p. 120; Ibn al-ʿAdīm, *Zubdat al-ḥalab*, ed. Dahān, vol. 2, p. 235, in *RHCHO*, vol. 3, pp. 654–655; also his *Bughyat*, in *RHCHO*, vol. 3, pp. 726–727; al-Bundārī, *Zubdat al-nuṣra*, pp. 144–145, attributing the murder to the Saljūq vizier al-Dargazīnī who had evidently converted to Nizārism in secret; Ibn al-Athīr, *al-Kāmil*, vol. 10, pp. 224–225, in *RHCHO*,

vol. 1, pp. 364–366; also his *al-Atābakiyya*, in *RHCHO*, vol. 2, part 2, p. 58; Sibṭ, *Mir'āt*, ed. Jewett, p. 71; Ibn Khallikān, *Biographical Dictionary*, vol. 1, pp. 227–228, and Ibn Taghrībirdī, *al-Nujūm*, vol. 5, p. 230. Rashīd, al-Dīn, p. 137, and Kāshānī, p. 157, include al-Bursuqī's name in the list of the Nizārī victims of Ḥasan-i Ṣabbāḥ's time.

107. Ibn al-Qalānisī, *Dhayl*, p. 213; tr. Gibb, pp. 175–176; tr. Le Tourneau, pp. 165–166.

108. On Bahrām's activities in Damascus and Bāniyās, see Ibn al-Qalānisī, *Dhayl*, p. 215; tr. Gibb, pp. 179–180; tr. Le Tourneau, pp. 167–168; al-ʿAẓīmī, p. 397; *Bustān*, p. 120; Ibn al-Athīr, *al-Kāmil*, vol. 10, p. 225, in *RHCHO*, vol. 3, pp. 366–368, and al-Qalqashandī, *Ṣubḥ*, vol. 1, pp. 121–122. On the site of Bāniyās, see Burckhardt, *Travels in Syria*, pp. 37–38, describing the castle as he found it in 1810; M. van Berchem, 'Le Château de Bāniās et ses inscriptions', *JA*, 8 série, 12 (1888), pp. 440ff., reprinted in his *Opera Minora*, vol. 1, pp. 265ff.; G. Le Strange, *Palestine under the Moslems* (London, 1890), pp. 418–419, and R. Dussaud, *Topographie historique de la Syrie antique et médiévale* (Paris, 1927), pp. 390–391.

109. Ibn al-Qalānisī, *Dhayl*, pp. 220–222; tr. Gibb, pp. 186–191; tr. Le Tourneau, pp. 177–180; al-ʿAẓīmī, p. 400; *Bustān*, p. 121; Ibn Muyassar, *Akhbār*, ed. Massé, p. 70; ed. Sayyid, p. 106; Ibn al-Athīr, *al-Kāmil*, vol. 10, p. 234, in *RHCHO*, vol. 1, p. 383; Sibṭ, *Mir'āt*, ed. Jewett, p. 72, and an anonymous Syriac chronicle translated in A. S. Tritton and H. A. R. Gibb, 'The First and Second Crusades from an Anonymous Syriac Chronicle', *JRAS* (1933), pp. 98–99.

110. On the debacle of the Nizārīs in Damascus, see Ibn al-Qalānisī, *Dhayl*, pp. 222–224; tr. Gibb, pp. 191–195; tr. Le Tourneau, pp. 181–184; al-Aẓīmī, pp. 400–401; *Bustān*, p. 121; Ibn al-Athīr, *al-Kāmil*, vol. 10, p. 234, in *RHCHO*, vol. 1, pp. 384–385; Sibṭ, *Mir'āt*, ed. Jewett, p. 80, in *RHCHO*, vol. 3, p. 567; Abu'l-Fidā, *al-Mukhtaṣar*, in *RHCHO*, vol. 1, pp. 17–18, and Ibn Taghrībirdī, *al-Nujūm*, vol. 5, p. 235. See also Grousset, *Croisades*, vol. 1, pp. 658ff.

111. Ibn al-Qalānisī, *Dhayl*, pp. 230 and 233; tr. Gibb, pp. 202–204 and 208; tr. Le Tourneau, pp. 192–193 and 197–198; al-ʿAẓīmī, p. 404; *Bustān*, p. 122; Ibn al-Athīr, *al-Kāmil*, vol. 10, pp. 239 and 243, in *RHCHO*, vol. 1, pp. 393 and 395–396; Ibn Khallikān, *Biographical Dictionary*, vol. 1, p. 274, and Ibn Taghrībirdī, *al-Nujūm*, vol. 5, p. 249, in *RHCHO*, vol. 3, pp. 501–502. These *fidā'*īs are named in the rolls kept at Alamūt; see Rashīd al-Dīn, p. 145, and Kāshānī, p. 167.

112. Al-ʿAẓīmī, p. 407; Ibn al-ʿAdīm, *Zubdat al-ḥalab*, ed. Dahān, vol. 2, pp. 251–252, in *RHCHO*, vol. 3, p. 665; Ibn al-Athīr, *al-Kāmil*, vol. 11, p. 3, in *RHCHO*, vol. 1, p. 400; Abu'l-Fidā, *al-Mukhtaṣar*, in *RHCHO*, vol. 1, p. 21, and Ibn Faḍl Allāh al-ʿUmarī, *Masālik al-abṣār fī mamālik al-amṣār*, ed. Ayman F. Sayyid (Cairo, 1985), pp. 132–133.

113. Qadmūs has remained a major Nizārī centre in Syria, and the circumstances surrounding the acquisition of that stronghold are still reflected in the traditions of the Nizārīs living there. In 1850, the Nizārīs of Qadmūs related to the British traveller Frederick Walpole (1822–1876) that their ancestors

had migrated to that place in large numbers from Damascus in mediaeval times; see F. Walpole, *The Ansayrii (or Assassins), with Travels in the Further East, in 1850–51* (London, 1851), vol. 3, pp. 299–303.

114. Ibn al-Qalānisī, *Dhayl*, pp. 273–274; tr. Gibb, p. 263; tr. Le Tourneau, p. 260; Yāqūt, *Muʿjam*, vol. 4, p. 556; Ibn al-Athīr, *al-Kāmil*, vol. 11, p. 30, in *RHCHO*, vol. 1, p. 438; Abu'l-Fidā, *al-Mukhtaṣar*, in *RHCHO*, vol. 1, p. 25; Usāma, *Memoirs*, pp. 177–178, and E. Honigmann, 'Maṣyād', *EI*, vol. 3, pp. 404–406.

115. On the Nizārī castles in the Jabal Bahrā' and their acquisition, see also Defrémery, 'Ismaéliens de Syrie', pp. 417–421; Le Strange, *Palestine*, pp. 36, 39, 80–81, 352, 468, 485 and 507; van Berchem, 'Épigraphie des Assassins', pp. 453ff. and 480–501, reprinted in his *Opera Minora*, vol. 1, pp. 453ff. and 480–501; also his 'Notes sur les Croisades', *JA*, 9 série, 19 (1902), pp. 442ff.; R. Dussaud, 'Voyage en Syrie (2e), Oct.–Nov. 1896: Notes archéologique', *Revue Archéologique*, 1 (1897), pp. 341, 343ff. and 349; Dussaud, *Topographie historique*, pp. 138–148; Cahen, *Syrie du Nord*, pp. 170ff., 347ff. and 352ff.; Hodgson, *Order*, pp. 106–107; Lewis, 'Ismāʿīlites and the Assassins', pp. 119–120, and also his *Assassins*, pp. 108–109. See also John G. Phillips, 'Qalʿat Maṣyāf: A Study in Islamic Military Architecture' (Ph.D. thesis, University of London, 1982), also his 'Mashhad Rāshid al-Dīn Sinān: A 13th-Century Ismāʿīlī Monument in the Syrian Jabal Anṣarīya', *JRAS* (1984), pp. 19–37.

116. Ibn al-Qalānisī, *Dhayl*, p. 301; tr. Le Tourneau, pp. 299–300, and Elisséeff, *Nūr ad-Dīn*, vol. 2, pp. 428–430.

117. Ibn al-Qalānisī, *Dhayl*, pp. 304–305; tr. Gibb, pp. 291–292; tr. Le Tourneau, pp. 305–306; Ibn al-ʿAdīm, *Zubdat al-ḥalab*, ed. Dahān, vol. 2, pp. 292ff.; Ibn al-Athīr, *al-Kāmil*, vol. 11, p. 54, in *RHCHO*, vol. 1, p. 476; Ibn al-Athīr, *al-Atābakiyya*, in *RHCHO*, vol. 2, part 2, pp. 177–178; Abu'l-Fidā, *al-Mukhtaṣar*, in *RHCHO*, vol. 1, p. 28; William of Tyre, *Historia*, in *RHC: Historiens Occidentaux*, vol. 1, pp. 771–773; Grousset, *Croisades*, vol. 2, pp. 275–278; Runciman, *Crusades*, vol. 2, pp. 325–326, and Elisséeff, *Nūr ad-Dīn*, vol. 2, pp. 430–432.

118. Ibn al-Qalānisī, *Dhayl*, p. 303; tr. Le Tourneau, pp. 302–303.

119. Ibn al-Furāt, *Ta'rīkh al-duwal wa'l mulūk*, ed. C. Zurayk (Beirut, 1936–1942), vol. 8, p. 79; William of Tyre, *Historia*, pp. 789–792; Sanudo, *Liber secretorum fidelium Crusis*, in *Gesta Dei per Francos*, vol. 2, p. 168; Grousset, *Croisades*, vol. 2, pp. 323–324, and Runciman, *Crusades*, vol. 2, pp. 332–333.

120. On the territorial structure and stability of the Nizārī state during the Alamūt period, see Hodgson, *Order*, pp. 115–120 and 244ff., and also his 'State', pp. 447–449 and 455–457.

121. On the reign of Muḥammad b. Buzurg-Ummīd, see Juwaynī, vol. 3, pp. 221–222; tr. Boyle, vol. 2, pp. 685–686; Rashīd al-Dīn, pp. 146–159; Kāshānī, pp. 168–181; Ḥāfiẓ Abrū, pp. 237–243; Mīrkhwānd; *Rawḍat al-ṣafā'*, ed. and tr. Jourdain, translation pp. 163–164, text pp. 221–223; Tehran ed., vol. 4, pp. 217–218; Khwānd Amīr, *Ḥabīb al-siyar*, vol. 2, pp. 470–471;

Hodgson, *Order*, pp. 143–146; also his 'State', pp. 450ff.; Lewis, *Assassins*, pp. 68ff., and Filippani-Ronconi, *Ismaeliti*, pp. 174ff.

122. Minhāj-i Sirāj Jūzjānī, *Ṭabaqāt-i Nāṣirī*, ed. ʿAbd al-Ḥayy Ḥabībī (2nd ed., Kabul, 1342–1343/1963–1964), vol. 1, pp. 349 and 350–351; English translation, *The Ṭabaḳāt-i-Nāṣirī: A General History of the Muhammadan Dynasties of Asia*, tr. Henry G. Raverty (London, 1881–1899), vol. 1, pp. 363 and 365, and C. E. Bosworth, 'The Early Islamic History of Ghūr', *Central Asiatic Journal*, 6 (1961), pp. 132–133.

123. Rashīd al-Dīn, pp. 160–161; Kāshānī, pp. 182 and 217–218, and Ḥāfiẓ Abrū, pp. 243–244.

124. Rashīd al-Dīn, pp. 146–147; also his *Āl Saljūq*, p. 115; Kāshānī, pp. 168–169; Ḥamd Allāh, *Ta'rīkh*, ed. and tr. Gantin, pp. 280–281; ed. and tr. Browne, vol. 1, pp. 363 and 465, and vol. 2, pp. 70 and 103; ed. Navā'ī, pp. 360–361 and 455; Ḥāfiẓ Abrū, p. 237; Ẓahīr al-Dīn Nīshāpūrī, *Saljūq-nāma*, p. 56; al-Bundārī, *Zubdat al-nuṣra*, p. 180; al-Rāwandī, *Rāḥat al-ṣudūr*, pp. 228–229; al-Ḥusaynī, *Akhbār*, p. 109; Ibn al-Athīr, *al-Kāmil*, vol. 11, p. 24, also his *al-Atābakiyya*, in *RHCHO*, vol. 2, part 2, p. 98, and Nakhjavānī, *Tajārib al-salaf*, pp. 302–303.

125. Rashīd al-Dīn, p. 155; Kāshānī, p. 176; Ḥāfiẓ Abrū, p. 240, and Ibn al-Athīr, *al-Kāmil*, vol. 11, p. 44.

126. Yāqūt, *Muʿjam*, vol. 3, pp. 534–535; tr. Barbier de Meynard, pp. 390–391, and Ibn al-Athīr, *al-Kāmil*, vol. 11, pp. 57 and 59.

127. See Ibn al-Athīr, *al-Kāmil*, vol. 11, pp. 75, 81, 84–85, 89–90 and 95.

128. On Ḥasan II's activities in Muḥammad b. Buzurg-Ummīd's time, see Juwaynī, vol. 3, pp. 222–225; tr. Boyle, vol. 2, pp. 686–688; Rashīd al-Dīn, pp. 162–163; Kāshānī, pp. 183–184; Ḥāfiẓ Abrū, pp. 251–252; Hodgson, *Order*, pp. 146–148; also his 'State', pp. 457–458; Lewis, *Assassins*, pp. 70–71, and Filippani-Ronconi, *Ismaeliti*, pp. 177–178.

129. On Ḥasan II and his short reign, see Juwaynī, vol. 3, pp. 225–239; tr. Boyle, vol. 2, pp. 688–697; Rashīd al-Dīn, pp. 162–170; Kāshānī, pp. 183–191; Ḥamd Allāh, *Ta'rīkh*, ed. and tr. Gantin, pp. 498–504; ed. and tr. Browne, vol. 1, pp. 522–523, and vol. 2, p. 129; ed. Navā'ī, pp. 522–524; Ḥāfiẓ Abrū, pp. 251–255; Mīrkhwānd, *Rawḍat al-ṣafā'*, ed. and tr. Jourdain, translation pp. 164–168, text pp. 223–228; Tehran ed., vol. 4, pp. 218–222; Khwānd Amīr, *Ḥabīb al-siyar*, vol. 2, pp. 471–473; Hollister, *Shīʿa*, pp. 310ff.; Hodgson, *Order*, pp. 148–159; also his 'State', pp. 458–460; Lewis, *Assassins*, pp. 71–75; Filippani-Ronconi, *Ismaeliti*, pp. 185–197; Ghālib, *Ta'rīkh*, pp. 275–276; also his *Aʿlām*, pp. 229–230; Ivanow, *Guide*, p. 102; also his *Ismaili Literature*, p. 132, and Poonawala, *Bio*, 257–258.

130. On the declaration of the *qiyāma* in the Nizārī community, see Juwaynī, vol. 3, pp. 225–230 and 237–239; tr. Boyle, vol. 2, pp. 688–691 and 695–697; Rashīd al-Dīn, pp. 164–166 and 168–169, and Kāshānī, pp. 184–186 and 188, all three chroniclers closely follow the same Nizārī sources, and Ḥāfiẓ Abrū, pp. 252–253. The doctrine of the *qiyāma*, as further developed under Ḥasan's son and successor, is discussed in a few later Nizārī texts, notably the *Haft*

bāb-i Bābā Sayyidnā, in *Two Early Ismaili Treatises*, pp. 19–24, 27, 30, 33, 36, 38, 40 and 41; English translation with commentary in Hodgson, *Order*, pp. 299–304, 312, 314, 316, 318, 319, 321 and 322, written by an anonymous author who had evidently been an eyewitness to the event at Alamūt, and al-Ṭūsī, *Rawḍat al-taslīm*, especially text pp. 62–63, 83–84, 101–102 and 128–149, translation pp. 68–70, 94–96, 115–116 and 149–175, which is, however, the chief source on the doctrine of the *satr* developed during the later Alamūt period. References to the doctrine of the *qiyāma*, with an important passage on the proclamation of the Resurrection at Alamūt, are contained also in Abū Isḥāq Quhistānī, *Haft bāb*, text pp. 19, 24, 38–39, 40–42 (describing the event), 43–44, 46–47, 53, 58 and 65, translation pp. 19, 23, 38, 40–42, 43–44, 46–47, 53–54, 58 and 65, a Nizārī treatise written at the beginning of the tenth/sixteenth century, and in Khayrkhwāh, *Kalām-i pīr*, text pp. 46, 51, 62–64, 65–66, 68, 90–92, 95–96, 100 and 112–113, translation pp. 38–39, 44, 57–59, 60–61, 64, 84–87, 91, 96, 109, and appendix pp. 115–116, containing Abū Isḥāq's original passage on the declaration of the *qiyāma*. The *Kalām-i pīr*, as noted, is a plagiarized and extended version of Abū Isḥāq's treatise. Of the secondary sources, see Ivanow's introductions to the *Kalām-i pīr*, especially pp. 27ff. and 59ff., and to the *Haft bāb-i Abū Isḥāq*, pp. 14–22; Hodgson, *Order*, pp. 148ff.; also his 'State', pp. 458–460; several of Henry Corbin's studies are relevant here including his *Étude*, pp. 20–25; 'Divine Epiphany', pp. 127ff., reprinted in his *Cyclical Time*, pp. 117ff.; 'Nāṣir-i Khusrau and Iranian Ismāʿīlism', pp. 529–531; *Histoire*, pp. 137–151; Persian translation, *Taʾrīkh-i falsafa-yi Islāmī*, tr. A. Mubashirī (Tehran, 1352/1973), pp. 123–135, and 'Huitième centenaire d'Alamūt', *Mercure de France* (February, 1965), pp. 285–304; see also Zāhid ʿAlī, *Taʾrīkh*, vol. 2, pp. 176ff.; L. V. Stroeva, 'Den' Voskreseniya iz mertvuikh i ego sotzial'naya sushchnost. Iz istorii Ismailitskogo gosudarstva v Irane XII v', *Kratkie Soobshcheniya Instituta Vostokovedeniya*, 38 (1960), pp. 19–25; also her 'Novuiy prizuiv Ismailitov kak ideologiya narodnogo dvizheniya v Irane v XI–XII vv' [*Ad-daʿwat al-djadida* of the Ismailites as an ideology of the people's movement in Iran in XI–XII centuries], *Palestinsky Sbornik*, 21 (84) (1970), pp. 199–213; Lewis, *Assassins*, pp. 71ff.; Filippani-Ronconi, *Ismaeliti*, pp. 185ff., and Jorunn J. Buckley, 'The Nizārī Ismāʿīlites' Abolishment of the Sharīʿa during the Great Resurrection of 1164 A.D./559 A.H.', *SI*, 60 (1984), especially pp. 142–157.

131. For some earlier spiritual interpretations of the Resurrection, Paradise, and Hell, by the Ismāʿīlīs see, for instance, al-Sijistānī, *Kashf al-maḥjūb*, pp. 83–96; also his *al-Yanābīʿ*, text pp. 67–69, translation pp. 88–89, and Nāṣir-i Khusraw, *Wajh-i dīn*, ed. Ghanīzāda, pp. 27–45; ed. Aavani, pp. 35–59.
132. *Haft bāb-i Bābā Sayyidnā*, p. 21; tr. Hodgson in *Order*, pp. 301–302, and al-Ṭūsī, *Rawḍat al-taslīm*, text pp. 148–149, translation pp. 173–175.
133. Rashīd al-Dīn, p. 165, and Kāshānī, pp. 185–186.
134. Juwaynī, vol. 3, p. 228; tr. Boyle, vol. 2, p. 690; Rashīd al-Dīn, p. 165; Kāshānī, p. 185, and Ḥāfiẓ Abrū, p. 253.
135. Juwaynī, vol. 3, p. 229; tr. Boyle, vol. 2, p. 690; Rashīd al-Dīn, p. 165; Kāshānī, p. 185, and Ḥāfiẓ Abrū, p. 253.

136. See al-Ṭūsī, *Rawḍat al-taslīm*, text pp. 113ff., translation pp. 129ff., and *Haft bāb-i Bābā Sayyidnā*, pp. 22–24, tr. Hodgson in *Order*, pp. 302–303.
137. See Azim A. Nanji, 'Assassins', in *The Encyclopedia of Religion*, ed. M. Eliade (London–New York, 1987), vol. 1, p. 470, and his 'Ismā'īlism', in *Islamic Spirituality: Foundations*, ed. S. H. Nasr (London, 1987), pp. 179–198.
138. Juwaynī, vol. 3, p. 239; tr. Boyle, vol. 2, p. 697.
139. Ẓahīr al-Dīn Nīshāpūrī, *Saljūq-nāma*, pp. 77–78; al-Rāwandī, *Rāḥat al-ṣudūr*, pp. 289–290; Rashīd al-Dīn, *Āl Saljūq*, pp. 164–166; Ibn al-Athīr, *al-Kāmil*, vol. 11, pp. 119–120; Ḥamd Allāh, *Ta'rīkh*, ed. and tr. Gantin, pp. 300–301; ed. and tr. Browne, vol. 1, pp. 471–472, and vol. 2, p. 105; ed. Navā'ī, p. 461; Mīrkhwānd, *Rawḍat al-ṣafā'*, Tehran ed., vol. 4, p. 339, and Khwānd Amīr, *Ḥabīb al-siyar*, vol. 2, pp. 530–531.
140. Ibn al-Athīr, *al-Kāmil*, vol. 11, p. 117.
141. Muḥammad II's long reign is briefly treated in Juwaynī, vol. 3, pp. 240–242; tr. Boyle, vol. 2, pp. 697–699; Rashīd al-Dīn, pp. 170–173; Kāshānī, pp. 192–198; Ḥāfiẓ Abrū, pp. 259–261; Mīrkhwānd, *Rawḍat al-ṣafā'*, ed. and tr. Jourdain, translation pp. 169–171, text pp. 228–232; Tehran ed., vol. 4, pp. 222–224, and Khwānd Amīr, *Ḥabīb al-siyar*, vol. 2, pp. 473–474; see also Hollister, *Shi'a*, pp. 315–316; Hodgson, *Order*, pp. 159ff., 180–184 and 210–217; also his 'State', pp. 466–468; Lewis, *Assassins*, pp. 75–78; Filippani-Ronconi, *Ismaeliti*, pp. 197–199 and 227ff.; Ghālib, *Ta'rīkh*, pp. 277ff.; also his *A'lām*, pp. 493–494; Ivanow, *Guide*, pp. 102–103; also his *Ismaili Literature*, pp. 132–133, and Poonawala, *Bio*, pp. 258–259.
142. See Juwaynī, vol. 3, pp. 180–181 and 231–237; tr. Boyle, vol. 2, pp. 663 and 691–695; Rashīd al-Dīn, pp. 79 and 166–168; Kāshānī, pp. 104 and 186–188; Ḥamd Allāh, *Ta'rīkh*, ed. and tr. Gantin, pp. 500–501; ed. and tr. Browne, vol. 1, p. 522, and vol. 2, p. 129; ed. Navā'ī, p. 522; Ḥāfiẓ Abrū, pp. 169–170 and 253–254; Mīrkhwānd, *Rawḍat al-ṣafā'*, ed. and tr. Jourdain, translation pp. 167–168, text pp. 227–228; Tehran ed., vol. 4, p. 221; Khwānd Amīr, *Ḥabīb al-siyar*, vol. 2, p. 472, and *Dabistān-i madhāhib*, vol. 1, pp. 263–264. Ibn 'Inaba gives a confused Nizārid ancestry for Jalāl al-Dīn Ḥasan III, the sixth lord of Alamūt, in his *'Umdat al-ṭālib*, p. 237, and *al-Fuṣūl al-fakhriyya*, ed. Jalāl al-Dīn Muḥaddith Urmavī (Tehran, 1984), p. 145. See also Hodgson, *Order*, pp. 160–162; Hollister, *Shi'a*, pp. 313–315, and Ivanow, *Alamut and Lamasar*, pp. 26–28.
143. See, for example, Abū Isḥāq, *Haft bāb*, text pp. 23–24, translation p. 23; Khayrkhwāh, *Kalām-i pīr*, text p. 51, translation p. 44, and Shihāb al-Dīn Shāh al-Ḥusaynī, *Khiṭābāt-i 'āliya*, ed. H. Ujāqī (Bombay, 1963), pp. 37–39. A more elaborate, but highly confused and anachronistic, account of the Nizārid Fāṭimid genealogy of Ḥasan II and the reign of his ancestors in Persia, is related by the modern Nizārī historian and poet Muḥammad b. Zayn al-'Ābidīn Khurāsānī, better known as Fidā'ī Khurāsānī (d. 1923), in his *Kitāb-i hidāyat al-mu'minīn al-ṭālibīn*, ed. A. A. Semenov (Moscow, 1959), pp. 104–111. Both Shihāb al-Dīn Shāh (d. 1884), the eldest son of the second Āghā Khān, and Fidā'ī relate that it was Nizār's son al-Hādī who was secretly brought to Alamūt. See also Tāmir, *al-Imāma*, pp. 192 and 217–219; Ghālib,

Ta'rīkh, pp. 259–274; also his *Aʿlām*, pp. 244–245, 417–419 and 484–486; Ivanow, 'Ismailitica', pp. 68–69, and also his *Brief*, p. 80. It suffices to mention here that the later Muḥammad-Shāhī and Qāsim-Shāhī Nizārīs accepted different ancestries for Ḥasan *ʿalā dhikrihi'l-salām*.

144. The doctrine of the *qiyāma*, as elaborated under Muḥammad II, is propounded in the anonymous *Haft bāb-i Bābā Sayyidnā*, in *Two Early Ismaili Treatises*, pp. 4–42. Composed around 1200 A.D., towards the end of Muḥammad II's reign, it is the only extant Nizārī source from the period of the *qiyāma*; its complete English translation with detailed commentary is to be found in Hodgson, *Order*, pp. 279–324. The doctrine, modified to various extents, is also represented in later Nizārī works, notably in al-Ṭūsī, *Rawḍat al-taslīm*; Abū Isḥāq, *Haft bāb*, text pp. 17ff., 30ff., 34ff., 45ff., 52ff. and 65–67, translation pp. 17ff., 30ff., 35ff., 45ff., 52ff. and 65–68, and Khayrkhwāh, *Kalām-i pīr*, text pp. 23ff., 46ff., 55ff., 58ff., 89ff., 94ff. and 112–116, translation pp. 19ff., 38ff., 49ff., 53ff., 84ff., 88ff. and 109–112. The best modern exposition of the fully developed doctrine of the *qiyāma* is contained in Hodgson, *Order*, pp. 162–180, and also his 'State', pp. 460–466.

145. Al-Ṭūsī, *Rawḍat al-taslīm*, text pp. 104–105 and 112, translation pp. 119 and 128–129; also his *Sayr va sulūk*, p. 51, and Badakhshānī, *Sī va shish ṣaḥīfa*, p. 51.

146. The spiritual resurrection of the Nizārīs is expounded in al-Ṭūsī, *Rawḍat al-taslīm*, text pp. 47–56, translation pp. 52–63.

147. *Haft bāb-i Bābā Sayyidnā*, pp. 8–14; tr. Hodgson in *Order*, pp. 284–293; see also al-Ṭūsī, *Rawḍat al-taslīm*, text pp. 115 and 128ff., translation pp. 133 and 149ff.; Abū Isḥāq, *Haft bāb*, text pp. 22 and 38–40, translation pp. 21–22 and 38–41, and Khayrkhwāh, *Kalām-i pīr*, text pp. 49 and 63–65, translation pp. 41 and 57–60.

148. See Vajda, 'Melchizédec dans la mythologie Ismaélienne', pp. 173–183, and Ivanow, 'Noms Bibliques dans la mythologie Ismaélienne', pp. 249–255.

149. The three categories, with their particular attributes, are explained in the *Haft bāb-i Bābā Sayyidnā*, pp. 24, 26–36 and 40; tr. Hodgson in *Order*, pp. 303, 308–318 and 321; al-Ṭūsī, *Rawḍat al-taslīm*, text pp. 42, 44–45, 73, 77, 82, 84, 98–99, 101–102 and 136, translation pp. 46–47, 49–50, 82, 87, 92–93, 95, 111–112, 115–116 and 159; Abū Isḥāq, *Haft bāb*, text pp. 21 and 46–48, translation pp. 20–21 and 44–48; Khayrkhwāh, *Kalām-i pīr*, text pp. 48–49, 90–92 and 106ff., translation pp. 40–41, 84–87 and 102ff., and Badakhshānī, *Sī va shish ṣaḥīfa*, pp. 35, 62–63 and 64. See also Ivanow's introduction to the *Kalām-i pīr*, pp. 46–47, and Hodgson, *Order*, pp. 172–174.

150. Ibn Isfandiyār, *Ta'rīkh*, vol. 2, pp. 142–147; tr. Browne, pp. 251–253; Āmulī, *Ta'rīkh*, pp. 143–149; Marʿashī, *Ta'rīkh-i Ṭabaristān*, ed. Dorn, pp. 74–78; ed. Tasbīḥī, pp. 27–29, and Rabino, 'Dynasties du Māzandarān', pp. 430–431 and 452.

151. Rashīd al-Dīn, pp. 170–173; Kāshānī, pp. 192–194; Ḥāfiẓ Abrū, pp. 259–261; Mīrkhwānd, *Rawḍat al-ṣafā'*, ed. and tr. Jourdain, translation pp. 169–171, text pp. 229–231; Tehran ed., vol. 4, pp. 222–224, and vol. 7, pp. 519–521; Khwānd Amīr, *Ḥabīb al-siyar*, vol. 2, p. 474, and Hodgson, *Order*, p. 183.

152. The only Nizārī biography of Rāshid al-Dīn Sinān is the so-called *Faṣl min al-lafẓ al-sharīf, hādhihi manāqib al-mawlā Rāshid al-Dīn*, a hagiographic work containing various anecdotes based on the oral tradition of the Syrian Nizārīs, written by a certain Abū Firās, now generally identified with the Syrian *dāʿī* Shihāb al-Dīn Abū Firās, who died towards the middle of the tenth/sixteenth century. This work was first published with French translation by S. Guyard under the title of 'Un Grand Maître des Assassins au temps de Saladin', *JA*, 7 série, 9 (1877), translation pp. 387–450, text pp. 452–489; Guyard had earlier published excerpts of this work, from an anonymous Ismāʿīlī collection, in his *Fragments relatifs à la doctrine des Ismaélîs*. The entire text of the *Faṣl* was republished by Mehmed Şerefüddin in *Darülfünun Ilahiyat Fakültesi Mecmuasi*, 2, no. 7 (Istanbul, 1928), pp. 45–71; and M. Ghālib produced a new edition of the text in his *Sinān Rāshid al-Dīn, Shaykh al-Jabal al-thālith* (Beirut, 1967), pp. 163–214. Our references to the *Faṣl* are to its text and translation contained in Guyard's article. Amongst the non-Ismāʿīlī sources, the most important biographical account of Sinān is related by Ibn al-ʿAdīm (d. 660/1262) in his *Bughyat al-ṭalab fī taʾrīkh Ḥalab*. The volume of the *Bughyat* containing Sinān's biography has not so far been recovered, but the bulk of its text has survived indirectly in at least three recensions in the works of Quṭb al-Dīn al-Yūnīnī (d. 726/1326), Shams al-Dīn al-Dhahabī (d. 748/1348), and Khalīl b. Aybak al-Ṣafadī (d. 764/1363). Al-Yūnīnī's text, the fullest of the three recensions, has served as the chief source for the edition produced by B. Lewis in his 'Three Biographies from Kamāl ad-Dīn', pp. 336–344; a better edition with English translation is contained in B. Lewis, 'Kamāl al-Dīn's Biography of Rāšid al-Dīn Sinān', pp. 225–267, reprinted in his *Studies in Classical and Ottoman Islam*. Of the secondary sources on the career of Sinān and his times, mention may be made of Quatremère, 'Notice historique sur les Ismaëliens', pp. 339–376; Defrémery, 'Ismaéliens de Syrie', *JA*, 5 (1855), pp. 1–32; Lewis, 'Ismāʿīlites and the Assassins', pp. 120–127; also his *Assassins*, pp. 110–118; Hodgson, *Order*, pp. 185–207; Mirza, 'Syrian Ismāʿīlīs', pp. 28ff., 40–77, 156–163 and 166–173; also his 'Rashid al-Din Sinan', in *Great Ismaili Heroes*, pp. 72–80; Filippani-Ronconi, *Isamaeliti*, pp. 201–222; ʿAbd Allāh b. al-Murtaḍā al-Khawābī, *al-Falak al-dawwār* (Aleppo, 1933), pp. 207–221; ʿĀrif Tāmir, *Sinān wa Ṣalāḥ al-Dīn* (Beirut, 1956); Ḥusayn, *Ṭāʾifat al-Ismāʿīliyya*, pp. 99–106; Ghālib, *Taʾrīkh*, pp. 278–283; also his *Aʿlām*, pp. 295–303; Poonawala, *Bio*, pp. 289–290; Ivanow, *Ismaili Literature*, pp. 169–170 and 173, and also his 'Rāshid al-Dīn Sinān', *EI*, vol. 3, pp. 1123–1124.

153. Yāqūt, *Muʿjam*, vol. 3, p. 275.

154. According to Abū Firās, *Faṣl*, translation pp. 391–394, text pp. 454–455, Sinān waited for seven years at Kahf, teaching children and healing the sick. This period of waiting seems to be long, unless, as Hodgson, *Order*, p. 186, has suggested, it is assumed that Sinān left Alamūt a few years before Ḥasan II's accession, perhaps fearing persecution by Muḥammad b. Buzurg-Ummīd. On this point, see also Lewis, 'Kamāl al-Dīn's Biography', p. 251.

155. On the acquisition, fortification and construction of castles by Sinān, see Abū

Firās, *Faṣl*, translation pp. 396–397, 419–421, 431–432, 433 and 449–450, text pp. 456–457, 471–472, 478–479 and 489.

156. William of Tyre, *Historia*, pp. 995–999. Walter of Map, writing in 1182 A.D., relates the same story in his *De Nugis Curialium* [Cymmrodorion Record Series, no. IX] (London, 1923), p. 37. See also Grousset, *Croisades*, vol. 2, pp. 598–603, suggesting that it was in fear of Nūr al-Dīn that the Nizārīs approached Amalric; Runciman, *Crusades*, vol. 2, pp. 396–397; Elisséeff, *Nūr ad-Dīn*, vol. 2, pp. 687–688; M. Melville, *La Vie des Templiers* (Paris, 1974), pp. 118–119, and J. Hauziński, 'On Alleged Attempts at Converting the Assassins to Christianity in the Light of William of Tyre's Account', *Folia Orientalia*, 15 (1974), pp. 229–246.

157. Ibn Khallikān, *Biographical Dictionary*, vol. 3, pp. 339–341; see also Ibn al-ʿAdīm, *Zubdat al-ḥalab*, ed. Dahān, vol. 2, p. 340; Abū Shāma, *Kitāb al-rawḍatayn fī akhbār al-dawlatayn* (Cairo, 1287–1288/1870–1871), vol. 1, pp. 228–230, and Lewis, 'Kamāl al-Dīn's Biography', pp. 254–256.

158. In 577/1181–1182, Saladin sent a letter to the caliph in Baghdād, accusing the Zangids of being in league with the heretical Nizārīs and the Crusaders; see Abū Shāma, *al-Rawḍatayn*, vol. 2, pp. 23–24, in *RHCHO*, vol. 4, pp. 214–215.

159. On Nizārī attempts on Saladin's life, see *Bustān*, p. 141; Ibn Shaddād, *al-Nawādir al-sulṭāniyya*, in *RHCHO*, vol. 3, pp. 62–63; Ibn al-ʿAdīm, *L'Histoire d'Alep*, tr. Blochet, in *Revue de l'Orient Latin*, 3 (1895), p. 563, and 4 (1896), pp. 145–146; Abū Shāma, *al-Rawḍatayn*, vol. 1, pp. 239–240 and 258; Ibn al-Athīr, *al-Kāmil*, vol. 11, pp. 158 and 163, in *RHCHO*, vol. 1, pp. 618–619 and 623–624; Sibṭ, *Mirʾāt*, ed. Jewett, pp. 207 and 212; Abu'l-Fidā, *al-Mukhtaṣar*, in *RHCHO*, vol. 1, pp. 46–47, and B. Lewis, 'Saladin and the Assassins', *BSOAS*, 15 (1953), pp. 239–245, reprinted in his *Studies in Classical and Ottoman Islam*.

160. See Abū Shāma, *al-Rawḍatayn*, vol. 1, p. 261, in *RHCHO*, vol. 4, pp. 183–184; Ibn al-Athīr, *al-Kāmil*, vol. 11, p. 165, in *RHCHO*, vol. 1, p. 626; Abu'l-Fidā, *al-Mukhtaṣar*, in *RHCHO*, vol. 1, p. 47; al-Maqrīzī, *Histoire d'Égypte*, pp. 72–73, and also his *Ayyūbid Sultans of Egypt*, pp. 54–55. According to Abū Firās, *Faṣl*, translation pp. 398–408, text pp. 458–463, it was Saladin, terrified by Sinān's supernatural powers and a Nizārī dagger placed at his bedside, who took the peace initiative.

161. Ibn Jubayr, *Riḥla*, ed. W. Wright, second edition revised by M. J. de Goeje (Leiden–London, 1907), pp. 249–250; English translation, *The Travels*, tr. Ronald J. C. Broadhurst (London, 1952), pp. 259–260; French translation, *Voyages*, tr. M. Gaudefroy-Demombynes (Paris, 1949–1965), vol. 3, pp. 287–288. See also Sibṭ, *Mirʾāt*, ed. Jewett, p. 208, and Abū Firās, *Faṣl*, translation pp. 418–419, text pp. 470–471.

162. *Bustān*, p. 142, places the event in 572 A.H.; Ibn al-ʿAdīm, *L'Histoire d'Alep* (1896), pp. 148–150; Abū Shāma, *al-Rawḍatayn*, vol. 1, pp. 274–275, in *RHCHO*, vol. 4, pp. 189–191; Ibn al-Athīr, *al-Kāmil*, vol. 11, p. 168; in *RHCHO*, vol. 1, pp. 631–632; Sibṭ, *Mirʾāt*, ed. Jewett, p. 219, and Muḥam-

mad b. ʿAlī al-Ḥamawī, *al-Taʾrīkh al-Manṣūrī*, ed. P. A. Gryaznevich (Moscow, 1963), p. 184, a chronicle completed in 631/1233 by a Syrian functionary of the Ayyūbids.

163. Abū Shāma, *al-Rawḍatayn*, vol. 2, p. 16.
164. *Bustān*, p. 136, under the year 561/1165–1166 reports that the Syrian Ismāʿīlīs changed their doctrine, ate and drank during the month of Ramaḍān, and stopped praying; and al-Ḥamawī, *al-Taʾrīkh al-Manṣūrī*, p. 176, records the same event under the year 560/1164–1165, naming Sinān as its instigator. Al-Dhahabī and Ibn al-ʿAdīm also relate that Sinān broke the fast of Ramaḍān and abolished the Sharīʿa; see Lewis, 'Kamāl al-Dīn's Biography', pp. 230, 241 and 261.
165. Lewis, 'Kamāl al-Dīn's Biography', pp. 231, 248–249 and 262.
166. Guyard, *Fragments*, text pp. 193–195, translation pp. 275–284; English translation in Hodgson, *Order*, pp. 199–201.
167. See Ibn Jubayr, *Riḥla*, p. 255; tr. Broadhurst, p. 264; tr. Gaudefroy-Demombynes, vol. 3, p. 294; Ibn Khallikān, *Biographical Dictionary*, vol. 3, p. 340; al-Maqrīzī, *Ayyūbid Sultans of Egypt*, p. 55, and ʿĀrif Tāmir, 'Sinān Rāshid al-Dīn aw Shaykh al-Jabal', *al-Adīb*, 23 (May, 1953), pp. 43–46.
168. See, for instance, Abū Firās, *Faṣl*, translation pp. 437–438, text p. 482; Guyard, *Fragments*, text pp. 247 and 249–250, translation pp. 391–392 and 395–398; Ibn Faḍl Allāh al-ʿUmarī, *Masālik al-abṣār*, pp. 77–78, and al-Qalqashandī, *Ṣubḥ*, vol. 13, pp. 238–239.
169. R. Dussaud, *Histoire et religion des Noṣairîs*, pp. 23, 34, 45, 54, 79ff. and 157–158; also his 'Influence de la religion Noṣairī sur la doctrine de Rāchid ad-Dīn Sinān', *JA*, 9 série, 16 (1900), pp. 61–69.
170. Ibn al-ʿAdīm, *L'Histoire d'Alep* (1896), pp. 147–148, and Lewis, 'Kamāl al-Dīn's Biography', pp. 230, 241–242 and 261.
171. For a survey of the occidental sources on this assassination, see R. Röhricht, *Geschichte des Königreichs Jerusalem* (Innsbruck, 1898), pp. 614–616; D. Schaffner, 'The Relations of the Order of the Assassins with the Crusaders During the Twelfth Century' (M.A. thesis, University of Chicago, 1939), pp. 39–49, and Hellmuth, *Die Assassinenlegende*, pp. 54–62. Amongst the Muslim sources, mention may be made of ʿImād al-Dīn's *al-Fatḥ al-qussī fi'l-fatḥ al-qudsī*, ed. C. Landberg (Leiden, 1888), pp. 420–422; Ibn Shaddād, *al-Nawādir al-ṣultāniyya*, in *RHCHO*, vol. 3, p. 297; Abū Shāma, *al-Rawḍatayn*, vol. 2, p. 196, in *RHCHO*, vol. 5, pp. 52–54, and Ibn al-Athīr, *al-Kāmil*, vol. 12, p. 31, in *RHCHO*, vol. 2, pp. 58–59. The accounts of ʿImād al-Dīn and Ibn al-Athīr are translated into English in F. Gabrieli, *Arab Historians of the Crusades*, tr. E. J. Costello (Berkeley, 1969), pp. 238–242. See also Grousset, *Croisades*, vol. 3, pp. 91ff., and Runciman, *Crusades*, vol. 3, pp. 64–65.
172. Abū Firās, *Faṣl*, translation pp. 408–412, text pp. 463–466; English translation in Gabrieli, *Arab Historians*, pp. 242–245.
173. *Bustān*, p. 151; Ibn al-ʿAdīm in Lewis, 'Kamāl al-Dīn's Biography', pp. 230 and 261; Sibṭ, *Mirʾāt*, ed. Jewett, p. 269, and al-Qalqashandī, *Ṣubḥ*, vol. 1, p. 122; the last two sources place Sinān's death in 588 A.H. See also Ibn al-

Dawādārī, *Kanz*, vol. 7, p. 120, and Ibn Taghrībirdī, *al-Nujūm*, vol. 6, p. 117.

174. Ibn Isfandiyār, *Ta'rīkh*, vol. 2, pp. 163 and 174; tr. Browne, pp. 255–256; Āmulī, *Ta'rīkh*, pp. 150–151; Marʿashī, *Ta'rīkh-i Ṭabaristān*, ed. Dorn, pp. 79 and 264; ed. Tasbīḥī, pp. 30 and 118, and Rabino, 'Dynasties du Māzandarān', pp. 432 and 453.
175. Al-Rāwandī, *Rāḥat al-ṣudūr*, p. 390; Juwaynī, vol. 2, pp. 43–44; tr. Boyle, vol. 1, pp. 312–313, and Ibn al-Athīr, *al-Kāmil*, vol. 12, p. 93.
176. *Ta'rīkh-i Sīstān*, p. 392; tr. Gold, p. 320; Jūzjānī, *Ṭabaqāt*, vol. 1, p. 396; tr. Raverty, vol. 1, p. 449; Juwaynī, vol. 2, p. 49; tr. Boyle, vol. 1, p. 316, and Ibn al-Athīr, *al-Kāmil*, vol. 12, pp. 65 and 73.
177. Jūzjānī, *Ṭabaqāt*, vol. 1, p. 403; tr. Raverty, vol. 1, pp. 484ff., Muḥammad b. Aḥmad al-Nasawī, *Histoire du Sultan Djelal ed-Din Mankobirti*, ed. and tr. O. Houdas (Paris, 1891–1895), vol. 1 (text), pp. 212ff., and vol. 2 (French translation), pp. 353ff., and the anonymous Persian translation of the same work, dating from the first half of the seventh/thirteenth century, *Sīrat-i Jalāl al-Dīn Mīnkubirnī*, ed. M. Mīnuvī (Tehran, 1344/1965), pp. 229ff. See also Juwaynī, vol. 2, p. 59; tr. Boyle, vol. 1, p. 326, and Ibn al-Athīr, *al-Kāmil*, vol. 12, pp. 82–83.
178. Al-Rāwandī, *Rāḥat al-ṣudūr*, p. 399; Juwaynī, vol. 2, pp. 45–46; tr. Boyle, vol. 1, pp. 313–314, and Ibn al-Athīr, *al-Kāmil*, vol. 12, p. 62.
179. Al-Nasawī, *Histoire*, vol. 1, p. 27, and vol. 2, pp. 47–48; ed. Mīnuvī, pp. 40–41.
180. Ibn al-Athīr, *al-Kāmil*, vol. 12, pp. 76–77.
181. Juwaynī, vol. 3, pp. 241–242; tr. Boyle, vol. 2, pp. 698–699; Rashīd al-Dīn, p. 173; Kāshānī, p. 197, and Ḥāfiẓ Abrū, p. 261.
182. On Jalāl al-Dīn Ḥasan III's reign and his doctrinal reform, see Juwaynī, vol. 3, pp. 243–249; tr. Boyle, vol. 2, pp. 699–704; Rashīd al-Dīn, pp. 174–178; Kāshānī, pp. 198–201; Ḥamd Allāh, *Ta'rīkh*, ed. and tr. Gantin, pp. 506–509; ed. and tr. Browne, vol. 1, pp. 524–525, and vol. 2, pp. 129–130; ed. Navā'ī, pp. 524–525; Ḥāfiẓ Abrū, pp. 264–266; Mīrkhwānd, *Rawḍat al-ṣafā'*, ed. and tr. Jourdain, translation pp. 171–174, text pp. 232–235; Tehran ed., vol. 4, pp. 224–227; Khwānd Amīr, *Ḥabīb al-siyar*, vol. 2, p. 475, and Ibn al-Athīr, *al-Kāmil*, vol. 12, p. 115. See also Hodgson, *Order*, pp. 217–225; also his 'State', pp. 468–472; Lewis, *Assassins*, pp. 78–81; Filippani-Ronconi, *Ismaeliti*, pp. 229–236; Tāmir, *al-Imāma*, pp. 192–194; Ghālib, *Ta'rīkh*, pp. 284–285, and also his *Aʿlām*, pp. 209–213.
183. Kāshānī, *Ta'rīkh-i Uljāytū*, pp. 57–58, extract in Schefer, *Chrestomathie Persane*, vol. 2, text pp. 95–96, translation p. 100, and in H. L. Rabino, 'Deux descriptions du Gīlān du temps des Mongols', *JA*, 238 (1950), pp. 328–329. See also Rabino, 'Rulers of Gilan', pp. 288–289; also his 'Dynasties locales du Gīlān', pp. 314–315, and Qazvīnī's notes to Juwaynī, vol. 3, pp. 418–424.
184. Jūzjānī, *Ṭabaqāt*, vol. 2, pp. 182–183; tr. Raverty, vol. 2, pp. 1197–1198.
185. Al-Nasawī, *Histoire*, vol. 1, pp. 212–213, and vol. 2, p. 355; ed. Mīnuvī, p. 230.
186. On the campaign against Mengli, see Juwaynī, vol. 3, pp. 245–246, tr.

Boyle, vol. 2, pp. 701–702; Rashīd al-Dīn, pp. 176–177; Kāshānī, pp. 199–200; Ibn al-Athīr, *al-Kāmil*, vol. 12, pp. 114, 116 and 118, placing the battle in 612/1215, and Qazvīnī's notes to Juwaynī, vol. 3, pp. 407–409.

187. Ibn al-Athīr, *al-Kāmil*, vol. 12, pp. 121–122; al-Nasawī, *Histoire*, vol. 1, p. 13, and vol. 2, p. 23; ed. Mīnuvī, p. 21; Juwaynī, vol. 2, p. 121; tr. Boyle, vol. 2, p. 391, and Qazvīnī's notes to Juwaynī, vol. 3, pp. 414–417.

188. On Muḥammad III and his deteriorating relations with his advisers and eldest son and successor Rukn al-Dīn Khurshāh, see Juwaynī, vol. 3, pp. 249–259; tr. Boyle, vol. 2, pp. 704–712; Rashīd al-Dīn, pp. 178–184; Kāshānī, pp. 201–206; Ḥamd Allāh, *Ta'rīkh*, ed. and tr. Gantin, pp. 508–511; ed. and tr. Browne, vol. 1, pp. 525–526, and vol. 2, p. 130; ed. Navā'ī, pp. 525–526; Ḥāfiẓ Abrū, pp. 268–272; Mīrkhwānd, *Rawḍat al-ṣafā'*, ed. and tr. Jourdain, translation pp. 174–176, text pp. 235–238; Tehran ed., vol. 4, pp. 227–229, and Khwānd Amīr, *Ḥabīb al-siyar*, vol. 2, pp. 475–476. See also Hodgson, *Order*, pp. 225ff., 244–246 and 250–262; also his 'State', pp. 476–480; Filippani-Ronconi, *Ismaeliti*, pp. 236–257; Ghālib, *Ta'rīkh*, pp. 286–288; also his *Aʿlām*, pp. 394–397; Lewis, *Assassins*, pp. 82–91, and his ''Alā'-al-Dīn Moḥammad', *EIR*, vol. 1, p. 780.

189. On the Ismāʿīlī affiliations and writings of Naṣīr al-Dīn al-Ṭūsī, see Shihāb al-Dīn ʿAbd Allāh b. Faḍl Allāh Shīrāzī, better known as Waṣṣāf, *Ta'rīkh-i Waṣṣāf* (Bombay, 1269/1853), pp. 20–30; al-Shūshtarī, *Majālis al-mu'minīn*, vol. 2, pp. 201–207; *Dabistān-i madhāhib*, vol. 1, p. 258; Muḥammad Taqī Mudarris Raḍavī, *Aḥvāl va āthār-i Abū Jaʿfar Muḥammad b. Muḥammad b. al-Ḥasan al-Ṭūsī* (2nd ed., Tehran, 1354/1975), pp. 3–16 and 83–93, and Muḥammad Mudarrisī Zanjānī, *Sargudhasht va ʿaqā'id-i falsafī-yi Khwāja Naṣīr al-Dīn Ṭūsī* (Tehran, 1335/1956), pp. 27–34, 54–56 and 125–130; Raḍavī and Mudarrisī, like other Twelver authors, categorically refuse to concede that al-Ṭūsī may have been temporarily an Ismāʿīlī, while M. Mīnuvī in the introduction to his edition of al-Ṭūsī's *Akhlāq-i Nāṣirī* (2nd ed., Tehran, 1360/1981), pp. 14–32, allows for this possibility, which is also admitted by M. T. Dānishpazhūh, the editor of al-Ṭūsī's *Akhlāq-i Muḥtashimī* (2nd ed., Tehran, 1361/1982), pp. 9–11 and 20; W. Madelung in his 'Naṣīr ad-Dīn Ṭūsī's Ethics between Philosophy, Shiʿism, and Sufism', in *Ethics in Islam*, ed. Richard G. Hovannisian (Malibu, Calif., 1985), pp. 85–101, discusses the Ismāʿīlī character of the *Akhlāq-i Nāṣirī* and argues that al-Ṭūsī joined the Ismāʿīlīs out of his philosophical concerns. See also W. Ivanow, 'An Ismailitic work by Nasiru'd-din Tusi', *JRAS* (1931), pp. 527–537, and his remarks in the *Rawḍat al-taslīm*, introduction pp. 23–26, suggesting that al-Ṭūsī may even have been born into an Ismāʿīlī family; Hodgson, *Order*, pp. 239–243; also his 'State', pp. 475–476; ʿĀrif Tāmir, *Naṣīr al-Dīn al-Ṭūsī* (Beirut, 1983), pp. 43–75; Ghālib, *Aʿlām*, pp. 587–588; R. Strothmann, *Die Zwölfer-Schīʿa* (Leipzig, 1926), pp. 17–24, 31 and 33ff., and also his 'al-Ṭūsī, Naṣīr al-Dīn', *EI*, vol. 4, pp. 980–981.

190. Al-Ṭūsī, *Sayr va sulūk*, especially pp. 38–42, 46, 51–52 and 54–55.

191. Ibid., p. 38.

192. Al-Ṭūsī's chief work dealing with the doctrine of the *satr* is the *Rawḍat al-*

taslīm, a detailed exposition of Nizārī thought after the *qiyāma* times, reflecting the modifications of Muḥammad III's period; a briefer treatment of the subject, designed for the ordinary members of the sect, is given in his *Maṭlūb al-mu'minīn*, ed. W. Ivanow, in *Two Early Ismaili Treatises*, pp. 43–55. Other works of al-Ṭūsī, especially his *Sayr va sulūk*, are also relevant here; see Mudarris Raḍavī, *Aḥvāl va āthār*, pp. 449–457, 558–560, 591–594 and 597; Ivanow, *Ismaili Literature*, pp. 134–136, and Poonawala, *Bio*, pp. 261–263. As noted, Ithnāʿasharī scholars in general reject the attribution of these Ismāʿīlī works to Naṣīr al-Dīn al-Ṭūsī. The best modern exposition of the doctrine of the *satr* may be found in Hodgson, *Order*, pp. 225–238, and also his 'State', pp. 472–475.

193. Al-Ṭūsī, *Rawḍat al-taslīm*, text pp. 62–63, 101–102, 110, 117–118, 143 and 145, translation pp. 69, 115–116, 126 and 136; Abū Isḥāq, *Haft bāb*, text p. 43, translation p. 43; Khayrkhwāh, *Kalām-i pīr*, text p. 67, translation pp. 62–63, and also his *Taṣnīfāt*, pp. 18–19.
194. *Rawḍat al-taslīm*, text p. 119, translation p. 138; Abū Isḥāq, *Haft bāb*, text p. 38, translation pp. 38–39, and Khayrkhwāh, *Kalām-i pīr*, text p. 63, translation p. 58.
195. *Rawḍat al-taslīm*, text p. 61, translation pp. 67–68; Abū Isḥāq, *Haft bāb*, text pp. 42–43, translation pp. 42–43, and Khayrkhwāh, *Kalām-i pīr*, text pp. 66–67, translation pp. 61–62.
196. *Rawḍat al-taslīm*, text pp. 61, 132–133, 147 and 149, translation pp. 67–68, 154–155, 173 and 175; see also Abū Isḥāq, *Haft bāb*, text pp. 11–12 and 39, translation pp. 11–12 and 39; Khayrkhwāh, *Kalām-i pīr*, text pp. 19 and 64, translation pp. 13 and 58–59, also his *Faṣl dar bayān-i shinākht-i imām*, ed. W. Ivanow (3rd ed., Tehran, 1960), pp. 1–2 and 28; English translation, *On the Recognition of the Imam*, tr. W. Ivanow (2nd ed., Bombay, 1947), pp. 18 and 43.
197. Al-Ṭūsī, *Rawḍat al-taslīm*, text p. 110, translation p. 126.
198. *Rawḍat al-taslīm*, text pp. 76, 82, 83ff., 100, 104–105, 122–123, 126 and 127, translation pp. 86–87, 92–93, 94ff., 114, 119, 143, 147 and 148; *Maṭlūb al-mu'minīn*, pp. 48–49; Abū Isḥāq, *Haft bāb*, text pp. 16, 17, 43 and 50, translation pp. 16, 17, 44 and 50, and Khayrkhwāh, *Kalām-i pīr*, text pp. 22, 26, 68 and 94, translation pp. 17, 21, 63 and 88.
199. *Rawḍat al-taslīm*, text p. 142, translation p. 166, and *Maṭlūb al-mu'minīn*, pp. 54–55.
200. *Rawḍat al-taslīm*, text pp. 42, 76–77 and 83–84, translation pp. 46–47, 87 and 94–95.
201. Jūzjānī, *Ṭabaqāt*, vol. 2, pp. 182–185 and 186–188; tr. Raverty, vol. 2, pp. 1197–1205 and 1212–1214.
202. On these interferences and the prosperous conditions of the Quhistānī Nizārīs at the time, see Jūzjānī, *Ṭabaqāt*, vol. 1, pp. 282–283 and 284–285, and vol. 2, pp. 184–185; tr. Raverty, vol. 1, pp. 195–197 and 199–201, and vol. 2, pp. 1203–1205, and *Ta'rīkh-i Sīstān*, pp. 393–395; tr. Gold, pp. 321–322.
203. Al-Nasawī, *Histoire*, vol. 1, pp. 70–71, and vol. 2, pp. 118–119; ed. Mīnuvī, p. 95.

204. Al-Nasawī, *Histoire*, vol. 1, p. 168, and vol. 2, pp. 280–281; the section dealing with the letter of Sirāj al-Dīn al-Muẓaffar, the Syrian Nizārī chief, sent to the Anatolian ruler, and a few other sections, were omitted in the anonymous Persian translation of al-Nasawī's *Sīrat-i Jalāl al-Dīn*.

205. The Indian Nizārī tradition on the commencement of the Nizārī *daʿwa* in India is analyzed in Azim Nanji, *The Nizārī Ismāʿīlī Tradition in the Indo–Pakistan Subcontinent* (Delmar, N.Y., 1978), pp. 50–69; see also Syed Mujtaba Ali, *The Origin of the Khojāhs and their Religious Life Today* (Würzburg, 1936), pp. 39ff.; Hollister, *Shiʿa*, pp. 339–355; Misra, *Muslim Communities*, pp. 10–12 and 54ff.; Ivanow, *Ismaili Literature*, pp. 174–177, and Poonawala, *Bio*, pp. 298–300.

206. See W. Ivanow, 'Shums Tabrez of Multan', in *Professor Muḥammad Shafiʿ Presentation Volume*, ed. S. M. Abdullah (Lahore, 1955), pp. 109–118, and Ghālib, *Aʿlām*, pp. 188–191 and 309–310.

207. See, for instance, Dawlatshāh, *Tadhkirat al-shuʿarāʾ*, p. 195; al-Shūshtarī, *Majālis al-muʾminīn*, vol. 2, p. 110, and A. Semenov, 'Sheikh Dzhelāl-ud-Dīn-Rūmī po predstavleniyam Shughnanskikh Ismailitov', analyzing the ideas of the Nizārīs of Shughnān on Jalāl al-Dīn Rūmī who is considered, by the contemporary Nizārīs of Central Asia and some other regions, to have been one of their co-religionists.

208. Al-Nasawī, *Histoire*, vol. 1, pp. 132–134, and vol. 2, pp. 219–223; ed. Mīnuvī, pp. 163–166, and Ibn al-Athīr, *al-Kāmil*, vol. 12, p. 182.

209. Al-Nasawī, *Histoire*, vol. 1, pp. 129–130 and 143–145, and vol. 2, pp. 215–216 and 237–240; ed. Mīnuvī, pp. 161–162 and 175–176; Juwaynī, vol. 2, pp. 204–205; tr. Boyle, vol. 2, pp. 471–472, and J. A. Boyle, 'Dynastic and Political History of the Īl-Khāns', in *Cambridge History of Iran*, vol. 5, p. 332.

210. Al-Nasawī, *Histoire*, vol. 1, pp. 145–146, and vol. 2, pp. 241–242; ed. Mīnuvī, p. 177.

211. Al-Nasawī, *Histoire*, vol. 1, pp. 157–158, and vol. 2, pp. 262–264.

212. Al-Nasawī, *Histoire*, vol. 1, p. 196, and vol. 2, p. 327.

213. Al-Nasawī, *Histoire*, vol. 1, pp. 212–216, and vol. 2, pp. 353–360; ed. Mīnuvī, pp. 229–233; see also Ibn al-Athīr, *al-Kāmil*, vol. 12, pp. 192–193.

214. Āmulī, *Taʾrīkh*, pp. 152–153; Marʿashī, *Taʾrīkh-i Ṭabaristān*, ed. Dorn, pp. 80–81; ed. Tasbīḥī, pp. 30–31, and Rabino, 'Dynasties du Māzandarān', p. 454.

215. Rashīd al-Dīn, p. 181, and Kāshānī, p. 205. According to *Dabistān-i madhāhib*, vol. 1, p. 265, this *shaykh* had secretly embraced Ismāʿīlism.

216. Juwaynī, vol. 1, pp. 205 and 213; tr. Boyle, vol. 1, pp. 250 and 258; Rashīd al-Dīn, *Jāmiʿ al-tawārīkh*, vol. 2, ed. E. Blochet (Leiden–London, 1911), pp. 243 and 248; also his *Jāmiʿ al-tawārīkh*, ed. B. Karīmī (Tehran, 1338/1959), vol. 1, pp. 568 and 570; English translation, *The Successors of Genghiz Khan*, tr. John A. Boyle (New York, 1971), pp. 181 and 184, hereafter cited as *Successors*.

217. Juwaynī, vol. 1, pp. 211–212; tr. Boyle, vol. 1, pp. 256–257; Rashīd al-Dīn, *Jāmiʿ al-tawārīkh*, ed. Blochet, pp. 247–248; ed. Karīmī, vol. 1, p. 570; *Successors*, p. 183.

218. Jūzjānī, *Ṭabaqāt*, vol. 2, pp. 181–182; tr. Raverty, vol. 2, pp. 1189–1197; Rashīd al-Dīn, *Jāmiʿ al-tawārīkh* (*Histoire des Mongols de la Perse*), ed. and tr.

Quatremère, pp. 118–128; also his *Jāmiʿ al-tawārīkh*, vol. 3, ed. A. A. Alizade (Baku, 1957), pp. 20–21, and also his *Jāmiʿ al-tawārīkh*, ed. Karīmī, vol. 2, pp. 684–685.

219. *Bustān*, p. 151; Sibṭ, *Mir'āt*, ed. Jewett, p. 261; Ibn al-ʿAdīm in Lewis, 'Kamāl al-Dīn's Biography', pp. 231 and 262, and Mufaḍḍal b. Abi'l-Faḍā'il, *Histoire des Sultans Mamlouks*, ed. and tr. E. Blochet, in *Patrologia Orientalis*, 12 (1919), p. 516.

220. On the general situation of the Syrian Nizārīs between Sinān's death and the fall of Alamūt, see Defrémery, 'Ismaéliens de Syrie' (1855), pp. 32–47; Lewis, 'Ismāʿīlites and the Assassins', pp. 127–129; also his *Assassins*, pp. 119–121; Hodgson, *Order*, pp. 207–209 and 246–250; Filippani-Ronconi, *Ismaeliti*, pp. 223–226, and Mirza, 'Syrian Ismāʿīlīs', pp. 78–105.

221. For the inscriptional evidence on the Syrian castles, see van Berchem, 'Épigraphie des Assassins de Syrie', pp. 455–457, 467, 478, 482, 488–489 and 495–499, also reflecting the information contained in Ibn Wāṣil's *Mufarrij al-kurūb*. Ibn Wāṣil (604–697/1208–1298), a native of central Syria was personally acquainted with Tāj al-Dīn Abu'l-Futūḥ, a Persian who came from Alamūt and led the Syrian Nizārīs at least from 637/1239–1240 to 646/1249. See also al-Ḥamawī, *al-Ta'rīkh al-Manṣūrī*, pp. 293–294, 330 and 340, and al-Nasawī, *Histoire*, vol. 1, pp. 132 and 168, and vol. 2, pp. 220 and 280; ed. Mīnuvī, p. 163.

222. Abū Shāma, *Tarājim rijāl al-qarnayn*, ed. M. Z. al-Kawtharī (Cairo, 1947), pp. 78 and 81; also his *al-Rawḍatayn*, in *RHCHO*, vol. 5, p. 159, placing the event in 609/1212–1213; Mufaḍḍal, *Histoire*, p. 517; Ibn al-Athīr, *al-Kāmil*, vol. 12, p. 115; Sibṭ, *Mir'āt*, ed. Jewett, p. 363; Abu'l-Fidā, *al-Mukhtaṣar*, in *RHCHO*, vol. 1, p. 86, and van Berchem, 'Épigraphie', pp. 475–477, quoting Ibn Wāṣil, *Mufarrij al-kurūb*, ed. J. al-Shayyāl (Cairo, 1954–1961), vol. 3, p. 211, and others.

223. See ʿĀrif Tāmir, 'Sinān Rāshid al-Dīn aw Shaykh al-Jabal', p. 45, and also his 'Furūʿ al-shajara al-Ismāʿīliyya al-Imāmiyya', *al-Mashriq*, 51 (1957), pp. 601–603.

224. Ibn al-ʿAdīm, *Histoire d'Alep* (1897), pp. 48–49; al-Maqrīzī, *Ayyūbid Sultans of Egypt*, pp. 159–160; Grousset, *Croisades*, vol. 3, pp. 195–196, and Cahen, *Syrie du Nord*, pp. 620–621.

225. Al-Ḥamawī, *al-Ta'rīkh al-Manṣūrī*, p. 340.

226. Ibid., p. 348.

227. Ibid., pp. 335–336.

228. Ibid., pp. 340–341.

229. Edwin J. King, *The Knights Hospitallers in the Holy Land* (London, 1931), pp. 216 and 234–235, reproducing the papal letter; see also Cahen, *Syrie du Nord*, pp. 344, 526, 620, 641 and 665, and J. Riley-Smith, *The Knights of St. John in Jerusalem and Cyprus* (London, 1967), pp. 138–140, 162 and 164.

230. In addition to Joinville's account in his already-cited *Histoire de Saint Louis*, which is the chief source on these dealings, see Defrémery, 'Ismaéliens de Syrie', (1855), pp. 45–46; van Berchem, 'Épigraphie', pp. 478–480; King, *Knights Hospitallers*, p. 249; Grousset, *Croisades*, vol. 3, pp. 516–518, and Runciman, *Crusades*, vol. 3, pp. 279–280.

231. On the operations of Hülegü's advance guards in Persia, see Rashīd al-Dīn, *Jāmiʿ al-tawārīkh*, ed. Quatremère, pp. 138 and 166–174; ed. Alizade, pp. 22–23 and 27–28; ed. Karīmī, vol. 2, pp. 686 and 689–690. Juwaynī, vol. 3, pp. 72 and 94–95; tr. Boyle, vol. 2, pp. 596 and 610, has only brief references here. See also John A. Boyle, 'The Ismāʿīlīs and the Mongol Invasion', in *Ismāʿīlī Contributions to Islamic Culture*, pp. 7–11, and also his 'Dynastic and Political History of the Īl-Khāns', pp. 340–342. On the participation of the Caspian rulers in the Mongol siege of Girdkūh, see Ibn Isfandiyār's continuator, *History of Ṭabaristān*, tr. Browne, pp. 258–259; Āmulī, *Ta'rīkh*, pp. 160–162 and 163–164; Marʿashī, *Ta'rīkh-i Ṭabaristān*, ed. Dorn, pp. 84–87; ed. Tasbīḥī, pp. 32–34; Mullā Shaykh ʿAlī Gīlānī, *Ta'rīkh-i Māzandarān*, ed. M. Sutūda (Tehran, 1352/1973), p. 50, and Rabino, 'Dynasties du Māzandarān', p. 455.

232. On Rukn al-Dīn Khurshāh's brief reign, during which the Nizārī state in Persia was destroyed by the Mongols, see Juwaynī, vol. 3, pp. 259–278; tr. Boyle, vol. 2, pp. 712–725; Rashīd al-Dīn, pp. 185–195, and Kāshānī, pp. 206–215, all three authors cover the events of Khurshāh's reign at the end of their histories of the Nizārīs. Hülegü's expedition against the Nizārīs is also covered separately in Juwaynī, vol. 3, pp. 89–142; tr. Boyle, vol. 2, pp. 607–640, and in Rashīd al-Dīn's history of Hülegü; see *Jāmiʿ al-tawārīkh*, ed. Quatremère, pp. 144ff., 174–220; ed. Alizade, pp. 24ff. and 29–38; ed. Karīmī, vol. 2, pp. 687ff. and 691–697. See also Jūzjānī, *Ṭabaqāt*, vol. 2, pp. 180ff. and 186; tr. Raverty, vol. 2, pp. 1187ff. and 1205–1211; Ḥamd Allāh, *Ta'rīkh*, ed. and tr. Gantin, pp. 512–515; ed. and tr. Browne, vol. 1, pp. 526–527, and vol. 2, pp. 130–131; ed. Navāʾī, pp. 527–528; Ḥāfiẓ Abrū, pp. 275–281; Mīrkhwānd, *Rawḍat al-ṣafā'*, ed. and tr. Jourdain, translation pp. 176–182, text pp. 239–248; Tehran ed., vol. 4, pp. 229–235, and vol. 5, pp. 228–234, and Khwānd Amīr, *Ḥabīb al-siyar*, vol. 2, pp. 477–479, and vol. 3, pp. 94–95. See also Constantin M. d'Ohsson, *Histoire des Mongols* (2nd ed., The Hague–Amsterdam, 1834–1835), vol. 3, pp. 188–202, the European classic on the subject, and Henry H. Howorth, *History of the Mongols* (London, 1876–1927), vol. 3, pp. 90ff. and 95–108. More recently, the late Professor John A. Boyle, the leading modern authority on the Mongol period of Persian history, treated the subject in his 'Ismāʿīlīs and the Mongol Invasion', pp. 11–22, and 'Dynastic and Political History of the Īl-Khāns', pp. 341–345; see also Hodgson, *Order*, pp. 263–271; also his 'State', pp. 480–482; Lewis, *Assassins*, pp. 91–96; Filippani-Ronconi, *Ismaeliti*, pp. 257–265; Ghālib, *Ta'rīkh*, pp. 289–290, and also his *Aʿlām*, pp. 289–292.

233. Juwaynī, vol. 3, pp. 102–103; tr. Boyle, vol. 2, pp. 615–616; Rashīd al-Dīn, *Jāmiʿ al-tawārīkh*, ed. Quatremère, pp. 180–181; ed. Alizade, pp. 29–30; ed. Karīmī, vol. 2, p. 691.

234. Juwaynī, vol. 3, p. 263; tr. Boyle, vol. 2, p. 714; Rashīd al-Dīn, p. 187; Kāshānī, p. 208, and Khwānd Amīr, *Dastūr al-wuzarā'*, p. 229.

235. This is the date given by Juwaynī, vol. 3, pp. 133 and 267, who witnessed Khurshāh's surrender. In his history of Hülegü, Rashīd al-Dīn places this event a day later, on 1 Dhu'l-Qaʿda/20 November, also quoting a chronogram composed to that effect by Naṣīr al-Dīn al-Ṭūsī; see *Jāmiʿ al-*

tawārīkh, ed. Quatremère, pp. 210–212; ed. Alizade, p. 35; ed. Karīmī, vol. 2, p. 695. However, Rashīd al-Dīn himself corroborates Juwaynī's date in relating the events of Khurshāh's reign in his *Jāmiʿ al-tawārīkh*; *qismat-i Ismāʿīliyān*, p. 190.

236. Juwaynī, vol. 3, pp. 186 and 269–273; tr. Boyle, vol. 2, pp. 666 and 719–721.
237. Juwaynī, vol. 3, p. 273; tr. Boyle, vol. 2, p. 721; Rashīd al-Dīn, p. 192, and Kāshānī, p. 213; see also Rashīd al-Dīn, *Jāmiʿ al-tawārīkh*, ed. Quatremère, p. 212; ed. Alizade, p. 35; ed. Karīmī, vol. 2, p. 695.
238. Juwaynī, vol. 3, p. 275; tr. Boyle, vol. 2, p. 723; see also Rashīd al-Dīn, p. 193, and Kāshānī, p. 214.
239. Hodgson, *Order*, pp. 259–260, and also his 'State', pp. 481–482.
240. Juwaynī, vol. 3, p. 137; tr. Boyle, vol. 2, p. 637.
241. Rashīd al-Dīn, *Jāmiʿ al-tawārīkh*, ed. Quatremère, pp. 218–220; ed. Alizade, p. 38; ed. Karīmī, vol. 2, p. 697.
242. Rashīd al-Dīn, *Jāmiʿ al-tawārīkh*, ed. Quatremère, pp. 212–213; ed. Alizade, pp. 35–36 and 140; ed. Karīmī, vol. 2, pp. 695 and 766, and Rashīd al-Dīn, *Ta'rīkh-i mubārak-i Ghāzānī; dar dāstān-i Abāghā Khān va Sulṭān Aḥmad va Arghūn Khān va Gaykhātū Khān*, ed. K. Jahn (Prague, 1941), p. 29, reprinted (The Hague, 1957), p. 29. See also Jūzjānī, *Ṭabaqāt*, vol. 2, p. 186; tr. Raverty, vol. 2, pp. 1206–1211, stating that the garrison of Girdkūh, reduced to one or two hundred men, was still holding out against the Mongols in 658/1260, when Jūzjānī was writing. Of the key Nizārī castles in Persia, Girdkūh is the one least studied in modern times. The rock of Girdkūh and the remains of its fortifications, including those of its three outer walls, visited in 1985 by the author, are indeed impressive. The ruins of the living quarters built by the besieging Mongols and the two different types of mangonel stones, used by the Nizārīs and the Mongols, which are still scattered on the northeastern slope of the Girdkūh rock, attest to the fierce and extended fighting that occurred during the siege of Girdkūh.
243. See Rashīd al-Dīn, *Ta'rīkh-i mubārak-i Ghāzānī; dāstān-i Ghāzān Khān*, ed. K. Jahn (London, 1940), pp. 30 and 56; also his *Jāmiʿ al-tawārīkh*, ed. Alizade, pp. 272 and 286–287; ed. Karīmī, vol. 2, pp. 860–861 and 883; extract in Dorn, *Auszüge aus Muhammedanischen schriftstellern*, pp. 132 and 137.
244. On the situation of the Syrian Nizārīs in the period between the fall of Alamūt and the subjugation of their castles by the Mamlūks, see Defrémery, 'Ismaéliens de Syrie', (1855), pp. 47–65; Guyard, 'Un Grand Maître des Assassins', pp. 373–377; Lewis, 'Ismāʿīlites and the Assassins', pp. 130–132; also his *Assassins*, pp. 121–124; Hodgson, *Order*, pp. 272–275; Mirza, 'Syrian Ismāʿīlīs', pp. 108–130, and Abdul-Aziz Khowaiter, *Baibars the First: His Endeavours and Achievements* (London, 1978), pp. 118–126.
245. Ibn Muyassar, *Akhbār*, ed. Massé, p. 68; ed. Sayyid, p. 102, and Abū Firās, *Faṣl*, translation pp. 415–417, text pp. 468–470.
246. Ibn Muyassar, *Akhbār*, ed. Massé, p. 68; ed. Sayyid, p. 102. Some sources give the name of this Nizārī leader as Riḍā al-Dīn; see Mufaḍḍal, *Histoire*, pp. 433–434.
247. S. Fatima Sadeque, *Baybars I of Egypt* (Dacca, 1956), translation pp. 138–139,

text p. 45, partial edition and English translation of Ibn ʿAbd al-Ẓāhir's *Sīrat al-Malik al-Ẓāhir*.

248. ʿIzz al-Dīn Muḥammad b. ʿAlī b. Ibrāhīm b. Shaddād, *Taʾrīkh al-Malik al-Ẓāhir*, ed. A. Ḥuṭayṭ (Wiesbaden, 1983), pp. 268–269; Mufaḍḍal, *Histoire*, p. 433; and Ibn al-Dawādārī, *Kanz al-Durar*, ed. U. Haarmann (Cairo, 1971), vol. 8, pp. 84–85.

249. Ibn Muyassar, ed. Massé, p. 68; ed. Sayyid, p. 102; Ibn Shaddād, *Taʾrīkh*, pp. 323, 327 and 358; Ibn Faḍl Allāh al-ʿUmarī, *Masālik al-abṣār*, pp. 132–133; al-Qalqashandī, *Ṣubḥ*, vol. 1, p. 121, and vol. 4, pp. 146–147; al-Maqrīzī, *Ittiʿāẓ*, vol. 3, p. 109, and W. Popper, *Egypt and Syria under the Circassian Sultans, 1382–1468 A.D.* (Berkeley, 1955–1957), vol. 1, pp. 17–19.

250. Ibn ʿAbd al-Ẓāhir, in Sadeque, *Baybars I*, translation pp. 171–172, text pp. 70–71, and al-Maqrīzī, *Histoire des Sultans Mamlouks de l'Égypte*, tr. Étienne Quatremère (Paris, 1845), vol. 1, part 1, p. 198.

251. Al-Maqrīzī, *Sultans Mamlouks*, vol. 1, part 2, p. 24, and Badr al-Dīn ʿAynī, *ʿIqd al-jumān*, extract in *RHCHO*, vol. 2, part 1, p. 223.

252. Al-Maqrīzī, *Sultans Mamlouks*, vol. 1, part 2, pp. 32, 40 and 42.

253. Abu'l-Fidā, *al-Mukhtaṣar*, in *RHCHO*, vol. 1, p. 153; Ibn al-Dawādārī, *Kanz*, vol. 8, pp. 143–144, and al-Maqrīzī, *Sultans Mamlouks*, vol. 1, part 2, pp. 79–80.

254. Ibn Shaddād, *Taʾrīkh*, p. 88.

255. On the final subjugation of the Nizārī strongholds in Syria, see Ibn Shaddād, *Taʾrīkh*, pp. 37, 60 and 323; Abu'l-Fidā, *al-Mukhtaṣar*, in *RHCHO*, vol. 1, pp. 153–154, and al-Maqrīzī, *Sultans Mamlouks*, vol. 1, part 2, pp. 87, 99–100 and 112–113.

256. See Ibn Faḍl Allāh al-ʿUmarī, *Masālik al-abṣār*, p. 77; Ibn al-Dawādārī, *Kanz*, vol. 8, pp. 157–158; al-Qalqashandī, *Ṣubḥ*, vol. 13, p. 245; al-Maqrīzī, *Sultans Mamlouks*, vol. 1, part 2, p. 100, and Ghālib, *Taʾrīkh*, pp. 292–293.

257. ʿAynī, *ʿIqd*, in *RHCHO*, vol. 2, part 1, p. 247; *Les Gestes des Chiprois*, in *RHC: Documents Arméniens*, vol. 2, pp. 775 and 779; Defrémery, 'Ismaéliens de Syrie', (1855), pp. 65–75; Grousset, *Croisades*, vol. 3, pp. 646–647 and 663; King, *Knights Hospitallers*, pp. 272–273, and Runciman, *Crusades*, vol. 3, p. 338.

258. Ibn Baṭṭūṭa, *Voyages d'Ibn Battūta*, ed. and tr. Ch. Defrémery and B. R. Sanguinetti (Paris, 1853–1859), vol. 1, pp. 166–167 and 171; English translation, *The Travels of Ibn Baṭṭūṭa*, tr. H. A. R. Gibb (Cambridge, 1958–1971), vol. 1, pp. 106–107 and 108–109; Persian translation, *Safar-nāma-yi Ibn Baṭṭūṭa*, tr. Muḥammad ʿAlī Muvaḥḥid (Tehran, 1337/1958), pp. 65–67.

7. *Post-Alamūt Nizārī Ismāʿīlism*

1. For descriptions of the few Muḥammad-Shāhī works recovered so far, see Ivanow, *Ismaili Literature*, pp. 165–167, and Poonawala, *Bio*, pp. 270–275, 278 and 280–281.

2. Ivanow, *Brief*, p. 29; also his *Ismaili Literature*, pp. 10–11; Corbin, *Histoire*, pp. 139–140, and also his 'La Philosophie Islamique depuis la mort d'Aver-

roës jusqu'à nos jours', in *Encyclopédie de la Pléiade, Histoire de la philosophie*, III (Paris, 1974), pp. 1142–1144.

3. See Ivanow's introductory remarks to his edition of Abū Isḥāq's *Haft bāb*, pp. 1–8; Ivanow, *Ismaili Literature*, pp. 141–142, and Poonawala, *Bio*, pp. 269–270.
4. See Ivanow's introduction to his edition of Khayrkhwāh's *Faṣl dar bayān-i shinākht-i imām*, pp. 5ff.; Ivanow, *Ismaili Literature*, pp. 142–144, and Poonawala, *Bio*, pp. 275–277.
5. See A. A. Semenov, 'Ismailitskaya oda, posvyashchennaya voploshcheniyam 'Aliya-boga', *Iran*, 2 (1928), pp. 1ff.; Ivanow's introduction to his edition of an abbreviated version of Khākī Khurāsānī's *Dīwān* (Bombay, 1933), pp. 1–15; Z. Jafferali, 'Khaki Khorasani', in *Great Ismaili Heroes*, pp. 95–97; Ivanow, *Guide*, pp. 109–111; also his *Ismaili Literature*, pp. 145–148, and Poonawala, *Bio*, pp. 279–280.
6. Mumtaz Tajddin Sadikali, 'Pir Shahabu'd Din Shah al-Husayni', in *Great Ismaili Heroes*, pp. 100–101; Berthels and Baqoev, *Alphabetic Catalogue*, p. 51; Ivanow, *Guide*, pp. 116–117; also his *Ismaili Literature*, pp. 149–150, and Poonawala, *Bio*, pp. 283–284.
7. Details on Fidā'ī's life and works were given to the author by his grandson, Ṣadr al-Dīn Mīrshāhī, who mentions some of this information in his unpublished biography of Fidā'ī as well as in the introduction to one of his collections of Fidā'ī's works. This collection, copied by Mr Mīrshāhī from autograph manuscript copies, includes the *Kashf al-ḥaqā'iq*, *Irshād al-sālikīn*, *Hidāyat al-mu'minīn*, and Fidā'ī's correspondence with Shaykh Sulaymān, a Syrian Nizārī leader from Salamiyya. I would like to express my gratitude to Mr Mīrshāhī for having given me a copy of this collection. Unfortunately, the original manuscripts of some of Fidā'ī's works have been taken by different persons from his descendants on the pretence of publishing them. On Fidā'ī, see A. A. Semenov, 'Ismailitsky panegirik obozhestvlennomu 'Aliyu Fedai Khorasanskogo', *Iran*, 3 (1929), pp. 51ff.; Semenov's introductory section to his edition of Fidā'ī's *Hidāyat al-mu'minīn*, pp. 5–24, reprinted recently (without Semenov's Russian introduction) with the same pagination (Tehran, 1362/1983); Ivanow's introduction to Khayrkhwāh's *Faṣl*, pp. 2–3; Ivanow, *Guide*, p. 117; also his *Ismaili Literature*, pp. 153–154, and Poonawala, *Bio*, pp. 284–285.
8. Corbin, *Étude*, pp. 11ff.; also his 'Nāṣir-i Khusrau and Iranian Ismā'īlism', pp. 525ff.; Ivanow, *Guide*, pp. 13–14, and his *Ismaili Literature*, p. 128.
9. Berthels and Baqoev, *Alphabetic Catalogue*, pp. 19–105. Five of the works recovered by this expedition, including *Āfāq-nāma*, *Umm al-khiṭāb* and *Uṣūl-i ādāb*, were subsequently published in a collection entitled *Panj risāla dar bayān-i āfāq va anfus*, ed. Andrei E. Berthels (Moscow, 1970).
10. See Ivanow's foreword to Suhrāb Valī Badakhshānī's *Sī va shish ṣaḥīfa*, pp. 9–15; Ghālib, *A'lām*, pp. 304–305, wrongly attributing a number of anonymous works to this author; Ivanow, *Ismaili Literature*, pp. 163–164, and Poonawala, *Bio*, pp. 267–268.
11. Ivanow, *Ismaili Literature*, pp. 172–173, and Poonawala, *Bio*, pp. 293–297.

12. See ʿĀrif Tāmir's introduction to his edition of Abū Firās Shihāb al-Dīn's *Kitāb al-īḍāḥ* (Beirut, 1965); Sami Makarem's introductory remarks to his edition of *al-Shāfiya*, pp. 13–20, an anonymous *qaṣīda*, originally composed by a Ḥāfiẓī poet and then revised by a Nizārī author, erroneously attributed to Abū Firās; see also Ghālib, *Aʿlām*, pp. 313–315; Ivanow, *Ismaili Literature*, p. 172, and Poonawala, *Bio*, pp. 294–295 and 350.
13. On the *ginān* literature of the Indian Nizārīs, see Ivanow, *Ismaili Literature*, pp. 11–12 and 174–176, and Nanji, *Nizārī Ismāʿīlī Tradition in the Indo-Pakistan Subcontinent*, pp. 7–24, hereafter cited as *Nizārī Tradition*.
14. For lists of the major *ginān*s, see Ivanow, *Ismaili Literature*, pp. 176–181; Zawahir Noorally, *Catalogue of Khōjkī Manuscripts in the Collection of the Ismailia Association for Pakistan* (Karachi, 1971); Poonawala, *Bio*, pp. 298–311, and Nanji, *Nizārī Tradition*, pp. 143–149. See also N. Tajdin, *A Bibliography of Ismailism* (Delmar, N.Y., 1985), pp. 162–170.
15. See N. Contractor, *Pirana Satpanth ni Pol* (Ahmedabad, 1926), pp. 152ff., and S. Kasimali Durveshali, *Satpanth Shastra* (Garhkampa, 1954), pp. 1–47.
16. Amongst these works, the most important are Ṣ. Nanjiani, *Khoja Vrattant* (Ahmedabad, 1892; 2nd ed., Ahmedabad, 1918); J. Rahimtoola, *Khoja Komno Ithihas* (Bombay, 1905); Ṣ. Pīrzāda Dargāhvālā, *Tawārīkh-i Pīr* (Navsari, 1914–1935), 2 vols.; Contractor, *Pirana Satpanth ni Pol*, and Alimahomed J. Chunara, *Noorum Mobin* (Bombay, 1936), representing the official view of the Nizārī Khojas. Our references are to the Urdu translation of this work, *Nūr-i mubīn* (Bombay, 1936). For further items in this category, see Misra, *Muslim Communities*, pp. 190–191.
17. Ḥamd Allāh Mustawfī, *Ta'rīkh-i guzīda*, ed. and tr. Browne, vol. 1, p. 583, and vol. 2, p. 143; ed. Navā'ī, p. 592; Rabino, 'Rulers of Gilan', pp. 293–294, and E. G. Browne, *A History of Persian Literature under Tartar Dominion* (Cambridge, 1920), p. 25.
18. On Nizārī Quhistānī, see Dawlatshāh, *Tadhkirat al-shuʿarā'*, pp. 231–234; Nūr al-Dīn ʿAbd al-Raḥmān Jāmī, *Bahāristān*, ed. and tr. O. M. Schlechta-Wssehrd (Vienna, 1846), text p. 100, translation p. 116; Mīrkhwānd, *Rawḍat al-ṣafā'*, Tehran ed., vol. 4, p. 193; Khwānd Amīr, *Ḥabīb al-siyar*, vol. 2, p. 457; Amīn Aḥmad Rāzī, *Haft iqlīm*, ed. J. Fāḍil (Tehran, n.d.), vol. 2, pp. 322–323; Ādhar, *Ātashkada*, Bombay ed., p. 106; Tehran ed., p. 104; Riḍā Qulī Khān Hidāyat, *Majmaʿ al-fuṣaḥā'* (Tehran, 1295/1878), vol. 1, p. 607; ed. M. Muṣaffā (Tehran, 1336–1340/1957–1961), vol. 3, pp. 1358–1359, and Shihāb al-Dīn Shāh, *Khiṭābāt*, p. 36. Amongst the secondary sources, see Browne, *A History of Persian Literature under Tartar Dominion*, pp. 154–155; the introductory comments of Y. E. Bertel's to his edition and Russian translation of Nizārī's *Dastūr-nāma*, in *Vostochniy Sbornik*, 1 (1926), pp. 37ff.; M. Mujtahidzāda Bīrjandī, *Nasīm-i bahārī dar aḥvāl-i Ḥakīm Nizārī* (Mashhad, 1344/1925); Muḥammad Ḥusayn Āyatī Bīrjandī, *Bahāristān dar ta'rīkh va tarājim-i rijāl-i Qā'ināt va Quhistān* (Tehran, 1327/1948), pp. 198–207; Tch. G. Baradin, 'Ḥakīm Nizārī Quhistānī', *Farhang-i Īrān Zamīn*, 6 (1337/1958), pp. 178–203; J. Durri, 'Baʿze maʿlumot dar borayi Nizori', *Sharqi Surkh* (1958–1959), pp. 140–154; Ghulām Riḍā Riyāḍī, *Dānishvarān-i*

Khurāsān (Mashhad, 1336/1957), p. 296; Muḥammad Bāqir Āyatī Bīrjandī, *Rijāl-i Qā'in*, in *Sih risāla dar ʿilm-i rijāl*, ed. S. Kāẓim Mūsavī (Tehran, 1344/1965), pp. 8–9; ʿAlī Riḍā Mujtahidzāda, 'Saʿd al-milla wa'l-dīn Nizārī Quhistānī', *Revue de la Faculté des Lettres de Meched*, 2 (1345/1966), pp. 71–100 and 298–315; Z. Ṣafā, *Ta'rīkh-i adabiyyāt dar Īrān* (2nd ed., Tehran, 1355/1976), vol. 3, part 2, pp. 731–745; Ch. G. Baiburdi, 'Rukopisi proizvedeniy Nizārī', *Kratkie Soobshcheniya Instituta Narodov Azii*, 65 (1964), pp. 13–24; also his *Zhizn i tvorchestvo Nizārī-Persidskogo poeta* (Moscow, 1966), a detailed study of the life and works of Nizārī with numerous selections of his poetry; J. Rypka, 'Poets and Prose Writers of the late Saljuq and Mongol Periods', in *Cambridge History of Iran*, vol. 5, pp. 604–605; also his *History of Iranian Literature*, pp. 255–256; Fakquir Muhammad, 'Hakim Nizari Birjandi Kohistani', in *Great Ismaili Heroes*, pp. 81–82; Ivanow, *Guide*, pp. 105–106; also his *Ismaili Literature*, pp. 137–138, and Poonawala, *Bio*, pp. 263–267.

19. This date is given in one of Nizārī's poems, cited in Baradin, 'Ḥakīm Nizārī', p. 191, and in Baiburdi, *Zhizn*, p. 90. Before setting off on this journey, Nizārī travelled widely in Quhistān, and he relates that many former Nizārī villages in Quhistān had remained deserted; see I. P. Petrushevsky, 'The Socio-Economic Conditions of Iran under the Īl-Khāns', in *Cambridge History of Iran*, vol. 5, p. 488, citing this information from a manuscript of Nizārī's *Kulliyyāt* preserved at the Institute of Language and Literature of the Academy of Sciences of the Tajik S.S.S.R., Dushanbe; see also A. M. Boldyrev et al., *Katalog Vostochnykh rukopisei, Akademii Nauk Tadzhikskoi S.S.S.R.* (Dushanbe, 1960–1970), vol. 2, pp. 142–145.

20. Cited in Baiburdi, *Zhizn*, pp. 158 and 162.

21. For a few biographical details on the Imām Shams al-Dīn, reflecting the oral tradition of the sectarians, see Shihāb al-Dīn Shāh, *Khiṭābāt*, p. 42; Fidā'ī, *Hidāyat al-mu'minīn*, pp. 117–118; Ghālib, *Ta'rīkh*, pp. 291–293; also his *Aʿlām*, pp. 311–312; Tāmir, *al-Imāma*, p. 196, placing Shams al-Dīn's death in the year 711 A.H.; Ḥusayn, *Ṭā'ifat al-Ismāʿīliyya*, p. 86; Ivanow, *Brief*, p. 18; Hollister, *Shīʿa*, p. 331, and the genealogical chart prepared by Sherali Alidina and published in Kassim Ali, *Ever Living Guide* (Karachi, 1955), facing p. 1.

22. On some poems by Abū Firās Shihāb al-Dīn and by a Syrian Mu'minī Nizārī *dāʿī*, al-Shaykh Sulaymān b. Ḥaydar (d. 1212/1797–1798), naming the Mu'minī Imāms from Mu'min Shāh until Amīr Muḥammad al-Bāqir, the last imām of this line, see Tāmir, 'Furūʿ al-shajara al-Ismāʿīliyya', pp. 596–597; also his *al-Imāma*, pp. 174–176, and Poonawala, *Bio*, pp. 295–296. For further details on the Muḥammad-Shāhī (Mu'minī) Nizārīs and their imāms, according to the Syrian sectarians, see Tāmir, 'Furūʿ al-shajara al-Ismāʿīliyya', pp. 581ff., and also his *al-Imāma*, pp. 157–158, 169–178, 192–196 and 197ff.

23. W. Ivanow was the first Western scholar who referred to these Muḥammad-Shāhī authors and to the schism in question, see several of his works, 'An Ismailitic Pedigree', *JASB*, NS, 18 (1922), pp. 403–406; *Concise Descriptive*

Catalogue of the Persian Manuscripts in the Collection of the Asiatic Society of Bengal (Calcutta, 1924), pp. 370–371; 'A Forgotten Branch of the Ismailis', *JRAS* (1938), pp. 57–58 and 64–76; *Brief*, p. 18; *Guide*, pp. 111–112, and *Ismaili Literature*, pp. 10, 165 and 166–167. See also Ḥusayn, *Ṭā'ifat al-Ismā'īliyya*, pp. 86–87; Ghālib, *Ta'rīkh*, pp. 294–295; also his *A'lām*, p. 312, supporting the claims of Qāsim Shāh, and Poonawala, *Bio*, pp. 270–271 and 281.

24. Abū Isḥāq, *Haft bāb*, text p. 24, translation p. 24, and Khayrkhwāh, *Kalām-i pīr*, text p. 51, translation p. 44.
25. On Kiyā Sayf al-Dīn and his pro-Nizārī activities in Daylamān, see Ẓahīr al-Dīn Mar'ashī, *Ta'rīkh-i Gīlān va Daylamistān*, ed. H. L. Rabino (Rasht, 1330/1912), pp. 64–67; ed. M. Sutūda (Tehran, 1347/1968), pp. 66–68; H. L. Rabino, *Les Provinces Caspiennes de la Perse: Le Guīlān* (Paris, 1917), pp. 281 and 403–404; Persian translation, *Vilāyāt-i dār al-marz-i Īrān: Gīlān*, tr. J. Khumāmī-Zāda (Tehran, 1350/1971), pp. 326 and 469–470; also his 'Rulers of Gilan', p. 295, and his 'Dynasties locales du Gīlān', pp. 316–317.
26. Mar'ashī, *Ta'rīkh-i Gīlān*, ed. Rabino, pp. 50–51, 67–68 and 74ff.; ed. Sutūda, pp. 52, 69–70 and 76ff.
27. On Khudāwand Muḥammad and his activities, see Mar'ashī, *Ta'rīkh-i Gīlān*, ed. Rabino, pp. 51–64 and 120–121; ed. Sutūda, pp. 52–66 and 123–124; Rabino, *Provinces Caspiennes*, pp. 402–403; tr. Khumāmī-Zāda, pp. 468–469; Rabino, 'Rulers of Gilan', pp. 293–294; also his 'Dynasties locales du Gīlān', pp. 315–316 and 317–318, and Sutūda, *Qilā'*, pp. 83–88, reproducing the relevant extracts from Ẓahīr al-Dīn Mar'ashī.
28. Mar'ashī, *Tar'īkh-i Gīlān*, ed. Rabino, pp. 79ff., 86–87, 118, 120 and 122–127; ed. Sutūda, pp. 81ff., 89, 121, 123 and 125–130; see also the following works of Rabino, *Provinces Caspiennes*, pp. 405 and 409–410; tr. Khumāmī-Zāda, pp. 471 and 475–476; 'Rulers of Lahijan and Fuman, in Gilan, Persia', *JRAS* (1918), pp. 88–89 and 94; 'Rulers of Gilan', pp. 287, 294 and 296, and 'Dynasties locales du Gīlān', pp. 318–320 and 322–323.
29. This is reported by Ẓahīr al-Dīn Mar'ashī in his *Ta'rīkh-i Gīlān*, ed. Rabino, p. 64; ed. Sutūda, p. 65, a work completed in 881/1476–1477 and later continued by its author to the year 894/1489.
30. See Mar'ashī, *Ta'rīkh-i Gīlān*, ed. Rabino, pp. 132ff., 165ff., 199 and 240–241; ed. Sutūda, pp. 135ff., 169ff., 204–205 and 247.
31. Shaykh 'Alī Gīlānī, *Ta'rīkh-i Māzandarān*, pp. 88–89 and 100. See also 'Abd al-Fattāḥ Fūmanī, *Ta'rīkh-i Gīlān*, ed. B. Dorn (St Petersburg, 1858), pp. 127–129 and 192–195; ed. M. Sutūda (Tehran, 1349/1970), pp. 164–166 and 241–244; Rabino, *Provinces Caspiennes*, p. 438; tr. Khumāmī-Zāda, p. 506, and Rabino, 'Dynasties du Māzandarān', pp. 472–473; Iskandar Beg Munshī, *Ta'rīkh-i 'ālamārā-yi 'Abbāsī*, ed. I. Afshār (2nd ed., Tehran, 1350/1971), vol. 2, pp. 399, 499, 503–504, 513, 521, 534 and 535–537; extracts in Dorn, ed., *Auszüge aus Muhammedanischen schriftstellern*, pp. 330–333, 341, 345–346 and 348–351; Riḍā Qulī Khān Hidāyat, *Rawḍat al-ṣafā-yi Nāṣirī* (Tehran, 1339/1960), vol. 8 (published as the continuation of the Tehran

edition of Mīrkhwānd's *Rawḍat al-ṣafā'*), pp. 299 and 303; Rabino, *Provinces Caspiennes*, p. 438; tr. Khumāmī-Zāda, p. 506, and Rabino, 'Dynasties du Māzandarān', pp. 472–473.

32. For instance, see Shihāb al-Dīn Shāh, *Khiṭābāt*, p. 42; Fidā'ī, *Hidāyat al-mu'minīn*, pp. 118–119; Ghālib, *Ta'rīkh*, pp. 294–300; also his *Aʿlām*, pp. 116–117, 427–429 and 445–446; Tāmir, *al-Imāma*, pp. 220–221, and Hollister, *Shīʿa*, pp. 332–334.

33. Niẓām al-Dīn Shāmī, *Ẓafar-nāma*, ed. F. Tauer (Prague, 1937–1956), vol. 1, p. 136; Sharaf al-Dīn ʿAlī Yazdī, *Ẓafar-nāma*, ed. Mawlawī Muḥammad Ilahdād (Calcutta, 1887–1888), vol. 1, p. 621; ed. M. ʿAbbāsī (Tehran, 1336/1957), vol. 1, pp. 443–444; ed. A. Urunbayev (Tashkent, 1972), p. 500; see also Mīrkhwānd, *Rawḍat al-ṣafā'*, vol. 6, pp. 211–212.

34. See Shāmī, *Ẓafar-nāma*, vol. 1, p. 128; Sharaf al-Dīn ʿAlī, *Ẓafar-nāma*, ed. Ilahdād, vol. 1, p. 577; ed. ʿAbbāsī, vol. 1, pp. 413–414; ed. Urunbayev, pp. 476–477; Mīrkhwānd, *Rawḍat al-ṣafā'*, vol. 6, p. 207, and John Malcolm, *The History of Persia* (New ed., London, 1829), vol. 1, pp. 294–295; Persian translation, *Ta'rīkh-i Īrān*, tr. I. Hairat (Bombay, 1323/1906; reprinted in Tehran, 1362/1983), vol. 1, p. 232.

35. See, for example, Ivanow, *Brief*, p. 18, and Corbin, *Étude*, pp. 23–24.

36. On Maḥmūd Shabistarī and his mystical poem, see Zayn al-ʿĀbidīn Shīrwānī, *Riyāḍ al-siyāḥa*, ed. A. Ḥāmid Rabbānī (Tehran, 1339/1960), pp. 89–92; Riḍā Qulī Khān Hidāyat, *Riyāḍ al-ʿārifīn*, ed. M. Garakānī (Tehran, 1344/1965), pp. 221–227; H. Ethé, 'Neupersische Litteratur', in *Grundriss der iranischen philologie*, vol. 2, pp. 299 and 301; Browne, *A History of Persian Literature under Tartar Dominion*, pp. 146–150; A. J. Arberry, *Classical Persian Literature* (London, 1958), pp. 301–305; Rypka, 'Poets and Prose Writers', p. 603; also his *History of Iranian Literature*, p. 254; Muḥammad ʿAlī Tarbiyat, *Dānishmandān-i Ādharbāyjān* (Tehran, 1314/1935), pp. 334–338; Ṣafā, *Ta'rīkh-i adabiyyāt*, vol. 3, part 2, pp. 763–766; B. A. Dar, 'Maḥmūd Shabistari, al-Jīli, and Jāmi', in *A History of Muslim Philosophy*, ed. Sharif, vol. 2, pp. 839–843, and J. T. P. de Bruijn, 'Maḥmūd Shabistarī', *EI2*, vol. 6, pp. 72–73. The first complete edition of the *Gulshan-i rāz* with a versified German translation was prepared by J. von Hammer-Purgstall under the title of *Rosenflor des Geheimnisses* (Pesth–Leipzig, 1838), and subsequently Edward H. Whinfield (1836–1922) produced a critical edition of the Persian text of the poem with a prose English version entitled *Gulshan i Raz: The Mystic Rose Garden* (London, 1880). Most recently, an edition of this poem was produced by Gurban-eli Memmedzade (Baku, 1973). Meanwhile, the text of the *Gulshan-i rāz* was lithographed in Bombay in 1280/1863, and elsewhere; a limited special edition of the poem was published by the Hamdami Foundation (Tehran, 1357/1978). The text of this poem also appears at the end of the edition of its commentary by Muḥammad Lāhījī, *Mafātīḥ al-iʿjāz fī sharḥ-i gulshan-i rāz*, ed. K. Samīʿī (Tehran, 1337/1958), pp. 723–771.

37. This anonymous Nizārī commentary entitled *Baʿḍī az ta'wīlāt-i gulshan-i rāz* has been edited and translated into French with commentaries by H. Corbin

in his *Trilogie Ismaélienne*, text pp. 131–161, translation pp. 1–174. See also W. Ivanow, 'An Ismaili Interpretation of the Gulshani Raz', *JBBRAS*, NS, 8 (1932), pp. 69–78, describing the work on the basis of a single manuscript transcribed in 1312/1895 and subsequently used by Corbin for preparing his edition; Ivanow, *Guide*, p. 99; also his *Ismaili Literature*, p. 164; Berthels and Baqoev, *Alphabetic Catalogue*, p. 83, and Poonawala, *Bio*, pp. 274 and 351.

38. See Khayrkhwāh, *Faṣl*, p. 13; tr. Ivanow, p. 29; Fidā'ī, *Hidāyat al-mu'minīn*, pp. 113–116 and 138; Ghālib, *A'lām*, pp. 187–191, 309–310 and 423–424; Corbin, *Étude*, pp. 7 and 13; also his *Histoire*, pp. 139–142 and 149–151; Ivanow, 'Ismailitskiya rukopisi', pp. 379–384; also his *Guide*, pp. 97, 104–105 and 118–119; and his *Ismaili Literature*, pp. 129–131, 155, 164 and 185, and Ivanow's introduction to his edition of the *Chirāgh-nāma*, a Ṣūfī poem preserved in the upper Oxus, published in *Revue Iranienne d'Anthropologie*, 3 (1338/1959), English pp. 13–17, Persian pp. 53–70.
39. See M. Molé's introduction to his edition of Nasafī's *Kitāb al-insān al-kāmil* (Tehran–Paris, 1962), especially pp. 20–27 and 34–36; Semenov, 'Opisanie Ismailitskikh rukopisei', pp. 2187–2188; Ivanow, *Guide*, p. 99, and Berthels and Baqoev, *Alphabetic Catalogue*, pp. 63–64 and 81–82. Al-Nasafī's *Zubdat al-ḥaqā'iq*, lithographed in Tehran in 1320/1902–1903, has been edited, on the basis of copies preserved in Badakhshān, in *Panj risāla dar bayān-i āfāq va anfus*, ed. Berthels, pp. 91–207.
40. Fidā'ī, *Hidāyat al-mu'minīn*, p. 107; Ghālib, *A'lām*, pp. 505–507, and Ivanow, *Guide*, p. 118.
41. On Ḥaydar Āmulī's thought and the relationship between Shī'ism and Ṣūfism in general, see al-Shūshtarī, *Majālis al-mu'minīn*, vol. 2, pp. 51–54; Corbin, *Histoire*, pp. 47ff., 56, 70–71, 88ff., 98, 141 and 300; and his *En Islam Iranien*, vol. 1, pp. 74–85, and vol. 3, pp. 149–213; Kāmil M. al-Shaybī, *Tashayyu' va tasawwuf*, tr. 'Alī Riḍā Dh. Qaraguzlū (Tehran 1359/1980), pp. 64–71 and 112–125, being a translation of al-Shaybī's *al-Fikr al-Shī'a wa'l-naza'āt al-ṣūfiyya* (Baghdad, 1386/1966), and J. van Ess, 'Ḥaydar-i Āmulī', *EI2*, Supplement, pp. 363–365, where further sources are cited. See also S. H. Nasr, *Sufi Essays* (London, 1972), pp. 104–120, and also his *Ideals*, pp. 121–146.
42. See, for instance, Ḥaydar Āmulī, *Jāmi' al-asrār wa manba' al-anwār*, ed. H. Corbin and O. Yahya, in a collection of Āmulī's treatises entitled *La Philosophie Shi'ite* (Tehran–Paris, 1969), pp. 47, 116–117, 216–217, 220–222, 238, 388 and 611–615; see also Ḥaydar Āmulī, *Asrār al-sharī'a wa aṭwār al-ṭarīqa wa anwār al-ḥaqīqa*, ed. M. Khvājavī (Tehran, 1982), pp. 5ff. and 23ff.
43. On the Ḥurūfīs and the Nuqṭawīs and their doctrines, which have barely been investigated, see the pioneering studies of E. G. Browne, especially his 'Some Notes on the Literature and Doctrines of the Ḥurūfī Sect', *JRAS* (1898), pp. 61–94; 'Further Notes on the Literature of the Hurufis and their Connection with the Bektashi Order of Dervishes', *JRAS* (1907), pp. 533–581, and *A History of Persian Literature under Tartar Dominion*, pp. 365–375 and 449–452. Clément Huart edited and translated into French a number of Persian Ḥurūfī texts in a collection entitled *Textes Persans relatifs à la secte des*

Houroûfîs (Leiden–London, 1909), also containing a study on the Ḥurūfī religion by Rizā Tevfīq, pp. 219–313. See also *Dabistān-i madhāhib*, vol. 1, pp. 273–278; English translation, *The Dabistān or School of Manners*, tr. D. Shea and A. Troyer (Washington–London, 1901), pp. 337–344; Elias J. W. Gibb, *A History of Ottoman Poetry*, ed. E. G. Browne (London, 1900–1909), vol. 1, pp. 336–388; John K. Birge, *The Bektashi Order of Dervishes* (London, 1937), pp. 58–62, 148–158 and 281–282; Ṣādiq Kiyā, *Nuqṭawiyān yā Pasīkhāniyān* (Tehran, 1320/1941); H. Ritter, 'Studien zur Geschichte der islamischen Frömmigkeit, II: Die Anfänge der Ḥurūfīsekte', *Oriens*, 7 (1954), pp. 1–54; Persian translation, 'Āghāz-i firqa-yi Ḥurūfiyya, tr. H. Mu'ayyad', *Farhang-i Īrān Zamīn*, 10 (1341/1962), pp. 319–393; Petrushevsky, *Islām dar Īrān*, pp. 322ff.; tr. Evans, *Islam in Iran*, pp. 260ff.; Naṣr Allāh Falsafī, *Zindagānī-yi Shāh ʿAbbās-i avval* (Tehran, 1334–1352/1955–1973), vol. 3, pp. 40–51; Nūr al-Dīn Mudarrisī Chahārdihī, *Sayrī dar taṣawwuf* (Tehran, 1359/1980), pp. 144–151; S. Amir Arjomand, *The Shadow of God and the Hidden Imam* (Chicago, 1984), pp. 71–74 and 198–199; Ṣafā, *Ta'rīkh-i adabiyyāt*, vol. 4, pp. 61–66; B. S. Amoretti, 'Religion in the Timurid and Safavid Periods', in *The Cambridge History of Iran*: Volume 6, *The Timurid and Safavid Periods*, ed. P. Jackson and L. Lockhart (Cambridge, 1986), pp. 623–625 and 644–646; Ivanow, *Ismaili Literature*, pp. 12–13 and 188–192; Cl. Huart, 'Ḥurūfī', *SEI*, pp. 141–142, and A. Bausani, 'Ḥurūfiyya', *EI2*, vol. 3, pp. 600–601.

44. Iskandar Beg Munshī, *ʿĀlamārā*, vol. 1, pp. 473–477; Hidāyat, *Rawḍat al-ṣafā-yi Nāṣirī*, vol. 8, pp. 273–276; Kiyā, *Nuqṭawiyān*, pp. 37–45, and Falsafī, *Zindagānī*, vol. 2, pp. 338–344.
45. See *Dabistān-i madhāhib*, vol. 1, pp. 298–299; Shāh Nawāz Khān, *Ma'āthir al-umarā'*, ed. Maulavī ʿAbd al-Raḥīm and Maulavī Mīrzā Ashraf ʿAlī (Calcutta, 1888–1891), vol. 3, pp. 285–290; English translation, *The Maaṣiru-l-umarā; being Biographies of the Muhammadan and Hindu Officers of the Timurid Sovereigns of India*, tr. H. Beveridge (Calcutta, 1911–1952), vol. 2, pp. 812–816, and Kiyā, *Nuqṭawiyān*, pp. 45–48.
46. Mīrkhwānd, *Rawḍat al-ṣafā'*, Tehran ed., vol. 6, pp. 691–694; Khwānd Amīr, *Ḥabīb al-siyar*, vol. 3, pp. 615–617; al-Shūshtarī, *Majālis al-mu'minīn*, vol. 2, pp. 44–47, and R. M. Savory, 'A 15th Century Ṣafavid Propagandist at Harāt', in *American Oriental Society, Middle West Branch: Semi-centennial Volume*, ed. D. Sinor (Bloomington, 1969), pp. 189–197.
47. See Amīn Aḥmad Rāzī, *Haft iqlīm*, vol. 2, pp. 431–432; ʿAbd al-Bāqī Nihāwandī, *Ma'āthir-i Raḥīmī*, ed. M. Hidayat Husain (Calcutta, 1910–1931), vol. 3, pp. 1497–1506; Hidāyat, *Riyāḍ al-ʿārifīn*, pp. 275–276; Mīrzā Ḥasan Fasā'ī, *Fārs-nāma-yi Nāṣirī* (Tehran, 1312–1313/1894–1896), vol. 2, pp. 142–143; Kiyā, *Nuqṭawiyān*, pp. 59–61 and 65–68; Falsafī, *Zindagānī*, vol. 3, pp. 44 and 45–46; Ivanow, *Guide*, p. 108; also his *Ismaili Literature*, pp. 144–145 and 189; Poonawala, *Bio*, pp. 277–278, and his 'Amrī', *EIR*, vol. 1, p. 996.
48. On Anjudān and its Nizārī antiquities, see W. Ivanow, 'Tombs of Some Persian Ismaili Imams', *JBBRAS*, NS, 14 (1938), pp. 52–56, and F. Daftary,

'Anǰedān', *EIR*, vol. 2, p. 77. Ibrāhīm Dihgān (d. 1984) who was a native of Arāk has many details on the geography and history of the area in his *Kār-nāma yā du bakhsh-i dīgar az ta'rīkh-i Arāk* (Tehran, 1345/1966), pp. 9–185.

49. Nāṣir al-Dīn Shāh Qājār, *Safar-nāma-yi 'Irāq-i 'Ajam* (Tehran, 1311/1893), pp. 44ff.

50. Ghālib, *Ta'rīkh*, pp. 301–303; also his *A'lām*, pp. 398–399; Tāmir, *al-Imāma*, p. 222, and Sherali Alidina's genealogical chart in Kassim Ali, *Ever Living Guide*.

51. The earliest lists of the Qāsim-Shāhī Nizārī Imāms of the Anjudān period are contained in Abū Isḥāq, *Haft bāb*, text p. 24, and in Khayrkhwāh, *Kalām-i pīr*, text p. 51; Khayrkhwāh's list has been continued for several generations by later scribes. The versified list given in the *Qaṣīda-yi dhurriyya* composed by 'Alī Qulī Raqqāmī Dizbādī, ed. Semenov in 'Ismailitskaya oda', pp. 8–13, is extended down to the forty-eighth imām, Sulṭān Muḥammad Shāh, Āghā Khān III, probably by Fidā'ī Khurāsānī; in some manuscripts, Raqqāmī's father Khākī Khurāsānī is named as the original composer of this poem. The imāms are listed also in Shihāb al-Dīn Shāh, *Khiṭābāt*, pp. 42–43 and 45. See also Ivanow, 'Ismailitica', pp. 67 and 69; Mujtaba Ali, *Origin of the Khojāhs*, pp. 54–58; Hollister, *Shī'a*, p. 332; Ghālib, *Ta'rīkh*, table 4 at the end of the book; also his *A'lām*, table 4; Tāmir, *al-Imāma*, pp. 159–161 and 178–179, and Nanji, *Nizārī Tradition*, pp. 141–142. The official list of the imāms currently circulating amongst the Āghā Khānī Nizārīs is cited, for instance, in Sherali Alidina's genealogical chart in Kassim Ali, *Ever Living Guide*, published by the Ismailia Association Pakistan, Karachi, reproduced in Poonawala, *Bio*, pp. 372–373, and at the end of the daily prayers recited regularly by the modern-day Nizārīs. The list appearing at the end of one of these *du'ās* was given to the author in 1985 at Mashhad by the leaders of the Persian Nizārī community of Khurāsān. Brief biographical notices on the imāms of the Anjudān period after Mustanṣir bi'llāh II, with few reliable details, are given in Ghālib, *Ta'rīkh*, pp. 304–319; also his *A'lām*, pp. 285–286, 332–335, 412–413, 491–492, 508–509 and 575–576, and Tāmir, *al-Imāma*, pp. 222–225. Fidā'ī, *Hidāyat al-mu'minīn*, pp. 133–140, has only praises for the imāms without supplying any particular biographical details.

52. On the political situation of Persia between the collapse of the Īlkhānid empire and the establishment of the Ṣafawid dynasty, see Hans R. Roemer's articles 'The Jalayirids, Muzaffarids and Sarbadārs', 'Tīmūr in Iran', 'The Successors of Tīmūr', and 'The Turkmen Dynasties', in *Cambridge History of Iran*, vol. 6, pp. 1–188.

53. Hodgson, *Venture of Islam*, vol. 2, pp. 493ff.

54. Cl. Cahen, 'Le problème du Shī'isme dans l'Asie Mineure turque préottomane', in *Le Shī'isme Imāmite*, pp. 118ff.

55. On the spread of Shī'ism through the Ṣūfī orders in pre-Ṣafawid Persia, and the activities of certain Shī'ī-related movements of social protest during this period, see al-Shaybī, *Tashayyu' va taṣawwuf*, pp. 155–340; Petrushevsky, *Islām dar Īrān*, pp. 371–398; tr. Evans, pp. 302–326; Hodgson, *Venture of Islam*, vol. 2, pp. 455ff. and 490–500; Michel M. Mazzaoui, *The Origins of the*

Ṣafawids: Šīʿism, Ṣūfism, and the Ġulāt (Wiesbaden, 1972), pp. 22ff., 37–40, 41ff., 63–71 and 83–85; Amir Arjomand, *Shadow of God*, pp. 66–84, and Amoretti, 'Religion in the Timurid and Safavid Periods', pp. 610–634.

56. On Muḥammad Nūrbakhsh and the Nūrbakhshī Ṣūfī order, see al-Shūshtarī, *Majālis al-muʾminīn*, vol. 2, pp. 143–156; Muḥammad Maʿṣūm Shīrāzī, better known under his Ṣūfī name of Maʿṣūm ʿAlī Shāh, *Ṭarāʾiq al-ḥaqāʾiq*, ed. Muḥammad Jaʿfar Maḥjūb (Tehran, 1339–1345/1960–1966), vol. 2, pp. 319–322, 334ff., and vol. 3, pp. 127–130, an important work on the Persian Ṣūfī orders and their leaders written by a member of a branch of the Niʿmat Allāhī order, and J. Ṣadaqiyānlū, *Taḥqīq dar aḥvāl va āthār-i Sayyid Muḥammad Nūrbakhsh Uvaysī Quhistānī* (Tehran, 1351/1972), containing some writings ascribed to Nūrbakhsh; see also the important studies of M. Molé, including his 'Les Kubrawiya entre Sunnisme et Shiisme aux huitième et neuvième siècles de l'hégire', *REI*, 29 (1961), pp. 61–142, and *Les Mystiques Musulmans* (Paris, 1965), pp. 99–122; ʿAbd al-Ḥusayn Zarrīnkūb, *Dunbāla-yi justijū dar taṣawwuf-i Īrān* (Tehran, 1362/1983), pp. 159–188; R. Gramlich, *Die schiitischen Derwischorden Persiens* (Wiesbaden, 1965–1981), vol. 1, pp. 13–26, and J. Spencer Trimingham, *The Sufi Orders in Islam* (Oxford, 1971), pp. 55–58 and 99ff.

57. On Shāh Niʿmat Allāh Walī and his *ṭarīqa*, see J. Aubin, ed., *Matériaux pour la biographie de Shāh Niʿmatullāh Walī Kermānī* (Tehran–Paris, 1956), containing the earliest biographies of this saint; Dawlatshāh, *Tadhkirat al-shuʿarāʾ*, pp. 333–336; al-Shūshtarī, *Majālis al-muʾminīn*, vol. 2, pp. 47–50; Shīrwānī, *Riyāḍ al-siyāḥa*, pp. 583–602; Maʿṣūm ʿAlī Shāh, *Ṭarāʾiq al-ḥaqāʾiq*, vol. 2, pp. 325–334, and vol. 3, pp. 1–48 and 84–104, and Javād Nūrbakhsh, *Zindagī va āthār-i Shāh Niʿmat Allāh Valī Kirmānī* (Tehran, 1337/1958), a book on the life and works of this saint written by the present master of one of the Niʿmat Allāhī branches in Persia. See also Browne, *A History of Persian Literature under Tartar Dominion*, pp. 463–473; N. Pourjavady and Peter L. Wilson, *Kings of Love: The Poetry and History of the Niʿmatullāhī Sufi Order* (Tehran, 1978), especially pp. 13–92; Zarrīnkūb, *Dunbāla*, pp. 189–200; Amir Arjomand, *Shadow of God*, pp. 116–118; Gramlich, *Die schiitischen Derwischorden*, vol. 1, pp. 27ff., and Trimingham, *Sufi Orders*, pp. 101–102.

58. Shāh Niʿmat Allāh has referred to his genealogy in one of his *risāla*s which remains unpublished, and in a poem; see his *Kulliyyāt-i dīwān*, ed. M. ʿIlmī (Tehran, 1333/1954), pp. 585–586. This poem and the genealogy derived from it are reproduced in near-contemporary biographies written by ʿAbd al-Razzāq Kirmānī (d. after 911/1505) and ʿAbd al-ʿAzīz Wāʿiẓī (d. after 839/1436), edited by Aubin in *Matériaux*, pp. 21–23 and 274–276, respectively. See also Zayn al-ʿĀbidīn Shīrwānī, *Bustān al-siyāḥa* (Tehran, 1310/1893), p. 526; also his *Riyāḍ al-siyāḥa*, p. 583; Maʿṣūm ʿAlī Shāh, *Ṭarāʾiq al-ḥaqāʾiq*, vol. 3, pp. 1–2, and Hidāyat, *Riyāḍ al-ʿārifīn*, p. 232.

59. See Berthels and Baqoev, *Alphabetic Catalogue*, pp. 32, 34 and 61–62, and N. Pourjavady and P. L. Wilson, 'Ismāʿīlīs and Niʿmatullāhīs', *SI*, 41 (1975), pp. 115–116.

60. See Muḥammad Mufīd Yazdī, *Jāmiʿ-i Mufīdī*, in Aubin, *Matériaux*, pp. 199–

268, and N. Pourjavady and P. L. Wilson, 'The Descendants of Shāh Niʿmatullāh Walī', *IC*, 48 (1974), pp. 49–57.

61. On the Ṣafawī Ṣūfī order and the background to the establishment of Ṣafawid rule in Persia, see Mazzaoui, *Origins of the Ṣafawids*, pp. 41–63 and 71–82; R. Savory, *Iran under the Ṣafavids* (Cambridge, 1980), pp. 1–26; H. R. Roemer, 'The Safavid Period', in *Cambridge History of Iran*, vol. 6, pp. 189–212, and Ghulām Sarwar, *History of Shāh Ismāʿīl Ṣafawī* (Aligarh, 1939), pp. 3–29; all four citing the primary sources on the subject.
62. Fidāʾī, *Hidāyat al-muʾminīn*, pp. 133, 136 and 140.
63. Mustanṣir biʾllāh II, *Pandiyāt-i jawānmardī*, ed. and tr. W. Ivanow (Leiden, 1953). On this work, see Hollister, *Shīʿa*, pp. 362, 383 and 407; Nanji, *Nizārī Tradition*, pp. 27, 65, 80–81, 85–86 and 89; Ivanow, *Guide*, pp. 106–107; also his *Ismaili Literature*, pp. 139–140; Ivanow's introduction to the *Pandiyāt*, pp. 1ff., and Poonawala, *Bio*, p. 268.
64. See *Pandiyāt-i jawānmardī*, text pp. 47 and 56, translation pp. 29 and 35.
65. Berthels and Baqoev, *Alphabetic Catalogue*, pp. 36–37, and Ivanow's remarks in *Pandiyāt-i jawānmardī*, introduction p. 17.
66. Mustanṣir biʾllah II, *Pandiyāt-i jawānmardī*, text pp. 31, 57, 87, 90, 91, 99 and 101, translation pp. 19, 36, 54, 55, 56, 61 and 62.
67. Ibid., text pp. 11, 26, 27, 32, 39, 65, 86 and elsewhere, translation pp. 7, 17, 20, 24, 40 and 53.
68. Ibid., text pp. 2–3, translation p. 2.
69. Ibid., text pp. 3, 11, 13, 14, 16, 21, 25, 27, 32, 36, 37, 39, 41, 42, 45, 46–47, 48–49, 50, 53, 57–58, 60, 62, 65–66, 67, 69, 70–71, 77, 80, 82, 86, 87, 93, 98, 99 and 100–102, translation pp. 2, 7, 8, 9, 10, 13, 16, 17, 20, 22, 23, 24, 25, 26, 28–29, 30–31, 33, 36, 38, 39, 41, 42, 43, 44, 48, 50, 51, 53, 54, 57–58, 60, 61 and 62–63.
70. Ibid., text pp. 34–36 and 54–55, translation pp. 21–22 and 34.
71. Ibid., text pp. 2, 11, 17, 21, 34, 60, 63–64, 70, 78, 82 and 88–89, translation pp. 2, 8, 11, 13, 21, 37, 39, 43–44, 48–49, 51 and 54–55.
72. See, for instance, Khayrkhwāh's *Taṣnīfāt*, p. 108, and *Faṣl dar bayān-i shinākht-i imām*, p. 33; English translation, *On the Recognition of the Imam*, tr. Ivanow, pp. 49–50; the latter treatise emphasizes the paramount importance of recognizing the sole legitimate imām of the time and his chief deputy or *ḥujja*.
73. Ivanow, *Ismaili Literature*, pp. 140–141, and Poonawala, *Bio*, p. 269.
74. This date is mentioned by Khayrkhwāh in one of his poems; see his *Taṣnīfāt*, p. 120.
75. Khayrkhwāh, *Risāla*, in his *Taṣnīfāt*, pp. 1–75.
76. Khayrkhwāh, *Risāla*, in his *Taṣnīfāt*, pp. 35ff.
77. Ibid., p. 51.
78. Ibid., pp. 45–46 and 55.
79. Ibid., pp. 46ff.
80. Ibid., pp. 34 and 50.
81. Khayrkhwāh emphasizes such internal quarrels throughout his *Risāla* and elsewhere; see, for instance, his *Qiṭaʿāt*, in his *Taṣnīfāt*, pp. 94ff.

82. Fidā'ī, *Hidāyat al-mu'minīn*, p. 135.
83. The relevant passage from the *Ta'rīkh-i alfī* is cited in Kiyā, *Nuqṭawiyān*, pp. 36–37, and in Falsafī, *Zindagāni-yi Shāh ʿAbbās*, vol. 3, p. 44. The part of the *Ta'rīkh-i alfī* containing this section was written by Jaʿfar Beg Āṣaf Khān (d. 1021/1612).
84. Qāḍī Aḥmad al-Qummī, *Khulāṣat al-tawārīkh*, ed. Iḥsān Ishrāqī (Tehran, 1359/1980), vol. 1, pp. 582–584; see also Hidāyat, *Rawḍat al-ṣafā-yi Nāṣirī*, vol. 8, pp. 145–146, and Dihgān, *Kār-nāma*, pp. 50–52.
85. Khayrkhwāh, *Risāla*, in his *Taṣnīfāt*, p. 52. Shihāb al-Dīn Shāh, *Khiṭābāt*, pp. 42–43, relates that the thirty-fourth imām, ʿAbbās Shāh, too, was obliged to live for some time away from his ancestral home, hence his epithet of Gharīb Mīrzā.
86. This is the latest date mentioned in his poems; see Khākī Khurāsānī, *Dīwān*, p. 19. In 1985, the author found access at Dizbād to what seemed to be a complete collection of Khākī's poetical works. Perusing through that manuscript, transcribed by Sayyid Badakhshānī and now owned by ʿAbd al-Sulṭān b. Mullā ʿAbbās, a descendant of Khākī Khurāsānī, the author did not come across any date later than 1056/1646.
87. Khākī Khurāsānī, *Dīwān*, pp. 10, 17, 67, 95 and 104.
88. Ibid., pp. 10, 12, 17, 19, 20, 21, 22, 23, 31, 54, 66, 76 and 101.
89. Ibid., pp. 9 and 68–69.
90. Fidā'ī, *Hidāyat al-mu'minīn*, pp. 136–139.
91. For references to the Qāsim-Shāhī *daʿwa* organization during the Anjudān period, see *Pandiyāt-i jawānmardī*, text pp. 41ff. and 62ff., translation pp. 25ff. and 39ff.; Abū Isḥāq, *Haft bāb*, text pp. 49–50 and 59, translation pp. 49–50 and 59; Khayrkhwāh, *Kalām-i pīr*, text pp. 44, 76–77, 93–94, 101 and 110, translation pp. 37, 72, 88, 97 and 106; also his *Taṣnīfāt*, pp. 3, 23, 58, and 113ff., enumerating the hierarchy in a poem, and his *Faṣl*, pp. 1, 7 and 32; tr. Ivanow, pp. 17, 24 and 48–49; see also Khākī Khurāsānī, *Dīwān*, pp. 47, 70, 76, 79 and 119.
92. Abū Isḥāq, *Haft bāb*, text pp. 11–12, 57, 60 and 62, translation pp. 10–12, 57, 60 and 63; Khayrkhwāh, *Kalām-i pīr*, text pp. 18–19, 98 and 102, translation pp. 12–13, 94–95 and 98; also his *Faṣl*, p. 28; tr. Ivanow, p. 43, and Khākī Khurāsānī, *Dīwān*, pp. 91 and 125–126. The Nizārī doctrine of the early Anjudān period, as propounded by Abū Isḥāq Quhistānī, is analyzed in Z. Haji, 'La Doctrine Ismaélienne d'après l'Oeuvre d'Abu Ishaq Qohestani' (Thèse de doctorat de 3ᵉ cycle, Sorbonne, Paris IV, 1975).
93. Abū Isḥāq, *Haft bāb*, text pp. 37 and 67, translation pp. 37–38; Khayrkhwāh, *Kalām-i pīr*, text pp. 72–73, 86, 104, 107 and 114–116, translation pp. 67–69, 80, 100, 103 and 111–112, and Khākī Khurāsānī, *Dīwān*, pp. 44–45, 55, 56, 58, 62, 103, 109 and 118.
94. Abū Isḥāq, *Haft bāb*, text pp. 19–20 and 67, translation pp. 19–20 and 67–68, and Khayrkhwāh, *Kalām-i pīr*, text p. 46, translation pp. 38–39; see also Khākī Khurāsānī, *Dīwān*, pp. 12, 14, 19, 33, 49, 61, 64, 66, 68, 69, 75, 106, 115–117 and 124–125.

95. Abū Isḥāq, *Haft bāb*, text pp. 53 and 58, translation pp. 53–54 and 58; Khayrkhwāh, *Kalām-i pīr*, text pp. 95–96 and 100, translation pp. 91 and 96, and also his *Taṣnīfāt*, pp. 18ff.
96. See Khayrkhwāh's *Taṣnīfāt*, pp. 1–35, and his *Faṣl*, pp. 11–32; tr. Ivanow, pp. 28–48.
97. Abū Isḥāq, *Haft bāb*, text pp. 33 and 50, translation pp. 33 and 50; Khayrkhwāh, *Kalām-i pīr*, text pp. 58 and 94, translation pp. 52 and 88; also his *Faṣl*, p. 9; tr. Ivanow, pp. 25–26, and Khākī Khurāsānī, *Dīwān*, pp. 72 and 84.
98. Khayrkhwāh, *Taṣnīfāt*, pp. 20, 26, 52, 77, 78, 82, 89–90, 100, 102, 116 and 120; and his *Faṣl*, pp. 11, 13 and 21–22; tr. Ivanow, pp. 28, 30 and 36–37, and Khākī Khurāsānī, *Dīwān*, p. 18.
99. *Pandiyāt-i jawānmardī*, text pp. 42–43, 44–45 and 64–65, translation pp. 26, 27–28 and 40; Abū Isḥāq, *Haft bāb*, text pp. 17–18, 43, 50 and 64–65, translation pp. 17–18, 43–44, 50 and 64–65; Khayrkhwāh, *Kalām-i pīr*, text pp. 26, 67–68, 111–112 and 116, translation pp. 21, 63–64, 107–108 and 112; also his *Taṣnīfāt*, pp. 3ff., 20, 23–24, 26, 53, 86, 118 and 127ff.; also his *Faṣl*, pp. 1–2, 6, 12, 21 and 23; tr. Ivanow, pp. 18–19, 22, 29, 36 and 38, and Khākī Khurāsānī, *Dīwān*, pp. 84 and 85.
100. Khayrkhwāh, *Taṣnīfāt*, pp. 19 and 92–93, and also his *Faṣl*, pp. 28 and 32; tr. Ivanow, pp. 43 and 48.
101. Abū Isḥāq, *Haft bāb*, text p. 43, translation pp. 43–44; Khayrkhwāh, *Kalām-i pīr*, text pp. 67–68, translation pp. 63–64, and also his *Faṣl*, pp. 2 and 4–5; tr. Ivanow, pp. 18–19 and 20–21.
102. On these categories and their particular characteristics, see Abū Isḥāq, *Haft bāb*, text pp. 21–22 and 48, translation pp. 20–21 and 48; Khayrkhwāh, *Kalām-i pīr*, text pp. 48, 92 and 106ff., translation pp. 40–41, 86–87 and 103ff.; also his *Taṣnīfāt*, pp. 2–3, 18, 22, 86, 89–90, 92–93 and 116ff., also *Faṣl*, pp. 6–7, 9, 11ff., 29–31 and 32–36; tr. Ivanow, pp. 22–23, 25–26, 28ff., 45–46 and 48–52, and Khākī Khurāsānī, *Dīwān*, pp. 84–85.
103. *Pandiyāt-i jawānmardī*, text pp. 48ff., 67, 81–82, 84, 96–97 and 98–100, translation pp. 30ff., 42, 51, 52, 59–60 and 61, also attacking those Shīʿīs, notably the Twelvers, who blindly followed their *ʿulamāʾ*; see also Khayrkhwāh, *Taṣnīfāt*, pp. 68 and 91, and also his *Faṣl*, pp. 32–33; tr. Ivanow, p. 49.
104. The best modern discussion of the spread of the Nizārī *daʿwa* on the Indian subcontinent during the early post-Alamūt and Anjudān periods may be found in Nanji, *Nizārī Tradition*, pp. 65–96, based on the *ginān* literature. The sectarian traditions are reflected also in the account of Misra, *Muslim Communities in Gujarat*, pp. 54–65. For earlier discussions on the subject, see W. Ivanow, 'Satpanth', in *Collectanea*: vol. 1, pp. 1–54; Ali, *Origin of the Khojāhs*, pp. 41–44, and Hollister, *Shīʿa*, pp. 353–362. See also Zawahir Noorally, 'Hazrat Pir Shamsuddin Sabzwari Multani'; J. H. Lakhani, 'Pir Sadar Din', and Abualy A. Aziz, 'Pir Hasan Kabiruddin', in *Great Ismaili Heroes*, pp. 83–86, 87–90 and 91–92; Enthoven, *Tribes and Castes of Bombay*,

vol. 2, pp. 217–230; A. Yusuf Ali, 'Khōdja', *EI*, vol. 2, pp. 960–962; W. Ivanow, 'Khodja', *SEI*, pp. 256–257, and W. Madelung, 'Khōdja', *EI2*, vol. 5, pp. 25–27.

105. The Indian Nizārīs have preserved genealogies (*shajaras*) and lists of their *pīrs*; see, for instance, ʿAlī Muḥammad Khān, *Mirat-i Ahmadi*, Supplement, Persian text, p. 123; Nanjiani, *Khoja Vrattant*, 1st ed., pp. 258–262; Pīrzāda, *Tawārīkh-i pīr*, vol. 2, pp. 23–24 and 265–272; Ivanow, 'Ismailitica', pp. 66–67; Ali, *Origin of the Khojāhs*, pp. 57–59, and Nanji, *Nizārī Tradition*, pp. 139–141.

106. Traditions concerning the initial phase of the Nizārī *daʿwa* in India are summarized in the *Jannatpuri*, a *ginān* attributed to Imām Shāh; this and other *ginān*s are translated into English in V. N. Hooda, 'Some Specimens of Satpanth Literature', in *Collectanea*: vol. 1, especially pp. 130ff.

107. For the relevant poems naming Qāsim Shāh, included in the so-called *Garbī ginān*s attributed to Pīr Shams al-Dīn, see Hooda, 'Some Specimens', pp. 60, 68, 70, 73 and 84.

108. Hooda, 'Some Specimens', p. 131.

109. Pīrzāda, *Tawārīkh-i pīr*, vol. 2, pp. 83–89, and Chunara, *Nūr-i mubīn*, pp. 495ff.

110. Hooda, 'Some Specimens', pp. 106, 114 and 131. According to Shihāb al-Dīn Shāh, *Khiṭābāt*, pp. 19–20 and 42, Ṣadr al-Dīn was a descendant of Muḥammad b. Ismāʿīl and he was sent to India from Sabzawār, Khurāsān, by Islām Shāh.

111. See Hamdani, *Ismāʿīlī Daʿwa in Northern India*, pp. 14–16, and Elliot and Dowson, *History of India*, vol. 1, pp. 483–497.

112. ʿAbd al-Ḥaqq Dihlawī, *Akhbār al-akhyār* (Delhi, 1891), pp. 204–205.

113. See W. Ivanow, 'The Sect of Imam Shah in Gujrat', *JBBRAS*, NS, 12 (1936), pp. 34 and 50–51. See also Pīrzāda, *Tawārīkh-i pīr*, vol. 2, pp. 99–101.

114. John A. Subhan, *Sufism, its Saints and Shrines* (Revised ed., Lucknow, 1960), p. 359.

115. The most detailed account of Imām Shāh and the sect named after him is contained in the already-noted *Manāzil al-aqṭāb*, written in Persian, which provides the main source for Ivanow's detailed study of the subject in his 'The Sect of Imam Shah in Gujrat', pp. 19–70. See also Pīrzāda, *Tawārīkh-i pīr*, vol. 2, pp. 103–108 and 121–126; Nanjiani, *Khoja Vrattant*, 1st ed., pp. 215–226; Chunara, *Nūr-i mubīn*, pp. 508ff., Abdul Hussain Nanjee, 'Syed Imamshah', in *Great Ismaili Heroes*, pp. 93–94; W. Ivanow, 'Imām-Shāh', *SEI*, p. 167, and A. A. A. Fyzee, 'Imām Shāh', *EI2*, vol. 3, p. 1163.

116. The account of this visit is related in the *Jannatpuri*, a *ginān* attributed to Imām Shāh and which is translated in Hooda, 'Some Specimens', pp. 122–137; the original text of this *ginān*, in Gujarātī written in Khōjkī script, was published in Bombay in 1905.

117. Khayrkhwāh, *Risāla*, in his *Taṣnīfāt*, pp. 54 and 60–61.

118. On this Imām-Shāhī revolt, see ʿAlī Muḥammad Khān, *Mirat-i Ahmadi*, Persian text, vol. 1, pp. 320–324; tr. Lokhandwala, pp. 286–289, and Ivanow, 'Sect of Imam Shah', pp. 52–54. See also Enthoven, *Tribes and Castes of Bombay*, vol. 2, pp. 150–157.

119. On different Mōmna groups and their history, see M. Nūrmuḥammad, *Ismaʿīlī Momin Komno Ithihas* (Bombay, 1936); M. Ibrāhīm, *Mashāyikh Chishti-nu Jiwancharita* (Bombay, 1372/1953); Enthoven, *Tribes and Castes of Bombay*, vol. 2, pp. 155–157, and vol. 3, pp. 62–64, and Misra, *Muslim Communities*, pp. 103–107.
120. Nanji, *Nizārī Tradition*, p. 93; see also Misra, *Muslim Communities*, pp. 64–65.
121. Nanji, *Nizārī Tradition*, pp. 99–130, and also his 'Towards a Hermeneutic of Qur'ānic and Other Narratives in Ismaʿili Thought', in *Approaches to Islam in Religious Studies*, ed. Richard C. Martin (Tucson, 1985), pp. 164–173; see also Ivanow, 'Satpanth', especially pp. 19–40.
122. See Nanji, *Nizārī Tradition*, pp. 144–145. The section on the tenth *Avatāra* contained in the version ascribed to Pīr Ṣadr al-Dīn, which is longer than Shams al-Dīn's version but shorter than Imām Shāh's version, is translated into English in Hooda, 'Some Specimens', pp. 112–115. The entire version ascribed to Imām Shāh and preserved by the Imām-Shāhīs is quoted and translated into English in Gulshan Khakee, 'The Dasa Avatāra of the Satpanthi Ismailis and Imam Shahis of Indo-Pakistan' (Ph.D. thesis, Harvard University, 1972), pp. 62–478.
123. See, for instance, S. C. Mukherji, *A Study of Vaisnavism in Ancient and Medieval Bengal* (Calcutta, 1966), pp. 207–219; J. Gonda, *Aspects of Early Visnuism* (Utrecht, 1954), pp. 124ff., and A. Danielou, *Hindu Polytheism* (New York, 1964), pp. 116ff.
124. See Tāmir, 'Furūʿ al-shajara', pp. 587ff., and also his *al-Imāma*, pp. 200ff.
125. On the origins and development of Nizārī Ismāʿīlism in the upper Oxus region, see *Ta'rīkh-i Badakhshān*, ed. A. N. Boldyrev (Leningrad, 1959), pp. 227ff. and 234ff., and a number of studies by Aleksandr A. Semenov, including his 'Iz oblasti religioznuikh verovany Shughnanskikh Ismailitov', pp. 523–561, and 'Istoriya Shughnana', *Protokoli Turkest. Kruzhka Liubiteley Arkheologii*, 21 (Tashkent, 1917), pp. 1–24; see also W. Barthold, *Guzīda-yi maqālāt-i taḥqīqī*, tr. K. Kishāvarz (Tehran, 1358/1979), pp. 326ff.; W. Barthold et al., 'Badakhshān', *EI2*, vol. 1, pp. 851–854, and V. Minorsky, 'Shughnān', *EI*, vol. 4, pp. 389–391, where the Russian sources are cited.
126. Firishta, *Ta'rīkh-i Firishta*, ed. J. Briggs (Bombay, 1832), especially vol. 2, pp. 213–231, and later editions (Cawnpore, 1301/1884), vol. 2, pp. 110–118; (Nawal Kishore, n.d.), vol. 2, pp. 110–118; English translation, *History of the Rise of the Mahomedan Power in India*, tr. J. Briggs (London, 1829), vol. 3, pp. 216ff. John Briggs (1785–1875) omitted the section about Shāh Ṭāhir from his almost complete translation and only the references to Shāh Ṭāhir's diplomatic mediations are contained in the section on Burhān Niẓām Shāh. Earlier, Jonathan Scott (1754–1829) produced a partial English translation of this work entitled *Ferishta's History of Dekkan* (Shrewsbury, 1794), but Scott, too, omitted the section about Shāh Ṭāhir and included, in vol. 1, pp. 363ff., merely references to his diplomatic services. The earliest reference to Shāh Ṭāhir appears in Sām Mīrzā, *Tuḥfa-yi Sāmī*, ed. V. Dastgirdī (Tehran, 1314/1936), p. 29; ed. R. Humāyūn-Farrukh (Tehran, 1347/1968), pp. 43–44, a biographical work on poets written in 957/1550 by one of the sons of the

Ṣafawid Shāh Ismāʿīl who was a contemporary of Shāh Ṭāhir. Shāh Ṭāhir and his sons are also mentioned in a few works written slightly earlier than the *Ta'rīkh-i Firishta*; see ʿAbd al-Qādir Badā'ūnī, *Muntakhab al-tawārīkh*, ed. Aḥmad ʿAlī et al. (Calcutta, 1864–1869), vol. 1, pp. 482–488 and 490–491; English translation, *Muntakhabu-t-tawārīkh*, tr. George S. A. Ranking and W. H. Lowe (Calcutta, 1884–1898), vol. 1, pp. 624–632 and 635–636; ʿAlī b. ʿAzīz Ṭabāṭabā, *Burhān-i ma'āthir* (Ḥaydarābād, 1936), pp. 251–270, 274ff., 281ff., 291, 308, 314, 324–326, 338–339, 361, 381, 433, 448–450, 452–454, 502–503, 505, 525, 557 and 584; abridged English translation, *The History of the Niẓām Shāhī Kings of Aḥmadnagar*, tr. Woseley Haig, in *Indian Antiquary*, 49 (1920), pp. 166–167, 177–188, 197ff., 217ff., and 50 (1921), pp. 1ff., 30, 196, 229–230, 231–232, and 51 (1922), pp. 34–35, and 52 (1923), pp. 35 and 259; Ṭabāṭabā was in the service of the Niẓām-Shāhs and began to compose his history in 1000/1592 at the request of Burhān Niẓām Shāh II; Amīn Aḥmad Rāzī, *Haft iqlīm*, vol. 3, pp. 203–207, and al-Shūshtarī, *Majālis al-mu'minīn*, vol. 2, pp. 234–240. Later works do not add any details to the accounts of Firishta, Ṭabāṭabā and al-Shūshtarī; see ʿAbd al-Bāqī Nihāwandī, *Ma'āthir-i Raḥīmī*, vol. 2, pp. 413–414; Khāfī Khān, *Muntakhab al-lubāb*, ed. Kabīr al-Dīn Aḥmad et al. (Calcutta, 1860–1925), vol. 3, pp. 162–182; Mīr ʿAbd al-Razzāq, *Bahāristān-i sukhan*, ed. S. Abdul Wahab Bukhari (Madras, 1957), pp. 403–406; Ādhar, *Ātashkada*, Bombay ed., pp. 238–239; Tehran ed., pp. 239–240; Hidāyat, *Riyāḍ al-ʿārifīn*, pp. 160–161; Maʿṣūm ʿAlī Shāh, *Ṭarā'iq al-ḥaqā'iq*, vol. 3, pp. 133–150; Shihāb al-Dīn Shāh, *Khiṭābāt*, pp. 40–41, and Fidā'ī, *Hidāyat al-mu'minīn*, pp. 119–132, confusing Shāh Ṭāhir with Muḥammad b. Islām Shāh, the thirty-first Qāsim-Shāhī Imām. Of the secondary sources, mention may be made of Ivanow, 'A Forgotten Branch of the Ismailis', pp. 57ff.; also his 'Ṭāhir', *SEI*, p. 560; H. Hosain, 'Shāh Ṭāhir of the Deccan', *New Indian Antiquary*, 2 (1939), pp. 460–473, reprinted in *A Volume of Indian and Iranian Studies Presented to Sir E. Denison Ross*, ed. S. M. Katre and P. K. Gode (Bombay, 1939), pp. 147–160; Masoom R. Kazimi, 'Shah Tahir-ul-Hussaini', *Indo-Iranica*, 18 (1965), pp. 41–49; R. Shyam, *The Kingdom of Ahmadnagar* (Delhi, 1966), pp. 63–64, 66, 72–76, 80–83, 84, 87ff., 93–94, 368, 379–380 and 392; ʿĀrif Tāmir, 'Ṭāhir Shāh al-Nizārī al-Alamūtī', *al-Dirāsāt al-Adabiyya* (al-Jāmiʿa al-Lubnāniyya), 1 (1959), pp. 83–93; also his *al-Imāma*, pp. 202–208; Ghālib, *Aʿlām*, pp. 321–322, and Ṣafā, *Ta'rīkh-i adabiyyāt*, vol. 5, part 2, pp. 662–670. See also Charles Rieu, *Catalogue of the Persian Manuscripts in the British Museum* (London, 1879–1883), vol. 1, pp. 393–396; Storey, *Persian Literature*, vol. 1, pp. 740–741, and Poonawala, *Bio*, pp. 271–275.

127. See several works by Ivanow, 'An Ismailitic Pedigree', pp. 403–406; 'A Forgotten Branch of the Ismailis', pp. 70–79; *Guide*, pp. 111–112; *Ismaili Literature*, pp. 166–167, and Poonawala, *Bio*, p. 281.

128. See Tāmir, 'Furūʿ al-shajara', pp. 597–598, and also his *al-Imāma*, pp. 208–216.

129. On Nizār II, see Shihāb al-Dīn Shāh, *Khiṭābāt*, p. 43; Fidā'ī, *Hidāyat al-mu'minīn*, pp. 140–141; Tāmir, *al-Imāma*, p. 225; Ghālib, *Ta'rīkh*, pp. 320–

322; also his *Aʿlām*, pp. 573–574; Ivanow, 'Tombs of Some Persian Ismaili Imams', pp. 56–59, describing Nizār's mausoleum at Kahak; also his *Ismaili Literature*, p. 148; Hollister, *Shīʿa*, pp. 335–336, based on Ivanow; Pourjavady and Wilson, 'Ismāʿīlīs and Niʿmatullāhīs', pp. 116–117, and Poonawala, *Bio*, pp. 281–282.

130. See Shihāb al-Dīn Shāh, *Khiṭābāt*, p. 43, and Aḥmad ʿAlī Khān Vazīrī, *Jughrāfiyā-yi Kirmān*, ed. M. I. Bāstānī Pārīzī (Tehran, 1353/1974), pp. 157 and 199, an important historical geography of Kirmān written in 1291/1874 and first published in *Farhang-i Īrān Zamīn*, 14 (1345–1346/1966–1967), pp. 5–286. For some references to Nizārī activities in Kirmān and adjacent regions during the subsequent decades, see Muḥammad Kāẓim Marwī, *ʿĀlamārā-yi Nādirī*, ed. N. D. Miklukho-Maklai (Moscow, 1960–1966), vol. 1, pp. 438 and 549ff.; ed. Muḥammad A. Riyāḥī (Tehran, 1364/1985), vol. 1, pp. 283 and 356ff.

131. The sectarian sources do not relate any particular details on this imām; see Fidāʾī, *Hidāyat al-muʾminīn*, pp. 141–142; Tāmir, *al-Imāma*, pp. 225–226; Ghālib, *Taʾrīkh*, pp. 323–325, and also his *Aʿlām*, pp. 159–160.

132. Aḥmad ʿAlī Khān Vazīrī, *Taʾrīkh-i Kirmān*, ed. Muḥammad I. Bāstānī Pārīzī (2nd ed., Tehran, 1352/1973), p. 542.

133. Vazīrī, *Taʾrīkh*, p. 543. The sectarian sources relate only some legendary and anachronistic details on Imām Ḥasan ʿAlī; see Shihāb al-Dīn Shāh, *Khiṭābāt*, p. 43, stating that Nādir Shāh persecuted this imām and eventually blinded him, a story repeated by Fidāʾī, *Hidāyat al-muʾminīn*, pp. 142–143; see also Tāmir, *al-Imāma*, p. 226; Ghālib, *Taʾrīkh*, pp. 326–328, and his *Aʿlām*, pp. 220–221.

134. See Shihāb al-Dīn Shāh, *Khiṭābāt*, p. 43; Fidāʾī, *Hidāyat al-muʾminīn*, p. 143; Tāmir, *al-Imāma*, p. 226; Ghālib, *Taʾrīkh*, pp. 329–330, and his *Aʿlām*, pp. 430–431, stating that Imām Qāsim ʿAlī married one of the daughters of Shāh Ṭahmāsp II (1135–1145/1722–1732), the last effective Ṣafawid ruler.

135. The most detailed account of this imām is contained in Vazīrī, *Taʾrīkh*, pp. 543–565; see also his *Jughrāfiyā*, pp. 72, 81, 86 and 157. Other chroniclers of the Zand and Qājār dynasties of Persia make briefer references to Imām Abu'l-Ḥasan; see the *Dhayl* (continuation) written by Mīrzā ʿAbd al-Karīm b. ʿAlī Riḍā al-Sharīf to Muḥammad Ṣādiq Nāmī's *Taʾrīkh-i gītī-gushāy*, ed. S. Nafīsī (Tehran, 1317/1938), p. 327; ed. ʿAzīz Allāh Bayāt (Tehran, 1363/1984), pp. 97–98; ʿAlī Riḍā b. ʿAbd al-Karīm Shīrāzī, *Taʾrīkh-i Zandiyya*, ed. E. Beer (Leiden, 1888), pp. 52–56; ed. Ghulām Riḍā Varahrām (Tehran, 1365/1986), pp. 74–77, based on Beer's edition; Muḥammad Ḥāshim Āṣaf Rustam al-Ḥukamāʾ, *Rustam al-tawārīkh*, ed. M. Mushīrī (Tehran, 1348/1969), pp. 378 and 415; Hidāyat, *Rawḍat al-ṣafā-yi Nāṣirī*, vol. 9, pp. 250, 252 and 255; Muḥammad Ḥasan Khān Iʿtimād al-Salṭana, *Taʾrīkh-i muntaẓam-i Nāṣirī* (Tehran, 1298–1300/1881–1883), vol. 3, pp. 53–54, and Ḥasan Fasāʾī, *Fārs-nāma-yi Nāṣirī*, vol. 1, p. 232; English translation, *History of Persia under Qājār Rule*, tr. H. Busse (New York, 1972), pp. 37–38. Shihāb al-Dīn Shāh, *Khiṭābāt*, p. 43, merely mentions this imām's name as Bāqir Shāh, while other sectarian sources relate few reliable details and omit the information

found in the Persian chronicles; see Hooda, 'Some Specimens', p. 111; Fidā'ī, *Hidāyat al-mu'minīn*, pp. 143–144; Chunara, *Nūr-i mubīn*, pp. 560ff.; Tāmir, *al-Imāma*, p. 227; Ghālib, *Ta'rīkh*, pp. 331–332, and also his *Aʿlām*, pp. 392–393. See also Malcolm, *History of Persia*, vol. 2, pp. 109–110; tr. Hairat, vol. 2, p. 416; the introduction of Sir H. Jones Brydges to his English translation of ʿAbd al-Razzāq Dunbulī's *Ma'āthir-i sulṭāniyya*, entitled *The Dynasty of the Kajars* (London, 1833), p. 123; Sykes, *Ten Thousand Miles in Persia*, p. 68; also his *A History of Persia* (3rd ed., London, 1930), vol. 2, pp. 284–285; Browne, *A History of Persian Literature in Modern Times*, p. 148; ʿAbbās Fayḍ, *Khulāṣat al-maqāl* (Qumm, 1330/1951), pp. 552–553; Hollister, *Shīʿa*, p. 336; Dihgān, *Kār-nāma*, pp. 40–42; Maḥmūd H. Kirmānī, *Ta'rīkh-i mufaṣṣal-i Kirmān* (1350/1971), pp. 215–227; M. Roschanzamir, *Die Zand-Dynastie* (Hamburg, 1970), pp. 105–106; Pourjavady and Wilson, 'Ismāʿīlīs and Niʿmatullāhīs', pp. 119–121; John R. Perry, *Karim Khan Zand* (Chicago, 1979), pp. 135–136; M. Bāmdād, *Sharḥ-i ḥāl-i rijāl-i Īrān* (Tehran, 1347–1350/1968–1971), vol. 1, pp. 37–38, and H. Busse, 'Abu'l-Ḥasan Khan Maḥallātī', *EIR*, vol. 1, p. 310.

136. On the revival of the Niʿmat Allāhī order in Persia and the renewed association between this Ṣūfī order and the Nizārī Imāms, see Vazīrī, *Ta'rīkh*, pp. 556–560; Maʿṣūm ʿAlī Shāh, *Ṭarā'iq al-ḥaqā'iq*, vol. 3, pp. 170–192; Pourjavady and Wilson, *Kings of Love*, pp. 93–135, citing further Niʿmat Allāhī sources; Michel de Miras, *La Méthode spirituelle d'un maître du Soufisme Iranien Nur ʿAli-Shah* (Paris, 1973), pp. 21–33, and M. Humāyūnī, *Ta'rīkh-i silsilihā-yi ṭarīqa-yi Niʿmat Allāhiyya* (Tehran, 1358/1979), pp. 36–74.

137. See Ivanow, 'Tombs of Some Persian Ismaili Imams', pp. 60–61. The grave attributed to Imām Abu'l-Ḥasan is still intact in one of the chambers of the Mushtāqiyya, but the mausoleum of this imām's relatives which was located near Mushtāqiyya, as reported by Ivanow, who visited the site in 1937, was no longer in existence when the author visited Kirmān in 1975. Imām Abu'l-Ḥasan was a learned man and a friend of the Ṣūfīs; he also patronized the local artists. The author possesses a copy of the *Dīwān* of the famous Persian poet Ḥāfiẓ, with several miniatures of the Zand period, produced for the private library of this imām.

138. Muḥammad Taqī Lisān al-Mulk Sipihr, *Nāsikh al-tawārīkh*; *ta'rīkh-i Qājāriyya* (Tabrīz, 1319/1901), vol. 1, p. 32; ed. Muḥammad Bāqir Bihbūdī (Tehran, 1344/1965), vol. 1, p. 70; hereafter cited as *Qājāriyya*.

139. On Shāh Khalīl Allāh III, see Hidāyat, *Rawḍat al-ṣafā-yi Nāṣirī*, vol. 9, pp. 551–553; Lisān al-Mulk, *Qājāriyya*, Tabrīz ed., vol. 1, p. 134; ed. Bihbūdī, vol. 1, pp. 292–294; Iʿtimād al-Salṭana, *Muntaẓam-i Nāṣirī*, vol. 3, p. 116; also his *Ṣadr al-tawārīkh*, ed. M. Mushīrī (Tehran, 1349/1970), p. 84; Shihāb al-Dīn Shāh, *Khiṭābāt*, pp. 43–44; Fidā'ī, *Hidāyat al-mu'minīn*, pp. 144–145; Chunara, *Nūr-i mubīn*, pp. 570ff.; Tāmir, *al-Imāma*, p. 227; Ghālib, *Ta'rīkh*, pp. 333–334, and his *Aʿlām*, pp. 287–288. We have already cited the references of the contemporary European travellers Rousseau and Fraser to Shāh Khalīl Allāh; see also Watson, *History of Persia*, pp. 191–192; Browne, *A History of Persian Literature in Modern Times*, p. 148; Fayḍ, *Khulāṣat al-maqāl*, pp. 553–556; Hollister, *Shīʿa*, p. 337; H. Algar, *Religion and State in Iran,*

1785–1906 (Berkeley, 1969), pp. 55–56, and Bāmdād, *Sharḥ-i ḥāl-i rijāl*, vol. 1, pp. 486–487.

140. On these Niʿmat Allāhī Sayyids, the maternal grandfather and uncle of Āghā Khān I, see Shīrwānī, *Bustān al-siyāḥa*, p. 530; Maʿṣūm ʿAlī Shāh, *Ṭarāʾiq al-ḥaqāʾiq*, vol. 3, pp. 190, 209 and 263–264, and Pourjavady and Wilson, 'Ismāʿīlīs and Niʿmatullāhīs', pp. 121–123.

141. See Masʿūd Mīrzā Ẓill al-Sulṭān, *Sargudhasht-i Masʿūdī* (Tehran, 1325/1907), p. 197. For Fatḥ ʿAlī Shāh's religious attitude and policy, see Algar, *Religion and State in Iran*, pp. 45–72.

142. Ḥasan ʿAlī Shāh, Āghā Khān I, wrote an autobiography, the *ʿIbrat-afzā*, relating the events of his youth and his encounters with the Qājār regime in Persia, culminating in his permanent settlement in British India. The *ʿIbrat-afzā* was lithographed in Bombay in 1278/1862, reprinted with numerous typographical errors by Ḥusayn Kūhī Kirmānī (Tehran, 1325/1946), and also published in M. Sāʿī, *Āqā Khān Maḥallātī va firqa-yi Ismāʿīliyya* (Tehran, 1329/1950), pp. 25–68. A Gujarātī translation of this work appeared in India soon after its first publication. According to Ivanow, *Guide*, p. 114, and also his *Ismaili Literature*, pp. 148–149, the *ʿIbrat-afzā* was actually written on behalf of the Āghā Khān by Mīrzā Aḥmad Viqār Shīrāzī (d. 1298/1881), son of the celebrated poet Viṣāl, who stayed briefly with the imām in Bombay in 1266/1850; see also M. Navābī, *Khānidān-i Viṣāl-i Shīrāzī* (Tehran, 1335/1956), pp. 56ff. and 74. Fidāʾī Khurāsānī devoted a large section of his *Hidāyat al-muʾminīn*, pp. 146–176, to the first Āghā Khān and his deeds. The sections on the Āghā Khāns appearing in the *Hidāyat al-muʾminīn* were evidently written mainly around 1328/1910 and added to Fidāʾī's original text by Mūsā Khān b. Muḥammad Khān Khurāsānī, who died in Poona in 1937. Mūsā Khān and his father were in the service of the first Āghā Khān and his descendants; see Daftary's review of the *Hidāyat al-muʾminīn* in *Nashr-i Dānish*, 4 (June–July, 1984), pp. 32–37. Shihāb al-Dīn Shāh, the eldest grandson of Āghā Khān I, who wrote his *Khiṭābāt* in Bombay during the latter part of his grandfather's imāmate, merely names this imām, pp. 44 and 45. For the notices of other Ismāʿīlī authors on Āghā Khān I, see Chunara, *Nūr-i mubīn*, pp. 583–623; Tāmir, *al-Imāma*, p. 228; Ghālib, *Taʾrīkh*, pp. 335–338, and his *Aʿlām*, pp. 214–219. See also Watson, *History of Persia*, pp. 331–334; Sykes, *Ten Thousand Miles*, pp. 69–70; Naoroji M. Dumasia, *A Brief History of the Aga Khan* (Bombay, 1903), pp. 66–95; also his *The Aga Khan and His Ancestors* (Bombay, 1939), pp. 25–59; Fayḍ, *Khulāṣat al-maqāl*, pp. 556–561; Muḥammad ʿAlī Muʿallim Ḥabīb Ābādī, *Makārim al-āthār* (Tehran, 1377–1397/1957–1977), vol. 3, pp. 662–672; Bāmdād, *Sharḥ-i ḥāl-i rijāl*, vol. 1, pp. 354–358; Ḥ. Maḥbūbī Ardakānī, 'Āqā Khān Maḥallātī', *EII*, vol. 1, pp. 111–112; H. A. R. Gibb, 'Agha Khān', *EI2*, vo.. 1, p. 246; H. Algar, 'Maḥallātī, Āghā Khān', *EI2*, vol. 5, pp. 1221–1222, and his 'Āqā Khan I Maḥallātī', *EIR*, vol. 2, pp. 170–172. The Qājār chronicles and modern sources dealing specifically with the first Āghā Khān's political activities in Persia will be cited further on.

143. Āghā Khān Maḥallātī, Ḥasan ʿAlī Shāh, *ʿIbrat-afzā*, ed. Kūhī Kirmānī, p. 7;

our subsequent references to the *ʿIbrat-afzā* are to this edition; Lisān al-Mulk, *Qājāriyya*, Tabrīz ed., vol. 1, p. 252; ed. Bihbūdī, vol. 2, p. 158; Iʿtimād al-Salṭana, *Muntaẓam-i Nāṣirī*, vol. 3, p. 161, and Aḥmad Mīrzā ʿAḍud al-Dawla, *Taʾrīkh-i ʿAḍudī*, ed. Ḥ. Kūhī Kirmānī (Tehran, 1328/1949), pp. 9 and 69; ed. ʿAbd al-Ḥusayn Navāʾī (Tehran, 1355/1976), pp. 21–22, 127, 310 and 319.

144. Āghā Khān I's governorship of Kirmān and his subsequent military confrontations with the Qājār regime are related in the *ʿIbrat-afzā*, especially pp. 9–56, reflecting the Āghā Khān's own version of the events. The same events, depicted as acts of revolt, are recorded in a number of Qājār chronicles; see especially Hidāyat, *Rawḍat al-ṣafā-yi Nāṣirī*, vol. 10, pp. 169, 249–253 and 259–261; Lisān al-Mulk, *Qājāriyya*, Tabrīz ed., vol. 2, pp. 291, 331, 338–341, 342–343 and 344; ed. Bihbūdī, vol. 2, pp. 248, 334–335, 350–356, 358–360 and 364; Iʿtimād al-Salṭana, *Muntaẓam-i Nāṣirī*, vol. 3, pp. 165, 167, 173–174, 175–176 and 177; and his *Mirʾāt al-buldān-i Nāṣirī* (Tehran, 1294–1297/1877–1880), vol. 1, pp. 539, 570, 578 and 579; ed. P. Nūrī ʿAlāʾ and M. ʿAlī Sipānlū (Tehran, 1364/1985), vol. 1, pp. 623, 653, 661 and 662; see also Muḥammad Jaʿfar Khūrmūjī, *Ḥaqāʾiq al-akhbār-i Nāṣirī*, ed. Ḥusayn Khadīv Jam (2nd ed., Tehran, 1363/1984), pp. 25 and 28–31; Vazīrī, *Taʾrīkh*, pp. 602–604 and 608–613; also his *Jurghrāfiyā*, pp. 64, 66, 106–107, 124, 162–163 and 191, and Yaḥyā Aḥmadī Kirmānī, *Farmāndihān-i Kirmān*, ed. M. I. Bāstānī Pārīzī (2nd ed., Tehran, 1354/1975), pp. 72–82, originally published in *Farhang-i Īrān Zamīn*, 12 (1343/1964), pp. 24–30. Amongst the works of modern Persian historians and writers dealing with the subject, mention may be made of F. Ādamīyat, *Amīr Kabīr va Īrān* (3rd ed., Tehran, 1348/1969), pp. 251–258; I. Rāʾīn, *Ḥuqūq bigīrān-i Ingilīs dar Īrān* (Tehran, 1347/1968), pp. 332–350, and M. I. Bāstānī Pārīzī, *Farmānfarmā-yi ʿālam* (Tehran, 1364/1985), pp. 305–323, 337–342, 345–346, 352–353 and 366. See also Zawahir Noorally, 'The First Agha Khan and the British, 1838–1868' (M.A. thesis, University of London, 1964); Nadia Eboo, 'The Revolt of the Āghā Khān Maḥallātī and the Establishment of the Nizārī Imāmate in India' (M.A. thesis, Victoria University of Manchester, 1979), and H. Algar, 'The Revolt of Āghā Khān Maḥallātī and the Transference of the Ismāʿīlī Imamate to India', *SI*, 29 (1969), especially pp. 61–81, the best modern account on the subject.

145. Ḥabīb Allāh Qāʾānī, *Dīwān* (Bombay, 1322/1904), pp. 54–55; ed. Muḥammad J. Maḥjūb (Tehran, 1336/1957), pp. 180–181.

146. Āghā Khān Maḥallātī, *ʿIbrat-afzā*, pp. 23–24. Āghā Khān's successor as governor, Fīrūz Mīrzā Farmānfarmā, who participated in the operations at Bam, recalls this incident in his *Safar-nāma-yi Kirmān va Balūchistān*, ed. M. Niẓām-Māfī (Tehran, 1342/1963), p. 7.

147. *ʿIbrat-afzā*, pp. 24–25.

148. Parts of the high walls and turrets encircling this compound are still in existence in Maḥallāt, in addition to a Ḥusayniyya built by Āghā Khān I. One of the buildings constructed by the Āghā Khān was later used as a residence by the Qājār governors of the locality; see A. Houtum-Schindler, *Eastern Persian Irak* (London, 1896), p. 92, and Nāṣir al-Dīn Shāh, *Safar-nāma-yi ʿIrāq-i ʿAjam*, p. 31, relating that many of the houses in the Āghā Khān's

compound were already destroyed when this Qājār monarch passed through Maḥallāt in 1309/1892.

149. *ʿIbrat-afzā*, p. 13.

150. *ʿIbrat-afzā*, pp. 12–16; Ẓill al-Sulṭān, *Sargudhasht-i Masʿūdī*, pp. 197–198; Shīrwānī, *Riyāḍ al-siyāḥa*, p. 690; Maʿṣūm ʿAlī Shāh, *Ṭarāʾiq al-ḥaqāʾiq*, vol. 3, pp. 280ff., 286, 327–328 and 390; Pourjavady and Wilson, 'Ismāʿīlīs and Niʿmatullāhīs', pp. 125–131; Pourjavady and Wilson, *Kings of Love*, pp. 147–151 and 155–158; Algar, 'Revolt of Āghā Khān', pp. 73–74; Humāyūnī, *Niʿmat Allāhiyya*, pp. 184–185 and 191, and Gramlich, *Die schiitischen Derwischorden*, vol. 1, pp. 50ff.

151. *ʿIbrat-afzā*, p. 25; Fidāʾī, *Hidāyat al-muʾminīn*, p. 153, and Lisān al-Mulk, *Qājāriyya*, Tabrīz ed., vol. 2, p. 331; ed. Bihbūdī, vol. 2, p. 335.

152. Muḥammad Maʿṣūm Shīrāzī (Maʿṣūm ʿAlī Shāh), *Tuḥfat al-ḥaramayn* (Bombay, 1306/1889), pp. 292–297, reprinted with the same pagination in Tehran in 1362/1983, and also his *Ṭarāʾiq al-ḥaqāʾiq*, vol. 3, pp. 399, 528 and 561.

153. *ʿIbrat-afzā*, pp. 25–26.

154. Ibid., p. 27.

155. On these documents, see Vazīrī, *Taʾrīkh*, pp. 608–609, and Bāstānī Pārīzī's comments therein, and Bāstānī Pārīzī, *Farmānfarmā-yi ʿālam*, pp. 305–306.

156. Āghā Khān I relates his account of this and subsequent campaigns in Kirmān in *ʿIbrat-afzā*, pp. 30–47.

157. See Ādamīyat, *Amīr Kabīr*, p. 255, citing a letter written in 1262/1846 by Ḥājjī Mīrzā Āqāsī to the British legation in Tehran.

158. *ʿIbrat-afzā*, pp. 47–54.

159. See *Correspondence Relating to Persia and Affghanistan* (London, 1839), pp. 36–37 and 64, citing also a relevant dispatch sent in 1837 by John McNeill, the British minister in Tehran, to Henry J. Palmerston, the foreign secretary in London.

160. The date of 17 Dhu'l-Qaʿda 1258 A.H., mentioned in Āghā Khān, *ʿIbrat-afzā*, ed. Kūhī Kirmānī, p. 56, and reproduced in Algar, 'Revolt of Āghā Khān', p. 77, is a misprint; it is inconsistent with the dates of the Āghā Khān's subsequent activities in Afghanistan. See also Isaac N. Allen, *Diary of a March through Sinde and Affghanistan* (London, 1843), pp. 200–205, relating interesting details on the situation of Āghā Khān I in Afghanistan.

161. Āghā Khān, *ʿIbrat-afzā*, pp. 59ff.; William F. P. Napier, *The Conquest of Scinde* (London, 1845), pp. 369, 372 and 404–405; also his *The History of General Sir Charles Napier's Conquest of Scinde* (2nd ed., London, 1857), pp. 224, 226 and 245; also his *History of General Sir Charles Napier's Administration of Scinde* (London, 1851), pp. 75–76, and his *The Life and Opinions of General Sir Charles James Napier* (London, 1857), vol. 2, p. 342, and vol. 3, pp. 45 and 127; see also J. Outram, *The Conquest of Scinde: A Commentary* (Edinburgh, 1846), pp. 186ff.; Richard F. Burton, *Scinde* (London, 1851), vol. 1, pp. 190–196; Frederic J. Goldsmid, *James Outram, A Biography* (London, 1880), pp. 293ff.; Dumasia, *A Brief History of the Aga Khan*, pp. 77–82; also his *The Aga Khan*, pp. 37–42, and H. T. Lambrick, *Sir Charles Napier and Sind* (Oxford, 1952), pp. 157ff.

162. Āghā Khān, *ʿIbrat-afzā*, pp. 64–65 and 70–73; Hidāyat, *Rawḍat al-ṣafā-yi*

Nāṣirī, vol. 10, p. 306; Iʿtimād al-Salṭana, *Mirʾāt al-buldān*, lithographed ed., vol. 1, pp. 589–590; ed. Nūrī ʿAlāʾ and Sipānlū, vol. 1, p. 673; Vazīrī, *Taʾrīkh*, pp. 612–613; Fīrūz Mīrzā Farmānfarmā, *Safar-nāma-yi Kirmān*, p. 30; Sykes, *Ten Thousand Miles*, pp. 78 and 105; Chunara, *Nūr-i mubīn*, p. 611; Fayḍ, *Khulāṣat al-maqāl*, pp. 560–561, and Abu'l-Ḥasan Buzurg-Ummīd, *Az māst kih bar māst* (2nd ed., Tehran, 1363/1984), pp. 15–16, written by Sardār Abu'l-Ḥasan Khān's grandson, Mukhbir Humāyūn (1878–1966), the younger brother of the author's maternal grandfather Nāṣir Qulī Āghā Khān Mukhbir al-Sulṭān (1873–1941). A warrior and an accomplished hunter, Sardār Abu'l-Ḥasan Khān was also a calligrapher; the author is in possession of an illuminated Qur'ān produced by him in 1291/1874 for his Qājār wife.

163. *ʿIbrat-afzā*, pp. 65ff. and 71ff.
164. See Ādamīyat, *Amīr Kabīr*, pp. 254–256, and Dumasia, *The Aga Khan*, pp. 43ff.
165. *ʿIbrat-afzā*, pp. 77–78, and Ādamīyat, *Amīr Kabīr*, pp. 256–257. See also Khān Malik Sāsānī, *Siyāsatgarān-i dawra-yi Qājār* (Tehran, 1338/1959), pp. 59 and 124.
166. *ʿIbrat-afzā*, pp. 80–81.
167. Iʿtimād al-Salṭana, *Muntaẓam-i Nāṣirī*, vol. 3, p. 306, and Buzurg-Ummīd, *Az māst*, p. 18, relating that yet another elephant was sent from India to Nāṣir al-Dīn Shāh by the Āghā Khān's family in 1304/1886–1887.
168. See Nāṣir al-Dīn Shāh Qājār, *Safar-nāma-yi ʿatabāt*, ed. Īraj Afshār (Tehran, 1363/1984), pp. 98, 118, 119, 128 and 146, and Muʿallim Ḥabīb Ābādī, *Makārim al-āthār*, vol. 3, pp. 670–672.
169. See Ali, *Origin of the Khojāhs*, pp. 45ff.; Hollister, *Shīʿa*, pp. 364–370, and Fyzee, *Cases in the Muhammadan Law of India and Pakistan*, pp. 530ff.
170. The long judgement pertaining to the case of 'Advocate General of Bombay v. Muhammad Husen Huseni', known as the Aga Khan Case, as noted, was reported in *Bombay High Court Reports*, 12 (1866), pp. 323–363, published separately in Bombay in 1867. The text of the judgement may also be found in Picklay, *History of the Ismailis*, pp. 113–170, and in Fyzee, *Cases in the Muhammadan Law of India and Pakistan*, pp. 504–549.
171. On Āqā ʿAlī Shāh, see Fidāʾī, *Hidāyat al-muʾminīn*, pp. 176–183 and 193; Tāmir, *al-Imāma*, pp. 228–229; Ghālib, *Taʾrīkh*, pp. 339–341; also his *Aʿlām*, pp. 373–376; Dumasia, *A Brief History of the Aga Khan*, pp. 96–99; also his *The Aga Khan*, pp. 60ff.; Hollister, *Shīʿa*, p. 371; Bāmdād, *Sharḥ-i ḥāl-i rijāl*, vol. 2, p. 379; Maḥbūbī Ardakānī, 'Āqā Khān Maḥallātī', *EII*, vol. 1, p. 112, and Algar, 'Aqā Khan II', *EIR*, vol. 2, pp. 172–173.
172. On Āghā Khān II's association with the Niʿmat Allāhī order, see Maʿṣūm ʿAlī Shāh, *Ṭarāʾiq al-ḥaqāʾiq*, vol. 3, pp. 328, 413, 434, 445–446 and 528; also his *Tuḥfat al-ḥaramayn*, pp. 295 and 297–298; Humāyūnī, *Niʿmat Allāhiyya*, pp. 194, 259, 267–270, 277–279, 285–287 and 289, citing Ṣafī ʿAlī Shāh's own unpublished account of his visit to Āghā Khān II in Bombay; Pourjavady and Wilson, 'Ismāʿīlīs and Niʿmatullāhīs', pp. 131–132, and Pourjavady and Wilson, *Kings of Love*, pp. 155ff. and 252–253.
173. Aside from Shihāb al-Dīn Shāh's already-noted *Khiṭābāt-i ʿāliya*, see his

unfinished *Risāla dar ḥaqīqat-i dīn*, ed. and tr. W. Ivanow (Bombay, 1933). Subsequently, Ivanow produced a facsimile edition of this *Risāla* from its autograph copy in 1947 (reprinted in 1955) in Bombay, published in the series of the Ismaili Society, Bombay; Ivanow's English translation of the *Risāla* entitled *True Meaning of Religion*, appeared in the same series in 1947 and 1956. Shihāb al-Dīn Shāh's *Risāla* has been translated also into Arabic, Gujarātī, Sindhī and Urdu; see Poonawala, *Bio*, p. 284.

174. Many details on Āghā Khān III's life and political career are contained in his own memoirs entitled *The Memoirs of Aga Khan: World Enough and Time* (London, 1954); French translation by Jane Fillion (Paris, 1955). Sulṭān Muḥammad Shāh has been the subject of a number of modern biographies; see especially Dumasia, *A Brief History of the Aga Khan*, pp. 100–154 and 168–176; and his *The Aga Khan*, pp. 62–338; Sirdar Ikbal Ali Shah, *The Prince Aga Khan: An Authentic Life Story* (London, 1933); also his *The Controlling Minds of Asia* (London, 1937), pp. 85–124; Harry J. Greenwall, *His Highness the Aga Khan: Imam of the Ismailis* (London, 1952); S. Jackson, *The Aga Khan, Prince, Prophet and Statesman* (London, 1952); Qayyum A. Malick, *His Royal Highness Prince Agakhan III, Guide, Philosopher and Friend of the World of Islam* (2nd ed., Karachi, 1969) and W. Frischauer, *The Aga Khans* (London, 1970), pp. 53–213. See also Fidā'ī, *Hidāyat al-mu'minīn*, pp. 183–189 and 193–199; Chunara, *Nūr-i mubīn*, pp. 631–760; Tāmir, *al-Imāma*, pp. 229–237; Ghālib, *Ta'rīkh*, pp. 342–401; also his *Aʿlām*, pp. 459–479; Ḥusayn, *Ṭā'ifat al-Ismāʿīliyya*, pp. 114–129; A. le Chatelier, 'Age Khan', *Revue du Monde Musulman*, 1 (1906), pp. 48–85; Hollister, *Shīʿa*, pp. 371–377; Maḥbūbī Ardakānī, 'Āqā Khān Maḥallātī', *EII*, vol. 1, pp. 112–113; Kenneth A. Ballhatchet, 'Aga Khan', *Encyclopaedia Britannica*, vol. 1, pp. 317–318, and H. Algar, 'Āqā Khan III', *EIR*, vol. 2, pp. 173–175.

175. Aga Khan, *Memoirs*, p. 34, and Hollister, *Shīʿa*, pp. 391–392.

176. Aga Khan, *Memoirs*, pp. 56 and 69ff.

177. Ibid., pp. 63–65.

178. Ibid., pp. 72–73.

179. See 'Hajji Bibi v. H.H. Sir Sultan Mahomed Shah, the Aga Khan', in *Bombay Law Reporter*, 11 (1908), pp. 409–495, and Aga Khan, *Memoirs*, pp. 79–80.

180. Aga Khan, *Memoirs*, pp. 35–36, 77–78, 114–116 and 120; M. S. Jain, *The Aligarh Movement* (Agra, 1965), pp. 65 and 156; Aziz Ahmad, *Islamic Modernism in India and Pakistan, 1857–1964* (London, 1967), pp. 65–66 and 87; Sheikh Mohammad Ikram, *Modern Muslim India and the Birth of Pakistan, 1858–1951* (2nd ed., Lahore, 1970), pp. 81–83, 103, 110, 138 and 182ff., and R. Gopal, *Indian Muslims* (Bombay, 1964), pp. 98–99, 102–103, 118–120, 209–210 and 329ff.

181. Aga Khan, *Memoirs*, pp. 130, 190–191 and 322, and M. Yegar, *The Muslims of Burma* (Wiesbaden, 1972), p. 46.

182. Aga Khan, *Memoirs*, pp. 142–143, and Sykes, *A History of Persia*, vol. 2, p. 447.

183. Aga Khan, Sulṭān Muḥammad Shāh, *India in Transition: A Study in Political Evolution* (Bombay, 1918).

184. Aga Khan, *Memoirs*, pp. 209–210.
185. Aga Khan, *Memoirs*, pp. 285–286, and Greenwall, *The Aga Khan*, pp. 190ff.
186. On the Nizārī Khojas of East Africa, and their organization and socio-economic progress, aside from the general sources investigating the East African Ismāʿīlīs, cited previously in connection with the Ṭayyibī Bohra settlers, see Hatim M. Amiji, 'The Asian Communities', in *Islam in Africa*, pp. 141ff., 145–155 and 168ff.; also his 'Islam and Socio-Economic Development: A Case Study of a Muslim Minority in Tanzania', *Journal, Institute of Muslim Minority Affairs, King Abdulaziz University*, 4 (1982), pp. 175–187; R. J. Bocock, 'The Ismailis in Tanzania: A Weberian Analysis', *British Journal of Sociology*, 22 (1971), pp. 365–380; Azim Nanji, 'Modernization and Change in the Nizari Ismaili Community in East Africa – A Perspective', *Journal of Religion in Africa*, 6 (1974), pp. 123–139, and G. Thompson, 'The Ismailis in Uganda', in *Essays on Ugandan Asians*, ed. M. Twadle (London, 1975), pp. 30–52. See also Habib Keshavjee, *The Aga Khan and Africa* (London, 1957); H. S. Morris, 'The Divine Kingship of the Aga Khan: A Study of Theocracy in East Africa', *Southwestern Journal of Anthropology*, 14 (1958), pp. 454–472, and his *The Indians in Uganda* (London, 1968), pp. 77–90, studying the Nizārīs in the wider perspective of the Ugandan Muslim community. In recent decades, a number of East African Nizārīs have written dissertations in Western universities on the conditions of their communities; see Aziz Esmail, 'Satpanth Ismailism and Modern Changes within it, with Special Reference to East Africa' (Ph.D. thesis, University of Edinburgh, 1971); Zarina G. Bhatia, 'Social Changes in the Ismaili Society of East Africa, with Reference to the Imamat of Four Successive Aga Khans' (B.Litt. thesis, Oxford University, 1974), and Shirin R. Walji, 'A History of the Ismaili Community in Tanzania' (Ph.D. thesis, University of Wisconsin, 1974).
187. See H. Amiji, 'Some Notes on Religious Dissent in Nineteenth Century East Africa', *African Historical Studies*, 4 (1971), pp. 603–615.
188. *Rules and Regulations of the Khoja Shia Imami Ismailia Council* (Zanzibar, 1905).
189. Aga Khan, *Memoirs*, p. 167.
190. See, for instance, *Kalām-i imām-i mubīn: Holy Firmans of Mowlana Hazar Imam Sultan Mohamed Shah the Aga Khan* (Bombay, 1950); Sherali Alidina and Kassim Ali, comp., *Precious Pearls: Firman Mubarak of Hazrat Imam Mowlana Sultan Mahomed Shah* (Karachi, 1954); *Message of H.R.H. Prince Aga Khan III to Nation of Pakistan and World of Islam* (4th ed., Karachi, 1968); *Majmūʿa-yi farāmīn-i mubārak-i Mawlānā Sulṭān Muḥammad Shāh* (Mashhad, 1363/1984), and A. K. Adatia and N. Q. King, 'Some East African Firmans of H.H. Aga Khan III', *Journal of Religion in Africa*, 2 (1969), pp. 179–191.
191. His Highness the Aga Khan Shia Imami Ismailia Supreme Council for Africa, *The Constitution of the Shia Imami Ismailis in Africa* (Nairobi, 1962); see also J. D. N. Anderson, 'The Ismaʿili Khojas of East Africa: A New Constitution and Personal Law for the Community', *Middle Eastern Studies*, 1 (1964), pp. 21–39, and also his *Islamic Law in Africa*, pp. 322ff.
192. See, for instance, His Royal Highness Prince Aga Khan Ismailia Federal Council for Pakistan, *The Constitution of the Councils and Jamats of Shia Imami Ismaili Muslims of Pakistan* (Karachi, 1962); Hollister, *Shīʿa*, pp. 400ff.; Sami

N. Makarem, *The Doctrine of the Ismailis* (Beirut, 1972), pp. 65–71, and H. Papanek, 'Leadership and Social Change in the Khoja Ismaili Community' (Ph.D. thesis, Harvard University, 1962), discussing the Nizārī community of Pakistan.

193. See Karim Goolamali, *An Open Letter to H.H. the Aga Khan* (Karachi, 1927); also his *An Appeal to Mr. Ali Solomon Khan* (Karachi, 1932); Aga Khan, *Memoirs*, p. 187, and Hollister, *Shīʿa*, pp. 372–373.

194. On the history and conditions of the Syrian Nizārīs since the beginning of the nineteenth century, see Tāmir, 'Furūʿ al-shajara', pp. 590–593; also his *al-Imāma*, pp. 171–173 and 214–216; Ghālib, *Taʾrīkh*, pp. 353–365 and 395–401; also his *Aʿlām*, pp. 27–28 and 62–81; see also Rousseau, 'Mémoire sur les Ismaélis et les Nosaïris de Syrie', pp. 280ff. and 290ff.; Muḥammad Amīn Ghālib al-Ṭawīl, *Taʾrīkh al-ʿAlawiyyīn* (Latakia, 1924), pp. 276–277 and 370; Mirza, 'Syrian Ismāʿīlīs', pp. 131–134, and Norman N. Lewis, 'The Ismaʿilis of Syria Today', *Royal Central Asian Journal*, 39 (1952), pp. 69–77.

195. The history of the Persian Nizārīs and the conditions of their community during the last one and a half centuries have not been adequately studied. W. Ivanow, who on his first visits to Persia spent a few years in Khurāsān during the 1910s, included some notes on the geographical distribution and social conditions of the Persian Ismāʿīlīs of the time in his 'Ismailitica', pp. 50–58. More recently, Rafique H. Keshavjee conducted field research in Iran investigating the progress made by the Nizārīs of Khurāsān; see his 'The Quest for Gnosis and the Call of History: Modernization Among the Ismailis of Iran' (Ph.D. thesis, Harvard University, 1981). The author has obtained much information on the present conditions of the Persian Nizārīs from the members of the community in Mashhad, Dizbād, Maḥallāt and Tehran. The leaders of the *jamāʿat* in northern Khurāsān and the members of the Āghā Khān Committee at Mashhad were particularly helpful in providing details on various socio-economic and religious aspects of the community and its oral traditions. Ṣadr al-Dīn Mīrshāhī, the librarian of the Ḥakīm Nāṣir-i Khusraw Library at the Mashhad *jamāʿat-khāna*, made a number of unpublished documents and Ismāʿīlī works available to the author, who is deeply indebted to him.

196. See Ivanow, *Guide*, pp. 112–113; also his *Ismaili Literature*, pp. 150–151, and Poonawala, *Bio*, pp. 282–283. Several of Mīrzā Ḥusayn's religious poems have been published in recent years by the Āghā Khān Committee in Mashhad.

197. These details are culled from an unpublished biography of Fidāʾī written in 1961 by his grandson, Ṣadr al-Dīn b. Mullā Shams al-Dīn Mīrshāhī.

198. For similar practices observed by the Nizārī Khojas, see Ali, *Origin of the Khojāhs*, pp. 63–73; Hollister, *Shīʿa*, pp. 384–394; Amiji, 'The Asian Communities', pp. 153–154; Lokhandwalla, 'Islamic Law and Ismāʿīlī Communities', pp. 384ff., and Fyzee, *Outlines of Muhammadan Law*, pp. 69ff.

199. Aga Khan, *Memoirs*, pp. 169–177 and 187ff.; see also Shihāb al-Dīn Shāh, *Khiṭābāt*, pp. 22–28, 32–33, 52ff. and 67ff., and his *Risāla dar ḥaqīqat-i dīn*, 1947 ed., pp. 65ff.; tr. Ivanow, 1947 ed., pp. 42ff.

200. Aga Khan, *Memoirs*, p. 324.

201. Ibid., pp. 180ff.

202. A full account of Āghā Khān IV's activities, including a detailed description of his various projects for the Nizārī communities of different countries, still needs to be written. For brief biographical notices on the present Āghā Khān, see Ghālib, *Ta'rīkh*, pp. 402–404; also his *Aʿlām*, pp. 434–436, and Frischauer, *The Aga Khans*, pp. 206–272. The Ismailia Associations have produced periodical publications on Āghā Khān IV and the events of his imāmate; see, for instance, Sherali Alidina, *Ten Eventful Years of Imamat of H.R.H. Prince Karim Aga Khan* (Karachi, 1967), and Ismailia Association for Kenya, *Speeches of His Highness Prince Karim Aga Khan* (Mombasa, 1964), 2 vols. There are also several collections of Āghā Khān IV's *firmans*.

203. See A. Nanji, 'The Nizari Ismaili Community in North America: Background and Development', in *The Muslim Community in North America*, ed. E. H. Waugh et al. (Edmonton, Alberta, 1983), pp. 149–164; R. N. M. Hallam, 'The Ismaili Community in Great Britain' (M.Phil. thesis, University of London, 1971); Peter B. Clarke, 'The Ismaili Khojas: A Sociological Study of an Islamic Sect in London' (M.Phil. thesis, King's College, London, 1975); also his 'The Ismailis: A Study of Community', *British Journal of Sociology*, 27 (1976), pp. 484–494; also his 'The Ismaili Sect in London: Religious Institutions and Social Change', *Religion*, 8 (1978), pp. 68–84, and Farida A. Rajwani, 'Development of Ismaʿili Religious Education in Canada' (M.A. thesis, McGill University, 1983).

BIBLIOGRAPHY

The bibliography does not include all the works cited in the notes; it lists some basic works of reference and a selection of the published sources cited most frequently in connection with individual chapters. The abbreviations used in the bibliography are the same as those used in the notes.

1. *Works of reference*

Atiya, Aziz S. *The Crusade: Historiography and Bibliography*. Bloomington, 1962.

Bacharach, Jere L. *A Near East Studies Handbook, 570–1974*. Seattle–London, 1974.

Bāmdād, Mahdī. *Sharḥ-i ḥāl-i rijāl-i Īrān*. Tehran, 1347–1350/1968–1971.

Beale, Thomas W. *An Oriental Biographical Dictionary*, new and revised edition by Henry G. Keene. London, 1894.

Berthels, A. and Baqoev, M. *Alphabetic Catalogue of Manuscripts found by 1959–1963 Expedition in Gorno-Badakhshan Autonomous Region*, ed. B. G. Gafurov and A. M. Mirzoev. Moscow, 1967.

Bosworth, Clifford E. *The Islamic Dynasties: A Chronological and Genealogical Handbook*. 2nd ed., Edinburgh, 1980. Persian trans. F. Badra'ī, *Silsilihā-yi Islāmī*. Tehran, 1349/1970.

Brockelmann, Carl. *Geschichte der arabischen Litteratur*. 1st ed., Weimar, 1898–1902; 2nd ed., Leiden, 1943–1949. *Supplementbände*. Leiden, 1937–1942.

Cahen, Claude. *Introduction à l'histoire du monde Musulman médiéval: VIIe-XVe siècle*. Paris, 1982.

Encyclopaedia Iranica, ed. E. Yarshater. London–Boston, 1982–

Encyclopaedia of Iran and Islam, ed. E. Yarshater. Tehran, 1976–1982.

Encyclopaedia of Islam, ed. M. Th. Houtsma et al. 1st ed., Leiden–London, 1913–1938.

Encyclopaedia of Islam, ed. H. A. R. Gibb et al. New ed., Leiden–London, 1960–

Encyclopaedia of Religion and Ethics, ed. J. Hastings. Edinburgh–New York, 1908–1926.

Encyclopedia of Religion, ed. M. Eliade. London–New York, 1987.

Gacek, Adam. *Catalogue of Arabic Manuscripts in the Library of the Institute of Ismaili Studies*. London, 1984–1985.

Ghālib, Muṣṭafā. *Aʿlām al-Ismāʿīliyya*. Beirut, 1964.

Goriawala, Muʿizz. *A Descriptive Catalogue of the Fyzee Collection of Ismaili Manuscripts*. Bombay, 1965.

The Great Ismaili Heroes, ed. A. R. Kanji. Karachi, 1973.

Handbook of Oriental History, ed. C. H. Philips. London, 1951.

Handwörterbuch des Islam, ed. A. J. Wensinck and J. H. Kramers. Leiden, 1941.

Hellmuth, Leopold. *Die Assassinenlegende in der österreichischen Geschichtsdichtung des Mittelalters*. Vienna, 1988.

Ivanow, Wladimir. *A Guide to Ismaili Literature*. London, 1933.

Ismaili Literature: A Bibliographical Survey. Tehran, 1963.

Justi, Ferdinand. *Iranisches Namenbuch*. Marburg, 1895.

Lane-Poole, Stanley. *The Mohammadan Dynasties*. London, 1894. Persian trans. ʿAbbās Iqbāl, *Ṭabaqāt-i salāṭīn-i Islām*. Tehran, 1312/1933.

Modarressi Tabātabā'i, Hossein. *An Introduction to Shīʿī Law: A Bibliographical Study*. London, 1984.

Pearson, James D. *Index Islamicus, 1906–1955*. Cambridge, 1958.

Index Islamicus, Supplement. Cambridge–London, 1962–

Poonawala, Ismail K. *Biobibliography of Ismāʿīlī Literature*. Malibu, Calif., 1977.

Sauvaget, Jean. *Introduction à l'histoire de l'Orient Musulman: Éléments de bibliographie*. Paris, 1946.

Introduction to the History of the Muslim East: A Bibliographical Guide, English translation based on the second edition as recast by Claude Cahen. Berkeley, 1965.

Sayyid, Ayman F. *Maṣādir ta'rīkh al-Yaman fi'l-ʿaṣr al-Islāmī*. Cairo, 1974.

Sezgin, Fuat. *Geschichte des arabischen Schrifttums*. Leiden, 1967–

Shorter Encyclopaedia of Islam, ed. H. A. R. Gibb and J. H. Kramers. Leiden, 1953.

Storey, Charles A. *Persian Literature: A Bio-bibliographical Survey*. London, 1927– . Persian trans. Yaḥyā Āriyanpūr et al., *Adabiyyāt-i Fārsī*. Tehran, 1362– /1983–

Tajdin, Nagib. *A Bibliography of Ismailism*. Delmar, N.Y., 1985.

Wüstenfeld, Ferdinand. *Genealogische Tabellen der arabischen Stämme und Familien*. Göttingen, 1852–1853.

Zambaur, E. de. *Manuel de généalogie et de chronologie pour l'histoire de l'Islam*. Hanover, 1927.

2. *Primary sources*

Abu'l-Faraj al-Iṣfahānī, ʿAlī b. al-Ḥusayn. *Maqātil al-Ṭālibiyyīn*, ed. A. Ṣaqr. Cairo, 1368/1949.

Abu'l-Fidā. *al-Mukhtaṣar ta'rīkh al-bashar*, extracts with French trans., in *RHCHO*, vol. 1, pp. 1–165.

Abū Firās, Shihāb al-Dīn al-Maynaqī. *Faṣl min al-lafẓ al-sharīf, hādhihi manāqib al-mawlā Rāshid al-Dīn*, ed. and tr. Stanislas Guyard, in his 'Un Grand Maître des Assassins au temps de Saladin', *JA*, 7 série, 9 (1877), pp. 387–489.

Abū Isḥāq Quhistānī. *Haft bāb; or, Seven Chapters*, ed. and tr. W. Ivanow. Bombay, 1959.

Abū Makhrama ʿAbd Allāh al-Ṭayyib. *Taʾrīkh thaghr ʿAdan*, ed. O. Löfgren, in his *Arabische Texte*, vol. 2, pp. 1–240.

Abū Shāma, Shihāb al-Dīn. *Kitāb al-rawḍatayn fī akhbār al-dawlatayn*. Cairo, 1287–1288/1870–1871. Extracts with French trans., in *RHCHO*, vol. 4, pp. 1–525, and vol. 5, pp. 1–287.

Ādhar, Luṭf ʿAlī Beg. *Ātashkada*. Bombay, 1299/1881–1882; Tehran, 1337/1958.

Āghā Khān Maḥallātī, Ḥasan ʿAlī Shāh. *ʿIbrat-afzā*, ed. Ḥusayn Kūhī Kirmānī. Tehran, 1325/1946.

Akhbār al-Qarāmiṭa, ed. Suhayl Zakkār. 2nd ed., Damascus, 1982.

ʿAlī Muḥammad Khān. *Mirat-i Ahmadi*, ed. and tr. S. Nawab Ali, Charles N. Seddon and M. F. Lokhandwala. Baroda, 1928–1965.

Āmulī, Awliyāʾ Allāh. *Taʾrīkh-i Rūyān*, ed. M. Sutūda. Tehran, 1348/1969.

al-Anṭākī, Yaḥyā b. Saʿīd. *Taʾrīkh*, ed. L. Cheikho et al. Paris–Beirut, 1909. Partial ed. and French trans. I. Kratchkovsky and A. A. Vasiliev, in *Patrologia Orientalis*, 18 (1924), pp. 699–833, and 23 (1932), pp. 347–520.

Arabische Texte zur Kenntnis der Stadt Aden im Mittelalter, ed. Oscar Löfgren. Uppsala, 1936–1950.

ʿArīb b. Saʿd al-Qurṭubī. *Ṣilat taʾrīkh al-Ṭabarī*, ed. M. J. de Goeje. Leiden, 1897.

al-Ashʿarī, Abu'l-Ḥasan ʿAlī b. Ismāʿīl. *Kitāb maqālāt al-Islāmiyyīn*, ed. H. Ritter. Istanbul, 1929–1930.

al-ʿAẓīmī, Muḥammad b. ʿAlī. *Taʾrīkh*, ed. Claude Cahen, in his 'La Chronique abrégée d'al-ʿAẓīmī', *JA*, 230 (1938), pp. 353–448.

Badakhshānī, Sayyid Suhrāb Valī. *Sī va shish ṣaḥīfa*, ed. H. Ujāqī. Tehran, 1961.

Badr al-Dīn Muḥammad b. Ḥātim al-Yāmī al-Hamdānī. *Kitāb al-simṭ al-ghālī al-thaman*, ed. G. R. Smith, in his *The Ayyūbids and Early Rasūlids in the Yemen*, vol. 1. London, 1974.

al-Baghdādī, Abū Manṣūr ʿAbd al-Qāhir b. Ṭāhir. *al-Farq bayn al-firaq*, ed. M. Badr. Cairo, 1328/1910. English trans., *Moslem Schisms and Sects*, part I, tr. K. C. Seelye. New York, 1919; part II, tr. A. S. Halkin. Tel Aviv, 1935.

al-Bharūchī, Ḥasan b. Nūḥ. *Kitāb al-azhār*, vol. 1, ed. ʿĀ. al-ʿAwwā, in his *Muntakhabāt Ismāʿīliyya*, pp. 181–250.

al-Bundārī, al-Fatḥ b. ʿAlī. *Zubdat al-nuṣra*, ed. M. Th. Houtsma, in his Recueil de textes relatifs à l'histoire des Seldjoucides II. Leiden, 1889.

Bustān al-jāmiʿ, ed. Claude Cahen, in his 'Une chronique Syrienne du VIe/XIIe siècle: Le *Bustān al-Jāmiʿ*', *Bulletin d'Études Orientales*, 7–8 (1937–1938), pp. 113–158.

Collectanea: Vol. 1, ed. W. Ivanow. Leiden, 1948.

Dawlatshāh b. ʿAlāʾ al-Dawla. *Tadhkirat al-shuʿarāʾ*, ed. E. G. Browne. London–Leiden, 1901.

al-Daylamī, Muḥammad b. al-Ḥasan. *Bayān madhhab al-Bāṭiniyya*, ed. R. Strothmann. Istanbul, 1939.

Fidāʾī Khurāsānī, Muḥammad b. Zayn al-ʿĀbidīn. *Kitāb-i hidāyat al-muʾminīn al-ṭālibīn*, ed. A. A. Semenov. Moscow, 1959.

Fragments relatifs à la doctrine des Ismaélîs, ed. and tr. S. Guyard, in *Notices et Extraits des Manuscrits*, 22 (1874), pp. 177–428.

Gardīzī, ʿAbd al-Ḥayy b. al-Ḍaḥḥāk. *Zayn al-akhbār*, ed. ʿA. Ḥabībī. Tehran, 1347/1968.

Gīlānī, Mullā Shaykh ʿAlī. *Taʾrīkh-i Māzandarān*, ed. M. Sutūda. Tehran, 1352/1973.

Gnosis-Texte der Ismailiten, ed. R. Strothmann. Göttingen, 1943.

Ḥāfiẓ Abrū, ʿAbd Allāh b. Luṭf ʿAlī al-Bihdādīnī. *Majmaʿ al-tawārīkh al-sulṭāniyya; qismat-i khulafāʾ-i ʿAlawiyya-yi Maghrib va Miṣr va Nizāriyān va rafīqān*, ed. M. Mudarrisī Zanjānī. Tehran, 1364/1985.

Haft bāb-i Bābā Sayyidnā, ed. W. Ivanow, in his *Two Early Ismaili Treatises*, pp. 4–44. English trans. M. G. S. Hodgson, in his *Order of Assassins*, pp. 279–324.

al-Ḥamawī, Abu'l-Faḍā'il Muḥammad. *al-Taʾrīkh al-Manṣūrī*, ed. P. A. Gryaznevich. Moscow, 1963.

Ḥamd Allāh Mustawfī Qazwīnī. *The Geographical Part of the Nuzhat al-Qulūb*, ed. and tr. G. Le Strange. Leiden–London, 1915–1919.

The Taʾrīkh-i Guzīda; or, 'Select History', ed. and tr. E. G. Browne. Leiden–London, 1910–1913; ed. ʿAbd al-Ḥusayn Navāʾī. Tehran, 1339/1960. Partial ed. and French trans. J. Gantin, *Târîkhè Gozîdè*. Paris, 1903.

al-Ḥāmidī, Ibrāhīm b. al-Ḥusayn. *Kitāb kanz al-walad*, ed. M. Ghālib. Wiesbaden, 1971.

Hidāyat, Riḍā Qulī Khān. *Rawḍat al-ṣafā-yi Nāṣirī*. Tehran, 1339/1960.

Riyāḍ al-ʿārifīn, ed. M. Garakānī. Tehran, 1344/1965.

al-Hidāyatu'l-Āmirīya, ed. Asaf A. A. Fyzee. London, etc., 1938.

Ḥudūd al-ʿĀlam, the Regions of the World, tr. V. Minorsky. 2nd ed., London, 1970.

al-Ḥusaynī, Ṣadr al-Dīn ʿAlī. *Akhbār al-dawla al-Saljūqiyya*, ed. M. Iqbāl. Lahore, 1933.

Ibn al-ʿAdīm, Kamāl al-Dīn. *Zubdat al-ḥalab min taʾrīkh Ḥalab*, ed. S. Dahān. Damascus, 1951–1968. Extracts with French trans., in *RHCHO*, vol. 3, pp. 571–690. Partial French trans. E. Blochet, *L'Histoire d'Alep*, in *Revue de l'Orient Latin*, 3–6 (1895–1898).

Ibn al-Athīr, ʿIzz al-Dīn. *Taʾrīkh al-kāmil*. Cairo, 1303/1885. Extracts with French trans., in *RHCHO*, vol. 1, pp. 187–744, and vol. 2, part 1, pp. 1–271.

Ibn al-Balkhī. *The Fārs-nāma*, ed. G. Le Strange and R. A. Nicholson. London, 1921.

Ibn al-Dawādārī, Abū Bakr b. ʿAbd Allāh. *Kanz al-durar*, ed. Ṣ. al-Munajjid et al., vols. 6–8. Cairo, 1961–1972.

Ibn Faḍl Allāh al-ʿUmarī, Shihāb al-Dīn. *Masālik al-abṣār fī mamālik al-amṣār*, ed. A. F. Sayyid. Cairo, 1985.

Ibn Ḥammād (Ḥamādu), Muḥammad b. ʿAlī. *Histoire des rois ʿObaidides*, ed. and tr. M. Vonderheyden. Algiers–Paris, 1927.

Ibn Ḥawqal, Abu'l-Qāsim. *Kitāb ṣūrat al-arḍ*, ed. J. H. Kramers. 2nd ed., Leiden, 1938–1939.

Ibn Ḥawshab, Manṣūr al-Yaman. *Kitāb al-rushd wa'l-hidāya*, ed. M. Kāmil Ḥusayn, in *Collectanea*: Vol. 1, pp. 185–213. English trans. W. Ivanow, 'The Book of Righteousness and True Guidance', in his *Studies in Early Persian Ismailism*. Leiden, 1948, pp. 51–83; 2nd ed., Bombay, 1955, pp. 29–59.

Ibn Ḥazm, Abū Muḥammad ʿAlī b. Aḥmad. *Kitāb al-fiṣal fi'l-milal*. Cairo, 1317–

1321/1899–1903. Partial English trans. I. Friedlaender, 'The Heterodoxies of the Shiites in the Presentation of Ibn Ḥazm', in *JAOS*, 28 (1907), pp. 1–80, and 29 (1908), pp. 1–183.

Ibn ʿIdhārī, Aḥmad b. Muḥammad. *al-Bayān al-mughrib*, ed. G. S. Colin and É. Lévi-Provençal. New ed., Leiden, 1948–1951.

Ibn ʿInaba, Jamāl al-Dīn Aḥmad b. ʿAlī. *ʿUmdat al-ṭālib fī ansāb āl Abī Ṭālib*, ed. M. Ḥ. Āl al-Ṭāliqānī. Najaf, 1961.

Ibn Isfandiyār, Muḥammad b. al-Ḥasan. *Ta'rīkh-i Ṭabaristān*, ed. ʿAbbās Iqbāl. Tehran, 1320/1941. Abridged English trans. E. G. Browne, *An Abridged Translation of the History of Ṭabaristān*, Leiden–London, 1905.

Ibn Khaldūn, ʿAbd al-Raḥmān. *Histoire des Berbères*, tr. W. MacGuckin de Slane, new edition by P. Casanova. Paris, 1968–1969.

Ibn Khallikān, Aḥmad b. Muḥammad. *Biographical Dictionary*, tr. W. MacGuckin de Slane. Paris, 1842–1871.

Ibn Mālik al-Yamānī, Muḥammad. *Kashf asrār al-Bāṭiniyya wa akhbār al-Qarāmiṭa*, ed. Muḥammad Z. al-Kawtharī. Cairo, 1939.

Ibn al-Ma'mūn al-Baṭā'iḥī, Jamāl al-Dīn. *Nuṣūṣ min akhbār Miṣr*, ed. Ayman F. Sayyid. Cairo, 1983.

Ibn Muyassar, Tāj al-Dīn Muḥammad b. ʿAlī. *Akhbār Miṣr*, ed. H. Massé. Cairo, 1919; ed. A. F. Sayyid. Cairo, 1981.

Ibn al-Nadīm, Muḥammad b. Isḥāq. *Kitāb al-fihrist*, ed. G. Flügel. Leipzig, 1871–1872. Persian trans. M. R. Tajaddud, *Kitāb al-fihrist*. 2nd ed., Tehran, 1346/1967. English trans. B. Dodge, *The Fihrist of al-Nadīm*. New York, 1970.

Ibn al-Qalānisī, Abū Yaʿlā Ḥamza b. Asad. *Dhayl ta'rīkh Dimashq*, ed. H. F. Amedroz. Leiden, 1908. Partial English trans. H. A. R. Gibb, *The Damascus Chronicle of the Crusades*. London, 1932. French trans. Roger Le Tourneau, *Damas de 1075 à 1154*. Damascus, 1952.

Ibn al-Ṣayrafī, Abu'l-Qāsim ʿAlī b. Munjib. *al-Ishāra ilā man nāl al-wizāra*, ed. ʿAbd Allāh Mukhliṣ, in *BIFAO*, 25 (1925), pp. 49–112, and 26 (1926), pp. 49–70.

Ibn Shaddād, ʿIzz al-Dīn. *Ta'rīkh al-Malik al-Ẓāhir*, ed. A. Ḥuṭayṭ. Wiesbaden, 1983.

Ibn Shahrāshūb, Abū Jaʿfar Muḥammad b. ʿAlī. *Kitāb maʿālim al-ʿulamā'*, ed. ʿAbbās Iqbāl. Tehran, 1353/1934.

Manāqib āl Abī Ṭālib. Bombay, 1313/1896.

Ibn Taghrībirdī, Abu'l-Maḥāsin Yūsuf, *al-Nujūm al-zāhira fī mulūk Miṣr wa'l-Qāhira*. Cairo, 1348–1391/1929–1972.

Ibn Ẓāfir al-Azdī, Jamāl al-Dīn ʿAlī. *Akhbār al-duwal al-munqaṭiʿa*; *La section consacrée aux Fatimides*, ed. A. Ferré. Cairo, 1972.

Idrīs ʿImād al-Dīn b. al-Ḥasan. *ʿUyūn al-akhbār wa funūn al-āthār*, ed. M. Ghālib, vols. 4–6. Beirut, 1973–1978.

Iʿtimād al-Salṭana, Muḥammad Ḥasan Khān. *Ta'rīkh-i muntaẓam-i Nāṣirī*. Tehran, 1298–1300/1881–1883.

Jaʿfar b. Manṣūr al-Yaman, Abu'l-Qāsim. *Kitāb al-kashf*, ed. R. Strothmann. London, etc., 1952.

Sarā'ir wa asrār al-nuṭaqā', ed. M. Ghālib. Beirut, 1984.

al-Jawdharī, Abū ʿAlī Manṣūr al-ʿAzīzī. *Sīrat al-ustādh Jawdhar*, ed. M. Kāmil Ḥusayn and M. ʿAbd al-Hādī Shaʿīra. Cairo, 1954. French trans. M. Canard, *Vie de l'ustadh Jaudhar (contenant sermons, lettres et rescrits des premiers califes Fātimides)*. Algiers, 1958.

Joinville, Jean de. *Memoirs of John Lord de Joinville*, tr. T. Johnes. Hafod, 1807.

Juwaynī, ʿAlā' al-Dīn ʿAṭā-Malik. *Ta'rīkh-i jahān-gushāy*, ed. M. Qazvīnī. Leiden–London, 1912–1937. English trans. John A. Boyle, *The History of the World-Conqueror*. Cambridge, Mass., 1958.

Jūzjānī, Minhāj al-Dīn ʿUthmān b. Sirāj. *Ṭabaqāt-i Nāṣirī*, ed. ʿAbd al-Ḥayy Ḥabībī. 2nd ed., Kabul, 1342–1343/1963–1964. English trans. Henry G. Raverty, *The Ṭabaḳāt-i-Nāṣirī: A General History of the Muhammadan Dynasties of Asia*. London, 1881–1899.

Kāshānī (al-Qāshānī), Abu'l-Qāsim ʿAbd Allāh b. ʿAlī. *Zubdat al-tawārīkh; ta'rīkh-i Ismāʿīliyya va Nizāriyya va Malāḥida*, ed. M. T. Dānishpazhūh, in *Revue de la Faculté des Lettres, Université de Tabriz*, Supplément no. 9 (1343/1964), pp. 1–218.

al-Kashshī, Abū ʿAmr Muḥammad b. ʿUmar. *Ikhtiyār maʿrifat al-rijāl*, abridged by Muḥammad b. al-Ḥasan al-Ṭūsī, ed. Ḥasan al-Muṣṭafawī. Mashhad, 1348/1969.

Kaykhusraw Isfandiyār. *Dabistān-i madhāhib*, ed. R. Riḍāzāda Malik. Tehran, 1362/1983. English trans. D. Shea and A. Troyer, *The Dabistān, or School of Manners*. Washington–London, 1901.

Khākī Khurāsānī, Imām Qulī. *An Abbreviated Version of the Dīwān*, ed. W. Ivanow. Bombay, 1933.

Khams rasā'il Ismāʿīliyya, ed. ʿĀrif Tāmir. Salamiyya, 1956.

Khayrkhwāh-i Harātī, Muḥammad Riḍā b. Sulṭān Ḥusayn. *Faṣl dar bayān-i shinākht-i imām*, ed. W. Ivanow. 3rd ed., Tehran, 1960. English trans. W. Ivanow, *On the Recognition of the Imam*. 2nd ed., Bombay, 1947.

Kalām-i pīr: A Treatise on Ismaili Doctrine, ed. and tr. W. Ivanow. Bombay, 1935.

Taṣnīfāt-i Khayrkhwāh-i Harātī, ed. W. Ivanow. Tehran, 1961.

Khwānd Amīr, Ghiyāth al-Dīn b. Humām al-Dīn. *Ḥabīb al-siyar*, ed. J. Humā'ī. Tehran, 1333/1954.

al-Kirmānī, Ḥamīd al-Dīn Aḥmad. *Kitāb al-riyāḍ*, ed. ʿĀrif Tāmir. Beirut, 1960.

Majmūʿat rasā'il al-Kirmānī, ed. M. Ghālib. Beirut, 1983.

Rāḥat al-ʿaql, ed. M. Kāmil Ḥusayn and M. Muṣṭafā Ḥilmī. Cairo, 1953.

al-Kulaynī (al-Kulīnī), Abū Jaʿfar Muḥammad b. Yaʿqūb. *al-Uṣūl min al-Kāfī*, ed. ʿAlī Akbar al-Ghaffārī. 3rd ed., Tehran, 1388/1968.

Lisān al-Mulk Sipihr, Muḥammad Taqī. *Nāsikh al-tawārīkh; ta'rīkh-i Qājāriyya*. Tabrīz, 1319/1901; ed. Muḥammad Bāqir Bihbūdī. Tehran, 1344/1965.

al-Majdūʿ, Ismāʿīl b. ʿAbd al-Rasūl. *Fihrist al-kutub wa'l-rasā'il*, ed. ʿAlī Naqī Munzavī. Tehran, 1966.

Majmūʿat al-wathā'iq al-Fāṭimiyya, ed. Jamāl al-Dīn al-Shayyāl. Cairo, 1958.

al-Malaṭī, Abu'l-Ḥusayn Muḥammad b. Aḥmad. *Kitāb al-tanbīh wa'l-radd*, ed. S. Dedering. Istanbul, 1936.

al-Mālījī, Abu'l-Qāsim ʿAbd al-Ḥakīm b. Wahb. *al-Majālis al-Mustanṣiriyya*, ed. M. Kāmil Ḥusayn. Cairo, [1947].

al-Maqrīzī, Taqī al-Dīn Aḥmad b. ʿAlī. *Kitāb al-sulūk*, partial French trans. E. Blochet, *Histoire d'Égypte*, in *Revue de l'Orient Latin*, 6–11 (1898–1908). Partial English trans. Ronald J. C. Broadhurst, *A History of the Ayyūbid Sultans of Egypt*. Boston, 1980.

Ittiʿāẓ al-ḥunafāʾ bi-akhbār al-aʾimma al-Fāṭimiyyīn al-khulafāʾ, ed. Jamāl al-Dīn al-Shayyāl and M. Ḥilmī M. Aḥmad. Cairo, 1967–1973; partial edition of volume one by H. Bunz. Leipzig, 1909.

Kitāb al-mawāʿiẓ wa'l-iʿtibār bi-dhikr al-khiṭaṭ wa'l-āthār. Būlāq, 1270/1853. Partial French trans. U. Bouriant and P. Casanova, *Description historique et topographique de l'Égypte*, in Mémoires publiés par les membres de l'Institut Français d'Archéologie Orientale du Caire. Cairo, 1895–1920.

Marʿashī, Ẓahīr al-Dīn. *Taʾrīkh-i Gīlān va Daylamistān*, ed. H. L. Rabino. Rasht, 1330/1912; ed. M. Sutūda. Tehran, 1347/1968.

Taʾrīkh-i Ṭabaristān va Rūyān va Māzandarān, ed. B. Dorn, in his Muhammedanische Quellen zur Geschichte der Südlichen Küstenländer des Kaspischen Meeres I. St. Petersburg, 1850; ed. M. Ḥusayn Tasbīḥī. Tehran, 1345/1966.

al-Masʿūdī, Abu'l-Ḥasan ʿAlī b. al-Ḥusayn. *Kitāb al-tanbīh wa'l-ishrāf*, ed. M. J. de Goeje. Leiden, 1894. French trans. B. Carra de Vaux, *Le livre de l'avertissement et de la revision*. Paris, 1896.

Murūj al-dhahab, ed. and tr. C. Barbier de Meynard and A. Pavet de Courteille. Paris, 1861–1876.

Maʿṣūm ʿAlī Shāh, Muḥammad Maʿṣūm Shīrāzī. *Ṭarāʾiq al-ḥaqāʾiq*, ed. M. J. Maḥjūb. Tehran, 1339–1345/1960–1966.

Mīrkhwānd, Muḥammad b. Khwāndshāh. *Rawḍat al-ṣafāʾ*. Tehran 1338–1339/1960. Partial ed. and French trans. Am. Jourdain, *Le Jardin de la Pureté*, in *Notices et Extraits des Manuscrits*, 9 (1813), pp. 117–274.

Miskawayh, Abū ʿAlī Aḥmad. *Tajārib al-umam*, [with its continuations by Abū Shujāʿ al-Rūdhrāwarī and Hilāl al-Ṣābi'], ed. and tr. H. F. Amedroz and D. S. Margoliouth, in *The Eclipse of the ʿAbbasid Caliphate*. Oxford–London, 1920–1921.

al-Muʾayyad fi'l-Dīn al-Shīrāzī, Abū Naṣr Hibat Allāh. *Dīwān*, ed. M. Kāmil Ḥusayn. Cairo, 1949.

al-Majālis al-Muʾayyadiyya, ed. M. Ghālib, vols. 1 and 3. Beirut, 1974–1984.

Sīrat al-Muʾayyad fi'l-Dīn dāʿī al-duʿāt, ed. M. Kāmil Ḥusayn. Cairo, 1949.

al-Mufīd, Abū ʿAbd Allāh Muḥammad. *Kitāb al-irshād*, tr. I. K. A. Howard. London, 1981.

Muḥammad ʿAlī b. Mullā Jīwābhāʾī. *Mawsim-i bahār fī akhbār al-ṭāhirīn al-akhyār*. Bombay, 1301–1311/1884–1893.

Muntakhabāt Ismāʿīliyya, ed. ʿĀdil al-ʿAwwā. Damascus, 1958.

al-Muqaddasī (al-Maqdisī), Muḥammad b. Aḥmad. *Aḥsan al-taqāsīm*, ed. M. J. de Goeje. 2nd ed., Leiden, 1906.

al-Musabbiḥī, Muḥammad b. ʿUbayd Allāh. *Akhbār Miṣr*, ed. A. F. Sayyid et al. Cairo, 1978–1984; ed. W. G. Millward. Cairo, 1980.

al-Mustanṣir bi'llāh, Abū Tamīm Maʿadd. *al-Sijillāt al-Mustanṣiriyya*, ed. ʿAbd al-Munʿim Mājid. Cairo, 1954.

al-Najāshī, Aḥmad b. ʿAlī. *Kitāb al-rijāl*. Bombay, 1317/1899.
al-Nasawī, Muḥammad b. Aḥmad. *Histoire du Sultan Djelal ed-Din Mankobirti*, ed. and tr. O. Houdas. Paris, 1891–1895. Anonymous Persian trans., *Sīrat-i Jalāl al-Dīn Mīnkubirnī*, ed. M. Mīnuvī. Tehran, 1344/1965.
Nāṣir-i Khusraw. *Dīwān*, ed. Naṣr Allāh Taqavī et al. Tehran, 1304–1307/1925–1928; ed. M. Mīnuvī and M. Muḥaqqiq. Tehran, 1353/1974.
Gushāʾish va rahāʾish, ed. S. Nafīsī. Leiden, 1950. Italian trans. P. Filippani-Ronconi, *Il libro dello scioglimento e della liberazione*. Naples, 1959.
Jāmiʿ al-ḥikmatayn, ed. H. Corbin and M. Muʿīn. Tehran–Paris, 1953.
Khwān al-ikhwān, ed. Y. al-Khashshāb. Cairo, 1940; ed. ʿA. Qavīm. Tehran, 1338/1959.
Safar-nāma, ed. M. Ghanīzāda. Berlin, 1341/1922; ed. M. Dabīr Siyāqī. 5th ed., Tehran, 1356/1977. English trans. W. M. Thackston, Jr., *Nāṣer-e Khosraw's Book of Travels (Safarnāma)*. Albany, N.Y., 1986; ed. and French trans. Charles Schefer, *Sefer Nameh, relation du voyage de Nassiri Khosrau*, Paris, 1881.
Six Chapters, or Shish faṣl, ed. and tr. W. Ivanow. Leiden, 1949.
Wajh-i dīn, ed. M. Ghanīzāda and M. Qazvīnī. Berlin, 1343/1924; ed. Gholam Reza Aavani. Tehran, 1977.
Zād al-musāfirīn, ed. M. Badhl al-Raḥmān. Berlin, 1341/1923.
al-Nawbakhtī, al-Ḥasan b. Mūsā. *Kitāb firaq al-Shīʿa*, ed. H. Ritter. Istanbul, 1931.
al-Nīsābūrī, Aḥmad b. Ibrāhīm. *Istitār al-imām*, ed. W. Ivanow, in *Bulletin of the Faculty of Arts, University of Egypt*, 4, part 2 (1936), pp. 93–107. English trans. W. Ivanow, in his *Ismaili Tradition Concerning the Rise of the Fatimids*, pp. 157–183.
Ithbāt al-imāma, ed. M. Ghālib. Beirut, 1984.
Niẓām al-Mulk. *Siyar al-mulūk (Siyāsat-nāma)*, ed. H. Darke. 2nd ed., Tehran, 1347/1968. English trans. H. Darke, *The Book of Government or Rules for Kings*. 2nd ed., London, 1978.
al-Nuʿmān b. Muḥammad, al-Qāḍī Abū Ḥanīfa. *Asās al-taʾwīl*, ed. ʿĀrif Tāmir. Beirut, 1960.
Daʿāʾim al-Islām, ed. Asaf A. A. Fyzee. Cairo, 1951–1961. Partial English trans. A. A. A. Fyzee, *The Book of Faith*. Bombay, 1974.
Iftitāḥ al-daʿwa, ed. W. al-Qāḍī. Beirut, 1970.
Ikhtilāf uṣūl al-madhāhib, ed. S. T. Lokhandwalla. Simla, 1972.
Kitāb al-himma fī ādāb atbāʿ al-aʾimma, ed. M. Kāmil Ḥusayn. Cairo, [1948]. Abridged English trans. J. Muscati and A. M. Moulvi, *Selections from Qazi Noaman's Kitab-ul-Himma; or, Code of Conduct for the Followers of Imam*. Karachi, 1950.
Kitāb al-majālis wa'l-musāyarāt, ed. al-Ḥabīb al-Faqī, I. Shabbūḥ and M. al-Yaʿlāwī. Tunis 1978.
al-Risāla al-mudhhiba, ed. ʿA. Tāmir, in his *Khams rasāʾil Ismāʿīliyya*, pp. 27–87.
Taʾwīl al-daʿāʾim, ed. M. Ḥasan al-Aʿẓamī. Cairo, 1967–1972.
al-Nuwayrī, Aḥmad b. ʿAbd al-Wahhāb. *Nihāyat al-arab*, ed. M. Jābir ʿAbd al-ʿĀl al-Ḥīnī et al., vol. 25. Cairo, 1984.
Pandiyāt-i jawānmardī, [Sermons of Imām Mustanṣir bi'llāh II], ed. and tr. W. Ivanow. Leiden, 1953.
Panj risāla dar bayān-i āfāq va anfus, ed. Andrei E. Bertel's. Moscow, 1970.

al-Qalqashandī, Aḥmad b. ʿAlī. *Ṣubḥ al-aʿshā fī ṣināʿat al-inshāʾ*, ed. M. ʿA. Ibrāhīm. Cairo, 1331–1338/1913–1920.
al-Qummī, Saʿd b. ʿAbd Allāh. *Kitāb al-maqālāt wa'l-firaq*, ed. M. J. Mashkūr. Tehran, 1963.
Rashīd al-Dīn Faḍl Allāh Ṭabīb. *Histoire des Mongols de la Perse*, ed. and tr. É. Quatremère. Paris, 1836.
Jāmiʿ al-tawārīkh, vol. 3, ed. A. A. Alizade. Baku, 1957.
Jāmiʿ al-tawārīkh, ed. B. Karīmī. Tehran, 1338/1959.
Jāmiʿ al-tawārīkh; qismat-i Ismāʿīliyān va Fāṭimiyān va Nizāriyān va dāʿīyān va rafīqān, ed. M. T. Dānishpazhūh and M. Mudarrisī Zanjānī. Tehran, 1338/1959.
Jāmiʿ al-tawārīkh; taʾrīkh-i āl Saljūq, ed. A. Ateş. Ankara, 1960.
al-Rāwandī, Muḥammad b. ʿAlī. *Rāḥat al-ṣudūr*, ed. M. Iqbāl. London, 1921.
al-Rāzī, Abū Ḥātim Aḥmad b. Ḥamdān. *Aʿlām al-nubuwwa*, ed. Ṣ. al-Ṣāwī and G. R. Aʿvānī. Tehran, 1977. Extracts in P. Kraus, 'Raziana II', *Orientalia*, NS, 5 (1936), pp. 35–56 and 358–378.
Recueil des Historiens des Croisades, [Académie des Inscriptions et Belles-Lettres]. Paris, 1841–1906, including *Historiens Occidentaux*. Paris, 1844–1895, and *Historiens Orientaux*. Paris, 1872–1906.
al-Shahrastānī, Abu'l-Fatḥ Muḥammad b. ʿAbd al-Karīm. *Kitāb al-milal wa'l-niḥal*, ed. ʿA. M. al-Wakīl. Cairo, 1968. Partial English trans. A. K. Kazi and J. G. Flynn, *Muslim Sects and Divisions*. London, 1984. Partial French trans. D. Gimaret and G. Monnot, *Livre des religions et des sectes*. Paris, 1986.
Shihāb al-Dīn Shāh al-Ḥusaynī. *Khiṭābāt-i ʿāliya*, ed. H. Ujāqī. Bombay, 1963.
Risāla dar ḥaqīqat-i dīn, ed. W. Ivanow. Bombay, 1947. English trans. W. Ivanow, *True Meaning of Religion*. 2nd ed., Bombay, 1947.
Shīrwānī, Zayn al-ʿĀbidīn. *Riyāḍ al-siyāḥa*, ed. A. Ḥāmid Rabbānī. Tehran, 1339/1960.
al-Shūshtarī, al-Qāḍī Nūr Allāh. *Majālis al-muʾminīn*. Tehran, 1375–1376/1955–1956.
Sibṭ Ibn al-Jawzī. *Mirʾāt al-zamān*, ed. J. R. Jewett. Chicago, 1907. Extracts with French trans., in *RHCHO*, vol. 3, pp. 511–570.
al-Sijistānī, Abū Yaʿqūb Isḥāq b. Aḥmad. *Ithbāt al-nubūʾāt*, ed. ʿĀrif Tāmir. Beirut, 1966.
Kashf al-maḥjūb, ed. H. Corbin. Tehran–Paris, 1949.
Kitāb al-iftikhār, ed. M. Ghālib. Beirut, 1980.
Kitāb al-yanābīʿ, ed. and tr. H. Corbin, in his *Trilogie Ismaélienne*, text pp. 1–97.
Tuḥfat al-mustajībīn, ed. ʿĀ. Tāmir, in his *Khams rasāʾil Ismāʿīliyya*, pp. 145–156; also in his *Thalāth rasāʾil Ismāʿīliyya*, pp. 10–20.
Some Specimens of Satpanth Literature, tr. Vali M. N. Hooda, in *Collectanea*: Vol. 1, pp. 55–137.
al-Ṣūlī, Muḥammad b. Yaḥyā. *Akhbār ar-Rāḍī billāh wa'l-Muttaqī billāh*, tr. M. Canard. Algiers, 1946–1950.
al-Ṣūrī, Muḥammad b. ʿAlī. *al-Qaṣīda al-Ṣūriyya*, ed. ʿĀrif Tāmir. Damascus, 1955.
al-Ṭabarī, Abū Jaʿfar Muḥammad b. Jarīr. *Taʾrīkh al-rusul wa'l-mulūk*, ed. M. J. de Goeje et al. Leiden, 1879–1901. English trans. by various scholars, *The History of al-Ṭabarī*. Albany, N.Y., 1985–

Ta'rīkh-i Sīstān, ed. M. T. Bahār. Tehran, 1314/1935. English trans. M. Gold, *The Tārikh-e Sīstān*. Rome, 1976.
Thalāth rasā'il Ismā'īliyya, ed. 'Ārif Tāmir. Beirut, 1983.
Trilogie Ismaélienne, ed. and tr. Henry Corbin. Tehran–Paris, 1961.
al-Ṭūsī, Abū Ja'far Muḥammad b. al-Ḥasan. *Fihrist kutub al-Shī'a*, ed. A. Sprenger et al. Calcutta, 1853–1855.
Rijāl al-Ṭūsī, ed. Muḥammad Ṣādiq Āl Baḥr al-'Ulūm. Najaf, 1381/1961.
al-Ṭūsī, Naṣīr al-Dīn Muḥammad b. Muḥammad. *Rawḍat al-taslīm, yā taṣawwurāt*, ed. and tr. W. Ivanow. Leiden, 1950.
Sayr va sulūk, in his *Majmū'a-yi rasā'il*, ed. M. T. Mudarris Raḍavī. Tehran, 1335/1956, pp. 36–55.
Two Early Ismaili Treatises, ed. W. Ivanow. Bombay, 1933.
'Umāra b. 'Alī al-Ḥakamī. *Ta'rīkh al-Yaman*, ed. and tr. Henry C. Kay, in his *Yaman, its Early Mediaeval History*, text pp. 1–102, translation pp. 1–137.
Ummu'l-kitāb, ed. W. Ivanow, in *Der Islam*, 23 (1936), pp. 1–132. Italian trans. P. Filippani-Ronconi, *Ummu'l-Kitāb*. Naples, 1966.
Vazīrī, Aḥmad 'Alī Khān. *Ta'rīkh-i Kirmān*, ed. M. I. Bāstānī Pārīzī. 2nd ed., Tehran, 1352/1973.
al-Walīd, 'Alī b. Muḥammad. *Tāj al-'aqā'id*, ed. 'Ārif Tāmir. Beirut, 1967. Summary English trans. W. Ivanow, *A Creed of the Fatimids*. Bombay, 1936.
al-Walīd, al-Ḥusayn b. 'Alī. *Risālat al-mabda' wa'l-ma'ād*, ed. and tr. H. Corbin, in his *Trilogie Ismaélienne*, text pp. 99–130, translation pp. 131–200.
William of Tyre. *Historia rerum in patribus transmarinis gestarum*, in *RHC: Historiens Occidentaux*, vol. 1. Paris, 1844.
Yaḥyā b. al-Ḥusayn b. al-Qāsim. *Ghāyat al-amānī*, ed. S. 'Abd al-Fattāḥ 'Āshūr. Cairo, 1968.
Yaman, its Early Mediaeval History, ed. and tr. Henry C. Kay. London, 1892.
al-Yamānī, Muḥammad b. Muḥammad. *Sīrat al-Ḥājib Ja'far b. 'Alī*, ed. W. Ivanow, in *Bulletin of the Faculty of Arts, University of Egypt*, 4, part 2 (1936), pp. 107–133. English trans. W. Ivanow, in his *Ismaili Tradition Concerning the Rise of the Fatimids*, pp. 184–223. French trans. M. Canard, 'L'autobiographie d'un chambellan du Mahdī 'Obeidallāh le Fāṭimide', *Hespéris*, 39 (1952), pp. 279–324.
Yāqūt al-Ḥamawī, Shihāb al-Dīn Abū 'Abd Allāh. *Mu'jam al-buldān*, ed. F. Wüstenfeld. Leipzig, 1866–1873. Partial French trans. C. Barbier de Meynard, *Dictionnaire géographique, historique et littéraire de la Perse*. Paris, 1861.
Ẓahīr al-Dīn Nīshāpūrī. *Saljūq-nāma*. Tehran, 1332/1953.

3. *Secondary sources*

Abdul Husain, Mian Bhai Mulla. *Gulzare Daudi*. Ahmedabad, 1920.
Abu-Izzeddin, Nejla M. *The Druzes: A New Study of their History, Faith and Society*. Leiden, 1984.
Aga Khan, Sulṭān Muḥammad Shāh. *The Memoirs of Aga Khan: World Enough and Time*. London, 1954.

Algar, Hamid. 'The Revolt of Āghā Khān Maḥallātī and the Transference of the Ismā'īlī Imamate to India', *SI*, 29 (1969), pp. 55–81.
'Āqā Khan', EIR, vol. 2, pp. 170–175.
Ali, S. Mujtaba. *The Origin of the Khojāhs and their Religious Life Today*. Würzburg, 1936.
Amiji, Hatim M. 'The Asian Communities', in *Islam in Africa*, ed. J. Kritzeck and W. H. Lewis. New York, 1969, pp. 141–181.
'The Bohras of East Africa', *Journal of Religion in East Africa*, 7 (1975), pp. 27–61.
Amir Arjomand, Said. *The Shadow of God and the Hidden Imam*. Chicago, 1984.
Amoretti, B. S. 'Religion in the Timurid and Safavid Periods', in *The Cambridge History of Iran*: Volume 6, pp. 610–655 and 1049–1051.
Arendonk, C. van. *Les débuts de l'Imāmat Zaidite au Yémen*, tr. J. Ryckmans. Leiden, 1960.
Assaad, Sadik A. *The Reign of al-Hakim bi Amr Allah (386/996–411/1021)*. Beirut, 1974.
Baiburdi, Ch. G. *Zhizn i tvorchestvo Nizārī-Persidskogo poeta*. Moscow, 1966.
Barthold, V. V. *Turkestan down to the Mongol Invasion*, ed. C. E. Bosworth. 3rd ed., London, 1968.
Becker, Carl H. *Beiträge zur Geschichte Ägyptens unter dem Islam*. Strassburg, 1902–1903.
Berchem, Max van. 'Épigraphie des Assassins de Syrie', *JA*, 9 série, 9 (1897), pp. 453–501.
Opera Minora. Geneva, 1978.
Bertel's, Andrei E. *Nasir-i Khosrov i ismailizm*. Moscow, 1959. Persian trans. Y. Āriyanpūr, *Nāṣir-i Khusraw va Ismā'īliyān*. Tehran, 1346/1967.
Bianquis, Thierry. *Damas et la Syrie sous la domination Fatimide, 359–468/969–1076*. Damascus, 1986.
'La prise de pouvoir par les Fatimides en Égypte (357–363/968–974)', *Annales Islamologiques*, 11 (1972), pp. 49–108.
Boyle, John A. 'The Ismā'īlīs and the Mongol Invasion', in *Ismā'īlī Contributions to Islamic Culture*, pp. 5–22.
Browne, Edward G. *A Literary History of Persia*. London–Cambridge, 1902–1924.
Cahen, Claude. 'Points du vue sur la Révolution 'Abbāside', in his *Les peuples Musulmans dans l'histoire médiévale*. Damascus, 1977, pp. 105–160.
'Le problème du Shī'isme dans l'Asie Mineure turque préottomane', in *Le Shī'isme Imāmite*, pp. 115–129.
'Quelques chroniques anciennes relatives aux derniers Fatimides', *BIFAO*, 37 (1937–1938), pp. 1–27.
La Syrie du Nord a l'époque des Croisades. Paris, 1940.
The Cambridge History of Iran: Volume 4, *The Period from the Arab Invasion to the Saljuqs*, ed. R. N. Frye. Cambridge, 1975.
The Cambridge History of Iran: Volume 5, *The Saljuq and Mongol Periods*, ed. J. A. Boyle. Cambridge, 1968.
The Cambridge History of Iran: Volume 6, *The Timurid and Safavid Periods*, ed. P. Jackson and L. Lockhart. Cambridge, 1986.
Canard, Marius. 'Fāṭimids', *EI2*, vol. 2, pp. 850–862.
Histoire de la dynastie des H'amdanides de Jazīra et de Syrie. Paris, 1953.

'L'impérialisme des Fatimides et leur propagande', *AIEO*, 6 (1942–1947), pp. 156–193.

Miscellanea Orientalia. London, 1973.

Casanova, Paul. 'Les Derniers Fāṭimides', *Mémoires de la Mission Archéologique Française du Caire*, 6 (1897), pp. 415–445.

'Monnaie des Assassins de Perse', *Revue Numismatique*, 3 série, 11 (1893), pp. 343–352.

Chunara, Alimahomed J. *Nūr-i mubīn*. Bombay, 1936.

Colloque international sur l'histoire du Caire. Cairo, 1972.

Corbin, Henry. 'De la gnose antique à la gnose Ismaélienne', in *Oriente ed Occidente nel medio evo: Atti del XII convegno Volta*. Rome, 1957, pp. 105–143.

En Islam Iranien: Aspects spirituels et philosophiques. Paris, 1971–1972.

'Épiphanie divine et naissance spirituelle dans la gnose Ismaélienne', *EJ*, 23 (1954), pp. 141–249.

Étude préliminaire pour le 'Livre réunissant les deux sagesses' de Nasir-e Khosraw. Tehran–Paris, 1953.

'Herméneutique spirituelle comparée (I. Swedenborg – II. Gnose Ismaélienne)', *EJ*, 33 (1964), pp. 71–176.

Histoire de la philosophie Islamique I: *Des origines jusqu'à la mort d'Averröes (1198)*; avec la collaboration de S. H. Nasr et O. Yahya. Paris, 1964.

'L'Initiation Ismaélienne ou l'ésotérisme et le Verbe', *EJ*, 39 (1970), pp. 41–142.

'Nāṣir-i Khusrau and Iranian Ismāʿīlism', in *The Cambridge History of Iran*: Volume 4, pp. 520–542 and 689–690.

'Rituel Sabéen et Exégèse Ismaélienne du rituel', *EJ*, 19 (1950), pp. 181–246.

Spiritual Body and Celestial Earth, tr. N. Pearson, Princeton, 1977.

Temple et contemplation. Paris, 1980. English trans. Philip Sherrard, *Temple and Contemplation*. London, 1986.

'Le Temps cyclique dans le Mazdéisme et dans l'Ismaélisme', *EJ*, 20 (1951), pp. 149–217.

Temps cyclique et gnose Ismaélienne. Paris, 1982. English trans. R. Manheim and James W. Morris, *Cyclical Time and Ismaili Gnosis*. London, 1983.

'Un roman initiatique Ismaélien', *Cahiers de Civilisation Médiévale*, 15 (1972), pp. 1–25 and 121–142.

'Une liturgie Shīʿite du Graal', in *Mélanges d'histoire des religions offerts à Henri Charles Puech*. Paris, 1974, pp. 81–99.

Crone, Patricia, and Hinds, Martin. *God's Caliph: Religious Authority in the First Centuries of Islam*. Cambridge, 1986.

Dachraoui, Farhat. *Le Califat Fatimide au Maghreb, 296–365 H./909–975 Jc*. Tunis, 1981.

'Les commencements de la prédication Ismāʿīlienne en Ifrīqiya', *SI*, 20 (1964), pp. 89–102.

Daftary, Farhad. 'The Bibliography of Asaf A. A. Fyzee', *Indo-Iranica*, 37 (1984), pp. 49–63.

'The Bibliography of the Publications of the late W. Ivanow', *IC*, 45 (1971), pp. 55–67, and 56 (1982), pp. 239–240.

'Carmatians, *EIR*, vol. 4, pp. 823–832.

'Marius Canard (1888–1982): A Bio-bibliographical Notice', *Arabica*, 33 (1986), pp. 251–262.

Dānishpazhūh, M. T. 'Dhaylī bar ta'rīkh-i Ismā'īliyya', *Revue de la Faculté des Lettres, Université de Tabriz*, 17–18 (1344–1345/1965–1966).

Defrémery, Charles F. 'Nouvelles recherches sur les Ismaéliens ou Bathiniens de Syrie', *JA*, 5 série, 3 (1854), pp. 373–421, and 5 (1855), pp. 5–76.

Derenbourg, Hartwig. *'Oumāra de Yémen, sa vie et son oeuvre*. Paris, 1897–1904.

Dumasia, Naoroji M. *The Aga Khan and His Ancestors*. Bombay, 1939.

A Brief History of the Aga Khan. Bombay, 1903.

Dussaud, René. *Topographie historique de la Syrie antique et médiévale*. Paris, 1927.

Elisséeff, Nikita. *Nūr ad-Dīn, un grand prince Musulman de Syrie au temps des Croisades (511–569 H./1118–1174)*. Damascus, 1967.

Engineer, Asghar Ali. *The Bohras*. New Delhi, 1980.

Enthoven, Reginald E. *The Tribes and Castes of Bombay*. Bombay, 1920–1922.

van Ess, Josef. *Chiliastische Erwartungen und die Versuchung der Göttlichkeit: Der Kalif al-Ḥākim (386–411 H.)*. Heidelberg, 1977.

Feki, Habib. *Les idées religieuses et philosophiques de l'Ismaélisme Fatimide*. Tunis, 1978.

Filippani-Ronconi, Pio. *Ismaeliti ed 'Assassini'*. Milan, 1973.

Fyzee, Asaf A. A. *Compendium of Fatimid Law*. Simla, 1969.

'The Ismā'īlīs', in *Religion in the Middle East*, ed. A. J. Arberry. Cambridge, 1969, vol. 2, pp. 318–329 and 684–685.

Outlines of Muhammadan Law. 4th ed., Delhi, 1974.

'Qadi an-Nu'man, the Fatimid Jurist and Author', *JRAS* (1934), pp. 1–32.

'The Religion of the Ismailis', in *India and Contemporary Islam*, ed. S. T. Lokhandwalla. Simla, 1971, pp. 70–87.

'The Study of the Literature of the Fatimid Da'wa', in *Arabic and Islamic Studies in Honor of Hamilton A. R. Gibb*, ed. G. Makdisi. Leiden, 1965, pp. 232–249.

Ghālib, Muṣṭafā. *Ta'rīkh al-da'wa al-Ismā'īliyya*. 2nd ed., Beirut, 1965.

Goeje, Michael J. de. 'La Fin de l'empire des Carmathes du Bahraïn', *JA*, 9 série, 5 (1895), pp. 5–30.

Mémoire sur les Carmathes du Bahraïn et les Fatimides. 2nd ed., Leiden, 1886.

Goldziher, Ignaz. *Introduction to Islamic Theology and Law*, tr. A. and R. Hamori. Princeton, 1981.

Muslim Studies, tr. C. R. Barber and S. M. Stern. London, 1967–1971.

Gramlich, Robert. *Die schiitischen Derwischorden Persiens*. Wiesbaden, 1965–1981.

Grousset, René. *Histoire des Croisades*. Paris, 1934–1936.

Halm, Heinz. *Die islamische Gnosis*. Zürich, 1982.

Kosmologie und Heilslehre der frühen Ismā'īlīya. Wiesbaden, 1978.

'Die Sīrat Ibn Ḥaušab: Die ismailitische da'wa im Jemen und die Fatimiden', *Die Welt des Orients*, 12 (1981), pp. 107–135.

'Die Söhne Zikrawaihs und das erste fatimidische Kalifat (290/903)', *Die Welt des Orients*, 10 (1979), pp. 30–53.

Hamdani, Abbas. 'The Dā'ī Ḥātim Ibrāhīm al-Ḥāmidī (d. 596 H./1199 A.D.) and his Book *Tuḥfat al-Qulūb*', *Oriens*, 23–24 (1970–1971), pp. 258–300.

'Evolution of the Organisational Structure of the Fāṭimī Daʿwah', *Arabian Studies*, 3 (1976), pp. 85–114.
The Beginnings of the Ismāʿīlī Daʿwa in Northern India. Cairo, 1956.
'The Ṭayyibī-Fāṭimid Community of the Yaman at the Time of the Ayyūbid Conquest of Southern Arabia', *Arabian Studies*, 7 (1985), pp. 151–160.
Hamdani, Abbas and de Blois, F. 'A Re-Examination of al-Mahdī's Letter to the Yemenites on the Genealogy of the Fatimid Caliphs', *JRAS* (1983), pp. 173–207.
al-Hamdānī, Ḥusain F. 'The Letters of al-Mustanṣir bi'llāh', *BSOS*, 7 (1934), pp. 307–324.
On the Genealogy of Fatimid Caliphs. Cairo, 1958.
'Some Unknown Ismāʿīlī Authors and their Works', *JRAS* (1933), pp. 359–378.
al-Hamdānī, Ḥ. F. and Maḥmūd, Ḥ. S. *al-Ṣulayḥiyyūn wa'l-ḥaraka al-Fāṭimiyya fi'l-Yaman*. Cairo, 1955.
al-Hammad, Ādala ʿA. *Qiyām al-dawla al-Fāṭimiyya bi-bilād al-Maghrib*. Cairo, 1980.
Ḥasan, Ḥasan I. *Ta'rīkh al-dawla al-Fāṭimiyya*. 3rd ed., Cairo, 1964.
Ḥasan, Ḥasan I. and Sharaf, Ṭāhā A. *al-Muʿizz li-Dīn Allāh*. 2nd ed., Cairo, 1963.
ʿUbayd Allāh al-Mahdī. Cairo, 1947.
Hinds, Martin. 'Kūfan Political Alignments and their Background in the Mid-Seventh Century A.D.', *IJMES*, 2 (1971), pp. 346–367.
Hodgson, Marshall G. S. 'How did the Early Shīʿa become Sectarian?', *JAOS*, 75 (1955), pp. 1–13.
'The Ismāʿīlī State', in *The Cambridge History of Iran*: Volume 5, pp. 422–482.
The Order of Assassins; the Struggle of the Early Nizārī Ismāʿīlīs against the Islamic World. The Hague, 1955. Persian trans. F. Badra'ī, *Firqa-yi Ismāʿīliyya*. Tabrīz, 1343/1964.
The Venture of Islam. Chicago, 1974.
Hollister, John N. *The Shiʿa of India*. London, 1953.
Ḥusayn, Muḥammad Kāmil. *Fī adab Miṣr al-Fāṭimiyya*. Cairo, 1950.
Ṭā'ifat al-Ismāʿīliyya. Cairo, 1959.
Idris, Hady R. *La Berbérie orientale sous les Zīrīdes, Xe–XIIe siècles*. Paris, 1962.
ʿInān, Muḥammad ʿAbd Allāh. *al-Ḥākim bi-Amr Allāh wa asrār al-daʿwa al-Fāṭimiyya*. 2nd ed., Cairo, 1959.
Miṣr al-Islāmiyya. 2nd ed., Cairo, 1969.
Islamic Civilisation, 950–1150, ed. D. S. Richards. Oxford, 1973.
Ismāʿīlī Contributions to Islamic Culture, ed. S. Hossein Nasr. Tehran, 1977.
Ismāʿīljī, Ḥasan ʿAlī Badrispresswala. *Akhbār al-duʿāt al-akramīn*. Rajkot, 1937.
Ivanow, Wladimir. *Alamut and Lamasar: Two Mediaeval Ismaili Strongholds in Iran*. Tehran, 1960.
The Alleged Founder of Ismailism. Bombay, 1946.
Brief Survey of the Evolution of Ismailism. Leiden, 1952.
'Early Shiʿite Movements', *JBBRAS*, NS, 17 (1941), pp. 1–23.
'A Forgotten Branch of the Ismailis', *JRAS* (1938), pp. 57–79.
Ibn al-Qaddah. 2nd rev. ed., Bombay, 1957.
Ismaili Tradition Concerning the Rise of the Fatimids. London, etc., 1942.
'Ismailis and Qarmatians', *JBBRAS*, NS, 16 (1940), pp. 43–85.

'Ismailitica', in *Memoirs of the Asiatic Society of Bengal*, 8 (1922), pp. 1–76.
'Ismāʿīlīya', *SEI*, pp. 179–183.
'The Organization of the Fatimid Propaganda', *JBBRAS*, NS, 15 (1939), pp. 1–35.
Problems in Nasir-i Khusraw's Biography. Bombay, 1956.
'Satpanth', in *Collectanea*: Vol. 1, pp. 1–54.
'The Sect of Imam Shah in Gujrat', *JBBRAS*, NS, 12 (1936), pp. 19–70.
Studies in Early Persian Ismailism. Leiden, 1948; 2nd ed., Bombay, 1955.
'Tombs of Some Persian Ismaili Imams', *JBBRAS*, NS, 14 (1938), pp. 49–62.
Jafri, S. Husain M. *Origins and Early Development of Shīʿa Islam*. London, 1979.
Jhaveri, K. M. 'A Legendary History of the Bohoras', *JBBRAS*, NS, 9 (1933), pp. 37–52.
Kohlberg, Etan. 'From Imāmiyya to Ithnā-ʿashariyya', *BSOAS*, 39 (1976), pp. 521–534.
Kraus, Paul. 'La Bibliographie Ismaëlienne de W. Ivanow', *REI*, 6 (1932), pp. 483–490.
'Hebräische und syrische Zitate in ismāʿīlitischen Schriften', *Der Islam*, 19 (1931), pp. 243–263.
Laoust, Henri. *Les Schismes dans l'Islam*. Paris, 1965.
Latham, J. Derek and Mitchell, Helen W. 'Bibliography of S. M. Stern', in S. M. Stern, *Hispano-Arabic Strophic Poetry*, ed. L. P. Harvey. Oxford, 1974, pp. 230–245.
Le Strange, Guy. *The Lands of the Eastern Caliphate*. 2nd ed., Cambridge, 1930.
Lev, Yaacov. 'Army, Regime, and Society in Fatimid Egypt, 358–487/968–1094', IJMES, 19 (1987), pp. 337–365.
Lewis, Bernard. *The Assassins: A Radical Sect in Islam*. London, 1967. French trans. A. Pélissier, *Les Assassins: Terrorisme et politique dans l'Islam médiéval*. Paris, 1982. Persian trans. F. Badraʾī, *Fidāʾīyān-i Ismāʿīlī*. Tehran, 1348/1969.
'Assassins of Syria and Ismāʿīlīs of Persia', in Accademia Nazionale dei Lincei, *Atti del convegno internazionale sul tema: La Persia nel medioevo*. Rome, 1971, pp. 573–580.
'The Ismāʿīlites and the Assassins', in *A History of the Crusades*, ed. K. M. Setton: Volume 1, *The First Hundred Years*, ed. M. W. Baldwin. 2nd ed., Madison, Wisconsin, 1969, pp. 99–132.
'Kamāl al-Dīn's Biography of Rāšid al-Dīn Sinān', *Arabica*, 13 (1966), pp. 225–267.
The Origins of Ismāʿīlism: A Study of the Historical Background of the Fāṭimid Caliphate. Cambridge, 1940.
'Saladin and the Assassins', *BSOAS*, 15 (1953), pp. 239–245.
'The Sources for the History of the Syrian Assassins', *Speculum*, 27 (1952), pp. 475–489.
Studies in Classical and Ottoman Islam (7th–16th Centuries). London, 1976.
Lokhandwalla, Sh. T. 'The Bohras, a Muslim Community of Gujarat', *SI*, 3 (1955), pp. 117–135.
Madelung, Wilferd. 'Aspects of Ismāʿīlī Theology: The Prophetic Chain and the God Beyond Being', in *Ismāʿīlī Contributions to Islamic Culture*, pp. 51–65.

'Bemerkungen zur imamitischen Firaq-Literatur', *Der Islam*, 43 (1967), pp. 37–52.
'Fatimiden und Baḥrainqarmaṭen', *Der Islam*, 34 (1959), pp. 34–88.
'Das Imamat in der frühen ismailitischen Lehre', *Der Islam*, 37 (1961), pp. 43–135.
Der Imam al-Qāsim ibn Ibrāhīm und die Glaubenslehre der Zaiditen. Berlin, 1965.
'Ismāʿīliyya', *EI2*, vol. 4, pp. 198–206..
'Ḳarmaṭī', *EI2*, vol. 4, pp. 660–665.
'al-Mahdī', *EI2*, vol. 5, pp. 1230–1238.
Religious Schools and Sects in Medieval Islam. London, 1985.
Religious Trends in Early Islamic Iran. Albany, N.Y., 1988.
'Shiism: Ismāʿīlīyah', *Encyclopedia of Religion*, vol. 13, pp. 247–260.
'The Sources of Ismāʿīlī Law', *Journal of Near Eastern Studies*, 35 (1976), pp. 29–40.
Mājid, ʿAbd al-Munʿim. *al-Imām al-Mustanṣir bi'llāh al-Fāṭimī*. Cairo, 1961.
Ẓuhūr khilāfat al-Fāṭimiyyīn wa suqūṭuhā fī Miṣr. Alexandria, 1968.
Mamour, P. H. *Polemics on the Origin of the Fatimi Caliphs*. London, 1934.
al-Manāwī, Muḥammad Ḥ. *al-Wizāra wa'l-wuzarā' fi'l-ʿaṣr al-Fāṭimī*. Cairo, 1970.
Marçais, Georges. *La Berbérie Musulmane et l'Orient au moyen-âge*. Paris, 1946.
Marquet, Yves. *La Philosophie des Ihwān al-Ṣafā'*. Algiers, 1975.
'Quelques remarques à propos de Kosmologie und Heilslehre der frühen Ismāʿīliyya de Heinz Halm', *SI*, 55 (1982), pp. 115–135.
Massignon, Louis. 'Esquisse d'une bibliographie Qarmaṭe', in *A Volume of Oriental Studies Presented to Edward G. Browne*, ed. T. W. Arnold and R. A. Nicholson. Cambridge, 1922, pp. 329–338.
'Ḳarmaṭians', *EI*, vol. 2, pp. 767–772.
Opera Minora, ed. Y. Moubarac. Paris, 1969.
Mélanges offerts à Henry Corbin, ed. S. Hossein Nasr. Tehran, 1977.
Minasian, Caro O. *Shah Diz of Ismaʿili Fame*. London, 1971.
Misra, Satish C. *Muslim Communities in Gujarat*. Bombay, 1964.
Molé, Marijan. 'Les Kubrawiya entre Sunnisme et Shiisme aux huietième et neuvième siècles de l'hégire', REI, 29 (1961), pp. 61–142.
Momen, Moojan. *An Introduction to Shiʿi Islam*. New Haven, 1985.
Nagel, Tilman. *Frühe Ismailiya und Fatimiden im lichte der Risālat Iftitāḥ ad-Daʿwa*. Bonn, 1972.
Najm al-Ghanī Khān. *Madhāhib al-Islām*. Lucknow, 1924.
Nanji, Azim. 'Modernization and Change in the Nizari Ismaili Community in East Africa – A Perspective', *Journal of Religion in Africa*, 6 (1974), pp. 123–139.
The Nizārī Ismāʿīlī Tradition in the Indo-Pakistan Subcontinent. Delmar, N.Y., 1978.
Nasr, S. Hossein. *Ideals and Realities of Islam*. New York, 1967.
O'Leary, De Lacy. *A Short History of the Fatimid Khalifate*. London, 1923.
Petrushevsky, Ilya P. *Islam in Iran*, tr. H. Evans. London, 1985. Persian trans. K. Kishāvarz, *Islām dar Īrān*. Tehran, 1351/1972.
Poonawala, Ismail K. 'Al-Qāḍī al-Nuʿmān's Works and the Sources', *BSOAS*, 36 (1973), pp. 109–115.

'A Reconsideration of al-Qāḍī al-Nuʿmān's Madhhab', *BSOAS*, 37 (1974), pp. 572–579.
'Al-Sijistānī and his Kitāb al-Maqālīd', in *Essays on Islamic Civilization Presented to Niyazi Berkes*, ed. Donald P. Little. Leiden, 1970, pp. 274–283.
Pourjavady, N. and Wilson, Peter L. 'Ismāʿīlīs and Niʿmatullāhīs', *SI*, 41 (1975), pp. 113–135.
Kings of Love: The Poetry and History of the Niʿmatullāhī Sufi Order. Tehran, 1978.
al-Qāḍī, Wadād. *al-Kaysāniyya fi'l-ta'rīkh wa'l-adab*. Beirut, 1974.
Quatremère, Étienne M. 'Mémoires historiques sur la dynastie des Khalifes Fatimites', *JA*, 3 série, 2 (1836), pp. 97–142.
Rabino, Hyacinth L. 'Les Dynasties du Māzandarān', *JA*, 228 (1936), pp. 397–474.
'Les Dynasties locales du Gīlān et du Daylam', *JA*, 237 (1949), pp. 301–350.
Les Provinces Caspiennes de la Perse: Le Guīlān. Paris, 1917. Persian trans. J. Khumāmī-Zāda, *Vilāyāt-i dār al-marz-i Īrān: Gīlān*. Tehran, 1350/1971.
'Rulers of Gilan', *JRAS* (1920), pp. 277–296.
Runciman, Steven. *A History of the Crusades*. Cambridge, 1951–1954.
Rypka, Jan. *History of Iranian Literature*, ed. K. Jahn. Dordrecht, 1968.
Ṣafā, Z. *Ta'rīkh-i adabiyyāt dar Īrān*. Various editions, Tehran, 1342– / 1963–
Sayyid, Ayman F. 'Lumières nouvelles sur quelques sources de l'histoire Fatimide en Égypte', *Annales Islamologiques*, 13 (1977), pp. 1–41.
Semenov, Aleksandr A. 'Ismailitskaya oda, posvyashchennaya voploshcheniyam ʿAliya-boga', *Iran*, 2 (1928), pp. 1–24.
'Iz oblasti religioznuikh verovany Shughnanskikh Ismailitov', *Mir Islama*, 1 (1912), pp. 523–561.
Shaban, M. A. *Islamic History: A New Interpretation*. Cambridge, 1971–1976.
Sharon, Moshe. *Black Banners from the East: The Establishment of the ʿAbbāsid State – Incubation of a Revolt*. Jerusalem–Leiden, 1983.
Le Shīʿisme Imāmite, Colloque de Strasbourg, ed. T. Fahd. Paris, 1970.
Silvestre de Sacy, Antoine Isaac. *Exposé de la religion des Druzes*. Paris, 1838.
'Mémoire sur la dynastie des Assassins', *Mémoires de l'Institut Royal de France*, 4 (1818), pp. 1–84.
Stern, Samuel M. 'Abu'l-Qasim al-Bustī and his Refutation of Ismāʿīlism', *JRAS* (1961), pp. 14–35.
'Cairo as the Centre of the Ismāʿīlī Movement', in *Colloque international sur l'histoire du Caire*, pp. 437–450.
'The Early Ismāʿīlī Missionaries in North-West Persia and in Khurāsān and Transoxania', *BSOAS*, 23 (1960), pp. 56–90.
'The Epistle of the Fatimid Caliph al-Āmir (al-Hidāya al-Āmiriyya) – its Date and its Purpose', *JRAS* (1950), pp. 20–31.
Fāṭimid Decrees: Original Documents from the Fāṭimid Chancery. London, 1964.
'Heterodox Ismāʿīlism at the Time of al-Muʿizz', *BSOAS*, 17 (1955), pp. 10–33.
History and Culture in the Medieval Muslim World. London, 1984.
'Ismāʿīlī Propaganda and Fatimid Rule in Sind', *IC*, 23 (1949), pp. 298–307.
'Ismāʿīlīs and Qarmaṭians', in *L'Élaboration de l'Islam*, Colloque de Strasbourg. Paris, 1961, pp. 99–108.

Medieval Arabic and Hebrew Thought. London, 1983.
'New Information about the Authors of the Epistles of the Sincere Brethren', *Islamic Studies*, 3 (1964), pp. 405–428.
Studies in Early Ismā'īlism. Jerusalem–Leiden, 1983.
'The Succession to the Fatimid Imam al-Āmir, the Claims of the Later Fatimids to the Imamate, and the Rise of Ṭayyibī Ismailism', *Oriens*, 4 (1951), pp. 193–255.
Strothmann, Rudolf. 'Kleinere ismailitische Schriften', in Islamic Research Association, *Miscellany*: Vol. 1. Bombay, 1949, pp. 121–163.
'Recht der Ismailiten', *Der Islam*, 31 (1954), pp. 131–146.
'Shī'a', *EI*, vol. 4, pp. 350–358.
Surūr, Muḥammad J. *Miṣr fī 'aṣr al-dawla al-Fāṭimiyya*. Cairo, 1960.
al-Nufūdh al-Fāṭimī fī bilād al-Shām wa'l-'Irāq. 3rd ed., Cairo, 1964.
Siyāsat al-Fāṭimiyyīn al-khārijiyya. Cairo, 1967.
Sutūda, Manūchihr. *Qilā'-i Ismā'īliyya*. Tehran, 1345/1966.
Sykes, Percy M. *Ten Thousand Miles in Persia*. New York, 1902.
Ṭabāṭabā'ī, Muḥammad Ḥusayn. *Shi'ite Islam*, ed. and tr. S. Hossein Nasr. London, 1975.
Tāmir, 'Ārif. 'Furū' al-shajara al-Ismā'īliyya al-Imāmiyya', *al-Mashriq*, 51 (1957), pp. 581–612.
al-Imāma fi'l-Islām. Beirut, n.d. [1964].
Trimingham, J. Spencer. *The Sufi Orders in Islam*. Oxford, 1971.
Vatikiotis, Panayiotis J. *The Fatimid Theory of State*. Lahore, 1957.
al-Walī, Ṭāhā. *al-Qarāmiṭa*. Beirut, 1981.
Walker, Paul E. 'Cosmic Hierarchies in Early Ismā'īlī Thought: The View of Abū Ya'qūb al-Sijistānī', *MW*, 66 (1976), pp. 14–28.
'Eternal Cosmos and the Womb of History: Time in Early Ismaili Thought', *IJMES*, 9 (1978), pp. 355–366.
'The Ismaili Vocabulary of Creation', *SI*, 40 (1974), pp. 75–85.
Watt, W. Montgomery. *The Formative Period of Islamic Thought*. Edinburgh, 1973.
Islamic Philosophy and Theology. Edinburgh, 1962.
Wellhausen, Julius. *The Arab Kingdom and its Fall*, tr. M. G. Weir. Calcutta, 1927.
The Religio-Political Factions in Early Islam, tr. R. C. Ostle and S. M. Walzer. Amsterdam, 1975.
Willey, Peter. *The Castles of the Assassins*. London, 1963.
Yād-nāma-yi Nāṣir-i Khusraw. Mashhad, 1355/1976.
Zāhid 'Alī. *Hamārē Ismā'īlī madhhab kī ḥaqīqat aur us kā niẓām*. Hyderabad, 1373/1954.
Ta'rīkh-i Fāṭimiyyīn-i Miṣr. 2nd ed., Karachi, 1963.
Zarrīnkūb, 'Abd al-Ḥusayn. *Dunbāla-yi justijū dar taṣawwuf-i Īrān*. Tehran, 1362/1983.
Ta'rīkh-i Īrān ba'd az Islām. 2nd ed., Tehran, 1355/1976.

INDEX

Main entries are arranged alphabetically; their sub-headings are arranged thematically rather than alphabetically. The Arabic definite article 'al-' is ignored for the purposes of alphabetization. In the alphabetization, no distinction is made between different Arabic letters which are represented by the same letter in transliteration: thus, *h* and *ḥ* are treated as one and the same. The abbreviation 'b.' for *ibn* ('son of') is alphabetized as written.

The letter 'n.' ('note') immediately following a page reference indicates the number of an endnote on that page (e.g. 642n.171), 'q.v.' ('*quod vide*') is used for cross-reference within the index, and '*passim*' indicates scattered references to the subject, not necessarily on consecutive pages.

Post-Alamūt Qāsim-Shāhī Nizārī Imāms are referred to as 'Nizārī Imāms'; but the full designation is used for Muḥammad-Shāhī Nizārī Imāms.

The glossary, genealogical tables and lists, plates and map have not been indexed.